Inside NetWare 4.1

Doug Bierer

New Riders Publishing, Indianapolis, Indiana

Inside NetWare 4.1

By Doug Bierer

Published by:
New Riders Publishing
201 West 103rd Street
Indianapolis, IN 46290 USA

Printed in the United States of America 3 4 5 6 7 8 9 0

Library of Congress Cataloging-in-Publication Data

Bierer, Doug
Inside NetWare 4.1 / Doug Bierer.
p. cm
Includes index
ISBN 1-56205-291-8
1. NetWare (Computer file) 2. Local area networks (Computer networks) 3. Operating systems (Computers) I. Title
TK5105.7.B54 1994
004.6'8—dc20 94-42918
CIP

Warning and Disclaimer

This book is designed to provide information about the NetWare computer program. Every effort has been made to make this book as complete and as accurate as possible, but no warranty or fitness is implied.

The information is provided on an "as is" basis. The author and New Riders Publishing shall have neither liability nor responsibility to any person or entity with respect to any loss or damages arising from the information contained in this book or from the use of the disks or programs that may accompany it.

Publisher *Don Fowley*
Associate Publisher *Tim Huddleston*
Product Development Manager *Rob Tidrow*
Marketing Manager *Ray Robinson*
Director of Special Projects *Cheri Robinson*
Managing Editor *Tad Ringo*

About the Author

Doug Bierer has been involved with NetWare since 1985. His first exposure to NetWare was when he had just finished writing a multiuser application program and was then told he had to go out and install the network. Many manuals, dozens of disks, and a couple of weeks later he had a NetWare 2.0A network up and running. He wrote his first program in 1971 and has written numerous applications since, using a variety of languages including BASIC, FORTRAN, PL/I, FORTH, C, Pascal, and dBASE. Doug has been involved in Novell training since 1988 and is a CNE as well as ECNE. He is a Senior Technical Instructor for Novell in San Jose, teaching NetWare and UnixWare courses. He can be reached through CompuServe at 73301,2020 or through the Internet at dbierer@novell.com.

Trademark Acknowledgments

Dedication

This book is dedicated to the memory of **Dan Elliott**. He was an inspiration and a compassionate human being. He was a mentor to me and "brought me into" the world of computers and high technology. His "can do" attitude is a model for all to follow. Dan was not only a master of computer technology, he was also a leader of men, a former commander in the U.S. Coast Guard, a first rate sailor, and deeply involved in the volunteer program at the YMCA. Dan, I salute you.

Product Director
Drew Heywood

Acquisitions Editor
Alicia Krakovitz

Production Editor
John Sleeva

Copy Editors
Amy Bezek
Fran Blauw
Sarah Kearns
Laura Frey
John Kane
Pete Kuhns
Cliff Shubs
Angie Trzepacz
Lisa Wilson
Phil Worthington

Technical Editors
Brad Dew
Brian Benson

Editorial Assistant
Karen Opal

Cover Designer
Dan Armstrong

Book Designer
Kim Scott

Production Team Supervisor
Katy Bodenmiller

Graphics Image Specialists
Dennis Sheehan
Clint Lahnen

Production Analyst
Dennis Clay Hager

Production Team
Carol Bowers, Michael Brumitt, Elaine Marie Brush, Jama Carter, Charlotte Clapp, Mary Ann Cosby, Judy Everly, Rob Nicolo Falco, Jr., Kimberly K. Hannel, Donna Harbin, Michael Henry, Aleata Howard, Louisa Klucznik, Ayanna Lacey, Shawn MacDonald, Cheryl Moore, Casey Price, Brian-Kent Proffitt
Erich Richter, SA Springer, Jill Thompkins, Scott Tullis, Jeff Weissenberger, Dennis Wesner

Indexers
Chris Cleveland
Greg Eldred

Acknowledgments

I would like to thank the following authors who contributed to this book:

Brian Benson is an independent training and database consultant from Boise, Idaho. He recently served six years at Novell, Inc. as Senior Instructor/Course Developer for NetWare 4.*x* products and as Product Marketing Manager for NetWare 3.*x* products. Before coming to Novell, he founded AccuGraph Inc., a software consulting firm specializing in accounting and inventory tracking systems. He received his Bachelor and Master of Science degrees from Brigham Young University where he worked as a database programmer/architect, designing, supporting, and managing information tools and networks.

Russ Clark is a lead instructional designer for the NetWare 4.1 curriculum for Novell. Russ designs and develops the courses for the Certified Novell Engineer (CNE) curriculum. He is a Certified Novell Instructor (CNI) and an Enterprise Certified Novell Engineer (ECNE). Russ has also presented at BrainShare the last two years on NetWare 4 and software distribution. Prior to Novell, Russ worked with Andersen Consulting as an instructional designer for the Network Solutions group and other new technology groups.

Al Sallette, a computer consultant originally from New York City, worked as an intructional designer for Novell in Sunnyvale, California. After a stint with Novell Technology Institute in San Jose, he now works for a technical marketing documentation group writing about new Novell products.

Christian M. Trahan is a LAN/WAN internetworking expert who has been working with NetWare since 1989 and has been a CNE since 1990. He has implemented a variety of enterprise networks ranging from a dozen to thousands of nodes. Christian's latest project was the design and implementation of Symantecs global network for voice and data containing over 240 file servers. Currently, Christian consults in the San Jose, CA area.

I would also like to thank the following people:

Eileen Bierer, my wife, for her caring and loving support through this endeavor. She kept our household from falling into chaos and ruins while I was buried in a mound of computer equipment and technical reference manuals. She was unswervingly supportive, even reminding me when it was time to eat.

Drew Heywood, for his patient guidance through the process of writing this book. He provided invaluable feedback and direction. He is also the "Magic Man," able to come up with the evaluation copies of some of the software mentioned in this book. Drew put a lot of his own time into the book, especially during the final phases of production.

Alicia Krakovitz, for keeping me on track and making great deals.

John Sleeva for his dedication and unending patience while I finished "this little part here" and "that little section there."

All the talented editors at New Riders who corrected my every little grammatical awkwardness.

Bill Lowrey for his patience and latitude at work, **Gary Clark** for his inspiration in being a "guiding light," and **Carolyn Rose** for her spirit and for setting a wonderful example.

Contents at a Glance

Table of Contents

Part Two: Examining NetWare 4.1's Benefits

Part Five: Building the NDS Structure

Part Six: Controlling the File System

Part Ten: Backing Up, Disaster Planning, and Troubleshooting

Introduction

Microcomputer networking has come of age. With the advent of such operating systems as Novell's NetWare 4.1, microcomputer networks can finally approach the level of service formerly available only in mainframe systems. This evolution stems from several factors:

- Faster and more powerful desktop computer systems
- Improved long-distance communications services
- Increased capacity and access speed of on-line storage devices
- Reliable and fast NICs (Network Interface Cards)
- Sophisticated technologies to connect smaller networks into large complex networks
- Network operating systems that enable you to easily manage complex networks

Along with this revolution in the computing industry comes a challenge: the need to keep up, the need to stay informed. Many industry pundits have said that the medium of exchange in the year 2000 will be information. This book addresses that issue.

This book is for people in the network industry who feel the need to keep pace with changing technology. This book is unique in that it focuses not only on Novell's latest network operating system, NetWare 4.1, but the diverse client systems that will connect to it. Desktop operating systems such as DOS, OS/2, Windows, Windows NT, and UNIX are addressed in the NetWare environment. *Inside NetWare 4.1* not only addresses NetWare, but the hardware and software that comprise a network. Topics as diverse as routers, repeaters, and network adapters are discussed along with software such as Novell's Network Management System (NMS), ARCserve by Cheyenne Software, and Symantec's Norton Anti-Virus for NetWare. This book brings together many diverse threads and weaves it into a comprehensive tapistry that will inform you and keep your interest peaked.

You should read this book if any of the following titles and situations apply to you now or will apply to you in the future:

- Network Administrator
- CNA, CNE, or CNI
- Professor or teacher involved in computer science
- College or university student studying NetWare
- Manager contemplating whether or not to buy NetWare 4.1
- MIS or DP professional
- Programmer working in the NetWare environment
- Technical writer
- Between jobs looking for a career change
- Up and coming executive who wants to add an impressive volume to the book shelf
- Anyone who is bored and looking for some alternative reading material

In addition to information and practical reference, this book provides numerous examples of screens you will see. There are dozens of examples of batch files, QBASIC programs, spreadsheet macros, and database programs that you can put to use immediately to make the task of managing a NetWare 4.*x* network easier.

How This Book Is Organized

The book is divided into 10 Parts. Each chapter in the book is half the size of a "normal" chapter. This is to give greater flexibility to the reader. Each chapter is easily digestible and can be finished quickly. The breakdown of the parts and chapters is as follows:

Part One—Understanding Complex Networks

In the first Part, you explore the elements and nature of complex networks. The first chapter, "Elements of a Simple Network," starts with an explanation of the nature and composition of a simple network. Topics include network interface cards, cabling, printers, and other aspects of a simple network. Chapter 2, "Elements of a Complex Network," discusses multiple protocols, wide area networks, and different types of lines and technology to connect networks (such as ATM technology). Chapter 3, "LANs and WANs," goes into the specifics of how different types of network interface cards access the network and other issues.

Part Two—Examining NetWare 4.1's Benefits

This Part gives you an idea of the capabilities of NetWare 4.1. NetWare 4.1 has hundreds of features. Some of these features will be of use to you as you manage your network. Other features may be of use to you at some future time—perhaps as your system grows and expands. Still other features you may find you will never use.

Chapter 4 examines features found in all NetWare versions since 2.10. Features examined include how network printing occurs, how the server works with its hard disk space, and some "fault tolerant" features.

Chapter 5 focuses on features added with NetWare 4.1. Chapter 6 examines NDS (NetWare Directory Services). NDS is new with NetWare 4.1. It is a global naming scheme that enables you to easily control and interact with the various objects, such as users or printers, in a network. Chapter 7 deals the security environment in NetWare 4.1. Chapter 8, the last chapter in this section, focuses on how older versions of NetWare stored information about network objects. Older versions used what are known as the *bindery files*. Chapter 8 explains how the bindery files work and how you can manage a network that uses both the bindery files and the NDS.

Part Three—Setting Up a New Network

Now that you have an understanding of some of the features and concepts of networks, this Part focuses on what is involved in setting up a new network. For those readers who have existing networks and are planning to upgrade to NetWare 4.1, this

Part serves as both a checklist and a reminder. The Part's purpose is to give you an overview of what is involved in setting up a network. Anything that this Part can suggest to you in advance saves you time and money. As the saying goes, "An ounce of prevention is worth a pound of cure."

Chapter 9 focuses on planning aspects and provides ideas on what to expect and how to prepare for the installation. Chapter 10 gives you an overview of the installation process itself. Many people lose sight of the big picture, focusing on the server installation alone. Chapter 10 covers not only the server, but all network components. Chapter 11 gives you tips and pointers on hardware configuration, including issues such as file server memory, disk drives, and peripherals. Chapter 12 steps you through a complete NetWare 4.1 operating system installation. Chapter 13 gives you tips and pointers on some issues that can come up during the installation.

Part Four—Activating and Using Clients

After your network is physically installed, and the file server is up and running, it is time to turn your attention to the clients. This Part discusses setting up various client systems. The clients, also known as *workstations*, are intelligent computers that utilize the services of the NetWare file server (and other types of servers, such as database servers and communications servers). Each client has its own independent operational environment. The chapters in this section focus on clients, one chapter per major operating system. The operating systems covered include the following:

- DOS
- Windows, Windows for Workgroups, and Windows NT
- OS/2
- UNIX
- Macintosh

Part Five—Building the NDS Structure

Part Five moves your attention to building the NDS (NetWare Directory Services) structure. This is a logical framework that shapes the network interactions of you and your network users. Chapter 19 discusses various NDS tree design considerations. This includes a look at how multiple trees affect the network, where to place objects, and managing the physical placement of the NDS database. The latter topic includes management of replicas and partitions. Chapter 20 gives you practical pointers on how to create objects using the DOS-based NETADMIN utility, or the Windows-based NWADMIN utility. Chapter 21 discusses a utilty that automates the creation of users:

UIMPORT. This utility enables you to take an existing database and convert it into a tool for adding users. Chapter 22 addresses the issue of *bindery services* (formerly called bindery emulation). You learn how to properly set up bindery services and how to deal with clients and utilities designed for previous versions of NetWare. Chapter 23 covers a feature that enables you merge two NDS trees together.

Part Six—Controlling the File System

After the network is installed and users have been added, the next step is to decide where to place files. Decisions addressed in this Part include a discussion of how the subdirectory structure on the file server should be designed. Design issues include what types of files users will be creating, what types of applications will be used, and where data is to be stored.

An important topic covered is that of the file system. *File system* is a term used to describe the logical process by which the file server manages files. Hardware used by the file system includes hard drives and host bus adapters (such as SCSI adapters). Workstations make requests for files, and the file services running on a NetWare file server respond. The file system is also involved in managing files. Part of this management process involves creating arbitrary subdivisions in the available disk space called *subdirectories.* The file system can be enhanced to provide support for different types of files. This support, referred to as *name space support,* involves loading a specialized NLM for each type of support desired. NetWare includes support for Macintosh and OS/2 file systems. With additional software, a NetWare file server can also support UNIX files using NFS (Network File System).

Chapter 24 covers how to create directories and how to manage directories and files. Chapter 25 discusses the implications and guidelines on installing applications on a NetWare file server. Chapter 26 gives you some tools with which to monitor the status of the file system.

Part Seven—Printing

This Part gives you practical techniques in setting up printing on a NetWare 4.1 network. Chapter 27 deals with the initial printing setup. Topics covered include quick printing setup, using the NWADMIN.EXE (Windows-based) utility to set up printing, starting print services, and dealing with printers directly connected to the network. Chapter 28 covers printing from DOS clients. It covers DOS-based printing utilities including CAPTURE.EXE and NPRINT.EXE. Chapter 28 also covers the utilities that enable you to specialize your printing environment: PRINTDEF.EXE, PRINTCON.EXE, PCONSOLE.EXE and PSC.EXE. Chapter 29 covers printing from Windows clients. In this chapter, you learn about printing from Windows and Windows NT clients.

Part Eight—Setting Up the User Environment

This Part focuses on setting up the user environment. Issues covered include assigning and viewing trustee rights for both the file system and the NDS. Chapter 33 covers the process of setting DOS (or OS/2 or Windows) drive letter assignments known as *drive mapping*. Chapter 34 goes into login scripts: what they are, when they are used, and what goes into a typical login script. Chapter 35 covers setting up custom user menus using NetWare 4.1's runtime version of Sabre menu and creating useful batch files.

Part Nine—Managing the File Server and the Network

In Part Nine, you learn how to manage a NetWare 4.1 file server and the network in general. This Part focuses primarily on commands and utilities that can be accessed through the file server console. It also discusses some of the NetWare Loadable Modules (NLMs) supplied with NetWare 4.1 that are used to manage and monitor the health and performance of a NetWare 4.1 file server.

Chapter 36, "Monitoring the File Server," focuses on various monitoring utilities. These include RCONSOLE, MONITOR, DSTRACE, TRACK, and CONFIG. You learn how to access the file server from another location using the RCONSOLE utility. The MONITOR utility enables you to monitor user connections and server performance. DSTRACE is used to monitor NetWare Directory Services on a file server. The TRACK utility is useful in monitoring communications between servers. The CONFIG utility gives you information on the configuration of your file server.

Chapter 37, "Making Configuration Changes," shows you how to make major (or minor) changes to the file server's environment. The INSTALL utility, which is used to make maintenance changes to the file server, is covered. Getting the latest drivers is a challenge that is discussed in this chapter. The INETCFG utility is introduced and its use in configuring network adapters is covered. Another part of this first chapter gives you pointers on managing file server hard drives and CD drives. The last part of this chapter shows you how to repair the NDS files on your file server using DSREPAIR.

Chapter 38, "Fine-Tuning the Server," discusses the several dozen SET commands that enable you to make fine adjustments to the server. By adjusting the SET parameters you can reconfigure a variety of aspects of file server operations from when it starts to compress files, to how often it collects free memory. In addition, using the SERVMAN utility to set parameters is explored along with its ability to control the filtering of network traffic.

Chapter 39, "Monitoring Network Performance," covers how to get a handle on the network in general. One of the most important tools defined and discussed in this chapter is a protocol analyzer. The accounting system also is discussed, as are other network management packages.

Chapter 40, "Auditing the Network," covers the AUDITCON utility. Network auditing enables you to monitor the usage of files, gather statistics to justify network purchases, and enhance the security of your network.

Part Ten—Backing Up, Disaster Planning, and Troubleshooting

There comes a time in the life of a network Administrator when a disaster occurs. The disaster could take many forms. In the Midwest, it might come in the form of a flood and the mud that accompanies the flood. In the East, it could be a bad storm that knocks down power lines. In the West, it could be an earthquake, damaging buildings. The disaster could be something as small as the cleaning staff chewing up network cabling or power cords with their vacuum cleaners.

The point of this section is to increase your awareness of how a disaster could impact the network and what types of preventative measures you can take to minimize the effect. Chapter 41 covers disaster planning, backups, mirroring servers (SFT III), and repairing the NDS. The Chapter 42 covers how to detect viruses and prevent them from infecting your network.

New Riders Publishing

The staff of New Riders Publishing is committed to bringing you the very best in computer reference material. Each New Riders book is the result of months of work by authors and staff who research and refine the information contained within its covers.

As part of this commitment to you, the NRP reader, New Riders invites your input. Please let us know if you enjoy this book, if you have trouble with the information and examples presented, or if you have a suggestion for the next edition.

Please note, though: New Riders staff cannot serve as a technical resource for NetWare or for related questions about software- or hardware-related problems. Please refer to the documentation that accompanies NetWare or to the applications' Help systems.

If you have a question or comment about any New Riders book, there are several ways to contact New Riders Publishing. We will respond to as many readers as we can. Your name, address, or phone number will never become part of a mailing list or be used for any purpose other than to help us continue to bring you the best books possible. You can write us at the following address:

New Riders Publishing
Attn: Associate Publisher
201 W. 103rd Street
Indianapolis, IN 46290

If you prefer, you can fax New Riders Publishing at (317) 581-4670.

You can send e-mail to New Riders from a variety of sources. NRP maintains several mailboxes organized by topic area. Mail in these mailboxes will be forwarded to the staff member who is best able to address your concerns. Substitute the appropriate mailbox name from the list below when addressing your e-mail. The mailboxes are as follows:

ADMIN	Comments and complaints for NRPs Publisher
APPS	Word, Excel, WordPerfect, other office applications
ACQ	Book proposal inquiries by potential authors
CAD	AutoCAD, 3D Studio, AutoSketch, and CAD products
DATABASE	Access, dBASE, Paradox, and other database products
GRAPHICS	CorelDRAW!, Photoshop, and other graphics products
INTERNET	Internet
NETWORK	NetWare, LANtastic, and other network-related topics
OS	MS-DOS, OS/2, all OS except UNIX and Windows
UNIX	Unix
WINDOWS	Microsoft Windows (all versions)
OTHER	Anything that doesn't fit the above categories

If you use an MHS e-mail system that routes through CompuServe, send your messages to:

mailbox @ NEWRIDER

To send NRP mail from CompuServe, use the following to address:

MHS: *mailbox* @ NEWRIDER

To send mail from the Internet, use the following address format:

mailbox@newrider.mhs.compuserve.com

NRP is an imprint of Macmillan Computer Publishing. To obtain a catalog or information, or to purchase any Macmillan Computer Publishing book, call (800)428-5331.

Thank you for selecting *Inside NetWare 4.1*!

Part I

Understanding Complex NetWorks

New Riders Publishing
INSIDE
SERIES

Elements of a Simple Network

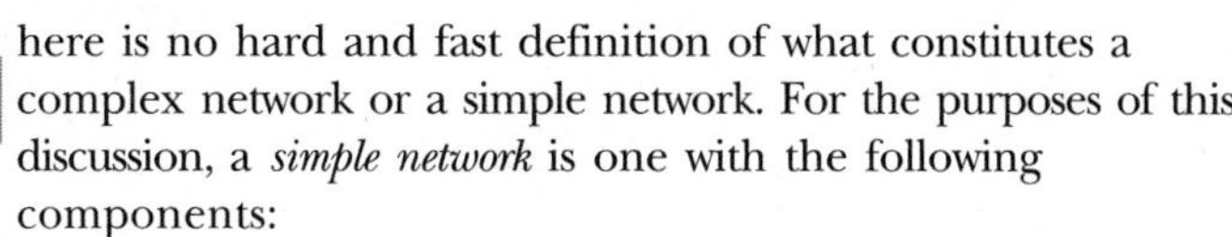

There is no hard and fast definition of what constitutes a complex network or a simple network. For the purposes of this discussion, a *simple network* is one with the following components:

- One file server
- One type of workstation (DOS-based)
- One type of network cabling (Ethernet)

Simple networks are found in small businesses and departments of large corporations around the world. This chapter examines some aspects of simple networks. This chapter will look at file servers, workstations, and network operating systems. It will also examine some of the major benefits of connecting computers together in a network. Finally, the different devices available for data storage and printing will be examined.

Introducing Client/Server Computing

The phrase *client/server computing* has been much used in the computer industry. This phrase refers to a relationship among computers that are connected together in a computer network. When one computer wants to use the resources of another computer, the computer that makes the request is referred to as the *client*. The computer that makes its resources available to the client is referred to as the *server*.

An analogy that might assist in illustrating this concept is that of a restaurant patron and a waiter. When you walk into a restaurant and sit down at a table, you become the client. The waiter, who is supposed to serve the food to you, becomes the server. You, the client, make requests. The waiter writes these requests down and takes them into the kitchen. The chef prepares the order as written. The waiter eventually retrieves the prepared food and serves it to you. A similar process occurs in a computer network. The client computer (often referred to as a *workstation*) requests a file. The server computer (in this case a *file server*) responds to the request and is responsible for searching the server's hard drive to locate the file. The server then serves the requested file to the client.

The following section discusses servers in more detail.

Servers: Providing Resources

The main job of a server is to provide resources to clients. Resources include the following:

- Disk storage
- Other online disk devices such as CD-ROM drives
- Tape backup units
- Printers
- Fax machines
- Modems

Servers are often referred to in reference to the service they provide. A server that provides access to the files on its hard drives is called a *file server*. A server that provides access to a fax machine is called a *fax server*.

A server can be a dedicated or nondedicated computer. The word *dedicated* indicates that this computer cannot be used for any other purpose. A *nondedicated* server can be used for other tasks while it is still acting as a server.

Some servers are integrated into a specialized piece of hardware. Novell markets a print server, for example, that is slightly larger than the size of an audio cassette tape. This print server has its own CPU (Central Processing Unit), its own RAM (random access memory), a parallel port to connect to a printer, and a network interface.

The server must be running some sort of software and must use a protocol to advertise its presence to the clients on the network. In the case of a file server on a Novell network, the software is called NetWare, and the protocol is called SAP (Service Advertising Protocol). Protocols are explained in more detail later in this chapter. In the case of a hardware print server, the software is often proprietary to the manufacturer and is embedded in a special memory chip known as ROM (read-only memory).

Clients: Working with Users

Client computers are often referred to as *workstations*. People who want to access network resources sit at their workstations, log in to the nearest file server, and proceed to do their work. The login process is explained in more detail in Chapter 14, "DOS Client Basics." A person who uses network resources is referred to as a *user*. The word "client" refers to the users' computers, not to the users themselves.

A client can be any of several things, such as the following:

- A computer connected to a network
- A specialized workstation (such as a Silicon Graphics workstation)
- A server temporarily acting as a client to obtain services from another server

In a typical network, a client is a computer with a network interface card (NIC) installed. The vast majority of clients in the NetWare networking world are PCs running DOS.

A *network interface card*, also called a *network adapter*, is a board that plugs into an empty slot in a PC. This adapter is then connected to the network. Using a network adapter and the NetWare client software, a user can communicate with network file servers and other network devices. For more information, refer to Chapter 3, "LANs and WANs."

Other client operating systems in a NetWare network can include the following:

- Windows NT
- UNIX

- OS/2
- Macintosh System 7

Before the client can communicate with a server, drivers that invoke the necessary protocols (such as IPX) must be loaded into memory. A DOS client requires a set of drivers collectively known as the *DOS Requester* to be loaded into memory. Once the client drivers are loaded, the client operating system sees the NetWare file server transparently. On a DOS client, for example, the NetWare file server appears as a series of additional drive letters. The local hard drive is drive C, and the file server's file system might be assigned as drive F.

Clients initially locate servers using SAP (Service Advertising Protocol). Clients access files on the server using NCP (NetWare Core Protocol) in conjunction with other protocols such as IPX (Internet Packet Exchange) and SPX (Sequenced Packet Exchange). These protocols are described in more detail in Chapter 2, "Elements of a Complex Network."

Connecting LANs at High Speed

This section looks at a LAN (local area network). The LAN is a localized version of the "information highway" that President Clinton and Vice President Gore have immortalized. A simple LAN consists of computers with NICs connected together using some sort of media. The LAN also requires a set of protocols that govern access to the LAN.

The LAN offers high-speed access to resources on remote computers. The data transfer rate of a well-tuned LAN can easily exceed that of parallel ports, or even, in certain cases, access to data on the computer's own hard drive. The final component is the network operating system, discussed in the section, "Network Operating Systems: Keeping Everything Working."

Media

The term *media* refers to the physical substance used to connect the computers on a LAN together. The most common type of media is a copper cable of some sort. Common types of copper cabling include twisted pair and coaxial. *Twisted-pair cabling* used in a LAN is similar to that used to connect your telephone to the wall outlet. Network *coaxial cabling* is similar to the cable used to connect your television set to the cable TV outlet.

Many other types of media are used to connect computer systems together in a LAN. A type of media that is fast growing in popularity is fiber optic cable. *Fiber optic* cable consists of a number of glass or high grade plastic optical strands in a tough cloth and plastic wrap. Fiber optic cables resemble coaxial cables from the outside. You might have seen fiber optic lamps in novelty stores, where colored lights are fed into optical strands, giving these lamps the appearance of having dozens of pinpoints of light. The same type of fiber optic is used in fiber optic cabling.

Another media that is gaining in popularity is no media at all. You might think that this is a strange statement to make in a book on the latest version NetWare. The types of networks using no media at all rely on network adapters that use radio waves or infrared to transmit data. Many major network vendors now offer wireless network adapters.

One way to determine whether or not a network can be classified as a simple network is that it usually uses a single type of media. When a network uses only one type of media, it is easier to troubleshoot and maintain. When you mix and match different types of media, difficulties arise. Mixed media requires a greater level of expertise and training on the part of the network support staff. When there is a problem on the LAN, the number of areas you must investigate increases exponentially.

A detailed discussion of media, along with the network adapters that make use of the media, is presented in Chapter 3, "LANs and WANs."

Protocols

A NetWare network can support many different types of protocols. According to the "Random House Dictionary," a protocol is defined as, "The customs and regulations dealing with diplomatic formality, precedence, and etiquette."

Protocols in the world of computer networking govern how computers exchange information. Protocols are designed using a layered approach. In other words, different types of functionality are assigned to different layers. All computer networks have the following basic elements in common:

- Physical and electrical (or optical) connections
- How and when any given computer can put data out onto the network
- How information is delivered from one network to another (internetworking)
- The format or appearance of the data

The OSI (Open Systems Interconnection) model is widely used in the computer networking industry to formally refer to these various layers. The OSI layers that correspond to the basic elements listed earlier are as follows:

- Physical layer
- Data link layer
- Network and transport layers
- Session, presentation, and application layers

For detailed coverage of the OSI model and the various layers, refer to the book *NetWare 4 for Professionals* (New Riders Publishing). Table 1.2 lists the various types of protocols used in a NetWare network. The IEEE (Institute of Electrical and Electronics Engineers) is a prominent organization involved in developing protocols and standards for the networking industry. Many of the protocols in the table were developed (usually based on a manufacturer's product) by the IEEE. Each of these protocols, and other important protocols such as TCP/IP, are discussed in greater detail in Chapters 2 and 3.

Table 1.2
NetWare Protocols in a Simple Network

OSI Layer	Protocol	Description
Physical and Data Link	IEEE 802.3 Ethernet	Ethernet protocol that controls how an NIC can place information on the network. This is also referred to as CSMA/CD (Carrier Sense with Multiple Access/Collision Detec tion). This protocol evolved from a type of network interface developed originally by Xerox, DEC (Digital Equipment Corporation), and Intel. One of the connectors on an Ethernet card, the DIX connector, was named after the initials of these three companies.
	IEEE 802.5 Token Ring	This protocol was developed from the Token Ring network interface developed by IBM. According to this protocol, each computer with a token ring card installed waits for a

OSI Layer	Protocol	Description
		special type of instruction known as a *token* to arrive before it can begin transmitting information across the network.
	ARCnet ANSI 878.1	This protocol was developed in the late 1970s by Datapoint Corporation. ARCnet stands for "Attached Resource Computer NETwork." This protocol proved very popular due to its robust design and extensive distance without having to introduce additional expensive hardware.
	FDDI	Fiber Distributed Digital Interface. This protocol was developed for high-speed networks using fiber-optic cable.
MAC Layer	Various 802.*x*	This layer is the bottom portion of the OSI data link layer. This layer defines how the network adapter accesses the media. The protocols defined at this layer are defined along with the specifications for the physical layer. The IEEE 802.3 specification, for example, consists of both a physical layer as well as a MAC layer specification.
Logical Link Control	IEEE 802.2	This layer, known as the LLC (logical link control), adds features that control the flow of information across the network. A high-speed file server can overwhelm a slower client with data. The LLC regulates how much data can be transmitted. The LLC also dictates what type of response is expected from a computer after receiving data.
Network and Transport Layers	IPX	Internet Packet Exchange. This Transport Layers protocol was developed from the original XNS (Xerox Network Standard) protocols as a means of regulating the

continues

Table 1.2, Continued
NetWare Protocols in a Simple Network

OSI Layer	Protocol	Description
		exchange of information from network to network (internetworking). The IPX protocol covers aspects of both the OSI network and transport layers.
Transport Layer	SPX	Sequenced Packet Exchange. This protocol was also developed from the XNS protocols. SPX is referred to as *connection-oriented,* meaning that a logical connection is established between the sending and receiving computers prior to the exchange of actual data. SPX maintains this connection throughout the transmission. This ensures high data integrity.
Session Layer	RIP	Routing Information Protocol. This protocol governs how routers exchange information in order to determine how to send a packet across an internetwork.
	NLSP	Novell has recently introduced an alternative protocol to RIP called NetWare Link State Protocol. This is backwards compatible to RIP, and can be configured on NetWare 4.1 servers and MultiProtocol Routers. NLSP offers superior routing performance and less network traffic than does RIP.
	SAP	Service Advertising Protocol. This protocol governs how servers announce their presence to the network. File servers, for example, inform clients of their availability using SAP.
Session, Presentation and Application	NCP	NetWare Core Protocol. This Presentation, protocol governs the reception of and Application data at the file server. Typical NCP requests

OSI Layer	Protocol	Description
		received from clients are requests for files and directory structure information.
	NDS	NetWare Directory Services. This protocol allows servers to coordinate services between themselves. NDS ties the LAN together, making it appear as one LAN to simplify network management. NDS provides lookup services for users of the LAN. Resources can be looked up using NDS. When a user needs to print to a certain printer, for example, NDS locates the printer and checks to see if the user is allowed to use it.

Network Operating Systems: Keeping Everything Working

The network operating system (NOS) is at the heart of the network. It consists of a software program running on one or more servers. The NOS coordinates LAN activities such as transferring files between computers and sending print jobs to network printers. NetWare 4.1 is the latest NOS offered by Novell.

The NOS is responsible for assigning and maintaining the names of network resources. NDS (NetWare Directory Services) is a tool used by NetWare 4.1 to store network resource naming information. The NOS is also responsible for the security of the network. Security is offered in the form of restricting access to the network by time or location. In addition, security can be assigned to allow or deny access to specific resources such as file server hard drives and network printers.

Sharing Programs and Data

One of the most important tasks of the NOS is to regulate access to programs and data stored on the file server's hard drive. This is known as *file sharing*. File sharing is one of the main reasons companies invest in a network. Companies save money by purchasing a single *network* version, instead of many *single-user* versions of a program. Placing data files created by the employees of a company on a file server also serves several other purposes, such as security, document control, and backup.

Documents are more secure on the file server than on individual computers. There is often limited or nonexistent security on individual computers. On the file server you will need to know a valid login name and have appropriate security rights to access a file.

Document control is critical in a company where a document could go through several revisions. In an architectural firm, for example, the design of a building might be done using a drafting program such as AutoCAD. The architects may produce several versions of the building plan as the client comes to a decision. If the plan was stored on the individual computers of each architect, at some point the firm might not know which is the most recent version of the plans. The wrong version might have a more recent date (because of a backup, for example). If the plan was saved on a file server, each architect would work on the same file. The file sharing would be regulated by the operating system.

A tape backup can be installed on the server, forming the heart of a centralized backup strategy. All files located on this (or other connected servers) can be backed up regularly. This strategy is much safer than relying on individual users to back up their workstations.

Sharing Resources

Much as file sharing allows companies greater economy, security, and integrity, other resources on the LAN can be shared. The most common example is shared printers. A graphic arts company with 20 artists, for example, can invest in one or two large, expensive printers rather than having to purchase a printer for each artist. An expensive CD-ROM unit with multiple drives (referred to as a *jukebox*) could be placed on a file server, enabling everyone in the company access to clip art.

Equipment shared on the LAN can be placed anywhere on the LAN. Printers, for example, no longer have to be placed within six feet of every computer. Printers can be placed strategically throughout the office and can be relocated as needs change.

This section covers some of the resources that can be shared on the LAN.

Communications

One of the fastest growing segments of the LAN industry is in the area of remote communications. This aspect will have increased importance with the growth of services offered by telephone and cable companies. The era of *telecommuting* is now a reality. More and more employees are able to work out of their homes. Using modems attached to home computers, shared *dial-in* resources on the network enable

remote employees to access the network as if they were in the office. This has a significant impact on the quality of life. By not having to commute to work each day, you gain productive time, decrease the stress introduced by driving in heavy traffic, and improve the environment.

Modem Servers

Modem servers or *dial-out* servers allow network users, from their workstations, to dial out to bulletin boards and remote hosts outside the office. Law firms, for example, might decide to subscribe to WestLaw, a service that maintains online documents of legal case law. The alternative is to purchase a set of books and keep them up to date. A big problem in a law firm is that there might be several people who need to access the same books at the same time. The online service not only allows multiple access to the same documents, but it also includes a search utility that allows legal researchers to quickly locate pertinent cases and to "clip" pertinent portions of the text.

There are several varieties of modem servers. Some devices consist of a software package that runs on a workstation with a modem. The software allows other network users to use the workstation's modem as if it were attached to their computer. Other workstations locate the shared modem through SAP (Service Advertising Protocol).

Some types of modem servers include software that is loaded on a file server (this software is referred to as an NLM—NetWare Loadable Module). The software regulates access to modems located on the file server itself or on remote workstations. Still other modem servers incorporate the modem, an NIC, and software in ROM, all contained in a single unit that directly connects to the network. Table 1.3 lists some of the more popular dial-out solutions.

An NLM (NetWare Loadable Module) is a name used to refer to a program that runs on a Novell NetWare file server. Most programs used on the network reside on the file server but do not run on the file server. When a user sits down at a workstation, logs into a file server, and runs a program, such as WordPerfect, the program actually runs on the workstation. The file server downloads the program to the workstation where it goes into memory and runs.

An NLM, on the other hand, is a program that runs on the file server. NLMs come in all different types. Certain NLMs are use to interface NetWare to its hardware. There are a series of NLMs used to manage the network adapters in the file server, for example. Other NLMs perform service functions. For example, you might load an NLM on the server to scan for viruses, or to monitor the battery backup unit attached to the file server.

Table 1.3
Modem Server Products List

Product	Vendor	List Price	Description
NetWare Connect	Novell	$2,495	Set of NLMs that regulate access to modems either on the file server or located on remote workstations.
NACS	Microdyne	$1,795 (8-port) $2,295 (16-port) $4,995 (32-port)	Set of NLMs that regulate access to modems either on the file server or located on remote workstations. 8- and 32-port versions enable you to set up a dedicated workstation to act as the modem server rather than tying up a file server.
Shared Access	US Robotics	$795 (single port) $1,395 (dual port)	Software package that installs on a nondedicated workstation. You can use either one or two of the workstation's serial ports (COM1 and COM2) to connect modems. The software sends SAP packets out advertising this workstation as a modem server.
LANFast Modem	UDS	$1,443 (Ethernet)	Intelligent network modem that provides dial in/out capabilities without the need for a dedicated PC. This stand-alone device connects directly to an Ethernet network.

The prices mentioned in the preceding table change frequently. Please consult your favorite computer reseller for a list of current prices.

Dial-In Servers

A dial-in server is the opposite of the dial-out server. The dial-in server enables you to dial the network from your home. Once connected through the modem, you can

then access the network as if you were using a computer in the office. All of the modem servers listed in table 1.3 have the capability to dial in. The way this works is that another workstation on the network must be running a host software package. When your home computer dials the modem server, it attempts to pass control to a host computer that uses SAP to advertise its presence. Once the host has accepted the connection, all processing is done on the host rather than on your remote computer. Your computer becomes little more than a dumb terminal. The modem server simply acts as a go-between. Figure 1.1 illustrates the use of a modem server to dial in.

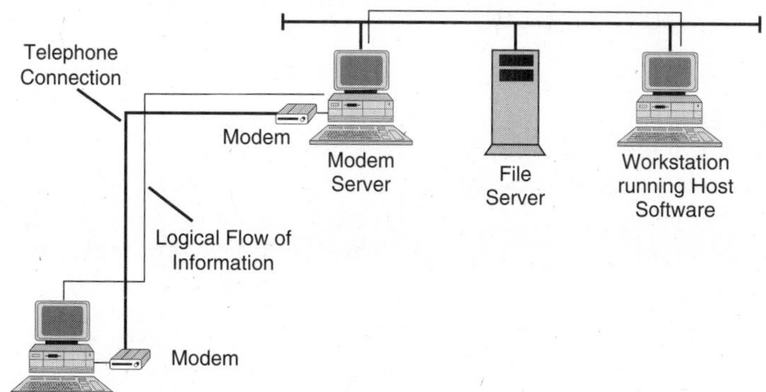

Figure 1.1

Using a modem server to dial in.

Other dial-server solutions feature either a hardware module or a software package running on a workstation. These solutions enable you to connect to the dial-in server and perform processing using the CPU of the dial-in server. As in the process described earlier, the processing is not done on your home computer. The advantage of this arrangement is that the only data traveling over the phone lines are keystrokes and screen updates.

A similar but less expensive solution is to run a software program that establishes a connection between a single home computer and a single computer in the office with a modem. The program you run at home dials in to the computer in the office and establishes a connection. The office computer is then turned into a host that performs all processing. Your home computer simply acts as a dumb terminal. This arrangement is ideal for situations where relatively few people need home access to the network. The solutions described earlier will handle dozens of dial-in users.

All solutions discussed in this section have a number of security features. Most include the capability to dial back. *Dial back* is where you program a list of user phone numbers and passwords. When a user dials in, the software consults the password, disconnects, and dials the user back. If an unauthorized user attempts to access your system, their phone number will not be dialed.

Table 1.4 lists vendors and dial-in solutions. Figure 1.2 illustrates some of these solutions.

Table 1.4
Dial-In Products List

Product	Vendor	List Price	Description
Access Server	Microdyne	$7,995 (4-port) $12,495 (8-port)	Includes a dedicated 386+ workstation. Can support up to 4 or 8 simultaneous connections. A network Administrator can monitor the status of these connections at any time.
80386 Processing Unit DX	J & L Information Systems	$2,195 $3,370	Consists of a PC on a board. The boards can plug in to an expansion chassis. 80486 Boards include highly integrated 80386 or 80486 complete computer systems. Each computer system has its own RAM and CPU. Use dial-in software (such as PC Anywhere or Carbon Copy) to enable you to access any one of the processors on any board.
Carbon Copy	Microcom	$199	This is a one remote computer to one network computer product. Your home computer, running the "Guest" software, connects to a computer in the office with its own modem running the "Host" software.
PC Anywhere	Symantec	$199	This is a one remote computer to one network computer product. Your home computer, running the "Customer" software, connects to a computer in the office with its own modem running the "Host" software.

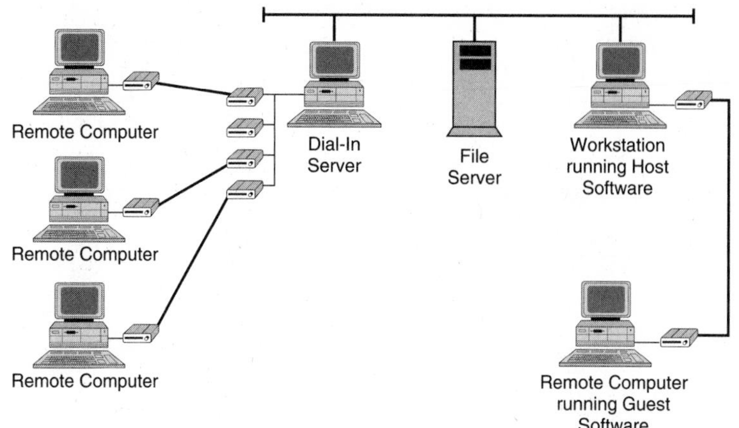

Figure 1.2

Dial-in solutions.

FAX Servers

Fax servers are very similar to dial-in and dial-out servers. These devices consist of either a software package running on a workstation equipped with a fax-modem, or an integrated hardware and NIC package. *Fax-modems* are modems with the added capability of sending and receiving fax transmissions.

Fax servers use SAP to advertise their presence to clients on the network. Special software running on the clients allows them to "print" documents across the LAN to the fax server. In the case of Windows client fax software, the fax server is identified as a printer. When you want to send a fax, you perform the same operations as you would to print the document. Instead of selecting a printer, you can select the fax server. A menu pops up asking you to supply a name and phone number.

Currently, one of the biggest problems with using a fax server for incoming messages is how to route the incoming fax to the appropriate user on the network. Many packages simply dump the incoming faxes into a common subdirectory on a host file server. An administrative assistant in the office must then sort through the incoming faxes periodically and either print and distribute them manually, or forward them (often through e-mail). Some of the more sophisticated services enable the person sending the fax to identify the e-mail address of the recipient, ensuring that the fax will arrive directly via e-mail. This is only possible, however, if your company has an e-mail gateway to the phone system, or to a public data network (such as CompuServe). A *gateway* is a software package that performs translations between dissimilar systems (such as translating between MHS e-mail, often used in Novell networks, and Profs e-mail, often used in IBM networks).

Table 1.5 lists some of the more popular fax server products.

Table 1.5
Fax Server Products List

Product	Vendor	List Price	Description
FaxPress	Castelle	$1,995 (single line) $4,295 (4 lines)	Integrated hardware solution that combines a fax-modem and NIC. Software enables administrative assistants to scan the cover page of a fax for distribution. Units are configured to handle from 1 to 4 phone lines.
MCI Mail	MCI	varies	Service offered by MCI. You can fax your document to a special number. MCI will route your fax anywhere in the world. They will either fax it directly or forward it as an e-mail message, in which case the recipient must also subscribe to the same service.

Storage

One of the most important decisions you can make when designing your network is what type of hard drive and how much disk space you need. There are many storage options available. Some options, formerly called *near-line storage,* are available immediately. Other options, often called *off-line storage,* are available after a period of time. Hard drives fall into the category of near-line storage. Tape backup or archival units fall into the off-line storage category.

The Speed/Capacity/Cost Trade-Offs

There are three classic trade-offs in computer system designs. These are as follows:

- Speed versus cost
- Speed versus capacity
- Capacity versus cost

Generally speaking, the faster the access to a storage device, the more it will cost. The second trade-off is not as straightforward. In the past, faster devices almost always had less capacity (were less dense) than slower devices. This is no longer a general rule. The last trade-off, capacity versus cost, still holds true. The more capacity a device has, the greater the cost. Table 1.6, at the end of this section, lists some of the more popular storage devices along with speed/capacity/cost information.

Speed of storage devices is measured in milliseconds (ms). A more accurate term for speed is access time. *Access time* for a hard drive, for example, is a combination of seek time and latency. *Seek time* is the time it takes the drive heads to move to the appropriate hard drive cylinder. *Latency* is the time it takes the disk to spin around to the proper sector.

Here are some common terms used in conjunction with disk drives:

- **Track.** A *track* is one of the concentric rings that logically subdivides each hard drive platter. Tracks are much like the grooves in an old style record. Previous recording technology physically cut grooves in a vinyl disk. The needle of the record player vibrated according to the depth of the grooves, which translated into sound waves. Unlike a record, however, a track on a disk platter does not spiral towards the center. Tracks remain the same distance from the center all the way around the disk platter.
- **Sector.** A *sector* is a subdivision of a track. A sector is like a slice of pie. Picture the hard drive's platter as if it were a pie. Cut rings into the pie starting at the center. Each ring would be analogous to a track. Slice the pie into pieces. Each piece is analogous to a sector.
- **Cylinder.** A *cylinder* consists of all tracks that are above or below each other. A cylinder is a logical, circular-shaped division of the hard drive. Cylinders consist of concentric ring-shaped divisions of the hard drive's platters.

Figure 1.3 illustrates these concepts.

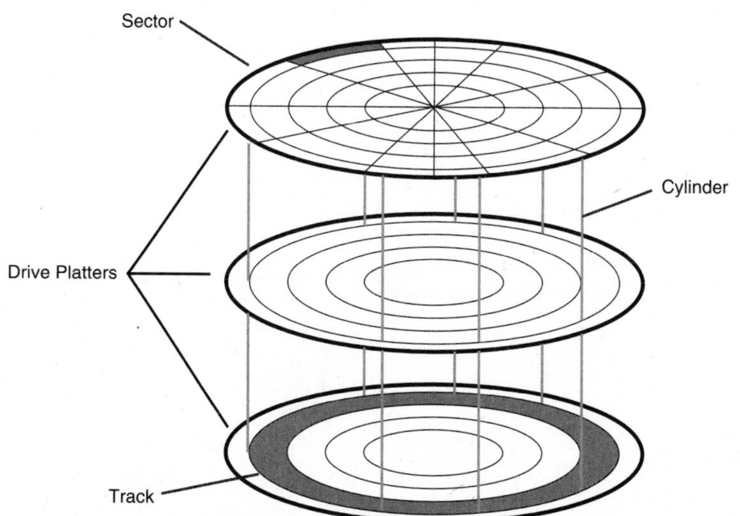

Figure 1.3

Hard drive concepts: tracks, sectors, and cylinders.

High-Speed Storage Systems

The highest speed storage is dynamic RAM (also called *DRAM*). Access time is measured in nanoseconds. The disadvantages of using RAM for storage are that it is expensive and will hold information only while electricity is applied. Current RAM prices range between $30 and $40 per MB.

The next fastest device available is the hard drive. Access time ranges from 4 to 60 milliseconds. Several different types of hard drives are available. The most popular types available now are IDE (Integrated Drive Electronics) and SCSI (Small Computer Systems Interface). Prices for IDE and SCSI drives are approximately 50 cents per MB (or less).

A nanosecond is a billionth (1/1,000,000,000) of a second. Access to disk drives is measured in milliseconds—thousandths of a second. The ratio between a nanosecond and a second is close to the ratio between a second and 32 years!

IDE Drives

IDE drives are fast and inexpensive. The electronics necessary to control the drive are integrated into the chassis of the drive itself. They are not fully standardized, so you might have difficulty putting drives of different vendors in the same computer. Most vendors of IDE drives have agreed on certain specifications, one of which limits the size of an IDE drive to 528 MB. Almost all IDE vendors plan to introduce models that exceed this limit. Because DOS and NetWare were written respecting the 528 MB limit, you have to use additional drivers provided by the vendors in the case of large IDE drives.

Another limitation of IDE drives has to do with how their controllers operate when more than one drive is placed in the same computer. IDE drives need additional supporting circuitry to operate inside a PC. This circuitry comes in two forms: a paddleboard (sometimes referred to as an IDE *controller*), or an integrated controller. The *paddleboard* is an inexpensive card that plugs into an expansion slot of a computer. The *integrated controller* is built into the motherboard of the computer.

Each paddleboard or controller can manage up to two IDE drives. You can have up to two paddleboards or controllers per computer, giving you a maximum total of four IDE drives. When you place more than one IDE drive in a computer, the electronics built into the drive chains itself to the first drive. Because of this arrangement, if the first drive were to fail, all drives chained to it would also fail. This problem negates the fail-safe mirroring you can set up in a NetWare file server. For more information on mirroring, please refer to Chapter 4, "Traditional Features of NetWare."

SCSI Technology

SCSI technology is not limited to hard drives. A number of devices use SCSI technology to communicate with the computer. SCSI devices include hard drives, tape drives, CD-ROM drives, and a number of other more esoteric devices beyond the scope of this book.

SCSI drives do not suffer from the drive-chaining problem mentioned in the previous section. Most SCSI drives, much like IDE drives, feature an *embedded SCSI controller.* The embedded controller consists of the circuitry needed to control the drive. A separate SCSI controller that plugs into an expansion slot in the computer is necessary to control SCSI devices. You create a SCSI bus when you daisy-chain several SCSI devices together and connect them to the SCSI controller in the PC. SCSI drives can be placed inside the computer or in an external box called an *expansion chassis.* Each SCSI controller inside a PC can control up to seven SCSI devices. Most computers will handle up to four SCSI controllers.

An extension to SCSI technology is what is known as RAID, which stands for Redundant Array of Inexpensive Devices. RAID technology chains SCSI drives together so that they function as a single unit. There are various levels of protection and performance available. A more detailed discussion of this technology is covered in Chapter 11, "Hardware Configuration."

CD-ROM

CD-ROM (Compact Disc-Read Only Memory) drives will not record data. These units will play back CDs programmed by the vendor. CDs are an efficient way to distribute large amounts of data. Most operating system vendors now ship their operating systems on CD. Novell, for example, ships NetWare 3.12, NetWare 4.1, and UnixWare on CD. Multimedia products, which feature software, sound, and graphics (sometimes full motion video clips), also ship on CD.

CD-ROM drives are much slower than hard drives. Typical access times range from 200 to 400 ms. This makes a CD-ROM drive 10 to 100 times slower than a typical hard drive. Capacity of a CD hovers between 500 MB and 1 GB (gigabyte, or 1 billion bytes). Most CD-ROM drives supported by NetWare are SCSI devices. You can attach them to a SCSI controller in the file server. CD-ROM drives can be daisy-chained to other drives. NetWare 4.1 has special drivers and procedures to provide access to CD-ROM drives. This is described in more detail in Chapter 11, "Hardware Configuration," in the section titled "Installing Server Peripherals."

WORM

WORM (write-once, read-many) drives are gaining in popularity as archival storage devices. Average access time is 200 ms, and capacity is currently around 1 GB. WORM drives are CD-ROM drives that can be written to one time only. Once written, they can be read but not rerecorded. Although this limits their use as online media, they are excellent for the purposes of archiving data or storing information such as the company's accounts for the last several years.

When writing information to the drive, the laser built into the drive head literally burns the new pattern onto the disk. Information is written to the disk one sector at a time until all sectors on the disk have been used. Information does not have to be written in one session. You could stretch the use of a single disk over several days, weeks, or months as needed.

Rewritable Optical

Some optical disk units enable you to both read and write. The most popular of such technologies is the *magneto-optical* drive. This drive has a read/write mechanism with both optical and magnetic heads. Typical access time of such devices is 100+ ms. The capacity is currently in the area of 650 MB.

Figure 1.4 illustrates the workings of the read/write mechanism. The disk is composed of a heat-sensitive magnetic material. When you want to write data to the disk, the laser heats the disk at the desired location. The magnetic head then changes the polarity of that location on the disk, thus changing it from a 1 to a 0 or the reverse.

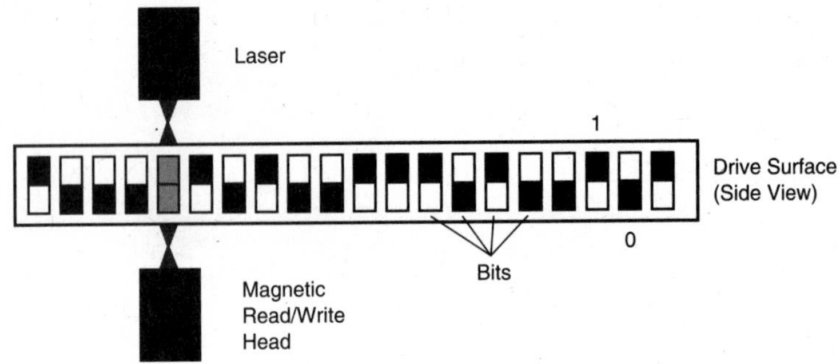

Figure 1.4

A magneto-optical drive read/write mechanism.

Other Removable Media

Several types of removable media are available. CDs, WORM disks, and magneto-optical disks fall into this category. Other sorts of removable media are variations of hard disk technology. There are two types of removable hard drive systems currently available. One technology, originally introduced as the Bernoulli hard drive system, featured a removable hard disk cartridge. The cartridges were almost twice the size of a VHS video tape. They plugged into a drive bay and originally furnished 20 MB of disk space per cartridge. This technology continues to be available, with the cartridges getting smaller and the capacity increasing.

In the other type of removable hard drive system, the cartridge is a completely self-contained hard drive. Systems typically feature IDE drive units that plug into a drive bay. The *drive bay* is little more than a connector that gains the drive access to the main bus of the computer. Access time and capacity match that of any other IDE drive.

TABLE 1.6
Sample Storage Products List

Product	Vendor	List Price	Average Access Speed	Capacity	Description
ST-11200N	Seagate	$1,195	12 ms	1.05 GB	Internal Fast SCSI-2 hard drive
LANstor 2Fast	Storage Dimensions	$2,085	9.5 ms	1.6 GB	32-bit EISA SCSI hard drive external storage subsystem
RAIDion Disk Array	Micropolis	$8,985	10 ms	2.7 GB	RAID 5 disk subsystem. Contains three 1.34 GB SCSI drives. Does not include SCSI adapter, which would plug into the file server.
External SCSI CD ROM Drive	Micro Designs International	$845	200 ms	600+ MB	CD-ROM drive
Internal SCSI WORM Drive	Micro Designs International	$2,495	200 ms	940 MB	WORM drive
—	HP, Teac, IBM, Panasonic Maxoptic	$1,500 (avg)	35-400 ms	128 MB to 1.3 GB	Magneto-Optical Drive
—	Syquest, Bernoulli	$500 (avg)	—	44-105 MB	Removable disk pack technology

Tape Backup Units

Tape backup units have the largest capacity of all devices discussed so far, but the slowest access speed. There are many different types of tape units, each of which is designed around a different type of tape. Most vendors also offer a tape unit that accommodates multiple tapes. These are referred to as *auto-loaders*.

The various types of tape backup units are summarized in table 1.7.

TABLE 1.7
Types of Tape Drives

Type of Tape	List Price Range	Vendors	Capacity	Description
DAT	$1,995 to $3,520	Emerald, Conner (ex-Maynard)	2-8 GB	Digital Audio Tape. Tape cartridges are approximately half the size of a standard audio cassette. The width of the tape is 4 mm.
8 mm	$7,495 to $9,495	Emerald, Conner	2-10 GB	8 mm tape units use a tape cartridge identical to that used in 8 mm video camcorders.
QIC	$495 to $2,120	Emerald, Conner, Colorado	250 MB to 4 GB	Quarter Inch Cartridge. The tape in one of these cartridges is 1/4" wide. The cartridge is almost the size of a VHS video tape. This is an older technology.

Network Printing

In one sense, the printed output from a network printer is the only tangible product of the network. Users want to log in to the network, do their work, and produce some sort of document, chart, graph, or other printed output. The printed page is generally what upper management sees, not the day-to-day workings of the network. As a result, an easy-to-use, fail-safe printing environment is essential to the existence of the network (and possibly the job of the network Administrator).

There are several types of printers available, and several ways in which these printers can be attached to the network. Chapter 4, "Traditional Features of NetWare," covers how to connect the printer to the network in the section titled" NetWare Printing." This section focuses on some of the different types of printers and where they might be used in your company.

Printers vary in speed, how the printed image is produced, the quality of the image, what type of paper is used, and, of course, cost. A printer's speed is measured in either cps (characters per second) or ppm (pages per minute). The image quality is measured in points or DPI (dots per square inch). A *point* is a term used in typesetting graphics to indicate the smallest dot of ink the printer can produce. The more dots per square inch the machine can produce, the higher the quality or resolution of the image.

Another measurement often used to categorize printer speed is *lines per minute.* This is a measurement often used with dot-matrix or line printers. This measurement has fallen into disuse with the rise in popularity of graphically oriented applications. A document produced in a Windows based word processing application, for example, is actually printed as a graphical image rather than as a stream of words and letters. Most Windows based programs use bitmapped graphics rather than a computer's built in character set. Bitmapped graphics refer to the way in which characters are defined as tiny images consisting of a varying number of bits. The size and printing density of a bit mapped image can vary widely depending on its size, the type of font, whether or not it is **boldfaced** or in *italics,* and so forth. Lines per minute was used when measuring the speed of older style printers where print jobs used evenly spaced characters.

Some of the devices used to physically produce the printed image include the following:

- Daisywheel printers
- Dot-matrix printers
- Thermal printers
- Laser printers
- Inkjet printers
- Line (or band) printers
- Bubble jet printers
- Plotters

Daisywheel printers were introduced in the early 1970s as an extension of electric typewriter technology. The *daisywheel* was named because if you look at it straight on, it has "spokes" somewhat like the petals of a daisy. The daisywheel is mounted on a print head that rotates the wheel to the proper letter under computer control. A pin inside the head pushes against the spoke containing the proper letter. The spoke presses against a ribbon that creates an image on the page. Daisywheel printers are slow and noisy compared to other technologies. The image quality is that of a typewriter, however, which caused daisywheel printers to be popular until laser printer technology matured.

Dot-matrix printers fire a row of pins in patterns against a ribbon that in turn produces an image on paper. Dot-matrix printers are the workhorses of the computer industry. The quality of the image rivals that of low-end laser printers, as does their speed. Relatively inexpensive, dot-matrix printers are typically equipped to handle tractor feed paper that comes in boxes of several thousand sheets. Tractor feed paper has holes at regular intervals on either side of the paper. Modern tractor feed paper features laser perforations that enable you to detach the strips on either side of the page, leaving paper that looks almost as good as standard typing paper. The disadvantages of dot-matrix printers are the noise produced by the print head, limits on speed, and limitations on print quality based on the physical size and arrangement of the pins.

Thermal printers, in contrast to dot-matrix printers, are whisper silent. The image is produced by applying heat to heat-sensitive paper. The technology first appeared in tiny printers that were attached to early calculators. Later this technology reappeared in fax machines. The main disadvantage to thermal printers is that you need special heat-sensitive paper, which does not age well and is expensive. A recent entry into this type of technology is a printer that places tiny multicolored dots of wax onto the paper. The wax dots melt into each other, forming a continuous image whose quality rivals that of a painting.

Laser printers use plain paper copier technology. The laser printer features a paper tray that holds standard typing or copier paper. A feeder mechanism pulls the paper out of the tray one sheet at a time. A laser inside a large cylinder, known as a *drum,* etches an image on the outside of the drum. Toner, a powdery substance, is attracted to the sheet of paper resting against the drum. The toner temporarily adheres to the paper according to the patterns etched by the laser. The paper, with toner, moves by a fusing area that heats the toner, causing it to melt onto the paper.

Laser printer technology has caught the purse strings of the computer industry. Laser printers can create any image that can be etched by a tiny laser. The speed of the printer is limited by how fast paper can be fed through the system. The main disadvantage to laser printers is that they are not capable of printing on multiple part forms. To get around this disadvantage, software publishers have created software that prints the entire form.

Inkjet printers spray a fine jet of ink in patterns onto the paper. Typical inkjet printers have a special cartridge that contains both the ink and the print head. Inkjet printers are quiet, fast, and inexpensive, with quality rivaling that of laser printers. As you will see when examining table 1.8, however, these printers are neither as fast as laser printers, nor is the quality quite as good. As with laser printers, inkjet printers cannot print on multiple part forms. Inkjet printers are excellent choices for the office workhorse, however, and are slowly replacing dot-matrix printers.

Line (or *band*) *printers* feature variations on dot-matrix technology. These are ultra high speed printers whose speed is measured in lines per minute. Line printers typically feature some combination of multiple tractor mechanisms to pull the paper through faster, multiple print heads, or a large array of print heads (a "band").

Bubble jet printers feature print heads with tiny tubes arranged in patterns much like the pins in a dot-matrix print head. Initially, the tubes are filled with ink. The tubes are selectively heated, which causes a bubble to form. Eventually the bubble bursts, causing a tiny drop of hot ink to spray onto the paper. The vacuum created by the departing ink refills the tube. Because the ink is hot, it dries quickly, minimizing the tendency of ink to bleed on the paper. Bubble jet technology has advantages and disadvantages over the other technologies. The image produced is better than that produced by an ink jet printer, but not quite as good as a laser printer. Bubble jet printers are quiet, but are slower than inkjet printers. As with inkjet printers, bubble jet printers can print on plain paper but not multiple part forms.

Plotters feature a rack of different colored pens that a mechanical arm moves horizontally back and forth across the paper. Another mechanism moves the paper vertically. Between the two mechanisms, any type of line can be drawn, from straight lines to smooth circles. Plotters are typically large scale and are designed to work with blueprint-sized paper. The images produced are of excellent quality. Plotters suffer from slow speed compared to other technologies, however.

Table 1.8 lists the different printer technologies along with their features. The figures listed in this table are averages based on a sample of printers of each type.

Table 1.8
Printing Technology—Average Figures

Method	Speed	Image Quality	Cost	Type of Paper	Vendors
Dot-matrix	311 cps	300 dpi	$370	Single Sheets, Tractor Feed, Multiple Part Forms	Epson, Star Micronics, Panasonic

continues

Table 1.8, Continued
Printing Technology—Average Figures

Method	Speed	Image Quality	Cost	Type of Paper	Vendors
Laser	12 ppm	300-1200	$3,620 dpi	Single Sheets	Hewlett Packard, Canon, Panasonic, Alps, Epson
Inkjet	180 cps	330 dpi	$320	Single Sheets	Hewlett Packard, Epson
Line/Band	372 lpm	N/A	$4,100	Tractor Feed	Alps, Output Technologies, CIE America
Bubble Jet	110 cps	360 dpi	$400	Single Sheets	Canon
Plotter	N/A	N/A	$2,500	Blueprint Paper	Calcomp, Houston Instruments, Hewlett Packard

Legend:

lpm Lines per minute

cps Characters per second

ppm Pages per minute

dpi Dots per square inch

How Network Printing Works

Network printing differs from local printing in the following two respects:

- A print job is first sent to a print queue on a NetWare file server.
- A print server redirects the job from the queue to a network printer.

The *print queue* is a subdirectory on one of the file server's hard drives that holds print jobs in the form of a file. When the job has been collected, or the signal to "time out" has occurred, the job is released to the print server.

The *print server* acts as a kind of printing traffic cop. The print server polls the print queue to see if there are any jobs ready for service. Ready jobs are received from the queue and redirected to a network printer.

While the job is in the print queue, the user who originated the job, or a network Administrator designated as a *print queue operator,* can put a hold on the job, change its priority in the queue, cause it to print at a later time, or remove the job from the queue. A network Administrator designated as a *print server operator* can similarly manage the print server. This person can start or stop printers, cancel jobs that the printer is servicing, redirect the printer to another queue, or "rewind" the printer so that information that did not print properly for some reason can be reprinted.

Figures 1.5, 1.6, and 1.7 illustrate the various ways a print job can be sent from the application program running at the user's workstation to a network printer. You will note that the network printer could be attached directly to the network, attached to another user's workstation, or attached to a file server.

In figure 1.5, a print job originates at a workstation and is sent to a print queue on the file server (1). The print server redirects the job from the queue (2) to a printer on the file server(3).

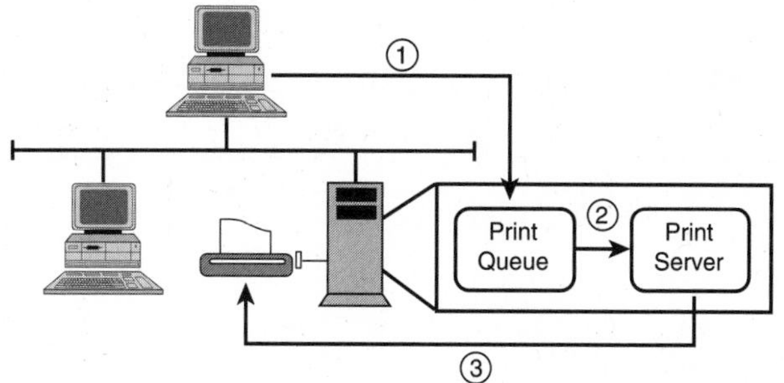

Figure 1.5

Sending a print job to a printer on a file server.

In figure 1.6, a print job originates at a workstation and is sent to a print queue on the file server (1). The print server redirects the job from the queue (2) to a workstation on the network (3). This workstation is running special software that makes its printer available to the LAN. The job is then sent, through the workstation, to its printer (4).

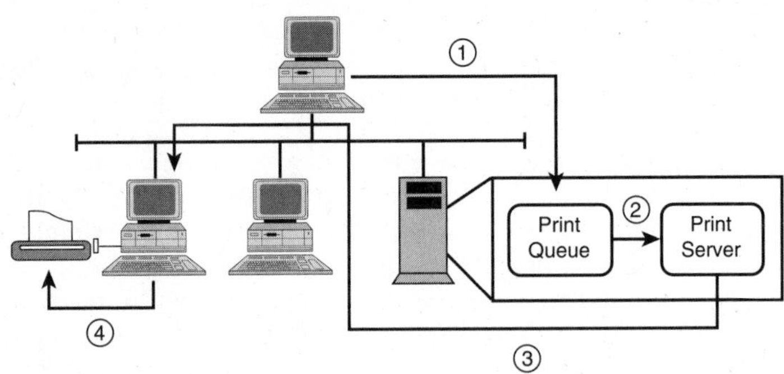

Figure 1.6

Sending a print job to a printer on a workstation.

In figure 1.7, a print job originates at a workstation and is sent to a print queue on the file server (1). The print server redirects the job from the queue (2) to a printer directly attached to the network (3).

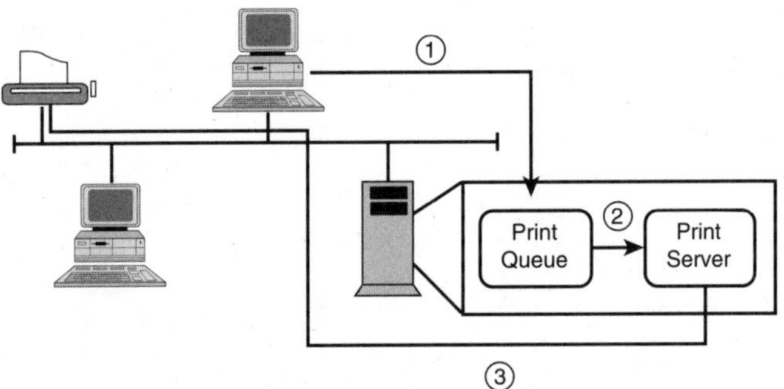

Figure 1.7

Sending a print job to a printer on the network.

Another important element of network printing is the software that redirects the printing from the local printer port on a workstation to the network print queue. This process is often referred to as *print capture.* Workstation software can be configured to "capture" print requests which are normally routed to a workstation's local printer port. The software involved in this process in a NetWare network is the *NetWare DOS Requester.*

Chapter 27, "Setting Up Printing," shows you how to set up and manage network printing. Chapter 28, "Printing from DOS Clients," shows you how to configure the NetWare DOS Requester software for printing.

Network Management

One of the major differences between simple and complex networks is the amount of management required. One of the primary advantages offered by NetWare 4.1 is its ease of management. This is accomplished through a mechanism known as *NDS* (NetWare Directory Services). In a simple network with a single file server, network management is very easy. When you need to make a change to a user's network environment, all you need to do is to login to the server and make the needed changes.

In a complex network, however, where you have multiple servers, management can be very difficult. Earlier versions of NetWare required that you make the changes for every server individually. This could entail quite a bit of work. If you need to change the access rights for a user in a network of 10 file servers, for example, you would have to login to each server individually to make the change. In NetWare 4.0, the NDS was introduced. The NDS is a distributed management database, pieces of which can reside on every server. If a server does not have a portion of the NDS database, it knows to consult a server that does have the relevant information.

Using NDS administration tools you can add network resources into areas of the NDS known as *Organizations* and *Organizational Units.* Network resources are called *leaf objects* and can include users, groups of users, file servers, file server hard drives, printers, print queues, and among other items. Organizations and Organizational units are also NDS objects referred to as *container objects.* The entire collection of container objects and leaf objects is known as a *tree.* (Evidently, someone at Novell was really into gardening.)

Container objects are much like subdirectories of a hard drive. Leaf objects are much like files. You can place all your files into a single directory. In the NDS you can place all network resource objects into a single organization container object. Alternatively, in DOS, you can subdivide your hard drive into subdirectories and place groups of similar files into appropriate subdirectories. You can divide up the NDS tree into a hierarchy of container objects, each with a number of leaf objects. (Yes, you guessed it, these are called *branches.*)

In contrast to earlier versions of NetWare, making changes to a network of 10 NetWare 4.*x* servers is no more difficult than making changes to a network of 100 NetWare 4.*x* servers. When you need to add a user to each server, you simply add the user to the tree. Because the tree is automatically distributed to each server, you have effectively added the user to each server.

You learn about the NDS, trees, container objects and leaf objects in more detail in Chapter 6, "NetWare Directory Services."

Summary

This chapter gave you an overview of the elements of a simple network. The beginning of the chapter gave you an idea of what the client/server relationship entails. As you discovered, one of the main reasons to install a LAN is to provide the ability of network users to share devices. You then read about the various devices used in a LAN, such as hard drives, printers, and communications devices. Network printing and printer technology was discussed. You were also given a brief exposure to the concepts behind managing a NetWare 4.*x* network: the NDS (NetWare Directory Services).

Elements of a Complex Network

Now that you have had a chance to examine the elements of a simple network, it's time to look at a complex network. As you learned in the Chapter 1, there is no clear boundary between simple and complex networks. For the purposes of this book, a *complex network* is one where any or all of the following elements are present:

- More than one file server
- Multiple protocols
- More than one LAN

A complex network consists of a series of simple networks connected together. This chapter will give you an overview of some of the devices used to connect LANs together. In addition, the impact of multiple file servers on the LAN and the use of different protocols will be covered.

Working with Multiple File Servers

Computer networks have a tendency to grow in size. Eventually, due to a number of factors, you will need to decide when to add another file server. This chapter first looks at why you would want to add additional file servers, and then examines the impact of multiple file servers on the network.

When To Add Another File Server

Several tools are available to monitor the performance of your file server and the network. These are discussed in Part Nine, "Managing the File Server and the Network." One of the tools discussed is MONITOR.NLM.

Although these tools and many more are available for you to use, the first warning that you might need to add an additional server will come from your users. People who use and depend on the network on a daily basis become extremely sensitive to its performance. When it takes longer than usual for them to access a file or send out a print job, you will be notified rather quickly.

Once you have determined that performance has dropped below a level acceptable to the network users, you have several options, one of which is to add an additional server. Before you do so, consider other sorts of remedial action. Other actions to take include the following:

- Upgrade file server components, including hard drives and NICs, to improve speed.
- Add additional network cards to the server and split up your network.
- Add additional RAM to the file server (improves file caching performance).
- Tune certain file server parameters using SERVMAN.NLM.

Additional details are available in Part Nine. If none of these actions yield better performance, you might want to consider adding another file server.

The Impact of Multiple File Servers

Several things take place when you add an additional file server to the network. First of all, you need to decide whether to add the new server to your existing NDS tree. If you decide to add it to the existing tree, you need to decide where in the tree to place the server.

Once the new server has been installed and positioned in the NDS tree, you need to make some administrative decisions. Adding a new file server has some similarities to adding a new hard drive to a DOS PC. You must decide which programs and files to move over to the new file server. You also have to modify login scripts, batch files and menu programs, and assign security rights.

Each server on the network adds administrative traffic to the network. The servers communicate NDS and SAP information between themselves. In addition, you will need to decide which servers are to provide time-synchronization information to the other servers.

Note *NDS*, as introduced in Chapter 1, stands for *NetWare Directory Services*. This is a distributed database which is used for network management.

SAP, discussed later in this chapter, stands for *Service Advertising Protocol*.

Time synchronization is a process used by NetWare 4.*x* file servers that participate in an NDS tree by which precise time is maintained across the network.

Geographic Considerations

In a complex network, geographic considerations can cause you to add additional file servers. If your company has offices in New York and Los Angeles, for example, it would be more efficient to have a server in each location. The local server would provide NDS information to users in that office. In addition, the programs and data needed by users in that office would be readily accessible. The two networks could be connected using dedicated lines so that file transfers and e-mail could occur between the two offices.

A *dedicated line* is a high-speed special line provided by the phone company. AT&T, Sprint, MCI, and local phone companies can provide you with a wide variety of phone lines to suit wide area network connectivity needs. These vary in the amount of data that can be transmitted per second, quality and integrity of the line, and cost. Data transfer rates for such lines vary from 1,200 bits per second all the way up to 45 million bits per second.

Understanding Multiple Protocols

Complex networks must suit the needs of their users. In a large company, the needs of its employees might not be met using a single workstation or network platform. In many companies, DOS-based clients and NetWare servers are all that is needed. In other companies this is not the case. A company that has been established for 15 years, for example, might have purchased many different types of data processing equipment over the years. The company might have started with a UNIX-based minicomputer. As the company developed, it could have upgraded its equipment, adding desktop PCs and finally LANs.

Other situations arise when companies merge. A computer games company primarily using Macintosh computers might have been acquired by a graphic design company using OS/2-based computers. In situations such as these, knowledge of different types of client operating systems and different protocols is essential.

This section examines different communications protocols, starting with the "native" NetWare protocols IPX and SPX. In reference to the OSI model mentioned in Chapter 1, these protocols operate at the network and transport layers. A discussion of different desktop operating systems takes place in Part Four, "Activating and Using Clients."

The IPX/SPX Protocol

As mentioned in Chapter 1, IPX stands for Internet Packet Exchange, and SPX stands for Sequenced Packet Exchange. These protocols evolved from the XNS (Xerox Network System) protocols.

The primary job of IPX is to provide a way of transmitting information across an internetwork. An *internetwork* is where there is more than one physical LAN. An example of a single physical LAN is the Ethernet network pictured in figure 2.1.

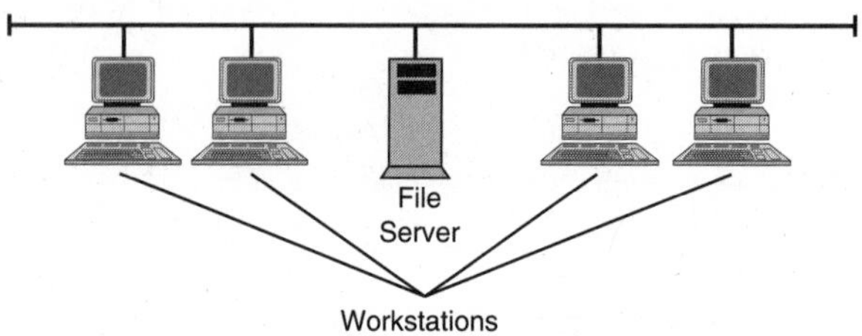

Figure 2.1
A single physical Ethernet LAN.

The various LANs are connected together in an internetwork using what is called a *router. External* routers are stand-alone units whose sole purpose is to route network information from one LAN to another. *Internal* routers use the NetWare file server's built-in routing capabilities to connect separate LANs together. Figure 2.2 illustrates an internetwork using routers. Routers are discussed in greater detail at the end of this chapter.

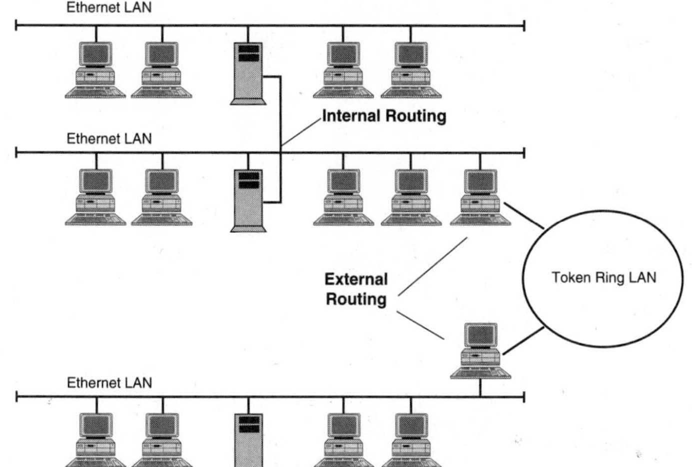

Figure 2.2
LANs joined in an internetwork using routing.

The IPX and SPX protocols are built into the NetWare operating system. The protocols simply need to be assigned to a network interface card. This is done at the server using the BIND statement. This is covered in greater detail in Chapter 12, "Installing the Network Operating System." At the client, IPX and SPX are enabled by loading a series of drivers. Once installed, the IPX and SPX protocols become transparent to the user. IPX carries information across the internetwork, across routers, and between clients and servers.

IPX is a way of packaging information traveling across the network. If Sue needs to save a file she has created on her workstation, for example, she simply designates a drive letter and directory assigned to her file server. The workstation IPX/SPX software breaks her file into smaller units known as *packets.* Each packet holds an initial header that identifies Sue's workstation as the source of the transmission and her file server as the destination. Following the IPX/SPX header is a portion of the original file.

The packets are transmitted out through the NIC in Sue's workstation across the LAN. Any routers between Sue and her file server will relay the packet, updating the IPX/SPX header if necessary. Finally, the packets arrive at Sue's file server. The packets are collected one-by-one and reassembled back into the original file. The file server then takes care of storing the file on its hard drive.

AppleTalk

AppleTalk protocols were first introduced in 1984 with the Apple Macintosh. These protocols were developed by the software engineers at Apple, Inc. AppleTalk itself is a comprehensive set of protocols governing the exchange of information between

Macintosh computers. It was originally designed for occasional file and printer sharing. AppleTalk has now gone through Phase II, which added several enhancements to the original AppleTalk protocols. The enhancements pertinent to this discussion add the capability of using Ethernet and token ring NICs in a Macintosh.

When placing Macintoshes on a Novell network, the first consideration is what type of NIC you are using. If your network uses Ethernet, you must install an Ethernet NIC in the Macintosh. Likewise, if you are using token ring, you must install a token ring NIC in the Macintosh. If you decide, for some reason, to use the built-in Macintosh network interface, you must place the Macintoshes on a separate LAN and use a router to connect them to the rest of the network. The built-in Macintosh network interface is known as *LocalTalk*.

One common misconception is that because the Macintosh uses a different set of protocols and a different operating system than DOS-based PCs, the Macintoshes must be on a separate physical LAN. Although you can set up your network in this manner, you can also place the Macintoshes on the same physical LAN as other computers, provided they all use the same type of NIC.

Ethernet NICs communicate with each other electronically regardless of which protocol is running at the upper layers. Ethernet is standardized to the point that an Ethernet NIC from one vendor will communicate with the Ethernet NIC of another vendor. The information that is physically traveling on an Ethernet LAN is in an Ethernet format. It is not until it arrives at the destination computer that the protocols being discussed in this section come into play.

Once you have installed the appropriate NICs and have connected the Macintoshes to the network, you must make provisions for translating the AppleTalk protocols into a format understandable to the NetWare file server. This is accomplished by installing a set of NLMs on the file server collectively known as *NetWare for Macintosh*. NetWare for Macintosh software comes standard with NetWare 4.1.

NetWare for Macintosh makes the Novell network appear as if it were an AppleTalk network to the Macintosh. The file server appears as an AppleShare server. AppleShare and AppleTalk are part of the original networking scheme defined on the original Macintosh and are continued in the present-day Macintosh computers. Directories on the file server's hard drive appear as Macintosh folders. Files appear as icons. The NetWare for Macintosh software allows the Macintosh user to print to a NetWare print queue.

TCP/IP

The Internet Protocol Suite is often referred to as TCP/IP (Transmission Control Protocol/Internet Protocol), after two of its most popular protocols. This protocol was developed by a number of organizations at the behest of the U.S. Government Department of Defense (DoD). Almost every major vendor of computer hardware and software has some sort of implementation of TCP/IP. This section gives a brief background of this set of protocols and where they fit into a Novell network.

History and Background of TCP/IP

TCP/IP was first introduced in the 1970s primarily to control the diverse systems of the DoD. At the time, the DoD had many different types of computer systems—most of which were not able to communicate between each other.

The suite was developed by a series of organizations and institutions, including the University of California at Berkeley and the Massachusetts Institute of Technology. By the early 1980s, the DoD had converted most of its systems to TCP/IP.

Along the way, the institutions, universities, and private companies involved in the development of the suite converted to TCP/IP themselves. These organizations eventually joined their networks together and thus formed the Internet. The *Internet* is a network of networks. It consists of a multitude of overlapping computer systems and networks. These systems are joined through a hodgepodge of phone connections, direct cabling, routers, and host computers. Computer systems on the Internet range from mainframes to minicomputers to microcomputer networks. At last count there were over 2 million systems connected together on the Internet.

In the early 1980s, a group of Univerisity of California at Berkeley graduates formed their own company, known as Berkeley Software Distribution (BSD). This company wrote the TCP/IP protocols into UNIX, which at the time was public domain. This spawned an extremely popular branch of UNIX called BSD UNIX. Since that time, most versions of UNIX use TCP/IP as their LAN protocol. Most major vendors offer TCP/IP implementations as well. These include, for example, Digital Equipment Corporation (DEC), Hewlett Packard, and IBM.

TCP/IP Protocol Basics

The TCP/IP Protocol Suite consists of a number of specifications. It is the job of the vendor to create a specific implementation of these specifications. This section provides a brief overview of some of the more important specifications and what you might expect from a vendor.

The TCP/IP specification that most closely matches IPX is a combination of two specifications: UDP (User Datagram Protocol) and IP (Internet Protocol). The IP protocol controls the transmission of data across an internetwork. It features routing protocols that allow IP packets to cross routers on the way to the receiving computer system. Each computer in a TCP/IP network is assigned an *IP address.* An IP address has four numbers separated by decimal points. An example of an IP address is 130.57.22.102.

UDP operates at the next layer above IP. This protocol was designed for speed. Information in the UDP header simply identifies the source and destination software of the next layer.

TCP (Transmission Control Protocol) operates at the same layer as UDP. This protocol corresponds to SPX in the NetWare environment. TCP maintains a logical connection between the sending and receiving computer systems. In this way, the integrity of the transmission is maintained. TCP detects any problems in the transmission quickly and takes action to correct the problem. The trade-off is that TCP is not as fast as UDP.

Higher-level protocols that are included in the TCP/IP Protocol Suite include *Telnet* and *FTP*. These two protocols are used extensively by TCP/IP users. Telnet (Terminal Emulation/Network) is a generic terminal emulation specification used on dumb terminals or workstations. This specification allows users to log in to a TCP/IP-based system no matter what type of hardware they are using.

FTP (File Transfer Protocol) is used to transfer files between systems. It contains a generic set of commands that allows users to view the contents of remote hard drives (referred to as *file systems*) and copy files back and forth. The beauty of FTP is that it can transfer files between *any* computer system that has a standard implementation of the TCP/IP Protocol Suite.

NetWare TCP/IP and Other Products

TCP/IP in the NetWare environment takes the form of a set of NLMs that can be loaded onto a file server. By setting up this environment, the file server can integrate into an existing TCP/IP network complete with an IP address. The NLMs that come standard with NetWare only enable the server to act as an IP router. Workstation software must be purchased separately.

Additional software is required if you want to access resources on the file server using TCP/IP. Two packages available from Novell enable you to transfer files using FTP and to print in either direction. These packages are Flex/IP and NetWare NFS. NetWare NFS also enables you to access the NetWare file server's hard drive directly using the UNIX mount protocol and the TCP/IP Remote Procedure Call (RPC) mechanism. The mount protocol makes the disk drives of the server appear as an extension to the directory structure of a remote UNIX (or other TCP/IP-based) system. RPC allows your remote system to perform actions on the NetWare server as if it were your own. Actions can include adjusting security rights and otherwise managing files and directories on the NetWare server.

Novell offers DOS, Windows, or Macintosh client software in the form of the LAN Workplace for DOS/Windows/Macintosh product line. This software enables clients to send and receive TCP/IP information using Telnet and FTP.

Understanding the OSI Reference Model

Open Systems Interconnection (OSI) is an organization under the auspices of the United Nations. This organization is responsible for producing standards for connecting dissimilar computer systems. It produced the OSI reference model used in the industry to compare different protocols. A detailed explanation of the OSI model is beyond the scope of this book. To properly configure file servers and workstations, a brief explanation of the workings of this model is necessary. This is especially true in an environment where there are mixed protocols (such as NetWare, AppleTalk, and TCP/IP).

The OSI model represents areas of functionality that must be present on two computers that want to communicate. These two computers might be a Macintosh and a NetWare file server, for example, or a DOS-based PC and a DEC Vax minicomputer. The functions that must be present in the client computer and the server computer are defined in seven different sets of specifications known as *layers*. Thus, the OSI model is referred to as a "seven-layer model." Figure 2.3 illustrates the seven layers on the client and server computers.

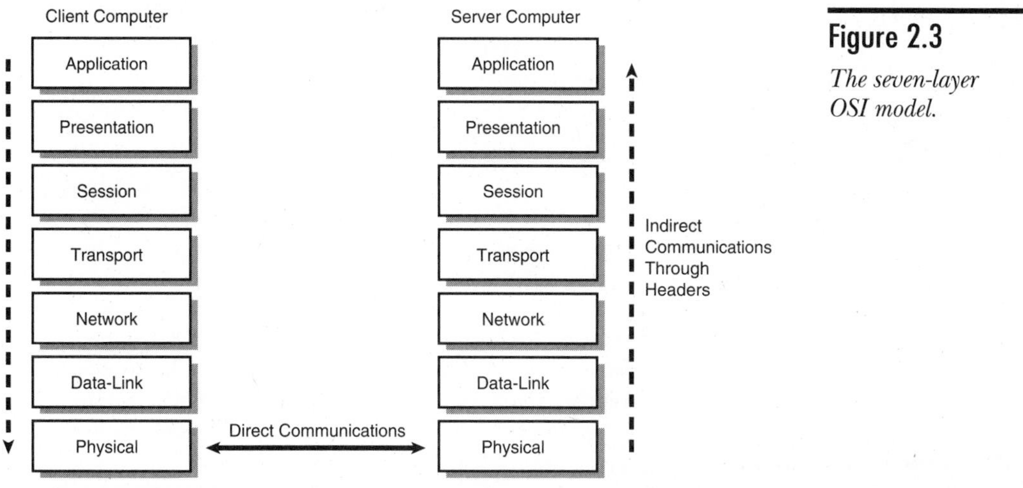

Figure 2.3

The seven-layer OSI model.

As you can see from figure 2.3, the layers communicate between themselves indirectly through a series of headers. The physical layers communicate directly through the LAN cabling, a phone connection, or a wireless transmission. A brief description of the functions defined for each layer follows.

The Physical Layer

The *physical layer* is where electronics specifications are defined. These specifications include voltage levels, the type of connector used, and the type of transmission method used, among other things. An example of a physical layer specification is the RS-232 interface found on most PCs. One of the important aspects of the physical layer for a network Administrator is the type of cabling to be used in the LAN. The 802.5 (token ring) specification, for example, which was adopted by the OSI from the IEEE, calls for twisted-pair cabling.

The Data Link Layer

The *data link layer* contains specifications regarding how information is placed on the network. An example of this is the CSMA/CD (Carrier Sense with Multiple Access/Collision Detection) specification used by Ethernet. In the case of Ethernet, the technique to place information on the networks has each Ethernet NIC wait until the network is free to begin a new transmission. A *collision* occurs if two or more NICs transmit at the same time. The specification includes an algorithm that causes the NICs involved in the collision to transmit a signal known as a *jam pattern* that notifies other NICs of the collision. The NICs then wait for an essentially random period of time before attempting to retransmit their data. The block of data being transmitted is often referred to at this layer as a *frame.*

The Network Layer

Specifications at the *network layer* are concerned with how information is to be transmitted across a large, complex network that consists of multiple LANs connected together using routers. (For a further discussion of routers, please see "Routers" in the section titled "Segmenting a Network" at the end of this chapter.) In a NetWare network, for example, the protocol that resides at this layer is IPX. IPX has provisions for assigning a number to each LAN known as the network address. The *network address* is a logical number assigned during the installation of a file server or router. When information has to cross several routers to reach a distant file server, each router must consult a *routing table,* which contains information on how to reach distant networks. The information is then sent using the most efficient route. Network layer information is grouped into *packets.*

The Transport Layer

The *transport layer* contains specifications that control how the information is sent. One of the functions at this layer is to maintain a logical connection between the client and server. The connection is identified by a number and is tracked to ensure the secure transmission of data. In the NetWare world, SPX is an example of a transport layer protocol. SPX is used in situations where reliable transmission of data

is needed. SPX sequences the packets of data. Missing packets or packets that do not arrive in the order they were sent are immediately detected. In addition, SPX offers *connection multiplexing*, which is used in the printing environment. Many accounting programs, for example, call upon the services of SPX to ensure that data is sent accurately.

Connection multiplexing is a term used to indicate where many source logical devices are attempting to communicate with many destination logical devices. In the example of a print server, for example, the print server takes jobs from several print queues. Jobs are then routed to printers. One print queue can send a job to many printers. One printer can be programmed to handle many print queues. To avoid sending a job, or worse, part of a job, to the wrong printer, each separate logical association between a print queue and and a printer is assigned a *connection identifier*. The print server handles many (multiple) connections.

The Session Layer

The *session layer* contains definitions regarding logging in, printing, and long-term logical connections between the client and server. In the NetWare environment, when you load the workstation network software (for example, VLM.EXE is the software used on a DOS workstation), you will see a message indicating that you are connected to a file server. The next step is to log in. Session layer specifications define how the connection is maintained and what types of connections can occur.

The Presentation Layer

Specifications at the *presentation layer* control the format and appearance of data. In the NetWare world, one of the primary protocols operational at this layer is the ASCII (American Standard Code for Information Interchange) specification for encoding letters and punctuation into binary code. On the NetWare file server, there are proprietary protocols governing data compression.

The Application Layer

The *application layer* is the portion of the OSI model that users see. In the DOS world, the application layer is the famous "C>" prompt. On a Macintosh, the application layer is the desktop. Major functions of the application layer include providing some sort of user interface and the ability to load and run application programs.

Putting It All Together

Figure 2.4 illustrates the working of the OSI model in the case of a DOS client sending a file to a NetWare file server. For the purposes of this book, the OSI model is used as a convenient means of referencing the functions of different protocols. There is a set of specifications and standards known as the OSI Protocol Suite. This is a collection of specifications gathered from other standards organizations (such as the IEEE), and some that were written by subcommittees. The United States government has made this set of standards the official standard for government agencies. Most vendors have endorsed the standards and made their networking products mesh with the standards. One hundred percent OSI products, however, are notably lacking in the industry.

Understanding Older Versions of NetWare

NetWare was originally a collaboration between a group of Brigham Young University graduates, who called themselves The Superset, and Novell Data Systems. They produced a product that allowed microcomputers to share printers and files. A proprietary design called ShareNet, based around the Motorola 68000 using an S-Net interface card, was released in 1983. Each S-Net board allowed six workstations to connect to the Novell 68 server directly. Each server supported a maximum of four boards, giving the network a maximum of 24 workstations. About a year later, ARCnet support was added. Each ARCnet card in the server could support a theoretical maximum of 254 workstations.

A version of NetWare known as NetWare 86 was released in the mid-1980s for the IBM PC-XT (a computer that used an Intel 8086 microprocessor). This was a major breakthrough for Novell in that the network operating system was independent of the hardware being used. This version of NetWare also marked the transition of Novell away from hardware to software.

A series of NetWare versions labeled NetWare 286 were released between 1985 and 1990. These included NetWare 2.0, 2.0A, 2.10 through 2.15E, and 2.2. These versions of NetWare were compiled using 16-bit compiler technology and could operate on an Intel 80286 or above microprocessor. These versions of NetWare required you to run an installation program that created a final operating system executable called NET$OS.EXE. The installation program installed the operating system and related files on the file server. When the file server booted up, the cold boot loader loaded the operating system into RAM and enabled the NICs and hard drives on the server. Any changes to the operating system required you to bring the server down, revise and reinstall NET$OS.EXE, and reboot the server. Memory management was a delicate balancing act in which server processes fought for working space in tiny (64 KB) memory pools known as *dynamic memory pools.* The operating system made full use of the services offered by the 80286 microprocessor and used less than 2 MB of RAM.

	The User	Creates a word processing file
		↓
Client	Application	Gathers filename and attributes
		Adds information about destination drive
		↓
	Presentation	Encodes data in ASCII format
		↓
	Session	Stores data in outgoing cache buffers
		Encodes user connection number
		Verifies security access to destination
		Negotiates with the file server to store the file
		↓
	Network	Breaks data into packets
		Adds network address information
		Negotiates with routers to transfer packets
		↓
	Transport	Adds a checksum for each packet
		↓
	Data-Link	Adds Ethernet frame header information
		Encodes address of Ethernet card
		Adds checksum at end of frame
		Listens to see if the network is busy
		↓
	Physical	Transmits data onto the LAN
		Listens for possible collision
		↓
Server	Physical	Receives data off the LAN
		↓
	Data-Link	Verifies that data is addressed to the server
		Verifies the checksum checks out OK
		Records the source Ethernet address
		↓
	Network	Organizes and stores data packets
		Orders received packets by number
		↓
	Transport	Verifies packet checksum
		↓
	Session	Authenticates user connection
		Places data from packets into cache buffers
		↓
	Presentation	Places data into DOS, Macintosh, or other
		name space format
		↓
	Application	Puts reassembled file into queue to be
		stored out to the file server's hard drive

Figure 2.4

The OSI model at work in the NetWare environment.

The first version of NetWare written exclusively for the Intel 80386 (or above) was NetWare 3.0, released in late 1989. It was followed quickly by NetWare 3.10. NetWare 3.11 was released in early 1991, and 3.12 in 1993. These versions of NetWare were originally referred to as *NetWare 386* after their use of the 80386. NetWare 3.*x* takes advantage of the 32-bit internal processing power and superior memory management capabilities of the 80386 microprocessor.

The major evolution in file server management was the NLM (NetWare Loadable Module) architecture. With NetWare 3.*x* you first boot your computer using DOS. Next you load the operating system kernel (SERVER.EXE). At this point the server is up and running. NLMs can now be loaded on an as-needed basis. When you want to upgrade an NLM, simply unload it and load the updated module.

Another major improvement was the ODI (Open Datalink Interface) architecture on both the file server and workstations. ODI provides you with multiple protocol support on one or more NICs. NetWare 3.*x* provides support for IPX/SPX, AppleTalk, TCP/IP, and the OSI protocols.

NetWare 4.1 builds upon the foundation of NetWare 3.*x*. The NLM and ODI architectures are used. Many of the improvements are described in Part Two, "Examining NetWare 4.1's Benefits."

Segmenting a Network

An important difference between a simple and a complex network is that a complex network consists of individual LANs connected together somehow. This section explores some important definitions and the different ways LANs can be connected.

The first word to define is segment. *Segment* is a term used to describe a portion of a simple LAN. The definition of a segment changes depending on what type of NIC you are using in your LAN. In a Thin Ethernet LAN, for example, a segment consists of all the RG/58 cabling between two terminators. A *terminator* is a connector with a 50-ohm resistor inside. The terminator serves the purpose of electrically ending the flow of electricity on that end of the cabling. On a Thin Ethernet segment, you might find "T" connectors that enable you to connect workstations, file servers, or other network devices.

In a token ring network, a segment consists of a series of MAUs (Multi Station Access Units, also referred to as MSAUs), and adapter cables to connect workstations, servers, or other network devices. Ethernet and token ring are discussed in greater detail in Chapter 3, "LANs and WANs."

Another new word in this discussion is node. A *node* is a device with some sort of network interface that could be a NIC or built into some sort of hardware. A workstation and a file server both qualify as nodes. Other devices such as printers that attach directly to the network, routers, and bridges can also qualify as nodes.

Another term that needs to be defined is topology. *Topology* refers to the layout of the network cabling system. There are three main topologies used in LANs: star, ring, and bus. *Star topology* is when all nodes connect to a central device such as a hub. *Ring topology* is when each node connects to its neighbor and the last node connects to the first node. *Bus topology* is when the network cabling runs (more or less) in a straight line from one node to the next.

Further details on the different types of NICs are available in Chapter 3. The next sections discuss devices that join segments into larger and larger networks.

Repeaters

A *repeater* is a self-contained unit with two or more network interface connections. A repeater operates strictly at the physical layer of the OSI model and contains electronics that serve several purposes, including the following:

- Boosting the signal back to its originally specified level
- Performing noise filtering to produce a clean signal
- Joining two or more segments together to extend the network
- Repeating the information received from one of its network interfaces to its other network interfaces
- Staying invisible to the nodes on the network

Other network devices have built-in repeater functions. These include token ring and FDDI (Fiber Distributed Digital Interface) NICs, concentrators, and hubs. Another device, a multiport repeater, connects more than two segments.

Token Ring and FDDI Repeater Functions

Token ring and FDDI NICs automatically repeat the information they receive. As a result, separate repeater units are not as common in these environments. Whenever a token ring or FDDI NIC receives information, the circuitry built into the NIC scans the data for certain types of information, and then places this data back out onto the LAN. The transmission is filtered to get rid of line noise and is boosted back to its original strength.

Concentrators and Hubs

The terms concentrator and hub are often used interchangeably. In the world of microcomputer LANs, *concentrator* refers to an Ethernet device that connects nodes to the network using twisted-pair cabling. Most vendors now refer to these devices as *hubs.*

An FDDI concentrator is used to connect FDDI nodes together rather than using the built-in repeater function. As its name implies, a concentrator "concentrates" the cabling in a single location. The FDDI concentrator changes the topology from ring to star. Even when a concentrator is used, however, FDDI NICs continue to send information logically in a ring.

There are two types of hubs in ARCnet networks: active and passive. An *active hub* contains active electronics that make it a repeater, which also splits the signal many different ways. A *passive hub,* on the other hand, simply splits the signal without the benefits of repeater functions. As a result, the length of cable permitted to and from a passive hub is limited to 100 feet, compared to a limitation of 2,000 feet going to or from an active ARCnet hub.

The definition of a segment changes when a hub is involved. The hub contains active electronics (an ARCnet passive hub being the exception), and the electrical signal is terminated internally. NICs designed to work with hubs are also designed with internal termination. As a result, the cable that goes between a NIC and a hub is terminated at both ends and becomes a separate segment. When an existing node is disconnected from a hub, or a new node is connected to a hub, the functioning of the network is not disrupted. If you add or take away a node from a Thin Ethernet bus, you would must disconnect the node's cable from the bus, thereby disrupting the bus. Figure 2.5 is a picture of an Ethernet hub.

Figure 2.5
An IBM Ethernet hub.

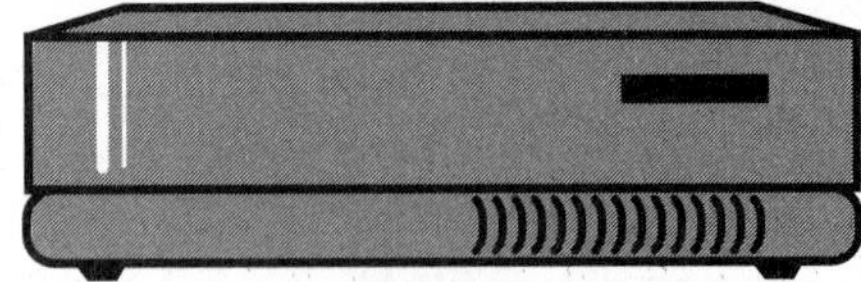

Multiport Repeaters

A *multiport repeater* is a stand-alone unit with multiple repeater connections. Seen primarily in the Thin Ethernet bus environment, these devices can be used to connect different segments together. A segment can be wired directly to the multiport repeater using its internal termination. Alternatively, the repeater can be somewhere in the middle of the segment just as you could place an ordinary repeater.

Bridges

A bridge has similarities to both repeaters and routers. Bridges operate at the data-link layer of the OSI model. A *bridge* consists of either a stand-alone unit with two network interfaces or a dedicated workstation with two NICs that runs specialized software.

The function of a bridge is to join two LANs together and perform intelligent filtering of traffic. The unit receives transmissions from one interface or the other and selectively retransmits the information "across the bridge." There are two primary types of bridges: *spanning tree* and *source routing*. The next subsections describe these two types.

Spanning Tree Bridges

A *spanning tree bridge* is used primarily in the Ethernet environment. The bridge builds an internal table whenever a node transmits information. This table contains Ethernet NIC addresses and where the NIC is located (on network A side or network B side of the bridge). Figure 2.6 illustrates this process. As you can see in the diagram, when Tom's workstation (address 00-B2-00-47-26-91) wants to communicate with file server FS1 (address 00-B2-00-34-18-56), both on network A side of the bridge, the bridge receives information but does not transmit. When Tom's workstation wishes to communicate with file server FS2 (address 00-B2-00-81-46-04), on network B side of the bridge, the bridge retransmits the information received from network A to network B.

Source Routing Bridges

Source routing bridges are found in the token ring environment. A *source routing bridge* transmits information to its other side based on routing information received from the originating node. Each token ring NIC builds a table in the memory of its host computer of connections to other computers and the best route to get there. Each workstation, for example, has information on how to reach the file servers it can connect to. When the workstation sends information to a file server, its token ring NIC builds routing information into the token ring frame header that precedes the data it wants to transmit. The source routing bridge reads this information and either forwards the information to its other side or repeats it on the same side, depending on the instructions in the token ring frame header.

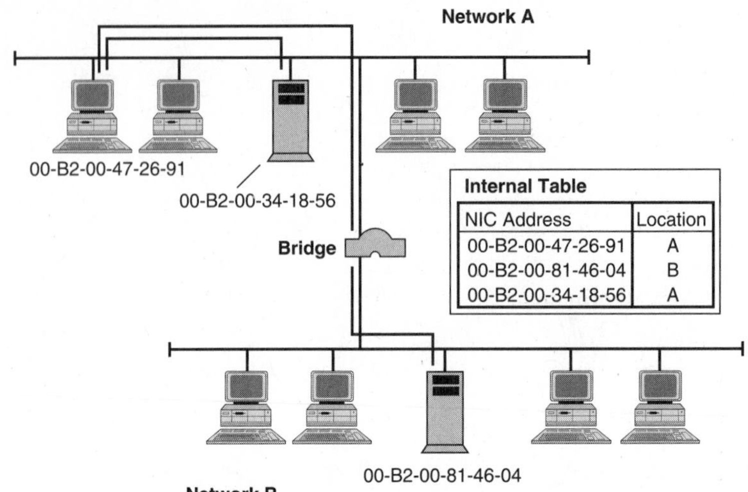

Figure 2.6
The function of a spanning tree bridge.

The result of this method of operation is that information can be forwarded quickly. The downside is that this process requires more overhead at each node. In a NetWare network, source routing support is provided by a driver ROUTE.COM, which is loaded into the workstation's memory, and the driver ROUTE.NLM, which is loaded on the file server.

WAN Bridges

WAN bridges have the capability to support long-distance connections. These bridges require additional hardware and the use of a dedicated phone line. Long-distance phone carriers such as AT&T, MCI, and Sprint offer specialized phone lines, called *dedicated lines,* or *leased lines,* that are used to transmit data between two locations. When you lease a phone line, there is no need to dial a number between the two locations. The line is preconnected and is available 24 hours a day, 7 days a week. Most leased phone lines have noise filtering built in. This makes such lines excellent choices for the long-distance transmission of data.

Leased lines are priced according to the amount of data you wish to transmit. Another term you will encounter is bandwidth. For the purposes of this book, *bandwidth* is the usable number of bits per second you can send through the line. Lines are often rated in kbps (kilobits per second), mbps (megabits per second), and gbps (gigabits per second).

Additional supporting hardware is often needed in conjunction with a leased line. Many leased lines offer different types of communications protocols at the OSI data link layer. Common communications protocols include the following:

- PPP (Point-to-Point Protocol)
- Frame Relay
- X.25
- SLIP (Serial Link IP)
- ISDN (Integrated Services Digital Network)

For further information about these protocols, see Chapter 3, "LANs and WANs."

The Use of Bridges

Bridges are used primarily for the following three purposes:

- To extend the distance of a LAN
- To add more nodes to the network
- To filter out extraneous network transmissions

The bridge does not simply repeat the transmission received but completely rebuilds the information frame and then retransmits. This allows the frame to travel farther than would be possible with simple repeaters. On the other hand, the repeater can transmit information at the speed of electricity (minus a small propagation delay). The bridge must perform some intelligent operations before retransmitting, which slows down overall throughput of data.

The repeater repeats all information received regardless of the destination or content. A bridge is much more selective in its transmissions. Consider figure 2.6, for example. Imagine that network A is used primarily by Accounting, and network B is used by Sales. You can place a bridge between the two segments to isolate traffic. The only traffic that will cross the bridge is when someone in Accounting needs to access data on the Sales side.

The usage of bridges is declining in favor of routers. Routers are capable of performing operations of much more intelligence and are less expensive and more flexible. Although the throughput of a bridge is about 10 times faster, there are other restrictions that negate the speed difference. The next section discusses routers.

Routers

Routers serve to extend the distance of a network based on network OSI layer information. Routers are dependent on the network layer protocol (such as IP or IPX). The router must read the protocol-specific information in the network layer header and make a decision on how to best route the packet to its destination. Each router typically maintains a *routing table* containing lists of network addresses and how long it takes to get there. The network layer protocol dictates what information routers maintain in their tables and how this information is acquired.

In a NetWare environment using the IPX protocol, for example, there is another protocol called RIP (Routing Information Protocol), which specifies what goes into the routing table. RIP causes each router to broadcast the contents of its routing table every 60 seconds. In this fashion, routers on the network exchange information. Another NetWare protocol, SAP (Service Advertisement Protocol), controls the exchange of server names and locations. A new routing protocol introduced by Novell is called NLSP. This is described in the next section.

NLSP—NetWare Link Services Protocol

The Novell Multiprotocol Router (MPR) uses a more advanced form of routing known as NLSP (NetWare Link Services Protocol). MPR is a routing product offered by Novell. Technology developed for the MPR is now being included in NetWare 4.1. NLSP is available for the 3.1*x* and 4.*x* environments as an NLM that can be loaded on the file server. NLSP provides both RIP and SAP information but in a more efficient format. The net result is that routers using NLSP need to communicate only new or changed information. Routers that use RIP and SAP communicate the entire contents of their tables every 60 seconds. Routers using NLSP send only updated information.

NLSP offers other performance enhancements over RIP and SAP. NLSP uses Link Services routing rather than the vector distance used by RIP. RIP uses a primitive means to determine the best route that involves a rudimentary timing parameter known as a *tick. Link state routing,* used in Novell's NLSP protocol, takes into account the time to reach a destination. NLSP also offers the following features:

- **Load balancing.** The router makes a decision when one route is being used too often.
- **Dynamic rerouting.** In case a router fails, other routers will figure out other paths.
- **Hierarchical routing.** The capability to designate primary and secondary routers.
- **Faster data transfer.** The capability to handle larger amounts of data at one time.
- **Backwards compatibility.** Routers using RIP and SAP will be able to work with NLSP.

How a Router Works

Routers are independent of the media and types of NICs used. The router reads information past the data link OSI layer, into the network layer. The data link layer is the domain of the NIC. The network layer is not at all concerned with what type of NIC is used. As a result, the router could be configured with an Ethernet card on side A and a token ring card on side B. When such a router receives an Ethernet transmission, it extracts the data and rebuilds it into a token ring frame to be transmitted on the token ring side.

Figure 2.7 illustrates the functioning of a router. Tom, sitting at his workstation, wants to log in to file server FS2. The software on his workstation sends a packet requesting a connection with file server FS2. The file server FS1 receives this packet and looks up FS2 in its server information table (maintained using SAP). FS1 discovers that FS2 is located on Network B. FS1 then consults its routing table and retransmits the packet to the router R1 through Network C. R1 consults its routing table and retransmits the packet onto Network B, where it is received by file server FS2.

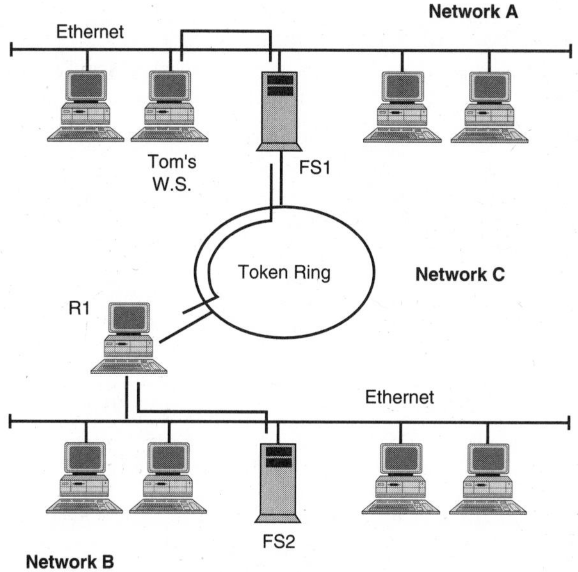

Figure 2.7

The function of a router.

A router operates much like a spanning tree bridge. It exchanges information with other routers on the network and builds its own routing table. The routing table contains a list of network addresses, a *hop count,* and some measurement of time. A "hop" is when a packet needs to pass through one router. If Network D is five hops away from Network A, this means a packet that originates on Network A would need to traverse five routers before reaching Network D. A typical measurement of time is the *tick.* A tick is 1/18 of a second. The number of ticks it would take to reach a destination network is often one more than the hop count. In the example cited earlier, if Network D is five hops from Network A, it will usually be six ticks. A tick count over 300 is a sign that the router has to traverse some sort of slow, dedicated phone connection.

Router Implementations

Routers are implemented in the following ways:

- Stand-alone units that connect to the network
- Software that runs on a dedicated workstation
- Software that runs on a file server
- Routing built into the operating system

Stand-alone units include those made by Cisco, a well-known router vendor. These units simply plug into the network and are ready to go. (There is a configuration program that you run to configure the router.)

One of the most common types of router is a software package that runs on a workstation (typically a dedicated workstation). A dedicated workstation can perform no other operations. The Novell Multiprotocol Router (MPR), for example, can run as software either on a file server or on a dedicated workstation. To install the MPR, you would place as many NICs as were appropriate for your situation (you need at least two NICs to make a workstation into a router), and load the software. The software installation includes the installation of a runtime version of NetWare. NetWare runtime is typically a stripped-down version of NetWare that has a two- to five-user limit. A configuration program enables you to assign network addresses to each NIC in the router.

Eiçon Technologies and Novell market router software that can run on a file server. This software makes use of the network operating system's internal routing capabilities. The routing software adds functionality to this built-in capability. Eicon's software, for example, adds the capability of PPP (Point-to-Point Protocol) and Frame Relay connectivity.

PPP and Frame Relay are high-speed, efficient communications protocols. They operate over dedicated phone lines at speeds ranging from 56 kbps to 2.048 mbps. To support these protocols, you will need additional hardware. This hardware could include the following:

- Synchronous connectivity cards that plug in to the file server (or router)
- DSU/CSUs (Data Service Unit/Channel Service Units)
- High-speed synchronous modems
- Specialized dedicated phone lines (such as the T1 line offered by AT&T)

Most versions of PPP also enable you to use conventional PC COM ports and asynchronous modems.

Most network operating systems offer limited routing capabilities. NetWare, for example, offers built-in IPX, AppleTalk, and IP routing. To route other protocols you need additional software or a separate router. UnixWare offers IP routing. To activate the built-in routing facility, you simply need to add additional NICs and assign network addresses. The commands used in NetWare are the LOAD and BIND commands, which are discussed in future chapters. Chapter 12, "Installing the Network Operating System," gives you a good idea of how to use the LOAD and BIND commands to enable IPX routing on the file server.

Most routers offer some sort of management capability. The router software includes a *network management agent*. The management agent responds to queries from some sort of network management software. Novell, for example, offers the NetWare Management System (NMS) package. This package enables you to manage, from your workstation, the entire network, including all routers, file servers, and workstations. You can gather performance statistics, and trigger alarms if certain error conditions arise. There is a detailed discussion of NMS in Chapter 39, "Monitoring Network Performance."

As with WAN bridges, most routers offer the ability to connect LANs through high-grade phone lines.

Gateways

A *gateway* is used when a complete protocol conversion is required. Gateways, which operate at all seven layers of the OSI model, are used to perform specialized tasks. The Novell NetWare for SAA product, for example, is a gateway that converts between the NetWare protocols and the IBM SNA/SAA protocols. You use NetWare for SAA when users on your LAN need to communicate with an IBM AS/400 minicomputer or a 9370 mainframe, for example.

Another example of a type of gateway is an e-mail gateway. E-mail gateways are used to convert e-mail from one format to another, transparent to both the sender and receiver. Fischer International Systems, for example, offers e-mail gateways that convert to and from Novell's MHS E-Mail format, to and from IBM's PROFS format, as well as conversions to and from X.400, SNADS, and SMTP.

Gateways often require additional hardware. Eicon offers an OSI gateway product that converts between the NetWare protocols and the OSI protocols. The product, OSI LAN Gateway, requires a specialized card, called an EiconCard, that supports high speed synchronous communications of up to 384 kbps, depending on the version.

Gateways usually work in conjunction with specialized workstation software. The workstation software often performs terminal emulation. *Terminal emulation* software turns the workstation into a dumb terminal (or ASCII terminal) from the standpoint of the remote host system.

Survey of Repeaters, Bridges, Routers, and Gateways

Table 2.1 summarizes some commercially available network connectivity products.

TABLE 2.1
A Survey of LAN Connectivity Products

Vendor	Product	List Price	Description
Novell	Multiprotocol Router Plus	$1,495	Routes IPX, AppleTalk, and IP. Supports all NICs supported by NetWare and PPP, Frame Relay, and X.25. Loads as a series of NLMs on a file server, or runs on a dedicated workstation using a runtime version of NetWare.
Eicon Technologies	SNA LAN Gateway	$1,195	Loads as an NLM on a NetWare file server. Requires an EiconCard ($1,095). Enables users on the LAN (using terminal emulation software) to access an IBM mainframe or mini-computer. Supports the

Vendor	Product	List Price	Description
			IBM protocols 3270, 5250, and APPC/LU6.2 and LU0.
	Router for NetWare	$995	Loads as an NLM on a NetWare file server. Requires an EiconCard ($1,095). Supports PPP, Frame Relay, and X.25. Features 4:1 data compression.
3Com	3C588 Modular Multiport Repeater	$1,295	Modular assembly that performs as a repeater to connect multiple segments of an Ethernet network. The unit supports up to 15 modules at $295 per module.
	3C1400-0 IsoLAN Primary Local Bridge	$2,400	Stand-alone bridge that connects Ethernet LANs together.
	3C5824 NETBuilder Remote Access	$4,995	Serves as a bridge or a router. Connects an Ethernet LAN to another via a dedicated phone line.
MicroCom	MBR-TR-6500 Token Ring X.25	$5,499	Serves as a bridge or router. Routes remote information from a token ring LAN through a remote connection. Supports X.25 and Frame Relay. Features 4:1 data compression.
Microdyne	NetWare SNA Gateway	$2,995	Allows workstations on the LAN using 3270 terminal emulation

continues

Table 2.1, Continued
A Survey of LAN Connectivity Products

Vendor	Product	List Price	Description
			software to access an IBM AS/400 or 3270 family mainframe system.
Newport Systems	LAN2LAN Mega Compression Router	$3,095	Supports HDLC, LAPB, X.25, PPP. Capable of routing IPX, AppleTalk, and IP. Features data compression on slow lines to improve overall throughput.

Advanced Program-to-Program Communications (APPC) is a set of specifications used by IBM to standardize communications between its systems. LU6.2 (Logical Unit 6.2) and LU0 (Logical Unit 0) are part of this specification. The LU (Logical Unit) software standardizes the interface between an outside entity and the SNA network environment.

High Speed Data Link Control (HDLC) is a data link layer protocol used extensively by the mainframe community. It is an extension of SDLC (Synchronous Data Link Control) used in the IBM mainframe environment.

Link Access Protocol Balanced (LAPB) is an improvement over HDLC. It is used as a standardized data link layer protocol over long distance phone lines.

Summary

This chapter provided you with an overview of the elements of a complex network. A complex network consists of multiple network segments that are connected together using any of a variety of devices. These devices include repeaters, bridges, routers, and gateways. Some bridges and routers feature long-distance communications capabilities.

A complex network features multiple file servers and protocols. This chapter gave you an idea of the impact of multiple servers on the network. In addition, different protocols were discussed. These included IPX/SPX, AppleTalk, TCP/IP, and OSI.

LANs and WANs

You are now familiar with some of the protocols and devices that comprise simple and complex networks. This chapter discusses the vehicles that make communications in LANs and WANs possible. In the LAN environment, this chapter explores different types of network interface cards (NICs). In the WAN environment, this chapter discusses the various technologies that facilitate communications across long distances. Finally, this chapter examines three case studies involving small, medium, and large companies.

Exploring LANs

LANs (local area networks) were originally designed to connect computers in a close geographic vicinity. LAN technology descended from the mainframe computer networks of the 1960s. At that time, a centralized host computer controlled a network of devices using proprietary hardware, software, and standards. Long-distance communications grew quickly in the 1960s. Because the host computers were so expensive, many smaller companies rented time on the systems owned by larger companies. Dial-in hardware, software, and protocols were developed to meet this need.

As minicomputers were introduced in the 1970s, more companies could afford to purchase computers of their own. Companies often purchased systems for several departments over the span of several years. Eventually the demand grew to connect the in-house systems together. Many companies worked to get LAN products to market. These companies included Xerox, Digital, Intel, IBM, DataPoint, and Hewlett Packard, among others.

This section presents you with a discussion of media followed by a discussion of the major types of network interface cards (NICs) pioneered by these companies. The major types of NICs include the following:

- Ethernet
- Token ring
- ARCnet
- FDDI

Before the discussion on NICs can begin, you must first learn about the media used to connect NICs together to form a LAN.

Media

The word *media* is used to indicate the physical connection between computers in a LAN. Media is not synonymous with cabling. Different NICs use different types of cabling. Some use no cabling at all. Table 3.1 lists some different types of media and the NICs associated with them.

Table 3.1
Media and NICs

Media	Associated NIC	Description
Coaxial Cable	Ethernet ARCnet	Coaxial cable was used in the original Ethernet specification. It is shielded from EMI (electromagnetic interference) and allows electrical signals to pass easily. Cable types associated with Ethernet include RG-11 (Thick Ethernet) and RG-58 (Thin Ethernet). Older Ethernet systems used RG-8. The resistance rating for Ethernet cabling is 50 ohms. The cable type associated with ARCnet is RG-62. The resistance rating for ARCnet cabling is 93 ohms.
Twisted Pair	Ethernet ARCnet Token ring	Twisted-pair cable consists of two pairs of wires (4 wires total—could be more in some cases) twisted around each other a certain number of times per foot. This type of cabling is very inexpensive and is often already installed in modern office buildings. There are two general types of twisted-pair: *shielded* and *unshielded.* Shielded twisted-pair includes an additional protective sheath of copper or aluminum that helps prevent EMI. Unshielded twisted-pair (UTP) is less expensive but less resistant to interference. Different types of NICs have different requirements for cabling and may have different types of connectors.
Fiber Optic	FDDI	Fiber optic cable is made of strands of glass fibers (or high-grade plastic). The cable is not stiff but is well protected by

continues

Table 3.1, Continued
Media and NICs

Media	Associated NIC	Description
		an outer layer of thickly woven mesh. Light travels through the cable in bursts, approximating the 1s and 0s that are the lifeblood of binary computers. This type of cable has a high band-width. This means that fiber optic cable can support extremely high speed data transmissions with room to spare for additional traffic (such as voice and video images). It is completely immune to EMI but tends to be more expensive than twisted pair.
Air	Wireless NICs	Some vendors (such as Motorola) offer wireless NICs. These feature miniature antennas on the back of the card that transmit and receive radio signals. Transmission rates are very good, and distances can sometimes extend to 5 miles or more. The advantage is that no wires need to be strung between computers. The disadvantage is that such systems are extremely vulnerable to EMI.

Electromagnetic interference (EMI) consists of electrically charged magnetic particles that appear on the media. EMI can be caused by a variety of sources, including the following:

- Electric generators
- Heavy duty equipment (such as an arc welder)
- Radio transmitters
- CB radios with linear amplifiers
- Transformers
- Power spikes

Working with Ethernet

Ethernet was developed by a consortium of companies that included Xerox, Intel, and Digital (DEC). The name Ethernet was coined after the term *ether.* The ancient Greeks proposed that a medium known as ether filled the upper regions of the sky and space. In the early 1900s, ether was a hypothetical substance thought to occupy all space. Marconi, in his experimentation with the "wireless" (which evolved into the radio), proposed that this substance accounted for the propagation of electromagnetic radiation through space. Like ether, Ethernet technology was hyped as a magical solution that would link all computers together.

Ethernet Background

When released in the late 1970s, Ethernet consisted of a computer interface that connected to a backbone. The backbone was a hefty RG-8 cabling segment that ran the length of the office or building. Nodes connected to the backbone using a drop cable, an external transceiver, and a vampire tap. A *drop cable* connects to the 15-pin DIX (the first initials of the three companies in the consortium, Digital, Intel, and Xerox) connector on the Ethernet interface and to the external transceiver at the other end. An *external transceiver* transmits signals out onto the backbone and receives incoming transmissions. The word "external" is used because later versions of Ethernet had a built-in ("internal") transceiver. The *vampire tap* is a clamp that looks something like a vice. It is bolted down onto the backbone. Sharp teeth bite into the cable; one goes all the way through to the center of the cable. The other only makes connection with the braided shield that surrounds the inner core of the cable.

RG-8 cable is a type of coaxial cable about the width of a garden hose. It is very thick, stiff, and heavy. An affectionate term used for this cable is "frozen garden hose." RG-8 cable is difficult to work with and is extremely expensive per foot compared with other types of cable. This, and other reasons, led to a broadening of the Ethernet specification.

Ethernet and the IEEE 802.3 Specification

The three companies involved in the development of Ethernet were also involved with the international electronics standards organization, the IEEE (Institute of Electrical and Electronics Engineers). In the early 1980s, several competing technologies, including ARCnet and token ring, were making headway in the marketplace. Ethernet was also becoming very popular in the budding computer network industry. In an attempt to make Ethernet the standard, and to possibly stave off the competition, the IEEE 802.3 workgroup was formed. The 802.3 specification was based on Ethernet but was broadened to include different types of cabling and different topologies.

The Institute of Electrical and Electronic Engineers (IEEE) is an international body that is responsible for a wide variety of standards. The standards for LANs were established as part of Project 802, so named because the project commenced in the second month of 1980. Several 802 standards have been developed, but only a few will be addressed in this book:

- 802.2 describes a Logical Link Control (LLC) standard that corresponds to the upper half of the data link layer in the OSI model. All other 802 standards utilize 802.2 LLC to interface with the network layer.
- 802.3 describes a CSMA/CD standard based on the original Ethernet standard. This standard corresponds to the lower half of the data link layer along with the physical layer of the OSI model. CSMA/CD stands for "Carrier Sense Multiple Access / Collision Detection" (described below).
- 802.5 describes a token-passing standard derived from IBM's Token-Ring technology. This standard also corresponds to the lower half of the data link layer along with the physical layer of the OSI model.

The 802.3 specification includes the following variations:

- 10BASE5—The original specification
- 10BASE2—Thin Ethernet
- 1BASE5—The original twisted-pair Ethernet based on AT&T's StarLAN
- 10BROAD36—Broadband Ethernet
- 10BASE-T—Twisted-pair Ethernet

The first number in the designation indicates the speed in mbps. The word indicates the type of transmission—baseband or broadband. *Baseband* is when only one type of signal (voice, video, or data) can be transmitted at one time on the cable. *Broadband* enables you to transmit mixed signals simultaneously. The number at the end of the designation indicates how many meters are allowed per segment. 10BASE5, for example, means that this interface can transmit at 10 mbps, uses baseband signaling, and can go up to 500 meters per segment.

A difference between the original Ethernet specification and the IEEE 802.3 specification is that the IEEE designed 802.3 to work with 802.2, which combines logical elements common to most of the IEEE 802.*x* specifications. 802.2, also known as the LLC (Logical Link Control) layer, occupies the top half of the OSI data link layer. LLC is concerned with how the data is transmitted, controlling the flow of data between the client and the server, and data integrity.

Figure 3.1 shows the relationships of these standards to the OSI model.

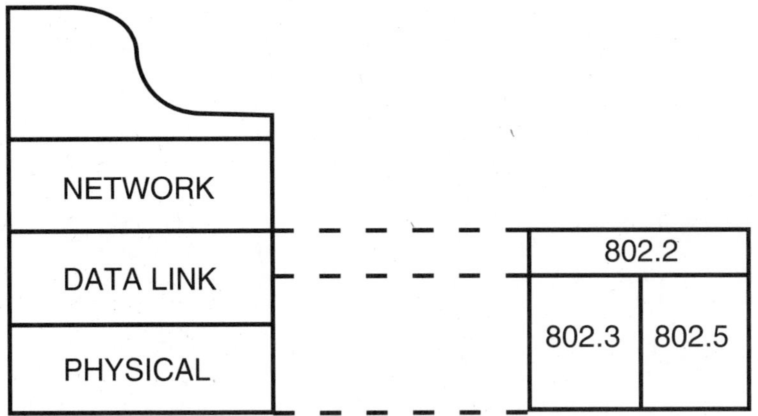

Figure 3.1

The relationship of several 802 standards to the OSI model.

Fast Ethernet Specifications

A number of Ethernet vendors have introduced "fast" Ethernet specifications. These are currently undergoing the scrutiny of the IEEE. One set of standards, proposed by Hewlett Packard, is called 10BASE-VG. These specifications push the transfer rate of Ethernet from 10 mbps to 100 mbps. This is accomplished in different ways, depending on the vendor. One technique is to use 8 wires instead of the 4 wires currently used by 10BASE-T. Another technique involves changing the signal encoding technique to improve efficiency.

How Ethernet Communicates on the LAN

Ethernet uses a technique known as CSMA/CD (Carrier Sense with Multiple Access/Collision Detection) to send and receive information. This simple technique has proven to be highly effective. The strategy is simple: When an Ethernet NIC wants to transmit data to the LAN, it first "listens" to see if the bus is busy. This is the Carrier Sense with Multiple Access (CSMA) phase. If another Ethernet NIC is accessing the network, your card will wait. When the network is free, your network card transmits. Other NICs wanting to transmit will wait until your NIC is done.

Network transmissions consist of precisely defined patterns of bits called *frames.* An Ethernet frame can consist of as many as 1,518 bytes and includes several types of information in addition to the data being transmitted. Among the items included are source and destination addresses and error checking information (called checksum information).

When two or more NICs transmit frames at the same time, a *collision* occurs. The Ethernet NICs on the same segment detect this due to excessive voltage on the cable. When an Ethernet NIC is transmitting, it keeps its voltage levels between +2.5 and -2.5 volts. When there is a collision, the voltage levels will exceed this threshold. The NICs involved in the collision back off for a period of time determined by a collision algorithm. The algorithm essentially produces a random timeout interval that increases with each successive collision. When the timeout period has expired, each NIC goes back into the waiting and listening mode to see if they can transmit.

Simply detecting the collision and backing off is not sufficient. As you can see in figure 3.2, suppose node B, on the other side of a repeater, is involved in a collision but is not aware of its involvement. The repeater will repeat any information it gains from the garbled collision but is not capable of producing improper voltage levels. Node B assumes that the transmission was successful. To prevent this situation from arising, each node involved in a collision generates a jam pattern immediately after detecting the collision.

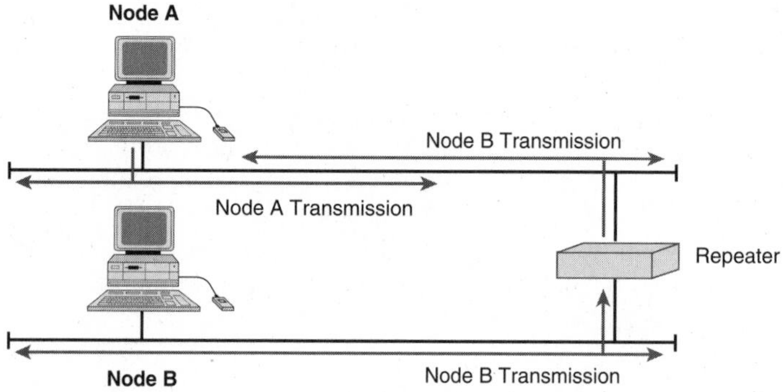

Figure 3.2
Ethernet collision detection.

The *jam pattern* is composed of a pattern of bits that do not correspond to a valid Ethernet data frame. This pattern is timed so that it will reach both ends of an extended Ethernet network before transmission completes, thus completely saturating the network. An extended Ethernet network consists of all segments connected through all repeaters. Segments connected through bridges or routers are not affected.

The jam pattern has two purposes. The first purpose is to make sure that all nodes on the network, including those separated by repeaters, know that a collision has occurred. The second purpose is to violate the normal delay time between Ethernet transmissions. Under ordinary circumstances, an Ethernet NIC is supposed to wait 9.6 microseconds between transmissions. This delay allows other NICs to get onto the network. Without this delay, one Ethernet NIC could "hog the bus." When network management tools on the other side of a repeater see an extended transmission with

no delay time, they assume there is a collision or some other problem and are, therefore, able to detect a collision.

Thin and Thick Ethernet Cabling

As you discovered in the preceding section, 10BASE2 is referred to as Thin Ethernet, and 10BASE5 as Thick Ethernet. These references are due to the fact that coaxial Ethernet NICs can support either RG-58 cable (Thin Ethernet) or RG-8 cable (Thick Ethernet).

To connect a node to a Thick Ethernet network, you need the following (see fig. 3.3):

- An Ethernet NIC
- A drop cable with 15 pin connectors at each end
- An external transceiver
- A vampire tap

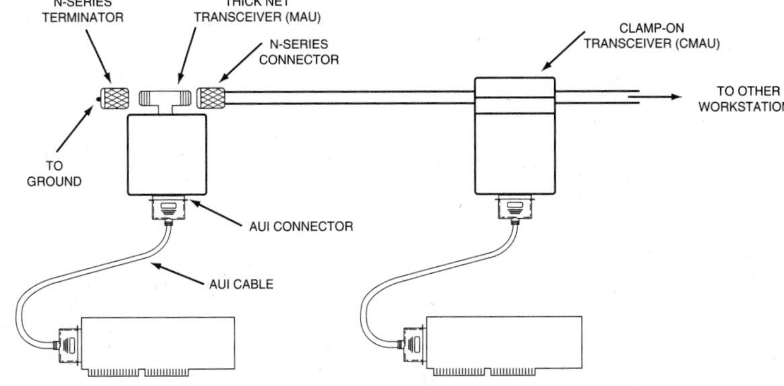

Figure 3.3
The components of a Thick Ethernet cabling system.

To connect a node to a Thin Ethernet network, you need the following (see fig. 3.4):

- An Ethernet NIC
- A "T" connector that connects to the BNC connector on the NIC

There are minor differences in setting up Ethernet networks using these two types of cable. Table 3.2 highlights some of the specifications relating to the two cable types. For further information, please see *NetWare: The Professional Reference,* also published by New Riders.

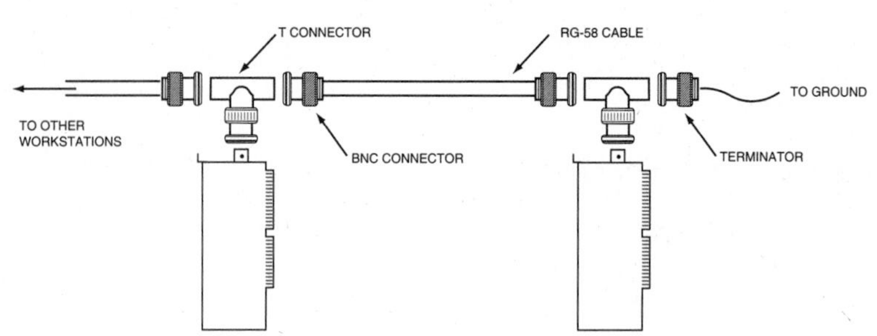

Figure 3.4
The components of a Thin Ethernet cabling system.

Table 3.2
Thin and Thick Cabling Specifications

Thin Ethernet	
Connector used	BNC
Internal or external transceiver	Internal
Maximum length of drop cable	N/A
Maximum nodes on entire network	1,024
Maximum nodes per segment	30
Maximum number of repeaters	4
Maximum segment length	185 meters
Maximum segments with active nodes	3
Minimum distance between nodes	0.5 meters
Resistance rating	50 ohms
Type of cable	RG-58
Thick Ethernet	
Connector used	DIX (15-pin)
Internal or external transceiver	External
Maximum length of drop cable	50 meters
Maximum nodes on entire network	1,024

Maximum nodes per segment	100
Maximum number of repeaters	4
Maximum segment length	500 meters
Maximum segments with active nodes	3
Minimum distance between nodes	2.5 meters
Resistance rating	50 ohms
Type of cable	RG-8

Twisted-Pair Ethernet

Twisted-pair Ethernet falls under the IEEE 802.3 10BASE-T specification. This type of Ethernet interface uses twisted-pair cable. The ends of the cable are capped with RJ-45 connectors, which resemble oversized modular phone jacks. The cable itself consists of from two to four pairs of 22-gauge wire twisted around each other.

Wiring a 10BASE-T Ethernet network requires one or more hubs (also referred to as concentrators). The twisted-pair cable is plugged into the RJ-45 jack of the NIC and then into one of the jacks in the hub. As you read in the preceding chapter, the hub and the 10BASE-T NIC terminate the connection forming an independent segment. You can plug in new nodes and unplug existing nodes without affecting the operation of the network.

Distances for 10BASE-T Ethernet are somewhat different than Thin or Thick Ethernet due to the use of hubs. A twisted-pair cable between a 10BASE-T Ethernet card and a hub can be up to 100 meters in length. Hubs can be daisy-chained; however, the rule specifying a maximum of four repeaters between any two nodes applies to twisted-pair repeaters as it does to Thin or Thick Ethernet repeaters. The preferred method of wiring hubs together is to use Thin Ethernet cabling between hubs. Some vendors, such as Synoptics, use a proprietary fiber-optic link between hubs.

10BASE-T Ethernet uses pins 1, 2, 3, and 6 in the RJ-45 connector. If you plan to wire your own cable, all you need is a specialized stripping and crimping tool, RJ-45 connectors, and twisted-pair cable. Cables that go between the 10BASE-T card and the hub should be wired straight through. Cables that go between two hubs need to wire pins 1 and 2 on the first end, to pins 3 and 6 on the second end. Likewise, pins 1 and 2 on the second end must be wired to pins 3 and 6 on the first end. This is known as a *crossover* cable. The 10BASE-T hub performs a crossover internally so that the send channel from the NIC goes to the receive channel in the hub. When going from hub to hub, you must invert the send and receive channels by using a crossover cable. Figure 3.5 illustrates 10BASE-T wiring.

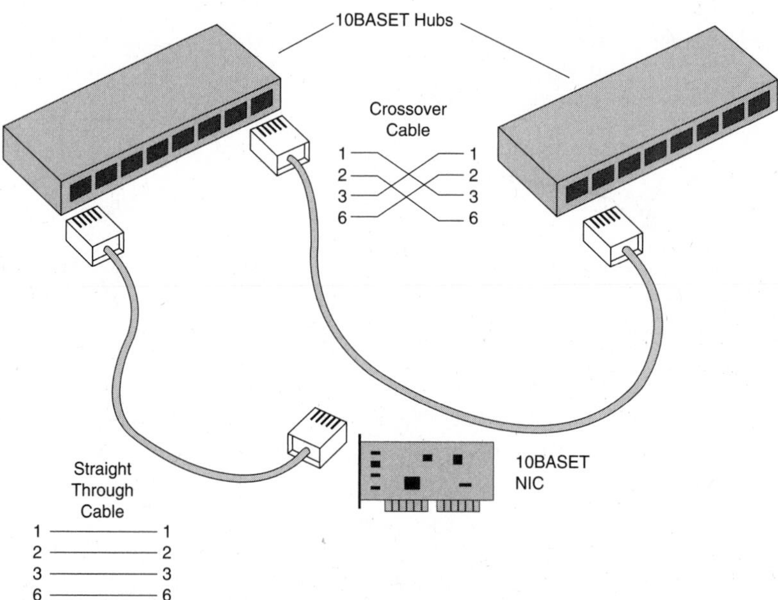

Figure 3.5
10BASE-T Ethernet wiring.

10BASE-T (or twisted-pair) Ethernet has gained in popularity over the past few years. Prices for these NICs have dropped substantially. The cables are easy to construct and cost very little compared to Thin or Thick coaxial Ethernet cable. Because nodes can be added or removed without affecting the network, management is easier. Most 10BASE-T hubs include a coaxial BNC connector that enables you to easily mix Thin or Thick Ethernet with twisted-pair Ethernet.

Mixed Protocols and Ethernet Frame Types

The development of Ethernet parallels the development of different protocols such as IPX or AppleTalk. Novell made certain key decisions in the design of the LAN card drivers it provides with NetWare. In the case of Ethernet, the IEEE was not ready to finalize the design of its 802.3 specification at the time the first releases of NetWare were to be introduced. As a result, Novell used features for its Ethernet drivers that would eventually be included in the final 802.3 specification.

Part of the job of the IEEE 802.3 Ethernet specification was to standardize how data is organized by the Ethernet NIC. This portion of the specification corresponds to the OSI data link layer. Data at the data link layer is referred to as a *frame.* This term is used to avoid confusion with data at higher layers (such as the network layer), which is referred to as a *packet.* The IEEE was interested in the structure of an Ethernet

frame. Items that go into the frame include a header, the data itself, and a checksum (actually a CRC—cyclic redundancy checksum). A *checksum* is an error-checking method that can determine whether errors occurred during a transmission.

The early Novell Ethernet drivers used what was called the Ethernet 802.3 "raw" frame type. It was understood that this frame type would be updated to be compatible with the IEEE 802.3 specification when it was to be introduced. There were minor differences in the frame header between the 802.3 "raw" and IEEE 802.3 frame types. Until NetWare version 4.0 was introduced, the "raw" 802.3 frame was the standard Ethernet frame type with all Novell networking products.

The latest NetWare NIC drivers support the IEEE 802.2 specification. Novell calls this frame type Ethernet_802.2, and this is the standard Ethernet frame type for NetWare 4.*x*. The Ethernet_802.2 frame type fully supports both the IEEE 802.3 and IEEE 802.2 frame information. The 802.2 information appears in the frame header immediately after the 802.3 information.

The Internet community introduced the TCP/IP set of protocols well before the IEEE started to work on the 802.*x* standards. The Internet community standardized first on the original Ethernet frame specification pushed by Digital, Intel, and Xerox. Later, a second revision was introduced and used extensively in the Internet community. Novell supports this frame specification in its TCP/IP driver set, calling it Ethernet_II.

A later Internet development introduced a set of Ethernet frame specification changes to support larger networks and other services. It is referred to by Novell as Ethernet_SNAP. SNAP stands for Sub Net Access Protocol. This later revision was also adopted for Ethernet NICs in the Macintosh.

Table 3.3 lists the different Novell Ethernet frame types and associated protocols.

TABLE 3.3
Novell Ethernet Frame Types

Type	Protocol	Notes
Ethernet_802.2	IPX	Fully supports IEEE 802.3 and 802.2 specifications. This is the default Ethernet frame type for NetWare 3.12 and 4.*x*.
Ethernet_802.3	IPX	Ethernet "raw" frame type. Introduced prior to and is compatible with the IEEE 802.3 specification. This is the default Ethernet frame type for NetWare 2.*x*, 3.0, 3.10, and 3.11.

continues

Table 3.3, Continued
Novell Ethernet Frame Types

Type	Protocol	Notes
Ethernet_II	TCP/IP IPX	Used with NetWare 3.1*x* and above.
Ethernet_SNAP	AppleTalk TCP/IP IPX	Used in conjunction with NetWare for Macintosh.

Before you can use a network card in a server, you must load a program known as a *LAN driver*, which enables NetWare to interface with the card's hardware. Frame types are assigned on the NetWare file server when you load the LAN driver. On the workstation you can specify the frame type in the NET.CFG file. For a more detailed explanation of frame types, see *NetWare: The Professional Reference*. For more information on loading LAN drivers, see Chapter 12, "Installing the Network Operating System."

Working with Token Ring

Token ring was developed by IBM and introduced in the mid-1980s. It was originally designed as a solution for connecting IBM mainframe computers, minicomputers, and terminals together. Token ring uses a controlled means of network access that allows each node an equal share of time on the network. It tends to perform very consistently even under heavy network loads. Token ring is very well-suited to manufacturing and robotics applications.

Token ring NICs transmit data at a rate of either 4 or 16 mbps. The effective rate of transfer is often in the range of 60 percent of the raw data transmission rate.

How Token Ring NICs Access the Network

The first token ring NIC to power up becomes the *active monitor*. The active monitor issues a special frame known as the *token*. The active monitor is also responsible for monitoring the ring for unusual activities, which include a break in the ring and when the same data frame circulates around the ring more than one time. When the active monitor goes off-line, a negotiation process takes place and another node assumes this role.

The token frame is passed from node to node in physical order. A node with data to transmit "seizes" the token and begins to transmit data for a certain amount of time. When this time period, dictated by the token ring specification, expires, the sending node must "give up" the token. The token passes to its "downstream" neighbor. In this fashion, the token circulates around the ring from one node to its downstream neighbor, indefinitely.

As you can see from this short description, each node in a token ring network is given equal access to the network. Because data is passed directly from one node to the next, collisions are not possible. Unlike Ethernet, when one node in a token ring network sends out data, only the downstream neighbor receives the data.

Each token ring NIC is also a repeater. Data received is filtered to remove noise and copied back onto the ring. Token ring NICs are capable of taking themselves off the ring to perform diagnostics. In addition, the token ring specification includes a number of self-test features that can be reported to network management software.

The token ring specification also allows for a prioritization scheme. This scheme allows one token ring NIC to assume a higher level of priority than other NICs. This NIC can "reserve" the token and transmit more frequently than other NICs.

Sixteen-mbps token ring cards utilize a feature known as *early token release*, among other techniques, to achieve an improvement in overall transmission rate. Early token release enables the node that sends data to release the token immediately after its transmission ends. Without early token release, the token ring sending node is supposed to wait until it receives its data back on the ring before releasing the token. Figure 3.6 illustrates how a 4-mbps token ring transmission occurs.

As you can see in the diagram, the sender receives the token in Step 1. In Step 2, the sender holds the token in a buffer and transmits data to the receiver. The receiver receives the data in Step 3, and repeats the data back onto the ring. Each intervening node also repeats the data, until it is returned to the sender. The sender, upon receipt of the data, releases the token in Step 4.

Token Ring Cabling

Token ring utilizes a special type of hub known as a Multi Station Access Unit (MAU, or MSAU). The function of the MAU is twofold as follows:

- It routes wiring from one port to the next
- It uses a relay that shuts when an attached node loses power

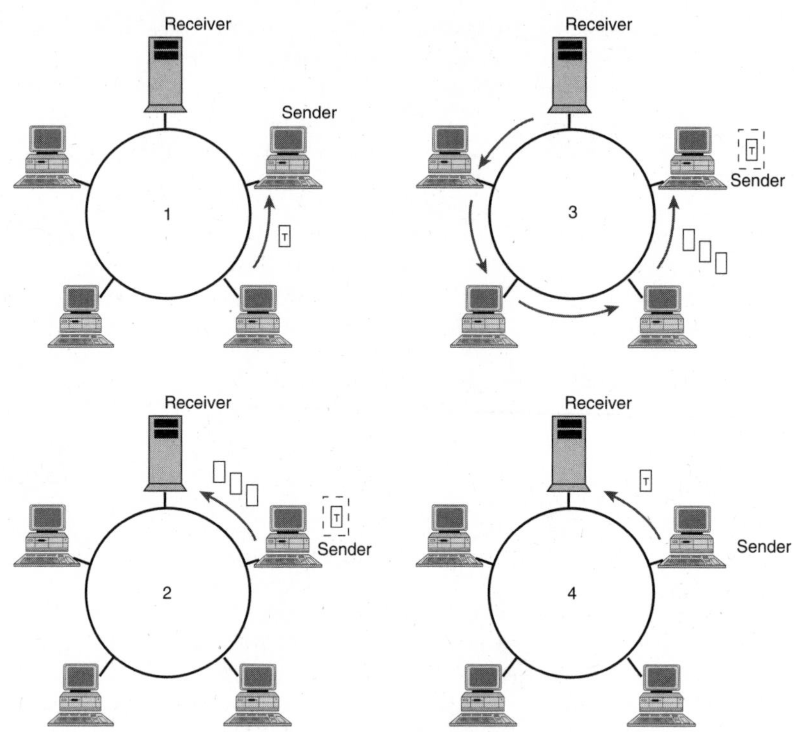

Figure 3.6
Token ring transmissions.

The MAU can be used to quickly disconnect any given node from the ring. The MAU gives token ring the appearance of a star topology. The MAU wires each port physically as a ring. A node connected to port 1, for example, will be directly wired to a node connected to port 2.

The cabling used in token ring is twisted pair. Two types of twisted-pair cabling can be used. Shielded twisted-pair cable supports the longest cable runs and has high resistance to electromagnetic interference but is bulky and high in cost. IBM calls shielded twisted-pair cable designed for token ring *Type 1 cable.* Unshielded twisted-pair cable has become increasingly popular with token ring now that many vendors have solved the problems associated with running 16-mbps data rates on unshielded cable. IBM calls unshielded twisted-pair cable that is suitable for token ring *Type 3 cable.*

The connectors for token ring are either a special data connector developed by IBM and used in their Type 1 cable, or a standard RJ-45 connector (as used in 10BASE-T Ethernet). A special type of cable known simply as *patch cable* is used to connect one MAU to another MAU. When connecting one MAU to another, the RO (Ring Out) and RI (Ring In) ports on the MAU are used. MAUs come in a variety of configurations, typically with 8 or 16 ports (not including RO and RI).

Table 3.4 lists some of the specifications you need to adhere to when wiring token ring networks.

TABLE 3.4
Token Ring Cabling Guidelines

	Maximum (1)	Recommended
Distance from one MAU to another	200 meters	120 meters
Distance from token ring NIC to MAU	300 meters	Up to 100 meters
Total distance of cabling between MAUs	1,000 meters	100 meters
Total number of NICs	260	(2)
Total number of MAUs	12	(3)

(1) The maximums listed in table 3.3 depend on what type of network you have. Many MAU units are rack mounted and are not designed to be easily moved. Other MAUs can easily be picked up and moved around. The type of cabling also affects the maximums. If you use Type 1 cabling, you can expect the maximums to increase. Type 1 cabling is shielded from EMI. Type 3 cabling, on the other hand, is unshielded.

(2) The number of NICs depends on what kind of network performance you expect. The more people who use the LAN, and the more they access files on the file server, the lower performance will be.

(3) There is no recommended number of MAUs.

Figure 3.7 illustrates token ring cabling. Note that *adapter cable* is used to connect the token ring NIC with a MAU, and that *patch cable* connects the RO and RI ports between two MAUs.

Mixed Protocols and Token Ring Frame Types

There are only two token ring frame types supported by NetWare. Unlike Ethernet, which was developed jointly by three different companies, and whose standardization was in the hands of a large number of organizations, token ring has been driven by one company: IBM. Other token ring vendors (such as Thomas Conrad, Proteon, and 3Com), follow IBM's lead.

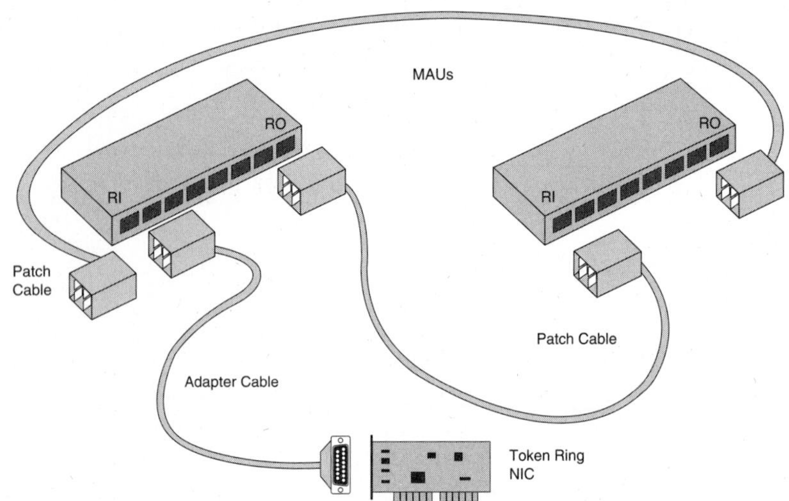

Figure 3.7
Token ring cabling.

The first frame type was originally developed by IBM and later refined by the IEEE. The IEEE 802.5 committee oversees token ring development. Novell refers to the standard token ring frame type as *Token-Ring*. This frame type is used with NetWare's IPX drivers.

The second frame type was developed at the same time as the Ethernet_SNAP frame type. This token ring frame accommodated certain needs of the Internet community. Novell refers to this frame type as *Token-Ring_SNAP*. It is used in conjunction with NetWare's TCP/IP drivers.

Working with ARCnet

ARCnet stands for Attached Resource Computer Network. This type of network interface card was developed by Datapoint Corporation in the 1970s. The first ARCnet cards were commercially available before Ethernet. ARCnet is a robust although low speed type of NIC. Cabling distances are relatively long compared to Ethernet or token ring. ARCnet uses a form of token passing but transmits data as on a bus. In a sense, ARCnet combines features of both Ethernet and token ring. Unlike the other two types of NIC, however, ARCnet enables you to set the address on the card through a *DIP switch*. A DIP (dual in-line package) switch is a block of tiny on/off switches that you can set with the tip of a pen.

Note A *bus* is a term for the network cabling when the network interface cards share the same physical media. In the case of thin Ethernet, for example, the bus is a series of

cables that connect the Ethernet nodes, capped on both ends by a terminator. In the case of ARCnet, the bus consists of a series of cables that connect the ARCnet nodes, including the hubs joining the cables together.

The raw transmission speed of ARCnet is 2.5 mbps. The actual throughput you can achieve in an ARCnet network is typically between 1 and 1.5 mbps.

How ARCnet NICs Access the LAN

ARCnet NICs, like token ring, must wait for a token frame before they are allowed to transmit data. Like Ethernet, when one node transmits, all nodes can receive the data. Collisions are controlled through the token mechanism.

When a new ARCnet card powers up and connects to the LAN, or when an existing ARCnet node powers down and disconnects from the LAN, the *reconfiguration* process occurs. This process is often abbreviated as *recon.* The recon process starts with the card with the lowest address. It sends out a series of broadcasts in an effort to find its next highest neighbor. The card adds 1 to its address until the next highest neighbor responds. The neighbor then starts sending out broadcasts until its next higher neighbor responds. This process continues until the highest communicates with the lowest.

Once the recon process has completed, the lowest NIC sends out a token. The token is received by the next higher NIC. This NIC has the choice to either send data or send the token to its next higher neighbor. The NICs continue to either transmit data or send the token around the network indefinitely.

Contrary to a myth circulating around the network community, ARCnet nodes do not have to be physically arranged in order of their address. There is no performance gain, because the ARCnet specification calls for a time of 31 microseconds between the sending of one token and the response of the next higher neighbor. This time period allows the token to travel electronically the entire distance of the network. The lowest ARCnet node could be at one end of the network, with its next higher neighbor at the opposite end of the network.

ARCnet Cabling

The ARCnet specification allows for a variety of cabling options. These options include the following:

- Coaxial cable (RG-62)
- Star topology using hubs
- Bus topology using "T" connectors and 93-ohm terminators

- Twisted-pair wiring
- Fiber-optic cabling

There are two types of hubs used in ARCnet cabling: active and passive. An *active hub* contains active electronics that perform noise filtering, signal boosting, and signal splitting. The connections to an active hub are self-terminating, meaning that you don't need to add external terminators to an ARCnet network that uses active hubs. A *passive hub* is a simple resistor network that splits the signal only. When you use a passive hub, the cabling distance decreases significantly. In addition, a 93-ohm terminator must be placed on unused connections on the hub. Otherwise, the signal strength will decrease to the point where the network will fail.

When you cable a series of ARCnet nodes in a bus, connect one end of the bus to an active hub (or an ARCnet card on a file server). You can then connect up to 10 ARCnet nodes together using "T" connectors. The maximum distance of such a bus can be no more than 1,000 feet. You must place a 93-ohm terminator at the end of the bus opposite the active hub.

Table 3.5 lists some of the ARCnet cabling maximums.

TABLE 3.5
ARCnet Cabling Maximums

From	To	Distance
Node	Node	2,000 feet
Active hub	Node	2,000 feet
Active hub	Active hub	2,000 feet
Anything	Passive hub	100 feet

Figure 3.8 illustrates some of the possible ways an ARCnet network can be wired.

Working with FDDI

FDDI (Fiber Distributed Digital Interface) was developed by a group of engineers from various NIC vendors and the American National Standards Institute (ANSI). This technology is designed to use fiber-optic cabling with a raw transmission speed of 100 mpbs. It was developed to serve as a backbone between file servers, or in a LAN that spans a greater distance than a single building within a city.

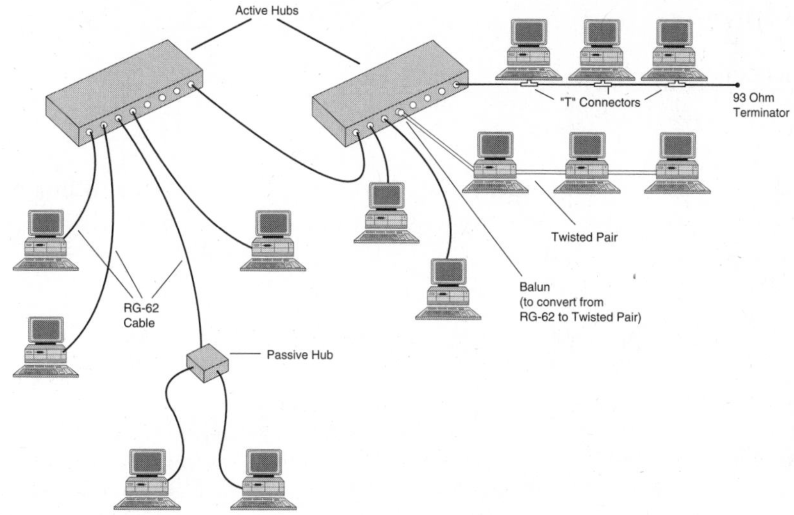

Figure 3.8
ARCnet cabling.

FDDI Characteristics

FDDI uses the same network access method as token ring. FDDI nodes wait for a token frame before transmitting data. In addition, FDDI provides for *asynchronous bandwidth allocation*, which allows FDDI nodes to transmit information "out of turn" (that is, asynchronously) as long as they do not interfere with the transmission of the token. In a certain sense, FDDI combines the best of Ethernet and token ring.

The fiber-optic cable required to cable an FDDI network allows for tremendous future expansion. Other types of signals, such as voice or video, can share the same cable as the FDDI nodes, provided that you wired the network using digital switches that accommodate multiple types of signals. An *ATM* (Asynchronous Transfer Mode) *switch* is an example of such a device.

Because FDDI uses optical signals, FDDI networks enjoy complete immunity from EMI. The use of optical signaling also dramatically increases the security of the network. Copper/electrical networks all transmit varying degrees of magnetic signals. Using relatively simple equipment, it is possible to pick up the electronic signals that emanate from a conventional LAN.

The cost of FDDI network interface cards has dropped considerably. Many major NIC vendors such as 3Com now offer FDDI interfaces.

Note Another specification, CDDI, is in the process of being standardized. This specification is similar to FDDI, except that it is designed for short distances over copper-based twisted-pair cabling.

FDDI Cabling

The cost of fiber-optic cable is much greater than that of coaxial or twisted-pair cable. The cost of the copper used in coaxial or twisted-pair cable is increasing, whereas the cost of the glass fibers is stable or dropping.

Fiber-optic cable itself is fragile. Most cable vendors wrap the fiber-optic strands in a resilient cloth fabric, resulting in a strength almost rivaling that of copper cable. There are easy-to-use kits available that simplify the process of placing connectors on fiber-optic cables.

Unlike copper cable, fiber-optic cable currently transmits signals one way only. The transmitter is typically either an injection laser diode or an LED (light emitting diode). The receiver is a photosensitive circuit. To properly cable a fiber-optic network, you must wire up one fiber-optic strand for sending and another for receiving. Most fiber-optic cable companies wire fiber-optic networks with 6-strand plenum cable. The word *plenum* refers to the space between a drop ceiling and the actual ceiling. Plenum cable is cable that passes building codes that govern cabling in the plenum. Building codes vary between localities. An example of a typical code is that cable which is passed across the plenum must be both fire-resistant and must not emit a noxious gas when burned. Six-strand cable is used for two reasons: if one of the strands breaks, another is available to take its place with minimum cabling effort. The other reason is that if your company wishes to use another strand for other purposes (such as voice or video signaling), the cabling is already in place.

FDDI networks can be cabled as SA (singly attached) or DA (doubly attached) networks. SA cabling is from node to node to form a ring. As with token ring, each FDDI node is a repeater. DA cabling involves an FDDI concentrator. The concentrator is similar to a token ring MAU. Each port contains a repeater and supports a dual ring architecture. Each DA node has two inputs and two outputs. DA FDDI networks have two rings: a primary and a secondary. If the primary ring fails, the FDDI nodes adjacent to the point of failure signal other nodes on the network to switch to the secondary ring. The change from primary to secondary rings is transparent to the user.

FDDI networks enjoy tremendous maximum distances. Table 3.6 lists some of the FDDI cabling maximum distances.

TABLE 3.6
FDDI Cabling Maximums

From	To	Distance
DA node	FDDI concentrator	1 km

From	To	Distance
SA node	SA node	2 km
Entire distance of a DA network		100 km
Entire distance of an SA network		200 km

Exploring WANs

WANs (wide area networks) are gaining in importance in the networking community. The original computer networks of the 1960s were often WANs. These early networks featured large, powerful (for the time) mainframes that had banks of dial-in connections. Users from all over the world would dial in to central data processing sites to handle their day-to-day computing needs.

The distinction between a WAN and a LAN has become blurred with advances in technology. The first part of this section deals with the differences between WANs and LANs. The following sections give you an overview of some of the different WAN technologies that are the counterparts of the LAN technologies described earlier.

Comparing WAN and LAN Communication

For many years the difference between a WAN and a LAN was that a WAN was a network that used telephone lines to communicate over widely dispersed geographic locations. The development of FDDI, bridges, and routers makes this simple definition no longer accurate. FDDI LANs can stretch up to 200 km (almost 120 miles). To further complicate the distinction, many LANs now feature the capability to dial in and dial out using modem servers and dial-in servers. To summarize: there is no clear distinction between a LAN and a WAN.

The IEEE makes a distinction at the OSI data link layer. LAN technology is defined by the 802.2 and lower level specifications. Lower level specifications include 802.3 (Ethernet), and 802.5 (token ring). WAN technology is defined by such specifications as X.25 and LAPB.

LAPB stands for Link Access Procedure Balanced. It evolved from HDLC (High speed Data Link Control), which in turn evolved from SDLC (Synchronous Data Link Control). SDLC was the original IBM specification that governed the high speed exchange of data between nodes in an IBM mainframe environment.

For the purposes of this book, a WAN is defined as a series of LANs joined together using leased analog or digital lines.

T1 and Other Leased Lines

Digital leased lines are communications channels leased from long-distance telephone carriers such as AT&T, MCI, and Sprint. The carrier guarantees a certain raw transmission speed. How the signal is transmitted within the long-distance carrier's system can vary. Typical media include long-distance fiber-optic trunk lines, microwave, satellite, and infrared, among other technologies.

Leased Lines

Leased lines have been in use in WANs for the last 20 to 30 years. Initially, companies relied upon analog lines. Data transmission rates 20 years ago were in the area of 150 bps for TTY (teletype) terminals, and up to 300 bps for some modems. CCITT (Consultative Committee for International Telephony and Telegraphy), an international organization, developed a series of telephone and modem standards of increasing speed and sophistication. The V.24 specification, for example, defined a rate of 2400 bps.

Long-distance carriers started to offer *digital circuits,* which were phone lines with extensive noise filtering. These lines could typically carry data at rates of up to 56 kbps.

T1 and T3

One type of leased digital phone line is known as T1. This is a technology developed and offered by AT&T. T1 lines are leased between two points and transmit digital data. The raw transmission speed of a T1 line is up to 1.54 mbps in the United States and Japan, and up to 2.048 mbps in Europe. Connections to a T1 line require a unit known as a DSU/CSU (Data Service Unit/Channel Service Unit). This device converts a high speed analog input (from a synchronous modem, for example) into a digital output acceptable to the T1 system.

T1 lines are often used to carry voice and video as well as digital data. If a company establishes a T1 line between two sites, for example, the T1 line is often tied into the company's phone system as well as its network. Partial T1 lines can also be leased, known as *fractional T1* lines. A fractional T1 line typically offers a raw transmission speed of 64 kbps. This allows you to run several different LAN connections over the same leased line.

The cost of a T1 line varies depending on the distance between the two sites. Costs can range anywhere from $100 a month within 1 mile to $2,000 a month for a distance of 500 miles.

Another type of leased line is the T3 line. The T3 specification was developed by AT&T shortly after the T1 specification. A T3 line guarantees a raw transmission speed of up to roughly 45 mpbs. T3 lines are for companies with the need for a great deal of bandwidth. T3 lines are most often used for multiple purposes: voice, video, and data transmissions.

SONET

SONET (Synchronous Optical Network) has recently been adopted as the physical layer for the B-ISDN (Broadband Integrated Services Digital Network). SONET was originally developed by Bellcore. The specifications for SONET are now accepted as an international standard by ANSI and CCITT.

SONET data rates are broken down into a hierarchy defined in terms of the Optical Carrier (OC) speeds and corresponding synchronous transport signals (STS). These divisions are in multiples of 51.84 mbps. OC-1 corresponds to a rate of 51.84 mpbs. OC-8 is 8 x 51.84, which amounts to 2,488.32 mpbs. The maximum rate according to this standard is OC-240, which corresponds with 12.4416 gbps (gigabits per second).

X.25

X.25 is another CCITT specification. This specification was designed to operate with packet switching networks. A *packet switching network* transmits across a network in packets. The packets are switched from one intermediate node to another to reach the destination. The operation of the packet switching network is designed to be transparent to its subscribers. X.25 specifications correspond to the OSI physical, data link, and a portion of the network layers.

The X.25 specification, introduced in the mid-1970s, was designed to allow LANs to communicate together in either a point-to-point or a multipoint connection. Speeds were typically 56 kbps, and up to 64 kbps in Europe. A *point-to-point connection* is when a single location connects to another single location. A *multipoint connection* is when you have many different locations and each can connect to the other.

On each LAN you want to interconnect, you will need an X.25 router or bridge. These devices are available as stand-alone integrated units, or as software that you would load on a dedicated workstation. The Novell MPR+ (Multiprotocol Router Plus), for example, is a software package that offers an X.25 connectivity option. In the case of the MPR+, you will need a synchronous adapter card to allow the file server or dedicated workstation, to connect to a synchronous modem. The modem connects to a leased line that in turn connects to the X.25 packet switching network. Figure 3.9 illustrates three LANs connected using X.25 routers.

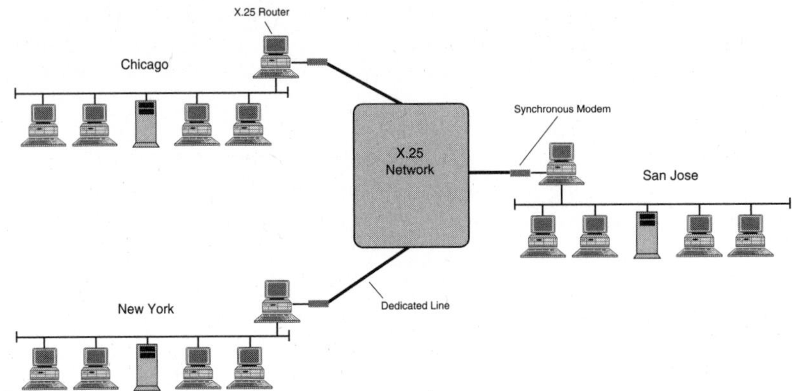

Figure 3.9
X.25 WAN connectivity.

PPP

Point-to-Point Protocol (PPP) was developed by the Internet community to provide WAN connectivity at T1 speeds. This protocol is based on HDLC (High-Level Data Link Control), which in turn is based on SDLC (Synchronous Data Link Control), developed by IBM. As with X.25, a PPP connection requires a router or bridge to connect to the LAN. A DSU/CSU is required to connect the router or bridge to the T1 line.

PPP was originally designed to transmit TCP/IP protocols over T1 lines. X.25 networks have transmission speeds of only up to 64 kbps. Using a PPP connection over a T1 line, you can achieve a raw transmission speed of up to 1.54 mbps (2.048 mbps in Europe).

PPP is a very flexible protocol. It can also be configured using standard serial ports and asynchronous modems. Novell's UnixWare, for example, enables you to configure a PPP connection using the COM1 or COM2 port and an asynchronous modem. Users can dial out of the UnixWare computer to a remote system on the Internet that is configured to accept PPP. The remote system sees the UnixWare computer as if it were directly connected on a LAN.

B-ISDN

B-ISDN (Broadband Integrated Services Digital Network) is a set of standards developed by the CCITT. This international group of specifications was introduced as the need grew for the integration of voice, video, and data. The B-ISDN model is beginning to replace the OSI model in the networking community.

One of the major differences between the OSI and B-ISDN models is that the latter is a three-dimensional model. Certain functions that are carried out at different layers of the OSI model are handled by different planes of the B-ISDN model. The difference lies in the fact that the OSI model was developed with baseband rather than broadband transmission techniques.

Baseband Transmissions

Baseband transmissions are transmissions in which only one type of signal (such as voice, video, or data) occupies the media at any given time. Examples of baseband transmissions are Ethernet NICs attached to a thin coaxial bus. When one NIC transmits, the other NICs wait. Only data can be transmitted in a Thin Ethernet network. Another example of baseband transmission would be token ring NICs in a token ring network.

To achieve some degree of network management, and to control the flow of data between client and server, the OSI model defines seven different layers, as discussed earlier. The data link layer, for example, includes the 802.2 or LLC (Logical Link Control) specification. The LLC controls how the flow of data between client and server is to be accomplished.

If the amount of data to be exchanged between client and server is too much for one or the other, the exchange of data must be interrupted while the data link layers of the two computers resolve the conflict. Likewise, if there is a problem in a token ring network, the NICs must negotiate between themselves to determine where the fault lies. This process occupies valuable time that could otherwise be used to transmit data. The OSI approach results in wasted time that results in lower actual throughput of data.

Broadband Transmissions

Broadband transmissions, on the other hand, allow many types of signals to be transmitted simultaneously. Signals are encoded onto the media using various techniques that are beyond the scope of this book. Voice, video, and data are all assigned different channels and can be transmitted at the same time.

Broadband transmissions techniques have been used for the last 10 to 20 years. Until recently, the major problem has been the limitations of the available media. Broadband techniques are especially useful in conjunction with fiber-optic cabling. Coaxial cable will support broadband, although the maximum data rates are limited by the media. Cable TV is an example of broadband transmissions, and many television signals can be transmitted over a single coaxial cable. (Now you know why the telephone companies are so interested in acquiring cable companies.)

The B-ISDN Model

The Broadband ISDN model has strong similarities to the OSI model. In a certain sense, it is a superset of the OSI model. As you can see in figure 3.10, SONET and ATM roughly correspond to the OSI physical layer. The IEEE 802.2 and Frame Relay specifications, along with the adaption layer, correspond to the OSI data link layer.

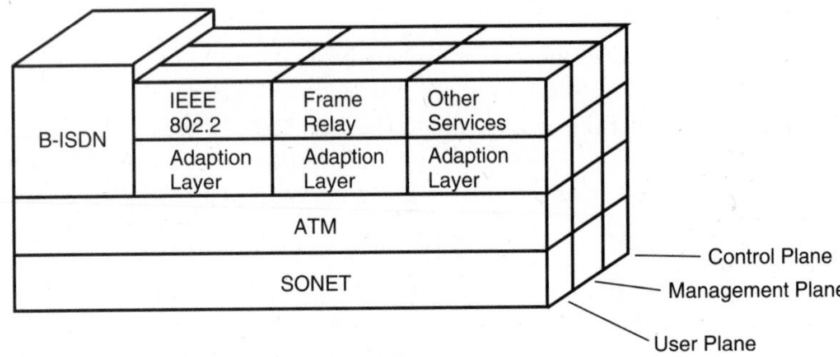

Figure 3.10
The Broadband ISDN model.

As you can see, the different planes give the B-ISDN model a three-dimensional aspect. The *user plane* is what network users utilize. This plane is for the transmission of user data. The *management plane* takes care of the flow of data between the sender and receiver as well as resolving transmission problems. The *control plane* handles signaling information.

ATM

Asynchronous Transfer Mode (ATM) has been adopted by the CCITT as the switching technology to support the B-ISDN model. As you can see in figure 3.10, ATM functions between SONET and the adaption layer.

ATM transmits data in 53-byte blocks known as *cells*. A cell is similar to a frame (such as an Ethernet frame) that consists of a 5-byte header and 48 bytes of data. The small cell allows ATM switches to easily intersperse voice, video, and data. An ATM switch is a device with an input that accepts voice, video, or data on one side, and a connection to the long-distance leased line on the other. An ATM network is formed when you have many leased lines that are connected to a series of ATM switches at various sites.

The ATM layer maintains a *virtual channel* between two points in the ATM switching network. A virtual channel is established on an as-needed basis. You can think of a virtual channel as a logical bus. The sending and receiving nodes will think they are directly connected and have exclusive use of the media. The ATM hardware makes this logical bus possible, while simultaneously handling hundreds or thousands of other transmissions.

The ATM management plane handles line problems and controls the amount of data flowing between switches. This arrangement frees the user plane to transmit data at tremendous speeds. A typical ATM network will allow data transfer rates of anywhere from 44 mbps to 600 mbps. The maximum transfer rate currently is in the area of 2.5 gbps.

ATM network interface cards are starting to make an appearance. There have been announcements from several major network vendors, including HP and IBM. The ATM NIC could potentially bypass the expensive ATM switch, allowing computers on a LAN to communicate directly with each other at speeds of between 45 mbps and 2 gbps. The ATM NIC gives each PC the potential to connect directly to the long-distance trunk lines. This means that LANs and WANs as you now know them might become one and the same. Vendors currently offering ATM cards include Cabletron, Digital Equipment Corporation (DEC), and Plexcom.

Frame Relay

Frame Relay is the WAN equivalent of an OSI data link layer specification such as 802.2 and 802.3. This technology was developed as a replacement for X.25. The protocols are very similar to X.25 without the management overhead.

Frame Relay currently offers anywhere from 56 kbps to 2.048 mbps transmission speed. Future implementations will work within the B-ISDN standards offering transmission speeds in the 2 to 3 gbps range.

Putting It All Together

The preceding sections discussed the technologies and equipment needed to implement a LAN or WAN. This section ties the preceding discussion together by presenting you with a series of case studies. The case studies start with a small office and then graduate to a campus of buildings and a large multinational company. In each case you read a description of the company, its data processing needs, and possible solutions.

Case 1: A Small Office

The law office of Stan Morgan and Lorraine Gonzalez is located in a suburban office complex. In addition to the two senior partners, there are three junior partners, four paralegals, eight secretaries, four word processors, and four administrative staff members. Each person has a computer on his desk. The office occupies a single floor and is approximately 6,000 square feet. The partners in the firm each have their own office. The office manager, who also manages the books, has her own office. All other employees have cubicles spread about the office.

The data processing needs for the firm are as follows:

- All computers have Microsoft Windows installed.
- All documents are produced using the WordPerfect for Windows word processing program.
- The attorneys' time is accounted for using the TimeSlips time accounting program.
- The books for the company are maintained using the Platinum accounting program.
- Several people maintain various spreadsheets using Excel.
- The paralegals and attorneys subscribe to WestLaw dial-up legal services.
- The attorneys are interested in being able to access the LAN after hours and on the road, using modems.

As you can imagine, the best solution for this case would be a simple LAN with a dial-in and dial-out server. The number of people and what they would be doing would not impose a severe load on the network. As a result, the company would be free to choose from Ethernet, ARCnet, or token ring. This decision will most likely hinge on what type of deal the firm can obtain through their nearest network reseller.

For this purpose, suppose they choose Ethernet. The next decision would be whether to use 10BASE2 (Thin coaxial Ethernet), or 10BASE-T (twisted-pair Ethernet). Thin Ethernet has a lower initial cost because there are no hubs to purchase. Coaxial cable costs more than twisted-pair cable, however, and is more difficult to troubleshoot and maintain.

At this point you need to know several additional factors:

- What types of EMI can be expected in the office?
- Is there any cabling already in place?
- How much growth is the firm expecting over the next few years?

If EMI is a problem, Thin coaxial Ethernet would be a better solution. If cabling is already in place, you will need to determine what type of cable and in what condition. If the company is expecting substantial growth, 10BASE-T would be a better solution.

As far as dial-in and dial-out solutions go, you will need to know the answers to the following questions:

- How many people will be dialing in or out at the same time?
- How often will dial-in or out take place?
- How much data will be transferred when dialing in or out?

Once you know how many people will be dialing in or out at the same time, you can order and configure the necessary hardware. If only one or two people will be dialing in or out, a solution such as the US Robotics Shared Access Modem, which uses the COM1 and COM2 ports available on any ordinary PC, would be a possible solution. If you find, on the other hand, that as many as 12 people might be dialing in or out, you might think in terms of the Microdyne NetWare Access Server, which can handle up to 15 dial-in users, and NetWare Connect, which can handle several dial-out users.

A hardware solution to both dial-in and dial-out is to use a Cubix system. These units offer the ability to plug in PCs on a card into a unit with a series of slots, power supply, and a common data bus. Each PC on a card has its own CPU, RAM, and separate COM ports. Cubix systems can be configured for both dial-in and dial-out. The advantage is that they do not require a dedicated computer and offer superior performance to software solutions. A disadvantage is the cost of such a system, which starts at $9,000.

You will also need to decide how many phone lines to order to service dial-in and dial-out. The amount of data being transferred might lead you to consider what types of modems to use. Generally speaking, the faster the modem, the more expensive it is.

Figure 3.11 shows you the layout of a possible solution to Case Study #1.

Case 2: A Campus of Buildings

The second case study involves a moderately sized software publishing company XYZ, which employs 400 employees. XYZ is located near a major city and has three buildings situated around a large parking lot. A fourth building is two blocks away. Building 1 houses the software engineers and quality assurance testing. It has a mainframe computer used for developing computerized models. There are several research and development labs. Each engineer needs access to the mainframe as well as access to e-mail and DOS-based programs. Each building has several NetWare file servers.

Building 2 houses the executives, accounting group, and sales staff. Everyone has a computer on his desk that is used for e-mail, maintaining spreadsheets, and word processing. There is a minicomputer that is used by Accounting. Building 3 houses education, technical writers who produce the documentation for the product, and shipping and receiving. Education and the tech writers use a UNIX-based desktop publishing program, Macintoshes for graphics, and PC DOS-based units for e-mail and DOS-based programs. Building 4 contains employees and equipment from a company recently purchased by XYZ. The employees use primarily DOS-based PCs. They need to communicate with the parent company via e-mail.

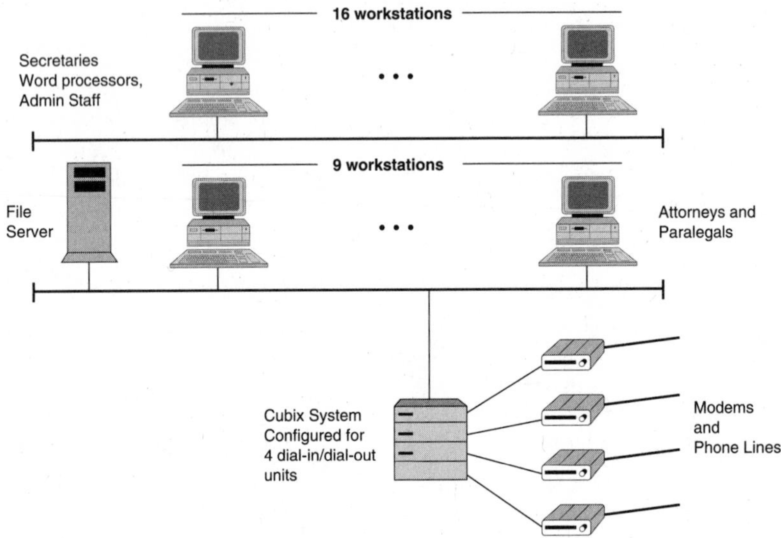

Figure 3.11

A possible solution to Case Study #1.

Solutions for this case study will vary widely. Much of the solution will depend on what equipment exists already. In a case like this, the company has been purchasing equipment throughout its existence. When a piece of equipment becomes obsolete it is replaced with the state of the art equipment at that time. In this case XYZ has a mixture of equipment: ARCnet, Thin Ethernet LANs, LocalTalk (for the Macintoshes), and token ring LANs. As Ethernet NICs and cable segments give out, they are replaced with 10BASE-T Ethernet. The 10BASE-T equipment is much easier to manage. Workstations can be added or moved at any time without disrupting the network as a whole.

NetWare file servers can be configured, using internal routing, to join the different types of LANs. A LocalTalk card enables a NetWare file server to support the Macintoshes using LocalTalk. The Macintoshes are slowly being upgraded and outfitted with 10BASE-T Ethernet adapters. This gives Mac users a tremendous increase in speed. LocalTalk allows a transmission rate of only 230 kbps, whereas Ethernet will give them a raw speed of 10 mbps.

The Ethernet segments can be isolated using bridges or routers to reduce traffic on any one segment. Protocol analyzers, such as Novell's LANalyzer for Windows discussed in Chapter 39, "Monitoring Network Performance," will give them statistics on the utilization of each segment.

An FDDI card can be installed in each file server and router, creating an FDDI backbone. FDDI will allow buildings 1, 2, and 3 to be connected together at a transmission rate of 100 mbps. FDDI has a maximum distance of 200 km if stations are wired using the Single Attachment mode.

The routers must be capable of handling multiple protocols. As you can see from the description of the needs of the company, there are at least three protocols used: IPX/SPX (the DOS/NetWare computers), TCP/IP (the UNIX computers), and AppleTalk (the Macintosh computers). In addition, the mainframe and minicomputer connections must be analyzed. A gateway might be needed to perform full protocol conversion between the LANs and the mainframe and minicomputer.

The amount of data that needs to be transmitted to building 4 needs to be analyzed. Eventually, the best course of action might be to make room for the employees of the newly acquired company in buildings 1, 2, or 3. In the meantime, if a small amount of data needs to be transmitted, an X.25 connection might be established. Alternatively, if a large amount of data needs to be transmitted between the buildings, it might be more practical to lease a T1 line.

The X.25 connection will give XYZ a rate of up to 64 kbps. The hardware needed would include an X.25 router with special PC adapters, synchronous modems, and a dedicated phone line. Rates are relatively low.

The T1 line will give them up to 2.048 mbps. A router that can handle PPP or Frame Relay will be needed, along with a special PC adapter and a DSU/CSU. The T1 connection will be substantially more expensive than an X.25 connection.

Figure 3.12 shows you the layout of a possible solution to Case Study #2.

Case 3: An International Company

Sparky Oil International is an international corporation with offices in almost every major city in the world. Corporate offices are in Houston, Texas. There are major research and development centers in Summit, New Jersey, and Los Angeles, California. Sparky has almost every type of computer in one of its offices, from IBM PC XTs to Sun Sparcs UNIX workstations, to minicomputers, to mainframes. The company currently has its own private TCP/IP Internet that spans the globe. NetWare LANs are located in most of its facilities.

Networking solutions for Sparky Oil International depend on various factors, such as budget, numbers of users, and external conditions. Ethernet is predominant because of its wide support. Token ring is used in the manufacturing facilities because of its deterministic nature. That is, in a token ring LAN, because of its use of the token to control transmissions, you can precisely determine when a given card can transmit.

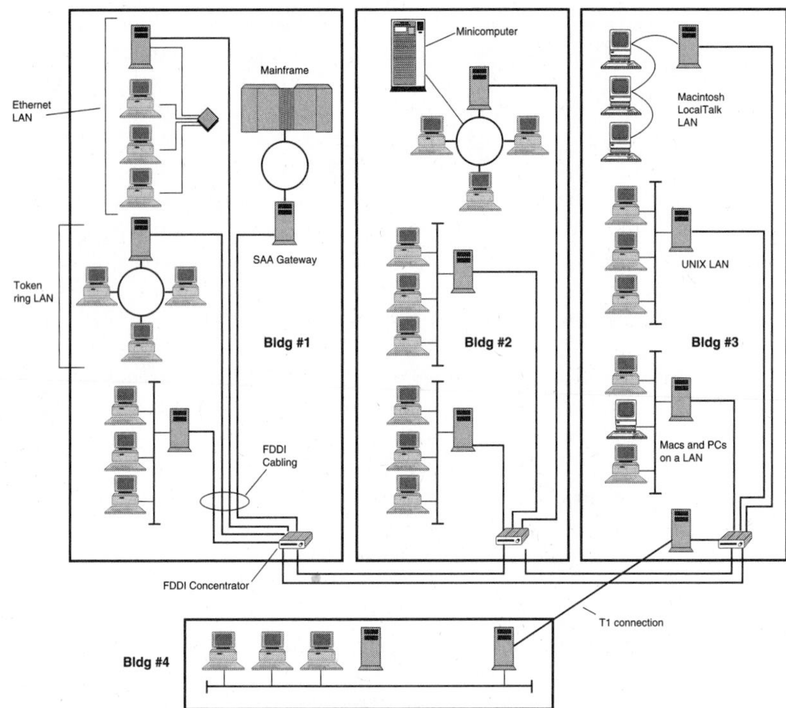

Figure 3.12

Possible solution to Case Study #2.

Multiprotocol routers are needed to tie the major systems together. TCP/IP is the predominant protocol in use. The reason for this is that this protocol has been around for as long as the company itself and is available on all the computer systems Sparky uses.

On the NetWare file servers, the TCP/IP command utilities are available at no extra charge. Each NetWare file server can be configured as an IP router. In addition, Novell offers a product, NetWare/IP, that allows DOS-based workstations to log in to a NetWare server using only the IP protocol (rather than IPX). This can simplify network management.

Many types of gateways are necessary at Sparky. Because of the diversity of mainframe and minicomputer systems, gateways are needed to convert protocols that are non-standard. The gateways attach to the LANs, allowing any user to access any minicomputer or mainframe. The users on the LAN will need to run terminal emulation software. This software allows the workstation to be seen as a terminal to the mainframe or mini host.

Summary

This chapter discussed the foundation technologies used in the WAN environment. The first discussion concluded that there is no clear distinction between a LAN and a WAN. For the purposes of this book, I define a WAN as a series of LANs joined together using leased analog or digital lines. Some of the LAN technologies discussed include Ethernet, token ring, ARCnet, and FDDI.

The next part of this chapter described the various technologies used in the WAN environment. Technologies that correspond to the OSI physical layer include leased lines, T1, T3, and SONET. As you discovered, T1 and T3 are older technologies developed by Bellcore that guarantee a certain rate of data. SONET, on the other hand, is specifically designed for optical cabling. On top of these technologies, an older protocol, X.25, was discussed. X.25 gives you a maximum data rate of only 64 kbps. A newer specification is ATM, which gives you a data rate of anywhere from 45 mbps to 2 gbps. PPP and Frame Relay are protocols based on T1 lines. Frame Relay will eventually be adapted to work with ATM and SONET under a new emerging standard, B-ISDN. The B-ISDN model is a three-dimensional model that will eventually supersede the two-dimensional OSI model.

Part II

Examining NetWare 4.1's Benefits

New Riders Publishing
INSIDE
SERIES

CHAPTER

Traditional Features of NetWare

NetWare 4.1 inherits a number of features that have become standard in Novell's line of network operating systems. These include safety features such as *mirroring* and *hot fix*, which protect the data on your file server. A discussion of bindery-based server management will give you a glimpse of how a file server running NetWare 4.1 views file servers running older versions of NetWare.

This chapter also gives you a look at file system features, including partitions and volumes. A discussion of network printing will give you a good overview of how printing occurs and can be controlled in a network. Other sections in this chapter look at how the file server manages memory and how it communicates with other devices on the network. Finally, there is a section dealing with clients of the file server. This section explains how clients (workstations) connect to the file server and also provides a picture of how different client operating systems interact with NetWare.

The History of NetWare Prior to NetWare 4.1

As you read in the first chapter, NetWare was first introduced in the early 1980s as a product known as ShareNet. The purpose of ShareNet was to enable PC users to share files and printers. Since that time, hardware-oriented versions of NetWare have been created, and finally, software-only versions. At present, Novell is positioned primarily as a software company.

NetWare is designed to work on Intel-based PCs. Other versions of NetWare, for example Processor Independent NetWare, are available for other platforms. These versions are beyond the scope of this book.

Although there are several versions of NetWare prior to NetWare 2.0, the following discussion begins with this version.

NetWare 2.*x*

There were a series of versions in the NetWare 2.*x* family of products. These versions were sometimes referred to as NetWare 286. This name comes from the fact that these versions were written for the Intel 80286 microprocessor. Because the NetWare 286 family was written for the 80286 microprocessor, the compilers used were 16-bit compilers and were limited by the memory management scheme available on the 80286.

The 80286 can perform operations on numbers up to 16 binary bits. This means that the maximum number that can be handled at any given time is 65,536 in decimal. If you need to handle a larger number, the parts of the number must be cycled in and out of the microprocessor in stages, slowing down overall performance.

The 80286 microprocessor is limited to 16 MB of RAM that it can directly address.

The installation process was similar for all NetWare 286 versions. First you ran an installation program. During this process, you selected various drivers for the NICs and hard drives on the file server. You also supplied configuration information regarding interrupts, I/O port addresses, and memory addresses.

An *interrupt* is a number assigned to a physical board in a computer. When the board needs to communicate information to the computer, it signals the computer using an *interrupt line*. The computer senses what interrupt line is being activated, performs a lookup in an *interrupt vector table* and jumps to a software program that services the interrupt. The interrupt vector table determines which program currently in the computer's memory can service interrupt *X*, where *X* is the number of the interrupt line being activated.

An *I/O port* is a number assigned to the circuitry on a PC's motherboard or a PC card such as a network interface card. The "port" is actually an address which the computer uses to send or receive information to or from the PC card.

Memory addresses are where the PC or the PC card can store information pertinent to the card. In some cases the PC card has a built-in ROM chip. The memory address is used to store some of all program instructions on the ROM chip. In other cases the memory address is a buffer where the PC card will store data coming in from the LAN, or going out to the LAN.

NetWare 2.0 and 2.0A

NetWare 2.0 was introduced in 1986. This version is software only and is designed to take advantage of the Intel 80286 microprocessor.

NetWare 2.0 features support for ARCnet, Ethernet, and token ring. It is sold in user license increments. If you want to have 50 users on a network, for example, you must purchase a 50-user license.

The software installation program is not very sophisticated. It enables you to install disk drivers, perform a low level format of the hard drive, and create a NetWare disk partition. A *low level format* is a procedure that analyzes and erases every byte of space on the hard drive. This type of format bypasses all the normal safety procedures built into operating systems such as DOS. A *disk partition* is a subdivision of the amount of disk space available. A partition is necessary when installing a new operating system such as NetWare. When NetWare is later installed on the hard drive, it will use space only in its partition. This way you can have several types of operating systems on a single hard drive.

With NetWare 2.0, network printers must be attached directly to the file server. You can have a total of five printers on any single file server. Printing uses a spooling process, a technique borrowed from the UNIX world, and printers are referred to by number rather than by name.

Note Later versions of NetWare, including NetWare 4.1, use a *print queue*.

Workstation software for NetWare 2.0 is limited to DOS-based computers. The workstation software consists of a single driver known as ANETx.COM. ANET2.COM is used for DOS 2.*x* and ANET3.COM for DOS 3.*x*. NetWare 2.0 is limited to the IPX/SPX protocol.

NetWare 2.1*x*

NetWare 2.10 was introduced in 1987. There are several versions that included a variety of new features. Some of the most successful features were the SFT (System Fault Tolerant) features. These included disk mirroring, disk duplexing, hot fix, and TTS (Transaction Tracking System).

The *disk mirroring* and *disk duplexing* features cause the operating system to write the same data to two drives. One of the drives is designated during installation as the *primary* and the other the *secondary*. Data is written to both drives simultaneously. If the primary drive fails, the secondary drive automatically takes over. Users will suffer no downtime. The difference between mirroring and duplexing is that duplexing uses additional redundant hardware for even more safety. The redundant hardware includes an additional disk controller and, in some cases, a redundant power supply.

Hot fix is a process that works in conjunction with read-after-write verification. Read-after-write verification takes place while the operating system is writing data to the file server's hard drive. The operating system keeps the data being written in the file server's memory. The operating system reads the data back again and compares it to the original. If there is any mismatch, the system tries again a couple of times. If the original data still does not match what is read back from the drive, the portion of the disk being written to is assumed to be bad. The data is then redirected to the hot fix area. The *hot fix area* is a reserved portion of the hard drive.

The *Transaction Tracking System* (TTS) is a feature that safeguards large data files. When a file is flagged as transactional by using the FLAG command, the operating system maintains a log file. The TTS log file tracks changes made to the file and maintains records in their original state prior to any changes. When a transaction is written to the hard drive and is verified by the read-after-write verification system, TTS erases the record of the transaction. If the system loses power or crashes during a transaction, the operating system consults the transaction log file and automatically *rolls back* the database to the last verified transaction. Once rolled back, the database is in a known good state prior to the last changes. The changes then can be reapplied.

The installation process for NetWare 2.1*x* is tedious and involved. SFT NetWare ships with approximately 45 disks! The disks are 360 KB in size, and installation requires a tremendous amount of disk swapping. The installation program is known as NETGEN. It features a maddening number of tiny menus that pop up in odd places across the screen and change in the number of available options depending on which options already are selected.

Printing in NetWare 2.1*x* is greatly improved. Print jobs are sent to a print queue that can be referred to by name. The workstation shell in NetWare 2.1*x* supports a command known as the CAPTURE command, which is still present (although modified) in NetWare 4.1. The CAPTURE command allows NetWare to transparently redirect printing from the workstation's local parallel port to a network print queue. This was a tremendous improvement that allows workstation software to print without being aware of the network.

The workstation shell is vastly improved in NetWare 2.1*x*. The IPX/SPX protocol component is separated out from the NETx shell. A new utility, SHGEN, was introduced, which simplifies the workstation shell generation process. SHGEN produces a file called IPX.COM that works with the NIC in the workstation and implements IPX/SPX on the workstation.

NetWare 2.1*x* went through approximately a dozen different revisions. The first release was NetWare 2.10. The last release in this product family was NetWare 2.15E. Table 4.1 lists different ways NetWare 2.1*x* is sold and associated features.

TABLE 4.1
NetWare 2.1*x* Versions

Version	Description
SFT NetWare	SFT (System Fault Tolerant) NetWare was functionally equivalent to Advanced NetWare. It could be installed only in nondedicated mode. This version of NetWare added disk mirroring and duplexing. In addition, TTS was offered.
Advanced NetWare	Advanced NetWare was sold in user-license packages ranging from 5 users to 100 users. This version could be installed in dedicated or nondedicated modes. When installed as nondedicated, the file server itself could also be used as a workstation.

continues

Table 4.1, Continued
NetWare 2.1*x* Versions

Version	Description
ELS Level II	ELS stood for Entry Level System. It had all the features of Advanced NetWare except for certain limitations. The limitations included the ability to support only one NIC in the file server. To get support for more users, you had to upgrade to Advanced or SFT NetWare.
ELS Level I	Level I had most of the features of ELS Level II NetWare, with certain exceptions. It had support for only one NIC in the file server. The file server that brought performance down was not dedicated.

NetWare 2.2

NetWare 2.2 was the final product in the NetWare 286 family. It had all the features of SFT NetWare version 2.15E. It incorporated all the patches and fixes that were available for previous versions of NetWare. The operating system was recompiled using newer optimizing compiler technology, and memory management was refined as much as possible given the 80286 microprocessor.

The installation procedure for NetWare 2.2 was greatly improved. A new installation program, INSTALL, was introduced to break down the procedure into four relatively simple steps. The 40 or 50 small input screens and menus were consolidated into two input screens, and the software was shipped on high-density disks, bringing the disk count down to 12–15 disks (depending on which options, such as NetWare for Macintosh, are counted).

The workstation shells were refined again, as well. A new utility, WSGEN, was used to generate the workstation software. The IPX.COM file that resulted was given new options that allow users to override the settings temporarily. The NET*x* shell was improved and could be unloaded from memory without having to reboot the workstation.

NetWare 3.*x*

NetWare 3.0, 3.10, 3.11, and 3.12 are sometimes referred to as NetWare 386. NetWare 3.0 was introduced in 1989. It is a 32-bit network operating system designed to take full advantage of the features of the Intel 80386 microprocessor. Portions of the operating system were written in 80386 assembly language to achieve speed. The

assembly language code includes portions designed to detect and take advantage of an 80486 chip.

NetWare 3.0 represents a radical departure from earlier versions of NetWare. It features a greatly improved memory management scheme. NetWare 3.0 is capable of allocating memory dynamically from a number of memory pools. Most of the memory allocated can be returned to the master memory pool when the process is unloaded.

The operating system acts like a software bus. Programs called NLMs (NetWare Loadable Modules) can be loaded on top of the operating system kernel. The NLM is dynamically linked to the operating system and makes additional commands and features available. When the NLM is no longer needed or has to be upgraded, it can be unloaded. When the NLM is unloaded, its memory can be released back to the master memory pool.

Another improvement is the incorporation of the ODI architecture, Streams, and multiple protocol support. *ODI* (Open Datalink Interface) allows NICs in the file server to send and receive multiple protocols. In addition to more than one protocol, each NIC can support more than one frame type. A single Ethernet NIC, for example, can be programmed to send and receive AppleTalk, TCP/IP, and IPX/SPX. The frame types for an Ethernet NIC can include Ethernet_802.3, Ethernet_802.2, Ethernet_II, and Ethernet_SNAP. The ODI interface is available in both the file server and the workstation.

Streams is a technology developed by AT&T and licensed to Novell. This technology allows more than one communications protocol to reside on the file server without conflict. Streams serves to "hide" the protocols from each other. Information entering the file server is first processed by STREAMS.NLM. Streams determines which protocol stack (for example, IPX/SPX or TCP/IP) is to process the information. Streams also facilitates the development of network applications by providing transport independence.

The NLM architecture of NetWare 3.*x* changed the installation procedure radically. Instead of generating the operating system using an installation utility, all you need to do is bring up the operating system kernel and load the appropriate NLMs. An installation procedure, INSTALL.NLM, allows you to format the hard drive and create NetWare partitions and volumes. Commands to load NLMs during system bootup are placed in two configuration files: STARTUP.NCF and AUTOEXEC.NCF.

Another difference between NetWare 3.*x* and NetWare 2.*x* is that 3.*x* does not include the 2.*x* cold boot loader. The *cold boot loader* is a PC bootup program that loads the operating system. This program took several hours to create and was difficult to maintain for all the new PC platforms being introduced (such as EISA, Micro Channel, and now computers based around the Pentium chip). Because the sole purpose of the cold boot loader was to boot up the PC and load the operating system kernel, the designers of NetWare 3.*x* decided to let the file server boot up under DOS and load the kernel as a DOS executable called SERVER.EXE.

Note NetWare 3.10 added support for TCP/IP and Macintosh, while NetWare 3.11 introduced several internal changes and improvements over 3.10. NetWare 3.12 introduced client software ported down from the NetWare 4.*x* environment and some of the NetWare 4.*x* tools (such as the DynaText online help system). NetWare 3.12 ships on disks or in CD-ROM format.

Bindery Files

Versions of NetWare before 4.*x* stored critical system information in a set of files referred to as the *bindery files.* In NetWare 2.*x* these files are NET$BIND.SYS and NET$BVAL.SYS. In NetWare 3.*x* the files were restructured and renamed as NET$OBJ.SYS, NET$PROP.SYS, and NET$VAL.SYS. In both NetWare 2.*x* and 3.*x* these files are stored on volume SYS in a directory SYSTEM.

Bindery files contain information about users, groups, and print queues. Any network entity that can be assigned security rights or a password is stored in the bindery files. When users at workstations log in to the file server, the operating system prompts them for a user name. The user name is verified in the bindery files along with the user's password.

The bindery files also are used to store information gathered through SAP (Server Advertisement Protocol). NetWare 3.*x* and 2.*x* servers exchange information about themselves through SAP. NetWare 4.1 does the same (for now) to maintain backward compatibility. Information obtained through SAP includes server names, network and node addresses, and the type of service provided.

The structure of the bindery files in NetWare 3.*x* matches that of a single NetWare 4.1 NDS container object. A *container object* is a point of reference in the NDS tree—it can "contain" other objects such as users, groups, or print queues. The structure of the NetWare 3.*x* bindery files is an object-oriented set of "flat" database files. The function of these files is detailed in table 4.2.

Table 4.2
NetWare 3.*x* Bindery Files

File Name	Function
NET$OBJ.SYS	This file contains references to objects. *Objects* include users, groups, and print queues. This file contains an identification number for the object (used internally) and a pointer to the NET$PROP file.

File Name	Function
NET$PROP.SYS	This file contains listings of *properties* of objects. The properties of an object vary depending on the type of object. Properties of a user include name, time restrictions, password restrictions, and station restrictions. Properties of a print queue include its name, what print server it was assigned to, and who could use the queue. Each reference to an object also contains a pointer to the next file, NET$VAL.SYS.
NET$VAL.SYS	This file contains values for properties. If the property were a time restriction, for example, values would include exactly what times the user could log in. If the property were a name, this file would contain the actual name.

Bindery-Based Resource Management

In NetWare 2.*x* and 3.*x*, server resources are managed through the bindery files. Various utilities give the system manager access to the bindery files. These included SYSCON and PCONSOLE. SYSCON is used to create users and group objects, and to assign values to each object's properties. When creating a user, for example, properties include the user's full name and the minimum length of his password.

This process works well in smaller networks, but with a network that includes 10 file servers, for example, you must do the following to give a user access to resources on each file server:

1. Log in or attach to a file server.
2. Run SYSCON.
3. Add the new user.
4. Assign security rights to the user.

This process must be repeated 10 times, which obviously, would lead to a management nightmare. A system manager might make a change to a login script for a user on file server number 4 and forget to repeat this change on the other servers. A user then might call saying she could not access a certain program, and the system manager would be hard pressed to track down the source of the problem.

There are utilities and techniques, however, to make the management of NetWare 2.*x* and 3.*x* easier. MAKEUSER, for example, enables you to add a new user by means of a script. The GRANT command can be issued from a DOS batch file. Third-party utilities, such as the Preferred Systems product Origene, enable you to create the user once, and on command, place this user into the bindery files of each server.

With NetWare 2.*x* and 3.*x*, the larger the network, the more difficult the management. As you will see in Chapter 6, "NetWare Directory Services," NetWare 4.1 provides for a much more comprehensive system of network management.

File System Features

File system refers to the physical and logical aspects of storing files on some media (such as a hard drive). This section discusses disk partitions, volumes, and fault tolerant features.

Disk Partitions

A *partition* isolates one operating system from another. Each different operating system uses a different partition on a hard drive. The partition information is recorded on the hard drive, typically in a reserved area on track 0 (the first track on the hard drive). Information read from the hard drive or written to it by UNIX, for example, will come only from the UNIX partition.

Note In the case of DOS or UNIX, the FDISK utility is used to display, create, and remove partitions. Windows NT has a utility Disk Administration under the Administration Tools program group.

Any changes made to a partition will result in the loss of all data contained in the partition. Such changes include the following:

- Increasing the size of a partition
- Decreasing the size of a partition
- Removing the partition

You can add a new partition to a hard drive that already contains a partition as long as you make no changes to the existing partition. You cannot, however, add a new partition that is larger than the amount of available disk space.

In the case of NetWare versions 3 and 4, a special NetWare partition is created during installation using the INSTALL.NLM utility. This utility is a NetWare Loadable

Module and can be invoked after the file server's kernel is loaded. NetWare will read and write only from the NetWare partition. Other partitions on the file server's hard drive (such as a DOS partition) are not normally accessible by NetWare.

The word *kernel* refers to an operating system's core functions. The kernel by itself is not useful. The kernel has a user interface and is capable of loading additional modules.

In the case of NetWare, the kernel is loaded when you run SERVER.EXE. You would need to load NLMs (NetWare Loadable Modules), such as LAN drivers and disk drivers to add functionality to SERVER.EXE.

A single hard drive can have one or more partitions. The size of any single partition can vary from 1 or 2 MB up to the size of the entire drive. Normally, a single partition cannot extend beyond one physical drive. The exception to this is if you have a drive array (using RAID technology). In the case of a drive array, all drives in the array will appear as a single drive to the operating system. This concept is discussed in greater detail in Chapter 11, "Hardware Configuration."

In the case of a NetWare file server, a DOS partition of 10 MB is recommended. The remainder of the drive should then be allocated to a NetWare partition.

There are different types of partitions for the different families of NetWare. NetWare 2.*x* has a type of partition referred to simply as NetWare 286. NetWare 3.*x* and 4 have a partition referred to as NetWare 386. Part of the rationale behind this naming scheme is that the partitions reflect the type of microprocessor required by the different families of NetWare. NetWare 2.*x* requires an 80286 microprocessor or above. NetWare 3.*x* and 4 require an 80386 or above.

When upgrading from NetWare 2.*x* to NetWare 3.*x* or 4, you will need to remove the NetWare 286 partition and create a NetWare 386 partition. This process erases all data on the old NetWare 286 partition.

Prior to beginning the upgrade, be sure to back up all data. Because all data will be erased during the upgrade from NetWare 2.*x*, you must have at least one viable backup of your data.

Another utility that can be used to upgrade from NetWare 2.*x* to 3.*x* is known as the In-Place Upgrade utility (2XUPGRDE.NLM). This utility changes the partition from NetWare 286 to NetWare 386 without requiring you to back up and restore data. The In-Place Upgrade utility requires 10–15 percent free disk space.

Volumes

A NetWare *volume* is a logical subdivision of the available disk space. Unlike a partition, a volume is independent of a physical hard drive. The size, names, and number of volumes are decided during installation. You can have as little as one volume, which can span multiple disk partitions, or you can have many volumes inside one disk partition. Volumes are created at the discretion of the network Administrator.

The capacity of a volume is fixed at the time it is created. Data on one volume will not spill over onto its neighboring volume. If you set volume SYS at 100 MB and VOL1 at 200 MB, for example, when volume SYS fills up, the space in VOL1 will not be used. You would have to manually move files to VOL1 to free space in volume SYS.

Assigning Volumes to Disk Partitions

Figure 4.1 illustrates three possible volume configurations for a file server with two hard drives.

Each of the examples in figure 4.1—A, B, and C—features a two-drive system. The first drive is 0, the second is 1. Drive 0 has two partitions: a DOS partition, and a NetWare 386 partition. In example A, each NetWare partition has its own volume. VOL1 is larger than SYS. In example B, the NetWare partition on drive 1 has three volumes: VOL1, VOL2, and VOL3. You will note that volumes do not have to be equal in size. In example B, VOL3 is larger than VOL1 and VOL2. In example C, volume SYS spans the NetWare partitions on drives 0 and 1. This capability was not available in NetWare 2.*x*.

Volumes are created according to the needs of your organization. Do not create more than one volume if there is no compelling reason to do so. It is easier to manage fewer volumes.

Volumes often are designated for political reasons within your organization. If a file server is used by many departments, for example, you might want to create a volume for each department. This way the information for the Sales department, for example, will not infringe on the space used by the Research department.

If you plan to have a single volume span many partitions (as in example C in figure 4.1), you should be aware that if one of the hard drives fails, you will lose the entire volume. There are several possible safeguards to prevent this from happening, including the following:

Drive Arrays	Invest in a drive array (using RAID 3 or 5 technology). Drive arrays have protection against single drive failures.

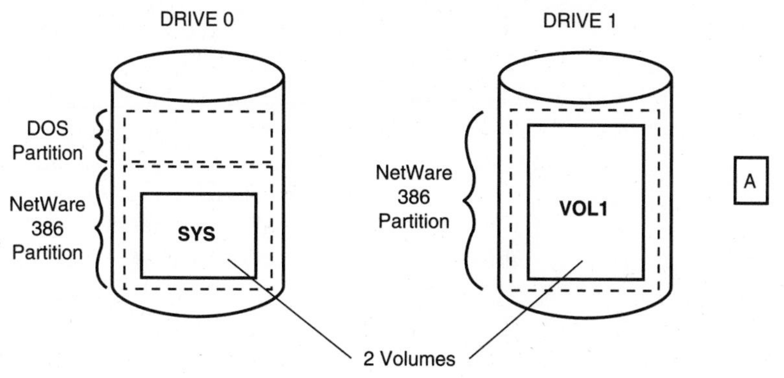

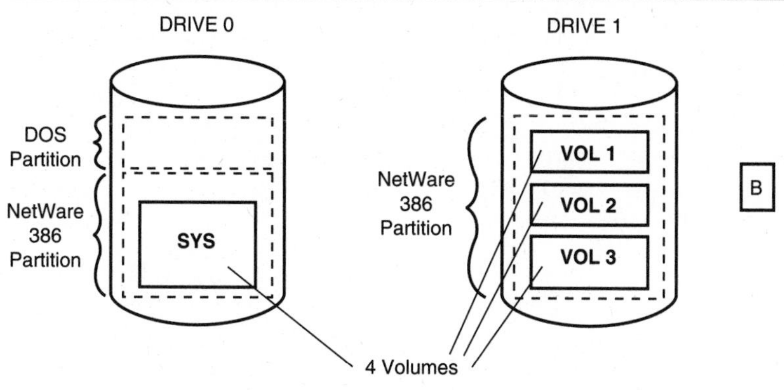

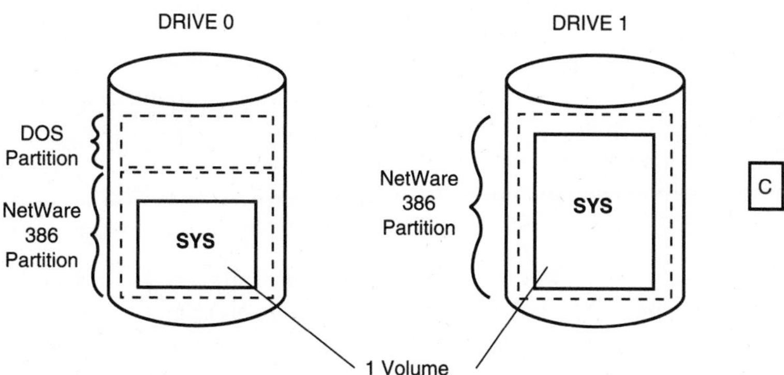

Figure 4.1
Possible volume configurations.

Mirroring	Mirror the drives using additional drives as a safeguard (see the section on fault tolerant features).
Separate Volumes	Assign a separate volume to each NetWare partition. This is the case with example A in figure 4.1. Although this technique does not protect you from losing data if a drive fails, it will minimize how much data you lose. In the case of example A, if drive 1 were to fail, you would lose VOL1 but not volume SYS.

Volume Segments

You can increase the amount of space available to a volume by adding additional volume segments. A *volume segment* is a portion of a NetWare partition that has been assigned to a volume. Referring to example B in figure 4.1, the NetWare partition on drive 1 has 3 volume segments. If you remove VOL3, for example, the volume segment assigned to VOL3 can be reassigned to any of the other volumes.

If you add a new drive to your file server, you would first need to create a NetWare partition on the drive. The new partition becomes an unassigned volume segment. You could then select any existing volume on that server and increase its space by adding the new unassigned volume segment.

When you increase the amount of space of a volume by adding a new volume segment, the data on the volume is not affected. You can even expand the capacity of a volume by adding a volume segment while people are logged in to the server. You will lose data in a volume by changing the NetWare partition, removing a volume, or decreasing the size of a volume.

Block Sizes

NetWare writes data to and reads data from the hard drive in *blocks* (also known as *disk blocks*). The size of a block can be configured when you create a volume. Block sizes may vary from volume to volume. NetWare 4.1 determines the size of a block based on the total size of the volume. The larger the volume, the larger the block size. Earlier versions of NetWare defaulted to the smallest block size: 4,096 bytes (note: 4,096 = 4 KB).

Block sizes can range from 4 KB to 64 KB. The larger the block size, the fewer blocks there are to manage. With fewer blocks to manage, the system can operate more quickly. Another argument in favor of a larger block size is *disk throughput.* Disk throughput is a measurement, typically in bytes per second, of how fast data can be transferred between the computer and the hard drive.

As you discovered in Chapter 1, hard drives are composed of disk platters and read/write heads. It takes a certain amount of time for the read/write heads to be posi-

tioned and the platter to spin around to the right place. After the heads are in position, data can be quickly transferred into the file server's RAM. If it were possible to transfer more data at one time, the overall disk throughput would increase. For this reason, larger block sizes will give you better disk throughput.

Prior to NetWare 4.1, a disadvantage was that larger block sizes wasted disk space. A disk block is the smallest unit of measure on a hard drive. If the users on a file server generate many small files (such as letters or e-mail messages), each file occupies an entire disk block. If you increase your block size to improve throughput, you waste disk space. If you decrease the block size to improve space utilization, you decrease throughput. NetWare 4.1 addresses this problem with its *block suballocation* feature (explained in the next chapter).

Fault Tolerant Features

Novell introduced a series of *system fault tolerant* (SFT) features with its SFT NetWare product. These features provide fail-safe mechanisms to safeguard data on the file server. Each additional SFT level provides additional redundancy to your system. The cost of adding redundancy to your system can be great. This cost must be measured against the cost of downtime. *Downtime* is when the computer system is unavailable for use. If your company has made provisions for downtime, your revenues may not be affected. Most companies are not in that position, however, and will lose revenue as a result.

Fault tolerant features are not a replacement for a good backup. SFT features will prevent the file server from going down, but there are no guarantees in the event of a catastrophic failure.

Note A firm in Los Angeles invested in drive duplexing. The day after the 1994 earthquake, the file servers, which had been mounted in a rack, were lying in pieces on the floor. A consultant, using the firm's off-site backup tape to rebuild the firm's system, was overheard to say that fault tolerance did not include geological faults.

SFT I: Hot Fix

When the NetWare partition is installed, a portion of that partition, known as the *hot fix table*, or *redirection area*, is set aside. The baseline amount is two percent of the size of the NetWare partition. This amount varies in NetWare 4.1 based on the size of the drive. The larger the drive, the smaller the percentage. The hot fix table is reserved on the inside portion of the drive—the area least subject to stress.

Hot fix works along with another feature known as read-after-write verify. These features come into play after data has been written out to the file server's hard drive. NetWare keeps the data in a cache buffer in memory until it can verify that the data has been written to the hard drive successfully. Here is how these two features work:

- NetWare reads back the data that was written in the last pass
- If the data is the same as the original, the data is cleared from the cache buffer and the operating system proceeds with the next operation
- If the data does not compare, NetWare will attempt to write the data out and read it back again two more times
- If the data is still not reading back the same as written out, NetWare will perform several operations, including the following:
    - Mark the block as bad
    - Redirect the data to a block in the Hot Fix area
    - Perform a read-after-write operation on the block in the Hot Fix area

Hot fix and read-after-write verify not only ensure data integrity but are performed dynamically. Users are not aware that their data has been redirected. System Administrators can gather information on redirection from the MONITOR.NLM utility.

SFT II: Transaction Tracking, Drive Mirroring, and Duplexing

SFT level II features such as TTS (Transaction Tracking System), mirroring, and duplexing were introduced with the NetWare 286 family product SFT NetWare. These features, along with hot fix and read-after-write verify, remain with the NetWare 4.1 product.

TTS

Transaction tracking provides a means of safeguarding database files. The file must first be registered with TTS using the FLAG utility. After a file has been marked as transactional, TTS will keep a log of changes to the file. When a user changes a record in a database file, TTS keeps an image of the record before the change. After the change has been written to disk and verified, the image is erased. If the system loses power or crashes before the change has been verified, TTS will back out all changes and restore the images when the server mounts the volume containing the data file. Note that this is true only when the application supports TTS.

It is important to understand the scope of a transaction. A transaction could be as little as a single change to a record in a database. On the other hand, a transaction could encompass a global database update. The beginning of a transaction occurs when a file lock or record lock is placed on a file. A lock is granted when an application, running at a user's workstation, requests exclusive access to a file or record in a file. The purpose of the lock is to prevent the changes made by one user from overwriting changes made by another user who is accessing the same file or record. The end of a transaction occurs when the last file or record lock is released.

The process of restoring a transaction-tracked database to its original condition is known as *rollback*. During a rollback, TTS restores the database to its last known good status. The database then is in the same condition it was prior to the last transaction. The user simply needs to repeat the process to update the database. This is an invaluable feature when several interrelated database files are being updated at the same time. The rollback process restores all files to their original state.

Some database systems perform their own version of TTS. In some cases, these custom-protection features are hampered by TTS. The default status for any file created on a NetWare server is nontransactional. The system Administrator must deliberately flag the file as transactional for TTS to track it. Conversely, the system Administrator can flag a file as nontransactional.

Because a transaction can involve the entire file, you must make certain you have free at least the amount of disk space the file occupies. TTS images are stored in a file called TTS$LOG.ERR. This file is located at the root of any volume where there are files marked transactional. When a transaction is completed, this file is not erased. The next time the system writes out an image, the file is erased and reused.

Mirroring and Duplexing

Mirroring and duplexing correspond to RAID (Redundant Array of Inexpensive Devices) level 1. In a mirrored system, the same data is written to two drives. Partitions on mirrored drives are paired together during installation. The operating system sees the two partitions as one logical partition.

Mirroring and duplexing are not to be confused with drive arrays. *Drive arrays* consist of a chain of SCSI drives that are viewed by the operating system as one drive. Most drive arrays commercially available use RAID levels 3 through 5. RAID technology is discussed in greater detail in Chapter 11, "Hardware Configuration."

When you mirror two partitions, you lose 50 percent of the disk space that would have been available without mirroring. If you mirror two partitions, for example, each with 500 MB of disk space, you could use only 500 MB rather than 1 GB of disk space.

The two drives involved in mirroring do not have to be physically identical. The data, not the physical hard drive, is mirrored. Hard drives develop bad blocks independently and have their own hot fix tables. The data may be physically stored in different places on the two drives.

Mirrored drives can have different capacities, although this is not recommended. The operating system will adjust the size of the hot fix area on the larger drive to make the data areas the same size. A 500 MB hard drive with a 2 percent hot fix area, for example, has a data area equal to 490 MB. A 600 MB hard drive with a 2 percent hot fix area has a data area of 588 MB. If these two drives were mirrored together, the installation procedure would resize the data area on the 600 MB drive to match the smaller drive. This would result in a loss of 98 MB of data space on the larger drive.

The advantage of mirroring is that if one of the drives goes down, the other takes over. There is a 15 to 30 second pause during the transition. Other than this relatively minor delay, users on the network will not experience any loss of service. An error message will appear on the file server's console indicating that a drive has failed. This message will also appear in the file server error log.

The disadvantage of mirroring is that the operating system must perform two disk write operations. This can be alleviated by using duplexing. *Duplexing* is the same process as mirroring except that the two disks are connected to two different disk controllers in the server. Duplexing often involves drives external to the file server. Such drives are known as *disk drive subsystems.* In this case, duplexing provides greater redundancy. If the disk controller fails, the other disk controller and drive subsystem can take over operations. If the power supply in one disk subsystem fails, the other disk subsystem continues to function.

Because duplexing involves another drive controller, there is no loss of performance during write operations. The operating system sends out the command to write data, and both controllers respond. Duplexing improves performance during read operations. Figure 4.2 illustrates typical mirroring and duplexing arrangements.

SFT III: Server Duplexing

The third SFT level was introduced as a separate product. Server duplexing employs a duplicate file server that serves as a backup to the mail file server. Computer failures can affect more than just the drives or controllers. SFT II, drive mirroring and duplexing, will not protect a network from downtime if the motherboard on a computer fails. SFT III, server duplexing, provides for complete redundancy.

The advantage of server duplexing is that you are protected from any type of component failure short of a failure of the network cabling system. As with drive mirroring or duplexing, the user is unaware of the failure of a file server save for a short delay.

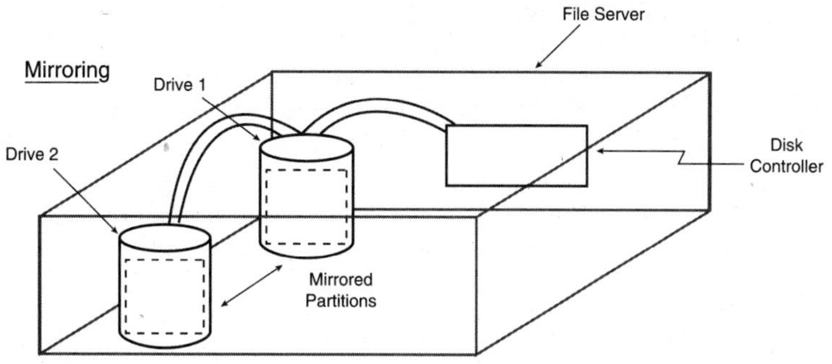

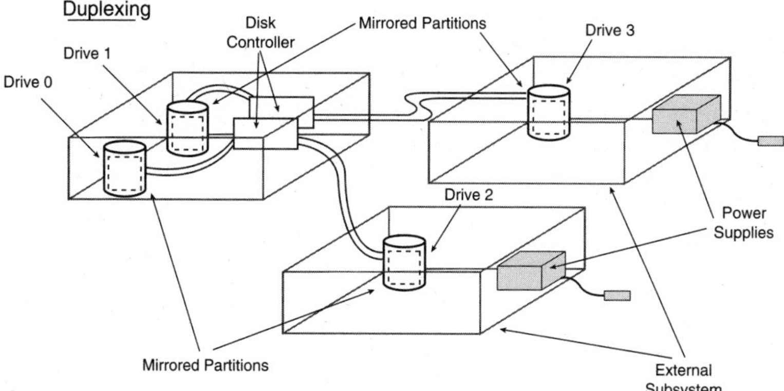

Figure 4.2
Typical mirroring and duplexing arrangements.

All data maintained on one server is duplicated on the other server. In addition, you can schedule disk drive maintenance during regular business hours because the other system is fully operational.

The disadvantage is that you must outlay additional capital to equip a second file server. You must also purchase special, expensive, boards which must be placed in each server and connected using a special fiber optic cable.

In environments where data integrity and downtime must be at a minimum, not only can the servers be duplexed, but the drives on each server can be duplexed. Such a system would have protection of the drives on each server, and duplicate servers as well. High volume mail-order businesses or the banking business, for example, often require such extreme measures. The rule of thumb is to determine whether the capital expense can be justified when compared to the cost of downtime.

Printing in NetWare

Printing in the NetWare environment involves print queues, printers, and print servers. Print jobs originate at a user's workstation when the user prints a document. The print job is redirected to a print queue that resides on a file server. From the print queue, a print server redirects the job to an assigned printer. The network Administrator is responsible not only for setting up the network printing environment, but maintaining it as well.

In many cases, printing problems can be traced to errors on the part of the user. User error is often the result of improper training. With a relatively small amount of training, users can learn what to expect when printing on a network. It takes quite a bit longer, however, to train users how to use the print functions of the application programs they use.

It is important for network Administrators to establish the bounds of their responsibility. In some cases the network Administrator must know how the network works as well as know how to use the application programs used in the office. In some instances, the sheer number of application programs in use precludes the possibility of being familiar with every one.

The NetWare printing environment can be set up and monitored using the following utilities:

- PCONSOLE.EXE
- NWADMIN.EXE
- PSERVER.NLM
- NPRINTER.NLM
- NPRINTER.EXE
- PRINTDEF.EXE
- PRINTCON.EXE
- CAPTURE.EXE
- NPRINT.EXE
- PSC.EXE

These utilities are discussed in greater detail in Part Seven, "Printing." This section discusses the function of the network in printing.

Print Jobs

The print job can be redirected to the network in several different ways. One method is through a NetWare-aware application. Such applications are designed for network use. They detect the presence of the network and are capable of placing the job directly into a print queue.

Another technique uses the print redirection capabilities that are built into the workstation Requester. The CAPTURE command is used to initialize the workstation print redirector. From that point on, any jobs destined for the workstation's parallel port are "captured" and placed in the designated print queue.

Yet another technique involves the NPRINT utility. This command can be used to place printer-ready files directly into a print queue. A printer-ready file can be created when the user has elected to print to a file from their application program. The file that is created contains printer control codes for a specific type of printer, in addition to the data that is to be printed. The printer-ready file might contain PCL codes for a Hewlett Packard LaserJet printer, or PostScript codes for an Apple LaserWriter. Because ASCII text files do not contain any printer codes, they can be printed on most printers and are another type of file that can be considered printer-ready.

Figure 4.3 illustrates the flow of a print job on the network. The following steps are illustrated in this diagram:

1. The print job is submitted from a workstation running the application "WP."
2. The print job is placed in the print queue "Q1."
3. The print job is directed to the print server "PS1."
4. The print server sends the print job to the printer "LJ1."

Print Queues

As you can see in figure 4.3, the print queue is located on a file server. In NetWare 4.1, the print queue is a subdirectory of a directory QUEUES. The QUEUES directory is off the root of the volume designated to hold the print queue. Print queues are assigned a random identification number when they are created. The number becomes the name of the subdirectory. Thus, if a print queue "Q1" is created, NetWare might assign a number 29400481. If the print queue is assigned to volume VOL1, the print queue subdirectory would be VOL1:QUEUES\29400481.QDR. Note that the extension QDR is added to indicate that this is a queue directory.

Figure 4.3
Network printing.

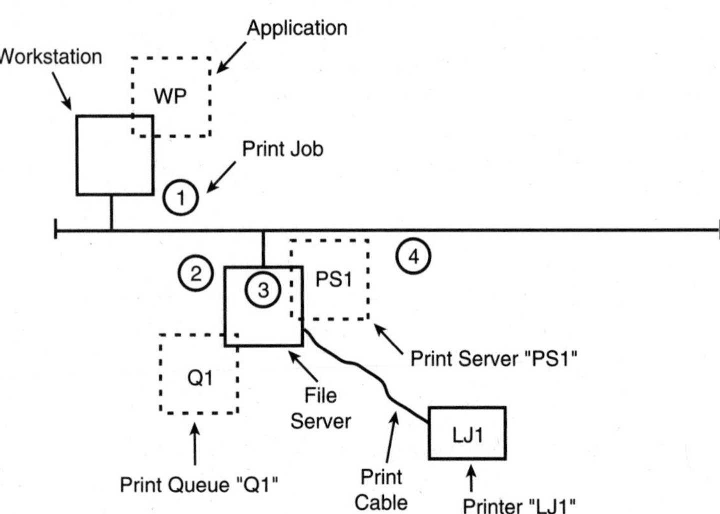

In earlier versions of NetWare, print jobs were *always* stored on volume SYS:. In NetWare 3.x, for example, print jobs are stored in print queue subdirectories off the SYS:SYSTEM directory. NetWare 4.x allows you to designate which volume print jobs are to be stored.

Print jobs are temporarily stored as files in the print queue directory. After the job has been successfully transmitted to a printer through a print server, the file is deleted from the queue directory.

Print jobs are serviced from the queue on a first-come first-served basis. This is also known as FIFO (First In First Out). Print jobs waiting in the queue can be viewed using the PCONSOLE or the NWADMIN (NetWare Administrator) utilities. These utilities are covered in greater detail in Part Seven, "Printing."

After a job is placed in the queue, further control is possible. A job can be controlled by either the user who originated the job or a print queue operator. The *print queue operator* is a user given this special status by the network Administrator. Possible operations on a print job by either the job owner or the print queue operator include the following:

- Deleting the job
- Changing the job's service sequence in the queue (moving it to first place, for example)
- Putting the job on hold

- Deferring the job to another date or time
- Modifying job parameters such as type and number of copies

Print jobs can assume different types of status. The status codes indicate the state of a print job at a given point in its cycle through the system.

Printers

Printers can be shared on the network through several different means, including the following:

- Attached to a file server
- Attached to a workstation
- Attached directly to the network

Printers that are attached to a file server are supported by a NetWare 4.1 utility called NPRINTER.NLM. This program is a loadable module that can be added to the file server's startup file (AUTOEXEC.NCF). In certain cases, the file server with the shared printer can also serve as the print server. In this case, NPRINTER.NLM is loaded automatically.

A printer attached to a workstation is supported by a utility named NPRINTER.EXE. This is a DOS executable that must be loaded into the workstation's memory. It is a terminate-and-stay-resident program (TSR) that communicates with an assigned print server. The workstation can still be used for other purposes. The NPRINTER program operates in the background.

When either NPRINTER.NLM or NPRINTER.EXE is loaded, you must identify the print server to which this printer is assigned. After this information is applied, the print server starts to communicate with the printer. Print jobs can be transferred from the queue to the printer, and the print server can make sure the printer is online.

NetWare supports a variety of different printer types. These include parallel, serial, and other/unknown. If the latter type is selected, the type of printer can be determined when NPRINTER is loaded. Other printer types include the following:

- UNIX printer
- AppleTalk printer
- XNP (Extended Network Printing protocol)
- AIO (Asynchronous Input/Output protocol)

The last two types of printer are not fully integrated. You should also note that if either of the first two types is selected, additional software is required. For a UNIX printer, you need one of the NetWare/UNIX products such as NetWare NFS, Flex/IP, or NFS Gateway. For an AppleTalk printer, you need NetWare for Macintosh.

Print Servers

The print server actually is a logical process running on a file server. The utility that activates a print server is PSERVER.NLM. The job of the print server is much like a traffic cop directing traffic at a busy intersection. The print server checks print queues to see if there are jobs waiting to be serviced. The print server also checks the status of printers to see if they can service print jobs. The print server then directs the print job from a queue to the right printer.

The functionality of the print server has been streamlined in NetWare 4.1. In NetWare 3, for example, the print server was designed not only to handle the tasks outlined earlier, but to service printers directly attached to the file server. In NetWare 4.1, the latter functionality has been removed. If a printer is directly attached to a NetWare 4.1 file server, NPRINTER.NLM now services the printer.

You can have as many print servers as you have file servers on the network. Each print server can process jobs going to as many as 255 printers.

The print server has its own monitor screen. This can be accessed directly from the file server or remotely using a utility such as RCONSOLE.EXE. (The RCONSOLE process is explained in Chapter 36, "Monitoring the File Server.") The print server lets you view the status of printers and jobs that are actively being serviced by printers.

From the print server screen you can control printers. Actions that you can perform include the following:

- Starting and stopping printers
- Rewinding a printer
- Pausing a printer
- Aborting a print job

Before you start the print server running, you must configure it by using PCONSOLE. The print server configuration has been greatly simplified in NetWare 4.1 using the Quick Setup option. This option, on one screen, enables you to create a print server, define printers, create queues, and assign the printers to queues.

Printers Directly Attached to the LAN

Many printers are now equipped with network interfaces. An example is the HP LaserJet 4si. This printer can be ordered with either an Ethernet or a token ring network interface. The interface also includes what amounts to a printer server in ROM (read-only memory). When the printer is attached to the network and powered on, it starts advertising itself as a print server. HP ships this interface with software to configure the print server. You simply need to assign a queue to the print server in ROM. Any job placed in such a queue will end up printing on the LaserJet.

Other examples of direct printing interfaces are the Castelle LANpress and the Novell/Eagle NPE400. These devices contain a parallel and a serial port along with a network interface. You plug them into the network on one side and then into a printer on the other side. These devices are configured much like a print server that runs on a file server using PCONSOLE. The difference is that the PSERVER software is contained in ROM. When the printer is powered up, the device starts advertising itself as a print server. Any job placed in a queue assigned to one of these devices will be redirected across the LAN to the attached printer.

Direct network printing devices offer superior performance compared to the traditional NetWare printing environment. They also take some of the burden off the file server. The disadvantage is that they represent an additional cost.

Understanding LAN Communication Features

As discussed earlier in this chapter, Novell introduced the capability to support multiple communications protocols with NetWare 3.0. The technology Novell intended to capture was TCP/IP.

NetWare TCP/IP was implemented as a series of NLMs. Part of the strategy included licensing the Streams driver from AT&T. The job of Streams was to hide the various competing protocols from each other. Novell's "native" protocols IPX and SPX had to be rewritten to accommodate Streams. The resulting modules, called IPXS.NLM and SPXS.NLM, are Streams-based versions of Novell's native protocols.

Additional support came in the form of the CLIB.NLM. This module consists of a library of C language function calls. This greatly simplifies the job of NLM developers. Instead of having to write NetWare function calls on their own, developers simply write functions that interact with the C library module supplied with NetWare.

When a protocol other than IPX is loaded, the following happen automatically:

STREAMS.NLM is loaded

CLIB.NLM is loaded

IPX and SPX are disabled

IPXS and SPXS are loaded

Associating LAN cards (NICs) with protocols was greatly streamlined in NetWare 3.*x*. This capability has been carried on in NetWare 4.1. To associate a protocol with a LAN card, you must do the following:

1. LOAD the LAN card driver
2. LOAD the protocol modules
3. BIND the protocol to the LAN card driver

More than one protocol can be bound to any given NIC, and more than one NIC can be bound to a protocol. To disassociate the NIC from the protocol, either UNLOAD the NIC driver or UNBIND the protocol. Further detail on loading LAN card drivers is available in Chapter 11, "Hardware Configuration."

Understanding Clients

NetWare client (workstation) support has improved with each successive version of NetWare. Another (perhaps distressing) trend is apparent as well. Each successive client shell (or *Requester* as the workstation software is referred to in NetWare 4 networks) has included more and more files. There are two reasons for this abundance of files: modularity and the demand for increased services on the part of the client software.

This section discusses traditional NetWare client support and features.

DOS Clients and the Workstation Requester

DOS client software consists of a number of memory resident programs that are loaded after DOS boots up. These drivers can be placed in the client's AUTOEXEC.BAT file to provide an automatic server connection when the client powers up.

The old client software (NetWare 3.11 and below) maintained an environment independent of DOS. The old software, referred to as a *shell*, had its own file connection table and working space for variables. The client software included with NetWare 3.12 and 4.*x* works more closely with services that have been built into DOS starting with MS-DOS version 3.1. The new software, referred to as a *Requester*, uses the DOS environment and shares DOS drive tables.

As mentioned earlier, the number of files in the DOS client Requester has increased. Table 4.3 summarizes this trend.

TABLE 4.3
NetWare DOS Client Shells/Requesters

Version of NetWare	Client Shell
NetWare 2.0	ANETx.COM
NetWare 2.1*x*	IPX.COM NETx.COM EMSNETx.EXE XMSNETx.EXE
NetWare 2.2 up to 3.11	IPX.COM NETx.COM EMSNETx.EXE XMSNETx.EXE LSL.COM IPXODI.COM
NetWare 3.12 and 4.*x*	LSL.COM IPXODI.COM VLM.EXE AUTO.VLM BIND.VLM CONN.VLM FIO.VLM GENERAL.VLM IPXNCP.VLM MIB2IF.VLM MIB2PROT.VLM NDS.VLM NETX.VLM NMR.VLM NWP.VLM

continues

Table 4.3, Continued
NetWare DOS Client Shells/Requesters

Version of NetWare	Client Shell
	PNW.VLM PRINT.VLM REDIR.VLM RSA.VLM SECURITY.VLM TRAN.VLM WSASN1.VLM WSDRVPRN.VLM WSREG.VLM WSSNMP.VLM WSTRAP.VLM

The client software provides several important features, including the following:

- LAN card initialization
- File server attachment
- Authentication (passwords, security check)
- Print redirection
- Drive mapping (providing drive letters that point to the file server's hard drive)

NetWare volumes are seen by DOS as hard drives. The drive mapping facility enables DOS to access files on a NetWare file server through one of these drive letters. The drive letters can be assigned by the system Administrator using a login script or a batch file. Login scripts consist of a series of commands that build an environment in which the client can operate.

The client Requester VLM.EXE is built upon the workstation ODI drivers. The ODI interface, explained in Chapter 1, works with the client NIC. It consists of three memory resident programs: LSL.COM, IPXODI.COM, and a driver for the NIC.

LSL.COM provides support for the IEEE 802.2 services. These services correspond with the upper portion of the OSI model's data link layer. LSL.COM provides an interface between the NIC driver (provided by the vendor of the card) and the protocol driver IPXODI.COM.

IPXODI.COM provides OSI network and transport layer services. This driver is responsible for converting data into packets and routing them through the LAN (or

WAN). IPXODI.COM also provides SPX services to the client. SPX, as you recall, adds reliability to the connection between the client and the server. The NIC driver activates the network interface card and talks with LSL.COM.

Windows Workstations

Support for Windows workstations falls into three categories:

- DOS workstations with Windows installed
- DOS workstations with Windows for Workgroups installed
- Workstations running Windows NT

DOS Workstations and Windows 3.1

The DOS workstation running Windows 3.1 is treated exactly like a DOS client. The only difference is that during the installation of the client software you can answer "Yes" when asked if you want to install support for Windows. The client installation program then proceeds to copy additional utilities, DLL files, and BMP files into the Windows directory. The WIN.INI and SYSTEM.INI files are modified, and NetWare drivers are copied over.

Windows users are presented with a new menu, NWUSER.EXE, when accessing resources on the NetWare file server. File Manager will have a new menu option under "Disk" labeled "Network Connections." Double-clicking on this option invokes NWUSER. In a similar fashion, the Print Manager will have an additional option allowing you to direct printing to a NetWare print queue.

The NWUSER utility provides the capability to add, edit, or remove network drive mappings, log in to a server, and manage network printing. This utility is described in greater detail in Chapter 15, "Windows 3.*x* and Windows NT Clients."

DOS Workstations and Windows for Workgroups

NetWare support for Windows for Workgroups (WFW) is a superset of the support for DOS/Windows 3.1 clients described earlier. Windows for Workgroups is a peer-to-peer network operating system based on Windows. WFW clients can access each other's hard drives directly as well as exchange e-mail. WFW uses Microsoft's communications protocol, NetBEUI (NetBIOS Extended User Interface). This presents a problem because NetWare uses IPX/SPX. Microsoft rewrote a driver originally provided by Novell that works on top of NetBEUI to provide IPX/SPX services. The drivers, MSIPX.SYS and MSNETX.SYS, could originally be called only from the CONFIG.SYS file. Later versions can be called in the AUTOEXEC.BAT file. Once loaded, the WFW workstation can communicate not only with its peers but the NetWare LAN as well.

WFW also provides an extra Network utility in the Control Panel. This utility enables you to add or remove NetWare support from a WFW client. The NWUSER utility cannot currently be used with a WFW client because support for the recent VLM Requester is not available. If WFW is configured for NetWare only, however, all NetWare 4.1 utilities are fully supported.

Windows NT Workstations

NetWare support for Windows NT workstations is provided by Microsoft with support from Novell. Microsoft engineers "camped out" at Novell for an extended period of time and have written IPX support into Windows NT. When you first install Windows NT, you are asked questions regarding which type of network adapter you have installed, and its settings. Once the product has been installed, you can add NetWare client support. The support is integrated into the operating system so that you can "connect" a network drive to either another Windows NT workstation, a Windows for Workgroups workstation, or a NetWare file server. In a similar fashion you can redirect printing to a NetWare print queue. The primary limitation of NetWare client support in Windows NT is that it is excluded from NetWare Directory Services. This means that the Windows NT client can only access services in the file server's bindery context. Bindery services is discussed in greater detail in Chapter 8, "Bindery Services."

Macintosh

Client software for the Macintosh consists of a set of utilities that allow the Macintosh user to administer a NetWare network. The software that manages the NIC in the Macintosh is provided by the vendor of the NIC. The Macintosh and Quadra computers currently support Ethernet, token ring, ARCnet, and FDDI. The Quadra can be ordered with a built-in Ethernet interface.

Software must be loaded on the NetWare file server to provide Macintosh support. A limited five-user version of NetWare for Macintosh is bundled with NetWare 3.12 and 4.0*x*. An optional upgrade that provides support for additional users is available at additional cost for these earlier versions of NetWare. A 50-user version of NetWare for Macintosh is included with NetWare 4.1.

After the software on the server is loaded, the network appears as an AppleShare network to the Macintosh user. The file server appears as an icon. When the Mac user clicks on this icon, a prompt appears asking for a login name and password. Once logged in, NetWare directories appear as Macintosh folders, and files appear as icons.

Another module that should be loaded on the file server is the MAC.NAM module. This module provides name space support. Macintosh file names contain information not supported by DOS. DOS is the default file name support provided by NetWare. Table 4.4 summarizes the types of information included in the different types of file names.

OS/2

Support for OS/2 workstations consists of a series of drivers much like the DOS software. Commands that invoke these drivers are typically placed in the CONFIG.SYS file on the OS/2 workstation. The OS/2 client software is referred to as the NetWare Client for OS/2.

NetWare 4.1 includes a set of utilities that allow the OS/2 user to administer the network using OS/2's Presentation Manager. The OS/2 workstation becomes a complete NDS (NetWare Directory Services) client. This means that the OS/2 user can manage the global network naming system, NDS.

A unique feature of the OS/2 client software is that it can support simultaneous NetWare sessions with different client operating systems. An OS/2 workstation can communicate simultaneously with the file server through a DOS window, a Windows application, and OS/2. This user also can communicate with an IBM 3270 family host computer at the same time.

As with the Macintosh, the network Administrator must load the OS2.NAM name space support module on the file server to ensure proper file name translation.

A product known as NetWare 4.1 for OS/2 allows an OS/2 computer to act as both a client and a NetWare 4.1 file server. This product consists of a series of drivers that allow the OS/2 software to run SERVER.EXE, the NetWare 4.1 kernel. The drivers include DSKSHARE.DSK.

UNIX

Support for UNIX clients comes in two versions: UnixWare and NetWare NFS. UnixWare is a Novell product that offers built in NetWare support using the IPX protocol. Other versions of UNIX can access NetWare servers using the TCP/IP protocol and the NetWare NFS product.

UnixWare

UnixWare was offered initially by a company called Univel. This company was a joint venture between Novell and UNIX Systems Laboratories (USL). In 1993, Novell purchased USL from AT&T. Eventually Univel was integrated into Novell under the UNIX Systems Group. The UNIX Systems Group is responsible for UnixWare, NetWare NFS, NetWare/IP, and other UNIX and TCP/IP products.

UnixWare is a full-blown version of UNIX System V Release 4.2 that runs on the Intel 80386 or above family of microprocessors. It comes in two versions: Application Server and Personal Edition. Both versions share a graphical desktop interface based on the Motif (X-Windows) specifications. They are both designed to integrate seamlessly with a NetWare network using the IPX communications protocol.

Personal Edition is designed as a two-user UNIX desktop system. It includes a limited set of System V commands as well as TCP/IP support. The Application Server allows unlimited logins. It includes a limited C compiler, TCP/IP and NFS support, and an extensive System V command set.

Computers running UnixWare can access NetWare file servers without additional support. They also can access the Internet world when TCP/IP is installed. They can access other UnixWare machines by using either the built-in IPX support or through TCP/IP.

NetWare NFS

NetWare NFS is a set of NLMs that are loaded onto a NetWare file server. These NLMs allow UNIX machines with TCP/IP support to use the disk space on the file server. The NLMs provide for translation between UNIX file permissions and NetWare Security rights. When the NFS.NAM name space module is loaded, UNIX machines can store files with standard UNIX file name support. As indicated in table 4.4, this includes up to 255-character file names, along with any characters (provided you follow the rules regarding UNIX regular expressions).

Currently, NFS clients can access a NetWare 4.1 file server only under bindery services. This means that NDS support is limited to the file server's bindery context only. NFS clients cannot access NDS resources outside of the file server's bindery context. This means that print queues defined in a context other than the file server's bindery context cannot be used. Bindery services is described in greater detail in Chapter 8, "Bindery Services."

Note Future versions of NetWare NFS will be fully NDS compatible.

The NetWare NFS product supports the following UNIX and TCP/IP utilities/protocols:

- ftp
- telnet (to access the file server's console remotely)

- mount (command to mount a NetWare directory as a UNIX directory)

As indicated earlier, the following table summarizes NetWare name space support.

TABLE 4.4
NetWare Name Space Support

Type of Name Space	NLM Required	Features
DOS	None	8.3 file name (up to 8 characters, a period, and a 3-character extension) Case insensitive Alphanumeric characters Some special characters DOS attributes (read-only, hidden) File owner name File size Dates (created, modified, last accessed)
Macintosh	MAC.NAM	32-character file name Alphanumeric and special characters Case sensitive Resource fork File owner name Dates (created, modified, last accessed) File Size Macintosh attributes
OS/2	OS2.NAM	255-character file name Alphanumeric characters Some special characters OS/2 attributes (same as DOS) File owner name Dates (created, modified, last accessed) File size
UNIX	NFS.NAM	255-character file name NFS (Network File System) naming support Any keyboard character supported File owner name Group owner name File type (file, directory, special)

continues

Table 4.4, Continued
NetWare Name Space Support

Type of Name Space	NLM Required	Features
		UNIX permission mask (User, Group, Other) Dates (created, modified, last accessed) File size inode (translates to closest equivalent)

Summary

This chapter discussed some of NetWare's traditional benefits. These benefits were introduced gradually into the NetWare product line, starting with NetWare 2.*x* and continuing through NetWare 3.*x* and now NetWare 4.1. The bindery files, which were used in versions of NetWare prior to NetWare 4.1, were discussed. In addition, this chapter discussed various file system features such as partitions and volumes. The System Fault Tolerant features, mirroring, duplexing, hot fix, and transaction tracking were explored. You learned how NetWare printing works and how to connect the printer directly to the LAN. An overview of how NetWare's DOS, Macintosh, OS/2, UNIX, and Windows clients connect to the network was also presented.

New Features of NetWare 4.1

The previous chapter covered features that NetWare 4.1 shares with older versions of NetWare. This chapter focuses on features that are new and specific to NetWare 4.1. Some of the new features center around improvements to the file system. Other features include changes to the client shell and network communications. One of the most striking features is NDS (NetWare Directory Services). The following section examines changes made to the file system.

Examining New Storage Features

NetWare 4.1 addresses storage problems that came to light in previous versions of NetWare. LANs are a relatively recent phenomenon. As LANs matured, the size and speed of disk drives increased. Certain features needed to improve speed resulted in a loss of space. The following features address these issues:

- File compression
- Block suballocation
- Data migration
- Read-ahead

File Compression

Data-compression techniques have been available for UNIX minicomputers and mainframes for quite some time. Data compression in the DOS environment has been available through tools such as SuperStor (DR DOS 6) and Stacker. These technologies compress and uncompress files as they are being accessed. The advantage of this immediate compression technique is that disk space is saved immediately. The disadvantage is that access to files is slower.

Another form of data compression involves compressing a file after it has been saved to the hard drive. In the DOS world, a utility called PKZIP can be used to compress a file anywhere from 10 to 90 percent once it has been saved. NetWare 4.1 embraces a disk-compression technology similar to PKZIP.

When a file has been saved on a NetWare 4.1 file server, the operating system automatically compresses it after a period of time. The series of parameters you can set to control various aspects of the compression technology includes the following:

- How many days NetWare will wait before compressing the file
- What NetWare will do when a file has been compressed and then uncompressed
- How much space savings is desired before compressing a file
- How much disk space must be free before uncompressing a file
- When data compression is to take place each day

In addition, you can set file and/or directory attributes that prevent compression. Additional information on settings for file compression is discussed in Chapter 12, "Installing the NetWare Operating System," and in Chapter 24, "Managing Directories and Files."

Disk Block Suballocation

Disk block suballocation is the process of subdividing a disk block into smaller storage units. Ordinarily, the smallest unit that NetWare can access on a volume is a disk block. As discussed earlier, the size of a disk block is decided during installation. In previous versions of NetWare, if a file was smaller than the size of a single disk block, the additional space in the block was wasted. Likewise, if a file occupies more than one disk block, the last portion of the file might not entirely occupy a single disk block, and the space would be wasted.

NetWare 4.1 allows portions of more than one file to occupy a single disk block. The blocks are divided into smaller units known as *suballocation units*. Disk blocks can range in size from 4 to 64 KB. Each suballocation unit is 512 bytes in size. Each disk block can therefore have anywhere from 8 to 128 suballocation blocks, depending on the size of the disk block selected during installation.

The main purpose for suballocation blocks is to store the last blocks of several files into a single disk block. Figure 5.1 illustrates the relationship between disk blocks and suballocation units. In the figure, three files are represented: FILE1.TXT, FILE2.TXT and FILE3.TXT. FILE1.TXT is 70 KB in size; FILE2.TXT is 80 KB in size; and FILE3.TXT is 60 KB in size. In previous versions of NetWare, if the block size were set to 64 KB, these files would have taken up five blocks. Five blocks at 64 KB each represents a total space of 320 KB. Because the files take up only 210 KB of space, 110 KB would have been wasted. In NetWare 4.1, the remaining portions of FILE1.TXT and FILE2.TXT are assigned to suballocation blocks in disk block #4, as you can see in the figure. Four KB remains in disk block #3 where FILE3.TXT resides. It is possible that a future write operation will rearrange the blocks so that the remaining space in disk block #3 is used by another file. As you can see in figure 5.1, four disk blocks were allocated, with 26 KB remaining to be suballocated to portions of other files. The greatest amount of space that could be wasted in NetWare 4.1 is 511 bytes.

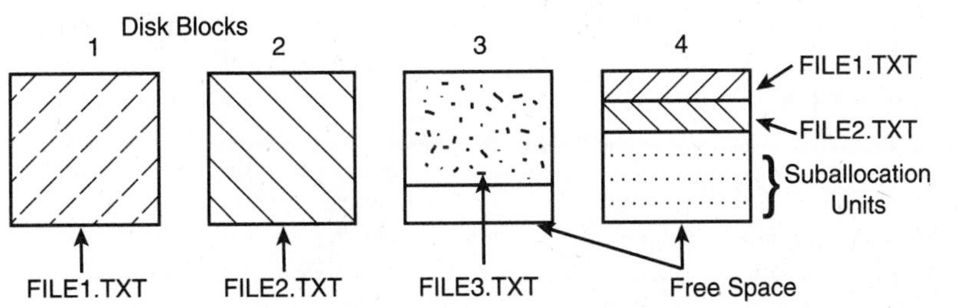

Figure 5.1
Disk blocks and suballocation units.

If, for some reason, you decide not to use suballocation, the feature can be disabled for any given volume. The default for disk suballocation is enabled. The primary reason for not using disk suballocation is if your server is short on memory. Suballocation increases the amount of RAM required to track the disk utilization.

Ordinarily the operating system has to allocate an amount of RAM to track each disk block. This process is known as *caching* the file allocation table (FAT). When disk suballocation is enabled, another table must be maintained in the file server's memory to track suballocation units.

Data Migration

Data migration is the capability of the operating system to automatically move files from its hard drive to another media (such as a read/write optical device). Files are moved based on age and when volumes reach a percentage of their total capacity that you set. NetWare keeps track of when a file is created, modified, or accessed. If a file has not been accessed within a time period you can set (such as six months), the data migration feature moves such files off the file server's hard disk and onto the media you designate. This process is performed automatically.

Files that have been migrated still appear in directory listings. They have a special attribute, "M," indicating that the file has been migrated. When a user tries to access a migrated file, the file server will automatically search for the file on the designated media and restore it to the hard drive. If the media is not mounted, the file server will indicate this with a console message.

As with the disk suballocation feature, data migration can be selected during installation. The default for data migration is off. In addition, you can set file and/or directory attributes that prevent files from being migrated.

Read-Ahead

The read-ahead feature causes NetWare to place the next block of a file into file cache buffers before the user asks for it. *File cache buffers* are reserved areas of file server memory where data going to or being read from the file server's hard drive(s) is stored. The read-ahead feature works only when the type of file access is sequential. An example of *sequential file access* is when a user calls up a large graphic image from the file server to his or her workstation. When the user accesses a database file at random, for example, the read-ahead feature is not used.

Read-ahead is especially useful when you have online databases stored on CD-ROM. An example of this is Novell's DynaText. DynaText is a CD that comes with NetWare 4.1 and contains all the product manuals. If you want to read one of the manuals, you can call up the DynaText and get to the desired manual. You can then scan through it by pressing the PgDn key. The read-ahead feature will anticipate your request for the next page by fetching it from the CD and caching it in RAM. When you go to the next page, the file server already has it ready to send across the LAN to your workstation. This makes access to the CD seem faster than it would if the CD were attached directly to your workstation.

The read-ahead process takes a certain amount of file server CPU (central processing unit) time. So as not to impair overall network performance, the read-ahead feature is assigned a low priority. This means that if the server is busy handling other requests (such as print jobs or sending files to users), the read-ahead process will not take place.

Understanding Improved Memory Management

The file server memory management used in NetWare 4.1 is much simpler than in previous versions of NetWare. NetWare 2.*x*, for example, is bound by the limitations of the 80286 microprocessor. Even though you can run NetWare 2.*x* on an 80386 or 80486, the code was originally designed for the 80286. NetWare 3.*x* incorporates several memory management improvements. NetWare 3.*x* features a series of memory pools. *Memory pools* are subdivisions of file server RAM that NLMs use for various purposes. NLM developers must follow strict rules regarding what memory can be returned to that pool.

This section discusses the following three important improvements in file server memory management:

- Memory pools
- The paging mechanism
- Memory protection

Memory Pools

NetWare 4.1 features a simplified memory management scheme: there is only one memory pool. All NLMs borrow memory from this pool and return it when they are finished. You can use MONITOR.NLM to view memory usage by selecting from three menu choices: Resource Utilization, Cache Utilization, and Memory Utilization.

NetWare 4.1 still reports statistics on the memory pools that were introduced with NetWare 3.*x*. This is to maintain compatibility with NLMs designed to work on a NetWare 3.*x* file server. In NetWare 4.1, an NLM can make a request for the *nonmovable* memory pool, for example. The operating system will grant the request. Unknown to the NLM making the request, the memory it receives for use actually originates from the main memory pool. The operating system hides this information from the NLM.

The down side to this approach to memory management is that when memory is returned to the main pool, it can be located in different sections of RAM. This problem is known as *fragmentation.*

Memory, from NetWare's viewpoint, is allocated in cache buffers. Each cache buffer is 4 KB in size. Fragmentation occurs when memory in noncontiguous buffers is freed by several NLMs. Contiguous free memory is memory that is available for use and is located in adjacent buffers. Noncontiguous memory is memory that is scattered all over the memory map.

When the operating system tries to allocate another block of memory, it doesn't know which memory buffer is available or where it is located. NetWare 4.1 uses a process known as *garbage collection* to account for available memory. The garbage collection process gathers together a list of available memory buffers in the form of a table. NetWare uses this table when making its memory allocations to NLMs. The garbage collection process can be controlled through a series of SET statements. You can control the following:

- How often garbage collection occurs
- How much memory must be available for garbage collection to occur
- How many times NLMs free memory before garbage collection should occur

For more information on tuning the file server's memory management, see Chapter 38, "Fine-Tuning the Server."

Memory Paging Mechanism

NetWare 4.1 uses the Intel *paging* mechanism in its memory allocation scheme. This mechanism is built into any Intel (or Intel-licensed) 80386 or above microprocessor. This scheme allows NetWare to parcel out memory in pages. Each page is a 4 KB contiguous block of memory. Pages of memory that have been allocated are recorded on page tables. *Page tables* are pointers to the pages of memory that are scattered all over the computer's memory map. To keep track of extremely large memory allocations, page tables are themselves grouped into *domains.*

What this means for the network Administrator is that the file server can assign RAM to NLMs in pages, and the NLM will think it is getting a contiguous block of RAM. Because this feature is hardware-based, it operates very quickly.

Ring Memory Protection

Another memory-related feature is that of *ring memory protection.* This feature is also referred to as *privilege level.* Memory in the NetWare 4.1 server is divided up into four

domains. Each domain is referred to in the Intel privilege level specification as a *ring*. There are four rings defined: 0 through 3. The NetWare 4.1 operating system kernel runs in ring 0. Other NLMs, by default, will also run in ring 0.

When you assign an NLM to a ring other than 0, it cannot access resources of the inner rings without making what is known as an *inter-ring gate call*. This process takes additional CPU time and protects processes running in the inner rings. If you have an NLM that has been known to crash, you can run it in ring 3, for example, to protect other NLMs. When an NLM running in a ring other than 0 crashes, it affects only itself, and possibly disallows access to that ring. Other rings are not affected. Figure 5.2 illustrates the process of running an NLM in ring 3. As you can see, if the NLM crashes, other NLMs are not affected.

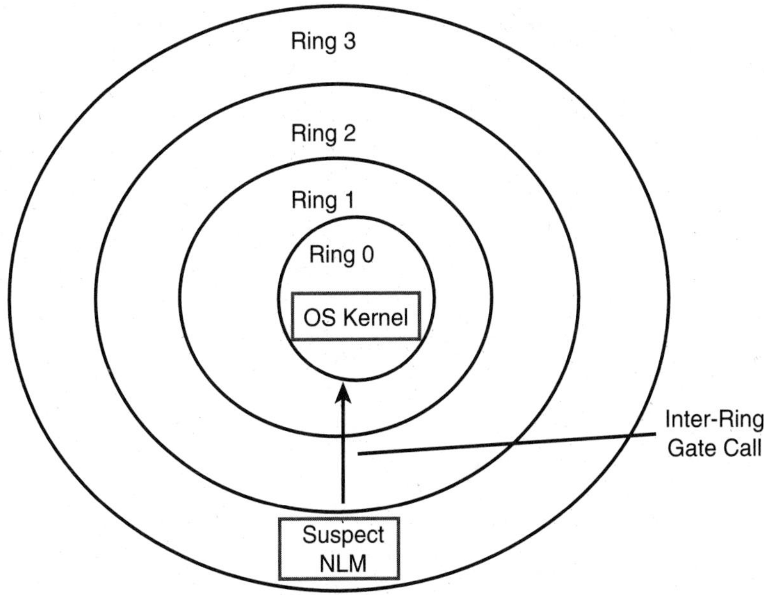

Figure 5.2

Ring memory protection.

Stop You can only load NLMs in Ring 3 (OS_PROTECTED domain) that are written to make inter-ring gate calls. Otherwise you can cause the operating system to crash.

NetWare 4.1 currently defines only rings 0 and 3. The software enables you to switch between all rings (0, 1, 2, and 3). If you load an NLM in ring 1, 2, or 3, however, it will load in the same domain.

Novell refers to the domain that comprises ring 0 as domain OS, referring to "operating system." The domain associated with ring 3 is called domain OSP or OS Protected, referring to "operating system protected." The domain ring protection feature is enabled by adding a command, LOAD DOMAIN.NLM, to the file server's

STARTUP.NCF configuration file. You can switch between domains using either the DOMAIN OS or the DOMAIN OSP commands from the file server console.

Understanding NetWare Directory Services

One of the most significant improvements offered by NetWare 4.1 is its global resource-naming structure, *NetWare Directory Services* (NDS). NDS is based on the CCITT's X.500 international directory services standard. NDS controls all interaction between the users and network resources. NDS is a distributed database, portions of which can reside on every server on the network. The distributed strategy means that the NDS is protected against the failure of any one file server. By distributing the NDS, you also can speed up access to network resources in a WAN environment. You can place file servers that have the desired portions of the NDS database on each side of a slow link, giving users better access to network resources.

Users need access to the NDS for a variety of reasons. The primary reason is for authentication. The *authentication* process occurs when NetWare asks a user for his login name and password, for example. When a user tries to log in, the nearest file server has to obtain NDS object information on that user.

This section provides a general overview of NDS. Chapter 6 deals with NDS in greater detail.

Objects, Properties, and Values

Network resources include any of the following:

- ◆ Users
- ◆ Volumes on a file server
- ◆ Shared printers
- ◆ Print queues
- ◆ Print servers
- ◆ Other types of servers (modem servers, fax servers, database servers)

Network resources are represented in the NDS as objects. An *object* is a collection of properties and values. You can think of an object as a record in a database. Most

companies, for example, have a personnel database. Each record in the database contains a certain type of information on the employees of the company. Each record is like an object. Types of information might include first and last names, an address, a phone number, or a title. When a clerk enters information into the database, a data entry screen is probably used. The data entry screen has a series of blank boxes—one box for each type of information. Some boxes will be filled in, and others might not be, depending on what information is available for that employee and what is applicable. The boxes themselves are like properties of the object. The data that is filled in is like the value of the property. Figure 5.3 illustrates this concept.

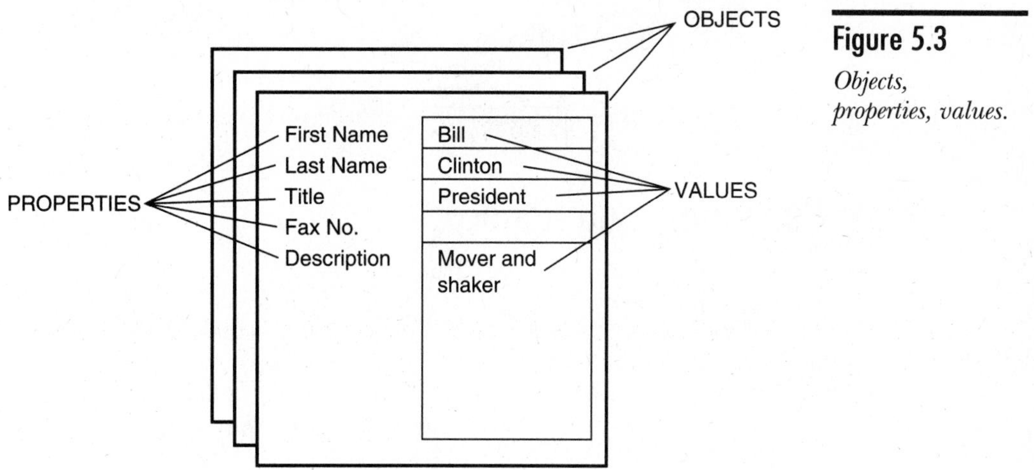

Figure 5.3

Objects, properties, values.

In addition to objects used to represent network resources, another category of objects is used to manage the network. Objects that represent resources are referred to as *leaf objects.* A leaf object is associated with a resource (such as a user or a print queue). Objects used for organizational purposes are known as *container objects.* Container objects "contain" either other container objects or leaf objects.

An analogy for container and leaf objects is the relationship between a DOS subdirectory and a file. A subdirectory can contain either other subdirectories or files. A file contains information but not files or subdirectories. A container object is like a subdirectory. A leaf object is like a file.

Container and leaf objects are used to model your company. Container objects are used to represent geographic locations, departments, subsidiaries, or divisions of your company. Leaf objects are used to represent file servers, volumes, printers, and users. Figure 5.4 illustrates a sample NDS structure for an international organization.

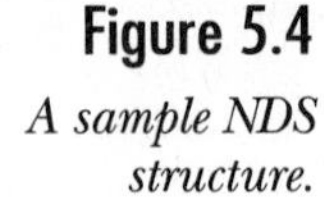

Figure 5.4

A sample NDS structure.

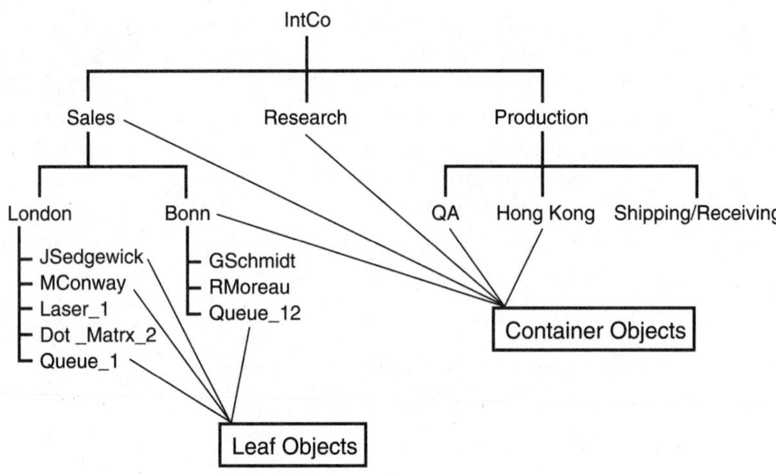

Trees, Partitions, and Replicas

The NDS is physically organized into trees, partitions, and replicas. These terms define the physical aspect of where and what type of NDS information is stored. A *tree* is the term used for the entire NDS structure. Each NDS tree starts with the [root]. [root] is the top of any NDS tree. All containers and leaf objects branch off the root. ([root] is also referred to as "the root.") Each NDS tree is given a name. This name is rarely referred to; users most often need to refer to a specific container or leaf object.

A *partition* is a subdivision of the tree. Partitions can be defined at any point in the tree. The partition consists of all NDS objects from the split point to the end of the tree. You can define a partition of a partition. In this case, the new partition is referred to as the *child* partition, and the partition it was split from is referred to as the *parent* partition. In a certain sense, the NDS tree itself is a partition that starts at the root. A partition that contains [root] is referred to as the *root partition.*

A *replica* is a copy of a partition that is stored on another file server. How many replicas you create, and where they are stored, strikes at the heart of successfully managing a NetWare 4.1 network. There are two primary decisions regarding how many partitions to create and where to store replicas:

- Safeguarding the integrity of the NDS tree
- Optimal local access to NDS information

Creating partitions and then replicating them is a trade-off between integrity and performance. In a single LAN, for example, there is no performance gain in splitting up the NDS. On the other hand, if the server that contains the NDS data goes down, you will have lost access to the entire network. It is advantageous in this situation to create a replica of the root partition on another file server.

In a WAN environment, it would be beneficial to create a replica of a partition on either side of the WAN link to improve performance. When a user in Bonn, Germany attempts to log in, for example, if there is no NDS object information for that user, the network must obtain that information from a server on the network. If that server is located at the other end of a WAN link, it will take a long time to log in. By placing a replica of the NDS partition that contains information on users in Bonn, you can tremendously improve network performance. Figure 5.5 illustrates the login process with and without a replica nearby.

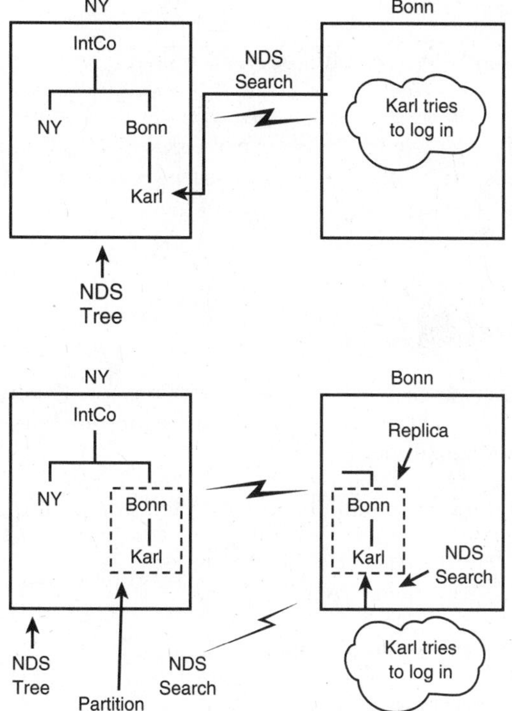

Figure 5.5

NDS replicas and the login process.

Network Management and NDS

The NDS scheme makes managing a large network much easier than previous versions of NetWare. Suppose, for example, that you have 12 file servers running NetWare 3.12. To grant a user access to a volume on every file server, you must go through the following steps—for each file server:

1. Log in or attach to the file server.

2. Run SYSCON, MAKEUSER, or USERDEF to create the user.

3. Use SYSCON, FILER, or the GRANT command to give the user trustee rights to the desired directory on the volume.

Because these steps must take place on each file server, you must perform the preceding three steps 12 times, for a total of 36 separate actions.

To perform the same operation in NetWare 4.1, you do as follows:

1. Log in to the NDS tree.

2. Create the user in the NDS tree.

3. Give the user rights to the desired volumes on each server.

Step 2 must be performed once for each server, giving you a total of 14 different actions. This is a difference of 22 actions. As your network gets larger and larger, the management difference between NetWare 4.1 and earlier versions of NetWare grows geometrically.

Printing Enhancements

Printing in NetWare 4.1 is very similar to printing in NetWare 3.*x*. The function of some of the printing utilities has changed. The basic procedure for sending a print job through the network remains the same:

- The job originates at the workstation and is redirected to a print queue on the file server.

- The job goes from the print queue to a print server.

- The print server directs the job to a printer.

PSERVER.NLM has been revised and streamlined. It can now handle up to 255 printers. One of the major differences between the new PSERVER and the one available in NetWare 3.*x* is that it is no longer responsible for servicing printers directly attached to the file server running PSERVER.NLM. As a result of this streamlining, PSERVER is able to do its job more efficiently and with fewer problems. You will notice that print jobs sent through the NetWare 4.1 PSERVER will print as much as 300 percent faster.

The appearance of PSERVER.NLM has changed from that in NetWare 3.*x*. You no longer see a screen with eight printers displayed. Instead, a menu appears in which you can choose from among the 255 supported printers. You can view a status screen for each printer much like the print server status/control screen in the PCONSOLE.EXE utility. PSERVER.NLM can now be unloaded from the menu

instead of having to toggle to the file server console command line and type UNLOAD PSERVER.

The PSERVER.EXE program that turned a workstation into a dedicated print server is no longer offered. Remote printing is now exclusively handled by a program called NPRINTER.EXE. NPRINTER.EXE has replaced RPRINTER.EXE from earlier versions of NetWare.

A change that corresponds to the changes in PSERVER.NLM is the introduction of the file server-based version NPRINTER.NLM. This NLM must be loaded once for each printer directly attached to a file server. NPRINT.NLM handles the physical printer management that was once part of PSERVER.NLM.

Another significant change to the overall printing environment has to do with the location of print queues. In older versions of NetWare, print queues are always set up as subdirectories under SYS:SYSTEM. Print jobs are temporarily placed as files into the subdirectories corresponding to their queues. When the print job is completed, the temporary file is erased. The problem with this system is that you are forced to estimate how much disk space is required for print jobs. You then must ensure that volume SYS had sufficient space.

In NetWare 4.1, you can designate which volume contains the print queue subdirectories. This gives you much more latitude and enables you to relocate queues onto another volume if disk space becomes a problem.

LAN Communications Improvements

Several communications improvements that were starting to appear as separate patches, fixes, and NLMs in the NetWare 3.*x* world are now built into NetWare 4.1. These include packet burst, LIP (Large Internet Packets), and a new release of the TCP/IP driver NLMs.

Packet Burst

Packet burst technology was offered on NetWare 3.0 to 3.11 file servers as a separate NLM called PBURST.NLM. This technology is built into the operating system kernel of NetWare 3.12 and NetWare 4.1. *Packet burst* is where several IPX/SPX packets are sent in a continuous string. The number of packets sent in one burst is first negotiated between clients, routers, and servers. When one computer sends a group of packets to another, the receiving computer can send an acknowledgment of the group instead of having to acknowledge each packet individually.

Before you can understand the benefits provided by packet burst, you must first understand the traditional communications approach offered by NetWare.

NetWare Core Protocol

NetWare Core Protocol (NCP) is a high-level protocol built into the NetWare operating system kernel. This protocol covers aspects of the session, presentation, and application layers of the OSI reference model. NCP has its own miniature language that programmers make use of when writing applications for the NetWare environment. The commands that NCP understands have to do primarily with access to files and directories on a file server. NCP commands are categorized as either a request or a response. An NCP *request* is sent from a client to a server. An NCP *response* is sent from the server back to the client.

The following is an example of an NCP request/response sequence:

Request	Workstation X requests a file from file server Z.
Response	File server Z grants the request.
Request	Workstation X sends the file specification Y to file server Z.
Response	File server Z sends back directory search information regarding filespec Y.
Request	Workstation X identifies the exact file Y.1.
Response	File server Z checks security access to file Y.1.
...	
Response	File server Z sends file Y.1 to workstation X in a group of 20 packets.

The problem arises in that every request and every response requires an acknowledgment. This is often called the *ping-pong effect.* Just as in the game ping-pong, for every ball you hit over the net, your opponent is supposed to hit it back. In some cases the request/response sequence depends on an answer from the client or server. In the preceding example, the first six requests depend on a response before continuing. When the file server actually sends the data, however, the workstation does not need to make any response other than to acknowledge receipt of the data.

The Benefits of Packet Burst

Packet burst offers an enhancement to NCP. When a large block of data is to be downloaded, the sender can organize the data into a block of packets. The receiver can then acknowledge the block of packets rather than having to acknowledge individual packets.

This arrangement offers the following two advantages:

- The sender does not have to wait for individual acknowledgments of each packet.
- The receiver needs to send only one acknowledgment per burst, which means less traffic on the LAN.

Packet burst is not advantageous if the majority of transmissions in your network consist of data that can fit into a transmission less than 10 packets (for example, exchanges of e-mail, one-page letters, or small spreadsheets). Depending on what type of NIC is used in your LAN, packet sizes can vary from 1.5 KB to 4 KB. Packet burst has a certain amount of overhead. As you read earlier, the sender and receiver negotiate on the maximum size of the packet burst. This negotiation process can end up accounting for an excessive amount of traffic.

Another situation in which packet burst is not useful is the type of traffic in which an acknowledgment is required before the sending computer can proceed. The first six actions in the example listed earlier fall into this category. When the workstation requests a file, it must wait for the file server to grant the request before proceeding. Figure 5.6 illustrates a transmission of 20 data packets with and without packet burst.

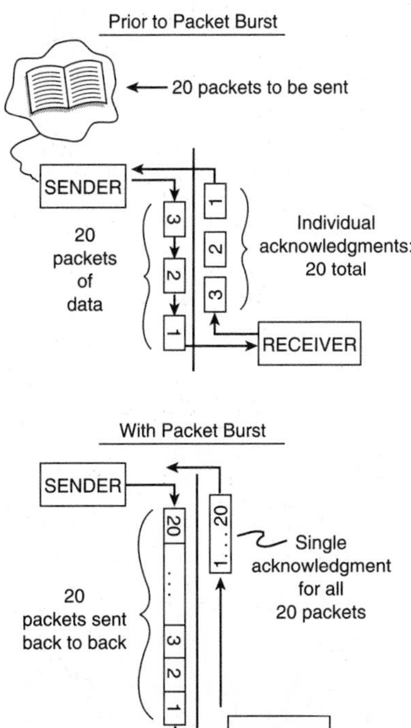

Figure 5.6

Data transmission with and without packet burst.

LIP

The Large Internet Packet (LIP) protocol was developed as an improvement over the way IPX/SPX routing used to occur. In the NetWare 2.*x* environment, and in the case when external routers were used, the routing algorithm dropped the packet size down to 576 bytes (512 bytes of data plus a 64-byte event control block). This was to accommodate older LAN cards that could handle only smaller packets. As a result of this drop in size, the efficiency of earlier NetWare routers suffered, and performance was noticeably slow.

It important to note that all routers involved must have LIP enabled or else the packet size drops back down to 576.

With LIP, the sender can negotiate with the router to obtain the largest possible packet size. Packets routed through a NetWare 4.1 file server, or a Novell Multiprotocol Router, for example, take advantage of LIP. Routers using LIP are extremely efficient and do not slow down the network.

External routers were created in the NetWare 2.*x* and NetWare 3.0, 3.10, and 3.11 environments using a program called ROUTEGEN. The word "external" is used to indicate that the routing is performed on a computer external to a file server. ROUTEGEN produces a DOS executable program called ROUTER.EXE that can be run on a workstation with two or more LAN cards. Depending on the memory available in the workstation chosen to act as a router, you can configure it in either dedicated or nondedicated modes. If dedicated mode is selected, the workstation can be used only as a router.

ROUTEGEN was created using the 16-bit technology used in NetWare 2.*x*. The program is designed for use with a wide range of LAN cards and assumes the worst-case packet size: 576 bytes. A router created using ROUTEGEN is not as efficient as a router that uses LIP.

TCP/IP Improvements

NetWare 4.1 features a new version of TCP/IP. It offers greater conformity to the standards proposed by the Internet community, controlled by the RFC process. The changes to TCP/IP have many internal changes and offer better performance.

RFC stands for *Request for Comment.* This is a process by which Internet users propose changes to Internet specifications. The Internet community is given a period of time in which to respond to the proposed changes. Usually an RFC goes through several drafts before acceptance.

A new NLM has been added: PING.NLM. This NLM implements the TCP/IP "ping" utility from the file server console. PING.NLM enables you to send a continuous stream of IP packets to another host. From the file server console, you type **LOAD PING *ipaddr***, where *ipaddr* is either the IP address or the host name of the target host. A screen appears, showing you the number of IP packets sent and the number of responses received from the target. If the number sent is the same as the number received, you have full IP communications.

As with previous versions of NetWare, to gain additional TCP/IP functionality you must purchase additional software. The list of software packages based on TCP/IP has increased. Table 5.1 summarizes the packages available.

TABLE 5.1
TCP/IP-Based Additional Software

Package	Description
NetWare NFS	Allows TCP/IP-based UNIX systems to utilize the hard disk space on a NetWare file server. Also provides file server console management and an ftp server agent for file transfers. Bidirectional printing support is provided.
NetWare Flex/IP	This package is a subset of NetWare NFS. Provides the ftp, console management, and printing features of the NFS product only.
NetWare NFS Gateway	Allows NetWare users to access files on remote NFS servers (usually UNIX hosts).
LAN Workplace	This family of products offers client support for the TCP/IP protocol suite. *Telnet* is provided for terminal emulation sessions on a remote host. *FTP* is implemented as an executable, enabling you to transfer files between a workstation and a host. You also can use this product to print jobs on the remote host. You must also purchase a LAN Workplace client package. Two are offered: NFS Client, which gains you access to remote UNIX computers via NFS, and TN3270, which provides access to the IBM 3270 family of products (mainframes and minicomputers). LAN Workplace version 4.2 includes the NFS Client and a Windows version of the TN3270 client package. The LAN Workplace products are offered for DOS, OS/2, and Macintosh.

continues

Table 5.1, Continued
TCP/IP-Based Additional Software

Package	Description
LAN Workgroup	This product family is the same as the LAN Workplace family except that you get a limited site license. The LAN Workplace family products are single-user only. The LAN Workgroup family starts with a 5-user package, and can go up to a 250-user package. The more users desired, the more expensive the package. There is a significant cost savings over buying the equivalent number of single-user packages.

Examining Changes to DOS Clients

NetWare 4.*x* introduces radically different DOS client software. As in NetWare 3.*x*, the ODI drivers form the foundation of the lower layers of the NetWare 4.*x* client software. ODI stands for Open Datalink Interface. The ODI software has been available for the last few years.

The new requester architecture has the following three major differences compared to the older software:

- It functions as a requester and works with the DOS environment.
- It is based on a modular concept utilizing modules called VLMs (Virtual Loadable Modules).
- It has greater connectivity (supports up to 50 simultaneous server connections).

This section provides an overview of the DOS requester and the VLM architecture. For more detailed information on which files to load and how to install the requester, please refer to Part Four, "Activating and Using Clients."

Comparing the DOS Requester to the NETx Shell

The NETx shell acts as an interceptor rather than as a requester. In its capacity as an interceptor, the NETx shell intercepts all commands before DOS had a chance to examine them. The NETx shell determines whether the command should be handled by NetWare or by DOS. NETx then passes the command either to DOS or to the file server.

The VLM requester, on the other hand, makes use of certain programming hooks that allow the requester to extend the functionality of DOS. The VLM requester uses the DOS environment and shares DOS tables. The VLM requester becomes an extension of DOS rather than an alternative to DOS.

Figure 5.7 illustrates the different approaches between NETx and VLM. Note that because the NETx shell is hidden from DOS, it maintains its own file handles table (among other tables).

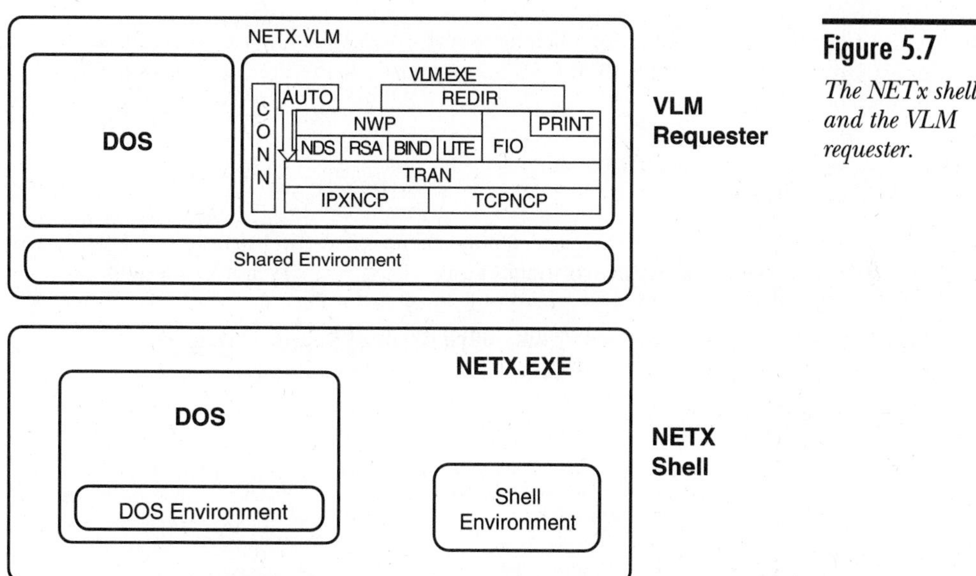

Figure 5.7
The NETx shell and the VLM requester.

VLM Architecture

The VLM architecture is modular in nature. Instead of placing all requester functions in a single program executable file, Novell split functions out into loadable modules. This is the same sort of change that NetWare 3.*x* and 4.*x* brought to the network world. On the file server you can load *NLMs.* On the workstation you load *VLMs.*

Different aspects of network functionality are represented by different VLM modules. The following list gives you an idea of the types of functionality available in the VLM modules:

- Printing
- Security

- Protocol support (IPX/SPX is the default)
- Automatic reconnection if the network connection goes down temporarily
- Access to the file system on a file server

VLMs are loaded when VLM.EXE is loaded. To unload one VLM you must unload them all. Which VLMs are loaded and in what order is specified in a file called NET.CFG, a configuration file generally stored in same directory as VLM.EXE.

The VLM requester makes very efficient use of workstation memory. If you have extended memory available, VLM.EXE automatically loads the VLM modules into extended memory.

Packet Burst

The VLM requester enables the packet burst protocol at the workstation. This means that your workstation is capable of negotiating with a file server how many packets it can send at one time. If, for reasons of efficiency (as discussed earlier), you want to disable packet burst, add the following command to the NET.CFG file under the new NetWare DOS Requester section:

PB BUFFERS = 0

Otherwise, the VLM requester will reserve three buffers for packet burst.

Authentication

The VLM requester supports an extended authentication process between the workstation and the authentication agent on the file server. There is an exchange of information between the file server and workstation prior to logging in. The process involves the following steps:

- The user issues the LOGIN command.
- The security agents in the client VLM requester send a request for authentication.
- The server responds with an encrypted private key.
- The user is prompted for a password.
- The VLM software decrypts the private key using the password.
- The VLM software builds a credential and a signature.

- The VLM software sends proof and request for continuation of the login process.
- The server checks the proof and sends confirmation if okay.

As you can see, the login process is somewhat complicated. The reason for this has to do with several security breaches that were discovered in the NetWare 3.*x* environment. Although the passwords in NetWare 3.*x* are encrypted before passing across the LAN, the user is authenticated only when he first logs in. If the user is a network Supervisor or equivalent, this fact is checked only when the user first logs in. From this point until the user logs out, the file server assumes every packet coming from that user's workstation has Supervisor access.

A potential NetWare 3.*x* security problem was exposed in Europe. Researchers used simple programming code that they devised, and network management tools, such as the LANalyzer, to discover the security breach. The researchers were able to fool the server into thinking that their workstation had the same address as that of the Supervisor. As a result, every command these users issued had Supervisor authority. Novell subsequently issued a security patch to solve this potential problem.

In NetWare 4.1, this is not possible. When a user first logs in, the file server sends the private key recorded with the user information stored in the NDS. The *private key* is an NDS data element created by NetWare when the user object is first created. A *credential* is constructed each time a user logs in, and it changes from session to session. The credential is constructed from the private key and the password that the user supplies upon login. The credential is constructed at the user's workstation and never travels across the LAN where it could be intercepted.

If high security is necessary, packet signatures can be enabled. This process requires the VLM software to add an additional, unique signature based on the credential and proof for every packet it sends to the server. A malicious user cannot capture this session and attempt to replay it later. Note that the packet signature option degrades network performance—the workstation software must take an extra set of steps as it prepares packets to send out across the LAN. For more detailed information on packet signature, see Chapter 14, "DOS Client Basics" and Chapter 38, "Fine-Tuning the Server."

Auditing the Network

Auditing is a new feature for NetWare 4.1. As in NetWare 2.1*x* and 3.*x*, NetWare 4.1 supports accounting. *Accounting* is a mechanism that tracks the usage of network resources (such as the amount of time logged in and the amount of disk space used).

Auditing, on the other hand, keeps track of any changes made to the NDS tree, and a vast number of file system events. Auditing is controlled with the new utility AUDITCON.EXE.

NetWare 4.1 allows for independent auditing of the network. Once auditing has been set up, the network Administrator can then turn over the auditing password to an independent auditor. This auditor can monitor the status of the network independent of the network Administrator. If the auditor chooses to change the auditing password, the network Administrator cannot access the auditing system.

The following are some of the NDS items that can be audited:

- ◆ When a user logs in
- ◆ When a user logs out
- ◆ Change of user security status
- ◆ Changes made to partitions
- ◆ Additions, deletions, or changes made to NDS objects

The file system events that can be audited include the following:

- ◆ Creation, deletion, or access to files
- ◆ Creation, deletion, or changes made to subdirectories
- ◆ Print queue volume and destination of print jobs
- ◆ File server events (such as bringing the server down)

File system events are logged in to an audit file that resides at the root of every volume. The maximum size of this file can be controlled through AUDITCON. NDS events are logged in to the NDS files themselves. To control the growth of these files you can set maximum sizes for both volume audit files and directory (NDS) audit files. In addition, three categories are available when tagging a volume event to be audited:

- ◆ Global
- ◆ User OR file
- ◆ User AND file

The first category allows any audited event into the audit file. The second option allows only events by tagged users OR (logical OR) tagged files. The third option is

the most restrictive—only events by the tagged users using the tagged files are allowed into the audit file. By controlling what goes into the audit file, you control the rate at which this file grows. By selecting Global, for example, the audit file will grow very quickly and may reach its maximum size sooner than anticipated. The last option, "User AND File" will slow down the growth of the file, but it limits the amount of information you can obtain.

The AUDITCON Report menu enables you to set up a filter. The *filter* acts much like the process of tagging events to be audited in the first place. You can create as many filters as you want and save them. When generating reports you can opt to use any of the filters you have created.

Auditing reports appear either on screen or in a file. If you choose to print the report to a file, you can then print it, in a separate step, to a printer.

Understanding Changes Specific to NetWare 4.1

The features discussed above are available in NetWare 4.0, 4.01, and 4.02 as well as in NetWare 4.1. This section will cover changes that are specific to NetWare 4.1.

Bindery Synchronization

A feature that is unique to NetWare 4.1 is bindery synchronization. *Bindery synchronization* is when up to 12 NetWare 3.*x* file servers are referenced to a NetWare 4.1 file server. This grouping of NetWare 3.*x* file servers and a NetWare 4.1 file server is known as a *NetSync cluster*. The bindery files of the NetWare 3.*x* servers in the NetSync cluster are combined into a single container in the NDS tree. The target container is the bindery context of the NetWare 4.1 file server.

Bindery synchronization is accomplished through two NLMs: NETSYNC3 through NETSYNC4. A problem with NetWare 4.0*x* is that NetWare 3.*x* file servers are recognized but not manageable through the NDS. With the bindery synchronization tools available in NetWare 4.1, changes made to the bindery files are propagated out to the NDS tree as well as to all other NetWare 3.*x* file servers in the same NetSync cluster.

The bindery synchronization process is reminiscent of a past product, the NetWare Name Service (NNS). NNS uses a process in which any changes made to the bindery files on one server are propagated out to all other servers in the domain. The difference between that product and the bindery synchronization tools available in NetWare 4.1 is that the new tools use the NDS itself to perform the propagation and do not attempt to involve any other 3.*x* file servers other than the one directly involved.

Using NetSync, NetWare 3.*x* servers can be integrated into the overall NDS network management framework.

Pruning and Grafting

With NetWare 4.1, you now have the ability to "prune" and "graft" entire branches of the tree from one location to another. In the past, when you needed to move a container and all its associated objects to another location in the tree, you had to create the new container and *move* objects to the new container. You then had to delete the old container. In NetWare 4.1, any container and its associated objects can be moved to another location in the tree. This process is accomplished by first designating the new container as a *partition.* As you learned earlier, a partition is a subdivision in the tree. After the partition has been designated, you can then perform the move operation. The entire partition is moved, moving all subsidiary objects along with it.

Merging NDS Trees

NetWare 4.1 introduces the DSMERGE.NLM utility. This is a utility that you can load at the file server itself and is used to merge two separate NDS trees into a single, combined tree. The merge operation occurs in four phases. Up to phase three you have the chance to back out in case you change your mind.

The process of merging two trees is similar to the "pruning and grafting" operation described above. The source NDS tree to be merged is made into a partition of the target tree. The merge process itself is quite simple: the root of the source tree is merged with the root of the target tree. The source tree now points to the root of the target tree. This process is discussed in greater detail in Chapter 23, "Merging Trees."

DynaText Online Help

The online help system in NetWare 4.1 has changed from Electro Text to DynaText. The DynaText help system includes all the NetWare 4.1 manuals. The system can be searched much like Electro Text. The main difference is that DynaText is two to three times faster than Electro Text.

DynaText help is also now included in NetWare 4.02 and NetWare 3.12. There are DynaText viewers available for Windows, OS/2, Macintosh, and UnixWare. For more information on the installation and operation of DynaText see Chapter 25, "Installing Applications."

Improved Macintosh Support

The Macintosh support for NetWare 4.1 now includes full NDS support. Users on a Macintosh can now see and log in to the NDS tree rather than individual servers as in the past. Macintosh users can also browse the tree and discern objects. Users on a Macintosh can access any resources in the tree, including volume and printing objects.

A 50-user version of NetWare for Macintosh is now included in NetWare 4.1 For information on installing this product and configuring the Macintosh client, see Chapter 18, "Macintosh Clients."

NLSP

NetWare 4.1 introduces the new routing protocol, NLSP (NetWare Link Services Protocol). This is an implementation of link-state routing as defined in the OSI protocols. NLSP offers backwards compatibility with IPX routers using RIP (Routing Information Protocol). NLSP has superior routing algorithms that route packets across an internetwork with greater efficiency. A NetWare 4.1 file server using NLSP maintains a map of the entire internetwork in RAM, and only broadcasts changes to the network. This enables the server to perform precise calculations in order to find the best route. By broadcasting only changes to the network, NLSP minimizes the excessive network traffic caused by IPX RIP. NetWare 4.1 gives you the ability to use either NLSP or the more traditional IPX RIP.

Summary

This chapter discussed features offered by NetWare 4 and features unique to NetWare 4.1. These include file system features such as file compression, disk block suballocation, data migration, and read-ahead. As you discovered, these features make the NetWare 4.1 file system faster and more efficient than previous versions of NetWare. This chapter also discussed issues such as memory management and LAN communications improvements. As you read, memory management is greatly simplified in that NetWare 4.1 uses only one memory pool. The paging mechanism and ring memory protection features enable the server to protect itself from misbehaving NLMs and to allocate memory even though it is fragmented. Communications improvements include support for packet burst, LIP, and improvements in the TCP/IP implementation.

NDS (NetWare Directory Services) was discussed briefly. You learned how the structure is built: objects have properties, which in turn have values. You saw that there are two different types of objects: container and leaf. You also learned how the NDS is divided up physically: into trees, partitions, and replicas.

Changes to the DOS client requester were discussed. As you learned, the VLM architecture works with DOS rather than against it, sharing common tables and memory. The VLM architecture is modular in nature and supports packet burst. The login process is much more sophisticated, offering considerable security improvements. Finally, you learned some of the capabilities available in network auditing. You learned that you can audit both file system events, such as accessing a file, and NDS events, such as when a user logged in. The bindery synchronization feature you learned about is available in NetWare 4.1 and enables 3.*x* file servers to be kept in sync with the NDS structure. As you saw, this new set of tools offers better performance than a similar tool, the NetWare Name Service.

Chapter 6 introduces much more detail about how NDS works in the NetWare 4.1 environment.

NetWare Directory Services

Chapter 5 included a general overview of NetWare Directory Services (NDS). This chapter takes a closer look at what exactly comprises an NDS network. The components of an NDS tree—trees, objects, partitions, and replicas—are examined. Concepts such as properties, values, and context are explored, and methods to address NDS objects through the NDS naming rules are investigated. Finally, issues on how NetWare 4.1 can best be put to use in a complex network are addressed. The first topic of discussion is the NDS tree.

Understanding Trees

The NDS tree represents the entire network. Design of the tree should not be taken lightly, yet it is very easy to overdesign the tree. When first setting up the network, look for simple solutions that work for your company. Changing the structure after the installation can be accomplished easily using the various network administration tools.

The name of the tree is assigned when you install the first NetWare 4.1 file server on the network. Once assigned, the only way of changing it is to use the DSMERGE utility.

The name of the tree can be up to 32 characters long. The name of the tree should be reflective of your organization as a whole. Once assigned, the name of the tree is not used, except as a reference that can be made on the workstation when logging in. Users can specify a *preferred tree* when logging in. This option, associated with VLM.EXE, enables users to log in to different trees. Alternatively, a user can log in to a specific file server, in which case they become part of the tree in which that file server participates.

One suggestion for a medium-sized company would be to name the tree after your company. Departments or divisions of your company could become the top level organizations. This would greatly simplify network management. All names would require less typing. Navigating the tree would be easier because you would have eliminated one level.

All NDS trees have a [root]. [root] is the top level object and is the primary container for the entire structure. You can have only one [root] per tree. [root] can be assigned rights just like any other container object. Rights assigned to [root] flow down and apply to every object in the tree. [root] cannot have any leaf objects as the next level in the structure; it can have only Organization, Country, or Locality container objects.

Figure 6.1 shows you a "map" of an NDS tree. In this figure, there are the container objects IntCo, NY, LA, and London. Leaf objects, representing users, print queues, volumes, and other objects, include JSmith, Laser3, RChavez, LA1_SYS, RJones, and Script_1.

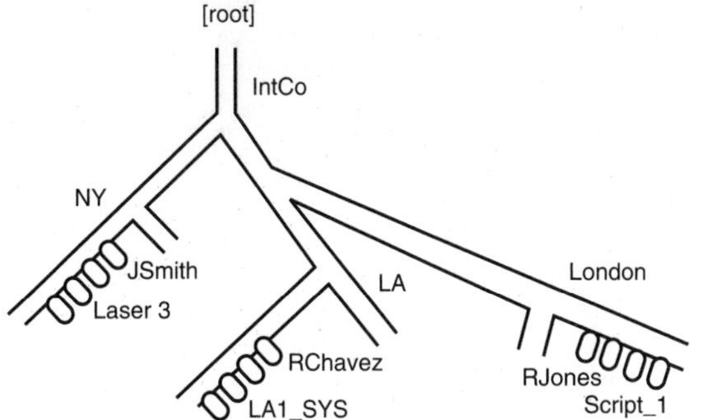

Figure 6.1

View of an NDS tree showing [root], container, and leaf objects.

The NDS tree is a hierarchical distributed database. Hierarchical database technology has been available for approximately 20 years. This method of implementing a database has been criticized for its lack of ability to model complex situations. On the other hand, hierarchical databases represent the fastest software technology in terms of searching and sorting. The hierarchical database achieves its speed because the order of a record in the database is determined by its position in the structure. As you create users, groups, and other NDS objects, the operating system (OS) is sorting them as it places them in the structure. When the OS needs to obtain information on an NDS object, it simply needs to refer to the name of the object to determine where it is in the tree. To enable the database to model complex situations, the designers of the NDS created an object known as an alias. The *Alias* object is a pointer that refers to another object in another part of the tree.

NDS trees do not communicate with each other. The primary purpose for installing a tree at all is to place the network under one structure. Trees assume that there are no others. This design decision extends into the realm of security. This way you can isolate networks from each other. If users log in to one tree, they get limited access to the resources of another tree.

Even though trees do not communicate with each other, users can still access the file systems of servers not on their tree. This is accomplished through *bindery services.* Users can attach or map drive letters to servers in another tree by attaching as a bindery user. Bindery services is a feature of NetWare 4.*x* that enables users from older NetWare environments to access resources on a NetWare 4.*x* file server. Bindery services is discussed in Chapter 4, "Traditional Features of NetWare," as well as later in this chapter.

The name of the tree can be viewed from the file server itself when the MONITOR utility is loaded. Tree names are also displayed, along with file server names, when you issue the DISPLAY SERVERS command from the file server console. Another command, TRACK ON, issued from the file server console will show you tree names. From a workstation, this command will give you a list of trees on your network:

```
NLIST /TREE
```

Each tree on the network advertises itself through the *Server Advertising Protocol* (SAP) process. The information being transmitted is the fact that this server supports name services (SAP type 632) and time services (SAP type 619). The name associated with these services is the tree name padded with underscore characters (_) to fill out the 32 character spaces reserved for tree names. In addition, a compressed network address is added.

You learn about using the file server console in Chapter 36, "Monitoring the File Server."

There is no theoretical limit to the size of a tree. The current limitations come from limits placed by the software engineers who created the NDS administrative utilities. NetWare 4.1, for example, expands the limit on the number of objects that can be placed in a single container from 1,500 to 40,000. The limit placed in NetWare 4.0*x* was due to limits in the administrative software, not to limits inherent to NDS. Practical limits include the following:

- How many servers do you have?

  The more servers you have, the more partitions you can create and distribute between the servers. A server needs to store physically only information contained in the partition it hosts. It is a very good idea to have one or two replicas of each partition. Novell recommends 3 or more. Replicas and partitions are discussed in more detail in Chapter 19, "NDS Tree Design Considerations."

- How many objects do you want any one server to keep track of?

  The more objects a single server is responsible for, the more CPU time it will spend performing lookups, authentication, and so forth.

- How much disk space is available on all servers to store the NDS database?

  As with any database, the NDS takes hard disk space. A rough rule of thumb is to estimate between 1 KB and 2 KB of space for each object. The more values stored for each object, the more disk space that will be required.

- How many replicas will there be? How much traffic is there on the LAN?

  Each Read Only or Read Write replica must check with its Master replica at a regular interval. This checking ensures proper update synchronization. If a change is being made to two replicas of the same partition, the timestamp for each change has to be sorted by the Master replica, and the changes must be applied in order. This creates a certain amount of additional traffic on the LAN.

Understanding Objects

Objects are used to represent network resources. As explained in the previous chapter, objects are like records in a database. Each object has properties, and properties can have values. This section discusses the concept of objects in greater detail. Also discussed are the various types of objects that are available and where they are appropriate.

Container Objects

Container objects are used to organize the structure of the tree. For those of you who have worked with previous versions of NetWare, container objects take the place of groups. Groups still exist in NetWare 4.1, but they are much less important.

Security rights of container objects are transferred to child objects, a characteristic of containers known as *inheritance.* A leaf object, such as a user, placed in a container object inherits these rights. Values can transfer only to objects with similar properties. A PRINTCON job template that you have created for a container is a value of the container's printcon job property. A User object also has the printcon job property. Thus, the container's printcon jobs would be accessible to a user object under the container. A Print Queue object, on the other hand, does not have a printcon job property and would not inherit the parent container's printcon job property value.

Figure 6.2 shows a view of a complex tree that includes Country, Organization, and Organizational Unit container objects.

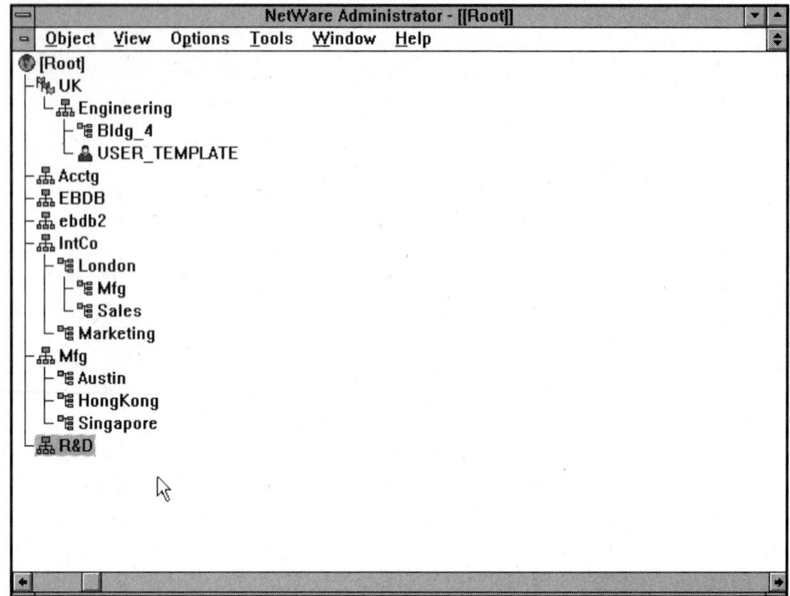

Figure 6.2
View of an NDS tree showing Country, Organization, and Organizational Unit container objects.

Table 6.1 summarizes and gives you characteristics of the various types of containers that are available.

Table 6.1
Container Objects

Object	Description
[root]	This is the top level container object. There are strict rules regulating [root]: ◆ There can be only one [root] per NDS tree. ◆ You cannot place a leaf object directly under [root]. ◆ Only Country and Organization objects can be placed under [root]. [root] is created when a new NDS tree is created (usually when the first file server is created). [root] cannot be renamed.
Organization	This object is designed to create a high level division in the structure of your NDS tree. Typically, the Organization is your company. In the case of a moderate-sized company, the

Object	Description
	name of the tree could be your company name, and Organizations could be created to represent branch offices, departments, or divisions. Organization must be placed under the [root], Country, or Locality container objects. You cannot place one Organization object under another (use Organizational Unit for this purpose). Leaf objects can be placed under an Organization object. You can have one or more Organizations off [root].
Organizational Unit	This object is a general purpose container object designed to allow easy subdivisions within the tree structure. Organizational Units can be placed under an Organization or another Organizational Unit. There is no limit to the depth of your structure, although you will experience a network mutiny if you have more than three levels with long names!
Country	The Country container object is provided to maintain compliance with the X.500 global naming specification. The X.500 specification is international and added this level to respect strong nationalistic feelings. In actual use, you might find the Country container object clumsy to use. Adding this level of complexity to your NDS structure may not be necessary. Organizations or Organizational Units can be used to represent a Country and offer greater flexibility. The rules governing the use of the Country object are as follows: ◆ Country objects can be placed only directly off the [root]. ◆ You can have as many Country objects as are desired.
Locality	This type of container object is used to distinguish the geographical location of an object. It is not recognized by the NetWare 4.*x* administrative utilities, although NDS will recognize its presence if created by some other means. The only way to create a locality object short of developing a custom program using the NDS API (Application Programming Interface) tools is during the initial installation. The use of this object is not recommended because NetWare 4.*x* NDS management utilities do not support it.

NDS Leaf Objects

Leaf objects are the end points of the NDS tree. They are used to represent network resources. Unlike a container object, a leaf object cannot contain other objects. Leaf objects have properties, and these properties have values. The properties of a leaf object do not inherit because the leaf object represents the lowest position in the tree at that point.

Figure 6.3 shows a view of a complex tree with a variety of leaf objects.

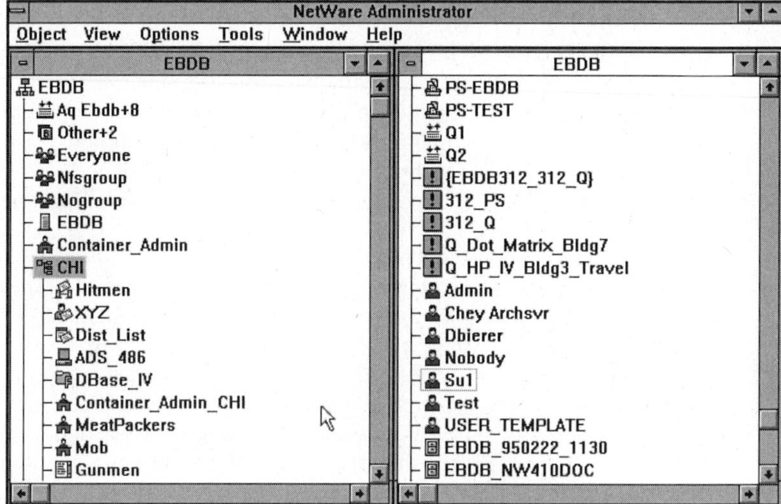

Figure 6.3
View of an NDS tree showing a variety of leaf objects.

Table 6.2 summarizes and gives you characteristics of the various types of NDS leaf objects that are available.

Table 6.2
NDS Leaf Objects

Object	Description
AFP Server	*Apple Filing Protocol* server. This leaf object represents a file server running NetWare for Macintosh.
Alias	An *alias* is a leaf object that points to other leaf objects. Once assigned to another object, it takes on the characteristics of that object. If you make an alias of a print queue, for

Object	Description
	example, the print queue icon will appear in the Windows-based NWADMIN utility. An alias is used to hide the true location of an object. Aliases also can be used to represent an object that might be awkward to represent using its full NDS name. The Alias object is used to work around the shortcomings of the hierarchical database structure. An alias is a method of allowing a single object to exist in several branches of the tree simultaneously.
Computer	The *Computer* object can be used to represent physical workstations. This object has properties that help you keep track of the physical makeup of a workstation, is for reference only, and serves no practical purpose other than to serve as a reference for inventory purposes. Assigning Security rights to this object, for example, can be done but serves no purpose. You cannot log in as a Computer object.
Directory Map	The *Directory Map* object is a method of providing an NDS reference to a subdirectory on a volume. This object can be used to hide the physical location of a directory. Once created, this object can be referenced using the MAP command, which can be used in a login script or a batch file. If the directory needs to change for some reason, you can simply reassign the directory map instead of having to change many login scripts or batch files.
Distribution List	The *Distribution List* object is designed for future implementations of e-mail and software that uses e-mail. This object has fields for the location of the messaging (i.e., MHS) server, department, description, and location. You can assign Users, Groups, Organizational Roles, containers, and other objects as members of the distribution list.
External Entity	This object is used as a "catch all" for objects you wish to manage from the NDS but do not have a specific NDS object to type assign. This object could be used to define an e-mail related entity (such as Lotus Notes), or an Internet host, for example.
Group	The *Group* object is used primarily to assign access rights to a number of users at the same time. The role of the Group object is greatly diminished in NetWare 4.1 compared to

continues

Table 6.2, Continued
NDS Leaf Objects

Object	Description
	earlier versions of NetWare. In NetWare 4.1 you would place similar Users into the same container. Access rights can then be assigned to the container. One use for a group in NetWare 4.1 is to give common Access rights to users in different containers.
Message Routing Group	This object is designed to enable you to identify a series of e-mail servers. It has common fields that you can fill in such as other name, description, location, department and organization. In addition, it has a *postmaster general* field, which can include any NDS User. This field can then be used by e-mail based applications. The other unique field for this object is *messaging server*. This is a multivalued field in which you can place a list of e-mail servers in the routing group. An example of this would be the names of a series of MHS servers you have defined for your network.
NetWare Server	The *NetWare server* object represents a file server in the NDS structure. The importance of the server object is not as great as a volume object. The server object is a leaf object as is the volume object. When you grant rights to the server object, you gain a degree of control over server management. The server object is created when you install NetWare 4.1 and NDS on a file server. During installation you specify a container that will contain the new server. The NetWare Server object will then appear under that container. You can move the NetWare Server object to another container at any time if you want.
Organizational Role	The *Organizational Role* object is similar to a group. You can assign users to the role by adding them to the list of role *occupants*. An organizational role is used to represent a position in a company rather than a specific person. For a clothing store, for example, a role might be "Men's Shoes Buyer." You can assign access rights to the role, and any occupants will acquire those rights. When a user changes positions within the company, you can easily remove them from the role and assign them to another.

Object	Description
Print Server	A *Print Server* object can be created using the NWADMIN administration utility or the DOS-based PCONSOLE utility. The print server redirects print jobs between print queues and printers.
Printer	The *Printer* object defines a printer. Its properties include the type of printer, the type of interface (parallel or serial), and what print queue it is assigned to. It can be defined using either the NWADMIN administration utility or the DOS-based PCONSOLE utility.
Profile	The *Profile* object is used to provide a common login script for a group of users. This login script is in addition to the container and user login scripts. To use a profile login script, users must be assigned to the profile.
Queue	The *Queue* object defines a print queue. When created, NetWare also creates off the designated volume a subdirectory called QUEUES, and another subdirectory under that using the queue object's ID number.
Top	This object represents all properties that are common to all objects. Think of the *Top* object as a wild card. It is not directly referenced by network Administrators or users. The Top object is used primarily when searching the NDS tree. You can use the Top object when you want to reference all objects.
Unknown	The *Unknown* object is designated by NetWare when it does not know how to reference an object. An Unknown object is created by the system to replace an object that has been moved to another container, for example, but not all servers with NDS data have been notified of the change. Another example is when you reinstall a file server. The file server's volumes become Unknown until they are reinstalled into the NDS.
User	The *User* object is used to represent people who use network resources. The User object contains information about network users, such as their name, phone number, fax number, and address. Users can be assigned *trustee rights,* which give them access to NDS objects or the file system on a NetWare file server. The User object name is the name a network user uses to log in.

continues

Table 6.2, Continued
NDS Leaf Objects

Object	Description
Volume	The *Volume* object represents a division of the available disk space on a NetWare file server. The volume contains directories and files. The relationship between the volume and the file server that houses it has changed in NetWare 4.1 compared with earlier versions of NetWare. In NetWare 3.1*x* and below, for example, the volume has a subsidiary relationship to the file server that holds it. In NetWare 4.1, the file server object serves only as a point of reference and does not even have to be in the same container as the Volume object.

The [public] Object

A special object referred to as [public] is defined in the NDS schema. *[public]* represents literally any entity connected to the network running NDS client software. You do not have to be logged in to belong to [public].

[public] cannot be managed directly. You can see references to [public] when assigning rights, but there is no option to manage its properties or values.

The function of [public] is like a Group object. [public] is assigned certain rights to the NDS tree to allow users who have not yet logged in to change context. If you do not know your complete NDS name, the rights assigned to [public] are necessary to see the tree.

The default rights assigned to [public] (discussed in next chapter, "NetWare 4.1 Security") could present a potential security breach. Because you do not have to be a valid user to acquire the rights of [public], any intruder could conceivably view your NDS tree. A member of [public] could view the names of any object in the tree, including containers, users, file server, and volumes.

Bindery Objects

Bindery objects are maintained by NetWare 4.1 to retain backwards compatibility with earlier versions of NetWare and NLMs written for the NetWare 3.*x* environment. Bindery objects are accessed through the file server's bindery services capability. Bindery objects reside in the file server's *bindery context.* This context is a container in the tree designated at the time of installation. Bindery clients can see only objects in this container.

Bindery objects are created either by bindery-based utilities or by the server when it attempts to recognize bindery-based clients. Bindery-based utilities include SYSCON.EXE (used to configure the system in NetWare 3.*x* and earlier) and management utilities from bindery-based NLMs. NUC.NLM is an example of the latter category, comes with UnixWare, and is used to configure UnixWare-based users, security rights transfers, and various tables.

The characteristics of bindery objects are the same as the characteristics of NDS objects. Bindery objects are NDS objects that happen to reside in the file server's bindery context. Each has properties but has no other status in the tree. The following bindery objects might get created through bindery services: Group, Queue, Server, User, and Volume.

Examining Properties

Properties define the characteristics of objects. Each type of object has a predefined set of properties. Two different types of objects will have different sets of properties. A User object, for example, has a property *last login.* The value for this property is the last time this user logged in to the network. A print server object, in contrast, does not have this property. It is not the nature of a print server to log in to the network. An example of a property for a print server would be default queue, which represents the print queue assigned to this printer by default.

Some properties are common to all objects. An example of this would be the Access Control List (ACL) property. Values for this property would be NDS names of objects and the Security rights they have for this object. The ACL property for an Organization object IntCo, for example, may have the following value:

```
.CN=JSmith.OU=Sales.O=IntCo   Create
```

This means that J. Smith, who is in the Sales Organizational Unit under the company IntCo, has the ability to create new objects under the Organization IntCo.

Other properties are common to certain categories of objects. An example of this would be the *common name* (CN) property, which is true for all leaf objects. The value of the CN property is the name of the object.

Figure 6.4 shows a diagram of an object and some of its properties.

Another property that is not defined in the NDS schema, but is implied, is *all properties.* This implied property refers to all properties of an object. It is used to assign default rights for all properties, saving you the time of having to select each property individually to assign access rights.

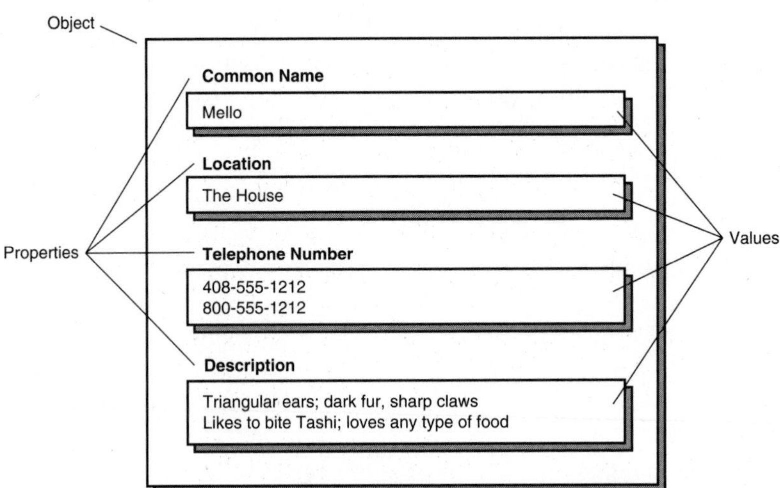

Figure 6.4

A diagram of an object and some of its properties.

Table 6.3 summarizes the NDS properties available to the User object. Following this table are two more tables. Table 6.4 summarizes the properties common to Organizations and Organizational Units. Table 6.5 summarizes miscellaneous other properties common to various objects.

Note Unfortunately, the NWADMIN (Windows-based) administrative utility, and NETADMIN, NLIST, and UIMPORT (DOS-based) utilities, do not agree on the names of properties. The tables that follow use the property names listed in the NLIST and UIMPORT utilities. You will find that the property names given in NWADMIN are very close, with minor differences.

TABLE 6.3
NDS User Properties

Property	Description
ACL	*Access Control List.* A list of objects that have security rights assigned to this user.
Account Balance	The user account balance hearkens back to the days of NetWare 2.10 and above. This property represents the total number of "units" the user has remaining. Units are subtracted based on accounting options such as connection time, files read from and written to the server, server activity on the account of this user, and disk space used. The account balance is effective only if the accounting

Property	Description
	options have been enabled. The accounting feature is discussed in Chapter 20, "Managing Objects and Properties."
Account Disabled	This property can have a value of Yes or No. This indicates if this user account is active. The account can be disabled by the system administrator or by the *Intruder Detection System.*
Account Has Expiration Date	This property has a value of Yes or No. If Yes, it also contains the date and time when this account is due to be no longer valid. After the given date and time, the user can no longer log in using this account name.
Allow Unlimited Credit	Values for this property can be Yes or No. If Yes, this option enables this user to have unlimited "credit" if accounting has been enabled. (See *Account Balance.*)
Allow User to Change Password	Values for this property can be either Yes or No. If you set this property to No, the user will not be able to change her password. This property is the same as the Password Allow Change property described below.
City	Used for mailing purposes.
CN	*Common Name.* The NDS name of the user. This is the name used when the user logs in.
Date Password Expires	This property contains the date the user's password is due to expire. When the date arrives, the user will receive a message indicating he should change the password.
Days Between Forced Changes	This property represents the number of days between password changes. If the value is 30, for example, the user has to change his password every 30 days.
Department	Used to describe the user's department. This property is for descriptive purposes and can be used at the network Administrator's discretion.
Description	The description property can contain anything that the system Administrator wants to add regarding this user. This field can be used to indicate the user's full name or capacity in the company.

continues

Table 6.3, Continued
NDS User Properties

Property	Description
Fax Number	Contains the fax number of the user.
Foreign E-Mail Address	E-mail address. Many companies use the Internet for e-mail. An example of a foreign Internet e-mail address is JSmith@Sales.IntCo.COM.
Grace Logins Allowed	This property holds the number of times this user can log in after the password has expired. When the password expires, and the user has remaining grace logins, the user will be asked, `Would you like to change your password?` Each time the user logs in after password expiration, one grace login is used. The count decrements. After the grace logins are exhausted, the user receives the message, `You must change your password.` If the user fails to change the password and no more grace logins remain, the user is denied access to the network.
Group Membership	This represents a list of groups this user belongs to.
Home Directory	This property records the volume and directory where the user can store personal files and works in progress. This is normally created at the time the User object is created.
Incorrect Login Attempts	If an illegal login attempt has occurred, this property tracks the number of such attempts. Same as *Login Intruder Attempts* property described soon.
Language	The default language for the user. The language is normally set in the NET.CFG file on the user's workstation. If you do not set the language in the NET.CFG file, this property will supply a default language for the user: English. Languages supplied with NetWare include English, Spanish, German, French, and Italian. Other languages are available at extra cost.
Last Login Time	The last time this user logged in.
Last Name	This property, which indicates the user's last name, is *mandatory*. This property and the Common Name (CN) property are used to form a unique key needed by the

Property	Description
	NDS to look up values for this user. This property is identical to the *Surname* property.
Location	Property used to describe the user's geographic location within the company. Network Adminstrators often use this property to store the user's building, floor, and office number.
Locked by Intruder	This property is set by the system. Values can be either Yes or No. If set to Yes, this indicates that someone has tried to log in using this user's Common Name, using an invalid password. If the User account has been locked by an intruder, the user will not be able to log in until the *Intruder Lockout Reset Interval* (a property of an Organization or Organizational Unit) has passed. The system Administrator can intervene and manually unlock the account by changing this value to No.
Login Allowed Time Map	This property has a "map" of the times in which this user is allowed access to the network. The time map covers a one-week period: Sunday to Saturday, 24 hours per day. Login times are specified in blocks of a half hour.
Login Diabled	Values for this property can be either Yes or No. You would set this to Yes when the user goes on vacation or will be out of the office for an extended period of time. When the login is disabled, no one will be able to log in using this user's name.
Login Expiration Time	This represents the date and time when this user will no longer be able to log in. You can set up a User with no expiration time if desired by leaving this property blank. This property is useful if you have a temporary worker who will be working on a company project for a limited amount of time. This can also be used if the user will be retiring at a certain time.
Login Grace Limit	The *Login Grace Limit* property indicates the number of times a user can log in after their password has expired. When the password expires, the user is presented with a message at the login prompt. The system will ask them to enter a new password. If you allow them a grace period, they will have that number of times to refuse to enter a

continues

Table 6.3, Continued
NDS User Properties

Property	Description
	new password. When the grace period is over, the system will indicate to the user that this is their last chance to change their password. If the user continues to refuse to change the password (which often happens!), the system will no longer enable him to log in (at which time your phone rings). This is the same as the *Grace Logins Allowed* property described previously.
Login Grace Remaining	The number of grace login attempts the user has until she is forced to change her password. This and the Login Grace Limit property are effective only if a password is required.
Login Intruder Address	This property is updated by the system if someone attempts to log in under a valid login name using an invalid password. At that time, it will contain the network address (address of a network segment) and physical workstation address (node address) where the invalid attempt occurred.
Login Intruder Attempts	If an illegal login attempt has occurred, this property tracks the number of such attempts.
Login Maximum Simultaneous	This property indicates the number of times a user can log in across the network using the same login name. This is a useful property for enforcing good network security. If you set this property to a value of 1, a user will need to log out of one workstation before being able to log in at another. You can set the value to unlimited, in which case a user can log in from many different workstations at the same time.
Login Script	The *login script* contains a set of instructions, much like a UNIX profile or a DOS batch file, that are executed when the user logs in. Login scripts are covered in greater detail in Chapter 34, "Creating Login Scripts."

Property	Description
Mailbox ID	An identification number used to connect the user with an e-mail server. This is used for networks that have e-mail installed, or use an e-mail related application.
Mailing Label Information	This property is used to indicate to which address packages and letters should be sent. This is also referred to as the *Physical Delivery Office Name* property.
Maximum Connections	This property indicates the number of times a user can log in across the network using the same login name. This is a useful property for enforcing good network security. If you set this property to a value of 1, a user will need to log out of one workstation before being able to log in at another. You can set the value to unlimited, in which case, a user can log in from many different workstations at the same time. Same as *Login Maximum Simultaneous* property described previously.
Minimum Account Balance	Controls the minimum amount of "credit" a user needs before their account is disabled. This property is associated with the account balance property described earlier.
Network Address	This property is automatically updated by the system when the user logs in. It contains the IPX network address and node address of the user's workstation.
Network Address Restrictions	In certain cases, you might want to impose a restriction on where the user can log in. You might have segments of the network that you want to restrict. You also might want to limit this user to a specific workstation. This property enables you to restrict the user to any or all of the following: ◆ Specific workstation ◆ A specific IPX network address (limits them to a network segment) ◆ Specific protocol (log in only using TCP/IP)
Password Allow Change	Values for this property can be either Yes or No. If you set this property to No, the user will not be able to change her password.

continues

Table 6.3, Continued
NDS User Properties

Property	Description
Password Expiration Interval	The password properties are effective only if the Password Required property is set to Yes. The password expiration interval property indicates the number of days between password changes. Same as *Days Between Forced Changes* property described previously.
Password Expiration Time	This property indicates at what date and time the current password will expire. Same as *Date Password Expires* property.
Password Minimum Length	Indicates the minimum amount of characters in this user's password. Novell recommends a minimum length of five for best security.
Password Required	Values for this property can be either Yes or No. If you set this property to No, the user does not have to have a password but can create one if they so desire. If set to Yes, the other password properties become effective.
Password Unique Required	This property specifies that the user's new password must be different from their old password. Values for this property can be either Yes or No.
Passwords Used	Contains a list of passwords the user has used in the past. If the Password Unique Required property is set to Yes, a user's new password is compared to this list. If the new password has already been used, the user will be asked to enter a unique password.
Physical Delivery Office Name	This property is used to indicate to which address packages and letters should be sent. This is also referred to as the *Mailing Label Information* property.
Postal Address	The street address of this user.
Postal Code	The ZIP code of this user (or other type of postal code).
Postal Office Box	This property can be used to store a PO Box for this user.

Property	Description
Print Job Configuration	The *print job configuration* property contains a series of print job templates that the user can use when printing. The job templates control printing parameters, such as the name of the print queue, the type of printer, the number of copies, and other printing parameters. Settings for this property are covered in great detail in Chapter 28, "Printing from DOS Clients."
Security Equals	The *Security Equals* property contains a list of objects to which this user has the same security rights. It also contains a list of groups the user is a member of. When a user belongs to a group, the user acquires the same security access as the group.
See Also	This property is used if you want to associate this User object with some other object.
Street Address	This is the user's actual address.
Surname	This property, which indicates the user's last name, is *mandatory*. This property and the Common Name (CN) property are used to form a unique key needed by the NDS to look up values for this user.
Telephone Number	This property indicates the user's phone number.
Title	This property indicates the user's title.

Organization and Organizational Unit objects have the following properties in common with User objects:

- Description
- Foreign E-Mail Address
- Fax Number
- Location
- Login Script
- Mailbox ID
- Mailing Label Information

- See Also
- Street Address
- Postal Code
- Postal Office Box
- State or Province
- Telephone Number

These properties were described for users in table 6.3. They serve the same purpose for organizations and organizational units except that they apply to the entire container rather than to an individual user. Table 6.4 describes other properties that are common to both organizations and organizational units.

Table 6.4
NDS Organization and Organizational Unit Properties

Property	Description
Detect Intruder	This property can have Yes or No values. If set to Yes, the operating system will keep track of all attempts to log in as a valid user with an invalid password. Someone who makes this attempt is called an *intruder*. The next four properties depend on the setting of this property. If this property is set to No, the following four properties are not accessible.
Foreign E-Mail Alias	This property can be used if you wish to set up an e-mail system where you can send to this alias to send to all users in this container.
Incorrect Login Count	This property sets the number of times someone can log in with a valid user name and an invalid password within the Intruder Attempt Reset Interval. A typical value is 6. In many cases, users mistype their own passwords, especially if it is a new password. A setting of 6 gives most users a fair chance to enter the password correctly.
Intruder Attempt Reset Interval	This property controls the amount of time from the first intruder detection before NetWare resets the intruder detection count back to zero. If you set the login intruder limit to 6 and the intruder attempt reset interval to 5 days, the system will enable an intruder to attempt to get into

Property	Description
	the system illegally a total of 6 times in 5 days. After 5 days, the count goes back to zero, and the intruder can try again. You will need to set this interval to a low value if the users on your network have difficulty typing the correct passwords.
Intruder Lockout Reset Interval	If you have set the Lock Account After Detection property to Yes, this property controls the amount of time the user account remains locked.
Lock Account After Detection	This property can have Yes or No values. If Yes, NetWare will lock a user account after the Login Intruder Limit has been reached. An account that has been locked by the system will remain locked until the Intruder Lockout Reset Interval has passed.
Login Script	This property is identical to the login script property of a user. In this case, the login script applies to any User who belongs to this container. This login script replaces the System Login Script used in NetWare 2.*x* and 3.*x*.
Print Job Configuration	As with users, organizations and organizational units can have print job configurations as well. These configurations supplement individual user configurations. If a user has no configurations of his own, he can use the configurations from the container he belongs to.

Table 6.5 summarizes and gives you characteristics of miscellaneous types of NDS properties that are available.

Table 6.5
Miscellaneous NDS Properties

Property	Objects	Description
ACL	All	The *Access Control List* of other objects and their security access rights to this object.
Back Link	All objects	Used internally by the system. It contains a list of servers that contain

continues

TABLE 6.5, CONTINUED
Miscellaneous NDS Properties

Property	Objects	Description
		a reference to this object. (See "Replicas and Partitions" later in this chapter.)
C	Country	Represents the name of a Country. This is included to maintain conformity with the X.500 naming rules. Its use is supported but not recommended.
Cartridge	Printer	This informational property can be used to store information about the type of cartridge used by this printer.
CN	All leaf objects	This is the Common Name of the object. This property is used as an identifier in a full NDS name.
Host Server	Bindery Queue, Volume	Contains the name of the file server that "hosts" this object. The value for this property is established automatically by NetWare.
L	All objects except Alias, Bindery Object, Country, Unknown	*Locality.* This is a feature included to maintain conformity with the X.500 naming conventions. It represents the physical location of the object. It is not recognized by some NetWare 4.1 utilities.
Login Script	Organization, Organizational Unit, Profile, User	The *Login Script* property can pertain to users, organizations, organizational units, and profiles. A user needs to be specifically assigned to a profile for that user to use the profile login script. The organization and organizational unit login scripts are assigned to any user under that container.

Property	Objects	Description
Member	Group	Contains a list of User objects belonging to the group.
Memory	Printer	This is an informational property that enables you to maintain data on the memory capacity of the printer.
Network Address	AFP Server, Bindery Queue, Computer, NCP Server, Print Server, Printer, Queue, User	Contains the exact location of the object on the network. The value for this property is filled automatically by the system. The network address consists of two parts: the *IPX Network Address,* which is the common address assigned to the network segment, and the *node address,* which is typically programmed into the network interface of the device.
Notify	Printer	A list of objects to be notified in case of printer problems.
O	All objects except Alias, Bindery Object, Country, Organizational Role, Organizational Unit, Unknown, User	Refers to the NDS name of an organization. This is an abbreviation used as an identifier in a full NDS name.
Operator	Bindery Queue, Computer, NCP Server, Printer, Print Server, Queue	The *Operator* property is a list of objects (usually users or containers) that can "operate" this object. If the object is a queue, for example, objects on this list can delete or edit print jobs.
OU	All objects except Alias, Bindery Object, Country, Organization, Unknown	Refers to the NDS name of an organizational unit. This is an abbreviation used as an identifier in a full NDS name.

continues

Table 6.5, Continued
Miscellaneous NDS Properties

Property	Objects	Description
Print Server	Printer	Identifies the print server that handles this printer.
Printer Configuration	Printer	Tracks configuration information about this printer. The information includes the port (parallel, serial), baud rate (for serial printers), and other information.
Private Key	AFP Server, NCP Server, Print Server, User	Used for RSA (Riva, Shamir, and Addleman—data security specialists who license their login authentication technology to Novell) *authentication,* which is the process where the file server determines what type of security clearance a particular process has. The *Private Key* is used solely by the operating system and is not available to user application programs.
Public Key	AFP Server, NCP Server, Print Server, User	The *Public Key* is similar to the private key but is made available to user applications.
Queue	Printer	Print queue. This is an object that represents the subdirectory on the file server used to hold user print jobs. Jobs are stored temporarily in this directory until they can be printed.
Role Occupant	Organizational Role	The *Role Occupant* is usually a User object who has assumed the position within the company. This property contains a list of users who occupy

Property	Objects	Description
		the role associated with the property. An example of this is a company with an organizational role of Sales Manager. Suppose you hire Joe Murphy to be the Sales Manager for the company. You would assign the User object Joe Murphy to be the Role Occupant for the Sales Manager organizational role.
See Also	All objects except Alias, Bindery Object, Unknown	The *See Also* property is used to refer to other objects. There is no transference of security rights nor does the system use this property in any way. It is intended merely as a form of cross-reference for the system Administrator.
Serial Number	AFP Server, Computer, Printer	This property is for your reference only. It is designed to contain the serial number for any of the devices associated with the objects indicated.
Status	AFP Server, Computer NCP Server, Printer, Print Server	The *Status* property contains an updated status of the object it is associated with.
Supported Typefaces	Printer	This informational property is a list of typefaces (also known as *fonts*) supported by this printer. This property is for your reference only.

Choosing Values

Values represent the actual data stored in the properties. Values come in various types, depending on how the properties are defined. Types of values can include the following:

- Yes or No
- Numbers
- Dates
- Time
- Object Names
- Text

The default values for a property can be changed. Default values for new users, for example, are stored in a special type of User object known as USER_TEMPLATE. When you create a new user, the system asks you whether to use the User Template. If you select Yes, the values of the properties for the User Template are substituted for the properties for the new user.

Not all properties have to have values. If the user has no fax machine, for example, you would not fill in the Facsimile Telephone Number property. Other properties are filled in by the system. The Last Login Time property for a new User you just created has no value. When that user logs in for the first time, the system will automatically update this property.

Understanding Context

As you work more and more with NetWare 4.1 networks, an understanding of context is critical. To understand context, you first must recall that an NDS tree is a hierarchy of objects. There are two types of objects: container and leaf. The leaf objects represent network resources. The container objects represent the structure of the tree.

You would use the word *context* when referring to either of the following:

- The position of an object in the tree
- Your particular position within the tree while you are logged in to the network

The last usage of context is sometimes referred to as *current context.*

Context represents either the position of an object or your position in the NDS tree. You can compare context to your position within a DOS directory structure. When referring to the position of a file on a DOS formatted hard drive, you would compose a complex name consisting of the drive letter, directory path, and file name. At the same time, you have a *current directory*, which represents your position in the DOS directory structure. Figure 6.5 illustrates a DOS directory structure.

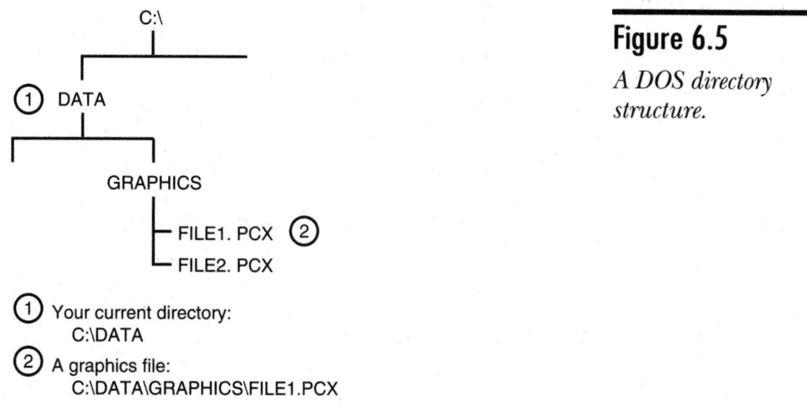

Figure 6.5

A DOS directory structure.

In figure 6.5, your current directory is C:\DATA. A file on the hard drive is C:\DATA\GRAPHICS\FILE1.PCX.

In a similar fashion, you can refer to an object in the tree and your current position using NDS naming (described in the next section). Figure 6.6 illustrates a sample NDS structure. In the example, your current context is the Organizational Unit London. The context of an object in the structure is JMurphy under the Organizational Unit Sales, under the Organizational Unit London, under the Organization IntCo.

You can change your context at any time (even if you are not logged in). The command to change context is CX. For example, assume that the User JMurphy is in the Sales department in London for the IntCo company. To change to the context that contains the user JMurphy, issue the following CX command:

CX .OU=Sales.OU=London.O=IntCo

The CX command is described in more detail in Chapter 14, "DOS Client Basics."

The default context can be set in two different ways:

- For individual workstations in the NET.CFG file
- For everyone on a file server, using the SET BINDERY CONTEXT command

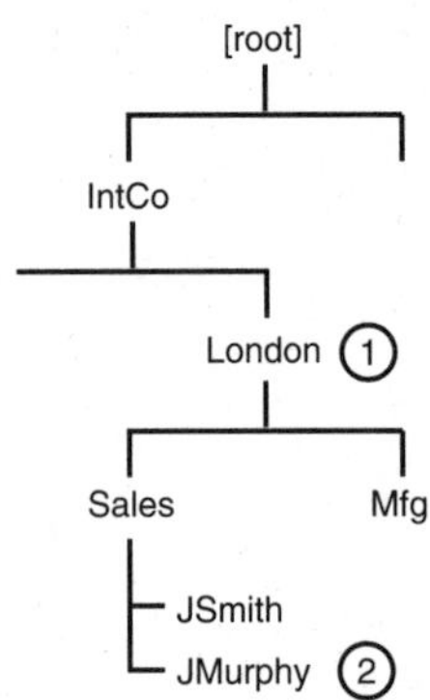

Figure 6.6
A sample NDS structure.

Set the default context for each user at their workstation to make it easier for them to utilize NDS resources. If the resource you want to refer to is in your current context, you do not need to specify a complete NDS name. You can instead refer to the object itself. Setting the context at the file server level not only serves to establish a default context for all users currently working with that file server, but it sets the NDS context where bindery clients can "see" and use network resources. For the purposes of bindery services you can include up to 16 different containers in the file server's bindery context. *Bindery clients* and the related concept of bindery services are described in greater detail in Chapter 22, "Using Bindery Services."

Using NDS Naming

Object names can be up to 64 characters in length. You must refer to objects by name when using NetWare utilities. Examples of such utilities include the following:

LOGIN.EXE	Used to gain initial access to the network (that is, to log in). You must know the NDS user name.
NWUSER.EXE	A Windows-based program that is used to gain access to network resources such as a volume on the file server, or to print to a print queue. You must know the NDS name of the volume or print queue.
CX.EXE	Used to change your context. When you change context, you change your view of the NDS tree to another container.

NWADMIN.EXE	A Windows program used by the network Administrator to manage the NDS tree. It can be used to create users or other NDS objects and to place them in the structure. You must know the NDS names of the various containers in the tree and objects that you want to manage.

Note You can include special characters and spaces in object names as long as you enclose the name in quotation marks ("). In some cases, you need to precede the special character with a backslash (\). In general, using special characters is not recommended. The following characters are used in DOS or for special purposes in NetWare commands and can cause problems when referencing the NDS name:

```
[ ] . = * ? + - %
```

Objects can be referred to in several ways. The possibilities include the following:

- Distinguished Names
- Nondistinguished Names
- Typeful Names
- Typeless Names
- Complete Names
- Partial Names

Combinations of the preceding types of names are possible. Table 6.6 covers these types of names.

Table 6.6
Types of NDS Names

Type of Name	Description
Distinguished Name	An NDS name that includes information about the location of the object in the structure. An example of a distinguished name was given earlier: `.CN=JMurphy.Sales.London.O=IntCo` The preceding name tells you exactly where JMurphy is located in the structure.

continues

Table 6.6, Continued
Types of NDS Names

Type of Name	Description
Nondistinguished Name	A name that refers to the object without information about the object's position in the NDS. Based on the preceding example, a nondistinguished name would be as follows: `JMurphy`
Typeful Name	Contains specifics that give you information about the objects that comprise the name. An example would be as follows: `.CN=HP_Laser.OU=Engr.O=Software.C=UK` This name tells you the following: CN = Common Name (`HP_Laser`—leaf object) OU = Organizational Unit (`Engr`) O = Organization (`Software`) C = Country Object (`UK`)
Typeless Name	Contains no information to indicate what type of objects are part of the name. Here is an example of a typeless name: `.DBierer.SJ.Novell` NetWare makes certain assumptions about typeless names, which are covered next. The only information you have is that DBierer is an object located under SJ, which is located under Novell.

Complete Name	Indicates the entire NDS structure and begins with a period. Here are a typeful complete name:
	`.CN=FS1_SYS.OU=SJ.OU=Sales.O=IntCo`
	Here is a mixed typeful and typeless complete name:
	`.JSmith.Sales.London.C=UK`
	In both cases, the name begins with a period, indicating a complete name. The leading period instructs the NDS to start its search from the root of the tree.

Type of Name	Description

Partial Name	Used to refer to a context based on the current context. NetWare appends the current context to the end of the partial name to construct a complete name. The following examples refer to figure 6.6. Assume the current context is OU=London.O=IntCo. The following command:
	`CX SALES`
	Changes your context to the following subsequent command:
	`.OU=Sales.OU=London.O=IntCo`
	And the following command:
	`LOGIN JSmith`
	Logs you in as the user:
	`.CN=JSmith.OU=Sales.OU=London.O=IntCo`

Typeless Name Assumptions

NetWare makes certain assumptions when building a typeful name out of a typeless name. The assumptions are as follows:

- When referencing a leaf object (for the purpose of logging in, for example), the leftmost object is assumed to be a leaf object and has "CN=" added to it.
- When referencing a container object (for the purpose of changing context, for example), the leftmost object is assumed to be a leaf object and has "OU=" added to it.
- The rightmost object is assumed to be either an organization or country and has "O=" or "C=" added to it.
- Objects in the middle are assumed to be organizational units or organizations and have "OU=" or "O=" added to them.

Thus the following name:

```
.DBierer.SJ.Novell
```

Would become the following:

```
.CN=DBierer.OU=SJ.O=Novell
```

If the name is mixed typeful and typeless, NetWare makes assumptions based on what typeful portions are indicated. If a country object is designated in typeful fashion, objects to its left are assumed to be an organization and organizational units. If an organization is identified, objects to its left are assumed to be organizational units. In other words, objects to the left of the object identified are assumed to be one level lower.

Here are some examples. The following mixed name:

```
.Laser3.Bldg_4.Engineering.C=UK
```

Would become:

```
.CN=Laser3.OU=Bldg_4.O=Engineering.C=UK
```

The following mixed name:

```
.CN=AParus.2ndFloor.O=KidsRMe
```

Would become:

```
.CN=AParus.OU=2ndFloor.O=KidsRMe
```

Period Rules

The use of the period in NDS naming has specific rules. The rules are as follows:

- ◆ Complete names must be preceded by a period.
- ◆ Objects in a name must be separated by a period.
- ◆ Each period added to the end of a name refers to one level higher in the structure.

Given the structure you saw in figure 6.6, the following are some examples of how to move around in the structure using the CX command.

From the following context:

```
.OU=Sales.OU=London.O=IntCo
```

The command:

```
CX OU=Mfg.
```

Would move you to the context:

```
.OU=Mfg.OU=London.O=IntCo
```

The trailing period refers to the next level up (OU=London).

From the context:

```
.OU=Mfg.OU=London.O=IntCo
```

The following command would move you to the root:

```
CX ...
```

Three trailing periods move you up three levels.

Here is the feedback you would expect from the file server from the commands mentioned above:

```
F:\>CX .OU=Sales.OU=London.O=IntCo
Sales.London.IntCo

F:\>CX Mfg.
Mfg.London.IntCo

F:\>CX ...
[root]

F:\>
```

Understanding Replicas and Partitions

As the network grows in size and complexity, there arises a need to safeguard the NDS tree. For performance reasons, you also might find a need to subdivide the tree. At this point, you must explore the concepts of replicas and partitions.

Partitions

A *partition* is an arbitrary subdivision of the tree. You can partition the tree at any container. The container becomes the split point for the partition.

The benefit to partitioning the tree is that searches can be made faster. Searching for an object through a large tree can become time-consuming (relatively speaking). By partitioning the tree, you limit the number of records the operating system has to traverse.

Novell recommends that you consider splitting the tree (or further subdividing a partition) when you approach 800 objects, although reports indicate that even trees with partitions of several thousand objects report no degradation in speed. The disadvantage to having too many partitions stored on a single file server is that the amount of maintenance increases.

When you install the first NetWare 4.*x* server in the network, the NDS tree is created. At this point, the only partition that exists consists of all objects in the tree. Because it is a partition that contains [root], it is called the *root partition.* When you install the first file server in your network, a root partition is created automatically.

The tools used for creating and maintaining partitions (and replicas) are as follows:

- PARTMGR.EXE (DOS-based)
- NWADMIN.EXE (Windows-based)

The use of these tools in creating and managing partitions is discussed in Chapter 19, "NDS Tree Design Considerations."

Replicas

Replicas are copies of partitions that are stored on other file servers. Creation of replicas is an essential part of making your NDS tree secure. In a network with a single file server, this is not a consideration. In a network with two or more file servers, consider creating at least one replica of each partition. Later, as the network grows, you might want to further partition the tree for performance reasons.

When you install a second and third file server in your network, NetWare will create replicas on the new servers automatically. Once the total number of any given replica reaches 3, NetWare will prompt you if you wish to create a replica on any additional file servers you install.

You have two choices when installing a second file server onto the same tree as the first file server. The first choice is to assign the new file server to an existing container. The second choice is to designate a container that does not exist.

Figure 6.7 illustrates the first case. Following is a list of what happens:

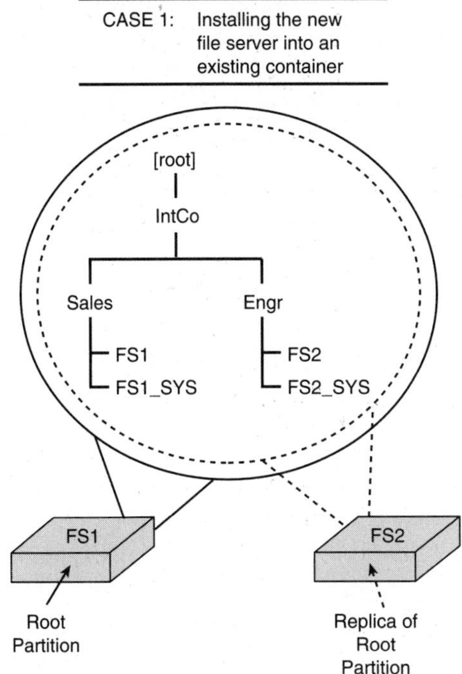

Figure 6.7

Installing a new file server into an existing container.

- File Server FS1 and volume FS1_SYS are located under Sales.
- File Server FS2 is installed and placed in existing container Engr.

  Volume FS2_SYS automatically appears under Engr as well.
- File Server FS1 retains its root partition.
- When FS2 is installed, NetWare checks to see if there are a total of three servers with replicas of this partition.

  If so, a prompt appears asking if you wish to add another replica on the new file server.

  If there are less than 3 replicas, NetWare will automatically add a Read/Write replica on the new server.

Figure 6.8 illustrates the second case. Following is a list of what happens:

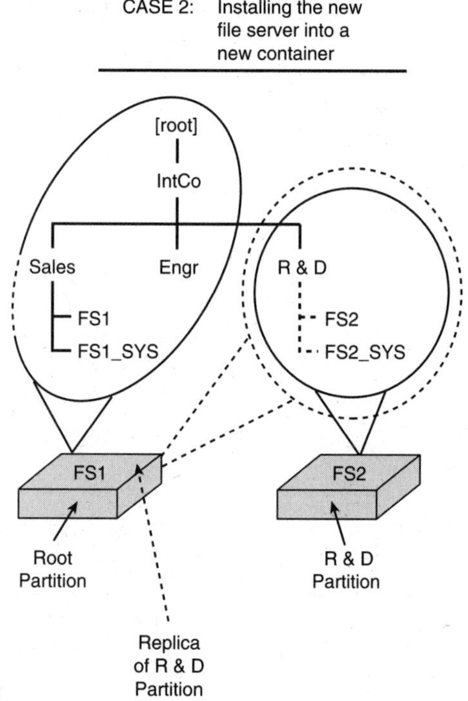

Figure 6.8
Installing a new file server into a new container.

- File Server FS1 and volume FS1_SYS are located under Sales.
- File Server FS2 is installed and placed in a new container R&D.

  Volume FS2_SYS automatically appears under R&D as well.
- File Server FS1 retains its root partition.
- A new partition is created at R&D and is stored on file server FS2.

You will note in case 2 that the root partition has not been replicated. To properly safeguard the tree, you should manually store a replica of the root partition on file server FS2.

There are three types of replicas:

- Master
- Read Write
- Read Only

A *Master* replica is the primary copy of the partition. The Master replica is responsible for keeping track of all updates during partitioning operations. A *Read Write* replica is a backup to the Master replica. It can answer queries and take updates. If a network link goes down or the file server containing the Master replica crashes, the Read Write replica can act as a Master. Replicas can be upgraded from Read Write to Master or downgraded using either of the partition managing utilities. The last type, *Read Only*, is for future enhancements and is not used.

Users in a NetWare 4.1 network need access to NDS information on a constant basis. When a user logs in, for example, the following NDS information is read or written:

- Lookup of the user name
- Password encryption using the Private Key
- Check for time restrictions
- Check for station restrictions
- Update the Last Login Time property

Using NetWare 4.1 in a Complex Network

LANs have a tendency to grow. LAN technology has become very stable over the years. After the first LAN is in place, companies tend to OK the budget for additional LANs. The individual LANs are connected together through bridges and routers. Finally, you have a complex LAN on your hands.

In a complex network, placement of replicas is critical. One of the reasons for creating a replica is for performance. If you have a dedicated line between two sites, a replica should be placed on either side of the line for performance and redundancy. If the line goes down, both replicas can service the needs of the network users on either side. When the line comes back up, the Master and Read Write replicas synchronize with each other, updating information as needed.

When you need access to NDS information, your computer draws its information from the nearest replica. Replicas on either side of the line provide fast response to the NDS needs of the users. If you did not have a replica on both sides of the line, your computer would have to send requests and get responses from across the dedicated line. Performance would suffer greatly.

As shown in figure 6.9, there are two LANs: one in New York and the other in San Jose. The server in NY contains the root partition. When user .CN=EBierer.OU=SJ.O=IntCo in San Jose attempts to log in, the NDS data must travel across the WAN link before she is allowed access to the LAN.

Figure 6.9
WAN without replicas.

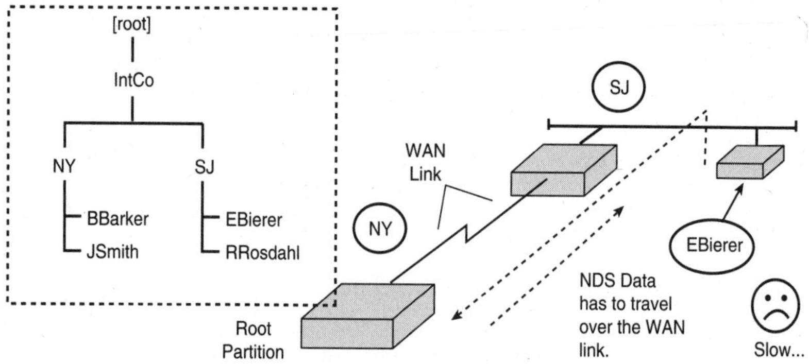

In figure 6.10, a Master replica of .OU=SJ.O=IntCo has been placed on the San Jose server, along with a Read Write replica of the [root]. The server in NY has a Read Write replica of .OU=SJ.O=IntCo, and a Master replica of the [root]. When user .CN=EBierer.OU=SJ.O=IntCo in San Jose attempts to log in, the NDS data has to travel only to the server on the same LAN.

Figure 6.10
Replicas on either side of a WAN link.

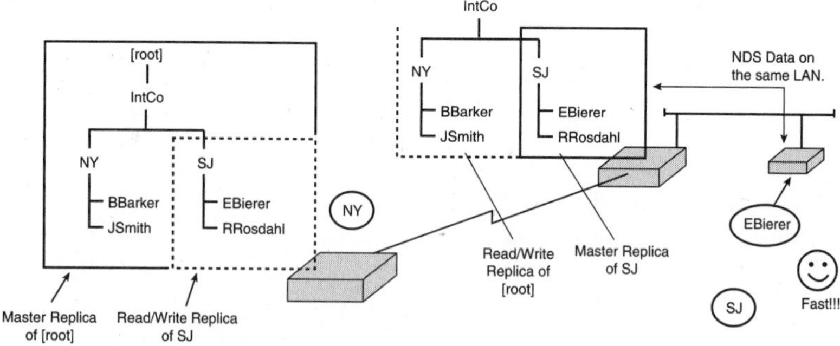

Summary

This chapter started with a discussion of NDS trees. As you discovered, a tree has only one [root]. [root] is a container object referred to as [root] or "the root." There are two types of objects: container and leaf. Container objects are used for structural purposes; leaf objects represent network resources.

You read about how objects have properties, and properties have values. The analogy that was drawn is that an object is like a database record, properties are like fields, and values are the actual data that gets filled into the fields. You were presented with lists of objects and properties. As you discovered, there are many different types of properties. Some objects share common properties. Other objects are quite unique.

You had an experience with NDS naming. You discovered that an NDS name has multiple parts separated with periods. There are several types of NDS names, including typeful, typeless, partial, and complete. You saw that CN designates a leaf object, OU is for an Organizational Unit, O is for an Organization, and C is for Country. You also learned about context and how an understanding of it is critical for proper network management.

The last section dealt with partitions and replicas. You learned that the entire NDS tree is a partition called the "root partition." Trees can be subdivided into smaller groupings known as partitions. Copies, or replicas, can be made of partitions. When you copy a partition, the original partition becomes the Master replica, and the copies are called Read Write replicas. A third type of replica, Read Only, is for future enhancements. You were shown an example of how placing replicas on both sides of a WAN link produces better response.

The next chapter, "NetWare 4.1 Security," shows how security access rights are assigned in NetWare 4.1. This chapter covers rights to both the NDS and the file system.

CHAPTER

NetWare 4.1 Security

This chapter provides an overview of NetWare 4.1 security. The first section gives you an understanding of what rights and trustee rights are. Next, the discussion on security focuses on NDS security and security for the file system. NDS security deals with rights to objects and properties in the NDS tree. File system security deals with Security rights to files and directories located on the volumes of file servers. Another section covers the Inherited Rights Filter (IRF) and its role in blocking the inheritance of Security rights from one level to the next. The last section shows you how to calculate what the effective rights are in various situations.

For detailed information on how to actually implement Security rights using the NetWare 4.1 system administration utilities, see Chapter 30, "Adding File System Rights," Chapter 31, "Adding NDS Trustee Rights," and Chapter 32, "Viewing Trustee Assignments." At this point, the discussion begins with an overview of trustee rights.

Using Trustee Rights

To fully understand what is meant by *trustee rights*, you must first analyze the two words themselves in the context of a network. According to the dictionary, a *trustee* is "a person... appointed to administer the affairs of a company, institution, etc." The definition of *rights* is multifaceted. The closest dictionary definition would be "a just claim or title..."

In NetWare, trustees need rights for several purposes. If a user is permitted to change the contents of a file, for example, he or she must be assigned the Write right for that file. To delete a file, a user must have the Delete right for that file. NetWare 4.1 has a wide variety of rights that enable system Administrators to fine-tune the capabilities of trustees on the network.

In NetWare 4.1, a trustee is an NDS object. Technically, any NDS object could be made a trustee of any other NDS object or of a file or directory in the file system. That is to say, any object can be given specific rights with regard to any other object in the tree. Practically speaking, this would not be appropriate. Trustees are usually one of the following objects:

- Any container object
- User
- Group

It would not make sense, for example, to make a printer object a trustee of the container .OU=Sales.OU=London.O=IntCo. The rights of inanimate objects such as printers are taken care of by the operating system. Making a user, or any object where a user is involved (such as a group or organizational role) will benefits from a trustee rights assignment.

Trustee rights are said to be *granted* for a certain object to another object. You could, for example, grant Read rights for the directory FS1_SYS:PUBLIC (file server FS1, volume SYS:, directory PUBLIC) to a user .CN=JMurphy.OU=Dublin.O=IntCo. For this reason, a trustee right that has been granted is sometimes called a *trustee assignment.* Other phrases used to indicate the same idea include *security assignment, rights assignment,* and *access rights.*

Trustee rights form a link between the trustee object and the target of the assignment. In the preceding example, a link is formed between FS1_SYS:PUBLIC and the user .CN=JMurphy.OU=Dublin.O=IntCo. Prior to the assignment, this user had no way to access this particular directory. When making a trustee assignment, there are always two components:

- The object of the assignment
- The user, group, or container object to be made the trustee

Understanding Inheritance

Trustee assignments at one level in the NDS tree are *inherited* at lower levels. Other phrases that you might see regarding trustee rights are that they "trickle down" or "flow down" the structure.

One analogy is to that of an irrigation system. If you punch a hole in a drip irrigation tube above the plant, the water flows down and provides the plant with water. The water cannot flow uphill (except in the famous "Mystery Spot," of course). Likewise, when assigning rights at one level of the NDS tree, or at one subdirectory in the file system, the rights apply to that level and all levels below that point.

Figure 7.1 illustrates the concept of inheritance. In this example, the user JWalker is assigned Browse rights to the container London (.OU=London.OU=R&D.O=IntCo). JWalker's authority inherits down the structure and applies to the following objects:

- .CN=FS1.OU=London.OU=R&D.O=IntCo
- .CN=Printer1.OU=London.OU=R&D.O=IntCo
- .OU=East_End.OU=London.OU=R&D.O=IntCo
- .CN=Printer3.OU=East_End.OU=London.OU=R&D.O=IntCo
- .CN=KJones.OU=East_End.OU=London.OU=R&D.O=IntCo
- .OU=West_End.OU=London.OU=R&D.O=IntCo
- .CN=Ptr4.OU=West_End.OU=London.OU=R&D.O=IntCo
- .CN=JMazlo.OU=West_End.OU=London.OU=R&D.O=IntCo

This assignment does not apply laterally, nor does it go "up" in the structure. Thus, IntCo, Sales, R&D, and Rochester are beyond the extent of this trustee assignment.

The inheritance mechanization is very effective when working with container objects. When you assign rights to a container, the rights assignment applies to all objects in the container. Not only that, but if there are any child containers in the parent container, all objects within the child container inherit the rights of the parent as well. If you were to give a trustee assignment to the [root] container, it would effectively apply to all objects in the tree.

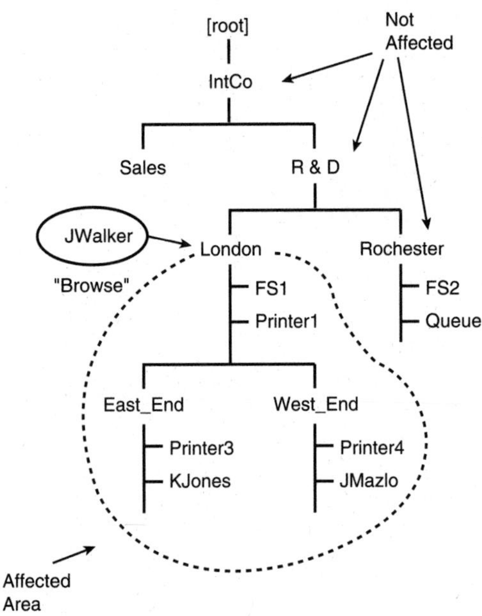

Figure 7.1

Inheritance of a trustee assignment.

Figure 7.2 illustrates the effect of granting a trustee assignment to a container object. In this example, the container .OU=MIS.O=IntCo is granted a trustee assignment of Create to the container .OU=R&D.O=IntCo. The trustee assignment trickles down to affect .OU=London.OU=R&D.O=IntCo and .OU=Rochester.OU=R&D.O=IntCo. Any objects in the .OU=MIS.O=IntCo container acquire the Create trustee assignment by virtue of belonging to the container. Thus, JMurphy, DBeaver, and MBierer all acquire the Create trustee assignment over the container .OU=R&D.O=IntCo.

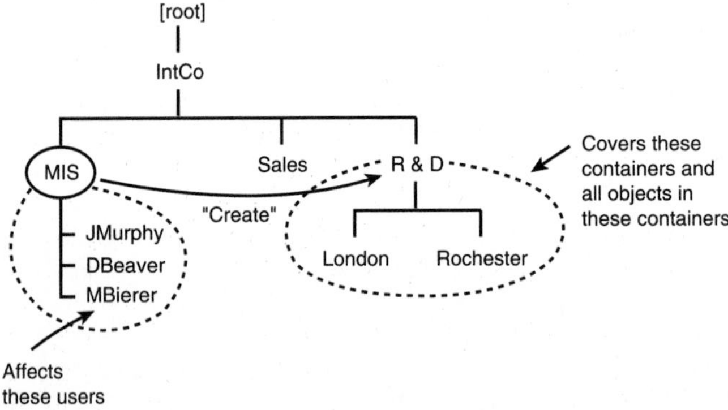

Figure 7.2

Granting a trustee assignment to a container object.

The inheritance mechanism enables you to simplify the number of trustee assignments you need to make to build an effective security system. Instead of having to make an assignment at every level of the structure, you just need to make a higher level assignment that inherits down to lower levels. Later in this chapter, ways to prevent this "trickle down" effect from occurring by using an Inherited Rights Filter (IRF) are discussed.

A trustee assignment at a lower level supersedes a higher level trustee assignment. If you assign a user Read and Write rights in a subdirectory, you could assign them Read, Write, Create, and Erase at a lower level. The rights assigned at the lower level could be greater or lesser than the rights assigned at higher levels. The lower level assignment negates the higher level assignment.

Figure 7.3 illustrates this principle in the file system. In this example, the user TRosa is granted Read and Write trustee rights to the file system, starting with the subdirectory DATA. These rights inherit to all directories underneath the DATA directory. Another assignment of Read is made for the user TRosa to the directory JONES. Starting with the JONES directory and including the two subdirectories below, the new assignment supersedes the higher level assignment. TRosa therefore has only Read in the JONES directory and the JONES\A and JONES\B subdirectories.

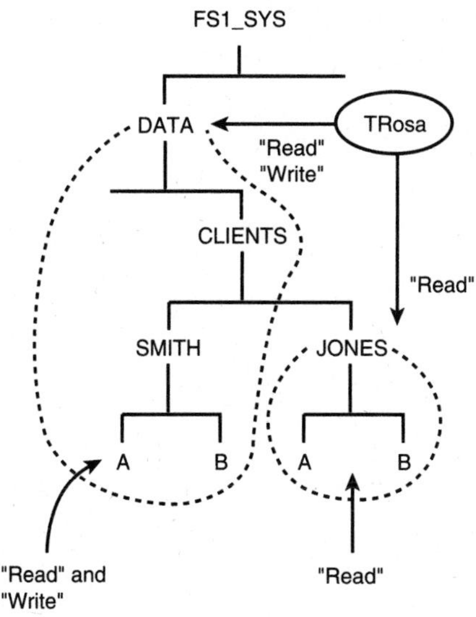

Figure 7.3
Lower level assignment supersedes a higher level assignment.

Examining File System Rights

Before proceeding to explain the security available for files and directories, the file system must be explained first. *File system* is a term used to indicate the logical and physical apparatus needed to store files on the file server. The file system encompasses many of the concepts covered in Chapter 4, "Traditional Features of NetWare." These include the following:

- A file server
- The hard drives attached to a file server
- Volumes
- Directory structure

When you assign file system rights, you can view the directory structure up to the directory where you assigned rights. Before you assign rights, the directory structure is invisible. After assigning even as little as File Scan rights to a file in a directory, the entire directory path up to the directory containing the file becomes visible. The structure from where you assign rights, and on down, is also visible unless blocked by a lower level assignment of *no rights* or by an IRF.

When you want to deny an object all rights in a directory, you can do either of the following:

- Block the rights with an IRF
- Assign the object an assignment of no rights

As the term implies, the latter possibility means simply granting the object a trustee assignment with no rights specified. This has the effect of blocking all rights for that object from that point down. The other choice—using an IRF—might be less attractive because the IRF affects all objects, in addition to the specific object you want to block.

An application program gains the rights of the user running the program. Thus, if user DSanto has Read and File Scan rights to a directory, any programs this user runs from that directory will also have Read and File Scan rights. If the program needs to create a temporary file, it will not be able to do so. For this reason, network Administrators set up a personal directory for each user (called a *home directory*), where the user has all rights. If users start the program and their current directory is their home directory, the program behaves properly.

The Relationship Between the File System and the NDS Tree

The file system is subordinate to the NDS tree. The file system ties into the tree in the volume object. In the network administration tool NWADMIN, for example, you can see the directory structure and files by double-clicking on the volume object icon.

NDS trustee rights do not flow down into the file system. If you give a user NDS rights to a container object that contains the volume object, these rights do not apply to the file system inside the volume. To give a user rights to a directory, you must make a separate file system trustee assignment.

There are certain exceptions to this rule, as follows:

- If you give a user Supervisor NDS rights to the file server object that contains the file system, the user becomes a *Supervisor* of the file server. The Supervisor of a file server by default gains all Security rights to any volumes, directories, or files on that file server.

- If you give a user Write NDS rights to the *Access Control List* (ACL) property of a volume object, this user gains Supervisor file system rights to the root of that volume.

It is important to note that to access the file system as an NDS user, the user must have at least the minimum NDS rights to the volume object—Browse. If a user is barred from access to the volume object in the NDS, this user cannot access the file system on that volume. Conversely, if a user has a limited set of NDS rights to the volume object, this user must also be granted file system rights to read or write files on that volume.

The exceptions to needing NDS rights to a volume object are the two listed earlier and whether the user chooses to access a file system through bindery services. If the latter is the case, the user needs only file system trustee rights or knowledge of the file server's Supervisor password. Bindery services is covered in detail in the next chapter.

Directory Trustee Rights

Directory trustee rights are granted to an object for a directory. The objects usually granted rights, as noted earlier, are users, groups, and containers.

Certain objects gain rights by default. These default directory trustee rights assignments are as follows:

- The container in which a newly installed file server is located gets Read and File Scan directory trustee rights to the PUBLIC directory on volume SYS:.
- The user name specified on the NDS installation screen when the file server is first installed becomes the Supervisor for the file server. The Supervisor gains all rights to all volumes, directories, and files on that file server.

Directory trustee rights apply to all files in the directory where the rights are granted. In addition, as mentioned earlier, these rights inherit down the directory structure and apply to all subdirectories and all files in those subdirectories.

The inheritance of rights may be blocked by either of the following:

- An Inherited Rights Filter (IRF)
- A lower level directory trustee assignment

File trustee assignments do not block a directory trustee assignment. Rather, file trustee assignments serve to augment a directory trustee assignment. If you grant a user Read directory trustee rights to directory ABC, for example, and Write file trustee rights to file XYZ, the user receives Read and Write rights to file XYZ in directory ABC.

Table 7.1 summarizes the directory trustee rights available. The rights are listed in order of importance. The first letter is boldfaced to emphasize that this is the abbreviation used to represent the right in the menu utilities.

Table 7.1
Directory Trustee Rights

Trustee Right	Description
Supervisor	The *Supervisor* right gives the object all rights at this point in the directory structure. Unlike the other rights, this particular right cannot be blocked at lower levels, which means that a lower level assignment or an IRF does not block the effect of this right. This right should be assigned to managers or "power users" who need full rights at a certain point in the directory structure. It could also be assigned to container objects to give rights to all users in that container.
Access Control	*Access Control* gives the object the capability to assign rights (except Supervisor) to any other object at this level or below. This right, as with the following rights, can be

Trustee Right	Description
	blocked by a lower level assignment or IRF. Access Control by itself does not give you additional rights; this is the right to assign rights. Knowledgable users with Access Control, for example, can assign themselves any of the rights below, but not the Supervisor right mentioned above. The Access Control right typically is assigned in a case where you need to delegate the ability to assign rights to a lower level manager, such as the lead word processor. Because this right can be blocked, you don't end up "giving away the ballgame."
Modify	The *Modify* right gives an object the capability to modify file or directory attributes. Attributes are explained later in this chapter. Attributes include, for example, Hidden and Read-Only. Users with this trustee right can change a read-only file to read-write, make changes, and then change its attributes back again. You often will need to assign this right to users running applications that need to assign or change attributes. Many applications, for example, rename files as they operate. If users do not have this right, the program will fail to operate properly. Another example is when you run a backup program. The backup program will change the "archive needed" attribute of a file that has been backed up from On to Off. This is how many backup programs determine which files need to be backed up.
Erase	This right gives users the ability to erase files. As with the Modify right, the Erase right may be needed to properly run certain application programs. Some programs create and delete temporary files as they operate.
Write	The *Write* right gives users the ability to make changes to existing files in a directory. This right is often assigned in conjunction with the Erase right. Users with Write can erase the entire contents of a file, for example, but not the name of the file itself. In so doing, the user would create an empty file. The Erase right would then be needed to erase the file name itself from the directory. Be careful not to confuse Modify with Write. Modify lets you modify file or directory attributes. Write lets you modify the contents of a file.

continues

Table 7.1, Continued
Directory Trustee Rights

Trustee Right	Description
Create	The *Create* trustee right gives users the ability to create new files or directories in this directory. This right is often needed when running an application that creates temporary files. WordPerfect, for example, creates temporary files when you first get into the program. If you do not have Create, you will not be able to run the program.
Read	The *Read* right gives you the ability to read the contents of a file. You can read the contents of a file even if it is hidden or you don't have File Scan rights, as long as you know the name of the file.
File Scan	The *File Scan* right gives you the ability to see the file name and attributes listed in the directory. You would need File Scan, for example, to use the Windows File Manager in any given directory. Note that even though you can see the name of the file, you cannot view its contents unless you also have Read rights. The File Scan right also gives you the ability to see a subdirectory. In addition, if a file or directory is hidden using the DOS *hidden* file attribute, the File Scan right allows you to view the file or directory using the NetWare NDIR utility.

File Trustee Rights

File trustee rights are similar to directory trustee rights. The difference is in inheritance. File trustee rights do not inherit to any further levels. If you grant a user ELobo Read and Write rights to the file XYZ.TXT, those rights do not carry down to another level, nor do those rights automatically apply to other files in the directory.

File trustee rights add to the rights already available as a directory trustee. For example, you might have Read and File Scan directory trustee rights, and Read and Write file trustee rights for the file ABC.TXT. You will have a total of Read, Write, and File Scan rights for the file ABC.TXT.

File trustee rights do not detract from directory trustee rights. You might have, for example, Read, Write, Create, Erase, and File Scan directory trustee rights, and Read

and File Scan file trustee rights to the file FILE1.DOC. Your rights to FILE1.DOC will be Read, Write, Create, Erase, and File Scan.

File trustee rights are used in situations where you need to assign additional rights to specific files in a directory, but have a more limited set of rights to other files in a directory. In this fashion you could control access to certain files. For example, MSchmidt is an accounts payable (AP) clerk, and WJurgens is an accounts receivable (AR) clerk. You could give the container that contains these users Read and File Scan directory trustee rights. You could then assign MSchmidt Write and Modify rights to the AP files, and WJurgens similar rights to the AR files. Figure 7.4 illustrates this situation.

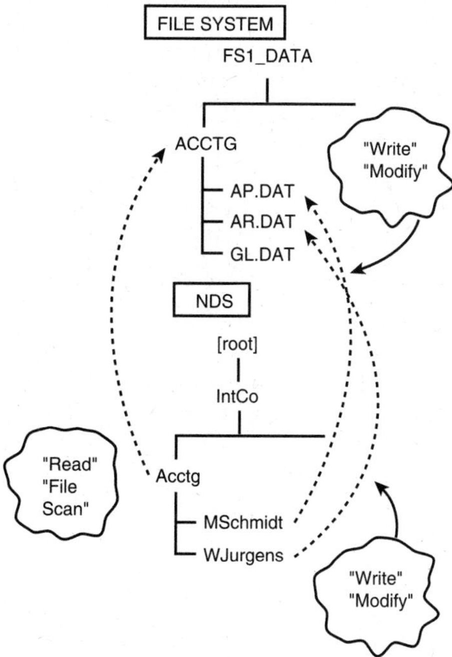

Figure 7.4

File trustee rights assignment example.

Table 7.2 summarizes the file trustee rights that are available. The rights are listed in order of importance. The first letter is boldfaced to emphasize that this is the abbreviation used to represent the right in the menu utilities.

Table 7.2
File Trustee Rights

Trustee Right	Description
Supervisor	The *Supervisor* right gives the object all rights to this file. This right is a quick way to assign all rights to a file.
Access Control	*Access Control* gives the object the capability to assign rights (except Supervisor) to this file. This is the right to assign rights. Knowledgeable users with Access Control, for example, can assign themselves any of the rights below, but not the Supervisor right.
Modify	The *Modify* right gives an object the capability to modify file attributes. Attributes include, for example, Hidden and Read-Only. Users with this trustee right can change the file from read-only to read-write. Often you will need to assign this right to users running applications that need to assign or change the attributes of this file. Many applications, for example, rename files as they operate. If users do not have this right, the program will fail to operate properly.
Erase	This right gives users the ability to erase the file.
Write	The *Write* right gives users the ability to make changes to the file. Be careful not to confuse Modify with Write. Modify lets you modify the attributes of the file. Write lets you modify the contents of the file.
Create	The *Create* trustee right gives an object the capability to salvage the file, should it be deleted. The SALVAGE utility will be covered in more detail in Chapter 26, "Monitoring the File System."
Read	The *Read* right gives you the ability to read the contents of the file. You can read the contents of a file even if it is hidden or you don't have File Scan rights, as long as you know the name of the file.
File Scan	The *File Scan* right gives you the ability to see the file name and attributes listed in the file. You would need File Scan, for example, to use the Windows File Manager with any given file. Note that even though you can see the name of the file, you cannot view its contents unless you also have Read rights.

File trustee assignments can be used extensively by certain file server-based applications. Examples of these applications are e-mail packages and packages such as NetWare NFS, which is a server-based application that enables UNIX users to access files and directories on a NetWare file server. UNIX security works in a different fashion from that of NetWare. In UNIX, the permissions associated with a directory are different from the permissions associated with files. In UNIX, when you want to prevent users from changing the contents of any files in a directory, you must apply a permissions mask to every file in the directory rather than to the directory itself. To mimic this behavior on files located on the file server, NetWare NFS creates a separate file trustee assignment for every file on the file server that is created or altered through UNIX.

File and Directory Attributes

Files and directories in NetWare have an additional security-related feature known as file and directory *attributes*, which are sometimes known as *flags*. Attributes are stored along with the file and directory names in a table known as the *Directory Entry Table* (DET). Attributes are the lowest level of access control for a file or directory. Attributes affect all users, including those with Supervisor rights.

Attributes can be assigned in several ways:

- The DOS ATTRIB.EXE command
- The Windows File Manager program
- The NetWare FLAG.EXE command
- The NetWare FILER.EXE utility

The use of these utilities is explained in Chapter 30, "Adding File System Rights."

NetWare extends the attributes present in DOS. DOS, for example, supports the Read-Only, Read-Write, Archive Needed, Hidden, and System attributes. NetWare adds additional attributes that correspond to network services that are offered. In addition, NetWare enables you to use certain attributes on directories as well.

Attributes are not a substitute for trustee rights. You must have the proper trustee rights before performing any operations on a file or directory. If a file attribute is *read-write*, for example, you cannot write to the file unless you have Write trustee rights.

Table 7.3 summarizes the NetWare 4.1 attributes that are available. Note that the second column ("Abbr.") contains the abbreviation used when setting the attribute. The third and fourth columns indicate whether this attribute applies to a file or to a directory. A "Y" indicates yes; an "N" indicates no. In some cases, the attribute will apply to both. Some attributes are set automatically by the system. Others are status attributes, for your information only, and cannot be changed. The footnote at the bottom of the table indicates how these attributes are designated.

Table 7.3
NetWare 4.1 Attributes

Attribute	Abbr.	Applies to File	Applies to Directory	Description
Archive Needed*	A	Y	N	The *archive needed* attribute is set by the system when a file has been changed. When you perform a backup of modified files, or a full system backup, the backup software will change this bit.
Can't Compress**	Cc	Y	N	This attribute is set by the system when the file cannot be compressed according to specifications you set at the file server's console. (For more information on the SET parameters, see Chapter 41.)
Compressed*	Co	Y	N	Indicates that the file has been successfully compressed by the operating system.
Copy Inhibit	Ci	Y	N	You can apply this attribute to a file to prevent Macintosh users from copying it. This was designed because certain DOS executable files executed on a Macintosh cause harm to the system.
Delete Inhibit	Di	Y	Y	Prevents users from deleting a file. If applied to a directory,

Attribute	Abbr.	Applies to File	Applies to Directory	Description
				the directory cannot be removed.
Don't Compress	Dc	Y	Y	Used to prevent the operating system from compressing a file. This is good in situations where you have critical files (such as accounting database files) that are accessed occasionally but must not be compressed. If applied to a directory, any files in this directory will not be compressed.
Don't Migrate	Dm	Y	Y	This attribute informs the operating system not to migrate the file to the designated online media. If applied to a directory, it protects any file in the directory from being migrated.
Execute Only	X	Y	N	Prevents a file from being copied by any user (Macintosh or other). Once applied, the only way to remove this attribute is to delete the file and reinstall it from another media (floppy disk). It is designed to prevent people from pirating programs off the network.
Hidden	H	Y	Y	Hides a file or directory from DOS commands such as DIR or DEL. NetWare commands enable users to see these files or directories, provided the user has File Scan rights.

continues

Table 7.3, Continued
NetWare 4.1 Attributes

Attribute	Abbr.	Applies to File	Applies to Directory	Description
Immediate Compress	Ic	Y	Y	Informs the operating system not to wait for the normal waiting period to compress the file. The file is then compressed when the operating system is not busy. If assigned to a directory, this attribute applies to all files in the directory.
Indexed**	I	Y	N	The operating system sets this attribute to indicate that this is a large file that occupies more than 64 entries in the File Allocation Table (FAT). If this is the case, the operating system creates an access table in RAM to expedite access to this file.
Migrated*	M	Y	N	This attribute indicates that the file has been moved to an online media (such as a read-write optical disk). The file still appears in a directory listing. Access to such a file will be slower because the system must go first to the online media to restore the file.
Normal	N	Y	Y	The *normal* attribute is a fast way to restore the default attributes. The default attribute for a file is read-write. All other attributes will be taken off.
Purge	P	Y	Y	The *purge* attribute is used to immediately purge the file

Attribute	Abbr.	Applies to File	Applies to Directory	Description
				after deletion. Otherwise, the file is available for salvage after deletion. This is useful for sensitive files. If applied to a directory, this attribute applies to all files in the directory.
Read-Only	Ro	Y	N	Can be used to prevent any changes being made to a file. The rename inhibit and delete inhibit attributes are also set. A read-only file cannot be deleted even if you have Supervisor trustee rights.
Read-Write	Rw	Y	N	This attribute is the opposite of read-only. A read-write file can be modified or deleted (assuming you have the necessary trustee rights).
Rename Inhibit	Ri	Y	Y	Prevents you from changing the name of a file. If applied to a directory, this directory cannot be renamed.
Shareable	S	Y	N	The *shareable* attribute causes the operating system to maintain data on who is accessing the file and whether the user has a file or record lock. The operating system does not maintain file or record locks—this responsibility falls on the application program. Shareable is used by the application program to keep track of the file. Some application programs have their own version of the shareable attribute.

continues

Table 7.3, Continued
NetWare 4.1 Attributes

Attribute	Abbr.	Applies to File	Applies to Directory	Description
System	Sy	Y	Y	The *system* attribute is identical in function to hidden. It is used by some software packages to track which files are program files.
Transactional	T	Y	N	This attribute, once put into place, causes NetWare to perform Transaction Tracking on this file. A *transactional* file can be recovered in case of a power failure or operating system crash. NetWare will perform a rollback to restore the file to its last known good condition.

*Indicates that the attribute is set by the system.

**Indicates that the attribute is set by the system and cannot be changed by you.

Examining NDS Security

NDS Security rights are similar to file system rights in the following respects:

- NDS rights inherit down the tree
- They are usually assigned to user, group, or container objects
- Container object rights, like directory rights, inherit down the structure
- Leaf object rights, like file rights, do not inherit further down the structure
- They can be blocked by a lower level assignment or an IRF

You should pay close attention to the last point. The ability to block the inheritance of rights includes the ability to block the Supervisor right. This ability is not true in the file system, as you read earlier. In the NDS structure, if the Supervisor right has been blocked, either through a lower level assignment or by an IRF, the user granted the rights loses her Supervisor authority.

NDS rights fall into two categories: object rights and property rights. The next sections discuss these two types of rights.

Object Rights

NDS object rights are granted to an object for another object. Object rights enable users, for example, to access network resources in NDS containers. Objects inherit the rights of their parent containers. Thus, if user JCallahan belongs to the container .OU=Marketing.OU=Education.O=IntCo, he acquires all the rights of the Marketing, Education, and IntCo containers.

Assigning Object Rights

When assigning rights to containers, you need to determine the minimum set of rights. The *minimum set of rights* is a collection of the lowest set of rights common to the users and other objects under the container. In figure 7.5, for example, you see an organizational unit MIS. Under it are users DNowell and CTrahan. Assume that DNowell is a technical manager in charge of all Domestic file servers, and CTrahan is in charge of International file servers. You want CTrahan or DNowell to be able to gather information on other file servers or install a new one in case one or the other is unavailable. One possible approach is as follows:

- Assign OU=MIS Browse and Create object rights at the level of OU=Sales
- Assign DNowell Supervisor object rights at the level of OU=Domestic
- Assign CTrahan Supervisor object rights at the level of OU=Intl

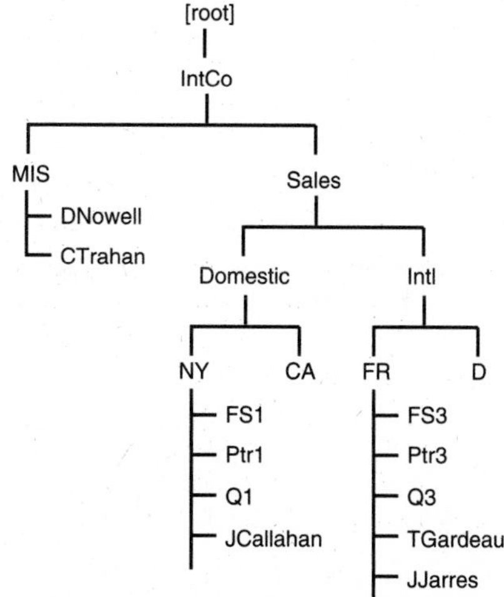

Figure 7.5
A sample NDS tree.

In this fashion, anyone in the MIS organizational unit could see objects and create new objects anywhere from OU=Sales down. DNowell has full rights from the level of OU=Domestic down. CTrahan has full rights from the level of OU=Intl. As illustrated in figure 7.6, following are the rights that each object would end up with:

	OU=MIS	CN=DNowell	CN=CTrahan
OU=Sales	BC	BC	BC
OU=Domestic	BC	SBC	BC
OU=NY.OU=Domestic	BC	SBC	BC
OU=CA.OU=Domestic	BC	SBC	BC
OU=Intl	BC	BC	SBC
OU=FR.OU=Intl	BC	BC	SBC
OU=D.OU=Intl	BC	BC	SBC

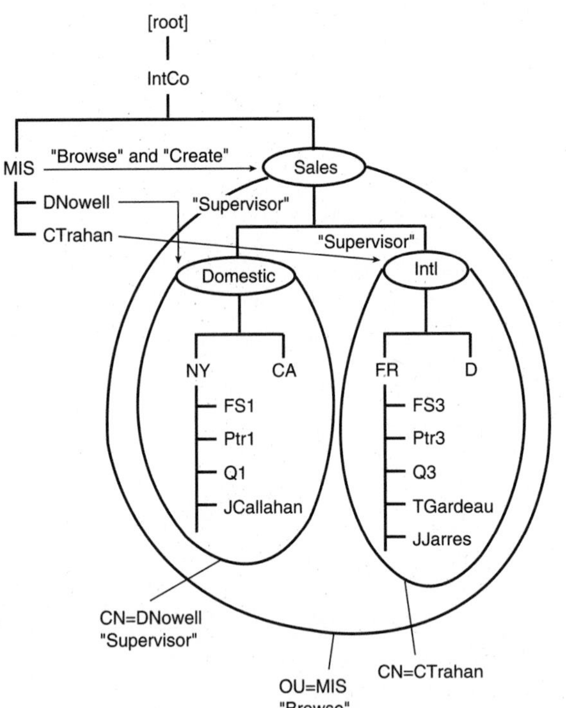

Figure 7.6

Sample rights assignments.

Summary of Object Rights

Object rights granted to an object for a container object inherit to all objects and containers below. Object rights granted to an object for a leaf object do not inherit further. If you were to grant user ECassidy Supervisor object rights for the file server object .CN=FS1.OU=NY.OU=Domestic.OU=Sales.O=IntCo, the rights would apply only to that one object. If you were to grant user ACamus Delete object rights for the container object .OU=FR.OU=Intl.OU=Sales.O=IntCo, this user would be able to delete the container OU=FR and any object under that container.

Table 7.4 summarizes the NDS object rights. The first letter is boldfaced to emphasize that this is the abbreviation used to represent the right in the menu utilities.

TABLE 7.4
NDS Object Rights

Right	Description
Supervisor	The *Supervisor* object right gives one object all rights to another object. In addition, the Supervisor object right automatically confers Supervisor property rights to all properties.
Delete	This right gives the trustee the ability to delete the object the right is granted for, as well as all objects below (if applicable).
Create	The *Create* right gives one object the capability to create a new object below the level the right is granted. This right applies only to container objects; leaf objects cannot have child objects created underneath them.
Rename	This right gives the trustee the ability to rename the object the right is granted for, and all objects below (if applicable).
Browse	This right gives the trustee the ability to see and gather information on the object the right is granted for, and all objects below (if applicable).

Default Object Rights

NetWare 4.1 defines certain default object rights. These rights ensure the easiest means of navigating the network when it is first installed. As you grow more comfortable managing the network, you might want, for security reasons, to revise the default rights. Table 7.5 summarizes the default object rights.

Table 7.5
Default Object Rights

Trustee Object	Target Object	Rights	Notes
[public]	[root]	Browse	Gives anyone the ability to browse the NDS tree. This is useful when users need to change their context prior to logging in. It also allows everybody to view the names of objects in the tree.
User who installs a new server	The new server	Supervisor	The user who installs a new file server is given Supervisor rights to the server object. This gives them Supervisor rights to all volumes, directories, and files on the server, as well.
The user who installs the first file server in the network	[root]	Supervisor	The default user when the network is first installed is .CN=Admin.O=*xxx* where *xxx* is the name of the top level organization. This user is given Supervisor object rights to [root]. This means that this user has full rights to the entire tree.
New user object	[root]	Browse	The [root] container is given Browse object rights to any user object when first created. This allows any user in the tree to see the name of the new user object.

Trustee Object	Target Object	Rights	Notes
New user object	The user who created the new user object	Supervisor	When you create a new user object, you are given Supervisor object rights to the new user.

You can block the default rights assigned to [public] through another assignment or by using an IRF. To do so, however, would mean that all users would have to either have their default context set for them or know their complete NDS name. Otherwise, users would not be able to view the tree or change their context.

Property Rights

As you learned in Chapter 6, "NetWare Directory Services," properties belong to objects. Each object has its own set of unique properties. Some properties are common to all objects.

Rights can be granted to a user for the properties of an object in two ways: selected property rights and the all-properties rights. *Selected property rights*, as the name implies, are trustee rights assigned to selected properties. A user, for example, could have a different set of rights assigned for each property of an object. The rights assigned for one property would not necessarily match the rights assigned for another property.

Another characteristic of selected property rights is that these rights do not inherit to lower level objects. If you assign the user JWalker Read rights to the Printcon Job Configuration property of the container object .OU=Sales, it would not inherit to lower level containers such as .OU=Intl.OU=Sales. Selected property rights override any rights assigned for all-properties.

All-properties rights are like defaults. If no selected property rights have been assigned to a given property, the rights a user acquires are the rights assigned for all-properties. Rights assigned to all-properties inherit to lower level objects. If you assign the user RCrowe Read rights to all-properties of the object .OU=Intl, RCrowe would also inherit Read for the objects .OU=FR.OU=Intl, and OU=D.OU=Intl.

Table 7.6 summarizes property rights. The first letter is boldfaced to emphasize that this is the abbreviation used to represent the right in the menu utilities.

Table 7.6
Property Rights

Property Right	Description
Supervisor	The *Supervisor* right gives the user all rights to the selected property, or all-properties.
Read	The user or other object with *Read* property rights can read the selected property or all-properties. If the property is, for example, a container login script, the user can read and execute the login script. Assigning the Read right automatically implies the Compare right.
Compare	*Compare* property rights give the user or other object rights to detect the existence of the selected property or all-properties. This is useful, for example, for users performing a scan of the NDS tree using the NLIST.EXE utility. If you have Compare property rights, you can use the NLIST utility to let you know whether an object has a password. Compare does not let you see any information about the object or its properties, just whether the property exists for that object.
Write	The *Write* right enables you to make changes to the selected property or all-properties. If you have Write rights to an object's ACL property, for example, you can control what objects have security access to that object. Assigning the Write right automatically implies the Add/Delete Self right.
Add/Delete Self	The user or other object with *Add/Delete Self* property rights can add themselves or delete themselves from the selected property or all-properties. This trustee right is applicable only where the property represents a list. If the object is a Group, for example, users with the Add/Delete Self right to the Group's Member List property can add or remove themselves from the Group.

Understanding the Inherited Rights Filter

The *Inherited Rights Filter* (IRF) is used to block the inheritance of rights. There is an IRF that corresponds to each type of right mentioned earlier. Following is a list of the IRFs and the rights they control:

Right	IRF
Directory Trustee	Directory IRF
File Trustee	File IRF
Object Trustee	Object IRF
Selected Property Trustee	Property IRF
All-Properties Trustee	Property IRF

The default IRF for any given object, directory, or file allows all rights to filter through. Therefore, by default, the IRF performs no filtering; rights are not blocked by default. With Administrator utilities such as NETADMIN.EXE, FILER.EXE, NWADMIN.EXE, or RIGHTS.EXE, you can change the IRF and remove rights. After a right has been removed from the IRF, that right is no longer inherited by lower level objects unless a trustee assignment is made that reinstates the right at a lower level. If a trustee assignment is granted for the same object, directory, or file where the IRF has been altered, the trustee assignment overrides the IRF. The effect of the IRF and other rights is explored in the last section of this chapter, "Examining Effective Rights."

The Function of the IRF

The IRF blocks the flow of rights down the NDS tree or down the file system directory structure. As the name implies, the IRF is a *filter* that filters rights that are inherited, allowing some through and blocking others. When you view an IRF, you can see only the rights that are allowed to pass. The rights that are blocked are not visible. Thus, if an IRF blocks "SWA" (Supervisor, Write, and Add/Delete Self) property rights, the rights that are visible are the rights that are allowed to pass: "RC" (Read and Compare).

Figure 7.7 gives you an example of the use of a file system directory IRF. The user JWalker is assigned "RFWCE" (Read, File Scan, Write, Create, and Erase) directory trustee rights in the subdirectory FS1_SYS:DATA. The IRF of the subdirectory

FS1_SYS:DATA\CLIENTS has been modified so that only "RF" (Read and File Scan) rights are allowed. JWalker's inherited rights in the FS1_SYS:DATA\CLIENTS\JONES subdirectory are restricted to "RF."

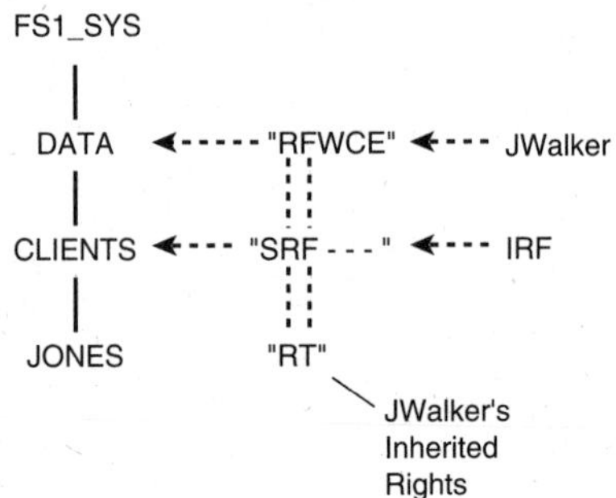

Figure 7.7
An example of the IRF filtering rights.

The IRF does not grant additional rights. As you can see in figure 7.7, even though the IRF allows "SRF" (Supervisor, Read, and File Scan) rights to be inherited, user JWalker does not acquire the Supervisor right. He ends up with no more rights than he started with based on the original trustee assignment in the DATA directory.

A lower level assignment can reinstate rights that have been blocked by an IRF. Figure 7.8 illustrates this principle with an example of NDS object rights. In the example, the group Sales_MIS is assigned "BCD" (Browse, Create, and Delete) object rights to the container .O=IntCo. The container .OU=Sales.O=IntCo has an IRF that is modified to allow only "B" (Browse) rights to pass. Normally, the group's rights to the .OU=Intl.OU=Sales.O=IntCo container would be Browse. In this example, however, another trustee assignment is granted to the group that gives it a different set of rights. In this example, the rights for the group Sales_MIS are Supervisor.

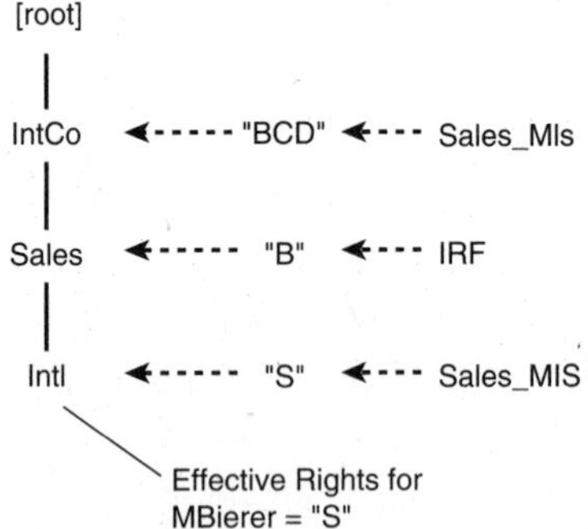

Figure 7.8
A lower level assignment changes inheritance pattern.

Figure 7.9 illustrates how a trustee assignment at the same level as an IRF overrides the normal effect of the IRF. In this example, the printer

.CN=Printer1.OU=Special.O=IntCo has an IRF that allows *no rights* to filter through. The container .OU=MIS.O=IntCo is assigned Supervisor object rights to the printer object. The container MIS therefore acquires Supervisor rights to the printer object. Because the rights are assigned to a container, any users who belong in the container MIS also acquire rights to the printer object.

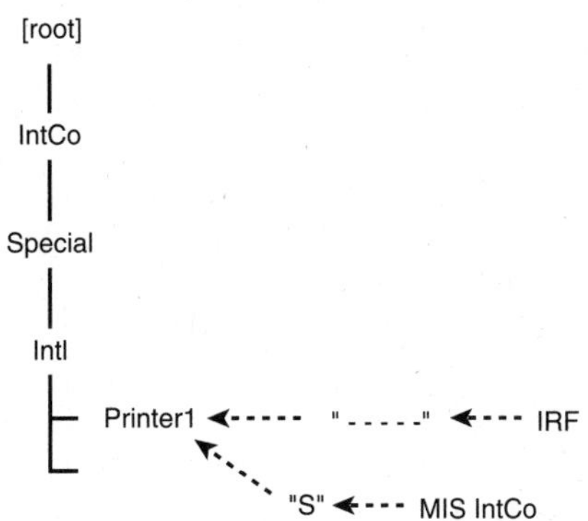

Figure 7.9

A trustee assignment overrides the IRF at the same level.

The IRF as a Bit Mask

As you gain some understanding of trustee rights and the IRF, you will come to realize that the IRF is a *bit mask*, which is used in binary operations to screen out incoming values. Operations performed against a bit mask are known as Boolean or logical operations. The Boolean operation you are concerned with here is the AND operation.

The *AND* operation is performed between two bits. *Bit* is an abbreviation for "binary digit." Because there are only two possible values for a bit—1 or 0—there are only four possibilities when two bits are compared. The outcomes are mapped into what is known as a *truth table*. The following is the truth table for the AND operation:

Bit Value	1	0
1	1	0
0	0	0

Reading the table in another way, following is a list of outcomes of the AND operation:

```
1 AND 1 = 1
1 AND 0 = 0
0 AND 1 = 0
0 AND 0 = 0
```

When applying this concept to a bit mask, you can see that if 1 is in the mask, an incoming value of 1 will come out of the AND operation as a 1. If 1 is in the mask, an incoming value of 0 will come out of the AND operation as a 0. In conclusion, if a 1 is in the mask, the value of the incoming bit will remain unchanged. If a 0 is in the mask, however, the result will always be 0. A 1 is used in a bit mask to *allow* a bit to pass unchanged. A 0 is used to *filter out* a bit.

In figure 7.10, if a directory trustee right granted is seen as a 1, and a right removed is seen as a 0, here's how a bit mask is applied.

Figure 7.10

Seeing a trustee assignment and IRF as a logical AND operation.

		Bit Mask S R C E W F M A
Trustee Assignment	" - RCEWF - - "	0 1 1 1 1 1 0 0
IRF	"SR - - - F - - "	1 1 0 0 0 1 0 0
Results	" - R - - - F - - "	0 1 0 0 0 1 0 0

As you can see from the figure, the resulting bit mask is 01000100, which translates (in the example) to directory trustee rights "RF" (Read and File Scan).

Examining Effective Rights

The term *effective rights* applies to the rights calculated after the cumulative trustee rights and IRF masking have taken place. Effective rights can be acquired from several sources in addition to a direct individual trustee assignment. For the purposes of the following list, the term *target* is used to refer to the object, directory, or file for which you want to determine effective rights (that is, the target of your calculations). The sources of your effective rights include the following:

- Assignments made to [public]
- Inheritance from the container you belong to
- Inheritance from the parent containers of the target (don't forget to include [root])
- Rights assigned to any groups you belong to
- Rights assigned to any organizational roles you occupy
- Security equivalencies assigned to you

- The effect of any IRF that blocks your rights
- Trustee assignments made directly to you

As you can see, rights in NetWare 4.1 can become complicated when you consider the many different possible sources.

To calculate effective rights, you need to trace the flow of rights down the structure. Include the effects of any lower level trustee assignments and IRFs and combine the rights acquired from the sources listed earlier. The cumulative sum total of rights are your effective rights.

Figure 7.11 illustrates effective rights for the user .CN=RJones.OU=MIS.O=IntCo for the file server object .CN=FS1.OU=Sales.O=IntCo. As you examine the figure, take note of the following:

- The container OU=Sales has an IRF that allows only Supervisor and Browse object rights to be inherited.
- The container OU=MIS has Browse and Create object rights to O=IntCo. These rights flow down to the container OU=Sales.
- Because of the IRF, the container OU=MIS has Browse rights only.
- The user CN=RJones is assigned Create and Delete rights directly to the container OU=Sales. The rights for CN=RJones as a user override the IRF at the same object level.
- The Create and Delete rights for CN=RJones flow down to the CN=FS1 object. These are combined with the Browse rights that CN=RJones acquires because he belongs to that container.

In figure 7.12, the user CN=BLowrey is a member of the group .CN=Sales_MIS.OU=Sales.O=IntCo. As you can see from its name, the group is under the container .OU=Sales.O=IntCo. The following property trustee assignments are made for all-properties:

- The container .OU=Sales.O=IntCo is assigned Read and Write property rights to itself.
- The group .CN=Sales_MIS.OU=Sales.O=IntCo is assigned Supervisor property rights to the container .OU=Sales.O=IntCo.
- The user CN=BLowrey is assigned Write, Compare, and Add/Delete Self to the container .OU=Intl.OU=Sales.O=IntCo.

Figure 7.11

An example of effective rights calculations for a user and the parent container.

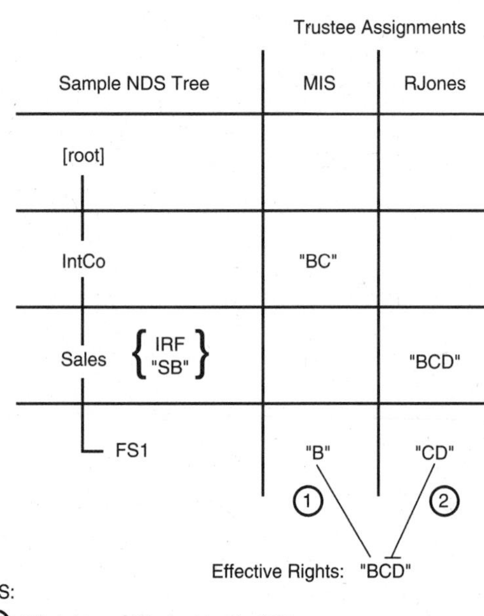

Figure 7.12

Effective rights of a user.

	IRF	Sales	Sales_MIS	BLowrey	BLowrey Effective Rights
IntCo					
Sales	- RWCA	- RW - -	S - - - -		SRW (C) (A)
Intl	- R - C -			- W - CA	RWCA

In this example, the container .OU=Sales.O=IntCo is assigned Read and Write property rights to itself. This overrides the IRF and gives these rights to any object under that container. Because the group .CN=Sales_MIS.OU=Sales.O=IntCo is under the container, it inherits Read and Write. As you recall from the Property Rights chart, Read implies Compare, and Write implies Add/Delete Self. These are indicated as effective rights in parentheses in figure 7.12 . In addition, the group .CN=Sales_MIS.OU=Sales.O=IntCo is assigned Supervisor rights to the container .OU=Sales.O=IntCo, which gives this group all rights. Because the user BLowrey is a member of the group, he inherits the rights of the group.

At the level of container .OU=Intl.OU=Sales.O=IntCo, there is an IRF that allows only Read and Compare rights to filter through. This blocks the rights assigned to the group Sales_MIS and allows only Read. By implication, the group also acquires Compare. The user BLowrey is explicitly assigned Write, Compare, and Add/Delete Self. He ends up with effective rights of Read, Write, Compare, and Add/Delete Self.

As you can see, calculating effective rights is not difficult, but it can become complicated when you consider all the possible sources of rights. When first setting up your system, it is advised that you keep security as simple as possible. Wherever possible, assign rights to containers so that the rights can inherit to objects below and save you from having to make elaborate trustee assignments.

Summary

This chapter discussed rights in both the file system and the NDS. File system rights include file trustee rights, file Inherited Rights Filters (IRFs), directory trustee rights, and directory IRFs. NDS rights include object trustee rights, object IRFs, property rights, and property IRFs. Two types of property rights include selected and all-properties rights. All-properties rights serve as a default for all properties of an object. Other default rights, file system, and object rights were discussed.

Most trustee assignments are inherited at lower levels. Selected property rights are not inherited, and all-properties rights are inherited. The inheritance of rights can be blocked either by another lower level trustee assignment or by an IRF. The Supervisor right cannot be blocked in this fashion in the file system.

You learned that the IRF filters out rights and does not give you any additional rights. The default IRF allows all rights to pass through. You also saw that the IRF is a bit mask against which rights are applied.

You learned about file and directory attributes. These represent lower level rights that affect all users on the system, including users with Supervisor rights. NDS rights do not ordinarily affect file system rights. Exceptions include when you assign a user Supervisor object rights to a file server object, or Write object rights to the ACL property of a volume object.

Chapter 8 discusses a topic of concern for system Administrators who have both 3.*x* and 4.*x* file servers sharing the same network: bindery services.

Bindery Services

As you discovered in Chapter 4, "Traditional Features of NetWare," older versions of NetWare stored information about their resources in a set of database files known as the *bindery files,* which consist of three related files. The first file stores object identifiers; the second contains information about the properties of objects; and the third contains the values of the properties.

As you saw in Chapter 5, "New Features of NetWare," NetWare 4.1 networks store information about network resources in a distributed database called the *NetWare Directory Services* (NDS). For a NetWare 4.1 network to coexist with earlier, bindery-based NetWare networks, there has to be a translation mechanism. This mechanism is known as bindery services (known in NetWare 4.0*x* as "bindery emulation"). *Bindery services* allows the NetWare 4.1 file server to offer information from the NDS in a bindery format. The bindery services mechanism allows the NetWare 4.1 file server to offer one container from its tree as a *pseudo bindery* to bindery-based file servers and processes. Through the bindery services mechanism, users logged into bindery-based file servers can simultaneously access the file system on a NetWare 3.*x* file server. NetWare Loadable Modules (NLMs) written for a NetWare 3.*x* file server that expect to get bindery information can run successfully on a NetWare 4.1 file server.

It is important to understand fully the bindery services mechanism. When upgrading a NetWare 3.*x* network to NetWare 4.1, or when integrating a NetWare 4.1 file server into a bindery-based NetWare network, the bindery services mechanism will be the only way the NetWare 4.1 file server can be seen and accessed by bindery-based file servers.

This chapter discusses various aspects of bindery services to increase your understanding of how to use bindery services to integrate NetWare 4.1 and bindery-based file servers.

Understanding Bindery Context

The key to understanding how the bindery services mechanism works is to understand the role of the file server's bindery context. As was discussed in Chapter 6, "NetWare Directory Services," *context* refers to either the location in the NDS tree of an object, or your current position in the tree. The bindery context is a place in the NDS tree where bindery-based servers or NLMs expect to find information in a bindery format.

The bindery context can be set using the following file server console command, where *.xxx* is a complete, typeful, NDS organization or organizational unit name:

```
<PX>SET BINDERY CONTEXT = .xxx [; .yyy]
```

(The SET commands are covered in more detail in Chapter 38, "Fine-Tuning the Server.") After the bindery context is set, the NetWare 4.1 file server immediately starts to respond to any bindery-based requests.

Optionally you can have a total of 16 different container objects in the server's bindery context. In the syntax noted above, *.yyy* is another complete, typeful container name. Container names are separated by a semicolon.

The bindery context can be any NDS organization or organizational unit. The objects in that container are seen as bindery objects by bindery-based systems accessing this server. For example, if your bindery context is set to .OU=Special.O=IntCo, and you have a user .CN=RJones.OU=Special.O=IntCo, bindery-based utilities see this user as RJones. If you are logged into a NetWare 3.*x* file server and run the bindery-based utility SYSCON.EXE, there is an option to see "User Information." If you change to the NetWare 4.1 file server from within SYSCON, you will see the user RJones on the list of users for the NetWare 4.1 file server. If you press Enter, you will see the properties and values for RJones.

Other objects in the file server's bindery context also appear as if they are in the bindery file. These other objects can include printers, print servers, print queues, and groups. Child container objects under the bindery context and objects under the child containers are not visible to bindery-based servers and services. You might recall from a discussion in Chapter 4 that the bindery files are *flat* databases, which is to say bindery objects are not arranged in a hierarchy. Bindery-based file servers and services (such as NetWare NFS) assume that all information needed is stored in the bindery. The top of the bindery hierarchy is the file server. If you need bindery access to another file server, the bindery client will make an attachment to the other file server and look at its binderies.

When setting more than one container in the server's bindery context, NetWare presents leaf objects in order of appearance. This is important to note if you have the same object names in different containers in the bindery context.

For example, suppose you set the bindery context as follows:

```
SET BINDERY CONTEXT = OU=Sales.O=EBDB; OU=MIS.O=EBDB
```

If a user GDees (Gary Dees) exists in OU=MIS, and a user GDees (Glenda Dees) exists in OU=Sales, bindery based clients will recognize the user *Glenda* Dees rather than the user *Gary* Dees. When the user *Gary* Dees goes to login, he will not have the correct password. One solution would be to create another user object for *Gary* Dees in the OU=Sales container. Another solution is to change both names to prevent duplication by including middle initials in both names.

If the bindery context is not set, bindery services will be effectively disabled for this file server. The file server will continue to act as a normal NetWare 4.1 file server, but will respond to requests for bindery information with invalid information.

NetWare 4.1 enables you to set different sets of bindery contexts. You must note, however, that when you change the current bindery context, the set of users that the bindery-based client will see changes. If you have a user who needs to be accessible no matter what bindery context is currently set, this user will have to be duplicated in each different bindery context.

The bindery context of a NetWare 4.1 file server also serves as its *default context.* The default context is used by the operating system when constructing complete NDS names. If the name you specify cannot be found in the current context, the file server next tries its default context.

Physical Location of Bindery Context Objects

Another factor comes into play when setting up a NetWare 4.1 file server to perform bindery services. The NetWare 4.1 file server must contain a replica of the partition that contains the bindery context. Another way of stating this is that the file server performing bindery services must physically store the objects represented in the bindery context.

A new file server, for example, probably has some sort of replica. The replica might be of a partition that does not contain the bindery context. If this is the case, bindery services fails. You need to locate the partition that contains the bindery context and create a replica of that partition on the file server that is to perform bindery services.

Tip: To simplify management of bindery services, set the file server's bindery context to the same container that contains the file server object.

Logical Location of the Bindery Context

Now that you have an understanding of bindery context, you must turn your attention to where in the NDS tree you should set the bindery context, and how this affects bindery services. There are two approaches you can take, as follows:

- Set the bindery context to the same container for all servers on the network.
- Set the bindery context to different locations in the tree for each server.

If you decide to set the bindery context the same, you might run into a situation where you have too many objects in a single container. Novell laboratories have reported that the speed at which a file server can search through the tree is noticeably slower as the number of objects in a partition approaches between 500 and 1,000 objects. On the other hand, if all file servers have the same bindery context, changes made to one container are automatically reflected in all file servers. This minimizes the amount of work you need to do to manage the network.

Different file servers in the tree can each have a unique bindery context. The advantage to this is that you can ensure that the bindery context for this file server is set to a container inside a replica stored on this file server. The disadvantage is from the

standpoint of network management—if all servers have a unique bindery context, you must query each file server separately when you need to find out where its bindery context is located in the tree.

Another alternative is to include two containers in the bindery context of each server. The first container could be the same for all servers. The second container could be unique for each server. This way, all servers have a common container to reference as well as a separate container for server-specific references.

The Impact of Bindery Services

Bindery services impacts many different areas and products in the NetWare world. These include the following:

- NetWare 2.*x* and 3.*x* file servers
- NetWare 4.1 file servers on a different NDS tree
- NLMs written for NetWare 3.*x*
- NetWare for SAA
- Server-based backup and other utilities
- Client software written for NetWare 3.*x* and older
- Login scripts and Printcon job configurations

This section discusses the impact of NetWare 4.1 and bindery services on these areas and products.

Interconnectivity with NetWare 2.*x* and 3.*x* File Servers

Although most critical network information is conveyed through the NDS, NetWare 4.1 file servers still send out periodic Routing Information Protocol (RIP) and Server Advertisement Protocol (SAP) broadcasts. Through these protocols, discussed in Chapter 2, NetWare 4.1 file servers announce their presence to other NetWare file servers. The IPX/SPX and NCP protocols provide the basic mechanism that allows access to resources between NetWare file servers. These protocols are used in both bindery-based and NDS environments.

NetWare 4.1 provides SAP and RIP by default. NLSP (NetWare Link Services Protocol), a more advanced protocol, can be configured. If NLSP is configured on your NetWare 4.1 file server, it provides SAP information for the purposes of bindery services. The version of NLSP provided with NetWare 4.1 is backwards compatible with SAP and RIP.

There are two major differences between these environments that affect connectivity: how the servers refer to resources (that is, how resources are named), and how security access is granted. In the bindery-based environment, resources are named in the bindery files. File server names are stored in the bindery as the NetWare 3.*x* or 2.*x* file server receives SAP information. Volume information is received from the file server itself. Most network resources are referenced through the bindery files. In the NetWare 4.1 environment, on the other hand, resources are referenced through the NDS. File server names, volume information, and other information is obtained through the NDS. Bindery services translates between NDS names and bindery names and vice versa.

When a NetWare 3.*x* file server wants to forward a print job to a print queue on a NetWare 4.1 file server, for example, it makes a request for bindery information on the print queue. The bindery services mechanism looks up print queue information in the bindery context to validate the request. The bindery emulator then provides the requested information, translating between the NDS format and the format expected by the NetWare 3.*x* server.

Security access is translated in a similar fashion. For example, when a user on NetWare 2.*x* file server FS22 maps a drive letter to a volume on NetWare 4.1 file server FS401, FS401 sends an authentication request to FS22. *Authentication* is the process by which a file server checks to ensure that the user making the request is valid and has the proper Trustee rights.

Mapping a drive letter is a process where you use the MAP.EXE command to assign a DOS drive letter to a volume on a file server. This process is similar to the DOS SUBST (substitute) command. Whenever you reference this drive letter, you actually are referencing a hard drive on a file server. For more information on this process, see Chapter 33, "Assigning Drive Mappings."

The authentication process used with NetWare 2.*x* is very different from the process used with NetWare 4.1. In 2.*x*, the server looks up the user name and password in the bindery files. In NetWare 4.1, the server looks up the user name and gets the private and public keys from the NDS. The keys are then used to decode authentication information returning from the client. FS401 asks the user on FS22 for a login name

and password. The user enters a login name in the bindery context of FS401. If the login name and password check out, FS401 grants a bindery connection to the user on FS22.

NetWare 4.1 File Servers on a Different NDS Tree

NetWare 4.1 file servers ordinarily communicate between themselves through the NDS. This is possible, however, only when the servers belong to the same tree. NetWare 4.1 file servers on different trees do not see each other through the NDS. Part of the reason for this is security. By placing servers on another tree, you essentially hide them from casual view. The preferred tree is specified in the NET.CFG file on each user's workstation. You also can specify the preferred tree when loading the VLM workstation shell. (For more information on setting up the workstation environment, see Chapter 14, "DOS Client Basics.")

When you map a drive letter to a volume on a NetWare 4.1 file server FS_TREE2 on another tree, for example, the bindery emulator on FS_TREE2 comes into play. At first, the NDS services running on FS_TREE2 tries to locate your file server in the tree. When it fails to see your file server, it passes the job to the bindery emulator. The bindery services process asks you for a bindery login name and password. When you enter this information, it looks up the user name in FS_TREE2's bindery context. If the information you supplied is valid, you are granted a bindery connection to FS_TREE2. In this fashion, you can gain access to volumes on servers that are not part of the tree just as you would to a NetWare 3.*x* or 2.*x* file server.

UnixWare, NetWare NFS, and NetWare for SAA Products

UnixWare, NetWare Network File System (NFS), and NetWare for Systems Application Architecture (SAA) all currently rely on bindery services. These products were designed for NetWare 3.*x* connectivity. All three products enable you to define users, groups, and levels of security access. To accomplish the complicated mapping between the security requirements of their respective host environments and that of NetWare, these products rely on access to information stored in the bindery files.

- **UnixWare.** Features built-in IPX connectivity and seamless integration to NetWare servers. The current connection is strictly bindery-based. UnixWare provides a utility NUC.NLM (NetWare Unix Client NLM) that loads on the file server and provides enhanced access rights for users in the file server's bindery context. UnixWare also ships with TCP/IP and NFS support and can be used in conjunction with NetWare NFS.

- **NetWare NFS.** Provides access to NetWare file servers to TCP/IP-based systems (usually UNIX host computers). The package supports a protocol developed by Sun Microsystems. NFS uses the External Data Representation (XDR) protocol to standardize the format of data transfers and a Remote Procedure Call (RPC) to carry out data transfers between the UNIX host and the NetWare file server.

- **NetWare for SAA.** Allows the NetWare file server to act as a node in an IBM SNA network. The LAN Workplace or LAN Workgroup software with a 3270 client package must be run on the workstations. NetWare workstations running 3270 emulation become SAA clients that enable users to log into IBM mainframes and minicomputers. The NetWare for SAA product supports connections to the IBM SNA environment through token ring, Ethernet, Synchronous Data Link Control (SDLC), and X.25 connections.

In the NetWare 4.1 environment, bindery services is necessary to provide these products with the necessary information. NetWare NFS and UnixWare, for example, maintain a list called NFSUSERS, which contains mappings between UNIX user ID numbers and NetWare user names. It is stored on volume SYS: in a directory ETC. The products are not designed to provide full NDS names and are not capable of asking the file server to search the NDS for user authentication. Instead, the user names in the NFSUSERS file must reside in the server's bindery context. When a UNIX user accesses the file server through the NFS mechanisms, a NetWare login name and password must be entered. The server uses the bindery services mechanism to look up and validate this information.

Note: Future revisions of NetWare 4.1 and the three products discussed in this section will provide full NDS client capabilities over the span of the year 1995.

Server-Based Backup and Other Utilities

Many file server-based backup utilities rely on bindery services. One of the critical issues when backing up a file server is what access to the files, subdirectories, and volumes should be allowed. Most tape backup utilities require that you have complete access rights to all files, directories, and volumes on your file server. In bindery-based systems, you needed Supervisor equivalence. The user Supervisor was a "super user" created automatically during the NetWare 2.*x* or 3.*x* installation process. This special user was given Supervisor trustee rights to all files, directories, and volumes on the file server. The role of the user Supervisor in bindery services is explained in more detail later in this chapter.

In NetWare 4.1, no user Supervisor is created as part of the NDS structure. The closest equivalent would be the user Admin, who is created under the first organiza-

tion you set up during installation. The Admin user is usually in charge of the entire network and is very likely not to get involved in backing up individual file servers. As a result, you might have to create file server Supervisors who have full rights to all files and directories on their file server. These users can then perform the backup of their file server. As you read in an earlier section, one quick way to give a user complete access to a file server is to grant them Supervisor object rights to the file server object.

Another issue is how to back up information about network resources. There are currently very few tape backup utilities that are aware of the NDS. Most major vendors of tape backup hardware and utilities will have NDS capabilities by the end of 1994. At this point, however, you are still faced with a decision of how to back up NDS information.

The first thing you need to do is to make sure each NDS partition has a replica stored on another file server. This way, if a file server fails, you will not lose access to any part of your network. The next step is to determine which tape backup vendors will back up NetWare 4.1 NDS data. Most backup software will back up NetWare 4.1 volumes; the volume structure for NetWare 4.1 is almost identical to that of NetWare 3.*x*. The problem is that not many vendors support backup of the NDS data files.

You can always use NetWare's SBACKUP.NLM utility to back up NDS data. Instructions on the use of SBACKUP are given in Chapter 41, "Protecting Your Network Files."

Most server-based utilities written for the NetWare 3.*x* environment will port successfully to NetWare 4.1. In some cases, however, you are required to supply a user login name. In this situation, the login name provided must be of a user residing in the server's bindery context. In addition, bindery services must be enabled by properly setting the file server's bindery context. An example of such a utility is the first version of Symantec's Norton Anti-Virus for NetWare software. This package protects your file server from viruses. When you want to run the workstation utility to manage the NAV.NLM utility running on the server, you are asked to supply a username and password. If you supply an NDS user name, you are not allowed to access the server software. If you enter the user Supervisor, for example, or the name of any user in the server's bindery context, you can gain access to the software.

Client Connections

Workstations running the following NetWare 3.*x* and 2.*x* shells are recognized as bindery services clients:

- NETX.EXE
- NETX.COM
- XMSNETX.EXE

- EMSNETX.EXE
- NET5.COM
- XMSNET5.EXE
- EMSNET5.EXE
- NET4.COM
- XMSNET4.EXE
- EMSNET4.EXE
- NET3.COM
- XMSNET3.EXE
- EMSNET3.EXE

The login sequence using any of these shells is the same as logging into a NetWare 3.*x* or 2.*x* file server. When logging in to a NetWare 4.1 file server, you cannot specify a complete NDS name. Furthermore, because the file server views your workstation as a bindery-based client, it looks only in the bindery context for login information. After you're logged in as a bindery client, you can access files, subdirectories, and volumes, depending on your security access rights. You cannot perform any operation that requires access to the NDS. Such actions include the following:

- Using any NDS network administration utility such as NETADMIN or NWADMIN
- Accessing any NDS resource outside of the server's bindery context

Some utilities, such as PCONSOLE.EXE, have a bindery mode. If this is the case, you can use these utilities when logged in as a bindery client. Also, if you have access to SYSCON.EXE (from an older version of NetWare), you can perform network management on objects in the server's bindery context. This includes adding, changing, or removing users. Other contexts in the NDS tree will not be accessible.

UnixWare workstations are also viewed as bindery clients. The client software provided on these systems precludes (at present) access to NDS resources outside of the server's bindery context. OS/2 workstations, on the other hand, have full and complete access to the NDS. NetWare 4.1 comes with a rich set of utilities for OS/2. The support for OS/2 is far better under NetWare 4.1 than in previous versions of NetWare.

Login Scripts

A *login script* contains a series of instructions that are activated when a user logs in to the network. A login script resembles a cross between a DOS batch file and a simplified version of the BASIC programming language. NetWare 4.1 supports three login scripts: a container login script, a profile login script, and a user login script. Refer to Chapter 34, "Creating Login Scripts," for more information on login scripts and how to create them.

NetWare 4.1 login scripts are stored in the NDS database. When an NDS user logs in, the server locates their NDS information. It then reads and executes their container login script and their profile login script if these exist. Finally, it executes their user login script. If the user login script does not exist, a preset login script called the *default login script* executes.

The operating system, on the other hand, expects the login scripts for bindery-based users to be located in a subdirectory on volume SYS: called MAIL. Each login script is stored as an ASCII text file in a subdirectory corresponding to the bindery user's internal ID number. The NetWare 4.1 bindery emulator creates a directory for a user in the bindery context who logs in as a bindery client. The personal login script for such a user is not created automatically; login scripts for bindery clients must be created and maintained manually. One technique is to use a bindery-based configuration utility, such as SYSCON.EXE, provided you have access to older versions of NetWare. Another technique is to find the user's directory under SYS:MAIL. This can be accomplished by logging in as that user and typing **RIGHTS SYS:MAIL**. The directory for which this user has rights becomes their directory. Use any text editor to create the login script, and store it in the correct subdirectory of SYS:MAIL. The file name must be "LOGIN."

Another potential login script problem is that NDS users run the login script of their container. If user .CN=CTrahan.O=MIS were to login, he would run the login script of the O=MIS container. A bindery user does not have access to this login script. To provide a common login script for bindery users, you need to create the login script in a text editor and save it with the following path and name:

```
SYS:PUBLIC\NET$LOG.DAT
```

Alternatively, assuming you have access to SYSCON.EXE from either NetWare 3.*x* or 2.*x*, you can create the System Login Script using the Supervisor Options menu.

Tip: Windows users can use the Copy and Paste feature to copy login scripts between NDS users and bindery users. Open the NetWare 4.1 Windows-based NWADMIN.EXE (NetWare Administrator) utility. (More details on how to access this utility are presented in Chapter 20, "Managing Objects and Properties.")

continues

Follow these directions:

1. Locate the user or container whose login script you want to copy.
2. Open up the object details dialog box for this user or container.
3. Select the Login Script property. Note that the user or container login script is displayed.
4. While holding down the Shift key, use either the PgDn or Down Arrow key to highlight the entire login script. Release the Shift key.
5. Press Ctrl+Ins to copy the script into a paste buffer.
6. Use Alt+Tab to switch to the Program Manager.
7. Select the Accessories program group and open up the Notepad.
8. Press Shift+Ins to copy the paste buffer into the Notepad.
9. Select the File menu and save the file as either of the following:
   - SYS:MAIL*nnn*\LOGIN for a user login script, where *nnn* is the user ID
   - SYS:PUBLIC\NET$LOG.DAT for the "system login script"

Printcon Job Configurations

Another area where NDS information and bindery information differ is the Printcon Job Configuration. PRINTCON.EXE is a DOS-based executable file that enables users to define characteristics of print jobs. The types of information you can enter into a Printcon job configuration include the following:

- The number of copies you would normally print (default is 1)
- Whether or not to print a banner page and what information is included in the banner
- Whether or not to add a page eject at the end of the print job

There are also various other types of information. More detail is available on Printcon job configurations in Chapter 28, "Printing from DOS Clients."

Printcon job configuration data for NDS users is stored in the NDS database. The same information for bindery users is stored in the same directory as their login script under the file name PRINTCON.DAT. As with login scripts, the Printcon job configurations for bindery users must be created and maintained separately. Unfortunately,

because these configurations are not stored in the form of an ASCII text file, you must create and maintain them through PRINTCON.EXE.

Bindery users do not have a common PRINTCON.DAT file like NDS users do. An NDS user can use any Printcon job configuration from their parent container. Bindery users must use their own file. You can log in as the bindery user Supervisor and copy configurations between users, but there is no facility to maintain common configurations for all bindery users.

In earlier versions of NetWare, there was a technique to enable all users on the system to access a common Printcon job configuration file. The technique involved the following:

- Creating a configuration for the user Supervisor using PRINTCON.EXE.
- Copying this configuration from Supervisor's mail directory (SYS:MAIL\1\PRINTCON.DAT) to SYS:PUBLIC.
- Modifying the search mode, using the SMODE.EXE utility, of various printing utilities so that they would find the common Printcon configuration file. The SMODE utility changes the way a DOS executable searches for information. You can have the utility not search the current directory first, for example, by selecting one of the SMODE search options.

This technique is not advised in NetWare 4.1. The last item on the preceding list causes problems with printing for NDS users.

Examining User Supervisor

NetWare 4.1's bindery services mechanism recognizes a bindery user *Supervisor*, which is a special user designed for programs and clients that need bindery-based full access to all volumes, directories, and files on a file server. If you attempt to locate this user through NDS utilities (such as NWADMIN.EXE or NLIST.EXE), you find that this user does not exist. If you examine the server using a bindery-based utility (such as SYSCON.EXE), the user Supervisor appears. It is safe to conclude that the user Supervisor is a pseudo-user.

To log in as the user Supervisor from a NetWare 4.1 file server, type the following:

LOGIN SUPERVISOR /B

The /B option forces the operating system to recognize you as a bindery-based user.

To log in as the user Supervisor from a NetWare 3.*x* or 2.*x* file server, type the following, where *fsname* is the name of the NetWare 4.1 file server you want to log into:

LOGIN *fsname*/SUPERVISOR

After you are logged in as the user Supervisor, you have complete access to all volumes, directories, and files on a file server. Because you are a bindery user, you do not have access to the NDS. If you have access to bindery-based utilities from older versions of NetWare, you can perform limited system administration.

If you are logged in as an NDS Admin user, you can actually create a user Supervisor in the file server's bindery context. Bear in mind, however, that this user does not correspond to the bindery user Supervisor.

The Supervisor's password is the same as the first password for the Admin user. It is very important to note the first Admin password assigned when you install the first NetWare 4.*x* file server in the tree. The first password for the Admin user remains the password for the pseudo-user Supervisor, even if the Admin password changes. If you need to change the Supervisor password, first login as the user Supervisor, and then issue the SETPASS command from the DOS prompt. If you do not know the Supervisor password and cannot login, you can use a bindery-based utility, such as SYSCON, to modify the Supervisor's password.

Comparing Bindery Mode and NDS

An NDS user can log in as a bindery user. Any user located in the file server's bindery context could potentially become a bindery user. Simply log in as a user under the bindery context using the /B login option. If a user DRosenfeld exists in the file server's bindery context and wants, for example, to log in as a bindery user, he could type the following:

LOGIN DROSENFELD /B

DRosenfeld would now be logged in as a bindery user. To log in as an NDS user, he should log in again and enter the complete NDS name. When he logs in a second time, the operating system closes down the previous login session and starts a new one.

Assigning Bindery Users Access to the File Server

Any user in the file server's bindery context could potentially log in as a bindery user. If you wanted to give a bindery user more access to the system, you could increase her trustee rights. Table 8.1 lists some possibilities.

TABLE 8.1
Bindery User Access Rights

To Give the User Complete Access to:	Perform These Actions:
The file server	Grant the user Supervisor object rights to the file server object.
A single volume	Grant the user Write property rights to the volume's ACL property.
A subdirectory	Grant the user Supervisor directory trustee rights to the desired subdirectory.
A file	Grant the user Supervisor directory trustee rights to the desired file.

Using NetWare 4.1 Utilities in Bindery Mode

Some utilities enable you to switch to bindery mode. The PCONSOLE.EXE utility, for example, has an option that enables you to switch between NDS and bindery modes. If you open the PCONSOLE utility while logged in as an NDS user, you can switch to bindery mode by pressing the F4 key. This option enables an NDS Admin user to manage objects that bindery users can see. Other utilities can be used when logged in as a bindery user. In this case, you are able to access the utility only in bindery mode.

Bindery Object Name Restrictions

Naming restrictions for bindery objects are much stricter than in the NDS. Although an NDS object can have a name up to 64 characters, bindery objects must have names of 47 characters or less. If you create an object with a name greater than 47 characters in the server's bindery context as an NDS Admin user, bindery-based utilities cuts off the name after the 47th character.

Embedded spaces in NDS names are replaced with underscore (_) characters. Also, the following characters are not allowed in bindery object names:

```
<PX>/ \ : , * ?
```

Synchronizing Binderies with Older Versions of NetWare

NetWare 4.1 offers a feature called *NetSync* that allows the bindery files of NetWare 3.*x* file servers to "synchronize" with the NetWare 4.1 NDS. To accomplish this, you can load NWSYNC3.NLM on the NetWare 3.*x* file server and NWSYNC4.NLM on the NetWare 4.1 file server. The NetWare 4.1 file server's bindery context becomes "synchronized" with the bindery on the NetWare 3.*x* file server. Any changes to this container are written out to the bindery files on the NetWare 3.*x* file server and vice versa.

In this fashion, up to twelve NetWare 3.*x* file servers can be synchronized per NetWare 4.1 file server. The bindery files of the NetWare 3.x file servers can be managed through NDS, providing great simplicity in network management. Any changes made to the 3.*x* file servers update the bindery context of the synchronized NetWare 4.1 server. All network management can be accomplished through the NetWare 4.1 management utilities such as NETADMIN.EXE or NWADMIN.EXE.

The bindery synchronization offered in NetWare 4.1 is a significant improvement over the NetWare Name Service (NNS) product offered for the NetWare 3.*x* and 2.*x* environments. NNS enabled you to synchronize the bindery files of designated file servers. What happened is that any changes made to the bindery of one file server were written out to the bindery files in all file servers in the same "domain." This caused a tremendous increase in network traffic, as well as timing problems.

Timing in NetWare 4.1 is provided through the NDS and is covered in greater detail in Chapter 13, "Upgrades and Other Installation Issues." NDS controls when a change to the NDS occurs and in what order. Each NDS change is date and time stamped. If two managers attempt to change the same object, their changes take place in the order received, based on the date and time stamp.

Rather than attempting to update all bindery files of NetWare 3.*x* file servers that are synchronized with the NDS, the NetSync NLMs update only the affected servers. The only NetWare 4.1 file servers that get notified of the changes are servers that contain a replica of the partition that contains the synchronized container.

Summary

This chapter covered the basic principles and pitfalls of bindery services. As you discovered, bindery services is built into the NetWare 4.1 operating system kernel. To enable bindery services, you simply need to set the bindery context. The bindery context is up to 16 containers in the NDS tree. Objects in the bindery context appear to bindery-based clients as if they were objects in a pseudo bindery file. One restriction to setting the bindery context is that the server on which you set the context must contain a replica of the partition that contains this context. Strategies for setting the bindery context could include setting the same context for all file servers in the tree or setting a separate context for individual servers. You also could have a combination of the two methods by setting two containers in the context: one common to all servers and one specific to each server.

This chapter covered the areas of impact of bindery services. These areas include the interconnectivity between bindery-based file servers and NetWare 4.1 file servers, NetWare 4.1 file servers on different trees, NLMs and products designed for the NetWare 3.*x* environment, server-based backup, client shells and software that perform bindery lookups, login scripts, and Printcon job configurations. In each case, possible problem areas were pointed out, and solutions were discussed.

The role of the pseudo user Supervisor was discussed. As you discovered, an NDS user located in the server's bindery context can log in as a bindery user. Methods of assigning such NDS users increased network access when logged-in bindery users were covered. Certain utilities enable you to switch between bindery mode and NDS mode, assuming you are logged in as an NDS user. The naming restrictions of bindery objects were examined. Finally, NetSync, which uses specialized NLMs available in NetWare 4.1 that enable you to synchronize the bindery files of NetWare 3.*x* file servers to the NDS, was discussed.

The next Part, "Setting Up a New Network," provides information leading up to installing a NetWare 4.1 network. This Part gives you an overview of the complete installation process, from physical installation issues such as cabling, to installing the file server, setting up workstations, creating the NDS tree, and defining users and login scripts.

Part III

Setting Up a New Network

New Riders Publishing
INSIDE
SERIES

Planning the Network

NetWare 4.1 is said to be *network-centric* rather than *server-centric.* In NetWare 3.*x* and earlier, the system Administrator focused on getting the file server up and running with little regard for the rest of the network. After the server was up and running, workstations, cabling, and other issues were secondary considerations. Many network installers assumed their job was done once the server was installed and delivered to the client site.

NetWare 4.1, by its very nature, is centered on the network as a whole; the file server is simply one aspect of the network. The purpose of this chapter is to bring up some network considerations and to give you an idea of what is involved in planning an entire network.

Planning the Physical Network

Network planning can be broken down into two main components: physical and logical planning. The *physical* planning portion involves such details as distances, how many locations are involved, and what type of cable should be used. *Logical* planning involves building a logical structure that best models your organization. Logical planning is covered in the next section.

The following is a questionnaire whose questions lead you to make decisions about the type of equipment you need for your network. After the questionnaire, the ramifications of each question are discussed in turn.

1. How many users will be on the network?

   ____

2. What type of growth do you estimate in your company? Over what period of time?

   ____

3. How many locations will be connected to the network?

   ____

4. What is the shortest distance between locations?

   ____

5. What is the longest distance between locations?

   ____

6. What is the average size file or document transferred between locations?

   ____

7. How frequently is data transferred between locations?

   A. Constantly Y [ ] N [ ]
   B. Hourly Y [ ] N [ ]
   C. Several times a day Y [ ] N [ ]

D. Once a day Y [] N []
E. Occasionally Y [] N []
F. Infrequently Y [] N []
G. E-mail only Y [] N []

8. What types of applications will be used and by what percentage of users?

A. Word processing Y [] N [] _____ %
B. Spreadsheets Y [] N [] _____ %
C. Database program Y [] N [] _____ %
D. Accounting program Y [] N [] _____ %
E. Presentation graphics Y [] N [] _____ %
F. Windows Y [] N [] _____ %
G. CAD/CAM Y [] N [] _____ %
H. Other Y [] N [] _____ %

9. What is the average size document or file your users produce?

____

10. How many new documents or files do your users produce on average per day?

____

11. What types of user desktop operating systems will you connect to the network?

A. DOS Y [] N [] _____ %
B. UNIX Y [] N [] _____ %
C. OS/2 Y [] N [] _____ %
D. Macintosh Y [] N [] _____ %
E. Windows NT Y [] N [] _____ %
F. Other Y [] N [] _____ %

12. Do your users dial out using modems? If so, how many users dial out on average per day? What is the average size of files your users download?

____

13. Do any users work at home or travel frequently?

____

14. Do you have any special connectivity needs?

A. IBM mainframe or mini	Y [ ]	N [ ]
B. Remote UNIX host	Y [ ]	N [ ]
C. Internet access	Y [ ]	N [ ]
D. Other access	Y [ ]	N [ ]

If yes, what type of other access?

____

15. On a scale of 1 to 10 (1 being least important, 10 being most important), rate the following:

A. Computer speed and performance?

1 2 3 4 5 6 7 8 9 10

B. Network security?

1 2 3 4 5 6 7 8 9 10

C. The ability to withstand disasters?

1 2 3 4 5 6 7 8 9 10

Now each question is examined to determine what your answers mean to your network plan.

How Many Users Will Be on the Network?

A question that's necessary to determine the number of nodes on the network. Also, you determine from this answer the number of network segments that are needed. You can expect a healthy network to handle anywhere from 20 to 40 nodes on a single segment. You are not fully able to determine the number of segments until you have determined the answer to question 8, "What types of applications...." Heavier applications create more traffic on the LAN. A segment with 10 database users could equal the traffic of a segment with 40 word processors.

Each additional segment in the network means adding a device to separate the segments. The devices could include repeaters, hubs, bridges, or routers. You could, for example, place additional network cards in the file server. Each card can handle its own segment. If this is the case, you use the file server's internal routing capability. Repeaters and hubs do not isolate network traffic. These devices are used mainly to add distance to a LAN segment.

Figure 9.1 illustrates this technique. In the portion of the figure labeled *Before*, you see a single file server with a single network interface card connected to the LAN. The LAN consists of 85 workstations on 5 separate segments connected using repeaters. The problem with this network is that since repeaters do not filter network traffic, all nodes have to contend with the traffic generated by the other nodes on the network.

In the portion of figure 9.1 labeled *After*, you see a simple solution to the problem of too much network traffic. Two additional network interface cards are placed in the file server. The network is then split into 3 fairly equal segments. Two of the segments have 28 workstations each. The third segment has 29 workstations. Each segment is directly connected to the file server. Not only does this cut the traffic on each segment to 1/3 of what it was before, but each workstation has a more direct path to the server.

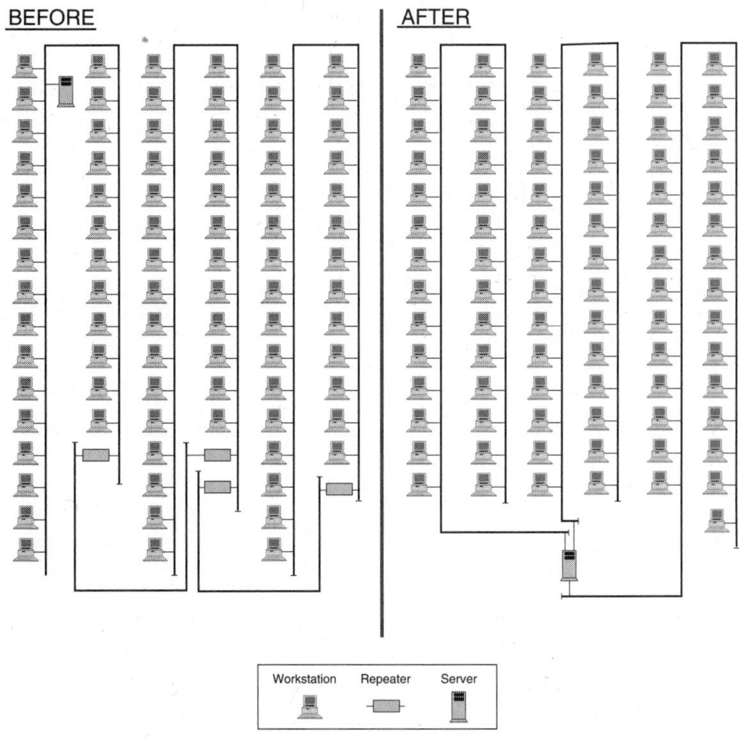

Figure 9.1

"Before" and "after" segmenting the network.

Note Even though NetWare 4.1 permits you to install 16 cards in a file server, it is not advisable to place more than four network cards in a single file server. Additional cards place a burden on the file server, which must process workstation requests

continues

coming in from each network card. Also, the file server hardware can become more and more difficult to configure. Each additional network card reduces the number of available interrupts, I/O addresses, and memory addresses on the file server.

If you find you need more than four NICs in a file server, consider adding an external router, an external bridge, or an additional file server.

What Type of Growth Do You Estimate in Your Company?

This question is tied to the first question. If you determine that your company will grow rapidly in the next several months, you need to plan for corresponding growth in the network. If the growth is limited or will take place over a long period of time, the need for more equipment and software is less critical.

How Many Locations Will Be Connected to the Network?

The answer to this question determines whether you need some sort of WAN connectivity. If there is only one location, you need to consider how much total distance is involved. A major law firm in San Francisco, for example, has one location. This location, however, spans several floors of a building that is a quarter of a mile long.

The next questions give you an idea of what type of WAN connection you might need.

What are the Shortest and Longest Distances between Locations?

If the longest distance is more than a couple of miles, you are getting beyond the range of typical Ethernet or ARCnet LANs. If the range is more than 100 miles, you are getting beyond the range of an FDDI network. Would it be feasible to consider cabling locations under 100 miles apart with fiber-optic cable? A state agency in Sacramento, California, for example, has two locations on either side of a busy interstate freeway. It was not possible for them to run cable between the two locations even though the distance was under a mile. They instead considered two alternatives: a microwave link or leasing a dedicated phone line. The initial cost of installing a microwave link would have been prohibitive, but was justified in the long run. Discussions with the phone company resulted in a substantial price break. In the end, this agency ended up leasing a T1 digital phone line.

What is the Average Size File or Document Transferred between Locations?

If the average size file or document is under 100 KB (100,000 bytes), the next question is how frequently files are transferred. If transfers are infrequent (once or twice a day or less) and the average size of the file is less than 100 KB, you would consider some sort of asynchronous package using standard dial-up phone lines. An example would be one of dial-in/dial-out solutions mentioned earlier, such as the U.S. Robotics modem server package or a simple terminal program that waits for someone to dial up (such as Procomm Plus). Another alternative is to equip users with an e-mail package with the ability to “attach” a file to a message.

On the other hand, if the average size file is over 100 KB and transfers take place constantly or several times a day, a more permanent solution might be desirable. Solutions for this sort of situation include remote bridges or routers and dedicated phone lines. Better access at higher speeds usually results in a substantial increase in cost.

How Frequently Is Data Transferred between Locations?

If you determine that the data transferred is only e-mail, you might want to consider one of several types of e-mail gateways. Products that meet this need include Novell’s Global MHS, or a competing product such as Lotus Development’s cc:Mail. Alternatively, you could subscribe to services such as MCI’s mail system.

Substantial and frequent data transfers, where the file sizes are over 100 KB and continuous access is required between locations, call for the more expensive solutions mentioned earlier (remote bridges, routers, and dedicated phone lines).

What Types of Applications Will Be Used and by What Percentage of Users?

The answer to this question determines what kind of load to expect on your network. Network “load” is an elusive item. This term describes the combined performance impact of network traffic and how fast the file server can pass information to and from its hard drives. The best way to monitor network traffic is using a network analysis tool (such as Novell’s LANalyzer for Windows). File server disk processing can be monitored using the MONITOR.NLM utility (described in detail in Chapter 39, “Monitoring the File Server”).

Network load cannot be defined precisely without a knowledge of these tools. For these purposes, a "load factor" is assigned based on a scale of 1 to 10, with 1 being the lightest and 10 being the heaviest. To determine the relative loads of different blends of users and applications, use the formula and factors listed in table 9.1. Add the results together for each application you use to compute your total load factor.

Table 9.1
Load Factors

Application	Load Factor
Word Processing	2
Spreadsheets	2
Database Programs	8
Accounting Programs	7
Windows (on the file server)	4
CAD/CAM	6
Presentation Graphics	5

Formula: Application Load Factor = Number of Users * Load Factor * Percentage of Use Total Load Factor = SUM of (Application Load Factors)

As an example, consider the two following scenarios:

Scenario 1

200 users

Word Processing: 80%

Spreadsheets: 20%

Windows: 60%

Database Programs: 10%

Using the formula once for each type of application, you get the following results:

```
Word Processing   = 200 * 2 * 80% =    320
Spreadsheets      = 200 * 2 * 20% =     80
Windows           = 200 * 4 * 60% =    480
```

```
Database Programs = 200 * 8 * 10% =    160
Total Load Factor =                   1040
```

Scenario 2

100 users

Word Processing: 80%

Spreadsheets: 80%

Database Programs: 50%

Accounting Programs: 50%

```
Word Processing     = 100 * 2 * 80% =    160
Spreadsheets        = 100 * 2 * 80% =    160
Database Programs   = 100 * 8 * 50% =    400
Accounting Programs = 100 * 7 * 50% =    350
Total Load Factor =                     1070
```

As you can see, even though Scenario 2 has half as many users as Scenario 1, the load factor is higher because the programs these users use place a heavier strain on the file server and network.

The load factor can be used to determine if a proposed mix of users and applications will work well on the new network you are in the process of installing. In order for the calculation of the load factor for your network to have any meaning, you must perform the load factor calculation for a "healthy" network first: you need a benchmark. Gather statistics on a network where users have few or no complaints.

Once you have determined the load factor for a network you consider to be performing well, you can use this as a measuring stick for any new network. If the load factor for the new network is 25% or more above the load factor for a healthy network, you know that you will have to take measures to compensate for the heavier load. These measures should be based on the healthy network.

- Decrease the number of users or change the applications mix by moving users or applications off the new network.
- Put a server on the new network with a faster and/or more powerful CPU. For example, use a computer with a Pentium chip running at 90 mhz instead of a 486 running at 66 mhz.
- Improve the disk performance by using a faster controller (use a SCSI-II instead of SCSI, for example) and/or a hard drive with faster access time.

- Add a better network adapter to the file servers. For example, you could add a network adapter with an internal cache buffer, or add an EISA network adapter instead of an ISA adapter.

What Is the Average Number and Size of Documents Produced?

The questions discussed here pertain to the average size document, how many are produced each day. The answers to these questions have an impact on the amount of disk space you will need. You can take the answer to the first question, along with the answer to the second question, and multiply it by the number of users on the network to determine disk requirements. It is also best to add a "fudge factor" of 5 MB per user. The final total should be doubled to leave room for expansion. Just think of the file server's hard drive like a closet—users will eventually fill it up completely.

Here is the formula for calculating the amount of disk space needed in a year:

> Disk Space = Average File Size * Average Number of Files per Day * Number of Users * 365

For example, in a company with 200 network users who produce an average of four documents of 5,000 bytes each, here is the amount of disk space they will consume in a year (assume 250 working days):

```
Disk Space     = 5,000 * 4 * 200 * 250    = 1,000,000,000
Fudge Factor   = 200 * 5,000,000          = 1,000,000,000
Subtotal                                  = 2,000,000,000
Total Space =     Subtotal * 2            = 4,000,000,000
```

As you can see, you must prepare for 4 GB of disk space in this situation. In some cases, however, you will find that users will not consistently produce new documents each day. Most of the time they will make changes to existing documents already stored on the file server. Some users make entries into a common shared database.

One of the jobs of the network Administrator is to monitor disk space. It often is necessary to migrate old files off the server from time to time to conserve disk space. NetWare 4.1 has an automatic data migration feature that saves you much time. In addition, NetWare 4.1 automatically compresses files which have not been accessed in 7 days. The default of 7 days can be adjusted down to 1 day. File compression will result in up to a 60% savings in disk space.

What Types of User Desktop Operating Systems Will You Connect to the Network?

This question gives you an idea of what type of software you might need on your file servers. If all your users use DOS and OS/2, the software to connect to the file server is already included with NetWare. If your users operate Macintosh or UNIX workstations, you might need additional software, depending on what type of access to the file server is required. A 50-user version of NetWare for Macintosh is included with NetWare 4.1. NetWare for Macintosh is not automatically installed when you install NetWare 4.1. Be sure to install this package if you have Macintosh users on the network. If the UNIX users are using UnixWare, NetWare connectivity is already included. You will have to install the NUC (NetWare Unix Client) software, which is included with UnixWare, on the NetWare 4.1 file server. Other UNIX users can access the NetWare server when you install NetWare TCP/IP (included with NetWare 4.1) and NetWare NFS (not included).

Questions Pertaining to Remote Access

Questions pertaining to remote access include the following:

- Do your users dial out using modems?
- If so, how many users dial out on average per day?
- What is the average size of files your users download?
- Do any users work at home or travel frequently?

The answers to these questions give you a picture of your dial-out and dial-in needs. You might need to consider purchasing modem server solutions to handle users working out of the office. Users in the office might need access to bulletin boards or on-line services. The average size of a file the users download impacts the amount of server disk space you need, and also the speed of the modems they require. Refer back to Chapter 1, "Elements of a Simple Network," for further discussion on dial-in and dial-out solutions.

Do You Have Any Special Connectivity Needs?

Special connectivity needs arise when you need to give users access to specialized equipment. This can include any of the following:

- **Mainframes.** There are many different types of mainframes in operation today. These range from the large super computers such as those made by Cray Manufacturing, to the "micro mainframes" which consist of dozens of microprocessors operating in parallel. Mainframe vendors include IBM, Amdahl, Cray, Tandem, and Hitachi.

- **Minicomputers.** Minicomputers enjoyed a decade of popularity in the 1970s. The dividing line between a minicomputers, mainframes, and microcomputers is blurred today. Many of today's microcomputers are as or more powerful than the minicomputers of the 1970s. Minicomputer vendors include IBM, Digital Equipment Corporation (DEC), and Hewlett Packard (HP).

- **Online services.** These services provide a variety of services. WestLaw, for example, provides an online legal research database. CompuServe provides various vendor forums, including Novell and Microsoft, as well as home shopping and travel services.

- **The Internet.** The Internet is a vast, public domain, network of networks. The Internet has literally thousands of user interest areas. Usenet, for example, provides the latest news. The World Wide Web (WWW) is a network of servers within the Internet that provides research and entertainment services including text, sound, and graphics. More and more companies are looking at ways of commercially exploiting this network of 21 million interconnected computer systems. The federal government is looking at ways of regulating it.

Special connectivity needs generally imply considerable added cost. You need to consider specialized hardware and software needed to connect to the other environments. Gateway software (such as NetWare for SAA) might be required to convert NetWare protocols to the protocols used by the remote systems. Connecting different environments also implies configuring the file server to handle multiple protocols. Refer to Chapter 2, "Elements of a Complex Network," for further discussion of the various types of hardware needed for special connectivity needs.

Speed, Performance, Security, and Disaster Recovery

Answers to these types of questions will give you an idea of what type of hardware to purchase. If computer speed and performance rank high, you will want to consider computers with high clock speeds, powerful microprocessors, and fast hard drives.

If network security is a big issue, you should look at network management and virus protection programs. You should also carefully document network security settings as you implement them. Security conscious networks also have Auditing enabled with strict criteria on what gets audited, and what types of audit reports are expected.

A high rating on the question on the ability to withstand disasters should lead you towards the purchase of *fault tolerant* systems. Look into mirroring, duplexing, or RAID drive arrays. You should also have a good backup system with a good rotation scheme where backup media is taken off-site on a regular basis.

Planning the Logical Structure (NDS)

Planning the structure of your NDS tree can be very simple or extremely complicated. A possible approach is to create the simplest possible structure. Many companies implementing NetWare 4.*x* networks have found that containers will support thousands of objects. Theoretically, there is no limit on the number of objects in a single container. The primary limit in NetWare 4.1 is that imposed by the software tools used to manage the NDS. The current limit imposed is 40,000 objects per container.

Remaining flexible and open to change is an important attribute for any network Administrator. It is important to have more than one plan ready. With this in mind you could design a very simple structure of one, or a few, key Organization or Organizational Units. Once this design has been accomplished, you can turn your attention to designing a more suitable and more manageable structure. If you run out of time before you must implement the structure, you can fall back to your simple design. Once the logical structure has been implemented, it is easy to move objects around. Even the most careful of plans can end up changed when confronted with the reality of implementing the network.

As you plan the tree, you might find that you want to involve more people in the company in the planning process. Remember that more people involved in the NDS planning process means that it will take longer. Studies have been done indicating that the time involved to reach a consensus on planning a project increases exponentially with each new person added. You might also ultimately lose control over the process entirely.

NDS Tree Planning Approaches

The NDS tree should model your company. You are putting an image of how your company operates onto the network. Highly structured companies end up with a highly structured tree. NDS tree planning techniques tend to center around either the organizational chart of the company or its geographical layout. The organizational chart approach organizes the tree according to the company's divisions, departments, and titles. The geographical approach favors how the company is physically situated.

As an example, take the United States government. Figure 9.2 shows you a sample NDS tree using the organizational approach. The tree is organized according to job titles and positions.

Figure 9.3, in contrast, shows you a sample NDS tree for the same organization, the U.S. government, using the geographical approach. This tree is organized according to the location of the various departments and entities rather than by titles and positions.

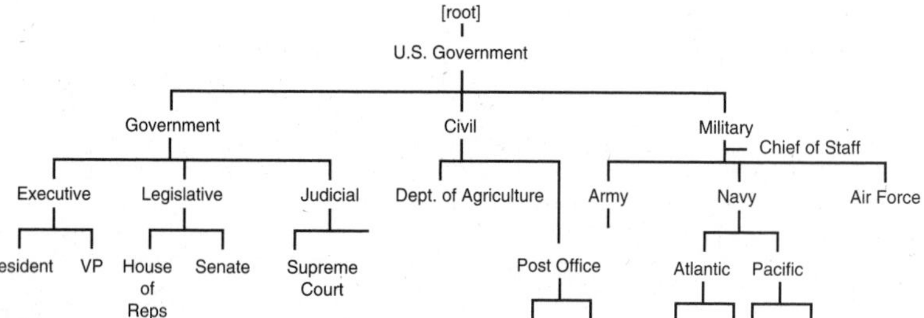

Figure 9.2

A sample NDS tree using the organizational approach.

Making Changes As You Go

The tree is not set in stone. As your network grows and progresses, you will find yourself making frequent adjustments and changes. Various requests will come in from different departments that you can consider and implement.

Leaf objects can be moved easily from one container to another. Tools that enable you to prune and graft the tree, unavailable in NetWare 4.0*x*, are available in NetWare 4.1. *Pruning* is where you can cut out entire branches of the tree. *Grafting* is where you can take the branch that has been cut off and move it to another location on the tree. NetWare 4.1 also includes tools that enable you to merge two NDS trees together.

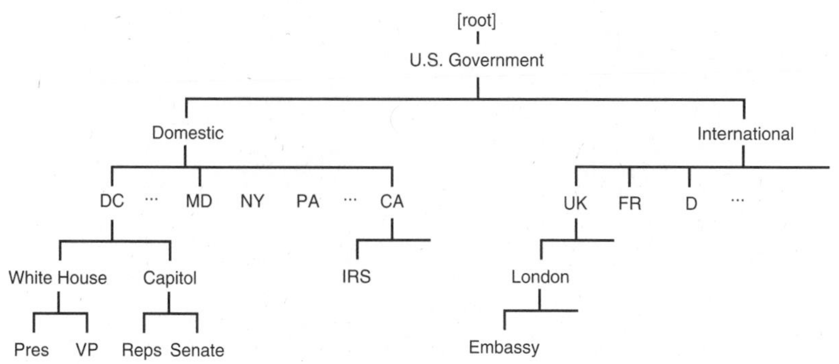

Figure 9.3

A sample NDS tree using the geographical approach.

The best tool currently available for making large scale changes to the tree is the Windows-based NWADMIN utility. This utility enables you to mark leaf and container objects and delete them at one time. This is much like pruning. To perform the equivalent of grafting, you have to use the PARTMGR, or the Partition Manager Tool in NWADMIN. The container to be moved must be designated as the start of a partition. Once this operation has been completed, the container can be moved. NWADMIN is explained in more detail in Chapter 20, "Managing Objects and Properties."

Some changes you make affect users on the network. Users are affected when you move their container or move them to another container. They need to know their new complete NDS name. You might need to change the default context specified in the NET.CFG file on their workstations. The users need to be informed of any changes to the objects in their containers, such as printers and print queues. Security rights access might have to be updated. Although changes can easily be made, the change should be carefully planned out.

The Simple Approach and the Complex Approach

As you are setting up your NDS tree, it is important to note that you can design either an extremely complicated and elaborate structure or a simple one. Remember that you can always make changes later. The simple approach should be favored when you do not have the time to completely plan and implement the structure. The manual operation of building the structure takes very little time. Documenting procedures, training users, and configuring workstations takes much more time.

The simple approach involves creating a small number of containers, with a large number of leaf objects in each. The complex approach involves a large number of containers, with a small number of leaf objects in each. Figure 9.4 shows you an example of the complex approach for a large law firm. Figure 9.5 shows you an example of the simple approach for the same firm.

As you can see from figure 9.4, the firm itself was represented as the top level organization (O=XYZ_Assocs). Each location was identified as an organizational unit under O=XYZ_Assocs. Thus OU=SF.O=XYZ_Assocs represents the San Francisco office. Each office is then divided into departments: Administrative, Word Processing, Paralegal, Secretaries, and Attorneys. The organizational unit OU=WP.OU=SF.O=XYZ_Assocs represents the Word Processing department in the San Francisco office. Leaf objects are then placed under these containers. The attorney Larry Ulm in NY is represented as the object .CN=LUlm.OU=Atty.OU=NY.O=XYZ_Assocs.

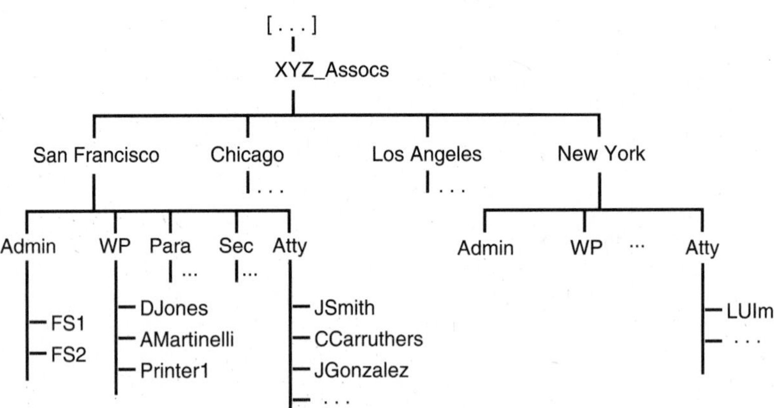

Figure 9.4
A sample NDS tree using the complex approach.

The example in figure 9.5 shows the same organization with a simplified structure. In this example, the top level organization has been removed. In its place, the name of the tree represents the organization. This makes sense because there is no need to have the organization name as the top level organization unless there are separate companies represented within the tree. General Motors, for example, has Chevrolet, Pontiac, Buick, and other companies under the parent organization. For the purposes of the law firm XYZ Associates, the branch office locations have been moved to the position of organizations. Thus, the office in Los Angeles is now simply O=LA. In figure 9.5, the subdivisions within each office have been eliminated. All leaf objects have been consolidated to one container. The attorney Juan Gonzalez in the San Francisco office is designated as .CN=JGonzalez.O=SF.

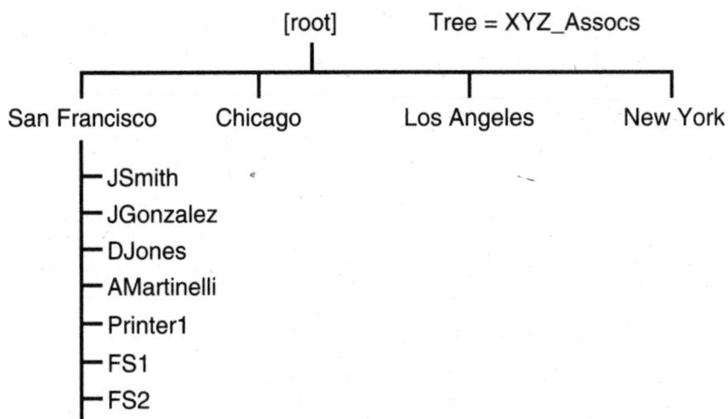

Figure 9.5

A sample NDS tree using the simple approach.

Taking Inventory of Necessary Equipment for the Network

Now that you have had a chance to grasp some of the major concepts behind network planning, both logical and physical, it is time to take inventory of the necessary equipment to properly implement your network. This section focuses on the network itself and workstations. The next section gives you some pointers on selecting equipment specifically for the file server.

Computers

At this point, you need to gather pricing and information on what kinds of computers you want to use as workstations. Recent price wars between hardware vendors have resulted in a buyer's market. Several issues need to be addressed. These include what level quality is needed, how much you have to spend, how much speed is needed at the desktop, and what kind of workstation disk space is needed. The initial discussion begins with a look at the "quality versus quantity" issue.

Quality versus Quantity

The issue of quality versus quantity is a classic one that is much discussed in many areas, including computer networking. As a general rule, the higher the quality, the higher the cost. If you need a large number of computers, can you afford high quality machines? One way to look at this issue is in terms of how long you need to use this equipment and the cost of a computer being down.

If you are working on a project that will last for a relatively short period of time, you might decide to forego quality to achieve lower prices. For example, if you are installing a network in a campaign headquarters for the next governor of Ohio, you know that the use of the computers is limited in duration for the next year or so. In this case, it might be more economical to purchase a lower quality, less expensive computer.

Some high quality manufacturers, on the other hand, offer substantial discounts on volume purchases. If you are purchasing a large number of computers, some vendors give you a price break that makes it more economical to purchase the high quality computer compared to a less expensive, lower quality model.

The advantage to having a large quantity of computers is that you could buy enough computers to have one or two spares. This way, if a computer breaks down, you can quickly replace it and send the defective unit out for repair or replacement.

When a computer is down, the computer user is not able to do her job as she did before. There is a cost associated with this user not working. At its simplest, the cost of a computer being down equals the cost to repair the computer, plus the salary of the computer user, plus the value of the work that person would have produced. For example, a mail order company might assign one computer to each order entry clerk. The company produces $60,000 worth of orders each day. Each clerk is paid $20,000 a year. The cost of a computer being down for one day would be

Cost of repairs	$100
Salary of the clerk	$76
Orders Produced	$10,000
Total Amount Lost	$10,176

Higher quality computers are more resilient and break down less often than lower quality computers. If you take proper precautions, however, you can extend the life of a lower quality computer. Precautions would include the following:

- Do not move the computer once installed.
- Prevent dust, dirt, and other contaminants from getting inside the computer.
- Ensure that your electrical system is properly grounded.
- Plug each computer into a computer-rated electrical surge protector.
- Run quarterly diagnostics.

Brand Names Versus Clones

The word "clone" is an interesting one in the computer industry. This word was not in popular use prior to the introduction of the IBM PC in 1981. A *clone* computer became a computer that matches the IBM specifications but is not manufactured by IBM. Since that time, several of the clone vendors have gained a reputation for quality. These vendors are generally known as "brand names." Brand name vendors include Compaq, AST, and Hewlett Packard. Other clone vendors have intensely loyal followings and may well have the same quality as IBM and the brand name vendors.

As with automobiles, you must carefully research the brand of computer you plan to purchase. The recent price wars have put many of the smaller clone vendors out of business and have resulted in a radical reduction in prices among the major vendors, including IBM. "Brand name" is no longer synonymous with "expensive." Computer magazines such as *Byte*, *PC Magazine*, and *PC Week* frequently have articles that analyze the performance, cost, and support issues of various computers. These magazines are a valuable source of information on the latest prices and features of the computers available.

386, 486, and Pentium

You will see the terms 386, 486, and Pentium bantered about quite liberally in computer magazines and ads. *386* refers to the 80386, and *486* refers to the 80486 Intel microprocessors. These two microprocessors are very similar in design. They feature a 32-bit internal architecture, meaning that they can process data 4 bytes in length. They can also address large amounts of RAM. The 80486 offers additional features over the 80386. The 80486 includes an area of cache memory used exclusively by the microprocessor for its internal calculations. The 80486 (except for the 80486 SX) also includes a *math coprocessor* that assists in calculations. The net result is that the 80486 offers a substantial speed improvement over a comparable 80386.

The Pentium microprocessor is actually an 80586. Due to recent court decisions, as well as marketing considerations, Intel decided to rename the series to Pentium. The Pentium offers a 64-bit internal data bus, as well as other improvements. A computer with a Pentium chip for its microprocessor offers a substantial improvement in speed over an 80486-based computer. Each microprocessor has the capability to run DOS-based applications and is backwards compatible with other Intel based microprocessors. Current software does not make a distinction between computers using an 80386, 80486, or Pentium microprocessor.

One issue is how much "horsepower" to place on users' desktops. The answer to this question depends on what types of applications you use and the expectations of your users (and management). If, for example, your primary applications are e-mail and word processing, a lower-powered computer, such as an 80386-based computer, might be sufficient. If, on the other hand, you use Windows or other graphics-based applications, an 80486- or Pentium-based computer is more appropriate.

The cost difference between an 80386- and 80486-based computer is negligible. Vendors are concentrating on producing 80486-based systems currently and are gearing up for Pentium-based systems. The sales of 80386-based computers are on the decline. The cost of a Pentium-based system is substantially higher than that of an 80486-based system. A typical 80486-based system, for example, runs anywhere from $500 to $2,000, depending on how much RAM, the size of the hard drive, and the type of monitor. A typical Pentium-based system ranges in price from $1,500 for a "barebones" system (1 MB of RAM, no hard drive, no monitor), to $3,000 or more. Prices are lower each day as more vendors produce more versions of the Pentium-based computer systems.

PowerPCs and RISC Computers

Many new computer technologies are now available. These include the PowerPC and the Reduced Instruction Set Computer (RISC) computer systems. The PowerPC is the result of a joint development effort between IBM, Apple, and Motorola. The result is a new microprocessor that promises more horsepower than a Pentium microprocessor. RISC microprocessors improve performance by reducing the number of instructions hard wired into the microprocessor itself. Both technologies offer considerable performance improvements over the classic Intel 80*x*86 series of microprocessors.

As with any new technology, there are problems. The major problem is compatibility with existing software. Companies over the years have actually invested more money in software than in hardware. The software for the microcomputer industry is primarily based on the Intel 80*x*86 series of microprocessors. A Pentium-based computer, for example, could run the same software designed for an IBM PC in 1981. The new systems offer (in some cases) a high degree of compatibility, but there are even problems with the software that is supposed to be compatible. If you decide you are interested in the performance of the new systems, such as RISC or PowerPC, you will need to investigate which software packages will work with these systems.

Systems based on the PowerPC offer the interesting capability of being able to run both Apple Macintosh and IBM PC-based software. If you are in a situation where you need access to both types of software, you might want to investigate these systems further.

With or Without Hard Drives?

Another question you need to decide is whether to equip each user's workstation with a hard drive, and what size hard drive you should buy. Installing workstations on a computer network gives you the option of installing literally no disk drives whatsoever, a configuration called a *diskless workstation.* There is a separate installation procedure you need to follow. When you are done with the installation, the diskless workstation boots from a file stored on the file server.

In some cases a diskless workstation offers tremendous advantages. These include lower price, better network security, and less individual workstation management. The disadvantage is in flexibility and the ability to work even if the network is down. The price difference is obvious. Many resellers, however, offer workstations preconfigured with hard drives at attractive prices. The same reseller offering a good price on a preconfigured system might actually charge more for a system without a hard drive. In terms of security, the diskless workstation prevents users from copying files to or from the file server. This helps control the spread of computer viruses and prevents the pirating of software.

Workstations with hard drives require more management. You will need to install, partition, and format the hard drives. You will need to install an operating system (DOS), build a directory structure, and install the network shell software. If you decide to upgrade the version of DOS running on a workstation, you will need to either instruct users in the procedure (dangerous), or go to each workstation and do it yourself. Diskless workstations get their version of DOS from a file stored on the file server. To upgrade DOS on diskless workstations, you would simply update the file on the server.

If the network goes down, the diskless workstation is rendered useless. A workstation with a hard drive, on the other hand, can continue to operate, provided single-user versions of the software are available. In the event of network failure, you could restore files onto individual workstations, allowing users to continue with their work until the network is restored.

Network Cards

You base your selection of a Network Interface Card (NIC) upon several considerations. The first question you need to investigate is what types of equipment and cabling already exist in your organization. You might very well find that one of the departments within your organization has already invested in a particular technology.

HP minicomputers, for example, were widely used to manage inventory and accounting. You might find that one of the groups within your company has a minicomputer with a number of terminals running on Ethernet or token ring.

You might find that one or more of the buildings within your organization is already wired with a certain type of cabling. RG-62 cabling was heavily used in the mainframe environment in the 1970s, for example. If this is the case, you might consider using the existing cabling with ARCnet network cards. If you find your building wired with twisted-pair wiring, you have the option of using either token ring or 10BASE-T Ethernet.

Another consideration is the speed required for your applications. You might want to review the preceding section on determining your network load to get an idea how much load you will place on the network. For the average office using primarily word processing and spreadsheet applications, ARCnet, Ethernet or token ring will do the job. If the network load is great, you might consider Ethernet or token ring, which will process information more quickly under heavier loads. Token ring is considered the most constant performer under heavy network loads; however, it is also the most expensive of the three.

Other types of network cards are available, depending on your needs. *Fiber Distributed Digital Interface* (FDDI) is a high-speed interface that uses a fiber-optic cable. Due to its efficient design, FDDI achieves speeds 10 to 20 times faster than Ethernet, and 5 to 20 times faster than token ring. The disadvantages of FDDI are that it requires a fiber-optic cable and the cost of the individual NIC is higher. Wireless NICs are available that require no cabling at all. Transmission speeds are comparable to ARCnet and are getting faster as the technology improves. Another new technology is fast Ethernet running at a raw transmission speed of 100 mbps. This technology uses a variety of wiring techniques, one of which is to use the standard RJ-45 connector (much like a large modular phone plug), with eight wires instead of the four required by 10BASE-T Ethernet. *Copper Distributed Digital Interface* (CDDI) is a copper-based technology derived from FDDI. This type of NIC uses standard token ring cabling and achieves a raw data transmission rate of 100 mbps.

You can mix and match different types of NICs. The only rule is that only one type of NIC can be used per physical cabling segment. For each type of NIC on the workstation, you must have the same type of NIC in either a file server or router to which the workstation is connected. Figure 9.6 illustrates a network of mixed types of NICs. The number of NICs on a physical network cabling segment depends on the rules of the type of cabling you have selected. This is covered in greater detail in *NetWare 4.1 for*

Professionals by New Riders Publishing. One suggestion to maintain the integrity of your network is to stay with one vendor for all NICs on a single physical cabling segment. If you decide on Ethernet, for example, and prefer 3Com, it is suggested that you use 3Com NICs on all nodes on a given segment. The reason for this suggestion is that each vendor has slightly different limitations and features on their products. When you mix vendors on a single cabling segment, you might find that some nodes work and others don't.

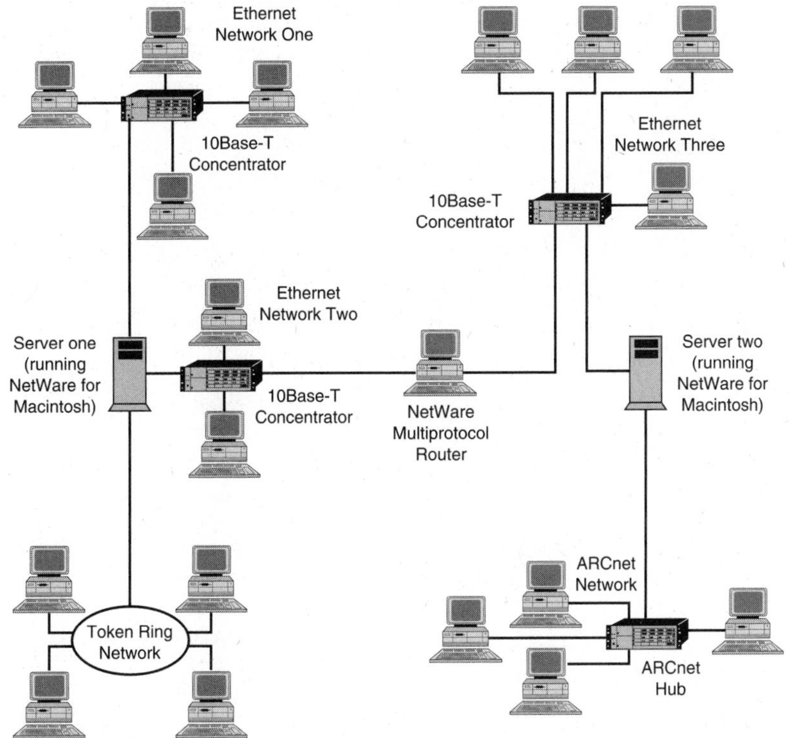

Figure 9.6
Mixed NICs in a network.

Probably the most important consideration is cost. In general, the faster the NIC, the more expensive it is. Table 9.2 gives you an idea of the types of NICs and their price ranges.

Table 9.2
Popular Types of NICs

Type of NIC	Price Range	Raw Speed	Vendors
Ethernet	$50 to $900	10 mbps	3Com, Accton, Intel, Novell/Eagle, Celan, SMC/Western Digital, Thomas Conrad, IBM, HP, Xircom, Cogent, D-Link, Dayna, Edimax, EFA, Interphase, Katron, MacNet, National Semiconductor, Olicom, Racal Interlan, Sureman, SVEC, Zenith
Token Ring	$270 to $1000	4–16 mbps	IBM, 3Com, Intel, Novell/Microdyne, Thomas Conrad, Proteon, SMC, Xircom, Cray Communications, DCA, Madge, Racal Interlan, Racore, SMC
ARCnet	$50 to $400	2.5 mbps	SMC, Thomas Conrad, Xircom, Datapoint, Xinetron
TCNS ARCnet	$350 to $1600	100 mbps	Thomas Conrad
FDDI	$800 to $6700	100 mbps	3Com, Microdyne, Cabletron, IBM, Madge, Network Peripherals, Rockwell, Syskonnect National Semiconductor
CDDI	$600 to $2000	100 mbps	IBM, Madge, Microdyne, National Semiconductor
Wireless	$395 to $10000	1 - 16 mbps	Alps, Schindler, AT&T, Cabletron, DEC, NCR, Photonics, Proxim, Windata, Xircom

Cabling and Connectors

The type of cabling you choose is tied to the type of NIC you select. Several factors influence the cable you select, including the following:

- Cost
- Distance
- Degree of EMI (Electromagnetic Interference)
- Existing cabling
- Type of existing NICs

The presence of existing cabling might persuade you to continue to use this type of cabling. The advantage is that you can save money otherwise spent in installing new cabling. The disadvantage is that you have no guarantees as to its condition.

If you contract the cabling to a company that specializes in it, you incur high costs, but the cabling is generally guaranteed. Cabling specialists get the cabling installed quickly and have the necessary permits. When you cable a building, various local, state, and federal government ordinances come into play. The cable must be fire retardant and must not emit a noxious gas if it burns. Cabling companies are prepared to deal with these rules and regulations. They charge on a per node basis, plus the cost of materials.

If the cable you buy is precut and premade, you will pay a higher price than buying cable in bulk. If you buy bulk cable, you must be prepared to manufacture your own connectors. This involves purchasing the endings and a special set of tools for wire cutting, stripping, and crimping.

There are many different types of cables. Coaxial cable can consist of either copper or aluminum. The center of the cable can be solid core or can consist of a series of strands wrapped around each other. The *shielding* is an outer metallic wrap between the outer plastic coating and the inner plastic coating. Figure 9.7 illustrates a cross-section of a coaxial cable. There are different types of shielding. One style features a copper braid, tightly meshed to protect against EMI. Another, less expensive, style features an aluminum foil wrap. Coaxial cabling is known for its high resistance to EMI. The cost of a coaxial cable can vary from 20 cents per foot to as high as $7 or $8 per foot, depending on the type of cable.

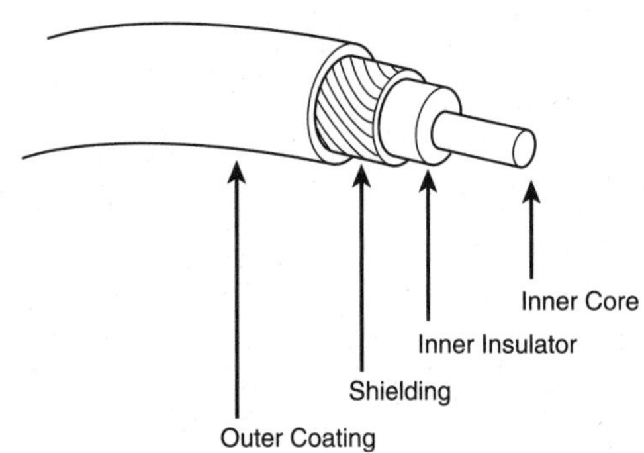

Figure 9.7

A cross-section of a coaxial cable.

Twisted-pair cable typically consists of two pairs of wires. Some cable installers prefer four pairs of wires in case one or more wires break. Each wire in a pair is twisted around its partner approximately seven times per foot. Each pair of wires is twisted around the other pair(s) three or four times a foot. The reason the wires are twisted is to prevent the buildup of EMI. When signal is traveling on the wire, it radiates electromagnetic energy. If the wires were not twisted, this energy would quickly build up into what is referred to as a *standing wave.* Essentially, the wire would turn into an antenna. The signals would start to travel and would interfere with the transmission and reception of data on the network.

Twisted-pair cable is used in 10BASE-T Ethernet, token ring, and CDDI. The cost of a twisted-pair wire ranges from 8 to 50 cents per foot, depending on how many pairs of wires and the nature and composition of the cable. Twisted-pair cable, even when shielded, is susceptible to EMI.

Fiber-optic cable is used for FDDI and other high-speed transmissions. It carries an *optical* signal instead of an electrical signal. Because fiber-optic cable carries patterns of light, it is completely immune to EMI. The optical fibers themselves are either glass or a high grade plastic. The signal currently travels in one direction only, so two strands are required for each NIC. FDDI specifications allow each NIC to support two rings, in which case four strands are required.

The fiber-optic strands are enclosed in a tough mesh often made of a material similar to that used in bullet-proof vests. The mesh is then enclosed in a plastic sheaf, giving the cable an appearance similar to a Thin Ethernet coaxial cable. Fiber-optic cable is often installed with multiple strands in case one of the strands is broken. Large installations install trunk cables with hundreds of strands to support data, voice, and video transmissions.

Fiber-optic cable is not designed for sharp bends, but most modern cable can support a bend of up to 10 times its diameter. Tool kits are available to assist you in attaching your own connectors or for splicing the cable. The cost of a typical 6-strand spool of fiber-optic cable is around $1.50 per foot.

Routers, Bridges, and Switches

After you have decided how many network segments you want to have on your network, you will need to add routers or bridges to connect the individual segments together. Routers and bridges are discussed in Chapter 2, "Elements of a Complex Network." For more information, please see another New Riders Publishing book, *NetWare 4.1 for Professionals.*

Routers are needed when the physical distance of the network exceeds the distance specified by the vendor of the NIC you have chosen. ARCnet networks, for example, specify that the network cannot exceed 20,000 feet. Although your building might not be 20,000 feet long, the distance is eaten up quickly when cabling. You might need to run cable across cubicles, up walls, over partitions, and across drop ceilings. Routers need to be placed at strategic locations to extend the distance of a network. You might end up using the routing capabilities of a file server rather than purchasing a stand-alone router.

In the case of a WAN, the router should be placed so that it can access the dedicated phone connection as well as the LAN. You need one router on each end of the dedicated phone connection. Most routers have a utility or command that can be issued to see if the connection is being made properly. Figure 9.8 illustrates a complex network with routers and other connections.

Bridge and router technology have started to blend. Bridges are now generally more intelligent to the point where they are almost routers. Bridges are used primarily where you need a fast connection between LANs that supports multiple protocols. Bridges have the advantage of being "plug-and-play." This means that when you buy a bridge, it is a self-contained unit the just needs to be plugged into the LAN and powered up. A certain amount of configuration is required in most cases.

Bridges also perform the function, unlike a repeater, of filtering network traffic, as explained in Chapter 2. Furthermore, multiple protocols do not interfere with the operation of a bridge. Because a bridge operates at the OSI data link layer, network protocols, which reside at the OSI network layer, are not visible to the bridge.

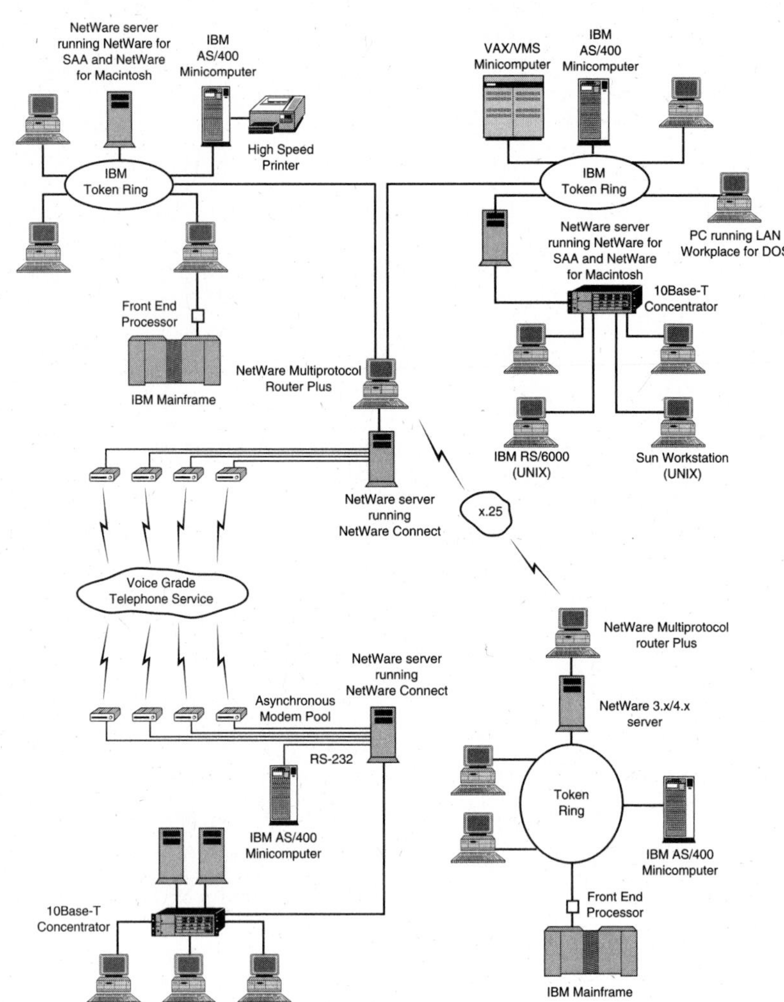

Figure 9.8
A complex network with routers.

Bridges are specific to the media and type of network adapter used. Prices range from $4,000 to $35,000. Vendors include 3Com, Accton Technology, Advanced Computer Communications, Allied Telesis, Andrew, Cabletron, Chipcom, Cisco Systems, Cray Communications, DEC, Fibronics International, Gandalf, HP, IBM, Madge Networks, Network Systems, RAD Data Communications, Retix, and Synoptics.

Most bridge vendors offer WAN connectivity options. In this case, the bridge connects two (or more) LANs across a WAN link. The protocols supported across the WAN link vary widely and can include V.35, T1, E-1, X.25, frame relay, and ISDN.

Another device for connecting LANs is called a *switch.* A switch is usually characterized by its capability to handle voice and video information along with data. Many switches are designed to accommodate ATM (Asynchronous Transfer Mode) at speeds in excess of 45 mbps. Switch vendors include Astarte Fiber Networks, Chipcom, Cisco Systems, DEC, HP, Hughes LAN Systems, IBM, Kalpana, LANnet, Network Equipment Technologies (NET), Networth, Plexcom, Synoptics, and XNet Technology. Prices for switches range from $3,000 to $100,000.

Printers

During the planning stage, you need decide on how many and what types of printers are needed for your network. You can review the different types of printers listed in Chapter 1, "Elements of a Simple Network." A good rule of thumb is one printer for every four network users. Your printing needs depend on what the users plan to do on the network. Some users are responsible for entering data and are not interested in printing. Managers, on the other hand, are often interested in generating printed reports. Word processing personnel are interested in printing letters and documents.

You also need to decide how to connect the printers to the network. As mentioned in Chapter 1, some printers can be ordered with a built-in network interface. An example is the HP Laserjet IV series of printers. You can order either an Ethernet or token ring interface and connect the printer directly to the LAN. If this is the case, your job is to create a print queue and connect the queue logically to the printer using HP-supplied utilities and the NetWare PCONSOLE utility. This utility and NetWare 4.1 printing are described in more detail in Part Seven, "Printing."

You need to decide where to place the printers in your company. One possibility is to place all printers in a common location. If this is the case, you can identify the printers with brightly colored labels. You can set up the NetWare printing environment to allow users to print to the next available printer. NetWare also notifies the users when a print job is completed and which printer was used.

Alternatively, you might decide to distribute the printers evenly throughout each office. In this case, the printers are most likely attached to various workstations. You can create queues for each of these printers and provide users access to the queue assigned to the printer closest to them.

Peripherals

Various peripherals are used in a network. These include devices for connecting network cable segments together and battery backup units. This section discusses each of these and gives you some ideas of what to expect when installing your network.

Concentrators, Hubs, Repeaters, and MAUs

The devices used to connect your network cable segments together depend on what type of NIC you decided to use, and what type of cabling. Each of these types of devices was described in greater detail in Chapter 2. Unlike bridges and routers, devices such as hubs do not create a separate network. A repeater, hub, or MAU extends the distance of a single network segment.

These devices come in a variety of configurations. An ARCnet passive hub, for example, supports four connections. HP has a hub, on the other hand, that supports 48 10BASE-T connections. Different devices support different types of cable. You can order one token ring MAU, for example, to support IBM Type 1 cable, or another to support twisted-pair cable using RJ-45 connectors. Table 9.3 gives you an idea of the types of devices, what they support, price ranges, and vendors.

Table 9.3
Repeaters, Hubs, and MAUs

Device	Price Range	Supports	Vendors
10BASE-T hub	$180-3,600	Twisted pair 8–48 ports	3Com, Intel, Ethernet, HP, GVC, CeLAN, Allied Telesis, Asante, SMC, Microdyne, Synoptics, Cabletron, Canary, D-Link, David Systems, DEC, Networth, XYPlex
Repeater	$230-1,200	Thin coax 2–8 ports	3Com, CeLAN, Ethernet, Allied Telesis
MAU	$220-5,000	Token ring 4–168 ports	IBM, Proteon, Thomas Conrad, 3Com, ACE/North Hills, Cabletron, LANnet, Madge, Fibronics
Token ring repeater	$1,200-2,000	Token ring	IBM
FDDI repeater	$1,450-4,000	FDDI 8 ports	3Com/Isolan

Device	Price Range	Supports	Vendors
FDDI hub/ concentrator	$1,800-16,000	FDDI 6–24 ports	3Com/Isolan, Synoptics, Cabletron, Cisco, Fibronics,IBM, Gandalf, LANnet, Synoptics
ARCnet hub	$25-995	Coax, twisted pair active, passive 4–16 ports	SMC, Thomas Conrad, Celan, Datapoint, Xinetron

Uninterruptible Power Supplies

An *uninterruptible power supply* (UPS) has become a de facto requirement for networks. You need to make a decision at this point on which devices should have a UPS. The most important device is the file server. You also might want to designate certain critical routers, hubs, and workstations. UPS units are rated according to how fast they come on line after a power failure, how much wattage they can produce and support, and how long their batteries last.

UPS vendors include NSSI (formerly Elgar), American Power Conversion (APC), and Tripplite. Most vendors have a range of products, ranging from those that can support a single workstation to units that support several file servers and peripherals. The less expensive devices have a battery that kicks in when a power outage has been detected. The more expensive devices provide continuous online power. The continuous units always supply power from their battery. The AC current charges the battery. As a result, a power outage does not affect your system.

Some of the additional features provided by UPS vendors include monitoring software that can install on a workstation or file server. The software monitors power continuously and can give you a graph of the surges and brownouts you experience over a period of time. It also includes diagnostics that let you determine the status of the UPS at any given time. The "smarter" units gauge the amount of time a brownout occurs. If the loss of adequate power extends beyond a given period of time (1 minute, for example), the unit will issue a warning. If power is restored within the given period, the smarter units will take no action. Some units can go so far as to shut down the file server in the event of a severe power outage.

In addition to providing battery backup, some UPS units also provide line conditioning. *Line conditioning* "smoothes out" power supplied to your computer. This prevents your computer from hanging up or rebooting. When the power is unsteady, faster computer systems will react badly. The faster systems are more sensitive to power swings. In many areas, power tends to surge above acceptable parameters or momentarily drop below the computer's acceptable range. This results in memory corruption. If you find that your computer reboots or hangs up for no obvious reason (that is, not because you have a software conflict), it could be due to uneven power.

Software

In the process of planning your network, one of the most important components is the software you plan to use. Software is broken into several different categories such as operating system, e-mail, and word processing. This section discusses the types of software and gives you some guidelines for software selection.

One important distinction you need to be aware of is that some software packages are available in single-user and network (or multiuser) versions. *Single-user* versions are a license for one person to use the software at a time. This type of software is designed for a stand-alone computer. *Network* or *multiuser* software is designed to be used by more than one person at a time. Network software will indicate with which type of networks it is compatible.

General considerations for network software include the following:

- Where is the program going to be located—which server, volume, and directory?
- How many users will be using the program? How many licenses will you need to purchase?
- Does the program create individualized user setup files? Where will these files be stored?
- What kind of Security rights access is required for a user to use this program?

These questions are best answered in the program's documentation. Unfortunately, there are no universal answers to these questions. You will need to consult your network users to determine their needs.

The next section begins the discussion of specific types of network and workstation software.

Desktop Operating System

One of the first decisions you might need to make is what type of desktop operating system software to use. In many cases, the operating system software comes with the computer. Sometimes, you have to purchase it separately. The most widely used desktop software is the *Disk Operating System* (DOS). DOS takes little disk space and

needs very little RAM, making it ideal for desktop computers based on the 80*x*86 series of microprocessors.

There are several versions of DOS. The most popular is Microsoft Disk Operating System (MS DOS). Produced by Microsoft, Inc., this version of DOS is installed on literally millions of IBM PCs and clones. The current revision level of MS DOS is version 6.2*x*. New versions of DOS appear at a fast pace—approximately every three to six months.

IBM and many of the major vendors manufacture their own version of DOS. IBM's version of DOS is known as IBM PC DOS. Many of the vendors license DOS from Microsoft and sell it with their computers with their own labels. An example is AST DOS.

A unique variant of DOS that is giving Microsoft a run for its money is Novell DOS 7 (NWDOS). NWDOS is fully compatible with MS DOS, which means that programs designed to run under MS DOS also run under NWDOS. It features a 32-bit architecture, multitasking, and networking software. The 32-bit architecture means that application programs designed to take full advantage of the 80386, 80486, and Pentium microprocessors are able to run unhindered under NWDOS. In contrast, MS DOS is designed with a 16-bit architecture so that applications designed for earlier Intel microprocessors can run properly.

Other types of operating systems include OS/2, Windows NT, Macintosh System 7, and UNIX. OS/2 and Windows NT are also based on 32-bit architecture. These two operating systems run programs specially designed to support their unique features, and also run standard MS DOS applications. Macintosh System 7 is designed specifically for the Macintosh. The Mac is based on the Motorola 68*xxx* series of microprocessors rather than the Intel microprocessors. Software designed for the Mac cannot run on an IBM PC or clone under DOS without specialized software or hardware.

UNIX is an operating system whose evolution began in the 1960s. It has a long and varied history. Some versions of UNIX can run on the Intel 80386 or above series of microprocessors. These include SCO (Santa Cruz Operations) UNIX, Sunsoft-Interactive UNIX and Solaris UNIX (both products by Sun Microsystems), and UnixWare (by Novell). Most PC-based versions of UNIX also support DOS and Windows applications. UNIX is a multiuser, multitasking, 32-bit operating system. UNIX supports multiple users using the same computer at the same time, through a LAN or through dial-up connections. The operating system can run many programs at the same time.

Windows NT, OS/2, and UNIX require much more memory and disk space than DOS. Windows NT and UNIX on an IBM PC require effectively 16 MB of RAM and anywhere from 80 to 140 MB of disk space. OS/2 requires 8 MB of RAM and 40 MB of disk space. DOS requires 512 KB of RAM and around 5 MB of disk space, although you could get away with less of both.

E-Mail

Electronic mail, or e-mail, is one of the most popular applications on the network. One of the primary reasons people network their computers is to exchange e-mail. Most e-mail packages offer the ability to perform the following actions:

- Read, create, and send messages
- Store and forward messages
- Maintain an address list of mail recipients
- Send messages to groups of people
- Attach a file to a message

Some e-mail packages are designed for a single LAN. Others offer complex solutions where users can dial in from remote sites to exchange mail. Novell offers a mail platform called the *Message Handling System* (MHS) that can call remote offices and exchange mail on a scheduled or on-demand basis. MHS also translates mail messages between different formats, which enables you to exchange mail between DOS, Macintosh, UNIX, and different mail packages. MHS does not, however, provide the "front end" user services listed earlier—it is strictly a transfer platform.

Table 9.4 gives you information on the two most popular e-mail packages available, including prices, vendors, and what operating systems are supported.

Table 9.4
Popular E-Mail Packages

E-Mail Program	Price Range	Vendor	DOS	OS/2	UNIX	Windows	Mac
cc:Mail	$180-895	Lotus Development Corp.	Y	Y	Y	Y	Y
DaVinci	$65-800	DaVinci Systems	Y	Y	Y*	Y	Y
FirstMail	Free**	Novell	Y	N	N	N	Y
MS Mail	$695/10	Microsoft	Y	Y	Y	Y	Y

*requires SMTP gateway

** FirstMail is included with NetWare 3.12, 4.1, and Global MHS

Word Processing

As with e-mail, competition in the word processing arena has narrowed the vast majority of the PC market down to two main competitors: Microsoft Word and Novell's WordPerfect. Word processing is also one of the most popular applications on the network. Features for both products could fill pages. For more information on either of these two programs, consult NRP's books *Inside Word for Windows 6* and *Inside WordPerfect for Windows 6.*

Many other word processing software packages are available, but the other packages do not have nearly the market share of Word or WordPerfect. The other packages often offer additional specialty features that make them popular in specific markets.

Word and WordPerfect enable you to create customized settings for individual users on the network. You might need to use special tools to create these files. In WordPerfect for Windows, for example, there is a tool called BIFEDIT that produces individual BIF files for users. Special techniques are used to indicate to the file server where these files are located. Word has its own peculiarities, including a device known as a "style sheet." This is a formatting template that enables you to standardize how people on the network format their documents.

Another consideration in the word processing environment is standardized documents, often called *boiler plates.* These documents are often set up by managers, supervisors, or lead word processors. They contain standard clauses necessary for your company to conduct business. An example would be a contract form. Whenever one of the sales people in your organization makes a sale, they could call up a master contract form to fill in. The completed form could then be saved to another directory.

The security rights for the forms directory will be different from the security for the completed forms. For the forms directory, you would generally assign a directory trustee right of Read and File Scan, enabling users to see a list of master documents and to read them in. Users would be granted directory trustee rights of Read, File Scan, Write, Create, and Erase for the completed forms directory.

Database

Database programs are used to store statistics, inventory, accounting, and other vital information for your company. You often will need to purchase a specialized database program developed for the niche market your company addresses. For example, there is a program called Metashop that is specialized for companies who manufacture products. Metashop enables you to keep track of parts on hand, orders pending, and finished products. Other programs are designed to keep track of accounting needs.

Networked multiuser database programs have special needs. In the case of a network, many people could be using the database at once. When many people read from the same database, there is no problem. The file server simply processes the Read requests one at a time. When two or more people try to write to the database at the same time, problems occur. In this case, the database program must be capable of establishing a file or record *lock*, which is when someone is planning to update a database file or a record in a file. The lock gives that user exclusive Write access to the file or record until they are finished, and then the lock is released. If another user attempts to write a change to a locked file or record, the database program prevents them from doing so and generates a warning message.

In other cases, you might need a database program you can customize for your own purposes or for ad hoc reports. These programs are available for all operating systems. Table 9.5 provides information on popular database packages available, including vendors and what operating systems are supported.

TABLE 9.5
Popular Database Packages

Program	Vendor	DOS	OS/2	UNIX	Windows	Mac
dBASE	Borland International	Y	Y	Y	Y	Y
Foxbase	Microsoft	Y	Y	N	Y	Y
Paradox	Borland International	Y	N	N	Y	Y
Access	Microsoft	N	Y	N	Y	N
Q&A	Symantec	Y	Y	N	Y	Y

Spreadsheets

Spreadsheet programs are used to build a financial picture, work with statistics, and perform calculations. Most current programs have some sort of programming capability so that you can create automated data entry forms and automate creating a contract. Most spreadsheet programs also have the capability to generate a chart or graph. Most popular spreadsheet programs have network versions. These are often sold as a bundle of user licenses.

The most popular spreadsheet program available is Lotus Development Corporation's 1-2-3. It is available for most operating systems, including DOS, Windows, UNIX, and the Macintosh. Microsoft has a program called Excel that is extremely popular. Novell (formerly Borland) has a competing product called Quattro Pro.

Spreadsheet programs do not tend to tie up network resources very heavily. Most of the work is done at the workstation. The network is used to download the program initially, to retrieve spreadsheets stored on the file server, and to print.

Graphics

Graphics programs are gaining in popularity. There are three general types of graphics programs used today: desktop publishing, presentation graphics, and programs that enable you to draw or "paint" unique artwork. Desktop publishing programs combine word processing with the capability to place graphics images on the printed page. Many companies publish their own internal newsletters that require graphics beyond the capabilities of most word processing programs. Most desktop publishing programs enable you to import documents and graphics image files from other programs. You thus can prepare a document in WordPerfect and scan in some graphics images using an HP Scanjet. The presentation graphics program enables you to create a layout of where you can place text and images on a mockup of the final printed page.

Presentation graphics programs are used to produce internal company reports, stockholder's reports, and training materials. Presentation graphics programs, as the name implies, are designed to enhance a presentation and are used extensively by salespeople preparing for a major product rollout. People who make presentations for conferences and seminars use such programs to emphasize their points. Trainers use presentation graphics for more effective training sessions.

"Paintbrush" or drawing programs are used to retouch scanned images or to create unique artwork. This artwork can be used in conjunction with desktop publishing or presentation graphics. There are many high-end photo retouching programs used by commercial advertising graphics companies. Some programs enable an artist to work with a scanned image at resolutions beyond the capacity of the human eye to perceive.

Some of the more popular graphics programs are summarized in table 9.6.

Table 9.6
Popular Graphics Packages

Program	Publisher	Notes
Harvard	Software Graphics Publishing	Designed for presentation graphics. Allows presenters to create slides for conferences and product rollouts.
Freelance Graphics	Lotus Development Corp.	Designed for presentation graphics.
PowerPoint	Microsoft	Designed for presentation graphics.
PageMaker	Aldus	Enables you to create layouts for publishing, newsletters, and documentation.
AutoCAD	AutoDesk	Used by designers, architects, and manufacturing design. Enables you to model complex products, buildings, and so forth.
Draw	Corel	Enhanced PC painting program. Designed for creating computer artwork or retouching scanned images.

Graphics programs require quite a bit of RAM on the workstation and tend to produce large image files, which must travel across the network when you want to save or print them, causing the network to be used heavily at these times.

Program Suites

A recent trend in the software publishing industry is that of bundling several applications into a single package known as a *suite*. There are three primary contenders in this arena: Lotus, Microsoft, and Novell. The advantage to this approach is that you save quite a bit of money over the price of each of these products offered separately. The disadvantage is that you often end up with a program you will rarely use.

The impact of this approach on the network is that of user licensing. Both Lotus and Microsoft, for example, count each copy of their suite as a single user license. Novell has a tiered approach offering separate licensing for individual products.

As with any program that is protected by copyright law, you must purchase one version of a program for each instance it is used simultaneously. If you have 20 people who use a program but only 12 use the program at the same time, you must purchase 12 copies of the program to remain within the bounds of the law.

Table 9.7 summarizes the three most popular program suites.

TABLE 9.7
Program Suites

Suite/ Publisher	Programs in the Suite	Type of Program
SmartSuite 2.1	Ami Pro	Word processing
Lotus	1-2-3	Spreadsheet
Development	Freelance	Presentation graphics
Corp.	Approach	Database
	Organizer	Information manager
	Application Manager	Menuing program
	Adobe Type Manager	Type fonts management
Office 4.0	Word	Word processor
Microsoft	Excel	Spreadsheet
	PowerPoint	Presentation graphics
	Access	Database
	Mail	E-mail program
	Office Manager	Menuing program
Novell	WordPerfect	Word processing
	Quattro Pro	Spreadsheet
	Paradox (by Borland)	Database program

User Interfaces

Another aspect of network software is what type of user interface you want your users to see when they log into the network. One possibility is to use NetWare's menuing utility which lets you create simple text-based menus that enable users to select from a number of options. Other possibilities include Microsoft's Windows or other front programs such as Novell/WordPerfect's PerfectOffice.

Windows has become extremely popular in the PC DOS world. Windows is a menuing program that offers additional features such as memory management, exchange of data between programs, limited background operations, and a series of utilities.

Windows offers programmers a common set of development tools minimizing the amount of time it takes to develop an application and standardizing the user interface. From the user perspective, there might be a high learning curve at first, but after one application is learned, other applications will not present as great a challenge. Due to the common environment, all Windows applications use the same set of tools.

As a network menuing system, Windows offers advantages and disadvantages. Because it can be easily customized, users tend to alter their "desktop" to suit their tastes. From the network support aspect, this presents challenges. If you allow your users to customize their Windows desktops, users will need Read and Write trustee rights to the Windows initialization files (commonly referred to as INI files after their extension, .INI). On the other hand, if you prevent users from making changes to the Windows desktop by denying them Write trustee rights, certain Windows programs that attempt to change an INI file will display error messages on the screen. For more detail on configuring a workstation for Windows, refer to Chapter 15, "Windows 3.*x* and Windows NT Clients."

Other user menu environments include such products as Novell/WordPerfect's PerfectOffice. PerfectOffice includes a menu and a set of utilities. As with Windows, the utilities include a calculator, a clock, and a calendar. The calendar is especially useful because it enables each user to quickly and easily store a running calendar charting out their daily, weekly, and monthly activities. PerfectOffice, designed with the LAN in mind, falls into the up and coming category of software known as groupware. *Groupware* is software designed for a LAN that enables a group of network users in an PerfectOffice to coordinate their activities. One of the features of the PerfectOffice calendar is the capability to schedule meetings and to check other users' calendars to see if they are free at a given time. Along with this facility is a built-in e-mail package.

Now that you have had a taste of some of the software packages typically used in the LAN environment, server hardware is now discussed.

Selecting Server Hardware

Many of the concepts discussed for workstation hardware also apply to the file server. The file server is a computer, just like the computer used at the desktop, but the file server has special needs—it is dedicated to serve one purpose: servicing user requests. User requests take the form of reading and writing files from the file server's hard drive, and jobs to be printed. The file server provides other services, as well: time synchronization, exchanging and updating NDS information, and providing other services in the form of third-party NLMs (tape backup, virus protection, power monitoring).

This section provides some guidelines for selecting file server hardware.

Storage Devices

Hard drives are discussed in Chapter 1. This section discusses other types of storage that you might want to install on the file server, including optical drives (CD-ROM drives) and backup devices.

CD-ROM Drives

There is an increasing need for optical storage on the file server. Many databases and programs are available that pack a tremendous amount of information onto a CD-ROM. A CD drive unit connected to the file server gives all network users access to this information. NetWare 4.1 includes CD-ROM file system support. A series of NLMs is loaded onto the file server, including the CDROM.NLM. These NLMs make the CD appear as a NetWare volume. Users can then map a drive letter to this volume to access information on the CD. Some CDs, such as Microsoft's Encarta, include an installation program that copies certain files onto the workstation to facilitate access to the information on the CD.

Some CD drive units come in the form of multiple players in a single unit. Micro Design International, for example, has an optical unit known as a *jukebox* that features seven CD-ROM drives in a single case. You can insert CDs into each of these drives and mount them as separate volumes. The unit attaches to a single SCSI host controller in the file server. Each CD drive unit is assigned a separate SCSI ID number from 0 to 6.

When NetWare mounts a CD as a volume, it needs to record certain information in RAM, which can result in a substantial amount of RAM required on the file server. The information placed into RAM as a CD is mounted includes its FAT (File Allocation Table), and portions of its DET (Directory Entry Table). As an example, in one installation, the file server (with 16 MB of RAM) initially had 83 percent available for file caching. This figure means that 83 percent of the file server's RAM was available to service user requests. After seven CDs were mounted in a jukebox CD drive unit, the amount of RAM available for file caching dropped to 23 percent. In other words, just mounting the CDs to make them available to network users used 60 percent of the file server's memory (9.6 MB)! The conclusion you can draw is that each CD mounted on the file server will require between 1 and 2 MB of additional RAM on the server for the CD's FAT and DET.

The NetWare 4.1 software comes in the form of a CD. In addition, the NetWare 4.1 manuals are available on a separate CD included with the product. You obviously need a CD drive unit to install the software initially, but it does not have to remain on the file server after NetWare has been installed. The manuals can be ordered separately, although the price of these manuals will lead you to reconsider using the manuals provided on CD.

At this point, you need to make inquiries of your network users. You must determine the level of interest in installing a CD drive unit on the file server. You initially might want to make the NetWare 4.1 manuals available through a CD drive unit on the file server. Not only are the manuals online, but a NetWare 4.1 tutorial is included. This can help decrease the initial learning curve as you get your users up and running on the network. Later, you might want to make additional CDs available to network users.

Backup Devices

During the planning stage, you need to decide how and where the backup devices should be located. Two options are available: on the file server or on a workstation. The advantage of a tape backup unit on the file server is that you can start the backup from anywhere on the network, it will not tie up a workstation, and it will proceed quickly. NetWare 4.1 includes a server-based backup utility, SBACKUP.NLM, that is adequate (but not necessarily elegant) for this purpose. Most server-based backup software packages enable you to back up the workstations, as well as the server.

The other choice is to install the backup unit on a workstation. The disadvantage to this approach is that the backup data must travel across the LAN, so you need to schedule the backup to take place at a time when the LAN is not heavily used. The advantage of a workstation-based backup unit is that you can still access your data if the file server is down.

Bus Types

The file server should be the most powerful computer you can afford. With this in mind, consider the different bus types available. The *Extended Industry Standard Architecture* (EISA) bus offers many advantages over the older *Industry Standard Architecture* (ISA) bus type found in the older IBM PC AT computers. The EISA bus can transfer 32 bits of data simultaneously, compared with 16 bits for the ISA bus. EISA bus cards give much better performance but are more expensive than ISA bus cards.

Another alternative is the *local bus*, which is a 32-bit bus designed originally for the purpose of moving video data off the main bus onto a separate "local" bus. Local bus computers are designed around a standard ISA or EISA bus with two or more additional local bus slots. Local bus cards for the computer look like ISA or EISA cards with an additional connector at the far end of the card. This connector fits into the local bus slot. For a file server, it would not make sense to get a local bus video adapter. Instead you might want to investigate getting a local bus hard disk controller. This would offer tremendous performance gains for the file server's hard drive(s).

Memory

A typical NetWare 4.1 file server has from 16 to 32 MB of RAM. The exact amount of RAM required in the file server can be calculated using the formula presented in Chapter 11, "Hardware Configuration." The formula requires that you know the following information:

- The number of users expected to use this file server
- The size of each volume you create on the file server's hard drive(s)
- The average size file your users will store on the file server
- The size required by the NLMs you will load on the file server

In addition to these factors, you also need to make decisions regarding the disk block size on each volume, the number of buffers used for incoming user requests (*packet receive buffers*), and the number of buffers used to store file name and attribute information (*directory cache buffers*). These concepts are explained in more detail in Chapter 11.

For now, there is one simple consideration: the minimum amount of RAM required to operate NetWare 4.1 itself is 8 MB. This amount is without any additional NLMs. Each NLM adds memory roughly equal to the file size of the NLM times 2. In addition, memory is needed to store file information for each volume. As you saw when discussing CDs, the amount of file server RAM is approximately 2 KB for each 1 MB of disk space. What memory is left is used to cache files needed by network users. The rule of thumb is to have at least 50 percent or more RAM free for the purpose of caching user files. Chapter 11 gives you a more precise memory formula.

NetWare places all files coming from and going to the LAN in file server RAM. As such, NetWare is very memory intensive. As a general rule, network performance can be improved by adding more RAM to your file servers.

Host Bus Adapters

Each disk controller in the file server is known as a *host bus adapter* (HBA). If the HBA is a SCSI controller, you can chain up to seven drives or other devices—such as a tape unit or a CD player—off one HBA.

There are several reasons to add additional HBAs to the file server. One reason is to support disk mirroring or duplexing. This concept was discussed in Chapter 3. Mirroring or duplexing enables you to write data to two drives at the same time, safeguarding data against hard drive failure.

Another reason to add additional HBAs is to increase the amount of disk space available to the server. When calculating disk requirements for your server, you can see that the amount of space you need might exceed the capacity of a single HBA. Additional HBAs enable you to add additional hard drives.

It is not a good idea to run too many disk drives from a single HBA. Just as in a LAN with too many workstations, when you have too many disk drives using the same HBA, performance drops. Wherever possible, distribute the load between multiple HBAs. If you decide you need six SCSI hard drives, for example, instead of running six drives off one HBA, you could buy a second HBA and run three drives off each one.

Network Interface Cards

The NICs on the file server should be the fastest and most reliable you can buy. If your file server has either an EISA or Local bus, buy EISA or Local bus NICs. An EISA network interface in the file server enables the server to send and receive information more efficiently. If the workstations have slower NICs, ISA, or even an original 8-bit PC bus NIC, the capability of these workstations to transfer data is affected. A slow NIC in the file server affects the entire network.

You must make sure the transmission speed of the NIC in the server matches the transmission speed of the NICs in your workstations. If you have a 4 mbps token ring NIC in your workstations, you cannot place a 16 mbps token ring NIC in the file server; the speeds will not match, and the network will not function. A more efficient NIC in the file server (an EISA card, for example) does not increase the transmission speed; that speed is set by the specification of the NIC itself. 10BASE-T Ethernet, for example, is set to transmit at 10 mbps regardless of whether it is an EISA card or not. The speed is in *throughput.* An EISA Ethernet card can move data faster between the file server and the network. After the data is placed on the network, it moves at the preset speed of the specification (10BASE-T Ethernet, for example).

CPU

Finally, as you saw, there are different kinds of microprocessors available. These are sometimes called *microprocessor units* (MPUs) or *central processing units* (CPUs). The CPU of the file server should be the fastest available. The Intel 80486 or Pentium MPUs are recommended. Various vendors have come up with other solutions that offer additional speed. One type of computer, the NetFrame, for example, offers a bus with multiple MPUs. The master MPU handles the calculations and logic processing; secondary MPUs handle the database and disk throughput. The technology used in the NetFrame was developed for mainframe computers 10 or 20 years ago and is now being used in the PC environment.

The 80486 is offered in several different varieties. These include the SX, the DX, and the DX2. Of these varieties, the SX is the slowest. The SX has certain functions disabled, including the math coprocessor. The math coprocessor is an auxiliary CPU that handles mathematical functions only. The DX and DX2 offer additional performance and power.

Unlike some operating systems, such as UNIX, NetWare is not particularly CPU intensive. Performance gains will be more noticeable when you upgrade the CPU of a workstation rather than the server.

Summary

In this chapter, you encountered guidelines to assist you in the physical and logical planning of your network. You learned some of the questions to ask when planning for the network. A list of questions was presented and reviewed. The purpose of these questions is to clarify the following:

- How many nodes you will need
- How much disk space
- How many network segments
- The nature and composition of your network

You had a chance to review some characteristics of popular network applications such as word processing and e-mail. You learned that different types of applications have different considerations and impacts on network utilization.

You had a glimpse of what is involved in planning the NDS tree for your network. As you learned, there are two basic approaches: organizational and geographical. Within these two approaches you can use either a simple or complex approach. The simple approach features less container objects and more leaf objects per container. The complex approach features more container objects with less leaf objects per container.

The last part of this chapter reviewed the physical components of the network. You were given some tips and pointers on what types of components are available and what to look for in the file server computer, for example. The various types of network software were reviewed, including the operating system software you plan to use on your workstations.

The next chapter, "Installation Overview," is a checklist and will give you a general overview of the installation process for all components and aspects of the network.

Installation Overview

This chapter presents you with a checklist of items to give you a general idea of what you will be doing when you install a network. Each item is explained in greater detail in the following chapters. Specific chapter references are given, along with a short explanation. You might want to use this chapter to double-check the process of installing your network.

Installing the Cabling

The first item generally installed in a new network is the cabling. Refer to the *Checklist for Installing the Cabling* later in this chapter to help you during this phase. During this phase, you will need to select the type of cabling to be used in your network. Remember from the discussions in Chapters 2 and 3 that the type of cabling is closely associated with the type of network interface card you plan to use.

During this phase you will also make a decision whether or not to employ an outside cabling company. If so, you will need to call around for pricing and to check references.

Many cabling companies are run by former electricians who have no knowledge of networking. Check the network references of potential cabling contractors carefully.

Installing the Computers

After the cabling is installed, you are ready to install the computers you will use in your network. The computers used include the workstations and file servers. You also might be using computers for specialized purposes such as routing, printing, or other network services.

Hard Drives and Storage Devices

At this point, you can take the cover off the computer and install the devices, starting with the hard drive. Use the *Checklist for Installing Hard Drives and Other Storage Devices* form later in this chapter.

After all cards have been installed in the computer, you need to run the setup program described in the following form. The setup program for the computer could be built into its BIOS. The setup program is often called the "CMOS Setup Program." In other cases, the setup program is on a separate disk shipped with the computer. For IBM PS/2 computers, for example, you need to run the program on the Reference Disk shipped with the computer. On some EISA computers there is an "EISA Configuration" utility you must run.

When installing IDE hard drives, you will need to set the drive jumpers to indicate if the drive is a single drive, or one drive of a pair of drives. Write down the settings for the IDE paddleboard as well. When installing SCSI hard drives, tape units, or CD drive units, you must set the SCSI ID and ensure that the SCSI bus is properly terminated.

Network Cards

At this point, you can install the NIC for this computer. Some NICs have jumpers and DIP switches that must be set. Other NICs have a software program you must run to configure the interface. Make sure that the settings on the NIC do not conflict with the settings of other cards or devices in this computer. Do not worry about the settings of the NICs in other computers. Use the *Checklist for Installing Network Interface Cards* provided later in this chapter during this portion of the installation.

Peripherals

There can be a variety of peripheral devices in a network. Refer to the *Checklist for Installing Peripherals.* Check any that apply, and add additional devices as needed.

Peripherals installed at this point include printers, tape backup units, and other devices. When connecting a printer, you will need to note several items. Is the printer a parallel, serial, or direct-connect type of printer? You will need to decide where the printer is to be connected. Choices include connecting to a file server, a DOS workstation, a Macintosh, or a UNIX host. In each case you will need to note the connection and load the appropriate software when it comes time to activate the printer.

Now that you have installed the printer, you need to ensure a proper paper supply, and have ink and/or toner cartridges on hand. The printer should be tested using its self-test feature. You can also do a DOS screen print for printers attached to DOS workstations.

When installing SCSI tape backup units, note the settings of the HBA as well as the SCSI ID of the tape drive. Test to see if the tape unit is recognized by the BIOS on the SCSI adapter. You will also need to ensure that a supply of tapes is on hand and that a sample backup has been performed.

Memory and Setup

All PCs based on the IBM PC architecture store setup information in battery-powered memory called *CMOS.* This memory retains the system settings even when the PC is turned off. Information stored in CMOS includes memory size, types of disk drives, and system date and time. The exact information depends on the design of the system, however.

To configure the CMOS data on older PCs, it usually was necessary to run a CMOS configuration program from a disk. Most newer PCs have built the CMOS configuration program into the system's BIOS, and you usually can enter setup mode by pressing one or more keys while the system is performing a cold boot.

Some computers require that you press a combination of keystrokes such as Ctrl+Alt+Esc or Shift+Ctrl+Insert. Some computers have you press a key during the computer's initial boot-up or when you press the Reset button. You might see a message such as the following:

```
Press DEL to Run Setup
```

Some Compaq computers have you press the F10 key during boot-up when the cursor shifts to the right side of the screen.

In addition to the CMOS configuration, EISA and Microchannel PCs require a configuration procedure for the bus itself. Most EISA bus computers have an EISA Configuration Utility. IBM PS/2 computers have a setup program on the Reference Disk. In most cases, these setup disks are bootable. You need to run the appropriate bus setup program on your PC after you finish configuring the CMOS.

You can use a form such as the *Checklist for Configuring a PC* to record the setup data for each of the PCs on your LAN. You should duplicate this form, fill it in for each system, and store the completed form with your LAN records.

Installing NetWare 4.1

After you have installed and configured the hardware for your network server, the next step is to install the NetWare 4.1 software on the server. Installing NetWare 4.1 is covered in more detail in Chapter 12, "Installing the Network Operating System." In this section, you learn about the preparations you need to make and the information you need to gather before you install NetWare. Here is the general procedure:

- Decide how to install NetWare: from a locally attached CD drive unit, or from another file server.
- Go to the installation directory on the local CD, or on the file server that contains the installation files. Go to the directory that contains the language you want to use during the installation.
- Run INSTALL.
- Create a DOS partition on the new server.
- Format the partition and make it bootable.
- INSTALL copies the server boot files to the DOS partition and runs SERVER.EXE.

- Load disk drivers.
- Load LAN drivers.
- Configure IPX network addresses.
- The INSTALL.NLM utility is loaded.
- Create NetWare partitions on each hard drive.
- Configure mirroring (or duplexing).
- Create NetWare volumes, as desired.
- Download files from your license disk.
- Copy initial operating-system files onto volume SYS.
- Create a new NDS tree or use an existing tree.
- Configure time-synchronization information.
- Designate the new file server's NDS context.
- Build NDS tree and create a replica, if appropriate.
- Create the AUTOEXEC.NCF and STARTUP.NCF files.
- Copy remaining operating-system files onto volume SYS.
- Install additional products (such as NetWare NFS or NetWare for SAA).
- Create the disks to install workstation software.

At this point, the new server is fully operational. To complete setup of the network, you need to have at least one operational client workstation, so setting up a workstation is the next step in configuring your network.

Installing the Workstation Software

The workstation software installation is covered in more detail in Chapters 14 through 18, as follows:

- Chapter 14, "DOS Client Basics," covers DOS workstations.
- Chapter 15, "Windows 3.*x* and Windows NT Clients," covers Windows and Windows NT.

- Chapter 16, "OS/2 Clients," covers OS/2.
- Chapter 17, "UNIX Clients," covers UNIX.
- Chapter 18, "Macintosh Clients," is on the Macintosh.

In this section, you get a general overview of the installation process.

DOS Workstations

The workstation software can be installed from a set of three disks created during the last phase of the file server installation. If the workstation is installed for an earlier version of NetWare, or if you have the workstation software on disk, you can connect to a file server containing the workstation software installation files.

The DOS workstations can be installed from either a set of client installation disks, or from the server. If installing from a server, you must have either a disk with the client software already loaded, or existing client software. Once you have changed to either the server or disk with the client software, run the INSTALL.EXE program. You will answer a series of questions regarding the placement of the software on your hard drive, if you have Windows installed, and which LAN driver you plan to use. Once these questions have been answered, INSTALL will create the necessary directories and copy files to your workstation. If you agree, the AUTOEXEC.BAT and CONFIG.SYS files will be modified to accommodate and call up the client software. In addition, the NET.CFG file will be created or modified.

Windows Workstations

The Windows product family consists of three products. *Windows 3.1* is a program that runs on top of DOS. *Windows for Workgroups 3.11* is a variation of Windows 3.1 that runs on top of DOS and has its own networking capabilities. *Windows NT (New Technology)* is a 32-bit operating system that resembles Windows for Workgroups 3.11. In this section, you get an overview of the installation procedures for each of these clients. For line-by-line details, see Chapter 15, "Windows 3.*x* and Windows NT Clients."

Windows 3.1 Client Installation Overview

The procedure for setting a DOS-based Windows 3.1 workstation is identical to that of setting up a DOS-based workstation. The major difference is that you need to specify Yes when asked if you want to install support for Windows. The INSTALL.EXE program copies certain files into the directory that contains Windows, as well as additional NetWare user utilities including NWUSER.EXE.

Windows for Workgroups 3.11 Client Installation Overview

The installation procedure for Windows for Workgroups 3.11 is substantially different from a Windows 3.1 installation. Windows for Workgroups (WFW) has its own peer-to-peer networking features. *Peer-to-peer networking* is when each node on the network can function as a client or a server (or both). A WFW node can share a file or printer with another WFW node.

The installation of a WFW client in a NetWare network changes depending on which types of networks you want to use. If you decide to use the built-in WFW networking features, you must install WFW as a network node and then select NetWare from the list of compatible networks. You can add NetWare after the installation by selecting the Networks option from the Windows Control Panel. Other networks supported include Microsoft's LAN Manager.

Installing WFW strictly as a NetWare client would be the same as installing a Windows 3.1 client.

Windows NT Client Installation Overview

Windows NT is a 32-bit operating system. The graphical interface looks like Windows 3.1 or Windows for Workgroups. The engine behind the interface, however, is radically different. NT incorporates a 32-bit operating system engine with many new features. The features that are of concern when using NT as a NetWare client are the file system and the built-in networking features. The preferred Windows NT file system is called NTFS (New Technology File System). NTFS features improved disk performance and elongated file name support (among other features).

Because a Windows NT computer is designed as both a client and a server, the built-in networking features enable access between NT nodes as well as Windows for Workgroups nodes. When installing a Windows NT client for a NetWare network, you will need to add the NetWare Client option. This is easily accomplished using the Control Panel. The primary disadvantage is that the NetWare client software provided by Microsoft does not support the NDS. Chapter 15 gives you more information about the procedures used to install the Windows NT (and Windows for Workgroups) clients.

OS/2 Workstations

Integration of OS/2 clients into a NetWare network is much simpler than that of Windows NT. OS/2 version 1.3 and below use the NetWare Requester for OS/2 software. OS/2 version 2.*x* uses the NetWare Client for OS/2 software. The NetWare Requester software is similar functionally to the NET*x* shell. The software provides for bindery attachments to the NetWare 4.1 file server only. The NetWare Client software provides full NDS support, along with documentation on CD-ROM in OS/2 standard format and support for diskless OS/2 workstations.

The installation procedure is documented in detail in Chapter 16, "OS/2 Clients."

UNIX Workstations

When allowing a UNIX client access to a NetWare network, you need to decide what type of access is desired. In the UNIX world, the term used for the computer running UNIX is the *host.* A UNIX host can be both a client and a server. There are several approaches:

- UNIX host accessing the NetWare server via TCP/IP and FTP
- UNIX host accessing the NetWare server via TCP/IP and NFS
- NetWare server accessing the UNIX host using NFS Gateway
- UNIX host accessing the NetWare server via IPX/SPX

The procedures for these strategies, along with an explanation of some of the concepts in the UNIX networking world, are presented in Chapter 17, "UNIX Clients."

Macintosh Workstations

As with UNIX, Macintosh workstations utilize a completely different file system and operating system. In order for the Macintosh workstations to access the NetWare file server, you need to install NetWare for Macintosh on the file server. This set of NLMs enables the NetWare file server to act as an AppleShare file server. Because the Macs come with networking features built into the operating system, no special client drivers need to be installed.

After you complete the NetWare for Macintosh installation, notice that a disk of Macintosh client utilities is supplied with NetWare. These utilities enable the Mac user to administer the NetWare file server. Details on the installation of the NetWare for Macintosh software are included in Chapter 18, "Macintosh Clients."

Testing the Physical Installation

After the cabling is installed and one or more file servers and workstations are installed, it is time to test the physical installation. This section gives you some tests to perform in order to make sure that the systems are talking with one another. The tests are divided into tests performed from a file server, tests performed from a workstation, and tests for the network in general.

Because many of the testing procedures require that the file server be up and running, testing is covered in more detail in Chapter 13, "Upgrades and Other Installation Issues." For suggestions on workstation issues, see Chapters 14 through 18. For more information on troubleshooting, see Part Ten, "Backing Up, Disaster Planning, and Troubleshooting."

Building the NDS Structure

After the network is installed physically and tested, it is time to build your logical organization. You need to add objects to the NDS tree and build up the directory on the volumes of your file servers. This section gives you a series of questions to answer to help you in the process of setting up the logical structure.

Adding Organizations and Organizational Units

The first task when setting up the NDS tree is designating which container objects you want to use. The most important container objects for the purposes of this section are organizations and organizational units. Other container objects include locality and country. Chapter 19, "NDS Tree Design Considerations," covers how to move from a conceptual view of your company's organization to an actual implementation of the NDS tree. Chapter 20, "Managing Objects and Properties," covers the actual mechanics of placing container objects in the tree.

[ ] How is your company organized (check all that apply)? By ...

  [ ] Division
  [ ] Department
  [ ] Workgroup
  [ ] Taskgroup
  [ ] Unit
  [ ] Project

[ ] How is your company situated geographically?

- [ ] In one room
- [ ] In one office
- [ ] In one floor
- [ ] In one building
- [ ] In one city
- [ ] In one metropolitan area (in the Los Angeles area, for example)
- [ ] In one state
- [ ] In one province
- [ ] In one country
- [ ] In one continent
- [ ] Worldwide
- [ ] Earth orbit or beyond (hey, you never know!)

[ ] Fill out the Organization/Location grid located at the end of this chapter. Note that this grid is included as a spreadsheet named ORG_LOC.XLS for Excel and ORG_LOC.WKS for Lotus 1-2-3 or Quattro Pro. You can download these files from the Macmillan Computer Publishing forum on CompuServe. After you access the Macmillan forum (GO MACMILLAN), you can find the files for this and other NRP networking books in the Networking and Comms library.

At this point, you then use an administrative tool such as NWADMIN.EXE (Windows based) or NETADMIN.EXE (DOS command-line based) to place the container objects in the tree.

Adding Users and Other Leaf Objects

After the organizational structure of the tree is determined, the next step is to add users and other leaf objects. You need to determine how to name your user objects. The following questions help you determine what type of naming scheme to use.

[ ] How many users will there be? _____

[ ] Do you already use e-mail? Y [ ] N [ ]

If the answer to this question is Yes, you might consider using people's e-mail names for their object names.

[ ] When people in your company send out memos, how are people addressed (check any that apply)? By...

[ ] First name
[ ] Last name
[ ] Full name
[ ] Title
[ ] Initials
[ ] First initial(s) and last name
[ ] First name and last initial(s)

The answer to this question gives you an indication of how you should designate object names. Bear in mind that there is a separate field for last name (surname) when creating user objects. The name this section is concerned with is the name of the leaf object, which is used to log in.

You might want to keep login names to a certain number of characters. If you keep names to eight characters, for example, this fits in neatly with DOS directory-naming restrictions. In addition, short login names can save your users typing time.

[ ] Fill out the *User Information Checklist* included at the end of this chapter. Note that this worksheet is included as a spreadsheet called USERINFO.XLS for Excel and USERINFO.WKS for Lotus 1-2-3 or Quattro Pro. You can download these files from the Macmillan Computer Publishing forum on CompuServe. After you access the Macmillan forum (GO MACMILLAN), you can find the files for this and other NRP networking books in the Networking and Comms library.

Other leaf objects could include any of the following:

- Organizational roles
- Profile objects
- Aliases

The reasons for creating these objects and the actual mechanics of creating objects are covered in detail in Chapter 20, "Managing Objects and Properties."

Creating the File System Directory Structure

The next step in the process of setting up your network is to create directories and subdirectories on each of the volumes on your file server. Here are some questions to assist you in deciding what directories to create.

[ ] Do you want to have a separate directory for each user on the network?
Y [ ] N [ ]

If Yes, which volume(s) will contain user directories?

____

____

____

____

____

____

If the answer to this question is Yes, you should create the directory for each user as you are creating the user object itself. This is an option that can be enabled in both the NETADMIN.EXE and NWADMIN.EXE utilities (explained in Chapter 20). By enabling this option, you not only create the user directory (called a *home directory*), but the system automatically grants the user full trustee rights.

[ ] How is your company's data organized (check all that apply)? By...

[ ] Client
[ ] Project
[ ] Date
[ ] Employee
[ ] Department

The answers to these questions lead you to create different subdirectory structures. If your data is organized by client, for example, you might want to create a directory called CLIENTS. Under this directory, you could create a separate directory for each client.

[ ] Where do you want application programs to be stored? For each application, you need to answer these questions:

File server: __________________

Volume: ____________________

Directory: ____________________

Name of application: ____________________

[ ] Fill in the *File System Checklist* included at the end of this chapter. Note that this worksheet is included as a spreadsheet FILESYS.XLS for Excel and FILESYS.WKS for Lotus 1-2-3 or Quattro Pro. You can download these files from the Macmillan Computer Publishing forum on CompuServe. After you access the Macmillan forum (GO MACMILLAN), you can find the files for this and other NRP networking books in the Networking and Comms library.

If the item described is an application, place an X in the Applic. column. If the item is a data directory, place an X in the Data column.

Creating Printing Objects

The next step in the network setup process is setting up printing. At this point, the printers should be set up and ready to go. Here are some questions that should help you decide what type of printing objects you need to create, and where to place them in the tree.

[ ] Minimum number of print servers needed: _____

Each NetWare print server can handle 255 printers. Divide the number of printers you need (or have) by 255 and round up to the next whole number. If you have 300 printers, for example, the number of print servers = 300/255 = 1.17 = 2 print servers needed. You may also decide to have more print servers based on geographic considerations.

[ ] How are printers shared (check any that apply)?

[ ] Not shared (users have their own private printers)
[ ] Every two users share a printer
[ ] Every _____ users share a printer
[ ] Each workgroup has its own printer
[ ] Each _____ has its own printer

[ ] Fill out the *Print Object Checklist* included at the end of this chapter. Note that this worksheet is included as spreadsheet PRINTING.XLS for Excel and PRINTING.WKS for Lotus 1-2-3 or Quattro Pro. You can download these files from the Macmillan Computer Publishing forum on CompuServe. After you access the Macmillan forum (GO MACMILLAN), you can find the files for this and other NRP networking books in the Networking and Comms library.

The Authorized Users column normally will be all users in that container (Organization or Organizational Unit). If this is not the case, list the users authorized to use this particular printer-queue set. Normally you would assign one printer per queue; however, there are other options. For more information, see Part Seven, "Printing."

Installing Application Programs

Application programs now can be installed on the file server. You need to be sure you have the software that is appropriate for your needs, as discussed in Chapter 9, "Planning the Network." You also have to ensure that you have network versions of the software with the appropriate number of user licenses.

Each software program has its own unique installation requirements. You will need to consult the manual for each particular application. In most cases, there will be a quick start or some sort of fast installation guide. In some cases, there will be a separate section for network installations giving you a list of specific requirements. For more details, see Chapter 25, "Installing Applications."

Here is a generalized checklist for installing network applications:

[ ] Log in as a user with full directory trustee rights to the directory to contain the application.

[ ] MAP a drive letter to the volume and directory to contain the application. Change to this drive letter.

Make a note of this drive letter. Some software programs require that this letter be present whenever the program is run. Some programs try to install themselves off the root. If this is the case, you can use the MAP ROOT command to create an "artificial" root. Please refer to Chapter 33, "Assigning Drive Mappings," for more information.

[ ] Install the program following the installation procedure outlined in the manual.

[ ] Test the program to ensure proper operation.

[ ] Use the FLAG command or the FILER utility to change program file attributes to Shareable, and possibly Read Only (depending on the requirements of the program).

[ ] Give users appropriate trustee rights through direct trustee assignments, granting rights to container objects or groups, or any other appropriate means.

[ ] Give users a search drive mapping to the program directory through their user login script, their container login script, a menuing program, or a batch file.

[ ] Log in as a user and test access to the program.

[ ] Add an entry for each application on the *File System Checklist* included at the end of the chapter. Note that this worksheet is included as spreadsheet FILESYS.XLS for Excel and FILESYS.WKS for Lotus 1-2-3 or Quattro Pro.

Setting Up User Access

The final set of tasks you must accomplish in setting up the network is giving users access to network resources. As you saw in the preceding section, one of the first tasks is to grant trustee rights to the files and directories containing programs. Other tasks include creating login scripts, menus, and batch files. Windows is a very popular menuing program for networks. It has its own traps and pitfalls, which are covered in general here. When you are done, you need to log in as each user and test each user's access to the network.

Assigning Trustee Rights

Most trustee rights should be assigned by container. The rights then will inherit down to all user objects in the container. With container rights you can create groups. The rights assigned to groups inherit down to all members of the group. A close alternative to a group is to create an organizational role. Rights can be assigned to the role. Occupants of the role inherit all the rights assigned to the role. These techniques minimize the amount of work for the network as a whole. If a user needs a different set of rights, you simply need to move him to another container, change his group membership, or move him between organizational roles.

On occasion, you might need to assign rights on an individual basis. Individual assignments are manageable on smaller networks (of less than 100 users, for example). Also, if the capability to assign rights has been delegated to a series of lower-level Administrators, individual assignments are a possibility. The problem with assigning rights to individuals is that after a while, you have difficulty keeping track of who has rights to which areas of the network.

Table 10.1 summarizes the sets of rights needed to perform various tasks.

Table 10.1
Standard Rights Assignments

Task to Perform	Type of Trustee Rights Assignment	Recommended Rights
Run a Program	File or Directory Rights	Read and File Scan rights for the program's directory
Access Shared Data	File or Directory Rights	Read, File Scan, Create, Write, and Erase
Assign Rights	File or Directory Rights	Supervisor
Manage Objects	Object Rights	Supervisor
Change a Login Script of an Object	Property Rights	Read rights to the Login Script property of the object
Create Leaf Objects in a Container	Object Rights	Create rights to the container
Assign Members to a Group	Property Rights	Compare, Read, and Write to the Group Membership property of the group object

To determine file-system rights you plan to assign to containers, groups, or organizational roles, you need to have an idea of which users need rights to which directories. The *Rights Worksheet* included at the end of this chapter assists you in this purpose. The name of the spreadsheet is RIGHTS.XLS for Excel and RIGHTS.WKS for Lotus 1-2-3 or Quattro Pro.

Fill out the names of the users on your network in the column labeled Usernames. Fill out the directory paths of applications and shared data directories across the top of the worksheet (columns labeled 1 through 9, and so on). Write down the target rights for each user and each application or shared data directory. After filling out this worksheet, you will see groupings of users. You can sort the spreadsheet in various ways to determine which users and which rights should be added to the various containers, groups, or organizational roles in your tree. Next, you can decide how to organize the users in terms of rights.

Assigning NDS rights is a similar process. You need to determine which users need to manage which objects. You can use the *Rights Worksheet* included at the end of this chapter. Instead of "Directory Paths," you can substitute "Objects." The default NDS object rights should be sufficient for most users. The users you need to be most

concerned with are those to whom you plan to delegate some sort of authority over portions of the tree.

Creating Login Scripts

The next step in the process is to create login scripts. Login scripts are much like UNIX profile scripts or DOS batch files. Much care should be taken when building container login scripts. These login scripts affect all users in that container. Login scripts common to a group of users can be associated with Profile objects. User login scripts can be created, but should be minimized to keep the network manageable. More information on creating login scripts and what should go into a login script is contained in Chapter 34, "Creating Login Scripts."

Creating Menus and Batch Files

The majority of network users encounter a menu system after they log in to the network. The menu is a way of controlling what the users see on the network. A menu keeps the users' attention focused on their work and prevents them from messing around on the network. Knowledgeable users (power users) might be proficient enough to merit letting them loose at the DOS prompt (or the prompt for whatever desktop operating system you are using). Most users will appreciate a good menuing system, however. Chapter 35, "Building Custom Menus and Batch Files," covers aspects of creating menus for users.

Most systems require at least a few batch files to automate network tasks. Batch files are used to supplement programs that require a series of setup commands prior to entering the program. An example is a program that uses Btrieve. To get into the program, you first need to load a Btrieve memory-resident program. A batch file can be used to load the TSR, load the program, and then unload the TSR when done. Batch files also can be used to supplement menu programs and Windows.

Setting Up Windows

If you plan to use Windows 3.*x* on your network, you need to make some decisions at this point on how to implement Windows. Chapter 15, "Windows 3.*x* and Windows NT Clients," gives you more detailed coverage on setting up Windows. Here is a series of questions that will start you thinking about how you want to implement Windows.

[ ] Will you have a need to access Windows outside of the network?
Y [ ]   N [ ]

If you answer Yes, you should consider installing Windows on each workstation, or those where users need access to Windows outside of the network. If you plan to do network analysis using LANalyzer for Windows, for example, you would want to access Windows outside of the network.

[ ] Do all workstations have hard drives?
Y [ ] N [ ]

If the answer to this question is No, you might want to install Windows on the network.

[ ] How much memory do your workstations have? _____MB

If the workstations have less then 4 MB, you should consider upgrading them. Windows requires about 4 MB of RAM in order to be effective. If you plan to run several applications simultaneously on the workstations, 8 MB or more is recommended. Additional RAM reduces the need for a swap file. This RAM greatly improves performance.

[ ] Do you want users to be able to customize their own Windows Program Manager screens?
Y [ ] N [ ]

If the answer to this question is No, you need to restrict trustee rights to the Windows *.GRP and *.INI files.

Testing User Access

When the network has been physically and logically set up, you need to log in as each user and test each user's access. Many network Administrators do not take this step. Many times you will not be given enough time. If you do not take the time to test, however, the result might be unhappy users. Your phone will ring off its hook, and you will take to hiding in dark places to avoid the wrath of disgruntled colleagues. Refer to the *User Access Checklist* at the end of the chapter.

Using Network Installation Checklists

This section contains a series of checklists referenced throughout this chapter. Feel free to duplicate the checklists to use for your own purposes.

Checklist for Installing the Cabling

☐ Select type of cabling:

○ Coaxial

☐ RG-58 (Thin Ethernet)
☐ RG-11 or RG-8 (Thick Ethernet)
☐ RG-62 (ARCnet)

○ Twisted Pair (10BASE-T Ethernet or token ring)
Number of wires (generally 4 to 8): ________

○ IBM Type 1 (Token-Ring)

○ Fiber optic (FDDI or TCNS ARCnet)
Number of optic strands (generally 6 and up): ________

☐ Contract cabling to a cabling company?

☐ Y ☐ N

If Yes, name of contractor: ________________________________

☐ Cables needed (one per workstation or server, and between hubs): ________

☐ Length of cable:

Total length of all cabling: ________

Shortest cable length (minimum distance between two nodes): ________

Longest cable length (maximum distance between two nodes): ________

☐ Connectors needed (enter 0 if not applicable):

BNC connectors (thin Ethernet or ARCnet: 2 per cable): ________

Fiber optic connectors (FDDI: 2 per cable): ________

T connectors (thin Ethernet: 1 per workstation or server): ________

Terminators (thin or thick Ethernet: one at the end of each physical segment):________

Terminators (ARCnet: one per unused port in passive hub only): ________

☐ Transceivers needed (thick Ethernet: one per node): ________

☐ Repeaters needed: ________

☐ Hubs needed (also called concentrators or wire centers):

Number of ports per hub (typically 8): ________

Number of hubs needed: ________

To obtain this number, divide the number of nodes by the number of ports per hub.

Checklist for Installing Hard Drives and Other Storage Devices

- ☐ **IDE drives or other IDE devices**
  - ○ Drive jumpers set for Drive 0 (1st drive)
  - ○ Drive jumpers set for Drive 1 (2nd drive)
  - ○ Data cable plugged in and oriented correctly
  - ○ Power cable plugged in
  - ☐ HBA
    - ○ Interrupt (IRQ: usually E or 14): ________
    - ○ Port (usually 1F0 or 170): ________
    - ○ Which HBA (could be 2 in the computer):
      - ○ Primary
      - ○ Secondary

- ☐ **SCSI drives, tape units, and CD drive units**
  - ○ SCSI ID set (0 for 1st drive, 1 for 2nd drive, and so on)
  - ○ Data cable plugged in and oriented correctly
  - ○ Power cable plugged in
  - ○ Terminating resistors removed if the drive is not at the end of the cable
  - ☐ HBA
    - ○ Interrupt (IRQ: usually B or 11): ________
    - ○ Port (generally between 200 and 3FF): ________
    - ○ SCSI ID (usually 7): ________

Checklist for Installing Network Interface Cards

- ☐ **Ethernet**
  - ○ Interrupt (IRQ: usually between 2 and 15): ________
  - ○ Port (I/O address: usually between 200 and 3FF): ________
  - ○ Memory (not applicable for all cards): ________
  - ○ Other settings: ________________________________
  - ○ Connector:
    - ☐ BNC (thin Ethernet)
    - ☐ 15-pin AUI port (thick Ethernet)
    - ☐ RJ-45 (10BASE-T)
- ☐ **Token ring**
  - ○ Interrupt (IRQ: usually between 2 and 15): ________
  - ○ Port (I/O address: usually between 0A20 and 3FFF): ________
  - ○ Memory setting 1 (not applicable for all cards): ________
  - ○ Memory setting 2 (not applicable for all cards): ________
  - ○ Other settings: ________________________________
- ☐ **ARCnet**
  - ○ Interrupt (IRQ: usually between 2 and 15): ________
  - ○ Port (I/O address: usually between 0A20 and 3FFF): ________
  - ○ Memory (usually between C0000 and DFFFF): ________
  - ○ Other settings: ________________________________
  - ○ Node address (between 1 and 254): ________
- ☐ **FDDI**
  - ○ Interrupt (IRQ: usually between 2 and 15): ________
  - ○ Port (I/O address: usually between 0A20 and 3FFF): ________
  - ○ Memory setting 1 (not applicable for all cards): ________
  - ○ Memory setting 2 (not applicable for all cards): ________
  - ○ Other settings: ________________________________
  - ○ Ring type:
    - ☐ Primary ring only
    - ☐ Dual ring

Checklist for Installing Peripherals

☐ **Printers**

- ○ Type of printer
  - ☐ Parallel ☐ Serial ☐ Direct connect to network
- ○ Printer connection
  - ☐ Connected to server
  - ☐ Connected to DOS workstation
  - ☐ Connected to UNIX host
  - ☐ Connected to Macintosh
  - ☐ Other connection: ________________________________
- ○ Paper supply for 2 weeks
- ○ Additional printer supplies for 2 months
  - ☐ Ribbons ☐ Toner cartridges ☐ Ink cartridges
- ○ Printer cable installed
- ○ Printer self test performed (see printer documentation)
- ○ Printer prints from DOS
  (*boot computer on DOS and press the Print Screen key*)

☐ **Tape backup unit**

- ○ HBA installed
  - ☐ Interrupt (IRQ: usually B or 11): ________
  - ☐ Port (generally between 200 and 3FF): ________
- ○ Tapes for 2 months purchased
- ○ Test backup and restore performed (see unit documentation)

☐ **Other Devices:**

____

____

____

____

____

Checklist for Configuring a PC

☐ PC identification: ____________________ ☐ Amount of RAM: ______ MB

☐ Type of video:

○ VGA ○ Super VGA ○ Other

○ Monochrome (often the file server or a dedicated computer)

☐ Floppy drive A:

○ 3 1/2-inch disk, 1.44 MB ○ 5 1/4-inch disk, 1.2 MB

○ 3 1/2-inch disk, 720 KB ○ 5 1/4-inch disk, 360 KB

☐ Floppy drive B:

○ 3 1/2-inch disk, 1.44 MB ○ 5 1/4-inch disk, 1.2 MB

○ 3 1/2-inch disk, 720 KB ○ 5 1/4-inch disk, 360 KB

☐ Ports:

○ COM1 ○ COM2 ○ LPT1 ○ LPT2 ○ LPT3

☐ Internal hard drives:

○ Type of controller

☐ IDE paddleboard ☐ SCSI

☐ IDE built into the motherboard of the computer

○ First hard drive type: ________ (set to 0 or None for SCSI)

Heads: ______________ Cylinders: ______________

Tracks per sector: ______________ Precomp: ______________

○ Second hard drive type: ________ (set to 0 or None for SCSI)

Heads: ______________ Cylinders: ______________

Tracks per sector: ______________ Precomp: ______________

☐ If this computer is a file server:

Name: __________________________ Location: ______________________

☐ If this computer is a workstation:

Name: __________________________ Location: ______________________

☐ Operating System and Version:

○ DOS ○ Macintosh ○ OS/2 ○ Windows NT ○ UNIX

Version: ____________________________

☐ Name of the computer (only applies to Macintosh, UNIX, Windows for Workgroups, or Windows NT):

____

User Access Checklist

- ☐ Successful login?

  Y ☐ N ☐

- ☐ Login script OK?

  Y ☐ N ☐

- ☐ Menu program OK?

  Y ☐ N ☐

- ☐ Successful execution of every application?

  Y ☐ N ☐

- ☐ Able to save and retrieve documents?

  Y ☐ N ☐

- ☐ Printing successful?

  Y ☐ N ☐

- ☐ Able to send and receive e-mail?

  Y ☐ N ☐

Location	→	Room	Floor	Building	City	State	Province	Country	Other
Organization:									

Organizational Structure Checklist

O or OU	User Name	Last Name	Phone	E-Mail	Location	Queue	Other Info

User Information Checklist

File Server	Volume	Directory	Applic.	Data	Description

File System Checklist

Print Server	O or OU	Printer	Queue	Location	Authorized Users

Print Object Checklist

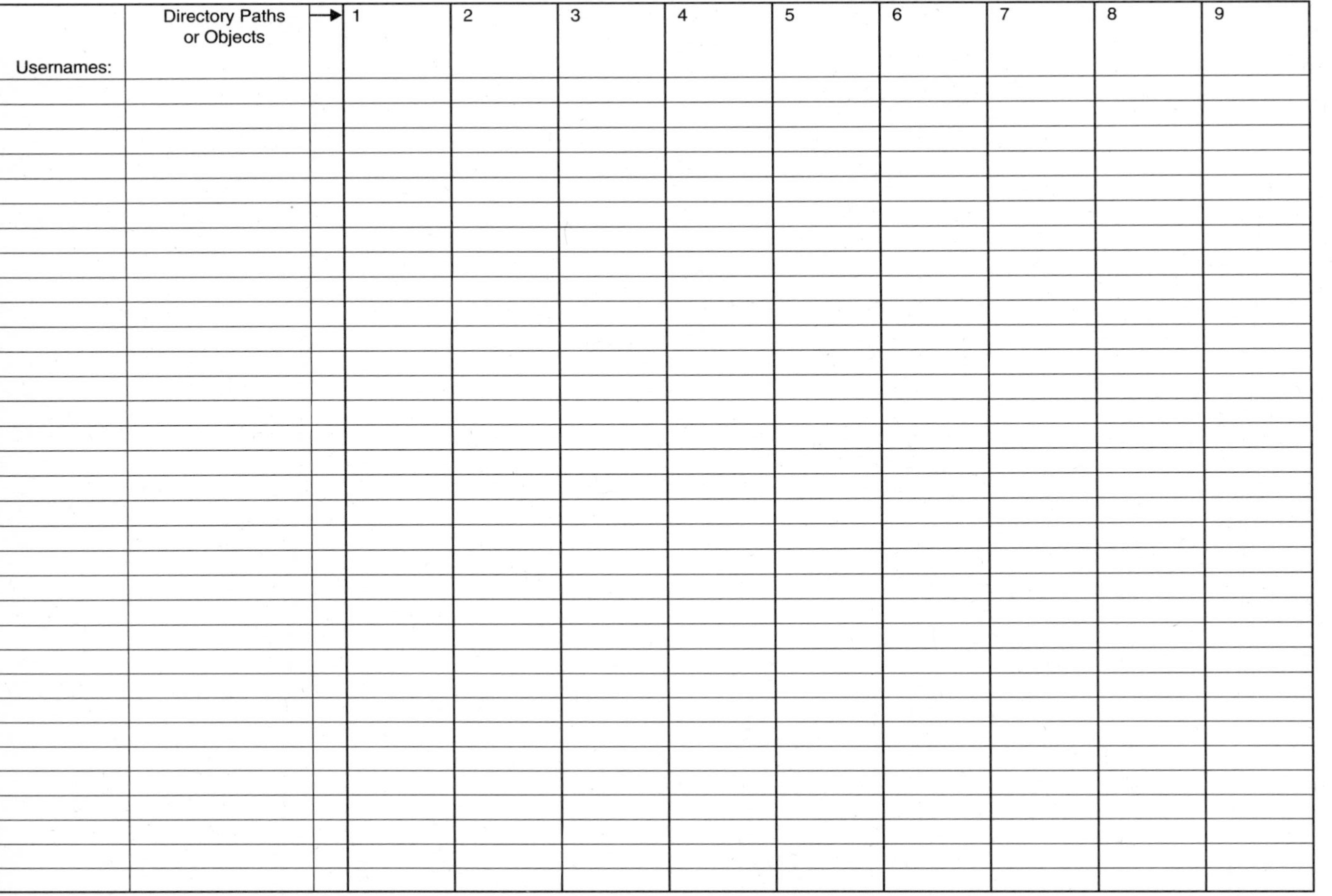

Usernames:	Directory Paths or Objects	→	1	2	3	4	5	6	7	8	9

Rights Worksheet

Table 10.2 summarizes the worksheets and their purposes.

Table 10.2
Worksheet Summary

Name of Worksheet	File Name (*.XLS and *.WKS)	Description
Organizational Structure Checklist	ORG_LOC.*	Provides a matrix of locations across the top (X axis), cross referenced by organizations, departments, units, workgroups, and so on, within your company.
User Information Checklist	USERINFO.*	Lists information on the users in your network. Information tracked includes users' NDS organization or organiza tional unit, user name, last name, and other information.
File System Checklist	FILESYS.*	Catalogs information on applications and shared data directories on the network. Information tracked includes the file server, volume, directory, and the type of listing (application or data).
Print Objects Checklist	PRINTING.*	Keeps track of network printing printing objects. The information tracked includes the name of the print server, the O or OU, printer, queue, physical location, and authorized users (or container/group).
Rights Worksheet	RIGHTS.*	You can use this worksheet to deter mine file system or NDS rights. Down the left column (the Y axis) you write down the names of users. Across the top (the X axis), write the names of directories of objects. Fill in the desired rights at the intersection of a username and directory (or object).

Summary

This chapter gave you an overview of the complete installation of a network. You were presented with a series of steps, all the way from physically installing the cable, to logically planning the NDS tree, to granting users access to applications and directories on the network.

Various questions were posed to help you plan for the physical installation of the network. These questions covered the areas of cabling, hubs, repeaters, MAUs, and so on; computer hardware and setup; and hard-drive configuration. You then were given an overview of the installation of NetWare 4.1, as well as DOS, Windows, OS/2, UNIX, and Macintosh clients. A series of tests were covered to give you an idea of how well the network is functioning. These tests can be performed from the file server, from workstations, and using network analyzers.

You also learned about planning the NDS tree, adding organizations and organizational units, and user objects. You were introduced to a series of worksheets to assist you in organizing your network.

The worksheets and questionnaires presented in this chapter will prove useful as documentation for your network. The worksheets also are provided in "soft" format on the disk provided with this book. Feel free to copy the worksheets and use them as needed. Do not use these worksheets with a presentation, product, or other commercial transaction (in other words, do not use these worksheets for your own financial gain).

The last sections in this chapter presented a brief overview of the remaining part of setting up a network: creating login scripts, batch files, and menus. Windows was discussed briefly, and a short section on testing user access was provided.

The next chapter covers hardware configuration in detail.

Hardware Configuration

Now that you have a general idea of what is required to install the network and have gone over the checklists presented in the preceding chapter, it is time to cover some installation con- cepts in detail. Chapter 12, "Installing the Network Operating System," covers NetWare 4.1 installation in detail. This chapter covers details of installing the file server computer and peripherals.

Planning Server Memory

Before you can install the file server computer, you must plan for a sufficient amount of file server RAM. This section covers what is involved in calculating the amount of RAM required in the file server. At the end of the section is a formula for you to use when calculating file server RAM.

Examining Resources and Memory Requirements

Various resources affect the amount of RAM required in the file server. These include the following:

- File caching
- File allocation table (FAT) caching
- Directory entry table (DET) caching
- Packet receive buffers
- The operating system kernel
- NetWare Loadable Modules (NLMs)

The largest usage of file server RAM should be for file caching. The file server makes a copy of each file as it comes in from the LAN to the file server's hard drive, or as the server reads a file from its hard drive and sends it out to a workstation on the LAN. Figure 11.1 illustrates the process of file caching: A file (1) is read from the file server's hard drive to RAM (2). From RAM, the file is sent through the file server's NIC (network interface card) out onto the LAN (3) in fragments known as *packets.* The packets are captured by the destination workstation and reassembled back into a file (4). In the meantime, another file is sent out across the LAN, fragmented into packets (5) from another workstation. The packets arrive at the file server's NIC, which transfers them into RAM (6). The packets are reassembled into a file that is then transferred to the file server's hard drive (7).

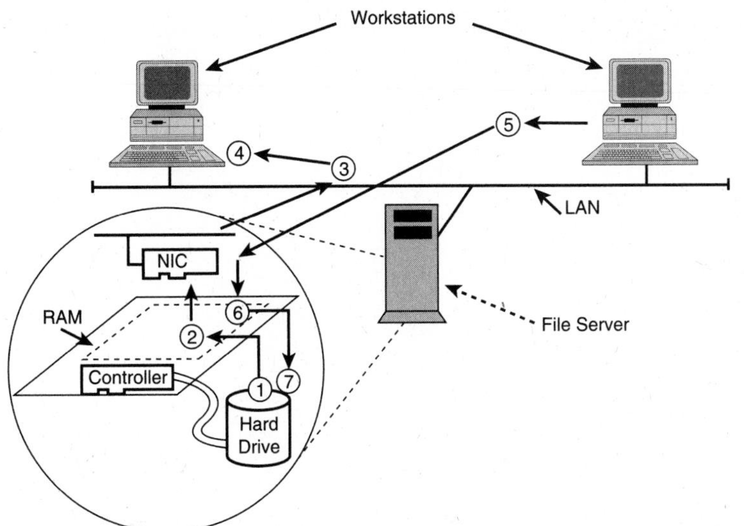

Figure 11.1
The file caching process.

FAT caching occurs as the file server is mounting the volumes on its hard drives and online storage (such as CD-ROM players). The mounting process involves copying the FAT from the hard drive (or online storage) to file server RAM. After the FAT is resident in file server RAM, the volume is made available to network users. The FAT is copied to RAM to increase the speed in which NetWare can access files on its hard drive(s) and online storage. When a user requests a file, NetWare consults the DET, which in turn points to the FAT. The FAT tells NetWare exactly where the file is located on the hard drive. NetWare then can organize the requests for files from network users in the order in which the files are physically stored on the hard drive. The result is a tremendous increase in efficiency and access speed.

The DET contains information about files stored on the file server's hard drive(s) and online storage. The information stored includes the following:

- File name
- File size
- File trustee rights
- Name of the user who created or last modified the file
- Date the file was created
- Date the file was last accessed
- Date the file was last updated

- Date the file was last backed up
- File attributes
- Pointer to the FAT

The DET also contains information about directories. The DET is not cached in its entirety in file server RAM; only the most recently used portions of the DET are cached. You can use SET commands from the file server's console to set the minimum and maximum number of buffers used to cache the DET. A *buffer* is a block of RAM (typically 4 KB) reserved for caching some sort of information. The SET commands are explained in great detail in Chapter 38, "Fine-Tuning the Server." The DET and FAT also are stored twice each in each volume on the file server's hard drive(s).

Packet receive buffers are specialized buffers used to store user requests coming into the file server from user workstations on the LAN. A packet receive buffer is set to the maximum physical packet receive size. This size can be adjusted using the SET MAXIMUM PHYSICAL RECEIVE PACKET SIZE command on the file server. The default size is 2,048 bytes.

The operating system kernel itself takes up approximately 7 MB of RAM. Additional NLMs will take additional RAM. Table 11.1 summarizes the various factors that affect the amount of RAM required in the file server. HD_CD_MB refers to the amount of hard drive space in megabytes you have available as well as the amount of space for CDs mounted.

Table 11.1
Calculating File Server RAM Requirements

Item	RAM Usage
NetWare 4.1 operating	7 MB system kernel
Memory for file caching	1 MB + (5 KB * HD_CD_MB)
Media manager	150 KB + (0.2 KB * HD_CD_MB)
User connections	2 KB * number of users logged in
Packet receive buffers	2.3 KB * buffer
Directory cache buffers	4.3 KB * buffer

Item	RAM Usage
Service processes	9 KB * service process
File compression enabled	250 KB
Volume Requirements: Add memory requirements for each volume (formulas on next few lines).	
Volume block (VB)	Volume size/block size
Number of files (NF)	Volume size/average file size
File allocation table	VB * 8.2 bytes
Block suballocation (if enabled)	(((block size * 2) – 1) * 4096 bytes) + (5 * NF)
Directory entry table	NF * 10 bytes
NLM Requirements: Add requirements for any NLMs you plan to load. Certain NLMs are listed later in the chapter.	
PSERVER.NLM	750,000
INSTALL.NLM	700,000
CLIB.NLM	500,000
TCPIP.NLM (plus SNMP.NLM — 48K)	480,000
IPXRTR, IPXTRNM, IPXFLT (NLSP)	580,000

Calculating Memory Requirements

Table 11.1 requires that you know certain parameters before calculating memory. This table has been placed into a worksheet for you to fill in and use in calculating server RAM. The worksheet is presented in table 11.2, and an example with values filled in appears in table 11.3.

Note You can download the file that contains this worksheet from the Macmillan Computer Publishing forum on CompuServe. After you access the Macmillan Computer Publishing forum (GO MACMILLAN), you can find the files for this and other NRP networking books in the Networking and Comms library. The name of the file is SPACE.XLS (Excel) or SPACE.WKS (Lotus 1-2-3 or Quattro Pro).

Table 11.2
File Server RAM Worksheet

Parameters		Values
Total hard disk + CD space in MB		0
Total number of users		0
Total number of volumes		0
Average file size in bytes		51,200
Total space for NLMs (see list)		3,010,000
Block size (if more than one, enter lowest)		64,000
Packet receive buffers		100
Directory cache buffers		100
Service processes		20
File compression enabled (Y/N)		Y
Block suballocation enabled (Y/N)		Y
Item	*RAM Usage*	*Total*
NetWare v4.1 operating system kernel	7 MB	7,000,000
Memory for file caching	1 MB + (5 KB * HD MB)	1,000,000
Media manager	150 KB + (0.2K * HD MB)	153,600
User connections	2 KB * number of users logged in	

Item	RAM Usage	Total
Packet receive buffers	2.3 KB * buffer	235,520
Directory cache buffers	4.3 KB * buffer	440,320
Service processes	9 KB * service process	184,320
File compression enabled	250 KB	256,000
Volume Requirements: Add memory requirements for each volume (formulas on next few lines).		
Volume block (VB)	Volume size/block size	_
Number of files (NF)	Volume size/average file size	_
File allocation tables	VB * 8.2 bytes	_
Block suballocation (if enabled)	(((block size * 2) – 1) * 4,096 bytes) + (5 * NF)	123,904 _
Directory entry tables	NF * 10 bytes	_
NLM Requirements: Add requirements for any NLMs you plan to load. Certain NLMs are listed below.		
PSERVER.NLM	750,000	750,000
INSTALL.NLM	700,000	700,000
CLIB.NLM	500,000	500,000
TCPIP.NLM (plus SNMP.NLM—48 KB)	480,000	480,000
IPXRTR, IPXTRNM, IPXFLT (NLSP)	580,000	580,000
NLM Subtotal	3,010,000	
TOTAL		12,403,664

Suppose you have the following system:

- One 1 GB hard drive and one 650 MB hard drive
- 100 users
- Average file size of 50 KB
- File compression enabled
- Block suballocation enabled
- Volume SYS is 650 MB with a block size of 16 KB
- Volume VOL1 is 1 GB with a block size of 64 KB
- Packet receive buffers are set to 300
- TCP/IP and NLSP are loaded

The worksheet with the preceding values filled in is illustrated in table 11.3. Note that because the block sizes for the two volumes are different, the lower of the two values is entered. Also note that when TCP/IP is loaded, CLIB is also loaded. This gives you the worst-case memory requirements.

TABLE 11.3
File Server RAM Worksheet with Sample Values

Parameters	Values
Total hard disk space in MB	1,650
Total number of users	100
Total number of volumes	2
Average file size in bytes	50*1024 = 51,200
Total space for NLMs (see list)	1,560,000
Block size (if more than one, enter lowest)	16*1024 = 16,384
Packet receive buffers	300
Directory cache buffers	100

Parameters	Values
Service processes	20
File compression enabled (Y/N)	Y
Block suballocation enabled (Y/N)	Y

Item	RAM Usage	Total
NetWare v4.1 operating system kernel	7 MB	7,000,000
Memory for file caching	1 MB + (5 KB * HD MB)	9,448,000
Media manager	150 KB + (0.2 KB * HD MB)	491,520
User connections	2 KB * number of users logged in	204,800
Packet receive buffers	2.3 KB * buffer	706,560
Directory cache buffers	4.3 KB * buffer	440,320
Service processes	9 KB * service process	184,320
File compression enabled	250 KB	256,000
Volume Requirements: Add memory requirements for each volume (formulas on next few lines).		
Volume block (VB)	Volume size/block size	105,600
Number of files (NF)	Volume size/average file size	33,792
File allocation tables	VB * 8.2 bytes	865,920
Block suballocation (if enabled)	(((block size * 2) – 1) * 4096 bytes + (5 * NF)	28,672 168,960
Directory entry tables	NF * 10 bytes	337,920

continues

Table 11.3, Continued
File Server RAM Worksheet with Sample Values

Item	RAM Usage	Total
NLM Requirements: Add requirements for any NLMs you plan to load. Certain NLMs are listed as follows.		
CLIB.NLM	500,000	500,000
TCPIP.NLM (plus SNMP.NLM—48 KB)	480,000	480,000
IPXRTR, IPXTRNM, IPXFLT (NLSP)	580,000	580,000
NLM Subtotal	1,560,000	
TOTAL		21,692,992

As you can see from table 11.3, the RAM requirements for this configuration are approximately 21.7 MB. Because RAM typically is sold in increments of 4 or 16 MB, the server would need 24 MB of RAM.

Installing Disk Drives

Several considerations are involved when installing hard drives. This section covers mirroring and duplexing issues, IDE and SCSI drives, RAID technology, and CD-ROM drives. The NetWare 4.1 operating system handles volumes rather than physical drives. It can handle a maximum of 64 volumes, and each volume can support up to 1,024 drives. This enables NetWare 4.1 to support a theoretical maximum of 65,536 drives. At the present time, no hardware technology is commercially available to support this many drives, but NetWare 4.1 is ready for the hardware when it arrives.

Duplexing and Mirroring

Setting up the file server to support disk mirroring requires that you install disk drives in pairs. Each mirrored drive should be mirrored with an identical drive. You generally can install two drives in the file server itself, but additional drives might require a separate external housing. Storage Dimensions, for example, is a company that specializes in selling external units. These drive units hold from two to four drives and can be stacked one on top of the other.

If you plan to duplex the drives rather than mirror them, you need to install additional hard drive controllers in the file server. The only difference between mirrored and duplexed drives is that the duplexed drives use separate disk controllers.

As you can see in figure 11.2, there are four drives connected to two controllers. If you mirror the two drives on each controller together, you will not achieve the performance gain realized by duplexing. Figure 11.3, on the other hand, shows the same configuration with drives mirrored across controllers. This is an example of duplexing.

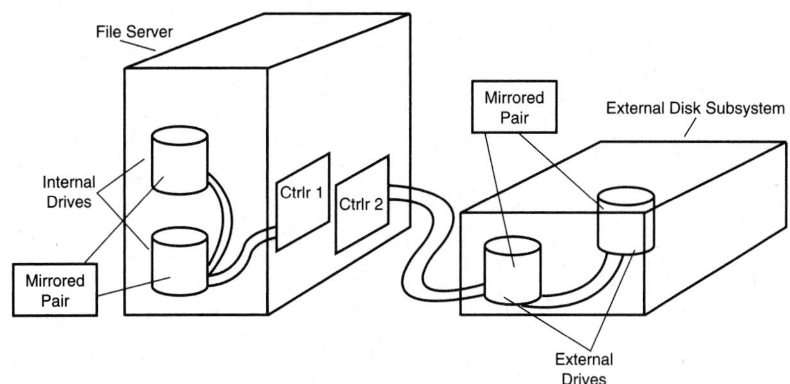

Figure 11.2

Drive mirroring.

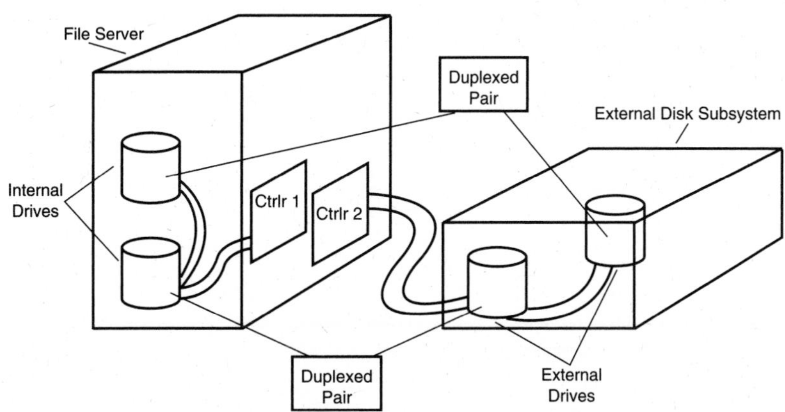

Figure 11.3

Drive duplexing.

IDE Drive Configuration

IDE (Integrated Drive Electronics) drives contain the drive controllers on the hard drive units themselves. This is also known as an *embedded controller*. On the computer's motherboard, you will need to either install a connecting device known as a *paddleboard* or locate an IDE connector integrated into the motherboard itself.

Each paddleboard can handle (currently) two IDE drives at most. It is possible to have two paddleboards in one computer, which will give you a maximum of four IDE drives.

Due to their nature, IDE drives do not support mirroring or duplexing. When two IDE drives are cabled together on the same paddleboard, the embedded controller on the second drive "slaves" itself to the controller on the first drive. The second controller essentially disables itself and defers to the controller on the first drive. If the first drive were to fail, the second drive would fail as well. This would defeat the mirroring mechanism, and the server would go down.

It is possible to duplex two IDE drives by setting up each drive as a master drive on its own IDE paddleboard. However, you should not use any slave drives with this configuration. Even when using dual paddleboards, the performance of duplexed IDE drives probably will not be as high as the performance of mirrored SCSI drives.

Here are some considerations when installing an IDE drive in a computer:

- ◆ You must make sure that pin 1 on the drive cable (it usually has a red stripe) is oriented correctly. You can use this as a guide to ensure that pin 1 on the IDE paddleboard (or on the motherboard when the IDE interface is built-in) is connected to pin 1 on the drive itself.

- ◆ Look for jumpers labeled C/D, DSP, HSP, and ACT. These jumpers are used to select which drive is the primary, which is the secondary, and a single drive. The settings for these jumpers will vary according to the vendor. Table 11.4 summarizes typical settings for most Conner IDE drives.

Table 11.4
Typical Settings for Conner IDE Drives

Drive Type	Settings
Single Drive (Drive 1 of 1)	ACT and C/D are jumpered
Primary Drive (Drive 1 of 2)	ACT, C/D, and DSP are jumpered
Secondary Drive (Drive 2 of 2)	HSP is jumpered

- You must run the computer's CMOS setup program and set the closest possible match for the drive type. Most computer BIOS chips store a series of drive types. These consist of a series of settings that consist of groupings of heads, cylinders, and tracks per sector. You need to consult the documentation provided by the drive vendor if unsure of these parameters. If you cannot find the proper drive type, you can do one of the following:
  - Look for a drive type called *auto sense.* This will read the drive type from the drive when the computer first boots up.
  - Look for a user-defined drive type. This setting enables you to enter the number of heads, cylinders, and so forth yourself. Enter the settings provided by the vendor, or the closest possible match.

If you are unsure of the drive parameters of an IDE drive when entering a new user-defined drive type, enter the closest match. The drive capacity you specify should always be less than the actual capacity of the drive. If you accidentally specify a drive capacity larger than the drive can physically handle, you run the risk of data corruption.

Figure 11.4 shows you a sample CMOS setup screen from which you can set the drive type.

```
           AMIBIOS SETUP PROGRAM - STANDARD CMOS SETUP
       (C)1992 American Megatrends Inc., All Rights Reserved

Date (mn/date/year): Sat, Apr 02 1994              Base Memory : 640 KB
Time (hour/min/sec): 14 : 05 : 37                  Ext. Memory : 7168 KB
                                    Cyln  Head  WPcom LZone Sect  Size
Hard Disk C: Type   : 47 = USER TYPE  723   13    65535 723   51    234 MB
Hard Disk D: Type   : Not Installed
Floppy Drive A:     : 1.44 MB, 3½"                 Sun Mon Tue Wed Thu Fri Sat
Floppy Drive B:     : Not Installed
Primary Display     : VGA/PGA/EGA                   27  28  29  30  31   1   2
Keyboard            : Installed
                                                     3   4   5   6   7   8   9

                                                    10  11  12  13  14  15  16
 FIXED type = 01...46, USER defined type = 47,
 For type 47 Enter: Cyln,Head,WPcom,LZone,Sec,      17  18  19  20  21  22  23
 (WPcom is 0 for ALL,  65535 for NONE)
                                                    24  25  26  27  28  29  30

                                                     1   2   3   4   5   6   7
 ESC:Exit ↓→↑Select F2/F3:Color PU/PD:Modify
```

Figure 11.4

A CMOS setup screen.

SCSI Drive Configuration

SCSI drives have considerations that are quite different from those of IDE drives. SCSI drives (or devices) can consist of hard drives, CD-ROM drives, tape drives, and other devices. Two of the most important issues when installing SCSI drives are setting the SCSI device ID and terminating the SCSI bus. This section addresses these and other important issues.

Host Bus Adapters

Each SCSI device has a built-in controller referred to as an embedded SCSI controller. The SCSI devices are cabled together to form a SCSI bus. The bus connects to the computer through an interface card known as a host bus adapter (HBA). HBAs are SCSI controllers in their own right that serve to interface other SCSI devices with a PC's data bus. Most SCSI controllers are capable of performing bus mastering, which enables the controller to seize control of the data bus and dump data directly into the computer's main memory without the intervention of the CPU.

The file server's SCSI hard drives should be on their own HBA. In many cases, you also will have a SCSI CD-ROM player and tape drive on the file server. If this is the case, you should place an additional SCSI HBA to service these units. Otherwise, you will find that these devices, which are substantially slower than hard drives, will slow down access to hard drives on the same SCSI bus.

SCSI ID

Each SCSI device has to be assigned an independent device ID. This ID typically is set by one or more jumpers on the device itself. Some external disk subsystems enable you to set the ID through an external rotary switch.

SCSI ID numbers range from 0 to 7, enabling you to have a total of eight SCSI devices/controllers on the same SCSI bus. The HBA typically is set to SCSI ID 7. Hard drives commonly start with 0 and are numbered sequentially upwards.

The device ID numbering starts fresh for each separate SCSI bus. The following is an example of a typical configuration:

HBA	Device	SCSI ID
First	The HBA itself	7
First	Hard drive 0	0
First	Hard drive 1	1
Second	The HBA itself	7

HBA	Device	SCSI ID
Second	CD-ROM player	0
Second	Tape drive	1

As you can see in the preceding example, even though there are four SCSI devices and two HBAs, the device numbering begins at 0 again for the second HBA.

Some SCSI adapters assume that SCSI ID numbers 0 and 1 are hard drives. If you have set your hard drives to an ID other than 0 or 1, and have problems, try setting them to 0 or 1 and see if the problem disappears.

SCSI Bus Termination

Each separate SCSI bus must be independently terminated. There are two types of termination: active and passive. *Active termination* (also referred to as *external termination*) uses a terminating resistor pack that is placed at the end of the cable. This typically is accomplished using a special connector that is plugged into the open SCSI port in an external SCSI drive subsystem or free-standing device (such as a CD-ROM player). *Passive termination* uses a set of terminating resistors, often built into the circuitry of the SCSI device, which pull the signal down to enable signals to travel on the SCSI bus reliably. Passive termination often is invoked by calling up a special setup routine. On an Adaptec SCSI HBA controller, for example, you can press Ctrl+A when first booting up the computer. This brings you to a special setup utility in the ROM on the controller. Between the two methods, active termination will give you the most reliable performance. This is especially true when you have more than two SCSI devices on a SCSI bus.

Figures 11.5 and 11.6 illustrate two types of termination scenarios. In figure 11.5, two internal drives and two external drives are connected to a single HBA. The outer two drives have termination; the inner two drives and the HBA itself have no termination.

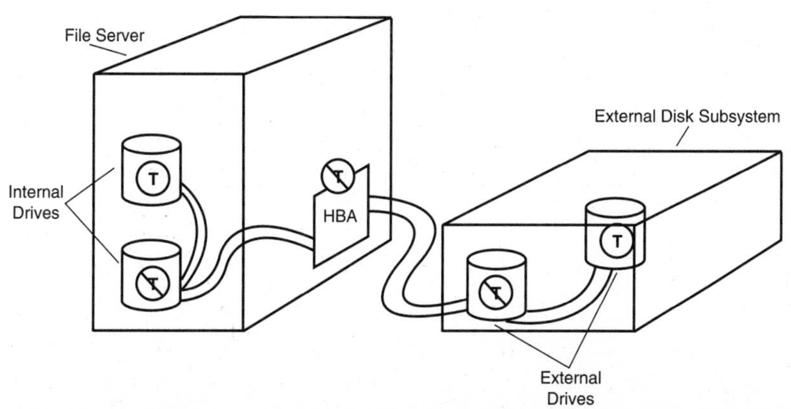

Figure 11.5

SCSI termination with four drives and one HBA.

In figure 11.6, there are two internal drives and two external drives connected to two HBAs. The outer drives in both SCSI buses have termination. The HBAs also have termination.

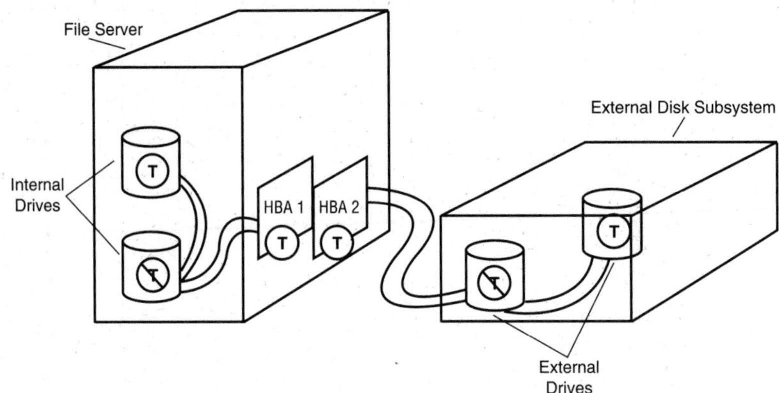

Figure 11.6
SCSI termination with two SCSI buses.

SCSI versus IDE

SCSI technology is more expensive than IDE. SCSI devices in a bus act independently, whereas secondary IDE drives use the controller of the primary drive. When SCSI drives are mirrored or duplexed and the primary drive fails, the secondary drive immediately takes over. There is no loss of service as with mirrored IDE drives.

When the file server sends a request to read or write data to a SCSI drive, the drive temporarily shuts itself off from the SCSI bus. The drive processes the data request and reestablishes access to the bus. In this way, the file server can put all SCSI drives to work on the bus without having to wait for any one drive to finish processing. IDE drives do not operate in this fashion. When an IDE drive receives a read/write request, it must entirely process the request before relinquishing control of the IDE bus.

Fast SCSI and SCSI-II

SCSI technology is developing in two directions: fast and wide. These two directions represent two different philosophies on the part of the SCSI manufacturers. The "fast" school proposes to improve SCSI technology by reading and writing data at a higher rate. The "wide" school proposes to transfer more bits of data at one time (using a wider bus). Some vendors are implementing variations of both.

Fast SCSI and SCSI-II are two specifications that are improvements over standard SCSI. Existing SCSI devices can, in most cases, work with the new controllers.

RAID Technology

RAID (redundant array of inexpensive devices) technology is generally built on a SCSI bus foundation. Some vendors, such as Micropolis, offer RAID systems that are hardware-based. If you purchase such a system you just need to plug the drive units together and connect them to an HBA supplied with the system. Other vendors, such as Adaptec, offer a software RAID utility that reprograms special Adaptec HBAs and turns them into RAID controllers.

An array of RAID drives is seen by the file server as a single drive. When you perform the NetWare installation, you will see only one drive on the list even though you may have 5 or 10 drives in the array. In the case of RAID systems you will not need to set up mirroring through NetWare. The redundancy is performed through the RAID system. When a drive in a RAID system fails, the system will continue to provide service to network users. The Administrator or network installer can then bring the system down at their leisure and the defective drive can be replaced. Some RAID systems have a hot swap feature that enables the defective drive to be replaced without turning off the disk drive subsystem or interrupting network services. In some cases a utility must be run to rebuild the data on the new drive. In other cases you just need to bring the server back up again, and the RAID system will rebuild itself.

CD-ROM Drives

CD-ROM drives on the file server are most commonly configured as SCSI devices. CD-ROM drives on workstations can be any of a variety of systems. The Sound Blaster card, for example, supports a proprietary CD-ROM drive interface. In this case, the Sound Blaster can provide for digitized sound as well as service a CD. SCSI CD-ROM drives tend to be faster than drives supported by other technologies such as the Sound Blaster.

Most vendors of SCSI HBAs provide additional hardware support for CD-ROM drives. Adaptec, for example, provides a driver ASPICD.DSK in addition to its other SCSI drivers (AHA1540.DSK and ASPITRAN.DSK, for example). This special driver must be loaded after the other drivers for the SCSI HBA.

Installing Server Peripherals

After the file server's hard drives, controllers, and so on are installed, it is time to look at installing additional peripheral devices. Of the many types of devices that can be installed on the file server, two of the most important are the UPS (uninterruptible power supply) and the tape backup unit. Other devices include modems, specialized adapters, and printers.

Uninterruptible Power Supplies

A UPS is a vital file server component, as explained in Chapters 1 and 9. Installing the UPS involves physically attaching the UPS to the file server and installing UPS monitoring software. The primary connection between the UPS and the server is the server's AC power cord. The file server computer is plugged into the power outlet on the back of the UPS so that the UPS can provide uninterrupted power.

In addition to the power connection, most UPS units include a connection that enables the UPS to inform the file server of a power outage. UPS monitoring software running on the file server receives such notification and takes the preprogrammed action. Some UPS vendors include a special card that you need to install in the file server and configure. Other vendors enable you to connect the UPS monitoring port to the file server's mouse port or serial port (COM1 or COM2).

UPS monitoring software varies in scope between vendors. At its simplest, the monitoring software provides the following features:

- The capability to bring the file server down gracefully after a power outage is detected.
- Giving the network Administrator the status of the UPS unit's internal battery.
- Enabling the network Administrator to change the amount of time between the loss of power and when the file server is brought down.

In addition to these capabilities, more sophisticated UPS units (and often, more expensive units), offer these capabilities:

- Power metering over a period of time. Some software includes utilities that enable you to graph the status of power being delivered to your office. Such software tracks when power surges take place as well as inadequate power and brownouts.
- Options to test the status of the internal battery.
- The capability to define the amount of time you consider to be a true power outage. In some situations you might experience a brownout that lasts for only 5 or 10 seconds (or less). In this case you might not want the UPS software to bring the file server down. With a sophisticated UPS you can define a power outage to be when you lose power for more than 10 seconds, in this case.

Read the installation notes provided by the UPS vendor carefully. Some vendors state that the UPS battery should be drained periodically for optimum performance. Other vendors state just the opposite—that if the battery is drained, the UPS unit will no longer operate.

Tape Backup Units

Most tape backup units supplied by network resellers are SCSI devices. As mentioned earlier in this chapter, you should be very cautious when attaching a tape drive to the same SCSI HBA as the file server's hard drives. If the backup takes place at a time when the hard drives are not being utilized, this is not a problem. Otherwise, the performance of the server will be affected.

Most tape backup units come with backup software. Most packages written for the NetWare 3.*x* environment will back up all files on the file server. The capability to back up the NDS is of greater concern. If you are not able to find suitable software compatible with the NDS, a good workaround is to use your existing NetWare 3.*x*-based software to back up files and directories on your servers. You then can use the SBACKUP.NLM utility provided with NetWare 4.1 to back up the NDS. SBACKUP is discussed in greater detail in Chapter 41, "Protecting Your Network Files."

Configuring Network Interface Cards

Network interface cards (NICs) are set in several different ways: jumpers, DIP switches, or through software. When configuring NICs, you can fill out the worksheet provided in the "Network Cards" section of Chapter 10, "Installation Overview." This section gives you an idea about what parameters need to be set, tools to use to determine which settings are in use, and how to go about setting the NIC.

Examining Parameters That Need To Be Set

NICs are like any other board that is installed in a PC—you need to configure the board to avoid conflicts with the settings of other boards in the computer. The parameters that need to be set on a NIC can include any or all of the following:

- Interrupts
- Input/output port addresses
- Memory addresses
- DMA channels
- Connector type
- Slot number (MCA and EISA)
- Node address (ARCnet)

This section discusses the parameters listed in this list. The following subsections discuss how to physically set the various parameters.

Interrupts

An *interrupt,* often abbreviated IRQ (for *interrupt request*), is the way NIC hardware physically signals the CPU. Microprocessors are designed with a number of pins designated as interrupt lines. Any NIC (or any PC board, for that matter) that requires periodic servicing by the CPU can send out an electrical signal on its interrupt line. The CPU senses the signal and stops what it is currently doing. Control passes to an *interrupt service routine,* a specialized software program designed to work with the NIC. After you set up the NIC and install it, you also will need to configure the software that drives the NIC with the appropriate settings.

Input/Output Port Addresses

The input/output port address is also known as *I/O address, port address,* or simply *port.* As the name implies, the port is an address from which the CPU can send and receive information from the real world. Each device in the computer that delivers output or receives input is assigned a port address. These devices range from the printer port, which delivers information to be printed to an attached printer, to the serial port, which could be used to send and receive information by modem. In the case of a NIC, the port address represents the memory address at which the CPU expects to find LAN information.

The port address is actually a range of addresses representing registers on an IC chip located on the NIC itself. A *register* is a type of storage circuit much like a single cell of RAM. The CPU thinks the address is somewhere in main memory. By setting the I/O address, what you actually are doing is redirecting this address from main memory to a register on a chip. The memory cells at this address are overlaid by the registers on the NIC.

The registers on the NIC are wired to the NIC's transmitter and receiver circuits. When data appears on the LAN that is addressed to the NIC, this data is pulled into the NIC through its receiver circuits. The data is then dumped into the storage registers on the NIC. The LAN driver on the file server causes its CPU to pull the information from the storage registers and place it in a packet receive buffer in main memory. The data is pulled in through the port one byte at a time until a complete data frame has been extracted off the LAN.

The port address represents the starting point of the series of locations reserved for the NIC's registers. The port address typically spans 8, 16, or 32 bytes of memory space. Figure 11.7 illustrates the process of receiving information through the I/O port.

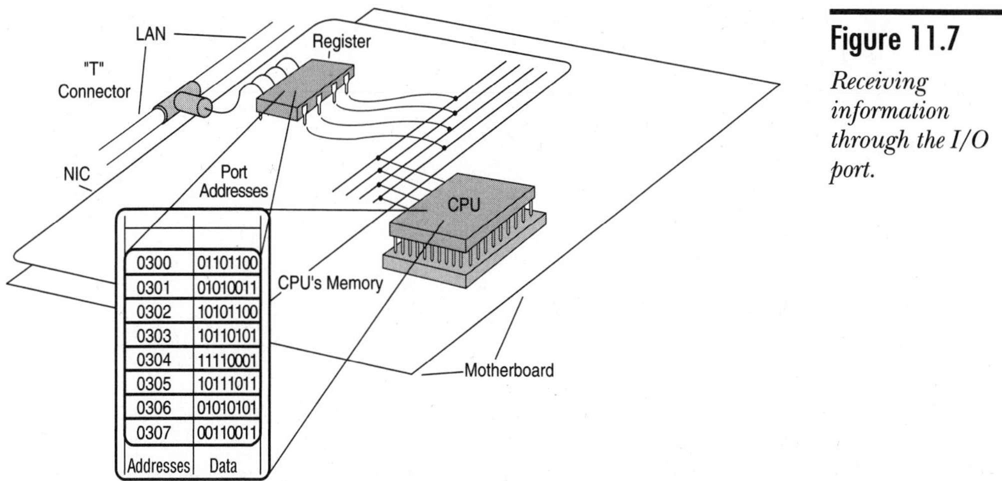

Figure 11.7
Receiving information through the I/O port.

Memory Addresses

Memory addresses serve several purposes depending on the NIC. In some cases the memory address serves to map a ROM chip on the NIC into the computer's memory scheme. The ROM chip contains software instructions that the LAN driver needs to access from time to time. When you program the memory address in this case, you instruct the LAN driver where to find the beginning of this instruction set. The computer's main memory is hidden, and the ROM chip is positioned at the memory address you program.

In other cases, the NIC needs a memory buffer that is taken from the host computer's main memory. In this case the memory address is a pointer to main memory where the NIC is allowed to store information coming in from the LAN or going out to the LAN.

Some NICs require two memory addresses: a memory buffer in main memory in addition to memory that enables the contents of a ROM chip to be mapped into the computer's memory. In other cases some NICs need two memory buffers in main memory: one for incoming information and another for outgoing information. Use of the memory address is controlled by the vendor of the NIC and varies considerably from vendor to vendor.

The area of main memory used for memory addresses is between the upper limit for DOS (640 KB) and the border reserved for extended memory (1 MB). This area of memory, often referred to as the *upper memory area,* is used for many other purposes (video adapters, for example). You need to exercise extreme caution when assigning memory in this area to a NIC. If you find that the NIC causes conflicts with other uses for memory on a DOS-based workstation, you might want to experiment with the

EXCLUDE option of the EMM386 driver. For more details, please see Chapter 14, "DOS Client Basics." This is not an issue on the file server because you should have no memory-resident programs running.

DMA Channels

DMA (direct memory access) is a technique used in place of bus mastering. The difference between DMA and bus mastering is that in the case of DMA, the NIC has to signal the CPU that it wishes to gain access to the bus using one of the DMA lines. If access is granted, the memory address lines of the CPU are shut off to prevent access to the bus. The NIC is then able to dump information directly into main memory. In the case of bus mastering, the NIC simply seizes control of the bus without notifying the CPU. Because one less step is involved in bus mastering, memory transfer is much faster with bus mastering than with DMA.

Eight DMA lines typically are available in an Intel-based PC. The lines are numbered 0–7. Most NICs that use DMA offer you the option of using a DMA channel from 1 through 7.

Connector Type

Some NICs have more than one connector that attaches the NIC to the LAN cabling. In the case of Ethernet, for example, NICs will offer a BNC connector and a 15-pin AUI (Attachment Unit Interface) connector. Twisted-pair Ethernet NICs often will offer an RJ-45 socket and a 15-pin AUI connector. Many new Ethernet NICs offer all three connectors.

On NICs that offer more than one connector type, you must select which connector you plan to use. The selection can be made through jumpers, DIP switches, or software. A common problem when installing networks is when the wrong connector type is selected. Many NICs now offer multiple connector types and can be selected with software. An NE2000 Plus, for example, has three types of connectors: twisted pair, thin Ethernet, and thick Ethernet. If you plug a cable into a connector that is not selected, you will not be able to log in to the network.

Node Address (ARCnet)

When installing ARCnet cards, you are required to set the physical address of the NIC. This address is known as the *node address,* or *MAC (media access control) address,* and is most commonly set on the NIC through a DIP switch. Each miniature switch on the DIP switch block represents one bit. There are eight bits in an ARCnet node address. An address of 00000000 (decimal 0) or 11111111 (decimal 255) should not be selected in accordance with ARCnet specifications. This leaves you with a range of addresses from 1 to 254 decimal, or 00000001 to 11111110 in binary.

Setting unique addresses for each different ARCnet NIC is extremely important. ARCnet uses the node address to determine the order in which the token should be passed. The token passing scheme is what enables nodes in an ARCnet network to communicate. If you have a duplicate set of node addresses, intermittent communications problems will crop up when both nodes are active at the same time.

Using Tools To Determine Available Settings

Many software publishers have tools to assist you in determining which interrupts, I/O addresses, and memory addresses are already in use on your computer. Popular packages include the Norton Utilities from Symantec and CheckitPro from Touchstone Software; other packages include Q&APlus, Manifest, and PC Tools. Microsoft DOS users have a diagnostic tool included with MS-DOS 6 (as well as with Windows 3.1*x*) called MSD (Microsoft Diagnostics).

Figure 11.8 shows a sample screen from the MSD utility. The workstation illustrated in the figure has the network shell loaded. The various menus give additional information on memory usage, which memory resident programs are in use, and which interrupts are used.

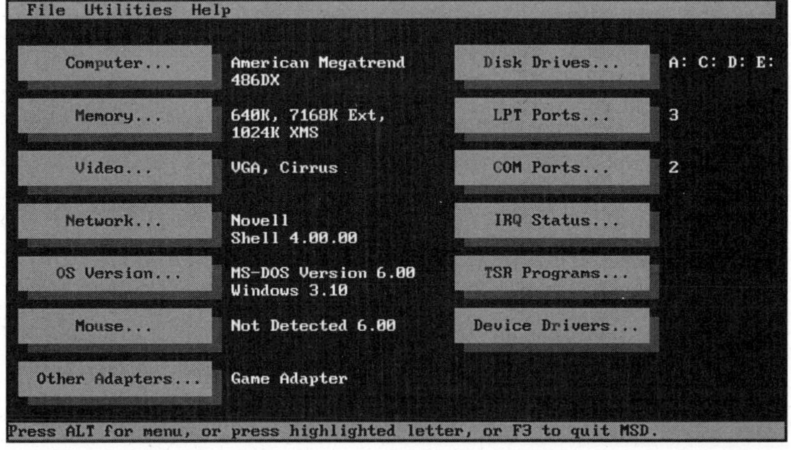

Figure 11. 8

The main menu of the MSD.EXE utility.

Unfortunately, you cannot rely on most such tools to detect all settings at all times. In the case of MSD, for example, interrupts might not be detected even though they are assigned to an NIC. In other cases, even though your computer has a COM2 port, if you do not have any devices attached to the port, the interrupt it normally uses can be used for other devices (such as an NIC).

Figure 11.9 shows the interrupt status for a workstation with an Intel EtherExpress 16 NIC installed. Note that the EtherExpress card is set to interrupt 10, and a Logitech

Scanner card is using interrupt 11. MSD reports that interrupt 10 is not detected; however, the EXP16ODI driver is identified at the right side of the figure. Interrupt 11 is reported as reserved, and no driver is identified for the scanner. Interrupt 12 is also reported as reserved, but no device is using this interrupt.

Figure 11.9

Interrupt information from the MSD.EXE utility.

```
File  Utilities  Help
                              IRQ Status
IRQ  Address    Description         Detected            Handled By
---  ---------  ------------------  ------------------  ----------------
  0  15F3:0543  Timer Click         Yes                 SAVE.EXE
  1  D676:185A  Keyboard            Yes                 Block Device
  2  0591:0057  Second 8259A        Yes                 Default Handlers
  3  0591:006F  COM2: COM4:         COM2:               Default Handlers
  4  DD75:3949  COM1: COM3:         COM1: Not Detected  LMOUSE.COM
  5  0591:009F  LPT2:               Yes                 Default Handlers
  6  0591:00B7  Floppy Disk         Yes                 Default Handlers
  7  0070:06F4  LPT1:               Yes                 System Area
  8  0591:0052  Real-Time Clock     Yes                 Default Handlers
  9  F000:EED2  Redirected IRQ2     Yes                 BIOS
 10  091E:01CB  (Reserved)                              EXP16ODI
 11  0591:00E7  (Reserved)                              Default Handlers
 12  0591:00FF  (Reserved)                              Default Handlers
 13  F000:EEDB  Math Coprocessor    Yes                 BIOS
 14  0591:0117  Fixed Disk          Yes                 Default Handlers
 15  F000:8DD0  (Reserved)                              BIOS

                                     OK
Press ALT for menu, or press highlighted letter, or F3 to quit MSD.
```

Setting Jumpers

Jumpers consist of a tiny piece of metal enclosed in a small plastic casing. The jumper is pushed over two metal posts protruding from the NIC. When the jumper is in place, the circuit is closed. When the jumper is not in place, the circuit is open.

In some cases, there are two rows of parallel posts. The pairs of posts typically are numbered JP1 through JP*nn,* where *nn* is the last numbered pair. Such sets of pairs are known as *jumper blocks;* they are used to represent a particular setting. Figure 11.10 illustrates a jumper block with jumpers in place that represent interrupt and I/O addresses. In this figure you will note that only the first pair of jumpers (JP1) is labeled.

Jumper blocks also can consist of sets of three posts. Early 3COM Ethernet NICs had such settings. They used the upper pair of the three to represent a binary 1, and the lower pair of the three to represent a binary 0.

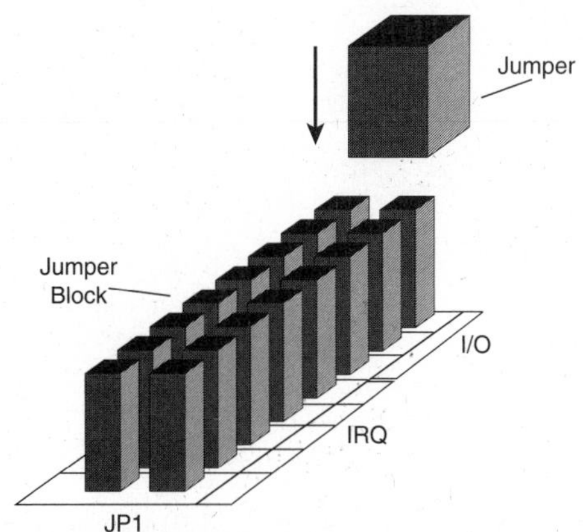

Figure 11.10

A jumper block representing IRQ and I/O address settings.

Setting DIP Switches

DIP (dual inline package) switches are, as the acronym suggests, a series of binary micro-switches. Each switch typically represents a bit (1 or 0). As with jumper blocks, DIP switches are used to represent a variety of settings, including interrupts, I/O addresses, and memory addresses.

There are two types of DIP switches: slide and rocker (see fig. 11.11). *Slide switches* have a raised portion that can be slid from one side to the other. *Rocker switches* have a raised portion that can be pushed down on one side or the other. In the case of a slide switch, the position of the raised portion indicates the setting of the switch. In the case of a rocker switch, the pushed-down portion indicates the setting of the switch.

DIP switches most often are marked OPEN or CLOSED on one side of the switch. In the case of a slide switch, for example, if the raised portion is toward the side marked OPEN, the circuit connected to this switch is open. If the manuals for your cards indicate that you should set switches on or off, set the switch to CLOSED for on and OPEN for off. Also, DIP switches often are marked SW1-1 or SW1-2. SW1 indicates "switch number 1," and the last digit represents the actual micro switch on switch 1.

Setting the switch with your fingers can be difficult. Any pointed instrument can be used to set the switch, with the exception of a graphite pencil. The graphite could flake off and get into the switch, creating a permanent closed setting. A ballpoint pen, for example, will work fine.

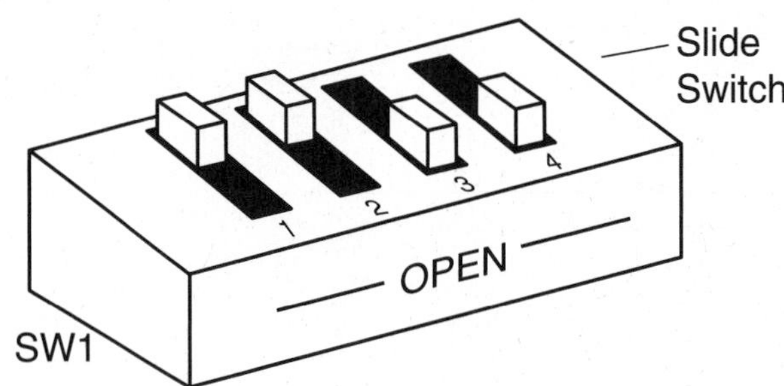

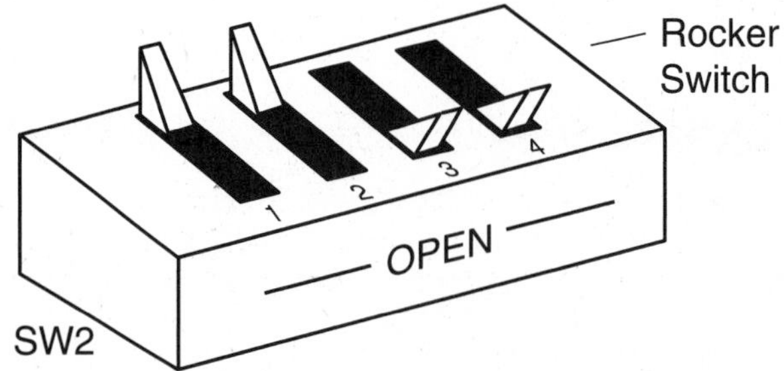

Figure 11.11
DIP switches.

Configuring Software

Many NICs now feature a software configuration program that can set the various parameters of the NIC. NICs that support this feature usually have some sort of nonvolatile RAM. Intel NICs, for example, feature "flash RAM." The settings are stored in this special RAM buffer and are true until the NIC is reset using the software configuration program.

Configuration programs often are DOS-based. To set the NIC on a file server, you must first boot the server using DOS. You then can run the software configuration program. Once the NIC is configured, you should document the configurations. The worksheet provided in Chapter 10 for configuring NIC cards will work fine for this purpose.

Figure 11.12 shows you the screen for the program used to set an Intel EtherExpress NIC.

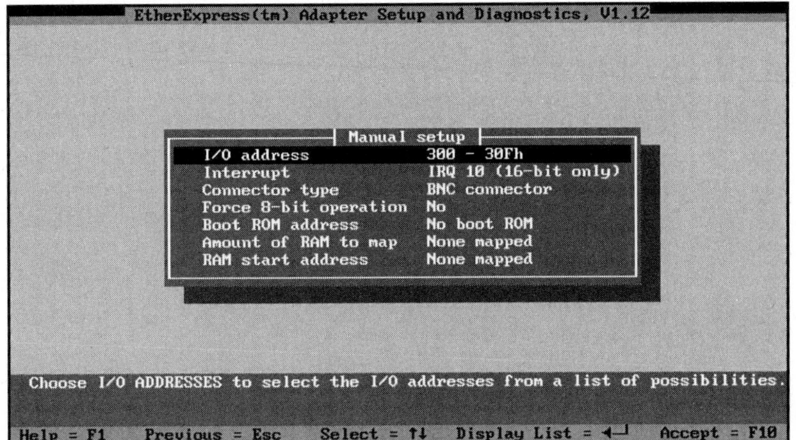

Figure 11.12
Intel EtherExpress software configuration program.

Summary

This chapter covered various aspects of hardware configuration and reviewed which factors affect the amount of RAM needed on the file server. You were given a worksheet and the formula to calculate the minimum amount of RAM needed for your needs. As you learned, the more files your server can store, the greater the RAM requirements to cache the FAT table. The amount of RAM remaining over and above this calculation is used for user file caching.

IDE and SCSI disk drives were discussed. As you learned, SCSI drives offer better service in terms of mirroring and duplexing. You learned that to properly duplex drives you need at least two host bus adapter controllers, and that the duplexing should occur across these controllers. Two major issues with SCSI devices are setting the SCSI ID and making sure the SCSI bus is properly terminated.

RAID technology was discussed from the installation standpoint. You learned that even though there may be several physical drives in an array, the server sees only one drive.

Two server peripherals were discussed: the UPS and tape backup units, with a focus on installation issues.

Finally, a section on configuring network interface cards was presented. You learned about the parameters used in NICs, including interrupts, I/O addresses, memory addresses, and DMA channels. The different ways a NIC can be set were discussed, including setting jumpers, DIP switches, and software configuration utilities.

Chapter 12, "Installing the Network Operating System," takes you through the installation of NetWare 4.1 itself.

Installing the Network Operating System

This chapter covers the NetWare 4.1 installation process. You will learn the various ways in which NetWare 4.1 can be installed. You will also learn about the various menu options you encounter during the installation process and the impact each choice has on your new file server.

Figure 12.1 illustrates the various steps and decisions that you need to make when you install NetWare 4.1. The following sections detail each step in the installation process.

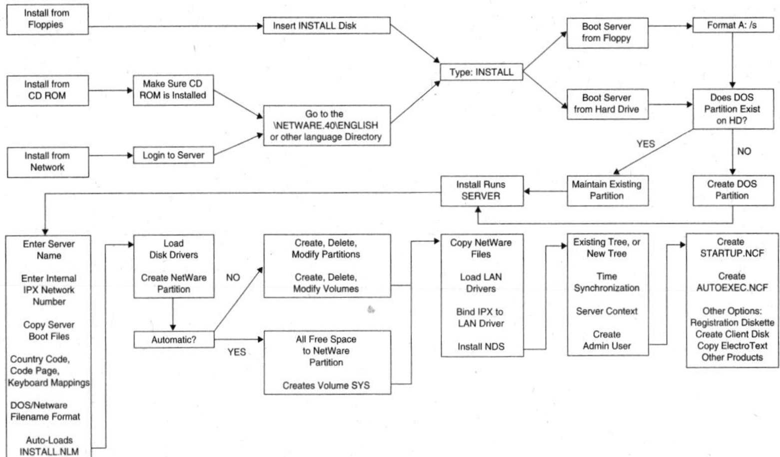

Figure 12.1
NetWare 4.1 installation steps.

Installing File Server Hardware

The first step in the installation is to install the file server hardware. You can consult the checklist of hardware and settings you prepared after reading Chapter 10, "Installation Overview." At this point in the installation you must open up the file server computer and add its RAM, hard drives, host bus adapter(s), and network interface card(s). You will need to run the CMOS setup program, which is built into the BIOS, or on a separate disk, to configure the computer. You may need to run setup routines that come with some network cards and host bus adapters. This is a good time to run diagnostics to determine that all components appear to be in operational order. Power up the computer and note whether or not it boots up properly. If there are any problems booting, you will need to resolve interrupt, port address, and memory address conflicts.

Preparing the File Server's DOS Partition

Unlike NetWare 2.*x*, UNIX or OS/2, NetWare 4.1 does not have its own cold boot loaders. To boot the server, you must boot from a DOS partition. The DOS partition

is a small area of the server disk. The total amount of space required for the server boot files will be a minimum of 5 MB. You should allocate at least 15 to 30 MB of space in the DOS partition to accomodate future drivers and utilities.

The files copied to the file server's DOS partition include disk drivers, LAN drivers, name space modules, the server boot file SERVER.EXE, and repair utilities. If you plan to load additional software onto the server's DOS partition, DOS anti-virus software, for example, be sure to allocate additional space.

You will need to boot the computer with the version of DOS supplied with your computer, and run the FDISK program. Create a primary DOS partition from 15 to 30 MB, depending on the how much room you decide to leave for future expansion. Make this parition active so that when you boot the computer it boots from the primary DOS paritition.

The NetWare 4.1 license disk comes with a limited version of Novell DOS 7. This disk is bootable and has FDISK as well as the FORMAT utility. If you do not have a legitimate version of DOS supplied with your file server computer, you can use the DOS on the license disk.

Once you exit FDISK, the computer will reboot. At this point you will once again need to boot from a bootable DOS disk. If you are using the DOS disk supplied with your computer, you do not need to install the complete version of DOS on the file server's DOS partition. Most DOS installation programs enable you the option of exiting the DOS installation menu by pressing a function key. In the case of MS-DOS, for example, you can exit the DOS installation program by pressing the F3 key.

You can now format the file server's DOS partition using the DOS FORMAT utility. Be sure to format the DOS partition as bootable and include the DOS system files. This can be accomplished with this syntax:

```
FORMAT C: /S
```

Once you are done formatting, reboot the file server computer and continue the installation.

Many computers come with the hard drive physically installed, with DOS preconfigured. If this is the case, the DOS partition is usually configured to occupy the entire hard disk space. You will need to use the FDISK utility to remove the DOS partition and create a partition that only occupies from 5 to 20 MB of disk space.

Choosing an Installation Method

You can use one of three installation methods: by using a floppy disk, by using a CD-ROM, or by installing through the network. The floppy installation method involves shuffling 60 to 70 floppy disks. The first disk is called Install. Insert this disk into the drive, type **INSTALL**, and you are on your way. Be prepared to swap floppies many times!

Installing from a CD-ROM drive involves loading the CD-ROM drivers and starting the installation from the CD. Installing through the network implies gaining access to another server with either the NetWare 4.1 CD mounted, or the intallation files copied onto one of the other file server's hard drives.

Installing from CD-ROM

If you ordered the CD-ROM version of NetWare 4.1, most of the NetWare files are included on the installation CD-ROM. You also receive a separate CD-ROM that contains the documentation, and a floppy disk that includes an individual server license number. As mentioned above, there is also a separate bootable disk with COMMAND.COM, FDISK and FORMAT.

If you choose to install your new file server using the CD, you can directly attach a CD-ROM player to your new server and load the DOS CD-ROM drivers. The drivers you require depend on your SCSI adapter and the version of DOS that you are using. Consult the documentation of your SCSI HBA for information about the drivers that are required and for the changes that must be made in your DOS CONFIG.SYS and AUTOEXEC.BAT files.

Note: Here is what you could add to the CONFIG.SYS file if you have an Adaptec 1542 SCSI adapter connected to a CD-ROM drive:

```
DEVICE=C:\ADAPTEC\ASPI4DOS.SYS /D
DEVICE=C:\ADAPTEC\ASPICD.SYS /D:ASPICD0
```

For a Future Domain TMC-1680 SCSI controller, add the following lines to the CONFIG.SYS file:

```
DEVICE=C:\PWRSCSI!\INT4BCAM.SYS
DEVICE=C:\PWRSCSI!\ASPIFCAM.SYS
DEVICE=C:\PWRSCSI!\FDCD.SYS /D:MSCD0001
```

The AUTOEXEC.BAT file will have to have a line added to run a driver that assigns the CD-ROM drive to the next DOS drive letter. This type of driver is known as a *CD Extension* driver. Here is an example using Microsoft's MSCDEX driver:

```
C:\DOS\MSCDEX.EXE /D:ASPICD0 /M:12 /S
```

Using Future Domain's *Power SCSI* CD drive support, here is what is added to the AUTOEXEC.BAT file:

```
C:\PWRSCSI!\CORELCDX.COM /D:MSCD0001 /M:10
```

Consult the documentation provided by the vendor of the SCSI controller, or by the vendor of the CD drive unit for further information. Many vendors provide an installation program that makes the changes to the CONFIG.SYS and AUTOEXEC.BAT files automatically.

To install using the default language (English) from the root of the CD-ROM drive, type **INSTALL.BAT**.

The Select the Type of Installation Desired menu appears. From this menu, select NetWare Server Installation. You are then launched into the server installation program.

To install using a language other than English, proceed as follows:

1. Move to the drive letter assigned to your CD-ROM drive unit. If the CD-ROM drive is assigned to drive D:, type **D:**.

2. Change to the \NW410\INSTALL directory. Note that this directory has a series of subdirectories that represent different langauges. Select the desired language directory and change to it. If you want to install in German, type the following:

   CD \NW410\INSTALL\DEUTSCH

3. From the \NW410\INSTALL*language* directory, begin the installation as follows:

   INSTALL

   You are then launched into the server installation program. The server installation menu is shown in figure 12.2.

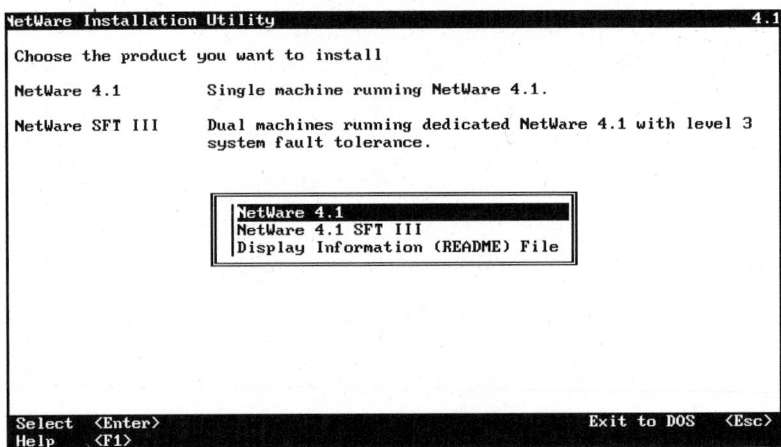

Figure 12.2
The NetWare 4.1 server installation menu.

Installing over a Network

If you choose to install NetWare 4.1 over the network, you need to prepare an existing NetWare file server of any type. The preparation varies depending on whether the version of NetWare 4.1 you purchased was shipped on floppy disks or CD.

Mounting the NetWare 4.1 Installation CD on a Server

NetWare 3.12 and 4.0*x* include CD support in the form of a driver CDROM.NLM. Make sure that the CD-ROM drive unit is connected to the server and that the proper driver for the HBA attached to the CD-ROM drive unit is installed and operating correctly.

At this point, you can issue server CD commands as described in Chapter 26, "Monitoring the File System." The following procedure mounts the NetWare 4.1 CD as a volume on an existing NetWare file server:

1. From the file server console, type:

   LOAD CDROM.NLM

   This command loads the CD support driver.

2. Find the number of the CD-ROM drive unit by entering

   CD DEVICE LIST

A list of CD-ROM drive units and the CD disks currently loaded will appear. The number of the CD-ROM drive unit is listed at the left side of this list. The name of the volume appears at the right side of the list. Write down both the drive unit number and volume name.

3. Mount the CD as a volume by entering

   CD MOUNT *number*

   where *number* is the number of the CD-ROM drive unit you found in step 2.

4. The NetWare 4.1 installation CD will now proceed to mount.

If you plan to install a series of NetWare 4.1 file servers, you may wish to copy the contents of the CD to a server hard drive with at least 400 MB of disk space. Mount the CD as a volume on the server with sufficient disk space. Make a directory on the server. You can then use the NCOPY utility to copy all files from the NetWare 4.1 installation CD to the directory you created on the server.

Connecting the New Server to the Existing Server

At this point you will need to connect the new server you plan to install to the existing file server with the NetWare 4.1 installation files. The first step is to install the NetWare client software on the new server. One technique is to copy the client files from an existing workstation onto a floppy disk. You can then either run the client software from disk, or copy the contents of the disk onto a subdirectory on the new server's hard drive.

You can use either the VLM requester or the NETX shell to perform a server installation over the network. Because you are installing a file server, it does not matter whether or not you can use NDS resources. You can use the NETX shell to establish a bindery connection with the server that has the NetWare 4.1 installation CD mounted.

Once you have run the NetWare client software, you now are ready to access the NetWare 4.1 installation files on the existing server. Temporarily using your new soon-to-be file server as a workstation, log into the existing file server and map a drive letter to the CD volume by entering the following command:

MAP NEXT *volume_name*:

Volume_name is the volume name assigned to the CD. Alternatively, if the existing server has the NetWare 4.1 installation CD files copied to a directory on one of its hard drives, map a drive letter to that directory. Change to the drive letter you mapped to the installation files.

To install using the default language (English), from the drive letter you mapped, type:

INSTALL.BAT

The Select the Type of Installation Desired menu appears. From this menu, select NetWare Server Installation. You are then launched into the server installation program.

To install using a language other than English, proceed as follows:

1. Change to the NW410\INSTALL directory. Note that this directory has a series of subdirectories that represent different languages. Select the desired language directory and change to it. If you want to install in German, proceed as follows:

   CD NW410\INSTALL\DEUTSCH

2. From the NW410\INSTALL*language* directory, begin the installation as follows:

   INSTALL

   You are then launched into the server installation program. The server installation menu is shown in figure 12.2.

Preparing for a Floppy Installation

To prepare for a floppy installation, you will need to make backup copies of all installation floppies. You can use the DOS DISKCOPY command to prepare the backup copies. When done, place your original disks in a safe place and perform the installation from the backup disks. Using the backups, you will have the originals available in case of problems.

Move to the new server you plan to install. Insert the first server installation disk into drive A and type:

INSTALL

You will then be launched into the server installation program.

Choosing the Type of Server Installation

From the server installation menu, select NetWare 4.1 to being the server installation. You are presented with the Select the Type of Installation You Are Performing menu. You have the following three choices:

- Simple Installation of NetWare 4.1
- Custom Installation of NetWare 4.1
- Upgrade NetWare 3.1x or 4.x

The Simple Installation option is designed for the network Administrator who wants to minimize the number of questions asked during the installation. The Simple Installation method is also the fastest of the three methods. This installation method makes the following assumptions:

- DOS is installed on the DOS partition.
- The server will boot from the DOS partition.
- There will be no mirroring or duplexing.
- All free space on the new server's hard drives will be allocated to NetWare.
- Each hard disk will contain one NetWare volume.
- The default randomly assigned IPX network address numbers will be accepted.
- No special drivers or changes are required for the STARTUP.NCF and AUTOEXEC.NCF files.
- The keyboard mapping will be standard U.S.
- The NDS tree will consist of a single container for all objects.
- Only the IPX protocol will be used.

The Custom Installation of NetWare 4.1 option is used when any of the assumptions listed above will not work for your environment. The last option, Upgrade NetWare 3.1x or 4.x is used when you need to upgrade any existing 3.1*x* or 4.0*x* file server to NetWare 4.1. The Upgrade option is covered in Chapter 13, "Upgrades and Other Installation Issues."

For the purposes of this book, the Custom Installation of NetWare 4.1 option is assumed. The Simple Installation option is a subset of the Custom Installation option. After you read this section you will be well equipped to perform either a Custom or Simple installation.

Performing a Custom Installation of NetWare 4.1

The steps involved in performing a Custom Installation NetWare 4.1 are outlined in this section.

Selecting the File Server Name

The next step is to enter a name for your new server. All servers on a multiserver NetWare internetwork must have a unique name that is used to identify the server from all other servers. The name—which can contain alphanumeric characters, hyphens (-), and underscores (_)—can have between two and 47 characters with no spaces. The first character, however, cannot be a period.

You should make the server name descriptive of the function it performs. Also, keep the server name to a reasonable length because it is used in many NetWare commands. Future network managers who are not fast and accurate touch typists will bless you for a reasonably short server name.

Enter a server name and press ENTER. The next screen that appears will ask you to supply an IPX number for your new server.

Assigning the Internal Network Number and Network Address

You must assign a unique internal number to identify the server process. This number must be different from all internal network numbers for other servers and the network addresses used to identify different cabling segments. The installation program will produce a unique number for you. If this number is suitable, press Enter. If you are not sure, go ahead and accept the number as the default. Figure 12.3 illustrates this screen.

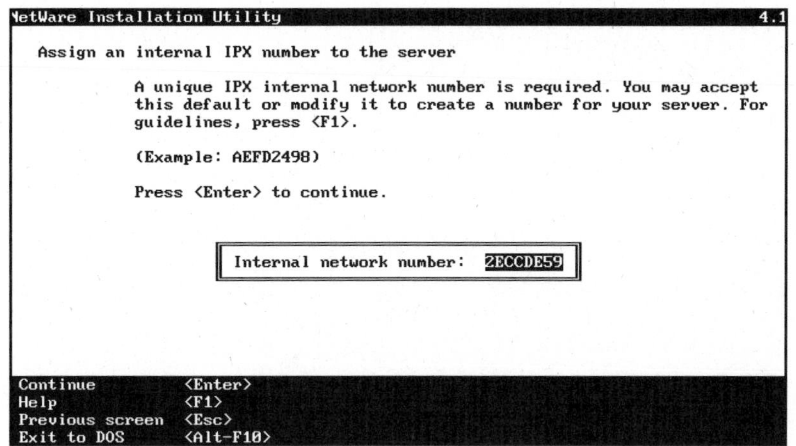

Figure 12.3

Assigning an internal IPX network number.

The internal IPX network address identifies the internal network in the file server itself. This internal network is used for routing between processes running on the file server. It is an important identifying number used for a variety of purposes. This number will appear in the routing tables of other file servers and routers.

The *internal IPX network address* is distinct from the *IPX network address* assigned for external network segments. The *internal address* is used within the server for routing between processes. The *IPX network address* is assigned to different cable segments connected to different LAN cards in the server.

Copying Server Boot Files

The next process copies initial boot files from the installation source (floppies, CDs, or across the network) to the DOS partition on the new file server's hard drive. These files include SERVER.EXE and language-support modules.

A screen appears indicating the source of the server boot files. If the source directory \NW410\INSTALL*language* is not listed or is not correct, press the F2 key and type the correct source path.

The default destination drive and directory is C:\NWSERVER. If this is not appropriate for your needs, press F4 and type the correct destination path.

Once you press Enter to continue, INSTALL copies the necessary files to the new server's DOS partition. A bar with a percentage of files copied appears at the top. This process ordinarily takes less than 2 minutes to complete depending on the speed of your hardware.

Choosing Alternative Keyboard Support

After the server boot files have been copied, you are asked to supply the correct country code, code page, and keyboard mapping. These numbers are to ensure that the proper characters and keyboard mappings for different languages are supported properly. If you are using a computer made in the United States, enter these defaults:

- Country Code = 001 (United States)
- Code Page = 437 (United States English)
- Keyboard Mapping = None

If you are using another type of computer or keyboard, press Enter at each of these choices. A list of alternative choices appears. Select the choice most appropriate for your system. Figure 12.4 illustrates this screen.

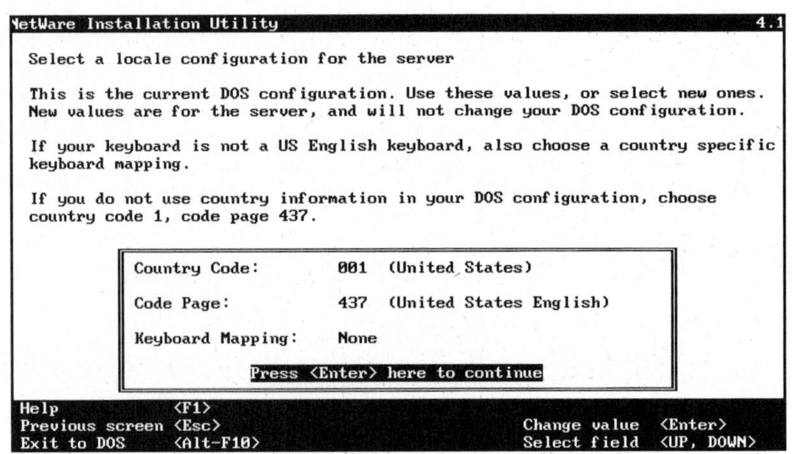

Figure 12.4
Selecting the Country Code, Code Page, and Keyboard Mapping settings.

When done, move the cursor to the bottom of the screen where it says:

```
Press <Enter> here to continue
```

Press Enter to continue with the installation.

Choosing the File Name Format

Next you see a screen that gives you a choice between the DOS Filename Format and the NetWare Filename Format. DOS Filename Format is the recommended choice, and matches standard DOS file-naming schemes. This format is compatible with the new VLM Shell, which is a DOS redirector. Figure 12.5 shows you this screen.

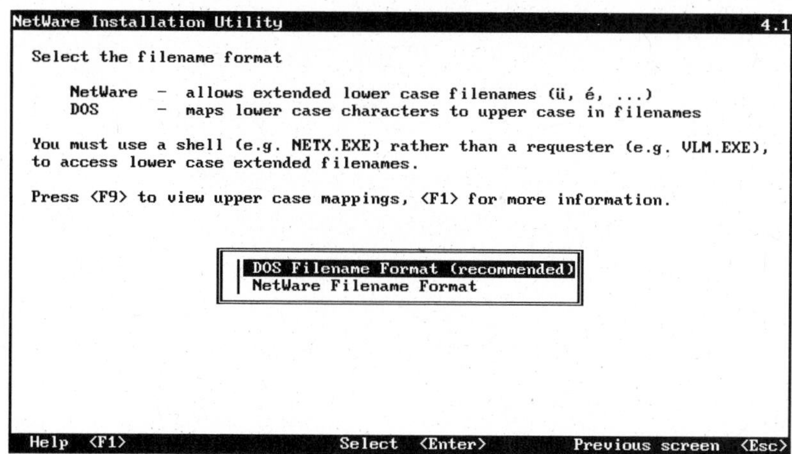

Figure 12.5
Choosing the file name format.

NetWare Filename Format supports alternative characters in a file name. With this format, you can have a file name such as the following:

hôtel.cté

The disadvantage to this format is that you no longer can use the redirector but must instead use the NETX.EXE Shell. Using this shell causes your workstation to be bound by the old restrictions of the shell (a maximum of eight server connections, for example), and also affects performance. When using the NETX Shell, your workstation is viewed as a bindery client. As a result, NETX Shell users cannot access the NDS or any NDS resources outside the file server's bindery context.

Select the desired filename format and press Enter.

Choosing Configuration Options Prior to Loading INSTALL.NLM

The next screen asks you whether there are any special commands that must be loaded into STARTUP.NCF. These commands can include special SCSI drivers or drivers for CD support. If this is the case, select Yes and type the commands you want to include in the beginning of STARTUP.NCF. Additional commands decided on during the remainder of the installation are added after the commands you type here. Otherwise select No and press Enter to continue the installation.

Next you are asked whether you want to have SERVER loaded in the AUTOEXEC.BAT file. If you select Yes, the install program updates or creates an AUTOEXEC.BAT file on the new file server's hard drive with the SERVER command.

INSTALL will now run SERVER.EXE. This is the main operating system kernel. The INSTALL.NLM utility is now automatically loaded with a script file. You are prompted to load disk drivers, create a NetWare partition, and so on.

Loading the Disk Driver Modules

At this point you will see the Disk Driver screen, as shown in figure 12.6. Disk drivers are written as NLMs and must be loaded so that the server can communicate with the disks. The installation process displays a list of available disk drivers. Choose the appropriate driver and press Enter. A configuration screen appears, enabling you to enter the data you documented when you installed the server's hard drive. (You did document these settings, didn't you?) The entries you make here eventually are recorded as a LOAD command in the STARTUP.NCF file. You also can enter these commands from the file server's console.

Note the upward and downward pointing triangles to the left of the list of drivers in figure 12.6. This indicates there are additional drivers above and below. Press either the PgUp or PgDn keys to access additional drivers. This technique works with other driver lists (such as LAN drivers) as well.

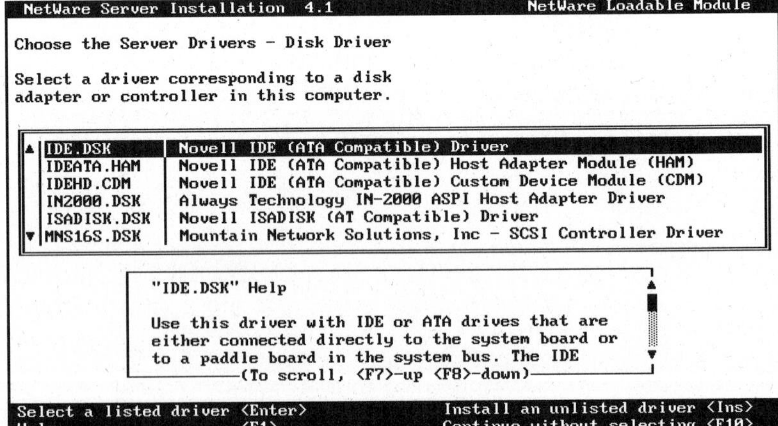

Figure 12.6
The Disk Driver screen.

Disk drivers are NLMs with the extension DSK. If you select the ISADISK.DSK (Industry Standard Architecture Disk) driver, for example, and specify the default settings, the following command is added to the STARTUP.NCF file, along with parameters for the interrupt and I/O port address:

```
LOAD ISADISK INT=E PORT=1F0
```

If more than one ISADISK controller exists on the server, you are given an option to enter the LOAD ISADISK command a second time. When the driver is loaded a second time, it loads itself reentrantly and accepts only an alternate set of parameters.

To specify the ISADISK parameters at the command line, select the Load ISADISK a Second Time option from the menu.

The PS/2 SCSI driver can be loaded four times, and it loads itself reentrantly. For Micro Channel Architecture, you must specify the SLOT parameter, such as in the following example:

```
LOAD PS2SCI SLOT=2
```

NetWare 4.1 includes a specialized driver for IDE drives called IDE.DSK. Use this driver if your file server has an IDE drive. There are a number of other drivers included in this menu, including drivers for Adaptec, Bustek, and Future Domain SCSI controllers, among other drivers.

A set of drivers that are unique to NetWare 4.1 represent the latest trend for NetWare device management. This set of drivers falls into the *Netware Peripheral Architecture* (NPA) specification. NPA uses a three-piece driver set that allows for greater control and support for devices. The architecture was originally introduced to provide better support for multiple CD-ROM drive units ("jukeboxes"). The driver set consists of the following three components:

- **NWPA.NLM** is the NetWare Peripheral Architecture driver. This is a generic driver that supports the architecture and contains library functions used by other drivers.
- **HAM** is the Host Adapter Module. An example of this is IDEATA.HAM, for IDE drives. The HAM drives the host bus adapter (HBA) installed in the new server.
- **CDM** is the Custom Device Module. This module is used to drive devices attached to the HBA. CDM detects devices attached to the HBA and binds itself to each device it can manage. CDM is automatically loaded by the HAM. In the case of an IDE drive, the module IDEHD.CDM will support up to 4 IDE drives in a server, if the server's hardware also supports 4 IDE drives.

Table 12.1 summarizes the drivers available on the Disk Driver screen.

TABLE 12.1
Disk Driver Modules Supplied with NetWare 4.1

Module	Description
ADAASPI.DSK	Always Technology ASPI device drive
AHA*.DSK AIC*.DSK	Designed for Adaptec's line of SCSI controllers. Controllers with numbers ending with 2 (such as 1542) contain floppy and hard drive circuitry. The AHA17*xx* and AHA27*xx* are designed for EISA motherboards. The AIC*.DSK drivers (including AIC777 and AIC7870) are more advanced drivers for EISA and Local Bus systems.
AL*.DSK	Always Technology ASPI HBA drivers
ASPICD.DSK ASPITRAN.DSK	CD-ROM support drivers for Adaptec SCSI controllers. Must be loaded after the other Adaptec support drivers. The ASPITRAN driver is usually automatically loaded by the Adaptec SCSI drivers listed above.
ASPIDAC4.DSK	Mylex DAC960 ASPI driver
BT*.DSK	Drivers for the BusLogic family of SCSI controllers. BT refers to BusTek (former name)
CDNASPI.DSK	CD-ROM support driver for Meridian Data CD-ROM drive units. As with the ASPICD.DSK driver, this must be loaded after other drivers are loaded for the SCSI controller.
DACNET4.DSK	Mylex DAC960 Controller Disk Driver
DAIFILTR.CDM	Emulates Netware 386 Device Driver Behavior
DPTSIM.DSK	NetWare DPT ASPI SIM
DTC*.DSK	DTC3280/DTC3270/DTC3250 ASPI manager and disk driver modules
FUT*.DSK	Future Domain ASPI and disk controller drivers
HPCHGR.DSK	NetWare ASPI Hewlett Packard AutoChanger Driver v4.0
IDE*.DSK	Driver for file servers with IDE drives. This series includes the self-contained IDE.DSK driver, or the NPA drivers IDEATA.HAM and IDEHD.CDM.

Module	Description
IN2000.DSK	Always Technology IN-2000 ASPI Host Adapter Driver
ISADISK.DSK	Generic driver for Industry Standard Architecture drives. This can be used in place of IDE.DSK, and for other older drive types.
MNS*.DSK	Mountain Network Solutions, Inc - SCSI controller, 8mm tape, and DDS DAT tape drive modules
NCR*.*	NCR 53C7xx SCSI HBA drivers and NPA drivers, 53C9x drivers, ASPI drivers, and other NCR SCSI drivers
PM*.DSK	Distributed Processing Technologies (DPT) ISA and EISA SCSI drivers
RFCHGR.DSK	NetWare ASPI Reflection Systems AutoChanger Driver v0.10
SCSI154X.HAM	Adaptec AHA-1540/42 Reference HAM Module
SCSI*.CDM	Novell SCSI NPA custom device driver modules
SIM*.DSK	Future Domain 18XX/36XX Series IC Future/CAM SIM Module and Future Domain 950/950 IC Future/CAM SIM Modules
TAPEDAI.DSK	NetWare 386 Tape Device Driver

Table 12.2 summarizes some of the drivers available from other vendors. The prefix generally used by the vendor is indicated, as well as sample driver file names. To access these drivers from the Select a Disk Driver menu, you need a disk supplied by the vendor. Press the Insert key and select the driver you want to load.

Table 12.2
Disk Driver Modules Supplied by Third-Party Vendors

Vendor	File Name Prefix	Sample File Names	Notes
3Com Corp.	3CN*.DSK	3CNDISK.DSK 3CNSCSI.DSK	Drivers for ESDI or SCSI controllers designed for the 3SERVER line of computers

continues

Table 12.2, Continued
Disk Driver Modules Supplied by Third-Party Vendors

Vendor	File Name Prefix	Sample File Names	Notes
Compaq Computer Corp.	CPQ*.DSK	CPQSDISK.DSK CPQDA386.DSK	Drivers for Compaq's SCSI and Drive Array technologies
Micropolis Corp.	RAID*.DSK	RAIDION.DSK	Drivers for the Micropolis *RAIDION* RAID level 5 drive array
NetFrame Systems, Inc.	NF*.DSK	NFDISK.DSK	Drivers for NetFrame computers
Storage Dimensions	LAN*.DSK	LANSTOR4.DSK LANSTOR5.DSK	Drivers for SCSI drive external subsystems
UltraStor Corp.	U*.DSK	U124_4X.DSK U14_4X.DSK U22_4X.DSK U24_4X.DSK	Drivers for Ultra Stor disk subsystems (both internal and external)

Loading NIC Driver NLMs

Once you have completed loading disk drivers, you will next see the Network Driver screen, as shown in figure 12.7. The network adapters (NICs) are activated by loading their NLM driver. You are presented with a screen that enables you to choose the LAN driver you want. The installation routine adds a LOAD command to the AUTOEXEC.NCF file later in the process.

LAN drivers also can be loaded from the console prompt. Press Alt+Esc to temporarily leave the INSTALL.NLM utility and go to the file server console prompt. When done loading the driver, press Alt+Esc to return to INSTALL.NLM. To load the TOKEN.LAN driver for token ring, issue the following command:

LOAD TOKEN

To load the Novell Ethernet driver for NE2000 and define a logical name ETHER for it, you need to use the same command, but in the following way:

LOAD NE2000 NAME=ETHER

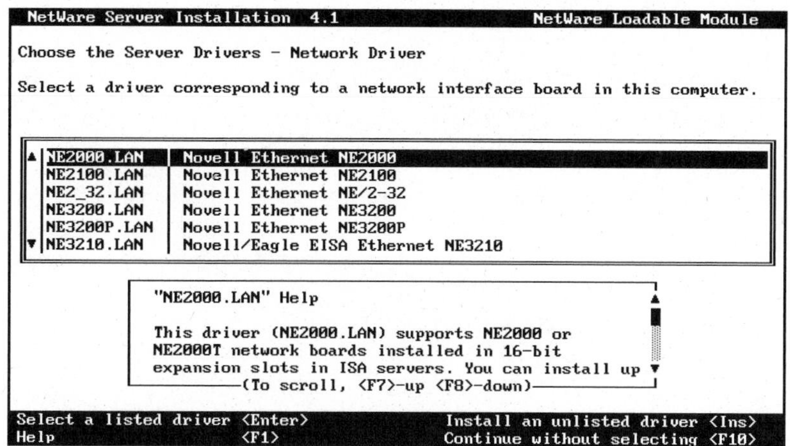

Figure 12.7
The Network Driver screen.

Because you can have multiple NICs in a server to form an internal router, you must issue the LOAD command for every NIC. Driver names enable NetWare to distinguish between several loaded instances of the same driver.

Hardware parameters, such as I/O port addresses and interrupt numbers, can be specified as parameters to the LOAD *diskdriver* command. If you do not specify hardware parameters, the NIC driver prompts you for values. If a LAN driver fails to load, check the settings on the NIC. The NIC must be installed, and its settings must match those you enter when loading the driver.

LAN drivers not supplied with NetWare must be loaded from a disk supplied by the vendor of the NIC. From the Network Driver screen, press the Insert key. NetWare searches for a driver with the extension LAN and attempts to load it.

Configuring Settings, Protocols, and Frame Types

Once you have chosen an NIC driver to load, you can configure its various parameters. The Network Driver Parameters screen enables you to make configuration decisions.

At the top of the screen are protocol choices. IPX is automatically chosen for you. You can select TCP/IP and AppleTalk by moving to those fields and pressing the spacebar. When you select TCP/IP, a configuration screen pops up where you can set the IP address and subnet mask for TCP/IP.

The *IP address* is the 4 byte address assigned to this server. You need to verify that the address you choose fits the IP addressing scheme established for your network segment. The *subnet* mask is a value assigned if the network segment where the server is located has been subdivided into subordinate networks.

The Parameters input box at the center of the screen enables you to enter pertinent parameters for your network interface card. To adjust the frame type for the NIC, press the F3 key. The Frame Type List input box appears. The frame types supported for this network adapter card appear in this list.

Different protocol stacks accept different frame types. A *frame type* is a specification for a type of NIC. Table 12.5 summarizes the frame types available in NetWare 4.1.

Table 12.5
NetWare 4.1 Frame Types

Frame Type	Type of NIC	Default For...
Ethernet_802.2	Ethernet	NetWare 4.*x* or 3.12
Ethernet_802.3	Ethernet	NetWare 3.0, 3.10, 3.11, or NetWare 2.*x*
Ethernet_II	Ethernet	TCP/IP-based systems, including UNIX
Ethernet_SNAP	Ethernet	AppleTalk, TCP/IP
Token-Ring	Token ring	NetWare 2, 3, and 4
Token-Ring_SNAP	Token ring	TCP/IP-based systems including UNIX, AppleTalk
RXNet	ARCnet	NetWare 2, 3, and 4, TCP/IP-based systems including UNIX, AppleTalk

Choose any frame type that is appropriate for your situation by selecting the desired frame type and pressing Enter. Press F10 to register your choices and return to the Network Driver Parameters screen. When done, select the Save Parameters and Load Driver option at the bottom of the screen.

Binding Protocol Stacks to NIC Drivers

The next screen to appear is the Bind LAN Driver to IPX screen. Before the file server can send and receive information from the LAN, you must specify which protocol stack (such as IPX/SPX or TCP/IP) the NIC is to use. This is done by a process called *binding*, in which an NIC driver is associated logically with a protocol stack.

The installation process displays a screen in which you can select the network address you want. If any network IPX addresses are already in use on your LAN, the address detected will be displayed. Otherwise, the address presented is a random IPX network address. The address you must assign at this point is an external address used to associate an NIC in the server with a cable segment.

If your new server is on a network with existing NetWare servers of any type, the installation routine detects network numbers that are being broadcast through RIP (Routing Information Protocol). If you choose a network number that does not match the network number of a server on the same physical cabling, a `Router Configuration Error` message appears.

A unique network address must be assigned to every cabling segment. NetWare 4.1 enables you to connect up to 16 LAN cards to a server. Each of these must have a unique number. This network address must be different from all other network addresses on all servers on the internetwork. The address is referred to as the *IPX network number* during the installation. The network address used in this context must not be confused with the address of the LAN card, which is referred to as the *node address.*

Figure 12.8 shows a LAN with three servers, with one server being used as a router. The internal network numbers of 4A20, 12345, and 3F are distinct from each other and from the network address of AA3B and BF17 used for the two cabling segments. The NICs attached to the same cabling segment have the same network address. Their node addresses (NIC card addresses) of 05, 06, 08, and 09 are distinct.

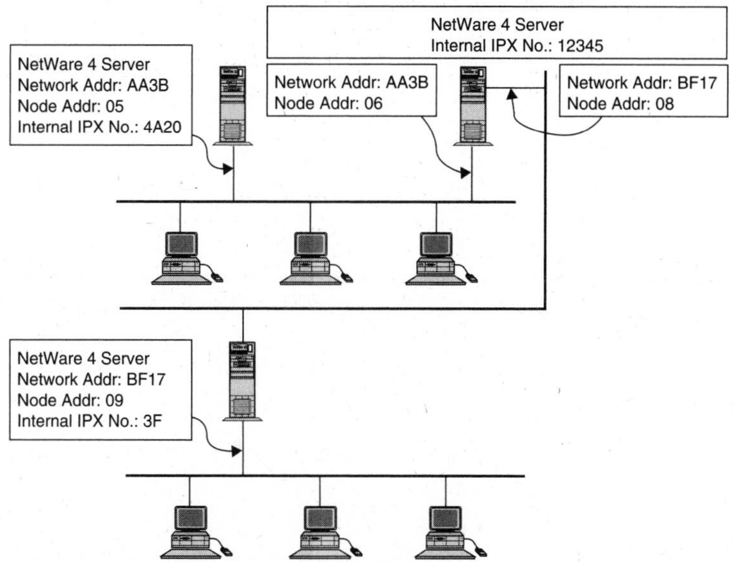

Figure 12.8

Assigning IPX network addresses.

Internal IPX network and network addresses can be eight-digit hexadecimal numbers. You can omit leading 0s when entering these values in the installation process.

After you select the network address for each card and frame type, the information is recorded in the AUTOEXEC.NCF file as a series of BIND commands.

One BIND command is placed in the AUTOEXEC.NCF file for every NIC in the server. If you have more than one NIC of the same type on the server, the BIND command needs to distinguish between the different driver instances. You can do this by including that driver's parameters along with the BIND command. You do not need driver parameters if you bind a protocol to a board name. To register a board name for the driver, it must be loaded by using the NAME parameter.

The AUTOEXEC.NCF file is created near the end of the installation. Here is an example of an AUTOEXEC.NCF file created for a file server with the following requirements:

- One Ethernet NIC
- One token ring NIC
- IPX protocols
- TCP/IP protocols
- Mixed NetWare 2, 3, and 4 file servers

Here is a sample AUTOEXEC.NCF File:

```
;
;    Loads Intel EtherExpress Ethernet NIC driver with
;     Ethernet 802.2 frame type
;
load EXP16 int=A port=300 frame=Ethernet_802.2 name=EXP16_1E_802.2
;
;     Loads EtherExpress Ethernet NIC driver again with
;     Ethernet 802.3 frame type
;
load EXP16 [int=A port=300] frame=Ethernet_802.3 name=EXP16_1E_802.3
;
;     Loads EtherExpress Ethernet NIC driver again with
;     Ethernet II frame type
;
load EXP16 [int=A port=300] frame=Ethernet_II name=EXP16_1E_II
;
;     Loads token ring NIC driver
```

```
;
load TOKEN port=A20 frame=token ring name=TOKEN_1T
;
;     Loads token ring NIC driver again with Token-Ring SNAP
;     frame type
;
load TOKEN [port=A20] frame=Token-Ring_SNAP name=TOKEN_1T_SNAP
;
;     Binds IPX protocols to Ethernet and Token ring drivers
;     Note the use of the board name rather than referencing the
;     driver name.
;
bind IPX to EXP16_1E_802.2 net=E102
bind IPX to EXP16_1E_802.3 net=E103
bind IPX to TOKEN_1T net=1101
;
;     Loads and Binds the TCP/IP protocol stack
;
load TCPIP
bind IP to EXP16_1E_II addr=130.57.3.101
bind IP to TOKEN_1T_SNAP addr=130.57.4.101
```

When you are done configuring the network interface card and assigning IPX network addresses, you will return to the Network Driver screen. You can continue to load additional network drivers at this point, or continue the installation.

If you choose to continue, the Summary screen appears, giving you the option of viewing and changing disk or LAN drivers. Select Continue Installation to continue to the next step.

Creating a NetWare Partition

The next screen to appear is the Create NetWare Disk Partitions menu. This menu asks you whether you want to create the NetWare partition on the new file server's hard drive manually or automatically. If you select Automatically, the following actions occur:

1. INSTALL creates a NetWare partition on the remaining free space on the hard drive.

2. A *hot-fix* area (a space reserved for bad blocks) is created. The target amount of space is 2 percent of the NetWare partition. This figure is decreased in inverse proportion to the size of the hard drive. A NetWare partition of 134 MB, for example, yields a 1.5 percent hot-fix area.

3. INSTALL creates volume SYS, which occupies the space remaining after the hot fix.

If you select Manually, you are given control over creating a new partition, deleting an existing partition, and adjusting the size of the hot-fix area. The Disk Partition Options menu appears, as shown in figure 12.9.

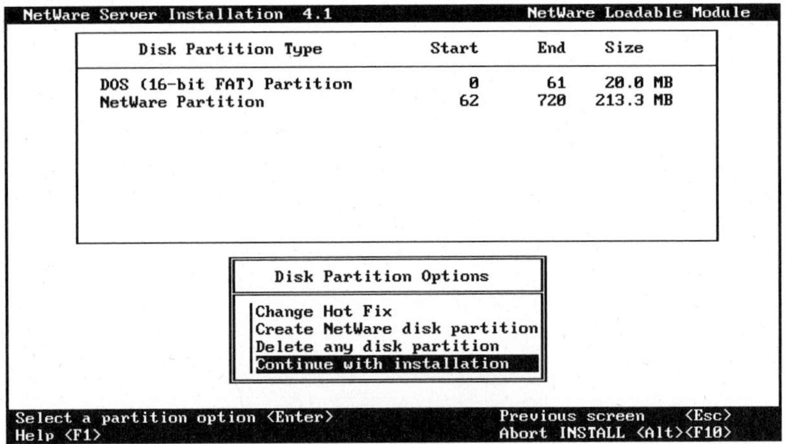

Figure 12.9
The Disk Partition Options menu.

From the Disk Partition Options menu, select Change Hot Fix to view or modify the amount of disk space reserved for Hot Fix. Select Create NetWare disk partition to create a NetWare partition. Select Delete any disk partition to delete an unwanted partition. When done, select Continue with installation.

Creating, Modifying, or Deleting NetWare Volumes

The next menu, the Manage NetWare Volumes menu, enables you to create, modify, or delete NetWare volumes. A NetWare volume is a subset of the total available disk space. A volume can span up to 32 physical hard drives. Alternatively, several volumes can be created on a single physical hard drive.

Volumes designations are arbitrary. There is no reason to create more than one volume. You might decide for reasons of your own to create additional volumes. Some of these reasons could include the following:

- You are following a company policy regarding the division of disk space between departments or workgroups.
- If you have more than one hard drive, and these drives are not set up as a drive array or mirrored, you might want to designate one volume per physical drive.

Now if one drive crashes, it only takes down one volume without affecting the other.

- Volumes are one way of separating files other than DOS files. Macintosh and UNIX users, for example, might be granted their own volumes.

Press F3 or the Insert key to view, add, or modify volume segments. Press Enter to modify the parameters for an existing volume.

Modifying or Adding Volume Segments

After you press the F3 or Insert keys, the Modify Disk Segments menu appears. A volume segment is the portion of a partition assigned to a volume. This is where you can create a volume that spans multiple physical hard drives. Table 12.3 lists the various parameters that are displayed in this menu. Table 12.4 lists the significant keystrokes.

TABLE 12.3
Add/Modify Volume Information Menu

Item	Description
Device Number	Refers to a physical hard drive. NetWare numbers the hard drives on your system sequentially.
Segment Number	Represents the segment number for the particular device number. You can assign from 0 (the first) to 31 (the last) segments of a single physical drive to a volume.
Size (MB)	Specifies the size in megabytes of this particular segment.
Volume Assignment	Specifies the volume to which this segment is assigned.
Status	Specifies one of four codes: E = Existing Volume S = System Volume (SYS) M = Mirrored Volume Segment N = New (not yet created)

Table 12.4
Add/Modify Volume Information Menu Significant Keystrokes

Keystroke	Description
F10 or Esc	Saves the changes you have made and returns you to the Manage NetWare Volumes menu.
Delete	Deletes the selected volume segment. When you delete a volume segment you will destroy all data on that volume.
Enter	Make free space into a volume or modify the size of a new segment (a volume segment with a status of "N").
F1	Help.

Press F10 or Esc to return to the Manage NetWare Volumes menu.

Modifying Volume Parameters

From the Manage NetWare Volumes menu, you can specify parameters for a volume. As a volume is created, you have the option of modifying certain parameters of this volume. These parameters are summarized in table 12.5.

Table 12.5
Modify Volume Parameters Menu

Parameter	Description
Volume Name	Specifies the name of the volume.
Volume Block Size	Specifies the size of a single disk block on this particular volume. The smallest size is 4 KB. The largest is 64 KB. If you enable suballocation, you gain performance without wasting disk space by selecting a 64 KB block size.
Status	Specifies the volume status: New = Not yet created Not Mounted = Volume created but not mounted Mounted = Volume is fully operational
File Compression	On (default) enables file compression; Off disables this feature.

Setting Time Configuration

The Time Configuration menu appears next (see fig.12.10). One of the most important underlying mechanisms behind NDS is its capability to determine precisely the time at which updates occur.

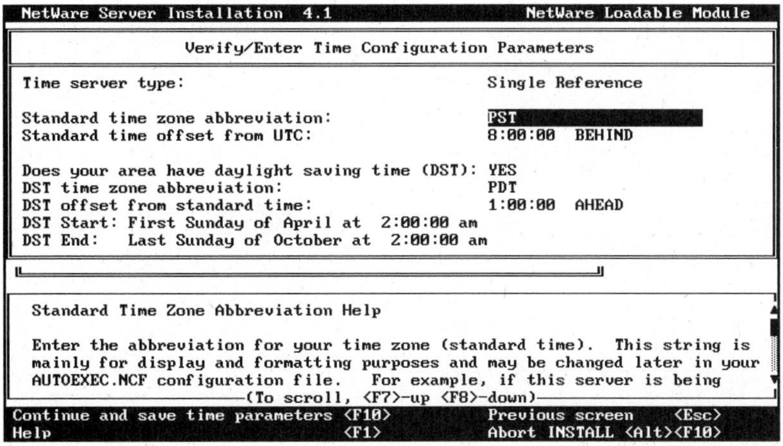

```
NetWare Server Installation  4.1                    NetWare Loadable Module
                Verify/Enter Time Configuration Parameters

 Time server type:                               Single Reference

 Standard time zone abbreviation:                PST
 Standard time offset from UTC:                  8:00:00  BEHIND

 Does your area have daylight saving time (DST): YES
 DST time zone abbreviation:                     PDT
 DST offset from standard time:                  1:00:00  AHEAD
 DST Start: First Sunday of April at  2:00:00 am
 DST End:   Last Sunday of October at  2:00:00 am

  Standard Time Zone Abbreviation Help

  Enter the abbreviation for your time zone (standard time).  This string is
  mainly for display and formatting purposes and may be changed later in your
  AUTOEXEC.NCF configuration file.  For example, if this server is being
                    (To scroll, <F7>-up <F8>-down)
Continue and save time parameters <F10>        Previous screen     <Esc>
Help                              <F1>         Abort INSTALL <Alt><F10>
```

Figure 12.10

The Verify/Enter Time Configuration Parameters screen.

You must enter the correct date and time. In addition, you need to specify the time zone, offset from Universal Time Coordinated (formerly Greenwich Mean Time), and daylight savings information, if applicable.

Several types of time server options are available. You need to determine which server is to provide the master time reference for other servers in a multiserver network. The first server you install becomes a master server. The default type is Single Reference server. Additional servers default to Secondary Time servers. This means that the first server provides time information to the other servers. Table 12.6 summarizes the types of time servers.

Table 12.6
Time Server Types

Time Server Type	Description
Single Reference	One server acts as the master time reference for other servers.
Reference	One server acts as the master time reference for other servers. This server has a special precision time clock installed, or is using an external time clock (such as an atomic clock used in many research laboratories).

continues

Table 12.6, Continued
Time Server Types

Time Server Type	Description
Primary	Several servers act as master time reference servers. To determine the correct time, these servers "vote" amongst themselves. This is a recommended option where one or more servers could go down, or across a WAN.
Secondary	A server that gets its time from one of the three earlier types in this table.

For further information on time synchronization see Chapter 13, "Upgrades and Other Installation Issues."

Establishing the Server Context

Next you can specify where the server appears in the tree. The Context For This Server screen enables you to specify an organization and up to three organizational units for the new server context (see fig. 12.11).

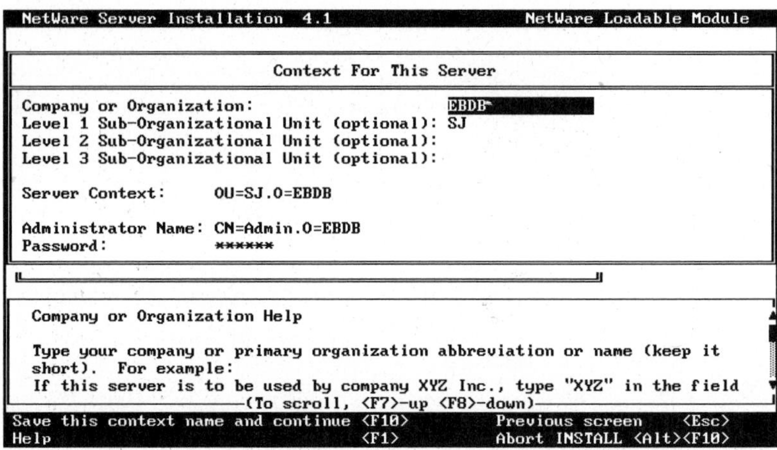

Figure 12.11
The Context For This Server screen.

If you want to insert a Country object, you must do so in the Server Context field. If your organization is XYZ and the first organization unit is Sales, for example, you would see this in the Server Context box:

```
Server Context: OU=Sales.O=XYZ
```

To add a Country container, add .C=*xx* after the last item. Replace *xx* with the two-letter Country code you want. To add Great Britain (GB), for example, enter the following:

Server Context: OU=Sales.O=XYZ.C=GB

Note that after you enter a Country code, typeless naming conventions do not work. (A *typeless* name is where you do not specify CN=, OU=, or O=.) When you enter a typeless name, the operating system assumes the following:

- ◆ The far left item is a leaf object (CN).
- ◆ The far right item is an organization (O).
- ◆ Intermediate items are organizational units (OU).

As you learned in previous chapters, the file server context is extremely important. It serves the following two major purposes:

- ◆ It sets the pointer for bindery emulation.
- ◆ It sets a default context.

When a user logs in or otherwise accesses NDS resources, the default context is searched if NetWare fails to find the complete or partial name specified by the user.

Viewing and Modifying the STARTUP and AUTOEXEC NCF Files

The last required step is to view and modify the STARTUP.NCF and AUTOEXEC.NCF files. The installation program creates these files for you based on information you have entered during the process. These files are presented to you one at a time. At this point, you can make any changes you want. Press F10 to save the file and move on to the next file.

Setting Other Installation Options

The server is now completely installed. You have a series of additional installation options, as shown in the Other Installation Options screen in figure 12.12.

- ◆ Create a Registration Diskette
- ◆ Upgrade v3.1*x* Print Services

- Create DOS/MS Windows/OS2 Client Install Diskettes
- Create NetWare UPGRADE/MIGRATE Diskettes
- Install NetWare for Macintosh
- Install NetWare MHS Services
- Configure Network Protocols
- Install an Additional Server Language
- Change Server Language
- Install Online Documentation and Viewers

These options are described in the following sections.

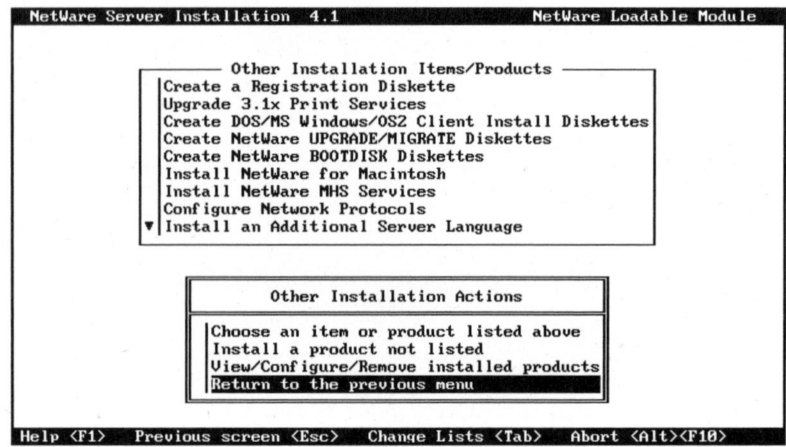

Figure 12.12
The Other Installation Options screen.

Creating a Registration Disk

You should select the Create a Registration Diskette option to register your copy of NetWare. This is especially important if you are participating in an upgrade program. This option presents you with a screen where you can fill out your reseller's name and information on your company. This information is written out to a floppy disk. Place the disk in the cardboard mailer provided with NetWare and mail it to Novell.

Upgrading 3.1*x* Print Services

The Upgrade v3.1*x* Print Services option runs PUPGRADE.NLM. This module converts the following print services items into NDS objects. These items are summarized in table 12.7. Note that print queues are converted to NDS print queue objects without selecting this option.

TABLE 12.7
Converting Print Services Items to NDS Objects

3.1*x* Print Service Item	NDS Object
Printer	Becomes an NDS printer object
Printer Definition	Becomes an NDS property of the Printer object
Print Job Configuration	Becomes NDS user object properties
Print Server	Becomes an NDS print server object

Create DOS/MS Windows/OS2 Client Install Diskettes

This option is used to create client installation disks. There are image files stored on the NetWare 4.1 installation CD that match the format of DOS or OS/2 for both 5.25" and 3.5" disks. By selecting this option, you have the choice of disk size and which client disk you want to create. Make your choice and insert disks as prompted. You can then use these disks to install clients. See Chapter 14, "DOS Client Basics," and Chapter 16, "OS/2 Clients," for more information.

Create NetWare UPGRADE/MIGRATE Diskettes

Use this option to create disks for upgrading a NetWare 2.*x* file server to NetWare 4.1. This process creates a bootable disk with the "In-Place Upgrade" utilities. You can then upgrade a 2.*x* file server to NetWare 4.1 using the same server throughout. This process will not work for NetWare 2.0A or older.

The Migrate process enables you to migrate bindery information and other data from a server running an older version of NetWare. You can move the information off to a workstation or onto an existing NetWare 4.1 file server. Once migrated, users can immediately login to the NetWare 4.1 file server and get to work while you then upgrade their server.

Consult Chapter 13, "Upgrades and Other Installation Issues," for more information on both Upgrade and Migrate.

Create NetWare BOOTDISK Diskettes

This option can be used to create a set of disks used to boot a server. Upon selecting this option, you will be asked to answer a series of questions pertaining to your installation. At the end of the process, you will end up with a set of disks that are bootable, and that contain SERVER.EXE, disk drivers, and LAN driver files. You can then use these disks to boot a file server from floppy. Once the server has been booted, you can then take the boot disks and lock them in a secure location.

The main reason for booting a server from floppies is for security reasons. You might want to control unauthorized access to a server that is not in a locked room. In such a situation, a server could be brought down and rebooted. An unauthorized user could bypass the server's AUTOEXEC.BAT file on its DOS partition. If the server is only booted from floppies, any time the server is brought down, the boot floppies must be brought out to bring it back up again.

Another use for boot floppies is a "spare" when you install a server for a remote site. Once the server has been installed, select this option to create a set of boot disks for the server. If the remote site experiences problems with the server's DOS partition, you can send this set of disks to the site.

Install NetWare for Macintosh

The Install NetWare for Macintosh option installs a 50-user version of NetWare for Macintosh, which ships with NetWare 4.1. Macintosh support includes a series of NLMs that load onto the server. These NLMs allow the Macintosh to see the NetWare server as an AppleShare server. Printer support is also provided. The client software allows the Macintosh to access the NetWare 4.1 server as an NDS client.

Install NetWare MHS Services

The Install NetWare MHS Services option installs what is known as "Basic MHS." MHS stands for Message Handling Services. MHS provides an e-mail delivery engine. This is useful in delivering e-mail messages between dissimilar platforms (for example between Macintosh and DOS machines). In addition to "Basic MHS," this package provides a DOS or Macintosh based front end utility, First Mail. This is a simple user front end that provides basic mail services such as sending and receiving messages, and attaching files. First Mail works with MHS.

Configure Network Protocols

The Configure Network Protocols option enables you to configure protocols other than IPX. This option calls the INETCFG.NLM utility. One of the major uses for this option is to configure TCP/IP. You can assign a protocol to any network interface

card in the server. This option is essentially a menu equivalent of the BIND command from the console prompt. In addition, there is an option to name a board to provide SNMP information to any SNMP managers you have running on your network. For more information on INETCFG.NLM, see Chapter 37, "Making Configuration Changes."

Install an Additional Server Language

The Install an Additional Server Language option installs the support files needed to provide support for languages other than the default language you selected when you first started the installation. The languages that ship with NetWare 4.1 include English, French, German, Italian, and Spanish. Support files for each additional language take approximately 5 MB.

Change Server Language

You can use the Change Server Language option to change the default language for the server. This option is useful when installing servers for a multinational company. You can perform the installation in one language and the change the server's default to another language. Before you can select an alternate langauge, you must first load the alternate language support files by selecting the Install an Additional Server Langauge option mentioned earlier.

Install Online Documentation and Viewers

The Install Online Documentation and Viewers option enables you to copy the DynaText viewer and book files to the hard drive of the new file server. The documentation is copied from the second installation CD provided with NetWare 4.1. Each language documentation set takes approximately 60 MB of hard drive space. Be careful to gauge the amount of space you have left.

If you select this option, the system creates a directory DOC off of volume SYS. Subdirectories exist under DOC for configuration data, help, and all the NetWare 4.1 manuals.

The viewer files are placed in a directory SYS:DOCVIEW. There are viewers available for DOS/Windows, Macintosh, and Unix based clients. For more information on how to install and use DynaText, refer to Chapter 25, "Installing Applications."

Summary

In this chapter, you learned how to install NetWare 4.1. You learned about the ways in which you can boot the file server—from a DOS partition on the file server's hard drive or from a bootable floppy. Different installation methods then were discussed, including installing NetWare from a floppy disk, CD-ROM, or another file server. You learned how to set up for each of these installation methods. The DOS partition on the server also was discussed, as well as what minimum files are required, and what additional files you can copy to the DOS partition.

You then learned the steps involved in a Custom Installation:

- Enter server name
- Enter server internal IPX address
- Decide on keyboard mapping and filename support
- Load and configure disk drivers
- Load and configure LAN drivers
- Create NetWare partition
- Create and configure volumes
- Install NDS
- Create STARTUP.NCF and AUTOEXEC.NCF files

NDS installation, as you learned, involves setting up the time-zone and time-synchronization information. You also can specify the first level organization and up to three levels of organizational units, as well as the Admin user and a password.

The last few sections in this chapter dealt with additional installation options, including creating a workstation installation disk, copying the online documentation, and installing other server software. The next chapter deals with upgrading and other installation issues.

Upgrades and Other Installation Issues

This chapter addresses issues that pertain to upgrades. The first is time synchronization, a critical issue in a NetWare 4.1 network. Actions that impact the structure of the NDS cannot take place without correct time synchronization. The first part of this chapter addresses time synchronization concepts, parameters, and how to set them.

The next major topic is upgrades. The MIGRATE.EXE utility is a tool you can use to smooth the transition from a bindery-based server to a network-based NDS tree. Upgrading a NetWare 2.*x* file server to NetWare 4.1 is discussed. A comprehensive discussion of the in-place upgrade shows you how to convert a NetWare 2.*x* file server to a NetWare 4.1 file server without additional hardware. The upgrade of a NetWare 3.1*x* file server to NetWare 4.1 is also covered.

The last portion of this chapter gives you ideas on how to perform simple tests to ensure that file servers and workstations are communicating after the installation or upgrade.

Time Synchronization

NetWare Directory Services uses *time synchronization* to ensure accuracy for the order in which replicas are updated. Every change to the directory is time stamped. The changes to the directory are made on a first-come, first-served basis, according to the time stamps. So, if two administrators in different locations change the same object, directory services applies the changes in the sequence of time recorded in the time stamps. Time synchronization is the way NetWare 4.1 ensures that all servers in a directory tree report the same time.

This subsection focuses on the four types of time synchronization. The NetWare 4.1 time synchronization server options are as follows:

- Single Reference time server
- Reference time server
- Primary time server
- Secondary time server

Each type of time server performs a different kind of time synchronization function. Single Reference, Primary, and Reference time servers are all time source servers. They provide a time to the network. Secondary time servers do not provide a time, they only receive a time from a time source server.

Single Reference Time Server

A *Single Reference time server* provides time to secondary time servers and to workstations—and is the only source of time on the network. Therefore, all other directory services servers must be able to contact it. Single Reference is the default when you install NetWare 4.1 (Secondary is the default if this is not the first server installed in the directory). Figure 13.1 illustrates a NetWare 4.1 network that has a Single Reference time server.

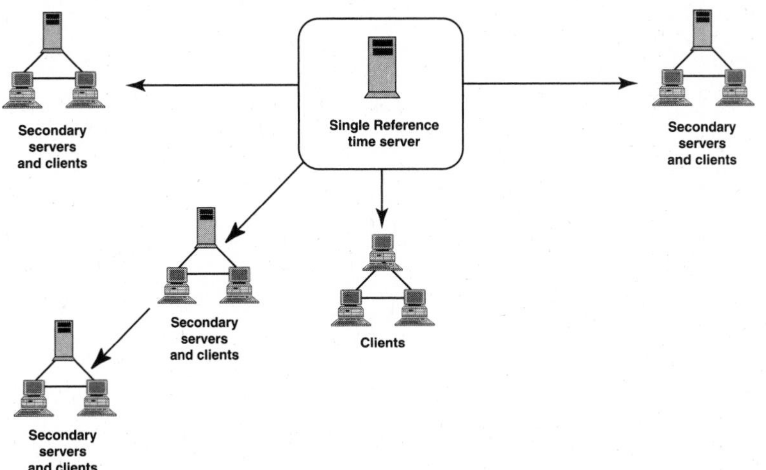

Figure 13.1

A Single Reference time server.

Reference Time Server

Reference time servers provide a time to which all the servers synchronize. You can synchronize reference time servers with external time sources such as atomic clocks. Reference time servers do not adjust their internal clocks; however, Primary time servers' internal clocks synchronize with the Reference time server. A network usually has only one Reference time server. A Reference time server must have at least one Primary time server. Whenever you have both Primary and Reference servers on a network, they must be able to contact each other for time synchronization. Figure 13.2 illustrates a NetWare 4.1 network that has a reference time server.

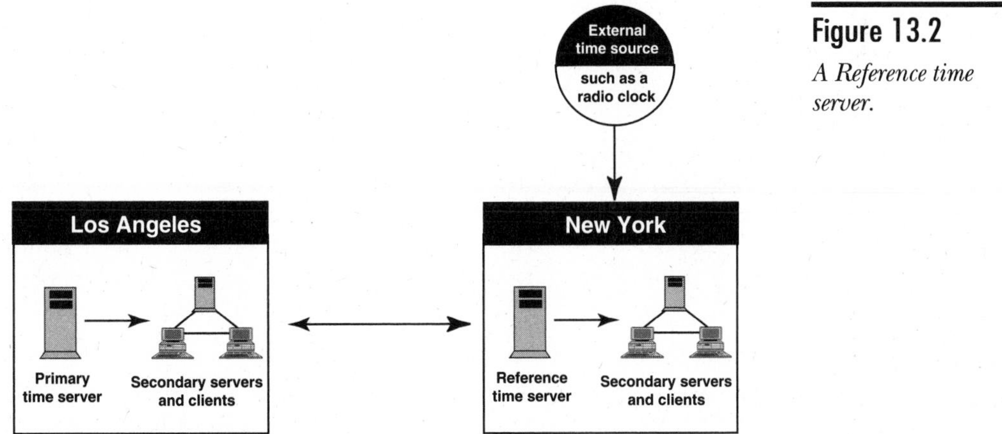

Figure 13.2

A Reference time server.

Primary Time Server

Primary time servers synchronize the time with at least one other Primary or Reference time server, and provide time to Secondary time servers and to workstations. On larger networks, Primary time servers increase fault tolerance by giving Secondary time servers multiple time sources. Also, you can put a Primary time server in each geographic location so that Secondary time servers need not use a wide area network (WAN) link. Figure 13.3 illustrates a NetWare 4.1 network that has a Primary time server.

Figure 13.3

A Primary time server.

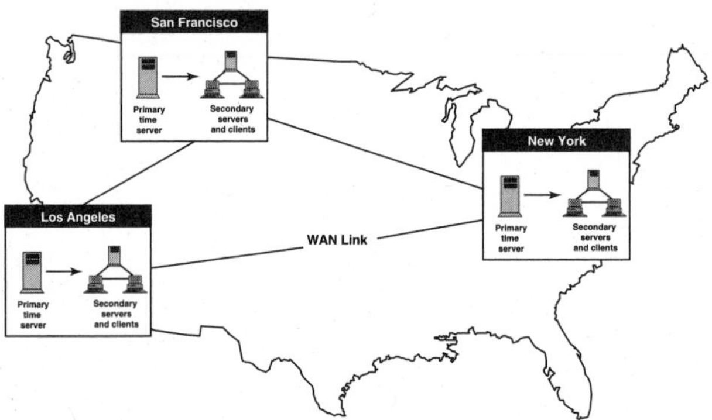

The only difference between a Primary and a Reference time server is that the Primary time server can accept its time information from other Primary or Reference time servers and can adjust its clock. A Reference time server cannot adjust its clock, whereas a Primary time server can adjust its clock by as much as 50 percent with respect to the time offered by an outside source. If the clock of a Reference time server was set to 10:20:30, for example, and the clock of a Primary time server was set to 10:20:28, the Primary would adjust its clock to 10:20:29. This represents a 50 percent forward adjustment.

Suppose you have two Primary time servers and one Reference time server. In this example, all three servers use configured time sources. Configured time sources are servers designated in the TIMESYNC.CFG file as time providers. Servers Primary 1 and Primary 2 are configured to exchange time information with each other. Primary 2 and the Reference also exchange time information. The polling intervals are set so that the time exchange between Primary 1 and Primary 2 takes place five minutes apart from the time exchange between Primary 2 and the Reference time server.

The time adjustments in this example are greatly exaggerated. Under normal conditions, time servers are set to adjust their clocks by no more than 2 seconds. For the

sake of illustration, assume that the time servers in this example are configured to adjust their clocks by a value of up to 3 minutes.

In the first polling interval, the following time values are exchanged:

```
Polling Interval: 14:00:00

Primary 1:        13:50:00
Primary 2:        13:54:00
```

Each Primary time server adjusts its clock by a factor of 50 percent. After the polling interval, Primary 1 adjusts its clock forward to 13:52:00 and Primary 2 does not adjust its clock backwards, but rather agrees to "wait" for a period of 2 minutes in order for Primary 1 to catch up.

During the next example polling interval, 5 minutes later, Primary 2 and the Reference server exchange time information. Here are the time values during this interval:

```
Polling Interval: 14:05:00

Primary 2:        13:59:00
Reference:        14:05:00
```

Here, the time difference between Primary 2 and the Reference is six minutes. Primary 2 adjusts its clock forward by a factor of 50 percent, or three minutes, which reduces the time difference. The Reference time server does not adjust its clock.

During the next polling interval, 5 minutes later, Primary 1 and Primary 2 exchange time information:

```
Polling Interval:      14:10:00

Primary 1:        14:02:00
Primary 2:        14:07:00
```

Here, Primary 2 is only three minutes off the Reference because of its last adjustment. Primary 1 is eight minutes off the Reference, and five minutes apart from Primary 2. Primary 1 adjusts its clock by 50 percent bringing it ahead two and a half minutes to a time of 14:04:30. Primary 2 does not adjust its clock backwards.

In five minutes, Primary 2 and the Reference exchange time as follows:

```
Polling Interval: 14:15:00

Primary 2:        14:12:00
Reference:        14:15:00
```

Here, the difference in time is three minutes. Primary 2 adjusts its clock ahead by 50 percent, which amounts to one and a half minutes. Primary 2 is now at 14:13:30. The Reference time server does not adjust its clock.

During the next polling interval, 5 minutes later, Primary 1 and Primary 2 exchange time information:

```
Polling Interval:     14:20:00

Primary 1:          14:14:30
Primary 2:          14:18:30
```

Here, Primary 2 is now only one and a half minutes off the Reference. Primary 1 is five and a half minutes off the Reference. The difference between the two is now four minutes. Primary 1 adjusts its clock ahead by 50 percent, which amounts to two minutes. Primary 1 is now at 14:16:30. Primary 2 does not adjust its clock backwards. Eventually, the two Primary servers adjust their clocks to match that of the Reference.

Secondary Time Server

Secondary time servers get the time from Single Reference, Primary or Reference time servers. They adjust their internal clocks to synchronize with the network time, and they provide the time to workstations. Unlike a Primary time server, a Secondary time server will adjust its clock by a factor of 100 percent. A Secondary time server does not participate in determining the correct time. You may choose to use the default time server type of Single Reference when you install the first NetWare 4.1 server. If you accept this default, all subsequent servers on the network will be Secondary time servers.

Time synchronization default settings are appropriate for most small networks. If you do not use the defaults, you should have a plan for the network that answers the following questions:

- What types of time servers do I need?
- What location on the network for the time servers would serve best to provide fault tolerance and keep network traffic to a minimum?

Provide the plan to the network supervisors who install NetWare 4.1 servers so they can designate the correct time synchronization function on each server they install.

By default, time synchronization messages are broadcast on the network. Optimize time synchronization by minimizing the number of routers and slow links between Secondary time servers and their Single Reference, Primary, or Reference time servers.

Customized Time Synchronization Options

The default SAP (Service Advertising Protocol) method of time synchronization enables you to install quickly and to easily make changes to the configuration. It does generate, however, a small amount of additional network traffic. You can determine time servers that a server should contact, but the cost is that you must then maintain time synchronization lists for each server.

At startup, NetWare 4.1 automatically loads the TIMESYNC.NLM to control time synchronization. The TIMESYNC.CFG file in SYS:SYSTEM contains the parameters for the TIMESYNC.NLM. You customize time synchronization by editing the TIMESYNC.CFG file.

You can also configure customized time settings by using SERVMAN.NLM from the file server console. To access these settings, from the file server console type the following:

LOAD SERVMAN

From the SERVMAN main menu, select Server Parameters. The Select a Parameter Category menu appears. From the Select a Parameter Category menu, select Time. The Time Parameters dialog box appears, as shown in figure 13.4.

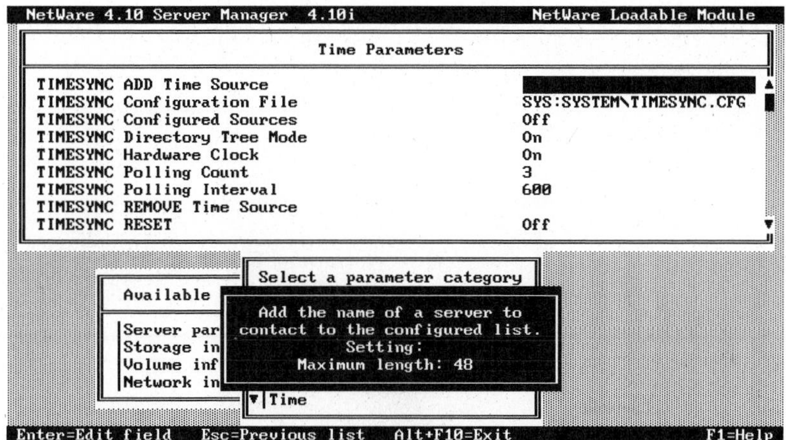

Figure 13.4

SERVMAN.NLM—Time Parameters dialog box.

Table 13.1 lists custom time synchronization options and their recommended usage.

Table 13.1
Time Synchronization Settings

SET Parameter	Recommended Usage
TIMESYNC ADD Time Source	To add a time source for this server. A *time source* is another server that this server consults to obtain the correct time. Not effective for a Reference or Single Reference server.
TIMESYNC Configuration File *Default =SYS:SYSTEM\TIMESYNC.CFG*	To identify the path and name of the time configuration file when it is not SYS:SYSTEM\TIMESYNC.CFG.
TIMESYNC Configured Sources *Default = OFF*	If set to ON, this server consults the TIMESYNC.CFG file for servers from which to get its time.
TIMESYNC Directory Tree Mode *Default = ON*	Turn this parameter OFF to allow SAP packets from other Directory trees to influence time synchronization on this server's Directory tree. Set to ON, this server gets time information only from servers in its NDS tree.
TIMESYNC Hardware Clock *Default = ON*	Turn this parameter OFF only if this server uses an external time source (such as a radio clock). All servers in the same tree should have the same setting for this parameter.
TIMESYNC Polling Count *Default = 3* (time packets)	To control the number of packets this server can exchange with other time servers when polling. Increase this setting to increase the accuracy of the time adjustments. By increasing this parameter,however, you also increase the number of SAP packets that are generated.
TIMESYNC Polling Interval *Default = 600* (seconds)	To control the amount of time between time exchanges with other time servers. To poll time servers

SET Parameter	Recommended Usage
	more often than every 10 minutes, decrease this setting. All servers in the same tree should have the same setting.
TIMESYNC REMOVE Time Source	To remove a time server from the time source list in the TIMESYNC.CFG file.
TIMESYNC RESET *Default = OFF*	To reset the values in the TIMESYNC.CFG file and remove the list of time sources, set to ON.
ON.TIMESYNC Restart Flag *Default = OFF*	To reload TIMESYNC.NLM without rebooting the server, set to ON, which causes the server to read the TIMESYNC.CFG file and register any changes.
TIMESYNC Service Advertising *Default = ON*	Turn this parameter OFF if you are using a custom-configured list of time sources. When set to ON, the server uses SAP to transmit time information. Note that Secondary time servers do not advertise time. If both this parameter and the TIMESYNC Configured Sources parameter are set to ON, the server will use both SAP and the source time servers indicated in the TIMESYNC.CFG file to obtain time values.
TIMESYNC Synchronization Radius *Default = 2000 (milliseconds)*	To allow a wider margin of error for time synchronization between servers, increase this parameter. If you decrease the radius too much (below 1,000), some time servers might not ever synchronize. This value represents the total time adjustment a server will make. This parameter does not apply to Reference or Single Reference time servers.

continues

Table 13.1, Continued
Time Synchronization Settings

SET Parameter	Recommended Usage
TIMESYNC Time Source	To add a time server or display the time source list in the TIMESYNC.CFG file.
TIMESYNC TYPE *Default = SECONDARY*	To change the time server type in the TIMESYNC.CFG file. Other choices include Primary, Reference, and Single Reference.
TIMESYNC Write Parameters *Default = OFF*	To change the settings in the TIMESYNC.CFG file.
TIMESYNC Write Value *Default = 3*	To control which parameters are written when you set the TIMESYNC Write Parameters value to ON (see above). The available options for this parameter are: 1 = Write internal parameters only (i.e., SET commands that affect only this server) 2 = Write configured time source parameters to the TIMESYNC.CFG file only 3 = Write both to the TIMESYNC.CFG file and the internal parameters
Time Zone	Abbreviated value which represents the time zone for this server. The format is ZZZn[DDD], where ZZZ is the time zone, n is the offset from UTC (Universal Time Coordinated), and DDD is optional and represents the Daylight Savings Time type. There are 24 possible time zone values, representing the 24 time zones around the world. Examples include PST for Pacific Standard Time, and EST for Eastern Standard Time. PST is an offset of eight hours from UTC. EST is an offset of five hours from UTC. An example of Daylight Savings

SET Parameter	Recommended Usage
	abbreviations is PDT (Pacific Daylight Savings Time). Thus, if the time zone is Pacific Standard Time and has an offset of eight hours from Greenwich (UTC), using Daylight Savings time, enter the following: **PST8PDT**
Default Time Server Type	Same as the TIMESYNC Type parameter (see above).
Start of Daylight Savings Time	To indicate when Daylight Savings Time starts in your time zone. A typical example follows: (APRIL SUNDAY FIRST 2:00:00 AM) This indicates that Daylight Savings Time is effective at 2:00 a.m. on the first Sunday in April.
End of Daylight Savings Time	To indicate when Daylight Savings Time ends in your time zone. A typical example follows: (OCTOBER SUNDAY LAST 2:00:00 AM) This indicates that Daylight Savings Time ends at 2:00 a.m. on the last Sunday in October. (Remember the old saying, "Spring Ahead Fall Back.")
Daylight Savings Time Offset	Time in hours to offset when Daylight Savings Time takes effect.
Daylight Savings Time Status	To indicate that you are currently on Daylight Savings Time, set to ON.
New Time With Daylight Savings Time Status	To indicate that the operating operating system should consult the Daylight Savings Time Status field, and offset all time calculations, set to ON.

You also can use the EDIT.NLM editor from the file server console, or any text editor from a workstation, to edit the TIMESYNC.CFG file located in the SYS:SYSTEM directory, rather than use SERVMAN to enter time parameters.

Time Synchronization Issues

Neither the Primary nor Secondary time servers adjust their clocks backward. If the clocks of your servers are running ahead of actual time, you need to adjust the time on your network manually. Do not adjust the CMOS clock or adjust time from the DOS prompt of any of the Primary or Reference time servers: this results in the error message, `Synthetic Time is being issued on server XYZ`, where `XYZ` is the name of the offending server. This message continues until the server with the backward time has caught up or a scheduled time adjustment takes place.

To schedule an orderly time adjustment, use the following command on the Reference or Single Reference server's console:

SET TIMESYNC TIME ADJUSTMENT = [+ | -] hh:mm:ss AT mm/dd/yy hh:mm:ss

This command schedules an orderly manual time adjustment that can then be distributed throughout the network using time synchronization. Use the plus (+) to push network time forward. Use the minus (-) to move network time backward. hh:mm:ss is the amount of forward or backward adjustment. mm/dd/yy hh:mm:ss is the date and time the adjustment takes place.

Be sure to schedule a time adjustment in advance. If the time adjustment is wrong, you can cancel it by using the following command, from the console of a Reference or Single Reference server:

SET TIMESYNC TIME ADJUSTMENT = CANCEL

You must issue a time adjustment cancellation before the scheduled time adjustment and from the same server from which the adjustment was first issued.

Another error message that you might see is when you have two servers configured as Single Reference servers. The message reads, `SINGLE servers are incompatible with REFERENCE and PRIMARY servers....` This prevents proper synchronization of time on your network. To fix the problem, change the TIMESYNC type of one of the Single Reference time servers to Secondary.

Upgrading to NetWare 4.1 from NetWare 3 and NetWare 2

You can upgrade your servers to NetWare 4.1 from any previous NetWare version or from several other operating systems. The following upgrade options are explained in this subsection:

- NetWare 3 to NetWare 4.1
- NetWare 2 to NetWare 4.1

Several methods work for performing the upgrades. Table 13.2 summarizes the advantages and disadvantages of the various upgrade options.

TABLE 13.2
Options for Upgrading to NetWare 4.1

Upgrade	Options Available	Advantages	Disadvantages
NetWare 3 to 4	Across-the-wire to an installed.	No risk of data loss. Can migrate multiple servers to a single installed server. Can choose what data you want to migrate. Can direct data to specific volume or directory.	Need a NetWare 4 server installed
	Across-the-wire on the same server.	Can select what data you want to migrate.	Some risk of data loss.
			Need to temporarily store files on a workstation or a tape drive. Need to use a third-party backup utility; NetWare backup tools are not supported.

continues

Table 13.2, Continued
Options for Upgrading to NetWare 4.1

Upgrade	Options Available	Advantages	Disadvantages
	In-place from NetWare 3.1*x* to NetWare 4.1	Need just the NetWare 3.1*x* server—no additional hardware needed.	Using this method, cannot upgrade from NetWare 3.0 server.
			If upgrade fails, you might have to restore server from backup.
NetWare 2 to NetWare 4.1	Across-the-wire to an installed NetWare 4.1 server.	No risk of data loss. Can migrate multiple servers to a single server. Can choose what data you want to migrate. Can direct data to specific volume or directory.	Need a NetWare 4 server installed.
	Across-the-wire on the same server.	Can select what information you to migrate.	Some risk of data loss.
			Need to temporarily store files on a workstation or a tape drive. Need to use a third-party backup utility; NetWare backup tools are not supported.
	In place in two steps from NetWare 2.1: (1) From NetWare 2.1 to NetWare 3.1*x*.	Need just one NetWare 2.1*x* server—no additional hardware needed.	Cannot upgrade from NetWare 2.0a. Cannot run on a 286 computer. Two step process.

Upgrade Available	Options	Advantages	Disadvantages
	(2) From NetWare 3.1*x* to NetWare 4		If upgrade fails, you might need to restore from backup.

The NetWare migration utility enables you to upgrade servers from NetWare 2 or 3 to NetWare 4.1 using one of three methods:

- **Across-the-wire to an installed NetWare 4.1 server.** You transfer your network information from a NetWare 2 or 3 server to an existing NetWare 4.1 server that is on the same network.
- **Across-the-wire to the same server.** You transfer your network information from a NetWare 2 or 3 server to an existing NetWare 4.1 server that is on the same network.
- **Upgrade-in-place.** You change your NetWare 2 or 3 server to a NetWare 4.1 server.

You need to complete several planning activities before you upgrade. First, select and prepare the NetWare 4.1 hardware. Choose the migration method. Collect information you need to perform the upgrade. Migrating file system rights and attributes, calculating RAM requirements, planning disk parameters (block size/suballocation, compression, data migration, and so forth), and reviewing directory structures are all matters you need to consider. Finally, prepare the existing server by doing a full backup and any necessary housecleaning: deleting obsolete bindery objects, running BINDFIX, cleaning up the file system, and so on.

In this chapter the term *migration* is used instead of upgrade because upgrading a program usually consists of deleting the original program and installing the new version, whereas migrating to NetWare 4.1 involves transferring bindery objects to corresponding Directory Services objects; upgrading file server volumes from NetWare 2 or 3 to 4.1 (while preserving their contents); installing new utilities, NLMs, and drivers; and installing new server software.

To avoid confusion later, know now that NetWare 4.1 has another type of migration: data migration. *Data migration* is a feature in which data that isn't accessed in a certain amount of time is moved to a storage device such as optical disk or tape, freeing up space on the server's hard drive.

Table 13.3 summarizes the changes to file system rights in NetWare 4.1.

TABLE 13.3
Upgrading Directory and File Rights

Right	Description	Changes in NetWare 4.1
Supervisory (v3.1*x*)	Grants all rights to the directory, its files, and its subdirectories.	Name changed to Supervisor. Note: do not confuse file system rights with NetWare Directory Services rights.
Create (all ver.) for dirs.	Assigned only if Open was also assigned.	Create now enables users to create directories without the and files need for the Access Control right.
Delete (v2.1*x*) Erase (v2.2-3.1*x*)	Deletes directories and files.	Same as v3.1x Erase.
Modify (v2.1*x*) Modify (v2.2-3.1*x*) directories and files	Renames files or changes their attributes.	Access Control is no longer required to rename directories and files or change attributes. Same as v3.1x Modify.
Open (v2.1*x*) directories and files	Opens directories and files	Open is no longer a separate right—included with Read, Write, and Create rights.
Parental (v2.1*x*) directories and files Access Control (v2.2-3.1*x*)	The Trustee Assignments and Inherited Rights Filter control how other objects can access the object.	All rights assigned to users with Access Control can be revoked at the file level. This file right no longer assigns the right to rename or create subdirectories.
Read and Open (v2.1*x*) file only	Reads and scans files.	A separate Open right is no longer required.

Right	Description	Changes in NetWare 4.1
Search (v2.1*x*) directories and files	Searches directories and files.	
File Scan (v2.2-3.1*x*) directories and files	Scans directories and files.	File Scan includes the right to search to the root files of the directory. File Scan is assigned automatically when any of the NetWare rights are assigned.
Write and Open (v2.1x) Write (v2.2-3.1*x*) directories and files	Enables the user write to files.	A separate Open right is no longer required.

Table 13.4 summarizes the changes to file attributes in NetWare 4.1.

TABLE 13.4
Upgrading File Attributes

Attribute	Description	Changes in NetWare 4.*x*
Can't Compress (Cc)	Indicates that a file cannot be compressed because of limited space savings. Cannot be set by the user.	New
Compressed (Co)	Indicates that the file is compressed. Cannot be set by the user.	New
Copy Inhibit (v3.1*x*)	Valid only on Macintosh workstations.	No change
Delete Inhibit (v3.1*x*)	Prevents file delete.	No change
Don't Compress (Dc)	Prevents the file from being compressed.	New

continues

Table 13.4, Continued
Upgrading File Attributes

Attribute	Description	Changes in NetWare 4.*x*
Don't Migrate (Dm)	Prevents the file from being migrated to a secondary storage device like an optical drive or tape drive.	New
Execute Only (v2.1*x*)	Prevents copying or backing up EXE or COM files.	Not available
Hidden	Hides files from file scans and prevents them from being copied or deleted.	No change
Immediate Compress	Sets the file to be compressed as soon as possible.	New
Indexed	Occurs automatically to files over 64 blocks. Large files don't need to be flagged by the user to be indexed.	This is now a status flag.
Migrated	Indicates the file is migrated. Cannot be set by the user.	New
Modified since last backup (v2.1*x*); Archive needed (v2.2-v3.1*x*)	Lists files since last backup. Automatically assigned.	Same as NetWare v3.1*x* Archive needed.
Purge (v3.1*x* and later)	Purges files marked for deletion.	No change
Rename inhibit (v3.1*x* and later)	Prevents renaming of files.	No change
Shareable (all versions)	Allows several users to open a file for update simultaneously.	No change
Non-Shareable (all versions)	Prohibits sharing of files.	No change from v3.1*x*—no

Attribute	Description	Changes in NetWare 4.*x*
		indication of this attribute is shown.
Read only (all versions)	Prohibits modification of files.	No change
Read Write (all versions)	Allows writing to files.	No change from v3.1*x*—on automatically when Read Only is not set.
System (all versions)	Hides system files.	No change
Transactional (all versions)	Activates Transaction Tracking System (TTS).	No change

Before you migrate a NetWare 2 or 3 file server to NetWare 4.1, you can take a number of preparatory steps to make the resulting Directory tree closer to what you plan.

Upgrading from NetWare 2.*x* to NetWare 4.1

Upgrading from NetWare 2.*x* to NetWare 4.1 is complicated because the NetWare 2.*x* partition is different than the partition used with NetWare 3.*x* or NetWare 4.x. An In-place upgrade process that changes the partition type is discussed in this section. This process is risky, however, and a good backup of all critical data on the NetWare 2.*x* file server is highly recommended.

The basic process is as follows:

- Clean up the NetWare 2.*x* file system
- Clean up the NetWare 2.*x* bindery files
- Perform two or more full backups

- Migrate the NetWare 2.*x* server
- Install NetWare 4.1
- Restore files as needed
- Recover login scripts
- Clean up the NDS tree

The next several sections cover the basic process.

Clean Up the NetWare 2.*x* File System

Because you are planning to upgrade to a new version of NetWare, now is the ideal time to clean up the file system on your NetWare 2.*x* file server. Take the time to remove old files that you no longer need or use. Get rid of temporary files that take up disk space. Remove subdirectories of users who are no longer on the system. The less clutter on your server, the faster and smoother the upgrade.

For an In-place migration, INSTALL needs about 50 MB free disk space on volume SYS for temporary storage during the migration process (less if you have few users and other bindery objects). While you free disk space for migration, you might want to delete any obsolete directories.

Another important attribute of a file server machine is that its internal clock should keep accurate time. With most computers this is not a problem, but because correct time stamps are so critical to the operation of Directory Services, you should verify the accuracy of your server's clock (before you install NetWare 4.1 on it) by comparing it to an accurate time source over a 24-hour period.

Because NetWare 4.1 is so different from previous versions of NetWare, migrating an existing NetWare network to version 4 is much like planning a new NetWare 4.1 network. For this reason, both processes are covered concurrently, and it is noted when different actions are required.

Clean Up the NetWare 2.*x* Bindery Files

Most of the preliminary steps you should take fall under the category of "cleaning up" the bindery. These steps are described in the following list:

- Change the names of users, printers, and print queues to conform to the standards you have set for Directory objects (if the standards are compatible with the naming requirements for bindery objects). Users can begin to become accustomed to the new object names before you migrate the server.
- Delete obsolete bindery objects: users who no longer exist, unused print queues, and so on. Two utilities, named PRINTUSR and PRINTGRP, are available on CompuServe's NetWire forum (GO NOVLIB) to help identify obsolete objects.
- Check for bindery objects that have the same name, but of different object type—for example, both a group and a print queue named MAC. We have provided a utility program that scans a server's bindery for duplicate bindery object names. You can download DUPBIND from NetWire (GO NOVLIB).
- Before you migrate your 2.*x* server, back up the file system and run BINDFIX. If BINDFIX repairs problems in the bindery, back up the file system again before you migrate.
- Check for users who have accounts on multiple 2.*x*/3.*x* servers. You will have to deal with this problem at some point during the migration.

During the migrate process, the bindery objects are moved to a single NDS container. The migrate process uses the MIGRATE.EXE utility, covered later in this chapter. Duplications of objects in the same container are not tolerated. Duplicate objects are renamed during the migrate process, by adding "+1" to the name of the first duplicate, "+2" to the second duplicate, and so forth, which might be inconvenient to track down later on.

In bindery-based versions of NetWare, bindery objects are organized by object type. Object types include the following:

- Users
- Groups
- Printers
- Print Queues
- Print Servers

Duplication between object types is allowed, but not within an object type. For example, the following objects are permitted:

Object Type	Name
User	Dallas
Group	Dallas
Print Queue	Dallas
Printer	Dallas
Print Server	Dallas

The following objects are not permitted:

Object Type	Name
User	Denver
User	Denver
Print Queue	Chicago
Print Queue	Chicago

Use SYSCON.EXE to review the contents of the bindery files. Check for duplications and make name changes as needed.

You do not have to change the names of duplicate objects because MIGRATE.EXE changes the names automatically. Duplicate objects, however, are imported as bindery objects and you cannot manage them by using NDS management tools such as NWADMIN or NETADMIN.

Figure 13.5 shows the list of users for NetWare 2.1 file server BOB.

To use SYSCON.EXE to change the name of an object, select the object name from the list and press F3. To rename a group object, for example, proceed as follows:

- From the SYSCON.EXE main menu, select Group Information.
- From the Group Information menu, select the name of the group you want to rename (do not press Enter yet!).
- Press F3 and change the name.

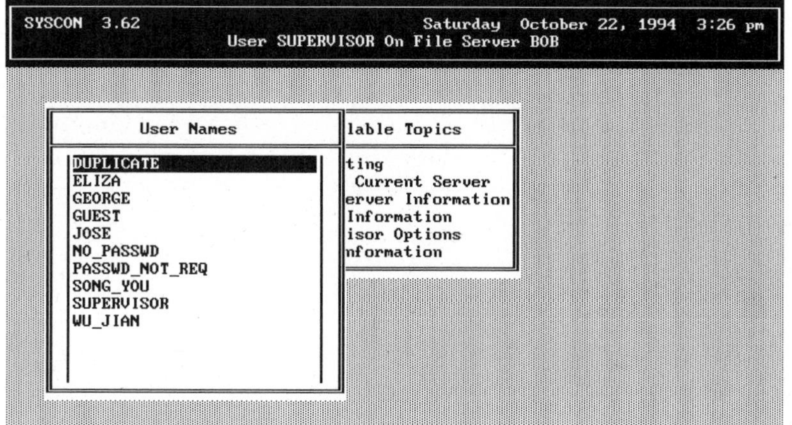

Figure 13.5
SYSCON.EXE—View of list of users for a NetWare 2.1 file server.

After you rename objects as necessary, the next phase of the bindery cleanup is to run the BINDFIX.EXE utility, which is located in the SYS:SYSTEM directory. BINDFIX goes through the bindery files and reindexes and resizes the files. Deleted objects are permanently removed. Inconsistencies are repaired. Figure 13.6 shows the progress of BINDFIX.

```
Discarding property NET_ADDRESS because object does not exists.
Discarding property OBJ_BACK_LINKS because object does not exists.
Discarding property NET_ADDRESS because object does not exists.
Discarding property NET_ADDRESS because object does not exists.
Discarding property OBJ_BACK_LINKS because object does not exists.
Discarding property NET_ADDRESS because object does not exists.
Discarding property OBJ_BACK_LINKS because object does not exists.
Checking objects for back-link property.
Checking set consistency and compacting sets.
Building avail lists and new hash tables.
There are 56 Object nodes and 0 Property Nodes free.
Checking user objects for standard properties.
Checking group objects for standard properties.
Checking links between users and groups for consistency.
Delete mail directories of users that no longer exist? (y/n): Y
Checking for mail directories of users that no longer exist.
Checking for users that do not have mail directories.
Delete trustee rights for users that no longer exist? (y/n): Y
Checking volume SYS.  Please wait.

Bindery check successfully completed.
Please delete the files NET$BIND.OLD and NET$BVAL.OLD after you have verified
the reconstructed bindery.

G:\SYSTEM>
```

Figure 13.6
The BINDFIX.EXE utility after repairing the bindery files.

Perform Two or More Full Backups

Now you must back up the NetWare 2.*x* file server. For more information on conducting a backup, consult the documentation that comes with your current backup system (you do have one, don't you?). Chapter 41, "Protecting Your Network Files," also has valuable information on backing up network files.

You should have at least two good backup copies of critical files, so if one backup is no good you have another copy. At certain points in the upgrade process, files on your NetWare 2.*x* file server are inaccessible or might be deleted entirely.

Before you proceed, a good way to ensure that you have a reliable backup is to choose a few files at random to do a sample restore. Remember to do the sample restore to a drive or directory that does not contain the original. If your backup is bad, you could overwrite the good copy with a bad copy.

Migrate the NetWare 2.*x* Server

The migrate process takes information from the NetWare 2.*x* file server and integrates it into an existing NetWare 4.1 file server, or stores it temporarily on the hard drive of a workstation. Before you can run MIGRATE.EXE, you must install it on the hard drive of a workstation, or on a file server other than the NetWare 2.*x* file server.

NetWare 4.1's server migration utilities focus on enabling a company to gradually switch a large network from 2 or 3 to 4. The idea is that a company will not try to upgrade over a weekend. You cannot change a large system in such a short period of time but shutting down long enough to do the upgrade is simply not feasible. In addition, network Administrators and users need time to get used to changes in the way the network operates.

Installing the MIGRATE Utility

You can install MIGRATE from disks that you must create or from the installation CD. You might want to create a set of MIGRATE disks if you plan to perform the migrate process on a number of installations. You need two disks, which you can then transport to any site and install on any file server or workstation.

To create MIGRATE disks, proceed as follows:

1. From the NetWare 4.1 file server console, load the INSTALL.NLM utility by typing **LOAD INSTALL**.

2. From the INSTALL.NLM main menu, select Product Options. The Product Options menu appears.

3. From the Product Options menu, select Create NetWare UPGRADE/MIGRATE Diskettes. You are prompted for the location of the installation media. The default is the volume of the CD used to first install NetWare 4.1 on this file server. Press Enter if the default is correct. If not, press F3 and enter the correct volume name. You need the following volume:

   ```
   volume:\NW410\INSTALL\ENGLISH
   ```

   volume is the name of the volume of the NetWare 4.1 installation CD.

4. INSTALL.NLM reads the installation CD and displays the Indicate Which File Groups You Want Included screen, as shown in figure 13.7.

   Choose the sections on this menu according to the following considerations:

   - Select 3.5 inch if your computer has 3.5 inch (1.44 MB) disks.
   - Select 5.25 inch if your computer has 5 1/4 inch (1.2 MB) disks.
   - Select UPGRADE if you plan to upgrade the same physical hardware from NetWare 2.*x* to NetWare 4.1. If you plan to install NetWare 4.1 on another physical computer, you do not need this disk.
   - Select MIGRATE to create the migrate process disks.

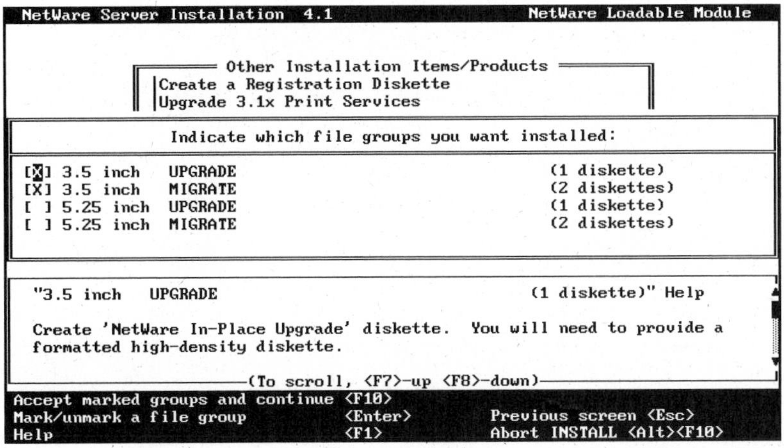

```
NetWare Server Installation  4.1                      NetWare Loadable Module

                 Other Installation Items/Products
              Create a Registration Diskette
              Upgrade 3.1x Print Services

                Indicate which file groups you want installed:

 [X] 3.5 inch   UPGRADE                              (1 diskette)
 [X] 3.5 inch   MIGRATE                              (2 diskettes)
 [ ] 5.25 inch  UPGRADE                              (1 diskette)
 [ ] 5.25 inch  MIGRATE                              (2 diskettes)

 "3.5 inch   UPGRADE                               (1 diskette)" Help

 Create 'NetWare In-Place Upgrade' diskette.  You will need to provide a
 formatted high-density diskette.
                    (To scroll, <F7>-up <F8>-down)
Accept marked groups and continue <F10>
Mark/unmark a file group          <Enter>     Previous screen <Esc>
Help                              <F1>        Abort INSTALL <Alt><F10>
```

Figure 13.7
Creating MIGRATE disks using INSTALL.NLM product options.

5. After you finish your selections, press F10 to continue. You are prompted to insert a blank, formatted, high-density floppy disk. INSTALL tells you what to label each disk.

6. After you have created the last disk, press Esc to return to the file server console prompt.

You can now install MIGRATE on a workstation or file server. To install MIGRATE from the disks you created in the preceding procedure, proceed as follows:

1. From a workstation or file server, create a directory to contain the MIGRATE utility files. The recommended directory is MIGRATE. For this example, assume that the files are installed on drive C in a directory named C:\MIGRATE.

2. Insert the first disk into drive A. Change your default drive to A and begin the installation by typing the following:

INSTALL A: ***destination***

destination is the drive letter and directory where you plan to install the MIGRATE utility. Assuming the directory \MIGRATE on drive C, type the following:

INSTALL A: C:\MIGRATE

3. The installation batch file copies files from the first disk to the destination. You are then prompted to insert the second disk and additional files are copied.

You can also directly copy the MIGRATE files from the installation CD if it is available. If so, proceed as follows:

1. Log in to a file server that has the NetWare 4.1 installation CD mounted, or move to a workstation that has a local CD ROM drive with the NetWare 4.1 installation CD mounted.
2. Make a directory to contain the MIGRATE files on the local workstation, or file server. Create a directory for the NLS (Native Language Support) files. Assuming you want to install on drive C, type the following:

   MD C:\MIGRATE

   MD C:\MIGRATE\NLS

3. Map a drive letter to the root of the installation CD. Change to that drive letter. For example, if the installation CD is mounted as volume NETWARE_410, do as follows:

   MAP G:=NETWARE_410:

   G:

   If mounted locally, move to the drive letter assigned to your local CD.

4. Copy the MIGRATE files from the installation CD to the destination directory as follows:

   COPY \MIGRATE________\MIGDISK1\CORE*.* ***destination***

   COPY \MIGRATE________\MIGDISK2\CORE*.* ***destination***

   COPY \MIGRATE________\MIGDISK2\NLS***language******.*** ***destination***

   COPY SYS:PUBLIC\NLS*.* ***destination*****\NLS**

   destination is the destination directory on your local workstation or on the file server. *language* is your preferred language (any of the following):

- DEUTSCH
- ENGLISH
- ESPANOL
- FRANCAIS
- ITALIANO

After you finish, you should have the following key files (among others) in your destination directory:

- MIGRATE.EXE
- LS10EXPO.EXE
- PCLPEXPO.EXE
- MIGPRINT.EXE

In addition, you will have a series of supporting files, including help files (*.HEP), message files (*.MSG) and overlay files (*.OVL). In the NLS subdirectory, you should have a series of files that begin with the prefix UNI*.

Running the MIGRATE Utility

To run the MIGRATE utility, move to the destination directory in which you installed the MIGRATE.EXE utility. Begin by typing the following:

MIGRATE

The MIGRATE main menu appears, as shown in figure 13.8.

During the migrate process, you can migrate from the NetWare 2.*x* (or 3.*x*) file server to an existing NetWare 4.1 file server—known as across-the-wire migration. If you plan to migrate files from a NetWare 2.*x* or 3.*x* file server and back again, select Same-Server Migration. If you use Same-Server Migration, you migrate bindery information to the destination directory in the form of a temporary file. After you upgrade the same server to NetWare 4.1, you can use MIGRATE to migrate the files back again.

To perform an across-the-wire migration, proceed as follows:

1. From the MIGRATE main menu, select Across-the-Wire Migration. The Select the Source LAN Type menu appears, as shown in figure 13.9.

2. From the Select the Source LAN Type menu, select NetWare 2.*x*. The Select the Destination LAN Type menu appears.

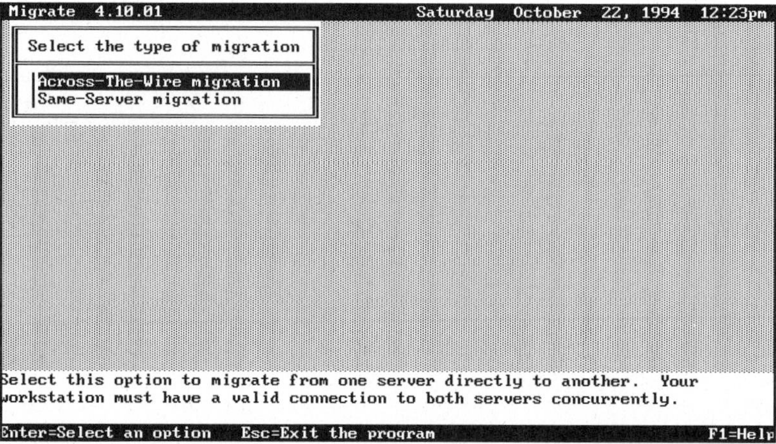

Figure 13.8
The MIGRATE main menu.

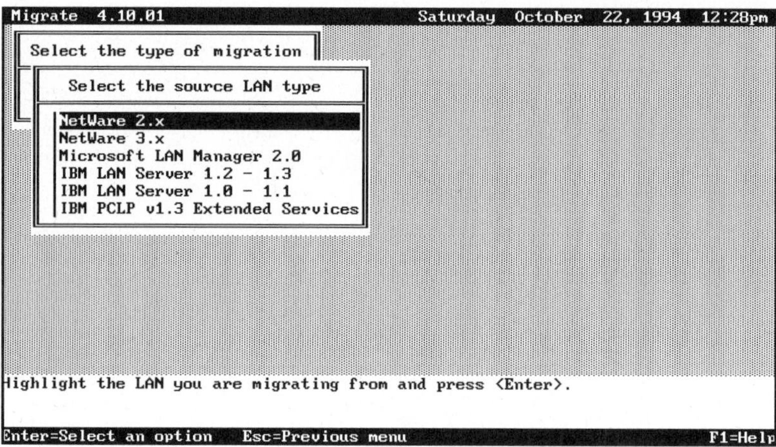

Figure 13.9
MIGRATE.EXE—Across-the-wire migration. The Select the Source LAN Type menu.

3. From the Select the Destination LAN Type menu, select NetWare 4.*x*. The Configure the Migration Utility menu appears. This menu, shown in figure 13.10, has three questions (filled in) you must answer.

   The various settings in the Configure the Migration Utility menu are summarized as follows:

- 1. Configure the Migration Utility
  - *Working Directory.* A directory that stores intermediate files and reports.
  - *Error/Warning Action.* Action to take if encounter an error. Default indicates that MIGRATE pauses on

every error encountered. Other choice is not to pause when errors occur.

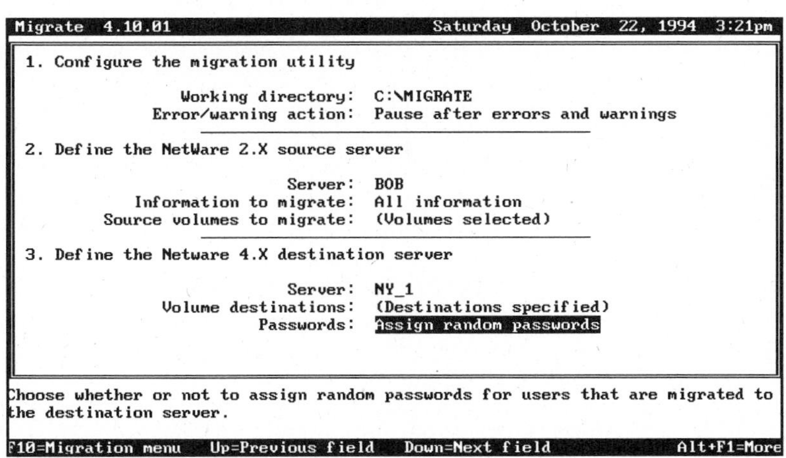

Figure 13.10

MIGRATE.EXE—The Configure the Migration Utility menu with questions filled in.

◆ 2. Define the NetWare 2.*x* Source Server

- ◆ *Server.* Field that contains the name of the NetWare 2.*x* file server from which the bindery information is obtained.

- ◆ *Information to Migrate.* When you select this option, the Select information to migrate menu appears, giving you a choice of what information to migrate (see fig. 13.11).

```
Migrate 4.10.01                                  Saturday October 22, 1994 3:33pm
 1. Configure the migration utility

             Working directory: C:\MIGRATE
          Error/warning ac
                            Select information to migrate
 2. Define the NetWare 2.X sou
                            All information
                       Se   Data files
        Information to mig  Trustee assignments
     Source volumes to mig  Users
                            User restrictions
 3. Define the Netware 4.X des  Groups
                            Default account restrictions
                       Se   Accounting information
         Volume destinat    Print queues and print servers
                    Passw   Non-Novell bindery objects

The default, 'All information' will migrate everyting below.  For specific
items only, select each item by highlighting it and pressing <F5>.
F5=Mark/unmark an option   Enter=Accept marked options               Alt+F1=More
```

Figure 13.11

MIGRATE.EXE - Select Information to Migrate Menu

To select all options, select the All Information option. To select more than one item but not all, select each item and press F5. The option appears in yellow (or boldface on a monochrome monitor). Options available are as follows:

- **All information.** Includes all information indicated on this list.
- **Data files.** Causes all directories, files and bindery information on the source server to be copied to the target. This option is not available when you perform a Same Server migration. In a Same Server migration, you must backup the data to a backup device. When you do an across-the-wire migration, the directories and files are copied to the destination server. If you do not want to combine the contents, indicate a directory on the destination server other than the root of volume SYS:. Otherwise, the contents of duplicate directories on the source and destination servers are combined. Files on the destination server are not overwritten by files on the source server where the name is the same.
- **Trustee assignments.** File and directory trustee assignments are transferred when you select this option in addition to the Data files option just described. If you do not select the Data files option, trustee rights are not transferred properly because trustee assignments are tied to files and directories and are recorded in the Directory Entry Table.
- **Users.** Causes user objects to be created in the destination server's bindery context by copying over basic user information. Information includes the following properties: full name, PRINTCON job information, login scripts (see Recover Login Scripts in this list), console operator status, workgroup or user account manager status, and security equivalencies.
- **User restrictions.** Causes user account restrictions to be migrated, including password, account balance, station, and time restrictions.
- **Groups.** Causes all group information to be migrated.
- **Default account restrictions.** Default account balance and restrictions are migrated, and information is placed in the USER_TEMPLATE. If current values are in the USER_TEMPLATE, this option causes them to be completely overwritten.
- **Accounting information.** Causes any accounting information from the source server to overwrite those of the destination server.

Sometimes you might not be using accounting on the destination server. In NetWare 4.1, you can obtain much of the same information from the

AUDITCON.EXE utility. If Accounting is installed on the NetWare 2.*x* source server, selecting Accounting Information enables Accounting on the NetWare 4.1 server.

- **Print queues and print servers.** Available only when migrating from a NetWare 4.1.0*x* to a NetWare 4.1 file server (or from one NetWare 4.*x* to another 4.*x* server). You must use the MIGPRINT.EXE utility to migrate printing objects from a NetWare 2.*x* file server.
- **Non-Novell bindery objects.** Causes all other bindery objects, such as objects created by Third Party utilities, to be migrated to the destination server.
- **Source volumes to migrate.** Enables you to specify which volumes to migrate, but is only effective when you also select the Data Files or All Information option from the Information to Migrate menu.

- 3. Define the NetWare 4.*x* Destination Server
  - *Server.* Enter the name of the destination NetWare 4.*x* file server.
  - *Volume destinations.* Brings up a list of source volumes as entered in the *Source* Volumes to Migrate field, and destination paths. You could, for example, migrate two different volumes on the source server to two separate directories on the destination server.
  - *Passwords.* Defines the fate of passwords.

If you select Assign No Passwords, all user objects migrated have no passwords on the destination server. Users can log in initially without a password. If a user must have a password, he or she is asked to enter a password after logging in.

If you choose the default, Assign Random Passwords, users are assigned a password at random. The usernames and passwords are listed in the file SYS:SYSTEM\NEW.PWD on the destination server. If users did not require a password on the source server, no password is assigned to the target.

Selecting the Accounting Information option causes the NetWare 4.1 server to start "charging" users. Eventually, user accounts are reduced to no credit, at which point they can no longer log in. If you do not plan to use the Accounting feature, do not select this option or the All Information option. If you want to migrate all options except this one, use F5 to mark all items except for All Information and Accounting Information.

4. After you fill in the Configure the Migration Utility menu, press F10 to begin the migration. The Select a Migration Action menu appears. Select Start Migration to begin the migration process.

5. After the migration is complete, you are returned to the Select a Migration Action menu. To view the migration report, select the View Migration Reports menu. Figure 13.12 shows the beginning of this report.

6. Select Exit to return to the DOS prompt.

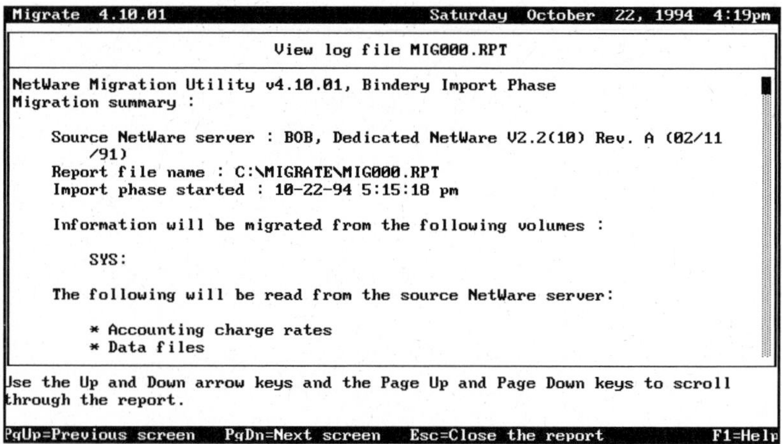

Figure 13.12
MIGRATE.EXE—Viewing a migration report.

You can view the random passwords assigned in the file SYS:SYSTEM\NEW.PWD on the destination server. A sample of that file follows:

```
F:\SYSTEM>type new.pwd
10-22-94 4:15:02 pm, PASSWD_NOT_REQ (user), password = PRQ
10-22-94 4:15:02 pm, GEORGE (user), password = ZXYFZ
10-22-94 4:15:02 pm, ELIZA (user), password = GUQNF
10-22-94 4:15:02 pm, WU_JIAN (user), password = HRVSQ
10-22-94 4:15:02 pm, SONG_YOU (user), password = CNMAR
10-22-94 4:15:02 pm, JOSE (user), password = QTJGT
```

Running the MIGPRINT.EXE Utility

The next step is to migrate printing objects, which you can accomplish by running the MIGPRINT.EXE utility, located in the same directory as MIGRATE.EXE. The syntax for this utility is as follows:

```
MIGPRINT /S=source_server /D=destination_server [/V=queue_volume] [/
➥O=output_file]
```

source_server is the name of the NetWare 2.*x* file server. *destination_server* is the name of the NetWare 4.1 server. If the volume you want to use to store print queues is not in the destination server's bindery context, you must specify the /V option and the name of the *queue_volume*. Use the /O option to specify the name of an *output_file* in which to store the output of the utility.

Here is a sample output file:

```
NetWare Printing Environment Migration Utility

Source NetWare server : BOB
Destination NetWare server : NY_1
Destination context : OU=NY.O=EBDB

Migrating print queues

  BOBQ1
    User : EVERYONE (Group)
    Print server : BOB (Print Server)

Migrating print servers

  BOB

    Migrating printers serviced by BOB

      LaserJet 4si
        Name changed to : LaserJet 4si000
        Type : Parallel port
        Starting form : 0
        Buffer size (KB) : 3
        Sampling interval : 15
        Banner type : Text
        Driver name : NPRINTER
        Default queue : BOBQ1
        Print server : BOB

          MIGPRINT.EXE-4.10.01-023: The program could not write the
          Print server attribute.

        Object to notify : (Job Owner)
        Print queue : BOBQ1
```

```
    Printer to service : LaserJet 4si000 (Printer)

      MIGPRINT.EXE-4.10.01-023: The program could not write the Printer
      to service attribute.

    User : EVERYONE (Group)


Migrating print job configurations


  GUEST
    Source configuration exists : No
    Print job configuration updated : No

  ELIZA
    Source configuration exists : No
    Print job configuration updated : No

  WU_JIAN
    Source configuration exists : No
    Print job configuration updated : No

  SONG_YOU
    Source configuration exists : No
    Print job configuration updated : No

  JOSE
    Source configuration exists : No
    Print job configuration updated : No
```

Install NetWare 4.1

The installation process can take several forms, as follows:

- Installing NetWare 4.1 on a physically different computer than the original NetWare 2.*x* file server
- Installing NetWare 4.1 on the same computer and using the backup to recover files
- Installing NetWare 4.1 on the same computer using the In-Place Upgrade process

The easiest technique is to install NetWare 4.1 on a different computer, in which you install NetWare 4.1 as a new installation. You then integrate the server into the existing tree (if any). Log in to the new file server and map a drive letter to the old file server. You can copy files from one server to the other, or you can use the MIGRATE utility and select All Information.

Another technique is to install NetWare 4.1 on the same computer but use the backup to recover files. First, migrate bindery information to a workstation. Then make a full backup of the server. Install NetWare 4.1 as a new file server. During this process, the NetWare 2.*x* partition is removed, which causes you to lose all data on the server. After you complete the installation, use MIGRATE to import bindery information into the NDS. Use the restore procedure as indicated, using your backup device to recover files.

The last technique is to perform an In-Place Upgrade.

Preparing for the In-Place Upgrade

An *In-place Upgrade* converts a NetWare 2.*x* file server temporarily to a 3.*x* file server, which sets the scene for a NetWare 3.*x* to 4.*x* upgrade installation. To prepare for the In-Place Upgrade you must create an UPGRADE disk. Follow the procedure outlined in the section, "Installing the MIGRATE Utility." Use the INSTALL.NLM on the file server and select the Product Options menu. From here, select the Create NetWare UPGRADE/MIGRATE Diskettes option to create the UPGRADE disk.

The UPGRADE disk is made bootable. The version of DOS created is Novell DOS 7. After the process is complete, the following files are copied to the UPGRADE disk:

COMMAND.COM

The DOS system files

Disk Drive NLM files (*.DSK)

2XUPGRDE.NLM (the In-place Upgrade utility)

SERVER.EXE (limited version of NetWare 3.*x*)

When you perform the upgrade, you need access to the NetWare 4.1 installation files. If the server you plan to upgrade has a CD-ROM drive, you can simply insert the CD into the drive and perform the upgrade. If you do have a CD-ROM drive, you need to add the following files to your UPGRADE disk, or copy them to a second disk:

- Both the NetWare and DOS driver for the host bus adapter for your CD drive (such as the AHA1540.DSK driver for an Adaptec 154x SCSI adapter, and MSCDEX.EXE for DOS)
- The ASPI driver for your host bus adapter (such as the ASPITRAN.DSK driver for an Adaptec for NetWare, and ASPI4DOS.SYS for DOS)

- The ASPICD driver for your host bus adapter and CD driver (such as ASPICD.DSK for NetWare, and ASPICD.SYS for DOS)
- NWPA.NLM (NetWare Peripheral Architecture) driver
- CDROM.NLM (NetWare CD-ROM driver)

If you have an existing network, you might want to first log in to the server using the installation files before you run the In-Place Upgrade. In addition to the files copied when you first create the UPGRADE disk, you might want to copy the following workstation software files:

- LSL.COM
- The driver for your network adapter (such as NE2000.COM)
- IPXODI.COM
- NETX.EXE (this driver is more convenient to use when booting with a floppy disk)
- NET.CFG file suitable for your network adapter

You must have NETX.EXE rather than NETX.COM because the version of DOS is Novell DOS 7, which is not compatible with NETX.COM if you don't have the SETVER.EXE utility. You could alternatively copy the VLM workstation software from an already configured workstation, which takes approximately 600 KB of disk space. If you want to use the VLM shell, you must create on the UPGRADE floppy a CONFIG.SYS file that includes the LASTDRIVE=Z statement.

If you have unusual hard disk requirements for your server, be sure to copy any necessary disk drivers to the UPGRADE disk as well.

Performing the In-Place Upgrade

Here are the steps necessary to perform an In-Place Upgrade:

1. Move to the NetWare 2.*x* file server's console. Bring the server down after performing migration and backup as needed.
2. Insert the UPGRADE disk (or any DOS boot disk) and reboot the file server as a workstation.
3. If you plan to install from an existing NetWare server that has the NetWare 4.1 installation files copied onto a hard drive, or that has the installation CD

mounted, load the network drivers and log in. You need to log in as the bindery user SUPERVISOR if you use the NETX.EXE shell. Be sure to map a drive letter to the volume or directory that contains the NetWare 4.1 installation files.

4. Change your default drive back to the UPGRADE disk and run the temporary SERVER program:

   SERVER

5. Enter the new file server name and IPX internal network address when prompted. The server comes up, as NetWare 3.12 with a 1 user license.

6. Load the disk drivers for your server. For example, if you have an IDE drive and are operating on an ISA computer, load the ISADISK.DSK driver.

7. Now you are ready to begin the In-Place Upgrade. Load the utility from the disk as follows:

   LOAD A:2XUPGRDE.NLM

   A screen appears that warns you that a recent backup is highly recommended before you continue. You must answer "Y" before you can continue.

8. The next screen to appear describes the phases of the In-Place Upgrade process (see fig. 13.13).

```
        In-Place Upgrade from NetWare 2.1x and 2.2 to NetWare 3.1x

                    >>>>> PHASE DESCRIPTIONS <<<<<

Phase #1: SYSTEM ANALYSIS
   Inventories each disk and each volume.  Also ensures that the system has
   enough memory and free disk space to successfully complete the upgrade.

Phase #2: DISK ANALYSIS
   Each disk is analyzed.  An image of the new NetWare 3.1x disk is built
   and stored into memory.  This phase is non-destructive, and will not
   damage the existing NetWare 2.1x or 2.2 file system.

Phase #3: DISK MODIFICATION
   The new NetWare 3.1x file system is written onto the disk, over-writing
   the existing NetWare 2.1x or 2.2 file system.  A disk failure during this
   phase may result in the irrecoverable loss of data on the server.

Phase #4: BINDERY
   Bindery objects, properties and values are updated, such as user accounts
   and passwords.  New user passwords are assigned if requested.

<Press ESC to terminate or any other key to continue>
```

Figure 13.13

The In-Place Upgrade screen showing the phases of this process.

9. The next screen prompts you as to whether you want to create a DOS partition. A DOS partition is the recommended way to start the NetWare 4.1 file server. You can enter the size of the new DOS partition in megabytes. The In-Place Upgrade utility accommodates a DOS partition from 0 to 32 MB. If you enter "0," the utility does not create a DOS partition. The default size is 15 MB.

10. The results of Phase #1, System Analysis, are shown in figure 13.14. This phase checks for sufficient RAM and disk space. You need 50 MB of free hard disk space on the server, and 4 MB of RAM more than the RAM required for the runtime version of NetWare 3.12.

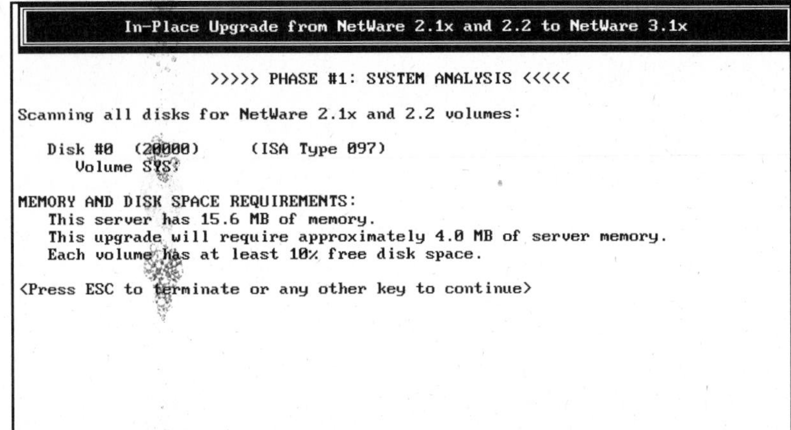

Figure 13.14
In-Place Upgrade Phase #1—system analysis display.

11. Figure 13.15 shows Phase #2, Disk Analysis, in progress. This phase prepares the hard drive for Phase #3, Disk Modification. After this is complete, you are prompted as to whether you want to continue with Phase #3. Phase #3 is permanent. Once you commit, failure is final—no recovery. This is your last chance to back out!

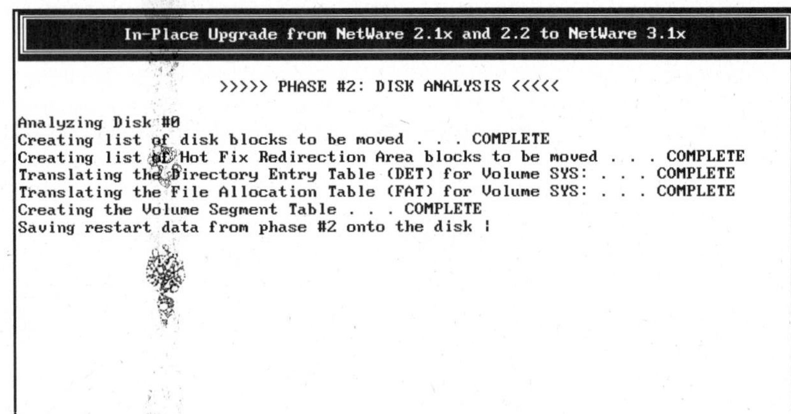

Figure 13.15
In-Place Upgrade Phase #2—disk analysis display.

12. The Disk Modification Phase (#3) can take some time. During this phase the NetWare 2.*x* partition is converted to a NetWare 3.*x* partition, disk blocks are moved, and the DET (Directory Entry Table) and FAT (File Allocation Table) are updated. After this phase is complete, you are prompted before phase #4, Bindery, takes place (see fig. 13.16).

```
In-Place Upgrade from NetWare 2.1x and 2.2 to NetWare 3.1x

                    >>>>> PHASE #4: BINDERY <<<<<

Mounting volume SYS
Initializing Transaction Tracking System

The In-Place Upgrade utility cannot transfer user passwords to the 3.1x
bindery.  Choose one of the following password assigning options:

       1) Do not assign any user passwords
       2) Assign a unique randomly generated password to each user
       3) Assign the same password to each user

New passwords are recorded in the file NEW.PWD in the SYS:SYSTEM directory.
The SUPERVISOR will not be given a password.

Enter your choice (1-3): 1
```

Figure 13.16
In-Place Upgrade Phase #4—Bindery, prompt screen.

Much as in the MIGRATE process, you have three choices: no passwords, random passwords, or one password for all users. Choose the option that suits your installation best.

13. After you select the appropriate password option, the bindery operation finishes and the NetWare 2.*x* bindery files are converted to NetWare 3.*x* format. After the entire process is complete, a status message appears, as shown in figure 13.17.

```
In-Place Upgrade from NetWare 2.1x and 2.2 to NetWare 3.1x

***** The In-Place Upgrade to the 3.1x File System is now complete *****

DISKS     VOLUMES                STATUS MESSAGES
Disk 0    SYS:                   Disk successfully upgraded.

Optional DOS Partition Size:  15 MB

The same password was assigned to each user.
They are recorded in SYS:SYSTEM\NEW.PWD.

<Press ESC to terminate or any other key to continue>
```

Figure 13.17
In-Place Upgrade—final status screen.

14. Press any key to continue. You are now ready to continue the upgrade as if it were an upgrade from NetWare 3 to NetWare 4.1.

Here is a quick overview of the NetWare 3 to NetWare 4.1 upgrade process:

- Bring the 3.*x* file server down and exit to the DOS prompt.
- If the CD is located on the file server machine, load the DOS CD drivers and move to that drive letter. If the CD is mounted on another file server, log in to that file server and move to the mounted CD volume.
- Type **INSTALL** to begin the installation procedure.
- Select Upgrade NetWare 3.x File Server.
- File server boot files are copied to the DOS partition of the server.
- The NetWare 4.1 SERVER.EXE is loaded.
- Disk drivers and LAN drivers are loaded.
- NetWare 4.1 operating system files are copied.
- NDS is installed.
- The AUTOEXEC.NCF and STARTUP.NCF files are updated.

For more complete information, see the section, "Upgrading from NetWare 3.*x* to NetWare 4.*x*," later in this chapter.

Recover Login Scripts

Login scripts in bindery-based versions of NetWare are maintained as physical files in the SYS:MAIL directory. Each user is assigned an ID number created as a subdirectory of the SYS:MAIL directory. In this subdirectory is a file called LOGIN, which is the user login script. The MIGRATE utility copies these files but does not import them into the NDS. MIGRATE does, however, create two files that you can use, in conjunction with the UIMPORT.EXE utility, to import the login scripts.

The names of the two files are UIMPORT.CTL and UIMPORT.DAT and they are located in the SYS:SYSTEM directory of the destination server.

UIMPORT.CTL is a control file. Here is a sample of the UIMPORT control file produced by MIGRATE.EXE:

```
F:\SYSTEM>type uimport.ctl
IMPORT CONTROL
  SEPARATOR=,
  IMPORT MODE=U
FIELDS
  Name
  Last Name
  Login Script
```

UIMPORT.DAT is a data file that contains instructions to import user login scripts. Here is a sample of the UIMPORT data file produced by MIGRATE.EXE:

```
F:\SYSTEM>type uimport.dat
GEORGE,,NY_1\SYS:MAIL\9010001\LOGIN
ELIZA,,NY_1\SYS:MAIL\B010001\LOGIN
```

Only users who have login scripts are represented in the data file.

To import login scripts, run UIMPORT from the SYS:SYSTEM directory as follows:

UIMPORT UIMPORT.CTL UIMPORT.DAT

The output of the preceding command looks like the following:

```
F:\SYSTEM>UIMPORT UIMPORT.CTL UIMPORT.DAT

**** Updating GEORGE ****

UIMPORT-4.20-991: An error occurred in NWDSModifyObject. Error code: FD77.
 User: .GEORGE.ny.ebdb
 Attribute: Last Name
 Value:
*** Done
**** Updating ELIZA ****

UIMPORT-4.20-991: An error occurred in NWDSModifyObject. Error code: FD77.
 User: .ELIZA.ny.ebdb
 Attribute: Last Name
 Value:
*** Done
```

The error messages occur because the user objects already exist and UIMPORT tries to create them. After the existing object is detected, UIMPORT updates any properties specified in the control file.

Clean Up the NDS Tree

The directory tree after the MIGRATE process is shown in figure 13.18.

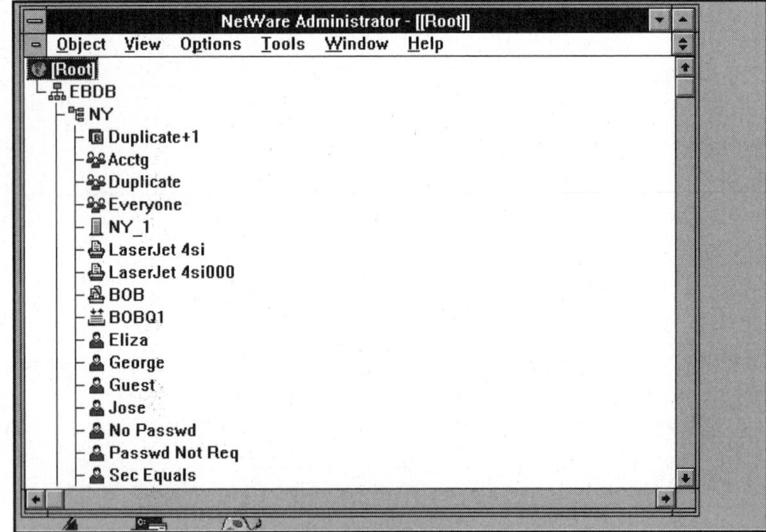

Figure 13.18
Viewing the migrated users in NWADMIN.EXE.

The group DUPLICATE was imported as a group object with no problem. The user DUPLICATE was imported as bindery object DUPLICATE+1. Unfortunately, +1 objects cannot be managed using any of the NDS management tools.

Figure 13.19 illustrates the Login Time Restriction property of the user TIME RESTRICTION. The time restrictions imposed on this user in the NetWare 2.*x* bindery files migrated successfully into the NetWare 4.1 NDS tree.

Figure 13.20 shows the way the User Account Manager feature of NetWare 2.*x* and 3.*x* migrates into the NDS. User UA_MGR was assigned as an Account Manager of user SONG_YOU. The Trustees of Object dialog box for the user SONG_YOU reveals that the user UA_MGR has Supervisor object rights.

Remaining cleanup tasks are to add any additional rights, create profile objects, and to move users and other objects around to different branches of the tree as appropriate.

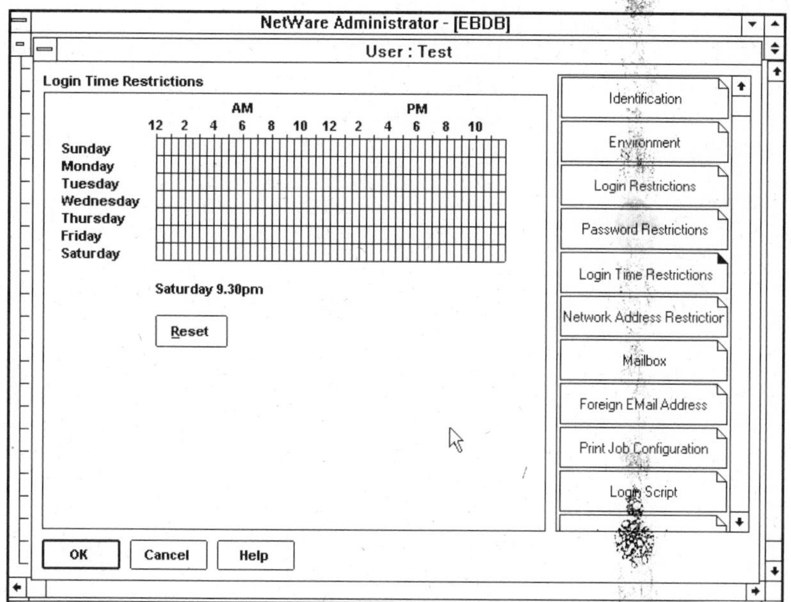

Figure 13.19

Viewing the time restrictions of a migrated user in NWADMIN.EXE.

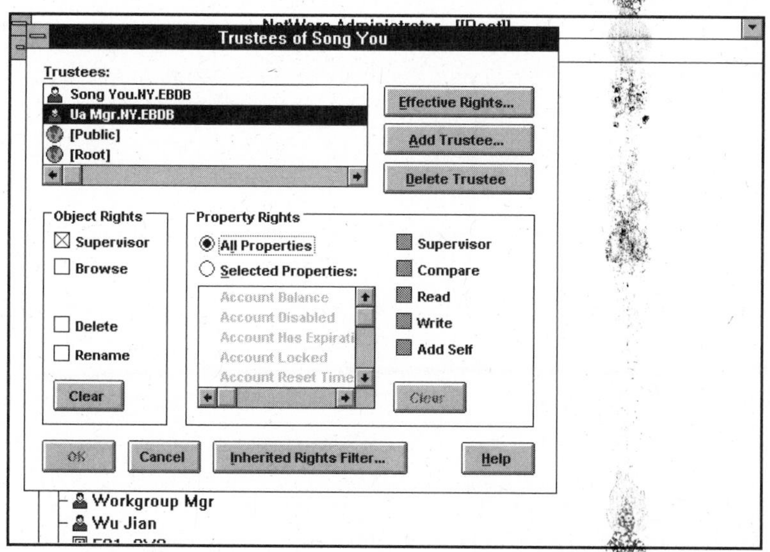

Figure 13.20

Viewing the NDS object rights for a User Account Manager in NWADMIN.EXE.

Upgrading from NetWare 3.*x* to NetWare 4.1

The upgrade from NetWare 3.*x* to NetWare 4.1 is less complicated than the upgrade from NetWare 2.*x*. NetWare 3.*x* uses the same partition as does NetWare 4.*x*. You have three upgrade options, as follows:

- Across-the-wire to an installed NetWare 4.1 server
- Across-the-wire on the same server
- In-place from NetWare 3.1*x* to NetWare 4.1

Across-the-Wire to an Installed NetWare 4.1 Server

Run the migration utility at a workstation attached to the original server (or servers) and a newly installed NetWare 4.1 server. Bindery information from the original server is migrated to the NetWare 4.1 server. Bindery objects are created as Directory objects in the NetWare 4.1 directory tree and placed in the same container that has the server and server volume.

This method is an excellent choice if you plan to get new hardware for your NetWare 4.1 servers. If you run NetWare 2 on a 286 machine, you need to upgrade to a 386 or 486 machine before you can run NetWare 4.1.

This method is also good if you want to merge data from several servers onto one server, or if you want to place bindery objects from several servers in one container.

Across-the-Wire on the Same Server

To use this method, you run the migration utility at a workstation that has enough hard disk space to temporarily hold your data. The data and bindery information are migrated to files on the workstation's hard disk. You then run the NetWare 4.1 installation on the server. After you install the new NetWare 4.1 server, you migrate the data to the server and the bindery information to the Directory.

The migration utility does both tasks automatically, but we have described it this way to keep the language consistent.

In-place Upgrade from NetWare 3.*x* to NetWare 4.1

The In-Place Upgrade from NetWare 3.*x* to NetWare 4.1 proceeds much like a NetWare 4.1 file server installation. To upgrade a NetWare 3.*x* file server to NetWare 4.1, proceed as follows:

1. Clean up the bindery files and file system of the NetWare 3.*x* file server as described in the section, "Clean Up the NetWare 2.*x* Bindery Files" earlier in the chapter.

2. Make two or more backups of critical data on the NetWare 3.*x* file server as a precaution.

3. Bring the NetWare 3.*x* file server down. Here, you can place the NetWare 4.1 installation CD in the CD-ROM drive located on the server or use NetWare client software to log in to a server that has the 4.1 installation CD mounted. If you need to log in to a server that has the 4.1 installation software, be sure to map a drive letter to the appropriate volume.

   Move to a local CD or a mapped drive letter that contains the NetWare 4.1 installation CD.

4. From the root directory of the 4.1 installation CD, type **INSTALL**. This starts the installation batch file, which takes you to the proper directory in which to begin the installation. The Select the Type of Installation Desired menu appears.

5. From the Select the Type of Installation Desired menu, select NetWare Server Installation. The Choose the product you want to install menu appears.

6. From the Choose the product you want to install menu, select NetWare 4.1. The Select the type of installation you are performing menu appears.

7. From the Select the type of installation you are performing menu, as shown in figure 13.21, choose Upgrade NetWare 3.1*x* or 4.*x*.

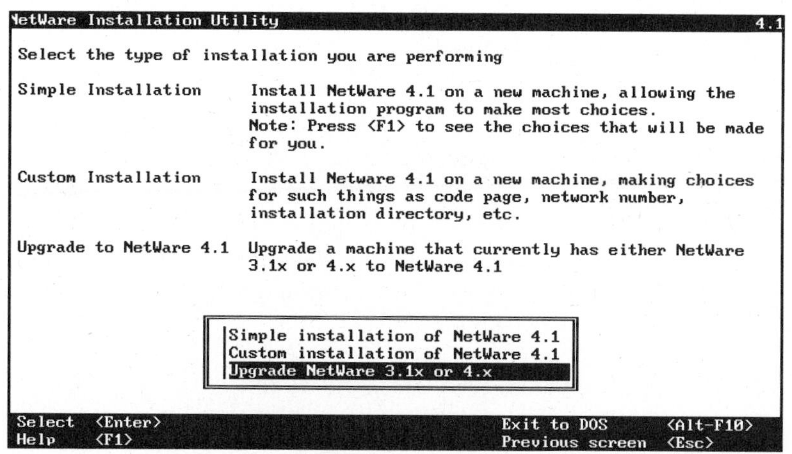

Figure 13.21

Upgrade—Select the Type of Installation ... menu.

The Copy files to the DOS partition input box appears. As with a new installation, the installation utility needs to copy the NetWare 4.1 file server boot files to the DOS partition on the file server computer. You are asked to supply the name of a directory on the file server's DOS partition. If this directory does not exist, the installation utility creates it.

If you want to conserve disk space on the server's DOS partition, choose the directory that contains your NetWare 3.1*x* server boot files. Enter the name of the desired directory and press Enter to continue.

8. You now see your choice of destination directory along with the current installation directory. If both choices are correct, press Enter to continue. Press F2 to change the source directory. Press F4 to change the destination directory.

9. You are now asked for the directory that contains the previous version of NetWare which is being upgraded. Enter the name of this directory. The installation routine looks here for the STARTUP.NCF file and other boot files. Press F8 if you do not want the installation routine to look at this directory (see fig. 13.22).

Figure 13.22

Upgrade—Prompt to enter the path to the existing SERVER.EXE file.

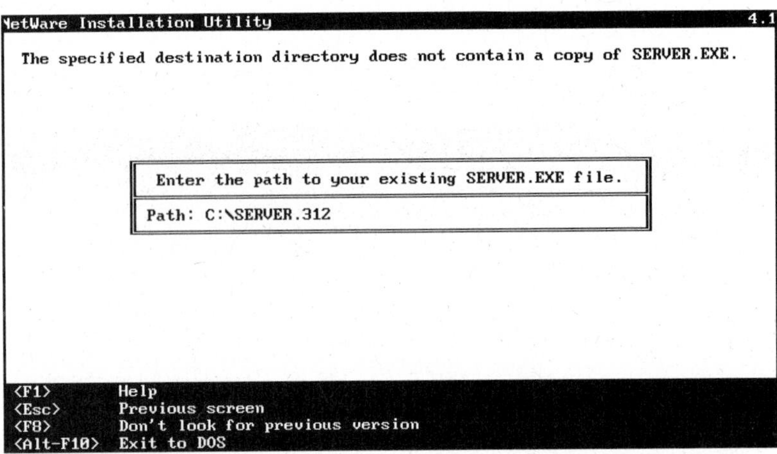

10. Server boot files are copied to the destination directory. Any files found but not updated are listed on the next screen. Press Enter to continue the upgrade. The Select a locale configuration screen appears.

11. Enter the Country Code, Code Page, and Keyboard Mapping information in the Select a locale configuration screen, as in a new installation. Press Enter after you are done. The Select the filename format screen appears.

12. Enter your choice of file format in the Select the filename format screen. As for a new installation, the DOS Filename Format option is recommended because the other option disables access to the NDS. Select your choice and press Enter to continue. Here SERVER.EXE loads along with your STARTUP.NCF file (if any was found). The Choose Server Drivers - Disk Driver screen appears.

13. From the Choose Server Drivers - Disk Driver screen, accept the driver currently loaded, or select Select an Additional Driver if you want to choose any other disk drivers. After you are done, select Continue Installation and press Enter.

14. A number of drivers, including the one selected, are copied to your file server's DOS partition. Any drivers found but not updated are indicated. The Select Optional NetWare Files screen appears next.

15. From the Select Optional NetWare Files screen, select the files to copy to the new server. By default, approximately 20 MB of basic system files are copied. The files on this screen are in addition to the basic files. Choices include DOS Utilities, OS/2 Utilities, MS Windows Utilities, UNIX Utilities, client installation files, and the MIGRATE utility files.

    After you finish marking file groups to copy, press F10 to continue.

16. Before the file copy can take place, you must specify the directory on the server's DOS partition that contains file server boot files. This is the directory where reside SERVER.EXE and STARTUP.NCF. Enter this directory when prompted, and press Enter to continue. The basic file copy operation takes place.

17. Next you are prompted to enter the name of the LAN driver used in your file server. Enter one or more drivers. When prompted, enter the parameters for the driver. Select Continue Installation after you finish. If any errors occur when loading the LAN driver, you are taken to the file server console where you can review and correct errors. A common error, for example, is to enter an interrupt value of "10" when the LAN driver expects a hexidecimal value of "A."

18. You now need to insert your NetWare 4.1 license disk into the disk drive on the server. If the license files are located in a path other than A, press F3 and enter the appropriate path. After a minute or so, the license is read. Press Enter to continue.

19. The NDS installation is next. If any NDS trees are located, their names will appear in the NetWare Directory Services Install screen. If you are sure that the network with which you want to connect has an additional tree, press Alt+Esc to toggle to the file server console prompt and ensure that your LAN driver is loaded with the correct values and frame type.

To see whether any other servers are found, you can issue the DISPLAY SERVERS command at the file server console prompt. You can use the CONFIG command to ensure that the IPX protocol is bound to the LAN driver. A common problem is setting a frame type other than that used by other servers on your network. NetWare 4.1 defaults to a frame type of Ethernet_802.2 for Ethernet network adapters. If you use FDDI, token ring, or ARCnet network adapters, the frame type is not usually a problem.

Press Insert to build a new tree. If you enter an existing tree, you are asked to supply a valid NDS username. This user must have, at minimum, Browse and Create NDS object rights to the container in which you plan to place the server.

20. You must now enter Time zone and Daylight Savings Time values. Enter the appropriate time zone from the list, and enter the time information in the Time Server Type dialog box.

21. You must now specify a context in the existing or new NDS tree. The Specify a Context ... screen enables you to enter a top level Organization and up to three levels of Organizational Units. In addition, in the Server Context field you can enter a context that does not otherwise fit on this screen. Press F10 to continue the installation.

22. The upgrade procedure will check the NetWare 3.*x* bindery files for conflicts and upgrade the bindery objects into the designated NDS tree. Volumes, files and directories will be identified by a pointer going into the NDS. The upgrade procedure will actually dismount and remount any volumes on this server.

23. After you finish, a final message appears that indicates the name of the tree, the name of the Admin user, and the server's default context.

24. Here the main file copy from the CD to the upgraded server takes place. If any files on the server are newer than those on the installation CD, the screen shown in figure 13.23 appears.

    Select Always overwrite newer files if you want to replace any files on the server with those on the installation CD. Select Never overwrite newer files if you want to retain any file on the server that is newer than those on the installation CD.

    The Main File Copy process takes approximately 15 to 30 minutes, depending on the speed of your computer and CD-ROM drive.

25. After the installation is complete, from the INSTALL.NLM main menu, select Product Options. From the Other Installation Options menu that appears, select Upgrade 3.1*x* Print Services.

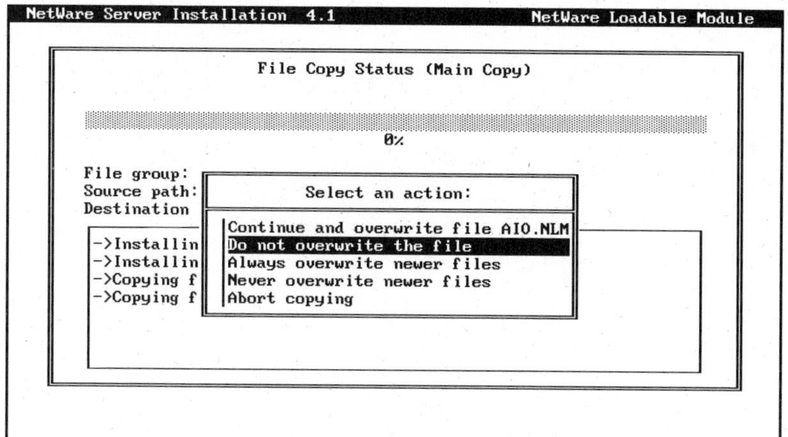

Figure 13.23

Upgrade—Message that appears when newer files exist on the server being upgraded.

Upgrade 3.1x Print Services upgrades printing objects in the NetWare 3.*x* bindery files into the NDS tree. Before the printing upgrade can occur, you must log in as the Admin user.

26. The last action is to upgrade the AUTOEXEC.NCF file, removing any NetWare 3.*x* specific commands and updating the file for NetWare 4.1. This operation occurs at the end of the upgrade process, or can be activated from INSTALL.NLM under the NCF Files Options menu. If the upgrade program determines that no changes need be made, the file is scanned and the upgrade continues without interaction on your part.

Figure 13.24 shows a sample new AUTOEXEC.NCF file.

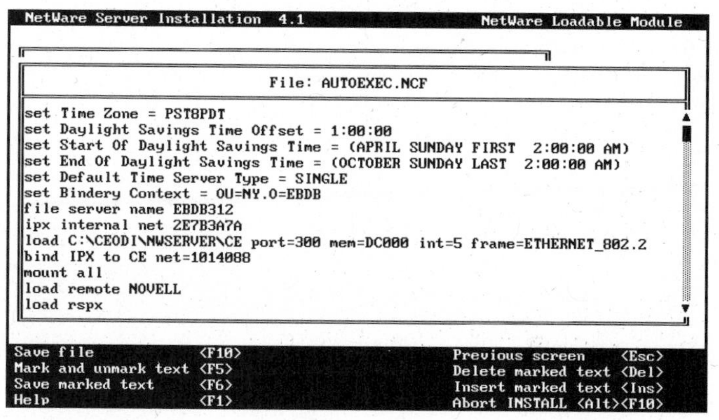

Figure 13.24

Upgrade—Sample upgraded AUTOEXEC.NCF file.

27. The installation is now complete. You should bring the new server down and reboot before you continue.

Bindery Services

Most organizations do not migrate their existing networks to NetWare 4.1 overnight, or even over a weekend. To accommodate the need for an extended period of time to make the transition, Novell includes some features in NetWare 4.1 that enable it to coexist on the same network with bindery-based versions of NetWare.

NetWare Directory Services can emulate the flat structure of the NetWare 2.*x*/3.*x* bindery, which enables clients to log in using NETX or the current Macintosh client software. When bindery services is on, bindery-based clients or utilities can see all leaf objects in the server's bindery context as if they were in a bindery.

The names of all objects in the container designated as the bindery context must conform to bindery conventions (up to 47 characters, no question marks, and so on).

The NetWare 4.1 INSTALL program enables bindery services by default by setting the server's BINDERY CONTEXT set parameter. You can turn off bindery services by executing the SET BINDERY CONTEXT= command at the file server console. You can add bindery-based (2.*x*/3.*x*) servers to the Directory tree as NetWare Server objects, which enables NDS users to access volumes on those servers the same as NetWare 4.1 volumes. Use NETADMIN or NWADMIN to create NetWare Server and Volume objects for the server you add to the tree.

After you start building your Directory tree, you might be tempted to set up user, printer, or other objects for a 2.*x*/3.*x* server before you migrate the server. If you do so, you might lose the login scripts, passwords, and rights that are stored in the bindery. You should let the NetWare 4.1 INSTALL program migrate bindery objects to the Directory.

For further information on bindery services, see Chapter 22, "Using Bindery Services."

Testing the Installation

Once the file server has been upgraded or newly installed, it is time to perform some simple connectivity tests. You can best test how well the server "talks" to nodes on the network using complicated network analysis tools, such as the LANanalyzer. This section shows you some commands that can be issued from the file server and from the workstation to ensure connectivity.

To perform some of these tests from the DOS workstation, you need to run the workstation software. If you followed the installation procedure outlined in the preceding chapter, the software starts automatically when you reboot the workstation. Otherwise, you can start the workstation software by changing to the NWCLIENT directory and running the STARTNET.BAT batch file.

The sequence of commands needed to load the DOS workstation software follows:

```
LSL.COM
NIC Driver (i.e. NE2000.COM)
IPXODI.COM
VLM.EXE
```

Tests Performed from a File Server

Tests performed from a file server require that you move physically to the file server computer. These tests should be performed on all file servers. Here is a checklist of tests to be performed.

[ ] Type:

DISPLAY SERVERS

Do you see a list of all file servers you installed?

Y [ ]   N [ ]

You will see some or all server names duplicated. This is OK. If you do not see a file server name listed, you need to troubleshoot the installation of that file server.

[ ] Type:

CONFIG

Do you see a list of all NICs on this file server?

Y [ ] N [ ]

If you do not see all NICs listed that you installed on this file server, you need to load INSTALL.NLM, select NCF Files Options, and check the AUTOEXEC.NCF file. In this file, you should see commands to LOAD the NIC drivers. Use the Alt+Esc keys to toggle between the AUTOEXEC.NCF file and the file server console prompt. Enter the command manually from the server's command prompt (:) and see whether the NIC driver loads. If it does not load, check the settings on the NIC.

If you see the command INITIALIZE SYSTEM in the AUTOEXEC.NCF file, the server was installed using the INETCFG.NLM utility. In this case, you will not see the commands to LOAD the NIC drivers. You can issue the command INITIALIZE SYSTEM from the file server console prompt to see if the NIC drivers load successfully. If not, consult Chapter 37, "Making Configuration Changes," for more information on INETCFG.NLM.

[ ] Type:

TRACK ON

You should see SAP and RIP information broadcast between all file servers. Each server broadcasts its name every 60 seconds. Within 60 seconds, you should see the names of all file servers. Note that the broadcasts are either in-bound or out-bound. Any servers that do not appear on this list might need further troubleshooting.

Tests Performed from a DOS Workstation

Tests performed from a workstation require that you move physically to the workstation computer. These tests should be performed on all workstations.

[ ] Load the workstation software manually. Do not rely on the AUTOEXEC.BAT or the \NWCLIENT\STARTNET.BAT files. When you load the VLM driver, use the following option:

VLM /V2

Do you get the message `Attached to server` *xxx* (where *xxx* is the name of one of your file servers)?

If you are not attached to a file server, you need to check to see whether the settings on the NIC match the settings recorded in the NET.CFG file. Check interrupts, port addresses, and memory addresses. Check to see whether the frame type matches the frame type on the file server. Also, you might be experiencing a cabling problem. Check the cabling, connectors, repeaters, hubs, MAUs, and routers.

[ ] If you are attached to a file server, type the following:

NLIST server /b

Do you see a list of all file servers installed?

Y [ ]   N [ ]

File servers require 60 seconds to update themselves. Make sure that you have left enough time for all file servers to appear on the server list. If you still do not see a list of all file servers installed, you might need to troubleshoot the cabling, connectors, repeaters, and so on between your workstation and the file servers you do not see. Also, you might want to check the installation of those file servers.

[ ] Log in to the file server as the Admin user you designated during the file server's installation. If you created an Admin user .CN=Admin.O=Novell, for example, log in as follows:

LOGIN .CN=Admin.O=Novell

Are you logged in?

Y [ ]   N [ ]

If not, check to see whether you have specified the proper context. Go to the file server and issue the following command:

SET BINDERY CONTEXT

This command returns the file server's default context. The Admin user should be a leaf object off the top level organization. If your bindery context comes back as OU=East_End.OU=Sales.O=Intco, then the Admin user most likely will be .CN=Admin.O=IntCo.

General Network Tests

At this point, you might want to test the network in general. Even though you can see all file servers and log in from all workstations, the network itself might be experiencing difficulties. Some general network tests can be performed from a file server. More comprehensive tests require network analysis tools such as the Sniffer or the LANalyzer.

[ ] From a file server prompt (:) type the following:

LOAD MONITOR

From the monitor screen select LAN/WAN Information. From the LAN/WAN menu, select each NIC, one at a time. If you see any errors recorded, consult Chapter 36, "Monitoring the File Server."

Note If MONITOR.NLM already is loaded, you can toggle to it by pressing Alt+Esc.

[ ] Using a network analyzer (such as the LANalyzer), look for the following:

[ ] Is the network utilization below 10 percent?

Y [ ] N [ ]

[ ] Are there any NIC errors?

Y [ ] N [ ]

If the answer to either of these questions is No, you need to troubleshoot the network cabling (including cabling, connectors, hubs, and so on) or look for a bad NIC.

Summary

Time synchronization was covered in detail in this chapter. The first part of this chapter gave you an overview of the types of time server types you can define on your NetWare 4.1 file servers. These types include Reference, Single Reference, Primary, and Secondary. As you discovered, the difference between a Reference time server and a Single Reference time server is that the former uses an external time source (such as the Internet), and the latter relies on its own internal system clock. The difference between a Single Reference server and a Primary is that the latter accepts

time changes and adjusts its clock by a factor of 50 percent. The Secondary accepts any time from the other three types of time servers without question and adjusts its clock 100 percent.

You can use SERVMAN.NLM from the file server console to adjust time parameters. You also can use any text editor to edit file SYS:SYSTEM\TIMESYNC.CFG. You can provide time by using regular SAP broadcasts, or you can configure the Time Source parameter in the TIMESYNC.CFG file, causing that server to "listen" only for time updates from the servers on the source list.

The second part of this chapter showed you how to upgrade a server from NetWare 2.*x* or NetWare 3.1*x* to NetWare 4.1. The basic procedure includes: clean up the file system, clean up the bindery files, perform two or more full backups, use the migrate procedure in some cases, install NetWare 4.1, restore files, recover login scripts, and clean up the resulting NDS tree.

You learned that a potential problem exists if duplicate objects are found during the migration. NetWare 2 or 3 allows a user and group to have the same name; for example, if left unchecked, the first object in the bindery is migrated properly. Duplicate objects are renamed and imported as unmanageable bindery objects.

You can install the MIGRATE.EXE utility from disk or by copying files from the installation CD. You learned that you must also create an NLS directory under the directory that contains the MIGRATE.EXE utility. When you run MIGRATE, you can choose Across-the-Wire or Same-Server. The former option assumes you have a NetWare 4.1 file server. The latter option assumes that you want to use the current directory on a workstation (or another server) to hold the bindery information until you can use MIGRATE to move the information back to the new server. The MIGPRINT.EXE utility, used to migrate printing objects from a bindery-based file server to an NDS tree, was also covered.

The In-Place Upgrade utility begins with a boot disk created from the installation CD mounted on a file server. This bootable disk contains a single user runtime version of NetWare 3.12, along with some basic disk drivers. You need to copy any additional disk drivers onto this (or another) disk. You might also want to copy NetWare client software if you plan to perform the installation from another file server.

To recover login scripts, you can run the UMIPORT UIMPORT.CTRL UIMPORT.DAT command from the SYS:SYSTEM directory. You also saw how the migrate process placed users in the destination server's bindery context. You saw the way User Account Managers were given certain rights.

You then learned about the process of upgrading from NetWare 3.1*x* to NetWare 4.1. You can use the MIGRATE utility to pull bindery information and transfer it to an existing NetWare 4.1 file server. Alternatively, you can upgrade a NetWare 3.1*x* file server in-place. The latter type of upgrade is very similar to the new file server installation covered in Chapter 12. Differences include upgrading the NetWare 3.1*x* bindery to NetWare 4.1 NDS, reading existing STARTUP.NCF and AUTOEXEC.NCF files, and upgrading printing objects.

The last portion of the chapter gave you some simple connectivity tests to perform on both the file server and workstation. The next chapter covers how to install the DOS client software and manage the user tools.

Part IV

Activating and Using Clients

New Riders Publishing
INSIDE
SERIES

DOS Client Basics

This chapter gives you an understanding of how to configure a DOS client workstation to log in to the server. This chapter covers how the NetWare DOS Requester works under DOS, some considerations for client LAN cards, and how to install the client software. In addition, this chapter covers the process of logging in and some utilities that will assist you during the login process.

Considerations for Client NICs

The physical installation procedure of a client NIC is identical to that of a server NIC. Only in rare instances does a vendor make an NIC that can be installed only in a workstation and not a server, or vice versa. In many cases, the NIC in the server is the top of the line for that vendor. The NICs in workstations are typically of a lesser quality. The NIC in the workstation does not need the same performance characteristics as an NIC in a server for the simple reason that it is not used as heavily.

Sixteen-bit NICs are generally regarded as adequate for use in workstations. However, 32-bit NICs are nearly essential for NetWare servers.

A consideration for a client NIC that is not a concern in a server is that workstations tend to have peripherals installed that you would not install in a server. These peripherals include scanners, printers, modems, and a mouse, among other devices. Because there may be more peripherals on a workstation, choosing a setting for an NIC that does not conflict with the settings of other devices can be difficult. Settings for jumpers can be found in a hardware reference manual or CD-ROM software like Micro House Technical Library. After you have made the correct settings, you will install the drivers to enable communication.

If you use a memory manager, you can load the driver into the upper memory area. The EMM386 memory manager is used on DOS computers to open up additional memory in the upper memory area (between 640 KB and 1 MB). Once the EMM386 driver is loaded, you can use the DOS LOADHIGH command in conjunction with the device driver. The LOADHIGH command loads device driver in the upper memory area if there is room. Because NICs often use a range of memory addresses in upper DOS memory, you might need to use an exclude setting when you load memory managers such as EMM386.EXE. If the memory used by a NIC is not safeguarded from other programs through an exclude option, the NIC might not function properly. The example illustrates the EMM386 command with an exclude option. If you are using a notebook, the drivers are based on a different standard.

Understanding PCMCIA Network Adapters

PCMCIA network adapters have become popular for use in notebook computers. PCMCIA adapters are often called *credit card adapters* because they are approximately the size of three credit cards stacked on top of each other. These tiny NICs plug into a special slot in the side of the notebook computer. An external cable is then

attached to a slot on the end of the card. The cable has the connection necessary to connect to the type of media used in your network. Intel Corporation and Xircom, Inc. are two vendors that make PCMCIA adapters. Figure 14.1 shows a diagram of how a Xircom CreditCard Ethernet Adapter is connected to a Thin Ethernet network.

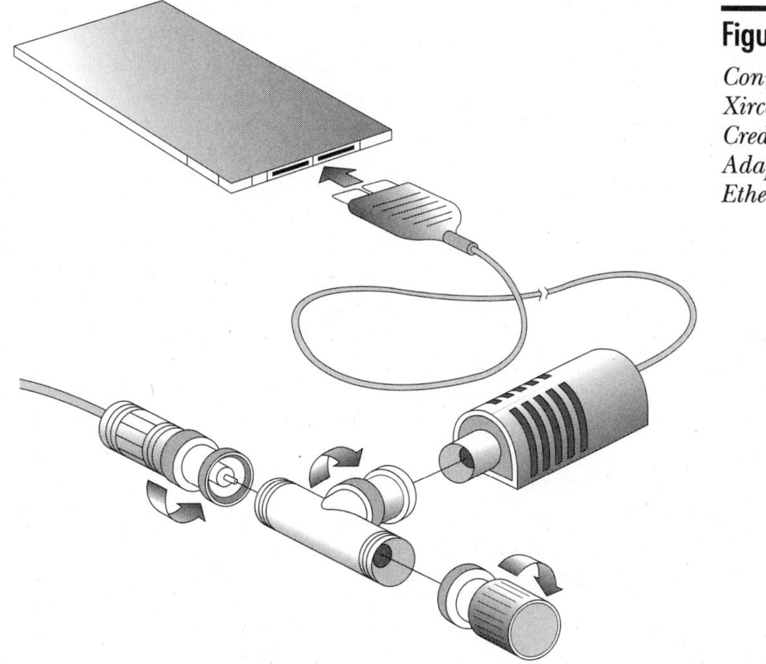

Figure 14.1

Connecting a Xircom CreditCard Adapter to a Thin Ethernet network.

The portable computer industry has evolved tremendously over the last several years. Here is a short summary of the terms used for computers that can be (relatively) easily carried with you:

- **Transportable.** A transportable computer, also affectionately known as a "luggable," is approximately the size of a medium suitcase or a sewing machine. Compaq Computer Corporation made its name with a model that could be carried around like a suitcase and could handle high resolution graphics (high resolution for the time). Another famous vendor of this style of computer was Osborne Computers. Transportable computers usually featured a 9-inch (or smaller) CRT, with a keyboard that folded into the case. Vendors usually placed two or three full-sized slots so that standard ISA bus PC cards could be placed inside. The power cord was stuffed into a panel in the side when traveling. These computers weighed upwards of 25 pounds.
- **Laptop.** The laptop computer features a flat screen display with either an early LCD panel or a gas-plasma screen. The flat screen display is folded down on top

of the unit, and a keyboard is placed underneath. These units typically have AC power connectors and two or three full-sized PC slots. Laptops weigh in at around 15 pounds. Laptop computers typically have limited expansion capability. Often it is necessary to use a special network adapter that connects through the unit's parallel printer port.

- **Notebook.** Notebook computers have flat LCD displays. The new units feature full color graphics with resolution rivaling that of a standard desktop VGA monitor. Notebook computers are extremely compact with 3.5" floppy drives built into the side of the unit. The LCD folds down on top of the keyboard. The key arrangement can be somewhat esoteric. Many units have a special function key to turn a portion of the standard keyboard into a numeric keypad. Hard drive technology has improved radically over the years. It is not uncommon for a notebook computer to have a 350 to 520 MB hard drive, as well as a full complement of RAM. New, fast CPUs are available that operate on three volts of DC power. Most notebooks have internal batteries that enable them to operate anywhere from two to six hours (depending on what power-saving features are used). A typical notebook computer weighs in at 7 pounds. Some notebook computers require printer-port network adapters, but PCMCIA adapters are rapidly becoming the adapters of choice for these computers.

- **Palmtop.** The palmtop computer is designed to be carried in the palm of your hand. It is small enough to fit into a suitcoat pocket. These tiny computers have a full key arrangement with the keys themselves miniaturized. Palmtops such as the HP Palmtop Computer run DOS and have 512 KB of RAM. There are no floppy or hard drives; however, these units often have a static RAM card that can be inserted into a slot and can act as a disk. The HP unit also features an infrared interface that allows it to communicate with a printer or another palmtop unit.

PCMCIA cards are also unique in that a management utility usually must be run for the notebook computer to recognize the card. The management utility is used to recognize and manage not only NICs, but other PCMCIA devices as well. Other devices include memory expansion cards and fax/modem cards. The management driver must be added to the CONFIG.SYS file before the PCMCIA card will initialize. The following shows the CONFIG.SYS file for a NEC Versa notebook computer with both a fax/modem and an Ethernet PCMCIA card:

```
DEVICE=C:\DOS\HIMEM.SYS
rem
rem    Note the "X=nnnn-nnnn" option after the DEVICE=EMM386.EXE command.
rem    This option causes EMM386 to "exclude" this range of memory.
rem    The Xircom Ethernet card uses memory address D0000-D1FFF
rem
DEVICE=C:\DOS\EMM386.EXE NOEMS X=DD00-DFFF X=E800-EFFF X=D000-D1FF
```

```
BUFFERS=10,0
FILES=99
DOS=UMB
LASTDRIVE=Z
FCBS=4,0
[COMMON]
DOS=HIGH
STACKS=9,256
DEVICEHIGH /L:2,12048 =C:\DOS\SETVER.EXE
SHELL=C:\DOS\COMMAND.COM C:\DOS /P
DEVICEHIGH /L:2,42592 =C:\NECUTILS\NECMOUSE.SYS
rem
rem  ============ PCMCIA2 Device Drivers ==============================
rem  == If PCMCIA Cards are not used in your system, these drivers
rem  == can be remarked to save system memory area.
rem  ==================================================================
rem  == This driver is loaded for "Loads the driver for an IDE type drive"
rem
DEVICEHIGH /L:2,8960 =C:\PCMCIA2\S_IDE.EXE /D:2
rem
rem  == This driver is loaded for "Driver for the Interface - must remain
rem  == for PCMCIA Support"
rem
REM DEVICEHIGH=C:\PCMCIA2\SS365SL.EXE /SIRM 0ABC /IIRM 02BC /PWRON 341 /PWROFF
➥9C4
rem
rem  == This driver is loaded for "Driver for Card Services - must remain
rem  == for PCMCIA Support"
rem
REM DEVICEHIGH=C:\PCMCIA2\CS.EXE /IRQ 0B
rem
rem  == This driver is loaded for "This is the memory card driver for
rem  == SRAM Support"
rem
rem DEVICEHIGH=C:\PCMCIA2\SCARD29.EXE /BAS D6 /SIZ 6
rem
rem  == This driver is loaded for "Driver for Client Device Driver - must
rem  == remain for PCMCIA Support"
rem DEVICEHIGH=C:\PCMCIA2\CIC.EXE /COM 2 /BAS D0 /SIZ 4 /CSBAS D4 /CSSIZ 8 /
➥NWBAS DC /NWSIZ 4
rem
rem  ============ PCMCIA Device Drivers ==============================
```

```
REM ================== Intel Card Manager Drivers =======================
DEVICEHIGH /L:2,8544 =C:\CARDMGR\SS365SL.EXE /ADA=0
DEVICEHIGH /L:1,43328 =C:\CARDMGR\CS.EXE
DEVICE=C:\CARDMGR\RTINIT.EXE /IO=300-30F
DEVICEHIGH /L:1,27536 =C:\CARDMGR\CMGRDRVR.EXE
REM ===================================================================
```

Understanding the ODI Drivers

To enable a PC to use its NIC to connect to the network, you must install drivers that add networking capabilities to the PC's operating system. Novell's current network driver technology is called the *Open Datalink Interface* (ODI). Novell and Apple developed the ODI specification to support multiple protocols in a workstation and a server. Network drivers for NIC cards can be written to this ODI specification, and this enables multiple protocol stacks to share the same network driver. NIC drivers for NetWare 4.1 workstations and servers are written to the ODI specification.

ODI offers a number of advantages, including the following:

- Multiple protocol support, such as TCP/IP, SPX/IPX, and AppleTalk, can be added to the same NIC driver without adding extra NICs.
- Sessions with a variety of servers and hosts using different protocol stacks at the workstation can be established. In general, you use a protocol stack at the workstation that the server or host understands.
- All protocol stacks written to the ODI specification can communicate with any NIC driver written to the ODI specification.
- Multiple protocol support is simplified because only one LAN driver exists. Improvements in the ODI LAN driver (or bug fixes) benefit all protocols that work with the improved LAN driver.
- More configuration choices are available through the NET.CFG configuration file. This makes it possible to change the workstation software configuration more easily.

The ODI Specification

On a DOS workstation, the three important components that make ODI work are as follows:

- LSL.COM (Link Support Layer)
- ODI LAN driver (MLID—Multi Link Interface Driver)
- Protocol stacks (IPX/SPX or TCP/IP)

The ODI drivers must be loaded in a specific order. The order is as follows:

1. LSL.COM
2. ODI LAN driver
3. Protocol driver

The same LSL.COM and protocol driver files can be used for all ODI-compatible PCs and NICs. Each NIC requires a custom driver program that is usually named for the NIC's model designation, however. If you have a Novell/Eagle NE2000 network card and are using the IPX protocol (the native NetWare protocol), for example, the load order is as follows:

```
LSL.COM
NE2000.COM
IPXODI.COM
```

In another example, if you have a workstation with an IBM Token-Ring NIC and plan to use the TCP/IP protocols, the load order is as follows. Please note that TCP/IP support at the workstation is available only through additional software such as Novell's LAN Workplace software. The following example assumes this software is installed:

```
LSL.COM
TOKEN.COM
TCPIP.EXE
```

ODI Driver Options

Each ODI driver has additional options that allow you to tailor your workstation setup. Each of the three drivers has the two options ? and U.

The ? option is an abbreviated help screen. This option displays the options available for that driver. The U option is for *unload*. Each ODI driver can be unloaded, with the following two provisions:

- ODI drivers must be unloaded in reverse order.
- ODI drivers cannot be unloaded if another TSR has been loaded at a later time.

The following illustrates the output after typing the command:

LSL /?

```
C:\NWCLIENT> lsl /?
NetWare Link Support Layer  v2.00 (920904)
(C) Copyright 1990, 1992 Novell, Inc.  All Rights Reserved.

Available command line options:
   LSL      -Installs the LSL
   LSL /U   -Removes resident LSL from memory
   LSL /?   -Displays this help screen

C:\NWCLIENT>
```

The protocol driver, IPXODI, has a few other options besides the /? and /U options. The IPXODI.COM file consists of the following three components:

- IPX (OSI network and transport layers)
- SPX (OSI transport layer)
- Remote Diagnostic Responder (OSI application layer)

Many applications do not need SPX or the Remote Diagnostic Responder. IPX is required for many applications, but many users will not require the SPX protocol. SPX is used to ensure communication between nodes through double checking the data. The Remote Diagnostic Responder is useful for some third-party applications that gather diagnostic information. By not loading these components, you can save workstation memory. SPX and the Remote Diagnostic Responder each take up roughly 4 KB of RAM. If you need more memory to run applications, IPXODI can be invoked using the A or D option.

Table 14.1 shows the amount of memory consumed when IPXODI is running with various options.

Table 14.1
IPXODI Options Memory Usage

Command	Meaning	Memory Used (Bytes)	Memory Saved (Bytes)
IPXODI	Loads IPX protocols with all options	15,904	N/A

Command	Meaning	Memory Used (Bytes)	Memory Saved (Bytes)
IPXODI /D	Loads IPX protocols without the diagnostic responder	12,272	3,632
IPXODI /A	Loads IPX only (without diagnostic responder and without SPX)	7,088	5,184

Two additional IPXODI options are summarized in table 14.2.

Table 14.2
Additional IPXODI Options

IPXODI Option	Description
IPXODI /C=*drive:\path\filename*	Enables you to specify the drive, directory path, and file name of an alternate NET.CFG file. (The use of this file is explained in the next section.)
IPXODI /F	Causes IPXODI to unload even if another TSR is resident. The "F" stands for Forced Unload. Note that the use of this *** option can cause your workstation to crash.

Understanding VLMs

The NetWare 4.1 client software (which was also offered with NetWare 3.12) consists of the ODI drivers and the Virtual Loadable Modules (VLMs). VLMs, a series of files with the extension VLM, are components of the client NetWare DOS Requester that are loaded by a loader module VLM.EXE. VLM.EXE hooks into DOS using a software interrupt. The end result is that DOS has additional commands and functionality added. The VLM modules serve to extend the functionality of DOS, sharing its tables and environment.

Several VLMs are provided with the ODI requester, and many workstations require different combinations of VLMs. The loading of VLMs is performed by a VLM manager, which also manages where the VLMs reside in memory. The VLM manager is capable of utilizing extended and expanded memory and automatically moves VLMs around in memory to reduce demand for conventional DOS memory. The VLM manager is implemented by a program named VLM.EXE.

VLM.EXE

VLM.EXE loads the component VLM files. VLM initializes a high level link with the server. It sends out a request to the server for a connection and provides for authentication. The *authentication* process is when the server asks the user for a login name and password. In addition to managing the login session, VLM also manages print jobs redirected from the workstation to the server.

VLM.EXE has several options that can be included on the command line (see table 14.3). These options can be combined together if needed.

Table 14.3
VLM.EXE Options

VLM Option	Description
VLM /?	Displays help screen.
VLM /u	Unloads VLM.EXE and all *.VLM files from memory. This option logs you out from any servers you were logged in to.
VLM /c=*drive:\path\filename*	Uses an alternate NET.CFG file (explained in the next section). The file is located on drive *drive*, in directory *path*, and the file name is *filename*.
VLM /*Mx*	Forces VLM to load VLM modules into the type of memory specified by *x*. *x* can be any of the following: C = Conventional Memory E = Expanded Memory (EMS) X = Extended Memory (XMS) (X is the default.)
VLM /*D*	Displays VLM diagnostics.

VLM Option	Description
VLM /*PS=server_name*	Forces VLM to look for a Preferred Server with the name *server_name*. If this server is not available, or if this option is not specified, the next available server is used. An available server is a server that is not busy and is able to respond to the workstation.
VLM /*PT=tree_name*	Forces VLM to look for a Preferred NDS Tree with the name *tree_name*. If a server that has a partition of this tree is not available, or if this option is not specified, the tree on the next available server is used.
VLM /*Vn*	Causes VLM to load with one of several "verbose" options according to the level specified by *n*. Each level includes the levels below it. The least amount of information is level 0 and the most is level 4. Verbose levels can be any of the following: 0 = Copyright and critical errors 1 = Warning messages 2 = Names of VLM modules loaded 3 = Configuration and file parameters 4 = Diagnostic messages

Explaining the *.VLM Files

Each VLM file represents a module that supports a specific function. Collectively they form the NetWare DOS Requester. Figure 14.2 illustrates the positioning of each VLM module and DOS.

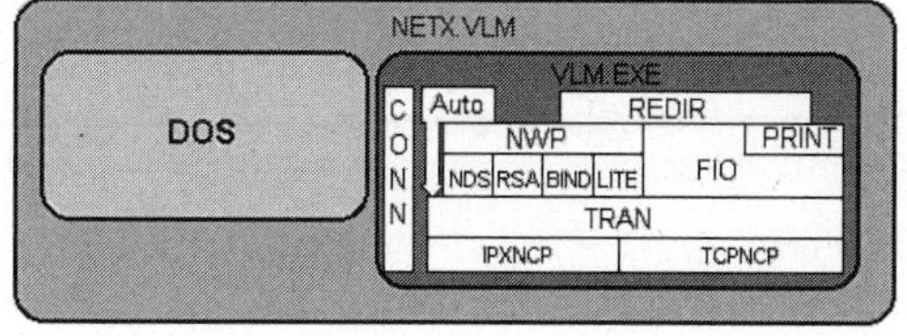

Figure 14.2

VLM architecture.

Some VLM modules are dependent on others. As you can see in figure 14.2, FIO.VLM is dependent on TRAN.VLM, TRAN.VLM is dependent on IPXNCP.VLM, and so forth. When you run VLM.EXE, VLM modules are loaded in their proper order. You can manually control which VLMs are loaded and in what order, however, by modifying parameters in the NET.CFG file. NET.CFG is a file used to configure the characteristics for the VLMs as well as for other ODI modules. Table 14.4 summarizes the VLM modules and their functionality. The table is organized by load order. Note that some VLMs, marked with an asterisk (*), are optional. If they are not loaded, however, their functionality will not be present in the shell.

Table 14.4
VLM Modules

VLM Module	Description
CONN.VLM	Connection manager. Manages connections between other VLMs.
IPXNCP.VLM	IPX and NCP (NetWare Core Protocol) protocol stacks.
TCPNCP.VLM*	Provides UDP/IP and NCP protocol stacks. Used with the NetWare/IP product.
TRAN.VLM	Transport services. Provides transport layer services that guarantee packet delivery and provide additional reliability of network communications.
SECURITY.VLM	General security function calls.
NDS.VLM	NetWare Directory Services module.
BIND.VLM	Provides bindery-based services.
NWP.VLM	NetWare Protocol Multiplexer. Redirects information coming from and going to the LAN to and from the proper protocol stack.
FIO.VLM	File Input Output. Manages redirection of files to or from the server and workstation.
GENERAL.VLM	General purposes VLM services.
REDIR.VLM	DOS Redirecter.
PRINT.VLM*	Provides printing redirection to a network print queue.

VLM Module	Description
NETX.VLM*	Emulates the old NETX.COM shell for backwards compatibility.
AUTO.VLM*	Responsible for automatically reconnecting the shell to the server in case the connection goes down.
NMR.VLM*	NetWare Management Responder. This module is to be used with future network management packages.

Configuring the NET.CFG File

Both the ODI drivers and the VLMs read a file called NET.CFG to obtain their parameter settings. Normally this file is located in the same directory as the ODI drivers and VLM.EXE. If you want to use a NET.CFG file in another directory, you must use the VLM C option described earlier.

NET.CFG is an ASCII text file that consists of a series of left-justified headings and indented parameter settings. The parameters should be indented from the left margin by at least one space. Each heading corresponds with either an ODI driver or VLM.EXE. The following example shows the format of the NET.CFG file:

```
Link driver NE2000
    INT 3
    PORT 300
    MEM D0000
    FRAME Ethernet_802.2
    FRAME Ethernet_II
Netware DOS Requester
    FIRST NETWORK DRIVE = F
    NETWARE PROTOCOL = PNW,BIND,NDS
    PREFERRED SERVER = ECORP
    name context = "O=EMA"
Link Support
    Buffers 8 1500
    MemPool 4096
    Max Stacks 8
```

For more options, view table 14.5, which lists headings that correspond with each driver program.

Table 14.5
NET.CFG Headings

Heading	Corresponding Driver
Link Support	LSL.COM
Link Driver *driver_name*	The ODI LAN driver *driver_name*
PARAMETER=value	Parameters that are left-justified (with no corresponding heading) are associated with IPXODI.COM. An example is IPX RETRY COUNT = 40
NetWare DOS Requester	VLM.EXE

If the NET.CFG file is not present, default settings are used. If a parameter is not specified under a certain heading, the default for that parameter is used. There are approximately 90 settings for all headings. Many vendors provide additional settings. Table 14.6 summarizes the more important parameters for the "Link Driver," and table 14.7 summarizes the more important parameters for the "NetWare DOS Requester" headings. The range of values is indicated in one column, followed by an explanation in the last column.

There is no reference here for the "Link Support" heading. The reason for this is that this heading is not used if you are using the IPX/SPX protocol on your DOS workstation. Because a discussion of TCP/IP on a DOS workstation is beyond the scope of this book, further reference to this heading is avoided. There are additional parameters associated with IPXODI.COM. The defaults will work fine under most circumstances. For this reason, there is no further documentation of these settings. Please consult *NetWare 4.1 for Professionals* by New Riders Publishing for a more complete reference.

Table 14.6
Important Link Driver NET.CFG Parameters

Parameter	Range of Values	Description
INT	2 to 15	Interrupt value (in decimal) for the NIC.
PORT	240 to 4AFF	I/O port address (in hex) starting value for the NIC.
MEM	8000 to EFFF	Memory address (in hex) for the NIC.

Parameter	Range of Values	Description
DMA	1 to 7	Direct memory access channel number for the NIC.
NODE ADDRESS	000000000000 to FFFFFFFFFFFE	Physical address of the NIC. Normally the address is burned in at the factory (except for ARCnet). This parameter lets you override that address.
SLOT	1 to *n*	Which slot in the PC the NIC is plugged in. This parameter is for microchannel (PS/2) and EISA computers. *n* depends on how many slots are in the PC.
FRAME	Ethernet_802.2 Ethernet_802.3 Ethernet_II Ethernet_SNAP Token-Ring Token-Ring_SNAP Novell_RX-Net	Different frame types can be loaded to work with different protocols you wish to use with your NIC. The default frame types for the IPX/SPX protocol in NetWare 4.1 are Ethernet_802.2 (Ethernet NICs), Token-Ring (Token Ring NICs), and Novell_RX-Net (ARCnet).

* The defaults for the Link Driver parameters depend on the NIC. A Novell/Eagle NE2000 Ethernet adapter defaults to interrupt 3, port address 300, for example.

Table 14.7
Important NetWare DOS Requester NET.CFG Parameters

Parameter	Range of Values	Default	Description
CACHE BUFFERS	0 to 64 buffers	5	This parameter sets how many cache buffers the requester uses for caching of nonshared, nontransactional files on the workstation. Increasing the value speeds up processing of files that are handled sequentially.

continues

Table 14.7, Continued
Important NetWare DOS Requester NET.CFG Parameters

Parameter	Range of Values	Default	Description
			Lower values decrease memory needed by VLM. The size of each buffer is set by the next parameter.
CACHE BUFFER SIZE	512 to 4,096 bytes	512 bytes	This parameter sets the size of each cache buffer. Larger values improve performance by allowing the workstation shell to cache larger portions of files passing across the LAN. The size should be adjusted to be equal to or less than the maximum packet size. If less than the maximum packet size, this parameter should be an evenly divisible increment so that it won't waste memory. For example, if your maximum packet size is 2,048, the cache buffer size might be 1,024 or 2,048.
CONNECTIONS	2 to 50 connections	8	The value represents the maximum number of logical network connections VLM.EXE will support. Larger values use more memory. The default of 8 is to maintain compatibility with the older NETX shell. Higher values might not be supported by software written for the NETX or below shell.

Parameter	Range of Values	Default	Description
FIRST NETWORK DRIVE	A to Z	First available drive	Sets the drive letter the user is assigned to initially access the file server. If you have a workstation with a floppy drive and one hard drive (with only a DOS partition), the first drive will be D. You do not need to specify the colon. To assign drive F as the first network drive, enter the parameter as follows: FIRST NETWORK DRIVE = F
LOAD LOW CONN	ON or OFF	ON	When set to OFF, this parameter causes CONN.VLM (the connection manager) to load into upper memory. This saves memory but degrades performance.
LOAD LOW IPXNCP	ON or OFF	ON	When set to OFF, this parameter causes IPXNCP.VLM to load into upper memory. This saves memory but degrades performance.
LOCAL PRINTERS	0 to 7 by BIOS	Determined	This value informs the shell how many printers are available locally on the workstation. If you have no printers attached locally to the workstation, enter a value of 0. A zero value prevents the system from locking up in case the user initiates a print job (by pressing the Print Screen key) without being captured to a network print queue. The BIOS will

continues

Table 14.7, Continued
Important NetWare DOS Requester NET.CFG Parameters

Parameter	Range of Values	Default	Description
			determine how many ports are available and will add one local printer for each LPT port.
MESSAGE TIMEOUT	0 to 10,000	0	This parameter controls the amount of time the ticks shell will wait before clearing broadcast messages. The default of 0 informs the shell to wait indefinitely until the user presses Ctrl+Enter to clear a broadcast message. A tick is 1/18 of a second. 10,000 ticks is approximately six hours.
NAME CONTEXT	*NDS Container*	[root]	This parameter enables you to enter the desired default NDS context for a user.
NETWORK PRINTERS	0 to 9	3	This parameter sets the number of printer ports the shell can capture. If you do not want to send any jobs to the network, and will print strictly locally, set the value to 0. Setting the value to 0 will cause PRINT.VLM to not load.
PB BUFFERS	0 to 10	3	This sets the number of buffers used by the Packet Burst protocol on the workstation. Setting this value to 0 disables packet burst on the workstation. Larger values will increase performance but will take additional memory on the workstation.

Range of Parameter	Values	Default	Description
PREFERRED SERVERS	*File Server Name*	Nearest available server	Forces the shell to attach to the specified server. If the PREFERRED TREE option is also used, the first server to make contact that meets either parameter will establish a connection.
PREFERRED TREE	*NDS Tree Name*	Tree on the NDS of the nearest available server	Forces the shell to attach to the specified partition NDS tree.
SIGNATURE LEVEL	0 to 3	1	Sets the level of security for the workstation. Each packet sent from the workstation can have a unique *signature* written. This prevents insertion of packets into the network from an unauthorized source. The values for *n* are described here: 0 = Disabled (no signature) 1 = Enabled but not preferred 2 = Preferred 3 = Required Each increasing level places a higher priority on the security signature process. With increased security, however, comes lower performance.

continues

Table 14.7, Continued
Important NetWare DOS Requester NET.CFG Parameters

Parameter	Range of Values	Default	Description
USE DEFAULTS	ON or OFF	ON	If set to OFF, you must specify which VLMs are to be loaded with the VLM = xxx parameter (described later).
VLM	*Complete VLM filename*	N/A	This enables you to load a specific VLM. You can include the path as well as the name of the VLM. You must indicate the complete file name, including the VLM extension.

Each parameter is followed by an equal sign (=) and then a value. You can have a space before and after the equal sign.

Installing a DOS Workstation

This section covers how to install the client software on your workstation. The installation process is automated by a program named INSTALL, which copies files from disks to the workstation and configures the required workstation files. INSTALL presents a data entry screen to be filled out. Once you have filled in the fields, the following actions are performed:

- The ODI drivers for the workstation's NIC are copied.
- A NET.CFG file is created with the settings you indicated.
- A batch file STARTNET.BAT is created. This file loads the ODI drivers and the VLM shell.
- The CONFIG.SYS and AUTOEXEC.BAT files are updated unless you have instructed INSTALL not to do so.
- If Windows support was indicated, Windows DLL files and utilities are copied to the appropriate Windows directories. In addition, certain INI files are copied.

Creating Workstation Installation Disks

The workstation installation program can be run directly from the NetWare 4.1 CD-ROM, from files that have been copied to a server, or from floppy disks. For a new network, you need to install client software on at least one workstation using the floppy disk or the CD-ROM method. Workstation installation disks can be created during the server installation process. You need to have the NetWare 4.1 CD available on a CD drive connected to the server or the software loaded on a server to create workstation installation disks. You can also use the Other Product options with the INSTALL.NLM.

Note: This process also can be accomplished at the end of an installation. After the server installation is completed, you will be placed in the Product Options menu of the INSTALL.NLM utility. You can create client disks at that time, or at any time, by following the steps presented here.

When you are done, you will have the following disks:

- WSDOS_1 (DOS installation files and LAN card drivers)
- WSDOS_2 (VLM files)
- WSDOS_3 (Windows DLL files and NLS language message modules)
- WSDOS_4 (Windows DLL files and Unicode files)
- WSDOS_5 (LAN card drivers and miscellaneous files)

To create DOS workstation installation disks, perform the following actions:

1. From any workstation, format and label five high density 3.5" disks as follows:

   WSDOS_1
   WSDOS_2
   WSDOS_3
   WSDOS_4
   WSDOS_5

2. Go to the server and press Alt+Esc to toggle to the server's prompt (:).

3. Load the INSTALL.NLM module as follows:

   LOAD INSTALL

If you receive a message indicating that this module is already loaded, press Alt+Esc to toggle to this module. The INSTALL Installation Options menu will appear.

4. From the Installation Options menu, select Product Options. The Other Installation Items/Products screen appears.

5. From the Other Installation Items/Products screen, select Create DOS/MS Windows/OS2 Client Install Diskettes. You will be prompted for the location of the NetWare 4.1 installation CD or the location of the installation files you have copied to a server. The Indicate File Groups screen appears, as shown in figure 14.3.

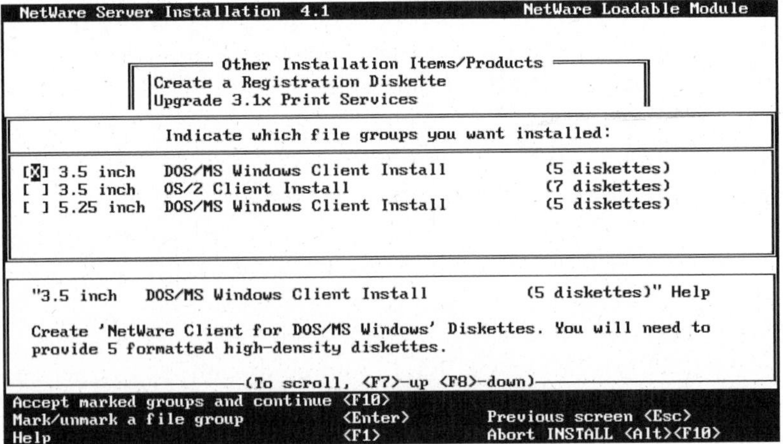

Figure 14.3
The Indicate File Groups screen.

6. From the Indicate File Groups screen, select the group of files you want to create. Move the cursor to the desired option and press Enter to make a selection. When an item is selected, an X appears between the square brackets ([X]). For this procedure, select the DOS/MS Windows Client Install file group. Figure 14.6 shows these options checked.

   Press the F10 key to start the disk creation process. The File Copy Status screen appears, prompting you to indicate the path to the installation files.

7. From the File Copy Status screen, press the F3 key and type the path to the installation files. For a CD mounted on the server, the path is the volume name of the CD. The default is the volume name of the NetWare 4.1 installation CD. If you are not sure of the volume name of the CD, use Alt+Esc to toggle to the server's prompt, and type the following:

   CD VOLUME LIST

You can also enter the name of another server where you have the NetWare 4.1 installation CD mounted or where the NetWare 4.1 installation files have been copied. If you are using RCONSOLE to access the server you have the additional option of pressing the F4 key to specify a locally mounted CD.

8. You are now prompted to insert one of the floppy disks created in Step 1. When finished, you have a set of DOS workstation installation disks.

Running the INSTALL Program

You can run the INSTALL program from the set of floppy disks you created in the preceding section, from a NetWare 4.1 installation CD, or from a server. To run the workstation INSTALL program from a server, the workstation must already contain a working set of NetWare shells. This option is available if you want to upgrade a series of workstations configured for an earlier version of NetWare.

Starting the Installation from Floppy Disks

To install a workstation from floppy disks, locate the disk labeled WSDOS_1 and place it in drive A of the workstation you want to install. Move to drive A by typing the following:

A:

Start the installation program by typing the following:

INSTALL

You are prompted for additional disks when the INSTALL program needs to locate drivers for the NIC in your workstation.

Starting the Installation from a NetWare 4.1 CD-ROM

If you are installing the NetWare DOS Requester to a workstation that has a CD-ROM drive, you can install directly from the NetWare 4.1 distribution CD-ROM. Move to the drive letter assigned to the CD-ROM drive (E, for example). Change to the installation directory by typing the following:

CD \CLIENT\DOSWIN

Start the installation program by typing the following:

INSTALL

Starting the Installation from a File Server

Before installing the client software from a server, you must first log in to the server. Load the existing client shell software and log in to the server that contains the client software. To install the client software from this server, you must have the NetWare 4.1 installation CD mounted on that server, or you must have selected the "Set up a Network Directory for Client Install" option during the installation of that server. See Chapter 12, "Installing the Network Operating System," for more information.

If you have a NetWare 4.1 CD mounted on the server, map a drive letter F to the volume name and directory containing the client files. If the volume name is NW41, for example, proceed as follows:

MAP F:=server_name\NW41:CLIENT\DOSWIN

Enter the name of the server in place of *server_name.*

If, on the other hand, you loaded the client software during the installation process, change to the client software directory by typing the following:

CD \PUBLIC\CLIENT\DOSWIN

Start the installation program by typing the following:

INSTALL

Completing the DOS Workstation Installation

Figure 14.4 shows you the INSTALL screen. The installation procedure consists of six numbered steps, which you must complete in turn. Use the Tab key to move from one step to the next, and complete each step as follows:

```
NetWare Client Install  v1.21 rc2            Monday  November  21, 1994  9:17am

 1. Enter the destination directory:
    C:\NWCLIENT

 2. Install will modify your AUTOEXEC.BAT and CONFIG.SYS files and make
    backups.  Allow changes? (Y/N):  Yes

 3. Install support for MS Windows? (Y/N):  Yes
    Enter MS Windows directory:   C:\WINDOWS
    Highlight here and Press <Enter> to customize.

 4. Configure your workstation for back up by a NetWare server running
    software such as SBACKUP? (Y/N):  No

 5. Select the driver for your network board.
    Highlight here and press <Enter> to see list.

 6. Highlight here and press <Enter> to install.

Install will add this path to AUTOEXEC.BAT if you allow changes to the DOS
configuration files.
Esc=Go Back   Enter=Edit/Select                                    Alt-F10=Exit
```

Figure 14.4
The DOS client software installation program.

1. Enter the name of the directory on the workstation that will contain the files needed to gain access to the server. The default is C:\NWCLIENT. Enter the desired path and press Enter.

2. The workstation software requires you to set your LASTDRIVE parameter in the CONFIG.SYS file to Z. If you select Yes for this option, the installation program makes this change for you. If not, you need to make this change yourself before attempting to access the server.

   The installation software creates a batch file called STARTNET.BAT that is placed by default in the C:\NWCLIENT directory. This batch file contains the commands needed to access the server. If you want to have your AUTOEXEC.BAT file configured so that STARTNET.BAT will run when the PC boots, answer Yes to this question.

   Answer Yes or No and press Enter.

3. Step 3 asks if you wish to "Install support for MS Windows?" Answer Yes to the question if you have Windows installed on your workstation. If so, the program copies a series of DLL, SYS, INI and GRP files to your Windows subdirectory.

   If you select Yes, you also need to supply the path where Windows is contained. The default is C:\WINDOWS.

   Another option of Step 3 is to customize the Windows client installation. Select the field which states, "Highlight here and Press <Enter> to customize." The Customize Support for Windows screen appears.

   When Windows is installed on a server, you can have users who need access to multiple country codes at the same time, using the same version of windows. If this is the case, answer Yes to the question, "Do you plan to use more country codes..."

   This screen also gives you a place to enter the path to the shared version of Windows on a server if you have Windows installed on a server.

4. Step 4 asks you if you want to "Configure your workstation for backup by a NetWare server running software such as SBACKUP?" Answer Yes if this is the case. The Configure TSA for Storage Management Services (SMS) screen appears.

   Enter the server name with the SMS backup software installed. You can assign a name for your workstation which will be recognized when the backup administrator goes to backup workstations. An optional password can be entered for security. You can assign from 1 to 30 buffers that are used during workstation backup. The more buffers you assign, the faster the backup will progress. Do not assign more than 1 or 2 buffers if workstation RAM is not freely available. The last parameter you can specify on this screen is a list of local hard drives to be backed up.

5. Press Enter to see a list of supported NICs. If you already have IPX.COM or the ODI drivers loaded for your card, the list appears on the screen. If not, select the desired card and press Enter. The NIC selection screen is shown in figure 14.5.

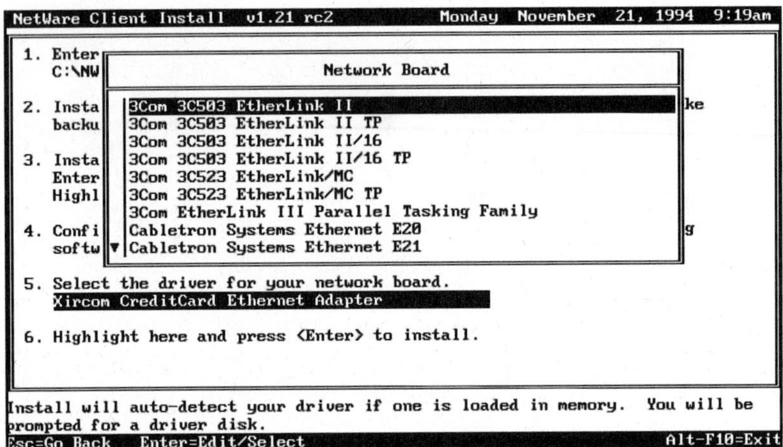

Figure 14.5
DOS Client Software Installation—NIC Selection.

The NIC drivers supplied with NetWare include drivers for the following NICs:

- 3Com Etherlink
- Cabletron
- Hewlett-Packard Ethertwist, MCA, and PC LAN adpaters
- Intel EtherExpress and 159x
- Madge Smart 16/4 token ring adapters
- Microdyne Ethernet
- National Semiconductor Ethernet
- NCR WaveLAN wireless
- Novell Ethernet NE/2, NE1xxx, NE2xxx, NE3200

- Novell Ethernet NTR2000 (token ring)
- Novell RX-Net (ARCnet)
- NSC Ethernet PCMCIA
- LANSUP (ODI support for IBM LAN Support Program)
- Olicom token ring
- Proteon p13xx, p18xx, p19xx token ring
- Racal Interlan Ethernet, Etherblaster
- Racal-Datacom Ethernet
- SMC PC 13x, PC5xx, PC6xx, PSx10 ARCnet
- SMC EliteFamily token ring
- Thomas-Conrad TCNS (ARCnet fiber optic)
- Thomas-Conrad Ethernet
- Thomas-Conrad token ring
- Thomas-Conrad ARCnet
- Xircom Credit Card and Pocket Adapters
- Zenith Data Systems Z-NOTE

If your NIC is not on the list, you must press the Insert key. You are prompted to insert a disk and/or indicate a directory that contains an ODI driver supplied by the vendor of your NIC. The INSTALL program reads the disk, searching for a suitable ODI driver, which is entered into the installation screen.

6. Once you have selected the desired NIC, you must supply configuration data. Figure 14.6 shows the screen for the Novell NE2000 card. When you select a field and press Enter, a list of supported choices for that field appears. Select the desired setting from the list of choices.

Ethernet drivers in NetWare 4.1 default to a frame type of Ethernet_802.2. Be sure to set the frame type of the workstation NIC to the same frame type as the server.

Figure 14.6

Novell NE2000 NIC configuration.

```
NetWare Client Install  v1.21 rc2          Monday  November  21, 1994  9:43am
                     Settings for Novell Ethernet NE2000
 Base I/O Port                         PORT 300
 Hardware Interrupt                    INT 3
 Media Frame Type(s)                   FRAME Ethernet_802.2
 Memory I/O Address

 Change the values above to match your network board settings.  Highlight the
 value and press <Enter>.  Press <Esc> when you are finished.  (Note: Avoid
 I/O Base Address 360 if you have a parallel printer, and Interrupt Request 3
 if you have a device using COM2, such as a fax, mouse or modem.)

 SPECIFIC HELP FOR THIS DRIVER:
 Please select the options that match your board's jumper settings.

Install will auto-detect your driver if one is loaded in memory.  You will be
prompted for a driver disk.
Esc=Go Back   Enter=Edit/Select   F10=Save                          Alt-F10=Exit
```

7. Move to Step 6 and press Enter. The installation program copies the needed files to the selected directory on your workstation.

At this point, the workstation software has been installed. You can now reboot the computer and test the software.

DOS Files Copied by the INSTALL Program

If, for some reason, the INSTALL program fails to run on your computer, here is a list of files and directories that are copied or created:

Directories created:

```
C:\NWCLIENT
C:\NWCLIENT\NLS
C:\NWCLIENT\NLS\ENGLISH
```

Files copied to or created in C:\NWCLIENT:

```
C:\NWCLIENT>dir /w

 Volume in drive C is DOUG
 Volume Serial Number is 2655-11F9
 Directory of C:\NWCLIENT
```

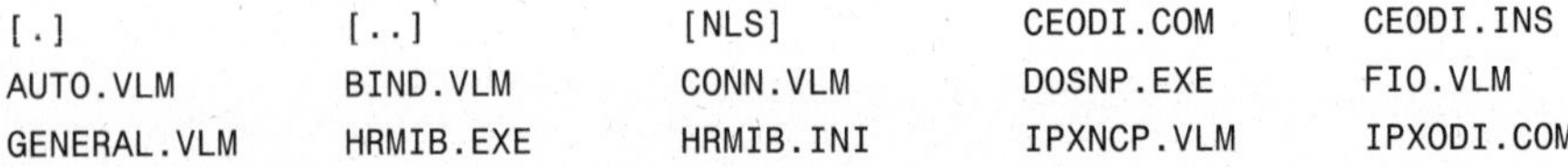

```
[.]            [..]           [NLS]          CEODI.COM      CEODI.INS
AUTO.VLM       BIND.VLM       CONN.VLM       DOSNP.EXE      FIO.VLM
GENERAL.VLM    HRMIB.EXE      HRMIB.INI      IPXNCP.VLM     IPXODI.COM
```

```
LSL.COM          MIB2IF.VLM       MIB2PROT.VLM     NDS.VLM          NESL.COM
NETBIOS.EXE      NETX.VLM         NMR.VLM          NWP.VLM          ODINSUP.COM
PNW.VLM          PRINT.VLM        REDIR.VLM        ROUTE.COM        RSA.VLM
RXMONSTK.COM     SECURITY.VLM     STPIPX.COM       STPUDP.COM       TRAN.VLM
TSASMS.COM       VLM.EXE          WSASN1.VLM       WSDRVPRN.MIB     WSDRVPRN.VLM
WSREG.VLM        WSSNMP.VLM       WSTRAP.VLM       STARTNET.BAT     NET.CFG
CONFIG.NEW       AUTOEXEC.NEW
       47 file(s)        541,791 bytes
                      10,162,176 bytes free

C:\NWCLIENT>

C:\NWCLIENT>dir nls\english /w

 Volume in drive C is DOUG
 Volume Serial Number is 2655-11F9
 Directory of C:\NWCLIENT\NLS\ENGLISH

[.]              [..]             DOSRQSTR.MSG     IPXODI.MSG       LSL.MSG
MIB2IF.MSG       MIB2PROT.MSG     NESL.MSG         NMR.MSG          README.TXT
READSNMP.TXT     READVLM.TXT      RXMONSTK.MSG     STPIPX.MSG       STPUDP.MSG
WSASN1.MSG       WSDRVPRN.MSG     WSREG.MSG        WSSNMP.MSG       WSTRAP.MSG
       20 file(s)         99,221 bytes
                      10,162,176 bytes free

C:\NWCLIENT>
```

All executables and VLM files can be found on the NetWare 4.1 installation CD in the \CLIENT\DOSWIN directory. The files are in compressed format. To manually install a workstation, you must uncompress the files using the NWUNPACK utility. This utility is also located in the \CLIENT\DOSWIN directory.

To manually unpack files to the workstation, proceed as follows:

1. Access the NetWare 4.1 installation CD by mapping a drive letter to the CD mounted as a volume on a server, or changing to the local drive letter if mounted locally.

2. Change to the \CLIENT\DOSWIN directory. Copy files that are not packed. You can distinguish a packed file by the underscore (_) character as the last character in the file extension.

3. Unpack files as follows:

```
\CLIENT\DOSWIN\NWUNPACK *.* C:\NWCLIENT
```

4. Change to the \CLIENT\DOSWIN\DOS directory. Locate the appropriate LAN driver and unpack it as follows:

```
\CLIENT\DOSWIN\NWUNPACK LAN_Driver C:\NWCLIENT
```

5. Make an NLS directory on your local drive:

```
MD C:\NWCLIENT\NLS
```

6. Change to the \CLIENT\DOSWIN\NLS directory on the installation CD. Copy NLS files from the CD to the local NLS directory:

```
COPY *.* C:\NWCLIENT\NLS
```

7. Make a language directory on your local drive. Language directories can be any of the following:

   Deutsch

   English

   Espanol

   Francais

   Italiano

   To create an ENGLISH directory, type the following:

   MD C:\NWCLIENT\NLS\ENGLISH

8. Change to the \CLIENT\DOSWIN\NLS*language* directory on the installation CD. Copy all unpacked files to the local language directory. Unpack all packed files to the *language* directory on the local drive. To unpack ENGLISH files, type the following:

   \CLIENT\DOSWIN\NWUNPACK *.* C:\NWCLIENT\NLS\ENGLISH

9. Create the C:\NWCLIENT\NET.CFG file. Refer to the discussion of this file later in this chapter.

10. Modify the C:\CONFIG.SYS file by adding this line:

    LASTDRIVE=Z:

11. You can optionally modify your C:\AUTOEXEC.BAT file to include the commands to start the workstation software. These commands will include the following:

```
rem
rem   Command to set the language environment
rem
SET NWLANGUAGE=ENGLISH
rem
rem   Command to start the Link Support Layer
CD \NWCLIENT
LSL.COM
rem
rem   Command to start the LAN driver NE2000
rem   Change this to select the driver for your card
rem
NE2000.COM
rem
rem   Command to start IPX
rem
IPXODI.COM
rem
rem   Command to load the VLM requester
rem
VLM.EXE
```

Network Connections and the NetWare User License

Once the client software is installed, you can proceed to activate the network connection to the server and log in. The STARTNET.BAT file, which is created in the C:\NWCLIENT directory by default, initiates the network connection. Here is a sample STARTNET.BAT file:

```
@ECHO OFF
C:
CD \NWCLIENT
SET NWLANGUAGE=ENGLISH
LSL
NE2000.COM
IPXODI
```

```
VLM
CD \
```

As discussed earlier, LSL, NE2000 (a LAN driver), and IPXODI form the ODI driver set. These drivers activate the NIC itself. VLM, as mentioned earlier, activates the logical attachment to a server.

When you run VLM.EXE, your workstation negotiates with the nearest server (or preferred server, depending on which switches or NET.CFG settings you used) for a connection. This connection is a logical attachment between your workstation and the server. The attachment does not count against your server user license until you actually log in and use resources on that server. It is possible to have an attachment to one server and not use its resources. In this case, the attachment does not count against your NetWare user license. One way to monitor connections is through the MONITOR.NLM running on a server. Under the Connection Information menu is a list of all connections to that server. Those marked with an asterisk do not count against the server license.

When a connection is established, the user at the workstation sees the message:

```
Attached to server: XYZ
```

where *XYZ* is the name of the server. If the user does not see this message, a problem has occurred. Check for the following:

- The settings in the NET.CFG file do not match the hardware settings of the LAN card.
- The LAN card is set to the wrong connector (for example, if you have a twisted-pair connection, the LAN card might be set to the thin Ethernet BNC connector).
- The frame type of the LAN card in the server does not match the frame type specified in your NET.CFG file.
- Network or cabling problems.

DOS Utilities

This section discusses the following DOS utilities, which you will find extremely useful when first logging in:

- LOGIN
- CX

- NLIST
- NETUSER

LOGIN, CX, and NLIST are located in the LOGIN directory; NETUSER is located in the PUBLIC directory, All utilities are installed on volume SYS:.

All DOS utilities have built-in command-line help, which can be accessed by typing a space and /? after the utility itself. To get help on CX, for example, type

CX /?

LOGIN, CX, and NLIST are examples of NetWare 4.1 command-line utilities. *Command-line utilities* in general can be issued from the DOS command line or from a batch file. They have a certain amount of syntax that must follow the command. NETUSER, on the other hand, is referred to as a *menu utility*. NETUSER has a main menu and online help that can be accessed at any time while in the utility. Menu utilities cannot be used in a batch file without user interaction.

LOGIN

The LOGIN.EXE command is used to log you in to the network. If you are already logged in, this command will first log you out, and then back in again. Before you can use any resources on any server, you must use the LOGIN command to authenticate your connection. Part of this process involves asking you for your login name and password. If you provide a valid complete or partial NDS name, and the correct password, the server grants you access to the network.

Another function of the LOGIN.EXE command is to invoke the login script(s) from the NDS database. There are several login scripts that can be executed, including the container, profile, user, and default login scripts. These are explained in greater detail in Chapter 34, "Creating Login Scripts."

The syntax for the LOGIN.EXE command is as follows:

```
LOGIN [server_name/][NDS name] [options]
```

If you omit the optional parameters, the LOGIN command prompts you for a user name and password. Table 14.8 summarizes the LOGIN.EXE command-line options.

Table 14.8
LOGIN.EXE Command Options

Parameter	Description
/NS	*No Script.* This causes the user to log in without running a login script. This command syntax replaces the ATTACH command from earlier versions of NetWare.
/CLS	*Clear Screen.* Causes the screen to clear prior to the execution of the login script.
/S *filename* | /S *objectName*	*Script.* Executes an alternative login script contained in the text file *filename* or the login script of NDS object *objectName.* This option bypasses all other login scripts. This is very useful when testing a new login script, to bypass a login script with bugs, or to execute another object's login script. If executing the login script of another object, you must have Read rights to that object's Login Script Property.
/B	*Bindery.* Logs in to a server using bindery emulation. This option is necessary when logging in to a 3.*x* server or below.
/TR *treeName*	*Tree.* Logs you in to a specific NDS tree *treeName.* This option is required if you have several NDS trees on an internetwork and you want to get into one or the other.
/SWAP	Swaps the LOGIN.EXE into extended or expanded RAM when running external commands from within the login script.
/NB	Login without displaying the initial login banner message.
/VER	Displays the version of the LOGIN.EXE utility.
/?	*Help.* Displays a syntax and help screen for the LOGIN command.

Here is an example of a standard LOGIN sequence for user EBierer:

```
LOGIN .EBIERER.NY.EBDB
```

This example is when you wish to force a login to a specific server EBDB:

```
LOGIN EBDB/.CN=Admin.O=EBDB
```

This example shows you a login sequence using an alternate login script:

```
LOGIN .EBIERER.NY.EBDB /S C:\TEMP\TEST.LOG
```

CX

The CX command is used to change or view context. This is the primary utility used to browse the NDS from the command line. The CX command has a tremendous resemblance to the DOS CD command. For the following examples, assume the NDS structure illustrated in figure 14.7.

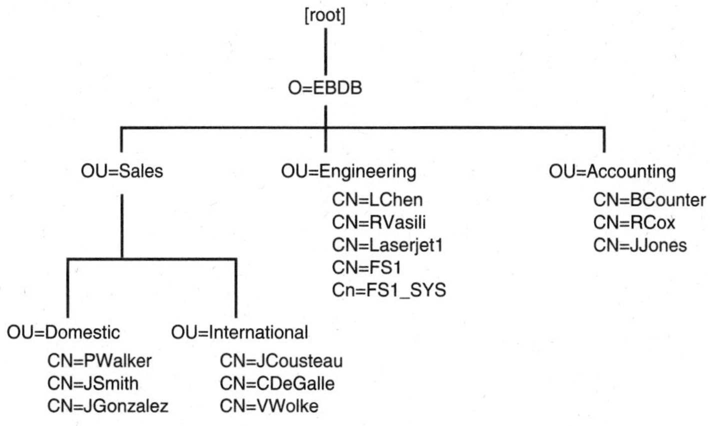

Figure 14.7
A sample NDS structure.

To change to any context, specify its complete NDS name. For example, to change to the International container from any other context, type the following:

CX .OU=International.OU=Sales.O=EBDB

To change to a context immediately above, use the trailing period. The trailing period indicates "parent container." To move from International to Sales, type the following:

CX .

To move to a container below the current container, type CX followed by the name of the container. This is a partial name. NetWare will add the current context to form a complete name. To move to Domestic from Sales, type the following:

CX Domestic

The following list summarizes the options associated with the CX command, along with an example:

/A This option displays names of *All* objects at the current context if used in conjunction with the /T or the /CONT options. If used with the /T option, displays all objects from the current context and all contexts below the current context. The /A option *must* be used in conjunction with either the /T or /CONT option.

Type **CX /T /A** to see figure 14.8.

Figure 14.8

The results of the CX /T /A command.

```
*** Directory Services Mapping ***

O=ebdb
   ├CN=EBDB
   ├CN=Admin
   ├CN=EBDB_SYS
   ├CN=Super
   ├CN=Q1
   ├CN=PS-ebdb
   ├CN=P1
   ├OU=Engineering
   │  ├CN=Doug
   │  ├CN=Bill
   │  ├CN=Hillary
   │  ├CN=Gary
   │  └CN=Belinda
   ├OU=Sales
   │  ├CN=Laura
   │  ├CN=Donna
   │  ├CN=Dale
   │  ├CN=Gordon
   │  ├CN=Log
   │  └CN=Jacques
   └OU=Accounting
F:\>
```

/T This option displays container objects below the current context. T stands for *Tree.*

Type **CX /T** to see figure 14.9.

Figure 14.9

The results of the CX /T command.

```
*** Directory Services Mapping ***

[Root]
   └O=EBDB
      ├OU=Engineering
      ├OU=Sales
      │  ├OU=International
      │  └OU=Domestic
      └OU=Accounting
F:\>
```

/R This option takes you to the [root] of the NDS tree. When the com mand finishes executing, you will see the message "[Root]" appear.

/CONT Use this option to view container objects only immediately below the current context, not the entire tree below.

Type **CX /CONT** to view figure 14.10.

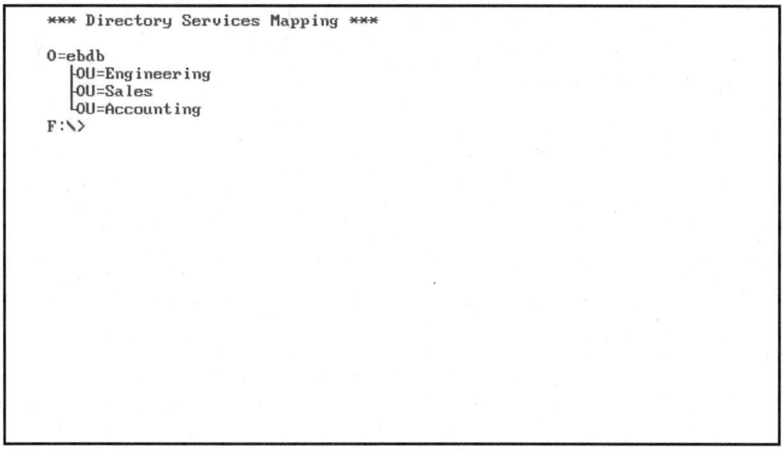

```
*** Directory Services Mapping ***

O=ebdb
   ├OU=Engineering
   ├OU=Sales
   └OU=Accounting
F:\>
```

Figure 14.10

The results of the CX /CONT command.

/C Continuous output. If your NDS tree becomes quite extensive, this option causes the output to display continuously. This must be combined with another option, such as /T.

The CX options can be used in any order. The commands

```
CX /T /A
```

and

```
CX /A /T
```

yield the same results. Single-letter option switches can even be placed together, as follows:

```
CX /TARC
```

NLIST

The NLIST.EXE utility is used from the DOS command prompt for browsing through the NDS tree. NLIST can be used to extract information about objects in the tree. The basic syntax for NLIST is as follows:

NLIST *object_class* [*property search option*] [*display option*] [*basic option*]

The next several subsections give you an overview of the various options associated with NLIST, followed by some examples. For the purposes of these examples, it would be easiest for you to change your context to the [root] by typing the following:

CX /R

Object Classes

To view all the objects in your NDS tree, be sure to change your context to the [root], and then type the following:

NLIST * /S

The /S option instructs NLIST to search the current context and all contexts below. As you can see, this command shows you object names and their object class, one context at a time. To get a list of all users in the tree, type the following:

NLIST user /S

The output from this command is shown in the following listing. Note that the output for different objects yields different information. In the following listing, login times and password expiration information are displayed along with the user name.

```
Object Class: user
Current context: O=EBDB
User name= The name of the user
Dis      = Login disabled
Log exp  = The login expiration date, 0 if no expiration date
Pwd      = Yes if passwords are required
Pwd exp  = The password expiration date, 0 if no expiration date
Uni      = Yes if unique passwords are required
Min      = The minimum password length, 0 if no minimum

User Name                                  Dis  Log Exp Pwd  Pwd Exp Uni Min
----------------------------------------------------------------------------
CN=Admin                                   No   0-00-00 No   0-00-00 No   0
CN=Super                                   No   0-00-00 No   0-00-00 No   0
A total of 2 user objects was found in this context.
```

```
Object Class: user
Current context: OU=Sales.O=EBDB
User Name                                  Dis  Log Exp Pwd  Pwd Exp Uni Min
----------------------------------------------------------------------------
CN=Laura                                   No   0-00-00 No   0-00-00 No   0
CN=Donna                                   No   0-00-00 No   0-00-00 No   0
CN=Dale                                    No   0-00-00 No   0-00-00 No   0
CN=Gordon                                  No   0-00-00 No   0-00-00 No   0
> > >  Enter = More   C = Continuous   Esc = Cancel
```

You also can use the object classes to include specific objects. You can either type in a specific object name or use an asterisk (*) before, after, or both before and after the search text. To view all printers that have the letters "laser" anywhere in their name, for example, type the following:

NLIST printer=*laser* /S

Basic Options

Basic options can be used in conjunction with the other options described in the preceding and following sections. Table 14.9 summarizes the basic options.

TABLE 14.9
Basic NLIST.EXE Command Options

Parameter	Description
/A	Displays active users or servers. To view users logged in, searching all contexts, type **NLIST user /A /S**
/S	Causes NLIST to search subcontexts in addition to the current context.
/R	Objects referenced from the [root].
/CO *context*	Changes where NLIST starts its search. Search begins at the specified *context*. To search the OU=Sales container, for example, type **NLIST * /CO .OU=Sales.O=EBDB**.
/C	Allows NLIST to present its output continuously rather than prompting you to press a key to continue.

continues

Table 14.9, Continued
Basic NLIST.EXE Command Options

Parameter	Description
/B	Displays bindery-based objects. This is useful for viewing NetWare 3.*x* or 2.*x* servers. To obtain a list of all NetWare servers on the network, type **NLIST server /B**.
/VER	Gives you the version of NLIST.EXE.
/TREE	Displays all NDS trees available on your network. To view NDS trees on your network, type **NLIST /TREE**.

Display Options

There are two main display options: /D and /N. The /D option causes NLIST to display detailed information about the object. The /N option causes NLIST to display the name of the object only.

To view detailed information on the user Dale, for example, type the following:

NLIST user=Dale /S /D

The following code illustrates the result of this command:

```
Object Class: user
Current context: OU=Sales.O=EBDB
User: CN=Dale
        Name: Dale
        Access Control List (ACL):
                Subject: Dale
                Property:  [All Properties Rights]
                Property Rights: [ R   ]
        Access Control List (ACL):
                Subject: Dale
                Property: Login Script
                Property Rights: [ RW  ]
        Access Control List (ACL):
                Subject: [Public]
                Property: Default Server
                Property Rights: [ R   ]
        Access Control List (ACL):
                Subject: [Root]
                Property: Group Membership
```

```
            Property Rights: [ R   ]
    Access Control List (ACL):
            Subject: Dale
            Property: Print Job Configuration
            Property Rights: [ RW  ]
    Access Control List (ACL):
            Subject: [Root]
            Property: Network Address
            Property Rights: [ R   ]
    Description: Sharp eyed and tireless
    Home Directory:
            Volume Name: CN=EBDB_SYS.
            Path: USERS\Dale
            Name Space Type: DOS
    Default Server: CN=EBDB.
    Object Class: User
    Object Class: Organizational Person
    Object Class: Person
    Object Class: Top
    Department: Marketing
    Last Name: Cooper
    Telephone Number: 333-4040
-------------------------------------------------------------------------------

One user object was found in this context.

One user object was found.
```

Property Search and Display Options

Some of the most complex yet useful aspects of the NLIST command are the property search and display options. There are two primary variations: NLIST...WHERE, and NLIST...SHOW. The *WHERE* option enables you to specify search criteria using equal to, greater than, less than, and other operators. The *SHOW* option displays the value(s) for the property you specify.

The following subsections provide some examples that illustrate the versatility of this powerful utility. The basic syntax for the NLIST...WHERE command is as follows:

```
NLIST object_type WHERE "property" operator "value"
```

Object type can be any of the object classes listed in the object type subsection. *Property* can be any valid property associated with that object. The list of property names is quite extensive (see table 14.10). Table 14.10 also shows you the type of value that can be associated with the search. *Operator* can be any of the operators listed in table 14.11. *Value* is a value appropriate to the property. If the property is a date, for example, the value should also be a date.

The basic syntax for the NLIST...SHOW command is as follows:

```
NLIST object_type SHOW "property"
```

The purpose of this variation is to enable you to see the values of various properties. If this particular property has no assigned value or, in the case of the WHERE option, if no objects meet the criteria, the following message appears:

```
No object_type objects were found.
```

Object_type refers to the type of object you specified in your NLIST command.

TABLE 14.10
NLIST Property Names

Object	Property Name	Values
User	Account Balance	Numeric
	Account Disabled	Yes/No
	Account Has Expiration Date	Yes/No
	Account Locked	Yes/No
	Account Reset Time	Numeric
	ACL	Text
	Allow Unlimited Credit	Yes/No
	Allow User to Change Password	Yes/No
	City	Text
	Date Password Expires	Date
	Days Between Forced Changes	Numeric
	Default Server	Object
	Department	Text
	Description	Text
	Foreign EMail Address	Text
	Fax Number	Text
	Grace Logins Allowed	Numeric

Object	Property Name	Values
	Group Membership	Object
	Home Directory	Text
	Incorrect Login Attempts	Numeric
	Language	Text
	Last Intruder Address	Exists
	Last Name	Text
	Location	Text
	Locked By Intruder	Yes/No
	Login Disabled	Yes/No
	Login Expiration Time	Date
	Login Grace Limit	Numeric
	Login Grace Remaining	Numeric
	Login Intruder Attempts	Numeric
	Login Intruder Reset Time	Numeric
	Login Maximum Simultaneous	Numeric
	Login Script	Exists
	Low Balance Limit	Numeric
	Mailbox ID	Text
	Mailing Label Information	Exists
	Maximum Connections	Numeric
	Minimum Account Balance	Numeric
	Minimum Password Length	Numeric
	Name	Object
	Network Address	Exists
	Network Address Restriction	Exists
	Password Allow Change	Yes/No
	Password Expiration Interval	Numeric
	Password Expiration Time	Date
	Password Minimum Length	Numeric
	Password Required	Yes/No

continues

Table 14.10, Continued
NLIST Property Names

Object	Property Name	Values
	Password Unique Required	Yes/No
	Post Office Box	Text
	Postal (Zip) Code	Text
	Postal Address	Text
	Profile	Object
	Remaining Grace Logins	Numeric
	Require a Password	Yes/No
	Require Unique Passwords	Yes/No
	Revision	Numeric
	Security Equals	Text
	Security Equal To	Object
	See Also	Object
	State or Province	Text
	Street Address	Text
	Telephone	Text
	Telephone Number	Text
	Title	Text
Computer	Name	Text
	Description	Text
	Location	Text
	Network Address	Exists
	Organization Name	Text
	Operator	Object
	Department	Text
	Owner	Object
	Revision	Numeric
	See Also	Object

Object	Property Name	Values
	Serial Number	Text
	Server	Object
Directory Map	Name	Text
	Description	Text
	Location	Text
	Organization Name	Text
	Operator	Object
	Department	Text
	Path	Exists
	Revision	Numeric
	See Also	Object
Distribution List	Department	Text
	Description	Text
	Foreign EMail Address	Text
	Foreign EMail Alias	Text
	Location	Text
	Mailbox Location	Object
	Mailbox ID	Text
	Members	Object
	Name	Text
	Organization	Text
	Other Name	Text
	Owner	Object
	Revision	Numeric
External Entity	ACL	Exists
	Description	Text
	External Name	Text
	Foreign EMail Address	Text
	Foreign EMail Alias	Text

continues

Table 14.10, Continued
NLIST Property Names

Object	Property Name	Values
	Name	Text
	Revision	Numeric
Group	ACL	Exists
	Member	Object
	Name	Text
	Revision	Numeric
Message Routing Group	ACL	Exists
	Department	Text
	Description	Text
	Location	Text
	Name	Text
	Organization Name	Text
	Owner	Object
	Revision	Numeric
	See Also	Object
Organization; Organizational Unit	ACL	Text
	City	Text
	Description	Text
	Detect Intruder	Yes/No
	Foreign EMail Address	Text
	Foreign EMail Alias	Text
	Fax Number	Text
	Incorrect Login Count	Numeric
	Intruder Attempt Reset Interval	Numeric
	Intruder Lockout Reset Interval	Numeric
	Location	Text
	Lockout After Detection	Yes/No
	Login Script	Exists
	Mailbox ID	Text

Object	Property Name	Values
	Organization Name	Text
	Post Office Box	Text
	Postal (Zip) Code	Text
	Postal Address	Text
	Revision	Numeric
	See Also	Object
	State or Province	Text
	Street Address	Text
	Telephone	Text
	Telephone Number	Text
Organizational Role	ACL	Text
	City	Text
	Department	Text
	Foreign EMail Address	Text
	Foreign EMail Alias	Text
	Fax Number	Text
	Location	Text
	Mailbox ID	Text
	Mailing Label Information	Exists
	Name	Object
	Occupant	Object
	Post Office Box	Text
	Postal (Zip) Code	Text
	Postal Address	Text
	Revision	Numeric
	See Also	Object
	State or Province	Text
	Street Address	Text
	Telephone	Text
	Telephone Number	Text

continues

Table 14.10, Continued
NLIST Property Names

Object	Property Name	Values
	Title	Text
Printer	Name	Text
	ACL	Exists
	Default Queue	Object
	Description	Text
	Notify	Exists
	Owner	Object
	Print Server	Object
	Printer Configuration	Exists
	Queue	Exists
	Revision	Numeric
Print Server	Name	Text
	ACL	Exists
	Description	Text
	Host Device	Object
	Network Address	Exists
	Operator	Object
	Printer	Exists
	Revision	Numeric
	SAP Name	Text
	Status	Numeric
	User	Object
Profile	Name	Text
	Description	Text
	Location	Text
	Organization Name	Text
	Department	Text
	Login Script	Exists

Object	Property Name	Values
	Revision	Numeric
Queue	Name	Text
	ACL	Exists
	Description	Text
	Device	Object
	Queue Directory	Text
	Operator	Object
	Revision	Numeric
	Server	Object
	Volume	Object
	User	Object
Volume	Name	Text
	Description	Text
	Location	Text
	Organization Name	Text
	Department	Text
	Revision	Numeric
	See Also	Object
	Host Resource Name	Text
	Host Server	Object

The Values are as follows:

Yes/No	You can use the values Yes or No only.
Numeric	You can use a numeric value.
Object	You can use a valid NDS object name only (complete, partial, typeful, typeless).
Text	You can use a text value, including wild cards (such as "A*" or "*net*").

Exists	You can use the "exists" or "nexists" (not exists). operators only.
Date	You can use a date value in the format *mm/dd/yyyy* or *mm-dd-yyyy*.

TABLE 14.11
NLIST...WHERE Operators

Parameter	Description
EQ	Equal to
NE	Not equal to
LT	Less than
LE	Less than or equal to
GT	Greater than
GE	Greater than or equal to
EXISTS	The property has a value assigned
NEXISTS	The property has no value assigned

NLIST...WHERE and NLIST...SHOW Examples

As you can imagine, the variations on the NLIST command are numerous. The following are some typical uses of the NLIST command. For the purposes of these examples, you can use the basic option "/R" or "/CO [root]" at the end of each command, or you could change your context to [root]. The latter approach will be taken to minimize the amount of syntax for you to type.

Change your current context to the [root] by typing the following:

CX /R

Example 1

You want to locate all users whose passwords will expire before January 1, 1996. Type the following:

NLIST user WHERE "password expiration time" LT 1-1-1996 /S

The following shows the result of this command.

```
Object Class: user
Current context: OU=Sales.O=EBDB
User name= The name of the user
Dis      = Login disabled
Log exp  = The login expiration date, 0 if no expiration date
Pwd      = Yes if passwords are required
Pwd exp  = The password expiration date, 0 if no expiration date
Uni      = Yes if unique passwords are required
Min      = The minimum password length, 0 if no minimum

User Name                                      Dis  Log Exp Pwd  Pwd Exp Uni Min
--------------------------------------------------------------------------------
Laura                                          No   6-01-95 No   5-26-95 No   5
One user object was found in this context.

Object Class: user
Current context: OU=Engineering.O=EBDB
User Name                                      Dis  Log Exp Pwd  Pwd Exp Uni Min
--------------------------------------------------------------------------------
Gary                                           No   0-00-00 No   5-26-95 No   5
One user object was found in this context.

A total of 2 user objects was found.
```

Example 2

You want to display the login scripts of all Organizational Units. Type the following:

NLIST "Organizational Unit" SHOW "Login Script" /S

The following shows you the result of this command.

```
Current context: O=EBDB
Organizational Unit: OU=Accounting
        Login Script:
WRITE "Accounting Login Script"
WRITE "-----------------------"
MAP INS S1:=.CN=EBDB_SYS.O=EBDB:APPS\PLAT
MAP G:=.CN=EBDB_SYS.O=EBDB:DATA\ACCTG

--------------------------------------------------------------------------------
```

```
One organizational unit object was found in this context.

Current context: OU=Sales.O=EBDB
Organizational Unit: OU=Domestic
        Login Script:
WRITE "Domestic Sales Login Script"
WRITE "-------------------------"
MAP INS S1:=.CN=EBDB_SYS.O=EBDB:APPS\SALEMAKR
MAP S:=.CN=EBDB_SYS.O=EBDB:DATA\SALES

------------------------------------------------------------------------------

One organizational unit object was found in this context.
A total of 2 organizational unit objects was found.
```

Example 3

You want to get a list of all servers that are down. To obtain this list, use the *status* property. A value of 2 indicates a healthy, running server. Any lesser value means trouble.

Type the following:

NLIST server WHERE "status" LT 2 /S

The following shows you the result of this command.

```
Object Class: server
Current context: O=EBDB
NetWare Server= The server name
Address       = The network address
Version       = The server version
Operator      = The network operator

NetWare Server                            Address  Version   Operator
------------------------------------------------------------------------------
EBDB                                    [2DA534C4]  Novell NetAdmin
One server object was found in this context.

One server object was found.
```

Example 4

You want to obtain all possible information on all objects in the tree. Type the following:

NLIST * /D /S

The following shows you the beginning of the output of this command:

```
Current context: [Root]
Top: [Root]
        Access Control List (ACL):
                Subject: Admin.EBDB
                Property:  [Object Rights]
                Entry Rights: [    S]
        Access Control List (ACL):
                Subject: [Public]
                Property:  [Object Rights]
                Entry Rights: [B    ]
        Access Control List (ACL):
                Subject: Super.EBDB
                Property:  [Object Rights]
                Entry Rights: [BCDRS]
        Convergence: 0
        Low Convergence Sync Interval:
                Days: 0  Hours: 0  Minutes: 15  Seconds: 0
        Object Class: Top
        Object Class: Partition
        Partition Creation Time: 10:28:17pm  2-05-06
        Replica:
                EBDB.EBDB
        Synchronized Up To: 12:32:50pm  4-16-94
-----------------------------------------------------------------------------
> > >  Enter = More   C = Continuous   Esc = Cancel
```

NETUSER

The NETUSER.EXE utility can be used by users for the following functions:

- ◆ Capturing printing to print queues or printers
- ◆ Sending messages to users or groups

- Mapping drive letters to directories on volumes
- Attaching to other servers
- Changing the current context

The following subsections discuss these functions.

You can exit the NETUSER utility at any time by pressing Alt+F10, or by pressing Esc from the main menu.

Capturing Printing

Before users can print on the network, you need to configure printers, queues, print servers, and so forth. Detailed procedures are covered in Chapter 28, "Printing from DOS Clients."

You can use NETUSER to redirect print jobs to a print queue or printer on the server. Before this discussion goes any further, recall the sequence of events when printing on a network. Print jobs originate at the user's workstation and are then routed to a print queue on a server. From the print queue, the print job is redirected to an assigned printer using the services of a print server. In NETUSER, you have the option of redirecting the printing from a local workstation parallel port to a network print queue or printer. If you select a printer, the job actually goes to the default queue assigned to the printer first.

To capture printing to a queue using NETUSER, perform these actions:

1. From the DOS prompt, type

   NETUSER

   Figure 14.11 displays the NETUSER main menu.

2. From the NETUSER menu, select Printing. From the Printing menu, you are shown a list of ports on your workstation. The ports listed are LPT1, LPT2, and LPT3. Select the desired port and press Enter.

3. Next a list of available options appears. The options include Print Jobs and Change Printers. Select Print Jobs to view and manage any of your print jobs currently queued to print. Select Change Printers to capture the selected port to the desired printer or queue.

   If the list of printers and queues is blank or not correct, you need to change context to the container object that contains the correct printer or queue. Press

the Insert key to change context. At this point, you can either type in the correct NDS complete name or press the Insert key a second time to browse through the tree. If you decide to browse the tree, highlight the correct context and press the F10 key to select the desired context. The selected context is displayed in the upper-left corner of the screen.

Once you have the correct context, press F10 to return to the Printers/Print Queues menu. Select the desired printer or queue and press Enter. Figure 14.12 shows the Printers/Print Queues menu.

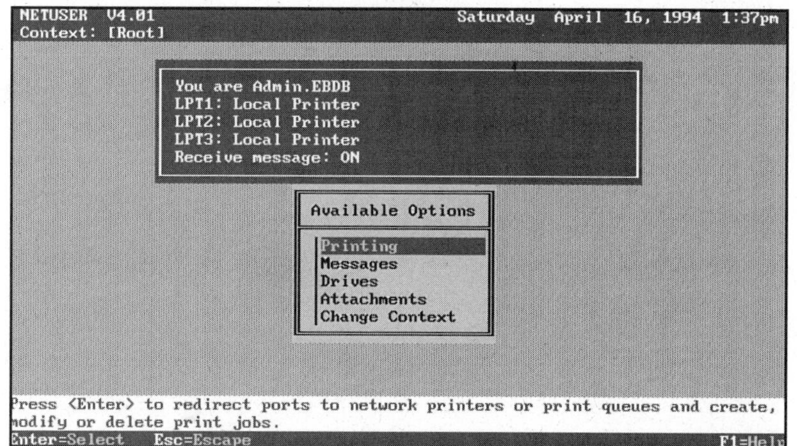

Figure 14.11

The NETUSER main menu.

Figure 14.12

The Printers/ Print Queues menu.

4. Once you have selected a printer or queue, the gray box at the top center of the screen changes to reflect your selection. You can now press Esc several times to return to the main menu.

5. To stop the print capture and return your LPT port to local printing, select Printing from the NETUSER main menu. From the Printing menu, highlight the port you want to stop the capture. Press Del. You will see a message asking you if you want to "disable LPT*x*," where *x* is 1, 2, or 3. Select Yes. This releases the port for local printing.

Sending Messages

You can use NETUSER to send messages to network users. In addition, you can send messages to groups of users or disable messaging altogether. To send a message to one or more users, perform the following actions:

1. From the NETUSER main menu, select Messages. The Available Options menu appears. The following options are possible:

    - Send Messages to Users
    - Send Messages to Groups
    - Set Receive Message: ON | OFF

2. From the Available Options menu, select Send Messages to Users. A list of current users logged in to the server appears, as shown in figure 14.13.

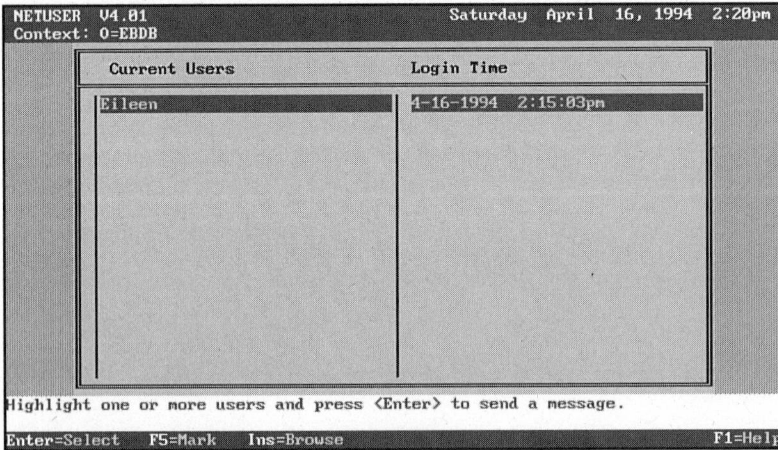

Figure 14.13
NETUSER—Send Messages to Current Users.

To send a message to a single user, highlight that user and press Enter.

To select multiple users, highlight a user and press the F5 key. Move to the next desired user, highlight that user, and again press the F5 key. Repeat this sequence until all desired users are selected. Press Enter when done.

3. When one or more users are selected, and you have pressed Enter, a message dialog box appears at the bottom of the screen. Type in your message and press Enter. The message is sent across the network and appears at the top of the screen of the recipient. When you receive a message, press Ctrl+Enter to clear the message display. Press Esc several times to return to the NETUSER main menu.

Mapping Drive Letters

NETUSER can be used to assign a drive letter to a directory on a volume. This assignment is valid only while you are logged in. To make a drive mapping permanent, issue the MAP command from your login script. The MAP command is covered in greater detail in Chapter 33, "Assigning Drive Mappings." Login scripts are covered in more detail in Chapter 34, "Creating Login Scripts."

To map a drive letter, perform these actions:

1. From the NETUSER main menu select Drives. A choice of either Drive Mapping or Search Mapping appears. The Drive Mapping option assigns a drive letter to a directory on a volume. The Search Mapping option does this as well as add the new assigned drive letter to your DOS PATH. Once added to the PATH, any application program executable in the PATH can be activated from any directory.

   Select Drive Mapping for the purposes of this exercise. A list of current drive mappings appears.

2. From the Current Drive Mappings list, press the Insert key to add a new drive letter to the list. NETUSER chooses the next available drive letter. If you want to assign another letter, use the Backspace key to erase the letter showing on screen, and then type in the desired letter.

   When you have selected the desired drive letter, press Enter. The Select Directory dialog box appears, prompting you to select a directory.

3. From the Select Directory dialog box, you can now either type in the proper NDS name of a volume and directory or press the Insert key to browse through the tree. When you have supplied the name of a volume and directory, as illustrated in figure 14.14, press Enter to finalize the selection. The Map Root dialog box appears.

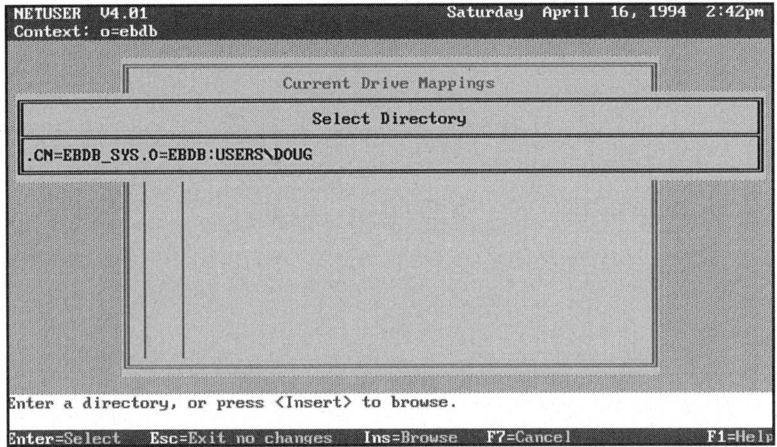

Figure 14.14
NETUSER—Select Directory dialog box.

4. The Map Root dialog box asks, "Do you want to map root this drive?" If you select Yes, NETUSER makes the selected directory appear as if it were a root directory. If you select No, you can see the directory path to the actual root of the volume. For the purposes of this exercise, select No. The new drive letter appears on the list of drive letters.

   Press Esc several times to return to the NETUSER main menu.

To remove a mapped drive letter, perform the following actions:

1. From the NETUSER main menu, select Drives. You then see a choice of either Drive Mapping or Search Mapping. Select Drive Mapping for the purposes of this exercise. A list of current drive mappings appears.

2. From the current drive mappings, select the drive mapping to remove. Press Del to remove the drive mapping from the list. Select Yes when prompted "Delete drive mapping?" Press Esc several times to return to the NETUSER main menu.

Attaching to Other File Servers

From time to time, you might want to switch to a server in another NDS tree, or even attach to a NetWare 2 or 3 server. Once attached to the other server, you can then map drive letters to directories on its volumes. The Attachments option of the NETUSER main menu enables you to do this.

To attach to another server, perform the following actions:

1. From the NETUSER main menu, select Attachments. A list of servers that are available appears. Select the desired server and press Enter. You are then prompted for a user name and password.

2. If the desired server is not on the list, press the Insert key. NETUSER searches the network for new servers. Locate the desired server on this list and press Enter. You are then prompted for a user name and password.

Changing Context

You can use both the CX and NETUSER commands to change context. Using the CX command can be difficult if you do not have intimate knowledge of your NDS tree, however. NETUSER can be used to browse the tree and change to the desired context.

To change context, follow these steps:

1. From the NETUSER main menu, select Change Context. You are presented with the Change Context dialog box prompting you to enter the desired context. At this point you can either enter in a valid NDS container name or press Insert to browse the tree. For the purposes of this discussion, press Insert. Figure 14.15 shows the screen that appears.

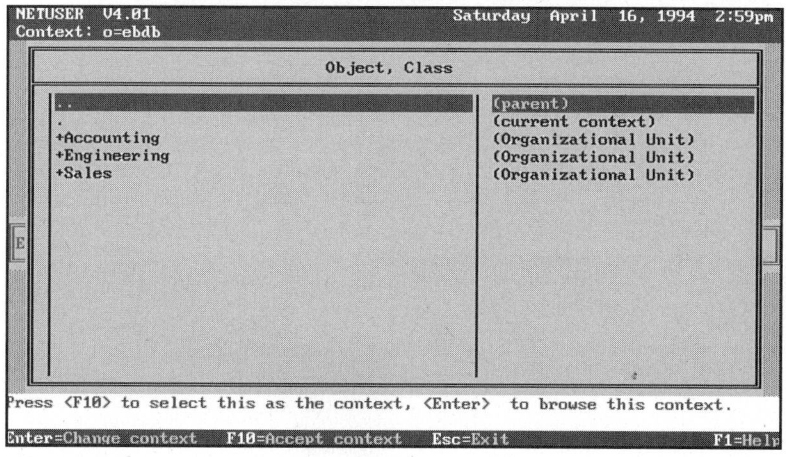

Figure 14.15
Using NETUSER to browse the NDS tree.

2. To change to the current context, highlight the single dot (.) and press the F10 key to accept. To change to a container immediately below the current context, highlight the name of that container and press the F10 key.

3. If you want to do further browsing, you can move either up or down the tree.

   To move up one level, highlight the double dots (..) and press Enter. This moves you to the parent container of your current context.

   To move down one level, highlight the name of the container you want to move down to and press Enter.

To change to that context, highlight either a container name or single dot (current container), and press the F10 key.

Summary

This chapter covered DOS client basics. It started with a discussion of issues you will encounter when installing a NIC in a client workstation. The CONFIG.SYS and PCMCIA cards in notebook computers were discussed. Following this was a discussion of the ODI drivers. You learned about the load order sequence and different options for LSL, IPXODI, and the driver for your NIC. The VLM shell architecture was discussed, along with the *.VLM files and VLM.EXE. Some parameters in the NET.CFG file pertinent to NetWare networks using the IPX protocol were also discussed.

The INSTALL program (and its options) that installs the NetWare shell software on a DOS workstation was covered. You learned how to create installation disks from the NetWare 4.1 installation CD, or how to install from an existing server. You learned exactly what files were copied by INSTALL, and into which directories.

The last part of this chapter covered various DOS utilities used during and after the login process. These utilities include LOGIN.EXE, CX.EXE, NLIST.EXE, and NETUSER.EXE. You learned what each of these utilities can do, and what options are important. LOGIN.EXE performs the initial login and authentication process. CX.EXE is used to view and change your NDS context. NLIST.EXE is used to gather information about NDS objects. NETUSER.EXE is used to redirect printing, map drive letters, send messages, and change context.

The next chapter covers Windows 3.*x* and Windows NT clients.

Windows 3.*x* and Windows NT Clients

This chapter covers the basics of installing a Microsoft Windows-based client. The versions covered in this chapter include Windows 3.1*x*, Windows for Workgroups, and Windows NT. More and more network workstations are running Windows. Surveys conducted by several computer magazines indicate that anywhere from 40 to 80 percent of all PCs attached to NetWare networks run Windows and Windows applications. Some installations use Windows 100 percent of the time.

Appendix A, "Windows: A Brief Tutorial," gives you an overview of how to operate within the Windows environment. Other chapters throughout this book cover aspects of NWADMIN.EXE, the Windows-based NetWare Administrator tool. In this chapter, you learn how to install and configure a Windows client on a NetWare network.

Understanding Windows and Windows for Workgroups

Windows is a graphical user interface that runs on top of DOS. It features extended memory management, pseudo-multitasking, a set of tools and utilities, and a common application interface.

Windows for Workgroups (WFW) is a superset of Windows. WFW includes the same interface, tools, and application interface as Windows. In addition, WFW includes peer-to-peer networking. In a peer-to-peer network, each WFW workstation contains both client and server network software. In this type of network, any WFW workstation can share files, printers, fax modems, or other resources, with other WFW workstations.

The primary disadvantages of WFW over NetWare are that (1) it runs on top of DOS, and (2) resource sharing must contend with the needs of the user sitting at that computer. DOS is not designed as a multiuser, multitasking operating system. In addition, the current versions of DOS (with the exception of Novell DOS 7) are designed for a 16-bit CPU. This means that DOS only uses 50 percent of the potential throughput of the 80386, 80486, or higher microprocessors. In an environment where a computer could be sharing files, printers, and other resources with other users, the performance of DOS is abysmal. For these and other reasons, Microsoft has announced future versions of Windows that eliminate DOS entirely and are designed to run on a 32-bit CPU.

WFW can be configured to coexist with NetWare. When WFW is installed in its "native" mode, it uses a set of network drivers that conform to the NDIS (Network Driver Interface Specification) standards. This is a specification for network adapters that is in competition with Novell's ODI standards. In addition, the networking protocols used by WFW in its "native" mode are based on the NetBEUI (NetBIOS Extended User Interface) specification. NetWare, on the other hand, uses the IPX/SPX protocol. When installing a WFW client in a NetWare network, you need to adjust the client configuration files so that the WFW workstation can accommodate both types of networks.

Installing a Windows Workstation

Installing a Windows workstation does not differ substantially from installing a DOS workstation. You need to run the workstation INSTALL program as with DOS.

To create the set of installation disks, from the server console:

1. Load INSTALL.NLM.
2. Select Product Options.
3. Select Create DOS/MS Windows/OS/2 Client Install Diskettes.
4. Select DOS/MS Windows Client Install.

The INSTALL utility will then prompt you for 5 disks. When done, you will have a working set of DOS/Windows client installation disks. These steps are covered in detail in Chapter 14, "DOS Client Basics," in the section entitled, "Creating Workstation Installation Disks."

When you are ready to install, either from floppy disks or from a directory or installation CD on a server, type INSTALL. The installation program described in the previous chapter starts. The major difference between installing DOS versus Windows support is that you need to answer "Yes" when you see the question, "Do you wish to install support for Windows?" You also need to supply the drive and path to the Windows directory. The installation program then proceeds to install the client software. Certain files are copied to the Windows directory, and certain Windows INI files are modified. These files are described in the next section.

Installing NetWare Files for Windows

The client installation program copies approximately 114 files to the Windows, SYSTEM, and the NLS directories. The NLS (Native Language Support) directory is created by the installation program. In addition to these files, the installation program modifies the WIN.INI, SYSTEM.INI, and PROGMAN.INI files. The original files are saved with the extension BNW (before NetWare).

Table 15.1 summarizes the files copied in to the Windows directories. The next section discusses modifications made to the Windows INI files. The table assumes a default Windows directory of C:\WINDOWS. If this is not the case on your system, substitute the appropriate directory.

Table 15.1
Windows Files Copied by the DOS/Windows Client Installation Program

Directory	File Name	Description
C:\WINDOWS	NETWARE.INI	Contains settings for the NWUSER.EXE utility.
	NOVELL.BMP	Novell logo. Appears as a 3D image of the Novell logo that appears to be carved in a granite slab on a marble floor.
	NOVLOGO1.BMP	Novell logo. 3D with a gray background.
	NWADMIN.INI	Contains settings for the NWADMIN.EXE utility. This feature, new with NetWare 4.1, causes NWADMIN to remember where you left off, and restores the utility to that state the next time you use it.
	NWRCON.PIF	A program information file (PIF) for the RCONSOLE.EXE utility.
	NW.GRP	NetWare Windows Program Manager group.
C:\WINDOWS\NLS		This directory contains native language support.
	UNI	Files with "UNI" in the filename are for *unicode* support. The *_UNI.??? files correspond with different code pages used for the proper display of characters. The file 850_UNI.033, for example, translates code page 850, country code 33 (France),

Directory	File Name	Description
		to unicode. File UNI_850.033 translates unicode to code page 850, country code 33. The UNI_MON.??? files handle monocasing (upper and lower case letters in different words), and the UNI_COL.??? files are for sorted lists.
C:\WINDOWS\NLS\ *language*		There will be a *language* directory (i.e. ENGLISH) that corresponds with the language setting for the workstation.
	NETWARE.HLP	General help for NetWare shell.
	NETWARER.DRV	NetWare Requester driver for Windows.
	TASKID.MSG	*language* text file for TASKID.COM (described below).
	TBMI2.MSG	*language* text file for TBMI2.COM (described below).
C:\WINDOWS\SYSTEM	NETWARE.DRV	NetWare shell driver.
	NETWARE.HLP	Same file as in the NLS*language* directory.
	NWCALLS.DLL	General NetWare API (Application Program Interface) calls library.
	NWGDI.DLL	NetWare device interface library.
	NWIPXSPX.DLL	IPX/SPX protocol library.

continues

Table 15.1, Continued
Windows Files Copied by the DOS/Windows Client Installation Program

Directory	File Name	Description
	NWLOCALE.DLL	Library that pertains to various locale-specific information. Locale settings include such considerations as time and date formats, representation of currency, and allowable characters in a file name.
	NWNET.DLL	NetWare network API library.
	NWPOPUP.EXE	Utility to display broadcast messages as a Windows dialog box.
	NWPSRV.DLL	Print Services API library.
	NWUSER.EXE	NetWare User Tools utility.
	PNW.DLL	Personal NetWare library (for peer-to-peer networking—outside of Windows for Workgroups).
	TASKID.COM	This is used for Windows 3.0 only. You must first load TBMI2.COM prior to starting Windows. See the circumstances where this utility is needed (see TBMI2.COM below). When you open a DOS session, run TASKID. This installs a task identifier that TBMI2 can use to control the flow of IPX/SPX information out of the network interface card. When the DOS session is over, unload TASKID and exit back to Windows.

Directory	File Name	Description
	TBMI2.COM	Task Buffer Manager Interface. This is started before you enter Windows under the following circumstances: 1. Your application bypasses the shell and makes direct calls to IPX/SPX, *and* 2. You are running Windows in standard mode (or real mode in 3.0), *and* 3. You plan to switch between multiple DOS sessions.
	TLI_SPX.DLL	Windows Dynamic Link Library containing SPX function calls for the workstation Transport Layer Interface. Works with the NetWare IPX/SPX protocol stack.
	TLI_TCP.DLL	Windows Dynamic Link Library containing TCP function calls for the workstation Transport Layer Interface. Works with the NetWare/IP protocol stack.
	TLI_WIN.DLL	Windows Dynamic Link Library containing general NetWare function calls for the workstation Transport Layer Interface.
	VIPX.386	Virtual IPX driver with support for Windows's 386 Enhanced Mode.
	VNETWARE.386	Virtual NetWare driver with support for Windows's 386 Enhanced Mode.

Modifying Windows INI Files for NetWare

The client installation program makes certain changes to the Windows INI files specified above. The original copies of these files are saved in the Windows directory with the extension .BNW. Changes to the WIN.INI file include the following:

```
[Network]
```

This section is where permanent drive mappings and printer assignments are stored. These assignments can be made through the NWUSER.EXE (NetWare User Tools) utility. Once you have mapped permanent drive letters and made permanent printer assignments, the [Network] section of WIN.INI might look like this:

```
[Network]
F:=\\EBDB\SYS \
G:=\\EBDB\NW410DOC \
LPT1:=\\EBDB\.CN=Q_Main.O=EBDB
LPT1-OPTIONS=8,1,8,10,0,Admin,LST:,16,0
```

In the preceding example, drives F and G are assigned to different volumes on server EBDB. LPT1: is captured to .Q_Main.EBDB. The options you see are encoded and represent autoendcap, timeout=10 seconds, no banner, and no form feed.

Under the [Windows] section, a command to load the NWPOPUP.EXE utility is added:

```
[Windows]
load= nwpopup.exe
```

Changes to the PROGMAN.INI file include the addition of a new group, NetWare Tools:

```
Group9=C:\WINDOWS\NW.GRP
```

Changes to the SYSTEM.INI file are summarized in table 15.2.

Table 15.2
SYSTEM.INI Changes by the DOS/Windows Client Installation Program

Section	Command	Description
[boot]	network.drv=netware.drv	Initializes the basic NetWare driver for Windows.

Section	Command	Description
[boot. description]	network.drv=Novell NetWare (v4.0)	Indicates which version of NetWare.
[386Enh]	network=*vnetbios, vipx.386, vnetware.386	Sets up virtual device for NetBIOS emulation. Also initializes virtual device support for IPX and NetWare in Windows 386 Enhanced Mode.
	TimerCriticalSection =10000	Specifies the amount of time in milliseconds before Windows is allowed to interrupt it. Decrease this value if network performance is not reliable. If you set the value to 0, the code that handles timer interrupts is not considered critical.
	ReflectDOSInt2A=*TRUE*	INT 2A is used primarily by NetBIOS applications. A setting of *TRUE* causes Windows to pass through interrupt 2A signals. You can set this to false if you are not using NetBIOS applications or your NetBIOS applications use INT 5C.
	OverlappedIO=*OFF*	When set to *OFF*, this parameter prevents Windows from placing I/O requests from more than one application on the disk I/O channel. This results in greater stability and data integrity, but slows performance. You might try experimenting by setting this value to *ON*. If users complain of corrupted data files, set the value to *OFF*.

continues

Table 15.2, Continued
SYSTEM.INI Changes by the DOS/Windows Client Installation Program

Section	Command	Description
	UniqueDOSPSP=*TRUE*	When set to *TRUE*, causes Windows to start each DOS virtual machine at a unique memory address. This allows the networking software to use each program's load address as an identifier.
	PSPIncrement=5	Tells Windows to reserve additional memory for each successive virtual DOS machine in increments of 5 16-byte blocks. This value is only used if UniqueDOSPSP is set to *TRUE*.

Deciding Whether To Install Windows Locally or on the Server?

One of the biggest debates in the networking industry is whether or not to install Windows on network servers. Advantages and disadvantages exist for each approach. This section presents you with some of the pros and cons.

Installing Windows Locally

In this option, you perform Windows installations on the local hard drives of workstations on the network.

Advantages:

- ◆ You have operational capabilities even if the network is down.
- ◆ Network traffic is minimized because Windows, and its numerous overlay files, are located on local hard drives.

- You can create a permanent swap file, which is much more efficient than a temporary swap file.
- It is advantageous for users with portable computers. For those users with notebook or other portable computers that go back and forth between the office and the field, a local Windows installation works best.

Disadvantages:

- Local Windows installation requires each workstation to have a hard drive with sufficient room to load Windows *and* the swap file.
- It is difficult to manage local Windows installations. If you want to make a global change, you must reconfigure each workstation independently.
- It is difficult to support local Windows installations. Users can customize their Windows desktops to a considerable degree. When you or your support organization attempts to help a user, you end up having to learn how that user has set up his or her desktop before giving support. This problem can be mitigated by purchasing some sort of Windows desktop control program. These include the Saber Menu for Windows or Norton Desktop.

Installing Windows on a NetWare Server

Please note that for the purposes of this section, installing Windows on a server refers to performing individual installations for the various computers in your organization, and actually storing the WIN.COM, INI, and GRP files, and so forth, on a server rather than on the local hard drive.

Advantages:

- It is easier to support large numbers of Windows users. Because the Windows files are on the server, you can make any changes or upgrades from one location rather than having to physically go around to the various workstations.
- You gain better security. Files on the server are protected through file and directory trustee rights assignments.
- Server installation makes use of file caching on the server. When Windows files are located on the server, font files, overlay files, and other Windows files are cached by the server before being distributed to workstations on the LAN. Over a period of time, most of the heavily used Windows files will be cached giving network users excellent response time when using Windows.

Disadvantages:

- You cannot have a permanent swap file on the server. The only option is to create a temporary swap file. This increases the time it takes to load Windows since the temporary swap file is created each time you go in to Windows.
- If you designate a temporary swap file on the server, considerable network traffic is introduced. Swapping to and from the permanent or temporary swap file occurs when the RAM required by the application's users' run exceeds the amount of RAM they have installed. When the swap file is located on the server, swapping occurs over the LAN, vastly increasing the amount of traffic. The solution is to specify a swap file on local hard drives.

You can mix server and local workstation Windows installations. You also can perform a SETUP /A operation that stores *all* Windows files in expanded format on a directory on the server. Once you have done a SETUP /A, you can perform Windows installations from this directory on either local workstation hard drives or to directories on servers.

As you can see, there are arguments that favor either situation. In the end, you have to make a decision which advantage or disadvantage is most compelling. In many cases, you end up with a mixture of both techniques.

Configuring Windows for Workgroups

Windows for Workgroups brings peer-to-peer connectivity to a NetWare network. The advantage to this arrangement is that you can share files and other resources between local workstations, as well as with the server. File access and transfer are slow with Windows for Workgroups. You can always shift critical files and applications to the server to enhance access speed. This section addresses how to configure a Windows for Workgroups client to access both NetWare and local resources.

Initial Installation Considerations

During the installation of Windows for Workgroups, the SETUP utility asks you for information on your network following the printer installation phase. The Network Setup screen appears, as shown in figure 15.1 (with the Advanced button pressed). If you start the installation with the NetWare drivers already loaded, the system reports that it has added support for Novell NetWare (Workstation Shell *xxx* and above) where *xxx* is the version of NetWare you are using. If you do not have NetWare drivers loaded, you have to click on the Networks button and specify Novell NetWare. Click on the Continue button to configure your network adapter.

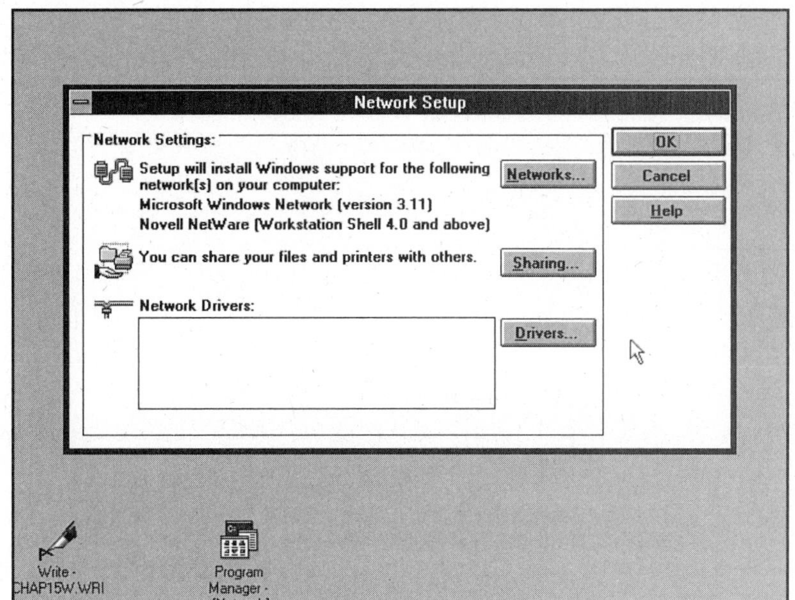

Figure 15.1

The Network Setup screen in Windows for Workgroups.

A warning message appears, warning you that you must install a NetWare/Windows driver (see fig.15.2). Click on the **Y**es button to proceed.

You now need to specify where the Windows/NetWare driver NETWARE.DRV is located. If you have the NetWare DOS/Windows client disks ready, enter drive A in the field prompting you for a path. Otherwise, if the NetWare Client for DOS and Windows is already installed, the file is already located in C:\WINDOWS\SYSTEM. This screen is illustrated in figure 15.3. Use the Sca**n** button to have SETUP locate the file for you on your hard drive. Use the **B**rowse button to manually locate the file.

The Windows for Workgroups setup utility might change the C:\WINDOWS\SYSTEM\NETWARE.DRV driver that the NetWare DOS/Windows Client installation installs. If you cannot access the NetWare User Tools, this is most likely the case. Reinstall the NetWare Client software. Specify the C:\TEMP directory as the target to install the software. If you specify the default C:\NWCLIENT, you end up having to answer a series of prompts warning you that the client files already exist. If the installation routine warns you about replacing the NETWARE.DRV or VNETWARE.386 files, allow it to replace whatever file is in the C:\WINDOWS\SYSTEM directory with the file supplied with the NetWare Client installation files (enter Yes when asked Replace File (Yes/No)?).

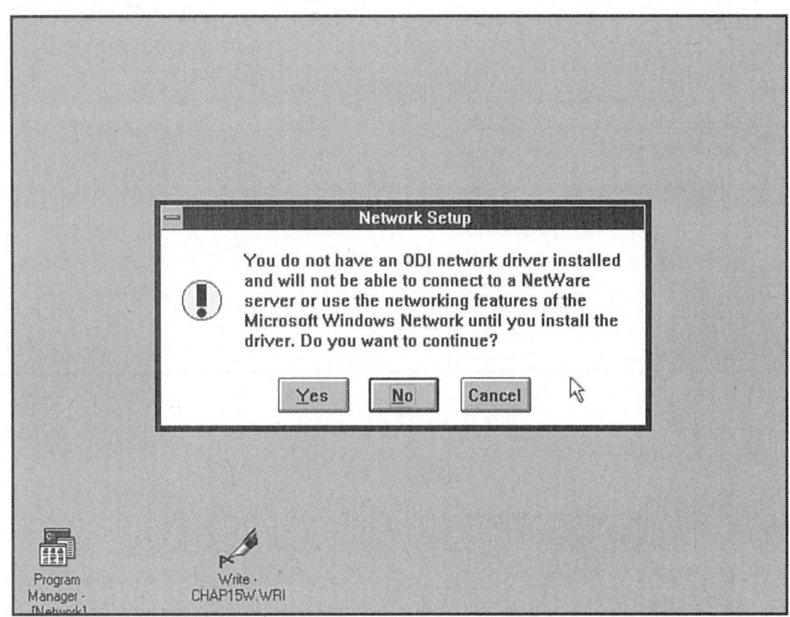

Figure 15.2
A warning message appears during Network setup.

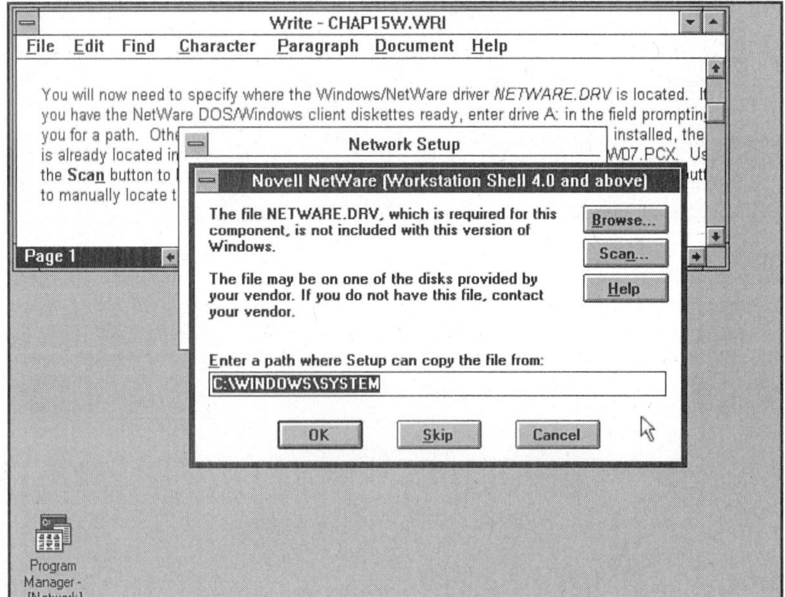

Figure 15.3
Specifying the location of the NETWARE.DRV driver.

Changes Made to Configuration Files

Installing or upgrading to Windows for Workgroups entails changes made to certain configuration files. The files changed include CONFIG.SYS, AUTOEXEC.BAT, NET.CFG, SYSTEM.INI, and the addition of a new file, PROTOCOL.INI. This section presents examples of these files. In the examples, the changes made appear in bold.

CONFIG.SYS

Certain changes are made to your CONFIG.SYS file. These include diverting any references to drivers such as HIMEM.SYS to the Windows for Workgroups directory. Windows for Workgroups includes drivers more current than the ones available under MS DOS 6.*x*. Also added is a command to load the IFSHLP.SYS, an interface support driver.

```
DEVICE=C:\DOS\SETVER.EXE
DEVICE=C:\WFW\HIMEM.SYS
DOS=HIGH
FILES=40
BUFFERS=10,0
SHELL=C:\DOS\COMMAND.COM /P /E:2048
STACKS=9,256
LASTDRIVE=Z
DEVICE=C:\WFW\IFSHLP.SYS
```

AUTOEXEC.BAT

Here are the changes made to your AUTOEXEC.BAT file:

```
C:\WFW\net start
@ECHO OFF
C:\WFW\SMARTDRV.EXE /X
C:\DOS\DOSKEY /INSERT
PROMPT $P$G
PATH C:\WFW;C:\DOS;C:\WINDOWS;C:\MOUSE;C:\NWCLIENT
SET TEMP=C:\DOS
SET COMSPEC=C:\DOS\COMMAND.COM
c:\MOUSE\MOUSE.COM CENHANCE
rem WIN
@CALL C:\NWCLIENT\STARTNET
C:\WFW\odihlp.exe
```

In this sample AUTOEXEC.BAT file, the NET START command starts up the local peer-to-peer Windows for Workgroups network. The new version of SMARTDRV.EXE is located in the Windows for Workgroups directory. This new version is a vast improvement over the older version. The new SMARTDRV can improve the speed of disk reads and writes by up to 50 percent. Another new driver that is loaded is ODIHLP.EXE. This driver provides support for the Windows for Workgroups local network over the Novell ODI drivers.

SYSTEM.INI

Here are the changes made to your SYSTEM.INI file:

```
[boot]
shell=progman.exe
network.drv=wfwnet.drv
mouse.drv=mouse.drv
language.dll=
sound.drv=mmsound.drv
comm.drv=comm.drv
keyboard.drv=keyboard.drv
system.drv=system.drv
386grabber=vga.3gr
oemfonts.fon=vgaoem.fon
fixedfon.fon=vgafix.fon
fonts.fon=vgasys.fon
display.drv=vga.drv
drivers=mmsystem.dll
secondnet.drv=netware.drv

[keyboard]
subtype=
type=4
keyboard.dll=
oemansi.bin=

[boot.description]
keyboard.typ=Enhanced 101 or 102 key US and Non US keyboards
mouse.drv=Microsoft, or IBM PS/2
language.dll=English (American)
system.drv=MS-DOS System
codepage=437
```

```
woafont.fon=English (437)
aspect=100,96,96
display.drv=VGA
network.drv=Microsoft Windows Network (version 3.11)
secondnet.drv=Novell NetWare (Workstation Shell 4.0 and above)

[386Enh]
device=*vpd
mouse=*vmd
ebios=*ebios
woafont=dosapp.fon
display=*vddvga
EGA80WOA.FON=EGA80WOA.FON
EGA40WOA.FON=EGA40WOA.FON
CGA80WOA.FON=CGA80WOA.FON
CGA40WOA.FON=CGA40WOA.FON
keyboard=*vkd
network=*vnetbios,*vwc,vnetsup.386,vredir.386,vserver.386
netheapsize=20
device=*vcd
device=*vpicd
device=*vtd
device=*reboot
device=*vdmad
device=*vsd
device=*v86mmgr
device=*pageswap
device=*dosmgr
device=*vmpoll
device=*wshell
device=*PAGEFILE
device=*BLOCKDEV
device=*vfd
device=*parity
device=*biosxlat
device=*vmcpd
device=*combuff
device=*cdpscsi
device=vtdapi.386
device=vpmtd.386
device=vcomm.386
```

```
device=serial.386
device=lpt.386
device=ifsmgr.386
device=vcache.386
device=vshare.386
local=CON
FileSysChange=off
COM3Irq=4
COM3Base=03E8
COM4Irq=3
COM4Base=02E8
PagingFile=C:\WFW\WIN386.SWP
MaxPagingFileSize=53248
InDOSPolling=FALSE
secondnet=vnetware.386
OverlappedIO=off
TimerCriticalSection=10000
ReflectDOSInt2A=TRUE
UniqueDOSPSP=TRUE
PSPIncrement=5
netmisc=ndis.386,msodisup.386
transport=nwlink.386,nwnblink.386,netbeui.386

[NonWindowsApp]
localtsrs=dosedit,ced

[vcache]
minfilecache=512

[mci]
WaveAudio=mciwave.drv
Sequencer=mciseq.drv
CDAudio=mcicda.drv

[drivers]
timer=timer.drv
midimapper=midimap.drv

[DDEShares]
CHAT$=winchat,chat,,31,,0,,0,0,0
SCHAT$=winchat,chat,,31,,0,,0,0,0
```

```
CLPBK$=clipsrv,system,,31,,0,,0,0,0
HEARTS$=mshearts,hearts,,15,,0,,0,0,0

[Network]
winnet=wfwnet/00025100
multinet=netware4
FileSharing=Yes
PrintSharing=Yes
LogonDisconnected=Yes
EnableSharing=Yes
PreferredRedir=FULL
UserName=DOUG2
Workgroup=EDUCATION
ComputerName=DOUG2
Comment=Doug Bierer

[NetWare]
NWShareHandles=FALSE
RestoreDrives=TRUE

[network drivers]
devdir=C:\WFW
LoadRMDrivers=No

[Password Lists]
*Shares=C:\WFW\Share000.PWL

[NWNBLINK]
LANABASE=1
```

Note that the changes to the SYSTEM.INI file pertain to the "first" network, which is the local Windows for Workgroups network, and the "second" network, which is the NetWare network.

PROTOCOL.INI

The new file PROTOCOL.INI is created during the installation or upgrade process. This file details what LAN adapters are installed and how the various protocols are to be handled. You will note that in the example used in this section, the Novell ODI drivers are used as a base. Two protocols are then stacked on top of the ODI drivers.

The IPX/SPX protocol is used for NetWare connectivity. The NetBEUI protocol is used for connectivity between Windows for Workgroup peers.

```
[network.setup]
version=0x3110
netcard=ms$ne2000,1,MS$NE2000,4
transport=ms$nwlinknb,NWLINK
transport=ms$netbeui,NETBEUI
lana0=ms$ne2000,1,ms$netbeui
lana1=ms$ne2000,1,ms$nwlinknb

[net.cfg]
PATH=C:\NWCLIENT\NET.CFG


[MS$NE2000]

[Link Driver NE2000]
data=Frame Ethernet_SNAP
data=Frame Ethernet_802.2
data=Frame Ethernet_II
data=Frame Ethernet_802.3

[NWLINK]

BINDINGS=NE2000
[NETBEUI]
BINDINGS=NE2000
LANABASE=0
SESSIONS=10
NCBS=12
```

NET.CFG

Here are the changes made to your NET.CFG file:

```
Link Driver NE2000
  Frame Ethernet_802.3
  Frame Ethernet_II
  Frame Ethernet_802.2
  Frame Ethernet_SNAP
```

```
        PORT 280
        INT 10
        MEM D0000
        FRAME Ethernet_802.2

NetWare DOS Requester
        FIRST NETWORK DRIVE = F
        PREFERRED SERVER = CLASS2-4X
        NAME CONTEXT = "O=NOVELL"
```

You will note from the example that the Windows for Workgroups installation program indiscriminately adds all four Ethernet frame types to the NET.CFG file, even though the desired frame type, Ethernet_802.2, has already been assigned. The four frame types added are in boldface type. The unwanted protocols have to be deleted to make the system work.

If left as is, the IPXODI driver would bind the IPX/SPX protocol to the Ethernet_802.3 frame type. Because the server defaults to Ethernet_802.2, unless you specified the Ethernet_802.3 frame type on the server manually, your workstation would never find the server.

Modifying the Windows for Workgroup Configuration

To modify the Windows for Workgroups network setup, proceed as follows:

1. From Program Manager, select the Network Program Group.
2. Select the Network Setup icon. The Network Setup dialog box appears, as illustrated in figure 15.4.
3. Select the Networks button to configure support for NetWare. The Networks dialog box appears, as shown in figure 15.5. Under Install Microsoft Windows Network select Other. Press the down arrow on the Other drop down box. Select the version of the NetWare shell most appropriate for your situation. For a NetWare 4.1 network, select Novell NetWare (Workstation Shell 4.0 and above). Although the workstation shell is actually revision 1.2, Shell 4.0 refers to the version of NetWare.

   If you only want to add support for NetWare, click on the Install Windows support for the following network only button, and indicate Novell NetWare (Workstation Shell 4.0 and above).

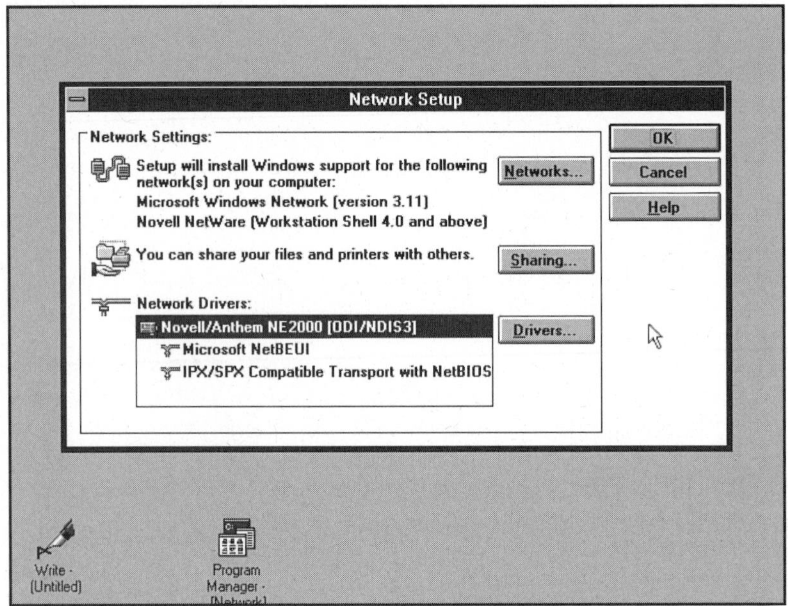

Figure 15.4

The Network Setup dialog box.

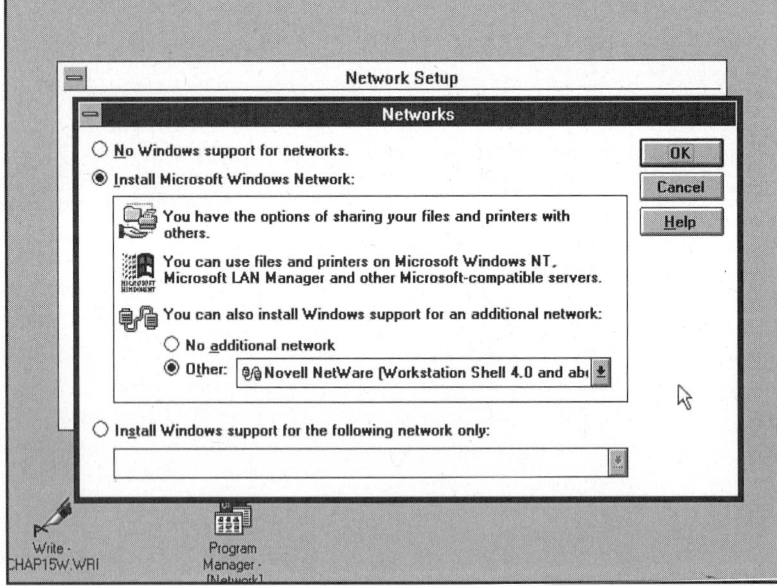

Figure 15.5

The Networks dialog box.

4. Click on OK when done. You then return to the Network Setup dialog box. To configure the network drivers, click the Drivers button. The Network Drivers dialog box appears, as indicated in figure 15.6.

   If you have no network adapters specified, click on the Add Adapter button. The Add Network Adapter list appears. Select the driver from the list that corresponds with your adapter and click on the OK button. Use the Detect option for adapters that are self-configuring or can be set through software.

   To add support for NetWare, be sure to select the IPX/SPX protocol. If you do not see IPX/SPX listed in the Network Drivers box, click on the Add Protocol button. The Add Network Protocol dialog box appears. Select the IPX/SPX Compatible Transport protocol for a standard NetWare network. Select the IPX/SPX Compatible Transport with NetBIOS protocol where you need NetBIOS support. Select either of these two protocols and click on the OK button when done.

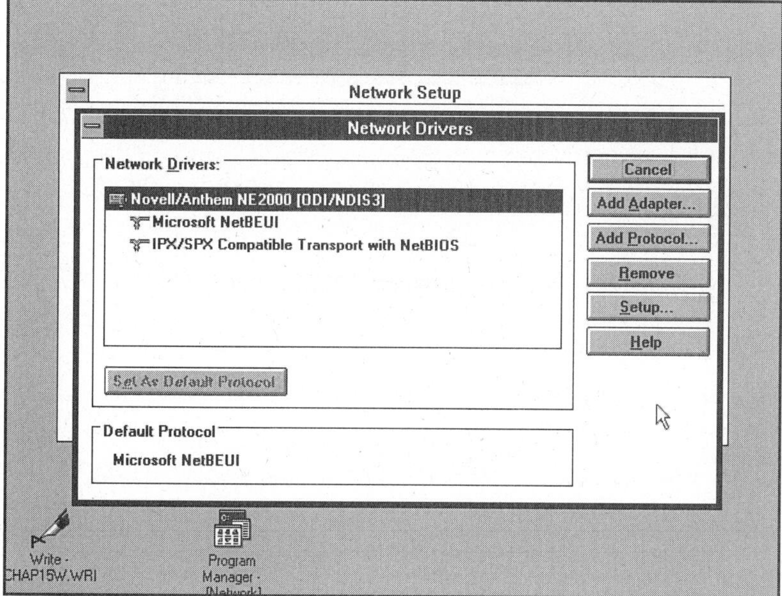

Figure 15.6
The Network Drivers dialog box.

The Detect option does not work with all adapters and might cause your machine to crash. Unfortunately there is no way to determine if your machine will crash in advance. Be sure to save any work in any other applications open at this time before proceeding.

5. To configure the network adapter, select the network adapter in the Network Drivers dialog box. Click on the Setup button. A dialog box specific to the network driver appears, as shown in figure 15.7. In the Hardware Settings box, select the appropriate Interrupt, Base I/O Port, and Base Memory Address. Other settings might appear depending on the type of network adapter in your computer. For network cards that can be configured through software, the setting might appear as Automatic or Unused.

   Select Driver Type to configure the network adapter for NDIS or ODI. Select ODI Driver for best performance in the NetWare environment. Other Windows for Workgroups workstations will be able to communicate together as long as they also use the same driver type.

Figure 15.7

An example of a specific network driver dialog box.

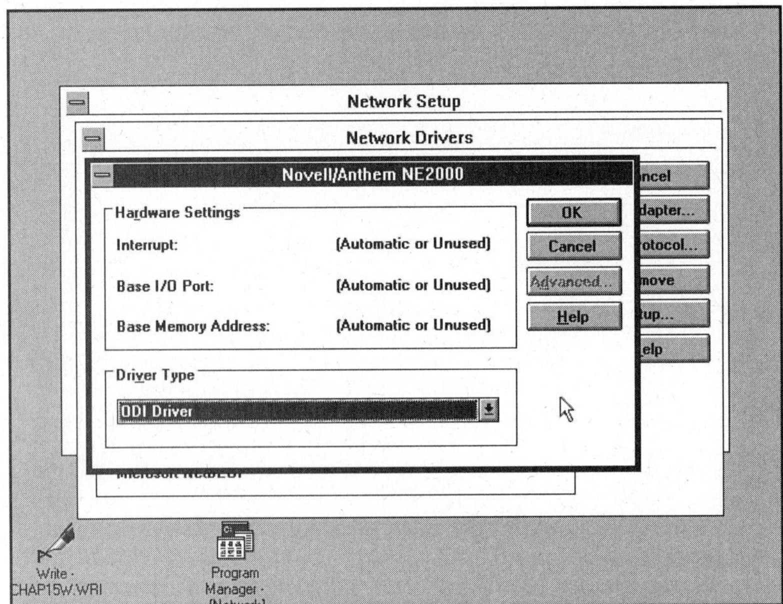

6. To configure the protocol, select the protocol in the Network Drivers dialog box. Click on the Setup button. A dialog box specific to the protocol appears, as shown in figure 15.8. When finished, click on the OK button.

7. When you are done configuring network drivers, select Close. Select OK to exit the Network Setup dialog box. You are notified that the following files are modified: NET.CFG, SYSTEM.INI, and PROTOCOL.INI. Old versions of these files are saved under the same prefix, with a 3 digit number for the file extension. The numbering starts at "001" and increments with each successive change. If you have made three changes, for example, the last saved version will have an extension "003."

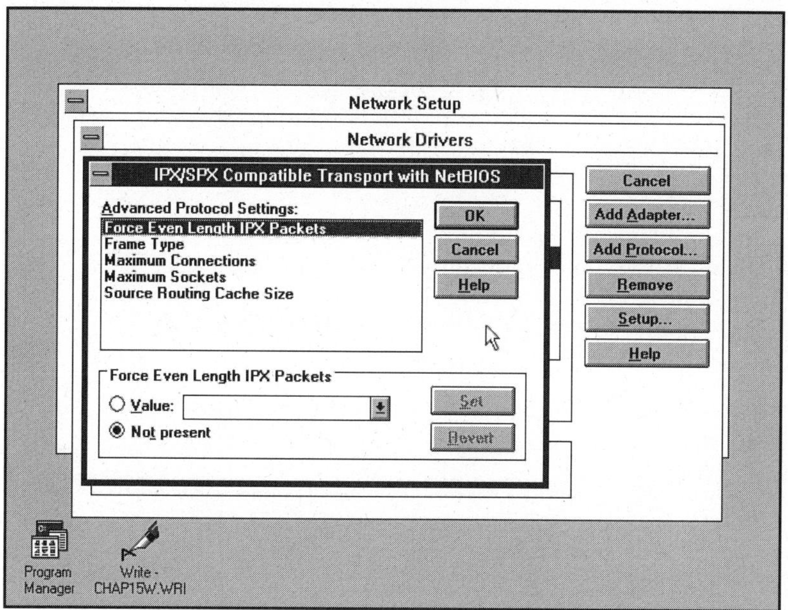

Figure 15.8

An example of a specific protocol setup dialog box.

8. To make changes effective, you need to reboot your computer. The Make Changes Effective dialog box gives you this option. Make sure all other windows are closed and all files are saved. From the Make Changes Effective dialog box click on Restart Computer to reboot.

When you finish installing and configuring Windows for Workgroups, you can access shared files on other Windows for Workgroups workstations or NetWare servers. Figure 15.9 shows the Connect Network Drive dialog box in the Windows for Workgroups File Manager. When you click on the NetWare button to access drives on NetWare servers, you are taken to the NetWare User Tools (NWUSER.EXE) utility. Figure 15.10 shows you the File Manager window where the following drive connections are displayed using tiled windows:

E:	\\DOUG2\WINDOWS	Windows for Workgroups Shared Directory
F:	\\\CLASS2-4X_SYS\...	Directory on a NetWare server
C:	C:\WFW	Local Hard Drive

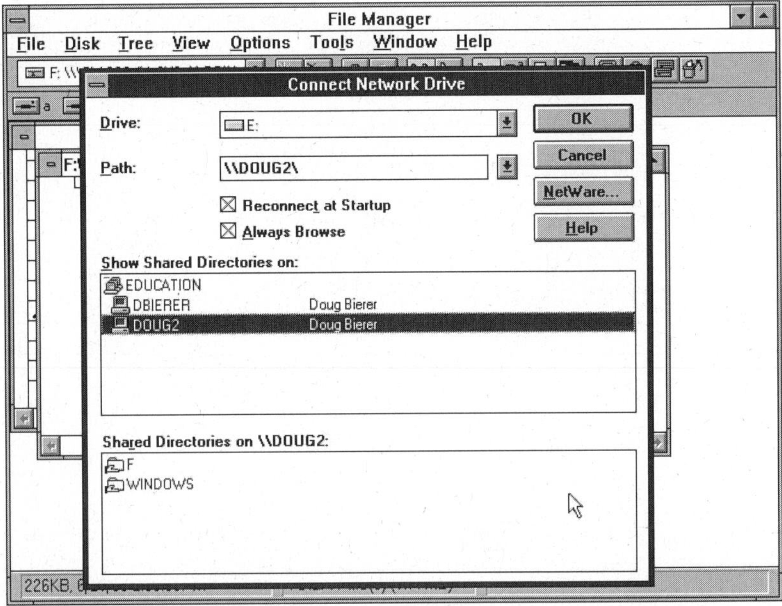

Figure 15.9

The Connect Network Drive dialog box.

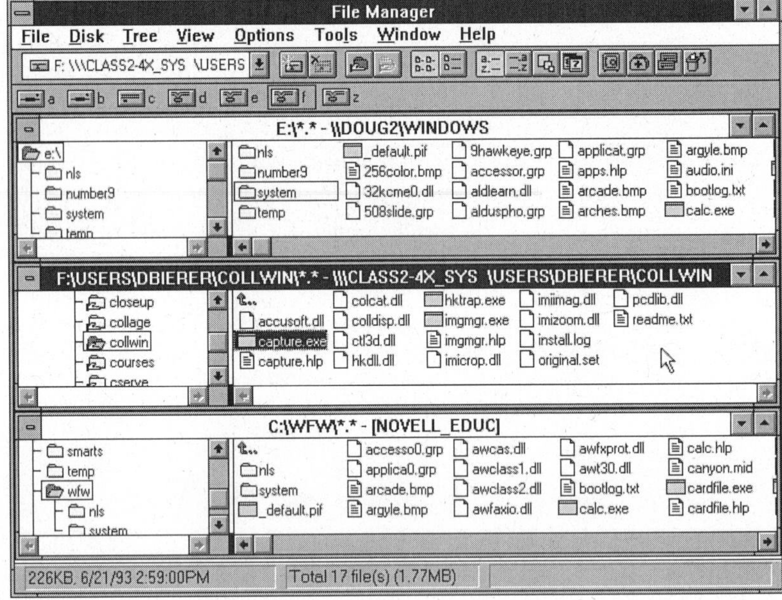

Figure 15.10

The File Manager window showing local and network drives.

Using NWUSER—the Windows Workstation Utility

The NWUSER.EXE utility, also called the User Tools or NetWare User Tools utility, was first introduced in NetWare 4.1.0. It is the successor to the NetWare Windows Workstation Toolkit introduced several years ago. This utility enables you to perform the following functions, all from within Windows:

- Drive mapping
- Print capture
- Log in and log out from NDS trees and bindery-based servers
- Send messages to other users
- Set various network settings

This utility is placed by default in to the NetWare Tools program group that is created after the Windows workstation client installation. You can move the icon in to another program group if that is more convenient. The NWUSER main menu is illustrated in figure 15.11.

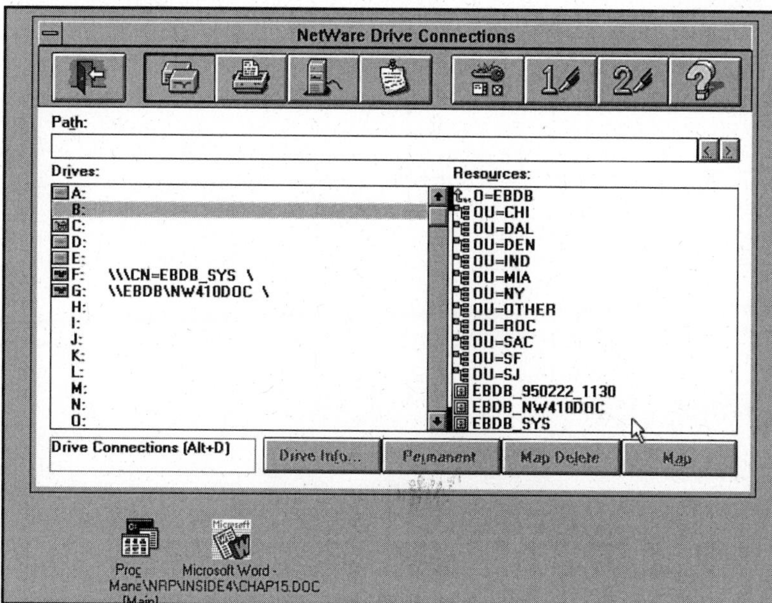

Figure 15.11

The NWUSER.EXE main menu.

Table 15.3 lists the action buttons available on the toolbar of the NWUSER utility, their function, and the hotkey that can be used to access them.

Table 15.3
NWUSER Action Buttons

Button	Hotkey	Description
	Alt+X	Exit
	Alt+D	Drive mappings
	Alt+P	Print capture
	Alt+C	Network connections (logins and logouts)
	Alt+M	Sending messages
	Alt+S	Network settings
	Alt+1	User-defined button #1
	Alt+2	User-defined button #2
	Alt+H	Help

Note that as you move the mouse pointer across these action buttons, the text in the box in the lower left corner of the main menu changes to reflect the action of that particular button. When you actually "press" a button by clicking once on it, the previously selected button is "raised." Once a button is pressed, the action buttons on the bottom change to reflect the currently selected action.

Mapping Drive Letters

To map a drive letter to a directory, first click once on the Drive Map action button, or press Alt+D. The NetWare Drive Connections dialog box appears, as was illustrated in figure 15.11. To map a drive letter, proceed as follows:

1. Select the desired drive letter in the Drives list box at the left side of the NetWare Drive Connections dialog box. If the desired drive letter is not shown, use the PgDn key or use the mouse to scroll down until the target drive letter is in view. Move the pointer to the drive letter and click once to select the drive letter.

2. In the Resources list box, locate the desired volume object. If necessary, double-click on container objects to expand your view so you can locate volume objects. Use the PgUp or PgDn keys, or use the mouse, to scroll up and down the tree. You can select the ".." entry to move to the next container level up the tree. Double-click on volume objects to expand the view to include directories on volumes.

3. As you continue to select items from the Resources list box, you will see the Path field change at the top of the NetWare Drive Connections dialog box. The path includes three backslashes (\\\) and the name of the volume object. Directories on the volume are separated by a backslash (\). Use the left arrow button located after the Path field to move the location of the root down towards the root of the volume. Use the right arrow button located after the Path field to move the location of the root away from the root of the volume. By default, the drive mapping performs a MAP ROOT operation.

When you map drive letters using the NWUSER utility, the root of the drive letter appears to be starting at the directory you specified. This is the equivalent of a MAP ROOT operation from the command line. To create a drive mapping that is not a fake root, use the left arrow button located to the right of the Path field. Click several times on the mouse button until a space appears immediately after the volume name.

4. Click once on the Map action button to finalize the drive mapping. You also can use the keyboard and press Alt+A.

Once the drive mapping operation is completed, you can click on the Drive Info action button to view your effective trustee rights to this directory and information regarding the location of the directory. The Permanent button records the drive mapping in the WIN.INI file. When you next go in to Windows, this drive mapping is in effect. A small red line appears on the drive map icon indicating a permanent drive mapping.

If you map a permanent drive mapping and go in to Windows without first logging in to the network, Windows actually prompts you for a username and password. If you use this technique, the system does not run any login scripts. You must rely on *permanent* drive mappings and print captures to give you access to network resources.

Use the Map Delete button to remove an unwanted drive mapping. If you click on the Map button again, the currently selected drive letter is re-mapped according to the current path.

The NetWare Drive Connections dialog box does not enable you to define search drive mappings. You have to either open a DOS prompt to create the mapping using the MAP command or define the search drive mapping prior to getting in to Windows. After the search drive mapping has been created from the DOS prompt, you can return to NWUSER and mark this mapping permanent. The drive icon for a search drive has tiny eyeglasses.

Capturing to Printers

To capture a printer port, first click once on the Printer Connections action button, or press Alt+P. The NetWare Printer Connections dialog box appears, as illustrated in figure 15.12.

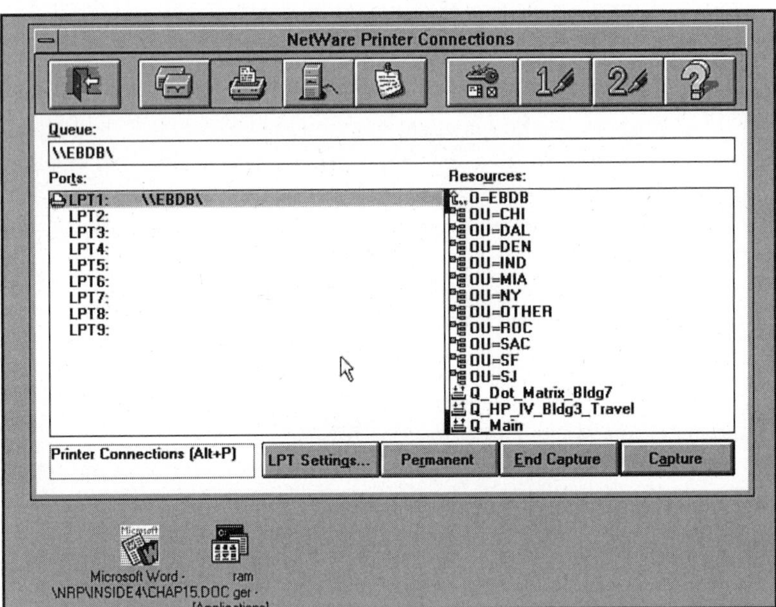

Figure 15.12 *The NWUSER.EXE NetWare Printer Connections dialog box.*

To capture a printer port, proceed as follows:

1. Select the desired printer port in the Ports list box at the left side of the NetWare Printer Connections dialog box. Click once to select the printer port.

2. In the Resources list box, locate the desired print queue. If necessary, double-click on container objects to expand your view so that you can locate print queues. Use the PgUp or PgDn keys, or use the mouse, to scroll up and down the tree. You can select the ".." entry to move to the next container level up the tree.

3. As you select items from the Resources list box, you will see the **Q**ueue field change at the top of the NetWare Printer Connections dialog box. The queue has three backslashes (\\\) and the name of the print queue.

4. Click once on the Capture action button to finalize the print capture. You also can use the keyboard and press Alt+A.

The Permanent button records the print capture in the WIN.INI file. When you next go in to Windows, this print capture is in effect. A printer icon appears next to the port indicating a "permanent" print capture. Use the **E**nd Capture button to remove any unwanted print captures. If you click on the Capture button again, the currently selected printer port is re-captured according to the current queue.

To adjust printer settings, click on the LPT Settings button. The NetWare Settings for LPT*x* dialog box appears, as shown in figure 15.13. The *x* is the number of the port you have captured.

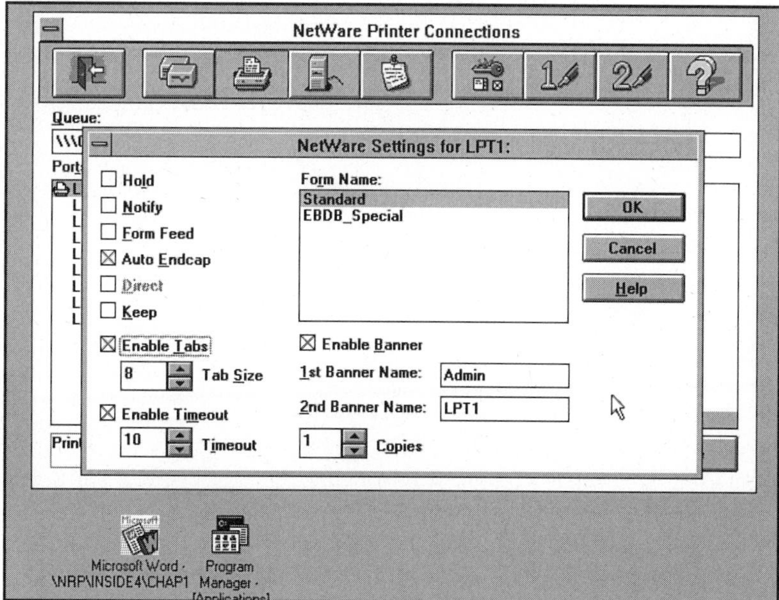

Figure 15.13
*The NWUSER.EXE NetWare Settings for LPT*x *dialog box.*

The settings illustrated in the figure correspond with settings for the CAPTURE command. For a complete description of each parameter, please refer to Chapter 28, "Printing from DOS Clients."

Login and Logout

To log in to a server, first click once on the Server Connections action button, or press Alt+C. The NetWare Connections dialog box appears, as illustrated in figure 15.14.

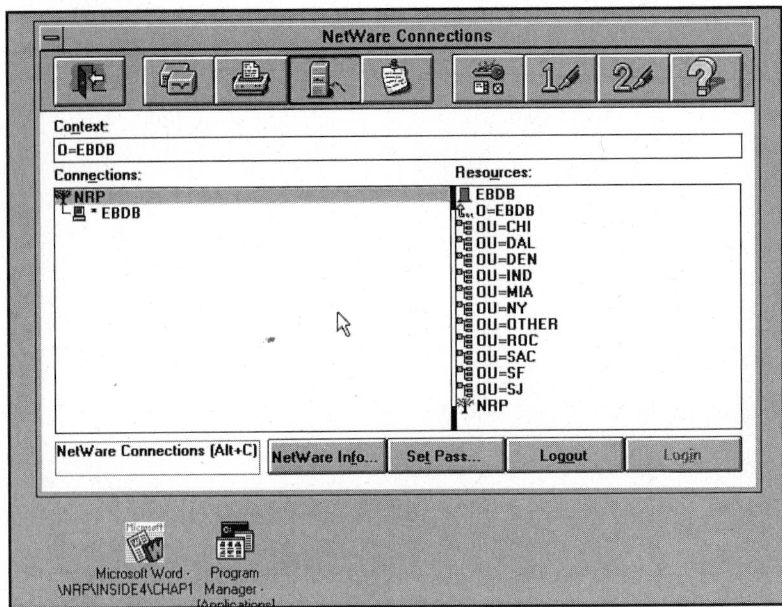

Figure 15.14 *The NWUSER.EXE NetWare Connections dialog box.*

To log in to a server, proceed as follows:

1. Select the desired server in the Connections list box at the left side of the NetWare Connections dialog box. Click once to select the server.

2. In the Resources list box, locate the desired server object. If necessary, double-click on container objects to expand your view so that you can locate server objects. Use the PgUp or PgDn keys, or use the mouse, to scroll up and down the tree. You can select the ".." entry to move to the next container level up the tree. Bindery-based server objects appear below the list of containers in your current tree.

3. As you select items from the Resources list box, the Context field at the top of the NetWare Connections dialog box changes. The context will have its proper NDS name.

4. Click once on the Login action button to finalize the login. You also can use the keyboard and press Alt+I.

To log in to an NDS tree, double-click on the tree icon in the Resources list box. To log out of a server (or tree), click once on the Logout action button. Click on the Set Pass button to change your password. The NetWare Info button gives you your login name for any given server or tree.

If you are logged in to an NDS tree, there is no need to log in to a specific server. By being in the tree you immediately have access to any server in the tree, depending on your security rights. The Login function is primarily to attach to bindery-based servers (NetWare 2.*x* or NetWare 3.*x* servers), or to access resources on NetWare 4.*x* servers not in your current tree.

Logging in through NWUSER does not run any login scripts. This is generally not a problem if you have established permanent drive mappings and print captures as described above.

Sending Messages

To send a message to one or more users on the network, proceed as follows:

1. Select the Send Messages action button by clicking once with the mouse or by pressing Alt+M. The NetWare Send Messages dialog box appears, as illustrated in figure 15.15.

2. From the NetWare Send Messages dialog box, select the desired server from the Connections list box in the left portion of the screen.

3. From the Resources list box, select the recipient user or group.

4. Enter the text of the message in the Message field at the top of the screen.

5. Click on the Send button. The message appears at the top of the screens of the targeted user, or members of the targeted group. If the user has Windows running, the message goes through the NWPOPUP utility and appears in a dialog box.

Use the NetWare Info button to gain information on the selected server. Information includes your login name and the version of NetWare on that server. The Hide Groups and Hide Users buttons prevent groups or users from being displayed in the Resources list box. This is if you have many users or groups in a container and want to limit which type of object you can view. When you click on either Hide Groups or Hide Users, those buttons change to Show Groups or Show Users.

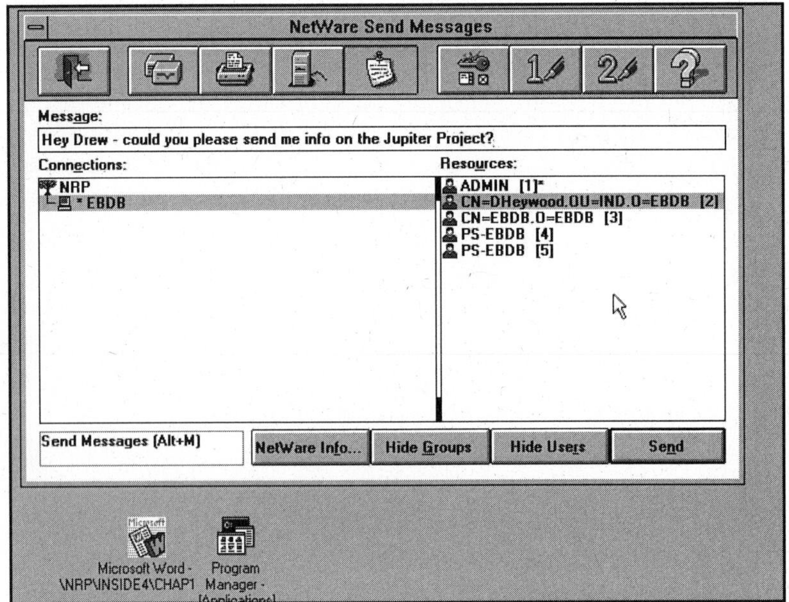

Figure 15.15 *The NWUSER.EXE NetWare Send Messages dialog box.*

Network Settings

The NetWare Settings dialog box can be used to change basic network settings. To access this dialog box, click once on the NetWare Settings action button or press Alt+S. The dialog box that appears is illustrated in figure 15.16.

Table 15.4 summarizes the different settings, showing you the name of the setting field (with the speed key underlined), default settings, and a description.

Table 15.4
NWUSER NetWare Settings Options

Setting	Default	Description
Broadcasts	Enabled	Controls whether or not you receive broadcast messages. When disabled, you receive no broadcast messages, which could potentially interfere with an application (especially communications sessions).

Setting	Default	Description
Network Warnings	Enabled	Controls whether or not you receive warning messages generated by the operating system. When disabled, you receive no warning messages, which could potentially interfere with an application (as mentioned above).
Maximum Jobs	50	Limits the number of network print jobs that can be displayed in the Windows Print Manager. Values range from 1 to 250 jobs.
Update Seconds	30	Number of seconds before Print Manager updates its display. Values can range from 1 to 65 seconds.
Restore During Startup	Enabled	Controls whether or not "permanent" connections, such as drive mappings or print capture settings, are restored when Windows first loads.
Disable Conflict Warnings	Disabled	If enabled, any conflict between current drive mappings and permanent drive mappings, for example, is not displayed. The default causes such conflicts to generate a warning message and a dialog box where you can take action to resolve the conflict.
Restore Now		This is an action button that causes any permanent settings to be restored upon pressing the button.
Enable Hotkey	Disabled	When enabled, you can set a hotkey (see next item in table).
Hotkey Value (when enabled)	F6	Defines a key that takes you immediately from any Windows application to the NetWare Tools (NWUSER) utility.

continues

Table 15.4, Continued
NWUSER NetWare Settings Options

Setting	Default	Description
Global Drives & Paths	Enabled	When enabled, this option causes all drive mappings to be reflected in all Windows applications and DOS sessions.
Bindery	Enabled	When enabled, causes bindery-based objects (such as NetWare 3.*x* servers) to be displayed.
Personal	Enabled	When enabled, causes Personal NetWare objects to be displayed. This assumes you have enabled Personal NetWare (comes with Novell DOS 7; used to be called NetWare Lite).
DS Objects	Enabled	When enabled, causes NDS leaf objects (such as users, groups, print queues, etc.) to be displayed.
DS Containers	Enabled	When enabled, causes NDS container objects (such as Organizations, Organizational Units, etc.) to be displayed.
Name Sort	Disabled	When enabled, objects are displayed sorted by name.
Type Sort	Enabled	When enabled, objects are displayed sorted by the type of object (for example, users are listed together, groups are listed together, etc.).

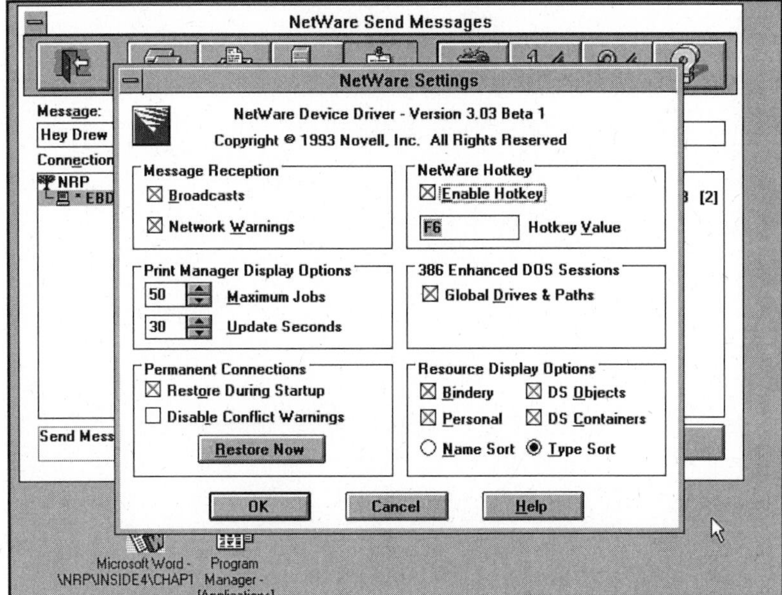

Figure 15.16
The NWUSER.EXE NetWare Settings dialog box.

User-Defined Buttons

NWUSER enables you to define two additional buttons with commands of your choice. To define an option for the customized buttons, press Alt+1 for the first button or Alt+2 for the second. The User Defined Path dialog box appears, as illustrated in figure 15.17.

In this example, the User Defined Path dialog box points to the file NLIST.PIF. This points to a Program Information File for the NLIST.EXE utility. The advantage to a PIF is that you have more control over the settings of DOS-based utilities. The settings for the PIF are illustrated in figure 15.18.

As you can see from the illustration, a question mark (?) is placed in the Optional Parameters field. This causes Windows to display a prompt box prior to executing the command. In the case of NLIST, you can enter any valid NLIST parameter. The search power of NLIST is now within your hands just by clicking on the user-defined button #1 in the NWUSER utility.

You also could define a PIF file for the MAP command using a question mark (?) in the Optional Parameters field. This way, when you execute the user-defined button, a prompt box would appear enabling you to perform a MAP SEARCH command.

Figure 15.17

The User Defined Path dialog box.

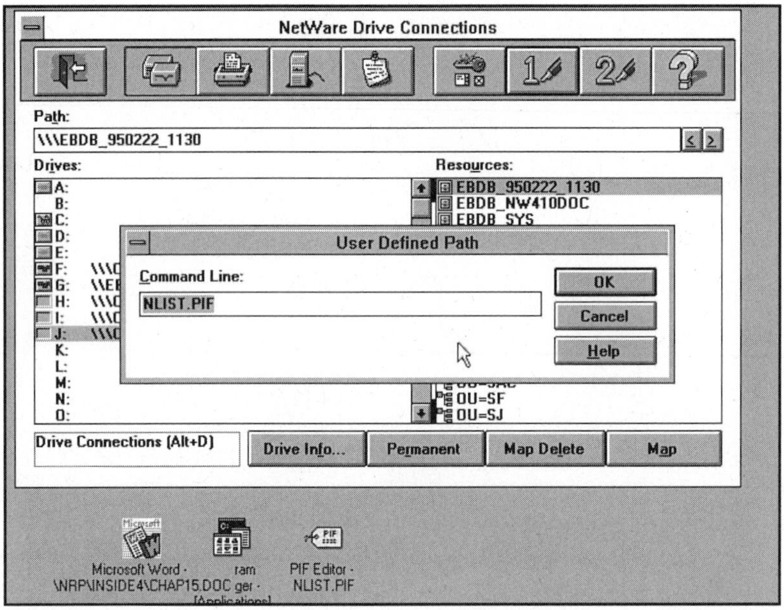

Figure 15.18

A Program Information File (PIF) for the NLIST utility.

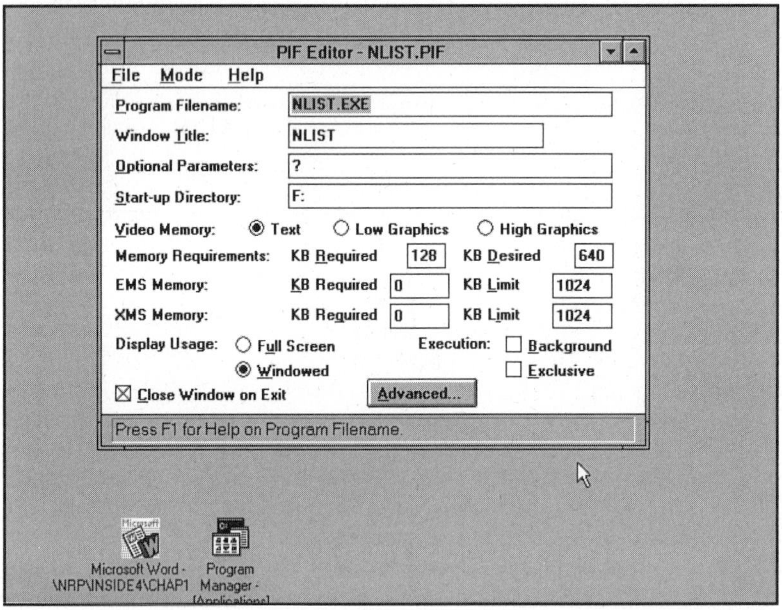

Configuring Windows NT

Microsoft has introduced a NetWare Client for Windows NT that allows a Windows NT workstation (or Advanced Server) to connect to NetWare servers. The client software integrates with other Windows features and behaves much as the first NetWare Client for Windows 3.0 software from a couple of years ago. Once the software is installed, you can map drive letters to NetWare servers and capture printer ports. The main disadvantage to the client software is that it currently does not support the VLM.EXE shell. As a result, the Windows NT client is supported through bindery services only.

Installing the NetWare Windows NT Client Software

During an Express setup of Windows NT, you can configure the settings for your network adapter. During this process, you also can configure native NT protocols and settings.

Determine which software is installed on your system as follows:

1. From the NT Program Manager, open the Control Panel from the Main program group.

2. From the Control Panel, select the Network icon. The Network Settings dialog box appears. Be sure that the NWLink IPX/SPX Compatible Transport has been selected.

   If this is not the case, click on Add Software to select this option. Click on Continue to return to the Network Settings dialog box.

3. To add the NetWare client software, from the Network Settings dialog box select Add Software. The Add Network Software dialog box appears.

4. Click on the Network Software drop down box button to obtain a list of network software drivers to add. Select the driver:

   ```
   Client Service for NetWare
   ```

   You will be prompted to insert a Windows NT installation disk, or the installation CD, depending on how you originally installed Windows NT. If you installed NT using floppy disks, insert any disk. The installation utility will read the disk and prompt you for the correct disk.

   Once the software has been copied, click on the Continue button. You will return to the Network Settings dialog box.

5. You are now ready to test the connection. From the Network Settings dialog box, click on the OK button. You must reboot your computer for the changes to take effect. When prompted to reboot, select Yes.

Configuring the NetWare Client for Windows NT

You can perform limited configuration on the NetWare Client for Windows NT. The items you can configure include the following:

- Network provider
- Preferred server
- Printing services

Network Provider

You can configure the order in which network services are provided. If you have followed the procedure outlined in this section, there will be at least two network service providers:

- Microsoft Windows Network
- NetWare Network

Windows NT supports a number of additional networks including TCP/IP and Ungerman-Bass, among others. To change the order in which NT searches for network providers, proceed as follows:

1. From the Control Panel, click on the Networks icon. The Network Settings dialog box appears.

2. From the Network Settings dialog box, from the Installed Network Software list, click once on Client Services for NetWare. Double-click on Configure. The Network Providers Search Order dialog box appears.

3. You can now select which network services you want Windows NT to search first. Click on your choice, and then click on OK to return to the Settings dialog box. Click on OK to return to the Control Panel.

Preferred Server and Printing Services

The preferred server is the server you communicate with most often. In the DOS client software, this is configured by editing the NET.CFG file. Printing services available for the Windows NT NetWare Client control how the print job is sent to the NetWare server.

To change the preferred server and print services settings for the NT client software, proceed as follows:

1. From the Program Manager, select the Control Panel from the Main program group.
2. From the Control Panel, select the Client Service for NetWare icon. At this point, the Client Service for NetWare dialog box appears.
3. Table 15.5 summarizes the options you can change in this dialog box. When done selecting options, click on OK. You will return to the Control Panel.

TABLE 15.5
Client Service for NetWare Settings

Setting	Description
Select Preferred Server	Displays a list of NetWare servers. You then choose the server you wish to attach to by default.
Add Form Feed	Adds an extra page eject at the end of print jobs sent to NetWare print queues.
Notify When Printed	Causes the NetWare server to send your workstation a broadcast message indicating the success of a print job and which printer the job printed on.
Print Banner	Sends your username and file name along with the print job. When the job prints, an initial page will precede the job with this information along with the date and time.

For more information on Windows NT to NetWare printing refer to Chapter 29, "Printing from Windows Clients."

Mapping Drive Letters to NetWare Servers

You can assign drive letters to directories on a NetWare server from either the Windows NT File Manager, or from a DOS session. When you create a drive mapping using either tool, the drive mapping becomes globally available to all Windows NT applications.

Windows NT clients access NetWare 4.*x* file servers using bindery services. You will only be able to access resources on servers where a valid bindery context has been set. NT clients are limited to volume and user objects in the bindery context.

To create drive mapping using the NT File Manager, proceed as follows:

1. From the Windows NT Program Manager, from the Main program group, select the File Manager. The File Manager main menu appears.

2. From the File Manager main menu, either click on the Connect Network Drive icon on the toolbar, or, select **D**isk, **C**onnect Network Drive. The Connect Network Drive dialog box appears.

3. From the Connect Network Drive dialog box, make the following choices:

   Click on the **D**rive drop down box to choose the drive letter to assign.

   Enter the NetWare username in the **C**onnect As box. The default is the username on the Windows NT workstation. Remember that you are limited to user objects in the bindery context of the server you plan to map to.

   Under the **S**hared Directories list double-click on the target file server. When you double-click on the server icon, a map of its volumes appears. Double-click on the target volume to reveal a map of its directories. Continue to double-click until you have selected the desired directory.

   Alternatively, you can manually enter the server, volume, and directory in the **P**ath box. The syntax is as follows:

   ```
   \\server\volume[\directory\...\directory]
   ```

   Server is the name of the NetWare server. Note the double backslashes (\\) that precede its name. *Volume* is the name of the target volume. *Directory* is optional. If unspecified, the chosen drive letter will be mapped to the root of the volume. Otherwise, you can specify a directory path.

   When you are done selecting the desired location on the NetWare server, click on OK. You will return to the File Manager main menu. A new drive letter icon appears. If you select this drive, you will see a listing of files on the NetWare server.

The files and directories you see on the NetWare server are in accordance with your NetWare file or directory trustee rights. You will not see files or directories where you have no trustee rights.

You can also map a drive letter from a DOS session. From the Windows NT Program Manager, from the Main group, click on the MS-DOS Command Prompt icon. This starts a Windows NT DOS session. To map a drive letter to a NetWare server, use this syntax:

```
NET USE letter: \\server\volume[\directory..\directory] [/user:username]
```

Letter is any available drive letter A – Z. *Server* is the name of the NetWare server. *Volume* is the name of the target volume. *Directory* is optional. If unspecified, the chosen drive letter will be mapped to the root of the volume. Otherwise, you can specify a directory path. *Username* is the name of the user on the NetWare server. The default is the username on the Windows NT workstation. Remember that you are limited to user objects in the bindery context of the server you plan to map to.

This example shows you how to map drive H to the root of volume *SYS* on server *Joshua*. The username used is the bindery user *Supervisor*.

```
C:\apps>net use h: \\joshua\sys /user:supervisor

Type the password for \\joshua\sys:
The command completed successfully.


C:\apps>
```

Here is what drive H looks like:

```
H:\>dir
 Volume in drive H is SYS
 Volume Serial Number is 0000-0000

 Directory of H:\

VOL$LOG  ERR                  64 11/07/94  08:22a
TTS$LOG  ERR                  82 11/07/94  08:22a
MYTREE   TXT                 260 11/07/94  02:36p
LOGIN         <DIR>              11/07/94  08:22a
SYSTEM        <DIR>              11/07/94  08:22a
PUBLIC        <DIR>              11/07/94  08:22a
MAIL          <DIR>              11/07/94  08:22a
ETC           <DIR>              11/07/94  08:28a
QUEUES        <DIR>              11/07/94  04:39p
               9 File(s)             406 bytes
                             108,904,448 bytes free

H:\>
```

You can use an asterisk (*) in place of a drive letter to map the next available drive letter. For example, this command maps the next drive letter to server *JOSHUA*, volume *ACCT*, directory *USER*:

```
G:\>net use * \\joshua\acct\user
Drive I: is now connected to \\joshua\acct\user.

The command completed successfully.


G:\>
```

Summary

This chapter discussed aspects of installing Windows NetWare client workstations. Versions of Windows discussed included Windows 3.*x* running on DOS workstations, Windows for Workgroups, and Windows NT workstations. The various NetWare/Windows files were covered and discussed in detail. Another part of this discussion included changes made to the WIN.INI and SYSTEM.INI files.

The next two subsections discussed the pros and cons of installing Windows on a server. The conclusion is that you should install Windows locally if you need to disconnect from the network from time to time. Otherwise, if you install on the server, Windows benefits due to the server's file caching ability. The swap file should be set to the local hard drive.

The next section discussed the NWUSER.EXE utility, also called the NetWare User Tools utility. You learned the main features of this relatively simple utility: how to map drive letters, capture printer ports, and log in to servers. You also learned how to send messages, configure print capture settings, and which hot keys can be used.

The last section dealt with Windows NT clients. You saw how to map drive letters in File Manager and from a DOS session. The next chapter discusses NetWare connectivity with OS/2 clients.

OS/2 Clients

This chapter provides an overview of the process of installing the NetWare Client software on an OS/2 workstation. You will learn how to obtain the OS/2 client drivers, how to install them on your OS/2 workstation, and how to use them once installed. In addition, you will learn about some configuration issues and how to make the integration with NetWare as smooth as possible.

Installing the NetWare Client for OS/2 Software

In this section, you will learn about installing the NetWare Client for OS/2 software. One of the primary considerations is how to obtain the software in the first place; this is explained in the first part of this section. The next portion of this section steps you through the installation process. The last part of this section covers changes made to the CONFIG.SYS and NET.CFG configuration files. The next section covers how to use the software once installed.

Creating NetWare OS/2 Client Disks

NetWare 4.1 maintains images of the NetWare Client for OS/2 installation disks on the installation media. If your installation media consists of floppy disks, you can use those disks to perform the client installation. If your installation media is CD-ROM, you will need to create the OS/2 disks from the CD.

To create the NetWare Client for OS/2 installation disks from a NetWare 4.1 installation CD mounted on a file server, proceed as follows:

1. Move physically to the server console itself. Alternatively you can use the RCONSOLE utility in the SYS:SYSTEM directory to access the file server console.

2. From the server console, load the INSTALL.NLM utility, as follows:

   LOAD INSTALL

   The INSTALL main menu appears. If the server is a NetWare 4.0*x* server, select Maintenance.

3. From the INSTALL main menu select Product Options. The Other Installation Items/Products menu appears.

4. From the Other Installation Items/Products menu, select Create DOS/MS Windows/OS2 Client Install Diskettes. You are prompted to indicate the location of the installation media. If the path indicated is not correct, press F3 and indicate the appropriate path to the installation CD. If you are using RCONSOLE to access the file server, you can also use the F4 key to indicate a locally mounted CD. The Indicate Which File Groups You Want Installed menu appears.

5. From the Indicate Which File Groups You Want Installed menu, you can use the Enter key to select or unselect options. Selected options have an X between

square brackets ([X]). Unselected options have a space between square brackets ([ ]). Select the OS/2 Client Install option and unselect all other options.

6. Press the F10 key to begin the installation onto floppy disks. A prompt asks which language you want to install. Select the appropriate language and press Enter.

7. INSTALL assumes you are copying to drive A:. If this is not correct, press F3 to add the correct path. If using RCONSOLE, you can also use the F4 key to indicate a local workstation path.

8. Insert blank disks as prompted. You end up creating the following disks:

   - WSOS2_1
   - WSOS2_2
   - WSOS2_3
   - WSDRV_1
   - OS2UTIL1
   - OS2DOC_1
   - VLMBOOT1

9. After INSTALL has finished copying disks, press Esc several times to exit the INSTALL utility.

Note NetWare creates the OS/2 client disks from images stored on the installation CD. The images are for 3.5-inch disks in 1.44 MB format. They are stored in the \CLIENT_______ directory and have the extension *.350.

Installing NetWare OS/2 Client Software from the Server

If your OS/2 workstation has an older version of the NetWare OS/2 Client software already installed, you can install the NetWare 4.1 client software directly from the server. For you to perform an installation directly from the server, you first must copy the software from the NetWare 4.1 installation media.

The NetWare OS/2 Client installation software can be copied to the server during the server installation process. Copying the OS/2 Client software is an option that appears at the end of the installation process. Refer to Chapter 12, "Installing the Network Operating System," for more information on the installation process.

If you have not copied the software during the installation, you can copy the OS/2 Client software to the server at any time by proceeding as follows:

1. Move physically to the server console itself. Alternatively you can use the RCONSOLE utility in the SYS:SYSTEM directory to access the file server console.

2. From the server console, load the INSTALL.NLM utility, as follows:

   LOAD INSTALL

   The INSTALL main menu appears.

3. From the INSTALL main menu, select Copy Files Option. You are prompted to indicate the location of the installation media. If the path specified is not correct, press F3 and indicate the correct path.

4. When prompted, enter the directory where the server boot files are located. This directory is not used for the purposes of this illustration, but you are required to specify the path. The default is C:\NWSERVER. The Indicate Which File Groups You Want Installed screen appears.

5. From the Indicate Which File Groups You Want Installed screen, you can see that all options are currently marked. Unselect the first option by pressing Enter. Continue moving down the list, pressing Enter to unselect all options. Note that unselected options do not have the letter X between the square brackets.

6. Select the Set up a Network Directory for Client Install option and press Enter. Make sure the letter X is between the square brackets. This option copies client installation files, including the NetWare Client for OS/2 files.

7. Press F10 to accept this selection and begin the file copy. When done, there will be a newly created directory SYS:PUBLIC\CLIENT\OS2 where you can find the NetWare Client for OS/2 files.

Obtaining the Client Files from CompuServe or the Internet

Part of the installation process is learning where and how to obtain the latest drivers. The primary source for the latest drivers is on NetWire. *NetWire* is Novell's bulletin board service, which is offered under CompuServe. NetWire files are mirrored on Novell's "ftp" server on the Internet. This section will show you how to obtain files from CompuServe, from the Internet, and how to move these files to floppy disks for installation.

Downloading Files from CompuServe

To access NetWire under CompuServe you must have a CompuServe account. Although you are not charged for downloading the NetWare OS/2 drivers, you will be charged for connect time. To download the files through CompuServe, proceed as follows:

1. Log in to CompuServe.
2. Type **GO NOVFILES**.
3. From the NOVFILES area, select Client Kits. You will see, among other choices, OS/2 and Windows NT. Select OS/2 Client Kit. From the OS/2 Client Kit area select NetWare Client v2.1 for OS/2.
4. From the NetWare Client v2.1 for OS/2 area, download the following files:

   WSOS21.EXE—the installation program

   WSOS22.EXE—Requester and RIPL files

   WSDRV1.EXE—Various drivers

   OSUTIL1.EXE—Utilities

   VLMBOOT1.EXE—OS/2 VLM support
5. You can also download the documentation and fixes by selecting, from the OS/2 Client Kit area, NetWare Client v2.1 for OS/2 — Documentation, or NetWare Client v2.1 for OS/2 — Fixes.
6. When the download is completed, type **BYE** to exit CompuServe.

Downloading Files from the Internet

A good alternative to CompuServe is through the Internet. To access the OS/2 client files through the Internet, you must establish a connection using FTP to the host FTP.NOVELL.COM. The IP address for this host is 137.65.1.3. To download the NetWare Client for OS/2 v2.1 files using the Internet, proceed as follows:

1. Open an FTP session with the FTP.NOVELL.COM host:

   ftp ftp.novell.com

2. Change to the directory containing the OS/2 client files:

   cd /pub/netwire/novfiles/client.kit/os2

3. Download the files to your local computer's current directory:

   mget *.EXE

If you have access to a version of Mosaic, you can access the files by opening a Uniform Resource Locator window. Type the following to get to the appropriate directory:

file://ftp.novell.com/pub/netwire/novfiles/client.kit/os2

You will see the OS/2 client files appear in the browser window. You then can click on them and download using Mosaic.

Moving the Downloaded Files to Floppy Disks

After you have downloaded the files, you need to decompress them to floppy disks. The simplest method begins with formatting blank disks and labeling them as follows:

WSOS2_1

WSOS2_2

WSOS2_3

WSDRV_1

OS2UTIL_1

VLMBOOT1

OS2DOC_1

Then, from the directory containing the downloaded files, decompress each file onto its own disk. Table 16.1 summarizes which file should be extracted onto which disk.

Table 16.1
Decompressing the NetWare Client for OS/2 v2.1 Files

Downloaded File	Corresponding Disk
WSOS21.EXE	WSOS2_1
WSOS22.EXE	WSOS2_2

Downloaded File	Corresponding Disk
WSOS23.EXE	WSOS2_3
WSDRV1.EXE	WSDRV_1
OS2UT1.EXE	OS2UTIL_1
VLMBOOT1.EXE	VLMBOOT1
OS2DC1.EXE	OS2DOC_1

Because the downloaded files are self-extracting ZIP files, to extract the contents, simply type the file name. To extract the WSOS21.EXE file to the disk labeled WSOS2_1, for example, insert the disk in drive A and type the following:

WSOS21 A:

When done, you will have disks containing the OS/2 client installation files.

Installing the NetWare Client Software on an OS/2 Workstation

Now that you have the disks containing the OS/2 Client software, you can install the software on an OS/2 workstation. Boot up the OS/2 workstation and proceed as follows:

1. Insert the WSOS2_1 disk in drive A (or B, if applicable) and click on the drive A icon to display the Drive A - Icon View window. Click on the menu button (top left) and select **O**pen, **D**etails View. You can see the Details View, illustrated in figure 16.1.

2. From the Details View, select INSTALL.EXE to display the NetWare Workstation for OS/2 Installation Utility screen. Review the text that appears on the screen, as shown in figure 16.2. To upgrade an existing NetWare OS/2 driver, choose **C**onfiguration, **T**his Workstation. To install a new OS/2 client, choose **I**nstallation, **R**equester on workstation.

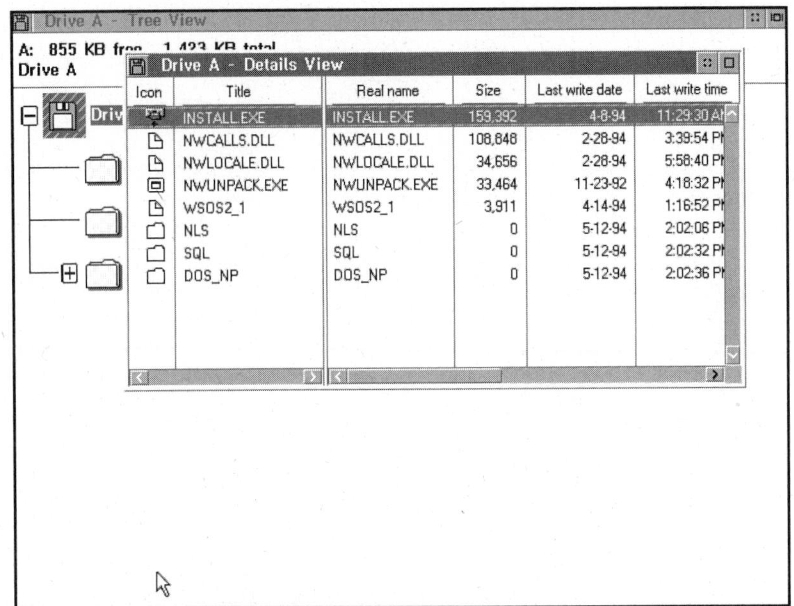

Figure 16.1

The WSOS2_1 Disk Details View.

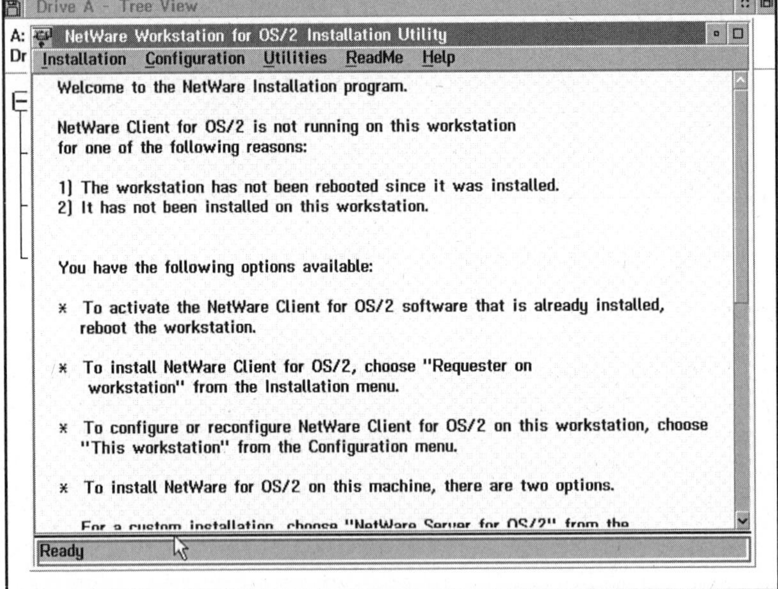

Figure 16.2

The NetWare Workstation for OS/2 Installation Utility main screen.

3. For the purposes of this section, assume that you will be installing new NetWare Client software, so choose Installation, Requester on workstation. The Select a target directory for the NetWare Client files dialog box appears, asking you where to place the client software. The default is C:\NETWARE. Type the appropriate directory and choose OK to display the Requester Installation dialog box. This dialog box offers the following choices:

   - **Edit CONFIG.SYS and Copy All Files.** Choose this option if you want to do a full NetWare Client for OS/2 installation. This option ensures that CONFIG.SYS is properly updated and all necessary files are copied.
   - **Only Edit CONFIG.SYS.** This option is available if the client software is already installed and you want only to make configuration changes to the CONFIG.SYS file.
   - **Only Copy Requester Files.** This option only copies the NetWare Client for OS/2 files without altering the CONFIG.SYS or other configuration files. Select this option to update an existing installation with the latest requester files.
   - **Only Copy ODI LAN Driver Files.** This option is similar to the preceding option except that only ODI driver files are copied. Use this option to update your ODI drivers.

4. For a full installation, select the Edit CONFIG.SYS and Copy All Files option. A series of "Step" dialog boxes appears at this point, the first of which is Step 1 - Choose the ODI LAN Driver. Click on the drop-down box arrow at the right of the blank field to display a list of available drivers. You are prompted to insert the WSDRV_1 disk or a disk with third-party drivers. Select the driver appropriate for your NIC and choose OK. This displays the Step 2 - Choose NetWare Support for DOS and Windows Applications dialog box, as shown in figure 16.3.

5. The two groups in this dialog box are IPX Support for DOS and Windows, and Default NetWare Shell Support. If you select Off for IPX Support for DOS and Windows, you will not be able to access a NetWare server through IPX from an OS/2 DOS or Windows session. You can still access the server from an OS/2 window. If you choose On, IPX support will be available for each DOS or Windows session.

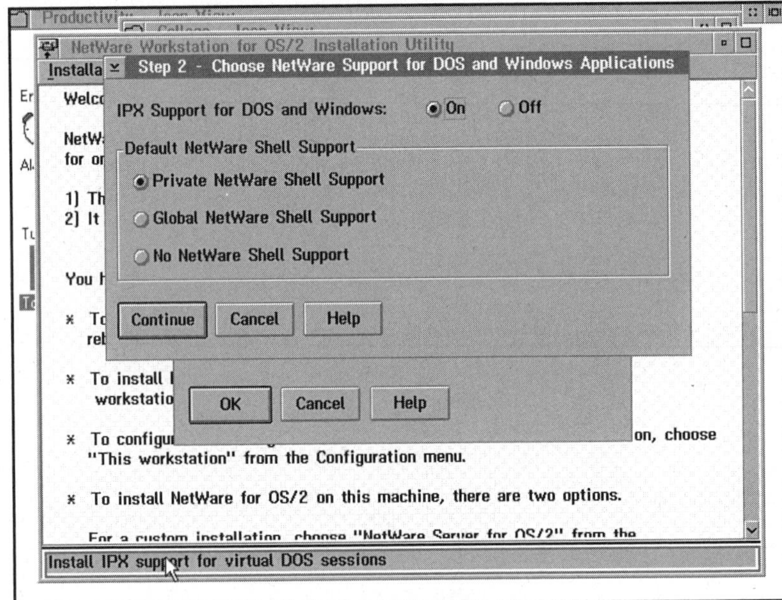

Figure 16.3
Step 2 of the client installation: the Choose NetWare Support for DOS and Windows Applications dialog box.

DOS or Windows sessions run the NETX shell. This means that when you log in through a DOS or Windows session, you do not have access to the NDS—you will be connected through bindery emulation. You will need to run an OS/2 session to access the NDS.

The exception to this is when you install the VMBoot option. This option boots a DOS image under OS/2 v2.11 that allows you to use the VLM Requester. In this case, you have full access to the NDS. See the section, "Installing the VMBoot Option."

The options for Default NetWare Shell Support are Private NetWare Shell Support, Global NetWare Shell Support, and No NetWare Shell Support. If you select Private NetWare Shell Support, each DOS or Windows session you run from OS/2 will have its own connection to the file server. OS/2 DOS or Windows sessions spawn *virtual machines,* which use the protected mode of the Intel microprocessor to create a protected, independent process. Separate DOS or Windows virtual machines do not share the environment of other OS/2 sessions. When Private NetWare Shell Support is selected, you will have a separate login session to the file server that is independent of your OS/2 login session. When you first open a DOS session, the NetWare Client for OS/2 software will run the equivalent of the ODI drivers and the NETX shell, giving you a connection to the file server. From there you must log in and gain drive mappings as would any DOS workstation.

If you select Global NetWare Shell Support (the default), logging in from any DOS, Windows, or OS/2 session affects all other sessions. In other words, all DOS, Windows, and OS/2 sessions share a single login to the network.

If you select No NetWare Shell Support, no network support will be available from any DOS or Windows session. You will need to use an OS/2 session to access the network.

6. For the purpose of this discussion, select Private NetWare Shell Support. Next you are asked if you want to load TBMI2.COM (which is required for Windows applications using IPX/SPX) and NETX.EXE (which is required for DOS/Windows sessions). These will be added to the AUTOEXEC.BAT file or other batch file you select. Another message regarding setting the DOS LASTDRIVE= parameter might appear. If so, this parameter should be set to Z:.

   Select the desired option and click on OK to continue.

7. The next step is the Step 3 - Choose Optional Protocols dialog box (see fig. 16.4). This dialog box enables you to add SPX and NetBIOS support for OS/2 sessions, and to select Remote Named Pipes support.

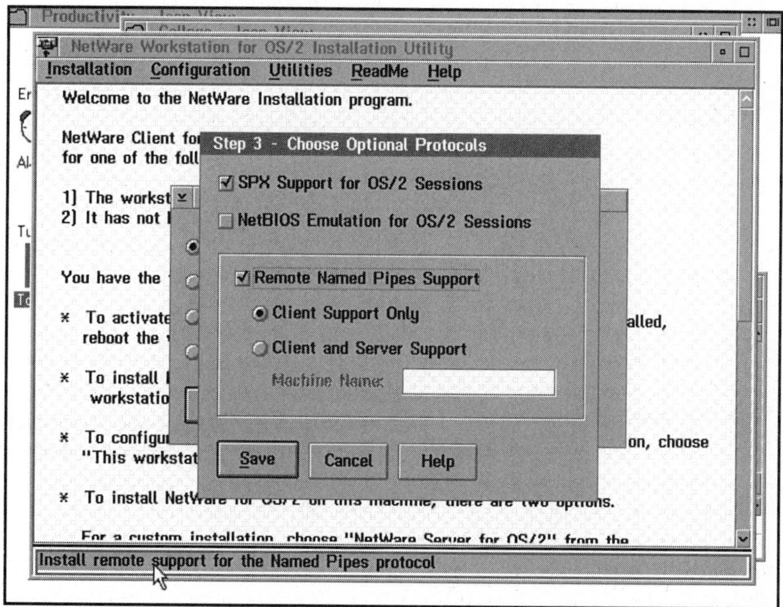

Figure 16.4

Step 3 of the client installation: the Choose Optional Protocols dialog box.

Choose SPX Support for OS/2 Sessions if you plan to run applications that make use of the Transport Layer Interface (TLI). Some printing utilities (such as NPRINTER.EXE) and the RCONSOLE.EXE utility require SPX support.

Choose NetBIOS Emulation for OS/2 Sessions if you will be using applications that use NetBIOS. These include applications that provide 3270 terminal emulation, for example, to gain access to mainframes.

Choose Remote Named Pipes Support if you plan to use this workstation as a Named Pipes application server or client. Choose Client Support Only if this workstation will use a Named Pipes application from another computer on the network. Choose Client and Server Support if this machine will be both a Named Pipes client and server. If this is the case, you also must enter a unique machine name for this workstation.

8. At this point, the installation utility adds the changes you have selected to the CONFIG.SYS file. Next the ODI driver you selected will be copied to the directory indicated above. After the ODI driver(s) has been copied, you will be prompted to reinsert the WSOS2_1 disk and then the remaining disks, WSOS2_2, WSOS2_3, OSUTIL_1, OS2DOC_1, and VLMBOOT1.

9. The installation is now complete. The CONFIG.SYS or the NET.CFG files might need additional configuration. The primary changes include setting the DOS LASTDRIVE in CONFIG.SYS and making changes to the NET.CFG file to suit your NIC. You are returned to the INSTALL main screen at this point. After making any desired changes to the CONFIG.SYS or NET.CFG files, close the screen by double-clicking on the menu button, or by pressing Alt+F4. Be sure to reboot your computer to make your changes take effect.

Installing the NetWare Client Software from a Server

The client installation procedure when installing the client software from a server is identical to the procedure from floppy disks indicated above. The exception is that you must have a way of initially accessing the server. This requires that you already have OS/2 client software available. This procedure is only useful when you need to upgrade existing OS/2 client software.

To install the NetWare Client for OS/2 software from a server, proceed as follows:

1. Using the existing NetWare client software, log in to the NetWare server with the OS/2 client installation files loaded.

2. Move to the directory where the client installation files are located. The default is SYS:PUBLIC\CLIENT\OS2.

3. Select the INSTALL.EXE icon.

The installation will then proceed as outlined previously. The difference is that you will not be asked to insert disks.

Installing the VMBoot Option

VMBoot stands for *Virtual Machine Boot.* The VMBoot function takes advantage of a feature of OS/2 version 2.11 that is not available under OS/2 version 2.10. This feature enables you to run a virtual DOS session, complete with its own environment, under OS/2 v2.11. In this section, you learn how to set up either a bootable DOS disk, or a bootable DOS image file on your hard drive. In the image file you can configure a complete, self-contained DOS environment, which will be referred to as a *VMBoot DOS session.* The VMBoot DOS session running under OS/2 v2.11 can be configured to load the VLM Requester, which gives the session complete access to the NDS. Using a VMBoot DOS session you can run NLIST, NETADMIN, or any other DOS NDS utility.

The VLMBOOT1 disk, which you created in the preceding section, contains a Novell DOS 7 image file that you can use to boot from. Alternatively, you can create an image file or boot disk using any other version of DOS. If you decide to create a boot disk, bear in mind that the VMBoot DOS session will load from a floppy disk, which is rather slow. An image file on your hard drive, on the other hand, boots quickly but takes up 1.5 MB of disk space.

Creating a Floppy VMBoot Disk

To create a VMBoot disk, proceed as follows:

1. Create a formatted, bootable floppy disk. You can use any version of DOS, v3.1 or greater.

2. Make a directory A:\NWCLIENT. Change to either the \CLIENT\DOSWIN directory on your NetWare 4.1 installation CD, or, if you copied the client installation files to your server, change to the SYS:\PUBLIC\CLIENT\DOSWIN directory. Unpack the VLM files to the A:\NWCLIENT directory, using the NWUNPACK utility:

   ```
   NWUNPACK *.VL_ A:\NWCLIENT
   ```

3. Unpack VLM.EXE using NWUNPACK:

   ```
   NWUNPACK VLM.EX_ A:\NWCLIENT
   ```

4. Change to the \CLIENT\DOSWIN\NLS directory on the NetWare 4.1 installation CD, or to the SYS:PUBLIC\CLIENT\DOSWIN\NLS directory on the server. Copy the unicode files to the floppy disk as follows:

   ```
   COPY *.* A:\NWCLIENT
   ```

5. Change to the directory \CLIENT\DOSWIN\NLS*language* on the 4.1 installation CD, or to the SYS:\PUBLIC\CLIENT\DOSWIN*language* directory on the server,

where *language* is DEUTSCH, ENGLISH, ESPANOL, FRANCIAS, or ITALIANO, depending on your needs. Unpack the message files to the floppy disk as follows:

```
..\..\NWUNPACK *.MS_ A:\NWCLIENT
```

6. Make a directory A:\VLMDLL directory. This directory contains the Windows support DLL files. Change to the \CLIENT\DOSWIN directory on the 4.1 installation CD (or to the same subdirectory under SYS:PUBLIC on a server) and unpack the following files:

```
NWUNPACK *.DL_ A:\VLMDLL
NWUNPACK *.DR_ A:\VLMDLL
NWUNPACK *.HL_ A:\VLMDLL
```

7. Copy these OS/2 MSDOS files to the root of the floppy disk, as follows:

```
COPY OS2_drive:\OS2\MSDOS\FSFILTER.SYS A:\
COPY OS2_drive:\OS2\MSDOS\HIMEM.SYS A:\
```

where *OS2_drive* is the OS/2 drive letter.

8. Copy the DOSVIPX.SYS file to the root of the floppy disk from the directory which contains the NetWare Client for OS/2 files, as follows:

```
COPY OS2_Client_Path:DOSVIPX.SYS A:\
```

where *OS2_Client_Path* is the OS/2 drive:\directory to the NetWare Client for OS/2 files.

9. Create an A:\CONFIG.SYS file as follows:

```
DEVICE = A:\FSFILTER.SYS
DEVICE = A:\HIMEM.SYS
DEVICE = A:\DOSVIPX.SYS
FILES = 114
LASTDRIVE=Z
```

10. Create an A:\AUTOEXEC.BAT file as follows:

```
PATH A:\VLMDLL;A:\NWCLIENT;OS2_Drive:\OS2\MDOS\WINOS2;
A:\NWCLIENT\VLM.EXE
```

where *OS2_Drive* is the OS/2 drive letter.

11. Create an A:\NWCLIENT\NET.CFG file as follows:

```
NetWare DOS Requester
        PB BUFFERS=0
        FIRST NETWORK DRIVE = F
```

where the *FIRST NETWORK DRIVE* can be "F" or any desired starting drive letter. The *PB BUFFERS = 0* setting disables packet burst under the VMBoot DOS session.

You must now move the NETWARE.DRV file from the OS2\MDOS\WINOS2\SYSTEM directory. This driver file is used by the WINOS2 session and is different from the NETWARE.DRV file used by the VLM requester. Proceed as follows:

1. Create a directory OS2_Drive:\NETXDLL.

2. Move the NETWARE.DRV and .HLP files from the OS2\MDOS\WINOS2\SYSTEM directory to this directory:

```
MOVE OS2_Drive:OS2\MDOS\WINOS2\SYSTEM\NETWARE.* OS2_Drive:\NETXDLL
```

3. Update the OS/2 PATH by editing the \AUTOEXEC.BAT file. Add this directory to the beginning of the PATH:

```
OS2_Drive:\NETXDLL;PATH
```

   where *OS2_Drive* is the OS/2 drive letter, and *PATH* is the existing PATH.

You can now run the VMBoot DOS session from the floppy drive by selecting "DOS from drive A:" from the the OS/2 system Command Prompts folder. If you experience problems running the VMBoot DOS session, check the DOS Settings notebook and verify the following settings:

```
NETWARE_RESOURCES    PRIVATE
VIPX_ENABLED         ON
```

Creating Your Own VMBoot Image on the Hard Drive

Running a VMBoot DOS session from the floppy drive can be slow. To speed up the process, you can create a boot image on your OS/2 hard drive. Proceed as follows:

1. Create a VMBoot disk as previously described.

2. Make a directory on your OS/2 hard drive as follows:

```
MD OS2_Drive:\VLMBOOT
```

   where *OS2_Drive* is your OS/2 drive letter.

3. Create an image file from the boot disk as follows:

```
VMDIS'K A: OS2_Drive:\VLMBOOT\VLMBOOT.IMG
```

where *OS2_Drive* is your OS/2 drive letter. This process takes the contents of the floppy and places them into a large (1.44 MB) file. This file is an *image* file. You will not be able to view the contents of this file. It is bootable.

4. Double click on the Templates folder on the OS/2 desktop. Drag and drop the Programs template onto the OS/2 desktop, holding the right mouse button down. The Settings Notebook screen appears.

5. From the Settings Notebook screen select the Program tab. For path and file name, enter the following:

   COMMAND.COM

6. From the Settings Notebook screen select the Session tab. Choose the DOS Full Screen button. Click on the DOS Settings button and fill in the following fields:

   DOS_STARTUP_DRIVE should be set to OS2_Drive:\VLMBOOT\VLMBOOT.IMG.

   NETWARE_RESOURCES should be set to PRIVATE.

   VIPX_ENABLED should be set to ON.

7. From the Settings Notebook screen, select the General tab. Change the title to reflect the function of the icon. An example is the following:

   ```
   VMBoot
   ```

You are now ready to run the VMBoot DOS session from an image file.

Using the Existing VMBoot Image

NetWare 4.1 provides a ready-made bootable image file, formatted with Novell DOS 7. The file resides on the VLMBOOT1 disk under the name VLMBOOT.IMG. To use this file, you can invoke the Rexx command file VLMBOOT.CMD, also located on the VLMBOOT1 disk. From an OS/2 window, change to the VLMBOOT1 disk and invoke VLMBOOT.CMD. The following listing documents this command file:

```
/*   */
/* Load REXXUTIL */
call rxfuncadd sysloadfuncs, rexxutil, sysloadfuncs
call sysloadfuncs

call CHKVER          /* VERIFY OS2 VERSION 2.11 */
call README          /* READ BEFORE CONTINUE */
call INPUT           /* GET INPUT FROM COMMAND LINE */
call SETUP           /* COPY TO OS2 DRIVE AND EDIT AUTOEXEC.BAT */
```

```
call VMBOOT          /* COPY VMBOOT IMAGE TO OS2 DRIVE */
call ICONBLD         /* BUILD THE VMBOOT ICON ON DESKTOP */

SAY ""
say "The extracted files are no longer needed and can be deleted."
say ""
SAY "VLM SUPPORT CAN NOW BE ACCESSED FROM THE VMBOOT ICON ON THE DESKTOP."
EXIT

CHKVER:
ver=SysOS2Ver()
if ver=2.11
 then return
ELSE
say "OS2 V2.11 IS REQUIRED FOR NETWARE DOS VLM SUPPORT UNDER OS2"
say "YOU HAVE VERSION "¦¦ver¦¦""
EXIT

README:
call sysCls
say "This REXX file will create an icon on the OS/2 DESKTOP that will"
say "enable NetWare Dos vlm support.(ie nwadmin.exe for windows.)"
say "Autoexec.bat is renamed to Autoexec.vlm before the Path is modified."
say "Two directories are created \VLMBOOT and \NETXDLL in Requester Directory."
say "OS2VLM.CMD must be executed from the directory it was extracted into."
say "!!IMPORTANT!! Close all Dos and WinOS/2 sessions before continuing."
say "Do you want to continue?  Y or N?"
PARSE PULL yorn
if yorn="y"
 then return
if yorn="Y"
 then return
if yorn="n"
 then EXIT
if yorn="N"
 then EXIT

EXIT



INPUT:
call sysCls
```

```
SAY "ENTER THE DRIVE WHERE OS2 BOOTS FROM? C, D or E etc. ?"
PARSE PULL OS2DRIVE
SAY "ENTER THE PATH WHERE NETWARE REQUESTER IS INSTALLED? C:\NETWARE ?"
PARSE PULL REQPATH

RETURN


SETUP:
rc = SysMkDir(""¦¦REQPATH¦¦"\VLMBOOT")
rc = SysMkDir(""¦¦REQPATH¦¦"\NETXDLL")

COPY "NETWARE.DRV "¦¦REQPATH¦¦"\NETXDLL"
COPY "NETWARE.HLP "¦¦REQPATH¦¦"\NETXDLL"

DEL ""¦¦OS2DRIVE¦¦":\OS2\MDOS\WINOS2\SYSTEM\NETWARE.DRV"
DEL ""¦¦OS2DRIVE¦¦":\OS2\MDOS\WINOS2\SYSTEM\NETWARE.HLP"


COPY ""¦¦OS2DRIVE¦¦":\AUTOEXEC.BAT "¦¦OS2DRIVE¦¦":\AUTOEXEC.VLM"
NNEPATH "/A "¦¦REQPATH¦¦"\NETXDLL PATH "¦¦OS2DRIVE¦¦":\AUTOEXEC.BAT"
return

VMBOOT:
COPY "VLMBOOT.ICO "¦¦REQPATH¦¦"\VLMBOOT"
COPY "VLMBOOT.IMG "¦¦REQPATH¦¦"\VLMBOOT"
return

ICONBLD:
Say " ";Say "Creating VLMBOOT Icon on Desktop Desktop..."
classname="WPProgram"
title="VLMBOOT"
location="<WP_DESKTOP>"
setup="OBJECTID=<VLMBOOTImage>;"¦¦,
      "ICONFILE="¦¦REQPATH¦¦"\VLMBOOT\VLMBOOT.ICO;"¦¦,
      "EXENAME=COMMAND.COM;"¦¦,
      "PROGTYPE=VDM;"
call charout , "Building: "title
result = SysCreateObject(classname, title, location, setup, "R")
If result=1 then call charout ,"...   Object created!"
Else                     call charout ,"...    Failed on create!  Return
code="result
```

```
Setup="SET DOS_STARTUP_DRIVE="¦¦REQPATH¦¦"\VLMBOOT\VLMBOOT.IMG;"¦¦,
      "SET DOS_LASTDRIVE=E;"¦¦,
       "SET NETWARE_RESOURCES=PRIVATE;"
result=SysSetObjectData("<VLMBOOTImage>",setup)
Say " ";
Return
```

Examining Changes Made to the OS/2 CONFIG.SYS File

The following listing shows additions made to the standard OS/2 CONFIG.SYS file by the NetWare Client for OS/2 v2.1 installation program. Table 16.2 gives you a summary of the commands added. Although you can directly edit the CONFIG.SYS file, it is recommended you make configuration changes through the INSTALL utility (in the Novell Icon View).

```
...
DEVICE=C:\NETWARE\VIPX.SYS
DEVICE=C:\NETWARE\VSHELL.SYS PRIVATE
...
REM --- NetWare Requester statements BEGIN ---
SET NWLANGUAGE=ENGLISH
DEVICE=C:\NETWARE\LSL.SYS
RUN=C:\NETWARE\DDAEMON.EXE
REM -- ODI-Driver Files BEGIN --
DEVICE=C:\NETWARE\CEODI.OS2
REM -- ODI-Driver Files END --
REM DEVICE=C:\NETWARE\ROUTE.SYS
DEVICE=C:\NETWARE\IPX.SYS
DEVICE=C:\NETWARE\SPX.SYS
RUN=C:\NETWARE\SPDAEMON.EXE
DEVICE=C:\NETWARE\NMPIPE.SYS
rem DEVICE=C:\NETWARE\NPSERVER.SYS
RUN=C:\NETWARE\NPDAEMON.EXE
DEVICE=C:\NETWARE\NWREQ.SYS
IFS=C:\NETWARE\NWIFS.IFS
RUN=C:\NETWARE\NWDAEMON.EXE
rem DEVICE=C:\NETWARE\NETBIOS.SYS
rem RUN=C:\NETWARE\NBDAEMON.EXE
DEVICE=C:\OS2\MDOS\LPTDD.SYS
REM --- NetWare Requester statements END ---
```

Table 16.2
NetWare Client Additions to the OS/2 CONFIG.SYS File

Command	Description
VIPX.SYS	This driver is used to produce virtual IPX support in DOS or Windows sessions.
VSHELL.SYS	This driver is used in DOS or Windows sessions to provide private, global, or no shell support, as described in the preceding section.
SET NWLANGUAGE	This command sets an environmental variable that adjusts the language used when accessing NetWare utilities. Choices include ENGLISH, FRANCAIS, DEUTSCH, ITALIANO, and ESPANOL. Additional choices are available with the purchase of additional software. Note that language support is provided only if such support was copied during file server installation.
LSL.SYS	A driver that supports the Link Support Layer, which forms the heart of Novell's ODI (Open Datalink Interface) specification. This driver implements the IEEE 802.2 specification.
DDAEMON.EXE	*Daemons*, as in UNIX, are programs that run transparently in the background, providing support for various processes. This utility provides support for drivers.
CEODI.OS2	This is an example of an OS/2 driver for a NIC; in this case, a Xircom CreditCard Ethernet adapter.
ROUTE.SYS	Support for source routing. This is used only if you have a token ring adapter installed on the workstation that needs source routing support. This would be the case, for example, where the workstation is attached to the nearest server through a series of source routing bridges.
IPX.SYS	The IPX protocol driver.
SPX.SYS	The SPX protocol driver.
SPDAEMON.EXE	This process is a daemon that provides SPX protocol support.

Command	Description
NMPIPE.SYS	The Named Pipe driver.
NPSERVER.SYS	This driver is loaded when the workstation functions as a Named Pipe server.
NPDAEMON.EXE	The Named Pipe daemon.
NWREQ.SYS	The NetWare Requester support driver, which provides NetWare services to OS/2.
NWIFS.IFS	IFS stands for Installable File System; NWIFS stands for NetWare Installable File System. This driver provides OS/2 with the necessary hooks to access the file system on the NetWare file server.
NWDAEMON.EXE	NetWare daemon, which provides the mechanism for accessing services on NetWare file servers.
NETBIOS.SYS	The main NetBIOS emulation driver.
NBDAEMON.EXE	NetBIOS daemon, which provides the mechanism for NetBIOS emulation.
LPTDD.SYS	Print redirection support. This driver makes it possible to send an OS/2 print job to a NetWare print queue rather than out a local port.

To make changes to the NetWare parameters in the CONFIG.SYS file, proceed as follows:

1. From the OS/2 Desktop, select the Novell Icon View. From the Novell Icon View, select the INSTALL utility.

2. From the INSTALL main menu, choose **I**nstallation, **R**equester on workstation to display the Select Target Directory dialog box.

3. Enter the directory path that contains the NetWare client files. The default is C:\NETWARE. The Requester Installation dialog box appears.

4. Select Only Edit CONFIG.SYS. You now will be taken through the "Step" dialog boxes described earlier in the section "Installing the NetWare Client Software on an OS/2 Workstation." Make any changes desired. When done, the CONFIG.SYS file will be automatically updated. You will have to reboot the workstation for the changes to take effect.

Exploring the OS/2 NET.CFG File

The NET.CFG file contains settings that affect the ODI drivers and the network connection. As with the CONFIG.SYS file, the NET.CFG file can be edited directly or through the INSTALL utility from the Novell Icon View. When editing the NET.CFG file through the INSTALL utility, online Help is immediately available. In addition, the INSTALL utility provides you with suggestions and examples of each setting. Figure 16.5 shows you how the INSTALL utility looks when editing the NET.CFG file.

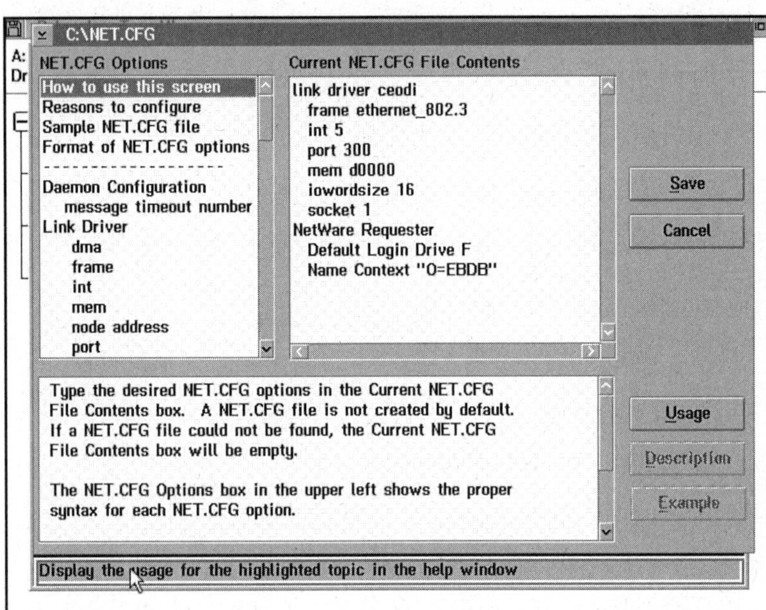

Figure 16.5

Using the INSTALL utility to edit the NET.CFG file.

The INSTALL utility can be accessed from the Novell Icon View. To edit the NET.CFG file using the INSTALL utility, proceed as follows:

1. From the Novell Icon View, select the INSTALL utility.

2. From the INSTALL utility main menu, choose **C**onfiguration, **T**his workstation to display the Default Location for NET.CFG File dialog box. Type the drive, path, and file name for the NET.CFG file. The default is C:\NET.CFG. Choose **E**dit when you are done to display the NET.CFG Edit Menu (refer to figure 16.5).

3. Scroll down the NET.CFG Options window to view various NET.CFG parameters you might want to include. Change to the Current NET.CFG File Contents window to make changes to your NET.CFG file. Choose any of the following three buttons to assist the process:

- **Usage.** Shows you how this parameter is used.
- **Description.** Gives you information on the parameter.
- **Example.** Gives you sample syntax for this parameter.

4. When done, choose Save to save the current contents of the NET.CFG file. You will have to reboot the workstation for the changes to take effect.

The following is a sample NET.CFG file created by the NetWare Client for OS/2 v2.1 installation program. Table 16.3, which follows the sample file, gives you a summary of the NET.CFG parameters added.

```
link driver ceodi
  frame ethernet_802.2
  int 5
  port 300
  mem d0000
  iowordsize 8
  socket 1
NetWare Requester
  Default Login Drive F
  Name Context "O=EBDB"
```

Table 16.3
NetWare Client for OS/2 v2.1 NET.CFG File Parameters

Section	Parameter	Default/ Values	Description
Daemon Configuration			Controls background processes.
	Message Timeout *nn*	Infinite	*nn* is how long, in milliseconds, you want to have pop-up messages stay on the screen. These messages can include other users sending you a message, or server broadcast messages. The default

continues

Table 16.3, Continued
NetWare Client for OS/2 v2.1 NET.CFG File Parameters

Section	Parameter	Default/ Values	Description
			specifies that the message stays in the screen indefinitely until you press Esc.
Link Support			Controls the behavior of the Link Support Layer (IEEE 802.2 specification). The parameters are the same as for DOS. For further information, see Chapter 14, "DOS Client Basics."
Link Driver			Controls NIC settings. Its parameters are the same as for DOS. For further information, see Chapter 14, "DOS Client Basics."
Named Pipes			Controls the behavior of this workstation with regard to Named Pipe applications.
	Advertise Board *nn*	1 / 1–16	Causes this workstation to advertise Named Pipe information for boards logically defined for this workstation. A *board* is a combination of physical NIC and a frame type. You can have one Ethernet NIC and four frame types assigned to the one NIC. In this case, there are four boards.

Default/ Section	Parameter	Values	Description
	Client Sessions *nn*	16 / 3–128	Controls the number of Named Pipe sessions allowed for this workstation. You need at least one session per Named Pipe connection. One application could spawn several connections. Sixteen usually is adequate.
	Machine Names *nn*	0 / 4–100	Controls how many Named Pipes server names are locally cached for faster access. The default of 0 causes the workstation to broadcast a query over the network for Named Pipes servers.
	Server Sessions *nn*	16 / 3–1,000	The number of sessions this machine can handle as a Named Pipes server. The number of SPX Sessions (discussed later in this table) must be one greater than this number.
NetWare Requester			Controls higher-level connection issues with the file server.
	Cache Buffers *nn*	8 / 0–30	Specifies the number of buffers maintained locally for network I/O. A higher number improves network throughput. More buffers use more local RAM. The NetWare Client software will not use more than 64 KB of RAM for Cache Buffers.
	Default Login Drive *letter*	L: / A–Z	Specifies the first drive letter to be assigned to a file server.

continues

Table 16.3, Continued
NetWare Client for OS/2 v2.1 NET.CFG File Parameters

Section	Parameter	Default/ Values	Description
	Display Hard Errors *boolean*	OFF or ON	If set ON, causes error messages (such as network errors) to appear on-screen, pausing all activity until resolved. If minor errors occur occasionally at your site that can be safely ignored, set this parameter OFF.
	Large Internet Packets *boolean*	ON or OFF	Adjusts whether the workstation is allowed to send large packets across IPX routers equipped with LIP (Large Internet Packet) protocol.
	Name Context *NDS Container*		Sets the default NDS context for this workstation. You also can accomplish this through a CX command in the STARTUP.CMD file.
	Packet Burst *boolean*	ON or OFF	Controls whether Packet Burst protocol is enabled for this workstation.
	Preferred Server *server*		Causes OS/2 to look for the named server instead of the first available server. If the preferred server cannot be located, the first available server is used.
	Preferred Tree *NDS Tree*		Causes OS/2 to connect to the named NDS Tree rather than the tree on the first available server. If the preferred tree cannot be located, the tree of the first available server is used.

Default/ Section	Parameter	Values	Description
	Request Retries *nn*	20 0–x	Instructs the NetWare for OS/2 Client to send a packet again in case of a communications failure. Increase this value if you are experiencing network errors but do not have time to locate the true source of the problem. The value of this parameter is theoretically unlimited. If the value is too large, however, the computer will appear to be locked up while the network driver repeatedly retries.
	Sessions *nn*	8 8–32	Limits the number of connections this workstation can have with all file servers. You must have three IPX sockets per connection.
	Signature Level *nn*	1 0–3	Sets the level of security across the network. The security offered by this process protects network packets from being intercepted and re-sent by a foreign workstation. 0 offers no security of this type. Level 3 offers the most security. The more security offered, the slower will be your network throughput.
Protocol Stack IPX			Controls IPX protocol parameters (including sockets).

continues

Table 16.3, Continued
NetWare Client for OS/2 v2.1 NET.CFG File Parameters

Section	Parameter	Default/ Values	Description
	Bind *driver*	First driver that loads	Associates the IPX protocol with the board initialized by *driver*.
	Router Mem *nn*	450	Specifies *nn* bytes allocated to routing requests to the network. The default of 450 accommodates 15 logical network boards.
	Sockets *nn*	64 9–128	Specifies the number of IPX sockets allocated. Should be at least three times the number of Sessions in the NetWare Requester section (see above).
Protocol Stack SPX			Controls the behavior of the SPX protocol on this workstation.
	Retry Count *nn*	20 1–255	*nn* represents the number of times SPX will retry in case of transmission error. This setting should be increased when experiencing difficulties with SPX-based applications (such as RCONSOLE). This can occur when you are going over several routers and network traffic is high.
	Sessions *nn*	16 9–1,000	Controls the number of SPX sessions allowed from this workstation. If you are using this workstation as a Named Pipes server, be sure

Default/ Section	Parameter	Values	Description
			that this setting is at least 1 greater than the number of Server Sessions under the Named Pipes section.

This table covers only common NET.CFG settings; the NET.CFG file contains many more settings.

Automating Your OS/2 Network Connection

After you have the NetWare for OS/2 Client software installed and properly configured, you might want to automate the login procedure. The most efficient way to accomplish this is to create a STARTUP.CMD file. This file contains commands that are executed before the OS/2 desktop is loaded. This file is similar to the DOS AUTOEXEC.BAT file. Bear in mind that there is an AUTOEXEC.BAT file in OS/2, but it is used for DOS sessions.

The STARTUP.CMD file is placed in the root directory and contains any valid OS/2 command. A common sequence of commands for the NetWare environment is as follows:

```
L:
CD OS2
CX .O=EBDB
LOGIN .cn=Admin.o=EBDB
MAP W:=SYS:APPS\WINWORD
C:
EXIT
```

The L: command moves to drive L, which is the first network drive, in the LOGIN directory on volume SYS:. The CD OS2 command changes to the SYS:LOGIN\OS2 directory, which contains OS/2-specific executables. The CX command changes this user to his default NDS Context. The LOGIN command supplies NetWare with a valid NDS user name. If this user has a password, NetWare will ask for it. The MAP command assigns drive letter W to the SYS:APPS\WINWORD directory on the file server.

The command file then moves the drive pointer back to drive C and exits. Without the final EXIT command, the OS/2 window that was used to invoke the STARTUP.CMD file will stay open on-screen.

Creating Shadows

A *shadow* in OS/2 is similar to a *link* in UNIX. The shadow file icon appears wherever you designate but is not the actual file itself. The shadow is actually a pointer to the actual file.

Creating shadows on your desktop of files on the file server can facilitate access to applications on the file server. The alternative is to go through either the Network icon or the Drives Icon View.

To create a shadow on your desktop of an application on the server, proceed as follows:

1. From the OS/2 desktop, choose either the Network icon or the Drives icon (from the OS/2 System - Icon View). From either of these two locations, select the drive letter assigned to the server volume that contains the desired application.

2. Move through the Tree View, clicking on directories as necessary, until the icon of the application's executable file is visible.

3. Click the right mouse button on the desired application icon. From the menu that appears, choose Create shadow to display the Create Shadow dialog box.

4. Select the desired target location for the shadow. If you want the shadow to appear on the OS/2 desktop, for example, select Desktop. Choose Create when you have selected the target location.

5. You now can close the Tree View windows and return to the desktop.

An icon that resembles the original application icon now appears in the desired location. You can continue in this fashion until the desktop (or other location on the workstation) is populated with shadows that point to the file server.

The shadow icons will appear even if the file server is not accessible. If you try to access an application when the file server is down or not accessible, you will receive an error message.

Exploring the Novell - Icon View

After the NetWare Client for OS/2 software is installed, a new icon view appears on your OS/2 desktop: the Novell - Icon View. This window is illustrated in figure 16.6. The following utilities are in the Novell - Icon View:

- ◆ NetWare Tools
- ◆ NetWare Client Documentation
- ◆ NetWare TSA
- ◆ NetWare Utilities Documentation
- ◆ NetWare Client Installation Utility
- ◆ Network Printer Utility (NPRINTER.EXE)

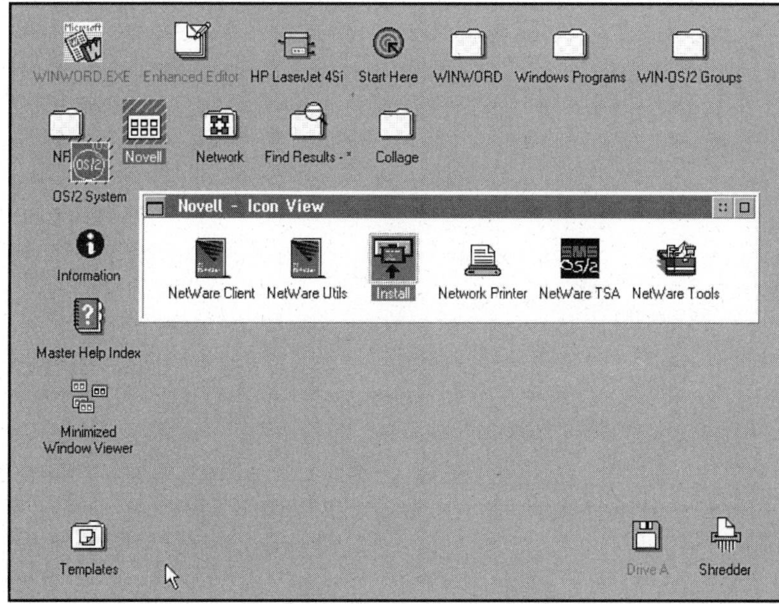

Figure 16.6

The Novell - Icon View.

This section discusses the various NetWare utilities provided in the Novell - Icon View.

Using the NetWare Tools Utility

The NetWare tools utility, which resembles the NWUSER.EXE utility provided for Windows clients, is a fast and easy way to use network resources (see fig. 16.7). Resources you can access include logging into the network, assigning drive letters to volume objects, redirecting printing to NetWare print queues, getting a list of users on the system, and browsing the NDS tree. This section explains some of the tasks you can perform by using this utility.

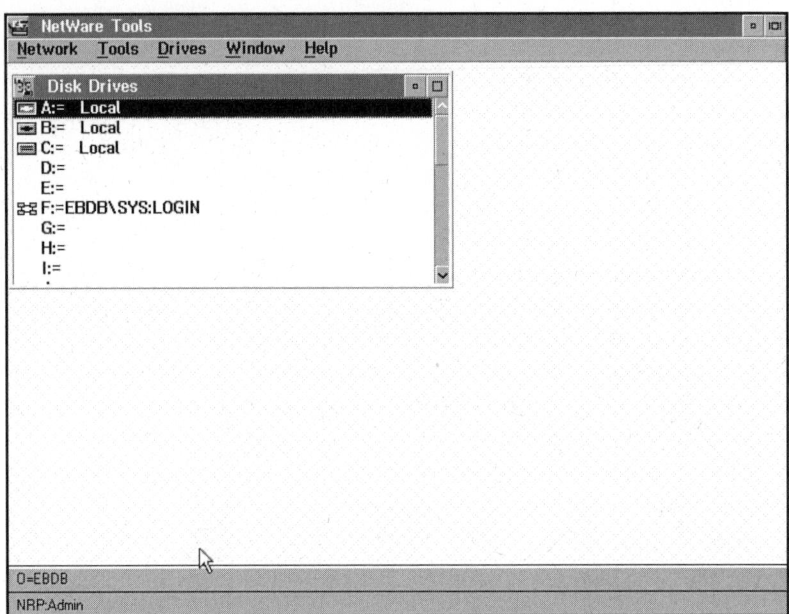

Figure 16.7
The NetWare Tools main screen.

Logging In to an NDS Tree

One of the first activities you will need to perform is to log in to the network. You can do so as follows:

1. From the NetWare Tools main screen, choose **T**ools, Di**r**ectory Tree to display the Directory Tree screen.

2. From the Directory Tree screen, press the Insert key. You will see the Log in to Directory Tree dialog box.

3. From the Log in to Directory Tree dialog box, you can choose **T**ree to log in to a specific NDS tree, or **S**erver to select a specific server. If you have several servers in a single tree and do not care which server you gain initial access to, choose **T**ree. Otherwise, select the specific server to which you want to log in. When you

log in to a server and supply a valid NDS name, you will be logged into the tree of which this server is a part.

If you need to log in as a bindery client, choose Server and supply a user name in the server's bindery context.

Alternatively, you can browse the tree, select the desired user name, and press Enter. You will be presented with the Log in to Directory Tree dialog box for that user.

Browsing the NDS Tree

You can use the NetWare Tools utility to browse the NDS tree. If you are not sure of the context or login name of your user identity on the network, you can use this tool to browse the tree. After you locate the proper user ID, you can double-click on the user object to pop up a login screen.

To browse the NDS tree, choose **T**ools, Directory t**r**ee. Figure 16.8 shows the resulting screen.

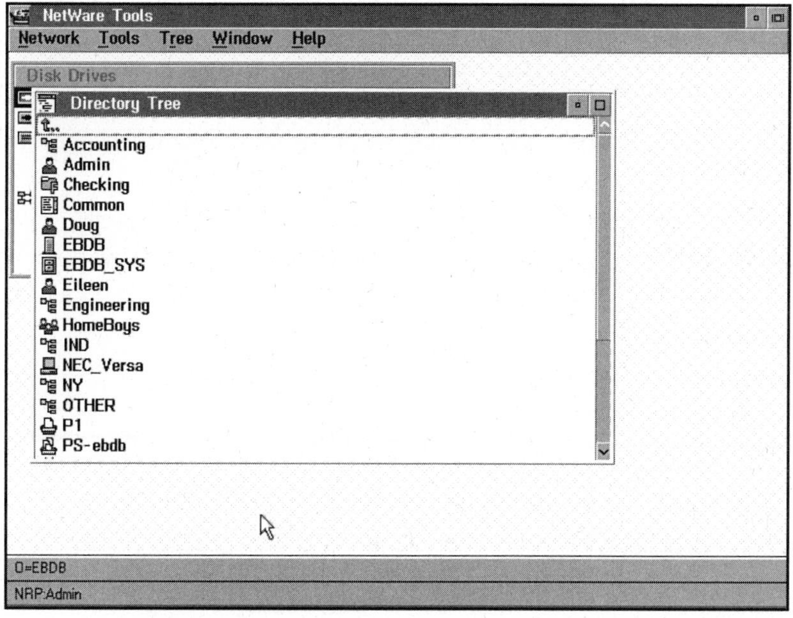

Figure 16.8

Browsing the NDS tree using the NetWare Tools utility.

Capturing a Printer Port

The NetWare Tools utility can be used to redirect printing to a NetWare print queue. To accomplish this, proceed as follows:

1. From the NetWare Tools main menu, choose **T**ools, **P**rinter ports to display the Printer Ports dialog box.

2. Select the desired LPT port to redirect. You can redirect a total of nine printer ports. Note that it does not matter whether these ports are physically available on your workstation. After you have selected the LPT port to redirect, the Capture LPT*x*:= dialog box appears, as shown in figure 16.9. *x* is the number of the port (1–9) that is captured.

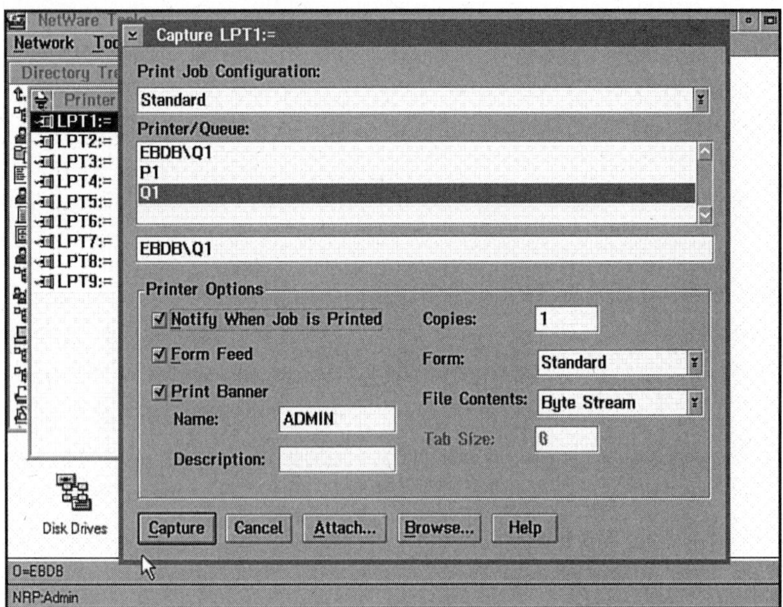

Figure 16.9
Capturing a printer port using the Capture LPTx:= dialog box.

3. From the Capture LPT*x*:= dialog box, you can enter the following information regarding the printer port redirection:

   - **Print Job Configuration.** This field is used to specify PRINTCON job configuration information, if available.

   - **Printer/Queue.** The top portion of this field lists all printers and queues visible on the network. You can scroll up and down this list until you locate the desired printer or queue. When you click on this printer or

queue, the bottom portion of the field will automatically be filled in. If you already know the name of the printer or queue, you can type it directly into the bottom field.

- **Notify When Job is Printed.** If this option is selected, you will be sent a broadcast telling you your job printed successfully, and on which printer.
- **Form Feed.** This option causes NetWare to add a page eject at the end of every print job. Some applications already do this, in which case you will end up wasting an extra sheet of paper after each print job.
- **Print Banner.** The print banner is used to identify the job owner, the file name of the print job, and the date and time printed. This is a valuable option in an office where printers are shared. If you have sole access to a printer, the office is small, or printing is infrequent, you might want to disable this option.
- **Name.** If this field is not filled in, your login name appears in the banner name field. This option enables you to override the default for a banner name.
- **Description.** The default description on the banner page is the file name. Again, you can override the default by filling in this field.
- **Copies.** This option represents the number of times the print job will print.
- **Form.** If you have used the PRINTDEF or NWADMIN utilities to create printer forms, you can select from these forms in the Form list box. The form number will accompany the print job. When the job reaches the print server and this form number is not currently mounted in the printer, the print server will cause the printer to pause. A message will be broadcast across the network instructing you, or the person on the notify list, to mount this form number. After this has been accomplished, use PCONSOLE or access the print server directly to instruct it that the proper form has been mounted. After this has occurred, the print server will restart the printer and your print job will appear.
- **File Contents.** This option should, in most cases, be set to Byte Stream. Byte Stream mode causes all printing to go to the printer unaltered. If Text mode is selected, tab characters will be replaced with the number of spaces indicated by the Tab Size field.

4. After selecting the print job capture information, click on the Capture button. If you are not attached to the network, you can use the Attach or the Browse buttons to connect with NetWare file servers containing print queues.

Accessing File Servers

The Servers tool enables you to perform actions on the selected file server. To access the Servers tool, choose **T**ools, **S**ervers from the NetWare Tools main menu. A list of NetWare file servers appears, as shown in figure 16.10. The Servers tool enables you to attach or detach from specific servers, change your password, and view users logged into a specific server.

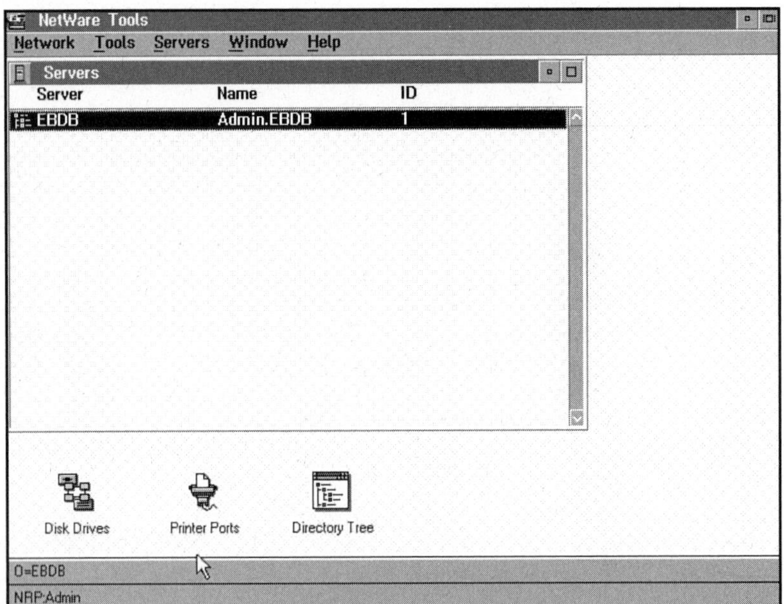

Figure 16.10
The NetWare Tools - Servers screen.

Viewing and Sending Messages to Network Users

For another way to view a list of users logged in to the network, choose **T**ools, **U**ser Lists. You will see a list of users logged into the network, as shown in figure 16.11. This list shows users on the network, as compared to users accessing individual servers, which was discussed earlier.

To send a message to one or more of the users on the list, select the user or users and proceed as follows:

1. Choose **U**sers, Send **M**essage to display the Send a Message dialog box.
2. Type the message in the Send a Message dialog box, and then choose **S**end. The message appears as a pop-up window in the recipient's screen. If the recipient is using DOS, the message appears on the first line of the user's screen.

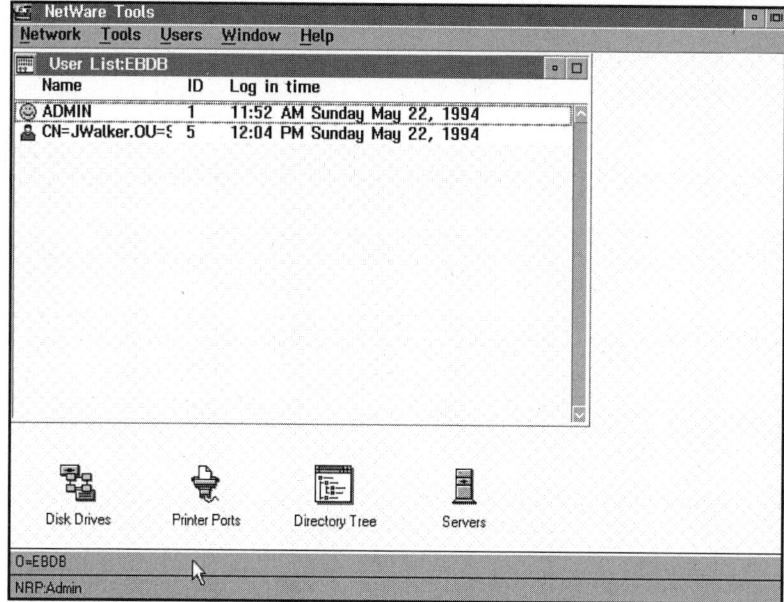

Figure 16.11
Users Tool screen showing a list of users logged in to the network.

Assigning Drive Letters

You can use the Disk Drives tool to assign drive letters to the file system on a NetWare server. This function parallels the Drive Mapping function of the Windows-based NWUSER utility discussed in Chapter 15.

To assign a drive letter to a NetWare directory, proceed as follows:

1. From the NetWare Tools main menu, choose **T**ools, **D**isk drives. The Disk Drives screen appears.

2. From the Disk Drives screen, double-click on the drive letter you want to map. The Map dialog box appears.

3. Fill in the following fields in the Map dialog box:

   Drive is the desired drive letter (A through Z) to map.

   Volume is the volume object to which you wish to map.

   Directory is the directory on the volume object.

   Path contains the server, volume, and directory. This field is automatically built up as you select items from the Volume and Directory fields.

4. You can use the following buttons to assist in the mapping process:

   Map actually performs the mapping.

   Cancel cancels this mapping operation.

   Attach can be used to connect you to another server.

   Browse lets you browse the tree for additional servers or volume objects.

   Help gives you online help.

5. When you choose the Map button to complete the operation, you are returned to the Disk Drives screen. The new drive mapping appears on the list.

Looking at the NetWare Tools Menu Structure

The following list charts the menu structure of the NetWare Tools utility. Note that some commands have alternate keystrokes that can be used. The underscored letter represents the hot key, which in conjunction with the Alt key enables you to access that menu or command. By pressing Alt+T, for example, you can access the Tools menu. Indented options are in a pull-down menu.

First two menus:

- Network
- Tools

    Disk drivers

    Printer ports

    Servers

    Directory tree

    User lists

    Print queues

The third menu option varies between one of the following:

- Drives

    Map (Ins)

    Delete map (Del)

    List all

    List mapped only

- **P**rinters
  - **C**apture (Ins)
  - **E**nd capture (Del)
  - **V**iew queue
- **S**ervers
  - **A**ttach
  - **D**etach
  - Change **p**assword
  - View **u**sers
  - De**t**ach all
  - L**i**st all
  - List attached **o**nly
  - **S**et primary
- **U**sers
  - Send **m**essage
  - **S**elect all (Ctrl+/)
  - **D**eselect all (Ctrl+\)
  - List **a**ttached only
  - List **f**ull name
- T**r**ee
  - Change t**r**ee
  - Change co**n**text
  - **L**og in (Ins)
  - Lo**g** out (Del)
  - Change **p**assword
  - View **u**sers
  - **M**ap
  - **C**apture LPT1

View queue

Attach server

- Queues

  Select all (Ctrl+/)

  Deselect all (Ctrl+\)

  Hold

  Release

  Delete (DEL)

The fourth and fifth menus follow:

- Window
- Help

Using NetWare Client for OS/2 v2.1 Documentation

The NetWare Client for OS/2 software includes two online manuals, *NetWare Client Documentation* and *NetWare Utilities Documentation.* The online manuals appear with a list box listing the table of contents of the manual; for example, the table of contents for the *NetWare Client Documentation* is shown in figure 16.12.

You can use keystrokes, menu selections, or mouse clicks to expand the topics that appear in the Contents list box. These actions are described in table 16.4.

Table 16.4
Keystrokes for the *NetWare Client Documentation* Manual

Keystroke	Menu Selections	Mouse	Action
+	Options, Expand one level	Click on any level with a plus (+) sign next to it	Expands this option by one level
*	Options, Expand branch	N/A	Expands this branch and shows all levels
Ctrl+*	Options, Expand all	N/A	Expands all branches and shows all levels

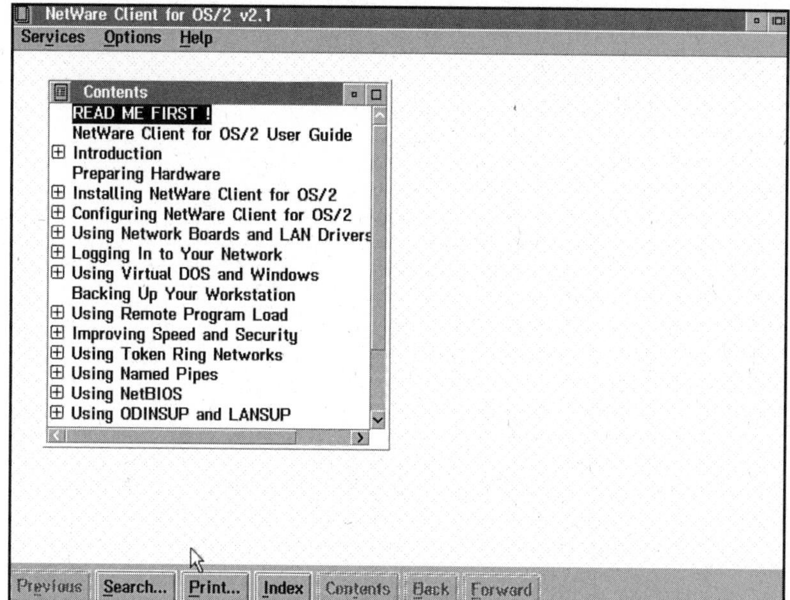

Figure 16.12
The Contents list box for the NetWare Client Documentation *manual.*

Double-click on any given item in the table of contents to go to that page in the manual. You also can access a word search by pressing Alt+S or choosing the **S**earch button. Type a word or words, and then select where you want to search. Choices include **T**his section, **M**arked sections, **A**ll sections, **I**ndex, Marked **l**ibraries, and All li**b**raries. When the search if completed, a "hit list" appears, showing you section titles that contain the target search string. Double-click on any of the listed items to be taken to that page in the manual.

NetWare Client Documentation gives you information on the workings of the NetWare Client software, configuration information, and NET.CFG file settings. *NetWare Utilities Documentation* gives you information on selected OS/2-specific utilities. These include CX, LOGIN, MAP, NLIST, and the Network Tools.

Using the NetWare TSA Utility

The NetWare TSA utility, available from the Novell Icon View window, loads a *Target Service Agent* (TSA). The TSA enables a NetWare file server using a *Storage Management Services* (SMS)-compliant backup system (including Novell's SBACKUP.NLM) to back up this workstation through a file server. There are several steps involved in loading the NetWare TSA utility. The TSA first must be loaded and initialized. You then must designate authorized users so that the files on your workstation are safeguarded from being accessed inappropriately. Finally, you need to designate which workstation resources are to be backed up. The initial TSA screen, once loaded, is shown in figure 16.13.

Figure 16.13

The NetWare SMS Target Service Agent for OS/2 screen.

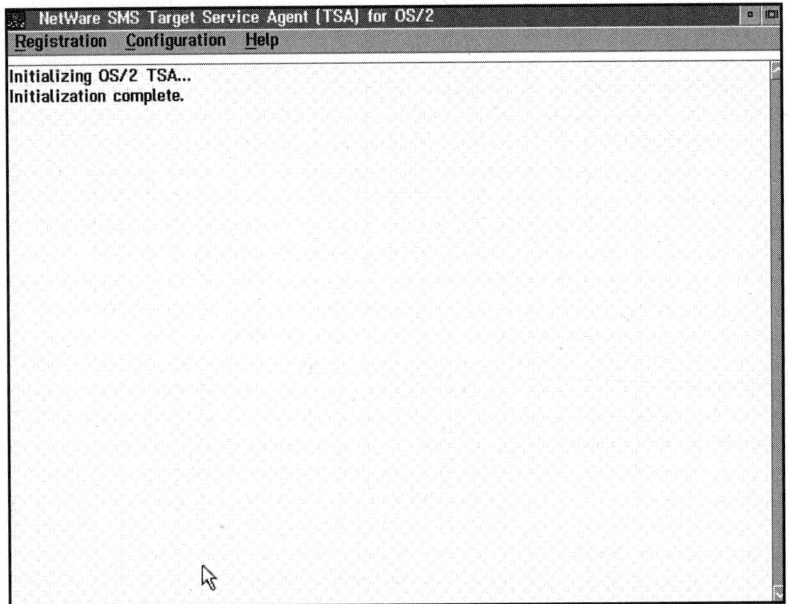

To add authorized TSA users, proceed as follows:

1. From the TSA main menu, choose **C**onfiguration, **U**sers to display the Authorized TSA Users screen.

2. Type the new user name and password, and then click on Add to add them to the list of authorized users. Click on Close when you are done adding to the list.

To enable the TSA to access workstation resources, proceed as follows:

1. From the TSA main menu, choose **C**onfiguration, **R**esources to display the Workstation Resources screen.

2. Place resources in the Available to TSA or Not Available to TSA lists, and then choose OK.

To give this workstation a name the server will recognize, from the main menu choose **R**egistration, WS **N**ame. Type the name of the workstation, and then click on OK.

To enable the file server to back up the workstation using SMS, choose **R**egistration, Register with Server to display the Register with server dialog box. Type the name of the host server, then select Register. The TSA is now loaded and available to the file server backup agent. Remember to load the necessary software at the file server to enable it to back up workstations.

Using the OS/2 NetWare Utilities on the File Server

OS/2 versions of the NetWare management utilities are available from the file server if you selected the OS/2 Utilities File Set during the file server installation. The utilities specifically written for OS/2 are located in the following directories on the file server:

SYS:PUBLIC\OS2

SYS:LOGIN\OS2

These utilities include EXE and CMD files. The EXE files are OS/2 executables. The CMD files are OS/2 command files and are used as reminders that these utilities are not supported in NetWare 4.1. The utilities in SYS:LOGIN\OS2 and SYS:PUBLIC\OS2 are shown in the directory listing that follows. The sample directory listing was drawn from a server with both English and French language files loaded.

```
[F:\OS2]dir

 The volume label in drive F is SYS.
 The Volume Serial Number is 2DEC:F8EF
 Directory of F:\OS2

 6-01-94    5:18p     <DIR>          0  .
 6-01-94    5:18p     <DIR>          0  ..
 6-01-94    5:18p     <DIR>          0  NLS
 9-01-94   12:12p     75328          0  MAP.EXE
 9-01-94   10:24a    129616          0  NLIST.EXE
 9-24-92   11:48a        26          0  SLIST.CMD
 8-09-94    3:23p     29584          0  TYPEMSG.EXE
 9-24-92   11:48a        27          0  ATTACH.CMD
 9-01-94   12:04p    128448          0  LOGIN.EXE
 8-11-94    4:07p     48304          0  CX.EXE
        10 file(s)      411333 bytes used
                      17072128 bytes free

[F:\OS2]
[F:\PUBLIC\OS2]dir /w

 The volume label in drive F is SYS        FAT16
 The Volume Serial Number is 439E:7CD9
 Directory of F:\PUBLIC\OS2
```

```
BRWSPREF.INI    CAPTURE.EXE     CASTOFF.CMD     CASTON.CMD      CHKDIR.CMD
CHKVOL.CMD      CX.EXE          DSPACE.CMD      ENDCAP.CMD      FLAG.EXE
FLAGDIR.CMD     GRANT.CMD       LISTDIR.CMD     GLCR20DP.DLL    GLCV30DP.DLL
GLFS20DP.DLL    LOGIN.EXE       LOGOUT.EXE      MAP.EXE         NCOPY.EXE
NCUPDATE.EXE    NDIR.EXE        NLIST.EXE       NPATH.EXE       NPRINT.EXE
NPRINTER.EXE    NSAPI.DLL       NVER.EXE        NWXTRACT.EXE    PSC.EXE
NWADMIN.EXE     NWC0BRWS.DLL    NWC0CORP.DLL    NWC0CTRL.DLL    NWC0DS.DLL
NWC0MOD0.DLL    NWC0MOD1.DLL    NWC0MPEW.DLL    NWC0PAR.DLL     NWC0PRNT.DLL
NWC0VIS0.DLL    NWC0VIS1.DLL    NWC0VIS2.DLL    PURGE.EXE       REMOVE.CMD
REVOKE.CMD      RIGHTS.EXE      SALVAGE.CMD     SEND.EXE        SESSION.CMD
SETPASS.EXE     SETTTS.EXE      SLIST.CMD       SMODE.CMD       SYSCON.CMD
SYSTIME.EXE     TLIST.CMD       TYPEMSG.EXE     UIMPORT.EXE     USERLIST.CMD
VERSION.CMD     VOLINFO.CMD     WHOAMI.EXE      ALLOW.CMD       ATTACH.CMD
ATOTAL.EXE      [NLS]
        67 file(s)    3918575 bytes used
                     17072128 bytes free

[F:\PUBLIC\OS2]
```

These utilities behave exactly as do their DOS counterparts. The major difference is that they have been optimized to run under OS/2. Figure 16.14 shows the NetWare Administrator running on OS/2.

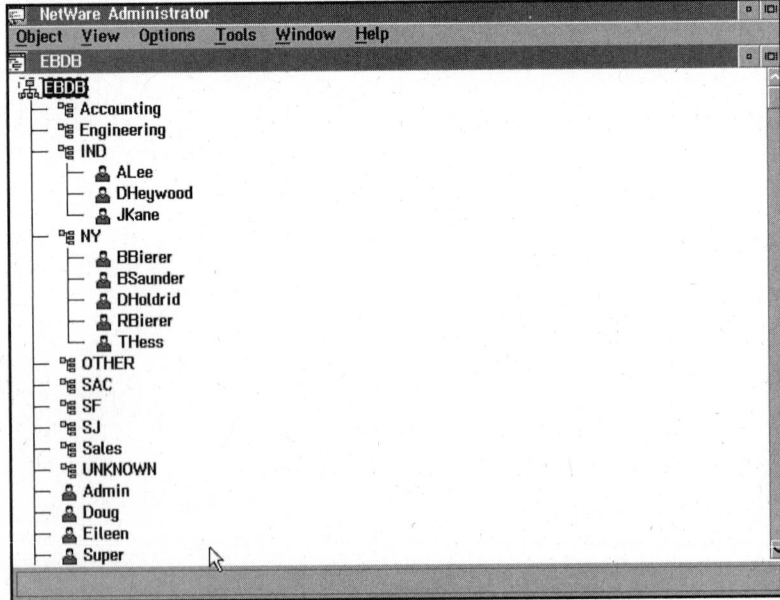

Figure 16.14
Running NWADMIN.EXE from SYS:PUBLIC/OS2.

Figure 16.15 shows a printout of the result of running ATOTAL.EXE from SYS:PUBLIC\OS2.

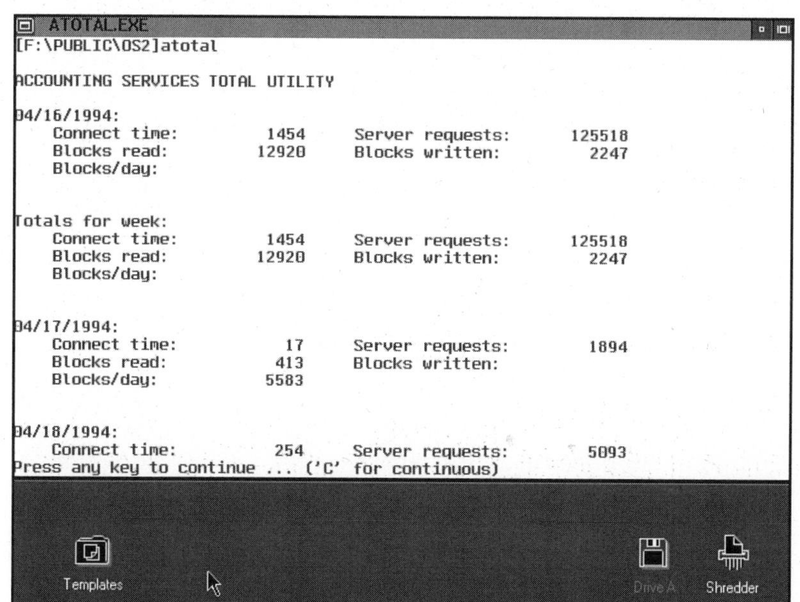

Figure 16.15
The results of running ATOTAL.EXE from SYS:PUBLIC/OS2.

Summary

This chapter gave you a detailed look at installing, configuring, and using the NetWare Client for OS/2 v2.1 software. The first part of the chapter showed you how to obtain the client software. Techniques included downloading the files through CompuServe and the Internet. Alternatively, you can obtain the client software through the INSTALL.NLM utility on a file server with the NetWare 4.1 installation CD mounted. The chapter proceeded to step you through moving the installation files to disk and performing the client installation. Changes to the OS/2 CONFIG.SYS and NET.CFG files were discussed in detail.

The next section discussed how to automate your workstation network connection. The two areas you learned about in this chapter include placing a LOGIN command in the STARTUP.CMD file and creating shadows of network applications for easy access.

The remainder of the chapter was devoted to some of the NetWare utilities provided with NetWare and the NetWare for OS/2 Client. You learned how to use the Network Tools utility, which enables you to capture a printer port to a network print queue, assign drive letters to directories on a file server volume, browse the NDS tree, and send messages to users. The client software includes two online manuals. The *NetWare Client Documentation* provides information on how the client software works and how to configure it. The *NetWare Utilities Documentation* provides information on NetWare utilities specifically designed for OS/2. You learned how to set up and configure the NetWare TSA that enables an OS/2 workstation to be backed up from a file server with SMS-compliant software. You also learned about utilities in SYS:LOGIN\OS2 and SYS:PUBLIC\OS2 that are optimized for OS/2.

UNIX Clients

There has been steady interest in UNIX since the 1960s when it was first introduced. UNIX is an operating system that operates on more hardware platforms than any other operating system in existence. UNIX was first developed at Bell Labs in the 1960s. It was written to provide a superior programming environment. UNIX was written in C language, and C language was developed using UNIX. It was the operating system of choice for major universities and scientific institutions. Many students first learned about computers using UNIX. When these same students went out into the business world and started using computers in the business environment, they demanded UNIX as their operating system. UNIX has successfully penetrated most international markets and is extremely popular in Europe and Asia.

The advent of the microprocessor was, in some respects, a severe blow to universal acceptance of UNIX. By the late 1970s and early 1980s, UNIX had grown in both size and power. The wimpy microprocessors and support circuitry available at this time were not able to handle the demands of UNIX. A less demanding operating system was required. Thus, DOS was born. Sporadic attempts to place UNIX on a microprocessor occurred throughout the 1980s. Success stories included Microsoft's XENIX, which ran on the Tandy/Radio Shack Model II. Another success was Sun Microsystem's version of UNIX, which ran on

Motorola 68*xxx*-based machines. As the popularity and importance of the IBM PC and its bevy of clones continued to grow, less and less of the overall computer market consisted of computers running UNIX.

UNIX has undergone somewhat of a resurgence in popularity due, oddly enough, to the increased hardware demands of competing operating systems such as OS/2, DOS machines running Windows, and Windows NT. PCs are now fully capable of supporting the demands of UNIX. PC users are becoming less enamored with DOS. The full 32-bit, preemptive multitasking environment of UNIX beckons once again. More and more NetWare LANs are linking to UNIX systems.

The following section gives you an overview of the different ways by which a UNIX client can be connected to a NetWare network.

For a thorough examination of UNIX, please see *Inside UNIX*, published by New Riders Publishing.

Understanding UNIX Client Access through IPX/SPX

Most UNIX systems connected to a LAN use the Internet Protocol Suite (often called TCP/IP, which represents two of the most popular of the Internet protocols). TCP/IP networks are difficult to configure and maintain, however, except to the most savvy of network Administrators. Successful administration of a TCP/IP network requires some knowledge of UNIX and the ability to modify a bewildering array of files often located in obscure directories. For this reason, recent attention has focused on solutions based on Novell's IPX/SPX protocol.

Novell's IPX/SPX protocol has a great deal of allure for network Administrators. Unlike TCP/IP, each client does not have to be separately configured with an address. IPX uses the hardware address built into the network interface card. The cabling segment is assigned an IPX Network Address at the file server. Each IPX-based client simply "listens" for the IPX network address broadcast periodically by NetWare file servers, and uses this address. In contrast, a TCP/IP-based client must either be configured with an IP address or must use Boot Protocol (BOOTP) or Reverse Address Resolution Protocol (RARP) to gain an IP address.

Most major UNIX players now offer some sort of IPX/SPX-based connectivity. Santa Cruz Operations (SCO) UNIX and Sun Microsystems are examples of "big names" in

the UNIX/PC industry that offer such connectivity. After the IPX/SPX connectivity package has been added to the base system, the UNIX client can now authenticate to the NetWare server, then proceed to mount portions of NetWare volumes as part of the local file system. The mount command enables the UNIX user to access subdirectories or files on the NetWare file server.

The mount Procedure

Hard disk space on UNIX systems is divided into subdivisions known as *file systems.* These file systems share a resemblance to a NetWare volume. You can divide the disk space of a NetWare server into independent volumes. Each volume is located on one (or more) hard drive and is allocated a finite amount of space. Likewise, the available disk space on a UNIX computer is divided up into file systems that are placed on various hard drives and allocated a finite amount of space.

Hard disk space on peripheral devices and remote computers on the LAN is viewed by the UNIX computer in terms of its file system. Thus, file systems exist for both CD-ROM drives (cdfs) and floppy drives (fdfs). Sun Microsystems developed a generic file system to give access to hard drive space on remote computers on a LAN. This generic file system is known as *Network File System* (NFS). NFS drivers are loaded on the remote computer system. UNIX computers also have NFS drivers installed. UNIX systems can then access any remote computer with NFS drivers using the TCP/IP protocol.

The procedure used to gain access to remote computers equipped with NFS drivers is the mount command. Here is the generic syntax for this command:

```
mount -F <file system> <options> <remote computer> <local directory>
```

The *file system* can be nfs, or some other file system that is appropriate for your level of connectivity. Used in conjunction with the *-F* parameter, the *file system* must be defined in the /etc/nfstab file of the UNIX host. (The name of this file varies from system to system.) An example of *options* is ro (read only). *Remote computer* typically includes the name of the computer as specified in your /etc/hosts file, a colon (:), and the directory path. The *local directory* is an empty subdirectory you create and is referred to as a *mount point.*

The following example mounts a file system nfs from a computer dallas, and a directory /data. The local mount point is an empty directory /mnt.

```
mount -F nfs dallas:/data /mnt
```

After this command has succeeded, changing to the /mnt directory places you on the computer dallas. If the /mnt directory on your local UNIX host is not empty before the mount command is issued, you are not able to access any of its files or directories after issuing the mount command. After the mount is reversed using the umount command, any files or directories under the local mount point directory are again visible.

Using UnixWare

UnixWare is a special version of System V Release 4.2 UNIX produced by Novell. UnixWare was originally a joint venture of Novell and Unix Systems Laboratories (USL). The company formed around this venture was called Univel. After Novell acquired USL in 1993, Univel was merged into Novell under the Novell Unix Systems Group.

UnixWare is designed to run on an Intel 80386-based (or higher) PC and comes in two versions: Personal Edition and Application Server. *Personal Edition* is a stripped-down version of the operating system designed for individual users. It comes equipped with a limited command set, an X-Windows-based graphical user interface, NetWare connectivity through IPX, and TCP/IP. *Application Server* includes the features of Personal Edition and allows unlimited logins (PE only enables two users to log in at one time), a C Compiler, a full UNIX command set, and NFS.

A UnixWare client can access a NetWare file server through either IPX or TCP/IP. When using TCP/IP, the UnixWare client uses the NFS file system and follows the mount procedure outlined above. UnixWare has the unique advantage of built-in NetWare connectivity using the IPX protocol.

Built into the UNIX kernel of UnixWare computers is the NetWare Unix Client (NUC). This module enables the UnixWare PC to issue NetWare Core Protocol (NCP) requests over the LAN using the IPX protocol. Several other components round out the picture. The NetWare Unix Client File System (NUCFS) component enables volumes on NetWare file servers to be seen as remote file systems much like nfs. The NetWare Unix Client Auto Mount Daemon (NUCAMD) constantly listens for requests for NetWare file services.

When the UnixWare client attempts to access a NetWare volume, UnixWare first handles the authentication process. After the user is authenticated, nucamd automatically mounts the desired NetWare volume onto a predefined special mount point, /.NetWare. File servers are viewed as directories with the extension .nws (NetWare Server). Volumes are viewed as directories with the extension .nwv (NetWare Volume). The next release of UnixWare eliminates the .nws and .nwv extensions.

Here is a sample listing of the /.NetWare auto-mount point:

```
$ cd /.NetWare
dabierer:[/.NetWare]
$ ls -l
total 30
dr-xr-xr-x  2 dabierer other    512 Dec 31 1994 ebdb2.nws
dr-xr-xr-x  2 dabierer other    512 Dec 31 1994 ebdb3x.nws
dr-xr-xr-x  2 dabierer other    512 Dec 31 1994 ebdb4.nws
dr-xr-xr-x  2 dabierer other    512 Dec 31 1994 ebdb5.nws
dr-xr-xr-x  2 dabierer other    512 Dec 31 1994 ebdb6.nws
dr-xr-xr-x  2 dabierer other    512 Dec 31 1994 ebdb7.nws
dr-xr-xr-x  2 dabierer other    512 Dec 31 1994 lab1.nws
dr-xr-xr-x  2 dabierer other    512 Dec 31 1994 nde.nws
dr-xr-xr-x  2 dabierer other    512 Dec 31 1994 NYC1.nws
dr-xr-xr-x  2 dabierer other    512 Dec 31 1994 NYC2.nws
dr-xr-xr-x  2 dabierer other    512 Dec 31 1994 NYC4.nws
dr-xr-xr-x  2 dabierer other    512 Dec 31 1994 NYC5.nws
dr-xr-xr-x  2 dabierer other    512 Dec 31 1994 NYC6.nws
dr-xr-xr-x  2 dabierer other    512 Dec 31 1994 chi1.nws
dr-xr-xr-x  2 dabierer other    512 Dec 31 1994 chi2.nws
```

After you change to a file server directory, you must authenticate to the file server before proceeding any further. The nwlogin command can be used for this purpose. The generic syntax for this command is:

```
nwlogin <file server>/<username>
```

You must supply a password. If the login name and password match, you can view the file server's volumes as follows:

```
$ nwlogin lab1/su1
dabierer:[/.NetWare]
$ cd lab1.nws
dabierer:[/.NetWare/lab1.nws]
$ ls -l
total 56
drwx------  2 dabierer other    512 Feb 1 1995 ed.nwv
drwx------  2 dabierer other    512 Jul 26 11:41 microhouse.nwv
drwx------  2 dabierer other    512 Feb 1 1995 sys.nwv
drwx------  2 dabierer other    512 Feb 1 1995 sys1.nwv
drwx------  2 dabierer other    512 Feb 1 1995 sys2.nwv
drwx------  2 dabierer other    512 Feb 1 1995 sys3.nwv
drwx------  2 dabierer other    512 Feb 1 1995 sys4.nwv
dabierer:[/.NetWare/lab1.nws]
```

UnixWare authenticates to NetWare servers as a *bindery* client. The NetWare account you use with the nwlogin command must be a user object in the file server's bindery context. The UnixWare client gains all the trustee rights of the user object authenticated. A user accessing a NetWare file server through UnixWare is not able to make use of any NDS services.

At this point, you can change to any of the volume directories. To get to volume SYS:, for example, proceed as follows:

```
$ cd sys.nwv
dabierer:[/.NetWare/lab1.nws/sys.nwv]
$ ls -l
total 320

drwx------  2 dabierer other     1 Feb 1 1995 etc
drwx------  2 dabierer other     1 Feb 1 1995 login
drwx------  2 dabierer other     1 Feb 1 1995 mail
drwx------  2 dabierer other     1 May 11 14:55 mhs
drwx------  2 dabierer other     1 Feb 1 1995 public
drwx------  2 dabierer other     1 Feb 3 15:44 queues
drwx------  2 dabierer other     1 Feb 1 1995 system
--w------  1 dabierer other   4228 Jul 26 11:39 tts$log.err
--w------  1 dabierer other   8396 Jul 26 11:39 vol$log.err
```

At this point you are at the root of volume SYS:.

The next release of UnixWare does away with the ".nws" and ".nwv" syntax. To access volume SYS on a server EBDB, for example, you can use this syntax:

```
cd /.NetWare/ebdb/sys
```

The Role of NUC.NLM on the File Server

Two NLMs must be loaded onto the NetWare file server to ensure proper UnixWare connectivity. They are NUC.NLM and NFS.NAM, and both are provided with UnixWare. NFS.NAM provides proper file naming conventions between NetWare and UnixWare. NUC.NLM is discussed in the following paragraphs. NFS.NAM is discussed later in this chapter.

NUC.NLM's function is to provide for the proper transference of UNIX permissions to NetWare trustee rights. NUC.NLM also provides a means of identifying UnixWare

users and mapping them to NetWare user accounts using the files described in the next section.

NUC.NLM's function is to provide UNIX User ID (UID) mapping to NetWare user objects. In addition, NUC.NLM controls the assignment of security rights. A UnixWare user may issue a chmod command, which changes the permissions on a UNIX file. NUC.NLM creates corresponding NetWare trustee rights. Table 17.1 summarizes the UNIX file permissions and corresponding NetWare trustee rights. Note that the rights are assigned to three NetWare objects: the user object, the group object, which is mapped by the NFSGROUP file (see next section), and the group object EVERYONE.

The chmod command is used in UNIX to change the permissions on a file or directory. This command is the equivalent of the NetWare RIGHTS command.

TABLE 17.1
UNIX File Permissions and NetWare Rights

Type of File	Permission	NetWare Rights
File	r	Read and File Scan
	w	Write
	x	N/A
Directory	r	File Scan
	w	Create
	x	N/A

Translation of UNIX Permissions to NetWare Trustee Rights

The translation of UNIX permissions to NetWare trustee rights is not precise. Table 17.2 summarizes the results when a UnixWare user issues the chmod command on a file located on a NetWare server. NUC.NLM provides the translation between the UNIX permission mask and NetWare trustee rights. NUC.NLM also provides feedback to the UnixWare user in the form of a UNIX permission mask.

The UNIX command to change permissions (a cross between a DOS attribute and NetWare trustee rights) is as follows:

```
chmod <permission mask> <filename(s) ¦ directory(s)>
```

The *permission mask* is an octal (base 8) number that sets the rights of the file owner, the primary group of the file owner, and all other users.

As you can see from the table, a UNIX command such as the following will have unexpected results:

```
chmod 700 test.file
```

TABLE 17.2
UNIX chmod File Operations Under NUC.NLM

chmod Mask	Resulting Mask	NetWare File Rights to Owner
700	-rwxrw-rw-	[SRWCEMFA]
600	-rw-rw-rw-	[SRWCEMFA]
500	-rwxrw-rw-	[SR CEMFA]
400	-rw-rw-rw-	[SR CEMFA]
300	-rwxrw-rw-	[S WCEMFA]
200	-rw-rw-rw-	[S WCEMFA]
100	-rwxrw-rw-	[S CEMFA]
000	-rw-rw-rw-	[S CEMFA]

If you were to perform the following command:

```
chmod 500 test.file
```

You should expect the following UNIX permission mask:

```
-r-x------
```

As you can see, however, if you have 7 or 6 in the chmod mask, the resulting mask is rwx. If you have 5 or 4, the Write right is removed. If you have a 3 or 2, the Read right is removed. If you have a 1 or 0, the Read and Write rights are removed. In all cases, the Supervisor right is granted, which results in all rights in any case.

chmod operations on directories are even more surprising. As you can see in table 17.3, if you have a 5, 4, 1, or 0 in the permission mask, the Create right is removed. Otherwise, the user gains full rights. Again, the Supervisor right is assigned, which gives the user full effective rights.

Table 17.3
UNIX chmod Directory Operations Under NUC.NLM

chmod Mask	Resulting Mask	NetWare Directory Rights to Owner
700	drwxrwxrwx	[SRWCEMFA]
600	drwxrwxrwx	[SRWCEMFA]
500	drwxrwxrwx	[SRW EMFA]
400	drwxrwxrwx	[SRW EMFA]
300	drwxrwxrwx	[SRWCEMFA]
200	drwxrwxrwx	[SRWCEMFA]
100	drwxrwxrwx	[SRW EMFA]
000	drwxrwxrwx	[SRW EMFA]

Consider the following sequence of events:

```
$ mkdir test
dabierer:[/.NetWare/ebdb5-sac.nws/sys.nwv]
$ ls -l
drwxrwxrwx  2 dabierer other    512 Aug 3 12:08 test
...
dabierer:[/.NetWare/ebdb5-sac.nws/sys.nwv]
$ cd test
dabierer:[/.NetWare/ebdb5-sac.nws/sys.nwv/test]
$ touch xyz
dabierer:[/.NetWare/ebdb5-sac.nws/sys.nwv/test]
$ chmod 765 xyz
dabierer:[/.NetWare/ebdb5-sac.nws/sys.nwv/test]
$ ls -l
total 0
-rwxrw-rwx  1 dabierer other     0 Aug 4 1994 xyz
dabierer:[/.NetWare/ebdb5-sac.nws/sys.nwv/test]
```

This example performed the following actions:

- A directory `test` was created.
- The owner is the user `dabierer`.

- The group of the directory is `other`.
- The permission mask of the directory is all.
- A file `xyz` was created.
- The `chmod` command changed the permissions to `rwxrw-rwx`.

Note that the chmod 765 xyz command should have changed the mask to rwxrw-r-x. Because the file is located on a NetWare server, the rights work differently. The file has the following attributes:

```
F:\TEST>ndir *.* /r
Files        = Files contained in this path
DOS Attr       = DOS file attributes
NetWare Attr     = NetWare file attributes
Status        = Compression/Migration status
Filter        = Inherited Rights Filter
Rights        = Effective Rights
Owner        = ID of user who created or copied the file

EBDB5-SAC/SYS:TEST\*.*
Files        DOS Attr  NetWare Attr   Status Filter   Rights
--------------- -------- ---------------- ----- ---------- ---------
XYZ        [Rw---A] [--------------]  --- [SRWCEMFA] [SRWCEMFA]


       0 bytes (0 bytes in 0 blocks allocated)
       1 File
```

The following NetWare file trustee rights were created:

```
F:\TEST>rights *.* /t
EBDB5-SAC\SYS:TEST\XYZ
User trustees:
   SU1                        [SRWCEMFA]
----------
Group trustees:
   OTHER                       [SRWCEMFA]
   EVERYONE                     [SR CEMFA]
```

The following NetWare directory trustee rights were created:

```
F:\>rights sys:test /t
EBDB5-SAC\SYS:\TEST
User trustees:
   SU1                           [ RWCEMFA]
----------
Group trustees:
   OTHER                          [ R   F ]
   EVERYONE                        [ R EMF ]
```

NUC support in the next release of UnixWare has radically changed. The permissions rights translation is much more accurate.

File Server Configuration Files

Three files must be maintained to provide for the mapping of UnixWare user IDs to NetWare user accounts. They are located in the SYS:ETC directory. The file names are as follows:

NFSUSERS

NFSGROUP

NFSPARAM

The NFSUSERS file contains a series of lines. Each line is in the following format:

```
<UNIX UID>             <NetWare Account>
```

The *UNIX UID* is the user ID number on the UNIX client. This number can be obtained for your own account by logging into the UNIX host and issuing the id command as follows:

```
$id
uid=100(dabierer) gid=1(other)
```

As you can see from this example, the UID of the user dabierer is 100. Alternatively, you can view the contents of the /etc/passwd file on the UNIX host. The following is a sample from such a file:

```
$ cat /etc/passwd
root:x:0:3:0000-Admin(0000):/:/usr/bin/ksh
daemon:x:1:12:0000-Admin(0000):/:
bin:x:2:2:0000-Admin(0000):/usr/bin:
```

```
sys:x:3:3:0000-Admin(0000):/:
adm:x:4:4:0000-Admin(0000):/var/adm:
uucp:x:5:5:0000-uucp(0000):/usr/lib/uucp:
nuucp:x:10:10:0000-uucp(0000):/var/spool/uucppublic:/usr/lib/uucp/uucico
nobody:x:60001:60001:uid no body:/:
noaccess:x:60002:60002:uid no access:/:
lp:x:7:9:0000-LP(0000):/var/spool/lp:/sbin/sh
listen:x:37:4:Network Admin:/usr/net/nls:/usr/bin/sh
sysadm:x:0:0:general system administration:/usr/sadm:/usr/sbin/sysadm
mhsmail:x:61:6:MHS Admin Processes:/var/spool/smf:/usr/bin/sh
dabierer:x:100:1::/home/dabierer:/usr/bin/ksh
smtp:x:102:6:SMTP Processes:/var/spool/smtpq:/usr/bin/sh
cisaacs:x:103:1::/home/cisaacs:/usr/bin/sh
```

Colons delimit fields in the /etc/passwd file. The first field is the UNIX user login name (or account name). The third field contains the UID. The user cisaacs on this host, for example, has the UID of 103.

The sequence of data in the /etc/passwd file is as follows:

<account name>:x:<UID>:<GID>:<comments>:<home directory>:<default shell>

The *account name* is the user's login name on the UNIX host. The letter *x* is a place holder for a password. In earlier versions of UNIX, this field actually contained the password. In System V Release 4.2 UNIX, this field is a place holder. The actual password is in the /etc/shadow file. The *UID* is the user's User ID number. The *GID* is the user's Group ID number. The name of the group can be found in the /etc/group file. The *comments* field usually contains the user's full name. There are no strict rules for what is placed in this field. The contents of the comments field vary widely. The *home directory* is the directory where the user is placed when first logging in. This is a directory in which the user has full rights. The *default shell* can be the Bourne shell (/usr/bin/sh), the C shell (/usr/bin/csh), or the Korn shell (/usr/bin/ksh). The shell varies depending on the desires of the users, ease of administration, and what types of scripts are available.

The NetWare account name must be the common name of a user object located in the file server's bindery context. When the UNIX user accesses files on the NetWare server, the security rights are those pertaining to the NetWare user object.

The NFSGROUP file, similar to the NFSUSERS file, contains a series of lines in the following format:

<UNIX GID>   <NetWare Group>

The *GID* corresponds to groups defined on the UNIX client. You can gather GIDs by viewing the /etc/passwd file. Another file, the /etc/group file, is shown next:

```
$ cat /etc/group
root::0:root
other::1:root
bin::2:root,bin,daemon
sys::3:root,bin,sys,adm
adm::4:root,adm,daemon
uucp::5:root,uucp
mail::6:root
tty::7:root,tty,adm
audit::8:root
nuucp::10:root,nuucp
daemon::12:root,daemon
cron::23:root
priv::47:root
nobody::60001:
noaccess::60002:
lp::9:root,lp
dos::100:
```

This file lists the group name, a blank field, the GID, then default members of the group. When a UnixWare user accesses a NetWare server, the user also gains the rights of their primary UNIX group.

The NFSPARAM file contains time zone information. A typical entry is as follows:

```
<TimeZone>          <Hours Offset from UTC>
```

The *TimeZone* could be any of the standard time zones such as Pacific Standard Time (PST), Eastern Standard Time (EST), or so on. The hours offset from Universal Time Coordinated (UTC—formerly called Greenwich Mean Time) would be eight hours for the U.S. West Coast and five hours for the U.S. East Coast.

Accessing NetWare Using the mount Command

The file system of a NetWare file server can be accessed using the standard mount command. The file system is NetWare UNIX Client File System (NUCFS). UnixWare also can use the Network File System (NFS) if you have TCP/IP installed on both the UnixWare client and the NetWare file server. To use an nfs mount, however, you have to install NetWare NFS on the file server. Use the resident nucfs to perform the mount command without NetWare NFS.

Before performing the mount command, you must first authenticate to the NetWare server. To do this, use the nwlogin (NetWare Login) command:

```
# nwlogin ebdb5-sac/su1
```

Note that you must be the root user to perform the mount command. If you are currently logged in as a regular user, you can change to the root user using the su (Substitute User) command. At this point, you now can issue the mount command:

```
# mount -F nucfs ebdb5-sac:sys /mnt
```

Issuing the mount command by itself shows you that volume SYS of the NetWare server ebdb5-sac has been mounted to the directory /mnt:

```
# mount
/ on /dev/root read/write/setuid on Wed Aug 3 20:40:07 1994
/proc on /proc read/write on Wed Aug 3 20:40:09 1994
/dev/fd on /dev/fd read/write on Wed Aug 3 20:40:09 1994
/stand on /dev/dsk/c0t0d0sa read/write on Wed Aug 3 20:40:10 1994
/home on /dev/dsk/1s1 read/write/log/setuid/mincache=closesync on Wed Aug 3 20:
40:20 1994
/.NetWare on /.NetWare read only on Wed Aug 3 20:41:01 1994
/mnt on ebdb5-sac:sys read/write/remote on Mon Aug 8 17:41:28 1994
```

To access files on the NetWare server, change to the /mnt directory.

Accessing NetWare with the Graphical Interface

Figure 17.1 shows the UnixWare desktop. UnixWare's graphical-user interface (GUI) is based on the X-Windows specifications. UnixWare 1.1 uses a MOTIF-like variation of Open Look. UnixWare 2.0 uses standard MOTIF. The UnixWare desktop is an iconified representation of the user's home directory. Files in the home directory appear as icons on the desktop. Operation of the GUI is very similar to the operation of Windows or OS/2. If you double-click with the mouse on an icon, the application associated with that icon runs. If the icon represents a subdirectory (a folder icon), double-clicking with the mouse causes a window to appear with the icons of that folder represented. To activate an icon using the keyboard, proceed as follows:

1. Use the arrow keys to select the icon.
2. Press the spacebar to select the icon. The icon appears as if it were pressed down.

3. Press Alt+F to activate the **F**ile menu.

4. Click on the **O**pen option.

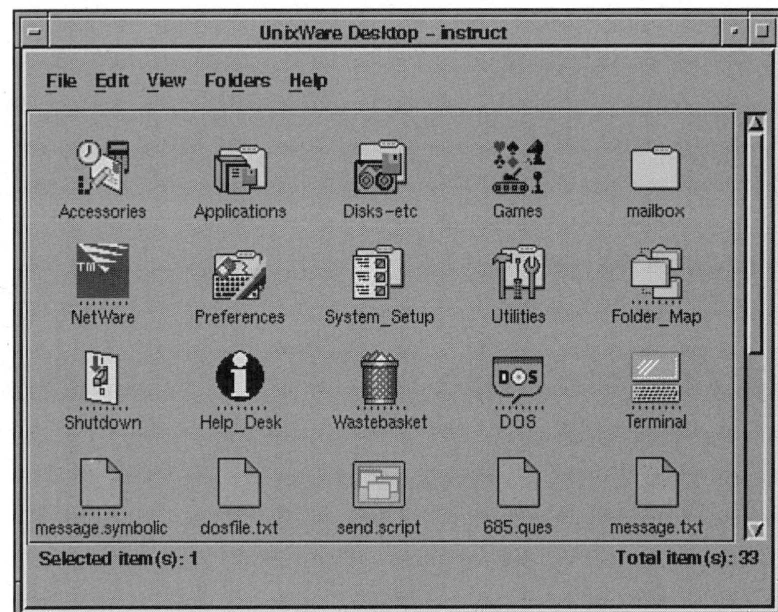

Figure 17.1
The UnixWare desktop.

To access the file system of a NetWare server through the GUI, proceed as follows:

1. From the UnixWare desktop, double-click on the NetWare icon with the mouse. If you are using the keyboard, use the arrow keys, the spacebar, Alt+F, and O as indicated above. The NetWare Servers window opens, displaying a list of NetWare servers (see fig. 17.2).

2. From the NetWare Servers window, select the server you want to access. After you activate the server icon, an authentication screen appears. Enter your login name and the password for that server. When successfully authenticated, the Volume window appears, showing the names of the volumes located on that server.

3. Activate the desired volume icon to see the Files window, showing the files and directories for that volume (see fig. 17.3).

4. At this point, the file server's volume has been auto-mounted from the NUCAMD (NetWare Unix Client Auto-mount Daemon) process. You can access the server's files by continuing to browse using the GUI. Alternatively, you can open a

terminal window and access the files through the command line. UNIX applications and files can be stored on a NetWare server. If you run an application stored on a NetWare server, the server downloads the application files to your UnixWare client, which runs the program.

5. When you're done accessing the server, close the windows either by double-clicking on the menu button at the upper left corner of the screen or by pressing Alt+F4.

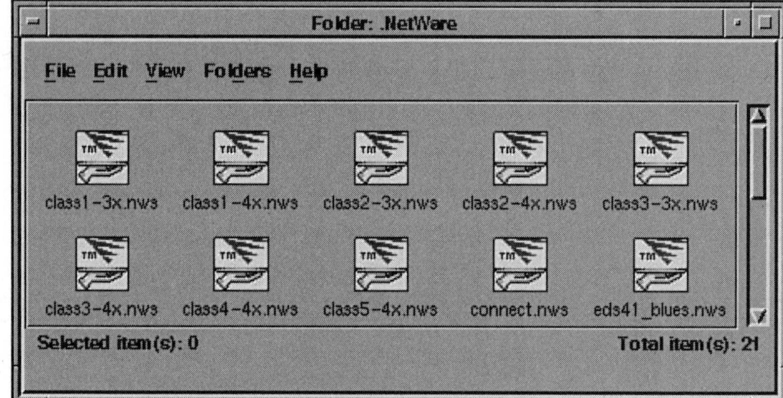

Figure 17.2 *The NetWare Servers window from the UnixWare desktop.*

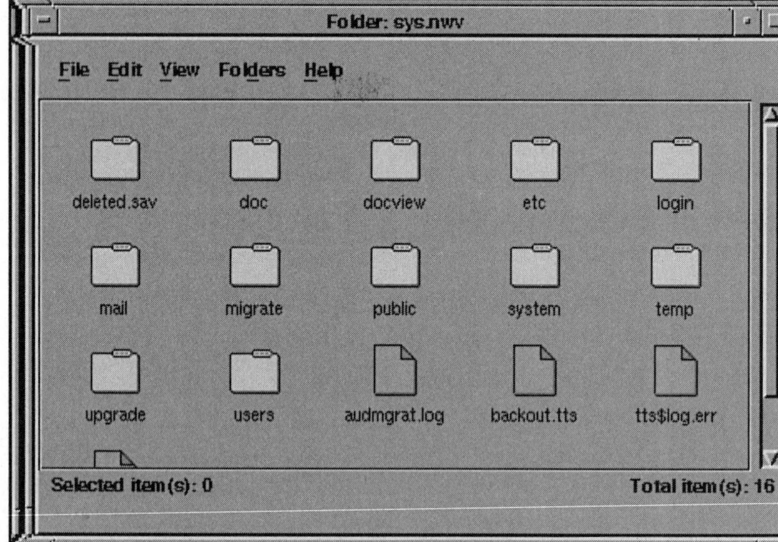

Figure 17.3 *The Files window from the UnixWare desktop.*

The NetWare Access utility enables you to log in and log out of NetWare servers without having to wait for the authentication screen to pop up. This utility is available from the UnixWare desktop by selecting the Utilities icon. From the Utilities window, activate the NetWare Access icon; the NetWare Servers screen that appears is shown in figure 17.4.

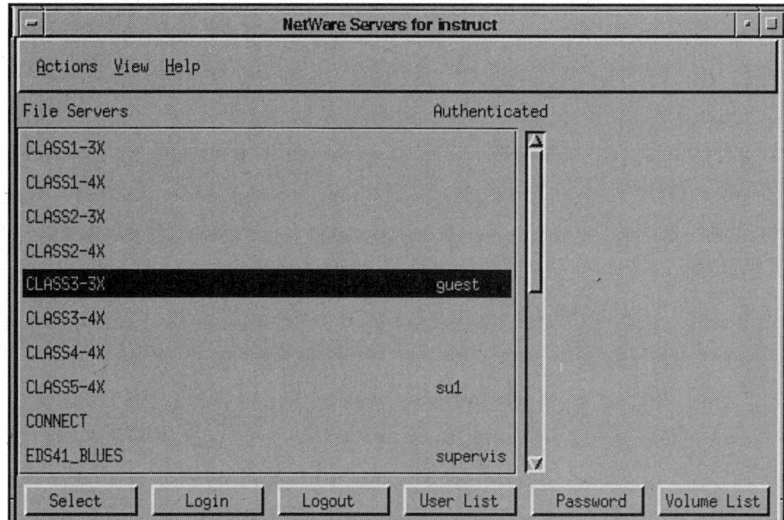

Figure 17.4
The NetWare Servers window from the UnixWare desktop.

To log in to a NetWare server, select the server from the list and double-click on it or press Enter. The authentication screen appears, and you can enter your login name and password on that server. Select Logout to log out from that server.

Note The screens shown in figures 17.1 through 17.4 are taken from UnixWare 1.1.2. The next release of UnixWare changes the graphical look of the NetWare access icons and windows. The functionality remains the same.

Understanding UNIX Client Access through NFS and TCP/IP

You can access NetWare file servers using the Network File System (NFS). The process for gaining access to the server's file system is similar to that used with the NetWare

UNIX Client File System (NUCFS). In contrast to NUCFS, however, NFS requires the following elements:

- TCP/IP must be installed and configured on the UnixWare client
- TCP/IP must be configured on the NetWare file server
- NetWare NFS must be installed and configured on the NetWare file server

Configuring NetWare NFS

After NetWare NFS has been installed on the file server, you must designate which files or directories should be made available for export. This is accomplished using the NFSADMIN.NLM utility. NFSADMIN is an NLM that is loaded on the file server from the file server console. From the main menu, select Tables. From the Tables menu, select Exports. In the Exported Path screen, shown in figure 17.5, press the Insert key to add additional files or directories to the exports list.

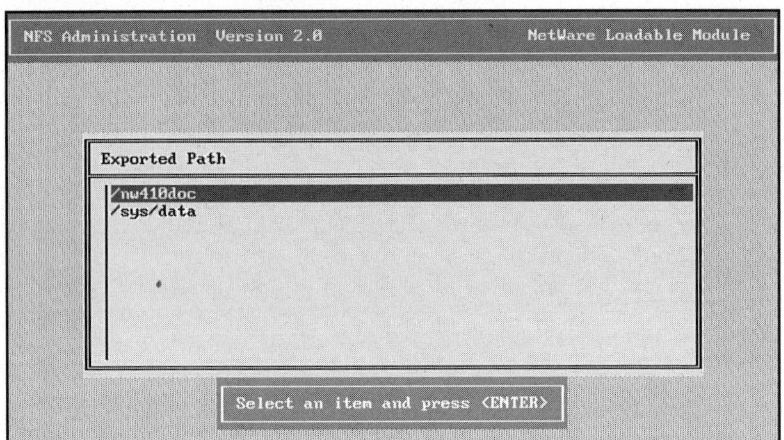

Figure 17.5
The NFS Exported Path screen.

Press Enter on any of the listed exports to perform further configurations. The resulting Exports File Options dialog box is shown in figure 17.6.

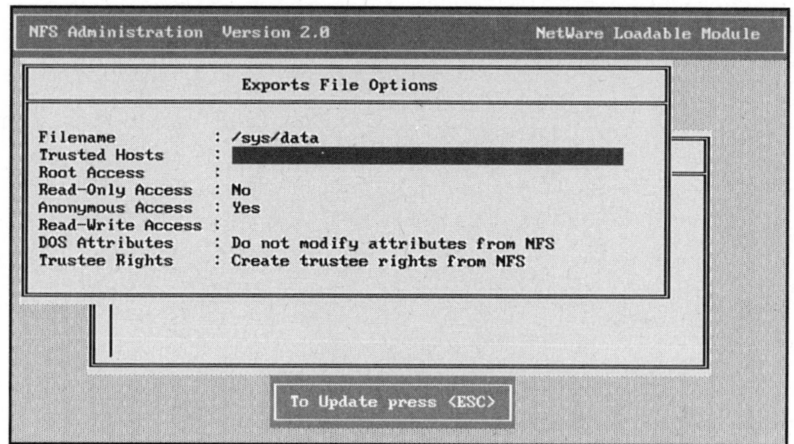

Figure 17.6
The NFS Administration Exports File Options dialog box.

Table 17.4 summarizes the options available in the Exports File Options screen.

TABLE 17.4
NFS Administration Exports File Options

Option	Default	Description
Filename		Name of the file or directory being exported.
Trusted Hosts		Any host name (selected from the names on the SYS:ETC\HOSTS file) on this list can access to the exported file or directory. If this is left blank (the default), *any* host can access this file or directory.
Root Access		Any host on this list can access the exported file or directory as the root user, meaning that such users have Supervisor file system rights to the file or directory exported. If left blank (default), no users are allowed root access.
Read-Only Access	No	If this option is set to Yes, all hosts, except those on the Read-Write Access list (see next table item), can only read from the exported file or directory.

continues

Table 17.4, Continued
NFS Administration Exports File Options

Option	Default	Description
Anonymous Access	Yes	Using the default setting (Yes), users with no corresponding account in the SYS:ETC\NFSUSERS file (described in the previous "File Server Configuration Files" section), are mapped to the NetWare user NOBODY. Such users have all the rights of this user.
Read-Write Access		This option is only valid if the Read-Only Access option is set to Yes. If this is the case, any host named on this list can both read and write to and from the exported file or directory. All other hosts can only read.
DOS Attributes	Do not modify...	If set to the default, UNIX users cannot change DOS attributes (such as Read Only, Hidden, System, and so forth) on the NetWare server. This affects UNIX users when creating files, and when issuing a chmod (Change Mode) command. Otherwise, UNIX users affect DOS attributes.
Trustee Rights	Create trustees	If set to the default, NetWare file and directory trustee rights are created when a UNIX user creates a file or makes a security permissions change (using the chmod, chown, or chgrp commands).

Another set of options you can adjust pertains to the defaults for exported files and directories. From the NFSADMIN main menu, you can set these options by choosing the Set File Information menu. Select the exported file or directory whose defaults you want to adjust (see fig. 17.7).

Filename refers to the exported file or directory. File Permission is the default UNIX permission mask assigned to this file or directory. File Owner and File Group are the default owner and group assigned to the exported file or directory. Recursion, if set to Yes, enables these permissions to apply to subdirectories, as well as to the exported directory. This option does not apply to exported files.

After you set the export options and defaults according to the needs of your system, you are ready to access the exported files or directories using NFS.

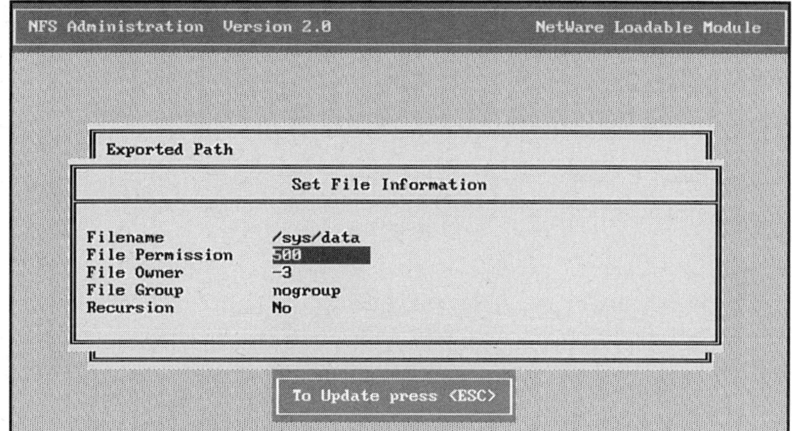

Figure 17.7
The NFS Administration Set File Information screen.

Accessing an NFS Volume

Prior to access, it is a good idea to verify TCP/IP connectivity and to verify that the name of the server you want to access has been properly entered into the /etc/hosts file on your UNIX system. One of the fastest ways to check is to use the ping command. The generic syntax for this command is as follows:

```
ping <hostname>
```

Here is an example using the ping command to check for a host ebdb2:

```
# ping ebdb2
ebdb2 is alive
```

When the ping command returns a positive response, *hostname* is alive. This confirms both TCP/IP connectivity and that the hostname is entered properly in the hosts file. To check which files or directories are available for export, use the dfshares command. The general syntax is as follows:

```
dfshares -F nfs <hostname>
```

The following example checks the host ebdb2 (the NetWare server):

```
# dfshares -F nfs ebdb2
RESOURCE                  SERVER ACCESS  TRANSPORT
   ebdb2:/sys/unixware          ebdb2 -      -
   ebdb2:/sys/login           ebdb2 -      -
```

As with NUCFS, use the mount command to gain access to the NetWare server. The following example mounts the directory unixware on volume SYS on the file server ebdb2 onto the directory /mnt:

```
# mount -F nfs -o soft,retry=4 ebdb2:/sys/unixware /mnt
```

Use the mount command by itself to verify that the operation took place properly:

```
# mount
/ on /dev/root read/write/setuid on Wed Aug 3 20:40:07 1994
/proc on /proc read/write on Wed Aug 3 20:40:09 1994
/dev/fd on /dev/fd read/write on Wed Aug 3 20:40:09 1994
/stand on /dev/dsk/c0t0d0sa read/write on Wed Aug 3 20:40:10 1994
/home on /dev/dsk/1s1 read/write/log/setuid/mincache=closesync on Wed Aug 3 20:
➥40:20 1994
/.NetWare on /.NetWare read only on Wed Aug 3 20:41:01 1994
/mnt on ebdb2:/sys/unixware soft/retry=4/remote on Mon Aug 8 17:55:01 1994
```

To access the file server, use the cd command to change to the mount point. The ls -l command shows you the files and directories on the file server:

```
# cd /mnt
# ls -l
total 45
drwxrwxrwx  2 dabierer other    512 Jul 31 11:31 dns
drwxrwxrwx  4 dabierer sys     512 Aug 3 05:25 goodies
drwxrwxrwx 14 dabierer sys     512 Aug 2 09:47 pkgs
drwxrwxrwx  2 dabierer sys     512 Jul 31 11:31 scenarios
drwxrwxrwx  2 dabierer sys     512 Aug 2 09:49 scripts
-rw-rw-rw-  1 4294967294sys      17 Jul 27 01:42 test.1
-rw-rw-rw-  1 dabierer other   19793 Aug 3 13:41 test.2
```

To release the mount point, use the umount command. Be sure to move off the mount point before issuing this command:

```
# cd /
# umount /mnt
```

Accessing a NetWare Server through FTP

NetWare NFS also offers an ftp server capability, which also is provided with Flex/IP, a stripped down version of NetWare NFS. You must first load and configure TCP/IP, then load INETD.NLM, which is the Internet Daemon that is supplied with NetWare

NFS. This module waits until a client issues a request using ftp. When such a request is received, FTPSERV.NLM is loaded dynamically. FTPSERV.NLM enables the NetWare server to act as an ftp server. It asks the user for a valid login name taken from the server's bindery context. A provision does exist for anonymous ftp access. If a user supplies the name anonymous, the file server can be programmed to accept or reject such requests.

The following series of lines shows a typical NetWare NFS ftp session. The first part shows you the login process:

```
# ftp ebdb2
Connected to ebdb2.
220 ebdb5-sac FTP server (NetWare v4.1) ready.
Name (ebdb2:root): su1
230 User SU1 logged in.
```

The next several lines show the process of changing to the unixware directory and viewing the files in that directory:

```
ftp> cd unixware
200 CWD command okay.
ftp> ls
200 PORT command okay.
150 Opening data connection for (130.57.88.58,1045).
- [RWCEAFMS] nobody      17     Jul 27 08:42  test.1
- [RWCEAFMS] su1         19793  Aug 03 20:41  test.2
- [RWCEAFMS] su1         58     Jul 14 08:27  dtinfo
d [RWCEAFMS] su1         512    Jul 31 18:31  dns
d [RWCEAFMS] su1         512    Jul 31 18:31  scenario
d [RWCEAFMS] su1         512    Aug 03 12:25  goodies
d [RWCEAFMS] su1         512    Aug 02 16:47  pkgs
d [RWCEAFMS] su1         512    Aug 02 16:49  scripts
226 Transfer complete.
```

The next several lines illustrate the process of copying a file from the server using the get command:

```
ftp> get test.1
local: test.1 remote: test.1
200 PORT command okay.
150 Opening data connection for test.1 (130.57.88.58,1047).
226 Transfer complete.
19 bytes received in 0.02 seconds (0.93 Kbytes/s)
```

Adding NFS Name Space to a CD

You might want to allow a UNIX user access to a CD mounted on a file server. Ordinarily, you would use the following command at the file server console:

```
add name space nfs to volume <volume name>
```

This command enables UNIX users accessing the server through NetWare NFS to view and set properly UNIX file permissions and file naming conventions. The process of adding name space modifies the Directory Entry Table (DET) that resides at the start of each NetWare volume. In the case of a CD, however, it is not possible to modify its DET for the simple reason that you cannot write to a CD.

NetWare 4.1 gets around this technical inconvenience by enabling you to record the desired name space at the time you first mount the CD. The name space is added as an option on the command line to mount the CD. Name spaces that can be added in this fashion include the following:

- ◆ NFS (/nfs)
- ◆ Macintosh (/mac)
- ◆ OS/2 (/os2)

NetWare 4.1 actually includes name space information in the file it builds for the DET of the CD. In the case of mounting a CD, you also should include the /R parameter, which informs NetWare that this device is read-only. The following example shows you the results when adding NFS name space when mounting a CD:

```
EBDB:cd mount 1 /nfs /R

 CDROM-4.10-018:
  NFS Name Space support enabled.

 CDROM-4.10-024: INFO:
  Mount Volume on device: 1

 CDROM-4.10-270: INFO:
  DO NOT turn on ComprGroup Access Rights: EVERYONE volume.


Creating CDROM Index [_] 100%

 CDROM-4.10-105: INFO:
  Adjusted Volume Capacity in Blocks (block size 64k):3169
```

```
Mounting Volume NW410DOC
** Reading In FAT
** Verifying Directory FAT Chain
** Scanning the Directory
** Checking Subdirectories
** Scanning Files with Trustee Nodes
** Scanning Deleted Files
** Linking the Name Spaces
** Shrinking the Extended Directory
EBDB:
```

Summary

This chapter showed you several ways to connect UNIX-based systems to NetWare file servers. Much of the chapter was devoted to Novell's UnixWare operating system. Other parts of the chapter dealt with Novell's NetWare NFS product. As you learned, many systems now offer connectivity through Novell's IPX/SPX protocols. IPX/SPX protocol support has the advantage of ease-of-management. Most UNIX systems access a NetWare file server's file system through the mount command—a process in which one or more NetWare directories are mapped over subdirectories in the UNIX system's directory structure. The result is that the NetWare file system appears as a subdirectory on the UNIX system.

UnixWare has an advantage over other versions of UNIX in that NetWare NCP calls can be made directly from the kernel. When a user wants to access the server, he can click on an icon, and an auto-mount daemon issues the equivalent of the mount command. You can do this through IPX/SPX without the added cost of NetWare NFS. UnixWare provides two NLMs to provide smooth translation between NetWare trustee rights and UnixWare file permissions: NUC.NLM and NFS.NAM. NUC provides security translation, and NFS provides UNIX name space support.

As you saw in this chapter, the security translation provided by NUC is not as finite as a UNIX user might imagine. The results of the UNIX chmod command do not exactly translate into NetWare trustee rights and file attributes.

You learned that the configuration files NFSUSERS and NFSGROUP are used to map Unix user IDs to NetWare accounts. The section then continued to show you how to access and authenticate to NetWare servers using the mount -F nucfs ... command, and the NetWare Access utility.

The last part of this chapter discussed how to access NetWare file servers using NetWare NFS, using the TCP/IP protocol. The mount -F nfs ... command was discussed as a way to gain access to NetWare files and directories. You also learned that a server configured with NetWare NFS includes an FTPSERV.NLM module, is loaded automatically by INETD.NLM, and provides ftp services.

The last section discussed and showed you an example of configuring a CD mounted on a file server for NFS name space.

The next chapter discusses how to install and configure NetWare for Macintosh, and how the Macintosh client can access a NetWare 4.1 network.

Macintosh Clients

NetWare 4.1 allows a Macintosh client to access Netware Directory Services, NDS. The Macintosh client can now become an equal citizen on the network. Prior to Netware 4.1, a Macintosh client had to use bindery emulation to access a Netware 4.0 server. Most networks are made up of multiple types of computer systems linked together in order to share resources and data. If your network has Macintosh clients installed, it is important that you understand how to integrate them into a Netware environment. This chapter explains how to integrate Macintosh computers into a Novell network, plus it explains Macintosh access to NDS.

First, Macintosh NLMs are reviewed and related network issues for AppleTalk are explained. The purpose of the explanations is to help you configure the Netware for Macintosh software. Additional AppleTalk protocol information can be found in the "AppleTalk Reference" section of DynaText. Second, the step-by-step installation procedure to get the Macintosh computers working on the network is covered. Then the focus is on the Macintosh client with which you are logging into the NDS tree. The installation procedure is covered for the client, along with descriptions of AppleTalk network software for the Macintosh client. By the end of this chapter, you will be able to load the NetWare software for Macintoshes, configure AppleTalk protocol for your network, and log into the NDS tree with a Macintosh client.

Understanding the AppleTalk File System

The AppleTalk file system modules allow the NetWare server to properly store Macintosh files and Macintosh file information. This file system is supported by loading the Apple Filing Protocol (AFP.NLM), which is a high level protocol allowing Macs to exchange files with a Netware server. When AFP.NLM is loaded, the server automatically loads the APPLETLK.NLM. The APPLETLK.NLM must be configured before AFP.NLM is loaded, or the Macintosh computers will not be able to log into the server. The installation steps outlined in this chapter will follow this path by explaining how to configure the APPLETALK.NLM.

In order for the AFP.NLM to store Macintosh files on a volume, the volume must have Macintosh name space added. This name space, called MAC.NAM, allows the volume to store Macintosh files. Macintosh files have what are called type and creator parts. The *type* identifies whether the file is an application or not. The *creator* identifies what application created the file. If this information stored on a NetWare volume ever gets corrupted or out of sync, the desktop on that volume will have to be rebuilt. This is done through the AFPCON utility. During a server crash, for example, the desktop files could be damaged to the point a rebuild would be necessary. During the install you will add the Macintosh name support to any volumes you wish to store Macintosh files.

AppleTalk Zone and Network Range Information

AppleTalk was designed as a client-server, or "distributed" network system. AppleTalk enables users to share network resources, such as files and printers, with other network users. AppleTalk defines four network elements, as follows:

- The *node* is any AppleTalk device, such as Macintosh computers and printers, connected to the network.
- A *network* is a single logical cable to AppleTalk.
- The *router* connects the different physical networks together into one or more logical networks.
- A *zone* is a logical group of one or more networks. A zone enables Macintosh users to view different Macintosh services within the same logical zone. An

example would be a zone called Marketing that contains servers and printers from different parts of the building, but logically groups them together within the zone Marketing.

A Macintosh node usually is attached to the network through LocalTalk, Ethernet or token ring. A node could be a work station, printer, server, or any other Apple device on the network. AppleTalk assigns dynamic addressing, unlike protocols such as IPX or TCP/IP. During boot-up, an AppleTalk node chooses an address and checks if any other AppleTalk node is using that address on that "network." This process repeats until a legal address is found. The protocol responsible for this service is *AppleTalk Address Resolution Protocol* (AARP) for EtherTalk and TokenTalk networks.

The first implementation of AppleTalk was called Phase I. Phase I is still built into Macintosh computers as LocalTalk, which uses twisted pair to connect each node. AppleTalk quickly entered larger network environments where built-in limitations needed to be upgraded. Apple created Phase II AppleTalk, which supports over 16 million nodes on an internetwork with up to 255 zones. A LocalTalk network is a non-extended network. A Phase II network, like EtherTalk or TokenTalk, is called an *extended* network. It is important for you to select the proper type of network during the AppleTalk NLM install for the server to properly function on the network. Different examples and tips will try to point out the distinction. If you are integrating this server into an existing AppleTalk network, please be sure to review the AppleTalk options with the AppleTalk network Administrator.

AppleTalk routers interconnect the AppleTalk networks. An AppleTalk router could be a NetWare server or a dedicated LAN router. This router contains network and zone information to route packets between the different network segments. Each router maintains tables in order to correctly route a packet to the proper network. These routing tables are maintained by the *Routing Table Maintenance Protocol* (RTMP).

Phase I networks have one cable range and a zone assigned to it by a router. All LocalTalk is a Phase I type network. Phase II networks allow for an extended cable range and multiple zones per network segment. The extended zone range was introduced by Apple to fix the problem of allowing only 253 nodes per network segment in Phase I. Many networks have a mix of Phase I and Phase II, called *transition routing*, and because of this will have certain limitations, as follows:

- Each extended network in a transition routing environment must have a range of one, as opposed to a range greater than one in a Phase II only environment. 10-10 is correct for a transition Phase II network but 10-11 is not correct.

- Each extended network can have only one associated zone name, as opposed to having multiple zones share that network segment.

These are important restrictions and can greatly affect the design of your AppleTalk network. An example of a transition network is given in figure 18.1.

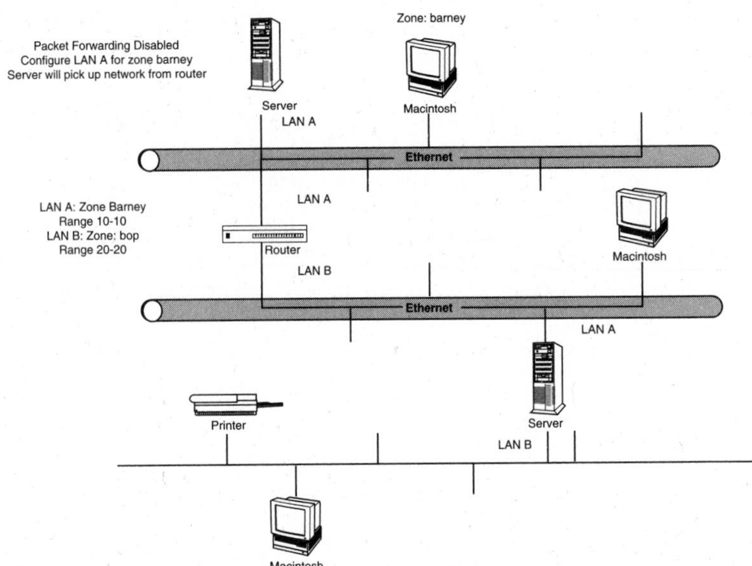

Figure 18.1
A transition (Phase I and Phase II) network.

Phase II networks support an extended cable range to handle more than 253 devices on each network. Network zones may extend over one or more networks to create a logical network. You must have unique zone ranges on each network throughout your internetwork. This uniqueness includes internal numbers for seed routers. Ranges cannot overlap whether or not it is a Phase I or Phase II network. Phase II networks are more difficult because of the introduction of ranges. The network Administrator should keep a list of all the current ranges on the network to avoid some problems and assist in tracking other problems. Figure 18.2 details a pure Phase II network with two routers showing possible network ranges.

Figure 18.2 has two zones that overlap one another on certain network segments. This design enables the network Administrator to select which zones have what services, regardless of the physical location of the device. Notice on the LAN-based router that Lan B does not have zone "bop" configured, but will capture that information from the seed router on the same network. The top two Macintosh computers see both zones in the Chooser. The printers on the bottom Ethernet network could be in either zone. Notice that LocalTalk was removed from this example. If LocalTalk needs to be integrated into a Phase II network, you must use transition routing. Transition routing is not pure Phase II and the limitations discussed above are enforced.

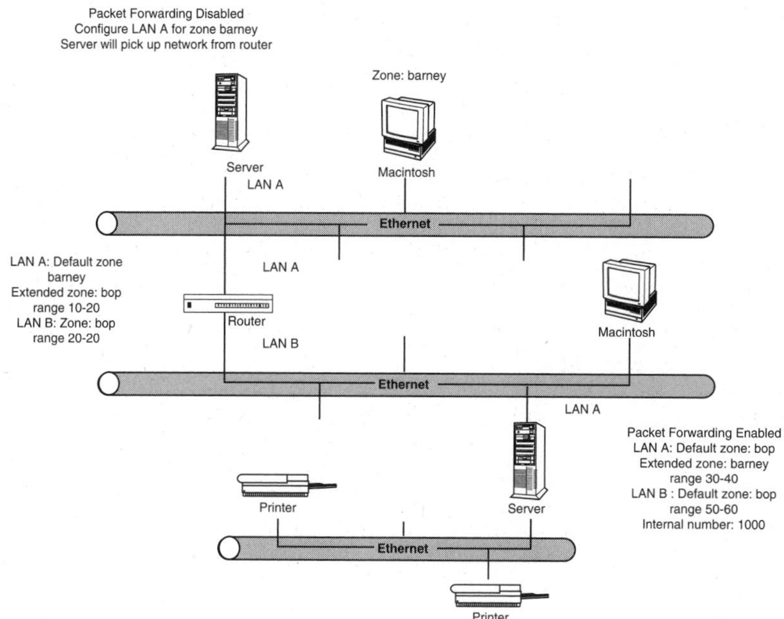

Figure 18.2

A Phase II extended network.

AppleTalk routers are either configured as seed routers or non-seed routers. A *seed* router is pre-configured with the network range and zone information during initial configuration. A seed router actively broadcasts this network information when it comes on-line. A *non-seed* router passively listens to the network for seed router information. Once a non-seed learns the network information, it will broadcast this zone and network range information until it is rebooted. You need at least one seed router connected to each network. Having more than one seed router does not cause any problems and many sites have multiple seed routers. Seed or non-seed is determined during software configuration. These two types of routers can be LAN-based routers or NetWare servers routing AppleTalk.

Zones enable the Administrator to group AppleTalk services the way the users would like them without regard to the way the network was set-up, cabled, and so on. Routers exchange zone information with the *Zone Information Protocol* (ZIP). You need a default zone for a NetWare server if it is configured to route AppleTalk packets between networks. This allows the server to know what zone to broadcast its services in. Servers with the packet forwarding option disabled have no default zone, and each interface card must be configured for the zone it is on. This is reviewed in detail in the installation section.

Be careful of upper- and lowercase spelling for zone usage. It is best to have zones match case. It is inadvisable, for example, to spell the zone "campbell" on one router and then spell it "Campbell" on another router. This will cause you headaches in managing the RTMP route tables on the network.

Understanding the NetWare for Macintosh Modules

This section lists the modules that are necessary to load for Macs to connect into and receive services from a NetWare server. Notice that ATPS and ATPSCON are used for Macintosh printing only. After you have installed the software and loaded the appropriate NLMs, you can type the following at the console prompt:

modules

The list produced can help you to verify what modules are loaded and can be very helpful in debugging problems. Table 25.1 lists the AppleTalk software modules with a description of each.

Table 25.1
NetWare Modules for AppleTalk Support

Module	Description
MAC.NAM (The Macintosh name space module)	This module needs to be added to every volume that needs Macintosh file support. This process is only done once per volume.
AFP.NLM (The AppleTalk Filing Protocol module)	AFP module allows the NetWare server to store Macintosh files and applications. These files can be shared with non-Macintosh users.
AFPCON.NLM (The AFP console utility)	AFPCON allows for the configuration of the AFP module.
ADSP.NLM (The AppleTalk Data Stream Protocol)	ADSP allows two programs to communicate through a full-duplex data stream.
APPLETLK.NLM (The AppleTalk module)	The AppleTalk protocol stack and router.

Module	Description
ATPS.NLM (The AppleTalk Print Services module)	This module enables Macintosh users to send print jobs to a network printer. Needed to support Macintosh printing using NetWare.
ATPSCON.NLM (The ATPS console utility)	This module is used to configure the ATPS module.
ATCONFIG.NLM (The AppleTalk config module)	Configures NetWare for Macintosh.

NetWare for Macintosh

NetWare for Macintosh allows Macintosh computers to work as equal "citizens" on a NetWare network. The suite of AppleTalk NLMs provides seamless network access and file and print services to a Macintosh from a NetWare server. They allow PCs and Macintoshes to exchange files and share printers and data.

NetWare for Macintosh enables Macintosh users on a network to access files on a NetWare server and to print to NetWare print queues, allowing the NetWare server to mimic an Appleshare server. The *AppleTalk Filing Protocol* (AFP) module provides the file services. The APPLETLK.NLM provides Macintosh network connectivity services by supporting AppleTalk Phase I and Phase II.

Memory Requirements

Supporting Macintosh computer access to a NetWare server increases the memory load of the server. Following is a review of some memory requirements for Macintosh support. Keep in mind that the more memory a server has, the better and more reliable it will run. Table 25.2 lists the memory requirements for different AppleTalk resources. Use this information to help gauge the amount of memory needed for your AppleTalk environment.

Table 25.2
NetWare for Macintosh Memory Requirements

Memory Required	Macintosh Services for NetWare
1 MB	This 1 MB relates to the Macintosh NLMs and BTRIEVE; BTRIEVE takes up about 500 KB of the 1 MB

continues

Table 25.2, Continued
NetWare for Macintosh Memory Requirements

Memory Required	Macintosh Services for NetWare
10 KB	Per Macintosh connection
12 KB	Per active AFP session
20 KB	Per ATPS print server
20 KB	Per ATPS spooler
10 KB	Per user currently printing to an ATPS spooler
20 KB	Per ATXRP printer

For example, an installation with AFP, ATPS, 200 Macintosh connections, four print servers, one ATPS spoolers, and five people printing at the same time requires roughly 3.2 MB for NetWare for Macintosh, as the following formula demonstrates:

$$1{,}000\text{ KB} + (200\times 10\text{ KB}) + (4\times 20\text{ KB}) + (4\times 20\text{ KB}) + (5\times 10\text{ KB}) = 3{,}210\text{ KB}$$

Installing NetWare for Macintosh on the Server

This section steps you through the install process for the Mac NLM on a NetWare server. The Macintosh software may be installed from the console, or through RCONSOLE, using a local or network storage device. If files have been copied from the distribution CD-ROM to a hard drive, ensure that all files are copied in their appropriate relative locations so the installer can locate them.

The first step is to run the RCONSOLE application if you are installing from a work station. RCONSOLE is located in the SYS:SYSTEM directory on the server. This application requires that the REMOTE.NLM and RSPX.NLM be loaded on the console. After these NLMs are loaded, type the following at the server console prompt:

load install

The NetWare Server Installation 4.1 screen appears, as shown in figure 18.3. Next, click on Product Options.

Next select the Install NetWare for Macintosh option to begin the install. Figure 18.04 displays this selection.

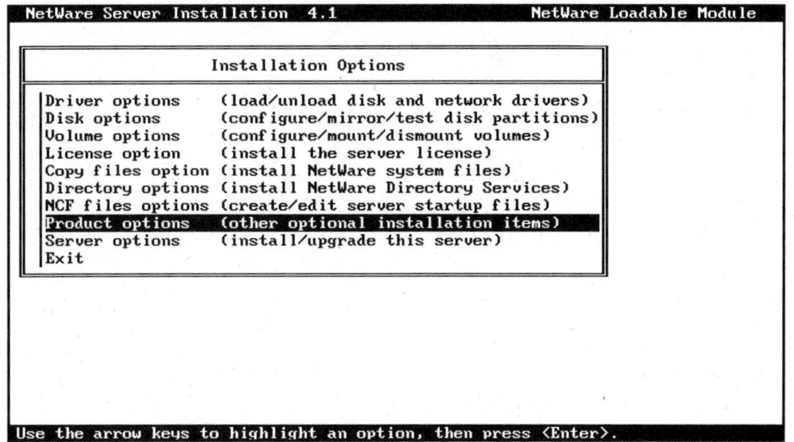

Figure 18.3

The NetWare Server Installation 4.1 options.

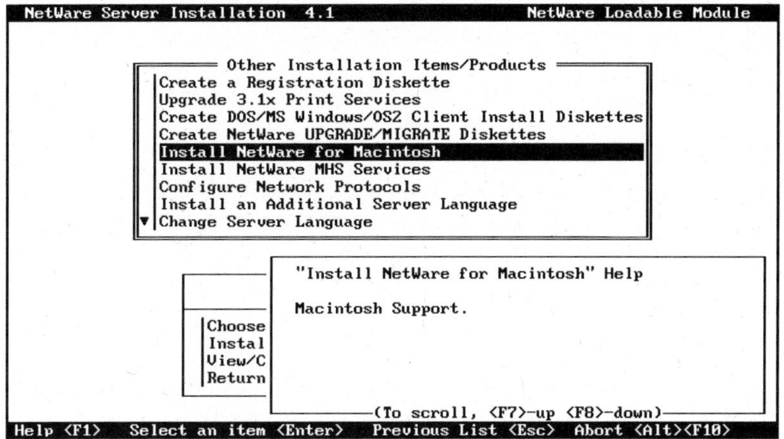

Figure 18.4

Selecting NetWare for Macintosh installation.

Path Selection for Install Files

The installation program will now try to locate the files for download to the server. If the installation files are not in the default location (D:\NW410\INSTALL\ENGLISH), an error message appears, and you must enter the correct path to the installation directory. Remember, if your CD ROM is set to drive letter E to reflect this on the install path.

If you are running this from a RCONSOLE screen with a locally attached CD-ROM, make sure you press F4 to inform the install program. Press F3 to change the path if the CD-ROM is directly attached to the server. The path in this case is not a DOS drive letter but is the following:

```
<vol_name>:\NW41\INSTALL\<language.dir>.
```

If you are experiencing trouble copying the files to the server from a work station running RCONSOLE, make sure you are not running a DOS session in Windows that is executing RCONSOLE. Try running RCONSOLE from DOS when RCONSOLE is trying to access the CD-ROM on the work station.

The next screen shown is Final Installation Options (see fig. 18.5). This screen enables you to configure final installation options, including volume selection and Macintosh support files.

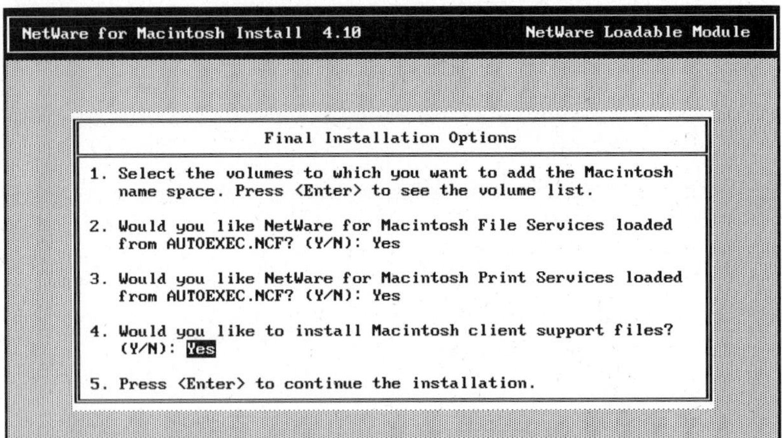

Figure 18.5
Choosing the Final Installation Options.

The Final Installation Options screen is not the final screen in this AppleTalk installation section. This screen is the last screen before the final file copy from the CD-ROM to the server. There are still many configuration options to work through.

The first option is used to select all the volumes on the server needed to store Macintosh files. Remember to adjust server memory as discussed in the "AppleTalk File System" section.

The next two options in the Final Installation Options screen let you decide if the AppleTalk Filing Protocol and AppleTalk Printing Service load automatically on server start up. These usually are set to Yes, so that when the server reboots, the Mac clients can log in.

If you select No to updating the AUTOEXEC.NCF file, then the server will not load the AppleTalk modules after a restart. The Macintosh users will not be able to log in.

The last selection in Final Installation Options loads the Macintosh client support files from the CD-ROM to the server in the SYS:PUBLIC\MAC\ENGLISH directory. This is a self extracting file for the Macintosh called macnds.sea and is discussed in "Working with Macintosh Client Files" later in this chapter.

After you exit the current screen, the install program copies the Macintosh related files from the CD-ROM to the server. When this is done, the INSTALL.NLM automatically launches the ATCONFIG.NLM. This modules opens the NetWare for Macintosh Configuration screen (see fig 18.6).

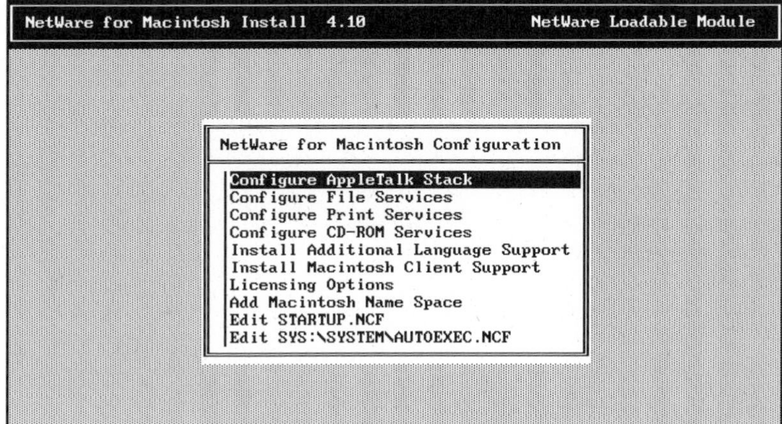

Figure 18.6

The NetWare for Macintosh Configuration screen launched from the ATCONFIG.NLM.

Selecting Configure AppleTalk Stack brings up the Internetworking Configuration screen.

The install procedure automatically launches the INETCFG module. In the future, you will independently launch this module from the server console to view or configure all internetworking settings, including AppleTalk.

Protocol Configuration Section

This section explains how to configure the AppleTalk protocol. The Protocol Configuration Section is used to configure the AppleTalk stack. AppleTalk provides the network connectivity between the Macintosh nodes and the NetWare server. The Protocol Configuration Section is in the Internetworking Configuration menu.

Click on the Protocols item from the Protocol Configuration Section. Figure 18.7 displays the different protocol choices. As you can see from this illustration, this is where you configure also the IPX and TCP/IP protocols.

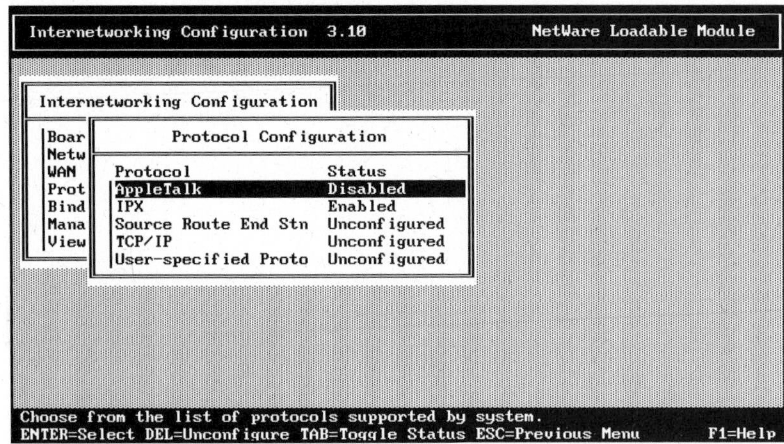

Figure 18.7
Protocol Configuration showing the AppleTalk selection highlighted.

Looking at figure 18.7, you can tell the state of a protocol. This relates to whether a protocol is configured, and also tells you if the protocol is enabled or not. During the initial install of the Mac NLM software, the status of the AppleTalk stack is unconfigured. After you have successfully completed the AppleTalk Configuration section the status should be enabled as indicated:

```
AppleTalk Status: Enabled
```

The AppleTalk status will be enabled after the protocol configuration is complete and the server has been rebooted so it can properly load the modules. This will happen at the end of the chapter. It is important to understand this status. If in the future the modules load incorrectly or if the modules do not load on server boot-up this status will be disabled.

Click on the AppleTalk protocol from the Protocol Configuration menu (see fig. 18.8). The next screen to appear is the main AppleTalk Configuration screen.

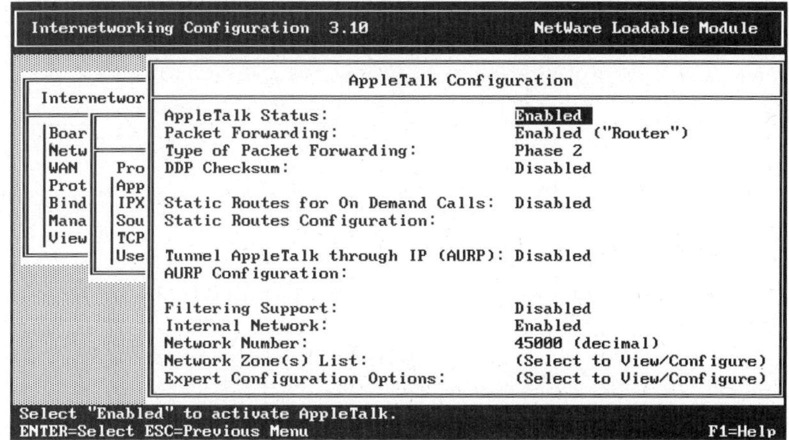

Figure 18.8
The AppleTalk Configuration menu.

The following bulleted list describes each option in figure 18.8. After each description the default setting is shown.

- **AppleTalk Status.** Enables and disables AppleTalk support during system initialization. Default: Disabled.

Disabling AppleTalk status and rebooting the server will not allow Macintosh clients to log into the server. The AppleTalk NLMs will load, but the protocol stack will be disabled.

If AppleTalk status is disabled, a Macintosh can still access the NDS tree if the Macintosh is running Mac IPX. The Macintosh cannot log in or mount any volumes tough in this configuration. The server console displays the following message if the AppleTalk stack is not bound to a network interface card:

```
AppleTalk DDP - AppleTalk clients open while stack is unbound
```

Macintosh client issues are discussed in the "Working with Macintosh Client Files" section later in the chapter.

- **Packet Forwarding.** By enabling packet forwarding, the server becomes an AppleTalk router on the internetwork. The server is responsible for forwarding or routing AppleTalk packets between the connected subnets. This would be the normal choice for a multiserver environment. In a NetWare 386 3.*x* environment, the server is usually set up to be a router. If you are upgrading from this type of environment, enable packet forwarding. Disablement causes the server to act only as a AppleTalk node. It will not forward or route packets. Default: Disabled.

- **Type of Packet Forwarding.** Configures the server to run in an AppleTalk Phase II only or AppleTalk Phase I and II transitional environment. Choose Phase II if you are using extended zones. Select the transition option if you are running LocalTalk along with Phase I on the network. For an explanation of extended and non-extended zones, review the "AppleTalk Zones and NetWork Ranges" section at the beginning of this chapter. Default: Disabled.

Packet forwarding allows the server to become an AppleTalk router. Disabling this feature makes the server act as an end node. Disabling packet forwarding disables all packet forwarding and routing between LAN cards in the server.

- **DDP Checksum.** Enables and disables Datagram Delivery Protocol checksums. Use only if DDP is enabled on other AppleTalk routers in the network. Default: Disabled.

- **Static Routes for On Demand Calls.** Enables static routing. Use this feature only if you have static routes or on-demand routes. Authentication parameter must be enabled from the INETCFG for on-demand links to operate properly. Default: Disabled.

- **Tunnel AppleTalk through IP (AURP).** Enable this only if you want to tunnel AppleTalk through IP. An example would be if you had an IP-only segment within the network, and AppleTalk needed to be routed between the two networks. By tunneling AppleTalk within IP, AppleTalk network information would travel between the two networks over the IP link. AppleTalk Update-Based Routing Protocol (AURP) is an enhancement over RTMP and allows tunneling of AppleTalk through IP. Default: Disabled.

- **Filtering Support.** Enabling this field sets the configuration of the AppleTalk filters in FILTCFG active. Default: Disabled.

To access the application to set the filters, type the following at the console prompt:

load filtcfg

- **Internal Network.** Enables you to configure an internal network on the router. This option does not need to be enabled to support packet forwarding or to support routing AppleTalk packets between LAN segments. This option only allows the server to be configured for more than one zone and advertises Apple services, such as the file server name, in more than one zone. Enable this option if you have a multiple-zone network, and you want the same services from the server broadcast in multiple zones. This will help the users because the AppleTalk services will be broadcast in multiple zones, although this will slightly increase network traffic and load on the routers. Default: Disabled.

- **Network Number.** If Internal Network is enabled, you must assign a network number for the server. This number can fall between 1 and 65,279 and must be unique on your AppleTalk network.

The internal network number cannot be between any zone ranges on any network segment anywhere on the LAN or WAN. It must be unique. This includes network ranges on the server currently being configured.

- **Network Zone(s) List.** This is where you enter your zone names. You must have a zone listed if you enabled the internal network number option. The zone you enter will become the default zone and will be broadcast within the range of the internal number selected. This means that Macintosh clients will be able to find the server within this default zone by using the Chooser application.

  Press Insert to add a zone to the list. You may have up to 255 zones each with up to 32 characters, and can include embedded spaces. Characters must be legal printing characters.

- **Expert Configuration Options.** This option enables you to view or configure AppleTalk running over X.25.

You will not be using this field for most installations. This relates only to the router communicating with another vendor's router using AppleTalk over an X.25 connection.

Exit the AppleTalk Configuration screen by pressing Esc and save the changes. You have now configured the AppleTalk protocol section of the install. You do not need to enter the IPX section of the Protocol Configuration screen to configure the AppleTalk section.

Exit to the Internetworking Configuration screen to begin the next section.

In the future, you can always view or modify these changes by typing the following at the server console:

load inetcfg

Bindings Configuration Settings

This section provides details of adding the configured AppleTalk stack to a LAN interface card. Applying the AppleTalk bindings to the LAN interface card is done through the INETCFG module, which is the same module used for the AppleTalk protocol configuration. This binding section, along with the previous section on protocol configuration, makes up the majority of configuring AppleTalk on the server.

Click on Bindings from the Internetworking Configuration menu. Figure 18.9 illustrates the current IPX protocol bound to a 3COM Ethernet card. Once AppleTalk is configured it will also appear in this screen.

Figure 18.9

The Configured Protocol to Network Interface Bindings screen.

Internetworking Configuration 3.10 NetWare Loadable Module

Internetworking Configuration

Configured Protocol To Network Interface Bindings

Protocol	Interface	Status	ID String
IPX	3C509_1	Enabled	FB44D1A2

Choose from list of protocol-to-interface bindings.
ENTER=Select INS=Insert DEL=Delete TAB=Toggle Status ESC=Previous Menu F1=Help

Press Insert in the Configured Protocol to Network Interface Binding windows to select the AppleTalk protocol. Press Enter while the AppleTalk protocol selection is highlighted. The next screen to appear lists the interface cards that are available to bind AppleTalk (see fig. 18.10).

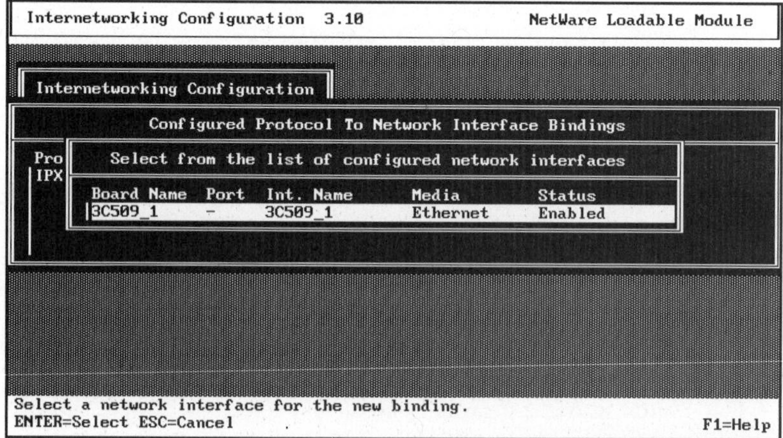

Figure 18.10

Select from the list of configured network interfaces.

The status for AppleTalk in the binding section will be enabled. Continue through with the bindings configuration. After you finish configuring the AppleTalk configuration for the first time, the server will need to be rebooted or reinitialized to properly load the AppleTalk NLMs and be available to Macintosh clients.

Highlight the interface card and press Enter. A smaller window appears asking whether you have an extended or non-extended network. Select the same option that you selected from the menu path in Internetwork Configuration—Protocol—AppleTalk—Type of Packet Forwarding. This selection was either Phase II or Transition (Phase I and II)and corresponds respectively to extended or non-extended networks.

Figure 18.11 shows the Binding NetWare AppleTalk to a LAN Interface screen.

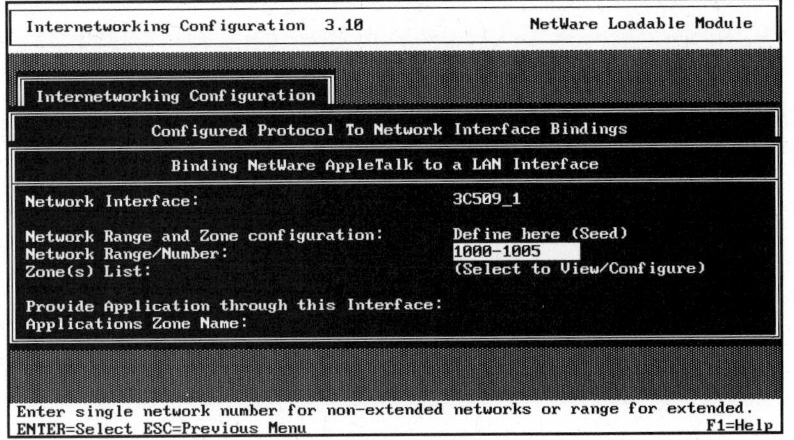

Figure 18.11

The Binding NetWare AppleTalk to a LAN Interface screen.

The following bulleted list explains the options in figure 18.11. The purpose of this screen is to link the range and zone information to a particular interface card.

- **Network Interface.** This is the LAN card you selected in the previous window.
- **Network Range and Zone configuration.** The two choices are seed or non-seed router configuration. There must be at least one seed router for AppleTalk on the network. A dedicated router on the network that is routing AppleTalk is an example of a seed router. A NetWare server can also be configured as a seed router. Seed routers inform all the other AppleTalk routers of network and zone information. When a non-seed router comes on-line, it learns about the network and acts as a seed router until it is rebooted. It is not a problem to have more than one seed router on a network. Generally a Netware server is configured as a seed router.

Select non-seed if there are other AppleTalk routers on the network that are performing this function. An example would be another NetWare server with the AppleTalk NLMs loaded configured as a seed router.

Select the seed option if there are no other routers on the network that are routing the AppleTalk protocol. The default: Learn from network (Non-Seed).

If there are other seed routers within the network, it is still permissible to add another seed router. The important step is to make sure that all seed routers have the proper cable range and network numbers for each of their network connections.

If the seed option is selected, the following two parameters become configurable:

- **Network Range/Number:** Enter a network number or range of numbers for this interface card that will be broadcast on this LAN segment.
  - If you selected Transition (Phase I and II) routing in the previous Protocol Configuration section, you must enter a unique number between 1 and 65,279. This number must not have a range (for example, 1000-1000).
  - If you selected Phase II routing in the Protocol Configuration section, you must enter a extended zone range between the range of 1 and 65,279 that is also unique (for example, 1000-1010).

Please review the section "AppleTalk Zone and Network Range Information" at the beginning of this chapter to help decide on proper network numbering.

- **Zone(s) List.** Enter the appropriate zone name in which the server will be broadcast. If you selected to enable packet forwarding ("Router") under the AppleTalk Configuration window in the previous section (see fig. 18.8), and you want the server to show up in that zone, then re-enter that zone name here. If packet forwarding was disabled ("End Node"), type the name of the existing zone on your network in which you want the server to show.

Zone names can be up to 32 characters, including embedded spaces. All characters for zone names must be valid printing characters. To insert a new zone, press Insert. After you insert the new zone name, a window appears, prompting for you to define the zone as the default zone or not.

If this server exists on a multiserver network and other NetWare servers are running the AppleTalk NLM software, you can query the AppleTalk routing tables, RTMP, on the other servers that are properly running AppleTalk to find legal network ranges.

At the server console running the AppleTalk NLMs, type the following:

load ATCON

Select Routing Table from the menu to view zone and network information. Select Network to view current AppleTalk ranges. This information is useful only if the server running the ATCON.NLM is on the same LAN as the server that is being configured for AppleTalk. Many problems with configuring AppleTalk are due to invalid network ranges. For information on selecting the correct network number, review the "AppleTalk Zone and Network Range Information" section earlier in this chapter.

The last two selections in figure 18.11 are only available if the Internal Network option is enabled in the AppleTalk Configuration screen (refer to fig. 18.8). If the Internal Network option is set to Disabled (under the AppleTalk Configuration menu), then you must configure each LAN card for AppleTalk application support. You must also select a zone for this LAN card to broadcast the application(s) in.

- **Provide Application through this Interface.** Determines if applications running on the server are able to be accessed through this interface.
    - By selecting Yes to the Application parameter and selecting a zone name described in next section, a Mac can connect to this server through this LAN card.
    - By selecting No, AppleTalk will not be broadcast from the server on this segment, and Macs will not be able to connect to the server through this interface.
- **Application Zone Name.** This selection instructs the server to broadcast the AppleTalk applications in the zone chosen by you. If this field is left blank, the default zone name is chosen.

  If this LAN interface is a seed interface, press Enter to display the already configured zone list. Select the zone that you want the applications to be advertised in.

  If the selected LAN interface is a non-seed interface, you must enter a zone that the applications will be broadcast in. Remember, by selecting non-seed, you are stating that there are other AppleTalk routers on the network broadcasting zone information. By leaving this field blank the server will select the default zone from the network. To enter a different zone press Enter and select the new home zone for this LAN card.

Tip: Remember, enabling Internal Network parameter under AppleTalk Configuration (see fig. 18.8) disables the Provide Application through this Interface and the Application Zone Name menu items. If the server has a unique internal network number, it will use this number as the address for the AppleTalk services. An internal network number simplifies configuration because the AppleTalk application does not have to be configured for every LAN interface on the server. After you bind AppleTalk to the LAN cards selected, the server activates AppleTalk over those LAN cards.

You have reached the end of the AppleTalk configuration. After these options are set, you may save changes and exit the install program completely. At the server console prompt, you may down and reboot the server to test the AppleTalk modules. The server should come up and automatically load the AppleTalk NLMs. If this does not happen, check the AUTOEXEC.NCF file and verify that the AFP.NLM is automatically loading during server boot-up.

After rebooting the server, run the Chooser application on a Macintosh to verify the server is a available. Make sure that you have the proper zone selected and that the proper network type is either Phase I or Phase II in the network control panel on the Macintosh. For detailed information on Macintosh NetWare configuration, review "Installing the Macintosh Client Software" section later in the chapter.

After the restart on the NetWare server, the Macintosh should be able to log in to the server as a valid NetWare user.

Working with Macintosh Client Files

NetWare 4.1 provides Macintosh connectivity to the server with the necessary software (called MacNDS) on the Macintosh client side. *MacNDS* enables a Macintosh running the System 7 operating system to access the NetWare Directory Services (NDS) on a NetWare 4.1 network.

This section explains the software pieces of the MacNDS client and how to install and configure them. It then covers Macintosh access to NDS, which is a new subject in NetWare 4.1, that will allow the Macintosh users to feel "equal" with their PC brethren on the NetWare network.

This section is intended for network Administrators to get their Macs "online" with this new NetWare 4.1 version.

Macintosh Requirements and MacNDS Client Components

To properly access this new NDS service with a Macintosh, certain requirements must be met. The client side consists of five software modules that provide NetWare connectivity. Once installed, the Macintosh will be able to access the NDS tree and network services. These software components are listed in table 25.3, which lists the component's name, description, and location on the Macintosh.

Table 25.3
Macintosh Client Software for NetWare Connectivity

Software Components	Description	Macintosh Location
AppleShare 3.5	AppleShare will automatically upgrade to 3.5 if your current version is older.	Extensions folder of local Macintosh
MacNCP	Allows directory service logins; the Directory Tree Login menu appears as a tree to the upper-right of screen.	Control Panel folder on a System 7.*x* Macintosh
NetWare UAM	NetWare User Authentication Method enables password encryption for the Macintosh.	AppleShare folder under the System folder
MacIPX	This is required for access into NDS; MacIPX allows a Macintosh to use the IPX protocol.	Control Panel folder on a System 7.x Macintosh
~NetWare Aliases	This extension enables you to log quickly into a server and launch frequently used applications.	Extension folder of local Macintosh

These programs are included in the MACNDS.SEA file, which is installed during the NetWare for Macintosh installation. The installation of this file onto the Macintosh is described in the next section.

Installing the Macintosh Client Software

This section details the installation of the Macintosh client software. You should by now have the NetWare for Macintosh server software installed and running. The Macintosh client should be network ready and able to log in to a NetWare 3.*x* or 4.0 network. After the MacNDS client software is installed and the Macintosh is rebooted, you will have access to NetWare Directory Services on the NetWare 4.1 server.

The NetWare User Authentication Method (NetWare UAM) should reside in the AppleShare Folder (inside the System folder) on a Macintosh client previously set up for logging into a 3.*x* server. If this file is not present, the Chooser will inform you that this server does not use a recognizable log on sequence. It will not be possible to connect to the server in bindery service mode or to continue installation of the MacNDS software with this error message. Make sure the NetWare UAM resides in the AppleShare folder.

1. To access the MacNDS install software, it is necessary to connect to the server running NetWare 4.1 in bindery service mode. This is accomplished by opening the Chooser (located under the Apple Menu) and selecting the AppleShare icon from the left hand window (see fig. 18.12). Highlight the NetWare 4.1 server from the right hand window and click on OK. Depending on your network, it might be necessary to select the proper zone from the lower left hand window of the Chooser.

Ensure that you are logged in as Supervisor for the following extraction step because you will need to create files on the server volume.

If you do not see a server available in the Chooser, check the following:

The Network control panel should be configured for the proper network connection. This is generally LocalTalk, EtherTalk, or TokenTalk. The Network control panel is located in the Control Panels folder inside the System Folder under System 7 and above. The Network control panel is located in the System Folder for System 6.

Select the AppleShare file and click on Get Info from the File menu in the Finder. Verify that it is version 3.5 or above. The AppleShare file is located in the Extensions folder inside the System Folder under System 7, but it's located in the System Folder for System 6.

Verify the link status and traffic indicators on your network cards and hubs. Also check your physical network cabling.

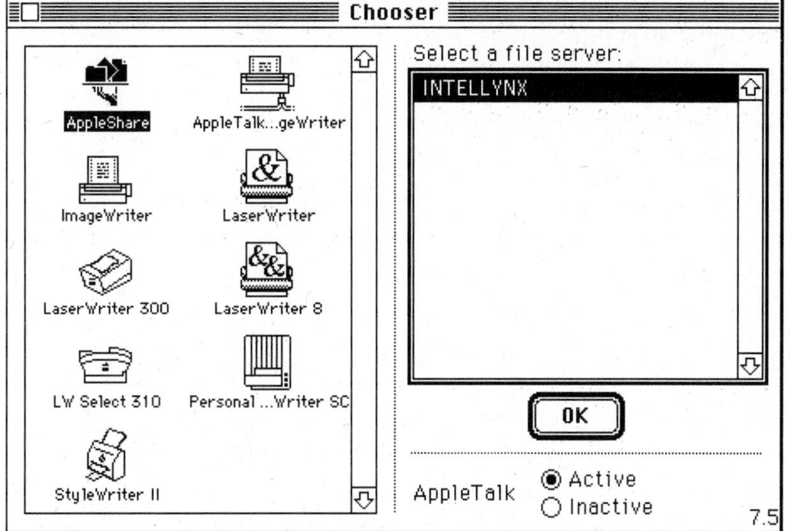

Figure 18.12
Selecting a NetWare server through the Chooser.

2. Mount the SYS: volume of the server onto the Macintosh desktop so you have access to the SYS:PUBLIC directory.

3. Next, open the English folder under the Public directory to view the MACNDS.SEA file (see fig. 18.13).

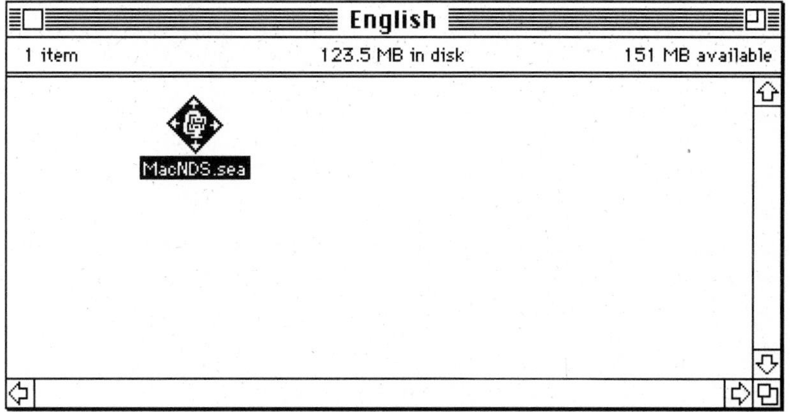

Figure 18.13
The folder showing the MacNDS.SEA file on NetWare volume.

If another language was installed during the initial installation, this language folder is located under the SYS:PUBLIC directory. Select the MacNDS file from the appropriate language folder.

4. Next, it is necessary to extract the installation software package from the original self extracting file (MACNDS.SEA). This is done by doubling-clicking the MACNDS.SEA file.

5. Launch the self-extracting archive by double-clicking it. You are prompted for a location into which to extract the files. These files should be placed on the server in a location of your choice. A good location for these files is under the Public directory in their own folder. This would allow any user read and file scan access to the files. The installation screen is illustrated in figure 18.14.

Note: Do not extract the files to the same Macintosh client that you will later run the Installer on because the Installer cannot modify the drive that it is launched from.

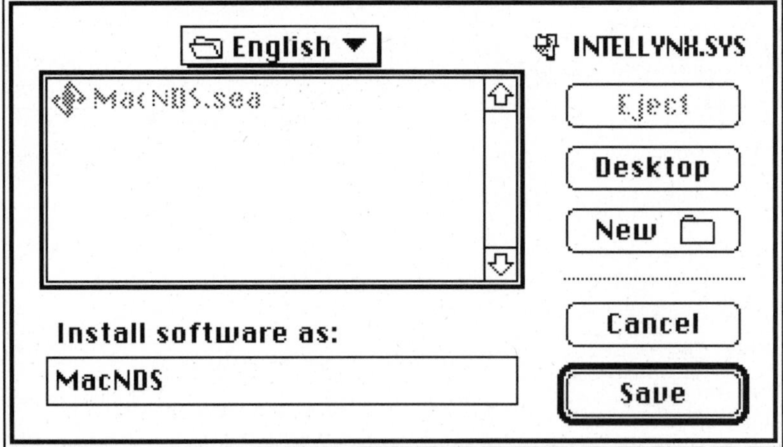

Figure 18.14
The installation screen of the self-extracting program.

The self-extracting archive reports `Installation was successful` after it has completed extraction. It is only necessary to extract the archive once. These new files will be used for all subsequent Macintosh client installations.

At this point, you have not installed the software on the Macintosh client. The self-extracting file has expanded and placed the new uncompressed client software in the location specified. Now you use the Macintosh Installer program to install these programs on the Macintosh client.

1. Open the MacNDS folder by double-clicking it (see fig. 18.15). This folder contains the Macintosh client software, as shown in figure 18.16.

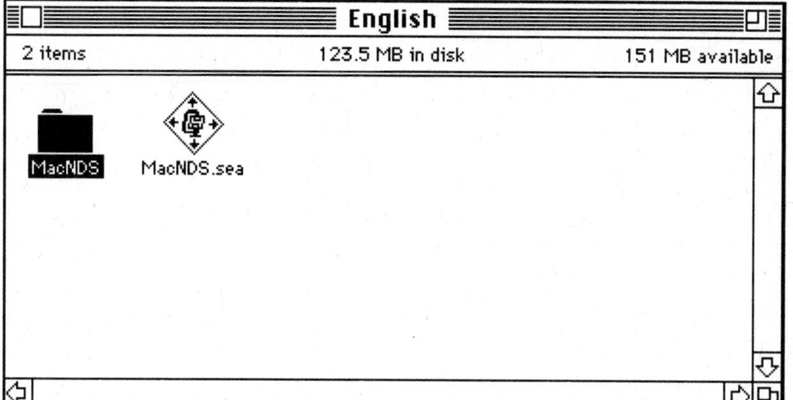

Figure 18.15
The MacNDS folder created on the NetWare volume.

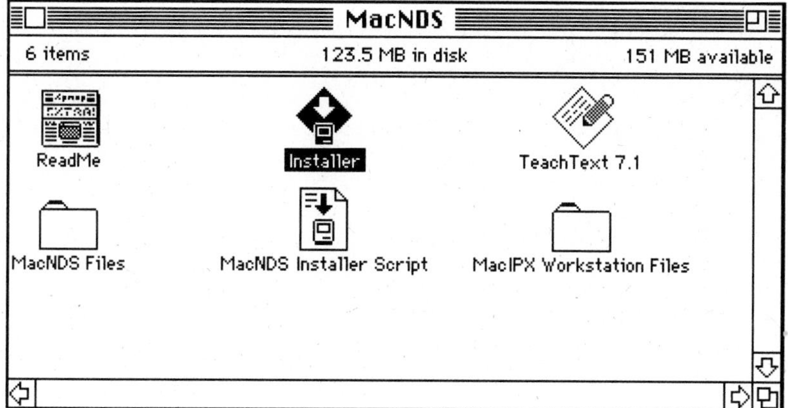

Figure 18.16
The contents of the MacNDS folder.

2. Double-click on the Installer icon.

   The installer program launches, presenting you with the opportunity to select install options and the location for the installation (see fig. 18.17). By default, it selects the Easy Install option (usually the best choice) and the drive from which the client Mac was started from (where the currently active System Folder resides).

Figure 18.17

The installation screen with default options selected

3. After the install, restart the Macintosh. The MacNCP icon appears on boot-up. If this icon is crossed out, it means it did not load properly, and you will not be able to log in to NDS.

MacNDS Control Panels Configuration

Configuring the NDS in Netware version 4.1 for the Macintosh client is made possible through the following two control panels:

- ◆ MacNCP control panel
- ◆ MacIPX control panel

MacNCP

The MacNCP program allows the Macintosh to "speak" the same language as NDS and therefore request services from NDS. The services provided by MacNCP are as follows:

- ◆ Capability to log in to the Netware Directory Services tree and retrieve Directory Services information like container, organization, and tree name.
- ◆ Access to other servers in the Directory tree is seamless because you are an authorized user within the Directory Services. Before this release, the user had to log into each Netware server from which he wanted services.

Settings in the MacNCP Control Panel

The MacNCP section reviews the different configuration values for the MacNCP software. This control panel enables a user to select default Directory Tree, Directory Context, and login name. It also provides the capability for a tree lookup facility, which would be helpful in larger LAN's with multiple trees.

The MacNCP program should load automatically when the Mac boots up. If you want to disable the load, hold down the mouse button. Holding down the mouse button during boot-up disables MacIPX and MacNCP. You are unable to log in to NDS without these loaded, but you can still log into a server with bindery services. Sometimes, during work station diagnostics, it is useful not to load certain control panel items.

To launch the MacNCP application, select the control panel option under the Apple symbol on the Macintosh desktop. Once you select the control panel option, you should see MacNCP and MacIPX each as a selection. Figure 18.18 illustrates the MacNCP application. The following bulleted list walks you through the MacNCP configuration screen.

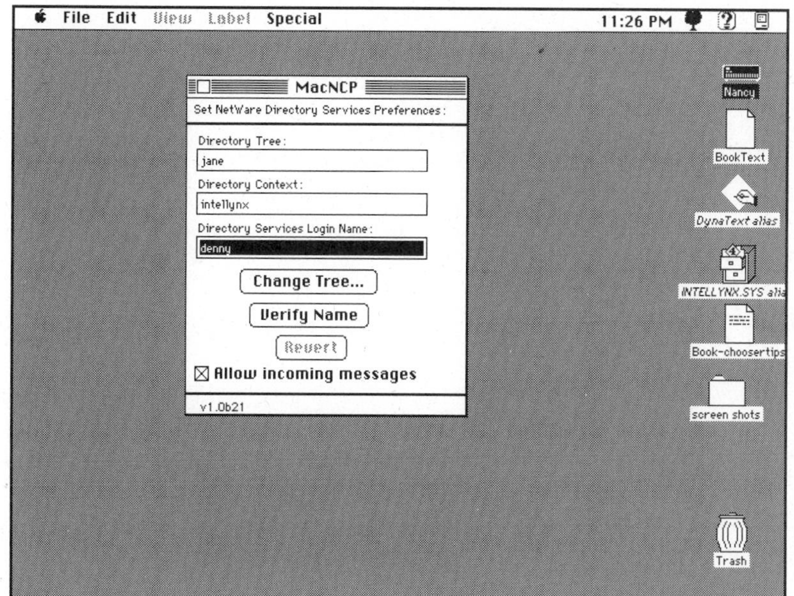

Figure 18.18

The MacNCP Client for Netware 4.10.

- **Directory Tree.** Signifies the name of the Directory tree MacNCP will log you into. This field may be up to 32 characters and is not case-sensitive.

  Click on the Change Tree button to perform a search on available trees to select from. Modifications in this field take affect after a reboot.

- **Directory Context.** Identifies default OU and O, along with your user name, to create the NDS login name. This field is not case sensitive. A type name or typeless name is legal. Following are examples of each of these two naming conventions:

  OU=inside.OU=sales.O=ACME (typeful name)

  inside.sales.acme (typeless name)

- **Directory Services Login Name.** Defines user name used to log into the Directory Services. You can change your name in the NDS login screen but this field will be the default. It is not case-sensitive.

- **Change Tree**. This button brings up a list of available trees on your network to log into. The current selection is highlighted. Additional information on searching for NDS trees is contained in the Using MacNDS Client for Netware in DynaText.

- **Verify Name.** This button enables you to identify quickly the validity of your user name within the specified tree and context. This operation verifies the following:

  - Directory Tree existence. If you are unsure of existing trees or need to check spelling, click on the Change Tree button.
  - Checks the Directory Context for existence.
  - Checks login name with each container specified.

  These fields are not case-sensitive. Be sure not to add a dot after the user in the Login Name field. This causes the verification to fail.

- **Revert.** This button enables you to return to the original configuration of MacNCP.

- **Allow Incoming Messages.** This check box turns on and off the receipt of messages from NetWare and AppleShare. An X enables messages to get to the user. Messages are denied when the X is removed.

MacIPX

The MacIPX section reviews the different configuration values for the MacIPX software. MacIPX allows the Macintosh to speak the IPX protocol. The MacIPX control panel works with MacNCP and provides MacNCP the ability to send requests to the server using NetWare native IPX protocol. It is through the IPX protocol that a Macintosh can access Directory Services. The MacIPX software and the associated network interface files were installed during the Macintosh client install.

Figure 18.19 illustrates the MacIPX application. To launch the MacIPX application, select the control panel option under the Apple symbol on the Macintosh desktop. Once you select the control panel option, you should see MacIPX and MacNCP each as a selection.

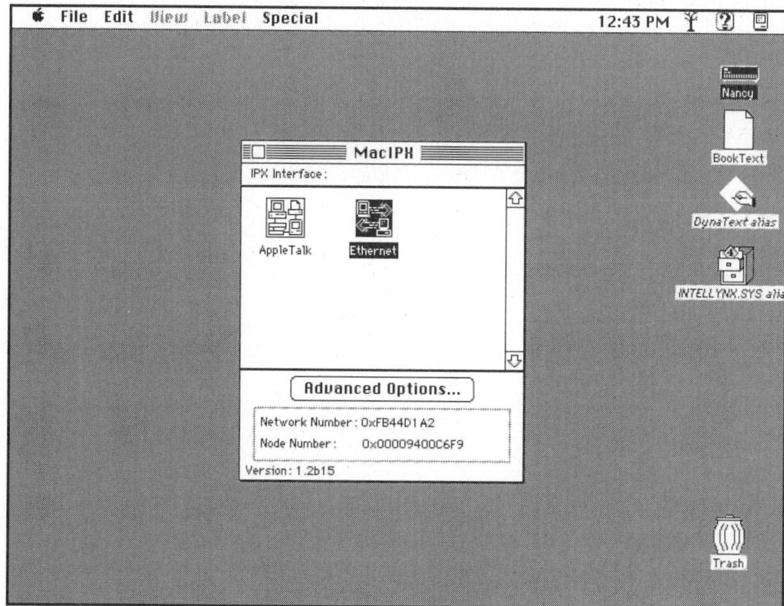

Figure 18.19
MacIPX Client for Netware 4.1.

The MacIPX program should load automatically when the Mac boots up. The same is true of MacNCP. If you want to disable the load, hold down the mouse button. Holding down the mouse button during boot-up disables MacIPX and MacIPX. Without these loaded you will not be able to log into NDS but will still be able to log into a server with bindery emulation. Sometimes, during work station diagnostics, it is useful not to load certain control panel items. The normal operation is to load these two modules, which are needed in order for a Macintosh to access the server. Sometimes it is possible for certain control panel items to conflict with one another, so it is always nice to have the option not to load them in certain cases.

Most network Administrators will not have to adjust these settings. Install the Macintosh client software first and work with it before trying to change the defaults.

Selecting an NIC

The MacIPX window enables you to select the proper interface card. If you have trouble activating the card with the supplied software driver, be sure to contact your card manufacturer. Click on an interface icon to check the frame type for your network. Figure 18.20 illustrates the Ethernet Access Configuration screen.

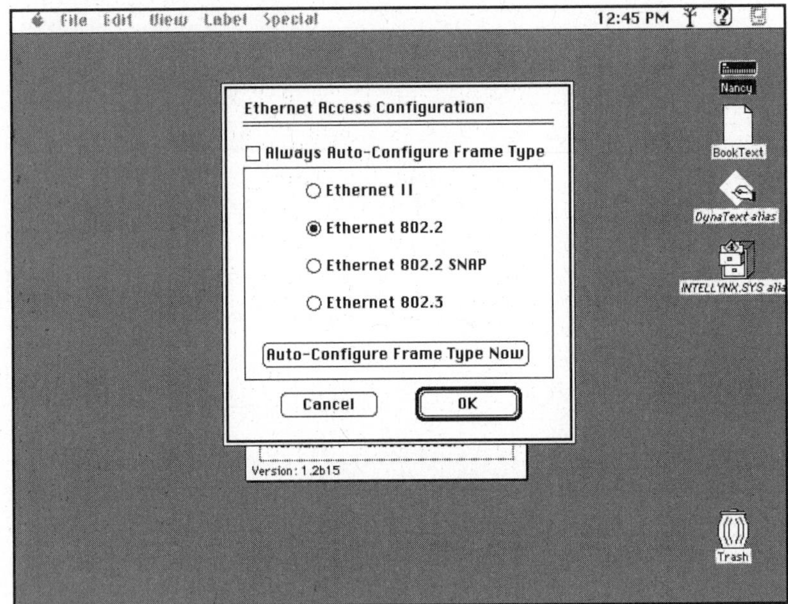

Figure 18.20
Configuring frame type for a Macintosh interface.

The default selection to auto-configure the frame type is probably fine. The network Administrator working with internetworking devices can also let you know the proper frame type for IPX. If you are running multiple frame types and the Macintosh is not working, then perform the following:

1. Deselect the auto-configure check box.
2. Select the proper frame type for IPX traffic. Remember, you can check the configuration on the server for this information.
3. Click on OK and check the network number on the MacIPX window.
4. If the network number is 0×0, repeat step 2.

AppleTalk Interface Selection

The AppleTalk selection in the MacIPX window allows a Macintosh to be connected to a network that does not support the proper framing. Examples of this are Macs connected to LocalTalk, Arcnet, or certain types of FDDI. In these cases, MacIPX encapsulates IPX into AppleTalk packets. You need an IPX gateway configured to route these packets to an IPX-supported network. This method should be used only if no other option is available. The best selection is either Ethernet or token ring extensions, depending on your network.

Preferences File for MacIPX

The preferences selected are stored in a file called MacIPX Preferences in a Preferences folder located inside the System folder. After properly configuring the MacIPX, copy this preferences file to the server. You may copy this file onto other Macs within their Preferences folder. The Macs must have the same network interface or the file will not work. You cannot copy a Ethernet preference file to a Mac with a token ring card and expect it to work. If Macs cannot access the network, copy the file to a disk for distribution. Reboot the workstation after copying the file.

Before the discussion of access methods to Netware 4.1, a review of terminology would be helpful. In Netware 3.*x*, a client would log in to the server through the bindery to gain access to services on that particular server. With the new DS access for Macintosh clients, Macs can log in to Directory Services directly, without being connected to a server. Therefore, the term *login* will be used for logging into Directory Services. The term *connect* will be used for connecting to a particular server only. Connecting to a server in 4.1 is the equivalent to logging in to a server in 3.*x*.

Remember, if you have MacNCP installed when you connect to a server, you will log in to Directory Services automatically. This is described in "Connecting to a Server through Chooser" later on in the chapter.

Logging in to Netware 4.1 with a Macintosh

Macintosh access to the NDS tree was not available prior to NetWare 4.1. With MacNDS software, a user can do the following:

- Log in to the Directory Services tree
- Log in to a specific server

- Connect to a specific server while logging in to NDS
- Connect to other server within the tree without being asked for a user name or password once he is logged in to NDS

You may not access NDS on a server prior to NetWare 4.1. A Macintosh running System 6 cannot access NDS, even with the MacNDS client software loaded.

Directory Services Tree Menu

There are four options available under the Directory Services tree icon. These menu options under the Directory Services tree icon include the following:

- **Get NDS Info.** This option describes the NDS tree information including login name, organization, and tree name.
- **Login.** Logging in to NDS directly is possible through the Directory Services Login window (see fig. 18.21). To open this window, click on the Directory Tree icon in the upper right hand corner. Select the login option. This tree will be bare if you are not logged in to Directory Services.

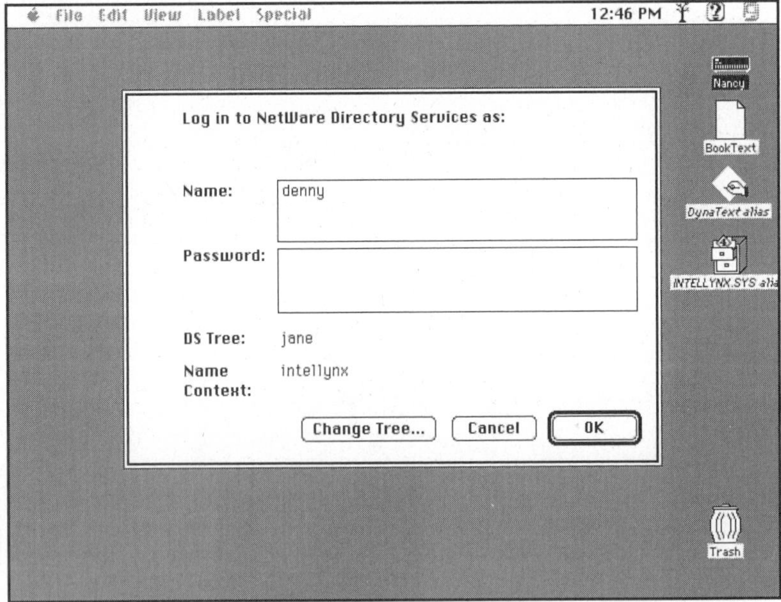

Figure 18.21
The Directory Services Login screen.

The following menu items explain the Netware Directory Services login screen as illustrated in figure 18.21.

- **Name.** Enter your user name for Directory Services.
- **Password.** Enter Directory Services password. This password is not case-sensitive.
- **Change Tree.** If the tree and context name need to be changed, click on this button to scan for other trees. Click on the OK button to log in after the fields are filled.

- **Change Passwords.** Use this to change your password in NDS.
- **Logout.** As the name implies, this logs you out of Directory Services.

Connecting to a Server through Chooser

This is the second method to log in to a server and also gain access to the Directory Services. The first method explained how to get into Directory Services only and did not connect you to any servers. The following method connects you to a server and logs you in to Directory Services.

1. Select the Chooser item under the Apple menu (see fig. 18.22).
2. Select the proper zone and highlight the server.
3. Click on OK.

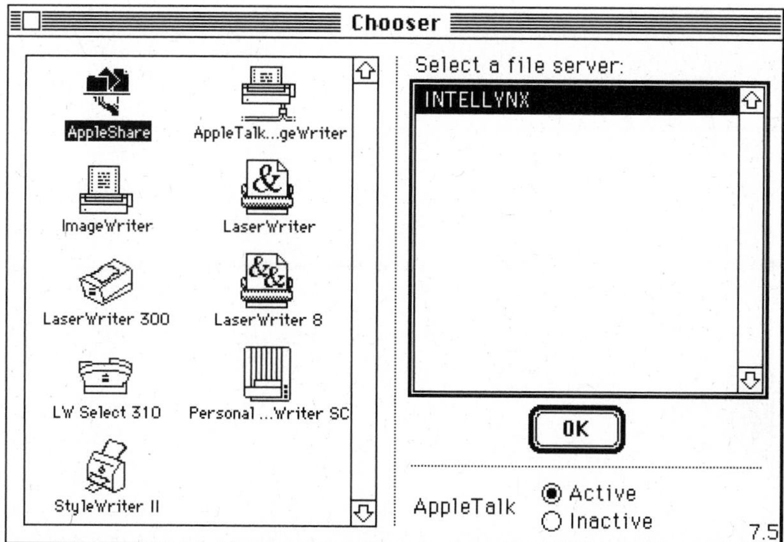

Figure 18.22
Using Chooser to log in to a server.

The next screen is the same login screen as the Directory Services Login screen in figure 18.19. From here, log in to the server, and you are connected to Directory Services. Following this, a screen appears asking which volumes from that server need to be mounted (see fig. 18.23).

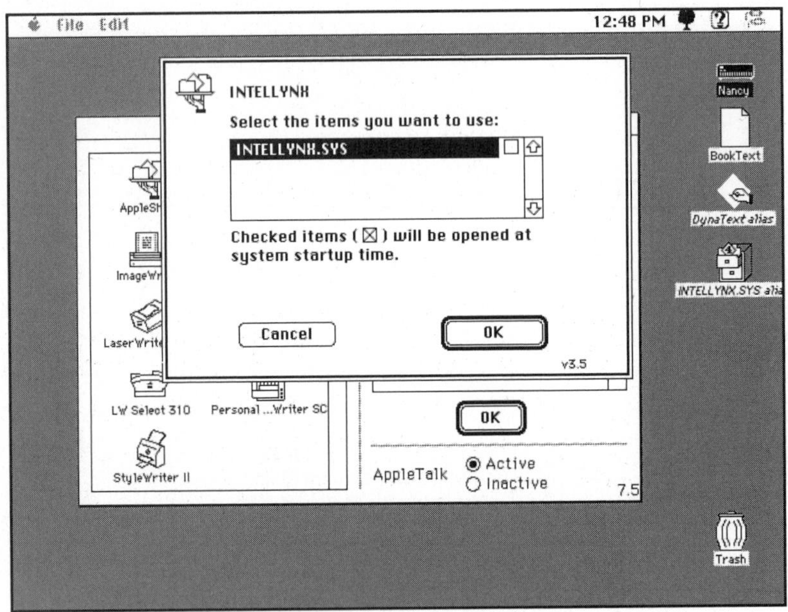

Figure 18.23

Selecting a volume to mount.

This is the same screen as in Netware 3.*x*, so Macintosh users should not see any additional screens beside the Directory Services Login screen. The advantage to Directory Services login is seamless access to other servers in the same tree.

After you have logged in to NDS, your Macintosh workstation can connect to any server in the tree with your access rights. Leaving a Macintosh logged into NDS unattended could pose a security risk.

Summary

Integrating the Macintosh into a Netware environment is not an easy task. This chapters focus was to show the Administrator a good overview with a step-by-step instruction for loading the server modules and client side software. The chapter

began with a Macintosh networking overview to try to familiarize the Administrator with key AppleTalk network terms. Key points in this section are the network ranges for Phase I and Phase II networks, transition routing concepts, and extended and non-extended zones.

Next the software modules that load on the NetWare server to support Macintosh connectivity were reviewed, followed memory requirements for these modules. Installation of the Macintosh NLM software modules was explained in detail with a step-by-step instruction given. Important points to know during this installation exercise are how your current AppleTalk network is configured and how to correctly install the server software into this network. As usual in networking, it more difficult to integrate something new into an existing network than start with a clean slate.

After the server install the chapter concentrated on the Macintosh client side. The key points in this chapter are installing the software from the server onto a folder on the server so a Macintosh can access it. Then the Macintosh has to run the install program to load the software onto the local hard drive. Key software components reviewed in detail are the MacIPX and MacNCP components. Each of these were illustrated with step-by-step configuration explained.

By now your NetWare server should be an active participant on the AppleTalk network, while you Macintosh community enjoys access to one of the most powerful network operating systems in the world.

Part V

Building the NDS Structure

New Riders Publishing
INSIDE
SERIES

NDS Tree Design Considerations

One of the first challenges that NetWare 4.1 Administrators must face is how to approach the design of the NetWare 4.1 NDS tree (or directory tree). NetWare 4.1 includes utilities that provide a great deal of flexibility in creating and modifying your directory tree design. Although NetWare directory design is not entirely a science, there are guidelines that you can follow to make your design and implementation closely match the needs of your organization. This chapter demonstrates some of the guidelines you can use to create an effective NDS design.

NetWare Directory Services, or *NDS*, is a network-wide database that regulates access to the network and its resources. NDS most easily is referred to and explained in two ways: the *directory tree*, which is the logical representation or view of the services connected to the network; and the *directory database*, which is the physical data that tracks, regulates, and grants access to network services. Both the directory and the directory database play an important role in the use of NetWare 4.1.

The network Administrator probably is the person responsible for designing and creating the NDS tree and database. Figure 19.1 represents the user accessing the directory database through the directory tree.

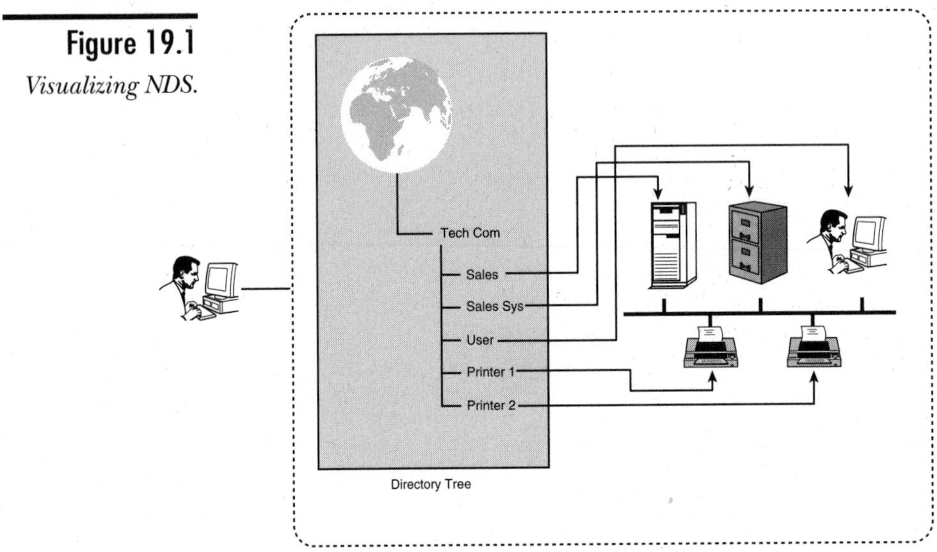

Figure 19.1
Visualizing NDS.

The directory tree provides the user interface to the directory database. The NDS tree enables you to organize and group resources in a logical fashion, just as you would organize files and applications in file-system folders or directories on your hard disk. The directory database, like the file allocation table of a file system, stores information about the resources such as their names, locations, security, and other useful information.

NDS design involves both the logical representation of the services and resources connected to the NetWare 4.1 network, and the strategic placement of the portions of the directory database on NetWare 4.1 servers throughout the network. Both phases of design require a small amount of planning in order for the design to meet fully your networking needs. An effectively planned directory maximizes the benefits you receive from NDS.

Planning NDS Trees

Some sources have overemphasized the need to plan the directory tree, which has caused some Administrators to feel reluctant to begin to upgrade to NetWare 4.*x*. Some Administrators fear that unless much time is invested beforehand into planning, the upgrade will fail to meet the organization's needs. Others feel that once the tree is designed and implemented, the structure cannot be changed. This chapter demonstrates the ease with which you can create and modify the configuration of the NDS tree to fit the evolving needs of your organization.

To begin, assume that the more complex the network you are trying to represent, or the more groups of network users or resources performing varied tasks, the more planning is required. A small company of 10 network users and a one-server, homogenous network might require only a few minutes to create an NDS system, for example. On the other hand, planning NDS for a multinational organization with hundreds of users, various geographic locations, and numerous workgroups with diverse needs might take several days. Although all NDS designs start with some planning, you do not need to spend weeks planning the structure before you begin. NetWare 4.1 includes tools that the simplest companies to the largest organizations can use to easily modify and fine-tune the configuration after implementation.

You should design the directory tree to meet two important goals:

- To minimize the initial shock and learning curve that network users might experience as a result of the upgrade
- To make the network administration easy to perform and track

You can use your organization chart as a general guide in designing the NDS tree. An NDS tree that is patterned after the way the organization looks and functions helps to familiarize the users and make them more comfortable with the new network setup.

Your users will appreciate the advantages of a single sign-on to the network; a graphical user interface; and the fact that they don't have to remember the names of servers to find file, print, or other services on the network. You will find that NetWare 4.1 is more flexible in assigning security and subadministrators. It also is better at displaying the resources on the network than before. These benefits combine to create a seamless, integrated network that can meet the needs of your users now and in the future.

After you have planned your directory tree and begun your implementation, you can change the structure to meet the needs of your organization. The guidelines provided here will help alleviate the apprehension Administrators might have. NDS can easily grow to meet the needs of the organization.

Deciding How Many Trees To Have

When you install NetWare 4.1, the operating system creates the directory database and the NDS tree. Each NetWare 4.1 server can be part of only one directory tree. With each server installation, you have a choice of creating a new NDS tree and database on the new server, or adding the new server to an existing directory tree. NetWare 4.1 enables you to place an unlimited number of NDS trees on the same segment or network. As a general rule, however, creating multiple trees unnecessarily complicates the network and its administration tasks. One directory tree per organization satisfies the needs of most installations.

The NetWare 4.1 installation program leads you through a set of forms that help you define how your server will function. One of the decisions you make during installation is how many NDS trees your network will use. As you contemplate the number of directory trees to create, consider the following advantages to having one NDS tree:

- You have fewer design decisions to make.
- You need to maintain only one user account per user on the network.
- Your users will have fewer problems logging into the network.

Deciding Whether To Use Multiple Trees

Naturally, more directory trees require more design decisions. As you build your NDS tree, you have to define organization and organizational unit levels for each directory tree you create. Each level of organization you add increases the amount of management and security that needs to be applied and checked.

Some Administrators feel that the extra security of having multiple NDS trees is worth the effort, however. Suppose that a law firm has a server called TOPSECRET. The server contains a critical history of judgments dating back to the establishment of the firm. To maximize the security of this server, the Administrator creates a separate directory tree on that server and disguises the server from NDS clients. The Administrator also can disable the servers service advertising protocol so that the server cannot be seen in a server list. When a user wants to log in to the server, the user has to perform one of the following procedures:

- Make a bindery attachment to the server by entering

  LOGIN TOPSECRET/*<username>* /B

  to grant a bindery attachment to the proper server. Then the user enters

  LOGIN *<distinguished name>*

  to authenticate to the NDS tree.

- The user specifies the preferred directory tree at login by entering

  LOGIN ***<distinguished name>*** **/P=*<tree name>***

Using multiple NDS trees to hide servers does not actually add security levels, but it does add steps that must be performed in addition to the normal login process. Network users who are unfamiliar with the existence of multiple directory trees within the organization might have difficulty discovering that another server or tree even exists.

Creating multiple user accounts defeats the purpose of having a directory service. NetWare 4.1 Directory Services is supposed to make it easier to find and use network resources than in prior versions, not more difficult. When you create multiple accounts, either in the same NDS tree or in different directory trees, you decentralize the information source and create more work than is necessary. A telephone directory for a city might contain references to the residents that live in the city, for example. Producing multiple versions of the telephone book does not help to communicate the information about the telephone users; it creates a confusing situation in which you might not know which telephone book to check in order to find a reference.

Managing redundant user accounts, security, groups, print queues, printers, and print servers, among the other objects that can be created in the NDS tree, could become a difficult situation to track. All the property values that can be set for a user are not easily transferable to another user. To change a password for a user with two NDS accounts would require the change to be made in each user account, for example. This also means that for two accounts, you as the Administrator would have to log in to the network twice—once in each directory tree in order to access the accounts.

With multiple directory trees on your network, a user belonging to one NDS tree could, during login, inadvertently attach to a server that belongs to a different directory tree than the one with his user account. Unless both NDS trees have a user with the same distinguished name and password, the network denies the user access. This is a frustrating situation for a user who does not understand why yesterday he could use the network, but today he cannot.

You can avoid this problem by entering

LOGIN ***<distinguished name>*** **/P=*<tree name>***

at the command line or in a batch file to ensure that the user attaches to the correct directory tree.

In addition, partitions and replicas might need to be created for each NDS tree. Each aspect of directory-tree management is impacted with the introduction of multiple NDS trees.

A side issue that affects the use of the directory tree when you have multiple NDS trees is that you can maintain only one directory connection from any one workstation (unless OS/2) at a time. If you log in to the Sales Directory tree, for example, and you want to retrieve information from another server in the Production NDS tree, the only connection you can make to the Production tree is a bindery attachment. You then can access the server in the Production tree as you would a NetWare 3.*x* server, but you cannot access any Directory Services information about the servers in the Production tree.

As a general rule, an organization should create and use only one directory tree.

Determining the Placement of Container Objects

In a new installation of NetWare 4.1, you must define the starting point or *trunk* of your directory. The top container in the tree is called the *organization.* All containers and terminal objects of the NDS tree are created inside the organization or beneath it.

All the branches of the directory fork downward from the trunk, just like in a real tree.

Keeping Your Tree Simple

As you begin creating your directory tree, try not to make the NDS tree too deep. A directory tree deeper than three levels can make it difficult for users to access objects in different containers. The more levels of containers created, the longer the distinguished name becomes.

The distinguished name for the user in figure 19.2, for example, is .hlopez.Marketing.CAMCON.Simulations. This string is prohibitive to use for login. If one or two of the NDS tree layers can be removed, you can reduce significantly the length of the object's name.

Do not lose sight of the fact that this new network also is new to the users you support as an Administrator. You should lay out the basic structure of your organization to look like something that is familiar to those that use it. The organization chart from your company is a good place to start, because most users are familiar with it.

Focus mostly on the common tasks performed by the workgroups in the company. Do you have an accounting group? Do you have a sales group? Individuals who perform similar tasks probably can be grouped into containers. Also, each group that performs a singular task probably has the same needs for resources and security.

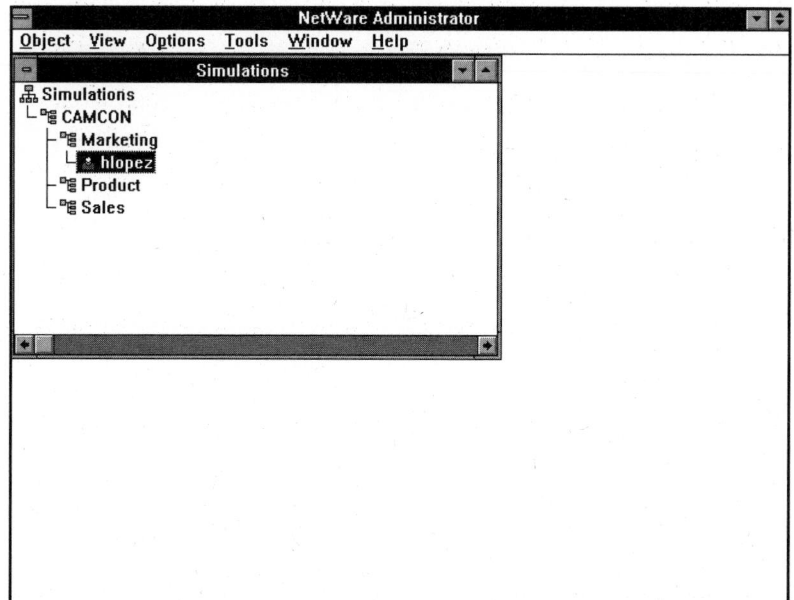

Figure 19.2
A deep NDS tree.

A Wide NDS Tree

Your network might also experience some performance degradation if you make your NDS tree too wide at the [Root]. Adding more than 5-6 organizations (or countries) at the [Root] will cause subordinate references to be created within each organization or country partition. A *subordinate reference* is like a read/write replica, but it cannot be viewed or deleted. The subordinate reference is used by NDS to facilitate browsing the NDS tree. As you add more organizations or countries at the [Root], you create subordinate references that may impact your network performance.

Deciding How Many Containers You Should Have

Because NDS has no practical limit on the number of containers you can create, it might be easy to make more containers than you really need to accomplish your design. You can approach the design using your organization chart, a workgroup chart, and a little common sense.

NDS containers act like groups. Objects within a container are subject to trustee assignments and other security restrictions, such as Inherited Rights filters. You can reduce greatly the administration task by using containers as groups, and by making rights assignments to the containers instead of to individuals.

The more containers you create, the more administration you must perform, but the more flexibility you have. If you can define and create your entire sales and marketing team within a single container because of the similar tasks with which they are involved, do so. You usually are better off with fewer containers than with too many.

Managing Partitions and Replicas

Partitions and replicas define how the directory database is distributed across the network. When you create a partition in the directory database, you define the boundary of a portion of the directory database that can be replicated, or copied, to other NetWare 4.1 servers on the network. Creating a partition does not change the structure of the database; it merely prepares the database for replication.

After defining partitions in the directory database, you can proceed to replicate the data to other NetWare 4.1 servers. This process of replication of the database provides two distinct benefits:

- Fault tolerance of the directory database
- Enhanced directory system performance

These benefits are discussed in the following sections.

Enhancing Fault Tolerance

Replication enhances the fault tolerance of the directory database by placing redundant Directory Services information on multiple servers. Suppose that a dentist's office has installed two NetWare 4.1 servers to track billing and work history. Server A and server B both have copies of each others' directory database information. If during the course of the day, server A becomes unavailable, the network users still can gain access to and log in to the network through server B, because their user accounts are known by more than one server. Even though the data and applications on server A are not accessible, users still can log in and access server B.

Improving Directory Access

The proper placement of replicas can enhance greatly the way your network performs. Placing replicas of the directory database on servers close to the people that use the information can help speed the access time to the directory database for authentication and other information needs.

You can effectively design a scheme for creating partitions and placing replicas if you have a basic knowledge of the segments on your network. Knowing which segments typically are slow helps you avoid spanning your design across a slow link, which might impede the performance of the network. The next sections examine some issues that you should consider when planning to partition and replicate your database.

Considering Geographical Factors

Organizations that have multinational offices probably have slower links spanning the ocean than the segments spanning a few local buildings. The slower lines are cheaper to maintain and generally are not tasked with the constant transfer of data. These slower network lines can have an impact on how the directory database communicates with other NetWare 4.1 servers in the network. You should consider the network links that cover large geographical distances when you design the layout of partitions and replicas.

Consider this example: InfoTech is a multinational organization that manufactures radio and television parts. The headquarters is in Sydney, Australia; and satellite offices are located in Frankfurt, Germany; Paris, France; and Tokyo, Japan.

Each branch office is connected to headquarters by X.25 over leased lines. With a geographic split like this and slow network links from one office to another, design considerations suggest that you should make each site a partition and replicate the partitions locally. Because replicas communicate with each other, it might take a large degree of bandwidth to span geographic locations with partitions. Therefore, identify the limits of your network and, if possible, create partitions and replicas so that they span the fastest links in the network.

NetWare 4.1 provides two utilities that manage partitions and replicas:

- PARTMGR.EXE (for DOS workstations)
- Partition Manager (for MS Windows workstations)

Both utilities have equivalent functionality.

Using PARTMGR.EXE

After you have considered the logical design of the directory tree, you should look at how to physically divide and distribute the portions of the directory database. PARTMGR.EXE is an NDS utility that enables you to partition and divide the directory database so as to enhance the fault tolerance and reduce the access time to the NDS system. PARTMGR.EXE works from DOS workstations that have a current connection to an NDS tree.

Creating a Partition

You must first use an NDS utility to divide, or partition the directory database before you can distribute the partitions. To utilize the benefits of fault tolerance and shorter access time to the database, you must first create a partition and then store or replicate the partition to another NetWare 4 server. Follow these steps to use PARTMGR to create a partition:

1. Enter **PARTMGR** from the DOS prompt. The main menu for PARTMGR appears, as shown in figure 19.3.

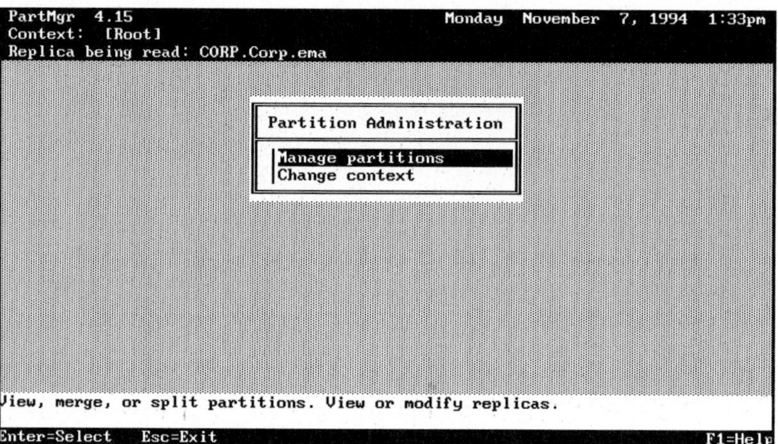

Figure 19.3
The PARTMGR main menu.

2. From the main menu, choose Manage partitions. This option enables you to walk the directory tree to view, create, or delete partitions.

3. From the Object, Class window, you can walk the NDS tree to find any available partitions. Figure 19.4 displays a partition already created.

4. To create another partition, highlight a container (an organization or an organizational unit). From the Object, Class window, press F10 to create a partition at the container you have highlighted. This action partitions this particular container and all container and terminal objects beneath it.

5. The utility asks whether you want to create a partition. Confirm the action, and within a few seconds, you have a partition created. Now your Object, Class window looks like the one shown in figure 19.5.

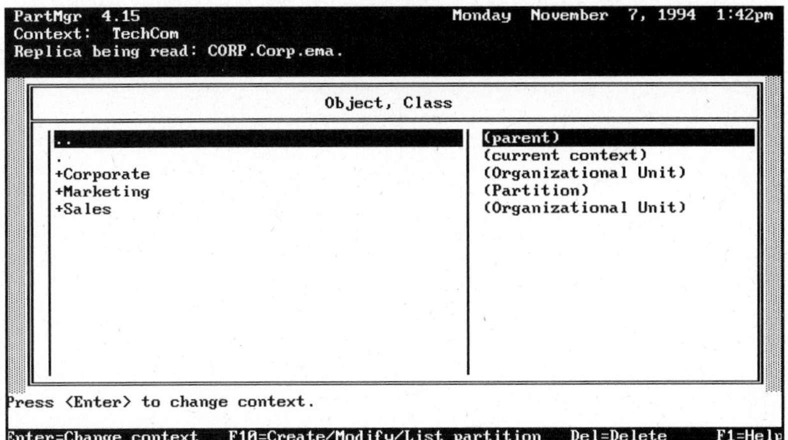

Figure 19.4

Locating a partition with PARTMGR.

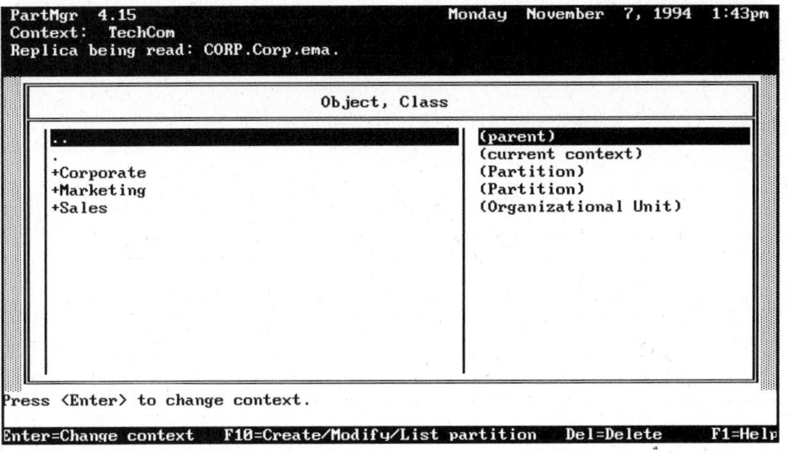

Figure 19.5

Creating a partition with PARTMGR.

Replicating a Partition

You can replicate the partition you just created by performing the following steps:

1. Enter **PARTMGR** from the DOS prompt, as you did in the preceding section to create a partition. The main menu for PARTMGR.EXE appears. Notice that at the top left corner a status line tells you your current context and the server from which the replica is being read (see fig. 19.6).

2. From the main menu, choose Manage partitions. Even though it does not mention replicas, this is the proper menu choice to use for replicas. If you have not created a partition, do so now by following the steps outlined in the preceding section.

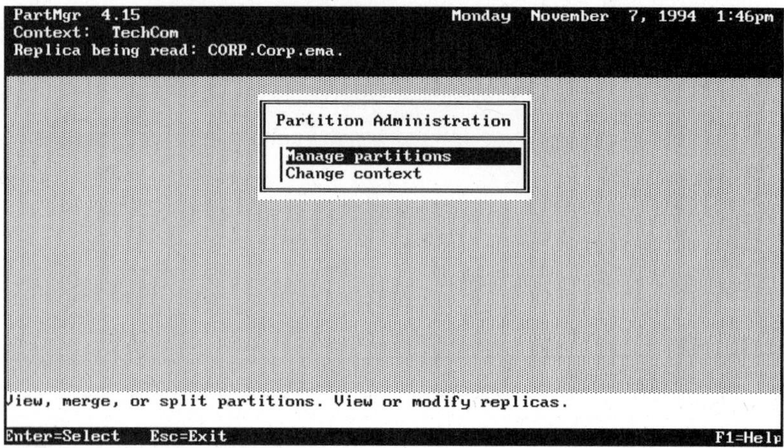

Figure 19.6
The status line for PARTMGR.

3. From the Object, Class window, highlight the partition that you want to replicate. This operation copies all the information from the partition to a NetWare 4.1 server.

4. Press F10. The Partition Management For box appears. Notice that the name of the partition you are working with appears in the box header (see fig. 19.7).

5. Choose the View/Edit replicas option. The name of the server on which the replica is stored appears, as shown in figure 19.8.

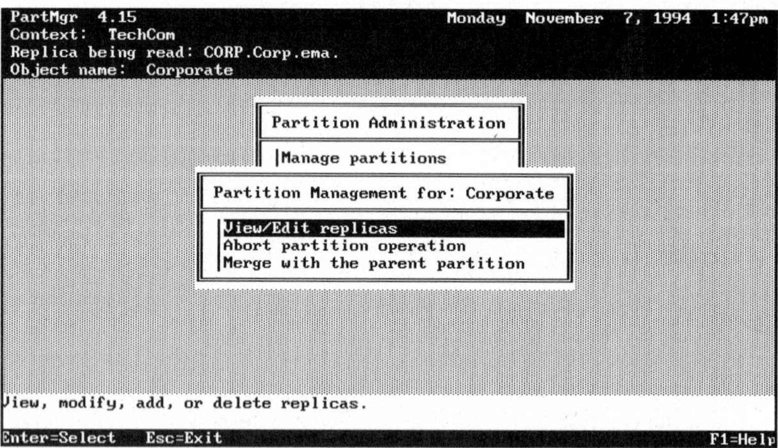

Figure 19.7
The Partition Management For box in PARTMGR.

6. From the Replicas stored on server box, press Ins to create a replica. The Add Replica box appears.

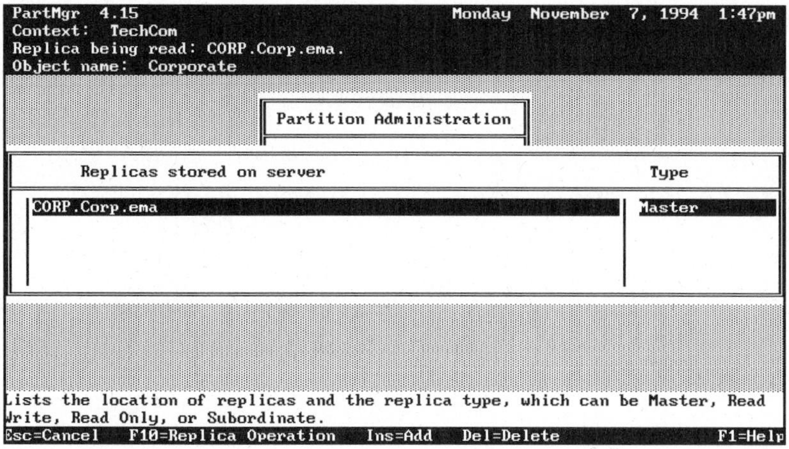

```
PartMgr 4.15                                  Monday November 7, 1994 1:47pm
Context: TechCom
Replica being read: CORP.Corp.ema.
Object name: Corporate

                    Partition Administration

      Replicas stored on server                                  Type
 CORP.Corp.ema                                                  Master

Lists the location of replicas and the replica type, which can be Master, Read
Write, Read Only, or Subordinate.
Esc=Cancel   F10=Replica Operation   Ins=Add   Del=Delete                F1=Help
```

Figure 19.8

The Replicas stored on server box in PARTMGR.

7. Press Enter to select the type of replica you want to create: a Read Write or a Read Only. Remember that the Read Only replicas have limited usage in the current version of NetWare 4.1, so use only Read Write replicas for now.

8. Move the cursor to the Store on Server field to specify on which server you want to create the replica. This action opens a field for you to specify the target server for the replica.

9. Type the distinguished name of the server, or press Ins to display the Object, Class window and browse the directory tree to find the target server.

10. From the browse box, locate the target server on which to place the new replica and press Enter. You return to the Replica to be stored on server box, with the distinguished name of the server displayed (see fig. 19.9).

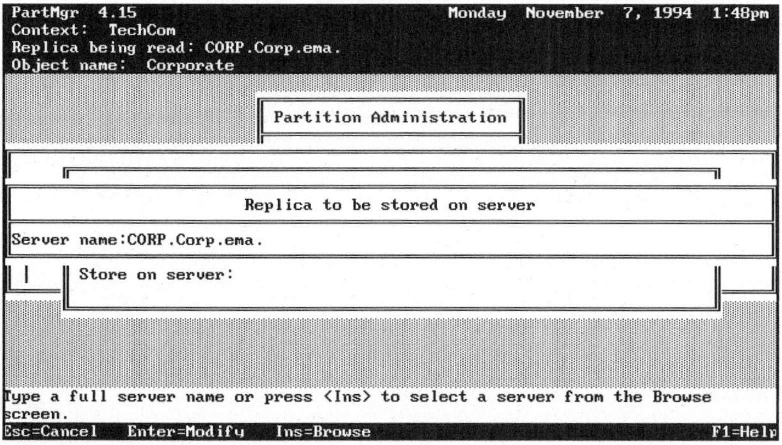

```
PartMgr 4.15                                  Monday November 7, 1994 1:48pm
Context: TechCom
Replica being read: CORP.Corp.ema.
Object name: Corporate

                    Partition Administration

                    Replica to be stored on server
Server name:CORP.Corp.ema.
      Store on server:

Type a full server name or press <Ins> to select a server from the Browse
screen.
Esc=Cancel   Enter=Modify   Ins=Browse                                   F1=Help
```

Figure 19.9

The target server for replica in PARTMGR.

11. Press F10 to save the replica.

12. After the replica is saved, you can exit from the utility by pressing Esc several times.

Using NWADMIN.EXE and Partition Manager To Manage Partitions and Replicas

NWADMIN.EXE, or more commonly referred to as *NetWare Administrator*, is a graphical user interface for NDS. You can use NetWare Administrator to create, delete, move, and change NDS objects. NetWare Administrator, however, will not allow you to move containers or view and manage partitions or replicas. Partition and replica management can be performed by launching another utility (Partition Manager) from the NetWare Administrator menu bar.

Under the Tools menu in NetWare Administrator, you will find the option for Partition Manager. Partition Manager is another GUI utility that enables you to partition and replicate the NDS database.

NetWare Administrator works from MS Windows workstations that have a current connection to an NDS tree. You must have the NetWare MS Windows client loaded to use NWADMIN.EXE.

Viewing Partitions

You can view the partitions defined in the NDS tree by performing the following steps:

1. Launch MS Windows.

2. From the Program Manager, find and open the program group NetWare Tools. This is where NetWare Administrator should be found.

3. From the NetWare Tools program group, start NetWare Administrator by double-clicking on its icon. The NetWare Administrator browser screen appears.

4. From the browser screen, open the Tools menu from the menu bar.

5. Choose Partition Manager. The Partition Manager screen appears.

In the Partition Manager screen, you can see the root of two partitions that have been created. The yellow and green partition icon and the name highlighted in red indicate a root of a partition (see fig. 19.10).

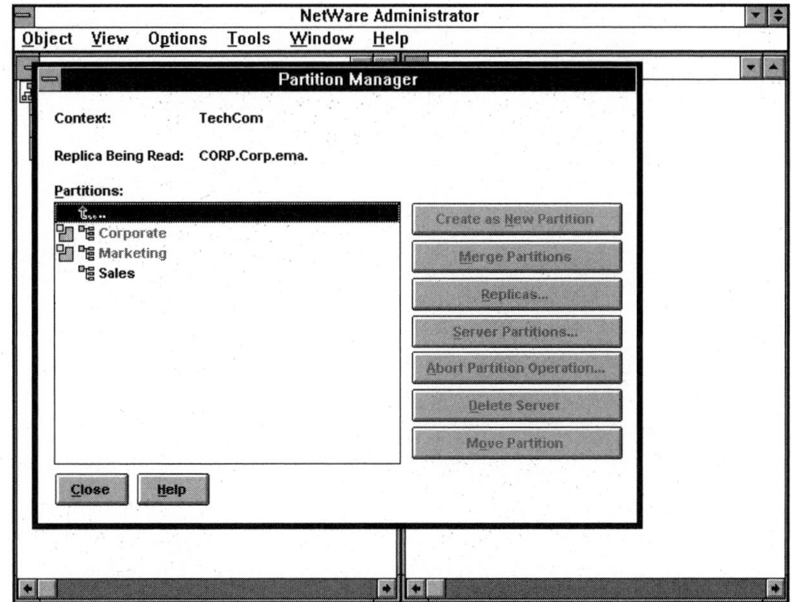

Figure 19.10
Viewing partitions in NetWare Administrator.

Viewing Replicas of Partitions on Servers

You can view the replicas stored on any NetWare 4.1 server throughout the network by executing the following steps:

1. Launch MS Windows.
2. From the Program Manager, find and open the program group NetWare Tools. This is where NetWare Administrator should be found.
3. From the NetWare Tools program group, start NetWare Administrator by double-clicking on its icon. The NetWare Administrator browser screen appears.
4. From the browser screen, open the Tools menu from the menu bar.
5. Choose Partition Manager. The Partition Manager screen appears.
6. Browse the directory tree until you find a NetWare server object, as shown in figure 19.11.

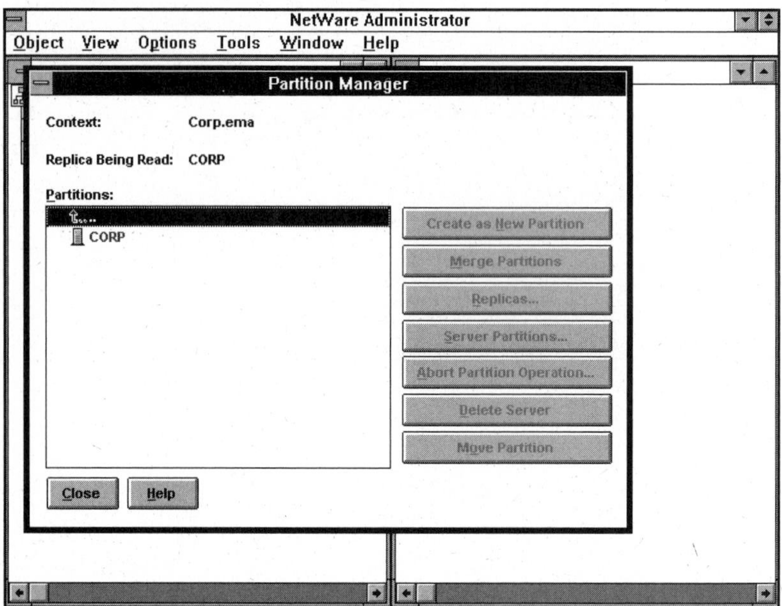

Figure 19.11
Viewing servers in NetWare Administrator.

At the Partition Manager screen, you can see that the server is displayed in blue. Click on the Server Partitions button to view the replicas that are stored on the server, as shown in figure 19.12.

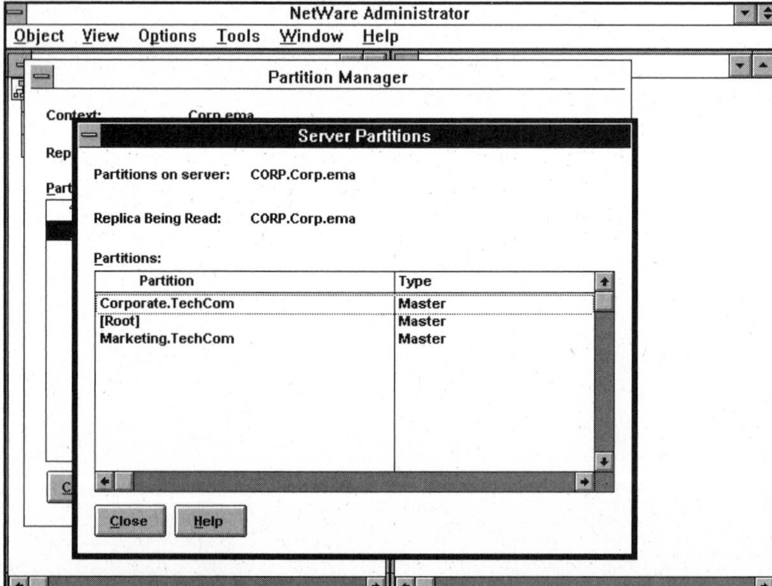

Figure 19.12
Viewing replicas in NetWare Administrator.

Summary

NDS design requires some brief but thoughtful planning to ensure that the design and implementation is a success. Typically, the design of the directory tree should pattern closely your organization or workgroup structure in order to minimize the learning curve to your users, as well as to minimize the network administration. Only one NDS tree per organization is suggested.

Container objects help you organize and group your network users and resources to make the network easier to use and navigate. Remember that although NetWare 4.1 places no limitation on the number of containers you can create, you should group your resources into the highest level of association possible, creating only as many containers as you need to reduce administration and enhance usability.

The appropriate use of partitions and replicas can enhance greatly the performance and availability of your NDS tree. Partitions define the segments of the directory tree that can be replicated. Replicating partitions, or segments, of the directory database ensures that the directory is readily available regardless of server unavailability. Strategically placed replicas also can enhance the performance of the network by making critical network resource data easier to access because the information is closer to the users. The PARTMGR.EXE and NetWare Administrator utilities facilitate partition and replica management.

The next chapter demonstrates how to use two NetWare 4.1 utilities to manage objects and assign useful properties that will make your network a more useful tool.

Managing Objects and Properties

This chapter includes procedures for managing objects related to users within NetWare Directory Services. Managing user objects is the most common task for the network Administrator. Other objects are available to coordinate and manage network services for the users. These objects help in creating users, organizing users, administrating users, and providing users access to resources outside of their immediate container. Each object contains unique properties that describe the characteristics of the objects.

NetWare 4.1 includes a graphical utility and a DOS text utility to create and manage objects. You perform these user tasks with the NWADMIN, a graphical utility, and NETADMIN, a DOS text menu utility.

Understanding Objects and Properties

NetWare Directory Services provides several objects that represent resources on your network. After designing the tree and creating the container objects, you create the objects within the containers that correspond to the network resources. The objects placed in the containers are known as *leaf objects*.

The leaf objects that represent users include user, user_template, group, computer, organizational role, profile, and alias. Other objects depict services available on the network: printing services comprise a printer, print server, and print queue objects; and file services include volume, server, AFP server, and directory map objects. You learn about the user-related objects in this chapter. The printing and file services objects are discussed in the respective chapters.

After you create the objects that represent the network resources in each container, you manage the resources by moving to each container or changing context. You can view different contexts with the graphical utility called NetWare Administrator, NWADMIN, (see fig. 20.1) or the DOS text utility called NETADMIN (see fig. 20.2). Changing current context is performed prior to entering the utilities using the Name Context entry in NET.CFG or the DOS command-line utility called CX (see fig. 20.3). These utilities also enable you to see the Directory tree structure and objects.

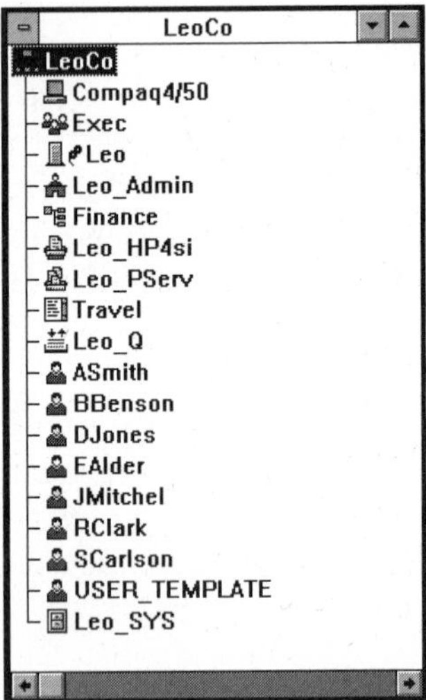

Figure 20.1
Viewing NetWare 4 Directory Objects in NWADMIN.

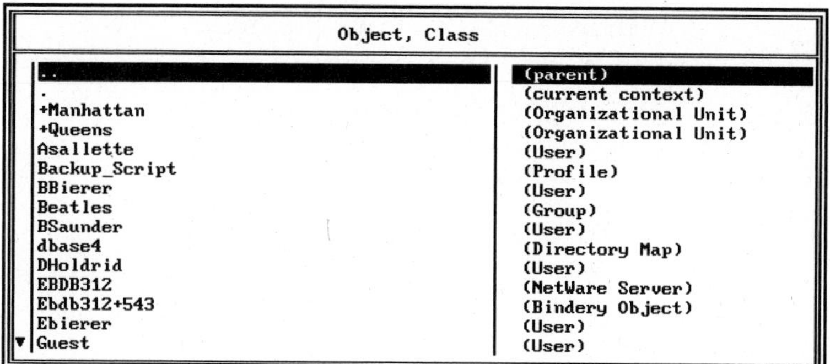

Figure 20.2

Viewing objects in NETADMIN.

```
*** Directory Services Mapping ***

[Root]
  └EBDB
      ├EBDB
      ├Admin
      ├EBDB_SYS
      ├EBDB_OTHER
      ├NY
      │   ├THess
      │   ├BSaunder
      │   ├Sales
      │   ├Asallette
      │   ├Ebierer
      │   ├EBDB312
      │   ├MIS_Script
      │   ├Guest
      │   ├USER_TEMPLATE
      │   ├BBierer
      │   ├DHoldrid
      │   ├LTelepho
      │   ├RBierer
      │   ├MIS
      │   ├Backup_Script
>>> Enter = More   C = Continuous   Esc = Cancel
```

Figure 20.3

Viewing Objects with CX.

Each object includes unique characteristics, called *properties.* When you create an object you fill in the mandatory properties before the object is created. For example, the mandatory properties for a user object are Login Name and Last Name, as shown in figure 20.4.

The dialog box that prompts you to create the object includes the mandatory properties as a minimum. Login Name and Last Name are the mandatory properties for the User object. Table 20.1 shows the mandatory properties for other user-related leaf objects.

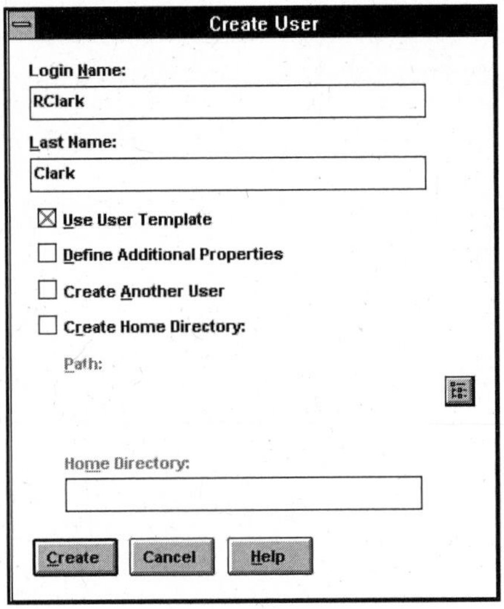

Figure 20.4

The dialog box for creating a user object.

Table 20.1
Mandatory Properties for User-Related Objects

Object Name	Required Property
Alias	Name Aliased Object
Computer	Name
Group	Name
Organizational Role	Name
Profile	Name

In addition to the mandatory properties, the creation dialog box includes other user object properties. Table 20.2 describes the other properties listed in the user creation dialog box.

Table 20.2
Properties for Creating a User Object

Property	Description
Login Name	The new user's login name (a manadatory property).
Last Name	The new user's last name (a mandatory property).
Use User Template	If you click in the box, the User Template that you can define at the creation of the container is used.
Define Additional Properties	If you click in this box, you view the pages of properties for this user object. This enables you to configure detailed characteristics of the user object. If you select this option, the Create Another User option is not available.
Create Another User	If you click on this box, you create more user objects after this one until you deselect the box.
Create Home Directory	If you click on this box, you create a directory with a specified volume and path. NetWare assigns the user RWDEMFA as a trustee assignment to this directory. To create this directory, you must have at least CREATE and ACCESS CONTROL rights to this volume and path.
Path	This option enables you to specify the volume for the user's home directory. (Valid only if you select "Create Home Directory.") You can select the volume object by clicking on the Browse icon, viewing the Directory tree, and selecting the volume. You also can type the volume object name in the field.
Home Directory	NWADMIN assumes you want the same name as the Login Name and uses the first eight characters. You also can enter the main subdirectory at the root of the volume if this is the first user. For example, MKTG_SYS:USERS where USERS is the new directory you created.

Naming Users

Prior to creating users, determine the types of naming standards for the properties. Companies usually have login names that correspond to e-mail addresses. As the network Administrator, you can determine the naming standards with properties for your users. If your naming standards are consistent, you increase the efficiency of administration. Here are some suggestions for naming conventions for login names:

- First Name
- Last Name
- Last Name and First Initial
- First Name and Last Initial
- Initials
- Numbers
- Alphanumeric

Consider the size of the organization, possibility of redundant names, actions in case of the same names, and ease of administration when naming users. For small LANs, you could get by with the first or last names. Larger organizations use the initial and names that are consistent with the e-mail conventions. You can use middle initials in the case of a name collision to maintain unique names. Colleges and university labs use social security numbers or alpha-numeric combinations due to the rapid turnover of users.

Adding Users

After entering the required properties, the object is created. You can finish configuring the user by entering the detailed property information that represents the needs for the user. If you need to create a few users, NWADMIN and NETADMIN can be used. For several users, UIMPORT provides a scripting language to add several users and their respective property information. UIMPORT is covered in the next chapter.

With earlier NetWare versions, you created a user on each server where a person needed network services. In NetWare 4, you create one user object that can have access to network services from several servers. As a result, the Administrator can manage one user object for more than one server rather than the same person being represented by an object for each server.

Creating User Accounts

After you provide the mandatory properties to create the object and select Define Additional Properties, the pages of the properties appear. The dialog box you see is shown in figure 20.5.

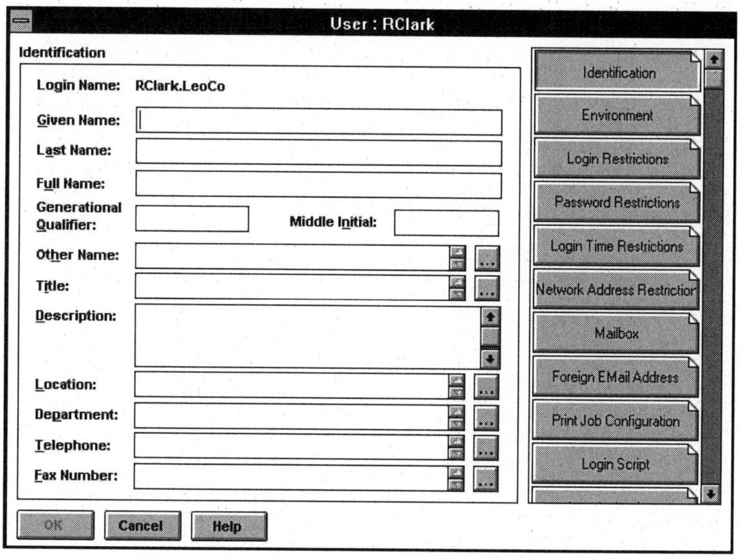

Figure 20.5
Property pages for the User object.

The User object is one of the most detailed Directory objects. This object contains several pages of properties. Names of all the pages that include properties for the User object are shown in the following list:

- Identification
- Environment
- Login Restrictions
- Password Restrictions
- Group Membership
- Login Time Restrictions
- Network Address Restrictions
- Account Balance
- Print Job Configuration
- Login Script
- Intruder Lockout
- Rights to Files and Directories
- Security Equal To
- Postal Address
- Mailbox
- Foreign EMail
- See Also

Properties are provided to customize the user's access to specific services provided on the network. For example, you can use the following limited set of values in table 20.3 for the properties of a user object.

TABLE 20.3
Property Values of a User Object

Property	Value
Login Name:	Rclark
Given Name:	Russell
Last Name:	Clark
Full Name:	Russell Clark
Generational Qualifier:	Sr.
Other Name:	Russ
Title:	Instructional Designer
Telephone:	(312)777-3333
FAX:	(312)777-3334
Foreign E-Mail:	rclark@Leo.com
Location:	Building C - Chicago
Department:	Professional Education
Language:	English (US)
Default Server:	CHI-EDUC
Home Directory:	CHI-EDUC_VOL1.Chicago: USERS\RCLARK

Gathering User Account Information

When you create a user, there are several values you can enter in the properties. Realistically, you will not use all of them. Plan to create and tailor a form that is unique to your company and users. This planning form would include the information you gather before entering the information on the newly created user. The User Information Form is included at the end of this chapter as an example.

It is important to keep both a hard copy and electronic copy of this information in a database. A log book with this type of information and other configuration information is invaluable to you as a network Administrator. The entire list of properties for a user is described in table 20.4.

TABLE 20.4
User Object Properties

Property Page	Property	Description
Identification	Login Name	User's relative distinguished NDS name (required).
	Given Name	User's first given name.
	Last Name	User's last name (required).
	Full Name	User's full name, usually written with middle initial.
	Generational Qualifier	Suffix that uniquely describes this person, as in Sr., Jr., etc.
	Middle	User's middle name.
	Other Name	Any other names by which you refer to this user. (For your information only.)
	Title	User's title (if any).
	Description	A description of this user.
	Location	This user's location.
	Department	User's department in the company.
	Telephone	User's telephone number.
	Fax Number	User's fax number.
Environment	Language	User's default language; can be changed by setting the NWLANGUAGE DOS variable to one of the languages supported on your server.
	Network	Read automatically when the user next logs in.

continues

Table 20.4, Continued
User Object Properties

Property Page	Property	Description
	Address	You cannot change this field. The Network Address is the address of the cabling segment and the network board IPX number from which the user logs in.
	Default Server	The NDS name of the server on which the user receives messages from a SEND command or a server broadcast.
	Home Directory	The volume and path of the user's home directory.
	Volume	The volume on which the user's home directory is located.
	Path	The exact subdirectory on the volume on which the user's home directory is located.
Login Restrictions	Account Disabled	If you select this option, this user will not be able to log in. This is generally done when the user is on vacation or extended leave of absence.
	Account Has Expiration Date	If you select this option, this account will no longer be valid after the determined date. This is useful when you set up accounts for temporary employees who will leave at a specified date.
	Expiration Date and Time	If you select this option, you can enter the expiration date.
	Limit Concurrent Connections	If you do not select this option, the user can log in to the network simultaneously, from different workstations, as many times as he wants. If you select this option, you can set a limit on the number of concurrent logins.

Property Page	Property	Description
	Maximum Connections	If the Limit Concurrent Connections is selected, you can enter the number of logins here. Values range from 1 to 32,000 inclusive. Note that you are limited by the number of user licenses your version of NetWare supports.
	Last Login	This field, which displays the last date and time the user logged in, cannot be modified.
Password Restrictions	Allow User to Change Password	If you deselect this option, the user cannot change her own password. If you leave the default setting, the password can be changed.
	Require a Password	If you do not select this option, the user can choose whether to have a password. If you select the option, the user must have a password. Users who do not have a password are asked to enter a new password the next time they log in.
	Minimum Password Length	Sets the minimum number of characters needed for the password; values range from 1 to 20. If you have users with Macintosh clients, you must limit the passwords to 9 characters.
	Force Periodic Password Changes	If you select this option, the user is prompted to change his password after a specified number of days.
	Days Between Forced Changes	The interval between forced password changes; values range from 1 to 365 days.
	Date Password Expires	You can "pre-expire" a password by setting a date in the past. Otherwise, you can set a limit on the user's current password. This option is useful when you set up new users.

continues

Table 20.4, Continued
User Object Properties

Property Page	Property	Description
	Require Unique Passwords	If you select this option, the system recalls the last eight passwords the user entered. Users cannot reuse a password until after the eighth password. Selecting this option will also require users to enter a password when users first log in.
	Limit Grace Logins	A grace login is the number of times a user is allowed to log in after her password has expired. If you select this option, the user must change the password when prompted.
	Grace Logins Allowed	The number of times the user can log in until he is forced to change the password; values range from 1 to 200 days.
	Remaining Grace Logins	This value reports the number of grace logins remaining for this user.
	Change Password	If this button is selected, the user can change the current password. The user must enter the existing password and the new password twice.
Login Time Restrictions		You will see a 7-day by 24-hour grid that enables you to set when this user can log in to the network. Time intervals are in half-hour segments. A white square indicates a time at which the user can log in; a filled in square indicates that a user cannot log in. You can clear the grid by clicking the Reset button.
Network Address Restrictions		A list of network cable segments and nodes from which the user can log in. This option prevents users from logging in to the network from

Property Page	Property	Description
		specific cable segments on the LAN. Suppose that you have a restricted area in your building. Ensure this area is off-limits by restricting users from this cable segment. If you limit a user to a particular node address, you effectively limit that user to one station.
Mailbox	Mailbox Location	This field specifies the messaging server where the mailbox resides.
	Mailbox ID	This field displays a unique name for this object's mailbox in the messaging database.
Foreign E-Mail Address		This entry identifies the e-mail address on a foreign messaging system. Only one foreign e-mail address can be entered. You can set or clear the address by clicking the respective buttons.
	Foreign E-Mail Aliases	This list box enables you to enter aliases for other foreign messaging services, such as X.400, CompuServe, and the Internet.
Print Job Configuration		This page shows the print job configurations you can use. Click on New to create the name and owner of the print job configuration. You can also modify, delete, or set the default by clicking on the respective buttons.
Login Script		This screen is a limited text editor that enables you to enter the user's login script.
	Profile	You can also select a Profile login script by clicking on Browse icon and selecting a Profile object in the Directory tree.

continues

Table 20.4, Continued
User Object Properties

Property Page	Property	Description
Intruder Lockout	Account Locked	If this option is selected, you know whether the Intruder Detection system (set up at the container level) has disabled this account.
	Incorrect Login Count	The number of times the intruder attempted to get in with an invalid password.
	Account Reset Time	The total amount of time the account is locked.
	Time Until Reset	The amount of time remaining before the account is unlocked.
	Last Intruder Address	The network and node address of the workstation at which the intrusion occurred.
Rights to Files and Directories	Volume	This shows the volume object name where this object has a file system trustee assignment. Use the Find button to locate a specific volume object. Use the Show button to display a specific volume object and use the Hide button to clear the volume object from the list.
	File and Directories	When you select a volume object, this list shows the specific files and directories that have trustee assignments. Use the Add button to include trustee assignments to more directories and files.
	Rights	When you select the files or directories, you will see the specific right this object has to the file system. The Effective Rights button enables you to select rights that have been removed or added from other sources of security rights.

Property Page	Property	Description
Group Membership	Memberships	This list shows which groups the user belongs to. Groups are objects that can be created when you want to assign trustee rights to users who need access to additional objects in the same container or in different containers. You can add or delete users by selecting them and then clicking on the appropriate buttons.
Security Equal To		User gains all the rights of any object you place on this list. This is a quick way to assign rights, but not the preferred method. By default, the user has the same level of security as his container.
Postal Address	Street	Street on which the user is located.
	Post Office Box	User's P.O. Box.
	City	City in which the user is located.
	State or Province	State or Province in which the user is located.
	Postal (ZIP) Code	ZIP code for the user.
	Copy to Label	If you click on this button, the preceding information is transferred to the Mailing Label section.
	Mailing Label	The previous five fields are part of a mailing label. Currently, this feature is not used. You use NLIST to extract this information and redirect it to an ASCII file, which then can be formatted and printed.
Account Balance		This figure, which represents the amount of credit in units remaining for this user, ties into the Account ing System in the server object. Values range from 99,999,999 to –99,999,999.

continues

Table 20.4, Continued
User Object Properties

Property Page	Property	Description
	Allow Unlimited Credit	If you select this option, this user is not affected if his credit goes below the Low Balance Limit. Otherwise, the user is locked out of the system when the credit balance is depleted.
	Low Balance Limit	The lower limit allowed before the user is locked out of the system. If a user is logged in and her Account Balance goes below this limit, the OS sends the user an `Out of Funds` message, giving the user five minutes to save work and log out.
See Also		Contains references to other objects to which this user might be related. (For your information only.)

Creating Users with NetWare Administrator (NWADMIN)

After determining naming standards for the mandatory properties, you are ready to create user objects. To create the user object with the NWADMIN, follow these steps:

1. Log in to your NetWare 4.1 server as a user with at least Browse and Create object rights to the new user's container.
2. Launch Microsoft Windows.
3. Run NWADMIN.
4. Change your context to view the container where you will create your user object.
5. Highlight the container object.

6. Either press the alternative mouse button to access the Create menu or select the Create option from the Object menu. The New Object dialog box for creating leaf objects appears (see fig. 20.6).

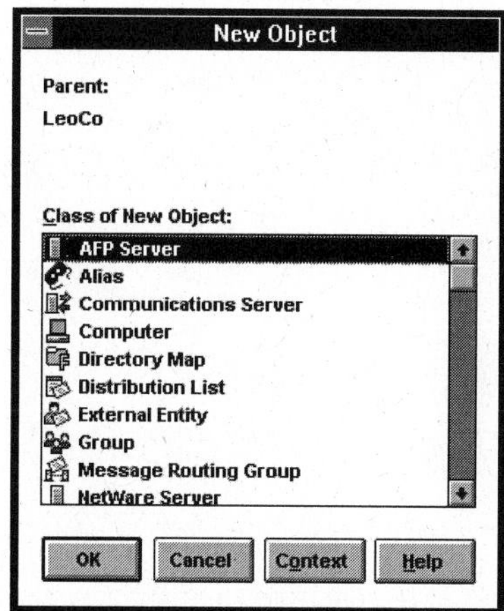

Figure 20.6
The New Object dialog box.

7. Select User. The Create User dialog box with the required properties appears. Notice the other options available: Use User Template; Define Additional Properties; Create Another User; and Create Home Directory.

8. Enter the value information in the property fields.

9. Select the boxes by the options you have chosen. A User_Template must exist in your container for you to select Use User Template. If you select Create Home Directory, use the following steps:

   a. Click on the browse icon. The browse window appears, as shown in figure 20.7.

   b. Double-click on the volume object in the right box.

   c. Click on the desired parent directory in the left box.

   d. Click on OK. Notice that the name of the path appears. NWADMIN also assumes that your home directory is the same as the first eight letters of your login name.

10. Click on OK to create the object. The Create User dialog box with user properties appears.

Figure 20.7
The browse window for creating a home directory.

11. Enter the values in the properties for each page of the Create User dialog box (refer to table 20.4).

    Be aware that if you click on Cancel while entering values in the pages of the properties, you will lose all previously entered information.

12. Click on OK to save the information in the properties.

Creating User-Related Objects

Procedures for creating the other related user objects are included in the following list:

- User_Template
- Group
- Organizational role
- Alias
- Profile
- Computer

Creating a User Template with NWADMIN

A *User_Template* enables you to create multiple users with a similar profile. The properties are the same as the user object. Enter the values in the properties that you want each user to include. Each user created using the User_Template has these values entered in the properties.

When you create a container, you have the option to create a User_Template. Figure 20.8 shows the Define User Defaults option when creating a container object.

Create Organizational Unit

Organizational Unit Name:

Finance

☐ Define Additional Properties

☐ Create Another Organizational Unit

☒ Define User Defaults

Create | Cancel | Help

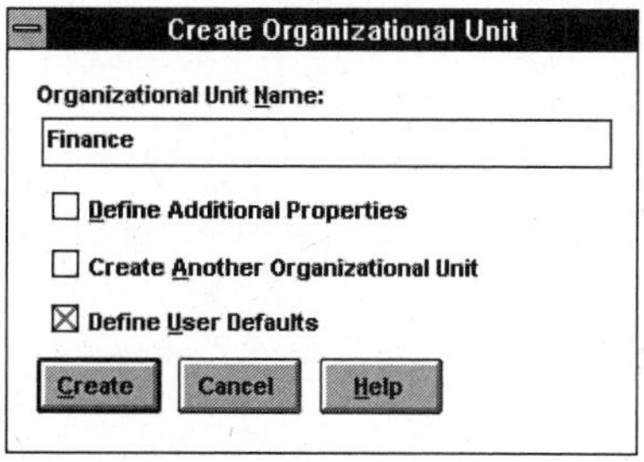

Figure 20.8

The dialog box for creating a container object.

Creating a Group with NETADMIN

Making users members of a specific group provides them access to a common network services. If you have users in a department or project team, create a group that represents this team. All members of the group have access rights to a similar set of network resources. In the Members page of properties, you can add the User objects that represent the members of the team.

For this illustration, you create a Group object with NETADMIN, the DOS text menu utility that is equivalent to the graphical NWADMIN utility. To create the Group object with NETADMIN, use the following steps:

1. Log in to your NetWare 4.1 server as a user with at least Browse and Create object rights to the container of the new group.

2. Type **NETADMIN** at the DOS prompt. The first menu for NETADMIN appears, as shown in figure 20.9.

3. Click on Manage objects.

4. Change to the context where you will create your Group object.

5. Press Insert. The list of leaf objects appears, as shown in figure 20.10.

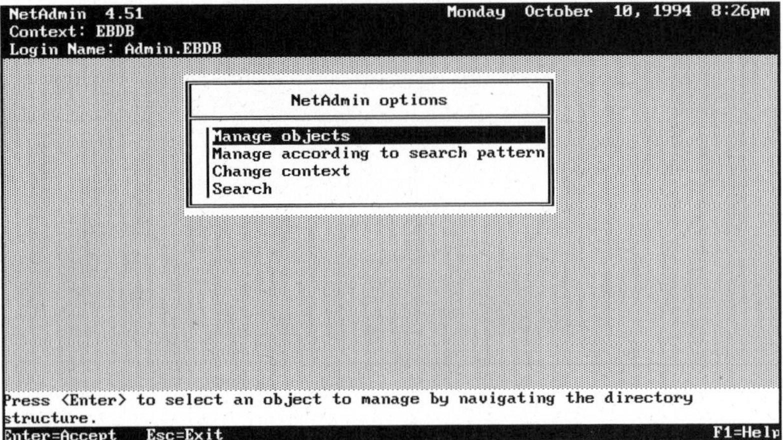

Figure 20.9
The main menu for NETADMIN.

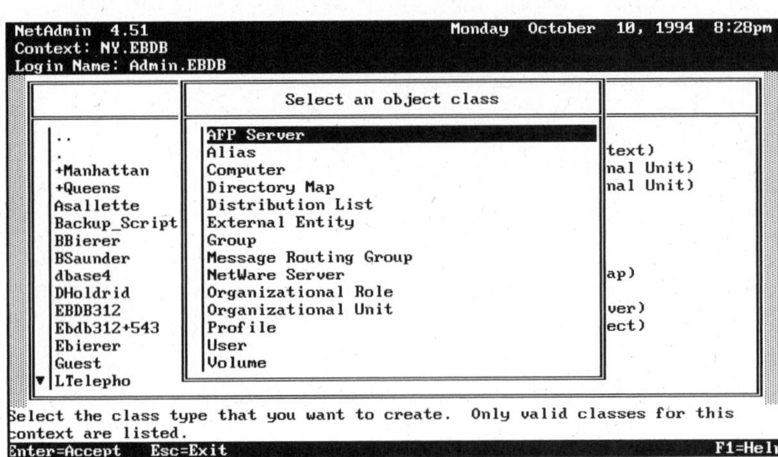

Figure 20.10
The list for creating leaf objects.

6. Select Group and press Enter. The Create Group Object dialog box appears.

7. Type in the Group name in the New Name field. Alternatively, you could enter a mailbox location for the group. This is not a required field. Press F10 to save the new group name.

8. Answer No when prompted to create another Group object. The Group object is now created. You return to the Object, Class list.

9. Select the new group and press Enter. The Actions for Group <*name*> menu appears. Select View or edit properties of this object. The View or Edit Group menu appears. The menu items represent different group properties, which you can edit. Table 20.5 provides an explanation of the Group properties.

Table 20.5
Group Object Properties

Property Page	Property	Description
Identification	Name	Group's relative distinguished NDS name (required).
	Other Name	Any other names by which you refer to this group. (For your information only.)
	Owner	Group's owner (if any).
	Description	A description of this group.
	Location	This group's location.
	Department	Group's department in the company.
	Organization	The organization to which the group belongs.
Group Members		A list of the members of this group. Options in this object affect these users.
Mailbox Information	Mailbox location	Provides the messaging server where the mailbox is stored.
	Mailbox ID	Name of the group mailbox.
	Foreign E-Mail Address	The unique e-mail address for this group.
	Foreign E-Mail Alias	The e-mail alias names for other messaging services.
Rights to Files and Directories	Volume	This shows the volume object name where this object has a file system trustee assignment. Use the Find button to locate a specific volume object. Use the Show button to display a specific volume object, and use the Hide button to clear the volume object from the list.

continues

Table 20.5, Continued
Group Object Properties

Property Page	Property	Description
	File and Directories	When you select a volume object, this list shows the specific files and directories that have trustee assignments. Use the Add button to include trustee assignments to more directories and files.
	Rights	When you select the files or directories, you see the specific right this object has to the file system. The Effective Rights button enables you to select rights that have been removed or added from other sources of security rights.
See Also		Contains references to other objects to which this group might be related. (For your information only.)

The Rights to File System and Directories is included as one of the property pages in NWADMIN. To perform the same tasks in NETADMIN for a Group object, you must select the option in the Actions for Group menu.

10. After entering the values for the properties, press F10 to save the information. You return to the View or Edit Group menu.

11. Continue to enter any additional information as appropriate.

12. Press Esc several times to return to the main menu.

Creating an Organizational Role with NWADMIN

An Organizational Role object defines a position that can be filled by more than one person. For example, an Organizational Role can be filled by a container Administrator, a team leader, a network backup operator, or printing specialist. Like the group object, you can grant specific rights to the object that affects those who are selected as occupants of the position.

The following steps show the process of creating an Organizational Role object:

1. Log in to your NetWare 4.1 server as a user with at least Browse and Create object rights to the organizational role's container.

2. Launch Microsoft Windows.

3. Run NWADMIN.

4. Highlight the container where you will create your user object.

5. Press the Insert key or with the mouse you can select the container object and click the alternate mouse button. A limited Object menu appears. Click on the Create option. The dialog box for creating leaf objects appears.

6. Select Organizational Role. The Create Organizational Role dialog box with the required properties appears. Notice that name is the only required property.

7. Type the name for Organizational Role. Place a checkmark next to the Define Additional Properties field so that you can define properties for the new object.

8. Click on Create. The Organizational Role: <*name*> dialog box with pages of the properties appears.

   Notice that the properties for this object are similar to the User and Group objects. The critical property for this object is the Occupant property.

9. Select the object for the Occupant property as follows:

   a. Click on the multi-value field icon next to the Occupant field. The Occupant dialog box for multi-value fields appears (see fig. 20.11).

   b. Click on Add. The Select Object browse window appears.

   c. Use the Directory Context list box to locate the context of the desired role occupant. Click on a User object in the Objects box (on the lower left).

   d. Click on OK. The name of the User appears in the Occupant dialog box. Press OK to return to the Organizational Role dialog box.

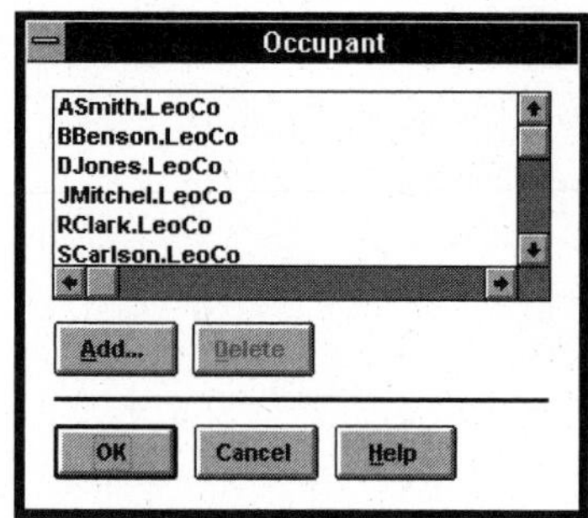

Figure 20.11

The window for selecting multiple values in a property field.

10. Finish entering the information in the other properties.
11. Click on OK to save the property information.

Creating an Alias Object for a User with NWADMIN

An Alias object refers to another object in the Directory. The aliased object inherits all the property information from the aliased object. Any changes made in either object affects the properties of the original aliased object. Logically, there is still only one object. The aliased object inherits all the property information from the aliased object.

To create an Alias object for a User, perform the following steps:

1. Log in to your NetWare 4.1 server as a user with at least Browse and Create object rights to the organizational role's container.
2. Launch Microsoft Windows.
3. Run NWADMIN.
4. Highlight the container where you will create your user object.
5. Press the Insert key. With the mouse, you can select the container object and click the alternate mouse button. A limited Object menu appears. Click on the Create option. The dialog box for creating leaf objects appears.
6. Select Alias. The Create Alias dialog box with the required properties appears. Notice that both Alias Name and Aliased Object are both required properties.
7. Type a name for the Alias object in the Alias Name field.

8. Select the object you want to alias from the Aliased Object as follows:

    a. Click on the browse icon next to the Aliased Object field. The Select Object browse window appears.

    b. Use the Directory Context list box to locate the context of the desired role occupant. Click on the User object you want to alias in the Objects box (on the lower left).

    c. Click on OK. The name of the User appears in the Aliased Object field.

9. Click on Create to create the object. The new aliased user object appears. Note the tiny mask next to the user icon. This indicates that the object is an alias of a user object.

10. Double-click on the new Alias object. The User <*username*> dialog box with pages for the properties appears. Notice that you are actually viewing the original user object. If you enter any changes, they affect the original User object.

11. Click on OK after viewing and changing any desired properties.

Creating a Profile Object with NWADMIN

A Profile object contains a profile login script that is utilized by users who need to use similar login script commands. The profile login script is executed after the container login script and before the user login script when a user logs in to the NetWare 4.1 server.

For a user to execute a profile login script, you must select the profile login script in the login script property page of the User object, as shown in figure 20.12. This user must have Read rights to the Profile object's login script property for the profile login script to execute.

To create a Profile object using NWADMIN, perform the following steps:

1. Log in to your NetWare 4.1 server as a user with at least Browse and Create object rights to the organizational role's container.

2. Launch Microsoft Windows.

3. Run NWADMIN.

4. Highlight the container where you will create your user object.

Figure 20.12

The window for selecting the profile login script for a user.

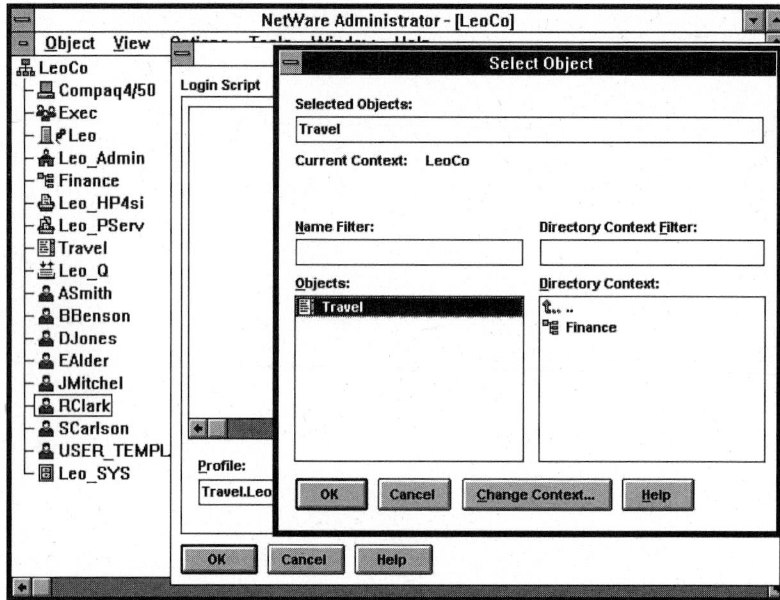

5. Press Insert. With the mouse, select the container object and click the alternate mouse button. A limited **O**bject menu appears. Click on the **C**reate option. The dialog box for creating leaf objects appears.

6. Select Profile. The Create Profile dialog box with the required properties appears.

7. Type a name for the Profile object in the Profile **N**ame field.

8. Place a checkmark next to the **D**efine Additional Properties option.

9. Click on OK. The Profile <*profile name*> dialog box for the Profile object appears. The properties for the Profile object are similar to other objects you have created. The critical property is the profile login script.

10. Click on the Login Script page. A dialog box for entering the Login Script commands appears.

11. Type the commands for the login script.

12. Click on OK to save the information.

Creating a Computer Object with NWADMIN

The Computer object represents a computer on the network. This object is for informational purposes only. You can enter description information as well as configuration information, like the network address.

To create a Computer object with NWADMIN, complete the following steps:

1. Log in to your NetWare 4.1 server as a user with at least Browse and Create object rights to the organizational role's container.
2. Launch Microsoft Windows.
3. Run NWADMIN.
4. Highlight the container where you will create your user object.
5. Press the Insert key. With the mouse, select the container object and click the alternate mouse button. A limited **O**bject menu appears. Click on the **C**reate option. The dialog box for creating leaf objects appears.
6. Select Computer. The Create Computer dialog box with the required properties appears.
7. Type a name for the Computer object in the Computer **N**ame field.
8. Select the **D**efine Additional Properties option.
9. Click on **C**reate. The Computer *<computer name>* dialog box with properties for the Computer object appears. The properties for the Computer object are similar to other objects you have created. The additional properties are the operators, serial number, and network address.
10. Type the information to describe the computer in the property pages.
11. Click on OK to save the information. The new Computer object appears in the Directory tree.

Summary

This chapter showed you information about the User and user-related objects: User_Template; Group; Organizational Role; Alias; Profile; and Computer.

Before creating users, you must determine what type of information you will collect about the users. You can use the properties of the user object to select the type of information you gather. You also need to determine the naming standards for specific types of information entered in the Directory database. Once you determine this information, you can create a planning sheet to fill in the information.

To create users, you use NWADMIN from Microsoft Windows or NETADMIN from DOS. This chapter showed the steps for creating users in NWADMIN and creating groups in NETADMIN. The rest of the procedures showed how to create the objects in NWADMIN.

The process of creating groups, organizational roles, profiles, and other user-related objects is very similar to the process of creating a user object. Once you gain skill creating user objects, creating other objects is much easier.

The next chapter covers how to create users on a large-scale, automated fashion, using the UIMPORT utility.

User Information Form

NDS Context: ______________________________

Login Name: ______________________________

Login Name: ______________________________

Given Name: ______________________________

Last Name: ______________________________

Full Name: ______________________________

Generational Qualifier: ______________________________

Other Name: ______________________________

Title: ______________________________

Telephone: ______________________________

FAX: ______________________________

Location: ______________________________

Department: ______________________________

Language: ______________________________

Default Server: ______________________________

Home Directory: ______________________________

Foreign E-Mail: ______________________________

User Information Form, Continued

Password Restrictions: ______________________________

Station Restrictions: ______________________________

Login Time Restrictions: ______________________________

Group Memberships: ______________________________

Profile Login Script: ______________________________

Security Equal To: ______________________________

Other Security Needs:

Volumes:

____
____
____

Directories:

____
____
____

Containers:

____
____
____

Object Rights:

____
____
____

Property Rights:

____
____
____

Importing Users

There are several methods of adding users to a NetWare 4.1 network. The two utilities discussed in the previous chapter, NWADMIN and NETADMIN, enable you to interactively add users to the network. These utilities are good for small numbers of users. When you are faced with installing a network consisting of several hundred or several thousand users, the task begins to take on gargantuan proportions. This is where the automated import utility UIMPORT.EXE comes into play.

This chapter discusses various aspects regarding importing users on a large scale.

Using the UIMPORT Utility

The UIMPORT utility is used to place users into a given context. It is a command-line utility and can be placed in a batch file. This utility uses two files during the import process; a control file and a data file. The *control file* controls which parameters are entered into the NDS database and how the updates to the NDS are processed. The *data file*, which must be in comma-delimited format, contains the raw data to be placed into the NDS. This section discusses the format of the two files as well as some restrictions to the UIMPORT utility.

The syntax of the UIMPORT command is as follows:

```
UIMPORT path:\control_file  path:\data_file
```

Path is the drive and/or directory to the file. *Control_file* is the name of the control file. The format of this file is discussed in the next section. *Data_file* is the name of the file containing raw data to be imported into the NDS. If you want to get more information on the utility, a help screen is available. Type the following:

UIMPORT /?

for general help. For a list of user properties supported by UIMPORT, type the following:

UIMPORT /? **ATTR**

Format of the Control File

The control file is used as a template, or filter, to control the information being inserted into the NDS by UIMPORT. The control file is an ASCII text file with the following two main sections:

- ◆ Import Control
- ◆ Fields

Each section has several parameters, each of which must be indented and on its own line following the section heading. *Import Control* gives UIMPORT instructions on how the data is to be processed and formatted. *Fields* contains a list of fields to be imported from the data file. The following shows you a sample control file:

```
Import Control
      Quote='
      Name Context="OU=Sales.O=EBDB"
      Replace Value=Y
      Create Home Directory=Y
```

```
    Home Directory Volume=".CN=FS1_SYS.OU=Sales.O=EBDB"
    Home Directory Path="USERS"

Fields
    Name
    Last Name
    Department
    Telephone Number
```

The Fields section of this file indicates that UIMPORT will import the Name (Login Name), Last Name, Department, and Telephone Number fields from the data file, in that order. The Import Control section indicates the following:

- A single quotation mark (') will be used to surround text strings.
- The default container will be "OU=Sales.O=EBDB."
- Existing properties will be overwritten.
- A home directory will be created on file server FS1, volume SYS, directory USERS.

Table 21.1 summarizes the possible Import Control parameters. Default values are specified in bold.

TABLE 21.1
UIMPORT Import Control Parameters

Parameter	Values	Description
Create Home	Y or **N**	When set to Y, this Directory parameter instructs UIMPORT to create a home directory for this user. The Home Directory Volume and Path parameters must also be supplied.
Delete Property	One or more characters	This parameter requires some character or combination of characters to tag the property or properties to be deleted. You must then place these characters in the data file instead of real data. The property associated with this

continues

Table 21.1, Continued
UIMPORT Import Control Parameters

Parameter	Values	Description
		data element will be deleted. See "Updating User Properties" for examples.
Home Directory	*dir1\dir2\..*	This parameter represents the Path directory path for the user's home directory on the volume indicated by Home Directory Volume. The path indicated here will become the parent directory of the new user home directory. The name of the user's home directory will be the login name.
Home Directory Volume	NDS Volume Object	The home directory volume is any valid NDS volume object. The home directory will then be created under a directory represented by Home Directory Path.
Import Mode	**B**, C, R, or U	This parameter controls how data is to be imported. The possible import modes are as follows: **B** If the user object exists, update existing values with values from the data file. If the user object does not exist, create it. This is the default mode. C Create new user objects only. If a user already exists, ignore any data for this object. R Remove any user objects listed in the data file. U Update data for existing objects only. If the object does not exist, skip to the next object in the data file.

Parameter	Values	Description
Name Context	*"NDS" "Container"*	The name context causes UIMPORT to import user objects into this context instead of the current context. Do not use a leading period when specifying the NDS container name.
Quote	Any character	This parameter changes the character used to surround string data. The default is a double quotation mark ("). In some cases the data itself might contain double quotation marks. If this is true, change the *quote character* to another character that will not appear as data.
Replace Value	Y or **N**	This parameter works in conjunction with Import Mode, but for multivalued properties only. When the Import Mode is set to B or U, the value of Replace Value is effective. If Replace Value is set to Y, new values specified for multivalued properties will be replaced or overwritten. If Replace Value is set to N, new values specified for multivalued properties will be added to the existing values. This is useful, for example, when you want to add several lines to the user's Postal Address or Telephone Number properties.
Separator	Any character	This parameter controls which character is used to separate data elements in the data file. The default is a comma. In some cases you may need to change this because of the way the data is formatted.

continues

Table 21.1, Continued
UIMPORT Import Control Parameters

Parameter	Values	Description
User Template	Y or **N**	When set to Y, the User Template object of the container object the user is to be placed into is used to give the new user a set of default values. When set to N, the User Template object is not used.

Format of the Data File

The data file must be in ASCII format. Any special characters produced by word processing or database programs must be removed. Most programs provide the capability to save the file in ASCII format. In WordPerfect, for example, you can save a file in "DOS Text" format. Microsoft Word provides the "Save As" feature. When using this feature, select the file type "Text Only." In dBASE IV, you can save a file using the COPY TO *filename* DELIMITED option. This causes a dBASE IV database file to be copied to a file specified by *filename* in an ASCII format with commas separating data elements.

Data elements in the data file correspond with the fields listed in the control file. Data elements include Name, Last Name, Telephone Number, and Department. Data elements do not have to be surrounded by the quotation character. Quotation characters are needed only if the separator character is included as data. The default separator character is a comma. If a data element contains a comma but is not enclosed in quotation marks, UIMPORT cuts the data element short and thinks that the text following the comma belongs to the next data element.

To illustrate possible problems, consider the control and data files shown in the following listings. The first listing contains a sample control file named TEST1.CTL:

```
Fields
      Last Name
      Name
      Description
```

The following listing contains a sample data file named TEST1.DAT with commas and quotes inside the data elements:

```
Last Name,        Login Name,        Description
Jones,            JJones,            3rd Division, 2nd Company
Howard,           MHoward,           12th Division, 4th Company, "Strike Force"
Sandiego,         CSandieg,          14th Cavalry, "EMI Specialist Grade"
```

In this example, there are both commas and quotation marks inside the Description field. In this case, the data file should be reformatted and new separator and quote characters must both be specified. Here are two listings that show the revised control and data files. The first example is a revised sample control file named TEST2.CTL:

```
Import Control
      Separator = ¦
      Quote = ^
Fields
      Last Name
      Name
      Description
```

This next example is the sample data file TEST2.DAT, with revised separator and quote characters:

```
Last Name¦         Login Name¦        ^Description^
Jones¦             JJones¦            ^3rd Division, 2nd Company^
Howard¦            MHoward¦           ^12th Division, 4th Company, "Strike Force"^
Sandiego¦          CSandieg¦          ^14th Cavalry, "EMI Specialist Grade"^
```

Restrictions on UIMPORT

UIMPORT is used to create users; it will not create any other NDS objects. Although UIMPORT can update the Group Membership property of a user, adding the user to a group, UIMPORT will not create the group. Likewise, UIMPORT will not create container objects. You must use another utility, such as NETADMIN or NWADMIN, to create the NDS structure, including any groups to which you want to assign users, prior to using UIMPORT.

UIMPORT can create a user home directory and will also assign the user full directory trustee rights to his home directory. UIMPORT will not create any other type of directory, nor will it assign other rights.

Another restriction to UIMPORT is that it works with only one container at a time. If you want to work with users in more than one container, there are two workarounds. You can create multiple data files and use a batch file to change the directory context by performing a CX command. Using this technique, you can have a batch file that changes to the contexts where you need to add or update users. After changing contexts, you could issue a UIMPORT command using the data file created for this context.

Another technique involves creating one large data file, ignoring which contexts the users are to be placed in. In conjunction with the large data file, you need a batch file to perform the CX command. Using this technique with an Update operation works but results in warning (nonfatal) error messages when UIMPORT does not find the user in a specific context. Using this technique when adding users results in all users being added to all contexts you change to. Another possibility is to add all users to a single context and then use the NWADMIN utility to perform mass move operations to move groups of users to their correct context.

User Properties Supported by UIMPORT

The Fields section in the control file indicates which data fields you want to add. Any or all of the fields listed in the following table can be used under the Fields heading in the control file. When you list a field, it must correspond with a data element in the data file. In addition, the fields listed must be in the order represented in the data file.

Table 21.2 summarizes the possible field names. The second column indicates if this field is single-valued (S) or multivalued (M). A single-valued field can have only one value. An example would be the person's login name (the Name field). An example of a multivalued field is Telephone Number. A person can have several phone numbers (fax, pager, cellular, office, home). The third column lists possible values for the field. A legend that describes the values follows at the end of the table.

Table 21.2
UIMPORT User Property Field Names

Property Name	Single/ Multiple	Values
Account Balance	S	Numeric
Allow Unlimited Credit	S	Yes/No
City	S	Text
Default Server	S	Object
Department	S	Text
Description	M	Text
E-Mail Address	M	Text
Facsimile Telephone Number	M	Text
Group Membership	M	Object

Property Name	Single/ Multiple	Values
Home Directory	S	Text
Language	M	Text
Last Name	M	Text
Location	M	Text
Login Disabled	S	Yes/No
Login Expiration Time	S	Date
Login Grace Limit	S	Numeric
Login Grace Remaining	S	Numeric
Login Maximum Simultaneous	S	Numeric
Login Script	S	Filename
Minimum Account Balance	S	Numeric
Name	S	Object
Other Names	M	Text
Password Allow Change	S	Yes/No
Password Expiration Interval	S	Numeric
Password Expiration Time	S	Date
Password Minimum Length	S	Numeric
Password Required	S	Yes/No
Password Unique Required	S	Yes/No
Post Office Box	S	Text
Postal (Zip) Code	S	Text
Postal Address	M	Text

continues

Table 21.2, Continued
UIMPORT User Property Field Names

Property Name	Single/ Multiple	Values
Profile	M	Object
Security Equals	S	Text
See Also	M	Object
Skip	S	—
State or Province	S	Text
Street Address	S	Text
Telephone Number	M	Text
Title	M	Text

LEGEND:

Date	*You can use a date value in the format mm/dd/yyyy or mm-dd-yyyy.*
Filename	*Valid DOS file name.*
—	*No values are associated with this field.*
Numeric	*You can use a numeric value.*
Object	*You can use a valid NDS object name only (complete, partial, typeful, typeless).*
Text	*You can use a text value, including wild cards (such as "A*" or "*net*").*
Yes/No	*You can use the values "Yes" or "No" only.*

The one field name that corresponds to no NDS property is Skip. Skip is used to indicate a data element that you do not want to import into the NDS. If your database contains home phone numbers, for example, you might not want to import this data into the NDS. If so, place the name Skip in place of a field name for this data element.

Adding Users

In this section, you see an example of adding users using every possible field. The sample control and data files contain examples of every possible parameter. The following code shows you the sample control file CTRL10.TXT used with the sample data file DATA10.DAT, shown in table 21.3. Because each line of data in DATA10.DAT stretches out to span several hundred characters, the sample data is

shown in tabular format.The following line contains the contents of the CTRL10.TXT control file, with all fields:

```
100000\YES\San Francisco\.CN=EBDB.O=EBDB\Obstetrics\Head Surgeon\...
```

The following is a listing of the sample data file DATA10.DAT shown in tabular format:

```
Import Control
     Create Home Directory=Y
     Home Directory Volume=".CN=EBDB_SYS.O=EBDB"
     Home Directory Path="USERS"
     Import Mode=B
     Name Context="OU=SF.O=EBDB"
     Quote='
     Separator=\
     Replace Value=N
     User Template=N
Fields
     Account Balance
     Allow Unlimited Credit
     City
     Default Server
     Department
     Description
     EMail Address
     Facsimile Telephone Number
     Group Membership
     Home Directory
     Language
     Last Name
     Location
     Login Disabled
     Login Expiration Time
     Login Grace Limit
     Login Grace Remaining
     Login Maximum Simultaneous
     Login Script
     Minimum Account Balance
     Name
     Other Names
     Password Allow Change
     Password Expiration Interval
     Password Expiration Time
```

```
Password Minimum Length
Password Required
Password Unique Required
Post Office Box
Postal (Zip) Code
Postal Address
Profile
Security Equals
See Also
Skip
State or Province
Street Address
Telephone Number
Title
```

Table 21.3
Sample Data File DATA10.TXT Shown in Tabular Format

Field	JJAVEZ	RDOAT	BSMITH
Account Balance	100000	500000	200000
Allow Unlimited Credit	YES	NO	YES
City	San Francisco	San Anselmo	San Rafael
Default Server	.CN=EBDB .O=EBDB	.CN=EBDB .O=EBDB	.CN=EBDB .O=EBDB
Department	Obstetrics	Gynecology	Optometry
Description	Head Surgeon	Research, Development, and Public Relations	Eye Care, Glasses, Contacts, and Prescriptions
EMail Address	JJavez@Obs .Mercy.COM	RDoat@RD .Mercy.COM	BSmith@Opto .Mercy.COM
Facsimile Telephone Number	415-111-2222	415-111-3333	415-111-4444
Group Membership	.CN=Managers .OU=Sales .O=EBDB	.CN=Research .OU=SF .O=EBDB	

Field	JJAVEZ	RDOAT	BSMITH
Home Directory	.CN=EBDB_ SYS.O=EBDB: SPECIAL	.CN=EBDB_ SYS.O=EBDB: SPECIAL	.CN=EBDB SYS.O=EBDB: SPECIAL
Language	ESPANOL	FRANCAIS	ENGLISH
Last Name	Javez	Doat	Smith
Location	Bldg 3, 4th Floor	Bldg 1, 7th Floor	Bldg 1, 2nd Floor
Login Disabled	NO	NO	NO
Login Expiration Time	1-1-1995	7-1-1996	
Login Grace Limit	10	6	
Login Grace Remaining	10	6	
Login Maximum Simultaneous	1	3	
Login Script	F:\PUBLIC \LOG.TXT	F:\PUBLIC \LOG.TXT	C:\LOGS \BSMITH.TXT
Minimum Account Balance	100	1000	1000
Name	JJAVEZ	RDOAT	BSMITH
Other Names	Juanita Javez	Robert Doat	Robert "Bob" Smith
Password Allow Change	YES	NO	YES
Password Expiration Interval	45	90	
Password Expiration Time	1-1-80	1-1-95	

continues

Table 21.3, Continued
Sample Data Rile DATA10.TXT Shown in Tabular Format

Field	JJAVEZ	RDOAT	BSMITH
Password Minimum Length	5	6	
Password Required	YES	NO	NO
Password Unique Required	NO	YES	NO
Post Office Box	PO Box 1248		PO Box 1571
Postal (Zip) Code	55432	55432	55432
Postal Address	Mercy Hospital	Mercy Hospital	Mercy Hospital
Profile CN=Opto.OU=SF_	.CN=Manager_ Script .OU=Sales .O=EBDB	.CN=R&D_ Script .OU=SF .O=EBDB	.O=EBDB
Security Equals	.CN=Dale .OU=Sales .O=EBDB	.CN=JJavez .OU=SF .O=EBDB	
See Also	.OU=Domestic .OU=Sales .O=EBDB	.CN=JJavez .OU=SF .O=EBDB	
Skip	Catholic	Catholic	Baptist
State or Province	CA	CA	CA
Street Address	1401 Taravel Street	1401 Taravel Street	1401 Taravel Street
Telephone Number	415-555-1212	415-555-1439	415-555-3947
Title	Surgeon	General Practitioner	Optometrist

If you need to add users where multiple values for properties exist (such as Postal Address), you need to specify the multivalued field as many times as are necessary in

your control file. In the data file, if users have a varying number of fields, you need to supply blank fields to satisfy UIMPORT. The following listings show you the sample control and data files used in the case where there is more than a single value for a field. In this example, the Group Membership and Postal Address fields have multiple values. Note that the data for each user appears on more than one line. This should not be done when producing actual data files. When you press Enter at the end of a line, UIMPORT assumes that this is the end of the record for this user. The second example is on more than one line for readability.

Here is the control file CTRL12.TXT with multivalued fields:

```
Import Control
        Create Home Directory=Y
        Home Directory Volume=".CN=EBDB_SYS.O=EBDB"
        Home Directory Path="USERS"
        User Template=Y
        Quote="
Fields
        Name
        Last Name
        Other Names
        Description
        Postal Address
        Postal Address
        Postal Address
        Group Membership
        Group Membership
        Login Script
```

Here is the data file DATA12.TXT with multivalued fields:

```
FDrake, Drake, Sir Francis Drake, "Poet, Adventurer, and Scholar",
      1214 Leeward Lane, Apartment 1222, "Radcliff, UK  S22",
      .CN=Seafarers.OU=Other.O=EBDB, , F:\NRP\INSIDE4\LOG12.TXT

QEliza, Elizabeth, Queen Elizabeth, Queen, Room 12, Buckingham Palace,
      UK  E14, .CN=Managers.OU=Sales.O=EBDB,
      .CN= Seafarers.OU=Other.O=EBDB, F:\NRP\INSIDE4\LOG12.TXT
```

Removing Users

UIMPORT provides a very simple method for removing users from the NDS database. You need to do the following:

1. Add the IMPORT MODE = R command under the Import Control section in the control file.
2. In the Fields section of the control file, add the following:
   - The login name of the user to remove (NAME)
   - The last name of the user to remove (LAST NAME)

The following two listings show you a sample control file and a sample data file, both of which are used to clean up some users created using the name and address example from the last section (see "Creating the User Database"). Note that there is no NAME CONTEXT reference in the control file. This is because the users to be cleaned up exist in different contexts.

Here is the sample control file:

```
Import Control
      Import Mode = R
Fields
      Name
      Last Name
```

Here is the sample data file.

```
KKouture, Kouture
"L105 (KI", "105 (KITS)"
"VSan Jos", "San Jose"
LTelepho, Telephoniste
```

The following is the batch file used to remove the users:

```
echo off
echo :
echo :  Title:  IMPORT14.BAT
echo :  Date:   5-8-94
echo :  Author: D. Bierer
echo :  Notes:  Batch file to remove unwanted user objects created by an
echo :          automated dBASE IV program CONVERT.PRG. Note that even
echo :          though user objects are located in different containers,
echo :          the same control and data files are used. This will
echo :          result in error messages but prevents having to create
echo :          separate data files.
echo :
echo on
cx .OU=NY.O=EBDB
```

```
uimport ctrl14.txt data14.txt
cx .OU=Other.O=EBDB
uimport ctrl14.txt data14.txt
cx .OU=SF.O=EBDB
uimport ctrl14.txt data14.txt
cx .OU=SJ.O=EBDB
uimport ctrl14.txt data14.txt
```

Note in the preceding example that even though the user objects to be cleaned up exist in different containers, the batch file calls the same control and data files. You can use this technique only when removing or updating user objects. UIMPORT does not address more than one container at a time. The batch file changes context and calls the control and data files CTRL14.TXT and DATA14.TXT. There is only one object per context to be removed. The result is that the one object out of the four listed in DATA14.TXT is removed, and you will see three error messages. This occurs for each container the batch file changes you to. When done, a total of four user objects in four different containers are removed. You see a total of 12 error messages. The error messages are not fatal; they simply inform you that some objects listed in the data file do not exist in this container.

Updating User Properties

In many cases you will need to update or remove user properties. The Telephone Number field is a good example of a field that may need to be updated on a regular basis. Network users change positions or change offices, each time resulting in a telephone change. In another situation, your company might decide not to keep track of certain information. Again, the Telephone Number field might become a sensitive area. Some companies keep track of the home phone numbers of employees. Your company might decide to remove the home phone number or postal address from the NDS database to maintain the privacy of its employees.

Sample Update of User Properties

The following two examples show the control and data files used to update the department, location, address, telephone number, and title of three users. Note that in the second example, the data is too long to fit on one line. Every other line of data is indented to indicate that it should be appended to the line above.

This first example is a sample control file to update user information:

```
Import Control
     Import Mode = U
     Name Context = "OU=IND.O=EBDB"
```

```
Fields
     Name
     Last Name
     Department
     Location
     Postal Address
     Postal Address
     Postal Address
     State or Province
     Street Address
     Telephone Number
     Title
```

This example is a sample data file to update user information:

```
ALee, Lee, Acquisitions, Main Headquarters, P.O. Box 1218, 1 First St.,
      "Indianapolis, IN 22222", IN, 1 First St., 317-555-1212, Vice President
DHeywood, Heywood, Management, Main Headquarters, P.O. Box 1219, 1 First St.,
      "Indianapolis, IN 22222", IN, 1 First St., 317-555-3333, President
JKane, Kane, Editing, Main Headquarters, P.O. Box 1220, 1 First St.,
      "Indianapolis, IN 22222", IN, 1 First St., 317-555-4444, Senior Editor
```

When you have a multivalued property, an update operation simply adds to the list of properties rather than overwrites properties. In this case you need to specify the control file under the Import Control section REPLACE VALUE = Y. The following examples illustrate control and data files where the phone number is replaced rather than simply updated.

This example shows a sample control file to update user information:

```
Import Control
     Import Mode = U
     Name Context = "OU=IND.O=EBDB"
     Replace Value = Y
Fields
     Name
     Last Name
     Telephone Number
```

This example shows a sample data file to update user information:

```
ALee, Lee, 317-555-1212
DHeywood, Heywood, 317-555-3333
JKane, Kane, 317-555-4444
```

The following syntax lines show the results of the update user information operation:

```
F:\NRP\INSIDE4>uimport ctrl19.txt data19.txt
Import context: OU=IND.O=EBDB
 Updated, ALee,+ Done.
 Updated, DHeywood,+ Done.
 Updated, JKane,+ Done.

F:\NRP\INSIDE4>nlist user show "Telephone Number" /co .ou=ind.o=ebdb
Object Class: user
Current context: ou=ind.o=ebdb
User: CN=ALee
        Telephone Number: 317-555-1212
User: CN=DHeywood
        Telephone Number: 317-555-3333
User: CN=JKane
        Telephone Number: 317-555-4444
A total of 3 user objects was found in this context.

A total of 3 user objects was found.

F:\NRP\INSIDE4>
```

Sample Removal of User Properties

User properties can be removed entirely from the NDS database. This can be done for several reasons. As stated in the previous section, properties might be removed to protect employee privacy. The following three listings are an example of how the Title property is removed from all three employees and the telephone number is removed from one.

The technique to remove a property is as follows:

1. In the control file, under the Import Control section, specify a special character as the Delete Property.
2. Place this character in the data file in place of the field to be deleted.

The following is a sample control file to delete user information:

```
Import Control
     Delete Property=*BYE*
     Name Context="OU=IND.O=EBDB"
```

```
Fields
     Name
     Last Name
     Telephone Number
     Title
```

The following is a sample data file to delete user information:

```
ALee, Lee, 317-555-1212, *BYE*
DHeywood, Heywood, *BYE*, *BYE*
JKane, Kane, 317-555-4444, *BYE*
```

Here are the results of the delete user information process:

```
F:\NRP\INSIDE4>cx .OU=IND.O=EBDB
OU=IND.O=EBDB

F:\NRP\INSIDE4>nlist user show "telephone number", "title"
Object Class: user
Current context: ou=ind.o=ebdb
User: CN=ALee
        Telephone Number: 317-555-1212
        Title: Vice President
User: CN=DHeywood
        Telephone Number: 317-555-3333
        Title: President
User: CN=JKane
        Telephone Number: 317-555-4444
        Title: Senior Editor
A total of 3 user objects was found in this context.

A total of 3 user objects was found.

F:\NRP\INSIDE4>uimport ctrl22.txt data22.txt
Import context: OU=IND.O=EBDB
 Updated, ALee,¦ Done.
 Updated, DHeywood,+ Done.
 Updated, JKane,- Done.

F:\NRP\INSIDE4>nlist user show "Telephone Number", "Title"
Object Class: user
Current context: OU=IND.O=EBDB
```

```
User: CN=ALee
        Telephone Number: 317-555-1212
User: CN=JKane
        Telephone Number: 317-555-4444
A total of 2 user objects was found in this context.

A total of 2 user objects was found.

F:\NRP\INSIDE4>
```

You will note in the last printout that the user with both Title and Telephone Number removed did not appear in the NLIST...SHOW "Telephone Number," "Title" scan because both of these properties had been successfully removed.

Creating the User Database

The UIMPORT utility is used to import large numbers of users from a comma-delimited ASCII file. As the name implies, the file is in ASCII format, with commas separating data items. In some cases, personnel files are readily available in the form of name, address, and phone number lists. Most companies maintain some sort of phone list.

Personnel database files come in a variety of formats. In most cases, the format is not ASCII comma-delimited. You must perform some sort of operation to get the data into this format. In the case of a list maintained using a word processing program, for example, you need to save the file as an ASCII text file. You might need to first perform some sort of global search and replace to insert commas between data elements. Most word processing programs enable you to do a merge in which you can merge the data from one document into a template you create in another document. The template can have commas separating the data fields.

In the case of a spreadsheet, most spreadsheet programs are capable of saving a file in a number of formats. Lotus 1-2-3 and Excel, for example, have a CSV (Comma Separated Values) format. The CSV format is ideal for use with UIMPORT. Most personnel files are maintained using a database program. In some cases the program is custom-made for your company, or perhaps incorporated into another program. Many accounting programs feature an employee database to go along with a payroll function. dBASE, Paradox, and Access are examples of database programs that are often used to maintain company personnel databases.

The following shows a portion of a name and address list maintained in a word processing document:

```
Jerry Lewis                   408-555-1212    281 French Ln., Bethesda MD  11223
Michelle Pfeiffer             916-888-9922    19 3rd Ave.  SF CA 94111
Michael Keaton                203-444-1234    Home Number
Co-Star Music Productions     415-333-5432    1900 Vicente St., SF CA 94101
```

The following listing shows a database NAMES.DBF in a dBASE IV format constructed to hold the database along with the definition of a database TEMP.DBF constructed to temporarily hold the text of the name and address list:

```
Structure for database: F:\NRP\INSIDE4\NAMES.DBF
Number of data records:       71
Date of last update   : 05/04/94
Field  Field Name  Type       Width    Dec    Index
    1  FIRST_NAME  Character     15               N
    2  LAST_NAME   Character     20               N
    3  LOGIN_NAME  Character      8               N
    4  PHONE       Character     12               N
    5  ADDRESS1    Character     30               N
    6  ADDRESS2    Character     30               N
    7  ADDRESS3    Character     30               N
    8  CITY        Character     20               N
    9  STATE       Character      2               N
   10  ZIP         Character     10               N
   11  DEPT        Character     20               N
   12  TEXT        Character     80               N
** Total **                     278


Structure for database: F:\NRP\INSIDE4\TEMP.DBF
Number of data records:       1
Date of last update   : 05/04/94
Field  Field Name  Type       Width    Dec    Index
    1  TEXT        Character     80               N
** Total **                      80
```

The name and address list must first be written out to an ASCII file PHONE.TXT. Once this is accomplished, the data is imported into the file TEMP.DBF. This file is then brought into the NAMES.DBF database through the common field TEXT, using the dBASE APPEND command. At this point the data in the TEXT field can be parsed out to fill in the other fields. As you can see from the sample file, there is little rhyme or reason to the structure of the data file in its original word processing format. The following listing shows you a sample dBASE IV program that performs manipulations on the TEXT field to parse the data into the other fields. This program does not produce a "clean" database. The most important fields for these purposes, the LAST_NAME and LOGIN_NAME fields, are accurately produced.

These are required fields when importing user information into the NDS:

```
*
*     Program:    CONVERT.PRG
*     Date:       5-6-94
*     Author:     D. Bierer
*     Notes:      Converts ASCII file PHONE.TXT to NAMES.DBF
*

*     Open temp file to contain text
use temp

*     Import text
append from PHONE.TXT type SDF

*     Bring text into NAMES.DBF file
use names
append from temp

*    Parse LAST_NAME, PHONE, ADDRESS, CITY, STATE and ZIP fields
*    Uses the "at()" function to locate key characters in each line
*    of the PHONE.TXT data file.  "chr(9)" is the ASCII code for a
*    TAB character.  The other key character is the ",".  Note that
*    the ADDRESS3 field contains CITY + STATE + ZIP
replace last_name with ;
     substr(text,at(" ",text)+1,at(chr(9),text)-at(" ",text)) all
replace phone with iif(val(substr(text,at(chr(9),text)+1,1))>0,;
     substr(text,at(chr(9),text)+1,12),"") all
replace phone with iif(val(substr(text,at(chr(9),text,2)+1,1))>0,;
     substr(text,at(chr(9),text,2)+1,12),phone) ;
     for val(left(phone,1)) = 0
replace address1 with substr(text,at(chr(9),text,3)+1,;
     at(",",text)-at(chr(9),text,3)-1) for at(chr(9),text,3) > 0
replace address2 with substr(text,at(",",text)+2,;
     at(",",text,2)-at(",",text)-2) for at(",",text,2) > 0
replace city with substr(text,at(",",text)+2,;
     at(",",text,2)-at(",",text)-2) for at(",",text,2) > 0
replace zip with right(trim(text),5) for val(right(trim(text),5)) > 0
replace address3 with trim(city) + "  " + state + "  " + zip all

*    The LOGIN_NAME is constructed from the first letter of the
*    FIRST_NAME field, and the first 7 characters of the LAST_NAME field
```

```
replace login_name with left(first_name,1) + left(last_name,7) all

*    The LOGIN_NAME and LAST_NAME fields have to be "cleansed" of
*    any TAB characters
replace login_name with left(login_name,at(chr(9),login_name)-1) ;
     for at(chr(9),login_name) > 0
replace last_name with left(last_name,at(chr(9),last_name)-1) ;
     for at(chr(9),last_name) > 0

*    The following series of statements fill in the DEPT field
*    based on the area code of the person's PHONE number
*    The dept "OTHER" is placed in all records initially.  Later,
*    different depts are filled in based on area code.
replace dept with "OTHER" all
replace dept with "SJ" for left(phone,3) = "408"
replace dept with "SF" for left(phone,3) = "415"
replace dept with "NY" for left(phone,3) = "716" .or. left(phone,3) = "212"
replace dept with "SAC" for left(phone,3) = "916"
replace dept with "IND" for left(phone,3) = "317"
replace dept with "UNKNOWN" for at("-",phone) = 0

*    A batch file IMPORT.BAT is created which changes context
*    to the department, and then does a UIMPORT command for that
*    department.
file1=fcreate("import.bat")

*    The database is indexed by Department and Login Name
index on dept+login_name to names

*    Process records from the TOP to bottom of the database
go top
do while .not. eof()

     *     Store the department code
m_dept = dept

*    Write out the CX and UMIPORT commands to the batch file
x=fwrite(file1,"cx .ou="+trim(DEPT)+".o=EBDB"+chr(13)+chr(10))
x=fwrite(file1,"uimport ctrl.txt +trim(DEPT)+".DAT"+chr(13)+chr(10))

*    Copy records for this department to a comma-delimited data file
dept_file=trim(dept)+".DAT"
copy to (dept_file) for dept=m_dept delimited fields first_name, ;
```

```
     last_name, login_name, phone, address1, address2, address3, ;
     city, state, zip,

*    Find the first record for this department and then
*    skip to the first record for the next department
x=seek(m_dept)
do while dept = m_dept .and. .not. eof()
     skip
enddo
enddo

*    Close out batch file and exit the program
x=fclose(file1)
return
```

Note the last manipulations: the first letter of the FIRST_NAME and first seven letters of the LAST_NAME fields are used to produce the user login name. The PHONE number field is parsed to produce the proper value for DEPT (department). The DEPT field is used to assign users to their proper NDS container. The following listing illustrates the batch file created by this program:

```
cx .ou=IND.o=EBDB
uimport ctrl.txt IND.DAT
cx .ou=NY.o=EBDB
uimport ctrl.txt NY.DAT
cx .ou=OTHER.o=EBDB
uimport ctrl.txt OTHER.DAT
cx .ou=SAC.o=EBDB
uimport ctrl.txt SAC.DAT
```

One of the data files created by this program is illustrated in the following example:

```
"Barbara","Bierer","BBierer","212-999-0011","777 Seventh Lane","Apt. 77",
      "Webster  NY  77777","Webster","NY","77777"
"Brad","Saunders","BSaunder","716-222-3333","111 First St.",
      "Rochester","Rochester  NY  11111","Rochester","NY","11111"
"Brad","Saunders","BSaunder","716-333-4444","","","","","",""
"Brad","Saunders","BSaunder","716-444-5555","","","","","",""
"Daryl","Holdridge","DHoldrid","716-555-6666","222 Second St.","",
      "Rochester  NY  22222","Rochester","NY","22222"
"Le","Telephoniste","LTelepho","101-222-3344","Rockford","PO Box 5555",
      "New York  NY  55555","New York","NY","55555"
"Ralph","Bierer","RBierer","716-667-7788","333 Third  St.",
      "Rochester","Rochester  NY  33333","Rochester","NY","33333"
```

```
"Ralph","Bierer","RBierer","716-777-8888","Lawrence Place","444 Fourth St.",
      "Rochester  NY  44444","Rochester","NY","44444"
"Tom","Hess","THess","716-888-9999","555 Fifth Ave.","",
      "Albany  NY  55555","Albany","NY","55555"
```

The UIMPORT control file CTRL.TXT used in this example is illustrated, as follows:

```
Import Control
      Create Home Directory = Y
      Home Directory Volume = .CN=FS1_DATA.O=IntCo
      Home Directory Path = HOME
      User Template = Y
Fields
      Other Names
      Last Name
      Name
      Telephone Number
      Postal Address
      Postal Address
      Postal Address
      City
      State or Province
      Postal (Zip) Code
```

Summary

This chapter discussed the importance of the UIMPORT utility. As you learned, UIMPORT can automate the process of adding users to the NDS. Various techniques using UIMPORT were demonstrated. You learned the format of the control file and the parameters associated with the Import Control and Fields sections. Some of the limitations of UIMPORT were discussed. These include only being able to add, remove, or modify user objects, and being able to work with only one context at a time.

Many examples of adding, updating, and removing specific properties were given. A complete list of parameters for the control file was given, along with a complete list of user object fields you can update or modify.

The last section detailed an operation with which you convert a name and address list into a UIMPORT file and import users in an automated fashion.

The next chapter covers aspects of bindery services.

Using Bindery Services

Bindery services is a hot topic in the NetWare 4 community. NetWare 3.*x* is a bindery-based operating system. Information about network resources is stored in a series of interconnected database files known as the *bindery files* or simply, the *bindery*. The NetWare 3.*x* bindery files are located in the SYS:SYSTEM directory, and are the following:

- **NET$OBJ.SYS.** Contains information on bindery objects. This information consists primarily of pointers to the other files and an object ID number. A bindery object can be a user, group, printer, print server, or other network resources.

- **NET$PROP.SYS.** Contains information on the properties of bindery objects. As in NetWare 4, each type of object has a set of associated properties. A user object, for example, has the properties of full name, password, time restrictions, and other properties. This file indicates what properties are defined for any given object in the NET$OBJ.SYS file, along with a pointer to the NET$VAL.SYS file.
- **NET$VAL.SYS.** Contains the actual values associated with the various properties. If a user has a password, for example, the NET$PROP.SYS indicates this, whereas the NET$VAL.SYS file contains the actual (encrypted) password.

The installed base of NetWare 3 systems is enormous (estimated in the millions). Many utilities are written for this environment, and many installed NetWare 3 clients exist.

When NetWare 4 was first introduced, it became evident that it is a radically different operating system. Although it has a great deal of resemblance to NetWare 3, the entire philosophical basis for the NetWare 4 operating system is different. NetWare 3 servers, with their individual binderies, are designed to serve as isolated servers. Although many users can and did place multiple servers on their LANs, the NetWare 3 servers are not designed for centralized management. NetWare 4, on the other hand, with its distributed NDS database, is designed for multiple servers on a LAN. It is only marginally more difficult to manage 100 NetWare 4 servers than it is to manage 8. This is not true for NetWare 3. Because the management of NetWare 3 servers is server centric, the time and difficulty of managing multiple servers increases exponentially with each additional server.

A problem arises when upgrading a NetWare 3 network to NetWare 4. This problem is how to handle clients still using the older workstation shells. In addition, when porting an NLM written for the NetWare 3 environment, what happens if the NLM requires access to the server's bindery files? The answer lies in *bindery services.*

Chapter 8 discusses the basic concepts behind bindery services. This chapter discusses how to implement and manage bindery services. In addition, this chapter addresses the issue of coordinating management of a mixed NetWare 3 and NetWare 4 network.

Setting Up Bindery Services

One of the key concepts behind bindery services is to set the server's bindery context. The bindery context can include up to 16 separate NDS containers and you can use from 1 to 16 at a time. These containers do not have any unique characteristics that set them apart from any other NDS container. Contrary to popular belief, the container does not have to contain a server or volume object.

The NetWare 4 server presents the objects in the containers in its bindery context as if they were bindery objects. The NetWare 4 servers *emulates* a NetWare 3 bindery. Bindery clients have access only to the containers in the NetWare 4 server's bindery context. Bindery clients do not see other portions of the NDS tree nor do bindery clients see many of the properties of NDS objects just login name, password, login script, and so forth. You only see what SYSCON enables you to see.

Figure 22.1 illustrates this concept.

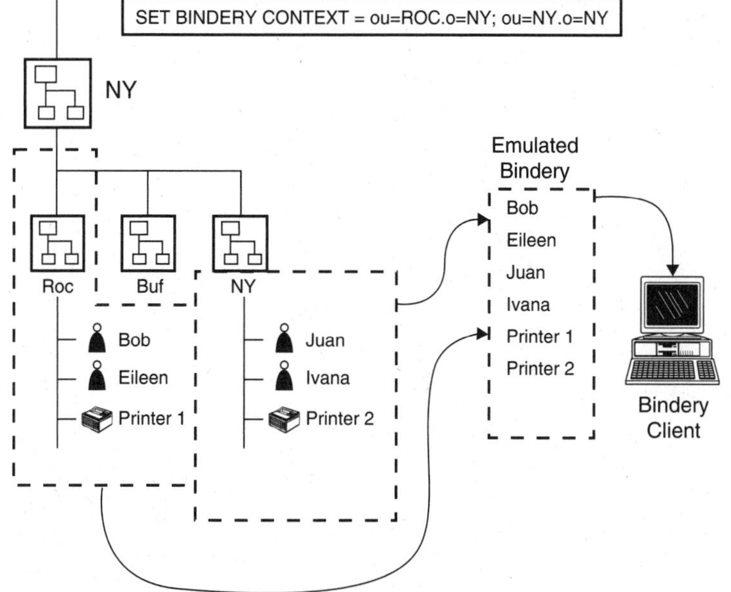

Figure 22.1
Visualizing the bindery context.

Setting the Bindery Context

The bindery context can be set on a NetWare 4 server using the following console command:

```
SET BINDERY CONTEXT = <NDS Container> [; NDS Container]
```

Alternatively, you can set the bindery context using the SERVMAN.NLM utility. To set the bindery context using SERVMAN, proceed as follows:

1. From the server console, load SERVMAN:

   LOAD SERVMAN

2. From the SERVMAN main menu, select Server Parameters. The Select a Parameter Category list appears.

3. From the Select a Parameter Category list, select Directory Services. The Directory Services Parameters dialog box appears.

4. From the Directory Services Parameters dialog box, move to the bottom of the box and select Bindery Context. The Bindery Context edit box appears.

5. From the Bindery Context edit box, you can enter in the desired bindery context. Enter up to 16 NDS container names separated by semicolons (;).

You *must not* use a leading period when specifying the bindery context of a server.

If you are not sure the bindery context you have specified is correct, toggle to the server's console prompt to see if there are any messages indicating the context was not correct. A message similar to this one appears if the bindery context is misspelled or does not exist.

```
Bindery context .NY.EBDB NOT set, entry not found.
```

6. Once the bindery context has been entered into the Bindery Context edit box, press Esc to exit the edit box and return to the Directory Services Parameters dialog box shown in figure 22.2. You can press Esc several times to exit SERVMAN. Be sure to update the AUTOEXEC.NCF file before leaving SERVMAN.

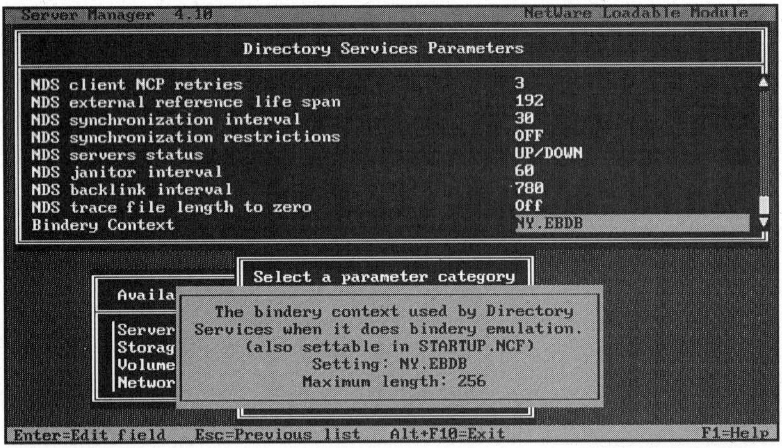

Figure 22.2
Setting the bindery context from SERVMAN.NLM.

Multiple Containers in the Bindery Context

If you choose to include more than one NDS container in the bindery context, add a semicolon (;) after the last NDS container specified, and add the desired additional container. You can have up to 16 containers in the bindery context of a single server. In the following example, the containers OU=NY, OU=SJ, and OU=CHI are placed in the server's bindery context:

```
SET BINDERY CONTEXT = ou=NY.o=EBDB; ou=SJ.o=EBDB; ou=Chi.o=EBDB
```

When more than one container is set as the server's bindery context, all objects in these containers are seen as a single bindery by bindery-based clients. A common complaint in earlier versions of NetWare 4 was that bindery services limited you to a single container. In some cases network Administrators were forced to place all objects in a single container so that bindery-based utilities and clients could see network users and other resources. Having the ability to place more than one container in the bindery context allows you to more easily administer the network without causing bindery clients to lose sight of needed resources.

If there is more than one object with the same common name, only the object in the first bindery context is visible to bindery clients. NetWare 4 searches multiple containers in a sequential fashion. Suppose, for example, that there is a user JWalker (John Walker) in the container UnixGurus. There is another user JWalker (Jim Walker) in the container OS2Gurus. Both containers are located under the organization XYZ_Corp. In this example, suppose the server's bindery context is set as follows:

```
SET BINDERY CONTEXT = ou=OS2Gurus.o=XYZ_Corp; ou=UnixGurus.o=XYZ_Corp
```

If user John Walker attempts to log in to the server from a UnixWare bindery-based client as the user JWalker, the server searchs the OU=OS2Gurus container first. It finds the user JWalker from the OU=OS2Gurus container and considers it a match. John Walker enters his password thinking he has been provided a login session. The server rejects his password as invalid (unless, by a long shot, John and Jim Walker have the same password). Workarounds to the hidden user problem include changing one name or the other or creating new user names and a separate container to be used as the bindery context.

NDS Partition Requirements

Before bindery services can take place, a requirement must be met. NLMs that make use of the bindery files expect there to be a physical location in which to write data. On a NetWare 3.*x* server, the physical location is in the SYS:SYSTEM subdirectory, where the three bindery files are physically located. On a NetWare 4 server, there is no equivalent. Bindery services in NetWare 4 satisfies this requirement when you have a Read/write replica of an NDS partition physically stored on the server that is to perform bindery services.

A *partition* is a subdivision of the NDS tree. A *replica* is a copy of a partition. The concepts behind replicas and partitions are discussed in Chapter 6, "NetWare Directory Services."

A further requirement is that the server must have a Read/write replica of a partition that contains the NDS containers in the bindery context. As you can see in figure 22.1, the containers OU=ROC and OU=NY are both located in the server's bindery context. If the server contained no replicas of any partitions, the SET BINDERY CONTEXT = ou=ROC.o=NY; ou=NY.o=NY would fail. If the server had a partition that contained only one container or the other, the SET BINDERY CONTEXT... statement also would fail. In this example, the server must have a Read/write replica of a partition that contains both containers OU=ROC and OU=NY.

The first step is to see if your bindery context is set. From the server console, issue this command to view the current setting of the bindery context:

SET BINDERY CONTEXT

You should see a response similar to the following:

```
EBDB:set bindery context
Bindery Context:  NY.EBDB
Maximum length:  256
   Can be set in the startup ncf file
   Description: The bindery context used by Directory Services when it does
                bindery services.
EBDB:
```

If the bindery context does not appear to be set, you must create a partition and store a Read/write replica on this server. Be careful with the preceding message, it could seem deceptive. Observe the following series of console commands:

```
EBDB:set bindery context = ou=xyz

Bindery context OU=XYZ NOT set, entry not found.
Bindery Context is set to: OU=XYZ
```

As you can see from the commands and response, the bindery context has been set to a container that does not exist or was not properly specified. If you issue the SET BINDERY CONTEXT command, all appears well even though the bindery context is not set:

```
EBDB:set bindery context
Bindery Context:  OU=XYZ
Maximum length:  256
   Can be set in the startup ncf file
   Description: The bindery context used by Directory Services when it does
                bindery services.
EBDB:
```

To view partitions and replicas on your server, you can use either the PARTMGR.EXE utility from the DOS prompt, or the NWADMIN.EXE utility from Windows. For the purposes of this section, the PARTMGR.EXE utility is used.

To view partitions and replicas on your server, follow these steps:

1. Log in to the network as a user with at least Supervisor object rights to the server object. From the DOS prompt, run PARTMGR.EXE. The PARTMGR main menu appears.

2. From the PARTMGR main menu, select Manage Partitions. You see the Object, Class list. From this list, select the container that contains the server object.

3. Once the server object has been selected, press F10 to view a list of partitions stored on the server. This is illustrated in figure 22.3.

```
PartMgr 4.14                              Thursday  September  29, 1994  7:37pm
Context:  O=EBDB
Replica being read: EBDB
Object name:  EBDB

                    Partition Administration

    Partitions stored on server                          Replica type
 NY.O=EBDB                                               Master
 SJ.O=EBDB                                               Master
 [Root]                                                  Master

Lists all the partitions that have a replica stored on the selected server.
Esc=Cancel                                                      F1=Help
```

Figure 22.3

Viewing partitions on a server using PARTMGR.EXE.

You need to create a partition and store a replica on this server if any of the following are true:

- ◆ The server does not contain any partitions at all
- ◆ The partitions stored on this server do not contain the bindery context

- The partitions are of type Read Only

4. Press Esc several times, or press Alt+F10, to exit PARTMGR.

For more information on partitions and replicas, please refer to Chapter 6, "NetWare Directory Services." For instructions on how to create a partition or replica, refer to Chapter 19, "NDS Tree Design Considerations."

Using NetWare 4 in Bindery Mode

Any bindery-based client can access the NetWare 4 server through bindery services. Bindery-based clients include the following:

- DOS workstations using the older (NETX.EXE or lower) shells
- NetWare 3 and NetWare 2 servers
- NetWare 4 servers in another NDS tree
- NLMs written for NetWare 3 that use the bindery files
- UnixWare clients
- Host access via NetWare for SAA
- Windows NT and OS/2 DOS sessions
- DOS workstations already logged into another Directory Tree and making an attachment

When you load the bindery-based NetWare client software, you attach to the server just as if it were a NetWare 3 or NetWare 2 server. Moving to drive F (in most cases), you can log in. The login name you specify does not have any NDS designations. The user .CN=KShoji.OU=Tokyo.O=EBDB, for example, would log in as KShoji, and the container OU=Tokyo must be in the server's bindery context.

Bindery services clients can perform most server functions that do not require access to NDS resources outside of the server's bindery context. Common actions for bindery-based clients include the following:

- Using the MAP command to map drive letters
- Using the CAPTURE command to redirect printing

- Storing files
- Running applications

In short, the NetWare 4 server acts just like a NetWare 3 server. You could even copy the SYSCON.EXE utility from a NetWare 3 server and manage user and group objects in the server's bindery context; however, using SYSCON limits you from from information unique to the Directory.

Coexisting with Older NetWare Servers

NetWare 4 enables you to manage bindery-based NetWare servers (NetWare 2.*x* or 3.*x* servers) through the NDS to a limited extent (without additional NLMs). You can define a NetWare 2.*x* or 3.*x* server as an NDS object anywhere in the tree. As long as you use the same name for the new object as the name of the server, you are able to view a certain amount of information on that server.

Adding a Bindery-Based NetWare Server to the Tree

The procedure for implementing this level of support is as follows:

1. Log in to the network as a user with at least Browse and Create object rights to the container that is to contain the new NetWare 2.*x* or 3.*x* server object.
2. Invoke either NETADMIN from the DOS prompt or NWADMIN from Windows. For the purposes of this illustration, assume the NWADMIN utility from Windows.
3. Select the desired container in which to place the server object, and press Insert. You see the New Object dialog box.
4. From the New Object dialog box, select NetWare Server, and then either press the OK button or press Enter. You see the Create NetWare Server dialog box appear.
5. From the Create NetWare Server dialog box, enter the name of the bindery-based server. Press the Create button when you are finished.

The name of the new server object and the name of the server you want to manage must match exactly.

The Server Login dialog box appears, as shown in figure 22.4.

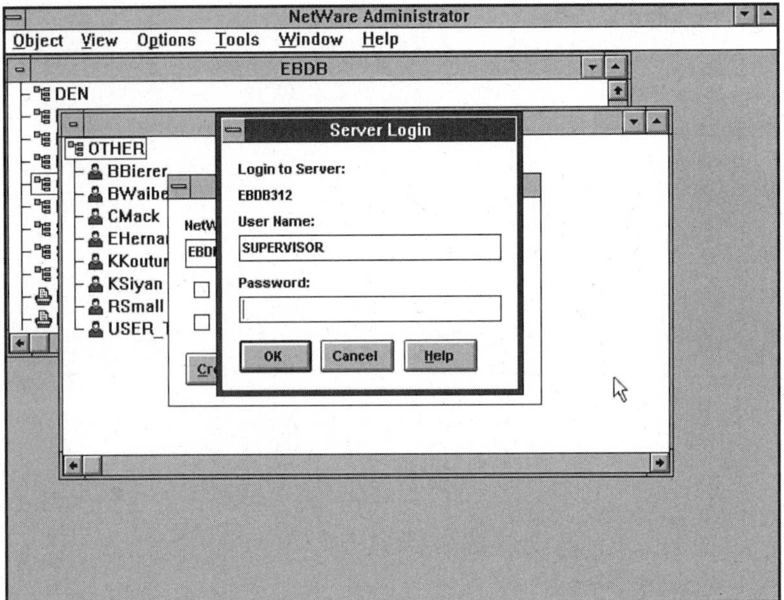

Figure 22.4
Adding a NetWare 2.x or 3.x server to the NDS.

6. From the Server Login dialog box, enter a valid login name and password of a user on the NetWare 2.*x* or 3.*x* server. You return to the NWADMIN NDS tree browse screen.

Viewing Bindery-Based Server Information

Now that the server is registered with the NDS, you can view some information on that server. If the user name is a Supervisor or equivalent, you can view the File Server Error Log.

To view a bindery-based server through the NDS, proceed as follows:

1. Log in as a user with at least Browse object rights to the bindery-based server object.

2. Invoke either NETADMIN from the DOS prompt or NWADMIN from Windows. For the purposes of this illustration, assume the NWADMIN utility from Windows.

3. Select the container in which the bindery-based server object is located. Select the server object and either double-click with the mouse or press Enter to bring up the NetWare Server information screen. The first screen is shown in figure 22.5.

   As you can see from the figure, the following information is available:

   Name This field shows you the server name followed by its NDS context.

   Net Address The IPX network address through which this server is visible.

   Version The version of NetWare for this server.

4. Click on the Error Log button at the right to view the server Error Log. This screen is shown in figure 22.6. The error log is useful in troubleshooting server problems.

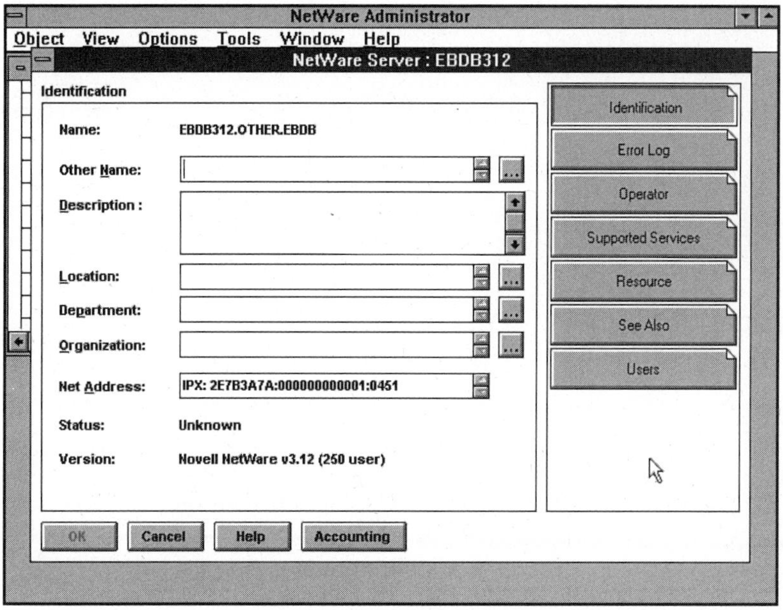

Figure 22.5

Viewing information on a bindery-based server through NWADMIN.

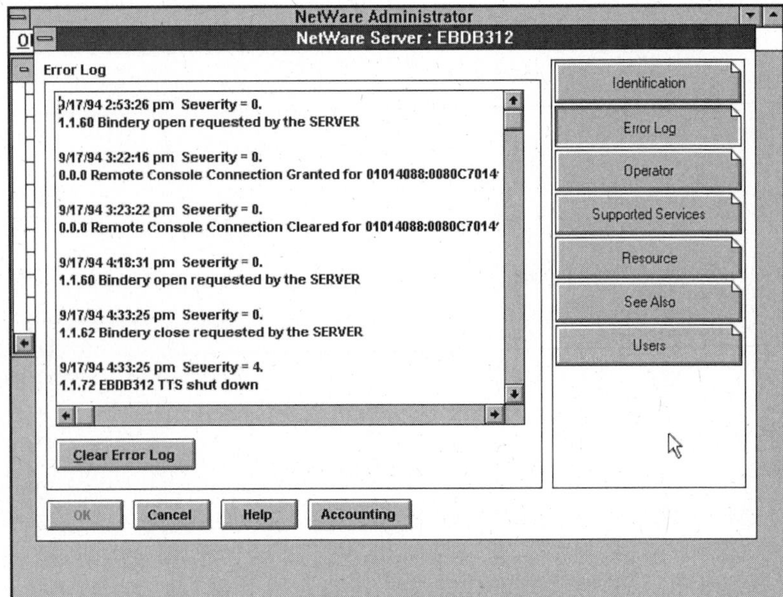

Figure 22.6
Bindery-based server Error Log as seen in NWADMIN.

Installing Accounting

You can install accounting on bindery-based servers, as well as NDS-based servers. Unlike auditing, the accounting system strictly reflects server resources. The accounting system is not selective by user or by NDS resource. You can set the parameters for the server in general but not unique parameters with specific users, files, or events. In other words, you enable accounting for all server resources.

The areas that can be accounted for are Blocks Read, Blocks Written, Connect Time, Disk Storage, and Service Requests. Table 22.1 summarizes these areas of accounting.

Table 22.1
Areas of Accounting

Accounting Parameter	Description
Blocks Read	A measurement of how many disk blocks have been read from or written to this server. The default block size in NetWare 2.*x* and NetWare 3.*x* is 4,096 bytes (4 KB). *Blocks Read* gives you an overview of how much information on that server's disk drives has been read. *Blocks Read* also is a measurement of network traffic from the server to clients.

Accounting Parameter	Description
Blocks Written	A similar parameter but measures blocks sent by the clients to the server.
Connect Time	Is in minutes and measures how long users have been logged in to this server.
Disk Storage	Is in disk blocks and measures how much disk space is in use by various users. Unlike the other parameters, which are tallied every 30 minutes, Disk Storage is tallied only once per day at a time period you determine.
Service Requests	This parameter is a measurement of overall demand for the services offered by this server. The primary request, of course, is for file services. This is a good measurement of how much usage is made of this server.

Once accounting is installed, it immediately starts tracking resources on that server. If you establish a charge for a specific area of accounting, this charge is decremented from user accounts and affects their account balance.

To install and configure accounting on a server, proceed as follows:

1. Log in as a user with Supervisor object rights to the server object. You also must log in to the bindery-based server. You can use NWUSER (NetWare User Tools) to accomplish this. Alternatively, you can select the bindery-based server icon. If you are not logged in, the Server Login dialog box appears, enabling you to enter a valid SUPERVISOR or equivalent login name and password.

2. Invoke either NETADMIN from the DOS prompt or NWADMIN from Windows. For the purposes of this illustration, assume the NWADMIN utility from Windows.

3. Select the container in which the bindery-based server object is located. Select the server object and either double-click with the mouse or press Enter to bring up the NetWare Server information screen.

4. From the NetWare Server information screen, click on the Accounting button at the bottom of the screen. You are asked if you want to install accounting on this server. Press the YES button. Accounting is now installed on this server.

5. To configure accounting, click on any of these buttons that appear on the NetWare Server information screen after accounting has been installed:

- Blocks Read
- Blocks Written
- Connect Time
- Disk Storage
- Service Requests

For the purposes of this section, suppose that you want to configure Connect Time.

6. From the NetWare Server information screen, press the Connect Time button. The Connect Time dialog box appears.

7. You must now determine a charge rate that is suitable for your purposes. Different network administrators establish different charge rates depending on their needs. A charge rate of 1/1, for example, is useful in determining baseline performance parameters for a server. You can run the accounting reporting utilities PAUDIT or ATOTAL (discussed later) once a week to generate performance statistics.

You may decide to establish other charge rates to determine how much to bill other departments for using your server. The charge rate hinges on what monetary value you want to recover and what baseline performance is considered normal for your server.

The formula for determining a charge rate for a particular area of accounting (blocks read, connect time, and so on) is: Amount to Recover / Baseline Figure.

For example, suppose that you want to recover the cost of your network over five years. If the cost of the network is $60,000, this means you want to recover $12,000 per year. The monthly figure would be $1,000 per month. You determine that a baseline figure for connect time should be 240,000 minutes.

The baseline is determined by monitoring the system using a charge rate of 1/1 for a month. It equals roughly 100 users at 8 hours a day, 5 days a week.

The charge rate should therefore be set at 1000/240000. Assuming the value of a *unit* is set at $1.00, this means that you are charging users $.0042 per minute. You can then monitor user accounts each month to determine how much to bill the other department.

8. After you have determined what charge rate to add, press the Add Charge Rate button from the Connect Time dialog box. Enter in the multiplier and divisor. The multiplier is the amount to recover. The divisor is the baseline figure. Click on the OK button when you are finished.

9. From the Connect Time dialog box, select this charge rate. Use the mouse to select a block of time from the weekly time grid at the top of the page. Figure 22.7 shows you the Connect Time dialog box with a block of time from Sunday at 8:00 AM to Saturday at 6:00 PM marked off.

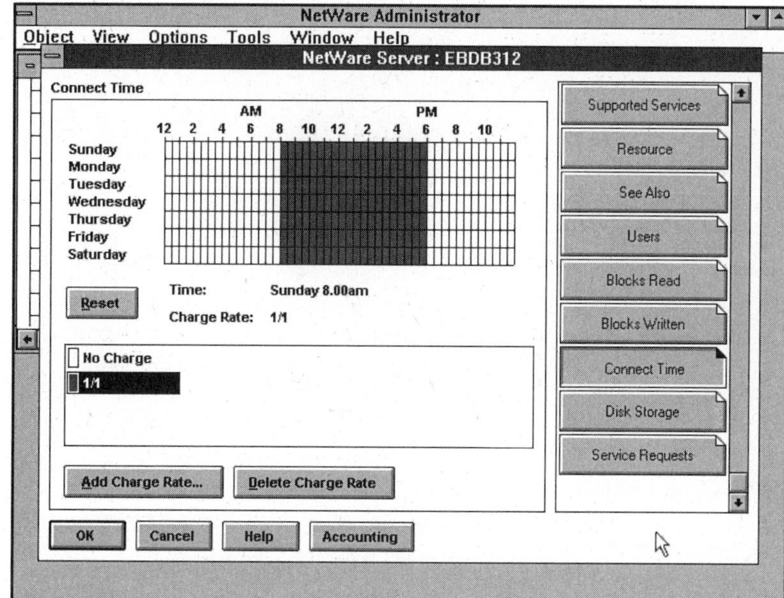

Figure 22.7

Server accounting as seen in NWADMIN.

10. When you are finished, click on the OK button. You return to the NDS Tree browse screen.

To view the effect of accounting on a user, view their account balance as follows:

1. From the DOS prompt, log in as a user with Supervisor or equivalent privileges to the bindery-based server.
2. Invoke the SYSCON utility from the DOS prompt.
3. From the SYSCON main menu, select User Information. A list of users in the bindery files of that server is displayed.
4. From the list of users, select the user you want to monitor, and press Enter. The User Information menu appears.
5. From the User Information menu, select Account Balance. This is where you can set and monitor this user's account balance. Figure 22.8 shows you settings where the account balance is zero and unlimited credit is allowed. This way the user is

not impacted by the accounting system. When the system starts to charge the user account, the account goes below zero by the amount charged. Each month you can log this figure and reset the account back to zero.

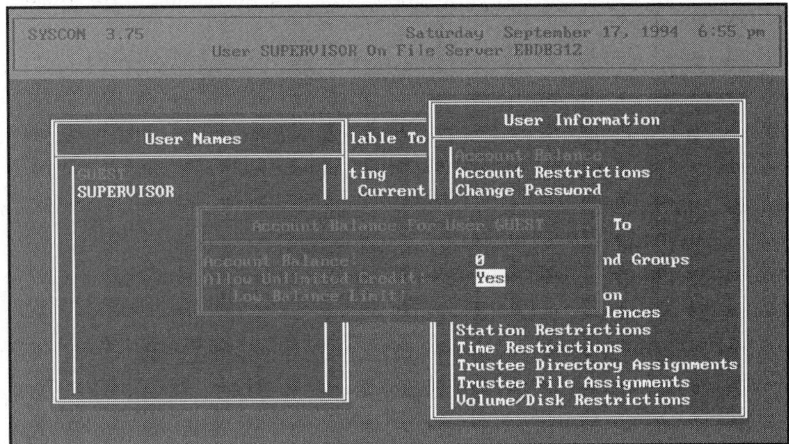

Figure 22.8
Using SYSCON to monitor a bindery user's account balance.

6. Press Esc to exit this screen. Press Alt+F10 to exit SYSCON.

Managing Bindery-Based Server Volumes

NetWare 4 also enables you to manage the bindery-based file system. You add a volume object, taking care to identify the bindery-based server object as the host for the volume. After you have made the object, you can view and manage the directory structure just as if the server were a NetWare 4 server. You also can view some statistics on the volume.

To add the volume object to the NDS, proceed as follows:

1. Log in to a NetWare 4 server as a user with Supervisor object rights to the server object. You also must log in to the bindery-based server. You can use NWUSER (NetWare User Tools) to accomplish this. Alternatively, you can select the bindery-based server icon. If you are not logged in, the Server Login dialog box appears, enabling you to enter a valid Supervisor or equivalent login name and password.

2. Invoke either NETADMIN from the DOS prompt or NWADMIN from Windows. For the purposes of this illustration, assume the NWADMIN utility from Windows.

3. Select the container in which the bindery-based volume object is located. Press the Insert key to add the volume to this container. You see the New Object dialog box.

4. From the New Object dialog box, select Volume and either click on the OK button or press Enter. You see the Create Volume dialog box appear.

5. From the Create Volume dialog box, enter the following information:

   Volume Name is the NDS name of the volume. This does not have to match the physical name of the volume on the bindery-based server.

   Host Server is the name of the bindery-based server. This must exactly match the server name as specified in the NDS tree.

   Physical Volume is the actual name of the volume as seen on the host server. You can click on the down-arrow button to the right of this field if you are unsure of the name.

   The filled-in dialog box is shown in figure 22.9.

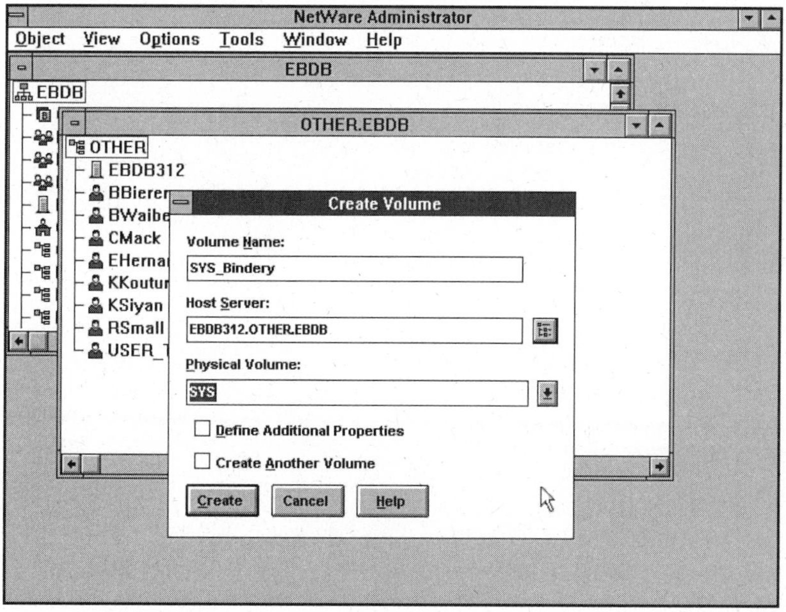

Figure 22.9

Adding a bindery-based volume to the NDS.

6. Click on the Create button when done. You return to the NDS browse screen. The new volume object appears as an NDS object.

Once the volume object has been added, you can select it as with any other NDS volume object. If you double-click on the object, its directory structure appears. You can press Insert to create a new directory, and Delete to remove a directory. Figure 22.10 shows you the directory structure of the bindery-based volume .CN=SYS_Bindery .OU=Other.O=EBDB.

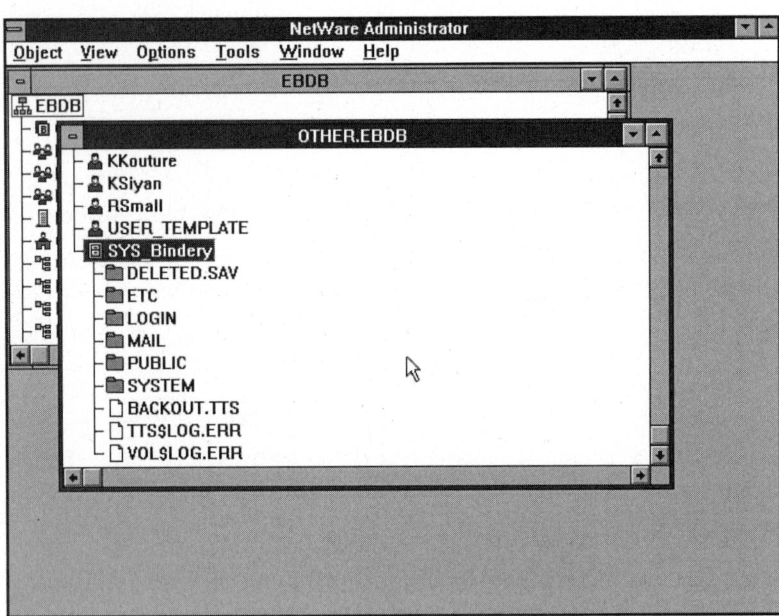

Figure 22.10
Viewing the directory structure of a bindery-based volume from NWADMIN.

You also can view some statistics on the volume by selecting the volume object icon in NWADMIN. The next screen you see is a Volume dialog box with several buttons at the right. Click on the Statistics button to view volume statistics. This screen is shown in figure 22.11.

As you can see from the figure, this volume is only 9 percent full. Out of 195 MB of disk space, 176 MB are available. The block size is 4,096 bytes (4 KB); 64 percent of the allocated directory entries are used; and there are 72 KB of space that could be reclaimed by using the PURGE command (observe the Purgeable Size parameter).

The next section discusses a feature available in NetWare 4.1 that allows more tightly integrated management of NetWare 3.*x* servers from within the NDS tree.

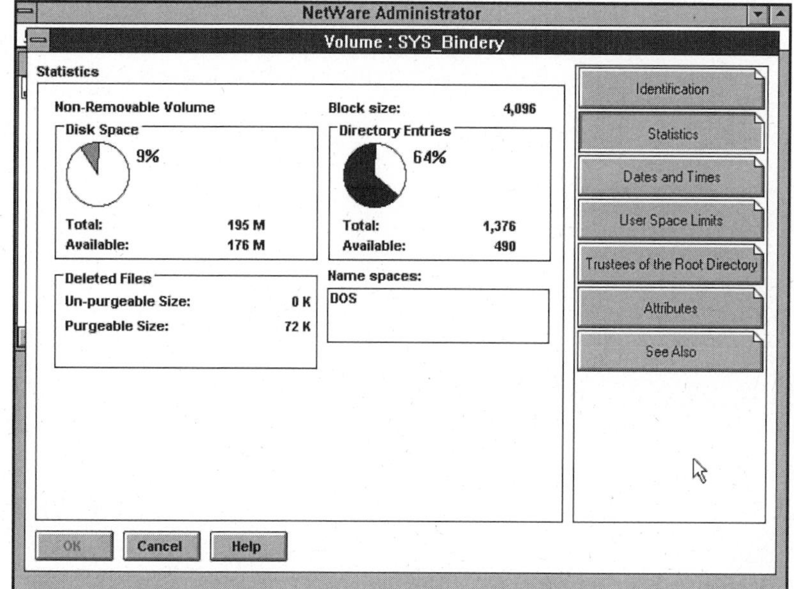

Figure 22.11
Viewing statistics of a bindery-based volume from NWADMIN.

Bindery Synchronization with NetSync

NetWare 4.1 includes a feature called NetSync that can be used to synchronize bindery information between the NDS and the bindery files of a NetWare 3.*x* server. This has an important impact on the network Administrator faced with the daunting task of managing both NetWare 4 and NetWare 3 servers.

As discussed early in the book, the problem with managing large networks that consist of NetWare 3.*x* servers is that each server is an island unto itself. Whenever you make a global change in a NetWare 3.*x* network, you must log in to each server in turn and make the change. When changing login scripts, for example, you would have to make the change for each successive server. This aspect of NetWare 3.*x* increases the amount of tedious management by a factor equal to the number of servers on your network.

For years many NetWare Administrators have been saying to themselves, “Wouldn’t it be nice if I could make a change in one place and have it be duplicated automatically on every server?” Many intermediate products offered tantalizing glimpses of a solution, including NetWare Name Services and Banyan’s Enterprise Management System for NetWare.

The NDS offers the possibility of making management of large, complex networks much easier. The only problem, to date, is that you were required to upgrade your NetWare 3.*x* servers to NetWare 4.*x*. With the advent of NetWare 4.1, the NetSync feature enables you to integrate the bindery files of NetWare 3.*x* servers into the NDS tree.

This section discusses these two NLMs and how to integrate the bindery file of NetWare 3.*x* into the tree.

Many people have characterized NetWare 4 as designed for large, complex networks. Actually, this is not necessarily the case. The disk block suballocation and file compression features alone would prove invaluable to small firms that are fighting for every byte of disk space on the server. In addition, in any network where you have more than two servers, the management capabilities of NetWare 4 make the job of the network Administrator that much easier. The more servers there are, the greater the gap in time required to manage the network between NetWare 3 and NetWare 4.

NetSync Overview

The NetSync feature consists of a series of NLMs, some of which are run on the NetWare 3.*x* servers, and another that is run on the NetWare 4.1 server. It is important to note that this feature supports up to 12 NetWare 3.*x* servers per NetWare 4.1 server. Thus, if you had 20 3.*x* servers, you would need to upgrade two of them to NetWare 4.1 to be able to use NetSync.

NetWare 3.*x* servers that are serviced by the same NetWare 4.1 server using NetSync are referred to as a NetSync Cluster. Once the feature is installed and running, bindery information for all 3.*x* servers in the cluster is managed through the NDS using NDS-based utilities (such as NETADMIN or NWADMIN). Updates to the bindery files of all servers in the cluster are replicated out to each server in the cluster. This way users on one server in the cluster have access to the resources of other servers in the cluster, depending on the security access rights you grant them.

Print servers from the 3.*x* servers in the cluster also are merged into a single print server running on the NetWare 4.1 server. This enables users based on servers in the cluster to access printing resources quickly and easily. In addition, once the print servers have been merged, you can administer printing through NDS-based management utilities (such as NWADMIN or NetWare 4.1 PCONSOLE). NetWare 3.*x* print queues still appear the same to users. The print queues are assigned to the print server on the NetWare 4.1 server acting as a host for the cluster. The installation process copies updated versions of the NetWare 3.*x* printing utilities that are used to allow NetWare 3.*x* users to print through NetSync.

Figure 22.12 gives you a visual image of how NetWare 3.*x* servers are managed using NetSync.

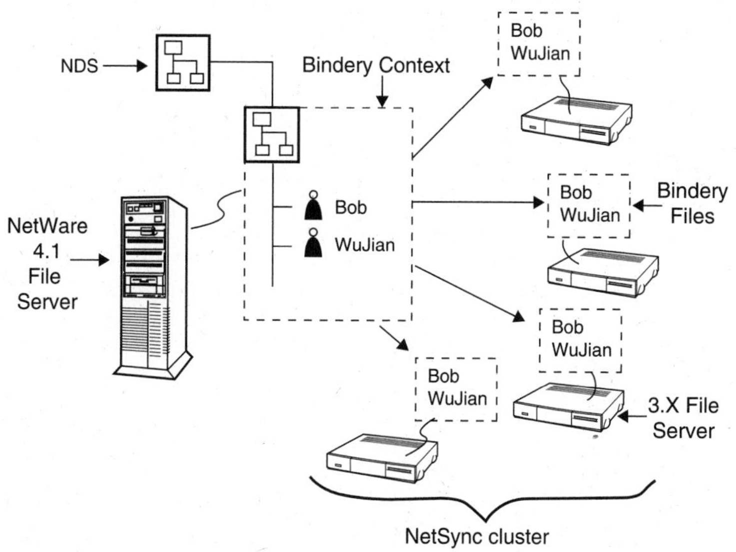

Figure 22.12
Management of a cluster of NetWare 3.x servers using NetSync.

Once the NetSync installation has been completed, the NetWare 3.*x* server dumps the contents of its bindery files onto the NetWare 4.1 server's bindery context in the NDS. Once this update has been completed, there is no need for further updates. All administration of the servers in the cluster should now be done using NDS-based management utilities such as NETADMIN or NWADMIN. Changes automatically are replicated out to the bindery files of the 3.*x* servers in the cluster.

It is possible to have more than one NetWare 4.1 server running NetSync with the same bindery context. If this is the case, all NetWare 4.1 servers, and all the NetWare 3.*x* servers in their NetSync cluster, are tied into one large network.

Table 22.2 summarizes which items are or are not synchronized by NetSync.

Table 22.2
Items Synchronized or Not Synchronized by NetSync

Item	Synchronized?	Description
Users	Yes	Bindery-based users are combined into the NetWare 4.1 server's NDS bindery context.

continues

Table 22.2, Continued
Items Synchronized or Not Synchronized by NetSync

Item	Synchronized?	Description
Passwords	Yes	User passwords are translated into the password property of a user object in the NDS.
Login Scripts	Yes	Login scripts are transferred into the NDS as login script properties.
GUEST	Yes	The user GUEST becomes an NDS user object.
Groups	Yes	All bindery-based groups become NDS groups.
EVERYONE	Yes	An NDS group EVERYONE is created. All users in the NetWare 4.1 server's bindery context are added to this group.
NNS Profiles	Yes	*NetWare Name Service* (NNS) profile login scripts (a profile is a group of servers running NNS) are brought into the NDS as a profile login script.
Account Balances	Yes	Bindery-based user account balances become NDS properties of their respective user objects.
PRINTCON Database	Yes	PRINTCON job configuration templates created on the NetWare 3.*x* server become properties of NDS user objects.
PRINTDEF Database	Yes	The PRINTDEF databases on the NetWare 3.*x* servers become the property of the container object that is the NetWare 4.1 server's bindery context.

Item	Synchronized?	Description
SUPERVISOR	No	The user Supervisor remains as a separate object on each NetWare 3.*x* server in the cluster with a separate and distinct password.
Accounting	No	The accounting system remains server-based. Accounting charge rates remain applicable only to the server in which accounting has been installed and configured.
Illegal Characters	No	NDS object names can be up to 64 characters long and permit any character that can be reproduced on the keyboard (provided you surround them with quotation marks). Any object names with characters not allowed by the bindery are not synchronized.
File System Trustee Rights	No	File system rights continue to be server-based. If you want a user on server FS1 to have rights to the file system on server FS2, you must make the assignment manually.
Home Directories	No	Home directories are not synchronized. If the user has a home directory on one of the 3.*x* servers in the cluster, a like directory is not created on any other server.

A final NetSync consideration is whether any of the NetWare 3.*x* servers to be synchronized are using NetWare Name Services (NNS). If you install NetSync on a NetWare 3.*x* server running NNS, NNS is deactivated (in fact, NNS is uninstalled). This server no longer participates in its previous NNS domain. To maintain NNS synchronization, you should install NetSync on all servers in the NNS domain at the same time. NNS and NetSync are mutually exclusive. You can run either one or the other, but not both.

NetSync Files and Directories

There are three primary NLMs involved in the NetSync process: NETSYNC4, NETSYNC3, and REMAPID. NETSYNC4.NLM runs on the NetWare 4.1 server. This NLM maintains the NetWare 3.*x* servers in its cluster. NETSYNC3.NLM runs on the NetWare 3.*x* server. It reports to NETSYNC4 and receives periodic bindery updates. REMAPID.NLM is responsible for maintaining password synchronization for users between servers in the cluster. All three NLMs should be running continuously on their respective servers for NetSync to work properly.

Other NLMs involved in the NetSync process include a series of updates to existing NLMs on the NetWare 3.*x* servers. The updated NLMs are CLIB.NLM, STREAMS.NLM, AFTER311.NLM (for NetWare 3.12 servers), NWSNUT.NLM, and PBURST.NLM. Another NLM, NWPSRV3X.NLM, is used to merge a NetWare 3.*x* print server into a print server running on the NetWare 4.1 host server.

The NetSync files are located initially on a directory SYS:SYSTEM\NETSYNC on the NetWare 4.1 server. A similar directory is created on all NetWare 3.*x* servers in the cluster during the NetSync installation process. This directory also is used to hold the NetSync log files. Initially, the log file is an ASCII text file named NETSYNC.LOG. The default maximum size is 500 KB. When the log file fills up, it is copied to a file NETSYNC.OLD, and a new NETSYNC.LOG file is started.

Although not covered during the installation process, it is recommended that you replace the NetWare 3.*x* LOGIN.EXE, MAP.EXE, and SETPASS.EXE utilities with the corresponding NetWare 4.1 program files. Make a subdirectory on each of the NetWare 3.*x* servers and copy the NetWare 3.*x* version of these utilities. Next, copy the NetWare 4.1 versions to the SYS:PUBLIC directory on each of the 3.*x* servers. This way user names created in the NetWare 4.1 environment that do not translate properly into the NetWare 3.*x* environment do not present a problem when the user wants to log in or access network resources. The primary place you see such problems is when creating a NetWare 4.1 user with a special character (such as an umlaut, used in several of the Scandinavian and European languages).

The Duplicate Name Problem

Prior to starting the installation of NetSync, you must review the bindery files of each server in the cluster to determine if there are duplicate names. Each bindery object becomes an object in the NDS tree. All objects reside in the same container—the bindery context container of the host NetWare 4.1 server. NDS does not allow duplicate object names in the same container.

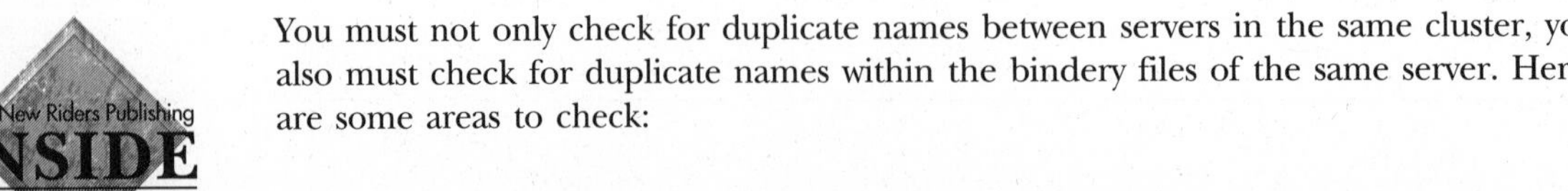

You must not only check for duplicate names between servers in the same cluster, you also must check for duplicate names within the bindery files of the same server. Here are some areas to check:

- Duplicate user and group names
- File server names that duplicate other bindery names
- Print queue names that duplicate other bindery names
- Volume names that duplicate other bindery names
- Duplicate names of any type between servers

If duplicate names are found between servers, the first server to be synchronized creates the NDS object. When the second server is synchronized, any duplicates in its bindery files are not created as NDS objects. If the duplication is deliberate, this might not be a problem. You might have servers Dallas and St_Louis where a user George needs access to both. Prior to installing NetSync, you might have created a user George on both servers to give one user access to both servers. When Dallas is synchronized, the user George is created in the NDS tree. When St_Louis is synchronized, the user George is ignored. On the other hand, if there is a user Sales on server Dallas, and a group Sales on server St_Louis, the user object Sales is created, and the group object Sales is not. That can cause a problem.

The duplicate name problem is compounded when there are multiple server bindery contexts. As mentioned earlier, you can place more than one container in the bindery context. NetSync does not allow duplicate object names to be seen. The reason behind this is that NetSync treats the server's bindery context as if it were a huge bindery file. The rules governing bindery files apply: you cannot have duplicate object names of the same type in the bindery files. Take the situation where the server has containers OU=Sales and OU=Accounting. In Sales there is a user RJones for Rick Jones. In Accounting there is a user RJones for Robert Jones. Suppose you place both containers into the server's bindery context as follows (assuming both containers are under the organization O=EBDB):

```
SET BINDERY CONTEXT = OU=Sales.O=EBDB; OU=Accounting.O=EBDB
```

When NetSync is installed, both containers are visible to all 3.*x* servers in the cluster. However, NetSync scans the containers in a serial fashion, starting with the first container. In this case, the first container is OU=Sales. This is the user .RJones.Sales.EBDB (Rick Jones). The user .RJones.Accounting.EBDB (Robert Jones) is invisible. Thus when Robert Jones goes to log in to one of the 3.*x* servers in the cluster, he ends up with the rights of Rick Jones and does not have rights to his own files and directories.

The only solution currently available is to review the bindery files and the server bindery context carefully. Ensure that there are no unintentional duplicate names. Be aware of the order in which the servers are synchronized. You also must be aware of the order in which containers are added to the server's bindery context.

Installing NetSync

The NetSync installation procedure is relatively simple. It consists of loading the NETSYNC4.NLM module on the host NetWare 4.1 server and authorizing NetWare 3.*x* servers. During the authorization process, NETSYNC3.NLM and updated NLMs are copied to the NetWare 3.*x* server. You then load NETSYNC3.NLM on the NetWare 3.*x* server. When NETSYNC3 first comes up, it transfers the contents of its bindery files to the NetWare 4.1 host. Once this process is complete, the NetWare 3.*x* server is synchronized with the NDS.

Here is a detailed look at the installation process:

1. From the NetWare 4.1 server's console (or using the RCONSOLE.EXE utility), load NETSYNC4.NLM as follows:

   LOAD NETSYNC4

   The NetSync Authorized 3.1*x* Servers menu appears as shown in figure 22.13.

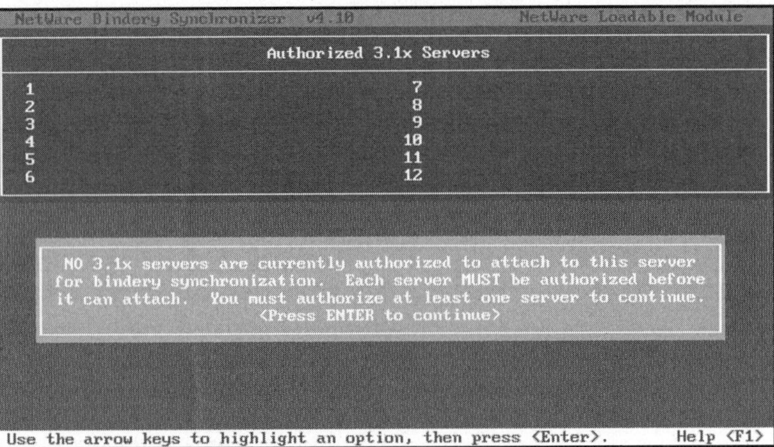

Figure 22.13
NetSync menu as seen from the NetWare 4.1 server console.

2. From the Authorized 3.1*x* Servers menu, press Enter to authorize NetWare 3.1*x* servers. The space for the first server is highlighted, and the NetSync Options menu appears. This menu is discussed in more detail later in the chapter.

3. From the Authorized 3.1*x* Servers menu, select a number from 1 to 12 to use for the server you plan to authorize. Press Enter to begin the authorization process. The Authorized Server Information input box appears, as shown (filled in), in figure 22.14.

4. From the Authorized Server Information input box, enter the following information:

3.1x File Server Name is the name of the NetWare 3.1*x* server you plan to add to the NetSync cluster.

NetSync Password is a password used for communications between the 3.1*x* server and the 4.1 host. This is not a user password. Do not use the SUPERVISOR or ADMIN password, due to possible security problems.

Install Files on 3.1x Server should be set to Yes if you want to have NetSync transfer files automatically to the 3.1*x* server. If you do not select this option, you must install the files on the 3.1*x* server manually.

Copy 3.1x Bindery to 4.1 should be set to YES to cause the NetWare 3.1*x* server to dump the contents of its bindery into the 4.1 server's bindery context.

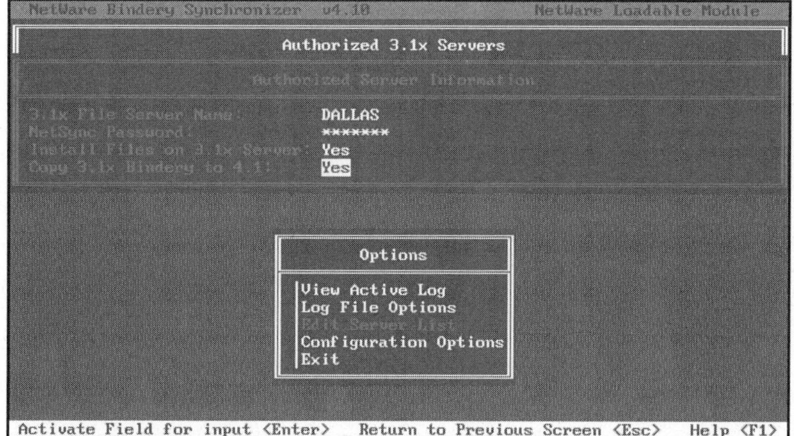

Figure 22.14
NetSync Authorized Server Information input box.

5. When you are finished with the Authorized Server Information input box, press Esc to continue with the installation. A warning message appears, notifying you that you must supply a user name and password. This user must have at least Read, Write, Modify, and Delete trustee rights to the NetWare 3.1*x* server's SYS:SYSTEM directory.

6. After you have supplied a valid user name and password with sufficient rights, you return to the Authorized 3.1*x* Servers menu. At the bottom of the screen you see displayed a list of files as they are copied to the 3.1*x* server (assuming you set the Install Files on 3.1*x* Server option to Yes).

7. After the file copy is completed, you see a warning message indicating that the 3.1*x* server's AUTOEXEC.NCF file will be modified. The command LOAD NETSYNC3 is added to ensure synchronization whenever this server is restarted. Press Enter to continue.

8. Next, you should see a message indicating a successful installation. It is recommended that you restart the 3.1*x* server, because certain NLMs have been updated.

9. The AUTOEXEC.NCF file of the host 4.1 server is updated next to ensure that the NETSYNC4.NLM module is loaded.

10. When these operations have been successfully completed, the NetWare 3.1*x* server appears on the list in the Authorized 3.1*x* Servers menu.

When you first restart the NetWare 3.1*x* server with the NetSync NLMs loaded, you need to configure the name of the NetWare 4.1 host server needed to synchronize. The initial synchronization request screen you see when first restarting the 3.1*x* server is shown in figure 22.15.

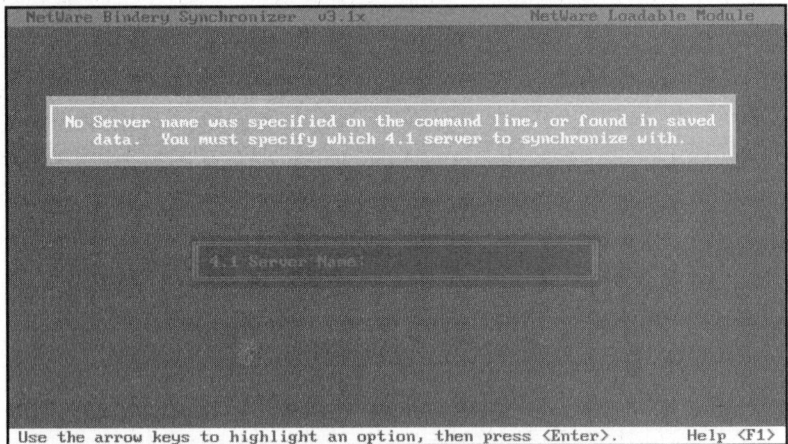

Figure 22.15 *Initial synchronization request screen on the 3.1*x *server.*

Enter the name of the NetWare 4.1 host server and the password defined earlier for communications between the 3.1*x* and 4.1 servers. You see the NetWare Bindery Synchronizer screen, as shown in figure 22.16.

Manually Installing NetSync on the 3.1*x* File Server

Manual installation of NetSync involves two steps:

- Preparing the installation disk
- Performing the installation on the 3.1*x* server

To manually install NetSync, proceed as follows:

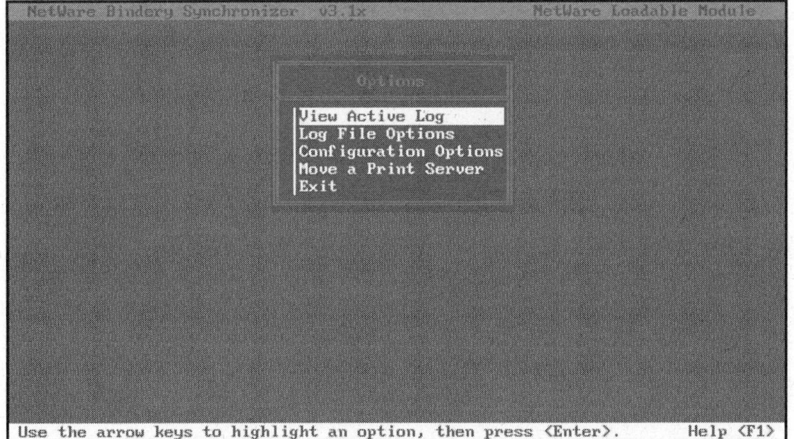

Figure 22.16
*NetWare Bindery Synchronizer screen on the 3.1*x *server.*

1. Log in to any NetWare 4.1 server as a user with at least Read and File Scan rights to the SYS:SYSTEM directory.

2. Change to the SYS:SYSTEM\NETSYNC directory.

3. Run the batch file to prepare the installation disk as follows:

   MAKEDISK A:

   This batch file copies the NetSync files to disk.

4. From the NetWare 3.1*x* server console, load the INSTALL utility as follows:

   LOAD INSTALL

5. From the INSTALL utility menu, select the Product Options menu. You see an Installed Products list. Any additional Novell products (such as NetWare NFS or NetWare for SAA) are listed. Press Insert to add NetSync to the list.

6. You are prompted to insert the disk prepared in Step 3. INSTALL reads the installation script on the disk and installs all necessary files.

7. When this process is completed, exit INSTALL and restart the server.

Resynchronizing Bindery Files and Other Maintenance

You can perform a limited number of maintenance tasks from the NETSYNC menu on the NetWare 4.1 server. These include the following:

- Viewing the Activity Log
- Setting Log File options

- ◆ Editing the Server List
- ◆ Setting Configuration options

The maintenance options are available from the main menu of the NETSYNC4 module. The Active Log option enables you to view activity that occurs pertaining to bindery synchronization. A typical screen is illustrated in figure 22.17.

```
NetWare Bindery Synchronizer  v4.10                    NetWare Loadable Module

09/18/94 15:50:39  **  EBDB312 Bindery Update Queued  **
AddObjectToSet, Name: EVERYONE, Prop: GROUP_MEMBERS, Mem: SUPERVISOR

09/18/94 15:51:38   **  Directory Event  **
VALCHG:  Name = EVERYONE, Prop = GROUP_MEMBERS

09/18/94 15:51:38  **  EBDB312 Bindery Update Queued  **
AddObjectToSet, Name: EVERYONE, Prop: GROUP_MEMBERS, Mem: SUPERVISOR

09/18/94 15:51:38   **  Directory Event  **
VALADD:  Name = EVERYONE, Prop = GROUP_MEMBERS

09/18/94 15:51:38  **  EBDB312 Bindery Update Queued  **
CreateProperty, Name: EVERYONE, Prop: GROUP_MEMBERS, Security: 31

09/18/94 15:51:38   **  Directory Event  **
VALADD:  Name = EVERYONE, Prop = GROUP_MEMBERS

09/18/94 15:51:38  **  EBDB312 Bindery Update Queued  **
AddObjectToSet, Name: EVERYONE, Prop: GROUP_MEMBERS, Mem: SUPERVISOR
Return to Options menu <Esc>                                         Help <F1>
```

Figure 22.17
NETSYNC4 options—Viewing the Active Log.

As you can see from the figure, this option displays the contents of the SYS:SYSTEM\NETSYNC\NETSYNC.LOG file. Each entry is date- and timestamped. In addition, the event is labeled and surrounded by asterisks (**). The second line of each entry contains the action (referring to the C++ language function called) and object and property information.

The Log File Options menu offers you the choices summarized in table 22.3.

TABLE 22.3
NETSYNC4 Log File Options

Option	Description
View Log File History	Press Enter to view the entire NETSYNC.LOG file. The View Active Log option shows you only events that are occurring right now.
Enable Log File	Set this to No if you do not want to have the system log synchronization activity. This might be the case if you want to minimize server activity or are short of disk space. The default is Yes.

Option	Description
Delete Current Log File	Set to Yes to erase the contents of NETSYNC.LOG, allowing the system to start again. The default is No.
Show All Events on LogScreen	Set to No to log only major events or errors. The default of Yes logs all bindery synchronization events.
Maximum Size of Log File	Sets the maximum size of the log file in bytes. You need to have at least twice this amount of disk space due to the OLD log filecreated after the current log file reaches maximum size.

The Configuration Options menu enables you to set configuration parameters. If you set Delete NetSync Configuration Data to Yes, the system returns to its defaults. Deleting NetSync configuration data requires that you reauthorize all 3.1*x* servers in the NetSync cluster.

The Watchdog Delay Interval is the maximum amount of communication time between the NetWare 4.1 host server and 3.1*x* servers in its NetSync cluster. The default is 300 seconds (5 minutes). If a 3.1*x* server does not respond within this interval, NETSYNC4 retries several more times within the next interval. If there is still no response, the connection to that server is terminated and it receives no more bindery updates until it comes back up. The Watchdog Delay Interval can be set from 30 seconds to 18 hours.

When you set the Synchronize Login Script Updates to Mail Dir option to Yes, a connection is made between the NDS login script and the login script file stored in the bindery user's directory under SYS:MAIL. When users log in using the NETX shell, the user login script in SYS:MAIL is executed (if it exists). If the user logs in using the VLM shell, the login script from the NDS user login script property is used. If you have users who change between shells or want to keep the two types of login scripts up to date, set this parameter to Yes. If you have no users using the NETX shell, set this to No to save processing time.

Note For help on any parameter in the NETSYNC4 menus, press Enter as if you plan to edit the field. Once the cursor appears in the field, press the F1 key. Context-sensitive help appears for that field.

To resynchronize the bindery files of a 3.1*x* server, you can reload NETSYNC3 on the 3.1*x* server. You also can force resynchronization from the console of the NetWare 4.1 host server. To do so, proceed as follows:

1. From the host NetWare 4.1 server's console, access the NETSYNC4 menu.
2. From the NETSYNC4 menu, select Edit Server List. The cursor moves to the top of the screen where the 12 servers in the NetSync cluster are listed.
3. Locate the server you want to update, and press Enter. The Authorized Server Information screen appears.
4. From the Authorized Server Information screen, change the Copy 3.1*x* Bindery to 4.1 field to Yes. Press Esc to save the change. This causes the 3.1*x* server to dump the contents of its bindery files to the 4.1 host.
5. Press Esc twice to return to the main menu. You can select View Active Log to confirm that the copy is taking place.

Managing Printing Between 3.1*x* and 4.1 Servers

The synchronization process does not update printing objects. Users on the NetWare 3.1*x* servers can print as usual by sending jobs to their usual print queues. The print servers running in the NetWare 3.1*x* environment continues to function as before. The disadvantage of this arrangement is that you lose the central management ability offered by the NDS. To manage printing from a single location, you need to merge the functions of the 3.1*x* print servers into a print server running on the 4.1 host server. This process then points the queues on the 3.1*x* servers to the print server on the 4.1 host server.

To merge printing, proceed as follows:

1. Log in to the NetWare 4.1 host server as a user with at least Browse and Create rights to the server's bindery context containers. You also must have access to the console of the 3.1*x* server whose printing objects you want to merge. You can execute the next steps physically located on the 3.1*x* server or by using the RCONSOLE.EXE utility.
2. From the console of the 3.1*x* server, select the NETSYNC3 menu shown in figure 22.18.

   Note that this menu is similar to that of NETSYNC4 located on the 4.1 host server.
3. From the NETSYNC3 menu, select Move a Print Server. You see a list of print servers defined on this server. Choose the desired print server to merge, and press Enter. If there is only one print server, you are asked to confirm the name of a print server.

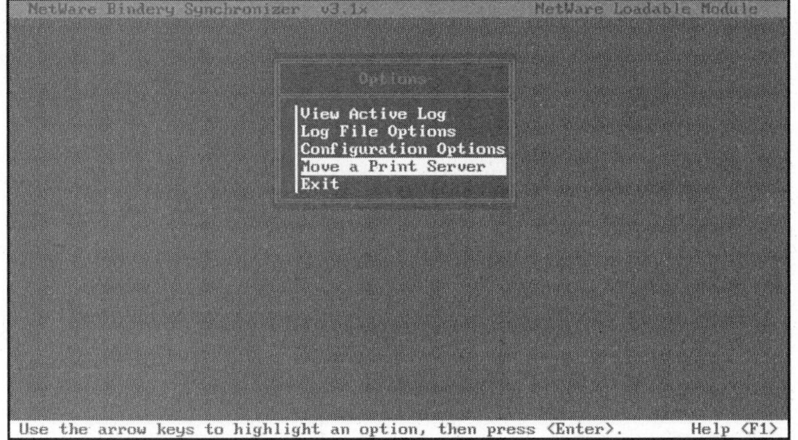

Figure 22.18
*The NETSYNC3 menu on a 3.1*x *server in the NetSync cluster.*

4. After supplying the name of the print server, press Enter to confirm the name. The print server is now merged into the printing environment on the host 4.1 server. Figure 22.19 shows you the activity log after the print merge activity has taken place.

```
NetWare Bindery Synchronizer  v3.1x                NetWare Loadable Module

09/19/94 19:05:25  **  EBDB Bindery Update Queued  **
Moving Print Server data for 312_PS (0 bytes) to 312_PS on EBDB
Completed SUCCESSFULLY

09/19/94 19:05:25   **  Status  **
EBDB bindery update request(s) processing complete.

09/19/94 19:05:25   **  Status  **
Received bindery update request.

09/19/94 19:05:25  **  EBDB Bindery Update Completed  **
CreateProperty, Name: 312_Q, Prop: Q_OPERATORS, Security: 21
Failed, status = 0100 (Property or value already exists)

09/19/94 19:05:25  **  EBDB Bindery Update Completed  **
AddObjectToSet, Name: 312_Q, Prop: Q_OPERATORS, Mem: 312_PS
Completed SUCCESSFULLY

09/19/94 19:05:25   **  Status  **
EBDB bindery update request(s) processing complete.
Return to Options menu <Esc>                                    Help <F1>
```

Figure 22.19
*NetSync log after merging a print server from 3.1*x *to 4.1.*

After the print merge has taken place, you must connect the imported printing objects as suits your situation. By going into NWADMIN (from Windows) or PCONSOLE (from the DOS prompt), you see that all the print queues and printers associated with the imported print server appear in the 4.1 server's bindery context. In addition, you see a special print queue object, as shown in figure 22.20.

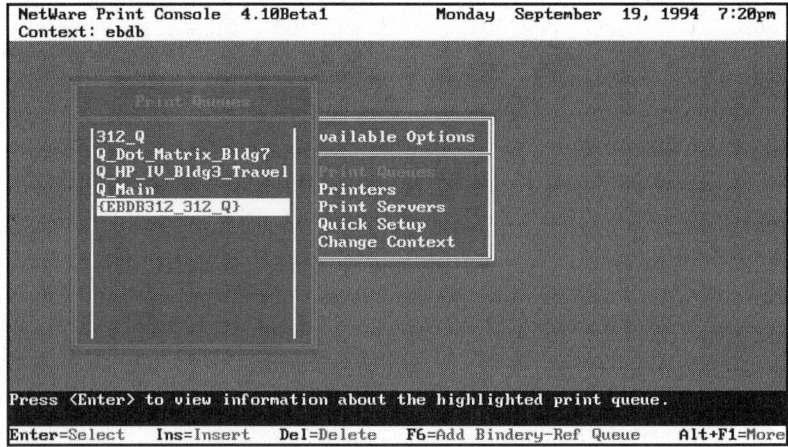

Figure 22.20
Imported print queues as seen in PCONSOLE.EXE.

As you can see from the figure, there are two print queue objects created from each 3.1*x* bindery-based print queue. The first object is 312_Q. This print queue physically resides on the 4.1 server. The other print queue object, {EBDB312_312_Q}, represents the same queue but physically resides on the 3.1*x* server. Both queues automatically are connected to the 3.1*x* printer object to which the original queue was assigned.

The only remaining task to complete the printing environment is to associate the imported 3.1*x* printer object to a 4.1 print server. The import utility does not know with which print server you want to connect this printer, and leaves this task to you. Select the desired print server and add the printer to the list. You are now ready to resume printing. NetWare 3.1*x* users on any of the servers in the NetSync cluster should notice no change in performance. If anything, they should notice an improvement, since the print server process in NetWare 4.1 has been greatly enhanced over that of NetWare 3.1*x*.

Note If you are using direct printer interfaces, for example the HP IVsi with a built-in Ethernet interface, performing the merge process is recommended, but associating the printer with a NetWare 4.1 print server is not.

Managing the Super Bindery Using NDS Utilities

When you install NetSync on a host 4.1 server and a cluster of NetWare 3.1*x* servers, the 3.1*x* servers dump the contents of their bindery files into the NDS database residing on the 4.1 server. The location of the 3.1*x* bindery objects is the 4.1 server's bindery context. This becomes a sort of *super bindery*.

NetWare 3.1*x* Administrators who are interested in the centralized management abilities inherent to NetWare 4 economically can have the best of both worlds by upgrading 1 server in 12 to NetWare 4.1. By installing NetSync on all servers, the NetWare 3.1*x* Administrator can manage all servers using NetWare 4.1 utilities.

All objects in the super bindery become visible to users of the NetWare 3.1*x* servers. Access to resources can be granted through appropriate assignment of both NDS and file system trustee rights. Any changes made to objects in the super bindery are replicated out to all 3.1*x* servers in the cluster.

There are few limits to the number of 3.1*x* servers whose binderies can be pooled. The only rule is that there must be one 4.1 host server running NETSYNC4 for every twelve 3.1*x* servers running NETSYNC3. Aside from this limit, there also is the practical limit of how many objects you want to manage in a single context. Experience suggests keeping the object count to under 3,000. Novell suggests a conservative limit of 1,000 objects.

Management of the super bindery is done through any NDS-based utility. From the DOS prompt you can use NETADMIN or PCONSOLE. From the Windows environment you can use NWADMIN.

It is important to note that objects imported from the bindery files of servers in the NetSync cluster are bona fide NDS objects. They can be treated like any other NDS object. The only restriction is that these objects must reside only in the 4.1 host server's bindery context. If you move an imported object, it disappears from the bindery files of the 3.1*x* servers in the cluster.

Do not manage NetWare 3.*x* servers using bindery-based utilities (such as SYSCON) after NetSync is installed and running. No damage or harm comes from using a bindery-based utility; however, any changes made to a server's bindery using a bindery-based utility are to be synchronized. This might cause a problem when attempting to debug a network access problem.

Figure 22.21 shows you a view of the super bindery maintained by the server .CN=EBDB.O=EBDB. In this example, the server's bindery context has been set to .OU=NY.O=EBDB. To view the super bindery, simply change contexts to the OU=NY container.

You can create a user just as if you were creating any other NDS user. A user created in the host 4.1 server's bindery context automatically appears in the bindery files of all 3.1*x* servers in the NetSync cluster.

Figure 22.22 shows the process of creating a user .CN=RSmall.OU=NY.O=EBDB using NWADMIN. The server's bindery context is set to OU=NY.O=EBDB.

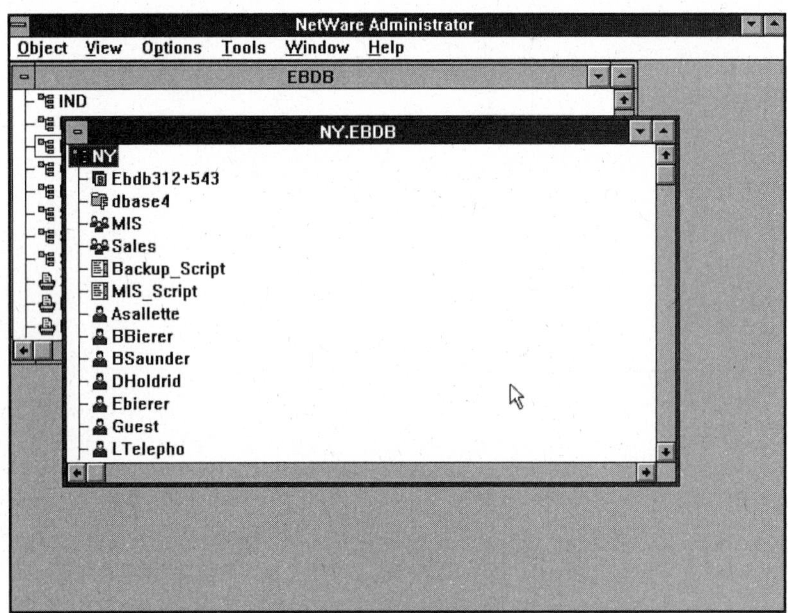

Figure 22.21

A sample super bindery as seen in NWADMIN.EXE.

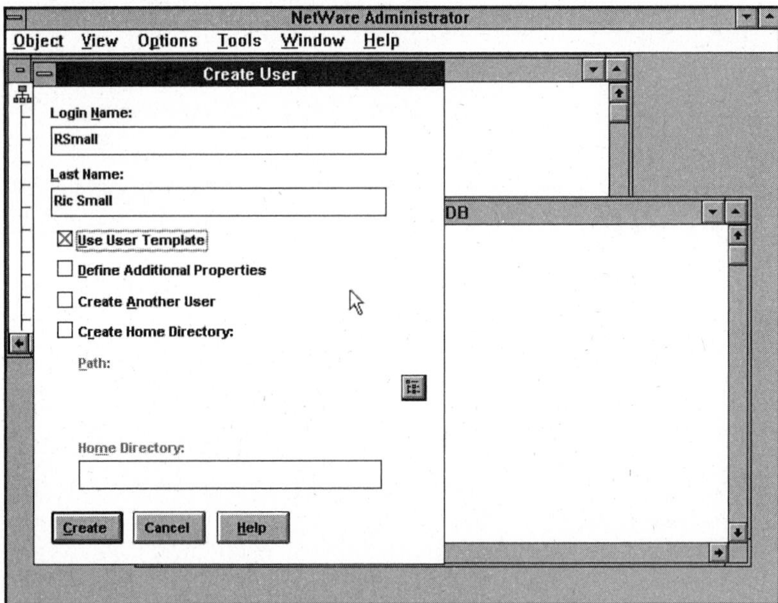

Figure 22.22

Creating a user RSmall using NWADMIN.

Figure 22.23 shows a view of SYSCON taken from the NetWare 3.12 server EBDB312, which is in the NetSync cluster of the NetWare 4.1 server EBDB.

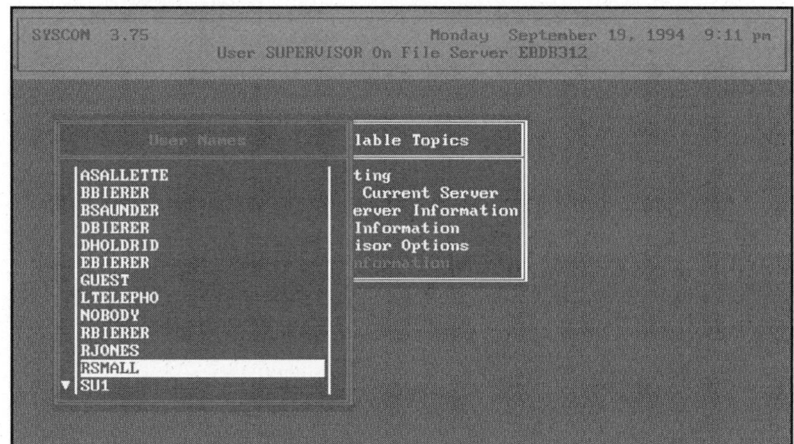

Figure 22.23
View of SYSCON from a NetWare 3.12 server in the NetSync cluster.

Note You must allow enough time for the synchronization to take place. If unsure, check the Watchdog Delay Interval from the NETSYNC3 or NETSYNC4 Configuration Options menu. This represents the maximum amount of time the synchronization process is allowed to take. In most cases the synchronization takes place as fast as an ordinary NDS update (generally within 60 seconds).

Creating a home directory for the user on a 3.1*x* server is more involved than just creating the user. To create a home directory for a user on a 3.1*x* server, proceed as follows:

1. You need to add the server to the NDS as outlined in the previous section "Adding a Bindery-Based NetWare Server to the Tree."

2. In addition, you need to add the 3.1*x* server's volumes as NDS objects.

3. Now you can select the volume object and manually make a directory for the user.

4. Assign the user directory trustee rights to the newly created directory.

As you can see in figure 22.24, the server EBDB312, its volume SYS (labeled SYS_Bindery in the figure), and the user RSmall are located in the super bindery (OU=NY.O=EBDB). The directory SYS:USERS\RSMALL has been created manually.

Directory trustee rights that include all possible rights are assigned to the user RSmall in the directory SYS:USERS\RSMALL using the NWADMIN utility, as shown in figure 22.25.

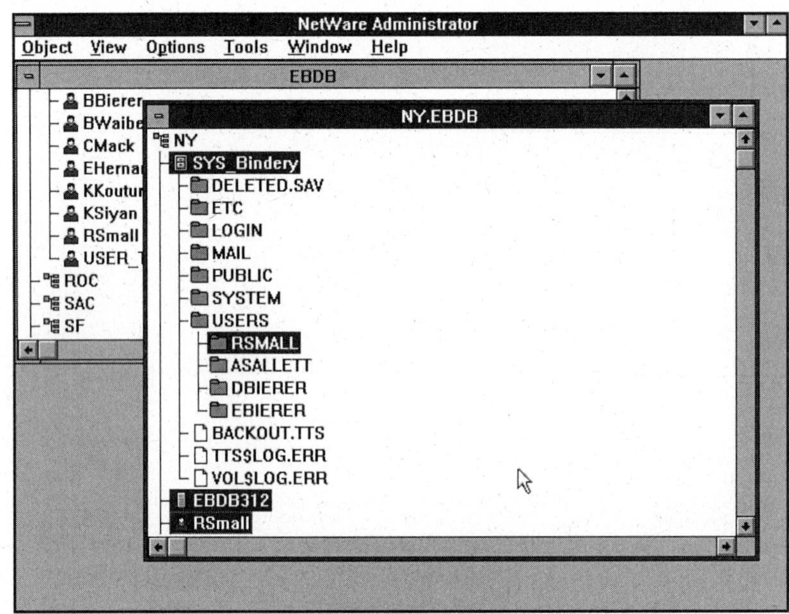

Figure 22.24

A view of the super bindery OU=NY.O=EBDB showing user and home directory.

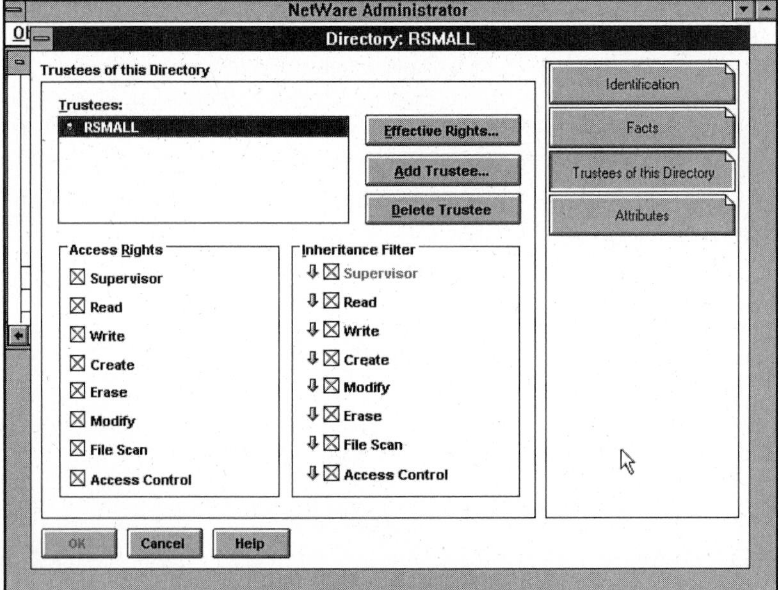

Figure 22.25

Assigning directory trustee rights for the home directory to the user.

Figure 22.26 shows a view of SYSCON on server EBDB312 showing the directory trustee rights of user RSMALL. As you can see from the figure, the rights administered from NWADMIN, an NDS-based utility, are replicated to the bindery of the 3.1*x* server EBDB312.

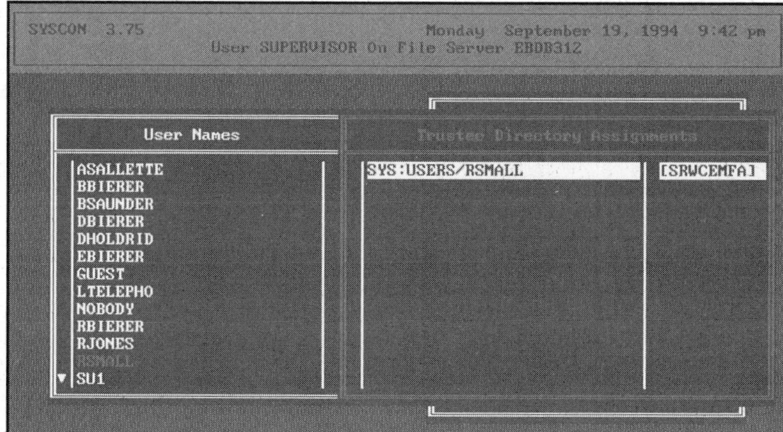

Figure 22.26

*Viewing directory trustee rights from SYSCON on the 3.1*x *server.*

Summary

This chapter covered various aspects of bindery services. The first part of the chapter covered how to set the server's bindery context. As you learned, you use the SET BINDERY CONTEXT server console command. Up to 16 NDS containers can be included in the bindery context as long as their names are separated by a semicolon (;). All containers are then viewed as a single bindery file to bindery-based clients.

As you learned, the NDS contexts are searched sequentially, so if there is a duplicate name in two or more containers in the bindery context only the first name is used.

It is necessary to have a physical partition stored on the servers you plan to use for bindery services. You learned how to use the PARTMGR.EXE utility to view the partitions on any given server.

Once bindery services has been set up, the NetWare 4 server acts like a NetWare 3 server from the client's viewpoint.

You then learned how you can manage NetWare 2 and NetWare 3 servers from NDS-based utilities by simply adding server objects where the name matches the actual name of the server. You also can add volume objects referencing the NetWare 2 or 3 servers. Limited viewing of statistics and management then can be performed using either the NETADMIN or NWADMIN utilities.

This chapter also gave you a brief overview of the accounting system.

The last part of this chapter covered bindery synchronization using the NetSync NLMs. The NetSync process enables you to manage the bindery files of NetWare 3 servers through NDS-based utilities. NETSYNC4.NLM is loaded on a NetWare 4.1 server that acts as a host to up to 12 NetWare 3 servers running NETSYNC3.NLM. This arrangement is referred to as a NetSync Cluster.

The bindery context of the NetWare 4.1 host server receives the contents of all binderies of the NetWare 3 servers in the cluster. Any changes made to the bindery context NDS container are then replicated out to the NetWare 3 servers in the cluster.

You also can merge printing objects on the NetWare 3 servers into a print server running on the NetWare 4 host. Print queue and printer objects are created in the host server's bindery context. You then can attach the printer objects to a print queue located on the host 4.1 server or on the original NetWare 3 server.

The next chapter covers how to merge NDS trees located in different NetWare 4 servers.

Merging Trees

NetWare 4.1 is the first version of NetWare to offer the ability to merge two NDS trees together. This feature was available in the Beta version of NetWare 4.0. The utility used to perform the merge, DSMERGE.NLM, was even documented in the original documentation set for NetWare 4.0. The utility had to be pulled from the final shipping version of the product, however, due to a variety of difficulties. It is not until version 4.1 was released that this utility was re-introduced.

The ability to merge NDS trees solves an enormous number of problems and greatly frees companies to convert existing networks to NetWare 4. Novell's original strategy was that corporations were to spend an amount of time designing their trees after which they were to upgrade all servers to NetWare 4. As you can imagine, this approach was naive at best. Very few companies were in a position to design and upgrade their entire enterprise network in one smooth, integrated transition. The reality was that different departments planned to upgrade at entirely different times. Also, there was very little agreement between departments in most companies over exactly how to design the master tree for the company. Political squabbles developed over who was above whom in the hierarchy. The situation quickly disintegrated and NetWare 4, for all of its benefits and features, was put on the shelves. Many departments upgraded anyway, only to discover that they could not merge their independently designed tree with that of a neighboring department.

NetWare 4.1 solves this problem. Now, networks can be designed and implemented independently. When two departments see the need, and have come to agreement, they can merge their two trees. Later, the expanded tree can be merged with that of another department. This process can continue indefinitely, until the entire company has been placed on a single tree.

Why Merge Trees?

One very good question that you must ask yourself during this process is, why merge trees? The answer to this question guides you in the process at your company. The following are two arguments in favor of merging trees:

- The only way to access resources in another tree is through bindery services.
- Once two trees are merged, you can manage the combined structure from a single network login.

The first argument is very compelling. When you have two different trees on the network, you only can be logged in to one at a time. Once logged in to a tree, you have access to any resources within that tree, depending on your trustee rights. If you wish to access resources on a server outside of the tree, you are limited to a bindery services connection only. This means that you only can access resources on servers with their bindery contexts set, and that have replicas of NDS partitions physically stored on them. Through bindery services, you only are able to see resources in the server's bindery context. This places a tremendous limitation on which resources you can use.

The second issue relates to management. When you wish to manage resources in a tree, you must be logged in to the tree as an NDS user. Once logged in, you can manage any resources in the tree depending on your trustee rights. If you want to manage resources on servers in another tree, you must first log in to the other tree. When you log in to one tree, you lose your login connection to the current tree. You can now manage resources on the second tree, but can no longer access resources on the first tree, except through bindery services.

Exploring Merger Considerations

Before getting in to the mechanics of merging NDS trees, you must first gain an understanding of the process as well as some insight in to what must be done before and after the merge. You need to bring together the two groups represented by the

two trees, and hammer out an agreement on the final appearance of the consolidated tree. Another consideration, which may seem minor but can have major political impact, is to decide which tree is to be merged in to the other.

Understanding the Merge Process

The merge process takes the tree on one server, removes the root, and makes it in to a partition. This partition becomes a child partition of the root on another server. All relationships, objects, properties and values within the partition are maintained. This includes object names, container objects, trustee rights, properties, and the structure itself. The old tree becomes a branch of the consolidated tree. The top of the old tree starts off the root of the consolidated tree.

The merge process involves two trees. For the purposes of this section, the tree that is being merged is called the *source tree.* The tree that is receiving the merge is called the *target tree.* The resulting tree after the merge is called the *consolidated tree.* In most cases the source tree is smaller than the target tree. This is not a requirement for the merge.

You must have Supervisor rights to the root object in both trees. During the merge process you are asked to supply valid NDS login names in both trees.

The merge takes place at the [root] of the target tree. Top level organizations of the source tree are placed immediately off the [root] of the target tree. Duplications cannot exist at any one level of an NDS tree. If the source and target contain the same name for an organization container that resides off the root, DSMERGE.NLM asks you to change the name of the source organization object which conflicts with an organization object on the target tree before the merge can take place. You can use either NETADMIN.EXE or NWADMIN.EXE to accomplish the name change.

Figure 23.1 shows you conceptually what the source, target, and consolidated trees look like.

As you can see in the figure, the source tree consists of [root], and organizations EBDB and R&D immediately off the root. EBDB has organizational units 1 and 2. The target tree has organizations Mfg and Acctg immediately off the root. In addition, there is a duplicate organization EBDB with organizational units 1, A, and B. After the merger, the consolidated tree is a combination of the source and target trees. The only difference is that the duplicate organization, EBDB, from the source tree has been renamed to EBDB2. During the merge process, the duplication is noted and you are prompted to make the name change. If you do not wish to change the name, your only other alternative is to move the duplicate container to another level of the tree.

EBDB in the source tree could be moved to become an organizational unit under R&D, for example. Note that duplicate organizational units do not cause a conflict. The main problem is if there are duplicate organization or country objects off the root.

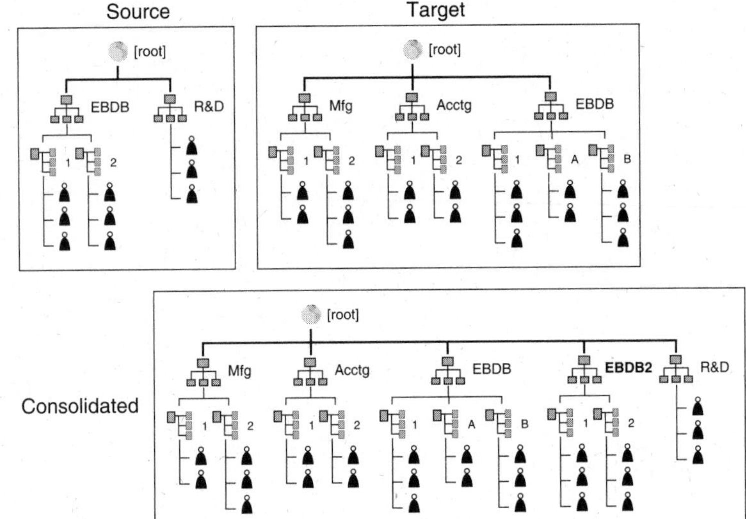

Figure 23.1
A conceptual view of the Source, Target, and Consolidated trees.

Before the Merge

Before the merge can begin, you need to make some decisions, and possibly take certain actions based on these decisions. The considerations before the merge are summarized in the following list:

- Decide how to deal with duplicate organization or country objects off the root of each tree.
- Perform a backup of each NDS tree.
- Rearrange time synchronization so that all servers in both trees have one SINGLE REFERENCE or REFERENCE server for a time source.
- Establish time synchronization in each tree before the merge can begin.
- Rename one of the trees if both have the same name before the merge begins.
- Locate which servers have the Master replica of the root partition for each tree. You need to run DSMERGE.NLM on these servers.

A backup of each NDS tree can be performed using either SBACKUP.NLM or another backup software package which is NDS compatible. Renaming or moving top level organization objects can be accomplished through the NWADMIN.EXE or NETADMIN.EXE utilities.

You must change duplicate names before beginning the merge process. Otherwise, DSMERGE stops the process after phase 1 (described in the following text).

Time synchronization already should be set up on your network. The main problem is that you probably have duplicate Reference or Single Reference servers. In order to properly merge the two trees you should change the time server types so that you have only one Reference or Single Reference time server for both trees. This is accomplished by using the SERVMAN.NLM utility, or by editing the TIMESYNC.CFG file. You need to change the TIME SERVER TYPE parameter. For more information on time synchronization, please refer to Chapter 13, "Upgrades and Other Installation Issues."

You can use the following command prior to the merge operation to force time synchronization:

```
SET TIMESYNC RESTART FLAG = ON
```

The following is an example of the file server console display after time synchronization has been established:

```
EBDB312:SET TIMESYNC RESTART FLAG = ON
TIMESYNC Restart Flag action was SUCCESSFUL.

10-26-94  4:34:06 pm:  TIMESYNC-4.10-138
   Time synchronization has been established.

EBDB312:
```

Any servers where the time server type was changed should then be brought down and back up again. Before beginning the merge process, wait until all servers report that time synchronization has been established. This is a message that appears shortly after a server has been brought up. In the case of a large network with many servers, this process could take upwards of an hour.

Renaming a Tree

If you discover that the two trees you plan to merge have the same name before the merge, you must rename one of the trees. The best choice of tree to rename is the source tree. Please note that under ordinary circumstances, renaming a tree could have a significant impact on your network. In this case, however, because the tree to be renamed disappears into the target tree, this operation has minimal impact on your network.

To rename a tree, proceed as follows:

1. Log in to the source tree as a user with Supervisor object rights to the [root].
2. Use either the PARTMGR.EXE or Partition Manager tools of the NWADMIN.EXE utility to determine which server has the master replica of the root partition. For the purposes of this discussion use NWADMIN.EXE.
3. From Windows, bring up NWADMIN.EXE.
4. From the NWADMIN main menu, select **T**ools, **P**artition Manager. The Partition Manager dialog box appears, as shown in figure 23.2.

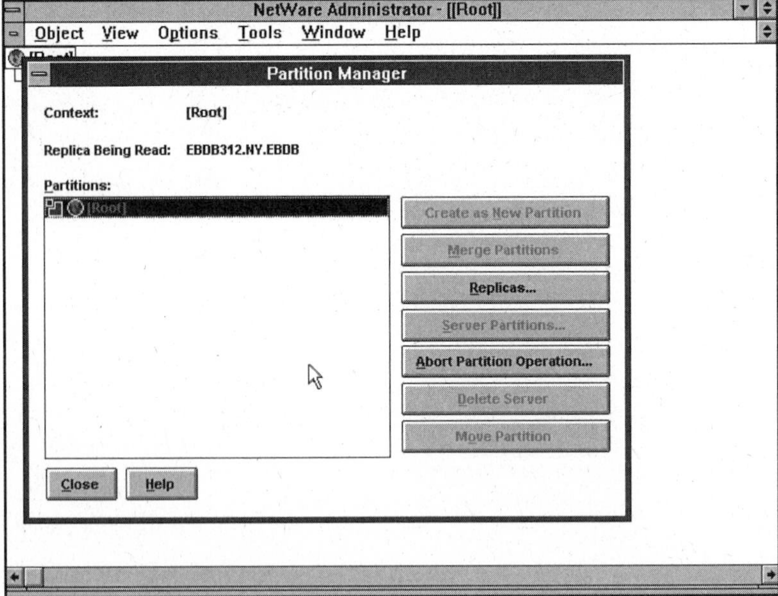

Figure 23.2
The Partition Manager dialog box.

5. From the Partition Manager dialog box, select the **R**eplicas button. The Partition Replicas screen appears, as shown in figure 23.3. Use this screen to view which servers have replicas and of what type. In the figure, you note that server EBDB312 has the Master of the [root] partition.

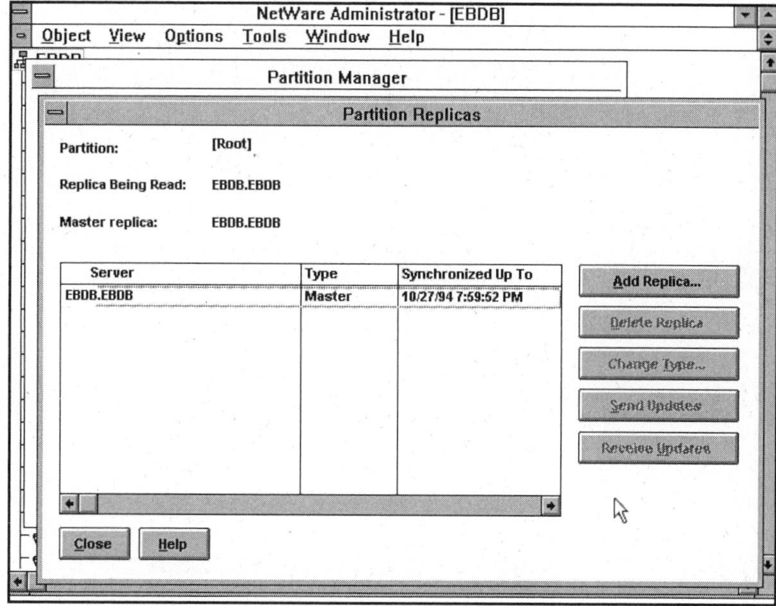

Figure 23.3

The Partition Replicas screen.

6. Select the **C**lose button a couple of times to return to the NWADMIN main screen. Exit the utility.

7. From the DOS prompt, run the RCONSOLE utility and access the file server console of the server with the master of the [root] partition. Alternatively, physically move to that server (if possible).

8. From the console of the server with the master of the [root] partition, load DSMERGE.NLM by typing the following command:

   LOAD DSMERGE

   The DSMERGE Available Options menu appears, as shown in figure 23.4.

9. From the Available Options menu, select Rename This Tree. The Rename Tree Information dialog box appears, as shown in figure 23.5. Enter the name of the user with Supervisor object rights to the [root] along with the appropriate password. At the bottom of this dialog box, you can enter the new name of the tree.

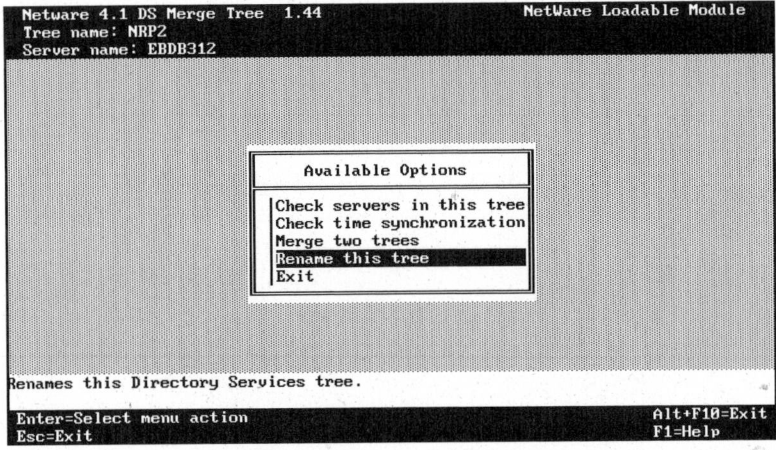

Figure 23.4

The DSMERGE.NLM main menu.

```
Netware 4.1 DS Merge Tree  1.44                          NetWare Loadable Module
Tree name: NRP2
Server name: EBDB312

                          Rename Tree Information

Local tree:               NRP2
Administrator name:       .admin.ebdb
Password:                 ******

New tree name:            NRP3

Enter the full Directory Services path (your complete name context). This user
needs the Supervisor object right to the Root object of this tree.
Enter=Edit this field           F10=Perform rename                 Alt+F10=Exit
Esc=Return to main menu         Down=Next field                    F1=Help
```

Figure 23.5

The Rename Tree Information dialog box.

10. When done filling in the Rename Tree Information dialog box, press the F10 key to perform the tree rename operation. You receive a warning beep along with a message warning you of possible dire consequences. In this situation, however, the renaming of the tree is only temporary. After the merge operation, the name you choose here disappears.

11. From the warning message, press Enter to continue. Select Yes when asked Rename Tree?. DSMERGE updates tree information on all servers in the tree. This process could take some time on a large network, especially if the tree spans a wide area network (WAN). Once completed, you see a message indicating the success of the operation. Press Enter to continue. You return to the main menu of DSMERGE.

After the Merge

After the merge process is complete, there are several housekeeping tasks that should be performed. These include the following:

- Clean up the consolidated NDS tree.
- Revise time server types as needed.
- Verify that all servers in the old trees are now properly represented in the consolidated tree.

The cleanup operation involves moving objects and possibly entire branches of the tree from one container in to another. Referring back to the conceptual view of the source, target, and consolidated trees, shown in figure 23.1, consider that objects from the new EBDB2 container should be moved in to the EBDB container. Once this has been accomplished, the EBDB2 container can be removed.

To move a branch of the tree, proceed as follows:

1. Log in as a user with Supervisor object rights to the source and target containers.
2. From Windows launch NWADMIN. From the main NWADMIN menu, select Tools, Partition Manager. The Partition Manager dialog box appears.
3. From the Partition Manager dialog box, browse through the tree until you find the container you want to move.
4. Once you locate the source container, select the Create as New Partition button. Answer Yes when prompted. This process could take a certain period of time to complete depending on the number of replicas of the parent partition, and what type of network connections you have (i.e. 56 kbps lines cause delays). If necessary, be prepared to wait upwards of an hour for this process to replicate.
5. Reselect the container. You note that it now has the icon for a partition next to it. Select the Move Partition button. The Move dialog box appears, as shown in figure 23.6,. Enter the target container in the Destination field.

   Select the Create Alias in Place of Moved Container option if you wish to retain an alias to make login scripts or other dependent operations workable. Select OK when ready.
6. The Move operation takes place and you are returned to the Partition Manager dialog box. Select Close to exit back to NWADMIN.

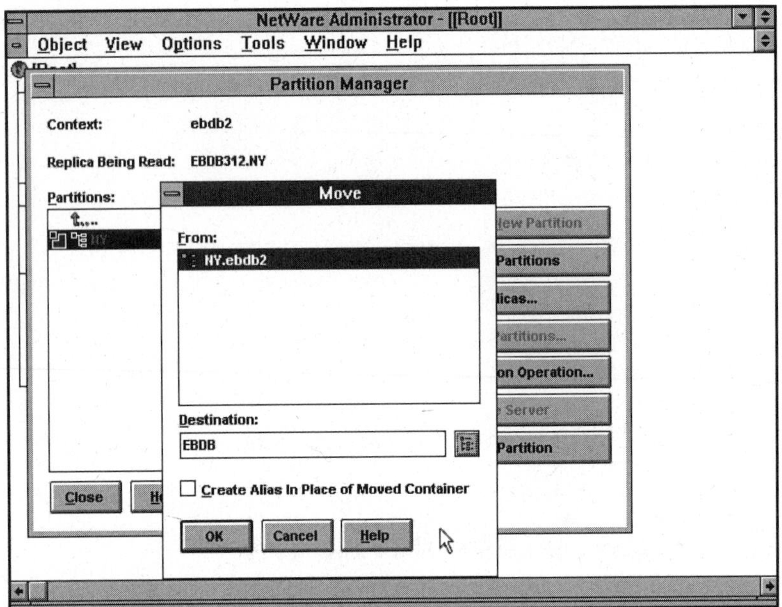

Figure 23.6
The Move dialog box.

Time server type issues should be resolved before you merge trees. After the merge has been accomplished, you may want to make further refinements. You may decide to upgrade some Secondary time servers from the old tree in to Primary time servers, or the other way around. Because the consolidated tree may be substantially larger, you may decide to move away from using SAP to provide time and switch to setting up custom time provider groups. For further information on time synchronization issues, see Chapter 13, "Upgrades and Other Installation Issues."

Another action that should be performed after the merge is ensuring that all servers in the consolidated tree recognize the same tree name. To perform this action, proceed as follows:

1. From the console of the file server that contains the master replica of the consolidated tree, load DSMERGE.NLM by entering the following command:

   LOAD DSMERGE

   The DSMERGE Available Options menu appears.

2. From the Available Options menu, select Check Servers in this Tree. The utility then sends a query to all servers in the tree and checks to see that they have the same tree name.

3. When this operation has completed, a status screen appears, as shown in figure 23.7.

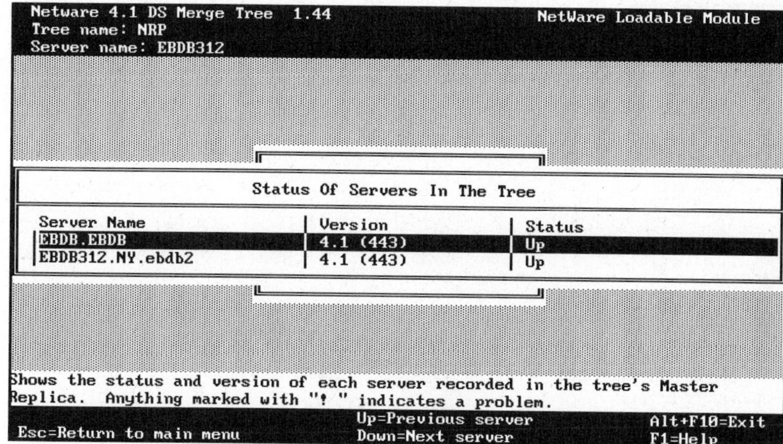

Figure 23.7

The Status Of Servers In The Tree screen.

Merging Trees With DSMERGE

Once all the preliminary tasks have been taken care of, you can perform the merge operation. You need to run DSMERGE.NLM from the console of the file server that contains the Master replica of the source tree. You can use PARTMGR or NWADMIN to locate this server.

To merge NDS trees, proceed as follows:

1. From the console of the file server that contains the Master replica of the consolidated tree, load DSMERGE.NLM by entering the following command:

   LOAD DSMERGE

   The DSMERGE Available Options menu appears.

2. From the DSMERGE Available Options menu, select Merge Two Trees. The Merge Trees Information dialog box appears, as shown in figure 23.8.

   The following fields need to be filled out:

   - Source tree is the name of the tree on the source server.
   - Administrator name is the name of the user with Supervisor object rights to the [root] of the source tree.
   - Password is the password for the Administrator.

- Target tree is the name of the tree the source tree is merged in to.
- Administrator name is the name of the user with Supervisor object rights to the [root] of the target tree.
- Password is the password for the Administrator.

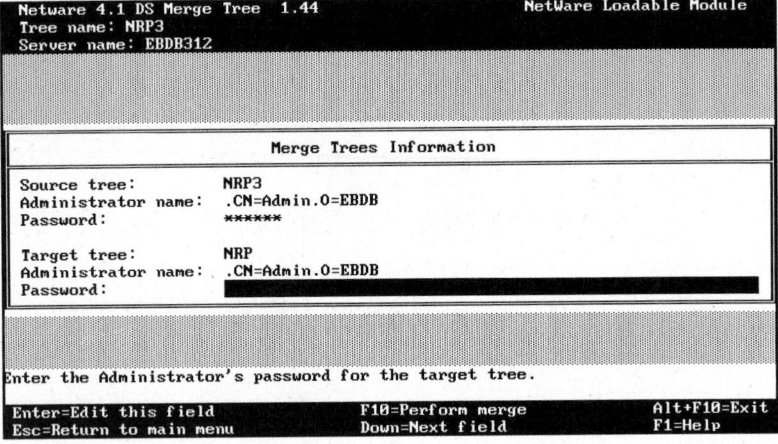

Figure 23.8
The Merge Trees Information dialog box.

3. Once the Merge Trees Information dialog box has been filled in, press F10 to start the merge. A message screen appears telling you about the 4 phases of the merge process. Table 23.1 summarizes these phases.

Table 23.1
The Four Phases of the Merge Trees Process

Phase	Description
Check	Checks both source and target trees for any problems which might prevent a successful merge. Does not change either tree at this point.
Preparation	Prepares the source tree. Changes at this point can be undone should you need to cancel the process and restore the original tree. Changes include the following: Creating separate partitions for each organization or country object off the [root]; All replicas of the [root] partition are deleted except for the Master.

Phase	Description
Merge	DSMERGE modifies the source and target trees so that the Master replica of the [root] of the source tree changes to a Read Write replica of the [root] of the target tree.
Completion	At this point, the process is not reversible. DSMERGE waits for synchronization to occur, and for all servers to recognize the new Read Write replica of the [root].

4. Press Enter a couple of times to get past the informative screen. DSMERGE proceeds with phase 1. Once you have moved successfully past phase 1, a dialog box appears asking you if you want to proceed and merge trees. This dialog box, along with the background screen for phase 1 is shown in figure 23.9.

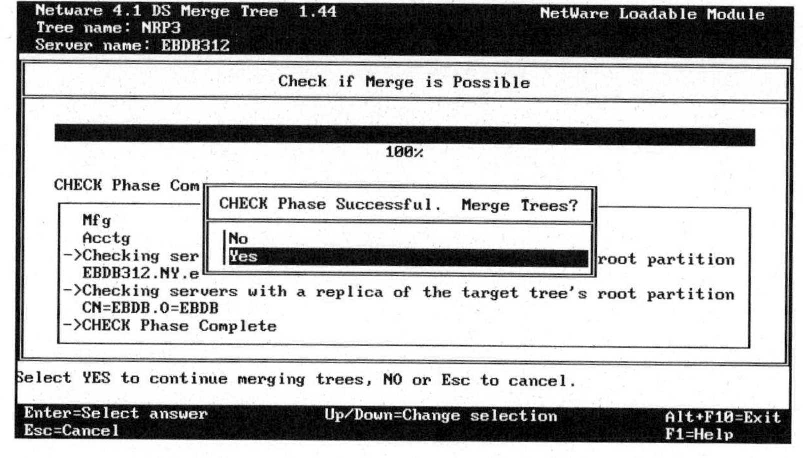

Figure 23.9

Phase 1 screen and prompt for next phase.

5. Select Yes to continue. The merge process continues. Server addresses are collected, and other information is processed. Upon completion of the operation, a message box indicating Merge Complete appears. Press Enter to continue. You are returned to the DSMERGE Available Options menu.

6. From the DSMERGE Available Options menu, select Check Servers in this Tree. This option verifies that all servers in the tree agree on the new tree name. If all servers report a status of UP, you are done and the operation was successful.

   If you do not see all servers, or the status is not UP for all servers, you might want to check the status of the network and make sure all routers are up and communications can take place.

> You also might want to check for time synchronization. It takes upwards of an hour for full synchronization of all replicas to take place. Use the Check Time Synchronization option from the Available Options menu. Try the Check Servers in this Tree process again in an hour. If still unsuccessful, consider running DSREPAIR.

After the merge operation and after merge operations discussed above have taken place successfully, you now can view the consolidated tree. Use the NETADMIN or NWADMIN utilities to browse through the new tree. You now can move objects and branches in order to complete the consolidation.

Figure 23.10 shows the consolidated tree created during the merge from the NWADMIN utility.

Figure 23.10

Viewing the consolidated tree from NWADMIN after a successful merge.

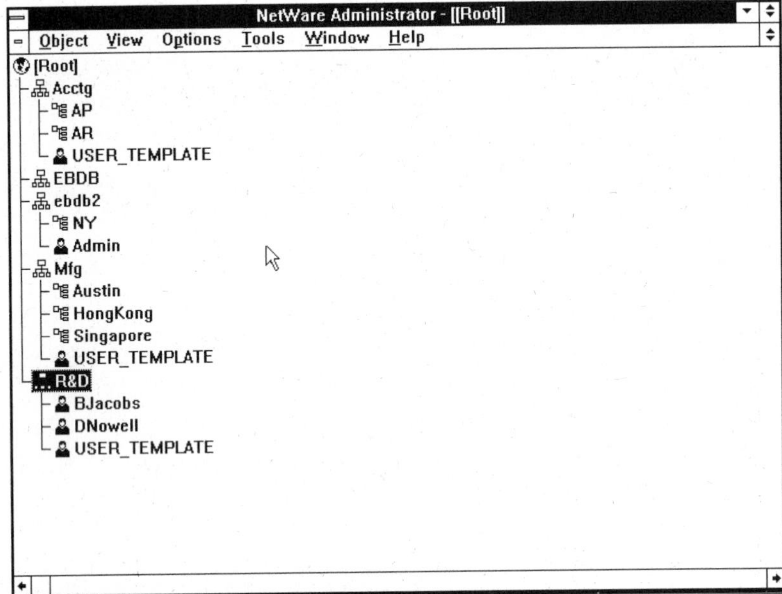

Summary

In this chapter, you learned what goes in to merging two NDS trees together. One of the first considerations discussed was the reasons for merging trees. As you discovered, the two main considerations are easier access to resources and management. You can only log in to one tree at a time. If you need to access or manage resources on another tree you can do so through bindery services, or by logging out of the first, and in to the second tree.

The next section dealt with merger considerations. As you learned, the tree to be merged is called the source tree. The tree that is to be merged in to is called the target tree. You saw an example of source and target trees.

You learned about what must take place before the merge. The most important issues are to make sure there are no duplicate objects off the [root], comparing both the source and target trees. Another important issue is time synchronization. As you learned, it is recommended that you set up a single source of time between the two trees prior to the merge. If the two trees happen to have the same name, the source tree should be renamed using DSMERGE.NLM. When renaming a tree you must first locate the server that contains the Master [root] replica. You learned how to do this using PARTMGR or from NWADMIN.

After the merge, the main tasks you face are to ensure that all servers see the same tree name, to revise time server types as needed, and to clean up the consolidated NDS tree. One of the operations you might end up performing is to move a branch of the tree. You learned how to do this using the Partition Manager tool from NWADMIN.

The actual merge process, as you saw, should be performed on the server that contains the Master [root] replica of the source tree. The utility used to perform the operation is DSMERGE.NLM. The merge operation takes place in four phases. The Check phase checks both source and target trees for any problems that might prevent the merge. The Preparation phase creates as separate partitions all branches of the source tree starting at the [root]. All replicas of the [root] partition of the source tree, except for the Master, are deleted. At this point, the merge process can still be stopped. The Merge process modifies the [root] partition of the source tree in to a Read Write replica of the [root] partition of the target tree. The Completion phase synchronizes all servers and updates them with the new partition information.

The next chapter shows you how to manage the file system.

Part VI

Controlling the File System

New Riders Publishing
INSIDE
SERIES

Managing Directories and Files

This chapter gives you some ideas on subdirectory design and how to manage the file system. The first part of the chapter covers basic design concepts, discussing what types of files and directories you can expect to store on a file server. The majority of this chapter covers creating and managing the file system. Some file management tools are also discussed, including FILER and the Windows File Manager.

Understanding Subdirectory Design

One of the first considerations when designing a subdirectory structure for your network is to decide which types of files you plan to use. The next step is to create a directory to hold these files. The following are the three basic types of files:

- Individual user directories
- Shared data directories
- Application program directories

In the first part of this chapter, you will learn about directories that contain each of these types of files. At the end of the chapter, you will be presented with several sample directory structures. Above all, please bear in mind that there is no one single directory structure that will suit all needs. The directory structure you decide on for your system will be the best structure to meet your needs.

Individual User Directories

There is considerable debate in the network community over placement of individual user files. Some companies make it a policy not to store individual user files on the corporate file server. The thinking in such situations is that any files that are placed on the file servers should be of interest to the company as a whole, not just to an individual user. In such situations, user files are often placed on the local hard drives of each user's desktop computer. In other cases, companies make it a policy to create directories for users on a file server. These directories are often referred to as *home directories.* Such a directory is a place where the user can start from (this directory is the user's "home" on the network).

The types of files stored in the user's home directory varies. In most cases, the user stores temporary works-in-progress. In the case of a law firm, for example, a paralegal working on a document for an attorney might temporarily store the document in the home directory. Once the document has been completed, a final copy might be stored in a shared data directory.

In other cases, users may install applications in their home directories. Such applications are typically specialized and are often single-user copies. In a software company, for example, one user may need to access CompuServe using the DOSCIM program. If nobody else in the company needs CompuServe access, a phone line and modem might be installed on this user's computer, and a copy of DOSCIM could be stored in a subdirectory off the user's home directory.

The advantage to having user home directories on the file server is twofold. First, individual user files can be backed up along with other important files. Second, the network Administrator gains additional control over the user environment. In the case of an application such as Windows, for example, you can economize on the amount of disk space required by placing a copy of Windows executable files in a shared application directory. The files that can be customized (WIN.INI, for example) can then be placed in the user's home directories. This enables users to create customized desktops reflecting their personal tastes in colors, arrangement of icons, and so forth. The advantage to this arrangement is that you can control which files each user can change to standardize the desktop company-wide. In addition, if an upgrade to the program is issued, it is much easier to upgrade executable files on the file server than it is on individual workstations.

The amount of control a user has over his or her home directory is yet another issue. In some cases, the user is awarded full rights to the home directory (Supervisor directory trustee rights). In other cases, the user is awarded considerable rights but lacks the rights to change file attributes or to reassign rights (all rights except Supervisor, Access Control, and Modify). For more detail, refer to Chapter 30, "Adding File System Rights."

Shared Data Directories

As the name suggests, shared data directories are designed to store data that is used throughout the company or department. These directories can contain several types of files, including the following:

- Order entry, inventory, or sales database files
- Files containing data pertaining to clients of the company
- Status sheets and reports
- E-mail mailboxes
- Accounting information such as accounts receivables or payables

A consulting firm XYZ Associates might want to create a directory CLIENTS. Under this directory, they might place a subdirectory for each client using the services of the firm. Any work done on behalf of a client Gloria Kwok, for example, would be placed in a directory CLIENTS/GKWOK. This would ease problems of finding client files when it came time to assess the amount of work done for this client and send a bill. Also, if one of the XYZ Associates partners is out of the office and the client calls, there is no harried searching to find her files.

Trustee rights to a shared data directory are often assigned to a group or to a container. This way all users in the group or container will have rights to the directory. Trustee rights for shared data directories typically include Read, Write, Create, Erase, and File Scan. One user or a management group is assigned Supervisor rights to the directory. This one user or management group is then responsible for the maintenance of the directory and its files.

Assigning Create and Erase rights might not be obvious. The reason for these rights is that applications that make use of the shared data directory will often create temporary files and then erase them when exiting the application. This is often the case when an application is generating a report. If users lack Create and Erase trustee rights, they might not be able to perform certain functions, including generating reports.

Shared data directories are also used as a transfer point when users want to copy files between themselves. If a user RickJ, for example, wants to make a file CDATA.DOC available to colleagues in another office, he could copy the file to a directory SYS:COMMON that the Administrator has created and has given [root] directory rights of Read and File Scan. Anyone on the network can then copy files from this directory. The SYS:COMMON directory becomes a transfer point to users outside of a particular department or workgroup.

Application Directories

Application directories contain executable and other application program support files. Application files should be separated from shared data files for reasons of security, integrity, and backup. Application files need to be backed up only when an application has been upgraded, or when doing a full system backup. User and shared data directories should be backed up as often as the amount of new data stored on the network merits, which could be once or more each day.

Trustee rights assignments to application directories are often only Read and File Scan, which are the minimum rights needed to locate and run an application. Some applications might require additional rights assignments. Some network-aware programs, for example, require that you set up a data file that maintains a list of users of the program. This file could be used both for user licensing restrictions and as a control file to maintain database integrity.

Still other programs require that you set up special directories to contain user setup files. In these cases, applications often enable you to place the user setup files in either their home directory or a directory other than the main application directory. The reason for placing setup files in other directories is that users will need to be able to both read and write to these files. If users had Read, Write, and Erase rights in the application directory, a vital program file might get accidentally erased or altered.

Where To Place DOS Files

The placement of DOS utilities and the COMMAND.COM program is another source of disagreement in the network industry. DOS and its supporting utilities are an application program, yet all DOS-based users need access to it. When fully loaded, DOS and its associated files can take upwards of 20 MB of hard drive space. This may overwhelm the capacity of the hard drives located on each workstation on the network. Furthermore, if DOS were placed on local workstations, it would be very difficult to upgrade workstations when a new version of DOS appeared.

On the other hand, placing DOS files on the file server only might cause problems if the network is down. Users unable to access the file server might need to run various DOS utilities such as disk formatting, antivirus, or file recovery programs. When you place all DOS files on the server, and only COMMAND.COM on the workstations, you may end up severely limiting users if the network goes down.

It is important to store DOS files on the file server in the situation where you have diskless workstations, or workstations that boot from a floppy disk. Once these types of workstations have booted up, you can place the appropriate DOS directory in the search PATH using the login script. The advantage to this arrangement is that users of these types of workstations will still be able to access all DOS utilities.

Placing DOS files on the file server does not affect the file server's operation in any way. DOS files are simply another set of utilities from the perspective of the file server. You can even place different versions of DOS files in different subdirectories without affecting the server's performance. The operating system of the file server is NetWare, not DOS.

At a minimum, you need to have COMMAND.COM and the DOS system files (IO.SYS and MSDOS.SYS are the hidden files for Microsoft DOS) on each workstation. These are the files needed to boot up the workstation. In addition, you need any system files called in the CONFIG.SYS or AUTOEXEC.BAT files to manage system hardware. An example of this is HIMEM.SYS, which manages extended RAM.

One solution is to load only COMMAND.COM and other potentially useful utilities onto individual workstations with hard drives. The DOS files users might need include the following: FDISK, FORMAT, EDIT (which also needs QBASIC.* in MS-DOS), MORE, DOSKEY, MODE, MSAV (or other antivirus program), ATTRIB, and SYS. A complete set of DOS files could then be placed in a subdirectory on the file server. When users log in, the container, profile, or user login script could place this directory in their search PATH.

Sample Directory Structures

When creating a directory structure using NetWare 4, it is important to think in terms of one network. Depending on security rights granted, users could have access to several file servers. Each file server could have several volumes. Each volume could have tens of thousands of directories and files. When charting out a directory structure, place the file server volumes at the top of the structure.

Directory Structure for a Small Firm

The first example is of a network for the law firm Wee, Cansoo, & Yu. The firm has four branch offices, all located in California. Each branch office has its own file server. The servers are all connected via routers and a T1 dedicated digital line. A decision was made to purchase identical software for each branch office. Otherwise, access to a server in another office, even across a fast line such as a T1 line, would be too slow for practical usage. The computer in the main office in Los Angeles has a centralized accounting database. This database keeps track of financial information, including payroll as well as time and billing. Each office maintains its own client information. Any office can access the client files from another office on a read-only basis if the need arises. A COMMON directory exists on volume SYS of each file server, giving users outside the office Read, Write, Create, Erase, and File Scan rights.

Figures 24.1, 24.2, and 24.3 show the NDS structure, followed by the directory structures for two offices. Note that the directory structures for the San Francisco and San Diego branches are similar to that of Sacramento except for the user names. Client directories are numbered according to the client number. Each office starts with a different digit. Clients out of the LA office are numbered starting with a 1, clients out of Sacramento with a 2, and so forth. User home directories are placed under a directory called HOME. The LA office has a separate volume FSLA_ACCT, where the accounting program and data are stored.

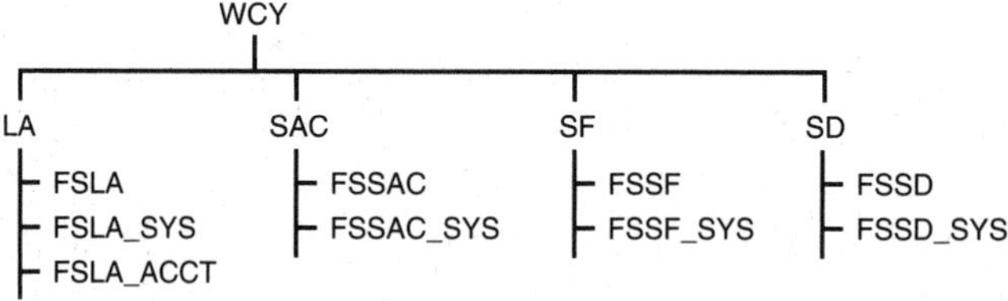

Figure 24.1

The NDS tree for WC&Y showing file servers and volumes.

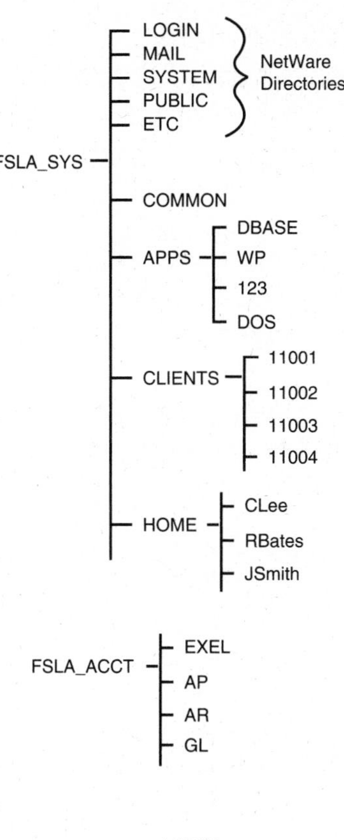

Figure 24.2

The directory structure for the LA office of WC&Y.

Figure 24.3

The directory structure for the Sacramento office of WC&Y.

Directory Structure for a Large Corporation

This example centers on the international corporation, International Engineering, Inc. This is a multinational construction firm that specializes in large projects such as building highways, dams, and bridges. The main headquarters are in Dallas, Texas. There are sales offices in 30 cities around the world. Major branch offices are located in New York, San Francisco, Buenos Aires, Hong Kong, Cairo, and Berlin. The sales offices connect to Dallas using 56 kbps X.25 connections. The major branch offices in New York and San Francisco are connected using a private fiber-optic T3 line with a raw throughput of 44 mbps. The other major branch office sites in Hong Kong, Cairo, and Berlin are connected through a private satellite network with an approximate data rate of 1 mbps.

The Dallas office has 11 file servers. Each major branch office has 8 file servers. Approximately half of the sales offices have their own file servers. Sales offices without their own file server are connected to the nearest major branch office using routers and dedicated phone lines with a speed of approximately 56 kbps.

Figure 24.4 shows you the NDS tree with file servers and volumes designated. Figures 24.5, 24.6, and 24.7 illustrate the directory structure for volumes in the Dallas, New York, and Paris sales offices.

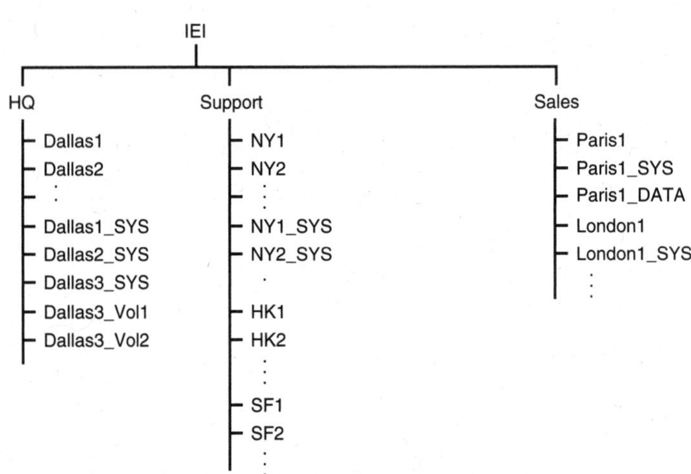

Figure 24.4

The NDS tree for IEI (International Engineering, Inc.), showing file servers and volumes.

As you can see in figure 24.4, there are three main divisions to the company's NDS tree: HQ (Headquarters), Support, and Sales. The file servers and volumes for each office are placed in their respective divisions. Servers are named after the city they reside in, followed by a number indicating which server they are.

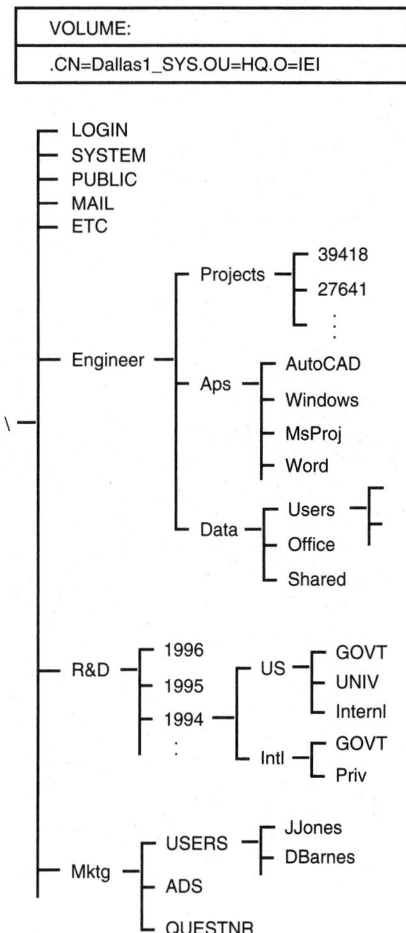

Figure 24.5
The directory structure for the IEI headquarters in Dallas.

Figure 24.5 shows a portion of the directory structure for volume SYS of the file server DALLAS1. As you can see from the figure, the Engineering, Research and Development, and Marketing divisions share space on this server. Engineering has subdirectories for its projects, by number, its applications, and data. R&D has directories by year. A directory for a year is further broken down into research coming through the U.S., or from international sources. In the U.S., for example, there is a further subdivision for Government-sponsored research, University-coordinated research, and Internal research. Marketing has directories for its Users, Ads that have been placed, and Questionnaires to be distributed.

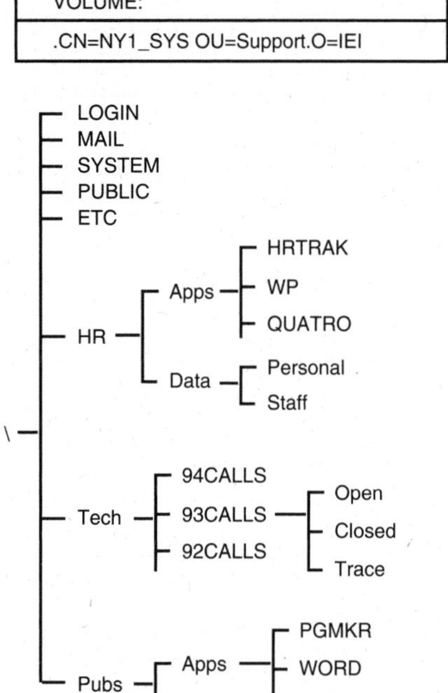

Figure 24.6
The directory structure for the IEI New York office.

As you can see in figure 24.6, as the office gets smaller, the subdirectory structure becomes less complex. One of the main functions of the NY major branch office is support. The Tech directory has subdirectories for calls taken in 1992 (92CALLS), 1993 (93CALLS), and 1994 (94CALLS). Each call directory by year has Open, Closed, and Trace subdirectories, each of which contain databases that track calls. The NY office also has a Human Resources (HR) department, as well as a Publications (Pubs) department. The Pubs directory is broken down into Apps, PR (Public Relations), Finance, and Home directories. HR has an Apps and a Data branch.

Figure 24.7 illustrates the subdirectory structure for the DATA volume of the PARIS1 server. This volume has directories for users in the office, including J. Thoreau and R. Sartre. An ADS directory tracks advertisements placed by year. The LEADS directory has databases that track sales leads by city. The major French cities have their own subdirectories. Paris has further subdirectories by arrondissement.

The next section covers the tools and techniques used to create and manage a directory structure.

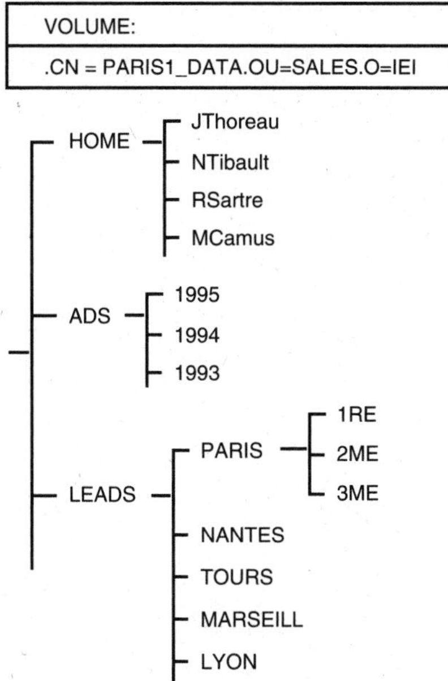

Figure 24.7
The directory structure for the IEI Paris office.

Creating and Deleting Directories from the Command Line

Using the DOS command line is a fast and easy way to create directories. The MD (Make Directory) command can be used to swiftly make a new directory. Likewise, the RD (Remove Directory) command can be used to quickly remove a directory. The RENDIR (Rename Directory) command can be used to change the name of a directory.

DOS commands can be placed into batch files, which gives you a way of creating many directories at one time and provides documentation and a template for future file servers.

Using the FOR Command

The DOS FOR command is a method of providing repetitive looping from the command line. The syntax of the FOR command is as follows:

```
FOR %<letter variable> IN ( <argument1 argument2 ...> DO <command>
```

The *letter variable* can be any letter from A to Z. When this command is used in a batch file, you must use two consecutive percent signs (%%) to indicate a letter variable. *Arguments* will be the names of directories in this case. Separate arguments with spaces. You can have as many arguments as you want as long as the entire command can fit in a single DOS command (127 characters in MS-DOS 5 or 6). The *command* following the keyword *DO* can be any valid DOS command. You can use the variable in this command as in the following listing, which uses the FOR command to create a client directory structure.

```
F:\DATA\CLIENTS>FOR %A IN (01 02 03 04 05 06 07 08 09 10 11 12 13 14 15 16 17
18 19 20 21 22 23 24 25 26 27 28 29 30) DO MD 10%A
F:\DATA\CLIENTS>MD 1001

F:\DATA\CLIENTS>MD 1002

...

F:\DATA\CLIENTS>MD 1028

F:\DATA\CLIENTS>MD 1029

F:\DATA\CLIENTS>MD 1030

F:\DATA\CLIENTS>DIR

 Volume in drive F is SYS
 Directory of F:\DATA\CLIENTS

1001          <DIR>          05-16-94   6:27p
1002          <DIR>          05-16-94   6:27p
1003          <DIR>          05-16-94   6:27p
1004          <DIR>          05-16-94   6:27p
1005          <DIR>          05-16-94   6:27p
1006          <DIR>          05-16-94   6:27p

...

1027          <DIR>          05-16-94   6:27p
1028          <DIR>          05-16-94   6:27p
1029          <DIR>          05-16-94   6:27p
```

```
1030          <DIR>          05-16-94   6:27p
       30 file(s)                0 bytes
                        65,536,000 bytes free

F:\DATA\CLIENTS>
```

As mentioned earlier, the variable used in the FOR command must be preceded by a double percent sign (%%) when used in a batch file. This is due to the fact that a percent sign (%) is used to identify a DOS environment variable in a batch file. The variable used with the FOR command is not an environment variable. The double percent sign prevents DOS from trying to use an environment variable. The following syntax line shows you a batch file used to create multiple directories using the FOR command.

```
FOR %%A IN (JONES SMITH GONZALEZ WU JURGENS HSU ASENZ) DO MD %%A
```

Using FILER To Create and Manage Directories

The FILER.EXE utility can also be used to create and manage directories. Although most network Administrators find FILER clumsy to use, it has the advantage of showing you the list of directories in a menu style utility as you are working with the directory structure. FILER also has the capability of moving or deleting an entire directory branch (including all files and subdirectories of the target directory).

This section shows you how to use FILER to create, delete, and move directories. In addition, you learn about deleting multiple files, as well as salvaging and purging files.

Moving between Directories

Before you start work in FILER, it is important to change to the desired volume in the correct context. You can do this by selecting either the Manage files and directories option or the Select current directory option from the Available options menu illustrated in figure 24.8.

To change to a target directory .CN=EBDB_SYS.O=EBDB:\DATA\CLIENTS, proceed as follows:

1. From the FILER main menu, select the Select current directory option. The Current directory path dialog box appears. Enter the desired directory or press the Insert key to browse the structure. If you press Insert, you will see a list of possible directories. If you select the double dots (..) and press Enter, you will change to the parent directory. If you were at the root of the volume, you will change from the file system to the NDS structure. The screen you will see is illustrated in figure 24.9.

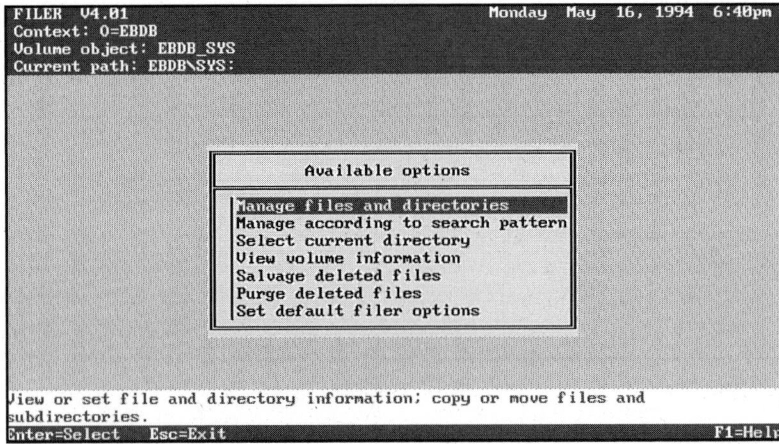

Figure 24.8
The Available options menu.

```
FILER V4.01                                    Monday May 16, 1994 6:45pm
Context: O=EBDB
Volume object: EBDB_SYS
Current path: EBDB\SYS:

                     Current directory path

                            Volumes
 [Additional Volume Objects]
 [Additional Servers]
 EBDB_SYS                              (DS Volume Object)

Press <Enter> to view the next level.  Press <F10> to select the path.
Enter=Next Level  Esc=Select  Del=Log out  F3=Change Username     F1=Help
```

Figure 24.9
Moving into the NDS structure with the Select current directory option.

To select additional volume objects, select [Additional Volume Objects]. You also can move to other server objects by selecting [Additional Servers]. If you select [Additional Volume Objects], you will be taken to a list of NDS container objects. Select the container that contains the desired volume object, and press Enter. Select the desired volume object and press Enter.

2. Once you have selected the desired volume, you will once again be working with the file system. You can move between directories by selecting the desired directory and pressing Enter. This action changes you to that directory. Pressing Enter on the double dots (..) moves you up one directory. As you move around

between directories, the directory displayed in the Current directory path dialog box will change. Once you have the desired directory in the Current directory path dialog box, press Esc to move your cursor back to the Current directory path dialog box. Press Enter to finalize your choice. Note that the new current directory will be displayed in the top left portion of the FILER menu next to the words "Current path."

Creating Directories

To create a directory using FILER, you must first move to the parent of the directory you want to create. If, for example, you want to create a directory under SYS:DATA\CLIENTS, you must first move to the SYS:DATA\CLIENTS directory. At this point, from the FILER main menu, you can select the Manage files and directories option. The Directory contents box appears, showing you a list of subdirectories of the current directory. To create a new directory, press the Insert key. Enter the name of the new directory in the New subdirectory name box that appears. You will return to the Directory contents box, and the name of the new subdirectory will appear on the list highlighted.

Moving or Deleting a Directory Branch

In the process of managing your network, you might decide to move an entire directory branch, including all files and subdirectories, to another location. This example moves a directory SYS:NRP from the root to the SYS:DATA directory. The new directory location is SYS:DATA\NRP.

To move a directory branch using FILER, proceed as follows:

1. From the FILER main menu, use either the Manage files and directories option or the Select current directory option to change to the parent directory. In this example, the parent directory of SYS:NRP is SYS: (the root of volume SYS:).

2. Once you have changed the current directory to the parent directory, select Manage files and directories from the FILER main menu. You will see the Directory contents box. From this box, highlight the directory you wish to move, and select it by pressing F10. The Subdirectory options box appears, as shown in figure 24.10.

3. From the Subdirectory options box, you will note that you can copy the subdirectory's files or the entire structure, as well as move them. For the purposes of this example, select Move subdirectory's structure, and press Enter. The Destination directory box appears.

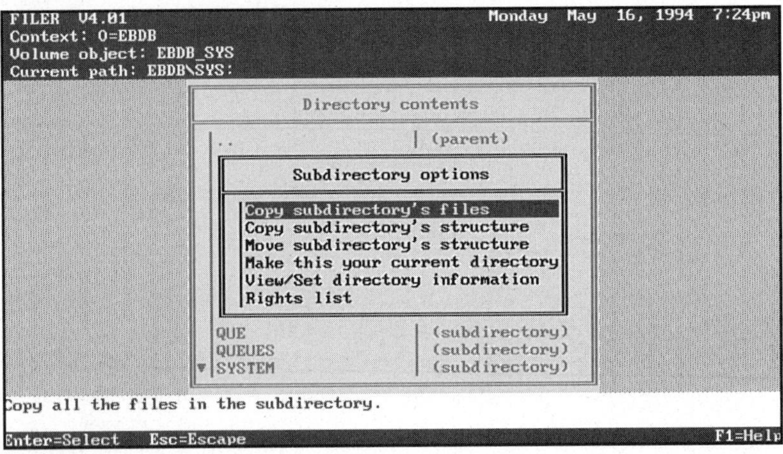

Figure 24.10

The Subdirectory options dialog box.

4. From the Destination directory box, you can either type in the name of the target parent directory or use the Insert key to browse the directory structure for a suitable parent directory. Note that you can even move the structure to another file server in another NDS container using this method. For the purposes of this example, enter **EBDB/SYS:DATA**. You will be prompted to enter a name for the destination directory under the target parent directory. The default is the current name of the directory.

   Enter a new name or simply press Enter to accept the default. You will return to the Subdirectory options box. Press Esc to return to the Directory contents box. Note that the directory no longer appears on the list. Press Esc again to return to the FILER main menu. You can press Alt+F10 at any time to completely exit FILER.

The technique to delete a directory branch is similar to the move operation. As an example, you will delete a directory SYS:TEST. To delete a directory branch, proceed as follows:

1. From the FILER main menu, use either the Manage files and directories or the Select current directory options to change to the parent directory. In this example, the parent directory of SYS:TEST is SYS: (the root of volume SYS:).

2. Once you have changed the current directory to the parent directory, select Manage files and directories from the FILER main menu. The Directory contents box appears. From this box, highlight the directory you want to delete. Press the Del key to delete the directory and its contents. Do not be alarmed—the directory has not been deleted just yet. The Delete subdirectory options box appears, as shown in figure 24.11.

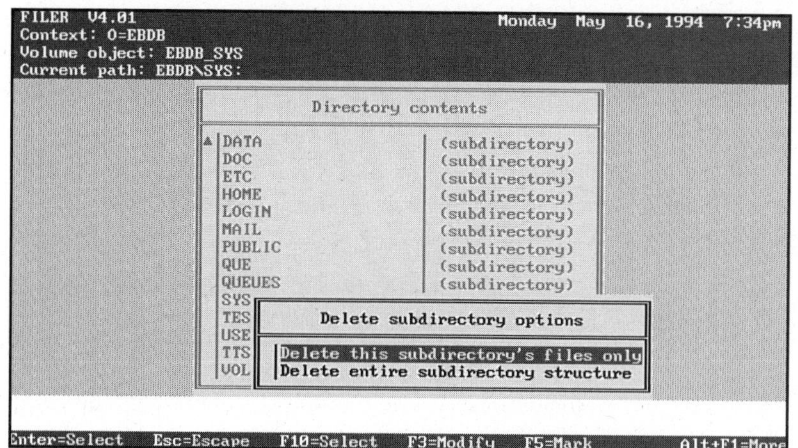

Figure 24.11
The Delete subdirectory options dialog box.

3. From the Delete subdirectory options box, you will note that you can delete the files of the directory by selecting the Delete this subdirectory's files only option. Alternatively, to delete not only the files, but all subdirectories and their files, select the Delete entire subdirectory structure option. If you select the latter option, yet another confirming prompt will appear, asking "Delete entire directory structure including subdirectories and files, YES or NO?". If you select YES at this point, the entire structure will be deleted.

You can use the Set default filer options option from the FILER main menu to change the way in which FILER prompts you. If you plan to delete a large series of directories, for example, you might not want to be prompted YES or NO each time FILER goes to delete a file in one of the directories being deleted. To turn off this prompt, select Set default filer options from the FILER main menu. You will see the Filer settings box. From the Filer settings box, change Confirm deletions to NO. When you delete directories, FILER will not stop to confirm individual file deletions.

4. If the directory structure you want to delete contains your current directory, you will be prompted. This could have an effect on which directory you are in when you exit FILER. If this is the case, FILER will display a box labeled "Delete default directory and its subdirectories?". When you exit FILER, the directory will still appear, temporarily. Once you change directories, the directory will no longer exist.

5. If the directory structure you want to delete contains read-only files or directories with the delete-inhibit attribute, a warning message will appear on screen. You have the option of continuing the operation only if you have either Supervisor or at least Modify trustee rights.

6. Once you have completed the desired deletions, press Esc to return to the FILER main menu.

Deleting Multiple Files

FILER has the capability to mark selected files in a list of files. Once they are marked, you can change attributes or other file-related values, or delete the files. To delete a series of files in a directory, proceed as follows:

1. From the FILER main menu, use either the Manage files and directories or the Select current directory options to change to the directory that contains the files you wish to delete. In this example, the directory is SYS:TEST\RDOAT.

2. Once you have changed to the desired current directory, select Manage files and directories from the FILER main menu. You will see the Directory contents box. From this box, highlight the first file you want to delete. Press the F5 key to mark the file. Marked files appear in yellow; unmarked files appear in white. Use the up and down arrows to move to the next file to delete, and mark it by pressing the F5 key. Continue in this fashion until all files to be deleted have been marked.

Note: If you press Enter after having marked a group of files, the Multiple file operations menu appears (see fig. 24.12). Operations that can be performed include copying, changing the owner's name, changing dates and file attributes, and setting the inherited rights filter for the marked files.

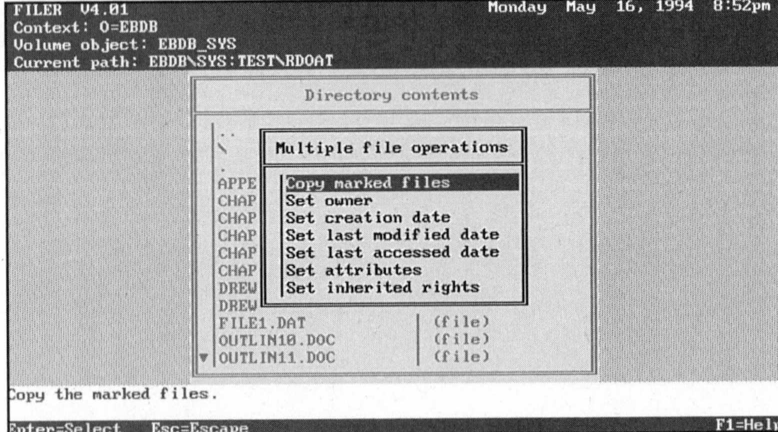

Figure 24.12

The Multiple file operations menu.

3. Press the Del key to delete the marked files. A screen appears asking if you wish to "Delete all marked files." Answer YES or NO. If you select YES, all files marked will be deleted. You are asked to confirm deletion a second time for any files with a read-only or delete-inhibit attribute. To delete files with either of these attributes, you need Supervisor or at least Modify trustee rights.

4. Once you have completed the desired deletions, press Esc to return to the FILER main menu.

Salvaging and Purging Files

Once files are deleted in NetWare 4, they are removed from any directory listing, and the space they occupy is reported as available. Until their disk space is needed, however, the contents of deleted files are retained. Deleted files can be recovered using the Salvage deleted files option from the main menu of FILER.

To salvage deleted files, follow these directions:

1. From the FILER main menu, use either the Manage files and directories or the Select current directory options to change to the directory where the files used to reside.

2. Once you have changed to the desired current directory, select the Salvage deleted files option from the FILER main menu. The Salvage menu appears, as shown in figure 24.13.

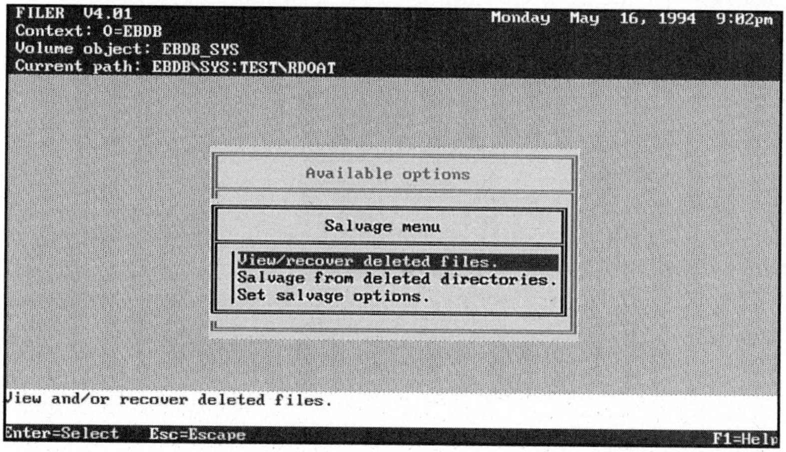

```
FILER  V4.01                                   Monday  May  16, 1994  9:02pm
Context: O=EBDB
Volume object: EBDB_SYS
Current path: EBDB\SYS:TEST\RDOAT

                     Available options

                       Salvage menu

                 View/recover deleted files.
                 Salvage from deleted directories.
                 Set salvage options.

View and/or recover deleted files.
Enter=Select   Esc=Escape                                          F1=Help
```

Figure 24.13
The Salvage menu.

3. The following options are available from the Salvage menu:

    ◆ **View/recover deleted files.** This option enables you to see which files have been deleted from this directory and recover them.

    ◆ **Salvage from deleted directories.** This option shows files whose parent directories have been deleted. Files that fall into this category are placed in a directory called SYS:DELETED.SAV.

    ◆ **Set salvage options.** Salvage options enable you to view deleted files in different sort orders. The types of sort order include by file name, size, deletion date, and deletor (user name of the person who deleted the file).

4. To recover a file from the current directory, select View/recover deleted files. At this point, you must enter either the name of the file you want to recover, or a pattern, in the Erased file name pattern to match box. The default is an asterisk (*), which is interpreted as "all files." A list of deleted files appears in the Salvageable files box. Highlight the file you want to salvage, or use the F5 key to mark multiple files to salvage. Press Enter when done. A box appears, giving information about the file deleted, including the name of the user who deleted the file and when the file was deleted (see fig. 24.14).

5. Enter Yes when prompted if you wish to recover the file or files. When you are finished, press Esc twice to return to the main FILER menu.

Figure 24.14

Salvaging a deleted file.

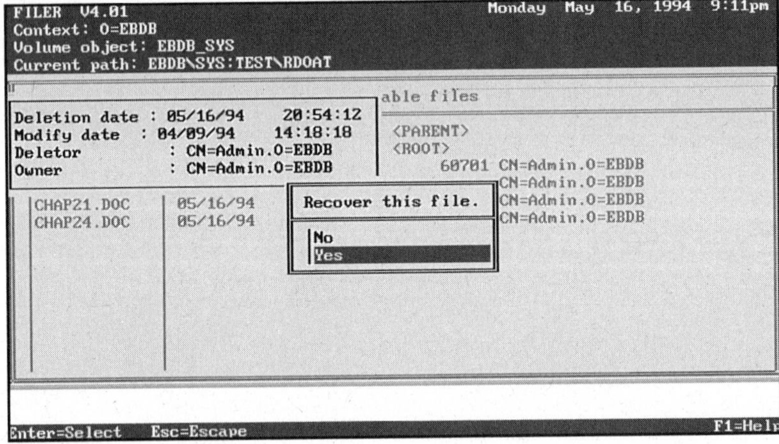

To purge deleted files, follow these directions:

1. From the FILER main menu, use either the Manage files and directories or the Select current directory options to change to the directory where you want to purge files.

2. Once you have changed to the desired current directory, select the Purge deleted files option from the FILER main menu.

   At this point, you must enter either the file name or pattern you want to purge. The default is an asterisk (*), which is interpreted as "all files."

3. Now you select the current directory or the entire subdirectory structure. After you select the option a screen will appear to show the files that were purged.

4. Press Esc to return to the main FILER menu.

Using NWADMIN To Create and Manage Directories

The NetWare Administrator (NWADMIN.EXE), the Windows-based network management tool provided with NetWare 4, can also be used to perform limited management of the file system. To manage directories or files, you must first select the target volume object.

Viewing the Directory Structure of a Volume

To view directories and files of a volume object, double-click on the volume object icon. The picture expands to show directories and files off the root of the volume object. Directories appear as green folders. Files appear as white pieces of paper with their edge folded over. Double-click on a directory, and its subdirectories appear. Figure 24.15 illustrates a volume object and its subdirectories.

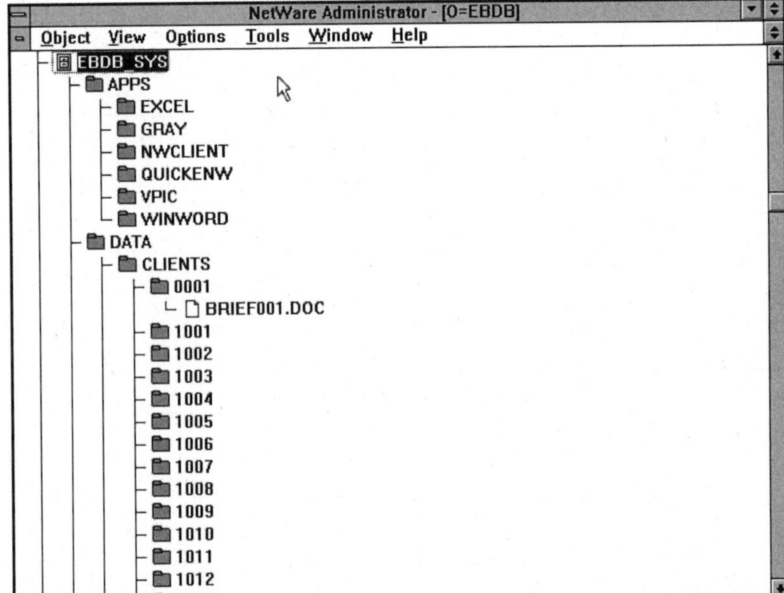

Figure 24.15
Viewing the directory structure of a volume.

Creating a Directory

Before you can create a directory using NWADMIN, you must first select the parent to the new directory. This can be accomplished by completing the following steps, in order:

1. Select the container that contains the volume object.
2. Select the volume object.
3. Select the parent directory.

Once this directory has been selected, proceed as follows to create a new directory:

1. With the parent directory selected, either press the Insert key, or from the Object menu select Create. The New Object dialog box appears. The only object that can be created under a directory from NWADMIN is a subdirectory. Select the OK button to create the new directory. The Create Directory dialog box appears.

2. From the Create Directory dialog box, enter the name of the new directory. Place a checkmark in the Create Another Directory box if you want to create another directory after the current operation is completed. Check the Define Additional Properties box to define directory attributes or assign trustees to this directory. Select OK when done. The new directory will appear under the parent directory.

Moving Directories and Files

To move a directory, directories, or one or more files, you must first select the desired objects. You can select a single object by clicking on it with the left mouse button. Using the keyboard, you can move to the object using the up and down arrow keys. The object can be selected using the keyboard by pressing the spacebar when you have moved the cursor to the desired object.

To select multiple files or directories in sequence, proceed as follows:

1. Select the first directory or file in the sequence.
2. Move the cursor or mouse pointer to the last directory or file in the sequence.
3. If you are using a mouse, click on the last directory or file in the sequence while holding down the Shift key. The sequence of files or directories will be selected. If you are using the keyboard, use the up or down arrow key while holding down the Shift key to select a sequence of files or directories.

To select multiple noncontiguous files or directories using the mouse, click on the desired directory or file while holding down the Ctrl key. Using the keyboard, press Shift + F8, then press the spacebar to select the file. Use the arrow keys to move to the next file and press the spacebar to select the next file. Continue the procedure until you have selected all the files.

To move or copy the selected files or directories, select Move from the Object menu. The Move/Copy dialog box appears. Under Operation, you can select either Move or Copy. The From box lists the files and/or directories to be moved or copied. Enter the target directory in the Destination box. If unsure of the location of the target directory, use the NDS browse button to the right of the field. Once the desired fields have been filled in, select OK. The Move/Copy dialog box is illustrated in figure 24.16.

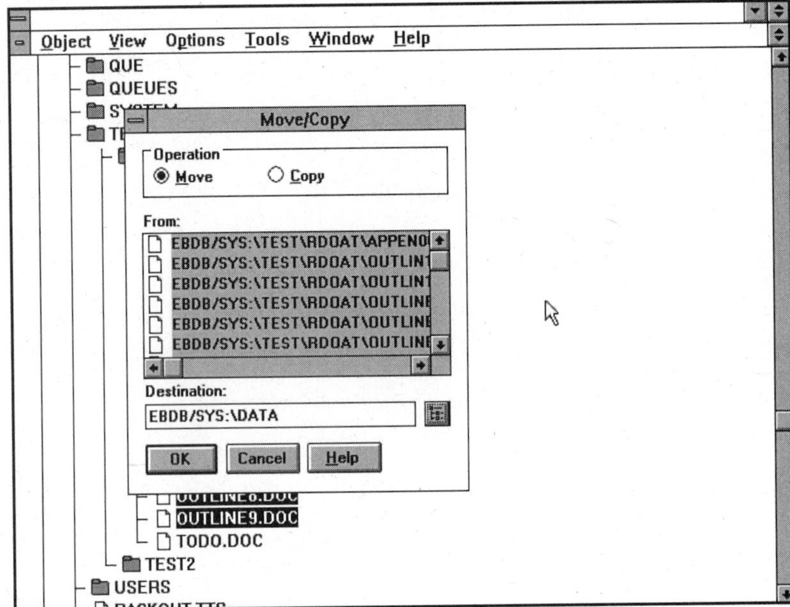

Figure 24.16
The Move/Copy dialog box.

Summary

This chapter covered directory design and management. The first part of the chapter gave you some pointers on what types of directories you will need to create on the file server. The major types include individual user directories (home directories), shared data directories, and application directories. The next topic discussed where and when to place DOS files on the file server. As you learned, it is most appropriate where you have diskless workstations or workstations that boot from a floppy disk. You saw that in situations where each workstation has its own hard drive, you can place a limited set of DOS files on each workstation, and place the entire set of DOS files on the file server. This way you end up saving disk space on the individual workstations. You then were presented with sample directory structures for a small firm and a large corporation.

The next part of this chapter covered creating directories. You were introduced to techniques from the command line, using the FILER utility and the NWADMIN Windows-based utility. From the command line you learned about the FOR command, which makes creating large numbers of directories very easy.

You then learned the basics of using FILER to create and manage directories. In FILER it is important to move to the parent directory first before getting into the management menu. The F5 key can be used in FILER to mark multiple directories or files. FILER can also move, copy, or delete entire directory structures.

The NWADMIN utility can be used to manage the directory structure when a volume object is selected. You learned that to create a directory you simply select the desired volume object and parent directory, and then press the Insert key. You also learned techniques for selecting multiple files or directories and performing move or copy operations.

The next chapter gives you pointers on installing network applications. Chapter 26 covers monitoring the file system.

Installing Applications

Although network applications seem similar to stand-alone applications, there are major differences. Network applications are ordinary applications, such as word processors, database management, and spreadsheets. A network application has the same appearance as a stand-alone application. The stand-alone application is designed to be used by a single user on a single computer; a network application is designed to run on a LAN. Network applications are installed on a file server. The user must have appropriate trustee rights and usually a drive mapping to the directory that contains the network application.

Network applications are typically licensed to be used by a certain number of users. You can typically purchase a copy of the application licensed for a given number of users. The numbers vary widely—from 5 users to 100 users. Purchasing user licenses for software is usually less expensive than purchasing an equivalent number of stand-alone versions. If the number of users who need to use an application increases, you must increase the number of users your license supports. Many vendors, including Novell, have an upgrade program that enables you to purchase an increased software license while giving you credit for a version with fewer licensed users. This policy is similar to trading in an older car for a new vehicle. Other vendors sell licenses in user packs: you continue to add users by adding user pack serial numbers to a central database.

Network applications may have expanded features that take advantage of the shared network environment. Microsoft sells Schedule+, for example, which uses e-mail and peer-to-peer network features so that you can coordinate meetings and events with the schedules of other users on the network. Lotus has an application called *Notes* that is revolutionizing the way information is disseminated across the networks of large organizations.

This chapter gives you an overview of what is involved in installing a network application. You will learn some tips and techniques, and what to expect in the installation process.

Installing a Network Application

The installation procedures for network applications are as varied as the applications themselves. The typical Novell application, for example, uses an INSTALL.EXE utility to perform the basic installation. The typical Microsoft application uses a utility SETUP.EXE. Most applications today are relatively easy to install. Installation programs are largely automated, and prompt you every step of the way. Friendly, informative messages appear, carefully explaining each step of the installation process.

Installation procedures vary according to the operating system. Windows and Macintosh applications are relatively uniform in installation. The graphical environment of these operating systems provides for enlightening (or at least entertaining) graphics. As you would expect, there are buttons to push, and windows that open along the way.

In UNIX, almost all applications use the pkgadd (Package Add) style. This includes a helpful installation script that largely automates the installation process. A UNIX installation can be as simple as issuing the following command:

```
pkgadd -d device
```

The parameter *device* represents the device where the installation media is located. cdrom1 is a standard device definition for the first CD ROM unit, for example, and ctape1 indicates the first tape drive.

DOS installations tend to be more varied. There is no standard for a DOS program installation. Installation procedures vary widely. The installation screens differ and keys are not standardized. The example used in this section is dBASE IV, a database management program from Borland International (formerly a product of Ashton Tate, Inc.).

Overview of the Installation Process

The steps involved in installing a DOS application apply to most other types of installations (Windows, OS/2, and Macintosh). The process for other workstation operating environments is, if anything, somewhat simpler. Here are the basic steps involved when installing a DOS network application:

1. Create a directory on a file server to hold application program files.
2. Install the software.
3. Test the installed software.
4. Assign file system trustee rights and set file attributes.
5. Create a directory map object corresponding to the directory that contains the application.
6. Add application to a menu, batch file, or a graphical icon.
7. Modify login scripts as needed.
8. Test access to the application as a user.

It is during installation that you notice most differences between stand-alone DOS applications and applications designed for operation on networks. Each application has its own unique set of requirements and procedures for installation. Many programs now feature a Quick Start guide, or a set of Release Notes. It is a good idea to peruse these reference materials, perhaps even the manual, before beginning the installation.

The method you use to provide users access to the application is another factor that varies between applications. Some applications require that certain directories be added to the PATH. For stand-alone DOS applications, this is typically performed in the AUTOEXEC.BAT file. Windows and OS/2 systems usually create a new folder or program group. In such graphical environments the new application will be accessible through a desktop icon.

Creating an Application Directory

Some application installation programs enable you to designate where on a drive letter and directory the new application is to reside. It is a good idea to choose a consistent drive letter for all applications installed on a specific volume object. If you start with drive F assigned to volume object .CN=APPS.OU=NY.O=EBDB, for example, continue to reference drive F for any additional applications installed into directories on this volume. Some applications may reference this drive letter through configuration files, scripts, or environment variables. If you attempt to run the program using another drive letter, some applications may fail.

Occasionally, you will come across applications that will not create a main program directory for you. You have to exit the installation program, create the directory, and restart the installation program. Other applications insist on installing themselves off the "root." Unless you do not mind a new directory off the root of the volume object, you can use the MAP ROOT command to create a "fake root" that can be used to install the application. Be aware that the application might require this "fake root" every time the program is used. If this is the case you must add the MAP ROOT command to a login script or batch file to provide proper access.

Many application installation programs provide you with a helpful set of defaults. Most will read the current drive letter and assume this is the drive you want to use. If you find an application that insists on installing itself on drive C, it is most likely not a network application. You can generally "fake out" such applications by mapping drive C to the desired directory on the NetWare volume object. Such mapping has the undesirable side effect of making the actual drive C unavailable until you use the MAP DEL C command to release the drive mapping. Any program that uses drive C as the default may give you problems further down the road and should not be installed on a network unless it is essential.

Another consideration when creating a directory is where to place the application in your network. You must analyze how the server is being used to help you decide where to place the application. Available disk space on volume objects is another consideration. You may have a volume object with just enough space. Many applications will create temporary files that may end up taking up all disk space on the volume.

Do not forget to document the location of the application after installation. On a large network it can become a management nightmare to remember on which volume any given application is located.

Installing the Software

After you have decided where to place the software and what drive letter to use, it is time to begin the software installation program. Before proceeding, be sure to read any release notes or README files. In this section, you will see the results of a dBASE IV installation. Figure 25.1 shows you the initial installation screen. As with many installation programs, the dBASE IV installation utility first warns you about the amount of disk space that will be required to complete the installation.

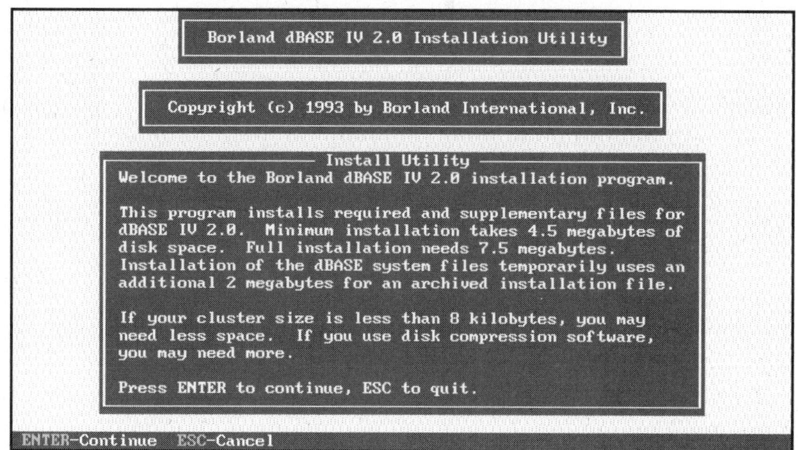

Figure 25.1

The initial dBASE installation screen.

As with many network applications, dBASE gives you the option of a stand-alone or network installation. The stand-alone installation assumes you want to place the application on drive C. The network installation uses the network drive letter from which you started. Figure 25.2 shows you the prompt for network installation.

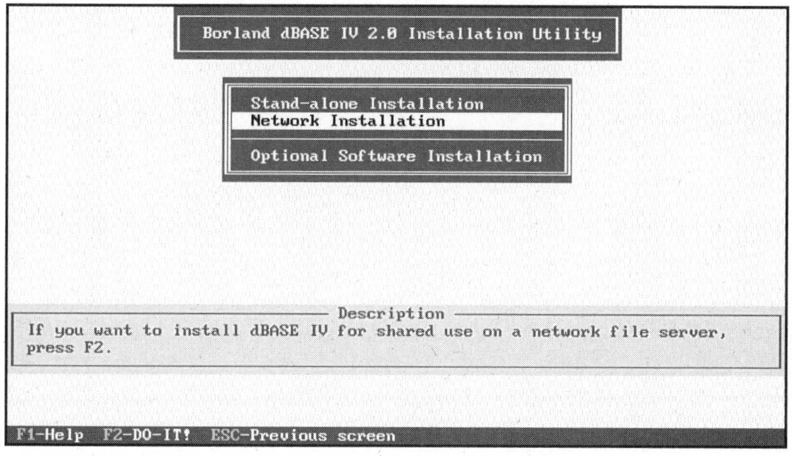

Figure 25.2

Application Installation Utility—The prompt for network installation.

Further along in the installation, you are asked for the drive letter and directory in which to place the application (see fig. 25.3). In this particular example, the dBASE installation utility creates the directory for you, and does not try to install itself off the root.

Figure 25.3
Application Installation Utility—Specifying the base directory.

```
Borland dBASE IV 2.0 Installation Utility

Directories...          [ F:\APPS\DBASE4 ]
Configuration...        [ dBASE ]
Install options...      [ KEEPDB4 SHIELDSQL ]

Description
INSTALL normally places the dBASE files in default directories.  Select this
option to place the files in other directories of your choice.

F1-Help  F2-DO-IT!  ENTER-Select  ESC-Previous
```

The remainder of the installation utility asks for the serial number, and then creates directories and copies files to the designated directories.

Testing the Software

Now that the software has been successfully installed, it is time to test the application. This initial test should be done while you are still logged in as the Admin user, or some user with full rights to the volume object. During this phase you may end up creating additional directories and modifying configuration files. The objective of this phase is to see if the application functions properly. (Testing user access is the last phase and is discussed in a later section.)

At this point, you should develop a series of steps that will test the features of the application that will be used most often. All applications should be tested to see if they can print (unless the application is not designed to produce printed output). The following sections give you examples of test suites for various types of applications.

Sample Test Suite for Database Applications

The primary purpose of a network database application is to provide users access to common data files. Database applications also need to search, sort, and print reports. It would be useful to create a large sample database of some 10,000 to 50,000 records. Most database programs can help you create large files. The database files do not have to have “live” data, although if you can convert an existing database this might be useful.

In dBASE IV, you can create a test database structure with the CREATE command. Use all possible data types in your test. Here is what a sample structure might look like:

```
Structure for database: F:\DATA\TEST.DBF
Number of data records:       0
Date of last update   : 09/05/94
Field  Field Name  Type       Width    Dec    Index
    1  FIRST_NAME  Character     15               N
    2  LAST_NAME   Character     20               N
    3  AMOUNT      Numeric       10      2        N
    4  DATE        Date           8               N
    5  LOGICAL     Logical        1               N
    6  NOTES       Memo          10               N
** Total **                      65
```

Here is a sample dBASE IV program that builds a database of 50,000 records based on the TEST.DBF structure:

```
*
*   Title:      CREATEST.PRG
*   Date:      8/26/94
*   Author:      D. Bierer
*   Notes:      dBASE program to build TEST.DBF
*         Before you begin, create three files,
*         "file.1," of 100 bytes, "file.2," of
*         1K bytes, and "file.3" of 10K bytes.
*
*   Open Database
*
use TEST
*
*   Set Up Random Variables
*
mfirstname="ABCDE"
mfirst_ascii=70
mlastname="BCDEF"
mlast_ascii=71
mamount=RAND(100001) * 10000
mdecimal=0
mdate=DATE() + MOD((RAND() * 1000000), 1000)
```

```
mlogical=.T.
mnotes1="file.1"          && 100 byte file
mnotes2="file.2"          && 1K byte file
mnotes3="file.3"          && 10K byte file
mnotes=mnotes1
mnotes_ptr=3
*
*   Set Outside Loop Control to 50,000
*
mloop=50000
DO WHILE mloop > 0
*
*   Add Record With Random Values
*
APPEND BLANK
REPLACE       first_name WITH mfirstname, ;
      last_name WITH mlastname, ;
      amount WITH mamount + mdecimal/100, ;
      date WITH mdate, ;
      logical WITH mlogical
APPEND MEMO notes FROM &mnotes
*
*   Update Random Values
*
*   Names are shifted to the left and the next ASCII
*   character is added to the right
*
mfirstname = RIGHT(mfirstname,4) + CHR(mfirst_ascii)
mfirst_ascii=IIF(mfirst_ascii < 91, mfirst_ascii + 1, 65)
mlastname = RIGHT(mlastname,4) + CHR(mlast_ascii)
mlast_ascii=IIF(mlast_ascii < 91, mlast_ascii + 1, 65)
*
*   Amount and Date values are assigned random values
*
mamount=RAND() * 10000
mdecimal=IIF(mdecimal < 100, mdecimal + 1, 1)
mdate=DATE() + MOD((RAND() * 1000000), 1000)
*
*   Logical value is given its opposite
*
mlogical=.NOT. mlogical
```

```
*
*   Notes field is pointed to one of three files
*   whose size varies from 10 bytes to 10K bytes
*
IF mnotes_ptr = 1
   mnotes = mnotes1
ELSE
   IF mnotes_ptr = 2
      mnotes = mnotes2
   ELSE
      mnotes = mnotes3
   ENDIF
ENDIF
mnotes_ptr = IIF(mnotes_ptr >= 3, 1, mnotes_ptr + 1)
*
*   Update Loop Counter
*
mloop = mloop - 1
ENDDO      && mloop > 0
```

After the sample database file has been created, you must run it through a series of tests that perform searches on random values, sorts, and print reports. Using TEST.DBF as an example, here is a program that performs these actions. Note that this test should be run on at least two workstations simultaneously to test for possible problems with multiuser access.

```
*
*   Title:      TEST.PRG
*   Date:      8/26/94
*   Author:      D. Bierer
*   Notes:      dBASE program to test performance of application
*
*   Record time in log file. Assumes log file and sample data
*   will be in default directory.
*
CLEAR
SET SAFETY OFF
mtestfile = LTRIM(STR(RAND(100001) * 1000000)) + ".LOG"
RUN echo "Start Test **********" >> &mtestfile
RUN systime >> &mtestfile
*
*   Open Database
*
```

```
USE Test
*
?
? "Perform Index Operation on Last + First Names..."
?
USE Test EXCLUSIVE
INDEX ON last_name+first_name TAG name
USE Test ORDER name
RUN echo "Index Test Completed..." >> &mtestfile
?
*
*   Loop Control for Search Test
*
x = 100
DO WHILE x > 0
*
*   Set up search variable
*
mlast="VWXYZ"
mlast_ascii=65
?
? "Search Number: " + TRIM(STR(x))
? "Perform Index Search for " + mlast
msearch=0
DO WHILE .NOT. EOF() .AND. SEEK(mlast)
   msearch=msearch + 1
ENDDO
? "Found " + TRIM(STR(msearch)) + " matches..."
*
x = x - 1
ENDDO
RUN echo "Search Test Completed..." >> &mtestfile
*
*   Setup for Sort Test
*
?
? "Sort Test..."
mfile = LTRIM(STR(RAND() * 1000000)) + ".TMP"
SORT ON date, amount, last_name TO &mfile
*
*   Setup for Report
*
```

```
USE &mfile
REPORT FORM test FOR amount < 5000 TO PRINT
*
*   Setup for Multiuser test
*
USE Test
COUNT TO mcount
mcount = mcount - 1
x = 100
DO WHILE x > 0
*
*   Test for File Lock conflicts
*
IF FLOCK()
   ? "Successful file lock achieved..."
   RUN echo "Successful file lock achieved..." >> &mtestfile
ELSE
   ? "Unsuccessful file lock attempt..."
   RUN echo "Unsuccessful file lock attempt..." >> &mtestfile
ENDIF
UNLOCK
RUN systime >> &mtestfile
*
*   Test for record lock conflicts
*
mrecno = MOD((RAND() * 1000000), mcount) + 1
GO mrecno
IF RLOCK()
   REPLACE amount WITH mrecno
   ? "Successful record lock achieved..."
   RUN echo "Successful record lock achieved..." >> &mtestfile
ELSE
   ? "Unsuccessful record lock attempt..."
   RUN echo "Unsuccessful record lock attempt..." >> &mtestfile
ENDIF
UNLOCK
RUN systime >> &mtestfile
*
x = x - 1
ENDDO
*
*   Finish Up
```

```
*
?
? "Test Completed..."
*
*   Log Stop Time
*
RUN echo "Stop Test ***********" >> &mtestfile
RUN systime >> &mtestfile
*
*   Display Test Log
*
? "Test Log Filename: " + mtestfile
?
TYPE &mtestfile
RETURN
```

Here is a sample log file for TEST.PRG:

```
"Start Test **********"
Current system time:  Monday 9-05-94 11:51:41 am
"Index Test Completed..."
"Search Test Completed..."
"Successful file lock achieved..."
Current system time:  Monday 9-05-94 11:51:46 am
"Successful record lock achieved..."
Current system time:  Monday 9-05-94 11:51:47 am
"Successful file lock achieved..."
Current system time:  Monday 9-05-94 11:51:49 am
"Successful record lock achieved..."
Current system time:  Monday 9-05-94 11:51:50 am
"Successful file lock achieved..."
Current system time:  Monday 9-05-94 11:51:51 am
"Successful record lock achieved..."
...
Current system time:  Monday 9-05-94 11:55:23 am
"Successful file lock achieved..."
Current system time:  Monday 9-05-94 11:55:24 am
"Successful record lock achieved..."
Current system time:  Monday 9-05-94 11:55:25 am
"Stop Test ***********"
Current system time:  Monday 9-05-94 11:55:26 am
```

Sample Test Suite for Word Processing Applications

The primary concerns with most word processing applications are the quality and speed of their printed output. Another area of concern, as with database software, is that of testing multiuser access to the same word processing document. Key test items for network word processing applications include:

- Print short documents
- Print long documents
- Print to all available printers
- Print using all possible fonts
- Print with graphics
- Does the application retain individual user setup parameters properly?
- How does the application react when two users access the same document at the same time?

Testing short documents is very straightforward. Your word processing staff should be able to supply you with sample short documents. You can also print short documents from multiple workstations at the same time to establish baseline timing requirements. It is not a bad idea to perform the word processing testing at the same time as other types of testing to get an idea of how the network will perform under full load.

Printing long documents may reveal quirks and flukes that are not visible when short documents are printed. Early versions of the NetWare 3.*x* RPRINTER software had strange glitches appear when documents larger than 100 KB were printed from Windows. Documents of less than 100 KB using the same printer and same queue had no problems. These glitches were fixed in subsequent update releases of the RPRINTER software. If you have no long documents readily available, you could combine several shorter documents; Windows also comes with some fairly sizable documents in Windows Write format. Most word processing packages now offer conversion from this format.

During your testing, be sure to send jobs to all available printers—you may have forgotten to configure one of your printers. You may also discover problems with the drivers supplied with the application. In most cases, you can download printer drivers from the bulletin boards provided by most word processing vendors. Many of the larger vendors, such as WordPerfect/Novell, Microsoft, and Lotus also have sections on CompuServe. Although this incurs the connect time from CompuServe, you can download files 24 hours a day, 7 days a week, without having to worry about the trials and tribulations of the smaller bulletin boards.

Another consideration is to print documents that use all possible fonts. You may have to create a test document with a font change each paragraph. Many problems with word processing applications occur because the program cannot compose a document with more than a certain number of fonts per page. You will also see if the word processing package is properly addressing the printer.

Printing with graphics is a common feature in today's popular word processors, and is a good feature to test. Create a 10 page document with graphics. Look at the size of the file on the volume object to gauge how much space documents with graphics will take up on the network volume objects. Print the document a couple of times to gauge the amount of time it takes the application to print. You may also want to monitor the size of the print file to get an idea of how much space is required on the volume object that contains the QUEUES directory. Under this directory will be a series of numbered subdirectories. Each numbered directory corresponds with the ID number of one print queue. It is in these directories that print jobs for print queues will be stored until printed.

Most network word processing applications enable you to set up and save user-specific parameters. These include desired color combinations, default fonts, margins, tab stops, and other customized parameters. Some applications store these settings in a central database. Other applications store settings in files in either the user's home directory, or in another directory that you created. It is important to create a couple different customized user settings and see if they save properly. You may need to login as a user to properly access this feature.

The last suggested test is to verify that the application properly handles two or more users accessing the same document at the same time. A typical scenario for a network word processing application is as follows:

1. User X opens document ABC at 10:00 a.m.
2. User Y opens document ABC at 10:01 a.m.
3. User Y receives notification that the document is already open. User Y should be able to open the document on a Read Only basis.
4. User X makes changes and saves the changes to document ABC at 10:15 a.m. User X now has a more recent version of document ABC.
5. User Y is unaware of any changes and still has the original version of document ABC from 10:00 a.m. open on a Read Only basis.
6. User X closes document ABC.
7. User Y attempts to save changes to document ABC but is not allowed to because of the Read Only status.

8. User Y closes document ABC and re-opens document ABC. In the process of re-opening the document, User Y now sees the changes made by User X. User Y now has Read/Write access to the document.

As you can see from this outline, the first user to access a document gains control over the document (has Read/Write access). Subsequent users are allowed access to the document on a Read Only basis. Another user cannot gain Read/Write access until the first user closes the document. The other user can then exit the Read Only document, and re-open the document on a Read/Write basis.

Sample Test Suite for Spreadsheet Applications

The test suite for spreadsheet applications is the same as for word processing applications—printed output has a high priority. When test printing, be sure to test a spreadsheet that requires more than one page of output. You need to know how your application handles the splitting of printed pages. As with word processing applications, you also need to know how your application handles multiple users accessing the same spreadsheet.

Sample Test Suite for Graphics Applications

The primary concern for graphics applications is to gather baseline performance statistics on printing. Most applications require large amounts of CPU activity on the workstation to "formulate" or "construct" the graphics page prior to printing. This process could cause the application to timeout, and the print job will be closed and printed if the CAPTURE timeout parameter is exceeded. The symptoms of an early timeout are partial pages of graphics. You may also see a partial page and then many pages of garbage output. To avoid this problem, you need to set the timeout parameter when issuing the CAPTURE command. In Windows, you can go to Print Manager and adjust the timeout in the Print Options menu. Please refer to Chapter 28, "Printing from DOS Clients," for further information.

Another consideration when printing graphics is that the print files generated can be quite large in size, often in the range of one or more megabytes per page. You need to monitor carefully the amount of disk space you have free on volumes that contain print queues. Print jobs will be automatically erased after they have printed. While the job is being collected on the server, however, a large amount of disk space could be consumed.

Design several graphics documents to test purposes. The larger the document the better. Have two or more users access the same document to see how the application handles conflicts. Print the documents several times. You can use the NDIR /VOL command to monitor disk space before, during, and after the documents have printed.

Assigning File System Trustee Rights and Attributes

After the application has been tested, the next step is to assign trustee rights and file attributes. File attributes normally assigned to applications are Read Only and Shareable. The Read Only attribute prevents a user (or the network Administrator) from accidentally erasing application files. If the application stops working after assigning this attribute the application may need to write to one of the files. You will need to determine which file is being written to, and change its attributes to Read/Write. If you have difficulty determining the file that needs its attributes changed, consider changing all file attributes back to Read/Write.

If the application fails because it needs to write to certain files, you can see which files are opened prior to the crash by using MONITOR.NLM on the file server. From the MONITOR main menu, select Connections. This program gives you a list of user connections to the file server. Locate your connection and press ENTER. You will see a list of files open at your workstation.

The Shareable attribute is useful for shared network application files. This attribute forces NetWare to provide file open and lock information to the application. To set the Read Only and Shareable attributes you can use the FLAG command. The following example sets all files in the EBDB/SYS:APPS\DBASE4 directory to Shareable (Sh) and Read Only (Ro). The /SUB parameter forces the system to flag all files in all subdirectories as well. The /C parameter causes the FLAG command to operate continuously rather than pause every 24 lines.

```
F:\APPS\DBASE4>FLAG *.* ShRo /SUB /C
EBDB\SYS:APPS\DBASE4
Files         = The name of the files found
Directories   = The name of the directories found
DOS Attr      = The DOS attributes for the specified file
NetWare Attr = The NetWare attributes for the specified file or directory
Status        = The current status of migration and compression for a file
                or directory
Owner         = The current owner of the file or directory
Mode          = The search mode set for the current file
```

```
Files                   DOS Attr NetWare Attr          Status Owner      Mode
-----------------------------------------------------------------------------
CONFIG.DB               [Ro----] [--ShDi--Ri----]      .Admin.EBDB       N/A
README.COM              [Ro----] [--ShDi--Ri----]      .Admin.EBDB       0
DRIVERS.EXE             [Ro----] [--ShDi--Ri----]      .Admin.EBDB       0
README                  [Ro----] [--ShDi--Ri----]      .Admin.EBDB       N/A
ASCII.PR2               [Ro----] [--ShDi--Ri----]      .Admin.EBDB       N/A
ADDUSER4.EXE            [Ro----] [--ShDi--Ri----]      .Admin.EBDB       0
ADDUSER4.RES            [Ro----] [--ShDi--Ri----]      .Admin.EBDB       N/A
DBASE.EXE               [Ro----] [--ShDi--Ri----]      .Admin.EBDB       0
DBASE.VMC               [Ro----] [--ShDi--Ri----]      .Admin.EBDB       N/A
DBASE1.RES              [Ro----] [--ShDi--Ri----]      .Admin.EBDB       N/A
...
```

You must also assign trustee rights so that users have access to the application. Trustee rights in NetWare 4 are typically assigned to an Organization or Organizational Unit. The rights assigned are directory trustee rights to the main directory that contains the application program files. At a minimum, you must assign Read directory trustee right. In most cases, you would also assign the File Scan right. These are the minimum rights required for a user to run the application.

Some users may need additional rights. In the case of a word processing application, for example, the word processor supervisor may be entrusted with creating and modifying user setup or configuration files. If this is the case, you can assign additional rights, such as Write, Create, Erase, and Modify to this person. Alternatively, you may decide to create an Organizational Role object below Lead Word Processor. You could assign the additional rights to the role, and assign the appropriate person as an occupant of the role.

In some cases, the application may write information back to the application directory. Some applications may create temporary files in their base directory. If this is the case, the application has the same rights as the user who is using the application. If the user does not have the rights to create temporary files, the application will not be able to do so either. If this is the situation, you may need to modify the application so that it writes to a directory where the user has the necessary rights, or you may need to increase the rights assigned to the application directory.

Figure 25.4 shows you the screen in the Windows NWADMIN utility where directory trustee rights for the application and data directories are assigned to the Organizational Unit *NY*.

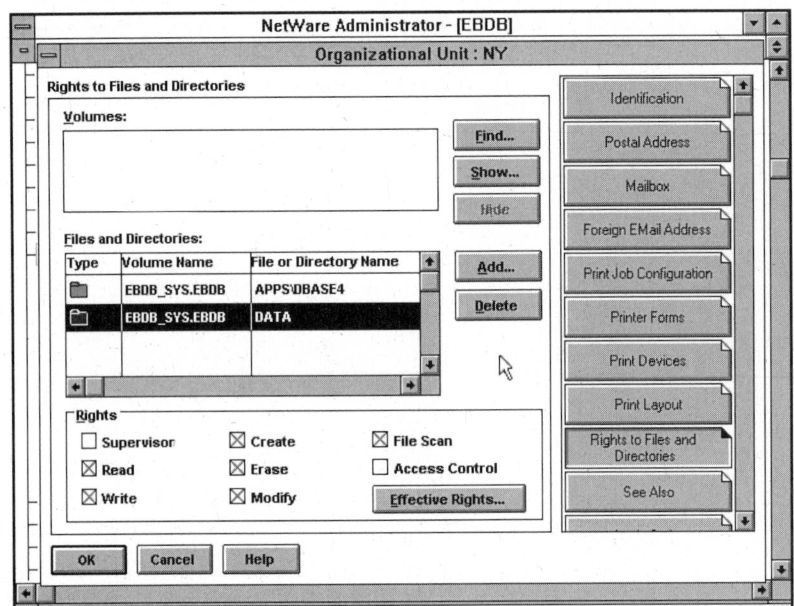

Figure 25.4

Adding Rights to OU=NY for the application and data directories.

Creating a Directory Map Object

It might be convenient to create a Directory Map Object (DMO) that points to the application directory. The DMO can then be used in a login script when assigning drive mappings. DMO's are convenient because you can see them in the NDS tree and thus make management of the location of applications easier. You can use NDS commands to locate your applications if there is a problem. DMO's also give you the freedom of changing the location of the application directory without having to change a series of login scripts and drive mapping statements.

For example, if your company uses Microsoft Word for a word processor, you might install the application in a directory WINWORD. You could create a DMO called WordProcessing and assign it to the WINWORD directory. Login scripts or batch files might then be created using the DMO WordProcessing to create drive mappings. If at some time in the future your company were to change to another word processor–WordPerfect, for example–you would install it in a directory WP. You could then change the directory of the DMO rather than have to change a series of login scripts or batch files. Figure 25.5 shows you the screen to create a DMO.

After you have created the DMO, you must also give users access to the object. The necessary rights are, at a minimum, Browse object rights, and Read property rights to the DMO's path property. Figure 25.6 shows the assignment of the container object NY NDS rights to the dBASE4 DMO.

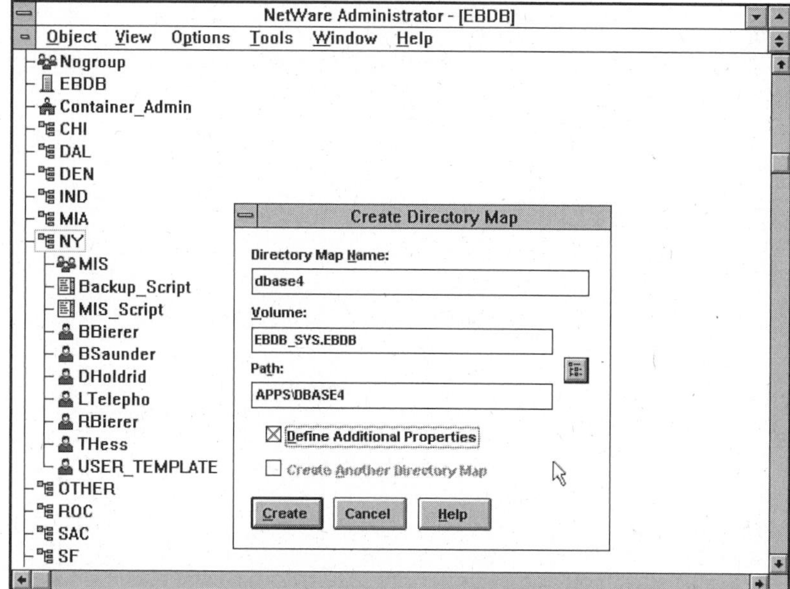

Figure 25.5

Creating a dBASE4 Directory Map Object.

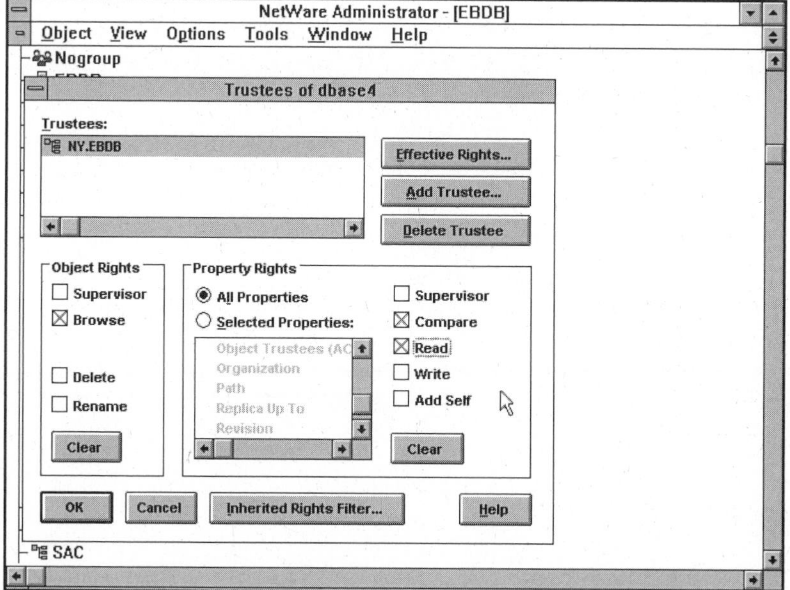

Figure 25.6

Giving the Container OU=NY NDS rights.

You can then verify that the rights have been assigned properly by checking the effective rights of a user object located in the container object. Figure 25.7 shows this screen.

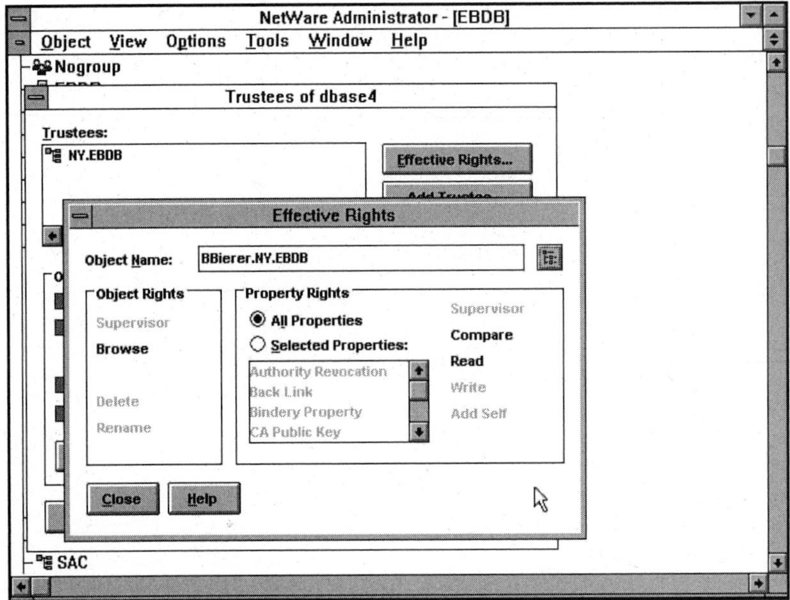

Figure 25.7

Checking user object's rights to Directory Map Object.

Modifying Login Scripts

It is a good idea to add a search drive mapping to the user environment to help access the newly installed application. Without a search drive mapping, the user will have to change to the application directory to execute the application. For further information on the nature and exact syntax for search drive mappings, please refer to Chapter 33, "Assigning Drive Mappings."

The statement to create the drive mapping can be placed in a menu, batch file, or login script. You can have only sixteen search drive mappings at one time. Because of this, you may decide not to add the mapping to the login script, but rather create a temporary mapping in a batch file or menu. These ideas are discussed in the next section.

The following example shows you where a search drive mapping might be placed in a login script. This could be in either a container, profile, or user login script:

```
MAP INS S1:=SYS:PUBLIC
MAP INS S2:=.CN=dbase4.OU=NY.O=EBDB
MAP F:=SYS:USERS\%LOGIN_NAME
INCLUDE SYS:PUBLIC\NY.LOG
```

The line in boldface is used to reference a directory map object that points to the application directory. Users can now execute the program from any directory.

Creating a Menu, Batch File, or Windows Icon

The next step in the process of installing a network application is to create an easy way for users to access the application. Typical techniques are to add the application to a menu, create a batch file that calls the application, or to place the application into a Windows program group.

To add the application to a menu, you should first review Chapter 35, "Building Custom Menus and Batch Files." You should consider where you plan to create a search drive mapping for the application. You may choose to create a search drive mapping in a login script. Bear in mind, however, that you may have many applications on the network, and may not want to create a search drive mapping for every single application. A good alternative is to create the search drive mapping in the menu program or in a batch file.

The following is an excerpt of a menu that creates a search drive to the directory map object and then calls dBASE:

```
MENU 01, Applications Menu
ITEM dBASE IV {BATCH}
   EXEC MAP INS S1:=.CN=dbase4.OU=NY.O=EBDB
   EXEC dbase
   EXEC MAP DEL S1:
```

The menu shown here first inserts a search drive 1 to the directory map object. Next, it calls up dBASE. The *{BATCH}* option causes the menu program to completely remove itself from RAM before executing dBASE; the last command erases the search drive.

A similar series of commands could be placed in a common batch file directory where users have both access rights and a search drive mapping. For example, if you place the batch file in a directory SYS:BAT, you could give the container Read and File Scan directory trustee rights. In the container login script, you could map a search drive to the SYS:BAT directory.

Here is the command to create the SYS:BAT directory and assign directory trustee rights:

```
cd SYS:
md \BAT
F:\>rights sys:bat R F /name=.ou=ny.o=ebdb

EBDB\SYS:
```

```
Directories                                                  Rights
------------------------------------------------------------ ---------------
BAT                                                          [ R     F ]

Rights for one directory were changed for .ou=ny.o=ebdb
```

Add a search drive mapping to the SYS:BAT directory to the container login script:

```
MAP INS S1:=SYS:PUBLIC
MAP INS S2:=SYS:BAT
MAP F:=SYS:USERS\%LOGIN_NAME
INCLUDE SYS:PUBLIC\NY.LOG
```

This is the contents of the *SYS:BAT\DB4.BAT* batch file:

```
echo :
echo :   Title:   DB4.BAT
echo :   Date:   9/5/94
echo :   Author:   D. Bierer
echo :   Notes:   Batch file to call dBASE IV
echo :
echo :   Add Search Drive to Directory Map Object
echo :
MAP INS S1:=.CN=dbase4.OU=NY.O=EBDB
echo :
echo :   Call the Application
echo :
DBASE
echo :
echo :   After Using the Application, Get Rid of the Mapping
echo :
MAP DEL S1:
echo :
echo :   Done...
echo :
```

Adding an Icon for the Application

To add the application program to Windows as an icon, proceed as follows:

1. From Windows Program Manager, select the target program group in which to place the new icon. From the File menu, select New. The New Program Object dialog box appears.

2. From the New Program Object dialog box, select Program Item. Press OK. The Program Item Properties dialog box appears.

3. From the Program Item Properties dialog box, enter the appropriate information in the following fields:

   Description is the name of the icon as you want it to appear in Windows.

   Command Line is the name of the executable. You can add a drive letter and the full path, or you can simply enter the executable itself with no path. If you do not enter a path, Windows will assume that the path for the executable is mapped as a search drive.

   Working Directory is the default directory where you want users to start before running the application.

   Shortcut Key allows you to specify a "hot key" combination that will call up the application from Windows.

Figure 25.8 shows you the completed Program Item Properties dialog box.

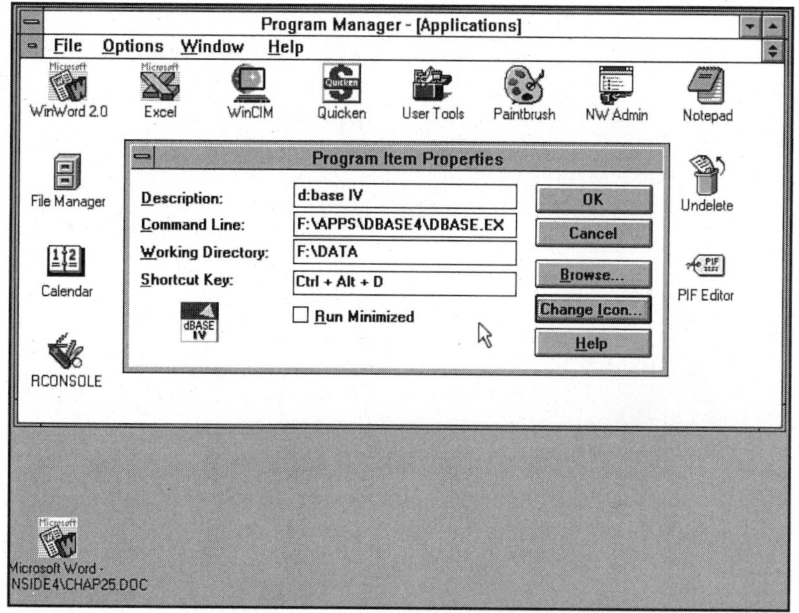

Figure 25.8

Adding an application icon to Windows.

4. Click on OK when done with the Program Item Properties dialog box. A prompt will appear indicating that "... the specified path points to a file that may not be available during later Windows sessions..." Press Yes to continue. The new icon will appear in the current Windows program group.

Some DOS applications, including dBASE IV, include a PIF (Program Information File) that sets the parameters of a DOS program running under Windows. If this is the case, specify the name of the PIF file in the Command Line field of the Program Item Properties dialog box.

Testing User Access

You are now ready to test user access to the new application. At this point, you must login as though you will be using this application. You will have a limited set of rights. If you are logged in as an Admin user, you cannot appreciate possible difficulties you would face as a user because you have a full set of rights to the NDS and volume objects.

Select the menu item, Windows icon, or run the batch file to access the program. Does the program appear to run properly? Do you notice any error messages or problems accessing the program? If so, login as an Admin user and make corrections. Now run the same test program or programs you ran as an Admin user. Does the application appear to function properly? Do you see any error messages? Did you receive proper output? If the answers to all the above questions are affirmative, you have successfully installed the program and can be reasonably assured that users will be able to run the application without difficulties. Otherwise, you must debug the work you have done and attempt the user test once again.

Installing the DynaText Online Documentation

One of the most important applications that comes with NetWare 4.1 is the DynaText online documentation. This is a Windows-based help system that contains all the NetWare 4.1 manuals in an online, electronic format. There are "viewers" available in the DOS/Windows, UNIX, and Macintosh platforms. This section discusses how to install the viewer for each platform.

DOS/Windows

The *DynaText* online help system is a Windows-based search engine and document viewer. All NetWare 4.1 manuals are included on the CD, which is separate from the

CD that contains NetWare 4.1 installation files. DynaText enables you to conduct rapid searches of the documentation to locate desired information. It shares some resemblance to the ElectroText of previous versions of NetWare 4, but is much faster.

You can access DynaText either off the original CD provided with NetWare 4, or you can copy the documentation to a hard drive. The documentation occupies approximately 50 MB per language.

Installing DynaText Files onto a File Server

If you want to copy the documentation files to a hard drive, follow these steps:

1. Go over to the file server and make sure all CD support drivers are loaded on the file server. These include SCSI drivers (if applicable), and any ASPI drivers for your controller card. To control the CD player on the server, be sure to load NWPA.NLM (NetWare Peripheral Architecture) and CDROM.NLM (NetWare CD ROM Support Module).

   To determine the volume name and device number for the currently mounted CD, enter the following:

   CD DEVICE LIST

   You will see a list of CD devices and volumes. This screen is illustrated in figure 25.5. On the left side is the number assigned to the CD device. Locate the device associated with the online documentation CD. Write down both the device number and volume name. The volume name shown in figure 25.5 is that of the online documentation.

```
  Version 2.10c   June 14, 1994
  Copyright 1994 Novell, Inc.  All rights reserved.
CDROM.NLM
  Netware CD-ROM Support Module
  Version 4.10s   May 24, 1994
  Copyright 1994 Novell, Inc.  All rights reserved.
REMOTE.NLM
  NetWare Remote Console
  Version 4.10c   June 14, 1994
  Copyright 1994 Novell, Inc.  All rights reserved.
RSPX.NLM
  NetWare Remote Console SPX Driver
  Version 4.10a   June 17, 1994
  Copyright 1994 Novell, Inc.  All rights reserved.
NWSNUT.NLM
  NetWare NLM Utility User Interface
  Version 4.10g   June 14, 1994
  Copyright 1994 Novell, Inc.  All rights reserved.
EBDB:cd device list

** CD ROM Device List
No. Act. Device Name                              Volume Name   Mounted
 1   Y   Device # 0 MEDIAVISCDR-H93MV    (8100000 NW410DOC         Y

EBDB:
```

Figure 25.9

The output from the CD DEVICE LIST command on the file server console.

2. After you have located the CD device number associated with the drive where you intend to place the documentation CD, enter the following command if you already have a CD mounted in the drive:

   CD CHANGE *n*

   n is the number of the target device. Wait for the CD to "spin down." The access light stops flashing when the CD is ready, and a message appears. You can now remove the existing CD, and insert the documentation CD. Wait for the CD to "spin up." When ready, press Enter. The server will now proceed to index the CD. After a short period of time, the CD will be ready for use.

3. If you do not have an existing CD in the drive, insert the documentation CD at this time. Type the following:

   CD MOUNT *n*

   n is the number associated with the target device. Wait for the CD to "spin up." When ready, press Enter. The server now proceeds to index the CD. After a short period of time, the CD will be ready for use.

4. Now that the documentation CD is ready for use, load the INSTALL utility on the file server as follows:

   LOAD INSTALL

   If you get a message indicating INSTALL is already on the server, press Alt+Esc until you come to the Installation Options screen. (If you are using RCONSOLE, press the Alt+F3 key until you reach this screen.)

5. From the Installation Options screen, select Product options. The Other Installation Actions menu appears.

6. From the Other Installation Actions menu, select Choose an item or product listed above. The cursor will jump to the Other Installation Items/Products screen. From this screen, select Install Online Documentation Database and Viewers (see fig. 25.10). Press Enter to continue.

7. INSTALL.NLM assumes you are installing an additional product, which is usually shipped on floppy disk. Because the source for the documentation is the CD, and not Drive A, you must press the F3 key to specify a different source path. The Specify a directory path input box appears.

8. From the Specify a directory path input box, enter the name of the volume associated with the CD—you wrote this down in Step 1 above (after the CD DEVICE LIST command). Be sure to enter a colon (:) after the volume name. When the correct path has been specified, INSTALL will read the CD. The Indicate which file groups... screen appears.

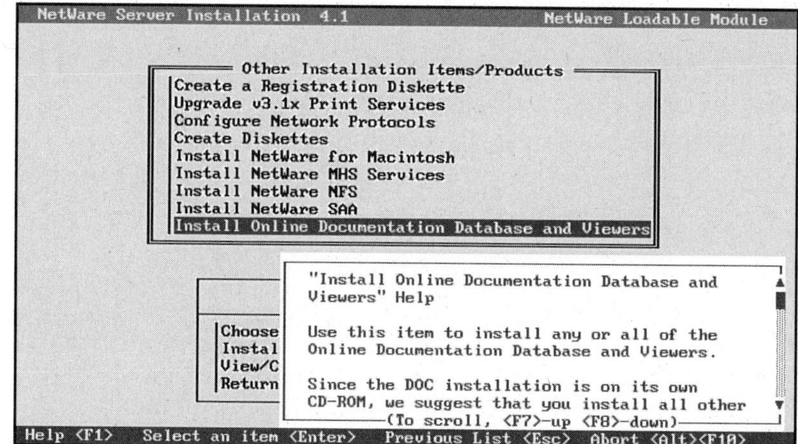

Figure 25.10
INSTALL.NLM—Install Online Documentation Database and Viewers option.

9. From the Indicate which file groups... screen, you can choose the database(s) and viewers you want to install. Databases are in different languages. The viewers are for different clients, including Windows, Macintosh, and UNIX. Press Enter to mark (or unmark) a file group. When done, press the F10 key to proceed with the installation.

   INSTALL will now copy the selected file groups to the server.

10. When this is finished, press Enter.

Configuring the DynaText Viewer

After you have decided where to place the online documentation database, you must configure the DYNATEXT.INI file that points to the location of the executable and data files. If the DYNATEXT.INI file is in a directory different from the database, changes will have to be made. Here are the important parameters in the DYNATEXT.INI file that must be set:

- **DATA_DIR.** This is the directory that contains DynaText data. This parameter points to the DTXTDATA directory. By default, this directory is a subdirectory of the directory that contains the viewer. If you copied the files to a server, and located the viewer in another directory, point this variable to a drive letter that will be mapped to the appropriate volume. The default is as follows:

  ```
  DATA_DIR=.\DTXT_DATA
  ```

- **COLLECTION.** The directory that contains the document collection. If the manuals specified in the SYSDOCS.CFG file (located in SYS:PUBLIC) are the only manuals to be made available, this variable is not necessary. Otherwise, you can indicate that sets of manuals are to be made available. This example lists three sets of manuals: NetWare 4, NetWare 3, and UnixWare:

```
COLLECTION=Z:\DOC\$NWLANGUAGE\NW410=NetWare 4.10
Manuals;Z:\DOC\$NWLANGUAGE\NW312=NetWare 3.12
Manuals;Z:\DOC\$NWLANGUAGE\UW20=UnixWare
2.0 Manuals
```

Unlike this example, however, the entire statement must be on a single line. No spaces are allowed around the semicolons (;) that separate the manual sets.

- **SYSCONFIG.** The system collection directory path. This indicates the location of the SYSDOCS.CFG file. This file identifies document collections available to everyone. The default is as follows:

  ```
  SYSCONFIG=\PUBLIC\SYSDOCS.CFG
  ```

- **PUBLIC_DIR.** Public notes directory path. This directory contains notes visible to everyone on the network. Users who will be allowed to create public notes need Read, Write, Create, Erase, and Modify trustee rights to this directory. The default is as follows:

  ```
  PUBLIC_DIR=\DOC\PUBNOTES
  ```

- **PRIVATE_DIR.** Private notes directory path, where users can store their own private notes. The default is a directory on the local hard drive:

  ```
  PRIVATE_DIR=C:\PRVNOTES
  ```

The remainder of the DYNATEXT.INI file contains configuration data that controls color settings and where the viewer appears on-screen.

Here is a sample SYSDOCS.CFG file:

```
[Unix]
collection /usr/public/doc/nw41=NetWare 4.1 Manuals;

[Windows]
COLLECTION=\DOC\$NWLANGUAGE\NW41=NetWare 4.1 Manuals;

[Mac]
Collection $(EXE_PATH)::::DOC:$NWLANGUAGE:NW41=NetWare 4.1 Manuals;
```

Using DynaText

Figure 25.11 shows you the main DynaText menu for a Windows client.

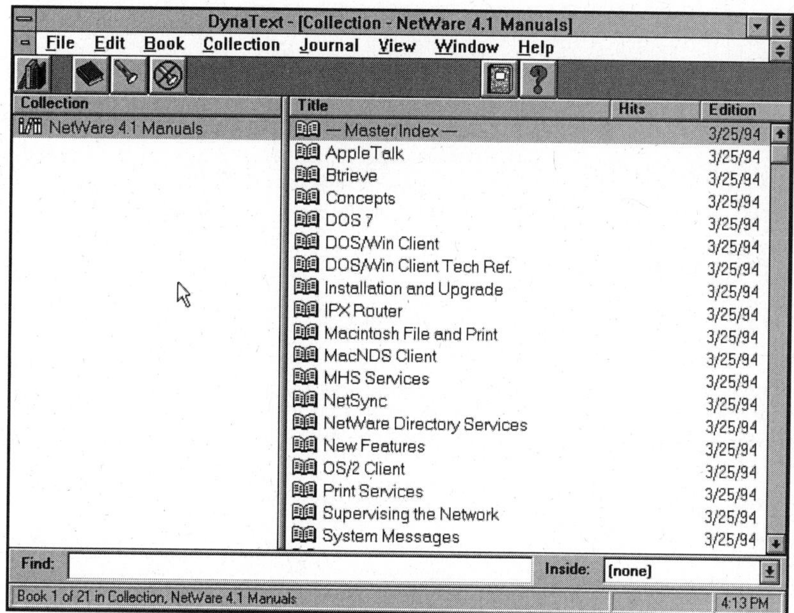

Figure 25.11

The DynaText main menu—Windows Client.

Table 25.1 summarizes the toolbar menu options.

TABLE 25.1
DynaText Windows Client Viewer Toolbar Options

Button	Menu	Description
	File Open Collection	Opens the selected collection of manuals.
	File Open Book	Opens the particular book that is selected.
	Collection Find	Performs a search across the collection.
		Cancels and clears search.

continues

Table 25.1, Continued
DynaText Windows Client Viewer Toolbar Options

Button	Menu	Description
	File Open Journal	Opens the journal utility. This utility enables you to "pre-record" a path across several manuals. Keeps the same timing you originally used when opening the path.

To open any given manual, select the manual from the list under Title. Either double-click on the desired manual or click on the book action button. To perform a search across a collection, enter the word or phrase in the Find input box. Press Enter or click on the flashlight action button. When the search is completed, the number of "hits" indicates how many times the search word or phrase was found in the manual.

After a book has been selected using the table of contents or a search, a new window opens. To switch between open documents, use the Ctrl+F6 key, or, from the Window menu, select the number that corresponds to the desired document. Figure 25.12 shows you the window for the Supervising the Network manual.

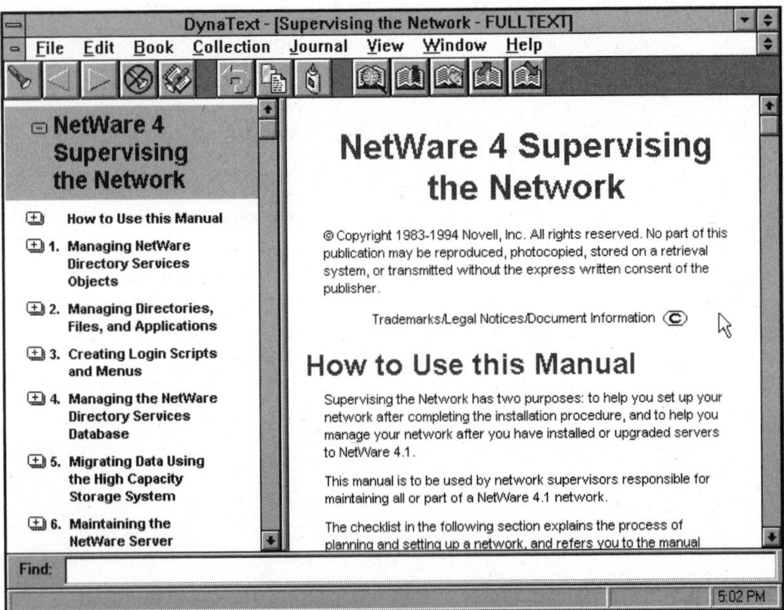

Figure 25.12
DynaText Windows client supervising the network manual window.

A new toolbar menu is available from any given manual. Table 25.6 summarizes the functions of this toolbar.

TABLE 25.2
DynaText Windows Client Viewer—Manual View Toolbar Options

Button	Menu	Description
	Book Find	Begins a search within the current manual.
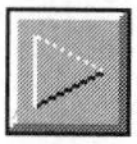	Book Next	Next occurrence of the search item in the text.
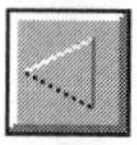	Book Previous	Previous occurrence of the search item in the text.
	Book Clear	Clears all search strings and markers.
	Book Search History	Lists a history of searches made during this session. You can then select from any of the previous search strings.
	Book Go Back	Returns you to your previous location in the manual.
		Copies selected text into the Find input box.
		Pastes the contents of the Clipboard into the Find input box.
	Window New Window	Opens a new window identical to the current window. Used to jump back and forth quickly between references.
		Places a bookmark in the current page in the manual.
	Book Create Annotation Create Note	Lets you place a note, either Public (assuming you have the rights to the directory containing Public Notes), or Private, at this point in the manual.
	Book Create Annotation Create Hyperlink	Starts a “hyperlink” to another collection, manual, or section.

continues

Table 25.2, Continued
DynaText Windows Client Viewer—Manual View Toolbar Options

Button	Menu	Description
	Book Create Annotation End Hyperlink	Ends a "hyperlink" to another collection, manual, or section.

Use the PgUp and PgDn keys to scan through the text. You can also use the scroll bar at the right side of the screen. Clicking on items in the Table of Contents window at the left side of the screen enables you to "jump" to that portion of the text. When done, press Ctrl+F4 to close a manual, or Alt+F4 to close the DynaText viewer entirely.

DynaText for Macintosh Users

A Macintosh client can access NetWare help information by using the DynaText viewer application. The DynaText application and data is downloaded to the NetWare server when NetWare for Macintosh is installed. The application, called DynaText, is under the SYS:DOCVIEW\DTAPPMAC\ENGLISH folder. Any NetWare client logged in to the NetWare 4.1 server has access to this application whether the client is on a Macintosh or PC. The file DYNATEXT.CFG contains information about the location of the data and application files if the Administrator needs to move them from their original location.

Double-click on the DynaText icon to launch the application. The program and data must download from the server, so it might take a few minutes. The DynaText application for Macintosh is very similar to Windows' DynaText. After the application loads, the first screen displays the titles of the twenty four chapters.

The DynaText chapters that concerned with Macintosh-specific information are as follows:

- AppleTalk (Book 2 of 24)
- Macintosh File and Print Services (Book 9 of 24)
- MacNDS Client (Book 10 of 24)

Administrators who want to familiarize themselves with Macintosh in a NetWare environment should read the AppleTalk section of DynaText, Book 2. This book covers NLM and server information, AppleTalk concepts, AppleTalk protocol and network information, SNMP concepts, and configuration parameters. The last section gives some examples of AppleTalk network configurations and shows the corresponding INETCFG settings.

Book 9, "Macintosh File and Print Services," is a good reference for AppleTalk file installation and configuration and AppleTalk printing services. This book also describes the AFPCON utility Administrators will use to manage the AppleTalk File Protocol running on the server. Many of the commands the Administrator had to type at the console are now built into the AFPCON utility. Another nice feature is the capability to check on desktop status. If the desktop information for a particular volume needs to be rebuilt, you can use the AFPCON utility. AFPCON, services, and troubleshooting hints are described in this book.

Book 10 covers Macintosh access to NDS, and discusses the Macintosh client side of this connection. Network Administrators should review this information and pay close attention to MacNDS and logging in to Directory Services.

To launch the DynaText application quickly, create an alias on the desktop. To create an alias on the desktop, follow these steps:

1. Open the English folder containing the DynaText application and highlight the application.
2. Under the File menu, select Make Alias. Drag the alias to the desktop.
3. Log out of the server and then test the alias.

You can now launch the DynaText application and automatically log in to the server if you are not already logged in.

DynaText under UnixWare

UnixWare version 2.0 features the DynaText help system for X-Windows. The appearance and operation of DynaText in UnixWare is almost identical to the Windows version. Because the configuration is nearly identical, to add NetWare help for UnixWare 2.0 users, you simply need to make changes to the DynaText configuration file. The file name is .ebtrc and is located in the /etc/opt/dynatext directory. To have this help system available, you must select the documentation set during the installation of your UnixWare system.

To configure and use DynaText for UnixWare 2.0, add a line to the /etc/opt/dynatext/.ebtrc file. In the following excerpt, the line added is the last line, in boldface:

```
# ---------------------------------------------
# System collection directory path specification
# ---------------------------------------------
#
# Document collections visible to everyone on a network are specified in
# publicly visible configuration files pointed to by the SYSCONFIG line.
```

```
# On a NetWare server, the default collection configuration file is
# SYS:PUBLIC\SYSDOCS.CFG. The default line below assumes that the
# directory containing sysdocs.cfg has been linked to /public. If this
# is changed, or if additional configuration files are added, the
# SYSCONFIG line will have to be modified.
#
# Default: SYSCONFIG /public/sysdocs.cfg
#
SYSCONFIG /public/sysdocs.cfg
COLLECTION      /usr/doc/Libraries/C/refman=Reference (UnixWare AS man pages)
COLLECTION      /usr/doc/Libraries/C/as=Use & Admin (UnixWare PE & AS guides)
#
#  The following line adds NetWare DynaText to the UnixWare collections
#
COLLECTION       /.NetWare/sf_1/sys/doc/english/nw41=NetWare 4.1 Manuals
```

The user must first log in to the server before opening DynaText. Server authentication under UnixWare 2.0 can be accomplished as follows:

1. From the UnixWare desktop, select Admin_Tools. The Admin_Tools window opens.
2. From the Admin_Tools window, select Networking. The Networking window opens.
3. From the Networking window, choose NetWare_Access. The NetWare Servers dialog box appears, as shown in figure 25.13.

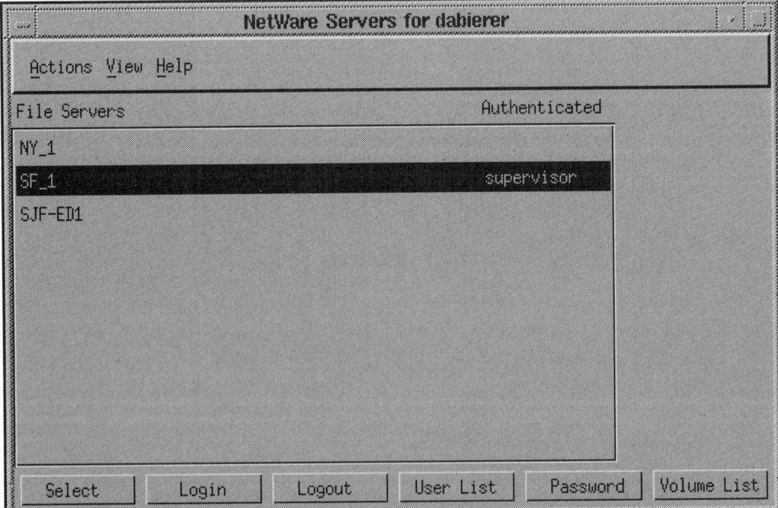

Figure 25.13
The UnixWare NetWare Access dialog box.

4. From the NetWare Servers dialog box, select the desired server and click on the Login button. You will be prompted for a user name and password on the selected server. After you have entered a valid user name and password, you will return to the NetWare Servers dialog box. Double-click on the menu button on the top left of the screen, or press Alt+F4 to close the window.

To use DynaText, open the Online_Docs icon, which is located in the Applications window on the desktop.

Installing the DynaText viewer for UnixWare 1.1 involves copying a tar file that comes with NetWare 4.1. The file is located in the unixware directory on the documentation CD. Copy the two files and extract their contents using the tar command, as shown here:

```
mount -F nucfs server:/volume/unixware /mnt
cp /mnt/dt*.tar /tmp
tar xvf /tmp/dtappuw.tar
tar xvf /tmp/dtdatuw.tar
```

Where *server* is the name of the server and *volume* is the volume where the UNIXWARE directory is located. After these two files are extracted, you can view the installation files for directions specific to your system.

Summary

The first part of this chapter described the process of installing an application on the network. There are many differences in the procedure for any given application.

You learned the basic steps when installing network applications:

- ◆ Create a directory
- ◆ Map a drive letter and use consistently
- ◆ Install the software
- ◆ Test the software
- ◆ Assign file system trustee rights. Minimum rights are Read and File Scan and should be assigned to containers.
- ◆ Create a directory map object
- ◆ Create a search drive mapping

- Create a menu item, batch file, or Windows icon
- Test user access

This chapter gave you a number of test suites to use for database, spreadsheet, word processing, and graphics applications. Included in this chapter is a sample dBASE application that can be used to test for network functionality.

The last part of this chapter covers the DynaText online documentation. You also saw a summary of commands and functions available in DynaText. You learned that it is a much faster version of online help than the previous version—ElectroText.

The last part of this chapter gave you details on how to configure Macintosh and UnixWare clients to use DynaText. The Macintosh DynaText viewer is available on the documentation CD. For Macintosh users it is recommended you create a desktop alias for ease of access. UnixWare 2.0 users already have DynaText included with their system. Adding access to NetWare DynaText help is simply a matter of editing the /etc/opt/dynatext/.ebtrc file. UnixWare users should authenticate to the server containing the documentation files before using the viewer.

Monitoring the File System

Now that you have some idea how to create directories and install applications, you will learn how to monitor the file system. The file system must be monitored as frequently as users on your network make changes to files and directories. In some cases you may need to monitor the file system on your file servers once a day. In other cases, when the changes are relatively infrequent, you may need to monitor the file system once a month.

When monitoring the file system, you need to observe several statistics, including the following:

- How much disk space do you have left on each volume?
- How many files haven't been used in the last several months?
- What is the status of the hard drives on each server?

In addition to the statistics listed here, you need to concern yourself with managing files using naming conventions other than DOS. This is known as *name space support*. This chapter covers various utilities that assist you in each of the areas mentioned.

Using NDIR To View the File System

NDIR (NetWare Directory) is an extremely useful utility used to gather information on files stored on a NetWare volume. NDIR is very similar to the DOS DIR command. NDIR is a superset of DIR. As with the DIR command, NDIR gives you the file name, date created or last modified, and size of the file. In addition, NDIR gives you the following information and features:

- File information:
  - File owner (User name of the user who created or last modified the file)
  - When the file was last updated
  - When the file was last archived
  - When the file was last accessed
  - File attributes
  - Alternative file names (if name space support for other operating systems is in effect)
  - File compression information
  - Version and checksum
- Directory information:
  - Directory IRF (Inherited Rights Filter)
  - Your effective rights in the directory listed
  - Information in subdirectories
  - Directory space limitation
- Volume information:
  - Volume space restrictions
  - Space used
  - Space available
  - Space saved through compression

In this section, you will learn some of the more common uses for the NDIR utility.

NDIR Command Syntax and Usage

The generic syntax for the NDIR utility is as follows:

```
NDIR [path\filespec] [/option [operator] [value]]
```

Path can include the name of the volume or a drive letter and any subdirectories.

Filespec can be the name of a single file or directory or can include wild cards. As in DOS, wild cards include an asterisk (*) to indicate one or more characters, and a question mark (?) to indicate a single character.

Option can include any of the following:

- Formatting options that control how NDIR results are displayed
- Display or NOT display files with certain attributes
- Sort the output using a specified NDIR field (file name, size, and so on)
- Apply output restrictions by owner, size, date, and so on
- Display only files or only directories
- Display subdirectories as well as the current directory
- Display volume statistics
- Other sorts of information, including disk space and the version of an executable file

Operator includes EQ (equal to), LE (less than or equal to), NOT (reverse of the restriction), and so forth.

Value is a value you enter at the command line. Values can include user names, dates, or numbers.

To get help with the NDIR command, type the following:

NDIR /?

To get help on all aspects of NDIR, type

NDIR /? ALL

Table 26.1 summarizes the NDIR options.

Table 26.1
Summary of NDIR Options

Category	NDIR Option	Description
Attributes	/RO, /RW, /Sy, /H, /A, /X, /T, /P, /Sh, /I, /Ci, /Di, /Ri, /Co, /Ic, /Dc, /Cc, /Dm, /M	Any file attribute can be listed as a search restriction by simply entering the *path\filespec* and then the desired attribute preceded by a forward slash (/). For example, to search for all shareable files in SYS:PUBLIC, type the following: **NDIR SYS:PUBLIC*.* /Sh**
Format	/DA	Modifies the output to show all dates maintained by the operating system. The dates include last update, last archived (backed up), last access (including just reading the contents of the file), and last created or copied. To view dates on all files with the extension DAT in the current directory, type the following: **NDIR *.DAT /DA**
	/R	Gives you rights information on the selected files or directories. File information displayed includes attributes, the status of the file (open, for example), the IRF for the file, and your effective rights to the file. Directory information includes directory attributes, the IRF for the directory, and your effective rights. If volume SYS: has been assigned to drive G:, to view the rights for files in the LOGIN directory, type the following: **NDIR G:\LOGIN /R**
	/D	This option gives you detailed information on files and directories. To view detailed

Category	NDIR Option	Description
		information in all user data directories on file server FS1, volume SYS:, type the following: **NDIR FS1/SYS:USERS/*.* /SUB /D**
	/MAC	Gives information specific to Macintosh files.
	/L	Gives long file names (if name space support for operating systems that support long file names has been added). You see a standard NDIR listing, with the DOS file name format displayed on the first line. One additional line per name space supported appears under each DOS file name. To view long file names on volume DATA, directory ACCT, type the following: **NDIR DATA:ACCT*.* /L**
	/COMP	Gives information on files that have been compressed. In addition to the file name, size, owner, and last update, this option tells you the original size of the file, its compressed size, and the percentage of space savings that occurred. To view compression information in the DOC directory of volume SYS, type the following: **NDIR SYS:DOC /COMP /SUB**
Miscellaneous	/FO	This option shows you information on files only. No directory information is displayed.
	/DO	This option shows you information on directories only. No file information is displayed. This syntax is useful to view the directory structure of any given volume.
	/SUB	Causes NDIR to display information for all subdirectories in addition to the current directory.
	/VOL	Gives you volume information. You can use NDS syntax when specifying the name of the

continues

Table 26.1, Continued
Summary of NDIR Options

Category	NDIR Option	Description
		volume. To view a volume object DATA in the container MIS, for example, type the following: **NDIR .cn=FS1_DATA.o=MIS /VOL** Information displayed includes the following: ◆ Total volume space available ◆ Space in use ◆ Space used for deleted files not yet purged ◆ Space remaining on the volume ◆ Space available to the user you are logged in as ◆ Information on the size of the DET (Directory Entry Table) ◆ Space used and saved by file compression ◆ Name space support loaded
	/C	Causes the NDIR output to scroll continuously rather than pausing every 24 lines.
	/VER	This option displays version and checksum information on a file. The checksum information can be used in conjunction with virus protection software. If you get different checksums at different times, know the file has been altered. The version information is useful when making upgrade decisions. Version numbers are available only for certain files. This feature was specifically designed for Novell operating system executables. To obtain the version of all executable files in PUBLIC, type the following: **NDIR SYS:PUBLIC*.EXE /VER**
	/SPA	Displays user space limitation information. The information displayed includes restric-

Category	NDIR Option	Description
		tions on your user account by volume and by specific directory.
	/FI	This option causes NDIR to search all files in your search drive directories for the specified file (that is, every directory in your PATH). If you want to find where any file starting with WIN is located in your PATH, type the following: **NDIR WIN*.* /FI**
	/SORT *sort_item*	This option is used to produce a sorted listing. The default *sort_item* is the file name. Other sort items are any of the restrictions OW, SI, AC, UP, CR, or AR. To sort the current directory by last Access Date, for example, type the following: **NDIR *.* /SORT AC**
	/REV SORT *sort_item*	This option is used to produce a reverse sorted listing. The default *sort_item* is the file name. Other sort items are any of the restrictions OW, SI, AC, UP, CR, or AR. To sort the current directory of drive Y: by most recent to oldest Update Date, for example, type the following: **NDIR Y:*.* /REV SORT UP**
Restrictions	/OW	Restrictions must be followed by an operator and then a value. The operators are summarized at the bottom of this table. This operator represents the file owner. This enables you to search for files that were last created or modified by a specific user.
	/AC	Specifies files by last access. An "access" could consist of a user opening a document to read it. Bear in mind that an access could also be recorded when a tape drive backs up a file.

continues

Table 26.1, Continued
Summary of NDIR Options

Category	NDIR Option	Description
		The value specified should be a date. Two date formats are acceptable, including 5-24-94 and 5/24/94. You can also specify the year using four digits—5-24-1994 and 5/24/1994 are both acceptable. Use the BEF or AFT operators to find files inside or outside of a specified date range. To find files that have not been accessed since February 1, 1994, for example, type the following: **NDIR *.* /AC BEF 2-1-94 /SUB**
	/SI	Specifies a restriction by size. You can use this option, along with the GR or LE operators, to locate files above or below a certain size. To locate executable files on your local C: drive that are greater than 1 MB in size, for example, type the following: **NDIR C:*.EXE /SI GR 1000000 /SUB**
	/AR	Restricts the search to files by archive date. The value must be a date. To locate files on file server FS2, volume DATA:, that have been archived since June 1, 1994, type the following: **NDIR FS2/DATA:*.* /AR AFT 6/1/1994/ SUB**
	/UP	This option restricts by last update. This date is the last time someone made changes to this file. The value specified must be in date format. To locate files that have not been updated since April 15, 1993, for example, type the following: **NDIR *.* /UP BEF 4/15/93 /SUB**
	/CR	This option, like UP and AC, requires a date value. The create option restricts files

Category	NDIR Option	Description
		presented in the NDIR output to files that have been created on, before, or after a certain date. To search for files in a directory on drive C: created on September 29, 1993, for example, type the following: **NDIR C:\DATA\A*.* /CR EQ 9-29-1993**
Operators (used with Restrictions)	LE	Less than or equal to
	EQ	Equal to
	GR	Greater than
	BEF	Before (same as LE)
	AFT	After (same as GR)
	NOT	Negates the restriction. To get a list of files where the user Admin is not the owner, for example, type the following: **NDIR *.* /OW NOT EQ ADMIN /SUB**

Common NDIR Examples

This section gives you examples of several common uses for the NDIR command.

Example 1: Finding a Lost File by Owner

Finding a lost file is a very typical network administrative operation. You might have a user call you and ask if you can locate a file he is sure he has saved somewhere on the network. Your first task will be to locate the most likely file server and volume to contain the lost file. In many cases the user will not be able to tell you the name of the file, where it is located, or even when it was saved (if at all). In a situation such as this, your best bet would be to search by owner. The following listing shows you the command and its resulting output. In this example, the user name is .CN=JWalker.OU=SJ.O=EBDB; the file server is EBDB; and the volume is SYS:.

```
F:\>NDIR EBDB/SYS:*.* /OW EQ JWALKER.SJ /SUB
Files              = Files contained in this path
Size               = Number of bytes in the file
Last Update        = Date file was last updated
Owner              = ID of user who created or copied the file

EBDB/SYS:\\HOME\JWALKER\*.*
```

```
Files                          Size Last Update      Owner
--------------- ----------- ------------- ----------------------
TEST2.TXT                        21  5-29-94  2:06p JWalker.SJ
XYZ.TXT                          20  5-29-94  1:44p JWalker.SJ


             41  bytes (131,072  bytes in 2 blocks allocated)
              2  Files


F:\>
```

When searching by owner, be careful who you specify. NetWare 4 records the NDS name of the user but leaves off the top-level organization. The user name specified must be a partial, typeless, NDS name without the top-level organization. To search for all files where the owner is .CN=Brenda.OU=90210.O=TV, you would specify the following:

```
NDIR \*.* /OW EQ Brenda.90210 /SUB
```

You can also use the GR (greater than) or LE (less than or equal to) operators to search for a range of user names. The disadvantage to this technique is that you also end up with a majority of undesired file names. In the preceding example, you could specify the following:

```
NDIR \*.* /OW LE Brenda /SUB
```

Example 2: Finding Files That Have Not Been Updated in the Last Six Months

This example shows you how to display a list of files that have not been updated in the last six months. This sort of activity is preparatory to archiving "old" files and removing them from the file server's hard drive. Network Administrators find themselves launching frequent "cleanup" campaigns in an effort to get users to clean up their unused files. In this example, two commands are used, one after the other. The first command scans by UPDATE date, and the second by ACCESS date. The problem with the ACCESS date is that most tape backup packages will change the access date as they back up files. The following listing shows the result of these commands.

```
F:\>NDIR SYS:*.* /AC BEFORE 2-1-94 /SUB
Files            = Files contained in this path
Size             = Number of bytes in the file
Last Update      = Date file was last updated
Owner            = ID of user who created or copied the file
```

```
EBDB/SYS:\LOGIN\*.*
Files                          Size Last Update     Owner
---------------- ----------- ------------- ------------------------
CMPQ_RUN.OVL                  2,815  1-19-93 10:33a [Supervisor]
ETHER.RPL                    16,272  4-09-93  8:30a [Supervisor]
F1ETH.RPL                    12,157  4-09-93  8:34a [Supervisor]
IBM_RUN.OVL                   2,815  1-19-93 10:33a [Supervisor]
PCN2L.RPL                    10,607  4-09-93  8:37a [Supervisor]
RBOOT.RPL                     7,542  4-23-93  3:42p [Supervisor]
TEXTUTIL.IDX                  9,170 12-10-90  1:37p [Supervisor]
TOKEN.RPL                    17,252  4-27-93  7:48a [Supervisor]
_RUN.OVL                      2,815  1-19-93 10:33a [Supervisor]


        81,445  bytes (589,824  bytes in 9 blocks allocated)
             9  Files

...


F:\>NDIR SYS:*.* /UP BEFORE 2-1-94 /SUB
Files            = Files contained in this path
Size             = Number of bytes in the file
Last Update      = Date file was last updated
Owner            = ID of user who created or copied the file

...

EBDB/SYS:\\TEST\RDOAT\*.*
Files                          Size Last Update     Owner
---------------- ----------- ------------- ------------------------
DREW01.DOC                    5,049 12-09-93  6:06p Admin
DREW02.DOC                    8,192 12-09-93  6:08p Admin
OUTLINE.DOC                  14,561 12-14-93  9:43p Admin
OUTLINE2.DOC                 11,345 12-09-93  8:27p Admin
OUTLINE3.DOC                 14,132  1-19-94  8:36p Admin
OUTLINE4.DOC                  6,010  1-19-94  8:36p Admin
OUTLINE5.DOC                 16,266  1-19-94  9:09p Admin
OUTLINE6.DOC                 16,244  1-20-94 10:01p Admin
OUTLINE8.DOC                 15,242  1-30-94  4:49p Admin
```

```
        107,041  bytes (589,824  bytes in 9 blocks allocated)
              9  Files

    125,989,718  bytes (332,333,056  bytes in 5071 blocks allocated)

           4631  Files

F:\>
```

Example 3: Creating a List of Files Sorted by Size

In this example, you produce a list of files sorted by size, going from the largest size to the smallest. This is useful when you want to find out which files are taking up the most room on the volume. The following listing displays the results of this command. Note that the results of this command are redirected to the file F:\TEMP\BIGFILE.TXT using the redirection symbol (>).

```
F:\>NDIR F:\APPS\*.* /REV SORT SI /SUB >F:\TEMP\BIGFILE.TXT
Directories      = Directories contained in this path
Filter           = Inherited Rights Filter
Rights           = Effective Rights
Created          = Date directory was created
Owner            = ID of user who created or copied the file

EBDB/SYS:APPS\*.*
Directories       Filter      Rights      Created          Owner
---------------- ----------- ------------ -----------------------
WINWORD           [SRWCEMFA]  [SRWCEMFA]  5-12-94  1:59p Admin
VPIC              [SRWCEMFA]  [SRWCEMFA]  4-08-94  9:29p Admin
QUICKENW          [SRWCEMFA]  [SRWCEMFA]  4-08-94  7:15a [Supervisor]
NWCLIENT          [SRWCEMFA]  [SRWCEMFA]  4-10-94  6:13p Admin
GRAY              [SRWCEMFA]  [SRWCEMFA]  4-08-94  9:21p Admin
EXCEL             [SRWCEMFA]  [SRWCEMFA]  5-12-94  2:14p Admin
             6  Directories

Files            = Files contained in this path
Size             = Number of bytes in the file
Last Update      = Date file was last updated
Owner            = ID of user who created or copied the file

EBDB/SYS:APPS\GRAY\*.*
```

```
Files                         Size Last Update      Owner
---------------- ----------- ------------- -----------------------
GRAY.EXE                   504,192  6-07-93  8:53a Admin
SCAN.EXE                   147,906 10-12-90  5:49p Admin
SETUP.EXE                   84,924  6-17-93  6:19p Admin
SAILBOAT.TIF                72,192 12-14-90  3:31p Admin
HALO.KRN                    54,960  5-15-92 10:55a Admin
PKUNZIP.EXE                 29,378  2-01-93  2:04a Admin
SETUP.TXT                   27,862  6-17-93  9:06p Admin
README.TXT                  19,211  6-17-93  6:37p Admin
SETUP.HLP                   14,968  6-17-93  6:57p Admin
HHSCAND.SYS                 10,816 11-07-91  1:24p Admin
SETUP.CNF                   10,501  5-19-93  4:10p Admin
README.EXE                   7,284  6-17-93 11:29a Admin
SIGNON                       5,014  6-17-93  8:27p Admin
GRAY.CNF                     2,925  4-08-94  9:28p Admin
SETUP.LST                      445  6-15-93 10:34p Admin
CHKLIST.MS                     162  4-08-94  9:33p Admin

...
```

Example 4: Gathering Volume Statistics

You can use NDIR with the /VOL option to gather volume statistics. The syntax for this command is as follows:

```
NDIR SYS: /VOL
```

The following listing shows the results of issuing this command.

```
C:\NRP\INSIDE4>NDIR SYS: /VOL

Statistics for fixed volume EBDB/SYS:
Space statistics are in KB (1024 bytes).

Total volume space:                              134,656  100.00%
Space used by 1,929 entries:                      73,600   54.66%
Deleted space not yet purgeable:                       0    0.00%
                                            ------------ --------
Space remaining on volume:                        61,056   45.34%
Space available to ADMIN:                         61,056   45.34%

Maximum directory entries:                        19,968
Available directory entries:                       8,200   41.07%
```

```
Space used if files were not compressed:        150,341
Space used by compressed files:                  62,937
                                           ------------
Space saved by compressing files:                87,404   58.14%

Uncompressed space used:                         40,359

Name spaces loaded: OS/2
C:\NRP\INSIDE4>
```

Using FILER To Monitor the File System

The FILER.EXE utility can be used to view volume information and statistics. To access this feature, select View volume information from the FILER main menu. A submenu appears, giving you several choices: Statistics, Features, and Dates and times. The Statistics option shows you information very similar to that gathered with the NDIR /VOL command. Features gives you information on the special "features" installed for this volume. Dates and times gives you information on when the volume was created and when it was last modified.

FILER Volume Statistics

This section discusses the FILER Volume statistics screen illustrated in figure 26.1.

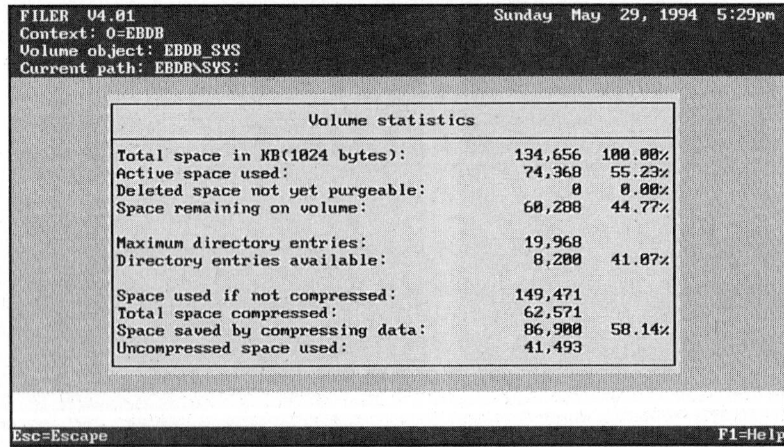

Figure 26.1
The Volume statistics screen.

Some statistics are represented as both an empirical number and a percentage. Table 26.2 summarizes the fields shown in the FILER statistics screen.

TABLE 26.2
Volume Statistics Descriptions

Statistic	Description
Total space in KB	This is the total amount of disk space available for this volume.
Active space used	Represents the amount of disk space in use through user and system files.
Deleted space not yet purgeable	Space used by deleted files that cannot yet be purged. The amount of time this space is taken up can be adjusted through a series of file server console SET commands that affect file purging. For example, the command SET MINIMUM FILE DELETE WAIT TIME affects the minimum time the system is required to wait before allowing files to be purged.
Space remaining on volume	Represents the available disk space on this volume.
Maximum directory entries	This figure is the current maximum size of the *Directory Entry Table* (DET). This number is increased when NetWare determines it needs more room in the table. Each directory entry contains the information extracted by NDIR as well as trustee rights information.
Directory entries available	Of the Maximum directory entries, this is the number of DET entries unused. When the server needs more entries, it allocates more automatically.
Space used if compressed	If file compression were not in effect, this is the not amount of disk space that would be required for the files on this volume.
Total space compressed	Represents the total space used by files that are compressed.

continues

Table 26.2, Continued
Volume Statistics Descriptions

Statistic	Description
Space saved by compressing data	Tells you how much space is saved through file compression.
Uncompressed space used	The amount of disk space used by files that were not compressed—either by setting the Dc (don't compress) attribute or where the percentage of compression gained fell below the minimum percentage required.

FILER Features, Dates, and Times

Figure 26.2 shows you the FILER Volume features screen.

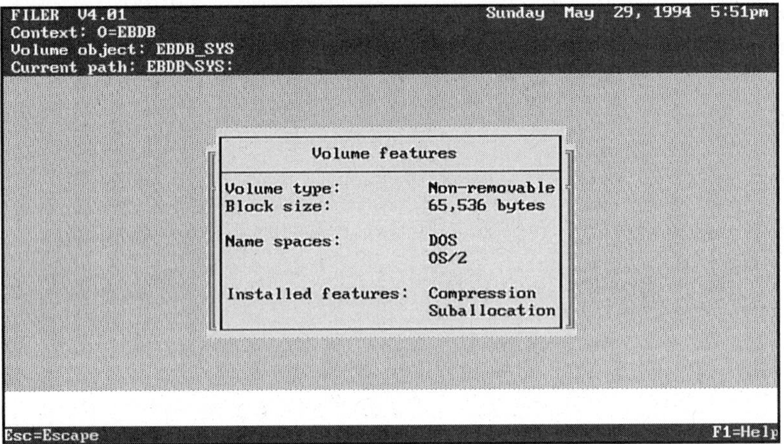

Figure 26.2
The Volume features screen.

The Volume type field shows you what type of volume you are examining. Choices include non-removable, which applies to fixed hard drives, or removable, such as CDs and Bernoulli drive packs. The Block size statistic tells you how the information on this volume is physically stored. Block sizes range from 4,096 (4 KB) to 65,536 (64 KB). The larger the block size, the better the throughput. Name spaces indicates what type of name space support has been added to this volume. Choices include DOS, OS/2, MAC (Macintosh), NFS (Network File System—used by most UNIX-based operating systems), and OSI (Open System Interconnection).

Installed features shows what special NetWare 4 file system features have been activated. Compression indicates that file compression has been enabled. Suballocation indicates the disk block suballocation feature has been enabled for this volume. Migration indicates the data migration feature has been enabled.

Figure 26.3 shows you the FILER Volume dates and times screen.

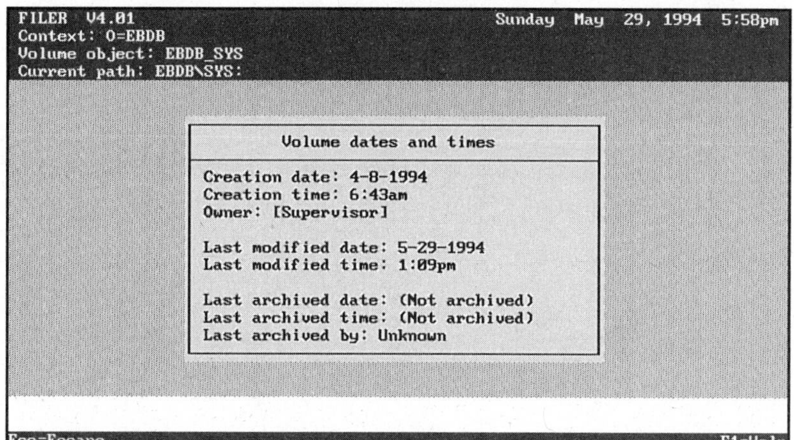

Figure 26.3

The Volume dates and times screen.

The Volume dates and times screen shows you information on the volume itself. Dates include the following:

- Creation date and time (the date and time the volume was first installed)
- Owner (the user who created the volume, usually the Supervisor)
- Last modified date and time (when the last change to the volume was made)
- Last archived date and time (the last time the entire volume was backed up)
- Last archived by (the user who last backed up the entire volume)

Note that volume modifications include name space support changes.

NWADMIN Volume Statistics

As with FILER, the NWADMIN.EXE utility features volume statistics. From the NWADMIN main screen, you need to locate the desired volume object. Once you have selected this object, select Details from the Object menu. A volume information dialog box appears. At the right side of the volume information dialog box, select Statistics. Figure 26.4 shows you the NWADMIN volume statistics screen.

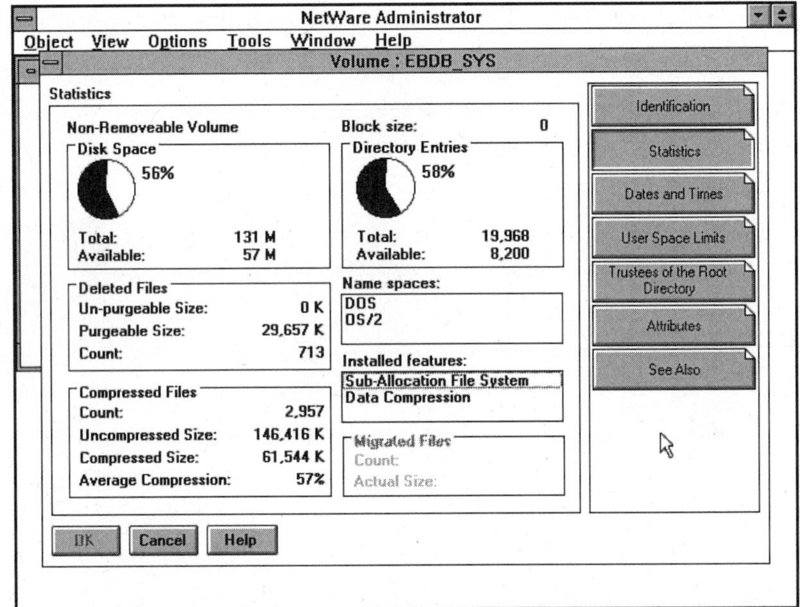

Figure 26.4
The NWADMIN volume statistics screen.

As you can see from the figure, this screen presents the same information as is found in FILER, presented in table 26.2. The NWADMIN volume statistics screen is graphical in nature and has a pie chart representing the total disk space used (solid color). On the right is another pie chart representing the directory entry table status.

Understanding Name Space Support

An important NetWare feature for the network with different desktop operating systems is that of *name space support.* The name of each file, when created, is added to the DET (Directory Entry Table). By default, the name and information for a file stored in the DET are based on DOS. As a result, by default, the file name and attributes of a file stored on a file server must follow DOS conventions. The information and restrictions imposed by DOS are as follows:

- File names are not case-sensitive.
- File names must be no more than eight characters, a period (.), and up to a three-character extension. This is called the "8.3 format."
- DOS attributes include Ro, Rw, H, Sy, and A.

- The file size is in bytes.
- DOS keeps track of the date the file was created or last modified.

NetWare preserves the information tracked by the workstation's "native" operating system. For DOS files, in addition to the information listed earlier, the following information and restrictions are available by default in the DET:

- NetWare attributes of Cc, Ci, Co, Dc, Di, Dm, Ic, M, P, Ri, Sh, and T
- File status (compressed, migrated, or normal)
- File owner's name
- IRF for the file
- File trustee rights
- Compression information
- Dates (date created, last accessed, last archived, last modified)

The following is a summary of DOS and NetWare attributes:.

Code	Attribute Name
A	Archive Needed
Cc	Can't Compress
Ci	Copy Inhibit
Co	Compressed
Dc	Don't Compress
Di	Delete Inhibit
Dm	Don't Migrate
H	Hidden
Ic	Immediate Compress
M	Migrated
P	Purge
Ri	Rename Inhibit
Ro	Read Only
Rw	Read/Write

continues

Code	Attribute Name
Sh	Shareable
Sy	System
T	Transactional

The problem with the default DET information is that it does not fully work for OS/2 files, and it certainly does not work for Macintosh or UNIX files. OS/2, for example, supports file names of up to 254 characters in length. To compensate for this inadequacy, NetWare provides a series of *name space support* modules. These modules are NLMs with a file name extension of NAM.

Adding Name Space Support

The following two actions must be performed before NetWare will support file information other than DOS:

- Load the name space module
- Add name space to the volume

Loading the name space module is simply a matter of issuing the LOAD command from the file server console and indicating the desired name space module. The name space modules provided with NetWare include MAC.NAM (Macintosh) and OS2.NAM (OS/2). The name space module NFS.NAM, which supports most UNIX systems, is available with additional software. NFS.NAM is included in Novell's NetWare NFS, Flex/IP, or UnixWare software packages. Other name space support packages include FTAM (File Transfer, Access, and Management, used for OSI-based system), and NT (New Technologies, used with Microsoft Windows NT-based systems).

To load the name space module for OS/2, for example, enter the following command from the file server's console:

LOAD OS2.NAM

In order to be effective, this command must be issued before the target volume has been mounted. To make this module available every time the file server boots up, add this command to the STARTUP.NCF file.

The next step is to add name space support to the volume. This action needs to be performed only once. What NetWare does when name space support is added is to add another entry in the DET for every existing file on the volume. This increases the

size of the DET by roughly 50 percent. The increased size of the DET will require more RAM on the file server when it caches the DET.

Think carefully about adding name space support to file servers that do not have sufficient RAM—you will end up with less RAM to service user requests, which might result in poor network performance.

The syntax for the command to add name space is as follows:

```
ADD NAME SPACE <name space module> TO <volume>
```

In place of *name space module*, you enter OS2, MAC, or NFS, for example. In place of *volume*, you enter the name of the volume to which you want to add name space. Figure 26.5 shows you the file server console screen where the commands to LOAD OS2 and to add name space have been issued.

```
EBDB:LOAD C:OS2.NAM
Loading module OS2.NAM
  Netware HPFS Name Space Support
  Version 4.00    February 1, 1993
EBDB:ADD NAME SPACE OS2 TO SYS
Adding a new name space may require up to 808K of available disk space.
At the present time the volume has only 62976K of available disk space.
If while adding the name space the server runs out of disk space then you
will be asked to either free up more disk space or dismount the volume.


Proceeding with the add name space.
OS2 name space support successfully added to volume SYS
EBDB:
```

Figure 26.5

Loading and adding OS/2 name space support.

What Happens When Name Space Support Is Added?

When name space support is added, the file server modifies the DET, adding a new entry for each existing file. The new entry has a translated file name that matches the convention of the target name space. In addition, other attributes associated with the target name space are entered in the DET. This process takes additional disk space and RAM on the file server. A warning message will appear, as displayed in figure 26.5, giving you an idea how much additional disk space will be used.

Each file now has two DET entries—one corresponding to the DOS operating system, and the other corresponding to the new name space module, OS/2, for example. NetWare detects which operating system your workstation uses and automatically gives you DET information based on that operating system. A DOS workstation sees DOS file information. An OS/2 workstation sees OS/2 information. If an OS/2 user creates a file, its OS/2 file name is translated into a DOS file name as well. If a DOS user creates a file, the name is translated into an OS/2 file name.

When NetWare cannot translate a file name exactly, it takes up to eight characters, adds a period, and then takes the next three characters. When the first eight characters of two different OS/2 files are the same, NetWare's name space support will take as many characters of the original file name as possible before adding random characters. NetWare will not allow two DOS or two OS/2 files with the same name.

OS/2 Name Space Support

OS/2 name space support offers many of the same features as the default DOS name space support. This module differs from DOS in the following ways:

- ◆ Support for OS/2's HPFS (High Performance File System)
- ◆ Named pipes support
- ◆ Support for long file names

The HPFS is an improvement over the method by which DOS manages files. The HPFS has an improved method of searching for files. DOS starts with the current directory and searches in a sequential fashion. HPFS uses a B-tree algorithm to improve the speed of searches. In DOS, the root directory is placed at either the beginning or end of the DOS partition. HPFS places the root directory at the "seek center" of the partition, which has the effect of speeding up searches.

Named pipes are a method of providing OS/2 workstations with a way of referencing resources without being aware of their physical location. You might have an OS/2 workstation managing a database. Other OS/2 workstations can access this data through the named pipes mechanism.

An OS/2 file name can be up to 254 characters in length. In addition, there are no restrictions in the number of periods in an OS/2 file name. OS/2 also allows spaces in a file name. As long as the OS2.NAM name space module is loaded on the server, and the ADD NAME SPACE OS2 TO *volume* command has been issued once, OS/2 workstations can save files using OS/2 naming conventions. The following shows you the result of the NDIR /L command in a directory containing OS/2 files.

```
F:\DATA\OS2DATA>NDIR /L
Files             = Files contained in this path
Size              = Number of bytes in the file
EA Size           = Extended attribute size
Last Update       = Date file was last updated

EBDB/SYS:DATA\OS2DATA\*.*
```

```
Files                                     Size       EA Size Last Update
-------------------------------- ----------- ----------- -------------
OS2.FIL                                    179             0  5-14-94  2:44p
 OS/2:   OS2.NET.CFG.File

THISISAL                                   355             0  5-12-94  5:08p
 OS/2:   ThisIsALongFileName

THISISAN.2EX                             2,784             0  5-12-94  5:13p
 OS/2:   ThisIsAnotherOS.2ExtremelyLongFilename


        3,318  bytes (196,608  bytes in 3 blocks allocated)
            3  Files

F:\DATA\OS2DATA>
```

The OS2.NAM name space module provides for HPFS or standard DOS/FAT file name support in conjunction with the NetWare Client for OS/2. Without the proper client support, the OS2.NAM module would not be able to provide proper OS/2 name space support.

Macintosh Name Space Support

Macintosh name space support includes support for features unique to the Mac environment. Mac file names can be up to 32 characters long. The names are case-sensitive and can have embedded spaces, unlike DOS. In addition, each Mac file name includes a pointer to the application that created the associated file. This pointer includes other information and is known as a *resource fork.* When the Mac user double-clicks on the file icon, the user expects to load not only the file, but the application that created it. The MAC.NAM name space support module includes support for the Mac resource fork.

UNIX Name Space Support

Most UNIX systems support NFS (Network File System). Novell's UnixWare Application Server 1.1, for example, supports NFS. In the case of UnixWare, you must first install the core product, then TCP/IP, and then NFS. All three packages are supplied on the distribution CD or tape. Other versions of UNIX, such as Sun or IBM's AIX, also support NFS over the TCP/IP protocol suite.

UNIX, using NFS, has a very different set of file-name features and requirements. Table 26.3 summarizes these features.

Table 26.3
UNIX File-Name Features

Feature	Description
Date and time	Date and time the file was created or last modified.
File name	The UNIX file name can be up to 256 characters in length. In some systems only the first 14 characters are significant. Any character can be used in the file name (including spaces, periods, and slash characters) as long as file names with special characters are referred to using quotes.
Group	The group name or GID (Group Identification number) of the primary group of the user who created or is the current owner of the file.
Inode	This is a pointer to the *inode* (information node) table. An inode contains the file's permission mask, UID, GID, size, date, and time. In addition, the inode contains a pointer to the starting location of the file on the UNIX file system. The name of the file is stored in the directory file.
Owner	The user name or UID (User Identification number) of the UNIX user who created or is the current owner of the file.
Permissions	UNIX permissions are a cross between DOS file attributes and NetWare trustee rights. There are 10 characters in a UNIX permission mask. The first character indicates the type of file (regular file, directory, or special file). The next three indicate the rights that apply to the owner of the file (the person who created the file). The next three are the rights that apply to the group that owns the file. The last three apply to any user who is neither the owner nor a member of the group. The permissions can be R (read), W (write), or X (execute). The meaning of the permissions changes depending on whether they apply to a directory or to a file.
Size	Size of the file in bytes. On some systems the size is referenced in disk blocks.

The NFS.NAM module provides the support summarized in table 26.3. In addition, NFS.NAM provides translation between UNIX file information and DOS file information.

NFS.NAM by itself does not provide UNIX connectivity. In addition to NFS name space support, you need modules that provide NFS file system support. This generally requires either specialized support on the UNIX workstation or additional software running on the file server. On the UNIX workstation side, most vendors provide some sort of NetWare connectivity option. Novell's UnixWare, for example, provides integrated NetWare support. On the file server side, Novell provides several options. NetWare NFS makes the file server appear as if it has an NFS file system that UNIX workstations can mount. Flex/IP provides the ability to transfer files using FTP (File Transfer Protocol). NFS Gateway allows NetWare clients to access the file systems on remote UNIX hosts.

Other Name Space Support

Other name space support includes FTAM and NT. The FTAM name space support is for OSI (Open Systems Interconnection) based systems. In the mid-1980s, the U.S. Government mandated that all government computer systems must adhere to the GOSIP (Government OSI Profile) standard by the turn of the century. Many vendors came out with modifications of their systems that adhered to these standards. Novell produced a package called NetWare FTAM. Sales of the product were dismal at best. This particular division was sold to an independent company. The product is compatible with NetWare, but Novell no longer sells, supports, or maintains this particular product.

Because Microsoft Windows NT provides a built-in capability of reading disks and other media using the traditional DOS FAT type of file name, NTFS name space support is not needed on the file server. When accessing a file on the file server, the Windows NT client will read from the server using the DOS FAT name space. When writing files to the server, the Windows NT client is limited to DOS naming conventions.

Removing Name Space Support

To remove name space support for a volume, several actions should be performed, as outlined here. Bear in mind that although this operation could be completed while users are logged in to the file server, it is not recommended. If users are using the volume from which you want to remove name space support, you will have to ask them to either log out or stop using applications or data on that volume.

To remove name space support for a volume, follow these steps:

1. Back up the volume. In some cases removing name space support causes damage to files or possibly the entire volume.

2. Load the VREPAIR name space support module for the name space you want to remove. They are as follows:

VREPAIR Name Space Module	Associated Name Space Support Module
V_MAC.NLM	MAC.NAM
V_OS2.NLM	OS2.NAM
V_NFS.NLM	NFS.NAM

   To remove OS/2 name space support, for example, from the file server console, type the following:

   LOAD V_OS2.NLM

3. The VREPAIR name space support module will automatically load VREPAIR.NLM. From the VREPAIR menu, select option 2, Set Vrepair Options. The VREPAIR options menu appears.

4. From the VREPAIR options menu, select option 1, Remove Name Space support from the volume. This menu is illustrated in figure 26.6. The Supported Name Space menu appears.

Figure 26.6
The VREPAIR options menu.

```
Current Vrepair Configuration:

     Quit If A Required VRepair Name Space Support NLM Is Not Loaded

     Write Only Changed Directory And FAT Entries Out To Disk

     Keep Changes In Memory For Later Update

     Retain Deleted Files

Options:

     1. Remove Name Space support from the volume

     2. Write All Directory And FAT Entries Out To Disk

     3. Write Changes Immediately To Disk

     4. Purge All Deleted Files

     0. Return To Main Menu

     Enter your choice:
```

5. From the Supported Name Space menu, select the name space support you want to remove. You are returned to the VREPAIR options menu. From this menu select option 0, Return to Main Menu.

6. From here you first need to toggle to the console prompt and dismount the volume whose name space you want to remove. You can do so by pressing Alt+Esc enough times to cycle through the menus until you return to the file server console prompt. If you are accessing the file server's console through the RCONSOLE.EXE utility, use the Alt+F3 or Alt+F4 keys to toggle to the console prompt.

7. From the console prompt, use the DISMOUNT *volume* command to dismount the target volume. To dismount volume SYS, for example, type the following:

   DISMOUNT SYS

8. Use the Alt+Esc (or Alt+F3 or Alt+F4 if using RCONSOLE.EXE) to return to VREPAIR. From the VREPAIR main menu, select option 1, Repair a Volume. Even though removing name space support may not appear to you as a "repair," the VREPAIR utility views it as such. VREPAIR will scan through the DET and remove name space support for each entry, starting with the root of the volume. Each time a DET entry is updated, VREPAIR records it as an error. You will get an error message for every file and directory on this volume. The first error message will be for the root of the volume, as displayed in figure 26.7.

```
Error at directory entry 0

Original Entry - Volume root directory entry
   Name: \
   The name space list is invalid
   The reserved area was not properly zero filled
   Supported name space list is invalid

Corrected Entry - Volume root directory entry
   Name: \
<Press F1 to change settings, or any other key to continue>
```

Figure 26.7

Removing name space support with VREPAIR—First error message.

9. From the error message screen, press the F1 key. Select option 1, Do not pause after errors. Otherwise you will have to press Enter after each file and directory on the volume. At this point you can select option 0, Continue with volume repair. A screen appears with a string of dots to signify that the operation is continuing. When the operation is completed, you see a screen similar to the one shown in figure 26.8.

Figure 26.8

Removing name space support with VREPAIR—The final screen.

```
Total errors: 10598
Current settings:
  Do not pause after each error
  Do not log errors to a file
Press F1 to change settings

Start  2:42:52 pm
Checking volume SYS

FAT blocks>..................................................................<
Counting directory blocks and checking directory FAT entries
Mirror mismatches>...........................................................<
Directories>.................................................................<
Files>.......................................................................<
Trustees>....................................................................<
Deleted Files>...............................................................<
Extended directory mismatches>...............................................<
Free blocks>.................................................................<

Done checking volume
Number of FAT repairs: 0
Number of directory repairs: 10598
Write repairs to the disk? (Y/N): y
```

10. A prompt appears, asking "Write repairs to disk? (Y/N)." Answer Y to this prompt, and the name space support is permanently removed. The hard drive on the server indicates a large amount of activity until this operation is completed.

11. At this point you are finished. Press Enter to return to the VREPAIR main menu. Select option 0 to exit out of VREPAIR and return to the console prompt. You now need to use the MOUNT *volume* command to bring the volume back on line without name space support. You can also remove the command to load the name space support module from your STARTUP.NCF file.

Working with CD-ROM Drives

After the drivers for the SCSI controller are loaded, another utility, CDROM.NLM, provided with NetWare 4.1, must be loaded. This utility enables CD-ROMs to act as NetWare volumes. CDROM.NLM commands are preceded by the letters *CD* and are issued from the file server console. Table 26.4 summarizes the CDROM.NLM commands.

TABLE 26.4
CDROM.NLM Commands

Command	Description
CD CHANGE *[number][volume]*	Use this command when changing a CD in a CD-ROM player on the server. The *number* or *volume* represents the CD player or volume name of the existing CD. When you change the CD, the old CD volume will be dismounted and the new CD volume will be mounted. You will notice a "Device Deactivated" message when this command is issued. This occurs between dismount ing the old CD and mounting the new CD, and is not a cause for concern.
CD DEVICE LIST	This command gives you a list of all CD-ROM drives detected by CDROM.NLM. This listing shows the device number assigned to each CD-ROM drive.
CD DIR *[number][volume]*	This command gives you a DOS-style directory listing of the contents of the CD. The CD can be referred to by volume name or number.
CD DISMOUNT *[number][volume]*	This command dismounts CD-ROM drive by *number,* or by *volume.* Once dismounted, the RAM allocated to cache the FAT and DET of the CD is released, and the CD is no longer available to network users.
CD HELP	This command gives you a list of the available CD commands and what actions they perform.
CD MOUNT *[number][volume] [/R]*	This command makes the CD indicated by CD player *number,* or by *volume,* available to network users. The MOUNT command might take some time to perform. NetWare will cache the FAT of the CD, as well as portions of its DET. Use the */R* parameter when mounting a CD that has been mounted before. This causes NetWare to reuse files created when it mounted this CD in the past. You will notice a tremendous speed increase in remounting the CD when this parameter is used.

continues

Table 26.4, Continued
CDROM.NLM Commands

Command	Description
	Make sure you have adequate file server RAM before issuing this command. You can verify how much RAM is used by loading the MONITOR.NLM and looking at the Resource Utilization menu, Cache Buffers parameter before and after mounting the CD. If the percentage of RAM used by cache buffers remains above 50 percent, you will experience no difficulties on your network. A figure between 20–50 percent will ensure baseline performance. A figure below 20 percent indicates a need for more RAM in your file server.
CD VOLUME LIST	This command gives you a list of volume names for all CDs loaded in CD-ROM drives detected by CDROM.NLM.

You can use one file server command and two utilities to test whether a CD has been properly mounted. The file server command is issued from the file server's console prompt (:). (You can switch to the console prompt from another NLM by pressing Alt+Esc until you reach the prompt.) Type **VOLUMES**. You should see the new CD volume listed along with the other NetWare volumes. In addition to the CD commands listed earlier, the other way to view the status of a CD-ROM drive is to use MONITOR.NLM or SERVMAN.NLM.

To access MONITOR.NLM, type the following from the file server's console prompt:

LOAD MONITOR

From the main menu, select the Disk Information menu. You will see a list of disk drives available on the file server. Locate the CD-ROM drive and press Enter. Note that you can gather statistics on the CD. The Drive Status field tells you whether the drive is active.

SERVMAN.NLM can give you even more information on the status of a CD-ROM drive. To load this utility, type the following from the file server's console prompt:

LOAD SERVMAN

From the main menu, select the Volume Information menu. You will see a list of "storage objects" available on the file server. Locate the CD-ROM drive and press Enter. You can gather information on the device driver for the HBA, the CD-ROM drive device itself, the partition on the CD, and the volume information. Move the cursor up and down these items to gather this information.

Summary

This chapter covered how to monitor and maintain the file system. The NDIR command was covered in great detail. The syntax and command-line options for the command were presented. As you learned, NDIR includes options that control the format of the output and restrictions on what information is presented. Examples given for NDIR included how to find a lost file by owner, which files have not been updated in the last six months, creating a list of files sorted by size, and gathering volume statistics. FILER.EXE and NWADMIN.EXE were also discussed. FILER has a volume statistics option, and NWADMIN enables you to view statistics on NDS volume objects.

You also learned about name space support issues. You were introduced to the concept and were shown how and why you would add name space support. Issues specific to OS/2, Macintosh, UNIX, and other types of name space support were presented. Finally, you were shown how to remove name space support from a volume using VREPAIR and a specialized name space support module.

The last part of this chapter discussed installing and managing CD-ROM drives on a file server. The CDROM.NLM was discussed, along with some of its parameters. You learned that the way to monitor the status of your disk drives is through MONITOR.NLM and SERVMAN.NLM.

Part VII

Printing

New Riders Publishing
INSIDE
SERIES

Setting Up Printing

This chapter shows you, step by step, how to set up printing on a NetWare 4 network. The first section gives you the "quick and dirty" method: using the PCONSOLE.EXE Quick Setup option. This is perhaps the fastest and easiest way to set up NetWare 4 printing. The next section shows you the process using the Windows-based NWADMIN.EXE utility. The following section covers how to start the print server and how to configure computers with printers attached. The last section covers printers with direct network connections.

Quick Setup with PCONSOLE

The PCONSOLE.EXE Quick Setup option is the fastest way to set up NetWare 4 printing. This option offers, in one screen, the ability to define all three basic objects of NetWare 4 printing:

- Print queues
- Printers
- Print servers

Not only does this option enable you to define these objects, but it creates the necessary links between the objects. When you are finished with this utility, all you need to do is start the print server and load the NPRINTER driver at each computer that has a network printer.

To access this option, you need first to log into the network as a user with sufficient rights to create printing objects under the desired target container. After you have done so, from a DOS command prompt, run PCONSOLE.EXE. From the main menu, use the Change Context option to change to the target container. This is the container under which you would like to place the new printing objects. After the current context is set to the appropriate container, proceed as follows:

1. From the PCONSOLE main menu, select Quick Setup. The Print Services Quick Setup menu appears, as illustrated in figure 27.1.

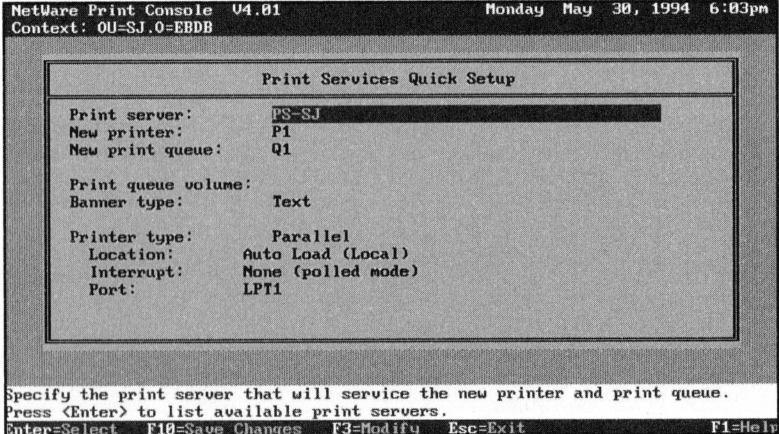

Figure 27.1
The Print Services Quick Setup menu.

2. From the Print Services Quick Setup menu you can now enter the basic parameters for the printing objects you plan to create. As you can see in the figure, there are three basic objects represented: the print server, a printer, and a queue. When you are finished with this screen, press F10. PCONSOLE creates these objects and associates the queue with the printer, and the printer with the print server. You then are presented with this screen again, with a new printer and queue. The numbers for the printers and queues continues to increment until you are ready to stop or the maximum number of printers (256) is reached.

Table 27.1 summarizes each field in the Print Services Quick Setup menu.

TABLE 27.1
Print Services Quick Setup Menu Fields

Field	Description
Print server	Name of the print server object. The default is *PS-container,* where *container* is the name of the current context container.
New printer	Name of the new printer you are currently adding. The default is *Pn,* where *n* is a number starting with 1.
New print queue	Name of the new queue you are currently adding. The default is *Qn,* where *n* is a number starting with 1.
Print queue volume	NDS name of the volume that will contain the print jobs temporarily until they can be printed. PCONSOLE will create a directory on this volume called QUEUES. Under this, directory will be a numbered subdirectory. The number will correspond with an internal identifying number assigned to this queue.
Banner type	This field can take on one of two values: text or postscript. Use text if the majority of your printing to this queue is on non-PostScript printers. If you plan to use primarily PostScript printers, select postscript. Selecting postscript ensures that a banner page, if printed, will not cause the printer to slip out of PostScript mode.
Printer type	Printer type can be any of these choices: *Parallel* is used for printers attached to any LPT port. *Serial* is for printers attached to any COM port. *Unix Printer* is for printers attached to UNIX workstations. *AppleTalk Printer* is for LaserWriters or other printers that use the AppleTalk printing protocols.

continues

Table 27.1, Continued
Print Services Quick Setup Menu Fields

Field	Description
	Other/Unknown is used when the type of printer is not known at this time. When a user or network Administrator attempts to connect this printer later, this menu will appear again, giving them these choices of printers: *XNP* is used for Xerox Network Protocol printers. *AIO* is for when your printer is connected through a remote connection (such as using NetWare Connect). Several hardware types are supported for AIO printing. These include COM ports, IBM Artic boards, ISDN controllers, NewPort Systems ANIC or WNIC, Hayes ESP boards, DigiBoard /X series boards, and Network Products Corporation boards.

3. Depending on the Printer type selected, other parameters might have to be entered. Table 27.2 summarizes the settings for different printer types.

Table 27.2
Print Services Quick Setup Printer Types

Printer Type	Parameter	Description
Parallel	Location	The default value is Auto Load (Local). This means that the printer is attached to the file server where PSERVER.NLM is running. NPRINTER.NLM, needed to initialize the printer, will be automatically loaded for this printer. The other possible value is Manual Load. As the name implies, you will need to manually load NPRINTER.NLM (for printers attached to file servers), or NPRINTER.EXE (for printers attached to workstations) to make the printer available.
	Interrupt	The interrupt for the parallel port on this computer. Values include all available interrupts (2 through 15) or None (polled mode). Using polled mode makes use of the computer's CPU that brings down performance of other processes running on that computer. On the other

Printer Type	Parameter	Description
		hand, polled mode allows certain software packages to coexist with NPRINTER (such as Windows).
	Port	Which parallel port. Choices include LPT1, LPT2, and LPT3.
Serial	Location	The default value is Auto Load (Local). This means that the printer is attached to the file server where PSERVER.NLM is running. NPRINTER.NLM, needed to initialize the printer, will be automatically loaded for this printer. The other possible value is Manual Load. As the name implies, you will need to manually load NPRINTER.NLM (for printers attached to file servers), or NPRINTER.EXE (for printers attached to workstations) to make the printer available.
	Interrupt	The interrupt for the parallel porton this computer. Values include all available interrupts (2 through 15) or None (polled mode). Using polled mode makes use of the computer's CPU that brings down performance of other processes running on that computer. On the other hand, polled mode allows certain software packages to coexist with NPRINTER (such as Windows).
	Port	Which serial port the printer is connected to. Choices include COM1, COM2, COM3, and COM4. You can select COM3 or COM4 only if your computer has the necessary hardware.
	Baud rate	Transmission speed the printer can handle. The larger the number, the faster the speed.
	Data bits	The number of bits in the data portion of each character sent to the printer.
	Parity	Method of parity error checking. Choices include Even, Odd, or None. This depends on the configuration of your printer.

continues

Table 27.2, Continued
Print Services Quick Setup Printer Types

Printer Type	Parameter	Description
	Stop bits	The number of bits per character sent to the printer used as a sort of "frame" around the character.
	Use X-ON/ X-OFF	This is a method of making sure too much data is not sent to the printer. If you set this option to YES, software sends a signal informing the print server when the printer's buffer has overflowed. If you set this to NO, hardware is used to control the flow of data using the CTS (Clear To Send) signal in the RS-232 connector.
Unix Printer	Host name	The name of the UNIX host that has the printer.
	Printer name	The name of the printer as defined on the UNIX host.
AppleTalk	AppleTalk name	The name of the printer as defined on the Printer AppleTalk side of the network.
	AppleTalk type	The type of printer. Choices include LaserWriter, ImageWriter, LQ, DeskWriter, DeskWriter 550C, PaintWriter XL, PaintJet XL300, and Other.
	AppleTalk zone	The name of the zone in which the printer has been defined. The default of asterisk (*) allows the printer to fit into any zone in most cases.
	Hide AppleTalk Printer	If you specify YES (recommended), Macs will not be able to send jobs to the printer directly. Instead they will have to send their jobs to the print queue, which will then redirect the job to the printer. If you select NO, Macs can send jobs directly to the printer, which might cause conflicts between jobs originating directly at a Macintosh and those originating at the NetWare print queue.
	Print error banners	This determines if error messages will appear on the error banner message page.

Printer Type	Parameter	Description
AIO	Location	Same as for Parallel.
	Hardware Type	This can be a value from 0 to 255. The types defined so far include the following: **Number** — **Hardware** 1 — COM1, COM2, and so on 2 — IBM's Artic board 3 — Gateway Communications WNIM+ 101 — AVM ISDN Controller-B1 102 — Newport Systems ANIC 103 — Newport Systems WNIC 104 — Hayes ESP board 105 — Digiboard DIGIXI series 106 — Digiboard DIGICX series 107 — Digiboard DIGIXM series 108 — Digiboard DIGIEP series 109 — Network Products Corp. NPCC
	Board number	The board number that the printer will use.
	Port	The port number assigned to the printer.
	Baud rate	Same as for Serial.
	Data bits	Same as for Serial.
	Parity	Same as for Serial.
	Stop bits	Same as for Serial.
	Use X-ON/ X-OFF	Same as for Serial.

If you select Unix Printer, AppleTalk Printer, or AIO printer, you must load additional software on the file server before these options can work. In the case of UNIX, you must load the printer gateways supplied with the NetWare NFS or Flex/IP packages. In the case of AppleTalk, you need to load the printing modules supplied with NetWare for Macintosh. AIO printers require a remote communications package such as NetWare Connect to operate.

4. Press the F10 key to register your configuration. This information will be entered into the NDS (which must synchronize the information to servers with replicas of the NDS partition). You will be returned to the PCONSOLE main menu.

5. If you want to continue to add printing objects in this context, from the main menu, select Quick Setup again and enter the new information. Note that the printer and queue numbers increment, enabling you to enter information rapidly. Continue in this fashion until all printing objects have been entered. Press Esc or Alt+F10 to exit PCONSOLE.

You can also enter printer, queue, and printer server objects separately by selecting the appropriate options from the main menu of PCONSOLE. If this is the case, you must make the connection between queue and printer, and printer and print server. To do so, follow these steps:

1. After the Queue, Printer, and Print Server objects have been defined, select Printers from the main menu of PCONSOLE. Select the target printer and press Enter. The Printer Configuration screen appears. Move your cursor to the option Print queues assigned and press Enter. You can see a list that starts with the words "Print Queue" at the upper left of the box.

2. From the Print Queue list, press Insert. Select the Print Queue object you want to assign to this Printer object. Press Enter to register your choice. Press Esc to exit this screen. You are returned to the Printer Configuration screen. Press Esc to return to the main menu of PCONSOLE.

3. From the PCONSOLE main menu, select Print Servers. Select the target print server and press Enter. The Print Server Information menu appears.

4. From the Print Server Information menu, select Printers. The Serviced Printers list appears.

5. From the Serviced Printers list, press Insert. Select the desired printer to add to this print server. Press Enter to register your choice. Press Esc several times or Alt+F10 to exit PCONSOLE when you are finished.

Using NWADMIN To Set Up Printing

When using the NWADMIN.EXE utility to set up printing, it is very important to remember the links between the three basic elements of printing. These connections are illustrated in figure 27.2.

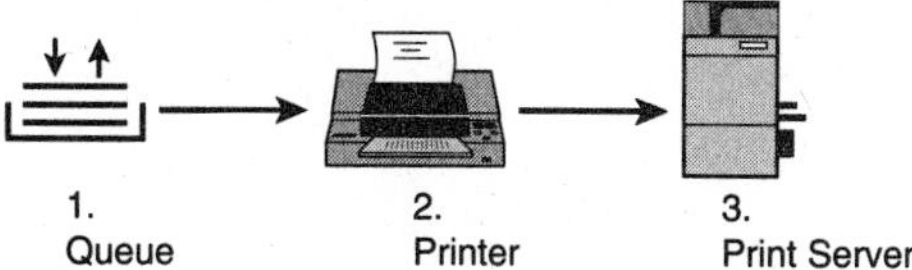

Figure 27.2
The connections between the three basic NetWare 4 printing objects.

As you can see in figure 27.2, first create the print queue object. Next, create the printer object. Finally, create the print server object. To make the association complete, assign the queue to a printer. The printer is then assigned to the print server. This section walks you through the process of creating queue, printer, and print server objects and shows you how to connect the three together to ensure smooth printing.

Creating Print Queue Objects

Before you can create a print queue object in the NWADMIN utility, you must first be logged in as a user with sufficient NDS rights to create objects in the target container. Once this is the case, get into Windows and click on the icon for NWADMIN.EXE (the NetWare Administrator utility). Select the desired container object, and proceed as follows:

1. After the desired container under which you plan to create printing objects has been selected, press the Insert key or select Create from the Object menu. The New Object dialog box appears. You can see a list of possible objects to create.

2. From the New Object dialog box, select Print Queue and click the OK button. The Create Print Queue dialog box appears, as shown in figure 27.3.

3. Fill in the name of the new print queue in the Print Queue Name field. Be as descriptive as possible. The print queue is what most users print to. The Print Queue Volume field should contain the NDS name of the volume to contain print jobs temporarily until printed. Place a checkmark in the Define Additional Properties box if you plan to add restrictions (such as print queue users) or other information to the print queue object. Otherwise, if you plan to create several queue objects at once, check the Create Another Print Queue box. When you are finished, press the Create button. The print queue object appears under the desired container, and you are returned to the view of the NDS tree.

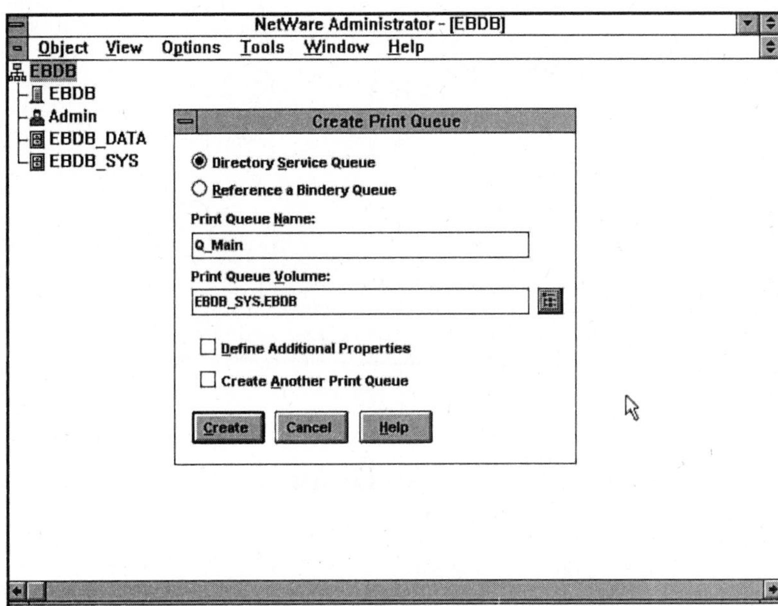

Figure 27.3
The Create Print Queue dialog box.

The Reference a Bindery Queue option is used if you need to manage a print queue on a NetWare 3.*x* or earlier (bindery-based) file server. If this is the case, enter the name you plan to use to represent the bindery-based queue in your NDS tree. Next, enter the name of the server and queue being referenced in the NetWare Server and Queue dialog box. Select OK to exit the NetWare Server and Queue dialog box and Create to add the queue. You can now manage the bindery-based queue from NWADMIN.

By default, the container becomes a print queue user. This means that all user objects and all objects below this container receive access to this print queue. If for some reason you want to restrict access to the queue, select the queue and press Enter, click on the right mouse button, or select **D**etails from the **O**bject menu. The Print Queue dialog box appears, as shown in figure 27.4.

From the Print Queue dialog box, select the Users button at the right side of the dialog box. Remove the container or user objects that are not desired, and select Add to add the desired objects. In this fashion you can control which objects have access to the print queue.

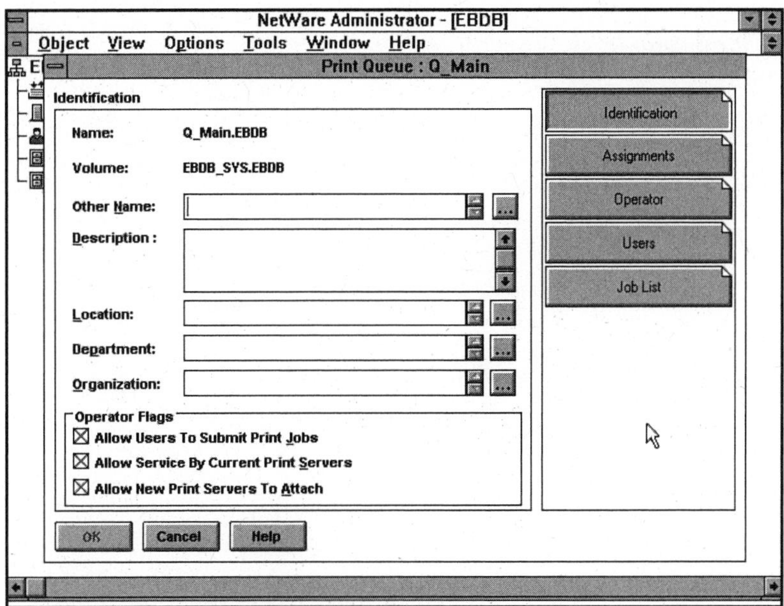

Figure 27.4

The Print Queue dialog box.

Creating Printer Objects

From the main NWADMIN menu, make sure you are in the container under which you want to add printer objects. To add printer objects, proceed as follows:

1. After the desired container under which you plan to create printing objects has been selected, press Insert or select Create from the Object menu. The New Object dialog box appears. You can see a list of possible objects to create.

2. From the New Object dialog box, select Printer and click on OK. The Create Printer dialog box appears, as illustrated in figure 27.5.

3. Fill in the name of the new printer in the Printer Name field. Place a checkmark in the Define Additional Properties box if you plan to add restrictions (such as print queue users) or other information to the print queue object. Otherwise, if you plan to create several queue objects at once, check the Create Another Printer box. When you are finished, press the Create button. The printer object appears under the desired container, and you are returned to the view of the NDS tree.

To configure the new printer object, select the printer object and press Enter, click on the right mouse button, or select Details from the Object menu. The Printer dialog box appears. The Configuration and Notification options are discussed in the following section.

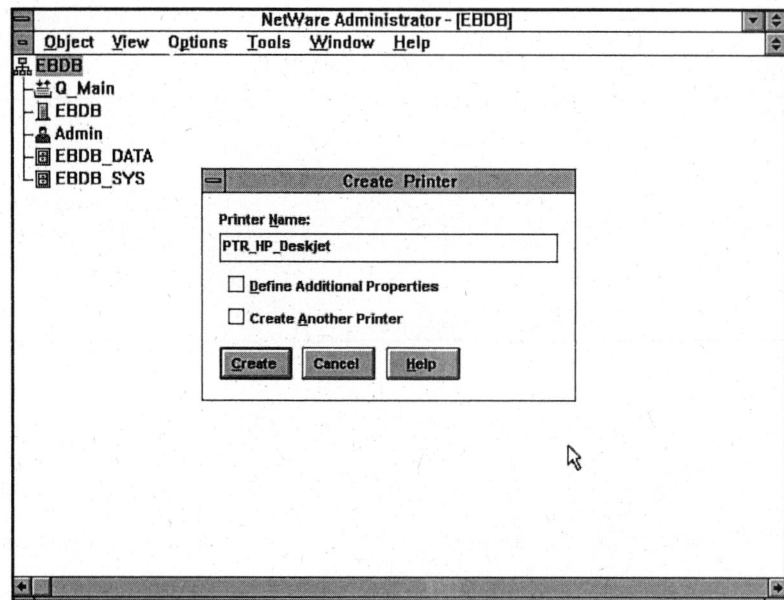

Figure 27.5

The Create Printer dialogbox.

Setting Configuration Options

The Configuration dialog box can be seen by selecting the Configuration button at the right side of the Printer dialog box. The printer configuration options are illustrated in figure 27.6. As you can see, the options presented in this dialog box are similar to those discussed in PCONSOLE Quick Setup.

The Printer Type field contains the same options you saw in PCONSOLE. These include Parallel, Serial, AppleTalk, Unix, XNP, AIO, and Other/Unknown. The Communication button can be pressed after the printer type has been selected to further configure this printer type. If you select Serial, for example, the options available in the resulting Serial Communications dialog box include the port (COM1, COM2, and so on), interrupts, baud rate, and data bits. These options are summarized in table 27.2. Table 27.3 summarizes the other options available in the Printer Configuration dialog box.

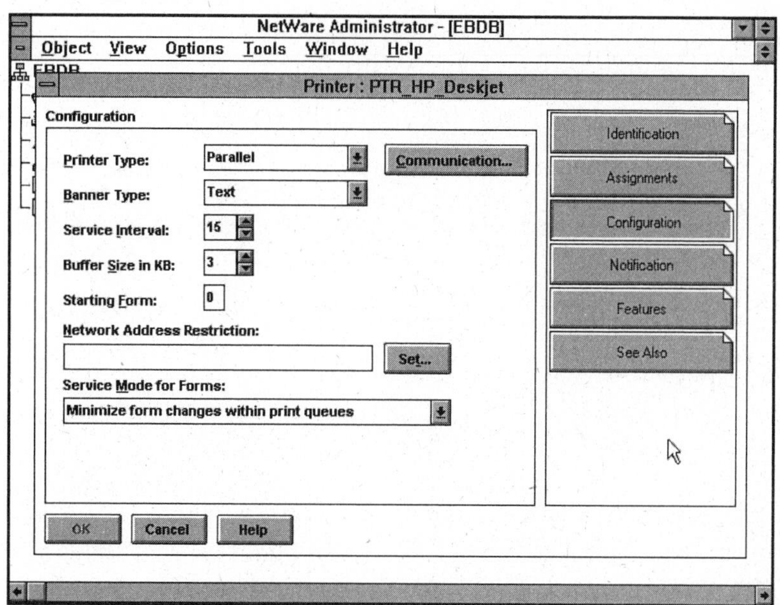

Figure 27.6

The Printer Configuration dialog box.

Table 27.3
Printer Configuration Dialog Box

Option	Description
Banner Type	The banner type can be either Text or Postscript.
Service Interval	This represents, in seconds, at what intervals the print server will check on the status of the printer. The shorter the interval, the quicker the response to the printer. Shorter intervals will take more CPU power, however.
Buffer Size in KB	This is the size of the buffer maintained by the printer server in sending information to the printer. The larger the buffer, the more control the print server has over sending jobs to the printer. In practice, the default buffer size of 3 KB is quite sufficient because the print job is queued as a file on the file server, and most printers have an ample buffer.
Starting Form	This represents the form number the printer is assumed to have mounted when first powering up.

continues

Table 27.3, Continued
Printer Configuration Dialog Box

Option	Description
Network Address Restriction	This field enables you to set a restriction on which cabling network the printer can be located. This prevents unauthorized users from placing a printer on a remote section of cabling and possibly capturing print jobs from print queues. Bear in mind that users who are this sophisticated most likely have high-paying jobs and will have neither the time nor the inclination to set up such a situation.
Service Mode for Forms	This represents the way in which the printer treats form changes. More information on forms and form changes is forthcoming in Chapter 28, "Printing from DOS Clients."

Setting Notification Options

Notification options can be viewed in figure 27.7. You can access this screen from the NWADMIN utility by selecting the Notification button at the right side of the Printer dialog box.

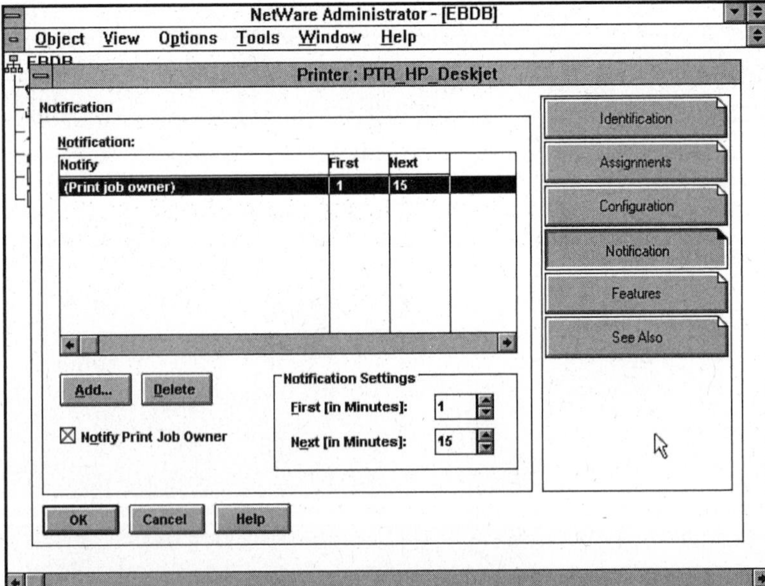

Figure 27.7
The Printer Notification dialog box.

There are two types of notification. The first type, which you can set from the Printer Notification dialog box, notifies a user if there is a problem. Problems include the printer off-line, out of paper, and form change needed. The other type of notification is established when a user first initiates a print capture. A *print capture* is a method of redirecting local printing to the network instead of to a local printer port. This type of notification informs the user when a print job has successfully printed and on which printer. Print capture notification is discussed in more detail in the next two chapters.

As you can see in figure 27.7, the print job owner (the user who originated the print job) is notified in the case of a printer problem. Under the Notification Settings group of parameters, adjust the First notification to the number of minutes you want to wait before a broadcast is sent out to the users on the Notification list. The Next time interval indicates when subsequent broadcasts are sent out.

Notification appears on the indicated users' workstations as a broadcast message. If you are running a DOS-based program, the notification appears at the top of the screen. In the case of Windows, OS/2, or Macintosh workstations, the notification is a dialog box that pops up on the screen. DOS-based users will have to press Ctrl+Enter to release the notification message. Windows, OS/2, or Macintosh users will have to press OK.

Because users have to take some sort of action to clear the notification message, you might want to disable this feature. In the case of DOS-based applications, for example, a notification broadcast message will freeze the application until the user presses Ctrl+Enter. If the user is performing an unattended backup, the backup program would not complete if a notification message appeared. To remove notification, select *(Print job owner)*, or any other user name, from the Notify column, and press the Delete button. To have other users added to the notification list (such as a print queue manager), select the Add button. Select the user object to add to the list and press the OK button.

Creating Print Server Objects

From the main NWADMIN menu, make sure you are in the container under which you want to add print server objects. To add print server objects, proceed as follows:

1. After the desired container under which you plan to create printing objects has been selected, press Insert or select Create from the Object menu. The New Object dialog box appears. You can see a list of possible objects to create.

2. From the New Object dialog box, select Print Server and click on the OK button. The Create Print Server dialog box appears, as illustrated in figure 27.8.

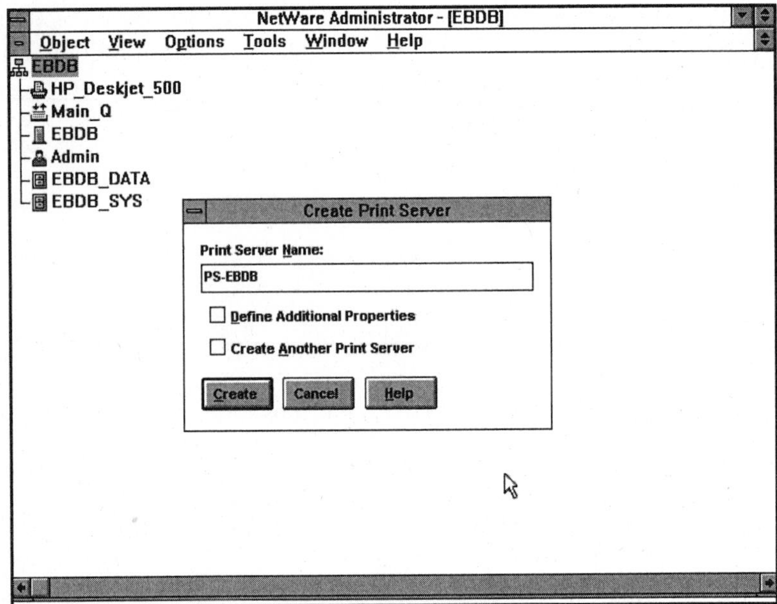

Figure 27.8

The Create Print Server dialog box.

3. Fill in the name of the new print server in the Print Server Name field. Place a checkmark in the Define Additional Properties box if you plan to add restrictions (such as print queue users) or other information to the print queue object. Otherwise, if you plan to create several queue objects at once, check the Create Another Print Server box. When you are finished, press the Create button. The print server object appears under the desired container, and you are returned to the view of the NDS tree.

Consider making the first letters reflective of the printer object. Printers could be *PTR_xyz*, Queues could be *Q_xyz*, and Print Servers could be *PS_xyz*, where *xyz* is some descriptive name. In this fashion, if you have an object PS_Dallas you would know that this is the Print Server for Dallas. PTR_HP3si would be an HP IIIsi printer.

Connecting the Three Types of Printing Objects

When the three types of printing objects have been created, it is time to connect them together. As you will recall from figure 27.2, the chain of events for printing is as follows:

Print Queue -> Printer -> Print Server

To associate a print queue with a printer, you will need to go into the Printer Details dialog box. To associate a printer with a print server, go into the Print Server Details dialog box. Before proceeding, from the main NWADMIN menu, make sure you are in the container under which you want to connect printing objects.

Here is the procedure to connect a print queue to a printer:

1. Select the target printer object. Double-click on the printer object, or press Enter, or select Details from the Object menu. The Printer dialog box appears.

2. From the Printer dialog box, select the Assignments button from the buttons at the right. The Assignments dialog box appears.

3. From the Assignments dialog box, select Add to associate a print queue with the printer. The Select Object dialog box appears. If necessary, use the Change Context button to select the context containing the desired print queue. When you have selected the desired queue in the Objects box in the Select Object dialog box, press the OK button. The completed Assignments dialog box is illustrated in figure 27.9.

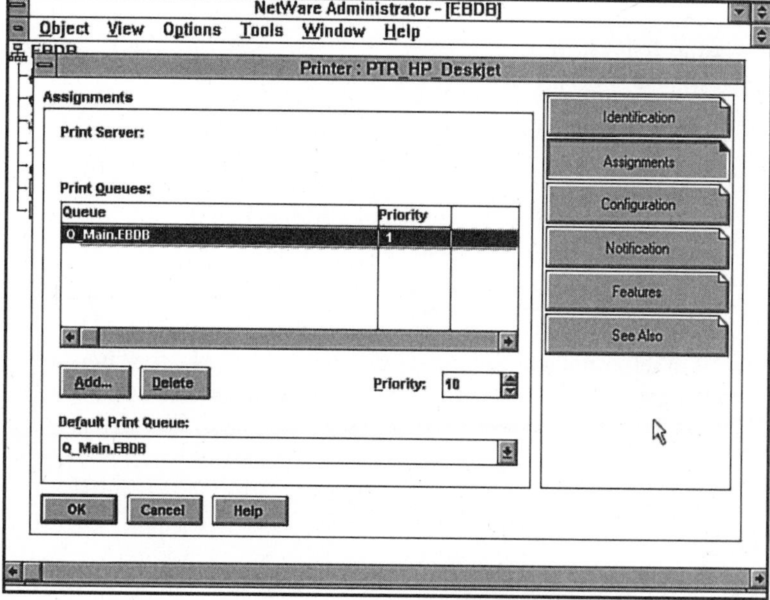

Figure 27.9

The Printer Assignments dialog box.

4. The first queue you assign to the printer becomes the default print queue. It is important to be sure that each printer has a default print queue. This queue appears in the **D**efault Print Queue field in the Assignments dialog box. This is the queue that will be used when users capture to the printer (rather than capturing to a queue, which is the normal course of action).

5. At this point you could add additional queues to the printer. When you are finished, press the OK button.

It is possible to assign more than one printer to a queue, and more than one queue to a printer. You might want to assign several printers to one queue when you have printers that are identical and you need high printer throughput. When multiple jobs arrive in the queue, the next available printer is put to use.

In the case where you have many jobs but need to prioritize them, you might want to assign more than one queue to a single printer. When this is the case, each queue can be assigned a *priority*. Jobs in a queue with a higher priority number will be serviced before jobs in queues with lower priority. The highest priority is 1.

The next step is to associate printers with print servers. To associate a printer with a print server, proceed as follows:

1. Select the target print server object. Double-click on the print server object, press Enter, or select **D**etails from the **O**bject menu. The Print Server dialog box appears.

2. From the Print Server dialog box, select the Assignments button from the buttons at the right. The Assignments dialog box appears.

3. From the Assignments dialog box, select **A**dd to associate a printer with the print server. The Select Object dialog box appears. If necessary, use the **C**hange Context button to select the context containing the desired printer. When you have selected the desired printer in the **O**bjects box in the Select Object dialog box, press the OK button. The completed Assignments dialog box is illustrated in figure 27.10.

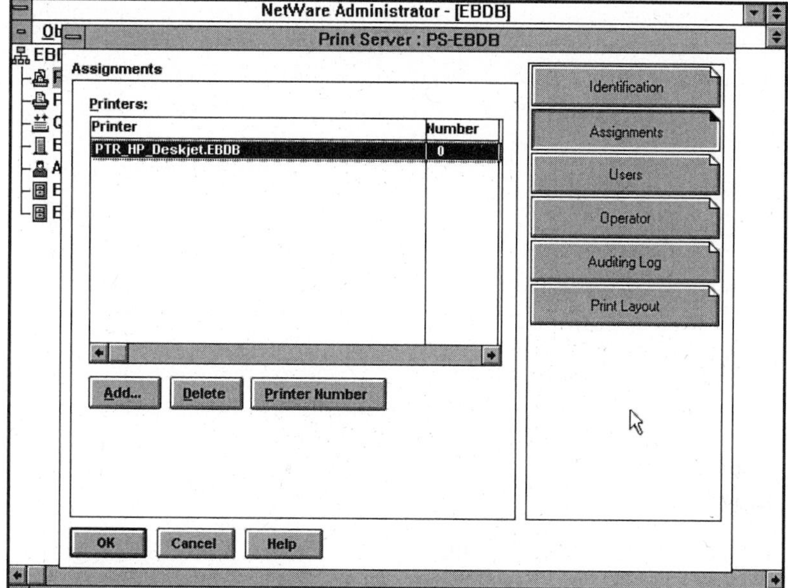

Figure 27.10

The Print Server Assignments dialog box.

Starting the Print Services

After the printing objects have been defined and connected, it is time to activate the printing system. This involves loading the print server on a file server and loading the management utility to handle the various printers. The print server driver is PSERVER.NLM. The printer management utility is NPRINTER. NPRINTER comes in two forms: NPRINTER.NLM and NPRINTER.EXE. This section discusses these utilities.

PSERVER.NLM

PSERVER.NLM is a NetWare Loadable Module that is used to start up a print server you have defined. Once the print server has started, it immediately starts advertising its presence. The advertising protocol used is SAP (Service Advertisement Protocol). Through SAP, other NetWare file servers, workstations, and other network devices become aware of the existence and location of the print server.

As mentioned in earlier chapters, the job of the print server is to redirect print jobs from queues to printers. In a sense the print server is like a switch in a railroad yard. The railroad switch redirects trains coming from one direction to another direction. One print server can be assigned up to 256 printers. You can have only one print server running per file server.

To load a print server, you need to gain access to the file server. You can either work directly from the file server's console, or you can use the RCONSOLE.EXE program to gain control over the file server's console. The print server process itself does not take a large amount of server resources. The more printers assigned to the print server, the heavier the load on the file server. If you have more than 16 printers assigned to the print server, you might want to consider loading it on a file server that is used less often.

To load the print server on a file server, proceed as follows:

1. Gain access to a file server either through RCONSOLE or by physically accessing the file server.

2. From the file server's console prompt, type

   LOAD PSERVER <*NDS_Print_Server_Name*>

   where *NDS_Print_Server_Name* is the NDS name of the print server. In the illustration that follows, the command used to load the print server was such:

   LOAD PSERVER .CN=PS-EBDB.O=EBDB

   The PSERVER main menu appears.

When the print server loads, several actions occur. First, the print server attaches to the network. If you look at the MONITOR.NLM utility (type **LOAD MONITOR**), and view Connection Information, you will note that the print server uses a licensed and an unlicensed connection. (A *licensed connection* counts towards the maximum number of users allowed on the file server. An *unlicensed connection* is used internally by the system and does not count towards your server license.) The print server then loads NPRINTER.NLM automatically for each printer defined as *autoload.* Figure 27.11 illustrates the PSERVER main menu.

You can see, by glancing at figure 27.11, that the PSERVER main menu shows you the NDS name of the print server and its status. If the status is anything other than Running, this indicates a problem.

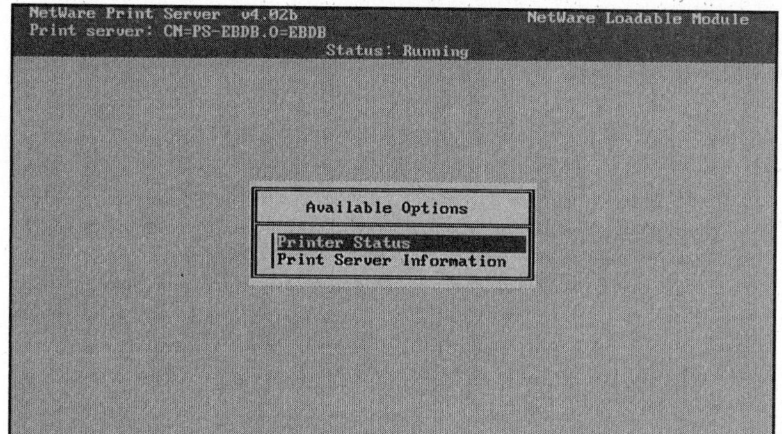

Figure 27.11
The PSERVER main menu.

If you have difficulty loading the print server, check out these possibilities:

1. You might have misspelled the NDS name of the print server.
2. Verify that the context that contains the print server is correct.
3. Make sure your file server has sufficient RAM to load the print server. You will need approximately 800 KB of file server RAM, plus approximately 4 KB for each printer defined. The RAM per printer varies depending on the buffer size you configured for the printer.
4. If you specified a password for the print server, you will need to enter it correctly when prompted.

PSERVER includes menu options that let you view the printer status for each printer assigned and information on the print server.

Printer Status

To view printer status, select Printer Status from the PSERVER main menu. You will see a list of printers identified by NDS name and an arbitrary number that PSERVER assigns as it loads. To view the status of a printer, select the desired printer and press Enter. Figure 27.12 shows the Printer Status screen with a print job in progress.

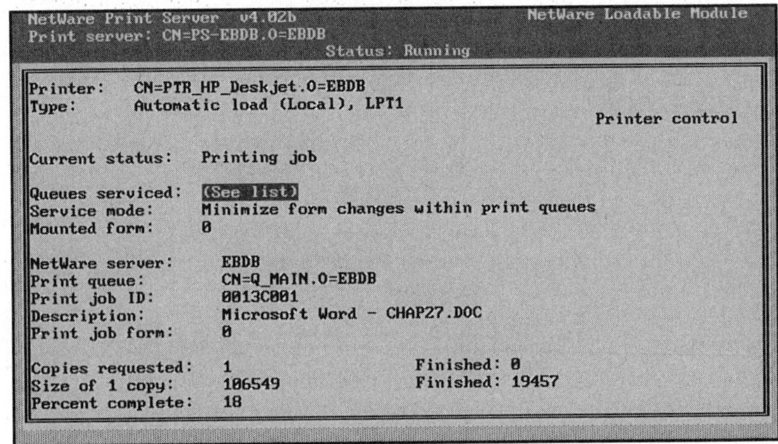

Figure 27.12
The PSERVER Printer Status screen.

Table 27.4 summarizes the fields visible on the Printer Status screen.

TABLE 27.4
PSERVER Printer Status Screen

Field	Description
Printer	The NDS name of the printer being viewed.
Type	The type of printer (automatic or manual load, parallel, serial, or Unix).
Printer control	Enables you to control the printer (discussed later). Controls include Abort print job, Form feed, Mark top of form, Pause, Start, and Stop.
Current status	Reflects the status of the printer. Status is affected by Printer Control setting. Also indicates printer problems, including out of paper and off-line.
Queues serviced	List of print queues assigned to this printer (discussed later).
Service mode	How form changes are handled by this printer (discussed later).
Mounted form	Number of the currently mounted form.

Field	Description
NetWare server*	From which NetWare server this print job originated.
Print queue*	Which print queue sent this print job.
Print job ID*	The ID number of this print job.
Description	A description of the job. NetWare-aware applications may show the document being printed.
Print job form*	The form number of this print job.
Copies requested*	How many copies were requested of this print job.
Copies requested/ Finished*	How many copies of this print job have been finished.
Size of 1 copy*	The size in bytes of a single copy of this print job.
Size of 1 Copy/Finished*	The number of bytes that have been printed for the current copy of this print job.
Percent complete*	What percentage complete is the current copy being printed of this print job.

*This field pertains to a particular print job currently being handled by this print server.

The Printer Status screen enables you to control the printer. There are four controls possible on this screen: Printer control, Queues serviced, Service mode, and Mounted form.

Note Changes made from this screen are only temporary. To make permanent changes, you need to go into either PCONSOLE.EXE or NWADMIN.EXE to make the desired changes. Changes made through either of these utilities are immediately reflected in PSERVER. You do not have to unload PSERVER and reload it as in previous versions of NetWare.

Table 27.5 summarizes the possible options for Printer control. This option is used to directly control the printer.

Table 27.5
PSERVER Printer Status Screen—Printer Control Options

Option	Description
Abort print job	This option stops the printer, deletes the print job from the queue, and restarts the printer.
Form feed	Causes the printer to do a page eject (or form feed). Useful to eject a page that printed only halfway and is now sitting in the printer.
Mark top of form	Causes a row of asterisks to appear where the printer thinks the top of the form is located. Useful when lining up new forms to see where the printer will start printing.
Pause printer	Causes the printer to print the contents of its buffer and then stop. The job remains in the queue, and users are allowed to continue to send jobs to this printer. Jobs sent after the pause will be stored in the queue until the printer has been started. When the printer is restarted using the start option, the job continues to print where it left off.
Start printer	Causes printer to restart after a pause or stop command.
Stop printer	Causes the printer to reject future jobs and sends a notification message to users on the printer notify list. The current print job remains in the queue. When the printer is restarted using the start option, the job continues to print where it left off.

The Queues Serviced screen gives you a list of print queues assigned to this printer. You can press Insert to add additional queues temporarily to this printer. This might be necessary if one printer needs maintenance and you want to assign its queue to another printer. You can also press Delete to temporarily remove a queue from a printer's list.

Table 27.6 summarizes the possible options for Service mode. This option controls how form changes are handled. For these options, please refer to figure 27.13, which illustrates multiple print jobs, forms, and queues assigned to one printer. In the diagram, the print queues Q_Main_1 and Q_Main_2 are both assigned to the printer Ptr_HP_Deskjet. Q_Main_1 has a priority level of 1; Q_Main_2 has a priority level of 2. For the purposes of this chart, assume that 12 different users have placed the documents listed in the queue at approximately the same time, in the order listed.

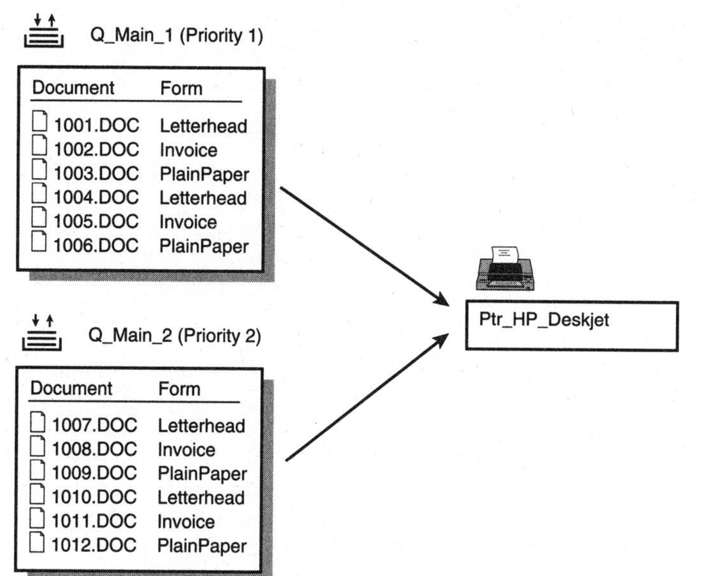

Figure 27.13

A diagram of multiple print jobs, forms, and queues serviced by one printer.

Table 27.6
PSERVER Printer Status Screen—Service Mode Options

Option	Description
Change forms as needed	The documents will print in the order indicated in figure 27.13. Documents 1001.DOC through 1006.DOC in Q_Main_1 will print first, followed by 1007.DOC through 1012.DOC in Q_Main_2. There will be a form change required before each document prints.
Minimize form changes across print queues	Documents will print by form, by queue. In figure 27.13, all documents with form Letterhead will print first (assuming this is the currently mounted form). 1001.DOC and 1004.DOC in Q_Main_1 will print first, followed by 1007.DOC and 1010.DOC in Q_Main_2. The form will change to Invoice, and 1002.DOC, 1005.DOC, 1008.DOC, and 1011.DOC will print next. Finally, the form will change to PlainPaper, and 1003.DOC, 1006.DOC, 1009.DOC, and 1012.DOC will print.
Minimize form changes within print queues	Documents will print by form inside the priority 1 queue before switching to documents in the priority 2 queue. In figure 27.13, the order of printing would be 1001.DOC, 1004.DOC, 1002.DOC, 1005.DOC, 1003.DOC, and

continues

Table 27.6, Continued
PSERVER Printer Status Screen—Service Mode Options

Option	Description
	1006.DOC. This completes the queue of documents in Q_Main_1. Because the form PlainPaper is currently mounted, this is the first type of document to be printed in Q_Main_2. Documents to be printed next are 1009.DOC, 1012.DOC, 1007.DOC, 1010.DOC, 1008.DOC, and 1011.DOC.
Service only currently mounted form	Only documents of the currently mounted form will be printed. In figure 27.13, assuming Letterhead is the currently mounted form, the following documents would print: 1001.DOC, 1004.DOC, 1007.DOC, and 1010.DOC. The remaining documents would remain in the queues until you manually specified the next form using either PCONSOLE or the PSERVER menu from the file server.

The Mounted form option enables you to specify manually which form the print server is currently servicing. You will need to change the currently mounted form when a document appears at the print server with a print header that calls for a certain form. This can be accomplished, for example, with the *form=* parameter in the DOS CAPTURE.EXE command.

Print Server Information

The Print Server Information option, from the PSERVER main menu, enables you to view information on the status of the print server. The screen that appears is illustrated in figure 27.14.

Version indicates the version of the PSERVER.NLM utility. The Type field indicates the type of print server. As you can see in figure 27.14, this is an NLM. The Advertising name shows the name of the print server as it will be advertised to other servers using SAP. Number of printers indicates how many printers have been defined for this print server. Queue service modes indicates how many different ways this module has to handle jobs with form changes originating from different queues, as explained earlier.

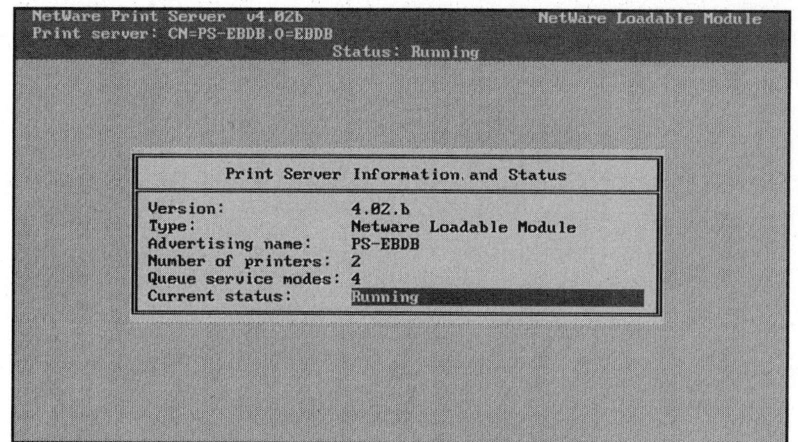

Figure 27.14

The PSERVER Print Server Information and Status screen.

Current Status

The Current Status option enables you to bring the print server down. A status of Running indicates that the print server is currently up and running. If you select the Unload option, the print server will stop functioning. Any jobs currently in the process of being printed will be canceled. Jobs still in the print queue will remain unaffected. If you select Unload after active print jobs, the job that is currently being printed will finish. After the active job has been printed, the print server will go down. Any jobs remaining in the queue will be unaffected. In the case of either of the Unload options, jobs remaining in the queue will not be printed until you either reassign the queue to another printer or bring the print server back up by issuing the LOAD PSERVER print_server_name command.

NPRINTER.EXE

NPRINTER.EXE is used to turn a locally attached printer into a network printer. This utility is a TSR (terminate-and-stay-resident) program that loads into the RAM of a workstation with a locally connected printer. When loaded by itself, with no command-line parameters, NPRINTER.EXE brings up the menu shown in figure 27.15.

As you can see from the figure, a list of active print servers appears. To make your local printer available to the network, select the desired print server and press Enter. A list of available printers on that print server will appear. Select the desired printer and press Enter. Your printer will now serve as the printer indicated. A successful loading of NPRINTER is accompanied by the following message where *xxx* is the name of the printer, and *n* is the printer number:

```
Network printer xxx (printer n) is installed.
```

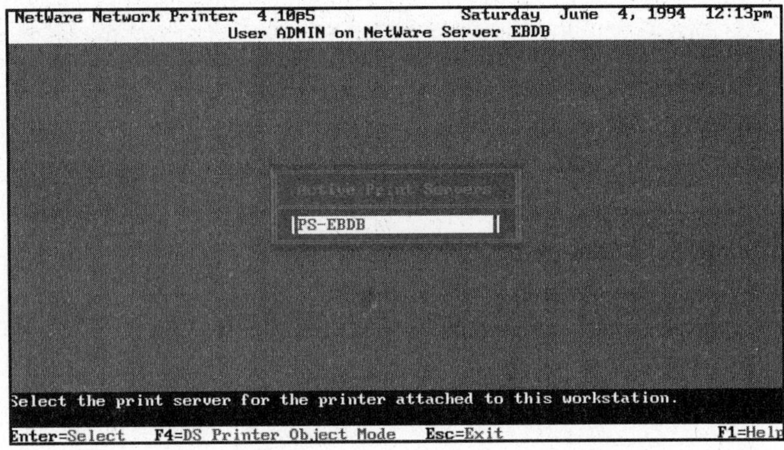

Figure 27.15
The initial NPRINTER.EXE screen.

The NPRINTER.EXE command can be placed in the user's AUTOEXEC.BAT file by specifying the name of the print server and the desired printer number as parameters following the NPRINTER command. The following command is an example of what might be placed in a batch file:

```
NPRINTER PS-EBDB 2
```

The preceding command connects the local printer to the advertising name of print server PS-EBDB as printer number 2. The following command loads a printer defined in your NDS tree:

```
NPRINTER .CN=PTR_HP_Laserjet_IVsi.OU=Sales.O=EBDB
```

NPRINTER.EXE can also be used to view the status of a printer and to unload one or more printers. The following command shows you the status of your NPRINTER.EXE printers:

```
NPRINTER /s
```

The following command unloads not only NPRINTER.EXE, but also any printers defined as network printers:

```
NPRINTER /u
```

The following command unloads the Bubblejet printer only.

```
NPRINTER .CN=PTR_Bubblejet.O=ABC /u
```

NPRINTER.NLM

NPRINTER.NLM is used to turn a printer attached to a file server into a network printer. NPRINTER.NLM can be loaded on the file server running PSERVER.NLM, or on another file server connected to the network. The command, issued from the file server console, is as follows, where *print_server* is the name the print server uses to advertise itself across the network, and *printer_number* is the number of the printer:

```
LOAD NPRINTER print_server  printer_number
```

Using Direct Connect Printers

Some printers, such as the HP IVsi, have an option where you can connect the printer directly to the LAN. Some vendors, such as Castelle, market devices with a LAN interface on one side and a parallel or serial port on the other side. If such is the case, the interface or installed printer option is viewed as both a printer and a print server. The firmware on the connecting device is geared to advertise itself as a print server using SAP. You will need to define a print server whose name matches the name assigned to the connecting device. In many cases the name corresponds to a serial number for the device.

Most vendors now offer a configuration utility that can be used to program the connecting device. The HP software included with the LAN interface, for example, enables you to define the name and certain other characteristics of the connection. Although such devices entail additional cost, they improve printing speed considerably. In some cases the improvement is 10 to 20 times faster.

To print to directly connected printers, you will need to create a print queue and assign it to a printer as defined by the firmware and setup software of the printing interface. Users will print to the queue. The queue will send its information to the print server in the printing interface. Implementations vary widely, and you will need to consult the documentation for your particular device.

Summary

This chapter gave you information about setting up the printing process in NetWare 4. Setup procedures covered included the Quick Setup option in PCONSOLE. As you saw, this is a quick and easy method of creating queues, printers, and print servers, as well as automatically establishing the right connections. Along the way you learned about the various printing parameters pertaining to queues, printers, and print servers.

The next part of this chapter covered setting up printing using NWADMIN. As you learned, using NWADMIN is not as easy as the PCONSOLE Quick Setup option. The relationship between the three basic printing objects was reviewed: queues connect to printers, which connect to print servers. The process of creating queues, printers, and print servers in NWADMIN was covered in detail. Notification was discussed. You learned that Printer Notification will notify the job owner or other users as assigned and will notify you in the case of a printer error. You then learned how to connect the three printing objects in NWADMIN.

The last part of this chapter covered how to activate the printer engines once defined. You learned that PSERVER.NLM is loaded on the file server. The PSERVER menu enables you to view and manipulate the printer status and gather print server information. You learned how to start, stop, and pause printers, among other actions. You also learned how to bring the print server down through the print server information option. You learned about NPRINTER.EXE and NPRINTER.NLM. These modules are used to initialize local printers and make them available to the network. A final discussion briefly described third-party hardware and utilities that allow a printer to directly connect to the LAN.

Printing from DOS Clients

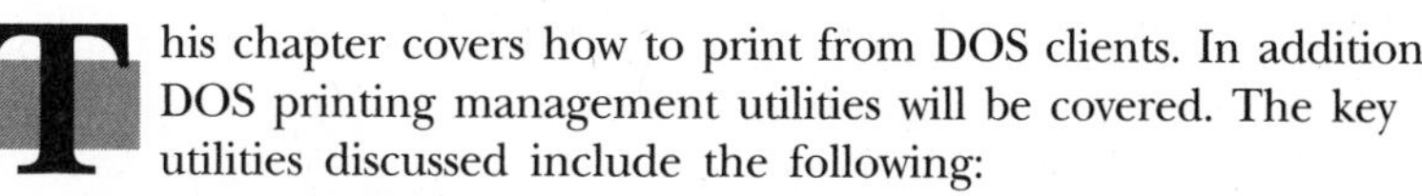

This chapter covers how to print from DOS clients. In addition, DOS printing management utilities will be covered. The key utilities discussed include the following:

- CAPTURE.EXE
- NETUSER.EXE
- PRINTCON.EXE
- PRINTDEF.EXE
- NPRINT.EXE
- PCONSOLE.EXE
- PSC.EXE

Chapter 29 discusses printing issues from Windows clients. Some of the DOS commands used to set up and configure the NetWare printing environment are menu-driven utilities. These include NETUSER, PRINTCON, PRINTDEF, and PCONSOLE. The other utilities mentioned in the preceding list are issued from the DOS command line and can be placed into batch files.

Using CAPTURE

The CAPTURE.EXE utility is critical when attempting to redirect print jobs from the local printer ports to a network print queue. The importance of the CAPTURE command has waned as the number of NetWare-aware applications has grown. Programs such as Windows and WordPerfect can be configured for a NetWare network. These programs are capable of recognizing NetWare print queues and can send print jobs to the queue without the intervention of CAPTURE (although they will also recognize printer settings made with CAPTURE). A study of the CAPTURE parameters is instructive, however, and is applicable to other environments, such as Windows. Novell supplies client software that interacts with the Windows printing interface and provides the same parameters as are available with the CAPTURE command.

DOS programs that are not NetWare-aware, or programs ported over from other environments, need assistance sending print jobs to NetWare print queues. Many vertical market programs are designed to print only to the local printer ports (LPT1, LPT2, and so forth). The function of the CAPTURE command is to "capture" print jobs headed for the local printer ports and redirect them to a NetWare print queue. Figure 28.1 illustrates the function of the CAPTURE command.

The CAPTURE command is not a memory-resident program, although its activities make it seem like one. The CAPTURE command programs the workstation's shell (either the NETX or VLM shells) to intercept all printing headed for a local printer port. The shell places a print header in front of the print job, a print tail at the end, and sends the entire job off to the designated NetWare print queue.

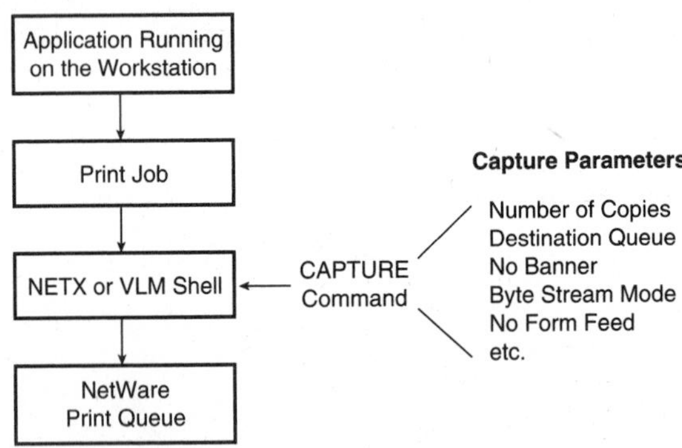

Figure 28.1

The role of the CAPTURE command.

The print header contains information regarding the formatting of the print job, whether to print a *banner page* that identifies the job originator, how many copies to print, and other information. The print tail generally contains a printer code to reset the printer once the job has completed.

The syntax for the CAPTURE command is as follows:

```
CAPTURE <options>
```

Capture options are summarized in table 28.1. Options are placed on the same line as the CAPTURE command. The order of the options is not important. A space or forward slash (/) should separate one option from the next. Abbreviations for parameters are indicated in the second column of the table. Another column indicates if this option is a default with an asterisk (*), or the default value (where applicable).

Table 28.1
CAPTURE.EXE Options

Option	Abbrev.	Default	Description
All	ALL		When combined with a CAPTURE /EC (End Capture) command, this option causes NetWare to stop the CAPTURE of all local printer ports and return them to local operation.
Autoendcap	AU	*	Causes all print jobs currently being added to the print queue through this CAPTURE session to be placed in ready mode. (Ready mode jobs can then be printed when they arrive at the top of the queue.)
Banner=*banner* which *name*	B	LPT or filename	Overrides the default banner name, appears at the bottom of the banner page. The default varies, depending on the nature of the capture. If you are printing a file, the file name will appear. If you are doing a screen capture, or some other form of redirecting output to the printer, LPT

continues

Table 28.1, Continued
CAPTURE.EXE Options

Option	Abbrev.	Default	Description
			will appear. Can be up to 12 characters. Enclose banner name in quotes if it contains spaces.
Cancel	CA		When combined with a CAPTURE /EC (End Capture) command, this option causes NetWare to cancel any print jobs for this user still queued up since the beginning of this CAPTURE session.
Copies=*n*	C	1	Specifies how many copies of the job you want to print. The value of *n* can be from 1 to 65,000.
Create=*path\filename*	CR		Causes print jobs to be sent to the file *filename* stored in the directory indicated by *path*.
Detail	D		Gives detailed information as the print CAPTURE is being initiated.
End Capture	EC		Stops the CAPTURE of the printer port indicated by the Local= parameter. If no Local= parameter is specified, LPT1 is assumed.
Form Feed	FF		Causes the printer to issue a page eject upon completion of the print job.
Form=*n*	F		Informs the print server that form *n* must be mounted to process the following print job. If printer notification has been enabled, the job owner or the designated user will receive a broadcast from the print server telling them to change the form. After the form has been physically mounted in the printer, you can use either PCONSOLE or PSERVER to modify the Mounted form field to match the form number requested using the CAPTURE Form=*n* parameter.

Option	Abbrev.	Default	Description
Hold	H		Sends print job to the queue and places the job on hold. The job will not print until the user releases the hold either through PCONSOLE or NETUSER.
Job=*jobname* PRINTCON job *[:container]*	J		Loads CAPTURE values from a template *jobname.* The job template can belong to the user or the user's immediate container. You can use a job template from another NDS container by specifying *:container.* Additional CAPTURE parameters specified on the command line after the Job=*jobname* option will override any conflicting parameters that exist in the PRINTCON job template.
Keep	K		This option ensures that the server will maintain what print data has been sent if the workstation locks up, loses power, or otherwise loses its network connection. The print job can then be redirected back into the queue by locating the print job and inserting the print file back into the queue. This can be accomplished using NPRINT from the command, or from PCONSOLE or NETUSER by going to the list of print jobs and pressing Insert.
Local=*n*	L	1	Causes CAPTURE to redirect the parallel port indicated by *n. n* can have a value from 1 to 9. If you want to capture more than three printer ports, you must increase the value indicated by NETWORK PRINTERS=*n* in the NET.CFG file under the NetWare DOS Requester section.
LPT*n*	LPT*n*		Has the same effect as the Local=*n* option. The value of *n* can be from 1 to 9.

continues

Table 28.1, Continued
CAPTURE.EXE Options

Option	Abbrev.	Default	Description
Name=*name*	NAM	Login	This option enables you to override the default *name* that is your user login name. The name appears at the top of the banner page just under the date and time section. Can be up to 12 characters. Enclose name in quotes if it contains spaces.
No Autoendcap	NA		Defeats the Autoendcap option.
No Form Feed	NFF	*	The job prints without an extra page eject upon completion.
No Notify	NNOTI	*	No notification takes place.
No Tabs	NT	*	No tab conversion takes place. This is also referred to as byte stream mode.
Notify	NOTI		Causes the print server to send the job owner a broadcast message when the print job has successfully printed. The message identifies the printer on which the job printed.
Printer=	P		Prints to the specified printer. The *printer* job is placed in the default queue for that printer.
Queue=*queue*	Q	defaults	Prints to the queue specified in the user's default PRINTCON job template.
Server=*server_name*	S	default server	Used to specify capturing to a bindery-based server. Could be a server in another NDS tree or a 3.*x* or below server.
Show	SH		Displays the current CAPTURE status.
Tabs=*n*	T		Inserts *n* spaces in place of any tab characters coming through the printing system. This option is rarely

Option	Abbrev.	Default	Description
			used these days. In the past, this option was available because many printers did not handle tabs properly. The value of *n* can be from 1 to 18.
Timeout=*seconds*	TI	0	Causes the printing system to wait the indicated number of *seconds* before placing a job into Ready status. If you do not specify a timeout value greater than 0 (the default), the printing system will keep adding to the current print job until one of the following events occurs: 1. You exit the current program, which invokes the AUTOENDCAP feature 2. You issue another CAPTURE command 3. You issue a CAPTURE /EC command (ENDCAP) 4. You log out of the network
Ver	V		Displays the version of CAPTURE you are using.

Certain options are mutually exclusive. The following list identifies these options.

Mutually Exclusive CAPTURE Options	
NOTI	NNOTI
P=*printer*	Q=*queue*
FF	NFF
B=*banner*, NAM=*name*	NB
T=*tab spaces*	NT
AU	NA

You can specify either NOTI (Notify) or NNOTI (No Notify), but not both. If you do so mistakenly, NetWare chooses the last option.

As with other DOS commands, CAPTURE displays built-in help when you specify the "/?" parameter. To obtain help on all aspects of the CAPTURE command, type the following:

CAPTURE /? ALL

The following listing shows you the result of typing **CAPTURE SHOW**:

```
F:\SYSTEM>capture show

LPT1  Capturing data to print queue CN=Q_Main
  Notify:               Disabled
  Automatic end:        Enabled
  Timeout count:        5 seconds
  Name:                 (None)
  Form feed:            Disabled
  Banner:               (None)
  Keep:                 Disabled

  Copies:               1
  Tabs:                 No conversion
  Form:                 0
  User hold:            Off

LPT2  Capturing is not currently active.

LPT3  Capturing is not currently active.

F:\SYSTEM>
```

The following example shows you a CAPTURE command that accomplishes the following:

- ◆ Redirects the output of LPT1 to the print queue Q_Main
- ◆ Sets up a timeout factor of 10 seconds
- ◆ Disables printing the banner page
- ◆ Prevents an extra form feed from taking place
- ◆ Specifies no tab formatting

```
F:\SYSTEM>CAPTURE q=q_main ti=10 nb nff nt
Device LPT1 re-routed to print queue CN=Q_MAIN.

F:\SYSTEM>
```

The following example illustrates setting up a CAPTURE to three different queues capturing three different local ports. Note the different flavors of the CAPTURE command. The third CAPTURE illustrates the use of the forward slash (/) as a separator, rather than a space. Note that you must include a space after an NDS object reference. In the third CAPTURE, note the space between "...O=EBDB" and "/nff/nb...." Also note that you can refer to printing objects by their common NDS name only if you are in the correct context. Otherwise you will have to specify a complete NDS name (as in the third CAPTURE).

```
F:\>capture LPT1 q=q_Main ti=10 name="Doug Bierer" nff
Device LPT1 re-routed to print queue CN=Q_MAIN.

F:\>capture Local=2 p=Ptr_Dot_Matrix_Bldg7 ti=10
Device LPT2 re-routed to printer CN=Ptr_Dot_Matrix_Bldg7.

F:\>capture /LPT3/q=.CN=Q_HP_IV_Bldg3_Travel.O=EBDB /nff/nb/ti=20
Device LPT3 re-routed to print queue CN=Q_HP_IV_BLDG3_TRAVEL.

F:\>capture sh

LPT1  Capturing data to print queue CN=Q_Main
  Notify:             Disabled
  Automatic end:      Enabled
  Timeout count:      10 seconds
  Name:               Doug Bierer
  Form feed:          Disabled
  Banner:             LPT1
  Keep:               Disabled
  Copies:             1
  Tabs:               No conversion
  Form:               Unknown
  User hold:          Off

LPT2  Capturing data to print queue CN=Q_Dot_Matrix_Bldg7
  Notify:             Disabled
  Automatic end:      Enabled
```

```
  Timeout count:      10 seconds
  Name:               (None)
  Form feed:          Disabled
  Banner:             (None)
  Keep:               Disabled
  Copies:             1
  Tabs:               No conversion
  Form:               Unknown
  User hold:          Off

LPT3  Capturing data to print queue CN=Q_HP_IV_Bldg3_Travel
  Notify:             Disabled
  Automatic end:      Enabled
  Timeout count:      20 seconds
  Name:               (None)
  Form feed:          Disabled
  Banner:             (None)
  Keep:               Disabled
  Copies:             1
  Tabs:               No conversion
  Form:               Unknown
  User hold:          Off

F:\>
```

Managing Workstation Printing with the NETUSER Utility

The NETUSER.EXE utility can be used to perform printing management on the workstation. The printing options of NETUSER are designed to perform many of the same functions as the CAPTURE command. Rather than requiring you to remember command line options, NETUSER provides help every step of the way. In addition, NETUSER provides print management functionality for the user previously reserved for the PCONSOLE.EXE utility. The NETUSER utility was introduced in Chapter 14, "DOS Client Basics." When you select the Printing option from the main menu, the Available Ports list appears, as illustrated in figure 28.2.

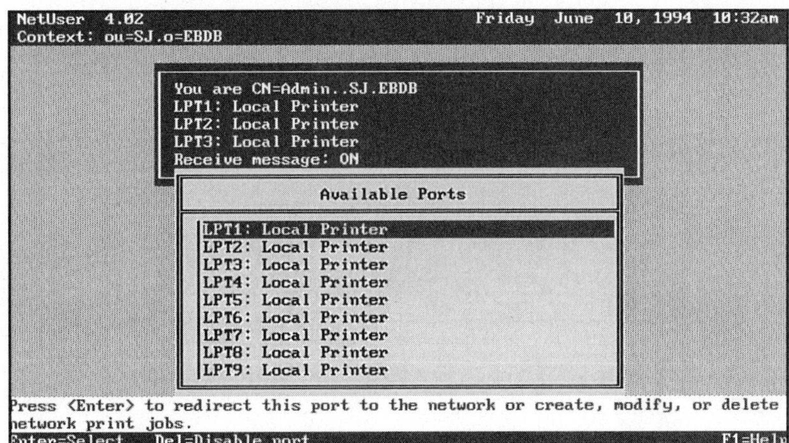

Figure 28.2
NETUSER.EXE printing—Available Ports screen.

As you can see from the illustration, the NET.CFG file on this workstation has specified, under the NetWare DOS Requester section, a setting of NETWORK PRINTERS = 9, giving this workstation a total of nine printer ports. As you can imagine, the workstation cannot physically accommodate nine ports—these ports are logical ports.

Capturing Printers with NETUSER

To assign a port to a queue, proceed as follows:

1. From the NETUSER.EXE main menu, select Printing. The Available Ports screen appears, as shown in figure 28.2.

2. From the Available Ports screen, choose which port you want to capture. The Available Options menu appears The two options at this point are Print Jobs and Change Printers. Use the Print Jobs option to view print jobs you have placed in the queue. Use the Change Printers option to initiate a print capture. For the purposes of the task at hand, select the Change Printers option. A screen showing currently captured printers or queues appears. If you have not yet selected a printer or queue to use, this list will be blank.

3. From the list of printers and queues, press Insert to select the desired network printer or queue. As with other NetWare 4 utilities, you must specify the NDS context that contains the target printer or queue. Either type in the complete NDS name of the printer or queue object or press Insert again to browse the tree.

4. Once the appropriate context has been selected, a list of printers and queues in that context appears. The Printers/Print Queues screen that appears is shown in figure 28.3.

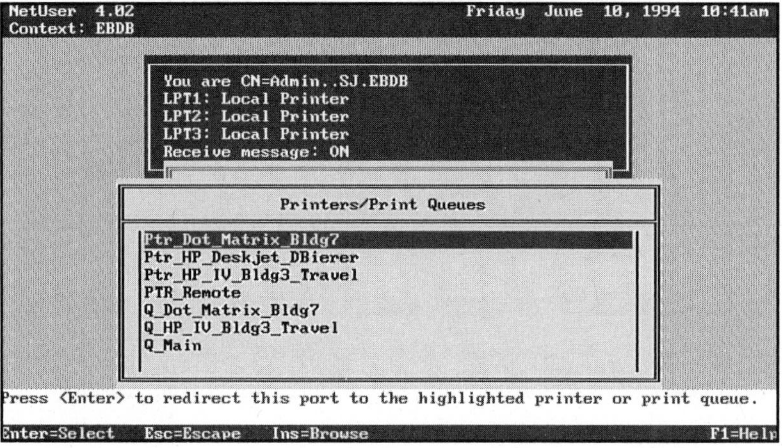

Figure 28.3
NETUSER.EXE printing—Printers/Print Queues screen.

5. As you can see from the figure, it is important to use a naming convention to distinguish a printer from a queue. It is not important which you select. If you select a printer, however, you lose control over which queue the job is sent to. When you select a printer, the job is placed in the default queue for that printer. If the default queue has a low priority, your job may end up being delayed.

   Select the desired printer or queue, and press Enter. The background screen changes to reflect the queue selected. Note that even if you elect to print to a printer, you are still printing to a queue. In the case where you select a printer, the default queue for that printer will be displayed on the background screen.

6. Press Esc several times to return to the main menu of NETUSER.

You can now exit the NETUSER utility and proceed with your printing. You can use NETUSER to capture printing in place of the CAPTURE command. NETUSER is interactive and controlled through menus. The CAPTURE command, on the other hand, can be placed in batch files or in a login script.

Managing Print Jobs with NETUSER

The NETUSER utility can also be used to manage print jobs submitted to the queue. This is a fast, effective tool that enables users to control their own jobs in the queue. An alternative is to use PCONSOLE. PCONSOLE is much more complicated and can be very confusing to novice network users.

To control a print job submitted, follow these steps:

1. From the NETUSER main menu, select Printing. The Available Ports list appears.

2. From the Available Ports list, select the desired port you want to control. The Available Options menu appears.

3. From the Available Options menu, select Print Jobs. A list of jobs you have currently submitted to this queue appears (see fig. 28.4).

```
NetUser  4.02                                     Friday  June  10, 1994  9:52am
Context: O=EBDB

 Seq Name          Description                    Status          Form  Job ID

  1 Doug Bierer  Paintbrush - FIG2707.PCX         Active           0   00156001
  2 Doug Bierer  Paintbrush - FIG2708.PCX         Ready            0   00158002
  3 Doug Bierer  Paintbrush - FIG2709.PCX         Ready            0   0015A007
  4 Doug Bierer  Paintbrush - FIG2710.PCX         Ready            0   0015C008
  5 Doug Bierer  Paintbrush - FIG2711.PCX         Ready            0   0015E009
  6 Doug Bierer  Paintbrush - FIG2712.PCX         Ready            0   0016000A
  7 Doug Bierer  Paintbrush - FIG2713.PCX         Ready            0   0016400B
  8 Doug Bierer  Paintbrush - FIG2714.PCX         Ready            0   00166003
  9 Doug Bierer  Paintbrush - FIG2715.PCX         Ready            0   00168004
 10 Doug Bierer  Microsoft Word - CHAP27.DOC      Adding           0   0016A005

Select a job to view its configuration. Press <Insert> to create new jobs. A
job can be changed or deleted by its owner or a queue operator.
Enter=Select   Ins=Ins   Del=Del   F5=Mark   Esc=Escape                 F1=Help
```

Figure 28.4

NETUSER.EXE printing—The Print Jobs list.

4. From the Print Jobs list, pick the job you want to control, and then press Enter. The Print Job Information screen appears, as illustrated in figure 28.5.

```
NetUser  4.02                                     Friday  June  10, 1994  11:08am
Context: EBDB
                              Print Job Information

 Print job:          0016C001             File size:          300
 Client:             CN=Admin[2]
 Description:        CTRL.TXT
 Status:             Print job is ready and waiting for the print server.

 User hold:          No                   Entry date:         6-10-1994
 Operator hold:      No                   Entry time:         11:06:22 am
 Service sequence:   1
                                          Form:               0
 Number of copies:   1                    Print banner:       No
                                          Name:
 File contents:      Byte stream          Banner name:
 Tab size:
                                          Defer printing:     No
 Form feed:          No                   Target date:
 Notify when done:   No                   Target time:

Enter up to 49 characters to describe the print job.

Esc=Escape   F10=Save                                                   F1=Help
```

Figure 28.5

NETUSER.EXE printing—The Print Job Information screen.

If the print job is not your own, you can see the Print Job Information screen for the job, but you will not be able to change any parameters. A *print queue operator* or a user with sufficient trustee rights (such as an Admin user) will also be able to administer the queue.

5. The fields in the Print Job Information screen are summarized in table 28.2. The defaults for these fields are set through the CAPTURE command or through the PRINTCON utility (discussed later in this chapter).

Table 28.2
NETUSER.EXE Print Job Information Fields

Field Name	Description
Print job	Random number assigned by NetWare to identify the print job.
File size	Size of the print job in bytes. Monitor this figure closely for graphics printing. This could impact the amount of disk space you have on the volume that contains the print queue.
Client	Name of the user who submitted the job. If a user name is followed by a number in brackets ([2]), this user is logged in to the network more than once. The number represents the network connection of that user.
Description	Description of the print job. If the job being printed is from an identifiable document, the file name of the document is listed. If the print job is from a screen print or some other form of print redirection, the description will be "LPT1" (or whatever port was used to capture the job).
Status	Current status of the job. This is also abbreviated in the previous print job list screen. Status can include any of the following: *Ready*—The print job is ready and waiting for the print server to move it to the printer. *Active*—The job is currently being printed. *Held*—The user or queue operator has placed a hold on the print job. *Adding*—The job is being added to the queue from a workstation.

Field Name	Description
User hold	Set this value to YES if you do not want to have the job print out when it reaches the top of the queue. The hold can be released at any time, in which case the job will become active when it reaches the top of the queue.
Entry date	Date the job was placed in the queue.
Operator hold	Similar to a User Hold except it is placed by a print queue operator.
Entry time	Time the job was placed in the queue.
Service sequence	The position of the job in the queue. The lower the number, the higher it is in the queue. If you change this number, the job will shift its position in the queue. Change the number to 1, for example, to place it at the top of the queue. NOTE: Only an Admin user or a Print Queue Operator can change the value in this field.
Form	The form number associated with this job.
Number of copies	The number of times this job will be printed.
Print banner	If set to YES, a banner page will precede the print job. If set to NO, no banner page will print.
Name	The name that appears on the top of the banner page.
Banner name	The name that appears at the top of the banner page.
File contents	Indicates whether tab formatting was selected. If not, the contents will read "Byte stream." Otherwise, this field will read "Text."
Tab size	The number of spaces that will be inserted in place of any tab characters encountered. This is applicable only when File contents is set to Text.
Defer printing	If set to YES, you can specify a date and time when you want this document to print. This is useful when you have a long print job and do not want to tie up the print queue (for fear of being mobbed by angry co-workers rushing to meet a deadline).

continues

Table 28.2, Continued
NETUSER.EXE Print Job Information Fields

Field Name	Description
Target date	The date a deferred print job is to print.
Target time	The time a deferred print job is to print.
Form feed	If set to YES, an extra page eject will occur after your job is finished printing. If set to NO, NetWare will not place an extra page eject after the job is done printing.
Notify when done	If set to YES, the print server will send the job owner a broadcast message indicating that the job printed successfully and specifying which printer.

When you are finished modifying parameters as necessary, press the F10 key to save any changes. You will return to the Print Job List screen. Press Esc several times to return to the main NETUSER menu.

Inserting a Print Job into a Queue

You can use NETUSER to directly insert a file into a queue to be printed. This technique is useful when you have an ASCII text file or other print-ready file you want to print. To insert a print job, proceed as follows:

1. From the NETUSER main menu, select Printing. The Available Ports list appears.
2. From the Available Ports list, pick a port that is captured. The Available Options menu appears.
3. From the Available Options menu, select Print Jobs. The current list of print jobs for this queue appears.
4. From the list of print jobs, press the Insert key. The Select Directory From Which To Print screen appears. Enter the name of the directory that contains the print file, or press the Insert key to browse the directory structure. Press Enter when the desired directory appears. A list of available files in that directory appears.
5. From the list of available files, pick the desired file, and press Enter. A list of print job configurations appears. In this list are the defaults as well as any PRINTCON job templates you have created. (PRINTCON is discussed in detail later.)

6. From the list of print job configurations, select (defaults) or the desired PRINTCON job template. Press Enter to choose the desired PRINTCON job template. You will see the Print Job Information screen discussed earlier. Make any desired changes to the fields and press F10 to save. You will be returned to the list of print jobs. Press Esc several times to return to the NETUSER main menu.

Stopping Print Capture

The NETUSER utility can also be used to stop print capturing. To do so, from the main menu, select Printing. The list of available ports appears. Select the port you want to stop print capture. Press Del. You are prompted, "Do you want to disable LPT*x*?" where *x* is the number of the selected printer port. If you answer Yes, printing is no longer redirected to the network.

Setting Up Print Jobs

This section gives you the basics on the PRINTDEF.EXE and PRINTCON.EXE utilities. PRINTDEF can be used to define print devices. Print devices consist of basic printing function codes you want to have inserted in front of certain print jobs, and groupings of these codes called *modes*. Definitions created in PRINTDEF can then be invoked using PRINTCON. In addition, PRINTCON can be used to group CAPTURE parameters into a series of print job templates.

Using PRINTDEF

The PRINTDEF.EXE utility is used to define a series of print devices and forms. Print device definitions consist of a series of basic printing *functions* that can be grouped into *modes*. Print forms are labels used to identify the various types of paper you might have in your printers. Forms could be defined for invoices, check stock, letterhead, and other types of printer paper.

PRINTDEF definitions are stored in the NDS in a specified container. Printer device definitions can be exported from one container to another using the Export and Import Device options. Print devices for one container are automatically available to any container below the one with the devices defined. Figure 28.6 shows you the main menu of PRINTDEF.

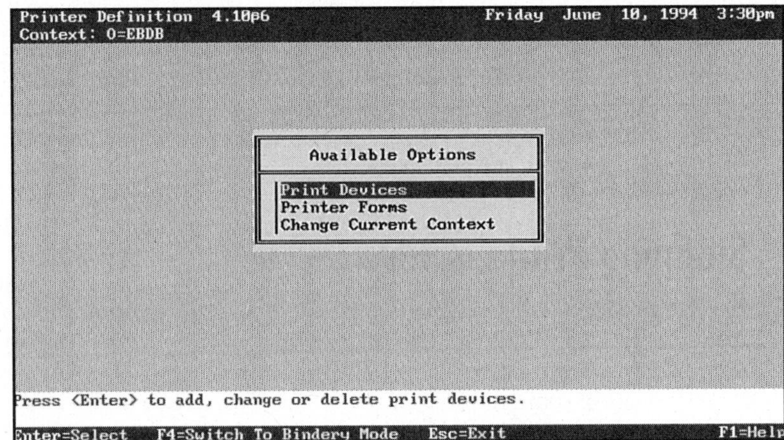

Figure 28.6
The PRINTDEF.EXE main menu.

Users can access PRINTDEF data associated with the container of the print queue they select in the PRINTCON job template. If you want to access PRINTDEF data in other containers, you need to create a print queue in the container you want to access and select this queue when defining a PRINTCON job template. PRINTCON does not allow you to select an Alias print queue.

As you can see from the PRINTDEF main menu, you can work with Print Devices and Printer Forms. As usual with the DOS-based utilities, there is an option to Change Current Context.

Before you can start defining devices or forms, you must change to the context where you want to begin. As mentioned earlier, print devices and forms are properties of container objects. The first item discussed will be forms, followed by a discussion of print devices.

Printer Forms

Printer forms are used in situations where you have one printer that prints using different forms or types of paper. A classic example is when you have an HP Laserjet or Deskjet printer with only one paper tray. If you need to print on letterhead, you can hope you can get the letterhead into the printer fast enough or before someone else starts printing, or you can use the printer forms option. Another example is a dot matrix printer that prints checks for two different business units within your company. You need to switch between the two types of checks. If the wrong information should accidentally print on the wrong set of checks, your company might end up missing payments of hundreds or thousands of dollars.

Printer forms are used by NetWare as labels. Even though you enter in the length and width of the form, these statistics serve no purpose. The form can be specified by name or number in the CAPTURE command. To specify a form Checks, for example, use the following syntax:

```
CAPTURE Q=Q1 TI=10 NB FORM=Checks
```

Forms can also be specified in the NETUSER utility or through a PRINTCON job template.

After the form has been registered with the print redirector using one of the preceding methods, all subsequent print jobs will have this form encoded into the print header that precedes each print job. The print job is then stored in the print queue until the print server signals that it is ready to process the job. The print server will then read the print header and check its internal buffer to see which form is currently mounted on the designated printer. If the printer's current form does not match the form requested in the print header, the print server sends a broadcast to everyone on the printer's notification list. The message is as follows:

```
<printer name> needs form <form name>
```

where *printer name* is the NDS name of the printer, and *form name* is the name of the form. A blinking message also appears on the Printer Status screen for the printer in question. The message is on the Status line and reads as follows:

```
Current status: Waiting for form to be mounted
```

Be sure that someone, preferably the job owner, is on the printer's notification list. If nobody is notified, all print jobs directed to that printer will stop until the form has been changed. In this case, the only notification that a form change is required is the blinking message on the status screen for the printer in question.

The next step is to physically change the form in the printer. This may consist of adding letterhead, placing the check stock in the printer, or whatever action is appropriate for the type of form requested. After the form has been changed, you need to notify the print server of the form change. This can be done from the file server console (or remotely through RCONSOLE) as follows:

1. Press Alt+Esc (or Alt+F3 from RCONSOLE) until the PSERVER menu is in view.
2. From the PSERVER menu, select Printer Status. The Printer List appears.
3. From the Printer List, select the printer whose form you changed. The Printer Status screen appears.

4. From the Printer Status screen, select Mounted form. Enter the form number that corresponds with the requested form. If unsure of the form number, consult PRINTDEF.

Once the form change has taken place, the document prints. Note that any future jobs might request a different form, and you need to go through the procedure again. The form change can be automated from the command line using the PSC.EXE utility (described later in the chapter).

To create a printer form, proceed as follows:

1. Change to the context for whose container you want to create forms. You can use the Change Current Context option from the PRINTDEF main menu to do so.

2. When the correct context has been established, select Printer Forms from the PRINTDEF main menu. The Forms list appears.

3. From the Forms list, press Insert to add a new form. The Form Definition screen appears, as illustrated in figure 28.7.

Figure 28.7

PRINTDEF.EXE—Form Definition screen.

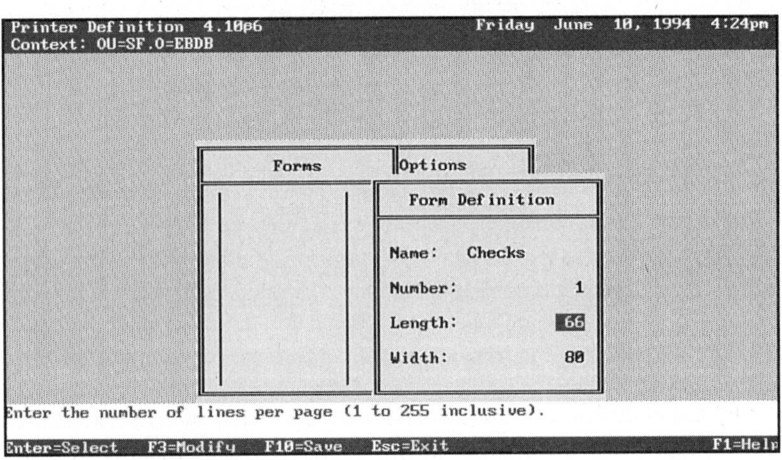

4. From the Form Definition screen, enter the form name, number, length, and width. As indicated earlier, NetWare does not make use of the length and width information.

5. When you are finished, press F10 to save the information. Press Esc to return to the PRINTDEF main menu.

To modify a printer form, select Printer Forms from the PRINTDEF main menu. Select the form you want to modify. If you want to remove the form, press Del. If you want to change the name, number, or other information, press Enter. To save changes, press F10.

Creating New Print Devices

The Print Devices option in PRINTDEF enables you define a custom print driver. A print device consists of functions. A *function* is one or more printer escape codes defined using the printer's manual. A function performs a single printer action. Examples of functions include changing the font to Helvetica, placing the printer in boldface mode, or altering the vertical line spacing. Functions are then grouped into modes. A *mode* is a collection of functions that occur in a specified order. You can define a mode, for example, that calls the functions to change the font to Helvetica, change the pitch to 10, and change the paper source to envelope.

To create a custom print device, proceed by first defining functions:

1. Change to the context for which container you want to create forms. You can use the Change Current Context option from the PRINTDEF main menu to do so.

2. Once the correct context has been established, select Print Devices from the PRINTDEF main menu. The Print Device Options menu appears.

3. From the Print Device Options menu, select Edit Print Devices. The Defined Print Devices list appears.

4. From the Defined Print Devices list, press the Insert key to create a new print device. Enter the name of your new print device in the New Device Name input box. You are returned to the Defined Print Devices list.

5. From the Defined Print Devices list, select the new device you just created, and press Enter. The Device Options menu appears.

6. From the Device Options menu, select Device Functions. The Functions for Device <*name*> appears, where *name* is the name of the new device you just created.

7. From the Functions for Device <*name*> menu, press Insert to add a new function. The Function Definition screen appears.

Create a function that will reset the printer. This can be inserted at the start of a mode (defined later) and ensures that the printer starts from an initial state.

8. From the Function Definition screen, enter the Name of the new function and the Escape Sequence. When entering the escape sequence, use the literal "<ESC>" or "\27" to represent the Esc code (ASCII code 27).

   ASCII control codes can be entered between the left and right angle braces (<>). Table 28.3 summarizes the pertinent ASCII control codes.

Table 28.3
Common ASCII Codes Used in Print Device Functions

Decimal Value	Letter Code	Description
8	BS	Back space
9	TAB	Inserts a tab character
10	LF	Line feed
11	VT	Vertical tab
12	FF	Form feed
13	CR	Carriage return. Note that for many printers, to have the printer jump to the next line, first position on the line, you will need to issue both a CR and an LF.
27	ESC	Escape
32	SP	Space

In addition, any ASCII code can be entered in decimal form using any of the following three methods:

- ◆ Angle braces (<>)
- ◆ Backslash (\)
- ◆ Carat (^)

ASCII codes are assumed to be in decimal. If you want to enter ASCII codes in hex, precede the code with the special prefix "0x". Here are some examples of escape sequences using ASCII codes:

```
\27\0x0A^254<ESC><CR><LF>
```

In addition to ASCII codes, letters and numbers can be freely intermixed. If this is the case, it is recommended you enclose any embedded ASCII codes in angle braces (<>). Here is an example of an HP control sequence that sets the font to PC-8/Courier and the number of dots per inch to 300:

```
<ESC>(10U<ESC>(s3T<ESC>*t300R
```

ASCII characters between 33 and 126 can be entered as they stand. For example, to enter a letter *A*, simply enter the letter *A* in the escape sequence. Other ASCII codes outside of this range must be delimited using any of the three methods mentioned earlier: ^ \ or <>. The escape sequence field can physically hold up to 256 characters.

9. When you are finished defining the function, press F10 to save the definition. You are returned to the Functions for Device <*name*> menu. Continue to press Insert and add new functions until all desired functions are added. When adding functions, be sure to minimize the task of a single function. For example, instead of having a function that changes the font to Helvetica and changes the vertical line spacing, create two functions: one that changes the font to Helvetica, and another that changes the vertical line spacing. Functions will be combined into modes later on.

10. When you are finished defining all functions, press Esc to return to the Device Options menu (see fig. 28.8).

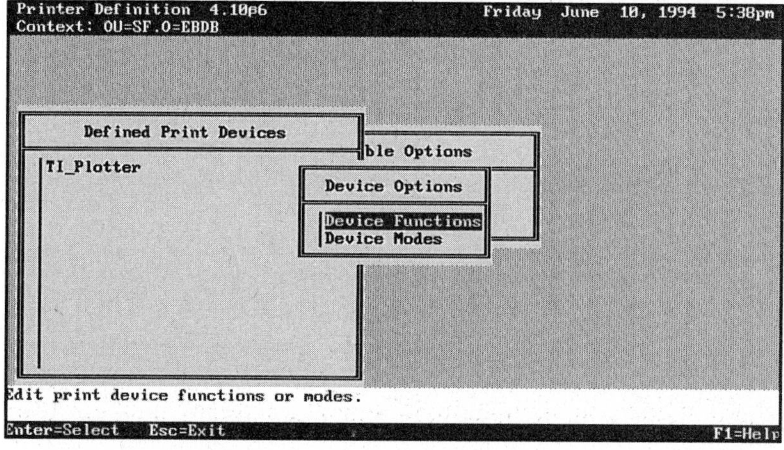

Figure 28.8

PRINTDEF.EXE—Device Options menu.

At this point you are ready to combine the functions created earlier into modes. You need to think carefully about what modes will be needed and which functions will reside in which modes.

To create a mode, proceed as follows:

1. From the Device Options menu, select Device Modes. The Modes for Device <*name*> list appears, where *name* is the name of the print device you are defining.

The default mode is *(Re-initialize)*. You should add the Reset function mentioned in the preceding Tip. The *(Re-initialize)* mode is placed into the Print Tail and executes after the print job finishes.

2. From the Modes for Device <*name*> list, press Insert to create a new mode. Enter the name of the new mode in the New Mode Name input box, and press Enter. You are returned to the Modes for Device <*name*> list.

3. From the Modes for Device <*name*> list, select the new mode just created, and press Enter. The Functions for Mode <*mode name*> list appear. *Mode name* is the name of the new mode just created. Press Insert to add a function to the mode. The order in which the functions appear can be critical. In the HP PCL (Printer Control Language), for example, if you enter a function for a font change, you must be sure you have first selected either the cartridge or the font family that contains that particular font.

   Figure 28.9 illustrates a function Bold Landscape Helvetica. Note that the setting for portrait must precede a font change in this case because the printer will select a different font set for portrait compared to landscape.

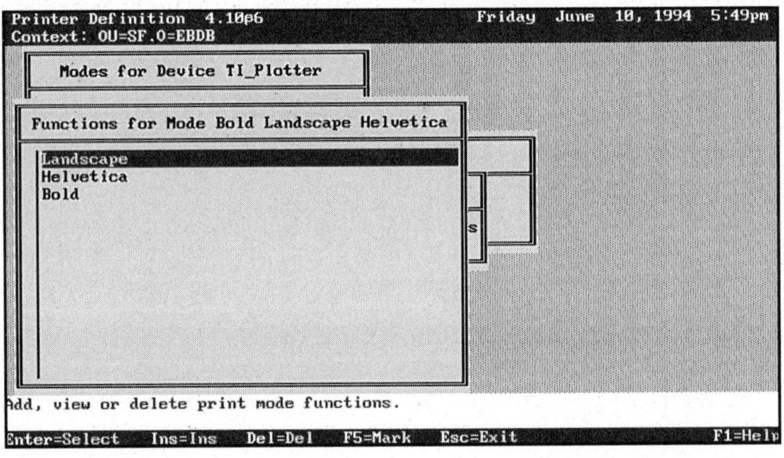

Figure 28.9
PRINTDEF.EXE Print Device Definition—Defining a mode.

4. Continue to create as many modes as desired. When you are finished, press Esc several times to return to the PRINTDEF main menu.

Importing a Print Device Definition

NetWare 4 comes with a set of predefined print device definitions. The definitions are stored in the SYS:PUBLIC directory and consist of a series of files with the extension PDF (printer definition file). To import a print device definition, proceed as follows:

1. Change to the context for which container you want to create forms. You can use the Change Current Context option from the PRINTDEF main menu to do so.

2. Once the correct context has been established, select Print Devices from the PRINTDEF main menu. The Print Device Options menu appears.

3. From the Print Device Options menu, select Import Print Devices. You are asked for a directory. Type in the directory that contains the desired PDF files, and press Enter. NetWare comes with a set of files in SYS:PUBLIC, for example. Figure 28.10 shows you the Available .PDFs screen that appears.

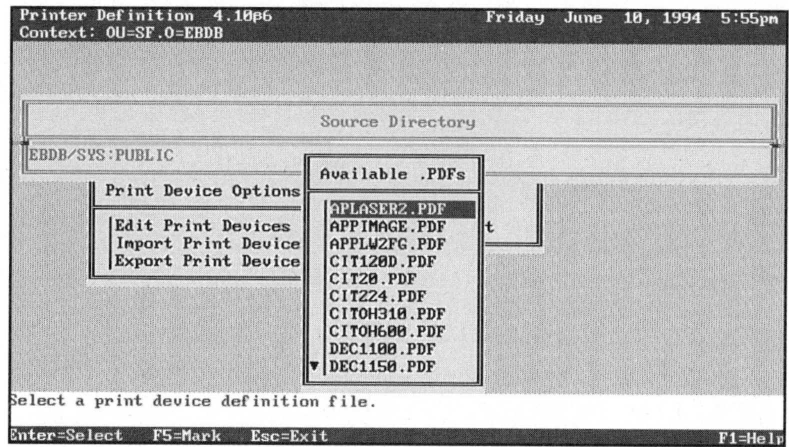

Figure 28.10

Importing a print device definition.

4. From the Available .PDFs screen, select the desired printer definition file, and press Enter. A delay occurs as the information is read from the PDF file and placed into the NDS. After the information has been read into the NDS from the PDF file, you are returned to the Print Device Options menu.

If the local file server to which you are logically connected does not have a replica that contains the container you are working with, a long delay could ensue. This is because NDS must locate a server that physically contains a replica defining this container. If such a server can be found only across a WAN link, the delay could be several minutes.

5. To verify that the import process occurred smoothly, select Edit Print Devices from the Print Device Options menu. The name of the printer that corresponds with the PDF file selected should now appear on the list. Figure 28.11 shows a list of some of the functions for an HP LaserJet 4SI-PCL printer.

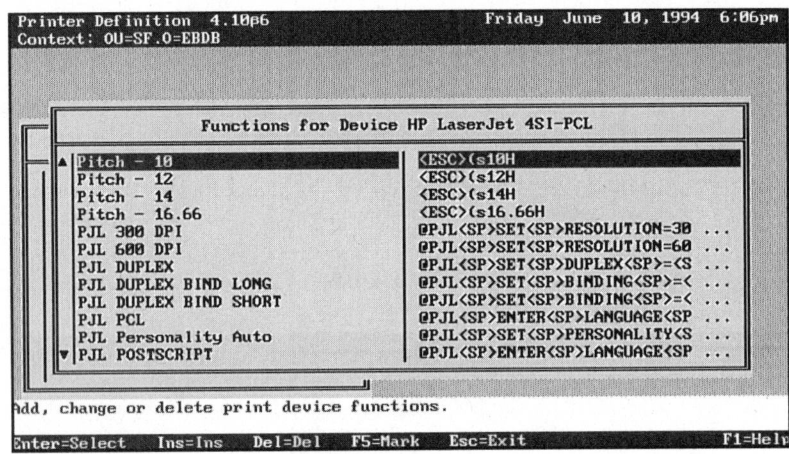

Figure 28.11

Functions for an HP LaserJet 4SI-PCL printer.

Exporting a Print Device Definition

When you have defined a custom print device, it is a good idea to export the device definition. Export serves as a type of backup and enables you to import the definition into other containers should the need arise. Remember that print devices defined for one container are automatically available to any child container. Use the export option to export a printer device definition to a container in another branch of the tree. To export a print device definition, proceed as follows:

1. Change to the context for which container you want to create forms. You can use the Change Current Context option from the PRINTDEF main menu to do so.

2. Once the correct context has been established, select Print Devices from the PRINTDEF main menu. The Print Device Options menu appears.

3. From the Print Device Options menu, select Export Print Devices. The Defined Print Devices menu appears.

4. From the Defined Print Devices menu, select the print device you want to export, and press Enter. You are asked for a destination directory. Enter the name of a directory. You can export to any of the following:

   - Another volume
   - Another file server's volume
   - Any local drives (C, A, and so on)

5. After you enter the name of a server, volume, or drive and directory path, press Enter. You are now asked to supply the name of the PDF file. Enter the eight-character file name, without the extension. PRINTDEF supplies the PDF extension. Press Enter when done. The definition is written out to the designated file, and you are returned to the Print Device Options menu.

Using PRINTCON

The PRINTCON.EXE utility is tremendously useful as a way of storing sets of CAPTURE parameters. Each set is referred to as a *print job configuration* or *print job template.* PRINTCON is also capable of bringing in forms and print device modes you created using PRINTDEF.

PRINTCON job templates are stored in the NDS. You can store templates for individual users or for a group of users. Print job configurations that you want to make available to groups of users are stored at the container level.

The PRINTCON main menu is illustrated in figure 28.12.

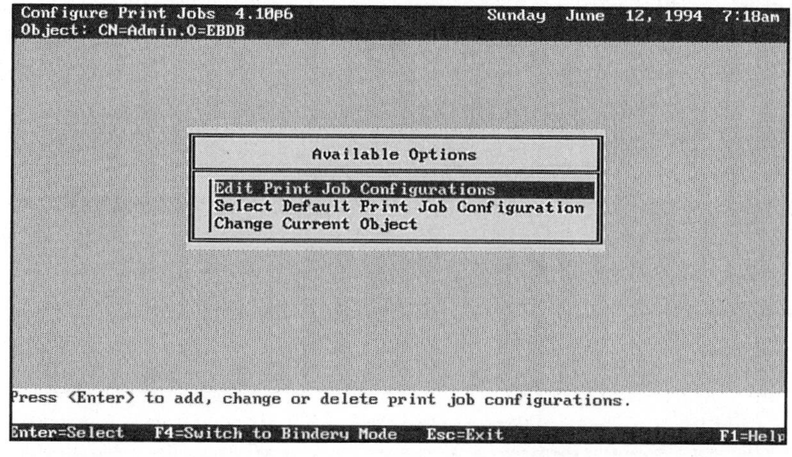

Figure 28.12
The PRINTCON main menu.

As with most DOS-based utilities, there is an option to Change Current Object. This is in place of the usual Change Current Context. PRINTCON works with the print job configurations of both user objects and container objects. When you change to another user object, current context is not applicable, so the term current object is used instead.

The Select Default Print Job Configuration option is used to select one of the configurations you have created as the default for the current object. The Edit Print Job Configurations option is used to add, delete, or modify print job configurations for the current object.

PRINTCON Print Job Configurations

To create a new configuration, first make sure you are working with the desired object to which you want to add a configuration. If this is not the case, use the Change Current Object option to change to another user or container object. From the PRINTCON main menu, select Edit Print Job Configurations. The Print Job Configurations list appears. Press the Insert key to add a new job configuration. The name of the new configuration appears on the Print Job Configurations list. Press Enter to modify the new configuration. The Edit Print Job Configuration "*xyz*" input screen appears, where *xyz* is the name of the new configuration. A screen with values filled in is shown in figure 28.13.

Figure 28.13

The PRINTCON.EXE Edit Print Job Configuration input screen.

```
Configure Print Jobs  4.10p6                    Sunday  June  12, 1994  8:41am
Object: O=EBDB

                  Edit Print Job Configuration "EBDB_HP"

Number of copies:       1                  Form name:          EBDB_Special
File contents:          Byte Stream        Print banner:       Yes
Tab size:                                  Name:               EBDB
Form feed:              Yes                Banner name:
Notify when done:       No

Local printer:          1                  Enable timeout:     Yes
Auto endcap:            Yes                Timeout count:      10

Printer/Queue:          CN=Q_Main.O=EBDB
  (Queue)

Device:                 HP LaserJet 4SI-PCL
Mode:                   Switch_to_PCL

Enter the number of copies (1 to 65,000 inclusive) to be printed.
Enter=Select   F3=Modify   F10=Save   Esc=Exit                          F1=Help
```

Table 28.4 summarizes the fields in the Print Job Configuration input screen. The defaults are listed in the middle column. Some fields have no defaults. The equivalent CAPTURE parameter (abbreviated) is also listed in this table.

Table 28.4
PRINTCON.EXE Print Job Configuration Fields

Field	CAPTURE Equivalent	Default	Description
Number of copies	C	1	Number of copies of each print job to be printed.
Form name	F		Name of form to be used when print job is sent.

Field	CAPTURE Equivalent	Default	Description
File contents	T, NT	Byte stream	A value of *byte stream* implies no tab formatting. A value of *text* requires a value for Tab Size. The number indicated by Tab Size is the number of spaces inserted in place of a tab character.
Tab size	T		The number of spaces used by tab expansion (only if File contents is set to *text*).
Print banner		Yes	Enter Yes if you want each print job to be preceded with a banner page.
Name	NAM	Login Name	Name of the user who originated the print job. This name appears at the top of the banner page.
Banner name	B	LPT	Name that appears at the bottom of the banner page. The default is the LPT port captured (for example, LPT1).
Form feed	FF	Yes	Eject a page after print job completes.
Notify when	NOTI	No	Notify job owner that the print job done printed successfully and specify which printer.
Local printer	L or LPT	1	Local printer port to be captured. Values can range from 1 to 9 depending on the Network Printers setting in your NET.CFG file.
Auto endcap	A	Yes	Causes all print jobs captured to be placed in ready mode when you exit an application.

continues

Table 28.4, Continued
PRINTCON.EXE Print Job Configuration Fields

Field	CAPTURE Equivalent	Default	Description
Enable timeout	TI	No	If set to Yes, this function causes print jobs that the workstation has finished sending to the queue to be placed in ready status mode.
Timeout count	TI		The number of seconds the queuing system is to wait after receiving the last character from the workstation before timing out and placing the job in ready status mode.
Printer/Queue	P or Q		The name or number of the printer, or name of the queue, to which print capture is to be redirected.
Device			The device name specified in PRINTDEF. Devices are available from the container of the print queue designated.
Mode			A device definition (created in PRINTDEF) containing function codes to be sent to the printer in advance of the print job. The function codes are placed in the print header.

Invoking PRINTCON Print Job Configurations

To invoke a PRINTCON job configuration that you have created, you have the option of simply typing CAPTURE or using the CAPTURE J=*xyz* option. When you type CAPTURE with no other parameters, your default print job configuration is invoked.

You can change your default by getting into PRINTCON, changing to the desired object, and using the Select Default Print Job Configuration menu option. Select the target job configuration from the list, and press Enter. An asterisk designates a default print job configuration.

Alternatively, to invoke a print job configuration other than the default, use the CAPTURE J=*job configuration name* option. If the job configuration is in another container, add a colon (:) and the complete NDS name of the container after the job configuration name. The following is an example of three cases using PRINTCON job configuration templates. In the first case you type CAPTURE with no other parameters. In the second case you specify the name of the job configuration using the J=*job configuration name* parameter. In the last example, the job configuration is pulled from another container.

```
F:\PUBLIC>CAPTURE
Device LPT1 re-routed to print queue CN=Q_MAIN..

F:\PUBLIC>CAPTURE J=EBDB_HP
Device LPT2 re-routed to printer CN=Ptr_HP_IV_Bldg3_Travel..

F:\PUBLIC>CAPTURE J=SF_SPECIAL:.SF.EBDB
Device LPT3 re-routed to printer CN=Ptr_Dot_Matrix_Bldg7..

F:\PUBLIC>CAPTURE SHOW

LPT1  Capturing data to print queue CN=Q_Main.
  Notify:              Disabled
  Automatic end:       Enabled
  Timeout count:       10 seconds
  Name:                (None)
  Form feed:           Disabled
  Banner:              (None)
  Keep:                Disabled
  Copies:              1
  Tabs:                No conversion
  Form:                Unknown
  User hold:           Off

LPT2  Capturing data to print queue CN=Q_HP_IV_Bldg3_Travel.
  Notify:              Disabled
  Automatic end:       Enabled
  Timeout count:       10 seconds
  Name:                SF
  Form feed:           Enabled
  Banner:              LPT2
  Keep:                Disabled
  Copies:              1
```

```
  Tabs:               8
  Form:               EBDB_Special
  User hold:          Off

LPT3  Capturing data to print queue CN=Q_Dot_Matrix_Bldg7.
  Notify:             Enabled
  Automatic end:      Enabled
  Timeout count:      30 seconds
  Name:               SF
  Form feed:          Enabled
  Banner:             LPT3
  Keep:               Disabled
  Copies:             1
  Tabs:               No conversion
  Form:               EBDB_Special
  User hold:          Off

F:\PUBLIC>
```

Using NPRINT

The NPRINT.EXE utility is used to place print-ready files into a print queue. NPRINT has many similarities to the CAPTURE utility, including the flags associated with it. You can, for example, use the NPRINT command with the J=*print job configuration* flag, specifying the desired PRINTCON print job configuration.

The differences between NPRINT and CAPTURE are as follows:

NPRINT	CAPTURE
Effective only when the command is issued.	Effective continuously until the command is revoked or changed.
Accepts only print-ready files as input.	Accepts any printable information files as input, including screen prints, TYPE commands, or printable output from applications.
Because only print-ready files are used, the NT and TI flags are not effective.	You can choose to use or not use the NT or TI flags, depending on what type of results you need.

The following NPRINT command sends the file FIG2807.TXT on drive C to the print queue Q_Main, with no banner and no extra form feed.

```
F:\SYSTEM>nprint c:FIG2807.TXT q=.CN=Q_Main.O=EBDB nb nff
The following files are being sent to print queue .CN=Q_Main.O=EBDB:
Local Drive C:\NRP\INSIDE4
   FIG2807.TXT  (Job ID=00144004)

F:\SYSTEM>
```

Because the input to NPRINT is limited to print-ready files only, its usefulness is limited. NPRINT is a good way to quickly print small batch or configuration files. NPRINT is also useful when you are in a situation where you cannot, or choose not to, print immediately. For example, NPRINT can be used to print files created using the CAPTURE cr=*path:\filename* command. This form of CAPTURE sends printing to a print-ready file. NPRINT can be used to send the file into a queue where it can be printed.

Managing Print Jobs

You have had a chance to see how to send jobs to a printer using CAPTURE or NPRINT. This section shows you how to manage the print jobs after they arrive in the print queue. The two tools you will learn about are PCONSOLE.EXE and PSC.EXE.

Using PCONSOLE

PCONSOLE.EXE is the primary utility used by DOS-based users to set up and manage the printing environment. Some of the functions of PCONSOLE are duplicated in other utilities, including NETUSER.EXE. This section focuses on how to manage print queues, printers, and print servers through PCONSOLE. PCONSOLE.EXE is located in SYS:PUBLIC, along with other NetWare utilities. You do not need any special rights (aside from Read and File Scan directory trustee rights to SYS:PUBLIC) to invoke PCONSOLE. To perform management tasks such as creating or deleting queues, however, you need the appropriate NDS rights to the container under which the queue resides.

Managing Queues

One of the primary printing management responsibilities that can be accomplished in PCONSOLE is the ability to manage print queues. Of the functions available in PCONSOLE, two options are used most often: monitoring print jobs and updating the print queue status.

To monitor print jobs from PCONSOLE, proceed as follows:

1. Move to the container that contains the printing resource you plan to manage. If necessary, use the Change Current Context menu option to accomplish this.

2. From the PCONSOLE main menu, select Print Queues. The Print Queues list appears. Select the desired print queue, and press Enter. The Print Queue Information menu appears, as illustrated in figure 28.14.

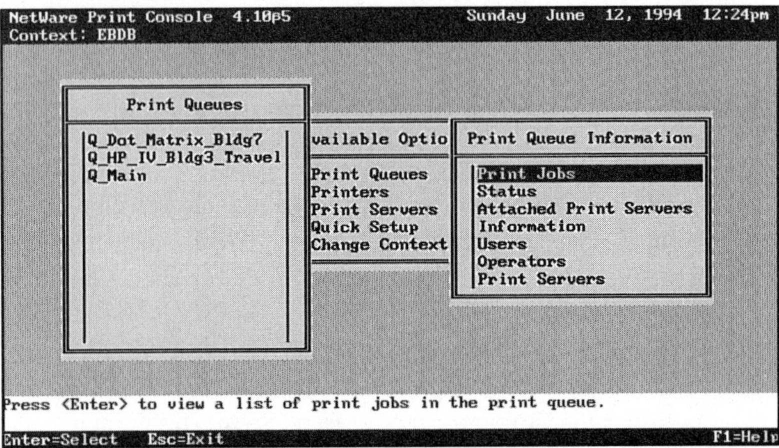

Figure 28.14
The PCONSOLE.EXE Print Queue Information menu.

3. From the Print Queue Information menu, select Print Jobs. The Print Job List screen appears. As you can see from the diagram, this is identical to the Print Job List you can obtain from the NETUSER utility (refer to fig. 28.4).

   The functions that can be performed at this point are identical to those for the NETUSER utility. They include the following:

   - Modifying print job parameters (press Enter)
   - Inserting a job into the queue (press Insert)
   - Deleting a job from the queue (press Del)

4. When you are finished working with the Print Job List, press Esc several times to return to the PCONSOLE main menu.

The Print Queue Status menu enables you to specify whether jobs can be placed in the queue in the first place, and whether a queue is allowed to release jobs to the print server. In some cases you might want to block all access to the queue in the first place. By doing so, users will be immediately notified that there is a problem. You might want to do this when performing extensive maintenance on the printer

associated with this queue. Send out a memo reminding users that the printer will be unavailable for an hour or so, and place a block on the queue. If users accidentally try to send a job to this queue, a warning message will be sent to them immediately. They can then send their print job again to another queue. The Print Queue Status menu option that controls this is the Allow users to submit print jobs operator flag.

On the other hand, you might want to allow users to send jobs to a queue but not have the jobs released until you specify. In this case, users can send jobs to the queue and will be unaware that their jobs are not being printed. When you release the flag, all jobs currently in the queue will start printing again. This is useful when creating queues where users can place large print jobs. At the end of each day you could release the queue so that long print jobs will print overnight. In the morning you could place a block on the queue so that large jobs can once again accumulate in the queue. The Print Queue Status menu option that controls this is the Allow service by current print servers operator flag.

Figure 28.15 illustrates the effect of these two operator flags.

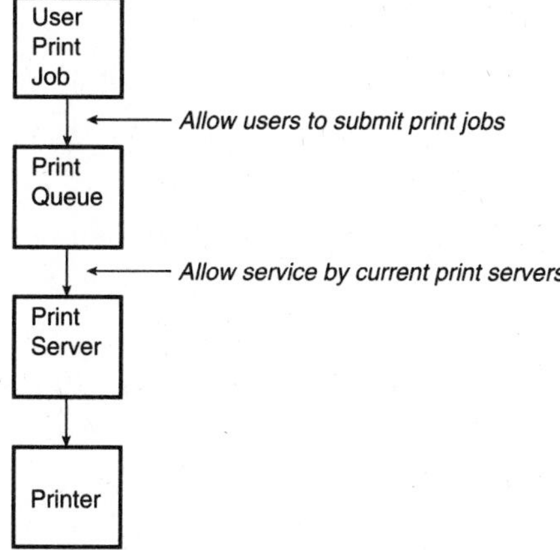

Figure 28.15

The effect of two print queue status operator flags.

To prevent users from placing jobs in a queue, proceed as follows:

1. Move to the container that contains the printing resource you plan to manage. If necessary, use the Change Current Context menu option to accomplish this.

2. From the PCONSOLE main menu, select Print Queues. The Print Queues list appears. Select the desired print queue, and press Enter. The Print Queue Information menu appears.

3. From the Print Queue Information menu, select Status. The Print Queue Status menu appears.

4. From the Print Queue Status menu, change the Allow users to submit print jobs operator flag to NO, and press Enter to register your choice.

5. Press Esc several times to return to the next menu you want to work with.

To allow users to send jobs to a queue but prevent any jobs from being released from the queue, proceed as follows:

1. Move to the container that contains the printing resource you plan to manage. If necessary, use the Change Current Context menu option to accomplish this.

2. From the PCONSOLE main menu, select Print Queues. The Print Queues list appears. Select the desired print queue, and press Enter. The Print Queue Information menu appears.

3. From the Print Queue Information menu, select Status. The Print Queue Status menu appears.

4. From the Print Queue Status menu, change the Allow service by current print servers operator flag to NO, and press Enter to register your choice.

5. Press Esc several times to return to the next menu you want to work with.

Managing Print Servers

The status of the print server can be monitored much as was discussed in Chapter 27, "Setting Up Printing." You can view certain pieces of information on the print server as follows:

1. Move to the container that contains the printing resource you plan to manage. If necessary, use the Change Current Context menu option to accomplish this.

2. From the PCONSOLE main menu, select Print Servers. The Print Servers list appears. Select the desired print server, and press Enter. The Print Server Information menu appears, as illustrated in figure 28.16.

3. From the Print Server Information menu, select Information and Status. The Print Server Information and Status menu appears.

4. The information you see displayed here is the same as in figure 27.14 in Chapter 27. You can see whether the print server is up and running by looking at the Current Server Status field.

5. Press Esc several times to return to the main PCONSOLE menu.

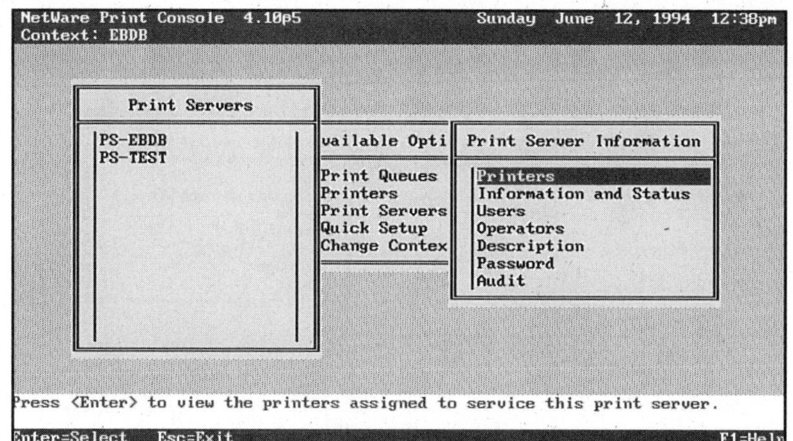

Figure 28.16

The PCONSOLE.EXE Print Server Information menu.

Managing Printers Through the Print Server Menu

PCONSOLE can be used to manage printers in the same fashion as you learned through the PSERVER menu on the file server in Chapter 27. The advantage to PCONSOLE is that you do not have to directly (or remotely, using RCONSOLE) access the file server console. The first action you need to perform is, from the main PCONSOLE menu, to change to the context that contains the printer you want to manage.

To manage a printer through PCONSOLE, proceed as follows:

1. From the PCONSOLE main menu, select Print Servers. The list of available print servers appears. Select the desired print server, and press Enter. The Print Server Information menu appears.

2. From the Print Server Information menu, select Printers. The Serviced Printers list appears, as illustrated in figure 28.17.

3. From the Serviced Printers list, select the desired printer, and press Enter. The Status of <*printer_name*> screen appears. This screen, and its values, is identical to those associated with figure 27.12 in Chapter 27.

4. When you are finished viewing or modifying the printer status, press Esc several times to return to the main PCONSOLE menu.

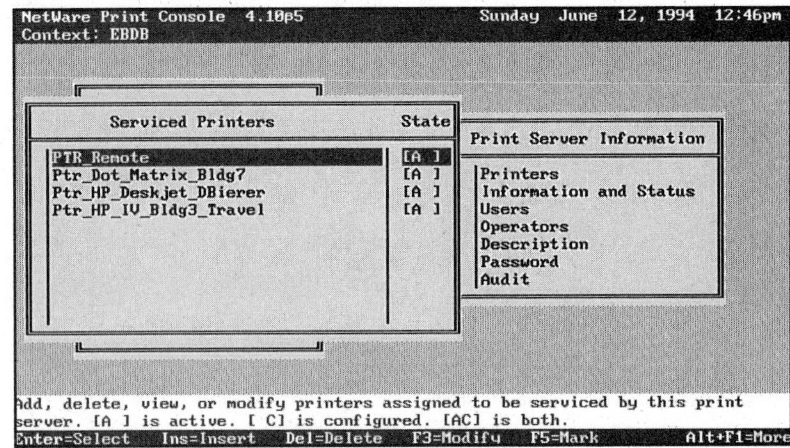

Figure 28.17
The PCONSOLE.EXE Serviced Printers screen.

Redirecting Print Jobs from One Queue to Another

You can use PCONSOLE to place a job that exists in one queue into another one. To perform this action, you need to know several pieces of information about the job you want to relocate and the print queue where it is currently residing, including the following:

- The volume where the print queue is physically stored
- The internal object ID number assigned to the queue
- The number assigned to the print job

To gather the preceding information, proceed as follows:

1. Move to the container that contains the printing resource you plan to manage. If necessary, use the Change Current Context menu option to accomplish this.

2. From the PCONSOLE main menu, select Print Queues. The Print Queues list appears. Select the desired print queue, and press Enter. The Print Queue Information menu appears.

3. From the Print Queue Information menu, select Information. An information screen appears, much like the one illustrated in figure 28.18.

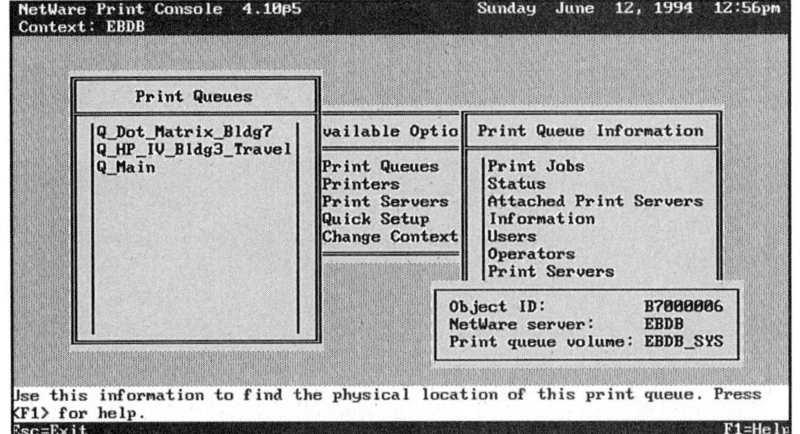

Figure 28.18
The PCONSOLE.EXE Print Queue Information screen.

4. From the Print Queue Information screen, write down the following information:

   ◆ Object ID

   ◆ NetWare server

   ◆ Print queue volume

5. To find the job number of the print job, press Esc to return to the Print Queue Information menu. From this menu, select Print Jobs. A list of print jobs for this queue appears. Locate the job you want to insert into another queue. If the job you want to relocate is not on this list, you might want to repeat the process from Step 1 until you locate the correct source queue.

6. When the print job has been located on the list, make a note of the job ID number recorded in the right column. Press Esc to return to the PCONSOLE main menu.

Once this information is in hand, you are now in a position to insert a job from one queue to another. The technique is as follows:

1. Move to the destination print queue by selecting Print Queues from the main PCONSOLE menu and pressing Enter on the destination print queue. Select the Print Jobs menu option. The print job list appears.

2. From the destination queue print job list, press Insert. You now need to locate the physical location of the source print job. Its location is on the file server and

volume you noted earlier. On the above-noted volume is a directory called QUEUES. Under this directory is a series of subdirectories with the extension QDR. The prefix is the print queue ID number. The screen you see is illustrated in figure 28.19.

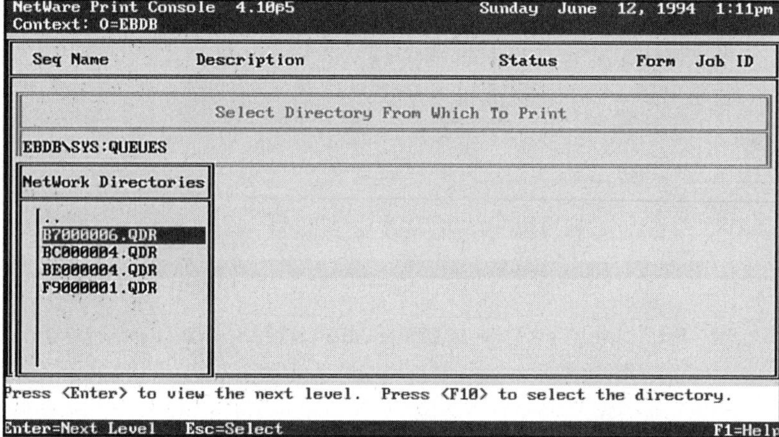

Figure 28.19
Inserting a job from a print queue directory.

3. Once you have entered the proper directory in the Select Directory From Which To Print input box, press Enter. The Available Files list for this directory appears. The file names listed have the extension Q and have a prefix that corresponds with their print job ID number.

4. Select the desired source file from the list, and then press Enter. You are asked to confirm the settings for the job, going through a list of print job configurations available for this queue, created in PRINTCON. Select the desired print job configuration, and press Enter. You see a data screen similar to that discussed earlier when creating a PRINTCON job configuration template.

5. From the job configuration sheet, press F10 to save your settings. The print job from the source queue now appears in the list for the destination queue.

A similar result could be obtained from the DOS prompt by changing to the file server/volume:queues\ print_queue_ID directory and using NPRINT to print the file to another queue. Files in queues are print-ready.

Using PSC

The PSC.EXE (Print Server Control) utility can be used to control certain aspects of printers on print servers. To use this utility, you must have either Supervisor effective rights to the print server object or be on the Print Server Operator list. PSC can be

used from the command line, or in a batch file, to perform operations similar to the Printer Status commands from the PSERVER menu on the file server console.

The general syntax for PSC is as follows:

```
PSC PS=<print server name> [P=<printer number>] [/<option>]
```

The *print server name* must be the NDS name for the print server object. If your current context does not contain the print server object, be sure to specify a complete NDS name. *Printer number* is the number of the printer you want to control. PSC *options* are summarized in table 28.5.

Table 28.5
PSC Options

Option	Abbrev.	Description
Abort	AB	Causes the print server to abort the current print job and to delete the job from the print queue.
Cancel Down	CD	Cancels the Unload after active print jobs option that can be issued from PSERVER or from PCONSOLE. This prevents the print server from going down.
Form Feed	FF	Causes the printer to eject the current page. If no current page, a blank sheet of paper will be ejected.
List	L	Lists the relationships between printing objects managed by this print server. The print server is shown at the top with its various printers the next level down. Print queues are shown branching off their respective printers.
Mark Char	M	Causes the printer to print a row of asterisks (*) where the printer thinks the current top of the form is located. Used to position the printer before printing complicated forms.
Mount Form=*form no.*	MOF	Informs the print server that the paper has been changed on the printer (that form *form no.* has been mounted).

continues

Table 28.5, Continued
PSC Options

Option	Abbrev.	Description
Pause	PAU	Causes the printer to stop printing after the current print buffer maintained by the print server (default 3K) has been printed. Does not affect current job in the queue.
Private	PRI	Causes a local workstation printer to be removed as a network printer. This can be done by the user of the printer (assuming the necessary NDS or operator rights are assigned) if that user wants to regain control of the local printer.
S=*server*		Enables you to specify a specific NetWare file server. This is useful when the print server resides on a file server accessible only through bindery emulation.
Shared	SHA	Places the local printer in Private mode back into Shared mode. The printer can once again be used by the print server as a network printer.
Start	STAR	Restarts a printer halted by either a Pause or a Stop command.
Status	STAT	Displays the status of the specified printer. If no printer is specified, shows the status for all printers.
Stop	STO	Causes printer to stop printing after the current print buffer maintained by the print server (default 3K) has been printed. Does not affect current job in the queue. Causes an error message to appear on the user's screen informing them that the printer is now unable to accept print requests.
Version PSC	V or Ver	Displays information about the version of the command.

```
F:\>PSC PS=.CN=PS-EBDB.O=EBDB /STAT
Printer Ptr_HP_Deskjet_DBierer (printer number 0)
      Status:Waiting for job

Printer PTR_Remote (printer number 1)
      Status:Not connected

Printer Ptr_Dot_Matrix_Bldg7 (printer number 2)
      Status:Not connected

Printer Ptr_HP_IV_Bldg3_Travel (printer number 3)
      Status:Not connected

F:\>PSC PS=.CN=PS-EBDB.O=EBDB /LIST

   .CN=PS-EBDB.O=EBDB                   (NetWare Server: EBDB)
       ├─CN=PTR_Remote                   (#1 - Not connected)
       ├─CN=Ptr_Dot_Matrix_Bldg7         (#2 - Not connected)
       │   └CN=Q_Dot_Matrix_Bldg7        (Volume: CN=EBDB_SYS)
       ├─CN=Ptr_HP_IV_Bldg3_Travel       (#5 - Not connected)
       │   └CN=Q_HP_IV_Bldg3_Travel      (Volume: CN=EBDB_SYS)
       └─CN=Ptr_HP_Deskjet_DBierer       (#6 - Not connected)
           ├CN=Q_Main                    (Volume: CN=EBDB_SYS)
           └CN=Q_Main_SJ.OU=SJ           (Volume: CN=EBDB_SYS)
F:\>
```

Figure 28.20

The results of the STAT and LIST commands.

Figure 28.20 shows you the results of the PSC.../STAT and PSC.../LIST commands.

Summary

This chapter covered the basics of printing from DOS clients. The utilities covered included CAPTURE, NETUSER, PRINTCON, PRINTDEF, PCONSOLE, and PSC. As you learned, the role of the CAPTURE command is to program the VLM shell with values regarding how printing should be redirected from local printer ports to NetWare print queues. A table summarizes the various CAPTURE parameters, and several examples were given showing you how to use the command.

The next section covered the NETUSER utility. This utility can be used not only to perform the equivalent of the CAPTURE command, but to manage print jobs once they reach the queue. NETUSER can be used to view jobs in the queue, change their order (assuming you have enough rights), and make other printing system changes.

The PRINTDEF and PRINTCON utilities were covered. You learned how to use PRINTDEF to create your own set of customized print drivers. You saw that printer definitions are called devices, and that they consist of functions that can be combined into modes. Printer functions can be programmed with any valid ASCII code as long as it is delimited using angle braces (<>) or preceded with a backslash (\) or a carat (^). PRINTCON can be used to create a series of print job configurations that can be stored in the NDS for individual users or for containers. Lower-level containers automatically inherit the PRINTDEF information from higher-level containers. You can use any PRINTDEF device or mode from the container of the print queue you specify in your PRINTCON print job configuration. PRINTCON job configurations can be invoked by typing CAPTURE or by using the J=*job configuration* option of the CAPTURE command.

The NPRINT utility can be used with many of the same flags as CAPTURE. It is used to place print-ready files into a print queue. PCONSOLE and PSC can be used to manage print jobs and printers. PCONSOLE can be used, like NETUSER, to view and modify jobs in the queue. In addition, PCONSOLE can be used to manage print servers and associated printers. You learned how to use PCONSOLE to insert a job from one queue into another. PSC is a command-line equivalent of the printer management portion of PCONSOLE. With PSC you can view the status and start and stop printers.

The next chapter covers printing from Windows clients.

Printing from Windows Clients

In Chapter 27, you learned how to set up a NetWare printing environment. In Chapter 28, you learned how to set up the printing environment for DOS-based clients. In this chapter, you learn about printing from Windows clients.

Most of this chapter covers printing from a Windows workstation to a NetWare network. Windows for Workgroups functions in a similar fashion to an ordinary Windows workstation when configured for a Novell network. Windows for Workgroups has its own method of printing peer-to-peer, which is not covered in this book. Windows NT printing to the network has many similarities to ordinary Windows; however, some variations exist, which are covered in this chapter.

Printing from Windows 3.1 Clients

Printing from a Windows client to NetWare is slightly more complicated than printing from DOS. In the DOS environment, you can issue the CAPTURE command to redirect all printing to an LPT port. DOS-based applications are unaware that printing has been redirected. In Windows, however, all printing is controlled by Windows itself. Windows applications are written to forward all printing to the Windows printing mechanism.

Windows printing uses its own print spooler, called Print Manager. *Print Manager* takes a print job and saves it as a file on the local hard drive. Print Manager then spools the job out to the locally connected printer as a background task. When a Windows client is connected to a NetWare network, this facility is not useful. Because NetWare is designed to spool the print job to a network printer, there is no need to spool the file locally.

Using NWUSER To Capture

The primary way to set up NetWare printing is through the NWUSER utility, which is installed in Windows when you specify that the DOS Requester should be installed for Windows. NWUSER also is called the *NetWare User Tools.* You can use this utility to perform the print capture, to alter print-capture parameters, and to mark a print setting as permanent. Permanent settings are effective upon loading Windows. The NWUSER utility also is hooked into the Windows Print Manager and the Printers option from the Control Panel. To access the NWUSER utility, choose Network Connections from the Options menu of the Windows Print Manager.

To capture an LPT port to a NetWare print queue, follow these steps:

1. Log in as any user and start Windows.
2. From Windows, run the NWUSER utility. The NetWare Drive Connections dialog box appears.
3. Select the Printer icon from the toolbar menu at the top (the third icon from the left) or press Alt+P. The NetWare Printer Connections dialog box appears.
4. Select the LPT port to capture in the Ports list. Under Resources, browse the tree and select the printer or print queue.
5. Click on the Capture button to issue the print capture. You see a screen similar to the one shown in figure 29.1.

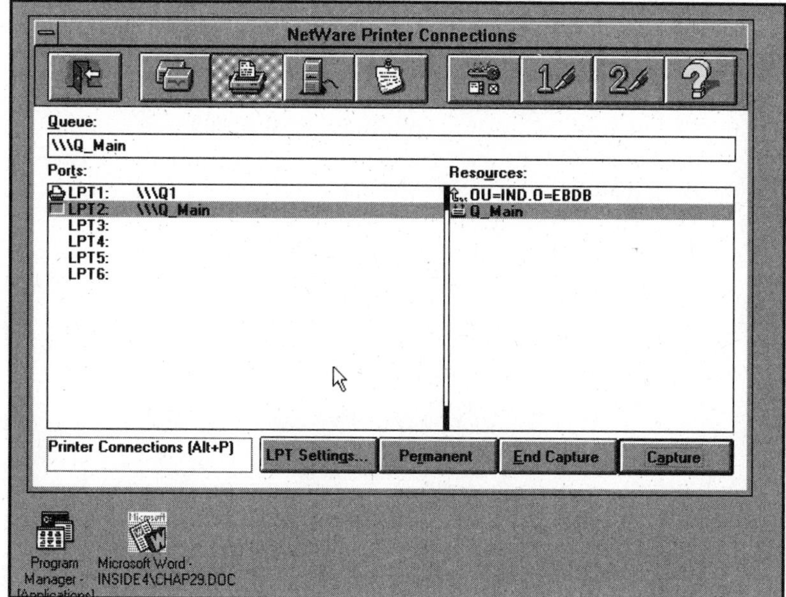

Figure 29.1
Using the Windows NWUSER.EXE utility to issue a print capture.

After you set up a print capture using NWUSER, you can make certain modifications. One option is to make the print capture permanent. This option causes NWUSER to write an entry to the WIN.INI file under the [Network] section. Click on the Permanent button to make a print capture permanent. The icon next to the LPT port changes from a nondescript rectangle to a tiny printer icon.

Setting a permanent print capture or drive mapping from NWUSER has a side effect if you enter Windows without logging in. When you first go into Windows, the NetWare client attempts to initiate the permanent drive mappings and print captures. If you are not logged in, you see a login dialog box where you can specify the username and password. After Windows authenticates these entries, it completes the permanent assignment.

Here is a sample of the [Network] section of the WIN.INI file:

```
[Network]
LPT1:=\\EBDB\.CN=Q1.O=EBDB
LPT1-OPTIONS=0,1,8,10,0,Admin,LST:,16,0
LPT2:=\\EBDB\.CN=Q_Main.OU=IND.O=EBDB
LPT2-OPTIONS=128,1,8,0,0,Admin,LST:,16,0
```

As you can see from this example, LPT1 is captured to file server EBDB and a print queue .CN=Q1.O=EBDB. LPT2 is captured to a queue .CN=Q_Main.OU=Ind.O=EBDB.

You also can alter the LPT settings of a print capture. First select the print capture with the settings you want to alter, and then click on the LPT Settings button. The NetWare Settings for LPT*n* dialog box appears, where *n* is the number of the LPT port (see fig. 29.2). Table 29.1 summarizes the possible options.

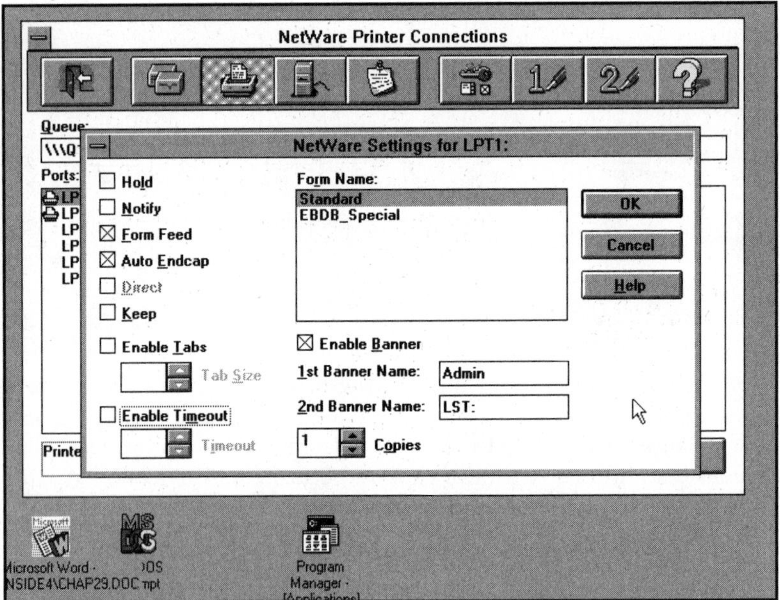

Figure 29.2 *The NetWare Settings for LPT1 screen in the NWUSER.EXE utility.*

Table 29.1
NWUSER NetWare Settings for LPT*n* Dialog Box Options

Option	Function
Hold	Places a hold on all jobs printed to this port. You can release the hold in Print Manager. This is useful when you have large jobs that would tie up the printer. When the printer is not busy, you can release the hold.
Notify	Sends back a message when the print job has printed successfully. The message is in the form of a Windows dialog box. The notification also tells you to which printer your job printed.

Option	Function
Form Feed	Adds an extra page eject at the end of your print job. This is useful when you have programs that do not automatically issue a page eject at the end of a print job.
Auto **E**ndcap	Causes the print job to print when you close an application. This option is useful if you have a print job that has not timed out or is not released by the application for some reason.
Direct	Enables you to print directly to a shared printer if there are no print jobs in the queue. This option is effective only if you also have Personal NetWare installed.
Keep	Causes print jobs to keep a copy of the job in the queue in the case of a print failure. A typical use for this option is when printing a long job overnight and your workstation hangs up or loses power. NetWare's normal response is to cancel the print job. Another use for this option is that the print file can be resubmitted to the print queue using the NPRINT command again and again. The disadvantage is that the print job is not deleted after printing, which means that eventually you will run out of disk space and have to delete the print jobs manually.
Enable **T**abs	Causes NetWare to replace any ASCII code-9 characters (the Tab character) with the number of spaces indicated by the Tab Size parameter. The problem with this parameter for a graphics print job is that a bit pattern that resembles an ASCII code 9 could be sent, causing a disruption in the bit stream. Select this option only if you plan to print from an application that does not handle tab formatting properly. A typical example is an application ported down from a mini or mainframe environment.
Tab **S**ize	Sets the number of spaces to be substituted for a Tab character. This parameter is effective only if the Enable Tabs option is enabled.
Enable Ti**m**eout	Causes a job to print after a certain time period (specified in the Timeout parameter) has elapsed at the end of a print job. NetWare normally waits to receive the entire print job in the queue before releasing the job to the print server. By default, there is no flag telling NetWare exactly when a print job has completed. NetWare waits for you to log out, recapture the port, or exit the application (invoking the Auto Endcap function)

continues

Table 29.1, Continued
NWUSER NetWare Settings for LPT*n* Dialog Box Options

Option	Function
	before printing. The Enable Timeout parameter tells NetWare to start a counter after each block of characters is received. If the count goes past the Timeout value, NetWare releases the job to be printed without the user having to perform any additional actions.
Timeout	Specifies the amount of time in seconds NetWare counts after receiving the last block of print characters in a print job. If the timeout value is too high, users will complain because printer response will slow down by at least this factor. If the timeout value is too low, NetWare could timeout too soon in the case of a print job that requires lengthy calculations on the part of the workstation. The symptom of a timeout that is too low is when you have partial pages of a report or a partial graphic image. Usually, the remainder of the report or image is on the next page.
Form Name	Specifies the name of a form to use when printing. The form can be defined in PRINTDEF.EXE (from the DOS prompt), or by using NWADMIN.EXE (from Windows). A print form is a property of a container object. See Chapter 27, "Setting Up Printing," for more details.
Enable Banner	Prints an identifying title page prior to the start of the print job. This option is useful when you have a printer that is shared by many people.
1st Banner Name	Places this value at the top half of the banner page. The default is your user login name.
2nd Banner Name	Places this value at the bottom half of the banner page. The default is the name of the file or the letters LST (indicates list device).
Copies	Specifies the number of copies of your print job you want to print.

Using the CAPTURE Command

The DOS CAPTURE command has an effect in Windows. If you have not set a permanent printing environment using the NWUSER.EXE utility, the parameters you specify in the CAPTURE command prior to entering Windows take effect. You also can issue a CAPTURE command from a DOS window and see the parameters take an immediate effect on the Windows environment.

Here is an example of a series of commands entered within a Windows DOS session:

```
F:\>CAPTURE L=2 Q=.Q_MAIN.IND.EBDB TI=20 B=XYZ
Device LPT2 has been re-routed to print queue Q_MAIN.IND.

F:\>CAPTURE SHOW

LPT1  Capturing data to print queue Q1.EBDB
  Notify:             Disabled
  Automatic end:      Enabled
  Timeout count:      10 seconds
  Name:               (None)
  Form feed:          Enabled
  Banner:             (None)
  Keep:               Disabled
  Copies:             1
  Tabs:               No conversion
  Form:               0
  User hold:          Disabled

LPT2  Capturing data to print queue Q_Main.IND.EBDB
  Notify:             Disabled
  Automatic end:      Enabled
  Timeout count:      20 seconds
  Name:               Admin
  Form feed:          Disabled
  Banner:             XYZ
  Keep:               Disabled
  Copies:             1
  Tabs:               No conversion
  Form:               Standard
  User hold:          Disabled

LPT3  Capturing is not currently active.

LPT4  Capturing is not currently active.
```

```
LPT5  Capturing is not currently active.

LPT6  Capturing is not currently active.

F:\>
```

As you can see, LPT1 already is captured. LPT2 now is captured to the print queue .CN=Q_Main.OU=Ind.O=EBDB, the timeout is set to 20 seconds, and the top half of the banner page is set to XYZ. If you now invoke the NWUSER utility and view printer settings for LPT2, you will see that the settings match those issued in the preceding CAPTURE command. This screen is shown in figure 29.3.

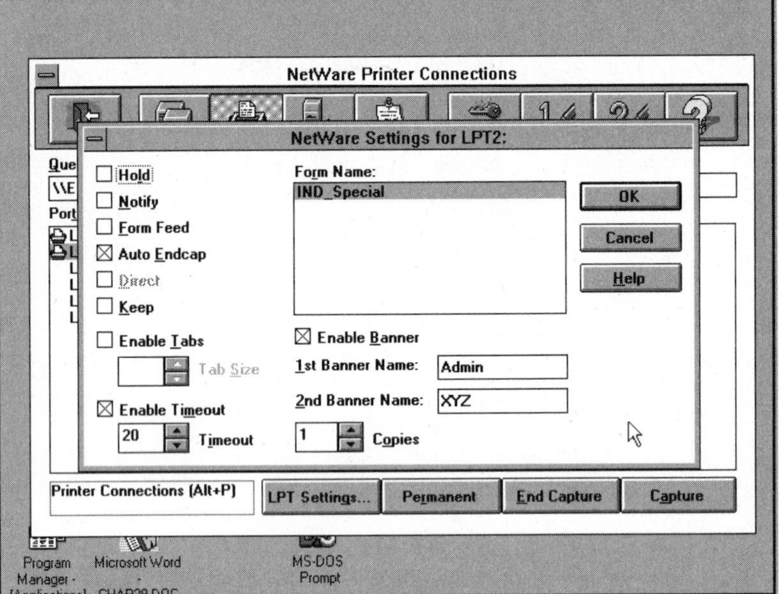

Figure 29.3
The NetWare Settings for LPT2 screen in NWUSER.EXE, showing CAPTURE effects.

You also can invoke the CAPTURE command before entering Windows. Any permanent print capture settings override the initial CAPTURE command. Any print capture not covered by permanent Windows settings takes effect. If only LPT1 was captured permanently from Windows, for example, and LPT2 was captured prior to entering Windows, you would see that LPT2 was captured in addition to the permanent capture set up for LPT1.

Any subsequent changes made in NWUSER override the initial CAPTURE. Any subsequent changes made at the DOS prompt using CAPTURE, while still in Windows, override the settings in NWUSER. Another way of looking at this is that the last setting takes effect.

Using Windows Print Manager

You can use the Windows Print Manager or the Printer utility from the Control Panel to make changes to network printer connections. The Network Connections option of both these utilities, however, takes you to NWUSER. Print Manager also offers the capability to control your print jobs. This feature is much more convenient than having to run PCONSOLE.EXE from the DOS prompt.

The NetWare client software automatically configures two important Print Manager network options. These options are Update Network Display and Print Net Jobs Direct. The Update Network Display option causes the Print Manager display to reflect the current status of the NetWare print queue to which this printer is captured. The Print Net Jobs Direct option causes all Windows printing to bypass the local spooling option and to pass immediately to the NetWare print queue. If you do not enable the Print Net Jobs Direct option, Print Manager spools the jobs locally before sending them to the network. Not only does this waste time, but it slows down workstation response tremendously.

To ensure that both of these options are enabled, follow these steps:

1. From Windows, run Print Manager. The Print Manager dialog box appears.
2. From the Options menu, choose Network Settings. The Network Options dialog box appears, as shown in figure 29.4.

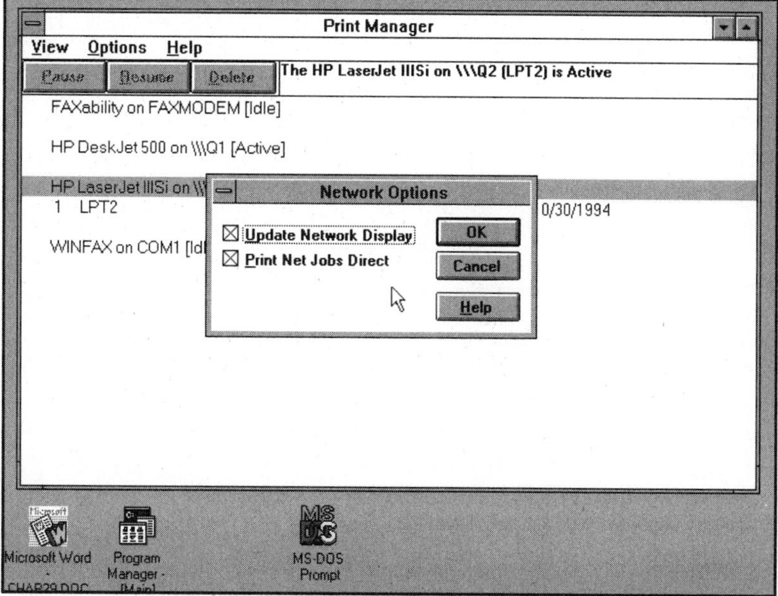

Figure 29.4

The Network Options dialog box.

3. Make sure that both settings are checked: Update Network Display and Print Net Jobs Direct. Press Esc to return to Print Manager.

Users also can use Print Manager to perform actions on their own print jobs. These actions follow:

- **Pause.** Enables users to stop their print jobs from being printed.
- **Resume.** Frees a paused print job so that it can continue to print.
- **Delete.** Removes a print job from the queue.

Setting Up Windows Printer Ports

You can adjust the number of printer ports available to Windows by adjusting two files: WIN.INI and NET.CFG. You use the WIN.INI file to adjust the number of printing ports available to Windows. You need to locate the [ports] section of this file. By default, you see the following:

```
[ports]
; A line with [filename].PRN followed by an equal sign causes
; [filename] to appear in the Control Panel's Printer Configuration dialog
; box. A printer connected to [filename] directs its output into this file.
LPT1:=
LPT2:=
LPT3:=
COM1:=9600,n,8,1,x
COM2:=9600,n,8,1,x
COM3:=9600,n,8,1,x
COM4:=9600,n,8,1,x
EPT:=
FILE:=
LPT1.DOS=
LPT2.DOS=
```

You can increase the number of printer ports available to Windows and its applications by editing the WIN.INI file and adding more LPT*x* settings, where *x* is a number from 1 to 9. You can "add" parallel ports, even though you do not physically have them. This changes Windows' capability to logically use these parallel ports. Windows does not check for the physical existence of the ports until it attempts to print. As long as the extra parallel ports are redirected to the network using the techniques described in this section, there will be no problem.

The following change to the WIN.INI file enables Windows to use six parallel printer ports. Note that the changes to the WIN.INI excerpt are in boldface:

```
[ports]
; A line with [filename].PRN followed by an equal sign causes
; [filename] to appear in the Control Panel's Printer Configuration dialog
; box. A printer connected to [filename] directs its output into this file.
LPT1:=
LPT2:=
LPT3:=
LPT4:=
LPT5:=
LPT6:=
COM1:=9600,n,8,1,x
COM2:=9600,n,8,1,x
COM3:=9600,n,8,1,x
COM4:=9600,n,8,1,x
EPT:=
FILE:=
LPT1.DOS=
LPT2.DOS=
```

The second change that you should make is to the NET.CFG file. Not only should you make printers available to Windows, but you also should increase the number of network printers. The setting in the NET.CFG file affects how many printer ports you can redirect, regardless of the setting in the WIN.INI file.

The setting in the NET.CFG file is in the NetWare DOS Requester section. The parameter follows:

```
Network Printers = n
```

Where *n* is a number from 1 to 9. This setting controls the maximum number of print captures you can have enabled simultaneously. The following excerpt from the NET.CFG file on the workstation sets the maximum number of network printers to six. This matches the changes made earlier to the WIN.INI file:

```
NetWare DOS Requester
     Name Context = "O=EBDB"
     Network Printers = 6
     Show Dots = ON
     First Network Drive = F
```

After saving the changes to both the WIN.INI and NET.CFG file, exit and restart Windows. You now have six printer ports and six network printers available. To confirm these settings, follow these steps:

1. From the Windows Program Manager, run the Control Panel.
2. From the Control Panel, select the Printers icon. The Printers dialog box appears.
3. Click on the Connect button. The Connect dialog box appears, as shown in figure 29.5.
4. Scroll down the Ports list to verify that all printer ports you defined appear. Click on the Cancel button in each dialog box to return to the Windows Program Manager.

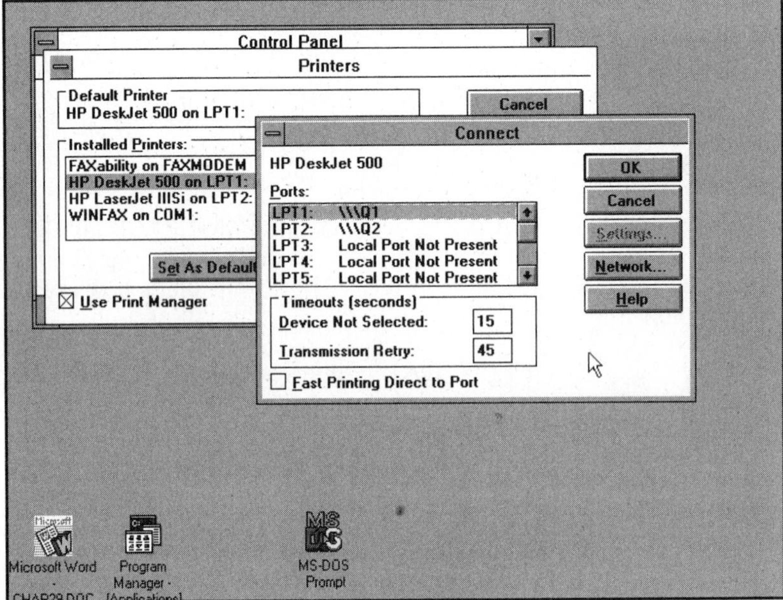

Figure 29.5
The Connect dialog box.

Printing with Windows NT Clients

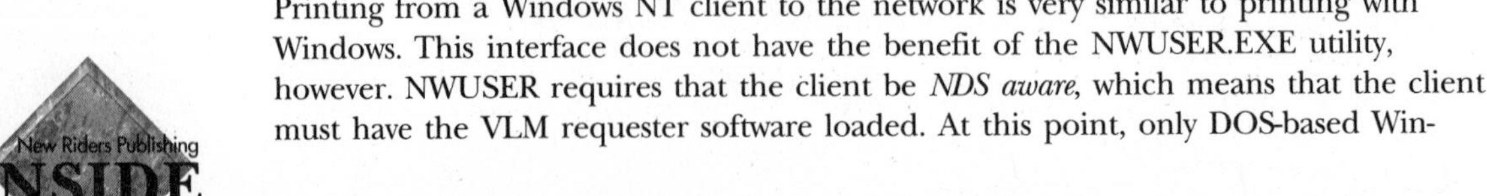
Printing from a Windows NT client to the network is very similar to printing with Windows. This interface does not have the benefit of the NWUSER.EXE utility, however. NWUSER requires that the client be *NDS aware*, which means that the client must have the VLM requester software loaded. At this point, only DOS-based Win-

dows clients, OS/2 clients, and Macintosh clients have this capability. The Windows NT client must print to the NetWare server using bindery emulation and the native network printing capabilities of Windows NT.

When printing to a NetWare server from a Windows NT client, you must decide which port you want to redirect and which queue and server to use. Because the NT client can access NetWare using only bindery emulation, you are limited to those servers that are running bindery emulation and the print queues in the bindery context.

You can use the Windows Print Manager or the NET USE command from a DOS prompt to make the connection. To redirect printing using Print Manager, follow these steps:

1. From the Main program group of the Windows NT Program Manager, select Print Manager. The Print Manager window appears and displays a list of defined printers.

2. From the **P**rinter menu, choose **C**onnect to Printer. Alternatively, click on the Connect to Printer toolbar icon. This icon is the third from the left on the toolbar, and resembles a printer with a cable underneath, with a starburst off the left corner. The Connect to Printer dialog box appears, as shown in figure 29.6.

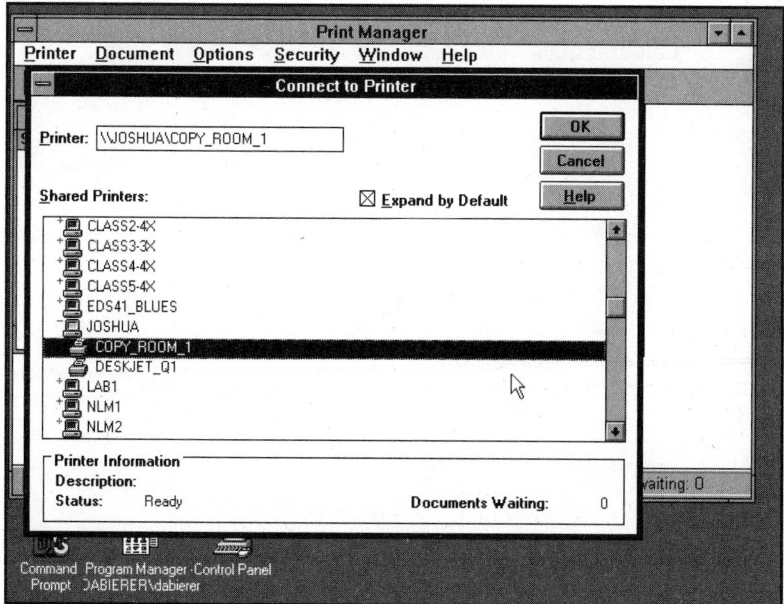

Figure 29.6

The Connect to Printer dialog box.

3. Select the file server you want. A list of print queues appears under the server icon. Select the print queue and click on OK. Note that you can view and use only print queues that are in the file server's bindery context.

Before you can use a NetWare print queue from Windows NT, you must add the Windows NT username to the server's bindery context. You also must make this user a print queue user. You can accomplish this by logging into the NetWare 4.1 file server as a bindery user. You can use the following command to do this:

```
LOGIN SUPERVISOR /B
```

Run PCONSOLE. You will be in bindery mode. From the PCONSOLE main menu, choose Print Queues. You see a list of print queues in the server's bindery context. Select the queue you want and press Enter. You see the Print Queue Information menu. Select Users, and then press Ins to add the Windows NT username to the list of users. Press Esc several times to exit PCONSOLE.

Now that the printer is connected, you can print to this printer by using the File Print option from your application. If you choose Print Setup from the File menu, you can select the printer from the list. This is illustrated in figure 29.7.

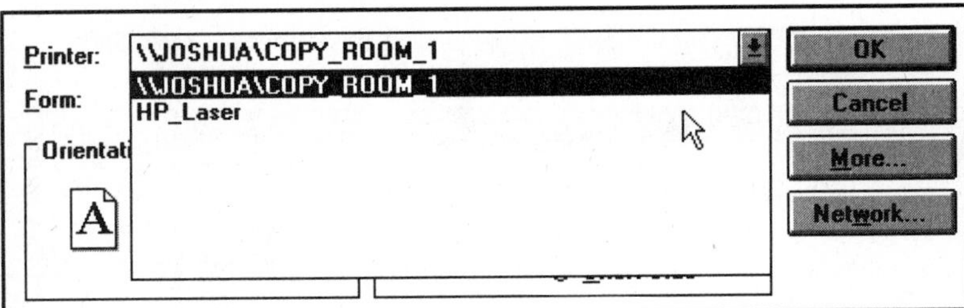

Figure 29.7
Using the Print Setup option to print to a NetWare print queue from an application.

If you click on the Network button, the Connect to Printer dialog box appears. Select the server and print queue from the list and click on the OK button. You now are ready to print to the NetWare print queue.

To redirect printing from a DOS prompt, follow these steps:

1. From the DOS command prompt, view the NetWare server name by entering the following command:

   NET VIEW /network:NW

   A list of NetWare servers appears:

```
G:\>net view /network:nw

Resources on NetWare Network

-----------------------------------------
\\CLASS1-3X
\\CLASS1-4X
\\CLASS2-3X
\\CLASS2-4X
\\CLASS3-3X
\\CLASS4-4X
\\CLASS5-4X
\\EDS41_BLUES
\\JOSHUA
\\LAB1
\\NLM1
\\NLM2
\\NLM4
\\NLM5
\\NLM6
\\NW1
\\NW2
\\NW4
The command completed successfully.


G:\>
```

2. To view the resources—including printing resources—on a specific server, use the following command:

   NET VIEW /network:NW \\<***servername***>

   Here is an example of this command:

```
G:\>net view /network:nw \\joshua
Shared resources at \\joshua

-----------------------------------------
Disk        \\joshua\ACCT
Print       \\joshua\COPY_ROOM_1
Print       \\joshua\DESKJET_Q1
Disk        \\joshua\SYS
```

```
The command completed successfully.


G:\>
```

3. To redirect printing, use the following command:

   NET USE *<port>* *<servername><queue>* [/USER:*<username>*]**

   The *port* can be LPT1, LPT2, or LPT3. The *servername* is the name of the NetWare file server. *Queue* is the name of the queue accessible in the server's bindery context. Use the /USER:*<username>* syntax to specify a user other than the username used at the Windows NT workstation. Here is an example of this command:

   ```
   G:\>net use lpt2: \\joshua\copy_room_1
   The command completed successfully.


   G:\>
   ```

Summary

In this chapter, you learned the ins and outs of printing to the network from Windows clients. The first part of the chapter covered the NWUSER.EXE utility. You learned how to set up a print capture using this utility, and how to mark a setting as permanent. The permanent setting updates the WIN.INI file and overrides any DOS CAPTURE you have set prior to loading Windows. If you are not logged in before entering Windows, a permanent setting causes the NetWare client to prompt you with the login name and password before Windows can complete the permanent assignment.

You learned about the LPT Settings dialog box in this chapter. You learned that these settings emulate those available using the CAPTURE command from the DOS prompt. You can issue a CAPTURE command before going into Windows, which affects the print capture settings visible in NWUSER. Permanent printer settings in NWUSER, on the other hand, override the DOS CAPTURE command. If you open a Windows DOS box and issue another CAPTURE command, those settings take effect.

The use of the Windows Print Manager in controlling jobs sent to the network was discussed. You learned how to increase the number of printer ports available to both Windows and the network. To increase the number of printer ports visible to Win-

dows, modify the [ports] section of the WIN.INI file. To increase the number of network print captures, add a parameter NETWORK PRINTERS = in your NET.CFG file.

When printing from a Windows NT client to a NetWare network, you use bindery emulation—only queues in a file server's bindery context are visible to the NT client. You can issue the print capture through the Windows NT Print Manager by selecting the Connect to Printer option. The NetWare server name is preceded by a double backslash (\\). The queue name follows. You also can use the NET USE command from a Windows NT DOS box. You can use the NET VIEW command to view available servers.

The next chapter covers how to add file system directory and file trustee rights.

Part VIII

Setting Up the User Environment

New Riders Publishing
INSIDE
SERIES

Adding File System Rights

This chapter covers how to grant and modify users' rights to the files and directories on the file servers in your network. A *file system* is the disk storage available to users on NetWare file servers. The file system is viewed logically as volume objects. *Volume objects* store files and are divided into directories. To access files on a volume object, users need browse NDS trustee rights to the volume object. NDS trustee assignments are discussed in more detail in Chapter 31, "Adding NDS Trustee Rights."

Two primary utilities are used to assign or modify file system rights: NETADMIN.EXE and NWADMIN.EXE. Utilities such as FILER.EXE and RIGHTS.EXE can be used as well, but are not as commonly used in the industry. DOS-based users will be inclined to use NETADMIN to assign rights. Windows or OS/2 users will use NWADMIN. This chapter gives you examples using both utilities.

Assigning Directory Trustee Rights

Directory trustee rights are assigned much more often than are file trustee rights. When you give a user, group, organizational unit, or other object a directory trustee assignment, not only do you give them rights to all files in that directory, you give them rights to files in subdirectories as well. Previous chapters covered where trustee assignments are best made, what rights you should assign, and who they should be assigned to. The purpose of this section is to show you how to make the assignment.

Using NWADMIN To Assign Directory Trustee Rights

A typical directory trustee rights assignment would be to assign container rights to SYS:PUBLIC. To assign the organizational unit .OU=SJ.O=EBDB rights to the PUBLIC directory on the volume object .CN=EBDB_SYS.O=EBDB using NWADMIN, proceed as follows:

1. To be able to assign file system rights to other objects, be sure that you are logged in as a user with sufficient rights in the volume object.

2. From Windows, run NWADMIN. A view of the NDS tree appears. Locate the desired volume object and expand the view (by double-clicking on the volume object) to include directories. Figure 30.1 illustrates what you might see at this point.

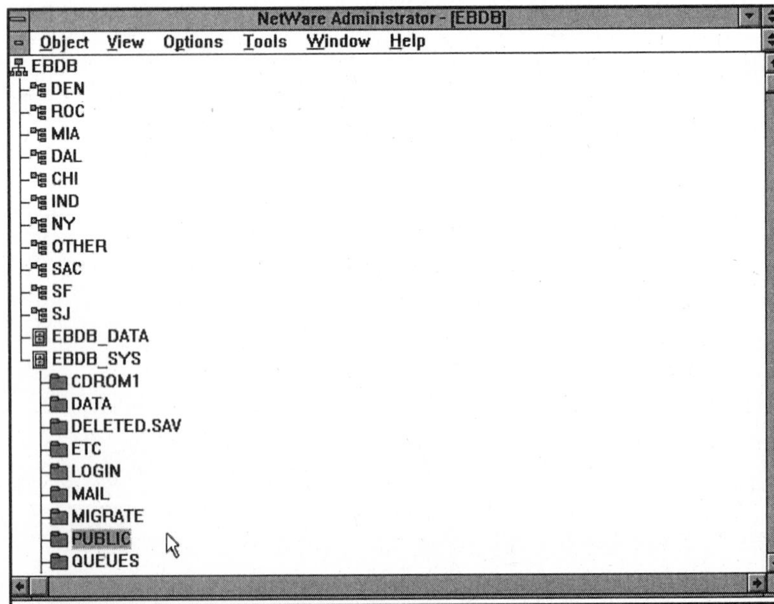

Figure 30.1

The NDS tree showing the directory structure under a volume.

When working with large NDS trees, it is useful to alter the view to include container objects and volume objects only. This can be accomplished as follows:

1. In the initial NWADMIN screen, click on Include in the View menu.
2. In the Included Object Classes list box, select Volume.
3. Click on the OK button.
4. Collapse the view of the tree by selecting Collapse in the View menu.
5. Expand the view of the tree by clicking on Expand in the View menu.
6. You now only see container and volume objects.

3. From the expanded directory tree of the volume object, select the desired directory. For the purposes of this example, select the PUBLIC directory. Press Enter or Details in the Object menu. The Directory:PUBLIC dialog box appears, giving general details on the volume you selected.

4. From the Directory:PUBLIC (or whatever directory you selected) dialog box, click on the Trustees of this Directory button to right. The Trustees of this Directory dialog box appears. At the top left of this screen is a list of trustees in the Trustees list box. Once you select a trustee in this list box, the Access Rights for this trustee will be clearly displayed. At the bottom right, the Inheritance Filter box lists the set of rights that are allowed in this directory. Removing the check mark from any of these boxes blocks the ability to perform that right.

Until you select a trustee from the list box in the Trustees of this Directory dialog box, the list of Access Rights remains grayed out, indicating that, because a specific trustee is not selected, the trustee rights are unknown.

5. From the Trustees of this Directory dialog box, select Add Trustee. The Select Object dialog box appears, as shown in figure 30.2.

6. In the Select Object dialog box, use the Directory Context list box to move up or down the NDS tree. From the Objects list box, select the desired object you want to add as a trustee. You can select more than one object.

The Select Object dialog box has many advanced features that facilitate selecting objects in large NDS trees. These features include the capability to select multiple objects and to filter which objects appear in the various list boxes. Table 30.1 summarizes the features found in this dialog box.

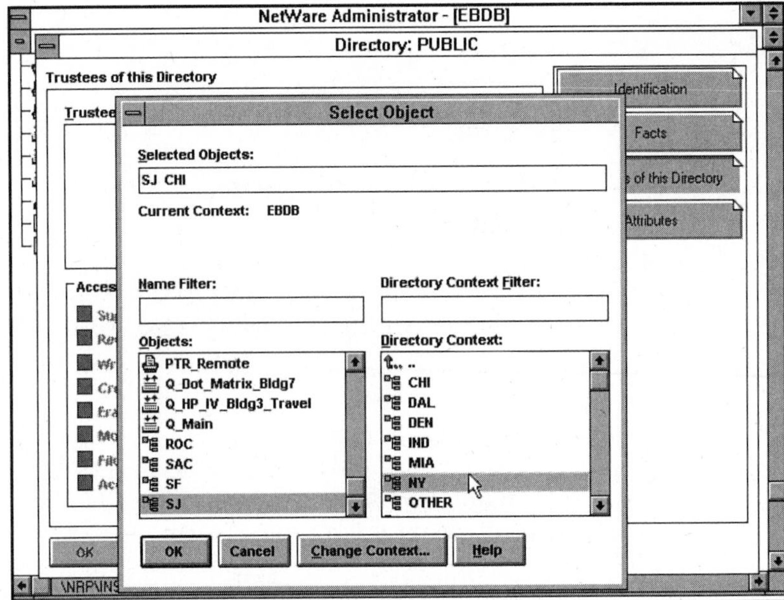

Figure 30.2

Adding trustees to a directory.

Table 30.1
The Select Object Dialog Box Option Fields.

Option Field, Window or Button	Description
Selected Objects	This field contains the objects you either type in (separated by spaces) or select from the Objects list box (described later).
Current Context	Informational field showing you your current context.
Change Context	Click on this button to enter a new current context.
Name Filter	This field limits the objects you see under the current context in the Objects list box. Wild cards are acceptable. For example, if you enter P* under Name Filter, you only see objects beginning with the letter P. Following the examples given in other chapters, if your printer names begin with PTR and your print servers begin with PS, entering P* shows you all those objects. If you limit names to PTR*, for example, you only see printer objects (assuming you followed this naming convention).

Option Field, Window or Button	Description
Directory Context Filter	This field places a limit on the container objects you can view in the Directory Context list box. This filter acts in a similar fashion to the Name Filter.
Objects	This window shows a list of objects to select. To select more than one object, press and hold the Ctrl key while clicking the left mouse button. Use the Shift+arrow keys if you're using the keyboard to select objects. Objects selected appear in the Selected Objects field.
Directory Context	Displays a portion of the NDS tree. Click on the ".." option (parent container) to move one level up the tree. Double click on any other container to move one level down. You cannot select objects from this list box; use the Objects list box instead.

7. When finished selecting object(s) to add as trustees, click on OK, and you return to the Directory:PUBLIC dialog box. From the Trustees list box, select the trustee object name you added. Note that the check boxes next to the eight rights in the Access Rights list change from gray to either blank or check marked. The default directory trustee assignment is Read and File Scan. Add or remove check marks to obtain the desired set of rights for this object. Click on OK when done.

You can also assign a directory trustee by working with the potential trustee object rather than first going to the directory. To assign a group .MIS.NY.EBDB rights to the PUBLIC directory on the volume object .CN=EBDB_SYS.O=EBDB using NWADMIN, proceed as follows:

1. To be able to assign file system rights to other objects, be sure that you are logged in as a user with sufficient rights in the volume object.

2. From Windows, run NWADMIN. A view of the NDS tree appears. Locate the desired trustee object. In this example, the group .CN=MIS.OU=NY.O=EBDB.

3. When the trustee object has been located, double click on it, press Enter or click on Details in the Object menu. The details dialog box for that object appears.

4. From the details dialog box for the object, select the Rights to Files and Directories button at the right side of the dialog box. The Rights to Files and Directories dialog box appears.

5. From the Rights to Files and Directories dialog box, select either **F**ind or **S**how to locate the volume object that contains the directory that you want to assign to this trustee. The volume appears in the **V**olumes list at the top of the dialog box. Select the **A**dd button to add the volume and directory to the **F**iles and Directories list for this trustee.

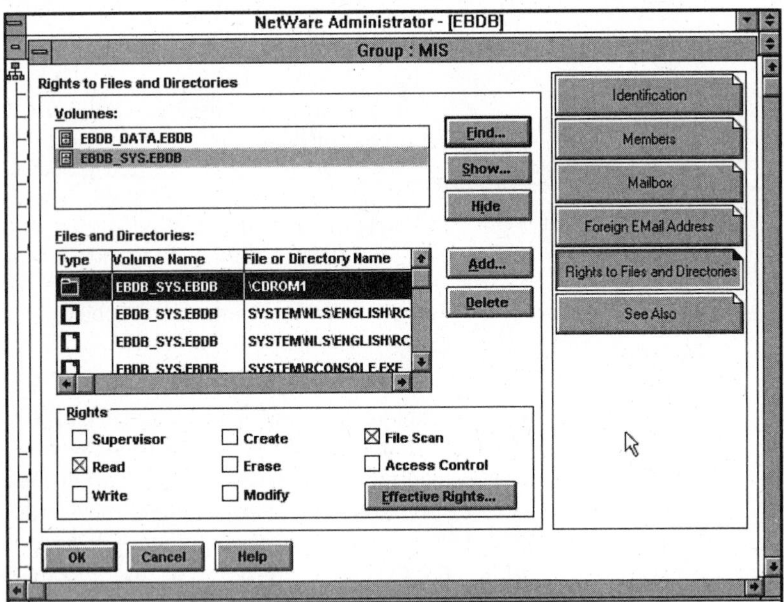

Figure 30.3

The Rights to Files and Directories dialog box.

6. After a volume and directory have been selected, place a check mark next to the desired trustee rights you want to assign in the **R**ights list. Figure 30.3 illustrates a completed Rights to Files and Directories dialog box.

7. Click on OK when finished, and you return to the NDS tree shown in the main screen of NWADMIN.

Table 30.2 summarizes the fields found in the Rights to Files and Directories dialog box.

Table 30.2
The Rights to Files and Directories Dialog Box Options

Option Field, Window, or Button	Description
Volumes	Shows the volumes you are currently working with to assign trustee rights.
Find	Automatically locates all volumes in a given container. Automatically displays trustee assignments for all volumes found.
Show	Brings up the Select Object dialog box. You can use Show to search manually for volumes in which trustee rights are to be assigned. Automatically displays trustee assignments for any volume chosen.
Hide	Removes a volume from the Volumes list. Use this option if there are too many volumes listed, and you want to work with only certain volumes.
Files and Directories	A list of volumes, directories, and files in which trustee rights are assigned. Three fields are represented are as follows: *Type* indicates the type of assignment (file or directory rights assignment). *Volume Name* indicates the name of the volume in which a trustee right is made. *File or Directory Name* lists the specific file or directory to which a trustee assignment has been made.
Add	Used to add a directory or file rights assignment for this trustee.
Delete	Removes the rights assignment selected.
Rights	Enables you to check mark specific rights for the item(s) selected from the Files and Directories list. If you select several items from the Files and Directories list, the rights you check mark are applied to the files and directories selected.
Effective Rights	Enables you to view effective rights of a trustee in a directory or file you specify.

Using NETADMIN To Assign Directory Trustee Rights

The NETADMIN.EXE utility can also be used to assign directory trustee rights. Unlike NWADMIN, however, NETADMIN only enables you to assign rights by first selecting the object to become the trustee, then specifying which file or directory you want to give rights to. NWADMIN enables you to use not only this approach, but also to go directly to the directory (or file) and add the trustee (see fig 30.4). Thus, to assign rights in NETADMIN, you must select the user, group, container, or other object that you want to make a trustee. You then must select the Rights to Files and Directories option and add a file or directory to the trustee list for the selected user, group, container, or other object. Note that FILER can be used to choose a directory, and then to assign rights to a user, group, container or other object.

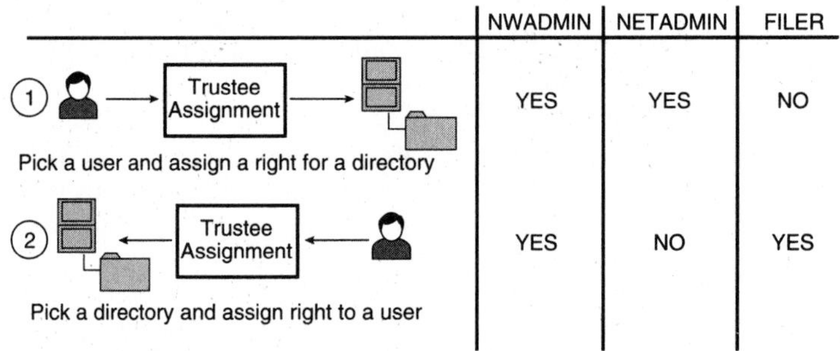

Figure 30.4
Comparing NWADMIN.EXE, NETADMIN.EXE, and FILER.EXE in assigning trustee rights.

To assign rights to an organizational role object for a directory using NETADMIN, proceed as follows:

1. To be able to assign file system rights to other objects, be sure that you are logged in as a user with sufficient rights in the volume object.

2. From the DOS prompt, run NETADMIN. From the NETADMIN main menu, use one of the following techniques to locate the object to which you want to give a trustee assignment:

   - Select Change Context to change to the context of the object, then select Manage Objects.

   - Select Manage Objects and move up or down the tree until the object to be managed is located.

   - Select Search from the main menu. Enter search criteria for the object and press F10 to begin the search.

3. After the desired object is located, press Enter to proceed. The Actions for *<object>* menu appears, where *<object>* is the name of the object selected.

4. From the Actions for *<object>* menu, select View or edit rights to files and directories. The Rights to files and/or directories screen appears.

5. In the Rights to files and/or directories screen, there are the following four options:

   - **Volume object name** contains the name of the volume object containing the file or directory you want to add the trustee rights to.

   - **Beginning Path** is a starting point for assigning file or directory rights. Enter a directory name in this field if you have a complex directory structure and do not want to start at the root every time you add an assignment.

   - **Directories/Files** is a switch. If the value is "Directory," then the trustee assignments you can view are limited to directory trustee rights assignments. If the value is "File," you can view file trustee assignments. If the value is "Directory and File," you can see both directory and file trustee rights assignments.

   - **Trustee Search Depth** can be "All subdirectories," in which case you can see listings of trustee assignments for all subdirectories. If the value is "Current directory only," you can see trustee assignments for the current directory only.

6. For the purposes of this discussion, enter the following values:

   Volume object name—set to volume SYS (which would be .CN=EBDB_SYS.O=EBDB)

   Beginning Path—leave blank (starts at the root of volume SYS)

   Directories/Files—set to Directory (displays only directory trustee assignments)

   Trustee Search Depth—set to All subdirectories

   The resulting screen is shown in figure 30.5.

7. Press F10 to view or assign rights after the Rights to files and/or directories screen has been filled in. The Trustee *<directory|file>* rights list appears, where *<directory|file>* is located.

8. From the Trustee <*directory|file*> rights list, you can take several actions, as follows:

    - ◆ Press Insert to add an additional trustee assignment.
    - ◆ Press Del to remove a trustee assignment.
    - ◆ Press Enter to modify a trustee assignment.

Figure 30.6 shows you the Trustee <*directory|file*> rights list with three trustee assignments.

Figure 30.5

The Rights to files and/or directories screen.

NetAdmin 4.36 Sunday June 19, 1994 8:51am
Context: EBDB
Login Name: Admin.EBDB
Actions for Organizational Role: Container_Admin
Rights to files and/or directories
Volume object name: EBDB_SYS
Beginning Path:
Directories/Files: Directory
Trustee Search Depth: All subdirectories
Press <Enter> to edit the volume name.
F10=Display list Esc=Exit F1=Help

Figure 30.6

The Trustee Directory Rights list.

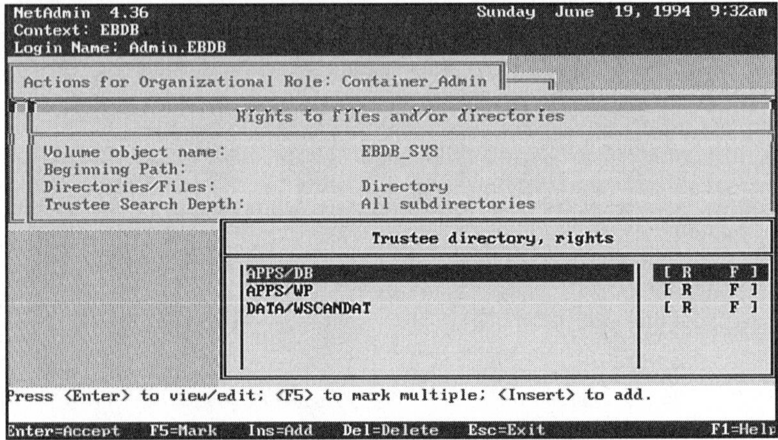

9. To modify a rights assignment, select from the Trustee <*directory|file*> rights list the trustee assignment you want to modify and press Enter. The Trustee rights granted list appears. Press Insert to add additional rights, or press Delete to remove a specific right. When adding or removing rights, the F5 key can be used to select multiple rights. After you mark multiple rights using F5, press Enter to add, or Delete to delete the rights. Figure 30.7 shows you the Trustee rights granted and the Trustee rights not granted lists. Press F10 to save the rights assignments and to return to the Trustee <*directory|file*> rights list.

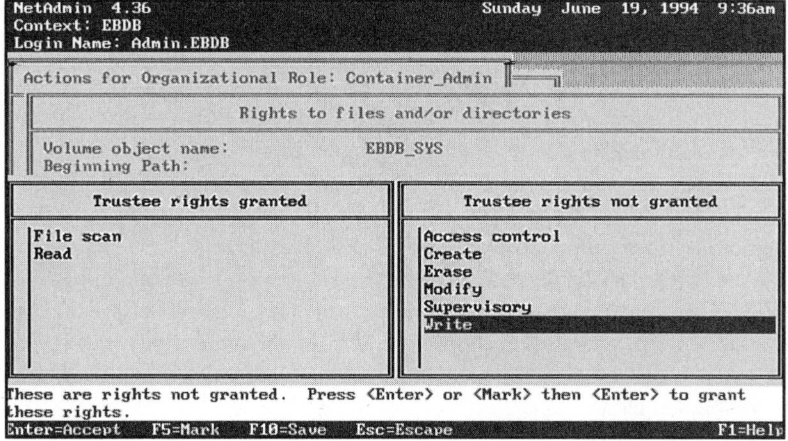

Figure 30.7

The Trustee rights granted and Trustee rights not granted lists.

10. Within the Trustee <*directory|file*> rights list, press F10 again to return to the Rights to files and/or directories screen. Now press Esc several times to return to the main menu of NETADMIN, or press Alt+F10 to exit the utility entirely.

Assigning File Trustee Rights

Assigning file trustee rights is the same process as assigning directory trustee rights, the main difference being that instead of assigning the trustee right for a directory to a user, group, container (or whatever) object, you would make the assignment for a file. File trustee rights do not filter down as do directory trustee assignments. As a result, file trustee assignments are much more limited in scope.

When making file trustee assignments, make sure that you assign rights to all the necessary files. If you want to assign an organizational person object rights to use the RCONSOLE utility, for example, you must assign rights to the following files:

SYS:SYSTEM\RCONSOLE.EXE

SYS:SYSTEM\TEXTUTIL.IDX

SYS:SYSTEM\NLS\ENGLISH\RCONSOLE.HEP

SYS:SYSTEM\NLS\ENGLISH\RCONSOLE.MSG

SYS:SYSTEM\NLS\ENGLISH\TEXTUTIL.MSG

Tip One method of finding out which utilities require which files is to use MONITOR.NLM from the file server's console. Log in as an Admin user to a workstation next to the file server that stores this utility. From the file server's console, load MONITOR.NLM. Go to Connection Information and locate the Active Connection, which corresponds to your Admin user. Press Enter to view the Files In Use. Return to the workstation and run the utility. You will see files being opened on the MONITOR screen on the file server. These are the files you need to give the user (or other object) rights to. Use NWADMIN or NETADMIN to grant the necessary file trustee rights. To test your configuration, log in as the user (or other) object and see if you can run this utility.

To give an organizational role object rights to use RCONSOLE using the NETADMIN utility, proceed as follows:

1. To be able to assign file system rights to other objects, be sure that you are logged in as a user with sufficient rights in the volume object.

2. From the DOS prompt, run NETADMIN. From the NETADMIN main menu, use one of the following techniques to locate the object to which you want to give a trustee assignment:

   - Select Change Context to change to the context of the object, then select Manage Objects.

   - Select Manage Objects and move up or down the tree until the object to be managed is located.

   - Select Search from the main menu. Enter search criteria for the object and press F10 to begin the search.

3. After the desired object is located, press Enter to proceed. The Actions for *<object>* menu will appear, where *object* is the name of the object selected.

4. From the Actions for <*object*> menu select View or edit rights to files and directories. The Rights to files and/or directories screen appears.

5. From the Rights to files and/or directories screen, enter the following options:

   Volume object name—set to volume SYS (which would be .CN=EBDB_SYS.O=EBDB)

   Beginning Path—leave blank (starts at the root of volume SYS)

   Directories/Files—set to File (displays only file trustee assignments)

   Trustee Search Depth—set to All subdirectories

   Press F10 to bring up the Trustee file, rights list.

6. From the Trustee file, rights list, press Insert to add a file trustee right. The Select a directory input box appears. For this discussion, enter **SYS:SYSTEM** as a directory name. Alternately, you could press Insert and browse the directory tree. The Select a file input box appears.

7. From the Select a file input box, press Insert. A list of files appears. From this list, locate RCONSOLE.EXE and press Enter. RCONSOLE.EXE now appears on the trustee list with Read and File Scan rights by default.

8. Continue to select files as in Steps 6 and 7 until all of the RCONSOLE files previously listed appear on the trustee list. Press F10 to save the list. Press Alt+F10 to exit the NETADMIN utility. You can now log in as the occupant of the organizational role to ensure this user has proper access to RCONSOLE.

Using FILER To Assign Rights

The FILER.EXE utility can also be used to assign trustee rights for a directory or file. FILER differs in perspective from NETADMIN. When using NETADMIN, you must first choose the object to become a trustee. From the Actions menu for that object, you can choose Rights to files and directories. When using FILER, you must first choose the directory. From the View/Set menu for that directory, you can access a list of trustees.

To make a directory trustee assignment using FILER, proceed as follows:

1. Log in as an Admin user or as a user with the right to assign rights to the file system.

2. From the DOS prompt type the following:

   FILER

3. From the FILER Available Options menu (the main menu), select Manage files and directories. The Directory contents list, a list of files and directories based on your current directory, is displayed.

   Select the double dots (..) and press Enter to move one level up in the directory structure. If you are already at the root (the top level directory), this option moves you into the NDS tree where you can select another volume object or another context.

   If you select another directory and press Enter, you change to that directory. To work with a directory, select it and press F10. To work with the current directory, select the single dot (.) and press F10. The Subdirectory Options menu appears.

4. From the Subdirectory Options menu, select View/Set directory information. The Information for directory *XYZ* screen appears, as shown in figure 30.8. The value for *XYZ* varies depending on which directory you have selected.

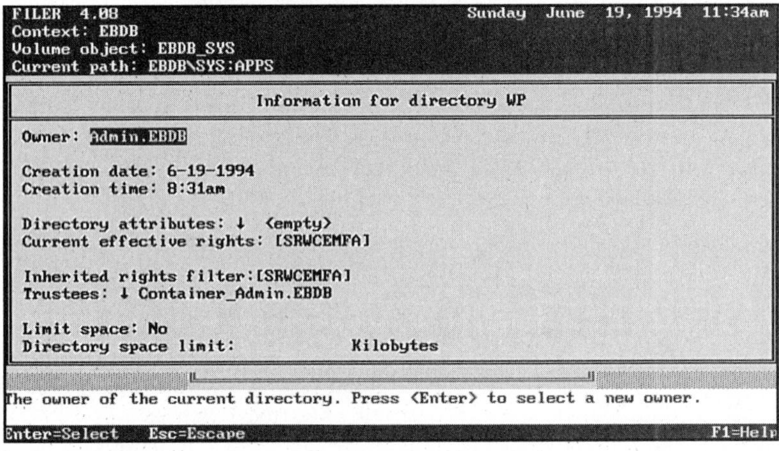

Figure 30.8

The Information for directory XYZ *screen.*

5. From the Information for directory *XYZ* screen, select Trustees and press Enter. The Trustee name list appears, listing the trustees for this directory—this is a list of objects that have rights to this directory.

To add another trustee to the list, press Insert.

To delete a trustee from the list, select the trustee in question and press Delete.

To modify the rights for an existing trustee press, select the trustee in question and press Enter.

6. To add a trustee to the list, press Insert. The Object, Class screen appears. You can browse the tree, searching for the object that you want to make a trustee. After that object has been located, press Enter. You return to the Trustee name list, and the selected object appears on the list. The default rights are Read and File Scan.

   To change the rights, press Enter. The Trustee rights screen appears.

   Press Insert to add other rights.

   Press Delete to remove a trustee right.

7. When you're done modifying the desired rights, press Esc several times to return to the FILER main menu.

To make a file trustee assignment, proceed as follows:

1. From the FILER Available Options menu (the main menu), select Manage files and directories. The Directory contents list, a list of files and directories based on your current directory, is displayed.

   Select the double dots (..) and press Enter to move one level up in the directory structure. If you are already at the root (the top level directory), this option moves you into the NDS tree where you can select another volume object or another context.

   If you select another directory and press Enter, you change to that directory. To work with a file, select it and press F10. The File Options menu appears.

2. From the File Options menu, select View/Set file information. The Information for file *XYZ* screen appears. The value for *XYZ* varies depending on which file you have selected.

3. From the Information for file *XYZ* screen, select Trustees and press Enter. The Trustee name list appears. This is a list of trustees for this file.

   To add another trustee to the list, press Insert.

   To delete a trustee from the list, select the trustee in question and press Delete.

   To modify the rights for an existing trustee, select the trustee in question and press Enter.

4. To add a trustee to the list, press Insert. The Object, Class screen appears. At this point, you can browse the tree searching for the object that you want to make a trustee. After that object has been located, press Enter. You return to the Trustee name list, and the selected object appears on the list. The default rights are Read and File Scan.

   To change the rights, press Enter. The Trustee rights screen appears. Press Insert to add other rights. Press Delete to remove a trustee right.

5. When you're done modifying the desired rights, press Esc several times to return to the FILER main menu.

Using RIGHTS To Assign Rights

The RIGHTS.EXE command is much more flexible and faster to use than NWADMIN, NETADMIN, or FILER. Because it only operates from the DOS command prompt, however, its usage is limited to DOS sessions, and the syntax must be remembered.

The generic syntax for assigning trustee rights using RIGHTS follows:

```
RIGHTS <directory or filename> <rights list> /NAME=<NDS Object>
```

Directory or filename is the name of the directory or file for which you want to add a trustee. You can include the drive letter and path, or you can supply a valid NDS volume object name and colon, followed by the directory or file name path.

Rights list should be a list of rights you want to assign. If you want to remove a right, precede it with a minus sign (-).

NDS Object is a valid NDS object name for the new trustee. This can be a user, group, container, organizational role, or other NDS object as desired.

The following output shows the results of a RIGHTS command to assign Read, File Scan, Erase, Write, and Create rights to the container .OU=NY.O=EBDB to the volume object .CN=EBDB_DATA.O=EBDB, in the directory \PROJECTS\R&D.

```
G:\>RIGHTS .EBDB_DATA.EBDB:\PROJECTS\R&D RWCEF /NAME=.NY.EBDB

EBDB\DATA:\PROJECTS
Directories                                             Rights
------------------------------------------------------- ---------------
R&D                                                     [ RWCE F ]
```

```
Rights for one directory were changed for .NY.EBDB
```

The following output assumes that you are on the file server that contains the volume DATA. This example removes the *Write, Create, and Erase* rights from a user .CN=ELOBO.OU=SAC.O=EBDB.

```
G:\>RIGHTS DATA:PROJECTS\R&D -WCE /NAME=.CN=ELOBO.OU=SAC.O=EBDB

EBDB\DATA:\PROJECTS
Directories                                          Rights
---------------------------------------------------  ---------------
R&D                                                  [ R     F ]


Rights for one directory were changed for .CN=ELOBO.OU=SAC.O=EBDB
```

Inherited Rights and the Inherited Rights Filter

You can establish an *Inherited Rights Filter* (IRF) to block the flow of rights through the file system. Filters can be established at both the directory and file system levels. When a filter is applied to a directory, it blocks the flow of directory trustee rights established at higher levels of the directory structure. When a filter is applied to a file, it acts as a file attribute, blocking access to that file.

The default IRF for both directories and files is ALL. This means that, by default, all trustee rights are allowed. The filter does not give rights that are not assigned through the techniques described previously; for an IRF to affect your rights, you must have a trustee rights assignment made for you at some level. If you have no rights assigned in the directory in question, or at any level above, the status of the IRF is irrelevant for you.

IRFs can be modified through NWADMIN.EXE, FILER.EXE, and RIGHTS.EXE. To modify the IRF of a directory using NWADMIN, proceed as follows:

1. To be able to assign file system rights to other objects, be sure that you are logged in as a user with sufficient rights in the volume object.

2. From Windows, run NWADMIN. A view of the NDS tree appears. Locate the desired volume object and expand the view (by double clicking on the volume object) to include directories. Under the list of directories, locate the directory whose IRF you want to change. Press Enter or click on Details in the Object

menu. The Directory: *XYZ* dialog box appears, where *XYZ* is the name of the directory you selected.

3. From the Directory: *XYZ* dialog box, click on the Trustees of this Directory button to the right. The Trustees of this Directory dialog box appears.

4. In the Trustees of this Directory dialog box, remove the check mark from the rights you want to block in the Inheritance Filter box. Figure 30.9 illustrates an IRF where Write, Erase, and Access Control have been blocked. Note that arrows with a line underneath indicate a right that has been blocked. An unimpeded arrow indicates an enabled right.

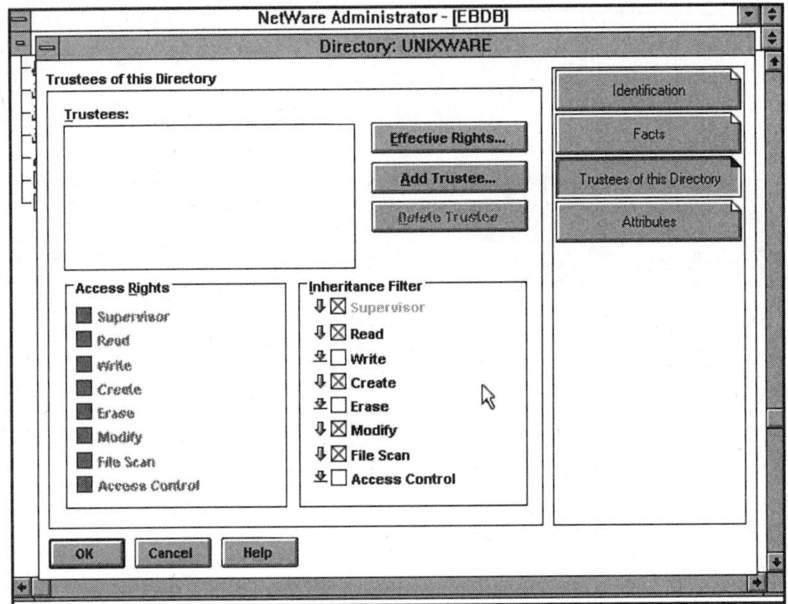

Figure 30.9
Modifying an Inherited Rights Filter.

5. When you've finished specifying changes to the IRF, click on OK to return to the main NDS tree view in NWADMIN.

To modify the IRF of a file using FILER, proceed as follows:

1. Log in as an Admin user or as a user with the right to assign rights to the file system.

2. From the DOS prompt, type the following:

   FILER

3. From the FILER Available Options menu (the main menu), select Manage files and directories. The Directory contents list, a list of files and directories based on your current directory, is displayed.

4. Within the Directory contents list, locate the target file and press Enter. The File options menu appears.

5. From the File options menu, select View/Set file information. The Information for file *XYZ* appears, where *XYZ* is the name of the file selected. Select Inherited rights filter and press Enter. The Inherited rights list for this file appears, as shown in figure 30.10.

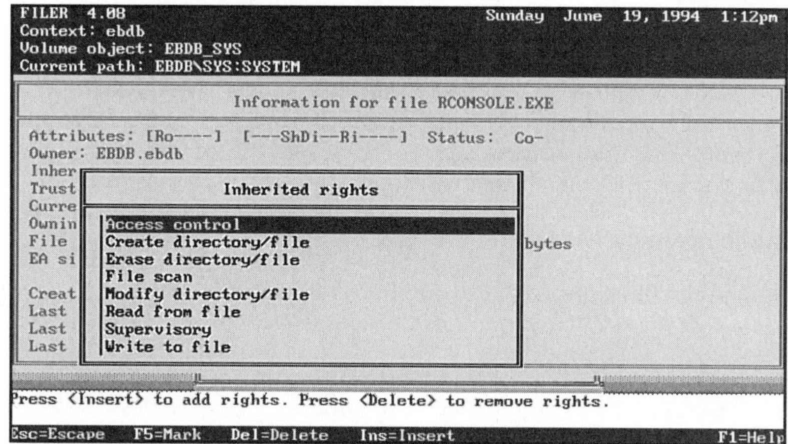

Figure 30.10

Modifying an Inherited Rights Filter for a file.

6. Use F5 to mark the rights you want to block. When done marking, press Delete. Answer yes to the prompt, Revoke all marked rights. Press Esc several times to exit this screen and to exit FILER.

To use RIGHTS to change the IRF of a directory, use the following syntax:

```
RIGHTS <directory> <rights list> /F
```

Directory is the volume object name and directory path.

Rights list is a list of rights to allow. Alternately, you could precede the rights list with a minus sign (–), in which case the list consists of rights to block. A right of ALL indicates all rights. A right of N indicates no rights. The following output demonstrates using the RIGHTS command to block all rights to inherit in a directory EBDB_SYS:DATA\TAX94.

```
F:\DATA>RIGHTS .EBDB_SYS.EBDB:DATA\TAX94 N /F

EBDB\SYS:\DATA
Directories                                               Rights
--------------------------------------------------------- ----------------
TAX94                                                     [S        ]
```

Modifying File and Directory Attributes

As with setting IRFs, the utilities NWADMIN.EXE and FILER.EXE can be used to change the attributes of a file. In addition, the FLAG.EXE utility can be used from the DOS command prompt. NetWare attributes are visible, as are the attributes pertinent to the specific name space available on that volume.

To modify file attributes using NWADMIN, proceed as follows:

1. To be able to assign file system rights to other objects, be sure that you are logged in as a user with sufficient rights in the volume object.

2. From Windows, run NWADMIN. A view of the NDS tree appears. Locate the desired volume object and expand the view (by double-clicking on the volume object) to include directories. Under the list of directories, locate the file whose attributes you want to change. Press Enter or click on Object, Details. The *volume:\directory\filename* dialog box appears, where *volume, directory,* and *filename* are pertinent to the file you selected (see fig. 30.11).

3. As you can see from the figure, there are two listings for the file: one for DOS and the other for OS/2. Select the desired item and click on the Attributes button to right. You can see a list of File Attributes and File Flags. Place a check mark next to the appropriate attribute(s) and click on OK. Note that the File Flags are informational only and cannot be changed.

4. At this point, you are back at the main NWADMIN menu.

To change file attributes using FILER, proceed as follows:

1. Log in as an Admin user or as a user with the right to assign rights to the file system.

2. From the DOS prompt type:

   FILER

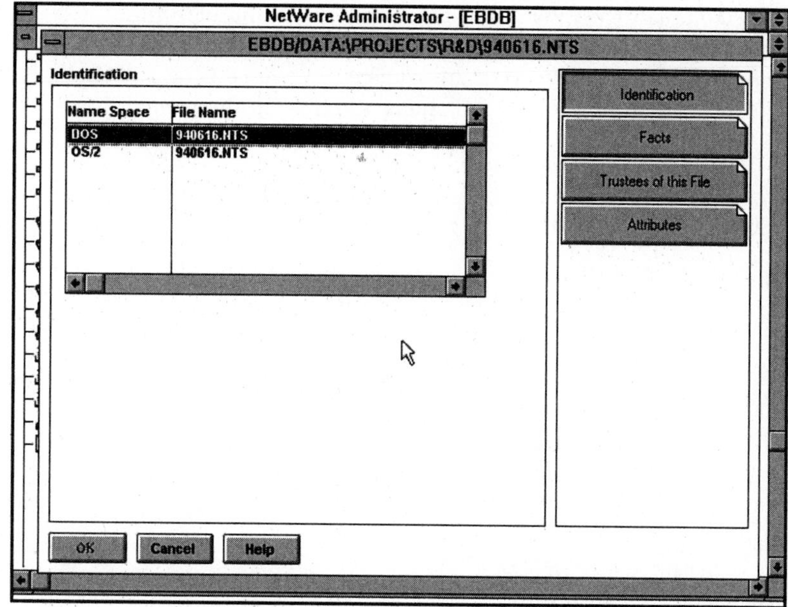

Figure 30.11

The volume:\directory\filename dialog box.

3. From the FILER Available Options menu (the main menu), select Manage files and directories. The Directory contents list, a list of files and directories based on your current directory, is displayed.

4. Within the Directory contents list, locate the target file and press Enter. The File options menu appears.

5. Click on File option, View/Set file information. The Information for file *XYZ* screen appears, where *XYZ* is the name of the file selected.

6. In the Information for file *XYZ* screen, select Attributes. The Current file attributes list appears.

7. From the Current file attributes list, press insert to add another attribute, or Delete to remove an attribute.

8. Press Esc to exit this screen after changes have been made. Press Esc several times to return to the main FILER menu.

The FLAG command can be used from the DOS command prompt to change file attributes. The general syntax for the FLAG command is as follows:

```
FLAG <filename> <attribute(s)> /FO
```

Filename includes the volume object name, directory name, and the file whose attributes you want to change. If you use wild cards within the file name (such as *.DAT), all file names matching that pattern are changed. If you add the /SUB option flag at the end of the command, FLAG changes all files in the named directory, as well as in all subdirectories.

The following output illustrates using FLAG to place an Immediate Compress (Ic) attribute on all files in volume .EBDB_DATA.EBDB.

```
F:\>FLAG EBDB/DATA:*.* IC /FO /SUB

EBDB\DATA:
Files         = The name of the files found
Directories   = The name of the directories found
DOS Attr      = The DOS attributes for the specified file
NetWare Attr  = The NetWare attributes for the specified file or directory
Status        = The current status of migration and compression for a file
                or directory
Owner         = The current owner of the file or directory
Mode          = The search mode set for the current file

Files                   DOS Attr NetWare Attr      Status Owner            Mode
-------------------------------------------------------------------------------
VOL$LOG.ERR             [Rw----] [----------Ic--]         .[Supervisor]    N/A

EBDB\DATA:\PROJECTS\R&D
Files                   DOS Attr NetWare Attr      Status Owner            Mode
-------------------------------------------------------------------------------
940616.NTS              [Rw----] [----------Ic--]         .Admin.ebdb      N/A

F:\>
```

Directory attributes can be changed in much the same way as for file attributes, the main difference in NWADMIN and FILER being that you must select a directory, then Directory Attributes, rather than selecting a file and File Attributes. When using FLAG, use the /DO option. The following output illustrates adding the Purge attribute to a directory. (The Purge attribute causes all files in that directory to purged immediately upon deletion.)

```
F:\DATA>FLAG .cn=EBDB_SYS.O=EBDB:\DATA\TEMP P /DO

Files         = The name of the files found
Directories   = The name of the directories found
DOS Attr      = The DOS attributes for the specified file
```

```
NetWare Attr = The NetWare attributes for the specified file or directory
Status       = The current status of migration and compression for a file
               or directory
Owner        = The current owner of the file or directory
Mode         = The search mode set for the current file

Directories             NetWare Attr   Owner
----------------------------------------------------------------------------
TEMP                    [--P--------] .[Supervisor]

F:\DATA>
```

Summary

This chapter showed you how to assign directory and file trustee rights. The two main utilities reviewed were NWADMIN.EXE (Windows or OS/2) and NETADMIN.EXE (DOS). Examples were given for each utility on how to add directory trustee rights using both utilities. A comparison was made between NWADMIN, NETADMIN, and FILER. You learned that NWADMIN can assign rights by first selecting a user, group, container, or other object to make into a trustee, or by first selecting the directory, then adding the trustee object. NETADMIN lets you work with the trustee object, and FILER lets you work with the directory. You also learned how to use the RIGHTS.EXE utility to assign rights from the command line.

A demonstration of how to assign file trustee rights followed. Again, examples using NWADMIN, FILER, and RIGHTS were used. As you learned, when assigning file trustee rights to a utility, you have to make sure you grant rights to all subsidiary files the utility calls when executing, otherwise, the user cannot properly use the utility.

You then learned how to use NWADMIN, FILER, or RIGHTS to make changes to the IRF. As you saw, the default IRF allows all rights to pass. When you remove a right from the mask, that right is blocked.

Finally, a section on file and directory attributes was covered. As you saw, NWADMIN, FILER, and the FLAG commands can be used to change file or directory attributes.

The next chapter, "Adding NDS Trustee Rights," covers assigning NDS rights.

Adding NDS Trustee Rights

NDS trustee rights (sometimes called *NDS assignments*) are the individual elements that make up the network security. The NetWare 4 Directory Services provides much flexibility in administering network security.

For the most part, you won't have to make many NDS rights assignments. NDS has various default rights that fit well in many situations. Customizing the NDS rights will mostly apply to assigning certain network users to act as sub-administrators. A *sub-administrator* could be someone to whom the responsibility of managing one or a few containers is given, or someone who would function as the network or container Administrator in the absence of the regular Administrator.

Figure 31.1 shows the graphical interface of the NetWare Administrator utility from which you can assign Directory tree rights.

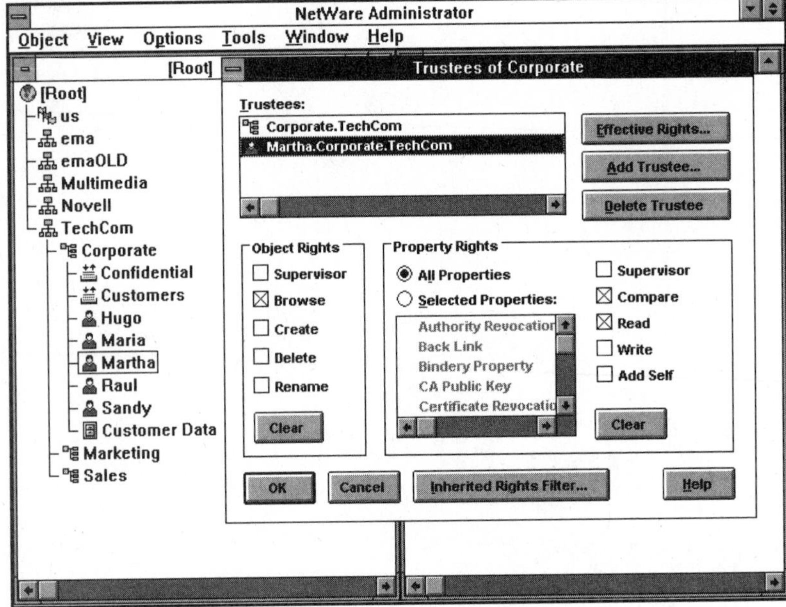

Figure 31.1
Assigning NDS trustee rights in the Trustees of Corporate dialog box.

NDS Rights Assigned by Default

This chapter demonstrates how NetWare 4 Administrators can customize the rights assignments in the Directory tree in great detail. But before showing how to customize rights, you must first have an understanding of the default rights that NetWare 4 provides. Default rights assignments can reduce the sometimes tedious task of managing network security. Table 31.1 shows some of the default rights assignments that are established.

Table 31.1
Default Rights Assignments

Situation	Trustee	NDS Default Rights	File System Rights
Installing NDS	Admin	Supervisor object right to [root]	No explicit file system rights, but Admin inherits Supervisor object right to the server object through the Supervisor object

Situation	Trustee	NDS Default Rights	File System Rights
			right to [root]. Thus, Admin receives Supervisor file system right to the root of each volume.
	Public	Browse object right to [root]	None
Creating a User Object	User	Browse object right to itself Read to All Properties Read and Write to Login Script Property Read and Write to Print Job Configuration property	Read, Create, Erase, Write, File Scan, Modify, and Access Control to own home directory Read, File Scan to the PUBLIC directory of any and all SYS: volumes existing in the target container

When you first install NDS, a user object named *Admin* is created by default. This Admin user is the *super-user,* the user with all rights granted. You must use this user object to create the structure and objects in your Directory tree. Do not delete this Admin object, or you could potentially lose all ability to modify the Directory tree.

[Public] is an element of the NetWare 4 Directory Services that works like a blanket group. Any rights that are assigned to [Public] are automatically assigned to all objects throughout the Directory tree. When you install NDS, the element [Public] receives, by default, the Browse right to the [root]. The Browse right assigned to [Public] gives all objects throughout the Directory tree the capability to browse any other object in the tree. This chapter later discusses the uses of the [Public] element.

If a user is created into a container that contains a SYS volume, the user automatically receives Read and File Scan rights to the PUBLIC directory on that volume. This way the user can immediately log into the Directory without further rights assignments.

Managing NDS Rights with NWADMIN

NWADMIN, referred to here as *NetWare Administrator*, is an MS Windows-based utility used to manage the NetWare 4 Directory tree. NetWare Administrator provides a *graphical-user interface* (GUI), which simplifies many administration tasks. The following paragraphs demonstrate how to use NetWare Administrator to perform some basic security functions.

Giving a User Rights to the Entire Tree

Granting a user rights to the whole Directory tree can be accomplished most easily by making the explicit right assignment at the highest place in the Directory, the [root]. The rights granted at the [root] filter down, or are *inherited* by all other objects in the Directory tree. The inheritance of these rights can be blocked with an Inherited Rights Filter, which is explained in Chapter 7, "NetWare 4.1 Security." In figure 31.2, a situation in which the Administrator grants Erik the Supervisor right to the [root] of the Directory tree is demonstrated.

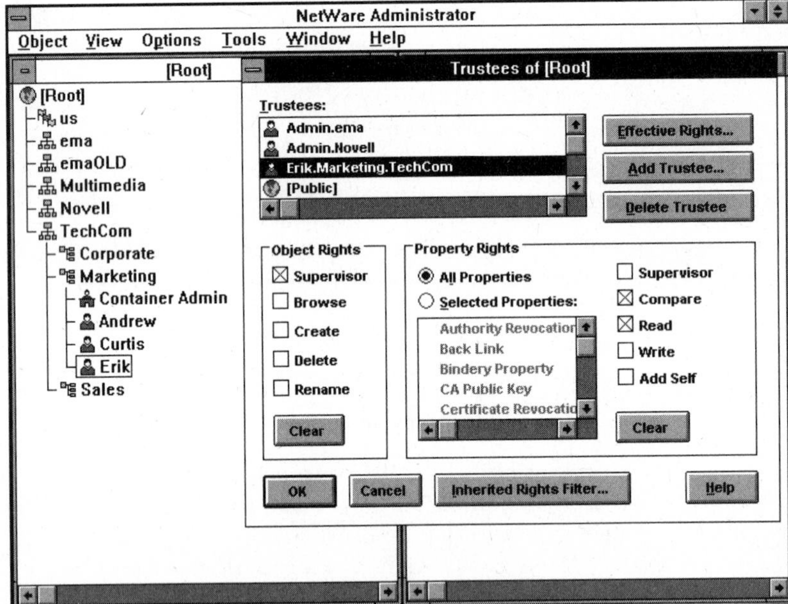

Figure 31.2

Using the Trustees of [root] dialog box to assign all NDS rights to a user.

By making this particular assignment, you have granted Erik an unqualified license to create, delete, or modify anything that exists or can exist in the Directory tree. Not only could Erik change containers and leaf objects, but he could change passwords, file system structures, and data that resides on any volume throughout the Directory tree. This assignment should *only* be made to someone in whom you have complete confidence.

Giving a Container Rights to Itself

Many rights assignments can be made in the Directory tree that might not make much sense, but one particular right assignment makes much sense when examined closely—that of giving a container object rights to itself. This single assignment can be a real time saver and can greatly reduce many individual assignments that might take its place.

What Is the Impact?

When you assign a container rights to itself, you have, with one assignment, given all the objects that reside within the container and underneath the container the same explicit rights assignment that the container has. For example, if you were to assign the container the Create object right to itself, every object inside that container (and objects underneath) would have the Create right within their own containers.

Why Would You Do It?

Consider the following scenario: You are the network Administrator over the Sales container. The 40 users whom you serve all have user objects created within the Sales container. The users all want to be able to look up each others' title and telephone number. When the users are created in the container, default rights assignments restrict the viewing of the Title and Telephone properties.

One way to meet the need of allowing title and telephone information to be shared is to create a group within the container and assign everyone in the container (all 40 users, each membership assignment being a separate and redundant task) as a member of the group. Then you would need to assign the proper access rights to the group for the members to access the information.

A better way to accomplish this objective is to assign the container rights to itself. The container already functions as a group, so there is no need to create a group within the container to assign rights that are equivalent for each user.

Consider now the same scenario. Because the 40 users need to access the titles and telephone numbers of other users in the container, make the Sales container a trustee of itself and assign the Read right to the Selected Properties (Title and Telephone).

How To Assign a Container Rights to Itself

Another example might be a similar situation in which the users in the Sales container all want access to a certain area on the server, such as a shared directory. The Administrator performs the following:

1. With NetWare Administrator running, locate the volume you want to share. Double-click on the volume object to reveal the directories and files.

2. From the browser that shows the directories and files, choose the directory that you want to share and access the Details screen by selecting **O**bject, **D**etails.

3. At the Details screen, locate and click on the Trustees of this Directory button to activate the Trustees screen.

4. With the Trustees screen up, click on the Add button to bring up the Select Object dialog box.

5. Within the Select Object dialog box, browse the Directory tree and locate the Sales container (the container that you want to assign as a trustee of the shared directory).

6. Select the container object and assign the appropriate file system rights by clicking on the boxes that represent the rights that can be granted.

The volume or server objects that your users want to share do not need to reside within the same container that the users reside. Figure 31.3 demonstrates assigning a container as a Browse object trustee to itself.

Yet another somewhat extreme example might be a company that has a branch in its Directory tree named Testing. This Testing container was created specifically for technicians to experiment with. The technicians all want to have the Supervisor right within that branch (the Testing container and subsequent containers).

As the Administrator, you assign the Testing container as a trustee to itself and assign the Supervisor object right. All objects within that container inherit the Supervisor object right from the container without making individual rights assignments.

One word of caution is that when you grant a container rights to itself, you have no way of restricting that rights assignment to a subset of objects. You should use this method only when the rights you want to assign apply to *every* object within the container.

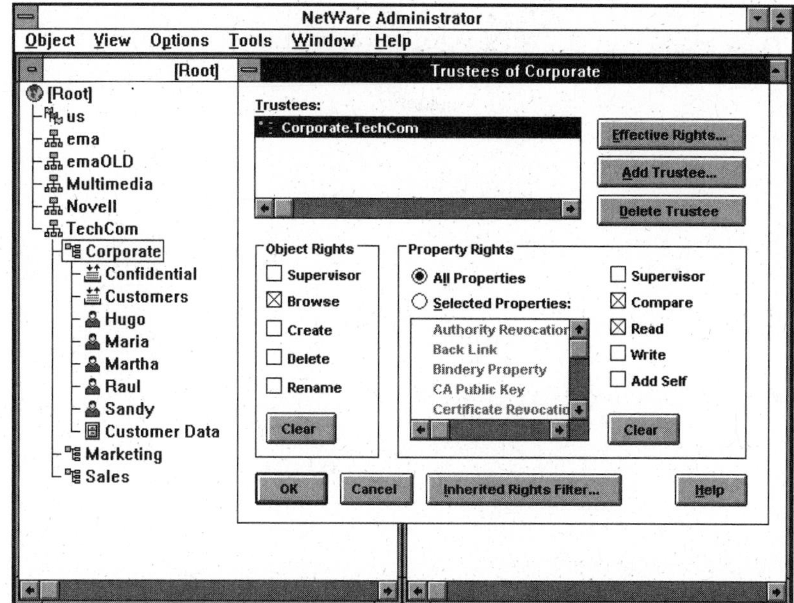

Figure 31.3

Assigning NDS rights to a container.

Managing NDS Rights with NETADMIN

NETADMIN.EXE is a text-based menu utility for DOS workstations that mirrors the functionality of NetWare Administrator. The next security function presented is performed using NETADMIN.

Giving a Container Rights To Manage Another Container

Because any NDS object can be a trustee of another, you might find occasion to grant an entire container rights to manage another container. For example, assume that you are a network Administrator over two containers: the Marketing container and the Tech Support container. The users in the Marketing group (whose NDS objects reside in the Marketing container) frequently call people in technical support (whose NDS objects exist in the Tech Support container) regarding problems with the network. As the managing network Administrator, you want to set up security so that the tech support personnel can manage and troubleshoot the Marketing network without having to come to you for access rights.

To grant the technical support people easier access to the Marketing container, you can assign the Tech Support container as a trustee of the Marketing container and assign Supervisor rights. Creating this assignment allows the technical support people to have access to the marketing people's NDS object, so that support is in a better position to provide help.

You can perform this task with NETADMIN using the following steps:

1. From the DOS prompt, load NETADMIN. The main menu appears.

2. At the main menu, choose the Manage Objects option. The Object, Class dialog box opens and shows the objects that exist in your workstation's current context. This Object, Class dialog box functions as a browser window, enabling you to browse through the Directory tree. As you notice the status line in the first three rows at the top of the screen, you can see that the utility shows the current context and the login name for this NETADMIN session.

3. Select the container that you want to be managed and press F10. This activates the Actions for Organizational Unit: dialog box. Notice that the container's name appears in the header.

4. From the Actions for Organizational Unit: dialog box, select View/Edit Trustees of this object.

5. At the Trustees of this Object dialog box, select Trustee Assignments. The Property, Rights, Trustee dialog box appears, displaying the current trustees of the container, as figure 31.4 demonstrates.

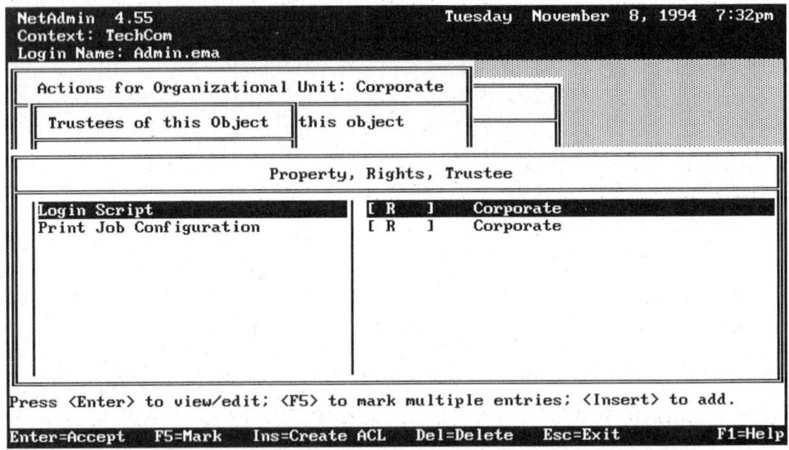

Figure 31.4
The current rights assignments for Corporate.

6. At the Property, Rights, Trustee dialog box, press Insert to open another dialog box that lets you choose which rights you want to assign to the trustee of the container.

7. With the Rights dialog box opened, choose [Object Rights].

8. In the Object Rights dialog box, select the Supervisor object right and press Enter to add the right to the active list. A field called Trustees opens, prompting for the name of the managing container (see fig. 31.5).

9. In the Trustees text box, enter the name of the managing container and press Enter, or press Insert to browse the Directory tree to find the container, then make your selection by pressing Enter. The Property, Rights, Trustee dialog box returns showing the trustee assignment that you have made (see fig. 31.6).

```
NetAdmin 4.55                                  Tuesday November 8, 1994 7:33pm
Context: TechCom
Login Name: Admin.ema

 Actions for Organizational Unit: Corporate
  Trustees of this Object   this object

                         Property, Rights, Trustee
                                 Trustees
 Enter trustee name: Sales

Type the object name or press <Insert> to browse for the object.
Ins=Add   Enter=Accept   Esc=Exit                                    F1=Help
```

Figure 31.5

Selecting the managing container.

```
NetAdmin 4.55                                  Tuesday November 8, 1994 7:34pm
Context: TechCom
Login Name: Admin.ema

 Actions for Organizational Unit: Corporate
  Trustees of this Object   this object

                         Property, Rights, Trustee
  [Object Rights]                      [     S]    Sales
  Login Script                         [ R    ]    Corporate
  Print Job Configuration              [ R    ]    Corporate

Press <Insert> to add other objects. Press <Enter> to edit. Press <F10> to
save.
Enter=Accept  F5=Mark  Ins=Create ACL  Del=Delete  Esc=Exit         F1=Help
```

Figure 31.6

The new NDS rights Assignment for Corporate.

This procedure makes one container and all its objects the manager of another container and all its objects.

Building a Rights Structure in Which No Single User Has Rights to the Entire Tree

Many organizations have departed from the one-Administrator design and have decentralized their network administration. Limiting the power of an overall Administrator and dividing the responsibility among other sub-administrators has some advantages:

- Sub-administrators do not have as much responsibility and power over the network. Limiting the power that any one person has over the network might help protect the network from malicious actions.
- Sub-administrators can, in theory, respond faster to network users' problems and needs than can an overall administrator. In large organizations, the sub-administrator might be one of the users in the workgroup.
- Sub-administrators can be granted specific responsibilities to preserve sensitive information.

NetWare 4 offers a way to make very specific and granular security assignments so you can design tiers of sub-administrators to match your network needs.

Designating "Sub" Admin Users

Granting rights to a network user to make her a sub-administrator is nothing more than merely granting either an NDS object or property right. In the following example, Rolf in the Sales container needs to participate as an Administrator over the TechCom container. Figure 31.7 shows the user's assignment to the TechCom container.

This action lets Rolf perform as the Administrator in the TechCom or lower containers. Remember not to delete the original Admin object as you create sub-administrators. You could lose supervisory access to the Directory tree.

Assigning Property Rights to an Organizational Role

One popular method of creating a sub-administrator in the Directory tree is to create an Organizational Role object. The Organizational Role functions somewhat like a NetWare group. You can assign rights to the Organizational Role just as you can to a user, and assign or add user objects to the Organizational Role's list. The net effect is that the users who are added to the Organizational Role gain security equivalence to the rights assigned to the Organizational Role. For example, examine figure 31.8.

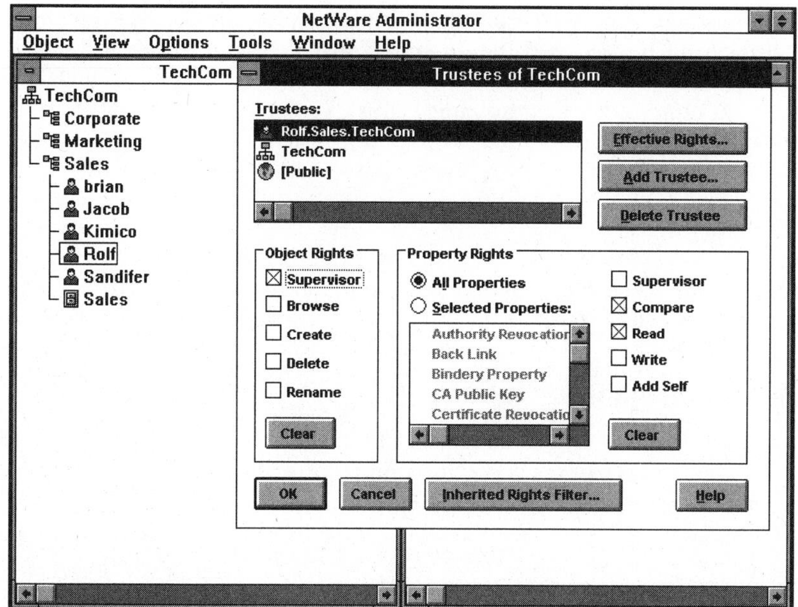

Figure 31.7

Assigning a user as a sub-administrator.

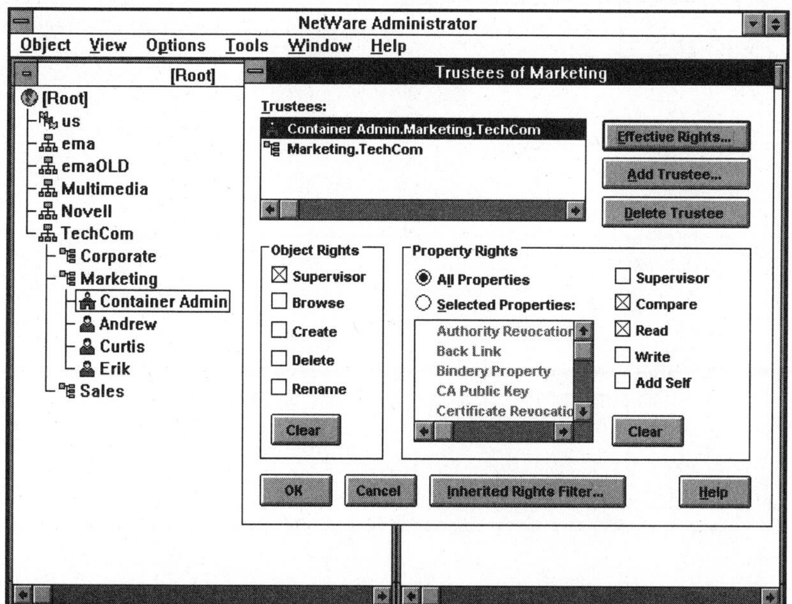

Figure 31.8

Adding NDS rights to an Organizational Role.

The network Administrator has created an Organizational Role object in the context .Marketing.TechCom and has assigned the Organizational Role as a trustee to the TechCom container. Now, when any user object is added into the Organizational Role's list of associates, the user gains the same rights that the Organizational Role has, plus any other rights explicitly granted to the user. In figure 31.8, each user added to the Organizational Role receives the Supervisor object right to the TechCom container.

The Administrator can easily swap user objects in and out of the Organizational Role's list. This facilitates using the Organizational Role as a means to assign sub-administrators in the Directory tree.

Assigning Rights to Organizations

Assigning a set of rights needed by the entire organization can save you time in security administration. Instead of assigning individual rights for the PUBLIC directory of a SYS volume in the Directory tree at the organizational unit levels, make the assignment at the organization level (see fig. 31.9).

Figure 31.9

Selecting a file system directory.

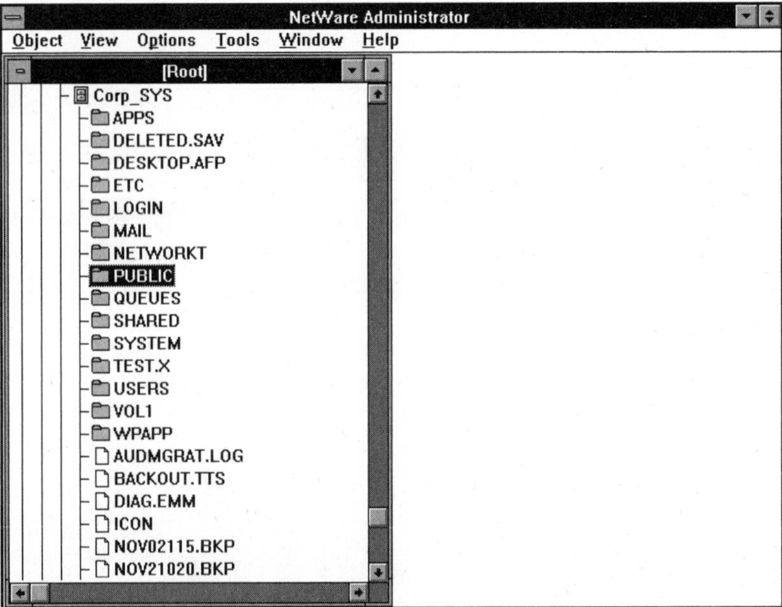

With NetWare Administrator, you can select a PUBLIC directory in a volume to which you want to have general access. Select the Details menu from the menu bar, then activate the Trustees of this Directory screen from the Details screen (see fig. 31.10).

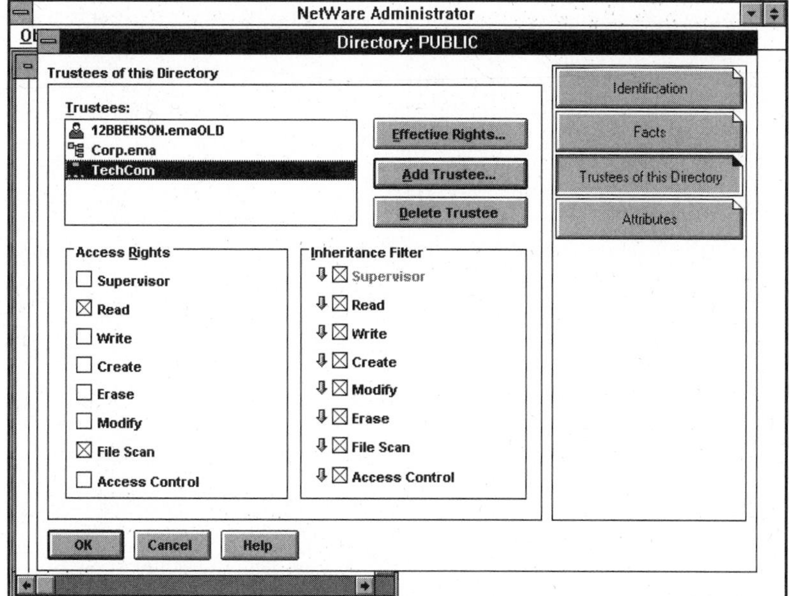

Figure 31.10

Assigning rights to the organization.

You can see how the container TechCom has been granted Read and File Scan rights to the PUBLIC directory. Every current and future object within the TechCom container or below is now automatically granted access to this file system directory.

Using the Inherited Rights Filter

Rights inheritance is a powerful way to perform security management. However, there are situations in which rights inheritance down to certain containers might be unwanted or unintended. NetWare 4 provides a way to block unwanted rights inheritance by setting an inherited rights filter.

The *Inherited Rights Filter* (IRF) can block rights inheritance from containers directly above. The IRF can block all rights, even the Supervisor object right. The IRF, however, does not block—nor can it limit—rights inherited by the objects in the same container where the rights are granted.

For example, Mary is a user in the .Sales.TechCom container. An explicit Browse object right is given at the TechCom container, and through inheritance from TechCom, Mary should receive the Browse right. If you place an IRF at the .Sales.TechCom container that blocks the Browse right, she will not inherit the Browse object right.

If the explicit Browse object right were made at the .Sales.TechCom container, however, Mary would receive the Browse right, even if an IRF is placed at the .Sales.TechCom container. The IRF *only* blocks rights that are inherited from containers above your own container.

Using an IRF To Block the Admin User's Rights

You can check or set the IRF at any level or container in the Directory tree. To set an IRF, perform the following steps:

1. Using NetWare Administrator, highlight the container on which you want to set the IRF.

2. From the Browser screen, access the Trustees of this Object menu.

3. At the Trustees of this Object menu, press the Inherited Rights Filter button. The figure 31.11 shows the screen of the IRF with all rights inheritance being blocked except Browse.

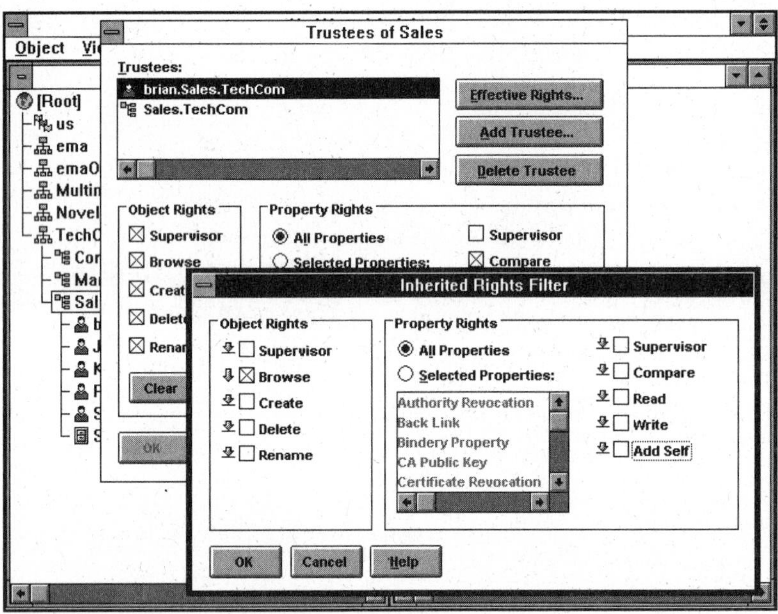

Figure 31.11
Blocking Supervisor rights inheritance.

You can actually cut off a branch from all access by setting an IRF. The NETADMIN and NetWare Administrator utilities permit you to block the Supervisor right at a certain container only if objects within that container or below are assigned the Supervisor right. But you can assign the Supervisor right to a user, block the

Supervisor right above, then delete the Admin object. This can potentially leave you unable to manage the part of the Directory tree above the IRF.

One thing to prevent this from happening is to create another object in the Directory tree and grant the user Supervisor rights to the [root]. That essentially creates another Admin object that can be used to manage the Directory tree if the original Admin is deleted.

Working with [Public]

The [Public] element of the Directory tree is a trustee to which all objects in the Directory tree are automatically security equivalent. The [Public] trustee can be assigned at the [root] or at any container within the Directory tree.

For example, when you assign the Browse right to the [Public] trustee at the TechCom container, you have granted the Browse right to the TechCom container and all subsequent containers to every object in the Directory tree. [Public] can be a very powerful security tool when used properly. Figure 31.12 shows the Browse object right and the Read right to All Properties being assigned to the user Brian in the Sales container.

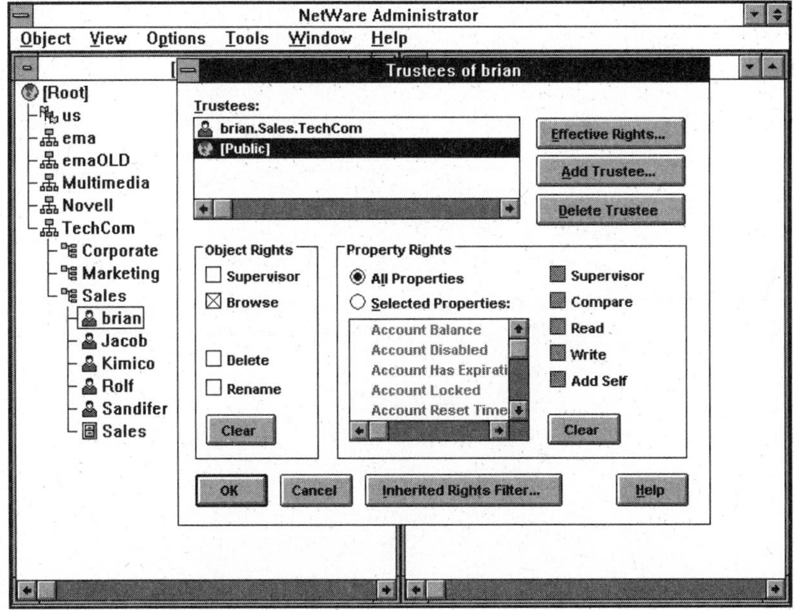

Figure 31.12
Assigning rights to [Public].

This would allow any user in the Directory tree to find the object that represents the network user Brian and read the values stored in his object's properties.

One practical example of using [Public] is to set up a paperless directory of all the users in your organization. You would make an assignment to the [Public] trustee at the organization level to Browse object and Read All Properties. This would enable anyone in the Directory tree to find any object and read the values stored in the properties.

What Rights Should Be Assigned to [Public]?

Any rights that you want all of the objects of the Directory tree to have can be assigned to the [Public] trustee. This could include Read and File Scan to a SYS volume, or other shared data or application directory, it could be the Browse right on a user, container, print queue, or other network resource.

The drawback of [Public] is that you don't have to be logged into the Directory tree to receive the rights granted to [Public]. For example, if S were assigned to [Public], anyone who has the CX.EXE utility could go anywhere in the tree.

How To Block Rights Assigned to [Public]

The rights assigned to [Public] can be blocked with an IRF. Refer to a previous example in which you created a paperless directory for all users in the Directory tree. By assigning the Browse and Read to All Properties to the [Public] trustee at the organization level, you granted access to all objects and the capability to browse and read all properties. But perhaps you have one department, Research, that does not want to have the information in their properties disseminated through the Directory tree. You can set an IRF blocking the Browse object and Read All Properties rights so that, even though the users can see down to the container above Research, the users cannot obtain information from objects residing in the container Research.

Working with [root]

The [root] element of the Directory tree is also a suggested place to assign rights that you want to have generally available throughout the Directory tree. Any rights assigned at the [root] level flow down to the containers below, unless blocked by an IRF.

Who Should Be Assigned Rights to [root]?

Regular network users should not be assigned rights (apart from Browse) at the [root]. Most installations don't need to let their users explore around the Directory tree.

Network services, such as general applications, login scripts, and profiles, are best suited for assignment at the top levels of the Directory tree so that the rights can affect the largest number of people with the least amount of administration.

What Happens When [root] Is Given Rights to Itself

Instead of assigning rights, such as Browse, to [Public] public why not assign the rights to the [root] itself. That way you have to be an authenticated user to get the rights.

Consider figure 31.13, which represents one extreme of assigning Supervisor rights to the [root].

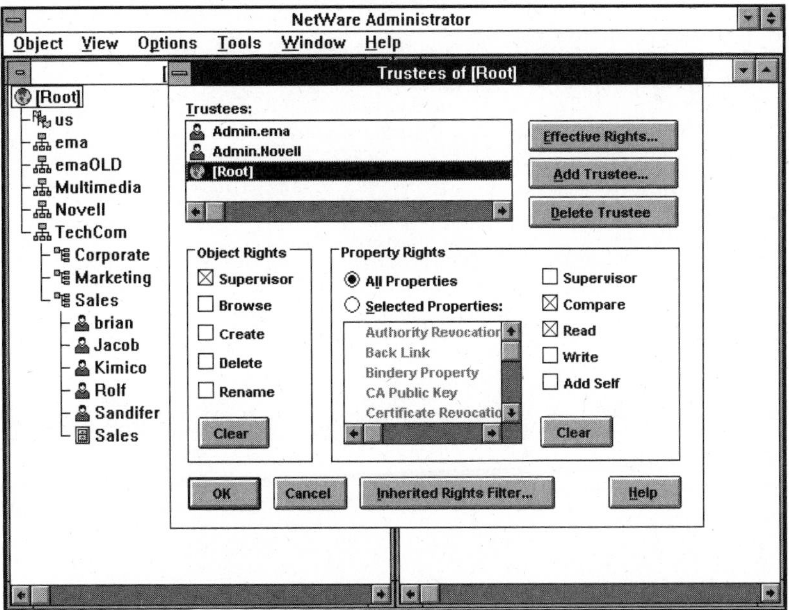

Figure 31.13

Assigning Supervisor rights to [root].

Making a Supervisor rights assignment at the [root] means that anything that is created in the Directory tree has Supervisor rights to everything else in the tree. *Any* object could modify the Directory tree, from the last terminal objects to the entire structure of the Directory. This example shows the extreme case of granting rights. Do not make this particular assignment unless you want to create an everybody-a-supervisor environment.

Figure 31.14 demonstrates an effective and useful way to assign rights to the [root]. Making the Browse assignment to the [root] permits every object in the Directory tree, such as users, to see every other object. But the user must be authenticated to the Directory tree before she can Browse the objects.

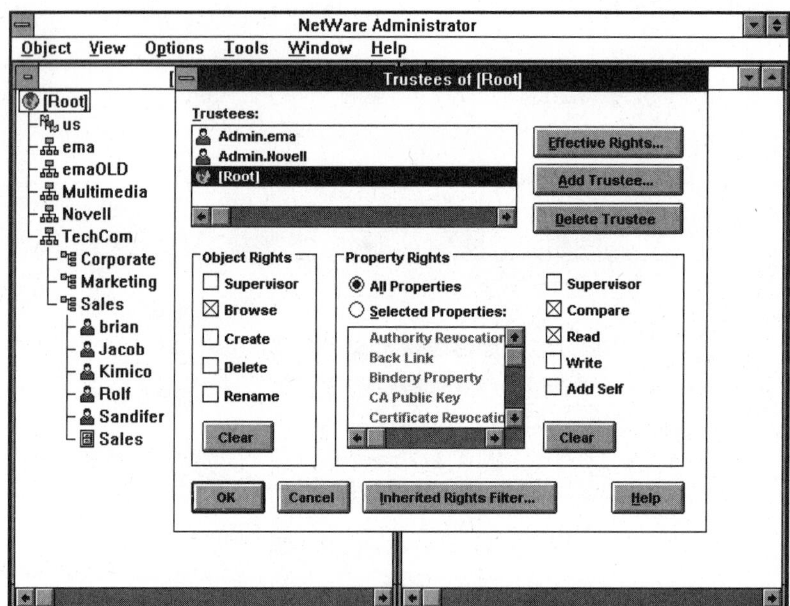

Figure 31.14
Assigning Browse rights to [root].

Summary

NetWare Directory Services provides much flexibility in administering network security. NetWare 4 has many default security rights that help reduce the tasks of administration, and you can customize the rights for your particular application.

Both NetWare Administrator and NETADMIN utilities can be used to regulate and assign network security. The utilities have equivalent functionality, so you may choose which environment best suits you and your users.

A successful Administrator knows how to plan, assign, and examine Directory tree rights. This chapter investigated various situations that can impact network Directory tree security. You saw the impact of giving one user all rights to the whole Directory tree, creating and using Organizational Role objects to manage containers, how to give one container rights to manage another, and the use of Inherited Rights Filters to block the unwanted inheritance of Directory rights.

You discovered the impact of assigning rights to [Public] versus [root]. Assigning rights to the [Public] object allows network users who are not authenticated to access the Directory tree. If you want to keep unauthenticated users from viewing your Directory tree, make [root] a trustee of itself and grant Browse or whatever level of rights is necessary for authenticated users to have to the complete Directory tree. The security needs of your organization shape the way that you assign rights to the [Public] and [root].

Although each installation has different security requirements, effective security design dictates assigning limited rights, such as Browse, high in the levels of the Directory tree. This is suggested for common access that is needed throughout the organization. Assigning Read and File Scan to the PUBLIC directory of a particular SYS volume is useful in many cases. The organization-wide rights can then be easily managed, without having to make any rights assignments to individuals or containers.

Chapter 32 demonstrates how to view trustee assignments.

CHAPTER

Viewing Trustee Assignments

This chapter introduces the five NetWare utilities you use to view trustee assignments and provides background information necessary to interpret the information that appears in these utilities.

Trustee assignments are stored in access control lists (ACLs). NetWare enables you to generate a list of who can use what resources and how they can use them for each type of file system or NDS resource, such as disk space in a directory or a print server in NDS. You can list users as individuals or as members of groups, so that when an individual tries to use a resource, NetWare compares that person's user ID to the list and permits access according to the assigned rights. So, you might request a print server to accept work from a certain user: NetWare first checks the access privileges, then permits that user use the print server. Or, an ordinary user might try to change the contents of the SYSTEM directory: NetWare checks the access privileges first, then denies the user access, thereby eliminating the opportunity to make changes.

NetWare 4.1 provides five utilities for viewing trustee assignments.

- **Rights.** The DOS command-line file system administration utility
- **Nlist.Exe.** The DOS command-line NDS viewing utility
- **Filer.Exe.** The DOS menu file system management and administration utility
- **Netadmin.Exe.** The DOS menu file system and NDS administration utility
- **Nwadmin.Exe.** The MS Windows file system and NDS administration utility

RIGHTS and FILER are utilities found in previous versions of NetWare. NLIST, NETADMIN and NWADMIN are new with NetWare 4. The DOS RIGHTS utility, however, is a consolidation of several previous utilities (namely, the NetWare 3.*x* functions ALLOW, GRANT, REMOVE, REVOKE, and RIGHTS, all of which were DOS command-line utilities).

You can use NLIST, in contrast to the other four utilities, only to view the NDS. You can use the other utilities to view and to modify trustee assignments.

Key Terms

You need to know the definitions of several key terms, including the following:

- Trustee
- Access control list
- Security equivalence
- [Public]
- Rights
- Effective rights

Definitions for these key terms follow. Be aware that most of the concepts discussed here are not specific to NetWare 4.1. Most of these concepts apply to NetWare 4.0, 4.01, and 4.02. The term *NetWare 4* indicates concepts that apply to all versions of NetWare 4.*x*. The term *NetWare 4.1* indicates a feature specific to NetWare 4.1.

Trustee

A *trustee* is an object that has access to a directory, file, or other object. The trustee has this access because it has a trustee assignment. A trustee assignment, in effect, says,

"This object (the trustee) can access this directory, file, or object, and can do so in these ways." You can make trustee assignments by using the RIGHTS, NETADMIN, or NWADMIN (NetWare Administrator) utilities.

In bindery-based versions of NetWare, you can grant rights to a user or group for only the file system. If multiple servers are involved, rights must be assigned individually for each server. Additionally, a user can be granted rights as a print queue operator or as a user account manager over another user; again, these rights are assigned separately for each server on the network. NetWare 4 simplifies these rights by separating them into two categories: file system rights and NDS rights. As discussed in earlier chapters, NDS rights are further broken down into object rights and property rights. When you assign an object rights to another object, NDS rights are involved. When you assign an object to a file or directory, file system rights are involved.

In NetWare 4, you can make any object a trustee of the file system or of another object. Technically, you can assign any object rights. Assigning rights to certain objects is clearly impractical. For example, it makes no sense to assign a printer object rights to the SYS:SYSTEM directory. FILER, NETADMIN, and NWADMIN do not even give you such a choice. The RIGHTS command, on the other hand, scans only for a valid object name, not its type.

Access Control List

Each directory, file, and object has a list of trustee assignments, called an access control list (ACL). This trustee list specifies who can access that directory, file, or object. An object's trustee list is a value of the object's Access Control List (ACL) property. When you use the utilities discussed in this chapter to view trustee assignments, you read the ACL property of the object you view.

Security Equivalence

If several users are to access a directory, file, or object, each user must have a trustee assignment. An alternative to making trustee assignments for each user is to create a Group object, which enables you to include the users in the group and assign rights to the group. Assigning rights to a group confers rights at once to all users who are members of the group.

Membership in a group is one example of the principle of security equivalence. Security equivalence is the transference of security rights, accomplished in several ways, such as the following:

- Group membership
- Direct security equivalence assignment

- Being the occupant of an organizational role
- Belonging to [Public]

Another security transference principle closely related to security equivalence is inheritance. *Inheritance* is the acquisition of rights assigned at a higher level or the acquisition of the rights of your container object and all parent container objects.

[Public]

[Public] is a special trustee that establishes the default rights for all users. You can use [Public] as the trustee of a file, directory, or object. If you try to access a directory, file, or object without any other rights, you at least have the rights granted to the [Public] trustee. You use [Public] only in trustee assignments and must notate it with square brackets. Rights you grant to [Public] are effective for any object in NetWare Directory Services, without exception. Granting rights to [Public] is similar to granting trustee rights to user GUEST or group EVERYONE in previous versions of NetWare.

One odd feature of [Public] is that you do not have to be logged in to acquire any rights granted to [Public], potentially a rather disturbing feature if you pay close attention to the ramifications. Recall that [Public] includes any user without exception, including users who simply load the VLM requester and access any NetWare 4 file server. If you were to assign Supervisor directory trustee rights to the root of volume SYS: to [Public], for example, you would grant all rights to any and all users who have the VLM requester loaded on their workstations.

Rights

Rights determine the type of access a trustee has to a directory, file, or object. For example, if you grant a user the Create trustee assignment (the right to create) to a directory, the user can create files in that directory. A trustee assignment grants an object specific rights to another object, file or directory.

Rights are granted within the object to which a trustee has rights, not within the trustee object. For example, to grant HARVEY the right to delete a Printer object, you would make HARVEY a trustee having the delete right, of the Printer object, not the Printer object a trustee of HARVEY.

Because directories, files, and objects contain such different types of information, the rights that control access to them must be set differently. Rights to directories and files and to other objects are controlled in different sections of the utilities. In NetWare 4, rights apply to four categories of resources:

- **Directories in the file system.** Directory rights control what a trustee can do with a directory. Directory rights also apply to files in the directory if file rights aren't granted and if the file's Inherited Rights Filter doesn't block the directory rights.

- **Files in the file system.** File rights control what a trustee can do with a file.

- **Objects in NDS.** Object rights control what a trustee can do with an object. These rights control the object as a single piece in the directory tree, but do not allow access to information stored within that object (unless the Supervisor object right is granted).

- **Property rights for information within an object in NDS.** Property rights control a trustee's access to information stored in the object's properties. Each object has several properties.

Default rights are granted to NetWare 4 resources when they are created. You can override the default rights by assigning trustee rights (adding to the access control list for a particular resource).

Effective Rights

Be sure to note the difference between the rights users have by being on an access control list and their effective rights. Each resource has default rights via the [Public] trustee and trustee rights that the system Administrator assigns to individuals or groups. These assignments cascade through the hierarchical file system and NDS structures in NetWare, but you can filter them out at any point in the hierarchy. In the absence of trustee assignments, a person's rights are the defaults that the Administrator assigns. If you are on the access control list, however, your trustee rights supersede the defaults. From a practical point of view, what you can do is called your effective rights, which are simply the default rights or the rights that supersede the defaults because you are on the access control list as an individual or because you have gained rights through a security equivalence.

NetWare calculates your effective rights to a directory, file, or object whenever you take an action, such as changing directories, mapping a drive letter, or changing contexts, among other possible actions. Effective rights to a file or directory are determined by the following criteria:

- An object's trustee assignments to the directory or file
- Inherited rights from an object's trustee assignments to parent directories
- Trustee assignments of Group objects to which a User object belongs
- Trustee assignments of objects listed in a User object's security equivalences list

If a user has a trustee assignment to a directory on a given level in the directory structure, and one on a higher level, the current trustee assignment overrides the higher one. Trustee assignments through a security equivalence, however, are added to individual user trustee assignments.

The RIGHTS, NLIST, FILER, NWADMIN and NETADMIN utilities enable you to view the trustee assignments for NetWare resources and the rights of those trustees. FILER and NWADMIN both have the capability to show you effective rights. The first utility we will look at is the RIGHTS DOS command-line utility.

Using the RIGHTS Utility

Use the RIGHTS DOS command-line utility at a workstation to do the following:

- View or modify object rights for files.
- View or modify object rights for directories and volumes.

The syntax for the RIGHTS command is as follows:

```
RIGHTS path [[+ ¦ -] rights] [/option...]
```

Table 32.1 lists rights parameters and usage.

TABLE 32.1
Rights Parameters

Parameter	Use To
no option	View the rights for the directory or file you indicate.
/VER	View the version number of the utility and the files it uses to execute.
path	Specify the path to the file, directory, or volume you want to modify or view rights to (if it's not the default). Could be a drive letter, a relative directory reference, a directory map object reference, file server/volume, or could use NDS syntax.

Parameter	Use To
rights	Specify one or more files or directory rights. For example, "+RF -W" is used to indicate add Read and File Scan rights, and remove Write rights. You can also specify ALL which adds RWCEMFA rights, but not S (Supervisor) rights. (Refer to Chapter 30 to refresh your memory on these rights.)
option	Specify one or more of the following options shown in table 32.2.

Table 32.2 lists rights options and usage.

TABLE 32.2
Rights Options

Option Syntax	Use To
/F	View the Inherited Rights Filter.
/GROUP= *group name*	Modify the rights for a group. Replace *group name* with the name of the group whose rights you want to modify.
/INHERITED	View the trustee and group rights that created the inherited rights and to view the source of the inherited rights. Can abbreviate as "/I".
/SUB	Modify subdirectories lower than the current level.
/TRUSTEE	View trustee assignments in a directory. Can abbreviate as "/T".
/NAME=*object*	Modify rights for the user listed. Replace *object* with the name of the object whose rights you want to modify.
/C	Scroll continuously through output.

continues

Table 32.2, Continued
Rights Options

Option Syntax	Use To
/? [option]	View online help. If you add an *option*, you can view specific types of help. Here is a list of available help options: T Trustee assignments F Setting the IRF I Viewing the IRF S Syntax O Miscellaneous

Figure 32.1 shows the help screen for the RIGHTS command.

```
RIGHTS                        General Help                              4.22

Purpose:  RIGHTS modifies or displays the trustee assignments or the
          inherited rights filter for volumes, directories, or files.

For help on:                                  Type:
  Trustee assignments                           RIGHTS /? T
  Setting Inheritance filter                    RIGHTS /? F
  Viewing Inherited rights                      RIGHTS /? I
  Syntax                                        RIGHTS /? S
  Miscellaneous options                         RIGHTS /? O
  All help screens                              RIGHTS /? ALL

For example, to:                              Type:
  See your effective rights                     RIGHTS

  Set user KIM's trustee rights
  in the current directory to Read              RIGHTS . R /NAME=KIM

F:\DATA>
```

Figure 32.1
The help screen for the RIGHTS command.

Here are some examples that illustrate using the RIGHTS command to view trustee assignments:

To display the rights assigned in a directory, type this command:

RIGHTS <*path*> /TRUSTEE

Remember that you can abbreviate the /TRUSTEE option as /T. Here is an example of this command in action:

```
F:\>RIGHTS F:\PUBLIC /T
EBDB\SYS:\PUBLIC
```

```
User trustees:
   THess.SC.EBDB                  [ RWCE F ]
   CTrahan.SJ.EBDB                 [ RWCEMFA]
No group trustees have been assigned.
----------
Other trustees:
   EBDB                      [ R  F ]
   NY.EBDB                     [ R  F ]


F:\>
```

The following example shows the source of user BBierer's inherited rights for SYS:DATA\SPECIAL\PAYROLL:

```
F:\>RIGHTS SYS:DATA\SPECIAL\PAYROLL /name=.BBierer.NY.EBDB /Inherited

Name= .BBierer.NY.EBDB
Path                                   Rights
-----------------------------------------------------------------------------
EBDB\SYS:\

Inherited Rights Filter:                         [      ]

Inherits from above:                          [      ]
                                   ---------
Effective Rights =                           [      ]
-----------------------------------------------------------------------------
EBDB\SYS:\DATA

Inherited Rights Filter:                         [SRWCEMFA]

Inherits from above:                          [      ]
                                   ---------
Effective Rights =                           [ R  F ]
-----------------------------------------------------------------------------
EBDB\SYS:\DATA\SPECIAL

Inherited Rights Filter:                         [SR  F ]

Inherits from above:                          [ R  F ]
                                   ---------
Effective Rights =                           [ R  F ]
-----------------------------------------------------------------------------
```

```
EBDB\SYS:\DATA\SPECIAL\PAYROLL

Inherited Rights Filter:                        [SRWCEMFA]

Inherits from above:                           [ R   F ]
Bbierer.NY                                 [ WCE   ]
                                        ----------
Effective Rights =                             [ RWCE F ]
--------------------------------------------------------------------


F:\>
```

The following example shows you how to view the settings of the Inherited Rights Filter (IRF) of a directory:

```
F:\DATA>RIGHTS \data\special /F

EBDB\SYS:\DATA
Directories                           Rights Filter
--------------------------------------------------------------------
SPECIAL                             [SR   F ]

F:\DATA>
```

Using NLIST.EXE To View Rights

The NLIST command is discussed in great detail in Chapter 14, "DOS Client Basics," and is used primarily to browse the tree for information about objects. One of the pieces of information that this powerful utility yields is the contents of the ACL of any given object. Before you can read the ACL of an object, you must have Read rights to an object's ACL property. If you are logged in as an Admin user, or as a user who has Supervisor object rights at a certain level, you can use NLIST to read the ACL properties of objects at that level and below.

The syntax for viewing rights assignments using NLIST is as follows:

```
NLIST <object> SHOW "ACL" /S [/CO <context>]
```

Replace *object* with the object class you want to browse. The *SHOW "ACL"* parameter causes NLIST to display the contents of the object's Access Control List property. If you are not in the context in which you want to start browsing, use the optional */CO* parameter to specify a starting context.

Here is the command to display the ACL of every object starting at the current context:

```
F:\>NLIST * SHOW "ACL" /s

Current context: [root]
Top : [Root]
    Object Trustees (ACL):
        Subject: Admin.EBDB
        Property: [Object Rights]
        Entry Rights: [  S]
    Object Trustees (ACL):
        Subject: [Public]
        Property: [Object Rights]
        Entry Rights: [B  ]
-------------------------------------------------------

Organization: EBDB
    Object Trustees (ACL):
        Subject: EBDB
        Property: Login Script
        Property Rights: [ R  ]
    Object Trustees (ACL):
        Subject: EBDB
        Property: Print Job Configuration
        Property Rights: [ R  ]
>>> Enter = More  C = Continuous  Esc = Cancel
```

The name of the object whose ACL appears at the left margin. Under the Object Trustees (ACL) heading is a specific trustee assignment. Subject identifies the name of the object assigned a right to the object being displayed. Property is the specific entity for which a trustee assignment was made. Entry Rights identifies the specific object right assigned. Property Rights shows the actual property right assigned.

In the first portion of the listing it can be seen that the user .Admin.EBDB has been assigned Supervisor object rights to [Root]. You can see in the next block that the organization EBDB is assigned Read property rights to its own Login Script property.

The following command displays the ACL of all user objects starting with the letter B, beginning at the O=EBDB container:

```
F:\>NLIST user=B* SHOW "ACL" /CO .O=EBDB /S

Object Class: User
```

```
Current context: NY.EBDB
User: Bsaunder
    Object Trustees (ACL):
        Subject: [Public]
        Property: [Object Rights]
        Entry Rights: [B  ]
    Object Trustees (ACL):
        Subject: Bsaunder
        Property: Login Script
        Property Rights: [ RW ]
    Object Trustees (ACL):
        Subject: [Public]
        Property: Default Server
        Property Rights: [ R  ]
    Object Trustees (ACL):
        Subject: [Root]
        Property: Group Membership
        Property Rights: [ R  ]
    Object Trustees (ACL):
        Subject: Bsaunder
        Property: Print Job Configuration
        Property Rights: [ RW ]
    Object Trustees (ACL):

User: Bbierer
    Object Trustees (ACL):
        Subject: [Public]
        Property: [Object Rights]
        Entry Rights: [B  ]
    Object Trustees (ACL):
        Subject: Bbierer
        Property: Login Script
        Property Rights: [ RW ]
    Object Trustees (ACL):
        Subject: [Public]
        Property: Default Server
        Property Rights: [ R  ]
    Object Trustees (ACL):
        Subject: [Root]
        Property: Group Membership
        Property Rights: [ R  ]
```

```
    Object Trustees (ACL):
        Subject: Bbierer
        Property: Print Job Configuration
        Property Rights: [ RW ]
>>> Enter = More  C = Continuous  Esc = Cancel
```

Using FILER.EXE To View Rights

You can see the effective rights a trustee has to a directory or file by using the FILER text utility. You use this utility from the DOS prompt to manage files and directories.

FILER works with the file system. It does not affect NDS objects. To view rights using FILER, you need DOS 3.30 or later, a minimum of 512K RAM available on the workstation, and the Access Control right to the file or directory.

Using FILER To View Directory Trustee Assignments

To view trustee rights assignments for a directory using FILER, proceed as follows:

1. At the DOS prompt, type the following:

   FILER

   The FILER Available Options menu appears. Your current context, Volume object, and path are shown in the upper left corner of the screen. Make sure you are in the correct path on the appropriate server and volume to complete this task.

Note If you receive the following error message while trying to load FILER, you may need to set the language variable on your workstation:

```
TEXTUTIL-4.00-577: The message file found is an incorrect version
of system message file TEXTUTIL.MSG. The correct version is 4.05.
See your network supervisor for assistance.
Program initialization failure - Execution terminated.
```

This problem and solution applies to any NetWare 4.1 DOS command-line utility. The solution is to first check the status of your NWLANGUAGE environment variable by using the DOS SET command, as follows:

continues

```
C:\COLLAGE>SET
PROMPT=$p$g
TEMP=C:\TEMP
COMSPEC=C:\COMMAND.COM
PATH=Y:.;X:.;Z:.;C:\DOS;C:\WINDOWS;C:\NECUTILS;C:\POPTERM;C:\NWCLIENT;
windir=C:\WINDOWS
```

As you can see in the first line of the preceding example, the NWLANGUAGE variable is not set. Set the variable to your preferred language (Deutsch, English, Espanol, Francais, or Italiano) as follows:

```
C:\COLLAGE>SET NWLANGUAGE=ENGLISH
```

You can now enter the desired DOS command-line utility successfully.

2. From the Available Options menu, select Manage files and directories. The Directory Contents menu appears. Here, you can browse up or down the directory structure of the volume.

3. From the Directory Contents menu, select the subdirectory you want to view and press F10. The Subdirectory Options menu appears.

4. From the Subdirectory Options menu, select Rights List. The Trustee name list appears, as shown in figure 32.2. From this list you can see which objects have been assigned specific trustee rights. In addition, a reference to an object, with its rights, will appear if the object inherits rights from a higher level trustee assignment. If the rights are assigned to a container, only the name of the container will appear, not every user in the container, even though users inherit the rights of their container.

5. Press Esc several times to return to the FILER main menu.

Using FILER To View File Trustee Assignments

To view file rights assignments for a file by using FILER, proceed as follows:

1. From the FILER Available Options menu, select Manage files and directories. The Directory Contents menu appears.

2. From the Directory Contents menu, find and select the subdirectory that contains the file you want by moving up and down the file system structure.

3. After you are in the directory that has the file you want to view, select the file and press F10. The File Options menu appears.

FILER 4.20
Tuesday November 8, 1994 6:54pm
Context: EBDB
Volume object: EBDB_SYS
Current path: EBDB\SYS:
Trustee name
Type
Rights
Dbierer.EBDB
MIA.EBDB
Nfsgroup.EBDB
Thess.NY.EBDB
User
Organizational Unit
Group
User
[RWCEMFA]
[R F]
[R F]
[SRWCEMFA]
Enter=Select Esc=Escape
F1=Help

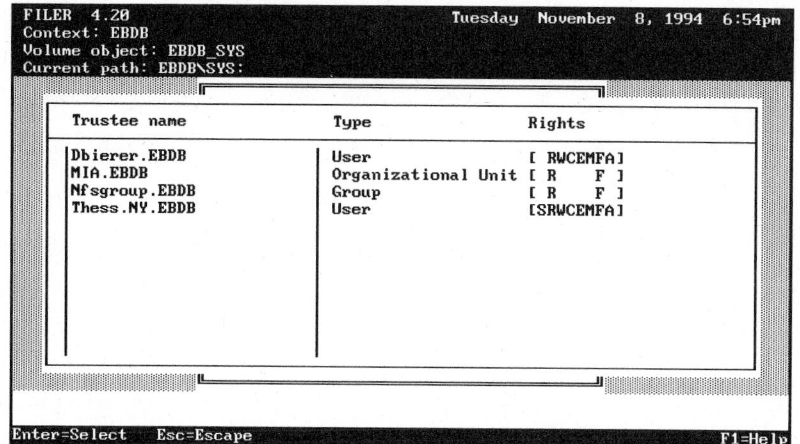

Figure 32.2

The Trustee name list of trustee assignments for a directory.

4. From the File Options menu, select Rights List. The Trustee name list appears, as shown in figure 32.3.

5. Press Esc several times to return to the FILER main menu.

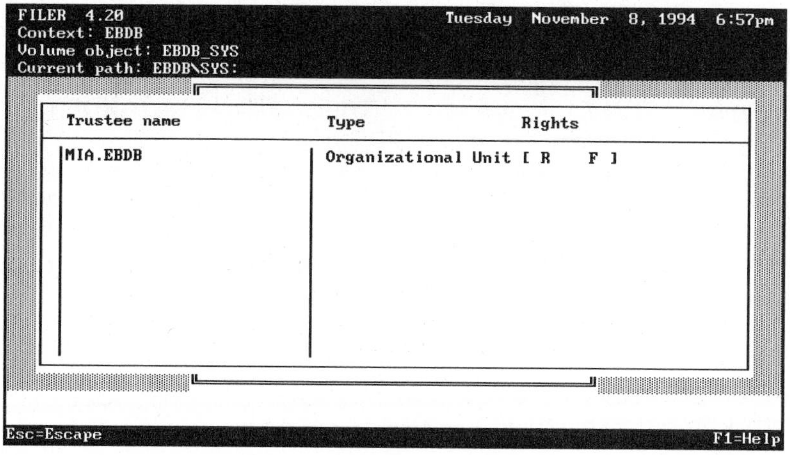

FILER 4.20
Tuesday November 8, 1994 6:57pm
Context: EBDB
Volume object: EBDB_SYS
Current path: EBDB\SYS:
Trustee name
Type
Rights
MIA.EBDB
Organizational Unit [R F]
Esc=Escape
F1=Help

Figure 32.3

The Trustee name list of trustee assignments for a file.

Viewing Trustee Assignments Using NETADMIN

NETADMIN and NWADMIN provide similar services. NETADMIN runs at the DOS prompt, and NWADMIN runs under Windows. Unlike NWADMIN, NETADMIN displays only the effect of assigning NDS trustee rights, not file system rights.

To view an NDS trustee assignment using NETADMIN, proceed as follows:

1. From the DOS prompt, log in as a Supervisor object rights, or at least Read rights to the ACL property of the leaf or container object you plan to view. The NetAdmin Options menu appears.

2. From the NetAdmin Options menu, select Manage Objects. The Object, Class list will appear. From this list you can browse the tree in search of the object whose trustee list you wish to view.

3. After you select the object, press F10. The Actions for ... menu for that object appears.

4. From the Actions for ... menu, select View or edit the trustees of this object. The Trustees of this Object menu appears.

5. From the Trustees of this Object menu, select Trustees. The Property, Rights, Trustee list appears, as shown in figure 32.4. The figure shows user .THess.SC.EBDB, with an assignment of Compare, Read, Write, Add or Delete Self, and Supervisor to all properties of the organization EBDB, which is being viewed. The same user also has all object rights. The container EBDB is assigned Read rights to its own Login Script and Print Job Configuration properties. [root] is assigned Read rights to the Printer Control property.

6. Press Esc several times to return to the main NetAdmin Options menu.

To illustrate how you use NETADMIN to view effective rights, establishing several hypothetical terms will be useful. For the sake of this illustration, assume the target object is the object for which you want to query. Assume that the trustee is the object whose effective rights (to the target) you want to view. When you view effective rights between objects, you must first select the target object. After you select the target object, you must call up the menu to view the effective rights of the trustee. What you see is a list of rights that the trustee effectively has to the target.

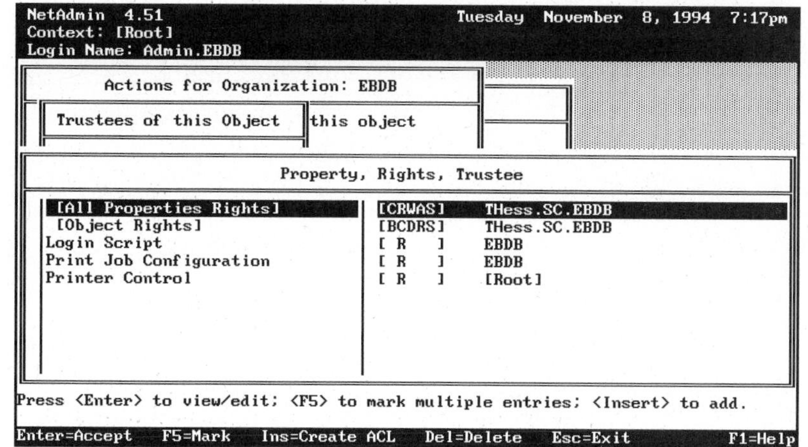

Figure 32.4
Viewing NDS trustee assignments for an object with NETADMIN.

For example, suppose you want to view the effective rights of the user .cn=BSaunders.ou=NY.o=EBDB for the container object .ou=MIA.o=EBDB. The user BSaunders is the trustee. The container object MIA is the target. You would need to select the target MIA and view the effective rights for the trustee BSaunders.

To view the effective rights of a trustee to a target object using NETADMIN, proceed as follows:

1. From the NetAdmin Options menu, select Manage Objects. The Object, Class list appears. You can browse the tree in search of the target object.

2. After you select the object, press F10. The Actions for ... menu for that object appears.

3. From the Actions for ... menu, select View or edit the trustees of this object. The Trustees of this Object menu appears.

4. From the Trustees of this Object menu, select Effective Rights. You are prompted to enter an object name. The name you enter is the trustee object name. You can enter the complete object name or press Insert to browse the tree. After you have filled the input box with a trustee object name, press Enter. The Effective Rights (object) list appears, as shown in figure 32.5. The user BSaunder has no All Properties rights, Browse object rights, and Compare and Read rights to the CA Public Key property. Press PgUp or PgDn to scroll through the list of effective rights.

5. Press Esc several times to exit NETADMIN.

```
NetAdmin 4.51                                   Tuesday November 8, 1994 7:51pm
Context: EBDB
Login Name: Admin.EBDB

   Actions for Organizational Unit: NY
  Trustees of this Object  this object

                     Effective rights (Bsaunder.NY)

 [All Properties Rights]                                          [      ]
 [Object Rights]                                                  [B     ]
 Authority Revocation                                             [      ]
 Back Link                                                        [      ]
 Bindery Property                                                 [      ]
 CA Public Key                                                    [CR    ]
 Certificate Revocation                                           [      ]
 Certificate Validity Interval                                    [      ]
 City                                                             [      ]
▼Cross Certificate Pair                                           [      ]

Press <Enter> to view effective rights details.
Enter=Accept   Esc=Exit                                                  F1=Help
```

Figure 32.5
Viewing NDS effective rights for an object with NETADMIN.

Using NWADMIN To View Trustee Rights

Much like NETADMIN, you can use NWADMIN to view rights. NWADMIN offers the additional ability of enabling you to view rights in the file system as well as rights to the tree. Unlike NETADMIN, the NWADMIN utility can show you effective rights by viewing the trustee or the target objects. This bidirectional ability applies only to the rights of objects to other objects, not the file system.

Before you can view trustee assignments or effective rights, you must log in as a user with at least Read rights to the target and trustee objects' ACL property. You obtain the best results if you have effective object rights of Supervisor to both objects.

The following section discusses the way to view rights using NWADMIN. After you log in as a user with sufficient rights, launch NWADMIN (the NetWare Administrator utility) from the Windows Program Manager.

Using NWADMIN To View File System Trustee Assignments

Before you can view the rights of the trustee object to a target file or directory, you must first select the target file or directory. You can view the trustee assignments and/or effective rights of the trustee from the details menu. The technique to view trustee assignments and effective rights for a file are the same as for a directory, except that the target you select is a file rather than a directory.

To view trustee assignments to a directory, proceed as follows:

1. From the main screen of NWADMIN, select the target directory. Press Enter, or, from the Object menu, select Details. The Directory:name dialog box appears.

2. From the Directory:name dialog box, click on the Trustees of this Directory button from the right. The Trustees of this Directory dialog box appears, as shown in figure 32.6.

3. Click on the Cancel button or press Esc to return to the main NWADMIN screen.

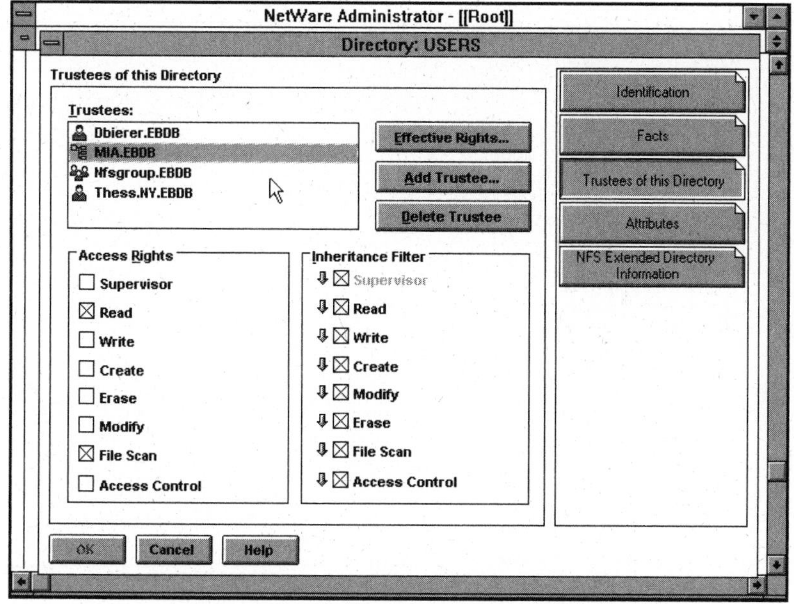

Figure 32.6
Viewing directory trustee assignments with NWADMIN.

To view effective rights to a directory, proceed as follows:

1. From the main screen of NWADMIN, select the target directory. Press Enter, or, from the Object menu, select Details. The Directory:name dialog box appears.

2. From the Directory:name dialog box, select the Trustees of this Directory button from the right. The Trustees of this Directory dialog box appears.

3. From the Trustees of this Directory dialog box, click on the Effective Rights button. The Effective Rights dialog box appears, as shown in figure 32.7. Click on the browse button at the right to select a trustee whose effective rights you want to monitor.

4. Click on the Close and then Cancel buttons to return to the NWADMIN main screen.

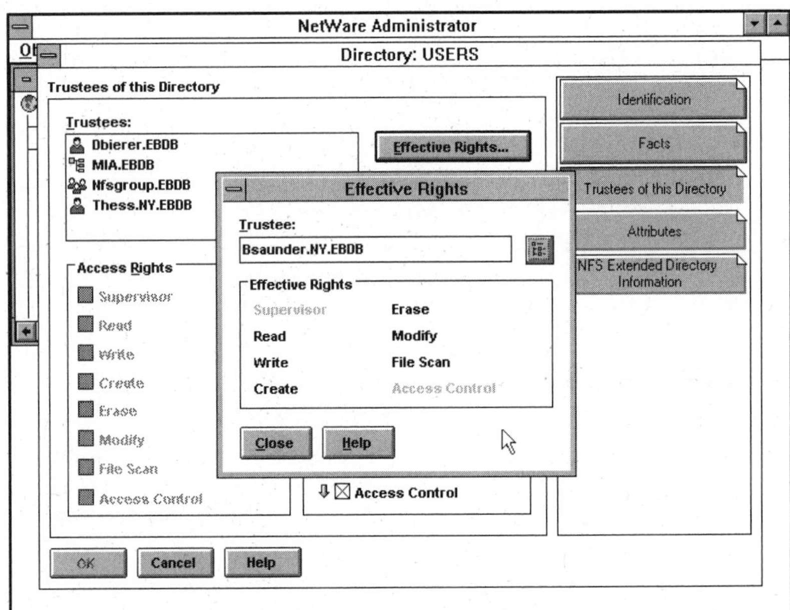

Figure 32.7
Viewing effective rights to a directory with NWADMIN.

Using NWADMIN To View NDS Trustee Assignments

To view NDS trustee assignments to an object, proceed as follows:

1. From the main screen of NWADMIN, select the target object. Press from the Object menu, select Trustees of this Object. The Trustees of <object name> dialog box appears, as shown in figure 32.8.

2. From the Trustees of <object name> dialog box, from the Trustees list, select the trustee whose rights assignments you want to view. The gray shading in the Object and Property rights at the bottom disappear and are replaced by a blank or a check-marked box. A gray box indicates an unknown status.

3. Click the Cancel button or press Esc to return to the main NWADMIN screen.

You can also view a trustee assignment by selecting the trustee and proceeding as follows:

1. From the main screen of NWADMIN, select the trustee object. From the Object menu, select Rights to Other Objects. The Search Context dialog box appears.

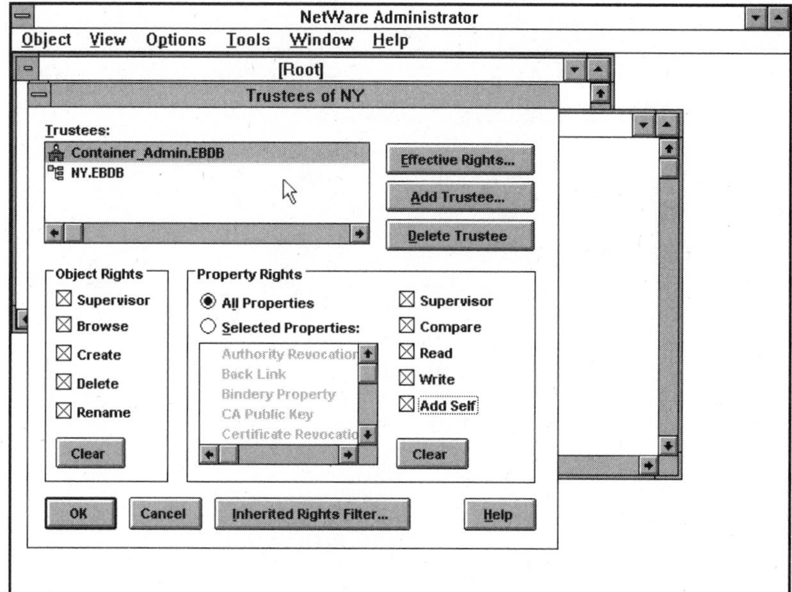

Figure 32.8
Viewing NDS Trustee Assignments with NWADMIN.

2. From the Search Context dialog box, enter the target object name or use the Browse button at the right to locate the target object name. When the target has been located, click on the OK button. The Rights to Other Objects dialog box appears, as shown in figure 32.9. The trustee object BSaunder has Browse, Create, Delete and Rename object rights and Compare and Read property rights to the Austin.MFG target object.

If you are unsure of the target to which the trustee object has rights assigned, checkmark the Search **E**ntire Subtree field. NWADMIN searches all objects below the Search Context for any rights assignments.

The technique for viewing effective NDS rights is very similar to the techniques discussed above. To view the effective rights of a trustee object over a target object, you can proceed in one of the following ways:

- Select the target object and from the **O**bject menu, select Trustees of this Object. Then click on the **E**ffective Rights button. Fill in the trustee object name in the Object **N**ame field. The effective object and property rights appear below in bold. Figure 32.10 shows the trustee object BSaunder and his effective rights to the target object ou=HongKong.o=MFG.

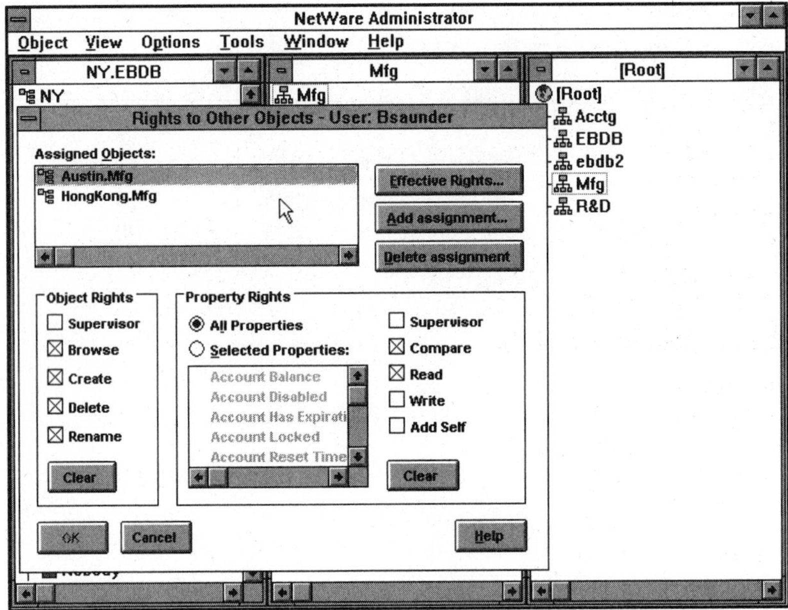

Figure 32.9
Viewing NDS trustee assignments from the trustee object's perspective with NWADMIN.

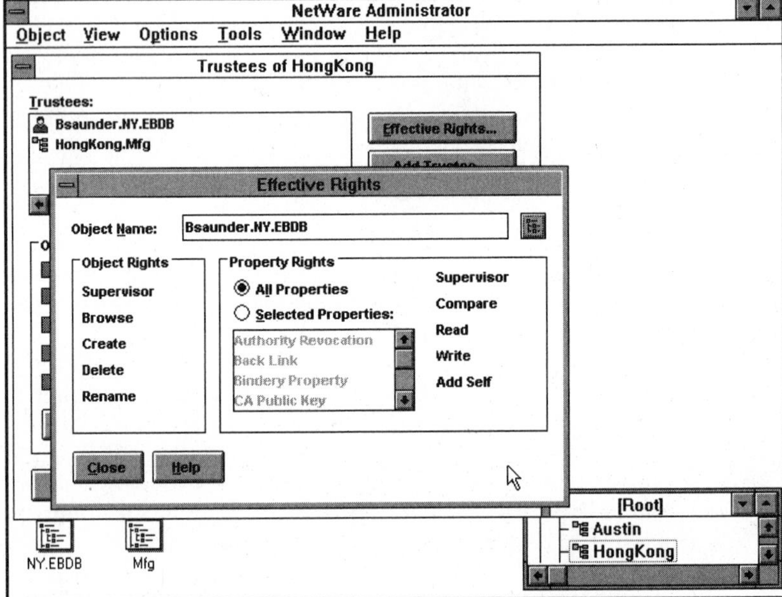

Figure 32.10
Viewing NDS effective rights by selecting the trustees of this object option.

- Select the trustee object and from the Object menu, select Rights to Other Objects. Click on the OK button and then the Effective Rights button. Enter the object name in the Object Name field. The effective object and property rights appear below in bold. Figure 32.11 shows the target object ou=HongKong.o=MFG and the effective rights of the trustee object BSaunder in bold.

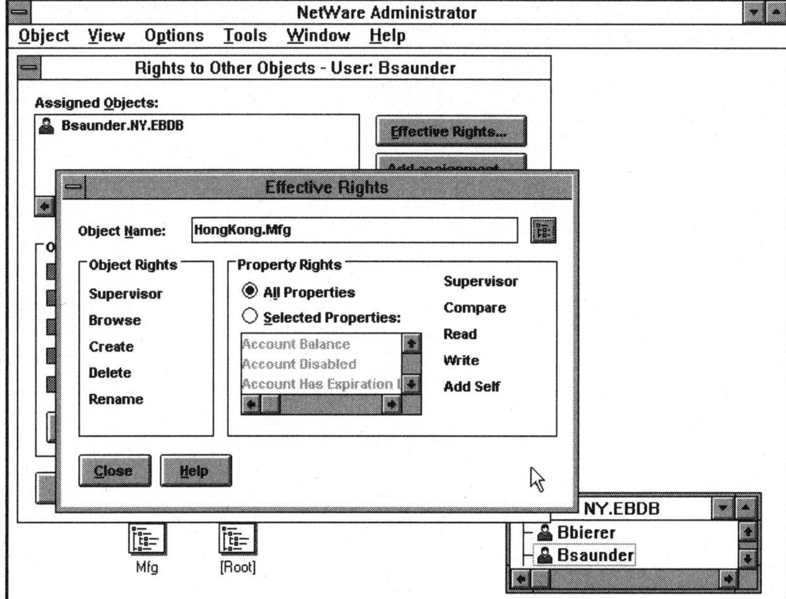

Figure 32.11

Viewing NDS effective rights by selecting the rights to other objects option.

Summary

This chapter covered viewing trustee assignments in detail. As you discovered, there are several types of assignments you might want to view:

- File system file and directory trustee assignments
- NDS object and property trustee assignments
- Effective rights

Five primary utilities are available for viewing rights: RIGHTS, NLIST, FILER, NETADMIN, and NWADMIN. You can use the first four from the DOS command prompt. NWADMIN is the Windows-based administration tool.

Key terms explained in the first part of the chapter included trustee, access control lists, security equivalences, [Public], rights in general, and effective rights. Toward the end of the chapter, you learned that when referring to the rights of an object to another object, a trustee object and a target object are involved. The trustee object is the object that receives rights to the target object.

You can use RIGHTS to view rights to the file system. It shows your effective rights in any given directory, the list of trustees assigned to a given directory, the setting for the IRF, and can trace the path of inherited rights. You can use NLIST to display the ACL property of the object(s) specified. FILER is for displaying trustee assignments and effective rights for both files and directories.

NETADMIN and NWADMIN are much more versatile when used to view rights. You can use NETADMIN to show trustee assignments and effective rights. Before you can use NETADMIN to view effective rights or trustee assignments, you must move to the target object. NWADMIN enables you to view rights by first selecting the target or the trustee object. You can also view rights to the file system by using NWADMIN.

The next chapter covers assigning drive mappings.

Assigning Drive Mappings

Once you have installed the applications you plan to use on your network and have assigned trustee rights, and the directory structure is in place, the next step is to gain access to the file system. The most convenient method of doing so is through drive mappings. This chapter explains what drive mappings are, and how you can create them from the DOS, Windows, and OS/2 operating systems.

Introducing Drive Mappings

A *drive mapping* provides to your local operating system a way to reference the file system on a NetWare file server. DOS, for example, is capable of reading or writing data on external drives. You can attach a CD-ROM player to your DOS computer, for example, and load a series of driver files. After rebooting your computer, DOS "thinks" of the external CD-ROM player as (perhaps) drive E. Likewise, you can have an external tape drive, or even an external hard drive. NetWare takes advantage of this DOS feature to allow DOS to reference a NetWare volume as if it were an external DOS hard drive. The actual drivers that allow DOS to access data on a NetWare volume are included in the workstation shell software. FIO.VLM (File Input/Output) works with REDIR.VLM (Redirecter) to allow DOS to import and export files through the network.

The Windows and OS/2 operating systems, which grew out of the DOS family of operating systems, maintain a similar structure for referring to external hard drives. In the case of OS/2, the NetWare shell drivers are called through the CONFIG.SYS file. In the case of Windows, additional drivers are called through the SYSTEM.INI file. Windows NT and Windows for Workgroups have NetWare drivers loaded through the CONFIG.SYS file.

The drive mapping itself is a drive letter assigned to a volume and directory. The following are some rules of DOS drive mapping; the rules for OS/2 and Windows are similar.

- The letters available for mapping go from A to the letter specified in the LASTDRIVE= parameter in the CONFIG.SYS file.
- If you choose to map a letter assigned to a physical device (such as drive A, which is assigned to your first floppy drive), the physical device becomes temporarily unavailable. You can use the MAP DELETE command to remove the drive mapping, which makes the physical device available again.
- The drive letter first assigned to the LOGIN directory on volume SYS of a NetWare file server is determined by the First Network Drive setting in the NET.CFG file under the NetWare DOS Requester section.
- Drive mappings are maintained individually per network connection. If users Bob and Mary, for example, logged in on their individual workstations, NetWare maintains a separate connection for each of them. Bob's drive letters do not interfere with Mary's drive letters in any way.

- Drive mappings can be added, deleted, or changed at any time while a user is logged in.
- If you make a drive mapping to an already existing drive mapping, the new mapping overwrites the existing mapping.
- When a user logs out, that user loses all drive mappings, except the initial mapping used to log in to a file server in the first place.
- Drive mappings can be assigned from the command line; from a batch file, menu, or login script; or through the NETUSER or NWUSER utilities.
- Drive maps only mark the last directory you are in. If you assign a drive letter G to a directory SYS:DATA\TEMP, for example, and then use the CD command to change to the SYS:DATA directory, the drive map will reflect the SYS:DATA directory rather than the initial assignment.
- To make DOS drive mappings available when you first log in, issue map commands in a login script.
- To make drive mappings available in Windows, use the "permanent" button in the NWUSER utility.

Types of Drive Maps

There are two types of drive maps available: regular and search.

A *regular drive map* is typically assigned to a directory where you store data. Assignments can include the following:

- The user home directory where personal files are stored
- A shared data directory used by a company or department-wide application
- Client data directories where data pertaining to certain clients is stored

Regular drive assignments are typically assigned starting with the first network drive letter (as assigned in the NET.CFG file). Subsequent assignments move down the alphabet. In most cases, start the assignments with drive F, followed by G, H, and down to Z.

A *search drive map* is how NetWare coordinates with the DOS PATH. The DOS PATH contains a series of drive:\directories separated by semicolons. The directories in the PATH contain executables that you want to use on a regular basis. As long as the directory is in the path, DOS searches the PATH to run a command you issue. It doesn't matter which current directory is yours, as long as the executable is in a directory that is in the PATH.

When you first log in to the network, you run one or more login scripts (explained in Chapter 34, "Creating Login Scripts"). The login script(s) contain a series of MAP commands that assign regular and search drive mappings. Prior to the login script, the LOGIN.EXE command automatically assigns any directory in your PATH to a search drive. If you want to preserve these assignments, use either the MAP INSERT or the MAP SEARCH16:= (abbreviated MAP S16:=) command.

You can convert any regular drive mapping to and from a search drive mapping by using the MAP CHANGE command. A regular drive mapping, which is placed in the DOS PATH automatically, becomes a search drive mapping. Conversely, if you take a drive mapping out of the PATH, it becomes a regular drive mapping.

Search drive mappings typically are made to directories that contain common executables. Just as with the DOS PATH, any command you issue is executed as long as it is in a directory referenced by a search drive mapping.

Search drive mappings do not "trickle down" as do directory trustee assignments. If you want to give a user access to executables in the following directories, you have to make three separate search mappings in this case. A single search map will not suffice.

SYS:APPS\WP

SYS:APPS\DB

SYS:APPS\SS

Using the MAP Command

The primary command used to make drive map assignments is MAP.EXE. The MAP command by itself displays the current set of drive map assignments. This section shows you the basic syntax for a regular and search mapping. The latter part of this section shows you additional MAP options.

Assigning a Regular Drive Mapping

The basic syntax for a regular drive map assignment is as follows:

```
MAP <letter>:=[NDS volume name:][\directory\...\directory]
```

Letter can be any letter from A to Z, with the warning about possibly hiding physical devices (such as drive A) as noted previously.

NDS volume name is the name of the volume object to which you want to make an assignment. Note that a colon follows the volume object name. If you leave off the volume object name, the current volume is assumed.

Directory is a directory that exists on the volume. If you attempt to map to a directory that does not exist or to which you have insufficient trustee rights, you receive an error message.

The following listing illustrates the result of a regular map assignment:

```
F:\>MAP G:=.CN=EBDB_DATA.O=EBDB:\

Drive G: = EBDB_DATA: \

F:\>MAP

Drives A,B,C,D,E map to a local disk.
Drive F: = EBDB_SYS: \
Drive G: = EBDB_DATA: \

      ----    Search Drives    ----
S1: = Y:. [EBDB_SYS: \PUBLIC]
S2: = X:. [EBDB_SYS: \]
S3: = Z:. [EBDB_SYS: \PUBLIC]
S4: = C:\NWCLIENT\
S5: = C:\DOS
S6: = C:\WINDOWS
S7: = C:\NECUTILS
S8: = C:\POPTERM
S9: = W:. [EBDB_SYS: \APPS\WP]

F:\>
```

There are some shortcuts you can use when assigning a regular drive mapping. If you plan to map to the volume your default directory and drive letter are using, you can leave off the NDS volume name. The results follow:

```
MAP H:=\DATA\TEMP
```

If you know the file server and volume names as assigned when the file server was installed, you can simply indicate those names, as in the following example:

```
MAP I:=EBDB/SYS:DATA\PRVNOTES
```

If you know the volume name and are working on the target file server, you can simply specify the volume name as installed. If unsure of the volume name, type the command **VOLUMES** from the file server's console. A sample command follows:

```
MAP J:=DATA:PROJECTS\R&D
```

DOS permits you to designate your current directory by merely entering a period as the directory name. To map the current directory to drive letter K, type the following:

MAP K:=.

Assigning a Search Drive Mapping

The basic syntax to assign a search drive mapping is as follows:

```
MAP SEARCH<number>:=[NDS volume name:][\directory\...\directory]
```

Number can be from 1 to 16. Lower numbers are searched before higher numbers. If you assign a number higher than the number of search drives currently assigned, NetWare assigns the next higher number.

NDS volume name is the name of the volume object to which you want to make an assignment. Note that a colon follows the volume object name. If you leave off the volume object name, the current volume is assumed.

When the search mapping takes place, a regular drive mapping is made first. The letter is picked from the first unassigned letter starting from the bottom of the alphabet, so the search drive letters assigned are Z, Y, X, and so on. This letter is placed in the path. The following listing illustrates the results of a search mapping and the impact on the PATH. Note in the list that a mapping to drive 16 was made. When the MAP command is typed by itself, notice that drive 16 became drive 9, the next higher search drive mapping.

```
F:\>MAP SEARCH16:=.EBDB_SYS.EBDB:APPS\WP

S9: = W:. [EBDB_SYS: \APPS\WP]

F:\>MAP

Drives A,B,C,D,E map to a local disk.
Drive F: = EBDB_SYS: \
Drive G: = EBDB_DATA: \
        ----    Search Drives    ----
S1: = Y:. [EBDB_SYS: \PUBLIC]
S2: = X:. [EBDB_SYS: \]
S3: = Z:. [EBDB_SYS: \PUBLIC]
S4: = C:\NWCLIENT\
S5: = C:\DOS
S6: = C:\WINDOWS
S7: = C:\NECUTILS
S8: = C:\POPTERM
S9: = W:. [EBDB_SYS: \APPS\WP]

F:\>
```

You can abbreviate the word SEARCH by using the letter S followed by the search drive number. If you want to assign search drive 5 to volume SYS:, directory APPS\SS, for example, you can type the following:

MAP S5:=SYS:\APPS\SS

The shortcuts mentioned previously regarding server name, volume name, or leaving them off also apply to search drives.

MAP Command Variations

A number of variations on the MAP command exist, including the ability to assign a "fake root" to change a mapping between regular and search, and so on. Table 33.1 summarizes these variations with examples of each.

Table 33.1
MAP.EXE Variations

MAP Variation	Description
INS	Enables you to insert one search drive above another, which protects existing search drives. Existing search drives are renumbered one greater. The following example inserts a search drive number 1 to directory PUBLIC on volume SYS on the current file server: `MAP INS S1:=SYS:PUBLIC`

DEL	Used to delete an existing drive mapping. You can delete by letter or by S<*number*>. The following example deletes a search drive G:
	`MAP DEL G:`
	The next example deletes search drive number 3. When done, higher number search drives are renumbered one less:
	`MAP DEL S3:`

drive:=	Enables you to map drive letter *drive* in conjunction with mapping a search drive. You gain control over which letter is assigned as a search drive by using this technique. If this option is not used, the next letter (moving backward through the alphabet starting with Z) is used. The following example maps a letter S as Search Drive 4: to the WORD directory: `MAP SEARCH4:=S:=SYS:APPS\WORD`
N	Maps the next regular drive letter. Starts lettering from the first network drive. If you have drive letters F, G, J, and K mapped, the following example chooses drive letter H `MAP N .EBDB_DATA.EBDB:\PROJECTS\SALES`
C	Changes the drive mapping from regular to search or vice versa. If the existing drive mapping is a regular drive, this command changes it to a search drive mapping. If the existing drive mapping is a search drive, this command changes it to a regular drive mapping. Following is an example that converts a search drive 3, assigned to drive X, from a search to a regular drive mapping. Search drives 4 through the end are renumbered one less: `MAP C X:`
R	Maps a regular or search drive as a "fake" root directory. The following code shows you the result of this operation. A sample syntax follows: `MAP R H:=EBDB/SYS:DATA\UNIX`

The following listing illustrates the result of the MAP ROOT command:

```
F:\>MAP R H:=EBDB\SYS:DATA\UNIX

Drive H: = EBDB_SYS:DATA\UNIX \

F:\>MAP

Drives A,B,C,D,E map to a local disk.
Drive F: = EBDB_SYS: \
Drive G: = EBDB_DATA: \
Drive H: = EBDB_SYS:DATA\UNIX \
Drive I: = EBDB_SYS: \DATA\PRVNOTES
Drive J: = EBDB_DATA: \PROJECTS\R&D
Drive X: = EBDB_SYS: \
       ----    Search Drives    ----
S1: = Y:. [EBDB_SYS: \PUBLIC]
S2: = Z:. [EBDB_SYS: \PUBLIC]
S3: = C:\NWCLIENT\
S4: = C:\DOS
S5: = C:\WINDOWS
S6: = C:\NECUTILS
S7: = C:\POPTERM
S8: = W:. [EBDB_SYS: \APPS\WP]

F:\>H:

H:\>
```

Note in this listing that the assignment for drive H has an extra backslash (\) at the end of the mapping. Also note that when you change to drive H, the prompt seems to indicate that it is the root. This feature is used to prevent users from getting confused in the middle of a complex directory structure. Using this technique, they only see the directory you have mapped them to and the subdirectories. If they execute a CD command to change to the "root," they are instead sent to the "fake root" you have assigned.

Stop The use of fake roots is not a replacement for proper security. Any user with a modicum of network savvy can "unroot" a "fake root." Following are some techniques for "unrooting" drive H.

continues

In the first technique, you simply change the directory to a directory name preceded by the volume name. Because DOS recognizes volume names, the command causes the fake root to self destruct.

```
H:\>CD SYS:DATA\UNIX

H:\DATA\UNIX>
```

Note that the prompt has now changed to reflect the fact that the directory is no longer mapped as a fake root.

The next technique involves using the MAP command to change the mapping of the current drive letter. As an alternative, any user could map another drive letter to any known directory where he has rights.

```
H:\>MAP H:=.EBDB_SYS.EBDB:DATA\UNIX

Drive H: = EBDB_SYS: \DATA\UNIX

H:\DATA\UNIX>
```

Using NETUSER To Assign a Drive Mapping

You can use the NETUSER.EXE utility to assign a drive mapping. The advantage of NETUSER is that you have help screens and can use the Insert key to browse the NDS tree and directory structure of the chosen volume. The disadvantage is that any mappings made in NETUSER are temporary and will not be in effect the next time you log in.

To assign a regular drive map, proceed as follows:

1. At the DOS prompt, execute the NETUSER utility by typing the following:

   NETUSER

2. From the main NETUSER menu, select Drives. The Available Options menu appears, giving you a choice of mapping a Drive Mapping (regular drive mapping) or Search Mapping (search drive mapping). For the purposes of this discussion, choose Drive Mapping. The Current Drive Mappings list appears, as shown in figure 33.1. This is a list of all local and regular drive mappings.

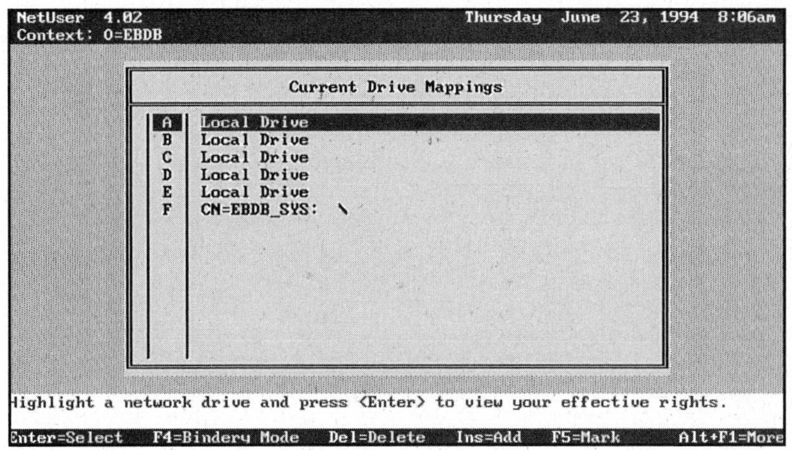

Figure 33.1

The Current Drive Mappings list.

3. In the Current Drive Mappings list, you can select a drive mapping and press F3 to modify the assignment. The F4 key switches to bindery mode. When in *bindery mode*, assignments are referenced by server and volume (as in NetWare 3.*x*), rather than by NDS volume objects.

   To add a new regular drive mapping, press Insert. NETUSER selects the next drive letter past your first network drive (the first network drive is set in your NET.CFG file and defaults to F). If you want to assign another drive letter, delete the drive letter presented to you and type in the desired letter. Press Enter to move to the next step. The Select Directory input box appears.

4. In the Select Directory input box, enter the volume object and the desired directory as follows:

   <NDS volume object name:><directory\...\directory>

   Alternatively, you can press Insert once again to browse the structure. If you select a directory, you move down the directory structure. Pressing Enter on the double dots (..) moves you to the parent directory (up the structure). If you move up past the root of the volume, you are taken into the NDS structure where you can select another volume object. As you browse, the name and path are built into the Select Directory input box. When the desired name appears, press Esc to exit the browse mode. You are returned to the Select Directory input box.

If you are in bindery mode, you can enter assignments in the Select Directory input box using the NetWare 3.*x*-style syntax, as follows:

<server name/><volume name:><directory\...\directory>

continues

For example, if the server name is FS_Chicago, the volume is DATA, and the directory is PROJECTS\SMITH, enter the following:

FS_Chicago/DATA:PROJECTS\SMITH

5. In the Select Directory input box and after the desired name has been entered, press Enter to finalize the drive mapping. A prompt box appears, asking the following:

   ```
   Do you want to map root this drive?
   ```

   If you want to establish a fake root, enter yes; otherwise, enter no. You return to the Current Drive Mappings list. The new drive mapping appears on the list. When you exit NETUSER, you will find that the drive mapping remains available until you change it or log out.

In a similar fashion, you can use NETUSER to assign search drive mappings. To add a search drive mapping, proceed as follows:

1. From the DOS prompt, execute the NETUSER utility by typing the following:

   NETUSER

2. From the main NETUSER menu, select Drives. The Available Options menu appears, giving you a choice of mapping a Drive Mapping (regular drive mapping) or Search Mapping (search drive mapping). For the purposes of this discussion, choose Search Mapping. The Current Search Mappings list appears, as shown in figure 33.2. This is a list of all local and search drive mappings in the DOS PATH. The number of the search drive appears to the left. To the right are the drive letter, NDS volume object, and directory.

3. In the Current Search Mappings list, you can select a drive mapping and press F3 to modify the assignment. The F4 key switches to bindery mode as discussed previously.

   To add a new search drive mapping, press Insert. NETUSER selects the next search mapping number in sequence. If you want to assign another number, delete the number presented to you and type the desired number. Note that if the number you select is already assigned, the assignment you now make is inserted above the number indicated; this is the equivalent of performing a MAP INSERT command.

   Press Enter to move to the next step. The Select Directory input box appears.

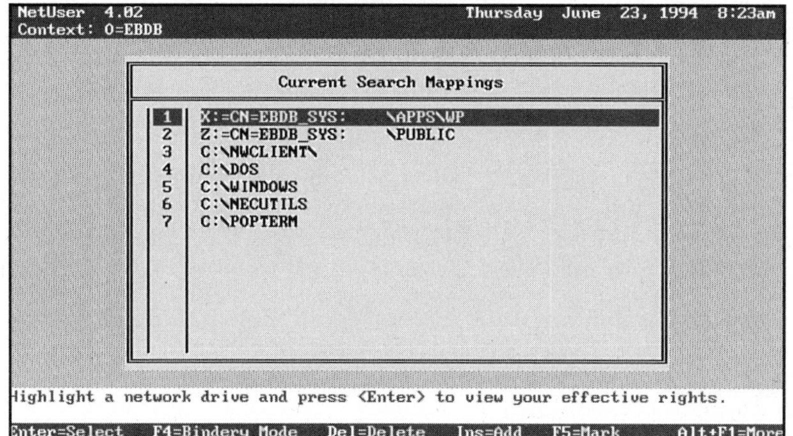

Figure 33.2

The Current Search Mappings list in NETUSER.

4. In the Select Directory input box, **enter** the volume object and the desired directory as follows:

   <NDS volume object name:><*directory*\...*directory*>

   Alternatively, you can press Insert again to browse the structure. If you select a directory, you move down the directory structure. Pressing Enter on the double dots moves you to the parent directory (up the structure). If you move up past the root of the volume, you are taken into the NDS structure where you can select another volume object. As you browse, the name and path is built up in the Select Directory input box. When the desired name appears, press Esc to exit the browse mode. You are returned to the Select Directory input box.

5. From the Select Directory input box, after the desired name has been entered, press Enter to finalize the drive mapping. A prompt box appears asking the following:

   ```
   Do you want to map root this drive?
   ```

   If you want to establish a fake root, enter yes; otherwise, enter no. You return to the Current Search Mappings list. The new search mapping appears on the list. When you exit NETUSER, you will find that the search drive mapping remains available until you change it or log out.

Assigning Drive Letters in Windows

Windows picks all drive letters assigned in your login script when you first log in. Once you are in Windows, you can assign additional drive letters through the NetWare User Tools utility NWUSER.EXE, which can be accessed directly from the Windows Program Manager or from File Manager.

To access NWUSER from the File Manager, select the **D**isk menu, then **N**etwork Connections. You are now in NWUSER in the NetWare Drive Connections dialog box.

Drive mapping assignments in NWUSER are made in the NetWare Drive Connections dialog box (see fig. 33.3).

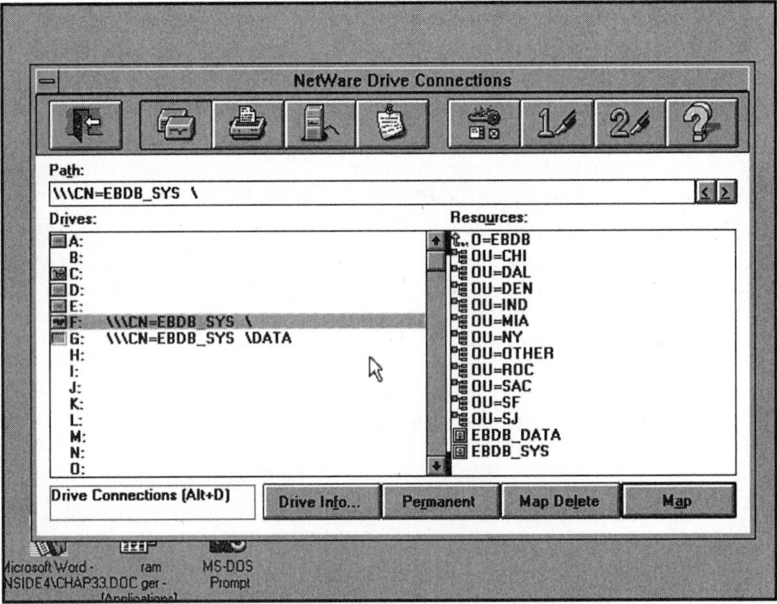

Figure 33.3
The NWUSER NetWare Drive Connections dialog box.

Table 33.2 summarizes the meaning of each of the drive icons that appear in the NetWare Drive Connections dialog box.

Table 33.2
NWUSER NetWare Drive Connections Drive Icons

Drive Icon	Description
	Local drive (which would be drive A, C, and so on)
	Temporary drive mapping assigned through NWUSER. This assignment is lost when you exit Windows.
	Search drive assignment picked up before you entered this dialog box. This assignment could be from your initial login script or, if you issue a command to create a search drive, from a DOS box while inside Windows. (This is only possible if you checkmarked Global Drives and Paths in the NetWare Settings dialog box.)
	Permanent drive mapping. These mappings are restored the next time you get back into Windows. (This is possible if you checkmarked Restore During Startup in the NetWare Settings dialog box.)

To create a drive mapping to a directory on a volume object within your NDS tree, using the NWUSER utility, proceed as follows:

1. From the Windows Program Manager, launch the NWUSER utility by clicking on the NetWare Tools icon.

2. In the NWUSER utility main menu, select the second icon from the left in the NWUSER toolbar to display the NetWare Drive Connections dialog box. You also can press Alt+D.

3. From the Resources list, select the desired NDS volume object, browsing the tree if necessary. Once the volume object is selected, an entry appears in the Path field. Double-click on the volume object in the Resources list to open the directory structure for that volume. Continue in this fashion until the desired directory is indicated in the Path field.

You can use the right and left arrows to the right of the Path field to change the position of the root in the drive mapping. When you click on the left arrow, the root moves down the structure. When you click on the right arrow, the root moves up the structure. Notice as you experiment with this function that the backslash and a preceding space move right and left in the path.

4. From the NetWare Drive Connections dialog box, select (under the Drives scroll box) the desired drive letter you want to map.

5. After the path and drive letter are finalized, click on the Map button to create the drive mapping. You can now make use of the drive mapping in other applications. Press the Exit icon (left side of the toolbar) to exit NWUSER, or press Alt+F4.

Other options in the NetWare Drive Connections dialog box are summarized in table 33.3. These include getting drive information, making a drive mapping permanent, and deleting a drive mapping.

Table 33.3
NetWare Drive Connections—Additional Options

Option Button	Description
Drive Info	This option gives you information on the selected drive mapping. The information given includes the following: *Server*—The name, revision level, and license information of the file server that contains the volume mapped. *Path*—The volume and directory path mapped. *User Name*—The name of the user connecting to this server. For servers inside your NDS tree, the user name will be the same. For servers outside of the tree (including NetWare 3.*x* or older), the name will be the user name initially used to attach to the server. You will also get a list of your effective rights in the directory mapped.
Permanent	Changes the icon from a regular mapping to the icon with a red "squiggle" in the center, representing a network connection. If you select Restore During Startup in the NetWare Settings dialog box (selectable from NWUSER), all permanent drive mappings are restored. If the server is not accessible, a warning message appears. If you are not already logged in to the network, you are asked for your user name and password before the mapping can be restored.
Map Delete	Removes the drive mapping. It has the same effect as performing the MAP DELETE command.

NWUSER can also be used to map drive letters to file servers and volumes outside of your NDS tree. Such mappings must be made through bindery emulation. To map a drive letter to a NetWare 3.*x* or 2.*x* server, or to a NetWare 4.*x* server outside of your tree, proceed as follows:

1. From the Windows Program Manager, launch the NWUSER utility by clicking on the NetWare Tools icon.

2. From the NWUSER utility main menu, click on the fourth icon from the left in the NWUSER toolbar to open the NetWare Connections dialog box. Alternatively, you can press Alt+C.

3. From the Resources list in the NetWare Connections dialog box, select the server that is outside of your NDS tree. Click the Login button, and the Login To NetWare dialog box is displayed, as shown in figure 33.4.

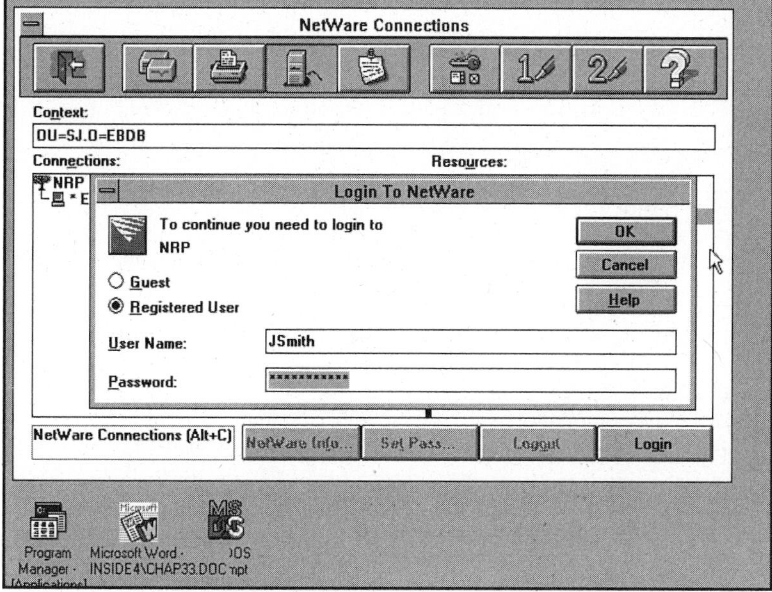

Figure 33.4

The Login To NetWare dialog box.

4. In the Login To NetWare dialog box, enter your login name and password. Click on OK to log in.

If you choose to log in to another NDS tree, you lose connections to all file servers in your current NDS tree. If you choose to log in to another NetWare 4 server outside your NDS tree, you are connected through bindery emulation and retain the connections to servers in your current tree. The same applies to NetWare 3.*x* or 2.*x* servers; connections to NetWare 4 servers in your current NDS tree are maintained.

5. Click on the second icon from the left on the NWUSER toolbar to display the NetWare Drive Connections dialog box. You also can press Alt+D.
6. In the Resources list, select the desired server and volume. After the server and volume are selected, an entry appears in the Path field. Double-click on the volume icon in the Resources list to open the directory structure for that volume. Continue in this fashion until the desired directory is indicated in the Path field.
7. Under the Drives scroll box, select the desired drive letter you want to map.
8. After the path and drive letter choices are finalized, click on the Map button to create the drive mapping. You can now make use of the drive mapping in other applications. Press the Exit icon (left side of the toolbar) to exit NWUSER, or press Alt+F4.

The NWUSER utility does not create search drive mappings. Windows normally does not need search drive mappings. If you find yourself in Windows needing a search drive mapping, there are two techniques that you can use:

- Use MAP to create a search drive mapping before going into Windows.
- Select the NetWare Settings icon from inside NWUSER and checkmark the Global Drives and Paths setting. Open the DOS prompt from the Windows Program Manager main group. At the DOS prompt, use the MAP command to create a search drive mapping.

Accessing the File System in OS/2

OS/2 views the network in a different conceptual fashion than does DOS. The network serves as an extension to the OS/2 High Performance File System (HPFS). The NetWare Client for OS/2 v2.1 allows the OS/2 workstation to seamlessly browse through the servers and volumes available in any given NDS tree.

Native OS/2 applications can use network resources as if they were part of the local HPFS. DOS or Windows applications running under OS/2 require you to map a drive letter. This section introduces you to both methods of accessing the file system on a NetWare 4 file server.

Accessing the Network Using Native OS/2 Methods

The network is available to an OS/2 workstation using the Network icon. Double-click on this icon to produce the Network - Icon View window. Here, you see icons for each type of network to which you are connected. Networks could include NetWare, SNA, or perhaps LAN Manager, for example. When you double-click on the NetWare icon, you see the NetWare - Icon View, as shown in figure 33.5.

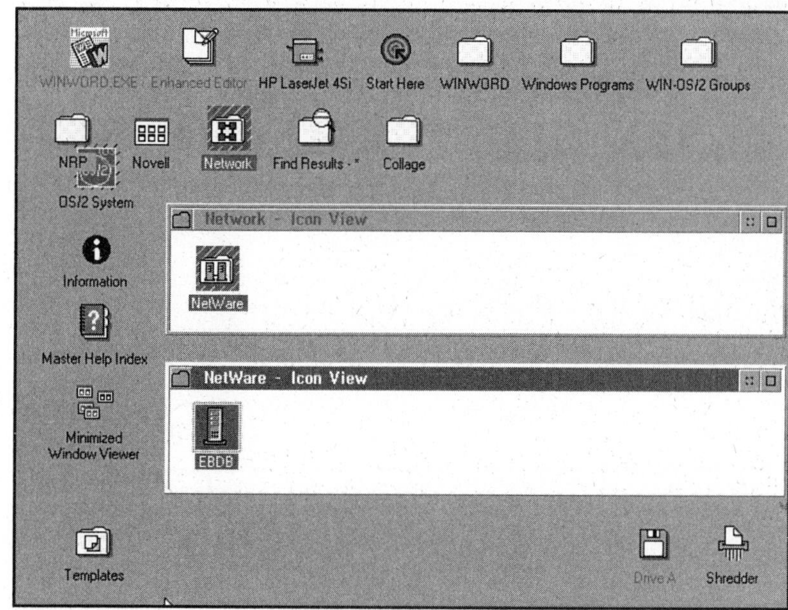

Figure 33.5
Network and NetWare Icon views in OS/2.

When you double-click on a server icon from the NetWare - Icon View window, you are asked to supply a login name and password (see fig. 33.6).

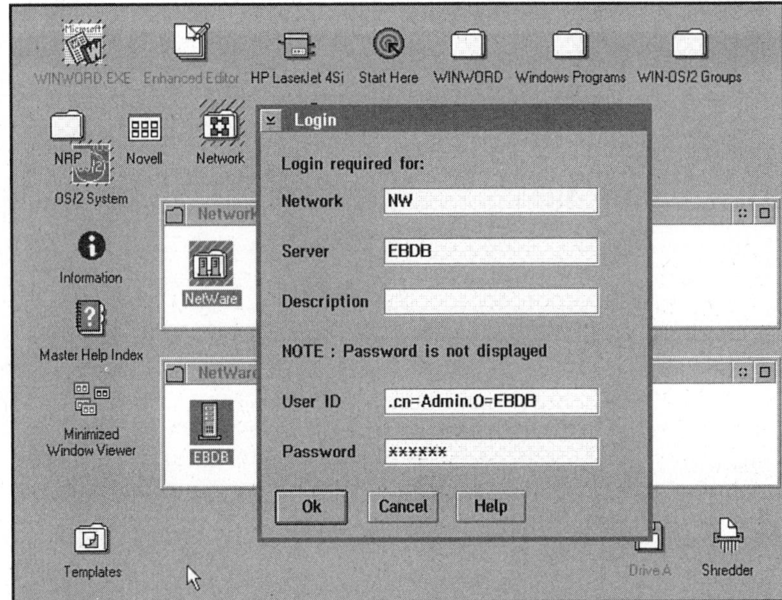

Figure 33.6
The NetWare Login screen.

After you have logged in successfully, you see an icon view window for that server. All volume and print queue resources associated with that printer are displayed. Double-click on a volume resource to browse the directory structure. Double-click on any directory for an icon view of that directory. To alter your view, as with any OS/2 icon view window, select the menu button at the upper left corner of the window. From the drop-down menu, select <u>O</u>pen. From the <u>O</u>pen menu, select the desired view. <u>D</u>etails view, for example, gives you a listing with file names, size, date, and time.

Assigning Drive Mappings in OS/2

To assign drive mappings used by DOS or Windows applications, there are several techniques. One method is to use a command prompt. Another involves the NetWare Tools utility provided with the NetWare Client for OS/2 v2.1.

To create a drive mapping using a command prompt, proceed as follows:

1. From the OS/2 desktop, select the OS/2 System - Icon View window.

2. From the OS/2 System - Icon View window, select Command Prompts. The Command Prompts - Icon View window appears.

3. From the Command Prompts - Icon View window, select the desired kind of command prompt: OS/2, WIN-OS/2, or DOS. You also have a choice of window or full-screen.

Drive mappings created in OS/2 windows are shared by all OS/2 applications and windows. Drive mappings created in WIN-OS/2 or DOS command prompts are *private* and are not shared.

4. From an OS/2 command prompt, enter the MAP command, exactly as described previously. The syntax for the MAP command from an OS/2 command prompt must follow the older NetWare 3.*x* syntax in which you specify a file server name, a volume name, and the directory path.

When executing commands on a file server from an OS/2 command prompt, remember that the commands located in PUBLIC are DOS commands. You can still execute them from OS/2, but OS/2 first creates a DOS shell and takes you in as a bindery client before executing the command. The best course of action is to either stick with the graphical interface or to execute OS/2-specific commands, such as those in the PUBLIC\OS2 directory.

5. From a DOS command prompt, you also can issue a MAP command, but the effect is limited to this window only. The DOS session uses bindery emulation. Before you can perform the MAP command you must first log in as a bindery user. The syntax for the MAP command must also use the file server/volume:directory mentioned previously for OS/2 command prompt mapping.

6. At a WIN-OS/2 command prompt, you need to use the Windows File Manager to create a drive mapping. Unlike the new NetWare client software, the WIN-OS/2 interface uses a NetWare 3.*x* interface. The current NetWare Windows drivers cause you to jump to the NWUSER utility when mapping a drive letter to a NetWare volume. In the WIN-OS2 interface, when you go to assign a drive mapping through File Manager, you have to Browse the network, Attach to a server, then perform the drive mapping. As with DOS, the WIN-OS/2 interface uses bindery emulation. Drive mappings are based on the file server/volume:directory style of drive mapping mentioned above.

Alternatively, you can create drive mapping using the NetWare User Tools, available by clicking the Novell icon, provided by the NetWare Client for OS/2 v2.1 shell. To assign a drive mapping using the tools, proceed as follows:

1. From the OS/2 desktop, select the Novell icon. From the Novell - Icon View window that appears, select the NetWare Tools utility.

2. From the NetWare Tools utility, click on **D**isk Drives from the **T**ools menu. You see the Disk Drives list box with a list of local and network drives.

3. From the Disk Drives list box, double-click on the drive you want to map or press Insert. The Map dialog box appears (see fig. 33.7).

Figure 33.7
The Map dialog box in NetWare Tools.

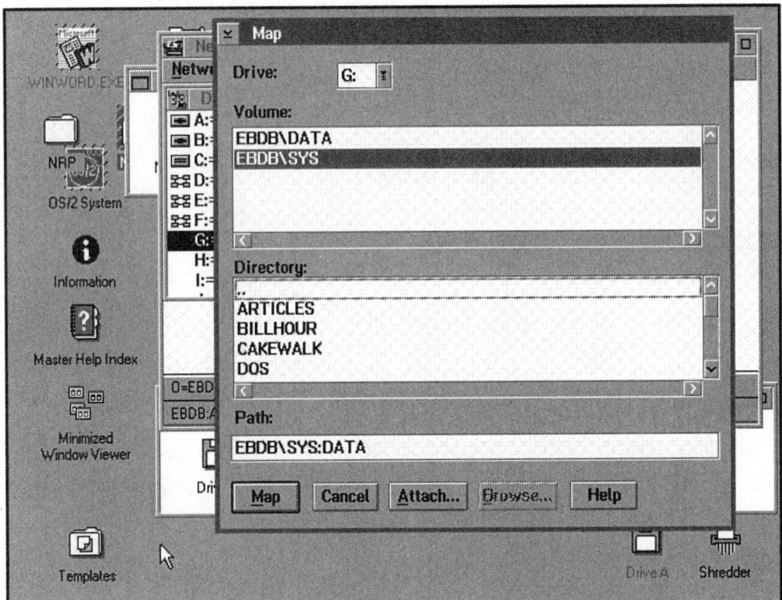

Change the desired drive letter by scrolling through the choices of letters in the Drive field. Select the desired volume in the Volume field. The Directory field contains a list of directories of that volume. The Path field continues to build up as you select directories.

4. When you are to finalize the mapping, select the **M**ap button. You are returned to the NetWare Tools - Disk Drives screen. You can continue to add drive mappings, or exit the utility. Drives mapped using the NetWare Tools utility are available for any OS/2 graphical window or command prompt.

Managing Drive Map Objects

Drive map objects can be used in conjunction with the MAP command. A *drive map object* is a method of representing a drive mapping in the NDS tree, and it becomes an intermediate point of reference that is used in a MAP command. When using a drive

map object, instead of making a direct assignment to a volume object and directory path on that volume, you must do the following:

- Assign a volume object and path to the drive map object
- Use the MAP command to assign a drive letter to the drive map object

Figure 33.8 illustrates this process.

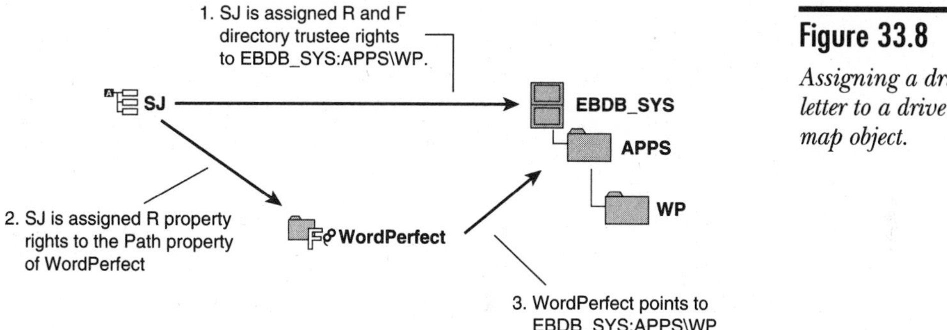

Figure 33.8

Assigning a drive letter to a drive map object.

This process might seem cumbersome, yet it has definite advantages. The main advantage is that when the directory map object is referenced in login scripts, the assignment can be changed through either of the NetWare Administrator utilities without having to change the login scripts themselves. Because you might end up placing this reference in hundreds of login scripts, using directory map objects could be quite a time saver.

To create a directory map object using NWADMIN, proceed as follows:

1. Log in as a user with sufficient rights to create the directory map object in the desired container.
2. From the Windows Program Manager, launch the NWADMIN utility.
3. Use the object browser or the scroll bar to locate the desired container.
4. Select the desired container and press Insert, or click on Create in the Object menu. The New Object dialog box appears.
5. From the New Object dialog box, select Directory Map. The Create Directory Map dialog box appears with values filled in, as shown in figure 33.9.

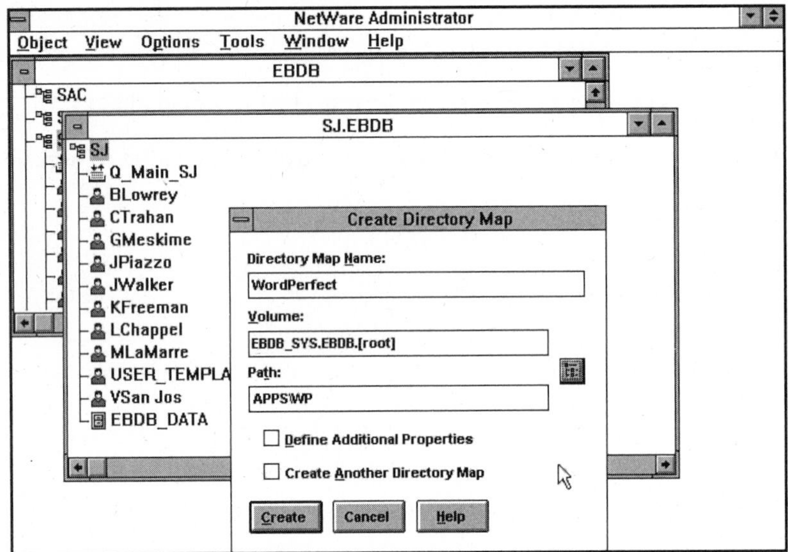

Figure 33.9
Creating a directory map object.

6. In the Create Directory Map dialog box, fill in the following fields:

   Directory Map **N**ame contains the NDS name of the new object.

   Volume is the volume where the directory is located.

   Pa**t**h is the directory the object is to point to.

7. Place a check mark in the **D**efine Additional Properties box if you immediately want to enter the Properties dialog box and make changes. Place a check mark in the Create **A**nother Directory Map box if you want to create another directory map object.

8. Press the **C**reate button when finished. The directory map object appears in the desired container.

To create a directory map object using NETADMIN, proceed as follows:

1. Log in as a user with sufficient rights to create the directory map object in the desired container.

2. From the DOS prompt, launch the NETADMIN utility.

3. Use the Manage Objects menu or the Manage According to Search Pattern menu to locate the desired container.

4. Select the desired container and press Enter to move within that container. Press Insert and the Select an Object Class box appears.

5. From the Select an Object Class box, select Directory Map. The Create Object Directory Map input box appears.

6. From the Create Object Directory Map input box, fill in the following fields:

   New Name contains the NDS name of the new object.

   Volume Object Name is the volume where the directory is located.

   Path on Volume is the directory the object is to point to.

   Name Space Type can be DOS, OS/2, NFS, Macintosh, or FTAM. This represents the type of name space on the desktop systems that will most likely use this object. If in doubt, or if there is more than one type of desktop system that might use this object, select DOS.

7. Press F10 when finished. You see a prompt box asking if you want to create another directory map object. Answer yes or no depending on what you plan to do next. When finished, the directory map object appears in the desired container.

After the directory map object has been created, you can use the MAP command to make use of it. Typically, you would place MAP commands in the container or in the profile login script so that a group of users has access to this directory. Note that the object using the directory map object must have directory trustee rights to the directory pointed to by the object. Assigning rights to the directory map object itself does not assign the proper rights.

You must assign directory trustee rights to the user, group, or in container for the directory itself, not the directory map object, before you can use it in a MAP command. If a user, for example, has no rights to the directory SYS:APPS\WP, this user will not be able to use the directory map object assigned to this directory. The directory map object is only a pointer and does not grant the entity using it any additional rights.

Note that you can assign rights to the directory map object itself. Doing so does not grant rights to the user of the object. You must make a separate trustee assignment for the user to successfully use the directory map object.

In addition to file system rights, you need to assign the users of the directory map object rights to the Path property of the directory map object. To do so using NETADMIN, proceed as follows:

1. Log in as a user with the rights to assign property rights to the directory map object.

2. From the DOS prompt, launch the NETADMIN utility.

3. Use the Manage Objects menu or the Manage According to Search Pattern menu to locate the container that contains the directory map object.

4. Select the directory map object and press Enter. The Actions for Directory Map...menu appears.

5. From the Actions for Directory Map... menu, select View or edit trustees of this object. The Trustees of this Object menu appears.

6. From the Trustees of this Object menu, select Trustees. The Property, Rights, Trustee list appears.

7. From the Property, Rights, Trustee list, press Insert. Enter the NDS name of the container, group, user, or other object to receive the rights. The Properties list appears.

8. From the Properties list, select Path and press Enter. The default right of Read appears, along with the property name Path and the name of the selected object receiving the rights. Press F10 to save your rights selection, and Alt+F10 to exit NETADMIN.

The following code illustrates a session that makes use of the directory map object through the MAP command:

```
F:\>NLIST "DIRECTORY MAP" /D
Current context: SJ.EBDB
Directory Map: WordPerfect
        Name: WordPerfect
        Access Control List (ACL):
                Subject: EBDB..
                Property: Path
                Property Rights: [ R    ]
        Host Server: EBDB_SYS.
        Object Class: Directory Map
```

```
        Object Class: Resource
        Object Class: Top
        Path:
                Volume Name: EBDB_SYS.
                Path: APPS\WP
                Name Space Type: DOS
-------------------------------------------------------------------------------

One DIRECTORY MAP object was found in this context.

One DIRECTORY MAP object was found.

F:\>RIGHTS .EBDB_SYS.EBDB:APPS\WP RF /NAME=.CTrahan.SJ.EBDB

EBDB\SYS:\APPS
Directories                                                   Rights
------------------------------------------------------------- ----------------
WP                                                            [ R    F ]


Rights for one directory were changed for .CTrahan.SJ.EBDB



F:\>LOGIN .CTrahan.SJ.EBDB

...

F:\>CX /T/A

*** Directory Services Mapping ***

SJ.EBDB
  +USER_TEMPLATE
  +BLowrey
  +CTrahan
  +GMeskime
  +JPiazzo
  +JWalker
```

```
  +KFreeman
  +LChappel
  +MLaMarre
  +VSan Jos
  +Q_Main_SJ
  +EBDB_DATA
  +WordPerfect

F:\>MAP S16:=WordPerfect

S9: = W:. [EBDB_SYS.: \APPS\WP]

F:\>
```

In the previous list, the following actions were performed:

- The NLIST command is used to display details on the directory map object WordPerfect. Note that the Read property right is assigned to the container .OU=SJ.O=EBDB.
- The user .CN=CTrahan.OU=SJ.O=EBDB is granted Read and File Scan directory trustee rights to the directory SYS:APPS\WP, which is pointed to by the directory map object.
- The user .CN=CTrahan.OU=SJ.O=EBDB logs in.
- CTrahan performs the CX command to view the contents of his current container.
- The user CTrahan performs a MAP command, assigning the directory map object WordPerfect to the last search drive. Because the user is in the container that contains the directory map object, he is not obliged to use the complete NDS name. This greatly simplifies the MAP command and makes the assignment more intuitive.

Summary

This chapter covered various aspects of creating drive mappings. The first part covered what a drive mapping is, and how it is used. Some rules of thumb regarding drive mapping were then covered. As you learned, there are two types of drive mappings: regular and search. Regular drive mappings are typically assigned to directories that contain data. Search drive mappings correspond to the DOS PATH and are assigned to directories containing program executables.

The syntax and usage of the MAP command was covered next. The MAP command can be used to create both types of drives from the DOS command line. You also learned about some variations to the MAP command, including MAP INSERT and MAP ROOT. The NETUSER utility also can be used to create drive mappings. It has the advantage of giving you helpful prompts along the way. The disadvantage is that mappings are only in effect until you log out.

The Windows equivalent to the MAP command and NETUSER is the NWUSER utility, which can be used to create regular, but not search, drive mappings. As you learned, mappings created in NWUSER can be made global so that other Windows applications and DOS sessions can make use of the mappings. The permanent setting can be configured so that Windows reconnects the drive mapping when you get back into Windows.

OS/2 has two different ways of accessing file system resources. One technique is to use the OS/2 graphical interface and the Network icon. With this technique, you can click on a series of icons until you reach the desired files and directories. Alternatively, the NetWare for OS/2 v2.1 client software provides the NetWare Tools utility, which lets you map drive letters. Drive letters mapped using the NetWare Tools are available in all OS/2 applications and command prompts. Drive letters mapped in a DOS session are private.

The last section discussed directory map objects and their use. As you learned, they point to a directory and are valid NDS objects. Directory map objects can simplify login script management and make mapping more intuitive to users in the same container. To set up a directory map object, you must also assign the user rights to the directory pointed to by the directory map object, and also Read rights to the Path property of the directory map object.

The next chapter shows you how to make drive mappings permanent. This can be accomplished by setting up a login script.

Creating Login Scripts

A *login script* is a series of instructions that the operating system executes when a user first logs in. A login script is much like a batch file in DOS. The DOS AUTOEXEC.BAT file, for example, executes when a PC initially boots up.

Login scripts are properties of user, profile, organizational unit, or organization objects. Login scripts, once created, are stored in the NDS. To use a login script, you must have both Browse object rights, and Read rights to the object's Login Script property.

Login scripts have their own language, which resembles a simple form of the popular BASIC programming language. One of the most important commands, the MAP command, is identical to the command described in the previous chapter. The first part of this chapter describes the kinds of login scripts that are available and how they are used. The commands that comprise the login script language are described in the last section of the chapter.

Understanding Types of Login Scripts

Although there is one login script language, there is more than one login script that can be executed. The types of login scripts include the following:

- Container login scripts
- Profile login scripts
- User login scripts
- The default login script
- External login scripts

Figure 34.1 is a flow chart that illustrates the order in which the various login scripts are executed.

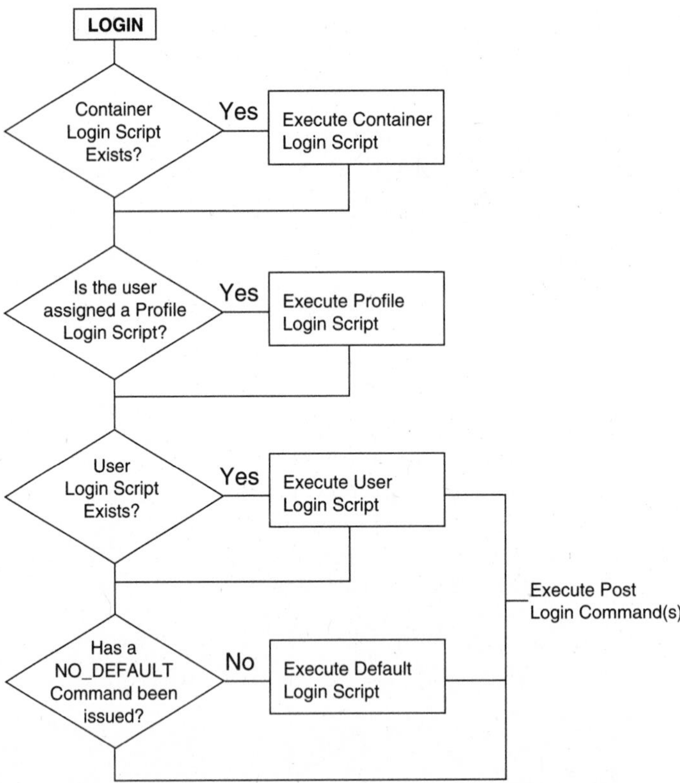

Figure 34.1

The order of login script execution.

Readers who are accustomed to NetWare 2.*x* or 3.*x* might feel disconcerted at the lack of a system login script. The closest equivalent in NetWare 4.*x* is the container login script. User objects of a given container will run the login script of their container. Commands that are common to users of this container should be placed in the container login script just as such commands were placed in the system login script in NetWare 2.*x* or 3.*x*.

As you can see from the figure, if a particular login script exists, NetWare executes it. Otherwise, control is passed to the next login script. The last check is for a user login script. If that exists, it is executed, otherwise, the system executes the default login script. A command NO_DEFAULT can be issued in the container or profile login scripts to bypass the default login script. In addition, you could issue an EXIT command, which exits the login script process altogether. These two commands are explained later in this chapter.

It is possible for the login script commands from one login script to override commands from another. Commands issued in the user login script, for example, occur last. As a result, you may accidentally have one drive mapping overwrite an earlier assignment. For this reason, it is important to document your login scripts and to carefully plan the sequence of events.

Container Login Scripts

Container login scripts are properties of container objects. The actual script itself, once created, is stored in the NDS. The container login script is used for common commands and drive mappings needed by all users in the container. This is where you would place a search drive mapping to SYS:PUBLIC, for example. In addition, if there are any applications all users in the container use (e-mail, for example), you can place necessary drive mappings, set DOS environmental variables, and so forth. Container login scripts replace the system login script used in previous versions of NetWare (3.*x* and older).

All user objects in the container run the login script of their parent container only. A user .cn=RJones.ou=Sales.ou=US.o=EBDB, for example, will run the login script for the ou=Sales container, not the ou=US or o=EBDB containers. If a user's parent container has no login script, the system moves on to a profile login script (if any).

To create a container login script using NETADMIN, proceed as follows:

1. Log in as a user with sufficient rights to Write to the container's Login Script property.
2. From the DOS prompt, run NETADMIN.

3. From the NETADMIN main menu, use the Search or the Manage Objects menus to select the desired container object. Once located, the Actions for Organization ... or Actions for Organizational Unit ... menu is displayed. From this menu, select View or edit properties of this object. The View or edit organization (View or edit organizational unit) menu appears.

4. From the View or edit ... menu, select Login script. If there is no login script for this container object, the following message appears:

   ```
   Script is empty. Copy script from another object?
   ```

   If you answer yes, you can select another object and copy its login script to this container. If you choose this, you can save a lot of time typing in the script. You are then placed in the Login Script screen where you can edit the script to add customizing features for this container.

   If you answer no, you are presented with a blank Login Script screen.

5. From the Login Script screen, you can edit and type the desired container login script. When finished, press F10 to save the login script. You can then press Esc several times or press Alt+F10 to exit the NETADMIN utility. The next time a user located in this container logs in, that user will execute the container login script that you have just created.

NETADMIN contains limited cut and paste editing features. To cut a block of text and paste it to another portion of the login script, proceed as follows:

1. Move your cursor to the beginning of the block of text.
2. Press the F5 key.
3. Move your cursor to the end of the target block of text. Your screen then looks something like you see in figure 34.2.
4. Press Del. The text disappears into the paste buffer.
5. Reposition the cursor to the new location.
6. Press the Insert key. The text in the paste buffer reappears.

To copy a block of text, proceed as follows:

1. Move your cursor to the beginning of the block of text.
2. Press the F5 key.
3. Move your cursor to the end of the target block of text.

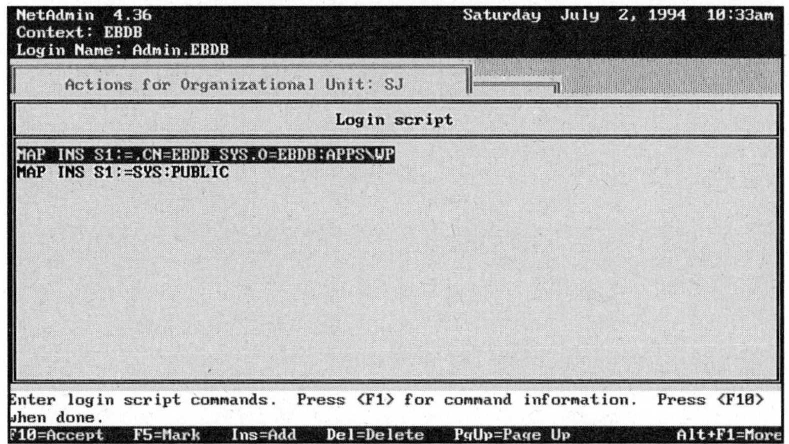

Figure 34.2
Marking a block of text in the NETADMIN login script editor.

4. Press Del. The text disappears into the paste buffer.
5. Press the Insert key. The text reappears.
6. Reposition the cursor to the new location.
7. Press the Insert key. The highlighted block is copied to the new location. You can continue to press the Insert key to make as many copies as you want.

Container objects are given Read rights to their own Login Script property. As a result, any object located under this container has the capability to use its login script. This is true due to security rights inheritance: objects in a container inherit the rights of the container. If you want to give a user or other object in another branch of the tree rights to a container's login script, you must assign the rights manually.

Profile Login Scripts

The *profile login script* was designed to serve as an intermediate login script between the container and user login scripts. NetWare customers have long demanded a "group" login script. The profile login script serves this purpose.

Typical uses for the profile login script are for drive mappings, messages, setting environmental variables, and other mechanisms needed by a group of people. Any user, in any container, can be assigned a profile login script. If the profile assigned is not in that user's container, you must ensure that the user has Browse object trustee rights and Read property rights to the profile object's login script property.

A profile login script can be created for all MIS personnel, for example. It can contain search drive mappings to network-management-related applications and directories.

To create and use a profile login script, you must take the following actions:

1. Create the profile object.
2. Create the profile login script.
3. Assign the user to the profile.
4. Give the user Read property rights to the login script property of the profile.

You must also ensure that the user has Browse object trustee rights to the profile object. This right is assigned by default to the object [public] at the [root], and may have been blocked by an IRF or an assignment which overrides the right. The Read rights to the profile's Login Script property is not automatically assigned. You must take action to ensure that users assigned to a profile have sufficient rights to read its login script.

To create a profile object and enter a profile login script using the Windows-based NWADMIN utility, proceed as follows:

1. Log in as a user with sufficient rights to create an object under a container and to assign rights to other users.
2. Scroll down the tree or use the search or browse features to locate the container under which you plan to create the profile object.
3. Press Insert, or from the Object menu, select Create. The New Object list appears.
4. From the New Object list, select Profile. The Create Profile dialog box appears, as shown in figure 34.3.
5. From the Create Profile dialog box, enter the desired name of the new profile object in the Profile Name field. Place a check mark in the Define Additional Properties field to jump immediately to the properties screen for the profile, enabling you to enter the login script immediately. Place a check mark in the Create Another Profile field if you want to continue creating profiles. Press the Create button when finished.
6. After the profile has been created, click on Details from the Object menu. You may have placed a check mark in the Define Additional Properties field, in which case the Profile: ... dialog box appears.
7. In the Profile: ... dialog box, click on the Login Script button at the right side to enter the login script for the profile. After you have completed the login script for the profile, click on OK. You are returned to the NWADMIN main menu.

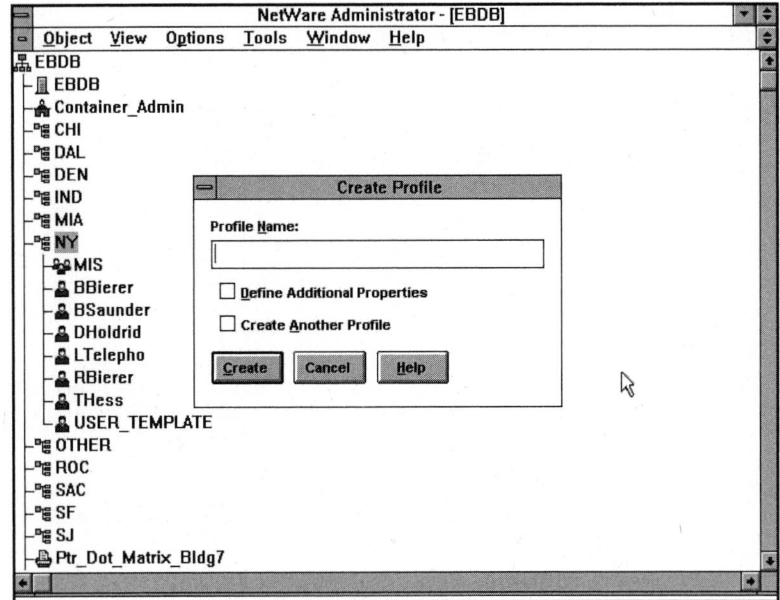

Figure 34.3

Creating a profile object in NWADMIN.

Now that the profile object has been created and a login script entered, you can assign a user to the profile script as follows:

1. Locate the user object you want to assign to a profile object by scrolling down the tree in the NWADMIN menu or by using the search or browse features.

2. Select the user object and press Enter, or click on Object, Details. The User: ... dialog box for this user appears.

3. On the right side of the User: ... dialog box, click on the Login Script button. The Login Script screen appears. At the bottom of the screen is the Profile field where you can assign this user to a profile.

4. Enter the name of the profile object in the Profile field by typing the name or using the browse button (see fig. 34.4). When finished with the assignment, click on the OK button. You are returned to the NWADMIN main menu. If the user has insufficient rights to use the profile object you just assigned, a warning message appears. Read the warning and click on Yes if you want to continue.

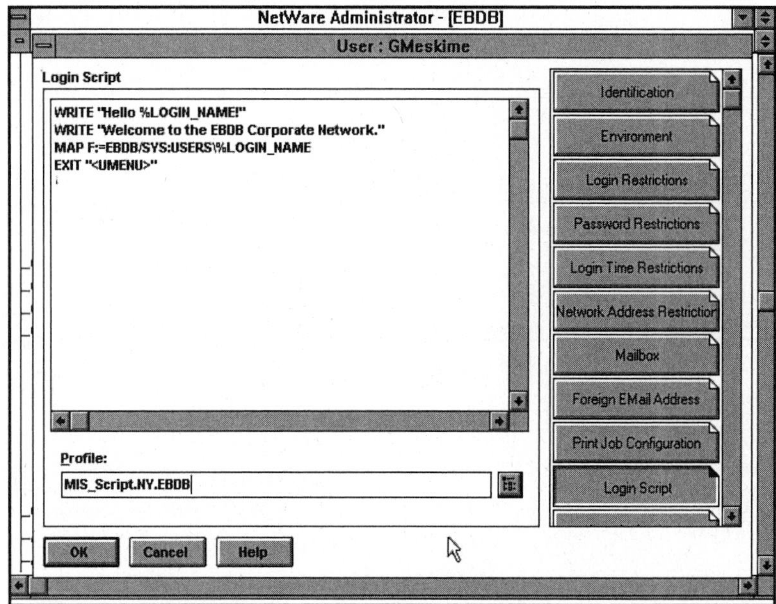

Figure 34.4
Assigning a profile object to a user in NWADMIN.

Now that the profile object has been created and assigned to a user, the last step is to grant the user Read rights to the profile's login script property, and to ensure that the user has Browse object rights. To perform these last steps, proceed as follows:

1. In the main NWADMIN menu, perform one of the following actions:

   - Select the profile object, click the right mouse button, and then select Trustees of this object.
   - Select the profile object, then click on Object, Trustees of this object.
   - Drag the user object and drop it on top of the profile object.

   The Trustees of ... menu appears, where the name of the object appears in place of "..."

2. If you used the drag and drop approach, the trustee name of the user is added automatically to the Trustees list. Otherwise, you need to click on the Add Trustee button and indicate which user is to be added as a trustee of the profile object. Once the user name appears in the trustees list, be sure to select that user to properly assign rights you see at the bottom of the dialog box.

3. After the user name has been added as a trustee and selected, place a check mark next to Browse under the Object Rights area in the Trustees of ... menu. This gives the user the ability to "see" the profile object.

Click on the Selected Properties radio button. From the selected properties list, locate and select the Login Script property. Place a check mark next to the Read property. The user now has the ability to read the login script from the profile object. When you finish you see a screen similar to that shown in figure 34.5.

If you want to allow this user to make changes to the login script, you can also place a check mark by the Write property.

4. Click on OK when you're finished assigning rights. You are returned to the main NWADMIN menu.

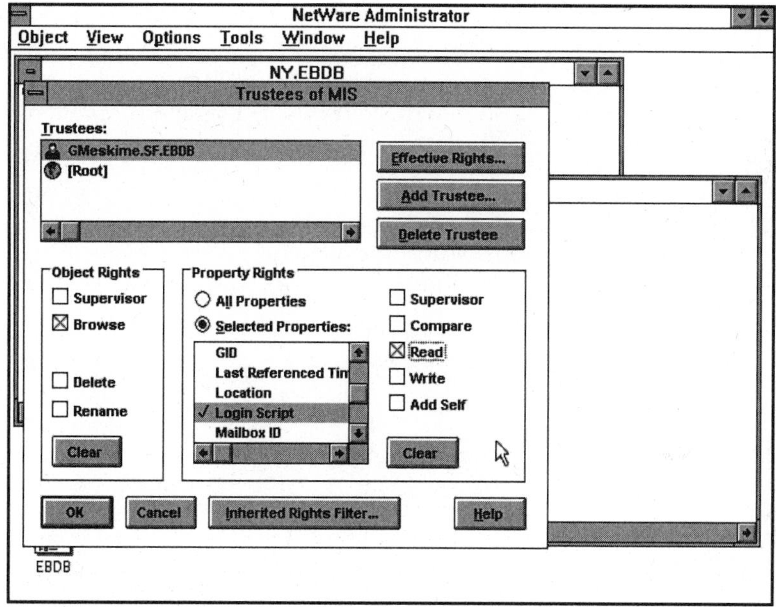

Figure 34.5

Assigning profile object rights with the Trustees of MIS dialog box.

User Login Scripts

User login scripts are used for drive mappings, environmental variables, and other settings specific to individual users. To avoid a management nightmare, place as many login script commands as possible in either the container or profile login scripts. User login scripts are a last resort. If your user login scripts become too elaborate, it takes quite a bit of time to edit them when you need to make a global change.

Ideally, you should not create user login scripts. More than 20 or 30 user login scripts are difficult to maintain. If you find that you need to use user login scripts, you should investigate using the INCLUDE statement described later in this chapter.

continues

With the INCLUDE statement in a user login script, you can have the user use the login script of a "dummy" user object. You can create a series of standardized login scripts in dummy user objects. The dummy user objects are used in this case strictly for their login script properties: the Account Disabled property set to TRUE. When a user moves to another department and their login needs change, change the INCLUDE statement in their login script to point to the dummy user object in the new department.

Users, by default, have the rights to Read and Write their own login scripts. If you do not want to enable users to make changes to their own login scripts, remove the Write right to the user's Login Script property.

To create a user login script using NETADMIN, proceed as follows:

1. Log in as a user with sufficient rights to Write to the user's Login Script property.
2. From the DOS prompt, run NETADMIN.
3. In the NETADMIN main menu, use the Search or the Manage Objects menus to select the desired user object. Once located, the Actions for User ... menu appears; select View or edit properties of this object. The View or edit user menu appears.
4. From the View or edit user menu, select Login script. If there is no login script for this user object, you are prompted with the following:

   ```
   Script is empty. Copy script from another object?
   ```

   If you answer yes, you can select another object and copy its login script to this user—doing this saves a lot of time typing the script. You are then placed in the Login Script screen where you can edit the script to add customizing features for this user.

   If you answer no, you are presented with a blank Login Script screen.
5. From the Login Script screen, you can edit and type the desired user login script. Press F10 when finished to save the login script. Then press Esc several times or press Alt+F10 to exit the NETADMIN utility. The next time this user logs in, he will execute the login script you have just created.

The Default Login Script

The default login script executes under the following conditions:

- There is no user login script.

◆ The NO_DEFAULT command has not been issued in the container or profile login script.

◆ An EXIT command has not been issued in the container or profile login script.

The default login script is located in the LOGIN.EXE file. As a result, you cannot change the default login script, but you can use a binary editor or other utility to view the default login script. Figure 34.6 shows you a portion of the default login script as viewed from the WordPerfect Program Editor.


```
HLOGIN.MSG (^@)^@%c-%d.%ds%c-%d.%ds^@^@ ^@^@^@,^@PATH^@:^@PATH^@\^@^@^@^A^@^A^
^@:^@^@^@Login Script^@Login Script^@r+t^@r^@r^@Login Script^@r+t^@r^@Profile^@
^@MAP DISPLAY OFF^@MAP ERRORS OFF^@MAP *1:=%FILE_SERVER/SYS:; *1:=%FILE_SERVER/
LOGIN-%s-%s
^@Password Expiration Time^@TZ^@LOGIN_CONTROL^@^@^@^_^@\^@^_^@^^^@^_^@^^^@^_^@
^@1^@0^@%02d^@%u^@%02d^@%d^@%02d^@%02d^@%01d^@%02.2X%02.2X%02.2X%02.2X^@%d^@%02
F:\LOGIN\LOGIN.EXE    File 1    Ln 2899    Pos 1
```

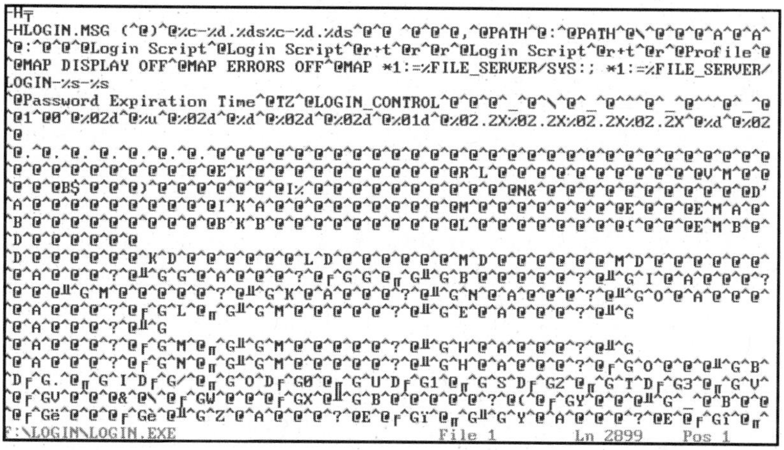

Figure 34.6

Viewing the default login script from the WordPerfect Program Editor.

The text of the default login script is documented in the following code:

```
MAP DISPLAY OFF
MAP ERRORS OFF
MAP *1:=%FILE_SERVER/SYS:;*1:=%FILE_SERVER/SYS:%LOGIN_NAME
IF "%1"="SUPERVISOR" ¦¦ "%1"="ADMIN" THEN MAP *1:=%FILE_SERVER/SYS:SYSTEM
MAP INS S1:=%FILE_SERVER/SYS:PUBLIC; INS S2:=%FILE_SERVER/SYS:PUBLIC/%MACHINE/
%OS/%OS_VERSION
MAP DISPLAY ON
MAP
```

The commands and syntax of the default login script are described in the "Login Script Commands" section later in this chapter.

External Login Scripts

You can use additional login scripts if you need to bypass the traditional login scripts described previously. External login scripts are a good way of testing to see if a login script will work—before storing it in the NDS. Techniques for implementing an external login script include the following:

- ◆ Using the LOGIN /S option to call an ASCII text file when first logging in
- ◆ Using the INCLUDE command to call a login script of another object or an ASCII text file

The LOGIN /S option is used to specify an alternate login script file when logging in. This option bypasses the other login scripts in favor of the script file specified. Use this option when testing a new login script or when an existing login script does not work. The syntax is as follows:

```
LOGIN [server/][username] /S <login script file>
```

The following code shows you a sample login script.

```
WRITE "Begin Alternate Login Script ---------------"
MAP INS S1:=SYS:PUBLIC
MAP F:=.EBDB_SYS.EBDB:
WRITE "Alternate Login Script Executed OK..."
WRITE "End Alternate Login Script ----------------"
```

The following code shows you a sample session where this file is used as an alternate to the standard login scripts.

```
F:\>LOGIN .ADMIN.EBDB /S C:\NRP\INSIDE4\FIG3408.TXT
Your current context is EBDB
Your current tree is: NRP
You are attached to server EBDB.
Begin Alternate Login Script ---------------
S1: = Z:. [EBDB_SYS: \PUBLIC]
Drive F: = EBDB_SYS: \
Alternate Login Script Executed OK...
End Alternate Login Script ----------------

F:\>
```

The INCLUDE statement can run either an external login script file or the login script of another object. If you want to run the login script of another object, you must have Browse object rights and Read rights to the object's Login Script property.

Figure 34.7 shows a login script for user CTrahan that uses the INCLUDE command to both run an external login script file and to run the login script of another object. Figure 34.8 shows the login script of the user object the INCLUDE statement references.

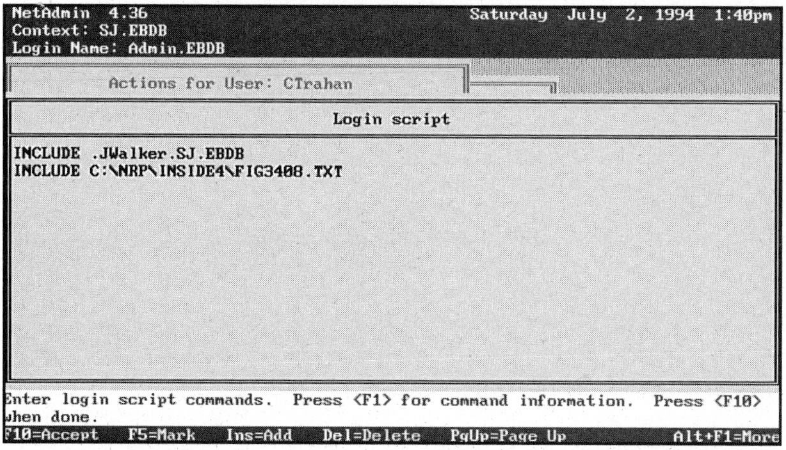

```
NetAdmin  4.36                                    Saturday  July  2, 1994  1:40pm
Context: SJ.EBDB
Login Name: Admin.EBDB

        Actions for User: CTrahan

                              Login script
INCLUDE .JWalker.SJ.EBDB
INCLUDE C:\NRP\INSIDE4\FIG3408.TXT

Enter login script commands.  Press <F1> for command information.  Press <F10>
when done.
F10=Accept   F5=Mark   Ins=Add   Del=Delete   PgUp=Page Up          Alt+F1=More
```

Figure 34.7

Viewing the login script for the user CTrahan.

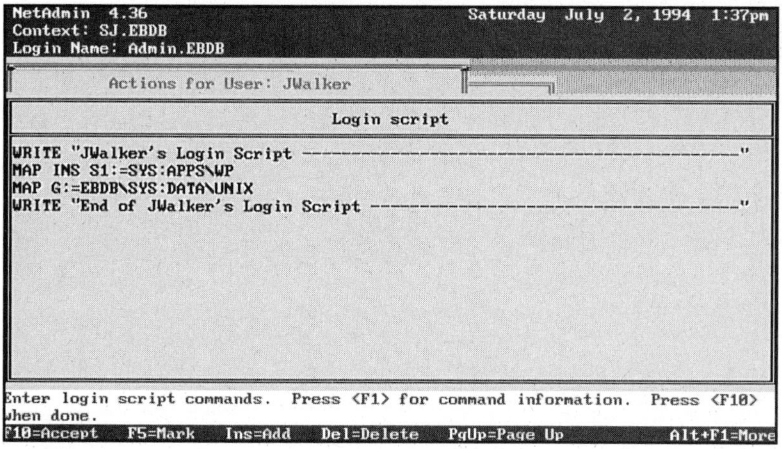

```
NetAdmin  4.36                                    Saturday  July  2, 1994  1:37pm
Context: SJ.EBDB
Login Name: Admin.EBDB

        Actions for User: JWalker

                              Login script
WRITE "JWalker's Login Script ------------------------------------------------"
MAP INS S1:=SYS:APPS\WP
MAP G:=EBDB\SYS:DATA\UNIX
WRITE "End of JWalker's Login Script -----------------------------------------"

Enter login script commands.  Press <F1> for command information.  Press <F10>
when done.
F10=Accept   F5=Mark   Ins=Add   Del=Delete   PgUp=Page Up          Alt+F1=More
```

Figure 34.8

Viewing the login script for the user JWalker.

The following code displays the results when CTrahan logs in. Note that the user CTrahan had to be given Read rights to the Login Script property for the user object JWalker.

```
F:\>LOGIN .CTRAHAN.SJ.EBDB
Your current context is EBDB
Your current tree is: NRP
You are attached to server EBDB.
S1: = Z:. [EBDB_SYS.: \PUBLIC]
S1: = Y:. [EBDB_SYS.: \APPS\DB]
JWalker's Login Script ------------------------------------------
S1: = X:. [EBDB_SYS.: \APPS\WP]
```

```
Drive G: = EBDB_SYS.: \DATA\UNIX
End of JWalker's Login Script -----------------------------------
Begin Alternate Login Script ---------------
S1: = W:. [EBDB_SYS.: \PUBLIC]
Drive F: = EBDB_SYS.: \
Alternate Login Script Executed OK...
End Alternate Login Script -----------------

F:\>
```

Note in the previous listing that the drive mappings that occurred prior to the start of JWalker's Login Script are from the container login script. Both the container login script and the alternate login script contain duplicate assignments of a search drive to SYS:PUBLIC.

Using LOGIN.EXE Command-Line Options

The LOGIN.EXE command, used to initially log in to the network, has command-line options other than the user login name. The /S option, as was shown previously, can bypass the other login scripts. Table 34.1 summarizes the LOGIN.EXE command-line options.

Table 34.1
LOGIN.EXE Command-Line Options

Option	Description
/B	Logs you in to a NetWare 4.1 file server in bindery mode. When in bindery mode, you can only log in as a user in the file server's Bindery Context. As a bindery user, you cannot administer NDS resources.
/CLS	Clears the screen before logging in.
/NS	The No Script option is used to simulate the ATTACH command used in previous versions of NetWare. You can use the LOGIN /NS option to log in to another server without logging out of the first, and without running another login script. This option is only useful

Option	Description
	when logging in to servers outside your NDS tree or when logging in to bindery-based servers (such as NetWare 3.*x* or older servers). To log in to a NetWare 3.*x* server 3X_UK as user George while remaining logged in to a NetWare 4.1 file server, type the following: **LOGIN 3X_UK/GEORGE /NS**
/S *path:\filename*	Executes the login script indicated by *path:\filename.*
/SWAP *[drive:\directory]*	Swaps the LOGIN.EXE process out to RAM or to a file on the specified *drive* and *directory*. When you run executables during the login process, a tremendous RAM overhead ensues. This option reduces the RAM overhead required by the LOGIN.EXE process itself to nothing, enabling you to run sizable programs while logging in. If you do not specify a *drive:\directory:*, NetWare will attempt to swap the LOGIN.EXE process to extended or expanded RAM. If there is not enough room, or you do not have extended or expanded RAM, NetWare will swap out to a file in the current directory. Specifying a *drive:\directory* overrides this behavior. The /SWAP option is only invoked when running external executables from inside a login script.
/NB	Prevents the screen from clearing and the initial NetWare login banner from appearing.
/TREE *treename*	Enables you to log in a NetWare 4.1 NDS tree with the name *treename.* This is useful if you have a network with multiple trees.
/VER	Displays version information about the LOGIN.EXE program.

The /SWAP option does not work when using DR DOS 6.0 and the EMM386 option. To get it to work properly, you must—prior to logging in—disable the upper memory area with the MEMMAX -u command.

Working with Login Script Commands

The following commands can be used in login scripts and are discussed in the following sections:

#	EXIT	PAUSE
ATTACH	FDISPLAY	PCCOMPATIBLE
BREAK	FIRE PHASERS	PROFILE
CLS	GOTO	REMARK
COMSPEC	IF ... THEN	SCRIPT_SERVER
CONTEXT	INCLUDE	SET
DISPLAY	LASTLOGINTIME	SET_TIME
DOS BREAK	MACHINE	SHIFT
DOS SET	MAP	SWAP
DOS VERIFY	NO_DEFAULT	TEMP SET
DRIVE	NOSWAP	WRITE

The # Character

When placed before an external command, the # character provides external program execution. The following is the general syntax of the command:

```
# [path:\filename] [parameters]
```

The *[path:\filename]* statement specifies the full path name of the external command. The # character must be the first character in the command line. Under DOS, you can execute any EXE and COM file. To execute a DOS batch file or a DOS internal command, you must invoke the command line processor by using the following command, where *<batch or internal>* is replaced by the name of a batch file or an internal command:

```
#COMMAND /C <batch or internal>
```

The DOS DATE command is shown in the following command:

```
#COMMAND /C DATE
```

When executing an external command, you must ensure that the proper drive mappings and search drives have been set, because the external command executes in the context of the NetWare environment set up at the time of execution. You must

have sufficient network rights in the directory where the program is located; minimum rights should be Read and File Scan.

When the external command is executed, the LOGIN.EXE program still is resident in RAM and is not released until termination of the login script processing. Therefore, do not load TSRs during login processing because it will leave a hole in memory (where the login program was) when login script processing terminates.

To avoid the RAM problem, use the /SWAP parameter when logging in. This causes the LOGIN.EXE program to be backed out of RAM entirely, leaving RAM free for any programs or TSRs.

A typical use for the # option is to enable print capture, as the following syntax shows:

```
#CAPTURE
```

This command invokes the print capture using the default PRINTCON job template for the user or the user's container.

To run a batch file SPECIAL.BAT in a directory SYS:APPS\BAT, enter the following into your login script:

```
#
#     Map to DOS and the BAT directories,
#     then run batch file SPECIAL.BAT
#
MAP INS S1:=SYS:APPS\DOS
MAP S16:=SYS:APPS\BAT
#COMMAND /C SPECIAL.BAT
```

The ATTACH Command

The ATTACH command, which can be executed as a NetWare command from the DOS prompt, enables you to attach to bindery-based servers (NetWare 3.*x* or older). The ATTACH command also can be used when connecting to a NetWare 4.1 server through bindery services. You can attach to the maximum number of connections specified in your NET.CFG file. (The default is 8 file server connections. You can specify up to 50.) ATTACH enables you to attach to other file servers without interrupting the current execution of the login script. The general syntax of the command is as follows:

```
ATTACH [fileserver/][username][;password]
```

If the *fileserver*, *username*, and *password* are not specified, you are prompted for them.

You need to be careful about including password information in the login script file. Anyone with read access to the login script property can read the password, which compromises the security of your network.

To attach to a NetWare 2.*x* file server DALLAS2 as user Dennis, enter the following:

ATTACH DALLAS2/Dennis

The BREAK Command

The BREAK command enables you to terminate the execution of your login script. The general syntax of the command is as follows:

```
BREAK [ON ¦ OFF]
```

If the command is set to BREAK ON, the command enables you to terminate the processing of your login script by pressing Ctrl+C or Ctrl+Break. The default value is OFF.

The BREAK command is different from the DOS BREAK command, explained in the following section.

The DOS BREAK Command

If DOS BREAK is set to ON, it enables Ctrl+Break checking for DOS. Whenever a program sends a request to DOS while the Ctrl+Break checking is enabled, you can terminate the program by pressing Ctrl+Break. This command is equivalent to the BREAK command, which is available under MS-DOS. Note that this command does not apply to OS/2 workstations.

The CLS Command

The CLS command clears the screen when the login script executes. The following example displays two consecutive text files, clearing the screen between displays:

```
#
#    Display File Number 1
#
MAP G:=.EBDB_DATA.EBDB:\MESSAGE
DISPLAY G:LOGIN.1
PAUSE
#
#    Clear Screen and Display File Number 2
CLS
DISPLAY G:LOGIN.2
```

The COMSPEC Command

COMSPEC specifies the directory that DOS should use to load the command-line processor COMMAND.COM. The general syntax is the following:

```
COMSPEC=[path]COMMAND.COM
```

You can use a command-line processor other than COMMAND.COM, but such implementations are rare. The COMSPEC command directly sets the COMSPEC DOS environment variable.

When DOS first loads, a transient portion of COMMAND.COM is loaded in the area of memory just below 640 KB. When a large program loads, it can overwrite the transient portion of DOS. When this program exits, the transient portion of COMMAND.COM needs to be restored. DOS makes use of the COMSPEC environment variable to obtain a copy of COMMAND.COM. If the COMMAND.COM in memory and the one indicated by COMSPEC are for different versions of DOS, the workstation will crash with an Invalid COMMAND.COM message. On a network, chances are that users are using different versions of DOS, and COMSPEC therefore might be pointing to an incorrect version of DOS. The COMSPEC variable should be set to the correct directory.

You need to set up directories for each version of DOS in use on your workstations. By default, NetWare assumes that you have the directory structure along the lines of that shown in figure 34.9.

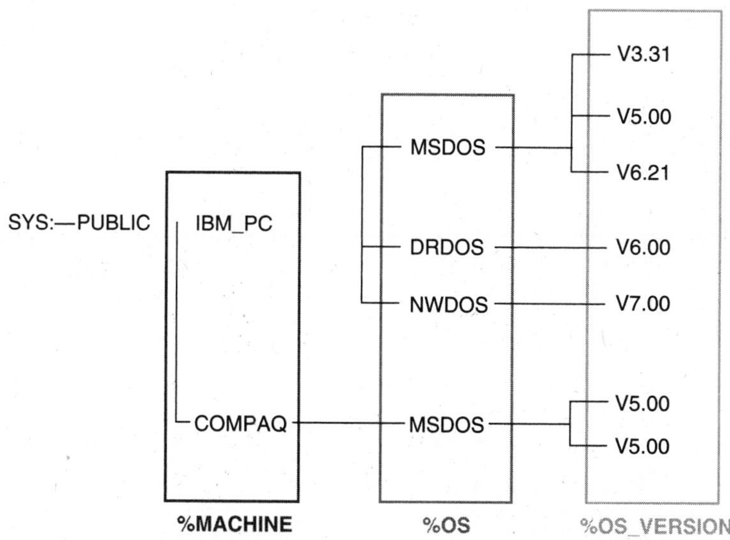

Figure 34.9

The default directory structure showing DOS directories.

The structure in figure 34.9 assumes you have different machines (such as IBM_PC and COMPAQ), different operating systems (such as MS-DOS and Novell DOS), and different versions of each operating system (v3.31, v6.22, and so on). If you choose to follow this model, create the directories appropriate for your environment and copy at least COMMAND.COM into the following directories: V3.31, V7.00, and so forth. Assuming you have done this, you can map a search drive to the appropriate directory in your login script using the following command:

```
MAP S2:=SYS:PUBLIC/%MACHINE/%OS/%OS_VERSION
```

You can then assign the COMSPEC to the appropriate version of DOS using the following command:

```
COMSPEC=S2:COMMAND.COM
```

If you have an IBM PC clone using MS-DOS 5, for example, the following search drive would be assigned:

```
SYS:PUBLIC/IBM_PC/MSDOS/V5.00
```

COMSPEC defaults to the root of the drive that you booted from. If you boot from a hard drive, for example, the COMSPEC defaults to C:\COMMAND.COM. If this is the case, you do not have to use the COMSPEC command in your login scripts, and your system will work just fine. If you have users who boot from floppy or have diskless workstations, it is extremely helpful (and highly recommended) to set the COMSPEC using a variation of the technique described previously.

If both DOS and OS/2 users use the same login script, the OS/2 users should reset the COMSPEC to a directory that contains the OS/2 command-line processor. This can be done in the OS/2 STARTUP.CMD file, for example.

The CONTEXT Command

The CONTEXT command sets the user's default NDS context. When the user exits the login script, their context will be whatever you set. This command is similar to the CX command, but is only able to set the context. The generic syntax is as follows:

```
CONTEXT NDS container object name
```

NDS container object name can be any valid NDS container. If you want to set the context to the container OU=SJ under the organization EBDB, for example, type the following:

CONTEXT .OU=SJ.O=EBDB

The DISPLAY Command

The DISPLAY command shows the contents of the specified file on the workstation screen. The exact characters are displayed, including any control codes for printer and word processing formats. The general syntax is as follows:

```
DISPLAY [pathname]file
```

The [*pathname*]*file* is the name of the file whose contents are displayed. If you have a company logo, created using DOS character graphics, stored in LOGO.TXT located in SYS:PUBLIC, for example, the following lines can be added to your login script:

```
;
;    Command to Display Logo File
;
DISPLAY SYS:PUBLIC\CO_LOGO.TXT
;
;    Pause the Display
;
PAUSE
```

The FDISPLAY Command

The FDISPLAY command shows the contents of the specified text file on the workstation screen. The text is formatted and filtered so that only the text is displayed. The general syntax is as follows:

```
FDISPLAY [pathname]file
```

The [*pathname*]*file* is the name of the file whose contents are displayed. FDISPLAY filters any unprintable characters, making it a safer alternative to the DISPLAY command. The syntax and usage is the same as the DISPLAY command, however.

The DOS SET or SET Command

This command can set a DOS environment variable from within a login script. "SET" or "DOS SET" are interchangeable commands. The general syntax is as follows:

```
[option] [DOS] SET name = "value"
```

The [*option*] parameter can be replaced by an optional keyword, such as TEMP, TEMPORARY, or LOCAL, to signify that the variable is set only during the login script processing and does not affect the DOS environment. Replace *name* with the name of the environment variable and *value* with its actual value. The value must always be enclosed in double quotation marks.

The following are examples of the use of the SET command:

```
#
#    Sets the DOS Prompt
#
SET PROMPT = "$P$G"
#
#    Removes the definition of the environment variable
#
SET FNAME =
#
#    Sets the value of "Y" to "1".
#
SET Y = "1"
#
#    Adds "1" to the current value of "Y"
#
SET Y = <Y> + "1"
#
#    Set a variable "UDIR" equal to the user's
#    home directory on the first network drive
#
SET UDIR = "*1:\\USERS\\%LOGIN_NAME"
```

Note that numeric operations are acceptable, but any value assigned to a variable, including numeric, must be enclosed in quotes. If you want to use the backslash character (\) in a string value, you must specify two backslashes, as shown in the following example:

```
SET FILENAME = "F:\\PUBLIC\\TEMP\\KSSFILE"
```

You need two backslashes because the single backslash character is used to indicate special character codes, as shown in the following list:

Code	Description
\r	Indicates a carriage return
\n	Specifies a new line
\”	Embeds quotation marks in string
\7	Generates a beep sound (bell)

The DOS VERIFY Command

When set to ON, the DOS VERIFY command verifies that the data copied to a local drive can be written without errors. The default is OFF and the general syntax is the following:

```
DOS VERIFY [ON ¦ OFF]
```

Other commands can verify, as well. The NCOPY command automatically does a read-after-write verify check and can copy files to floppy disks. If you want to use the MS-DOS COPY command, you should have the following command in your login script for added reliability in making copies to floppy disks:

```
DOS VERIFY ON
```

The /V option also can be used with the MS-DOS COPY command to produce the same effect.

The DRIVE Command

The DRIVE command can specify which network drive is the default drive. The general syntax is as follows:

```
DRIVE [driveletter: ¦ *n:]
```

Replace *driveletter* with a drive letter and **n* with the network drive number, such as *1, *2, and so on. The first network drive, *1, is the default drive, but you can change this by specifying the new default drive in the DRIVE command.

The EXIT Command

Normally, execution of the login scripts terminates at the end of processing the individual user login script. The EXIT command can prematurely terminate the login script processing or specifies the command to be executed on termination. The general syntax is as follows:

```
EXIT ["post login command"]
```

Replace the *post login command* statement with the program name, plus arguments of any command to be executed after the login script terminates. If you see an error message about the command string being too long to be executed, you can try to minimize the characters in the command string by leaving out file extensions. This variation of the EXIT command causes NetWare to place the characters inside quotes in the keyboard buffer. There is a limit of 15 characters inside quotes. NetWare automatically appends a carriage return/linefeed after the post-login command.

The following example terminates the login process:

```
EXIT
```

The following example executes the NetWare menu utility and calls the menu SALES:

```
EXIT "NMENU SALES"
```

The following code executes the batch file USEREXEC.BAT, located in the user's home directory, with an argument to the batch file, WP:

```
MAP F:=SYS:USERS\%LOGIN_NAME
DRIVE F:
EXIT "USEREXEC.BAT WP"
```

The FIRE PHASERS Command

The FIRE PHASERS command produces sound effects of firing phasers. It does not work from the DOS command line. The general syntax is as follows:

```
FIRE PHASERS <n> TIMES
```

Replace *n* with a number from 1 to 9. Some examples of this command follow:

```
;
;    Fires 4 phaser sounds
;
FIRE PHASERS 4 TIMES
;
;    Fires as many phaser sounds as is the day of the week
;    Note the abbreviation: FIRE n
;
FIRE %NDAY_OF_WEEK
```

The GOTO Command

Use the GOTO command to repeat processing of portions of the login script. The following is the general syntax:

```
GOTO <label>
```

You can replace *label* with an identifier, but it must be specified in the current login script. The following example shows how to use the command:

```
SET X = "1"
*
```

```
* The line below shows how labels can be defined
*
LOOP:
   *
   * The indentation shown below is for purposes
   * of clarity and readability of the login script.
   * It is not a requirement.
   * Placing <> around X tells the login processor
   * that this is an environment variable whose value
   * needs to be evaluated.
   *
   SET X = <X> + "1"
   *
   * Do whatever login script processing
   * that needs to be repeated, here.
   *
   WRITE "Processing Loop Number: %<X>"
   *
*
* Place a condition for terminating the loop, otherwise
* you will repeat this loop indefinitely!
*
IF <X> < "9" THEN GOTO LOOP
```

Set BREAK ON in the login script before experimenting with loops, just in case you need to break out of a loop you create by accident.

Numerical comparisons do not work in login scripts as they do in ordinary programming languages. Environment variables are evaluated as text, even though you can perform limited arithmetic functions on them. Thus, the syntax indicated previously is only valid for loops of 9 passes or less. When you place a value of 10 in the IF statement, the system only processes the loop twice.

The reason follows. Suppose the IF statement read as follows:

```
IF <X> < "10" THEN GOTO LOOP
```

When the value of *X* is 1, it is considered less than 10. When the value of *X* reaches 2, it is considered greater than 10. The values are not compared as numbers, but as text. The first digit of *X* is 2. The first digit of 10 is 1. Because 2 is greater than 1, the login processor returns a value of FALSE after reaching the IF ... THEN statement, and continues with the remainder of the login script.

The moral of this story is to use single digit loops whenever possible and to use the < operator rather than <=.

The IF ... THEN ... ELSE Command

The IF ... THEN ... ELSE statement enables you to execute certain commands conditionally. The general syntax is as follows:

```
IF <conditional(s)> [AND¦OR¦NOR] [conditional(s)] THEN
   <command>
   [command]
[ELSE
   <command>
   [command]]
END
```

The general syntax for a *conditional* is as follows:

```
<variable ¦ NDS property> <operator> <"value">
```

Variable can either be an Identifier variable (described in more detail later) or a DOS environment variable. DOS environment variables must be surrounded with angle braces (<>). The following operators can be used:

Operator	Meaning
=	Equals
<>	Does not equal
>	Is greater than
<	Is less than
>=	Is greater than or equal to
<=	Is less than or equal to

Values are enclosed in quotation marks and must be a type appropriate to the identifier variable or NDS property. If the property is a date, for example, the value must be in English style date format: mm/dd/yyyy or mm-dd-yyyy.

Tip A table of NDS properties is provided in Chapter 21, "Importing Users." A quick way to get a list of possible NDS properties from the command line is to type the following:

UIMPORT /? ATTR

The following example checks the value of a DOS variable *bdate*, which has been set in the user's AUTOEXEC.BAT file.

```
IF <bdate> = "%MONTH/%DAY" THEN
    WRITE "Happy Birthday, %LOGIN_NAME!!!"
    FIRE 4
END
```

The following code checks to see if a user is a member of the group MIS. If so, the user is given certain drive mappings. If not, other drive mappings are given.

```
IF MEMBER OF "MIS" THEN
    MAP S16:=SYS:SYSTEM
    MAP S16:=SYS:APPS\NMS
ELSE
    MAP NEXT EBDB/DATA:
    MAP S16:=SYS:APPS\DB
END
```

The following example uses an IF ... THEN statement to test the number of grace logins remaining:

```
;
;    Display an informative message if the number of
;    grace logins falls below 7 and the days before the
;    password expires is zero.
;
IF "%LOGIN_GRACE_REMAINING" < "7" AND "%PASSWORD_EXPIRES" = "0" THEN
    ;
    ;    Display the number of remaining grace logins
    ;
    WRITE "Number of Logins Remaining: %LOGIN_GRACE_REMAINING"
    WRITE "Days Before Password Expiration: %PASSWORD_EXPIRES"
    WRITE "Your password must be changed today."
    WRITE "Get a handle, dude: type SETPASS today!"
END
```

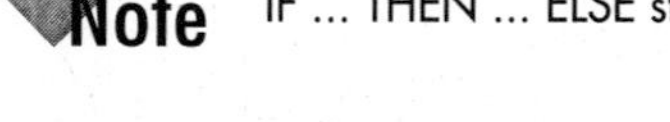

IF ... THEN ... ELSE statements can be nested up to ten levels deep.

The INCLUDE Command

The INCLUDE command indicates a level of indirection for processing login scripts. The content of the file specified in the INCLUDE statement is to be processed next, after which processing returns to the statement following the INCLUDE command. Instead of a file, INCLUDE also can call the login script of another NDS object. The general syntax is as follows:

```
INCLUDE <[pathname]filename ¦ NDS object>
```

The *[pathname]filename* is the location of the file to be processed. The *NDS object* is the name of an NDS object. The object must be one of the following:

- ◆ Organization
- ◆ Organizational Unit
- ◆ Profile
- ◆ User

You can nest INCLUDE commands up to any level, limited only by the memory available for processing. For practicality, do not use more than two levels of nesting or other users will have trouble deciphering your login script. You must have a minimum of Read and File Scan file trustee rights to the INCLUDE file. If the login script is in another NDS object, you must have Browse object trustee rights and Read rights to the object's Login Script property.

The following example uses a login script located in SYS:PUBLIC:

```
INCLUDE SYS:PUBLIC\SALES.LOG
```

The following uses a login script from a container object:

```
INCLUDE .OU=SJ.O=EBDB
```

The LASTLOGINTIME Command

The LASTLOGINTIME command displays the last time a user logged in. When included in a login script, the output looks like the following:

```
F:\USERS\THESS>LOGIN .THESS.NY.EBDB
Your current context is [Root]
Enter your password:
Your current tree is: NRP
You are attached to server EBDB.
S1: = Z:. [EBDB_SYS.: \PUBLIC]
Drive F: = EBDB_SYS.: \USERS\THESS
Sample Login Script -------------------------------
Last login occurred at: 7-03-94 5:06:31 pm.
End Sample Login Script ---------------------------
```

The MACHINE Command

The MACHINE command sets the machine type to the name specified. The syntax for this command follows:

```
MACHINE = <machine type>
```

Machine names also can be set in the NET.CFG file. Names can be up to 15 characters. Some older programs, such as those written for NETBIOS specifications, make use of this value.

The following example sets the MACHINE to a type identified by a DOS environment variable MACHINE_TYPE set earlier in an AUTOEXEC.BAT file:

```
MACHINE = "%<machine_type>"
```

The MAP Command

The MAP command has the same syntax and meaning as the NetWare MAP command found in the SYS:PUBLIC directory, with only a few extensions. Use the following extensions to the MAP command for login script processing:

```
MAP DISPLAY [ON¦OFF]

MAP ERRORS [ON¦OFF]
```

The MAP DISPLAY ON command shows the drive mappings when you log in. ON is the default setting. To disable the MAP processing, messages, use MAP DISPLAY OFF.

MAP ERRORS ON displays error messages that occur, for example, if the path to which you are mapping does not exist (cannot be relocated). The default setting is ON. To disable the display of MAP errors, you can use MAP ERRORS OFF. You should leave the MAP ERRORS command to its default setting of ON. For further information on the MAP command, refer to Chapter 33, "Assigning Drive Mappings."

The NO_DEFAULT Command

The NO_DEFAULT command, which can be placed in either the container or profile login scripts, prevents the login processor from executing the default login script. There are no parameters; the command is entered in the login script as follows:

```
NO_DEFAULT
```

The NOSWAP Command

The NOSWAP command modifies the normal behavior of the LOGIN.EXE processor. Ordinarily, when an external command is executed from within a login script with the # character, the LOGIN.EXE process is swapped out to extended or expanded RAM. Alternatively, if you used the LOGIN /SWAP [*path:\directory*] argument for logging in, LOGIN.EXE swaps itself out to the *path:\directory* specified in the form of a swap file. If this is the case, the NOSWAP command prevents this from occurring as well. The NOSWAP prevents LOGIN.EXE from being swapped out of memory. There are no parameters for this command; the syntax is as follows:

```
NOSWAP
```

The PAUSE or WAIT Command

Use either the PAUSE or the interchangeable WAIT command to pause the execution of the login script. The general syntax is the following:

```
PAUSE
```

or

```
WAIT
```

These commands can be used to pause the execution of the login script so that messages do not scroll by before you have time to read them.

The PCCOMPATIBLE or COMPATIBLE Command

Either the PCCOMPATIBLE or the interchangeable COMPATIBLE command is used to indicate that the workstation PC is IBM PC-compatible. The general syntax is as follows:

```
PCCOMPATIBLE
```

or

```
COMPATIBLE
```

If your machine is IBM PC-compatible, but you have changed the long machine or short machine name by using the LONG MACHINE TYPE= or SHORT MACHINE TYPE= statements in the NET.CFG file, you must use the PCCOMPATIBLE command to indicate to the shell that your machine is IBM PC-compatible. If you do not do this, DOS-based NetWare utilities, such as NETADMIN and FILER, will not work correctly.

The REMARK or REM Command

The REMARK command places comments in the login script file to enhance the readability of the login script. You can use the word "REMARK" or "REM" "*" or ";". The general syntax is as follows:

```
REM [text]
```

or

```
* text
```

or

```
; text
```

The SCRIPT_SERVER Command

The SCRIPT_SERVER command enables users to designate a NetWare 3.*x* or 2.*x* server from which their bindery-based user login scripts can be read. This has no effect on NDS users. The syntax is as follows:

```
SCRIPT_SERVER <file server name>
```

The *file server name* can be any valid NetWare 3.*x* or NetWare 2.*x* file server.

The SET_TIME Command

The SET_TIME command disables the automatic update of the clock of your workstation from the file server. Normally, when you log in, the software clock of your workstation is updated to match the time on the file server, a similar function as the DATE command in DOS. The general syntax for this command is as follows:

```
SET_TIME <ON ¦ OFF>
```

If you specify SET_TIME OFF when you log in, the time on your workstation is not updated to the file server's time.

The SHIFT Command

The SHIFT command can be used to process variables passed as parameters of the LOGIN command. These variables are referred to as %0, %1, %2, and so on. Variable 2 is considered to be "to the right" of variable 0. Variable 0 is considered to be "to the left" of variable 2. When you use the SHIFT 2 command you are shifting 2 variables "to the right." That is to say you are processing a variable that is 2 greater than the previous variable.

In the LOGIN command, you might have typed something like the following:

```
LOGIN WE_SERVE/LYDIA PUBS GRAPHIC
```

The following shows how the variables of the general syntax are replaced with statements in the preceding command:

```
%0    =    WE_SERVE
%1    =    LYDIA
%2    =    PUBS
%3    =    GRAPHIC
```

The %0 variable always is assigned to the file server being logged in to, even if the file server name is not explicitly specified in the LOGIN command. The %1 variable always is mapped to the user's login name. The %2 variable and other variables are mapped to the additional arguments on the LOGIN command line.

The SHIFT command shifts the variable assignments. Its general syntax is as follows:

```
SHIFT [n]
```

The *n* variable can be a positive number for the number of variables you want to shift to the right, or it can be a negative number for shifting to the left. If *n* is left out, the default value of 1 is assumed.

The primary use of SHIFT is to sequence through the parameters specified in the command line. The following loop, for example, can assign %2 to each of the parameters specified in the LOGIN command line after the user name.

```
LOOP:
   IF "%2" = "VAL1" THEN
        Command
   END
   IF "%2" = "VAL2" THEN
        Command
   END
   IF "%2" = "VAL3" THEN
        Command
   END
   SHIFT 1
IF "%2" <> "" THEN
    GOTO LOOP
END
```

The preceding loop checks each of the parameters against a specific value and, if a match is found, performs the action specified. The SHIFT 1 command causes the %2 variable to be assigned to the next parameter to the right until no more parameters are left to process. When no more parameters are left, the conditional expression in the IF statement evaluates to false, and execution proceeds to the statement following the IF statement.

The SWAP Command

As with the LOGIN /SWAP option, SWAP instructs the login processor to swap LOGIN.EXE into extended or expanded RAM, or to a file during execution of an external program. It is the opposite of the NOSWAP command. The syntax is as follows:

```
SWAP [path:\directory]
```

If you specify the *path:\directory*, the LOGIN.EXE process is swapped to a temporary file in the indicated directory.

The WRITE Command

WRITE displays a text message on the screen. Its general syntax is the following:

```
WRITE "text"
```

You can use the semicolon to concatenate text strings. The following two WRITE commands, for example, result in the same output:

```
WRITE "Good " ; GREETING_TIME ; "," ; LOGIN_NAME ; "."

WRITE "Good %GREETING_TIME, %LOGIN_NAME."
```

Using Login Script Identifier Variables

An important part of the login script language is the identifier variable. The *identifier variable*, also known as *login script variable*, or simply, *variable*, is used to identify, in symbolic format, a network resource that varies. Identifier variables are categorized into their various functions. Categories include the following:

- Date
- Time
- User-Related
- Network
- Workstation

- DOS Environment
- NDS Objects

The rules of usage for identifier variables include the following:

- Identifier variables should be all uppercase to ensure they are interpreted as such.
- If used inside quotation marks ("") or in a directory path (as with a MAP command), precede the identifier variable with a percent sign (%).

You must have a firm understanding of which variables are available and how to use them to create meaningful, powerful login scripts. Table 34.2 summarizes the identifier variables available in login scripts.

Table 34.2
LOGIN.EXE Identifier Variables

Variable	Description
**n*	Used to assign the next drive letter, starting with the letter assigned in your NET.CFG file as the *FIRST NETWORK DRIVE*. *1 is usually drive F, *2 would be G, and so on.
<>	Enables you to use any DOS environment variable as a string.
ACCESS_SERVER	Displays TRUE if access server is functional. Displays FALSE if not functional.
AM_PM	Displays the time as day or night, using a.m. or p.m.
DAY	Displays the day from 01 to 31.
DAY_OF_WEEK	Displays the day of the week.
ERROR_LEVEL	Displays the number of errors. If 0, no errors are found.
FILE_SERVER	Displays the name of the file server.
FULL_NAME	Displays the full name of bindery-based users.
GREETING_TIME	Displays the time of day as morning, afternoon, or evening.

Variable	Description
HOUR	Displays the time of day in hours, from 1 to 12.
HOUR24	Displays the hour in 24-hour time, from 00 to 23.
LAST_NAME	User's surname.
LOGIN_CONTEXT	Context where user is located in the tree.
LOGIN_NAME	Displays the user's login name.
MACHINE	Displays the machine for which the shell was written, such as IBMPC.
MEMBER OF *group*	Displays TRUE if the user is a member of a specified *group*. Displays FALSE if the user is not a member of the specified group.
MINUTE	Displays the minute from 00 to 59.
MONTH	Displays the month from 01 to 12.
MONTH_NAME	Displays the name of the month.
NDAY_OF_WEEK	Displays the numeric value of the weekday.
NETWARE_REQUESTER	Version of the VLM requester, or the NetWare Client for OS/2.
NETWORK_ADDRESS	Displays the network number of the cabling system in eight hexidecimal digits.
NOT MEMBER OF *group*	Group the user is not assigned to.
OS	Displays the workstation's operating system, such as MS-DOS.
OS_VERSION	Displays the DOS version of the workstation.
P_STATION	Displays the station address or node address in twelve hexidecimal digits.
PASSWORD_EXIRES	Number of days before user password expires.
REQUESTER_CONTEXT	The current context at the time the LOGIN.EXE process was started.

continues

Table 34.2, Continued
LOGIN.EXE Identifier Variables

Variable	Description
SECOND	Displays the seconds from 00 to 59.
SHELL_TYPE	Version of the workstation's DOS shell. Supports VLM as well as NetWare 2 and 3 shells.
SHORT_YEAR	Displays the year in short format, such as 92, 93, and so on.
SMACHINE	Displays the name of the machine in short format, such as IBM.
STATION	Displays the connection number.
USER_ID	Displays the ID number of each user.
YEAR	Displays the year in full format, such as 1992, 1993, and so on.

In addition to the list summarized in table 34.2, you can use any NDS property as a variable. If there are spaces in the property name, it must be enclosed in quotation marks.

For a list of properties associated with users, type the following command:

UIMPORT /? ATTR

For a more complete list of all properties, see Chapter 14, "DOS Client Basics."

Summary

This chapter gave you a detailed look at login scripts. You learned about the different types of login scripts (container, profile, user, default, and external), and their order (container then profile then user or default). You learned that to use the profile or the login script of another object, you need Browse object rights and Read rights to the object's Login Script property. You were shown how to create each of the different types of login scripts using NETADMIN from the DOS prompt or NWADMIN from Windows. You learned about external login scripts, which are ASCII files containing login script commands. These files can be called using the LOGIN /S option, or from within a login script using the INCLUDE statement.

Various LOGIN.EXE command-line options were discussed. The LOGIN /SWAP option, for example, causes the login processor to completely swap itself out of conventional memory to free memory for applications executed from within a login script.

The second half of this chapter discussed in detail each of the commands in the login script language. The syntax of each command was displayed in general format. Following the syntax were precise examples of the usage of each command. At the end of this chapter you were shown the identifier variables along with a brief explanation of their usage. You learned that any NDS property can be used as a variable. The UIMPORT /? ATTR command is used to view a list of variables for users that can be used.

Chapter 35 shows you how to build custom menus and batch files.

CHAPTER

Building Custom Menus and Batch Files

NetWare comes with its own menu generation facility. The menuing program is a runtime version of the Saber Menu system licensed from Saber Software Corporation. The menus you can create with this system are fast and do not allow users to break out of them. This chapter discusses this menu facility and shows you examples of how to build your own menus.

In addition, any network with DOS workstations could benefit from customized batch files. In this chapter, you learn about how batch files can be constructed for the NetWare environment, as well as some samples of useful batch files.

Understanding the NetWare 4.1 Menu Program

The runtime menu program uses a tokenized menu file that you must create. The runtime module interprets the menu file to produce a menu on screen. The menus you end up with resemble the menuing interface to the various NetWare DOS-based menu utilities such as NETADMIN or PCONSOLE. The menu system produces a box on the screen. At the top center is the menu title. Inside the menu box are choices. The user can use the up and down arrow keys to scroll through the choices. Pressing Enter on any choice causes the commands tied to that choice to execute.

The steps required to produce the tokenized menu file resemble the steps you would take to produce and compile a C language program or a database program such as FoxBase. The steps needed to produce a working menu are as follows:

1. Enter the menu titles and executable statements into an ASCII source file.
2. Run the MENUMAKE utility to convert the ASCII source file into a tokenized menu file.
3. Run the NMENU batch file that sets up the environment and runs MENUEXE.EXE.
4. MENUEXE.EXE interprets the tokenized menu file, producing the menu you see on screen.

You are limited to 12 choices per menu. To gain additional choices, you can divide your menu into smaller menus. One menu called from another is referred to as a *submenu.* The first menu you define in your source menu file is the *main menu.* You can call a submenu from the main menu, and then another submenu from the first submenu, and so forth. The submenu *depth* cannot exceed 11 (the main menu plus 10 submenus). Although this seems like a severe limitation, bear in mind that each menu choice can call a submenu. Each submenu can have 12 choices, each of which in turn can call a submenu. The limit of 11 limits the depth of the menu structure, not the breadth. You can have a total of 255 menu screens altogether. Submenus can be defined in the source menu file or from an external file.

Menus can execute any command that can be executed from the DOS prompt. You can call batch files and even Windows from a menu. When running applications from a menu, the menu processor backs itself out and leaves a small kernel (approximately 32 KB) in memory. If you are running applications that require maximum available memory, an ITEM...{BATCH} option is available that instructs the menu processor to back itself out of RAM completely.

Menus can prompt users for input. You can establish defaults that become effective if a user presses the Enter key without supplying any information. Information supplied from a user prompt can be made to be required. If a user does not supply information for a required prompt, the system does not let them exit the prompt input box until they enter the required information. In the case of passwords, the menu system lets you hide the information that the user types.

Menus produced in this fashion are designed to run from the DOS prompt. If you want to bring the menu files you create into Windows, Saber Software produces a Menu System for Windows. Saber also produces a complete developer's edition of the DOS Menu System.

Creating a Menu File

The original menu file can be created using any ASCII text editor. Windows Notepad, WordPerfect Program Editor, and the MS-DOS EDIT utility are all examples of ASCII text editors. This section describes the various commands that go into a menu file. They are broken down into two categories: flow commands and executable commands. The *flow commands* affect the overall flow of the menu. *Executable commands* affect the actual operation of the menu.

Tip

You also can use any word processing software to create or modify menu source files. When you save the source file, be sure to save it as an ASCII text file with no formatting.

Menu Flow Commands

Menu flow commands affect which menus appear and in what order. The two flow commands are MENU and ITEM. The MENU command is used to identify the start of a menu. The first MENU command in the menu source file is the main menu. Subsequent menus in the menu source file are identified by the keyword MENU and a number. The ITEM command is used to identify a menu choice. As mentioned earlier, you can have a maximum of 12 items per menu. This section discusses these two commands and their parameters.

The MENU Command

The MENU command is used to identify a menu. The generic syntax for the MENU command is as follows:

```
MENU <number>, <title>
```

Number is used for reference and can be from 1 to 255. *Title* appears at the top center of the menu box that appears on screen. The title can be up to 40 characters in length. An example of the use of this command is

```
MENU 21, Image Copy Menu
```

The ITEM Command

The ITEM command identifies a menu choice. The generic syntax for this command is as follows:

```
ITEM [^character]<name> [{option [option]}]
```

The *^character* is any single character that you wish to have appear in front of the item name, followed by a period and a space. The *name* of the menu item can be up to 40 characters. Options control the behavior of the executables for this item. You can have no options, one, two, three, or four options, in any combination. Options are placed after the ITEM name and are enclosed in curly braces ({}). If you have more than one option, spaces separate them. An example of this command is the following:

```
ITEM ^1D:Base IV {BATCH CHDIR}
```

In this example, the following text would appear on screen:

```
1. D:Base IV
```

^1 causes the numeral 1 to appear, followed by a period and a space. The name of this item is D:Base IV. BATCH causes the menu program to back itself out of memory when D:Base is executed. CHDIR ensures that the menu system returns to the default directory after program execution.

The options are summarized in table 35.1.

TABLE 35.1
MENU System ITEM Options

Option	Description
BATCH	This causes the menu program to remove itself from workstation RAM. This way you can run programs that use a lot of memory. When the user exits the program, the menu program reloads itself.
CHDIR	This changes the default directory back to the current directory in which the command was first executed. This way you can be assured that you start and finish in the same directory.

Option	Description
PAUSE	As in DOS batch files, this option causes the program to stop until the user presses a key. This saves you having to put the PAUSE command at the end of your menu options.
SHOW	This displays the name of the program being executed in the upper-left corner. This is useful to show the user that something is happening. Otherwise, when loading large programs, users tend to panic and reboot their computer before the program has a chance to load.

Menu Flow Commands Example

The following example shows you a simple menu with two submenus:

```
MENU 1,Main Menu
ITEM ^1Lotus 1-2-3 {BATCH CHDIR SHOW}
      EXEC 123
ITEM ^2WordPerfect {BATCH CHDIR SHOW}
      EXEC WP
ITEM ^3Print Menu
      SHOW 2
ITEM ^4DOS Menu
      SHOW 3
ITEM ^XExit to DOS Prompt
      EXEC exit
ITEM ^LExit and Logout
      EXEC logout

MENU 2,Print Menu
ITEM Print Console
      EXEC pconsole
ITEM Print Job Configuration
      EXEC printcon
ITEM Print Management
      EXEC netuser

MENU 3,DOS Menu
ITEM View Contents of Home Directory {PAUSE}
      EXEC NDIR F:
```

```
ITEM Execute DOS Shell {CHDIR}
      EXEC prompt Type 'EXIT' to Return $_$P$G
      EXEC command.com
      EXEC prompt $p$g
```

Figure 35.1 shows you what the menu looks like when run.

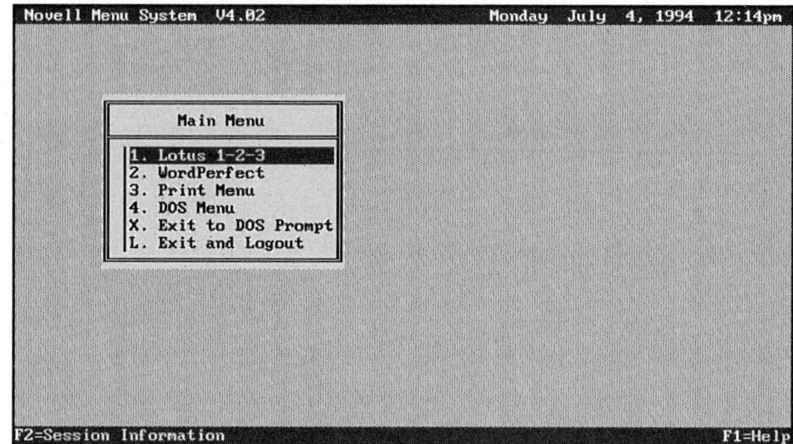

Figure 35.1
A sample menu file.

Menu Executable Commands

You can place within each menu ITEM a series of executable commands. There is no limit to the number of executables for any given ITEM. There are four executable commands: EXEC, LOAD, SHOW and GET*x*. The EXEC command is placed in front of an executable command or batch file. The LOAD and SHOW commands are used to call submenus. The GET*x* commands (GETO, GETR and GETP) are used to obtain user input. This section gives you detailed information on these commands, as well as examples of their use.

The EXEC Command

The general syntax for EXEC is as follows:

```
EXEC <command> ¦ <CALL ¦ DOS ¦ EXIT ¦ LOGOUT>
```

This option executes the *command*. The command can be a DOS program called from the DOS command prompt (including Windows). In addition, NetWare supplies several menu-specific EXEC commands. These are as follows:

- ◆ EXEC CALL calls a DOS batch file from within a menu.

- EXEC DOS creates a DOS shell.
- EXEC EXIT exits from the menu.
- EXEC LOGOUT logs you out of the network.

This example demonstrates the various uses of the EXEC command:

```
MENU 2,Applications Menu
ITEM ^1Order Entry {SHOW}
      EXEC MAP INS S1:=SYS:\APPS\ORDERS
      EXEC MAP G:=SYS:DATA\ORDERS
      EXEC G:
      EXEC OE
      EXEC F:
      EXEC MAP DEL G:
      EXEC MAP DEL S1:
ITEM ^2Run a Batch File {PAUSE}
GETO Enter Name of Batch File {} 40, \LOGIN\SLIST, {.BAT}
EXEC CALL %
ITEM ^3DOS Shell
      EXEC PROMPT Type 'Exit' to Return $_$p$g
      EXEC DOS
      EXEC PROMPT $p$g
ITEM ^XExit Menu to the DOS Prompt
EXEC EXIT
ITEM ^LExit Menu and Logout
EXEC LOGOUT
```

The LOAD Command

This command loads an external tokenized menu file. Use this command to call a submenu where the submenu file is external to the current menu file. The path to the source file must be specified and must be accessible through a drive letter. To load a file SALES.DAT in the PUBLIC\MENU directory, enter the following:

```
MENU 1, Main Menu
ITEM Sales Menu
     LOAD F:\menu\sales.dat
```

The SHOW Command

This command invokes a submenu defined inside the current menu file. You can have up to 255 menus within one menu file. For more menus, use the LOAD command. To show an ACCOUNTING menu, enter the following:

```
MENU 1, Main Menu
ITEM ^AAccounting Menu
     SHOW 2
...

MENU 2, Accounting Menu
ITEM ...
```

The GETO, GETR, and GETP Commands

The GET*x* series of commands is used to gather user input. The last letter refers to the status of the input as follows:

- **R** is required input. The user must enter something.
- **O** is optional input. The user can press Enter to bypass the input dialog box. If any defaults were defined, they are accepted.
- **P** assigns a variable to the input. The first GETP command is assigned to the variable %1, the second GETP is assigned to the variable %2, and so forth.

When using the GETO or GETR commands, the percent sign (%) is the generic variable used to represent the input from the command. The first command following a GETO or GETR command using the percent sign (%) as input prevents you from re-using the user input. When the GETP command is used, the variables are numbered (%1, %2, and so on). Values input using the GETP command stick and can be re-used again and again for the same ITEM. Otherwise, the usage of these commands is identical.

The user input from the GETO and GETR commands is valid only for a single command following the input command. If you need to use the input several times, use the GETP command instead.

The general syntax of the GET*x* commands is as follows:

```
GETx prompt {before} length, default, {after}
```

prompt is the text you want to have appear when the input box is displayed. You can have up to 40 characters for your prompt.

{before} is information you wish to have appear in front of whatever input the user supplies. Typically, this is a drive letter and a path. It is inserted in front of the text the user types automatically, saving him extra typing.

length is how many characters the user is allowed to input.

default is the default value when using GETO or GETP. If the user presses Enter without typing in anything, this value appears.

{after} is what is appended after the user enters information. This could be a file extension, for example.

The following example shows you the usage of the GETP input command.

```
MENU 1,Name and Phone Number List
ITEM ^1Add Name to List
      GETP Enter Last Name {} 30,, {}
      GETP Enter Login Name {} 30,, {}
      GETP Enter Area Code {} 3,, {}
      GETP Enter Phone Number {} 8,, {}
      EXEC ECHO "%1 %2 %3 %4" >>F:\DATA\PHONE\PHONE.LOG
ITEM ^2Find Name in Phone List
      SHOW 2
ITEM ^3Display Entire Phone List {PAUSE}
      EXEC type F:\DATA\PHONE\PHONE.LOG
ITEM ^XExit Menu to the DOS Prompt
      EXEC EXIT
ITEM ^LExit Menu and Logout
      EXEC LOGOUT

MENU 2,Search Phone List
ITEM ^1By Last Name {PAUSE}
      GETP Enter Last Name {} 30,, {}
      EXEC echo Searching For: %1
      EXEC find /I "%1" F:\DATA\PHONE\PHONE.LOG
ITEM ^2By First Name {PAUSE}
      GETP Enter First Name {} 30,, {}
      EXEC echo Searching For: %1
      EXEC find /I "%1" F:\DATA\PHONE\PHONE.LOG
ITEM ^3By Area Code {PAUSE}
      GETP Enter Area Code {} 3,, {}
      EXEC echo Searching For: %1
      EXEC find /I "%1" F:\DATA\PHONE\PHONE.LOG
ITEM ^4By Phone Number {PAUSE}
      GETP Enter Phone Number {} 8,, {}
      EXEC echo Searching For: %1
      EXEC find /I "%1" F:\DATA\PHONE\PHONE.LOG
```

Figure 35.2 shows you what the Add Name to List option of the preceding menu looks like when run.

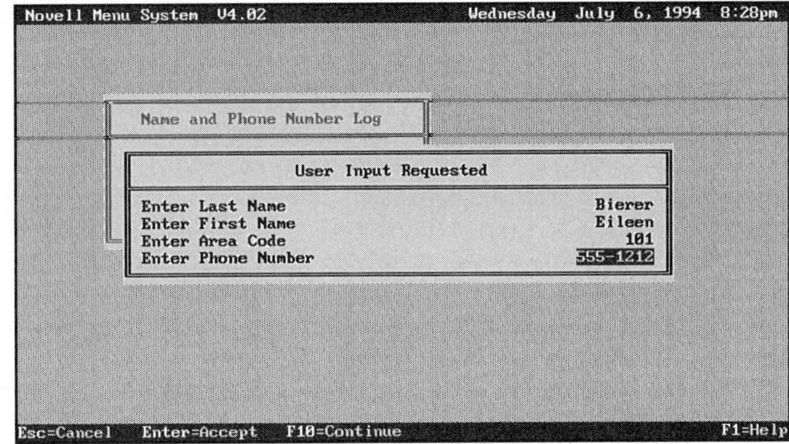

Figure 35.2
Name and phone number menu example—Add Name to List function.

MENUCNVT

The MENUCNVT utility can be used to convert NetWare 2.*x*- or 3.*x*- style menus into Saber menu format. NetWare menus prior to NetWare 4.1 had a preferred extension of MNU. The style and content of the menus are similar to those of NetWare 4.1; however, the command syntax and functionality have minor variations. The MENUCNVT utility can be used to convert an earlier style NetWare menu into a Saber menu SRC file. You must then run the MENUMAKE utility to tokenize the file and make it acceptable for the NMENU.BAT process to run.

The steps involved in converting a NetWare 2.*x* or 3.*x* style menu into NetWare 4.*x* format are as follows:

1. Convert the menu into a NetWare 4.1 SRC format as follows:

   MENUCNVT ***<old style menu filename>***

2. Tokenize the SRC file:

   MENUMAKE ***<.SRC filename>***

3. Run the tokenized menu:

   NMENU ***<.DAT filename>***

Creating Foreground/Background Color Palettes

You can use the COLORPAL.EXE utility to create colorful foreground/background color combinations for the menus you create.

Figure 35.3 shows the COLORPAL main menu.

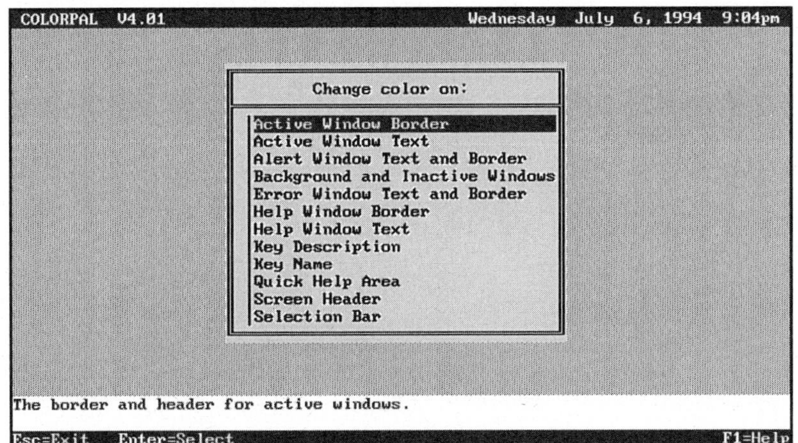

Figure 35.3
The COLORPAL main menu.

When you select any of the items from the COLORPAL main menu, you see a color chart. Choose the color that best suits your needs, and press Enter. The main menu of COLORPAL changes to reflect your choice.

Executing a Menu

The MENUMAKE.EXE utility is used to convert your menu source file into a tokenized menu file that can be executed. You can use the NMENU.BAT utility to launch your tokenized menu file. The NMENU.BAT command can be placed after the EXIT command in a login script to take users from their login script to menus you have created. Another aspect of menu execution discussed in this section is what security access rights and environmental changes users need to successfully launch menus.

MENUMAKE

The MENUMAKE.EXE utility is used to convert ASCII source text files into tokenized binary menu executable files. The file extension of the source files is assumed to be SRC. The file extension of the tokenized executable is DAT.

The syntax of the command is as follows:

```
MENUMAKE <source filespec>
```

If *source filespec* contains wildcards (such as *.SRC), MENUMAKE proceeds to tokenize all files that match the specification. When it is finished, a corresponding file with the extension DAT is produced. Here is what the output from this command looks like:

```
F:\DATA\NRP\INSIDE4>MENUMAKE fig3504
Novell Menu Script Compiler v4.01 (940202)
(c) Copyright 1993, Novell, Inc.  All rights reserved.
F:\DATA\NRP\INSIDE4\FIG3504.SRC:
F:\DATA\NRP\INSIDE4\FIG3504.DAT written.

F:\DATA\NRP\INSIDE4>
```

NMENU

The NMENU.BAT utility is used to execute a tokenized menu file. The NMENU.BAT batch file is located on volume SYS;, in the PUBLIC directory. You must understand two DOS variables you can set in the user's DOS environment. The two variables are the following:

```
S_FILEDIR
S_FILE
```

S_FILEDIR controls in which directory temporary files are located. S_FILE controls the name of the temporary files. One suggestion is to create a common directory on the file server where users can store temporary menu files. This must be a directory where users have at least Read, File Scan, Write, Create, Modify, and Erase directory trustee rights. The S_FILEDIR variable can be set to this directory. The S_FILE variable could be set to the workstation's file server connection number.

If you plan to use the SET command to set these variables in a user login script, you must use a double backslash (\\) when indicating subdirectories. The login script interpreter takes the first backslash to mean that the interpreter should treat the character immediately after the backslash literally.

In the user's login script, add the following commands:

```
*
*     This sets the location of temporary menu files
*     to the F:\COMMON directory
```

```
*
SET S_FILEDIR="F:\\COMMON"
*
*     This command makes sure that each user's temporary
*     filenames are unique by using value of the identifier
*     variable STATION, which records the workstation's
*     connection number with the file server.
*
SET S_FILE="%STATION"
*
*     This command exits to a menu specific to
*     this user.
*
EXIT "NMENU %LOGIN_NAME"
```

The contents of NMENU.BAT are as follows:

```
@ECHO OFF

IF "%1"== "/?" GOTO HELP
MENURSET
IF ERRORLEVEL == 1 GOTO EXIT
IF "%S_FILE%" == "" GOTO STDNAME
%S_FILEDIR%$%S_FILE% %1 %2 %3
:STDNAME
%S_FILEDIR%MENU_0 %1 %2 %3
GOTO EXIT
:HELP
MENURSET /?
:EXIT
```

The first line checks to see if the user has entered a "/?" that calls for the help screen. The MENURSET.EXE utility in the second line creates a temporary batch file MENU_O.BAT (or a batch file with the file name assigned by the variable S_FILE). In the third line, if the outcome of the MENURSET indicates a problem, the batch file is exited. The next line checks to see if the S_FILE variable has not been set. If so, the batch file jumps to the label STDNAME. Otherwise, the batch file located in the directory indicated by S_FILEDIR, of the name indicated by S_FILE, is executed. If S_FILE has not been assigned a value, the default temporary batch file, MENU_O.BAT, is executed.

The contents of the temporary batch file (MENU_O.BAT by default) are as follows:

```
REM Temporary batch file (MENURSET)
```

```
ECHO OFF
MENUEXE %1 %2 %3 %4 %5 %6 %7 %8 %9
MENU_X
```

MENUEXE is the main menu interpreter. It is a runtime version of Saber menu. When the menu is done, the MENU_X.BAT file, also located in SYS:PUBLIC, is executed. This batch file deletes the temporary menu batch file.

Giving Users Access to Menus

To give users proper access to menus you have created, you need to do the following:

1. Give the users at least Read trustee rights to either the menu file or the directory in which it resides.

2. Designate a place where the menu system can store temporary files. This can be the temporary directory indicated by the S_FILEDIR variable, or the current directory.

3. Give the users at least Read, File Scan, Write, Create, Modify, and Erase trustee rights to the directory where temporary menu files are to be stored.

4. Map a search drive to SYS:PUBLIC. This is the directory that contains, besides NetWare executables, NMENU.BAT, MENURSET.EXE, MENUEXE.EXE, and MENU_X.BAT.

In most cases, if you plan to use the Novell menu utility, you can place a command in the user login script that exits the user to a menu. An example of this is illustrated in the previous section. Place the NMENU command in quotes after the EXIT command.

Creating Batch Files

Batch files can be created and placed on the file server to serve various user needs. In some cases a simple batch file menu system might meet the needs of your network users. Batch files take up very little RAM and disk space. Complex batch files unfortunately can easily go astray. Bear in mind that a wide range of users with various levels of computer knowledge may be using batch files you create. Place as much error-checking into the batch file as possible.

Several considerations should go into the creation of batch files. One consideration is to decide who needs access to the batch file. Depending on the answer to this question, you need to grant at least Read trustee rights to either the batch file itself or the

directory where it resides. In addition to trustee rights, you need to either change to the directory containing the batch file or map a search drive to this directory.

If you decide to create more than five or six batch files, consider creating a special directory just for batch files. You could create a directory BAT off the root of volume SYS:, for example. In this directory, place all network batch files. You could grant Read and File Scan trustee rights to the container where users of the batch files are located, and map a search drive to this directory in the container login script.

Once the batch files are created and tested, another consideration is to change their attributes to Shareable and Read Only. Changing the attributes of the batch files protects them from being deleted or modified accidentally. The Shareable attribute is necessary where multiple users may be accessing the same batch file at the same time.

A Simple Batch File Menu System

The following sample batch files illustrate how a simple batch file menu system might work. The following commands could be placed in the user's login script:

```
*
*     Maps drive letter L: to the batch file directory
*
MAP ROOT L:=SYS:BAT
*
*     This command places the user on drive L:
*
DRIVE L:
*
*     Exit the login script and run the batch file menu
*
EXIT "L:BMENU.BAT"
```

Here is the BMENU.BAT batch file menu:

```
@echo off
rem
rem   Title:      BMENU.BAT
rem   Date:       7/11/94
rem   Author:     Doug Bierer
rem   Notes:      Batch File Menu System
rem
cls
type L:BMENU.TXT
rem
rem   At this point the batch file ends.  The user chooses any of
```

```
rem   the options listed, which are themselves batch files.  Each
rem   option batch file calls this file.
rem
```

As you can see, the batch file simply displays the contents of the BMENU.TXT file to the screen. Here is what this text file looks like:

```
-------------------------------------------------------------------
:                                                                 :
:       XXX       XXX      YYY       YYY      ZZZZZZZZZZZZZ       :
:        XXX     XXX        YYY     YYY                ZZZ        :
:         XXX   XXX          YYY   YYY                ZZZ         :
:          XXX XXX            YYY YYY               ZZZ           :
:           XXXXX              YYYYY               ZZZ            :
:          XXX XXX              YYY              ZZZ              :
:         XXX   XXX             YYY             ZZZ               :
:        XXX     XXX            YYY            ZZZ                :
:       XXX       XXX           YYY           ZZZZZZZZZZZZZ       :
:                                                                 :
:              C O R P O R A T E      M E N U                     :
:                                                                 :
:-----------------------------------------------------------------:
:                                                                 :
:   Enter any of the following choices:                           :
:                                                                 :
:      1 - WordPerfect               2 - Lotus 1-2-3              :
:      3 - dBASE IV                 4 - Inventory Control        :
:                                                                 :
:      L - Log out of the Network                                 :
:                                                                 :
-------------------------------------------------------------------
```

The options listed in the text file are actually batch files in and of themselves. Option 1, for example, corresponds with the batch file 1.BAT. Option L corresponds with the L.BAT file. Here is what the 1.BAT file looks like:

```
@echo off
rem
rem   Title:       1.BAT
rem   Date:        7/11/94
rem   Author:      Doug Bierer
rem   Notes:       Option #1 of the Batch File Menu System
rem                Calls WordPerfect
```

```
rem
rem   Maps search drive to the WordPerfect directory
rem
map INS S1:=SYS:APPS\WP
cls
echo :
echo :      Loading WordPerfect...
echo :
wp
echo :
echo :      Returning to Main Menu
echo :
rem
rem   Gets rid of the search drive created above
rem
map del S1:
rem
rem   Remaps drive L: just in case it has changed
rem
map root L:=SYS:BAT
cls
L:
type L:BMENU.TXT
```

1.BAT, as with the other batch files that correspond to options, does the following:

1. Maps search drive 1 to the application directory
2. Calls the application
3. Gets rid of search drive 1
4. Remaps drive L: to the batch file directory
5. Moves to drive L:
6. Displays the menu text file to the screen

In this manner, the batch file menu appears to be in control. In reality, each option is a batch file that returns to the batch file directory each time. Each option batch file clears the screen and redraws the original menu text file.

Multiuser Control Batch File

This example shows you how to use batch files to set up a multiuser control system.

This is ideal for applications that do not do a good job of checking for multiuser access. In this example, users want to run a special Order-Entry program that is not multi-user. The container login script for the users of this program sets a DOS variable ID to the user's login name, network connection number, and node address. The batch file checks for the existence of a file LOG.TXT. If this file exists, the batch file assumes the Order-Entry program is in use and warns the user to try again later. It displays the login name, network connection, and node address of the user who is using the program. If the LOG.TXT file does not exist, the batch file creates it and runs the program. When the user exits the program, the batch file erases the LOG.TXT file.

Here are the commands placed in the container login script:

```
*
*     Map a drive letter O: to the Order-Entry directory
*
MAP O:=.CN=EBDB_DATA.OU=SJ.O=EBDB:\OENTRY
*
*    Set a DOS variable ID1 = Login Name
*                       ID2 = Connection
*                       ID3 = Node Address
*
SET ID1="%LOGIN_NAME"
SET ID2="%STATION
SET ID3="%P_STATION"
```

The batch file OE.BAT is called up whenever users wish to run the Order-Entry program. Here is what that batch file looks like:

```
@echo off
rem
rem   Title:         OE.BAT
rem   Date:          7/11/94
rem   Author:        Doug Bierer
rem   Notes:         Calls the Order Entry Program
rem
rem   Moves to drive O: which was mapped in the container login script
rem
O:
rem
rem   Checks for the LOG.TXT file
rem
if exist LOG.TXT goto BUSY
rem
```

```
rem   If not busy, create the LOG.TXT file
rem
echo : >LOG.TXT
echo :                User Name:     %ID1% >>LOG.TXT
echo :       Network Connection:     %ID2% >>LOG.TXT
echo :             Node Address:     %ID3% >>LOG.TXT
echo :       Time: >>LOG.TXT
systime >>LOG.TXT
rem
rem   Run the Order Entry Program
rem
cls
echo :
echo :       Loading the Order Entry Program...
echo :
OE.EXE
rem
rem   When done, erase the LOG.TXT file
rem
del LOG.TXT
goto DONE
rem
rem   If someone is using the Order Entry program, display warning
rem
:BUSY
echo :
echo :       Warning: the Order Entry Program is in use.
echo :
type LOG.TXT
pause
:DONE
echo :
echo :       Exiting the Order Entry Program
echo :
```

If another user is using the program, the following message pops up:

```
:
:       Warning: the Order Entry Program is in use.
:
:
:                User Name:     LChappel
:       Network Connection:     2
```

```
:              Node Address:     0080C7014103
:         Time:
Current system time:  Tuesday 7-12-94 10:29:33 pm
Press any key to continue . . .
```

Summary

This chapter gave you detailed information about creating menus and batch files for your network. As you learned, the NetWare menu utility is a runtime version of Saber Menu. The source menu file is an ASCII text file containing a series of menuing commands. This file is then converted into a tokenized version using the MENUMAKE utility. The NMENU.BAT batch file executes the menu. The utility MENUCNVT can be used to convert NetWare 3.*x* or NetWare 2.*x* menus into the Saber Menu format.

Menu commands include MENU, which identifies a menu; ITEM, used to indicate a menu choice that appears on screen; and EXEC. The EXEC command precedes an executable command associated with an ITEM. The GET*x* commands are used to gather user input. Extensive examples of each of these commands were illustrated in this section.

The second part of this section covered batch files. Batch files are best used to augment the command set that comes with NetWare. Any repetitive sequence of commands could be facilitated by creating a batch file. As discussed, you could create a directory where all batch files could reside. A sample batch file menu system was presented, along with a sample multi-user control batch file. As you learned in this section, batch files are often supplemented with commands placed in user or container login scripts. In the login script you can SET a series of DOS variables that can be used in a batch file.

The next chapter covers ways in which you can give remote users access to the network.

Part IX

Managing the File Server and the Network

New Riders Publishing
INSIDE
SERIES

Monitoring the File Server

There are many things that should be regularly monitored on a NetWare 4 server. These include memory utilization, communications, and NDS activities. In addition, it is important to be able to monitor user connections and server configuration.

The server console is where the server is managed. It is important to remember that when you are operating on the server, you are interacting directly with NetWare. Server console commands form a limited command set available only from the console. This chapter gives you some familiarity with the more important console commands and utilities.

Operating from the Server Console

When operating from the server console, only certain commands are available. The term *server console* originated in mainframe computer systems. On a mainframe, there is no monitor or keyboard. The mainframe computer is a refrigerator sized unit with a series of peripheral devices (such as disk drive units and communications controllers) connected to it. To enable the mainframe computer operator to directly communicate with the mainframe, a dumb terminal is connected to a special port on the mainframe. This dumb terminal, consisting of little more than a screen and keyboard, is called a *console.*

Most servers are IBM PC's or clones typically equipped with large hard drives and 16 MB or more of RAM. A PC has its own monitor and keyboard. The server's monitor and keyboard are referred to as the *server console.*

The server console displays a colon (:) as a prompt. The rationale behind using the colon is to remind you that you are operating from the server's console rather than from some other operating system, such as DOS.

DOS function keys (such as F3) are not used on the server's console. The F1 key is used to obtain online help. Table 36.1 summarizes the keys that are available to assist you when entering commands at the server console.

Table 36.1
Server Console Command Keys

Command Key	Description
Up Arrow	The up arrow is used to retrieve the last 100 commands that have been issued at the server console. When more than 100 commands have been issued, only the most recent 100 commands are saved. The up arrow moves through the last 100 commands in the order of the most recent command to the oldest command.
Down Arrow	The down arrow enables you move down the list of commands. The down arrow moves through the last 100 commands in the order of oldest command to most recent command.
Right Arrow	The right arrow enables you to move horizontally to the right when you are editing the command currently on the command line. Characters are not erased while using the right arrow.

Command Key	Description
Left Arrow	The left arrow enables you to move horizontally to the left when you are editing the command currently on the command line. Characters are not erased while using the left arrow.
Home	The Home key moves you to the beginning of the command currently on the command line.
End	The End key moves you to the end of the command currently on the command line.
Backspace	The Backspace key is used to move horizontally to the left of the command currently on the command line while erasing characters.
Del	The Del key deletes the character currently above the cursor.
Esc	The Esc key clears the command line, canceling any command you have typed.
Enter	The Enter key executes the command currently on the command line.

You can create server batch files that execute a complex series of commands. On the server console, any ASCII text file that ends with the extension NCF is treated like a DOS batch file. You can place any valid server console command, or use the LOAD command to load any NLM in such server batch files.

These files should be placed in the SYS:SYSTEM directory to be accessible from the server console immediately. If you place them in another directory, either include the path when invoking the batch file or add the directory to the server's search path using the SEARCH ADD volume:directory command.

Please note that if you issue the SECURE CONSOLE command, you can only load NCF files and NLMs from the SYS:SYSTEM directory.

Using RCONSOLE

The RCONSOLE.EXE (Remote Console) utility is a DOS-based utility that enables you to access the server's console from a workstation. This utility is located in the SYS:SYSTEM directory of the NetWare 4 server. RCONSOLE takes your keystrokes and transmits them to the server console. In return, it transmits the server console screen to your workstation.

If you are running RCONSOLE on your workstation—accessing a server console—while another network Administrator is accessing the same server console, your keystrokes may interfere with the keystrokes issued by the other user. This effect is the same as if you were both typing on the same keyboard. If you are both in different server utility screens, your keystrokes do not conflict, but if you are both at the server console prompt, there could be a problem.

Configuring the Server to Run RCONSOLE

Before you can use RCONSOLE from a workstation, you must configure the server to enable remote access. This involves loading a series of NetWare Loadable Modules (NLMs) on the server and determining what type of connection is desired.

Three types of connections are available for remote users. These options are illustrated in figure 36.1 and are labeled 1, 2, and 3. Option 1 is a direct asynchronous connection between a remote computer and the server. Option 2 is a connection across the LAN. Option 3 is a connection where a remote computer takes over a computer on the LAN.

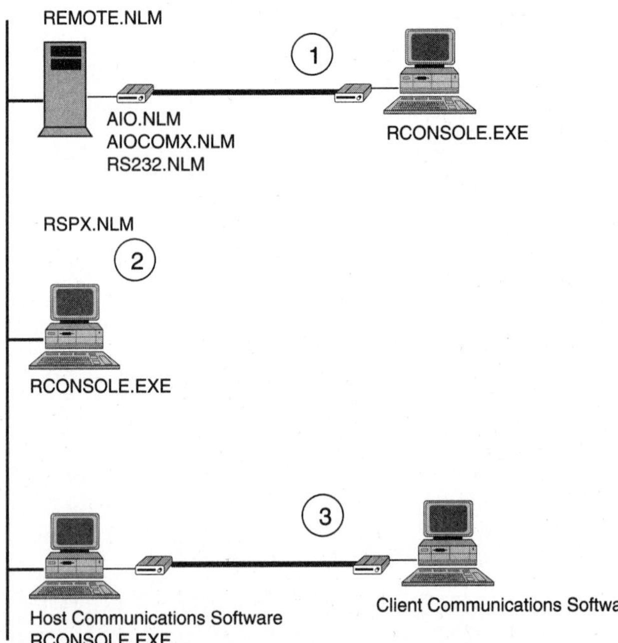

Figure 36.1 *Three RCONSOLE connection options.*

Loading the REMOTE Utility

In all three cases, you first need to load REMOTE.NLM on the server. This module controls the remote access sessions. When you enter the following command you are asked to supply a password. If you do not supply a password, an error message appears indicating that a password must be entered.

LOAD REMOTE

The REMOTE utility can produce an encrypted password for your use. This encrypted password then is placed in a file called LDREMOTE.NCF, which is used to load REMOTE with the encrypted password. The advantage here is that if a user happens to view the password, it is meaningless. The original password must be entered and REMOTE interprets the encrypted password to enable access.

The following is a sample session where REMOTE is used to produce an encrypted password:

```
EBDB:remote encrypt


Enter a password to encrypt
>
To use this password use the command:
     Load REMOTE -E 7326149766119133993 3D3
Would you like this command written to SYS:SYSTEM\LDREMOTE.NCF? (y/n)
```

If you answer Yes to the prompt above, a file LDREMOTE.NCF is created and saved in the SYS:SYSTEM directory.

REMOTE has the additional parameters LOCK OUT and UNLOCK. The LOCK OUT parameter locks out additional remote users. The advantage to this is that there are no other users who can interfere with a session on the server console. The UNLOCK parameter re-enables remote access.

To disable other users from accessing the server through RCONSOLE, type the following:

REMOTE LOCK OUT

To re-enable RCONSOLE access, type the following:

REMOTE UNLOCK

Unlike NetWare 4.0*x* or NetWare 3.*x*, NetWare 4.1 does not accept the SUPERVISOR password in place of the REMOTE password.

Establishing a Direct Asynchronous Connection

As you can see from figure 36.1, option 1 involves the server, 2 modems, a phone line, and a remote computer. When using option 1, you need to load REMOTE.NLM, RS232.NLM, and the appropriate asynchronous drivers on the server. At the workstation, you run RCONSOLE and select the Asynchronous option.

The asynchronous drivers selected are AIO.NLM and AIOCOMX.NLM. These drivers come with NetWare 4.1. The AIO driver is a runtime module used in conjunction with remote routing. It is designed to enable the server to handle asynchronous input/output (I/O) traffic. The AIOCOMX driver is designed for the COM ports on the server. If the server is equipped with other asynchronous hardware, such as a WNIM+ (Wide Area Network Interface Module) adapter, the driver for this board is loaded in place of AIOCOMX.

Finally, the RS232.NLM module is loaded to enable REMOTE.NLM to accept console through the RS-232 port (or other asynchronous ports) on the server. When you load RS232 you are asked for the port number and speed (baud rate) of the modem attached to the server's asynchronous port.

The following is a sample session on the server console configuring the server for a direct asynchronous connection:

```
EBDB:load remote
Loading module REMOTE.NLM
  NetWare Remote Console
  Version 4.10e   August 24, 1994
  Copyright 1994 Novell, Inc.  All rights reserved.

Enter a password for Remote Console
>
Remote Console successfully loaded
EBDB:load aio
Loading module AIO.NLM
  NetWare 4.0x Runtime Asynchronous I/O Library
  Version 2.00    February 14, 1994
  Copyright 1991-1993, Novell Inc. All rights reserved.
EBDB:load aiocomx
Loading module AIOCOMX.NLM
  NetWare 3.x AIO COMX Driver
  Version 2.00    December 17, 1992
  Copyright 1992, Novell Inc. All rights reserved.
For AIOCOMX Driver Load Information, Enter 'LOAD AIOCOMX ?'
Installed I/O Address 0x3F8 (Interrupt Number 4) as Board 0, Port 0
```

```
8250/16450 device detected: Driver rated at 2400bps
EBDB:load RS232
Loading module RS232.NLM
  NetWare Remote Console RS232 Driver
  Version 4.10    August 24, 1994
  Copyright 1994 Novell, Inc.  All rights reserved.
Available COM ports:
#1 -  hardware type:1  board:0  port:0
Please choose a COM port
COM Port: 1
Please enter the baud rate (2400 - 38400)
Baud Rate: 9600
```

The RS232.NLM has these additional options:

```
LOAD RS232 [com port] [modem speed] [N] [C]
```

The *com port* can be COM1 or COM2. On some computers you also can specify COM3 or COM4. The *modem speed* is from 2400 to 38400 bits per second. The letter *N* indicates you are using a *null modem* cable. This is a cable used to directly attach a dumb terminal or another computer to a COM port. The letter *C* indicates that you want to have the server call back a preselected number. The authorized phone numbers should be stored in an ASCII text file CALLBACK.LST you create and save in the SYS:SYSTEM directory. This file contains phone numbers. When the remote computer dials up, the server records its phone number and hangs up. If the phone number is the same as a phone number in the list, the server dials back this phone number and establishes an RCONSOLE session.

Establishing an RCONSOLE Session across the LAN

To establish an RCONSOLE connection across the LAN, you need to load two NLMs on the server: REMOTE.NLM and RSPX.NLM. RSPX, as the name implies, uses the SPX protocol to ensure a reliable connection. From the workstation, you only need to run RCONSOLE.

The following is a sample session on the server console configuring the server for RCONSOLE access across the LAN:

```
EBDB:load remote
Loading module REMOTE.NLM
  NetWare Remote Console
  Version 4.10e   August 24, 1994
  Copyright 1994 Novell, Inc.  All rights reserved.
```

```
Enter a password for Remote Console
>
Remote Console successfully loaded
EBDB:load rspx
Loading module RSPX.NLM
  NetWare Remote Console SPX Driver
  Version 4.10a   August 24, 1994
  Copyright 1994 Novell, Inc.  All rights reserved.
```

Accessing the Server Using Other Remote Communications Software

As option 3 in figure 36.1 illustrates, you can access the server console through a workstation already on the LAN. This option requires the following hardware and software modules:

- On the server, you must load REMOTE.NLM and RSPX.NLM.
- On the LAN workstation, you must load the host communications software.
- The LAN workstation must have a modem and access to a phone line.
- The remote computer must have a modem and access to a phone line.
- The remote computer must run client communications software.

The communications software must be of the type where you connect two computers over a phone line, and the client computer takes over the host computer. Examples of this type of software include the following:

- Carbon Copy by Microcom
- PC Anywhere by Symantec
- Closeup by Norton Lambert
- Windows for Workgroups (Microsoft), Remote Access option

Communications software such as the preceding transmits only keystrokes from the client to the host, and only screen updates from the host back to the client. The host computer runs all applications. This communications setup is very efficient and enables you to access programs on the LAN as well as run RCONSOLE. Once you run RCONSOLE on the host computer, you have access to the server console (provided you know the REMOTE.NLM password).

Using RCONSOLE

To use RCONSOLE, proceed as follows:

1. Log in to the network as a user with at least Read file trustee rights to SYS:SYSTEM\RCONSOLE.EXE and its supporting files.

2. From the SYS:SYSTEM directory, or any other directory if a search drive is mapped to SYS:SYSTEM, issue the following command:

   RCONSOLE

   The RCONSOLE Connection Type menu appears.

RCONSOLE might not function correctly if you run it under a Windows DOS session. In most cases this is not a problem. On some machines there can be conflicts, causing the session to terminate abruptly. When running RCONSOLE from Windows, a warning message appears telling you that there can be problems. You can proceed and test access on your computer.

3. Select Asynchronous from the Connection Type menu if you are using a direct asynchronous connection to the server (as in option 1 in figure 36.1). Select SPX if your connection is through the LAN (options 2 and 3 in figure 36.1).

   If you selected Asynchronous, you see the Asynchronous Options menu. Select Configuration to configure the phone number and characteristics of your modem. The Current Modem Configuration dialog box appears as in figure 36.2.

```
Remote Console  4.10                    Saturday  October  1, 1994  3:20pm

                        Current Modem Configuration

Select Device                           Hayes Compatible Modem
Select com port                         COM1
Select baud rate                        19200 Baud

Modem Reset Command                     ATZ\r~
Modem Initialization Command            ATQ0V1X4\r
Modem Reconnect Command                 ATH0Q0V1X4S0=1
Modem Dial Command                      ATDT
Modem Hangup Command                    ATH0\r~

User Connection ID                      Doug
Call Back Number                        555-1212

<F1> Help
```

Figure 36.2
The Current Modem Configuration dialog box.

Table 36.2 summarizes the options in this dialog box.

Table 36.2
RCONSOLE Current Modem Configuration Options

Option	Description
Select Device	Choices include Hayes Compatible Modem or Null Modem. If you are using a modem, select Hayes Compatible Modem. If your connection is direct using a null modem cable, select this option. (If your modem is not Hayes compatible, you may want to check your budget and consider making a purchase.)
Select com port	Select the COM port to which your modem is connected.
Select baud rate	Select the desired modem speed, from 2400 bps (bits per second) to a maximum of 38,400 bps.
Modem Reset Command	The command string used to reset your modem.
Modem Initialization Command	The command string used to initialize your modem.
Modem Reconnect Command	The command string used to reconnect your modem.
Modem Dial Command	The command string used to cause your modem to dial.
Modem Hangup Command	The command string used to cause your modem to hang up.
User Connection ID	An identifying name used by the server to track who you are.
Call Back Number	The number for the server to call back. This assumes that you have enabled the callback option (see RS232.NLM options).

4. The next step for an asynchronous connection is to select the Connect to Remote Location option from the Asynchronous Options menu. The Location/ Phone Number list appears. Press Insert to add a phone number to the list. Enter the name and phone number for the server location, as shown in figure 36.3. Press Esc to save the change and return to the Location/Phone Number list. Continue to add names to the list as appropriate. Press the F3 key to modify an entry.

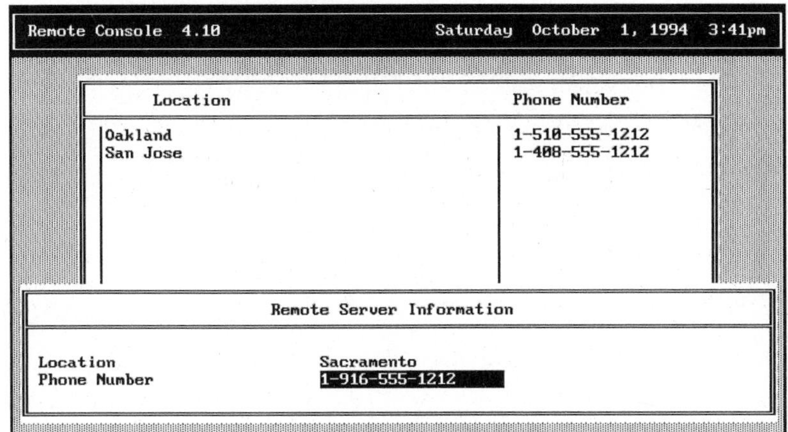

Figure 36.3
RCONSOLE Asynchronous Options—Location/Phone Number list.

When you finish entering names in the list, from the Location/Phone Number list select the target server and press Enter. RCONSOLE dials the location and creates a connection.

5. If you selected SPX from the RCONSOLE Connection Type menu, you see a list of servers. This list also appears when you make an asynchronous connection. Choose the target server from the list and press Enter to access the server console. You next see a screen asking you for the REMOTE password. Enter the password and press Enter. You now see the server console screen.

If the desired server does not appear on the list, the proper REMOTE and other NLMs might not be loaded on that server. You can go to the server (if available) and load these NLMs. When you return to your workstation, press Esc and answer No to the question, "Exit Remote Console?" When you return to the Available Servers list, the server checks the LAN for additional servers running REMOTE, refreshing the list.

The RCONSOLE Menu and Keystrokes

RCONSOLE has its own menu that you can access by pressing Alt+F1 (see fig. 36.4).

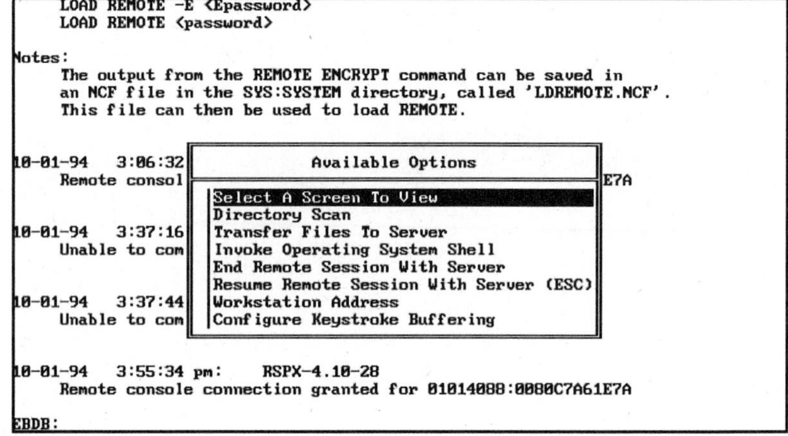

Figure 36.4
The RCONSOLE Available Options menu.

Table 36.3 summarizes the options for the RCONSOLE Available Options menu.

Table 36.3
RCONSOLE Available Options Menu Options

Option	Description
Select A Screen To View	Brings up a list of screens used by the various NLMs you have loaded on your server. You then can select which screen to view and press Enter to jump to that screen.
Directory Scan	Enables you to view a list of files and directories on the server. This includes a view of the server's DOS partition and any floppy disks that may be in its floppy drive(s).
Transfer Files To Server	Enables you to transfer files to the server.

Option	Description
Invoke Operating System Shell	Takes you to the DOS shell where you can perform any DOS command. When you type **EXIT** you are returned to the RCONSOLE session. This is especially useful when transferring files or getting a directory listing.
End Remote Session With Server	Exits the server console. You also can press Alt+F2 to exit the server console.
Resume Remote Session With Server	Returns you to the server console, closing the RCONSOLE menu.
Workstation Address	Gives you the workstation network and node address (useful for viewing connection information). You also can press Alt+F5.
Configure Keystroke Buffering	Enables you to control when your keystrokes appear on the server console screen. This is useful when there is a process running on the server or a series of error messages that prevent you from seeing your own keystrokes.

The options for Configure Keystroke Buffering are as follows:

- *No keyboard buffering* (the default) does not perform buffering.
- *Keystroke delay* sends keystrokes when the console keyboard is idle.
- *Manual keystroke send* stores your keystrokes until you press Alt+F8 at which time they are sent to the console.
- *On demand buffering* does not buffer keystrokes unless you press Alt+F9, at which time an input box appears enabling you to enter buffered keystrokes. Pressing Enter enters buffered keystrokes from the input box onto the server console.

You can view directly the NDS files using RCONSOLE. From the RCONSOLE menu, select Directory Scan. When you are asked for a directory name, enter SYS:_NETWARE. When you press Enter, you see the names, dates, and sizes of the NDS database files physically stored on this server.

RCONSOLE has the following keystrokes available (some of which have been mentioned already):

Keystroke	Function
Alt+F1	Brings up the RCONSOLE menu.
Alt+F2	Exits the server console.
Alt+F3	Toggles to the next server console screen. If you have MONITOR.NLM and INSTALL.NLM loaded, for example, repeatedly pressing Alt+F3 toggles from the console prompt to MONITOR, then to INSTALL, and then back to the console prompt.
Alt+F4	Toggles to the previous server console screen. If you have MONITOR.NLM and INSTALL.NLM loaded, for example, repeatedly pressing Alt+F4 toggles from the console prompt to INSTALL, then to MONITOR, and then back to the console prompt.
Alt+F5	Displays the network and node address of your workstation.
Alt+F8	Sends buffered keystrokes to the console if Manual keystroke send keyboard buffering is selected. (See Configure Keystroke Buffering from the RCONSOLE menu.)
Alt+F9	Sends buffered keystrokes to the console if On demand buffering keyboard buffering option is selected. (See Configure Keystroke Buffering from the RCONSOLE menu.)

Using MONITOR

The MONITOR.NLM utility is an excellent tool for viewing the status of the server at a glance. The main menu and status display screen for MONITOR are shown in figure 36.5. The MONITOR screen appears when you first load the utility by typing the following:

LOAD MONITOR

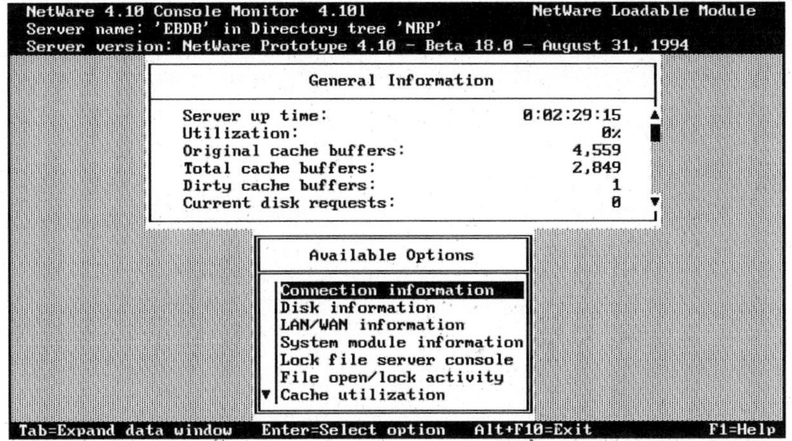

Figure 36.5

The MONITOR main menu and display screen.

MONITOR can be loaded with two parameters: L and N. The L parameter causes MONITOR to load with the server console keyboard automatically locked. The password for the bindery user SUPERVISOR can be used to unlock the console (this password is the original password assigned to the Admin user, unless changed). The LOAD MONITOR L command can be placed in the AUTOEXEC.NCF file. The N parameter causes MONITOR to load without the screen saver.

If you leave MONITOR running with no keyboard activity for 10 seconds, the General Information display screen expands to that shown in figure 36.6. You can use the Tab key to toggle between normal and expanded sizes. Another 10 minutes of inactivity causes MONITOR to invoke the screen saver, which consists of a series of consecutively lighter squares displayed on the screen.

```
NetWare 4.10 Console Monitor  4.101                NetWare Loadable Module
Server name: 'EBDB' in Directory tree 'NRP'
Server version: NetWare Prototype 4.10 - Beta 18.0 - August 31, 1994

                     General Information

      Server up time:                            0:02:32:55
      Utilization:                                       0%
      Original cache buffers:                         4,559
      Total cache buffers:                            2,849
      Dirty cache buffers:                                1
      Current disk requests:                              0
      Packet receive buffers:                            50
      Directory cache buffers:                           26
      Maximum service processes:                         40
      Current service processes:                          5
      Maximum licensed connections:                     250
      Current licensed connections:                       1
      Open files:                                        24

                    Lock file server console
                    File open/lock activity
                    Cache utilization
Tab=Shrink data window   Alt+F10=Exit                            F1=Help
```

Figure 36.6

The expanded MONITOR General Information screen.

Table 36.4 summarizes the fields in the MONITOR General Information Screen. Most values can be adjusted using the SERVMAN utility or by issuing a SET command from the server console. These commands are covered in the next chapter.

Table 36.4
Fields in the MONITOR General Information Screen

Field	Description
Server up time	The amount of time in Hours:Minutes:Seconds the server has been up.
Utilization	Percentage of CPU utilization of the server.
Original cache buffers	The number of cache buffers (4 KB each) available when the server first booted, before any NLMs were loaded.
Total cache buffers	The number of buffers remaining after the various NLMs and memory allocations have taken place. This is the amount of RAM available to cache files requested by users. The ratio of Total cache buffers to Original cache buffers should be 50 percent or greater. If not, you may want to load fewer NLMs or add more memory. If the ratio goes below 20 percent, the operation of the server is severely affected.
Dirty cache buffers	The number of buffers with data waiting to be written to the hard drive(s). If the ratio of Dirty cache buffers to Total cache buffers is greater than 75 percent, there is cause for concern. This means that there is a bottleneck getting data written to the hard drive. You can set a parameter: set Maximum disk cache writes to a higher value, or look at improving your disk hardware.
Current disk requests	The number of requests for data to or from the hard drives.
Packet receive buffers	The number of buffers reserved for processing requests between the server and client. The server continues to allocate packet receive buffers above the minimum number you set on an as-needed basis. If users report a slowdown in response, check if the server has allocated its maximum. If this is the case you can increase this value by issuing the Set Maximum Packet Receive Buffers command.

Field	Description
Directory cache buffers	The number of buffers allocated for directory caching. The target for data cached in this buffer space is the Directory Entry Table (DET), which uses another portion of RAM. When users need to access the DET frequently, the server allocates additional directory cache buffers to meet the needs.
Maximum service processes	The maximum number of service processes (task handlers) currently allocated to fill user requests. Each service process takes care of a file system request (such as reading files from or writing files to the server). When the task is completed, the service process is put to sleep.
Current service processes	The number of task handlers currently activated. This number represents the maximum currently made available by the server. The number of service processes actually working may be lower. If you notice that the number of current service processes equals the maximum service processes you should increase the maximum using the Set Maximum Service Processes parameter.
Maximum licensed connections	The number of user or other connections which are allowed by your version of NetWare.
Current licensed connections	The number of connections currently in use which count against your NetWare license.
Open files	The total number of files open on the server.

The following sections describe some of the MONITOR menu options. Because the options are too numerous for coverage in this chapter, only the items which have the most critical impact on your system are covered.

Connection Information

The Connection information menu gives you a view of users and logical processes that are using this server. When you select this menu, you see the Active Connections list (see fig. 36.7). Entries preceded with an asterisk (*) indicate a connection which is in use that does not count against your NetWare license. The number to the left of each active connection represents the connection identification number.

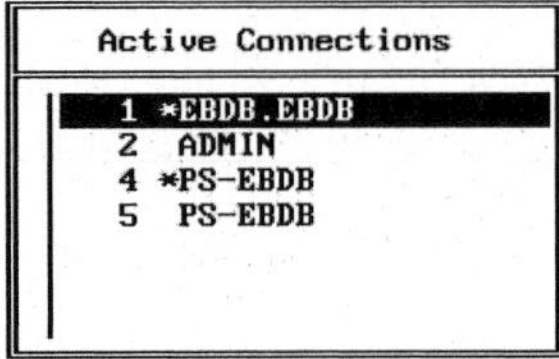

Figure 36.7
The Active Connections list.

A *connection* is a logical designation used by the server to track a communications session. When you first load the VLM shell on a DOS workstation, for example, you see an initial message, "Attached to Server *X*," where *X* is the name of the server. This attachment is assigned a connection number. If you look at the Active Connections list at this point, you see the connection number followed by the name `NOT-LOGGED-IN`. Once you login, your login name replaces `NOT-LOGGED-IN`.

If you press Enter after selecting a connection on the Active Connections list, you see the Connection Information screen as shown in figure 36.8.

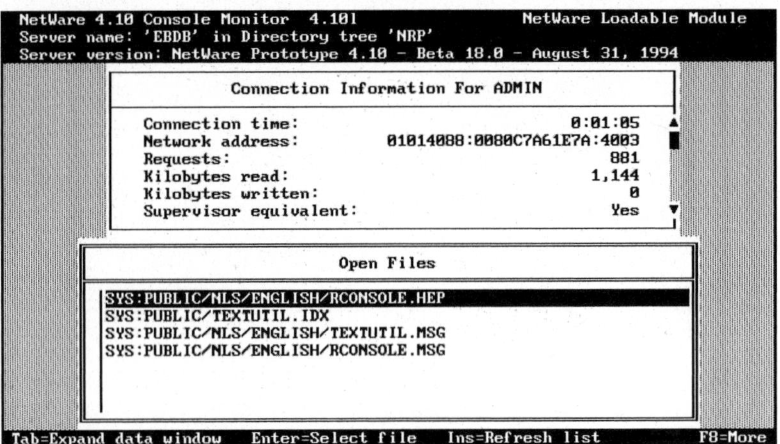

Figure 36.8
The Connection Information screen.

As you can see from figure 36.8, the Connection Information screen gives you information on the activities of this particular connection. You can see which files are currently open. This information is useful when the user is running a process that terminates and locks up the workstation for no apparent reason. By monitoring this user's connection information you can see which files are open at the time of the lockup.

Other information recorded includes the following:

- **Connection time.** The established amount of time for this connection.
- **Network address.** The network, node, and socket addresses for this connection.

- **Requests.** The number of service requests made by this connection. This is a good measurement of the level of activity generated by this connection.
- **Kilobytes read.** The number of bytes in 1,024 increments transferred from the server to this client.
- **Kilobytes written.** The number of bytes in 1,024 increments transferred to the server from this client.
- **Supervisor equivalent.** Whether or not this connection has SUPERVISOR equivalency. This is useful from a security standpoint.

When you press Enter on any open file, you can see its file or record lock status. If you press Del after selecting a connection from the Active Connections list, you can clear the connection. This causes any files opened by this connection to close, and logs the user out of this server.

Disk Information

The Disk information menu gives you information on hard disk or CD-ROM drives attached to the server. When you select this menu option from the MONITOR main menu, the System Disk Drives list appears, as shown in figure 36.9.

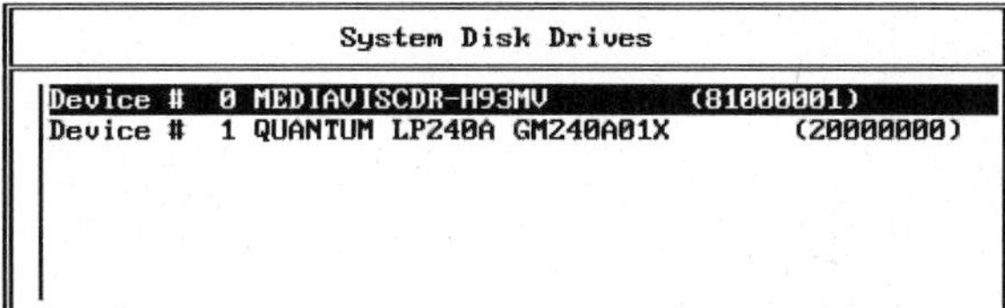

Figure 36.9

The System Disk Drives list.

Hard disk or CD-ROM drives are assigned device numbers. Following the device number is a description of the device giving you manufacturer and model information. In the figure you see device 0, "MEDIAVISCDR-H93MV," and device 1, "QUANTUM LP240A GM240A01X." Device 0 is a MediaVision CD-ROM drive, model CDR-H93MV. Device 1 is a Quantum IDE hard drive, model ProDrive LPS 240AT. The number following each device in parentheses is an internally generated device identifier. It consists of a manufacturer driver ID number, card number, controller number, and drive number. For example, the ID assigned to the Future Domain driver (a SCSI adapter used to drive the MediaVision CD-ROM in this example), is 81.

When you select a device in the System Disk Drives list, additional information appears. You can press the Tab key to expand the top screen. The resulting Drive Status screen is shown in figure 36.10.

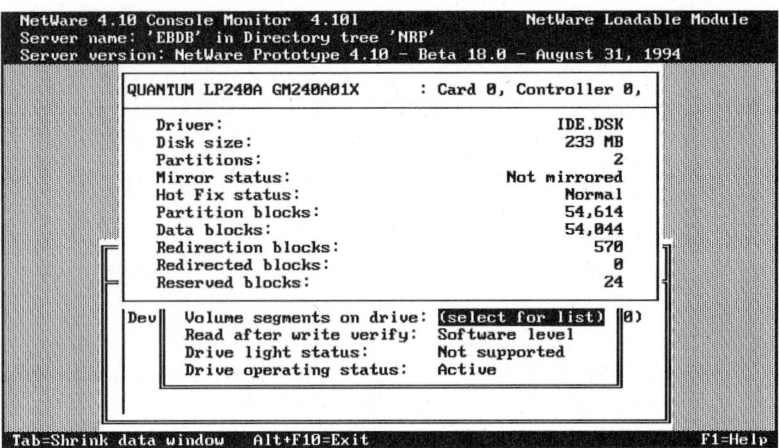

Figure 36.10
The Drive Status screen.

At the top of the Drive Status screen are the driver description and the card, controller, and drive numbers. The bottom screen is discussed later. Table 36.5 summarizes the contents of the top screen.

Table 36.5
Fields in the Drive Status Screen

Field	Description
Driver	The NLM loaded to drive this device.
Disk size	The size of the device.
Partitions	The number of partitions on this device. Partitions can include DOS, NetWare, OS/2, UNIX, Windows NT, or other operating system partitions.
Mirror status	Indicates if this device is part of a mirrored set.
Hot Fix status	If this field shows Normal, then Hot Fix is enabled and functioning normally. Hot fix is the process by which bad blocks are marked bad and data is diverted into the hot fix area.
Partition blocks	The number of disk blocks available in the NetWare partition. The block size used in this screen is 4,096 (4 KB).
Data blocks	This represents the number of data blocks out of the total number of partition blocks.

Field	Description
Redirection blocks	The number of blocks reserved for hot fix, out of the total number of partition blocks.
Redirected blocks	This is a critical number. This is the total number of blocks, out of the redirection blocks, used because bad blocks were detected. This number equals the number of bad blocks found on the NetWare partition of this drive.
Reserved blocks	The number of redirection blocks reserved for the hot fix process.

At the bottom of the Drive Status screen is a separate list. The most interesting aspect of this list comes into play when the drive is a CD-ROM drive, or has removable disk cartridges. In this case, the Drive Status list at the bottom changes, adding two additional parameters: Removable Drive Mount Status and Removable Drive Lock Status. If you want to dismount a CD, for example, you change the Removable Drive Lock Status to Not Locked. You then change the Removable Drive Mount Status to Dismount. This causes the CD to dismount. This technique is not recommended, however, and a better technique is to use the following command:

```
CD DISMOUNT <volume>
```

volume is the name of the volume to dismount. This command assumed you have CDROM .NLM loaded. For more information on dismounting CDs, see Chapter 37, "Making Configuration Changes."

LAN/WAN Information

The LAN/WAN information menu gives you information on network adapters in your server. When you select this menu, the Available LAN Drivers list appears. You see each network adapter in your server identified on this list by board name, driver, and settings for this driver. If you see the same driver listed multiple times it is most likely that the driver is configured for multiple frame types.

A *frame type* is a particular format used to send and receive data from this network adapter. Certain protocols are geared towards certain frame types. The TCP/IP protocol suite, for example, is oriented towards the Ethernet_II, Ethernet_SNAP, or Token-Ring_SNAP frame types. See Chapter 3, "LANs and WANs," for more details.

When you press Enter after selecting a particular LAN driver, a statistics screen appears, as shown in figure 36.11.

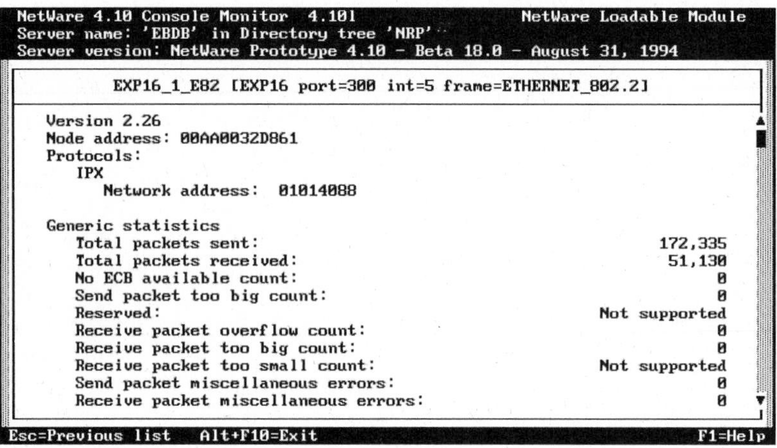

Figure 36.11
The LAN/WAN Driver Statistic screen.

A detailed discussion of every parameter is beyond the scope of this book. Table 36.6 summarizes some of the general statistics you should monitor.

Table 36.6
LAN/WAN Statistics To Monitor

Statistic	Description
No ECB available count	An *ECB* is an Event Control Block. This is an engineer's term for a packet receive buffer. If you see this statistic increase, check if the packet receive buffers statistic on the main MONITOR screen has reached its maximum. If this is the case, increase the maximum using the SET MAXIMUM PACKET RECEIVE BUFFERS command.
Receive Packet Too Big	This indicates the number of times a frame of data was received which was too large for the packet receive buffer to handle. If this number is large in proportion to the total (more than 1 or 2 percent of the total), increase the size of the packet receive buffers using the SET MAXIMUM PHYSICAL RECEIVE PACKET SIZE command.
Receive Packet Too Small Miscellaneous Errors Checksum Errors	Any of these errors can point to a bad network adapter. A network that is going bad sends out frames of data which are too big, too small, or which have internal errors. This also could be a sign of a cable which is intermittently shorting out, or a loose connector.

Statistic	Description
Adapter Queue Depth	If this statistic increases it is a sign that the network adapter in the server is having difficulty getting data onto the LAN. A possible cause is a busy LAN (perhaps too busy). Look at the total number of packets sent and received, and check if the consensus among users is that the network is slow. You can segment the network by breaking up the physical cabling and placing routers between segments. This decreases the traffic on each segment. Another possible cause is that the adapter on the server is insufficient for its job. You may consider replacing it with an adapter with internal buffering or with better throughput. If the adapter is a 16 bit ISA bus adapter, for example, consider replacing it with a 32 bit EISA adapter (if this is appropriate for your system).
Excess Collisions	A *collision* occurs when two or more network adapters transmit on an Ethernet network at the same time. Excess collisions, on the other hand, indicate that the network is either too busy and needs to be segmented, or that you have a bad network adapter which is sending out spurious transmissions.
Abort Delimiter	Specific to token ring, an excessive number of this error indicates that the active monitor in a token ring environment had to reinitialize the ring. This can indicate a bad cable, faulty MAU, or a network adapter going on and off line frequently.
Frame Copied Error	In a token ring environment this indicates the number of times the destination station received a transmission which another station had already copied. This can indicate physical wiring problems—a line hit by EMI (electromagnetic interference), for example, or a duplicate node address.

System Module Information

The System module information menu gives you a list of NLMs loaded on this server. You can scan down the list and press Enter for more information on any given module. When you press Enter, the Resource Tags list appears showing you system resources used by this NLM. At the top is a screen showing the amount of RAM used by this NLM and its file name. Pressing Enter on a resource gives you even more specific information on that resource. The System module information menu is shown in figure 36.12.

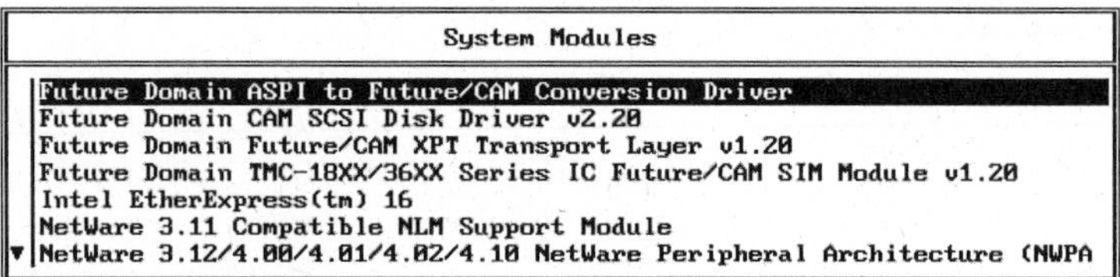

Figure 36.12
The System module information list.

Lock File Server Console

The Lock server console menu is used to assign a password to the server console, over and above the RCONSOLE password. You must enter the password to unlock the server console. If you are accessing the console through RCONSOLE, you come to this screen and can proceed no further until you enter the password. This is a useful security feature to prevent anyone with physical access to the server from tampering with the system.

File Open/Lock Activity

The File open/lock activity menu enables you to browse through the file system on this server. You can scan through by volume and directory until you find the file you want to examine. The information you can view on open files is shown in figure 36.13.

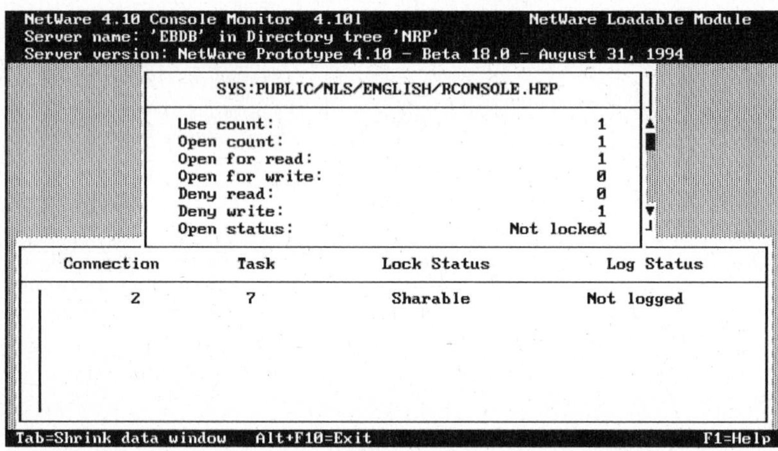

Figure 36.13
The File open/lock activity file status screen.

This is especially useful when you have problem applications that lock up workstations, or where users are experiencing problems deleting, modifying, or changing attributes of files. If a file is considered open, it cannot be deleted or modified in any way until closed.

The statistics screen shows the Use count and the Open count parameters. These parameters are the number of connections that have this file open and in use. The Open for read and Open for write parameters display the number of connections that have this file open for either reading or writing. When more than one connection has a file open for write, a possible conflict can arise unless the application in use is capable of controlling multiuser write access. The Deny read and Deny write parameters indicate how many connections want to prevent others from reading from or writing to the file. The Open status parameter indicates the current status of the file when opened.

At the bottom of the screen you see a list of connections that have the file open. If you need to close down this file for any reason, you can go to the Connection information screen and clear those connections with the file open. Clearing connections also logs that user out.

Cache Utilization

When you select Cache utilization from the MONITOR main menu, the Cache utilization menu option displays the status of the caching system on the server. The caching system is what is used to service user requests for files. When a file is read from the server's hard drives, it is first stored in cache before being sent to the workstation. When a file is written to the server's hard drives, it likewise is temporarily stored in cache. The Cache Utilization Statistics screen is shown in figure 36.14.

```
                 Cache Utilization Statistics

  Short term cache hits:                          100%
  Short term cache dirty hits:                    100%
  Long term cache hits:                            92%
  Long term cache dirty hits:                      94%
  LRU sitting time:                           40:34.1
  Allocate block count:                        48,832
  Allocated from AVAIL:                         9,058
  Allocated from LRU:                          39,774
  Allocate wait:                                    0
  Allocate still waiting:                           0
  Too many dirty blocks:                            0
  Cache ReCheckBlock count:                         0
```

Figure 36.14

The Cache Utilization Statistics screen.

Some terms you see on this screen include the following:

- **Cache hit.** This indicates that a block of data was available in cache when needed by the workstation. (The block is put into cache by an earlier workstation request.)
- **Dirty hit.** This occurs when a cache block has data to be written to the hard drive.
- **Short term.** This indicates activity within the last second.

- **Long term.** This indicates an average of accumulated statistics since the server has been up.
- **LRU.** Least Recently Used. This is the oldest cache buffers: the buffers that were allocated and have been sitting around for a long time (relatively speaking).

The statistic to watch on this screen is Long term cache hits. This figure should be above 90 percent. If it falls below 80 percent, network users notice a slowdown in network performance. If the situation continues to deteriorate, you should add RAM to the server.

When the LRU sitting time is large, the oldest allocated cache block is idle and has not been re-used. This is an indication that either your server is not busy, or you have ample RAM.

For information on the other statistics, use the F1 key for help.

Processor Utilization

The Processor utilization menu gives you an idea of how CPU time is being allocated. When you select this menu item, a list of Available Processes and Interrupts appears. You can use the F3 key to view all processes on the list. The F5 key enables you to mark selected processes. Press Enter to view the relative utilization of selected or all processes. In figure 36.15, the Interrupt 0 through Interrupt 15 processes were selected and displayed.

NetWare 4.10 Console Monitor 4.101 NetWare Loadable Module
Server name: 'EBDB' in Directory tree 'NRP'
Server version: NetWare Prototype 4.10 - Beta 18.0 - August 31, 1994

Process Name	Time	Count	Load
Interrupt 0	4,155	18	0.35%
Interrupt 1	0	0	0.00%
Interrupt 2	0	0	0.00%
Interrupt 3	0	0	0.00%
Interrupt 4	0	0	0.00%
Interrupt 5	12,361	16	1.06%
Interrupt 6	0	0	0.00%
Interrupt 7	0	0	0.00%
Interrupt 8	0	0	0.00%
Interrupt 9	0	0	0.00%
Interrupt 10	0	0	0.00%
Interrupt 11	148,598	74	12.77%
Interrupt 12	0	0	0.00%
Interrupt 13	0	0	0.00%
Interrupt 14	85,073	252	7.31%
Interrupt 15	0	0	0.00%

Esc=Previous list Alt+F10=Exit F1=Help

Figure 36.15

Processor utilization—Interrupt 0 through Interrupt 15 processes.

In the figure you can see activity for interrupts 0, 5, 11, and 14. In this example, a workstation copies files from the CD-ROM drive to the server's hard drive. Interrupt 0 is the system clock. Interrupt 5 is used by the Intel Ethernet adapter on the server. Interrupt 11 is used by the SCSI controller to which the CD-ROM drive is attached. Interrupt 14 is used by the server's hard drive controller.

Note It is important to note that the Load Factor you can see in figure 36.15 is a percentage of the current CPU utilization. This statistic is visible from the main MONITOR General Information screen next to the Utilization parameter.

Resource Utilization

The Resource utilization menu gives you information complementary to the System module information. When you select this menu, the Tracked Resources list appears at the bottom, and the Server Memory Statistics screen appears at the top (see fig. 36.16).

```
NetWare 4.10 Console Monitor  4.101                NetWare Loadable Module
Server name: 'EBDB' in Directory tree 'NRP'
Server version: NetWare Prototype 4.10 - Beta 18.0 - August 31, 1994

                    Server Memory Statistics

   Allocated memory pool (bytes):               3,195,120    16%
   Cache buffers (bytes):                      10,813,440    53%
   Cache movable memory (bytes):                1,007,616     5%
   Cache non-movable memory (bytes):                4,096     0%
   Code and data memory (bytes):                5,287,696    26%
   Total server work memory (bytes):           20,307,968   100%

             Tracked Resources

 AES Process Call-Backs                           tion
 Alloc Memory (Bytes)                             ole
 Alternate Debugger Handlers                      ty
 Alternate Key Handler
 Cache Memory Below 16 Meg (Bytes)
 Cache Movable Memory (Bytes)
▼Cache Non-Movable Memory (Bytes)

Tab=Expand data window   Enter=Select option   Alt+F10=Exit          F1=Help
```

Figure 36.16

The Tracked Resources and Server Memory Statistics screens.

The Tracked Resources list displays all the system resources that are tracked by this option. When you press Enter, the Resource Tags list appears showing you which NLMs are making use of this resource. A *tag* is a name assigned when an application (an NLM) requests, and is granted, a resource by the operating system.

At the top of the screen you can see a breakdown of server memory in the Server Memory Statistics screen. The Cache buffers parameter is of the most interest to network Administrators. This represents the percentage of memory available for user file caching. If this figure is above 50 percent your server is in good shape. If the figure is between 30 and 50 percent the amount of RAM is marginal to adequate, with little or no reserves. If the figure drops below 30 percent, you should add more RAM to the server. Usually your network users report a slowdown in performance by the time this figure drops below 30 percent.

Memory Utilization

The Memory utilization menu shows you the status of allocated memory. *Allocated memory* is memory used by the various NLMs and processes running on the server. When you first go into this menu you see the Allocated Memory For All Modules screen as well as a System Modules list (see fig. 36.17). Pressing the Tab key expands the top screen (as shown in the figure).

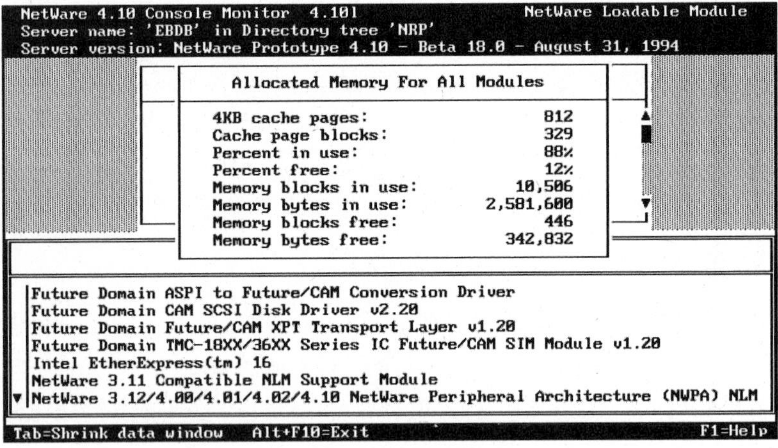

Figure 36.17
The Allocated Memory For All Modules and System Modules screens.

In the figure, a little more than 2.5 MB is in use from the allocated memory pool. You can go through the System Modules list one NLM at a time and press Enter to get an update on allocated memory usage for that particular module.

Some modules may allocate large blocks of memory for a short period of time and then drop down in use. In this case, the Percent free parameter represents memory which can be used in the user file caching memory pool. The *garbage collection* process takes unused memory (in 4 KB pages) and returns it to the main memory pool (the user file caching memory pool). You can force this process to take place for a particular module by proceeding as follows:

1. From the MONITOR main menu, select Memory utilization. The System Modules screen appears.

2. From the System Modules screen, select the offending module and press Enter. A breakdown of how many 4 KB cache pages are in use, along with the Percent free parameters, appears at the top.

3. Press the F3 key to force garbage collection for this module.

Garbage collection can only release memory in 4 KB pages. If the module only has allocated one cache page, and any percentage of that one page is in use, then garbage collection cannot occur for this module. For example, the Future Domain CAM SCSI Disk Driver has allocated one 4 KB cache page. The Percent in use parameter shows 1 percent. The Percent free parameter shows 99 percent. When you press F3 you notice that there is no change. The reason is that garbage collection does not release memory if it is less than 4 KB.

Pressing the F5 key when the Allocated Memory For All Modules screen is expanded performs garbage collection for all modules. Otherwise, the garbage collection process takes place at regular intervals. See Chapter 38, "Fine Tuning the Server," for more information on using the SET commands to adjust parameters such as garbage collection.

Scheduling Information

The Scheduling information menu displays information on processes scheduled to run on the server's CPU. This screen shows you all processes running (and tracked) on the server. MONITOR takes samples approximately every 2 seconds and displays statistics generated during the sample period. The last several processes and the totals are shown in figure 36.18.

NetWare 4.10 Console Monitor 4.101 NetWare Loadable Module
Server name: 'EBDB' in Directory tree 'NRP'
Server version: NetWare Prototype 4.10 - Beta 18.0 - August 31, 1994

Process Name	Sch Delay	Time	Count	Load
TCP Timing Loop	0	2,552	54	0.07%
TCP/IP 0	0	295	3	0.00%
TCP/IP 1	10	8,497	3	0.24%
TCP/IP Packet	0	0	0	0.00%
TCP/IP Utility	0	0	0	0.00%
TCP/IPX QRunner	0	0	0	0.00%
TimeSyncMain	0	164	3	0.00%
UDP Timing Loop	0	151	3	0.00%
UDP/IPX QRunner	0	0	0	0.00%
Interrupts		17,755	74	0.50%
Idle Loop		3,370,023	62	96.18%
Work		22,101	230	0.63%
Total sample time:		3,538,916		
Histogram overhead time:		35,116	(0.99%)	
Adjusted sample time:		3,503,800		

+=Increase delay -=Decrease delay Esc=Previous list F8=More

Figure 36.18

The Scheduling information screen.

Table 36.7 summarizes the data available in this screen.

Table 36.7
Scheduling Information Statistics

Statistic	Description
Process Name	The name of the process being monitored.
Sch Delay	The delay factor used when scheduling a process. The default is 0, which means no delay. You can press the plus key (+) at the right side of the console keyboard to introduce a delay in a process.
Time	The time the CPU spent servicing this process.
Count	The number of times this process was serviced in this sampling interval.
Load	Percentage of CPU time spent on this process.
Interrupts	The combined total time, count, and load spent servicing interrupt processes.
Idle Loop	The time the CPU spent not doing anything at all. This represents the margin of CPU power available to you. Subtract this value from 100 percent to arrive at the total time the server's CPU spent working.
Work	Other miscellaneous processes.
Total sample time	Total CPU time measured during this sample.
Histogram overhead time	The overhead associated with the Scheduling information process itself.
Adjusted sample time	The amount of time minus the Histogram overhead time.

You might find that certain processes are "hogging the CPU." This means that they are using more CPU time than is desirable. The more time a process spends on the CPU, the less time is available for other processes. You might want to introduce a delay to a process deliberately. To do so, select the process and press the plus key (+) at the far right side of the console keyboard (use the numeric keypad plus key). The Sch Delay parameter increments. Each time you increase the Sch Delay, you

cause the CPU to schedule this process less often. A value of 2, for example, causes the CPU to schedule this process 1/2 as often as a process with a delay of 0 (there is not an option of 1/1). A value of 10 causes the process to be scheduled 1/10 as often as a process with a delay of 0.

When you use the numeric plus key (+) to introduce a scheduling delay, it is only temporary. To introduce a permanent scheduling delay, use the SCHDELAY.NLM utility. The syntax is as follows:

```
LOAD SCHDELAY [process = value]
```

This causes *process* to be delayed by *value*. To make scheduling delays permanent, add the SCHDELAY command to the AUTOEXEC.NCF file. To delay the REMOTE process by a factor of 2, for example, issue the following command:

```
EBDB:load schdelay remote = 2
Loading module SCHDELAY.NLM
  NetWare 386 Scheduling Delay Control
  Version 1.02    February 1, 1993
  Copyright 1993 Novell, Inc.  All rights reserved.
  Debug symbol information for SCHDELAY.NLM loaded
  Setting "Remote" Scheduling Delay to 2.
EBDB:
```

To determine process names, load SCHDELAY with no parameters.

Using TRACK

The TRACK utility tracks communications between servers and other processes. You invoke the TRACK utility by issuing the following command:

TRACK ON

You see the output screen, as shown in figure 36.19.

You can press any key to pause the display, and any key to resume the display. Press Alt+Esc from the server console (or F3 from RCONSOLE) to move to another screen. To unload the TRACK screen issue the following command:

TRACK OFF

This screen displays Server Advertising Protocol (SAP) and Routing Information Protocol (RIP) information being passed between servers. Table 36.8 summarizes the information presented in the TRACK screen.

```
IN    [2DECF8EF:000000000001]  4:45:11 pm   PS-EBDB         1
IN    [2DECF8EF:000000000001]  4:45:12 pm   EBDB            1
OUT   [2DECF8EF:FFFFFFFFFFFF]  4:45:15 pm   2E7B3A7A  2/3       01014088  1/2
OUT   [01014088:FFFFFFFFFFFF]  4:45:15 pm   2DECF8EF  1/2
IN    [2DECF8EF:000000000001]  4:45:20 pm   NRP__________   1
IN    [2DECF8EF:000000000001]  4:45:26 pm   NRP__________   0
IN    [01014088:0080C7A61E7A]  4:45:27 pm   EBDB312         1   EBDB312         2
IN    [2DECF8EF:000000000001]  4:45:39 pm   EBDB            1
OUT   [2DECF8EF:FFFFFFFFFFFF]  4:45:45 pm   EBDB312         3   EBDB312         2
        NRP__________   1   NRP__________   1   PS-EBDB         1   EBDB            1
        EBDB            1
OUT   [01014088:FFFFFFFFFFFF]  4:45:45 pm   NRP__________   1   NRP__________   1
        PS-EBDB         1   EBDB            1   EBDB            1
IN    [01014088:0080C7014103]  4:45:48 pm   Get Nearest Server
OUT   [01014088:0080C7014103]  4:45:48 pm   Give Nearest Server EBDB
IN    [01014088:0080C7014103]  4:45:48 pm   Route Request
IN    [01014088:0080C7014103]  4:45:48 pm   Route Request
IN    [01014088:0080C7014103]  4:45:48 pm   Route Request
IN    [01014088:0080C7014103]  4:45:51 pm   Route Request
OUT   [01014088:0080C7014103]  4:45:51 pm   2DECF8EF  1/2
IN    [01014088:0080C7014103]  4:45:51 pm   Route Request
OUT   [01014088:0080C7014103]  4:45:51 pm   2DECF8EF  1/2
IN    [2DECF8EF:000000000001]  4:45:54 pm   EBDB            1
<Use ALT-ESC or CTRL-ESC to switch screens, or any other key to pause>
```

Figure 36.19
The TRACK ON output screen.

TABLE 36.8
Information from the TRACK Screen

Item	Description
IN	Indicates inbound information (originating outside of this server).
OUT	Indicates outbound information (originating from this server going out across the LAN).
[*nnnnnnnn:mmmmmmmmmmmm*]	*nnn...* is the network address and *mmm...* is the MAC (Media Access Control) or hardware address for either inbound or outbound information. A MAC address of *FFFFFFFF* indicates a broadcast (a transmission going to all nodes on the network).
hh:mm:ss [am | pm]	Time in *hh* = hours, *mm* = minutes, *ss* = seconds.
servername number	SAP information. You see server names (including servers, print servers, and other types of servers) and a number. The number represents how many hops the server is from this server. Each router counts as a hop.

Item	Description
nnnnnnnn hops/ticks	RIP information. *nnn...* represents a network address. The number following this is the number of hops to reach this network. Ticks is a time parameter where one tick = 1/18 of a second.
Get Nearest Server	This is a broadcast from a client seeking a connection from a server. This is a useful message when you are checking to see if a workstation is making a connection to a server.
Give Nearest Server	This is the server's response to a Get Nearest Server broadcast.

Using CONFIG

You can use the CONFIG utility to determine the current settings for the server. The information you see includes LAN information, the name of the server, the name of the NDS tree, and the server bindery context(s). The following is an example of the output produced when the CONFIG command is issued:

```
EBDB:config
File server name: EBDB
IPX internal network number: 2DECF8EF
     Node address: 000000000001
     Frame type: VIRTUAL_LAN
     LAN protocol: IPX network 2DECF8EF
Server Up Time:  22 Hours 59 Minutes 38 Seconds
Intel EtherExpress(tm) 16
     Version 2.26    May 20, 1993
     Hardware setting: I/O ports 300h to 30Fh, Interrupt 5h
     Node address: 00AA0032D861
     Frame type: ETHERNET_802.2
     Board name: EXP16_1_E82
     LAN protocol: IPX network 01014088
Intel EtherExpress(tm) 16
     Version 2.26    May 20, 1993
     Hardware setting: I/O ports 300h to 30Fh, Interrupt 5h
     Node address: 00AA0032D861
```

```
     Frame type: ETHERNET_II
     Board name: EXP16_1_EII
     LAN protocol: ARP
     LAN protocol: IP  address 192.112.14.97  mask FF.FF.FF.C0  interfaces 1
Tree Name: NRP
Bindery Context(s):
     NY.EBDB
     EBDB
EBDB:
```

Table 36.9 summarizes this information.

Table 36.9
Information from the CONFIG Utility

Item	Description
File Server Name	The name of the server.
IPX Internal Network Number	The number assigned to the internal network used for communications inside the server and unique identification of the server.
Node Address	The internal address or the hardware address of a network adapter.
Frame Type	The format of data sent or received by the internal driver or by a network adapter.
LAN Protocol	The protocol assigned to this device. This field indicates various protocols including IPX, and IP (including ARP).
Hardware Setting	The interrupt, I/O port address, memory address, DMA channel, and other settings pertinent to this board.
Board Name	The name assigned when loading a LAN driver with a specific frame type. When you assign two different frame types to a single LAN driver, for example, it is very useful to designate two different board names.

Item	Description
Server Up Time	The amount of time the server has been up.
Tree Name	The name of the NDS tree in which this server participates.
Bindery Context(s)	The NDS containers in this server's bindery context.

Use the CONFIG command when trying to determine the IPX or IP address of a network adapter in the server. If you have problems communicating with the server, check if a LAN protocol is not assigned to a particular board.

Using DSTRACE

The DSTRACE utility is used to monitor NDS replica-related activities. DSTRACE, which stands for Directory Services Trace, monitors synchronization activities in the NDS tree.

To activate DSTRACE, issue the following command from the server console:

SET DSTRACE = ON

You receive a confirmation at the server console prompt, `DS Trace is set to: ON`. You can view NDS trace activities by using the Alt+Esc keys from the server console, or Alt+F3 when using RCONSOLE, to toggle to this screen.

Different partitions of the NDS tree advertise in separate synchronization messages. The following example shows you three partitions, [Root], OU=NY.O=EBDB, and OU=SJ.O=EBDB:

```
(94/10/03 08:00:03)
SYNC: Start sync of partition <[Root]> state:[0] type:[0]
SYNC: End sync of partition <[Root]> All processed = YES.
(94/10/03 08:00:03)
SYNC: Start sync of partition <NY.EBDB> state:[0] type:[0]
SYNC: End sync of partition <NY.EBDB> All processed = YES.
(94/10/03 08:00:03)
```

```
SYNC: Start sync of partition <SJ.EBDB> state:[0] type:[0]
SYNC: End sync of partition <SJ.EBDB> All processed = YES.
```

As you can see, the date in year/month/day format, as well as the 24 hour time, is indicated in parentheses. The next line, SYNC: Start sync ... indicates the start of a synchronization interval. A state of [0] indicates a normal synchronization check. The next line, SYNC: End sync ... indicates the end of the synchronization interval. The message *All processed = YES* indicates that all updates were successfully incorporated into the master replica of this partition.

The next example shows activity when a partition is created or a partition is merged back into its parent. Notice that the state goes to [40]:

```
(94/10/03 08:20:40)
SYNC: Start sync of partition <NY.EBDB> state:[40] type:[0]
SYNC: End sync of partition <NY.EBDB> All processed = YES.
(94/10/03 08:20:40)
SYNC: Start sync of partition <[Root]> state:[40] type:[0]
SYNC: End sync of partition <[Root]> All processed = YES.
(94/10/03 08:20:40)
SYNC: Start sync of partition <NY.EBDB> state:[40] type:[0]
SYNC: End sync of partition <NY.EBDB> All processed = YES.
(94/10/03 08:20:40)
SYNC: Start sync of partition <[Root]> state:[40] type:[0]
SYNC: End sync of partition <[Root]> All processed = YES.
```

Any message at the end of a synchronization interval that does not indicate *All processed = YES* is a possible cause for concern. If you see such a message, wait for an hour and check again. Remember that there can be many replicas of partitions on your network, and the servers can be communicating through relatively slow links (56 kbps phone links). If you still are seeing error messages at the end of an hour you might consider checking the status of your network. The following are some questions to ask:

- Is the network functional: can all servers see each other? From the server console type **DISPLAY SERVERS** to see other servers.
- Are all routers on your network up and functional?
- Is there more than one network Administrator performing partitioning and replication on the same NDS tree at the same time?

The DSREPAIR.NLM utility can be used to perform repairs on the NDS data stored on this server if you cannot resolve the problem by other means. For more information on this utility, please refer to Chapter 37, "Making Configuration Changes."

Summary

This chapter covered several aspects of how to monitor the server. You learned what the server console is, and how to operate at it. You learned that the RCONSOLE.EXE utility can be used to remotely access the server console either through a direct LAN connection, or remotely from a PC with a modem. You learned about the RCONSOLE menu and its special capabilities. As you saw, you can use the directory scan option of RCONSOLE to actually view the NDS database files.

The next portion of this chapter dealt with the MONITOR.NLM utility. You learned about the primary menu options available in MONITOR as well as some statistics to watch.

You then learned about other utilities available from the server console. These included the TRACK utility which monitors SAP and RIP exchanges. The CONFIG utility shows you the current server configuration. The DSTRACE utility shows you NDS partition synchronization activity.

This chapter showed you how to monitor a server and view current settings. The next two chapters cover how to make changes to these settings.

Making Configuration Changes

Networks mirror the modern world, where changes are taking place constantly. In order to continue to serve the information needs of your organization, the servers also must change. As new technology develops you need to install updates and new drivers. The updates and new drivers in turn cause problems with older modules that require patches. As users continue to make use of the server, you constantly must monitor disk usage and be prepared to add additional hard drives. As the network itself changes you may need to modify the network communications parameters.

This chapter gives you techniques and procedures on making configuration changes to the server. The following major topics are discussed:

- Using INSTALL.NLM to make changes
- Making changes to LAN communications using INETCFG.NLM
- Obtaining the latest drivers, patches, and updates

Most of the utilities and techniques discussed in this chapter are used at the server console. The last part of this chapter, which discusses how to get the latest drivers, patches, and updates, involves both a workstation and a server.

Using INSTALL

The INSTALL.NLM utility is available from the server console. This is the utility used to initially install the server. Once the server is up and running, INSTALL can be used to make changes to the system.

To access the INSTALL utility, from the server console, enter the following command:

LOAD INSTALL

The INSTALL main menu appears, as shown in figure 37.1.

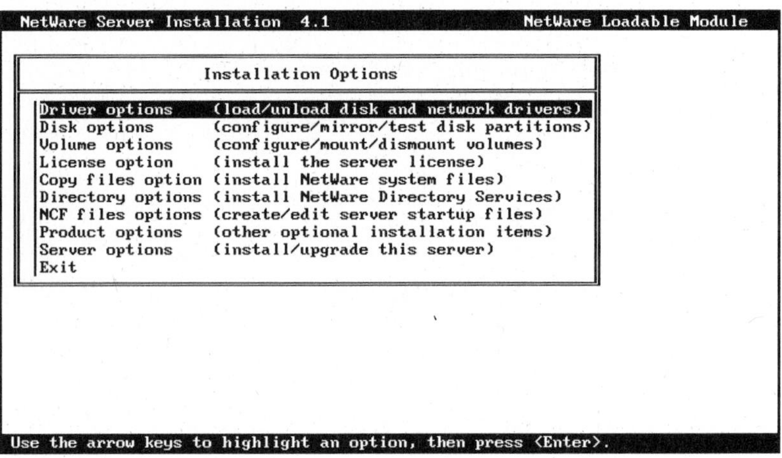

Figure 37.1
The Installation Options menu.

The next several subsections discuss each of the INSTALL menu options and how they relate to configuration changes.

Driver Options

The Driver options menu enables you to load and unload disk drivers and LAN drivers. When you press Enter, the Driver options menu appears. To load a disk driver, select the first option, Configure Disk and Storage Device Drivers. The

Selected Disk Drivers screen appears at the top, showing you which drivers are currently loaded. At the bottom of the screen is the Additional Driver Actions menu. This screen and menu are shown in figure 37.2.

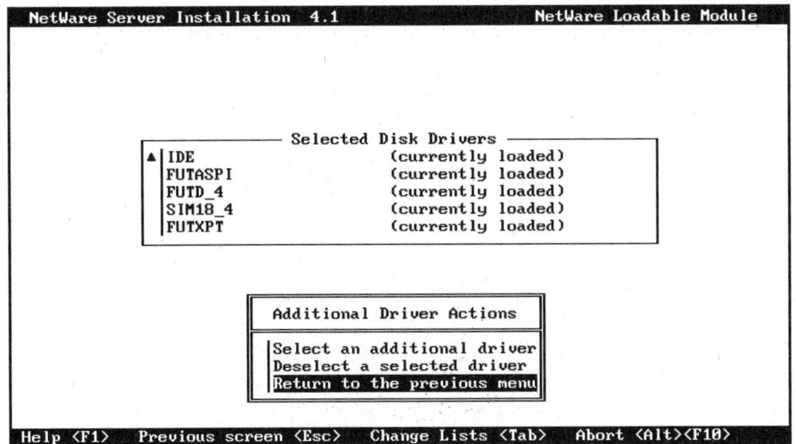

Figure 37.2

The Selected Disk Drivers screen and Additional Driver Actions menu.

As with most server console utilities where two screens are visible, you can use the Tab key to move to and expand the top screen. Note that the top screen is surrounded by a single line border. This indicates that it is an informational screen only and no changes are possible. When you press the Tab key, the border changes to a double line indicating changes are now possible, or that you can move to another menu one level deeper.

Loading and Unloading Disk and Storage Device Drivers

If you add an additional SCSI or other type of controller card to your server, you must load another disk driver (even if it is only to load the same driver twice). To load another disk driver, from the Additional Driver Actions menu, select Select an Additional Driver. The Select a Driver list appears as shown in figure 37.3.

Select the desired driver and press Enter. You next see a screen where you can enter settings appropriate to the hardware associated with the driver. Settings include interrupts, I/O port addresses, and other settings. When done choose the Save Parameters and Load Driver option. At this time the hardware is checked to verify settings. If there is a problem you can use Alt+Esc (or Alt+F3 from RCONSOLE) to toggle to the console to view any error messages. In most cases, error messages cause INSTALL automatically to toggle to the console when you press Enter. Otherwise, the driver loads and you are now ready to process the device appropriately.

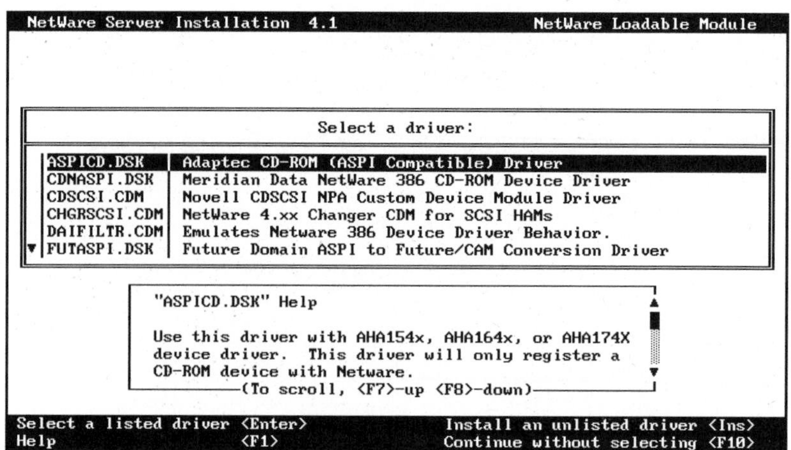

Figure 37.3
The Select a Driver list.

NetWare 4.1 uses the NPA (NetWare Peripheral Architecture) to access devices. Newer device drivers now consist of two modules. The first module has an extension HAM (Host Adapter Module). This module is adapter specific and drives the hardware. The second module has an extension CDM (Custom Device Module). This module addresses storage devices attached to the host bus adapter. This architecture grew out of difficulties that arose from the earlier convention. Earlier versions of NetWare used one module with an extension DSK (Disk), which drove the hardware. The problem arose when CD-ROM drives and other removable media became popular. The early NetWare device drivers were designed for fixed disks. CDs can be removed and created certain design considerations causing problems when users wished to change CDs on the server.

To use the new architecture, load the *.HAM module. This automatically loads NWPA.NLM (the NetWare Peripheral Architecture module), and associated *.CDM modules.

To unload a currently selected disk driver, proceed as follows:

1. From the INSTALL main menu, select Driver options. The Driver options menu appears.

2. From the Driver options menu, select Configure Disk and Storage Device Drivers. The Selected Disk Drivers screen and Additional Driver Actions menu appears.

3. From the Additional Driver Actions menu, select Unload a Selected Driver. The cursor jumps to the Selected Disk Drivers screen. Select the driver to unload and press Enter.

Loading and Unloading LAN Drivers

The Driver options menu also enables you to load and unload LAN drivers. If you install a new LAN adapter in your server, you can use this menu to load the new driver.

To load a LAN driver, proceed as follows:

1. From the INSTALL main menu, select Driver options. The Driver options menu appears.

2. From the Driver options menu, select Configure Network Drivers. The Selected Network Drivers screen and the Additional Driver Actions menu appears, as shown in figure 37.4.

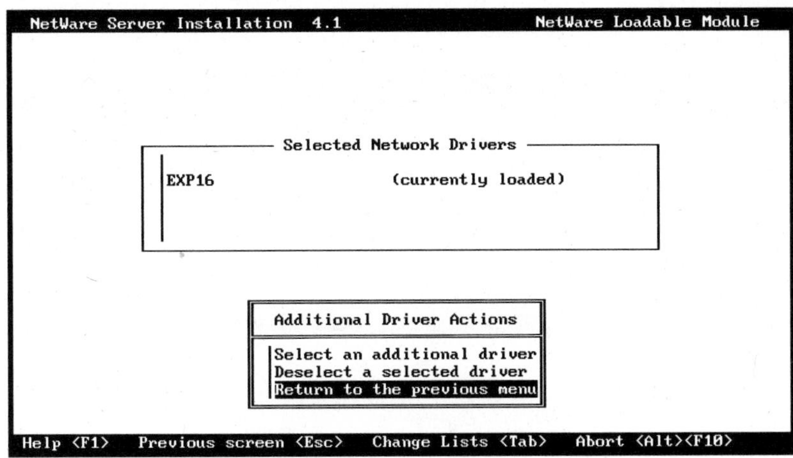

Figure 37.4

The Selected Network Drivers screen.

3. From the Additional Driver Actions menu, select Select an additional Driver. The Select a Driver list appears. Note that this list only contains drivers selected for the current installation. NetWare 4, unlike NetWare 3.*x*, only copies drivers for selected network adapters. To access additional drivers press the Insert key. You are prompted either to insert a manufacturer's disk, or mount the original NetWare installation CD. Press F3 to specify the path to the desired files.

   If you are using RCONSOLE, you have the option of mapping a drive letter to another location (such as a locally mounted CD). NetWare 4.1 also enables you to map to another server directly from INSTALL.NLM.

   Note that when working with the NetWare 4.1 installation CD, the LAN drivers are located in the directory \NW410\LANDRV.

4. Once INSTALL has read the disk or CD, the Select a driver to install list appears as shown in figure 37.5.

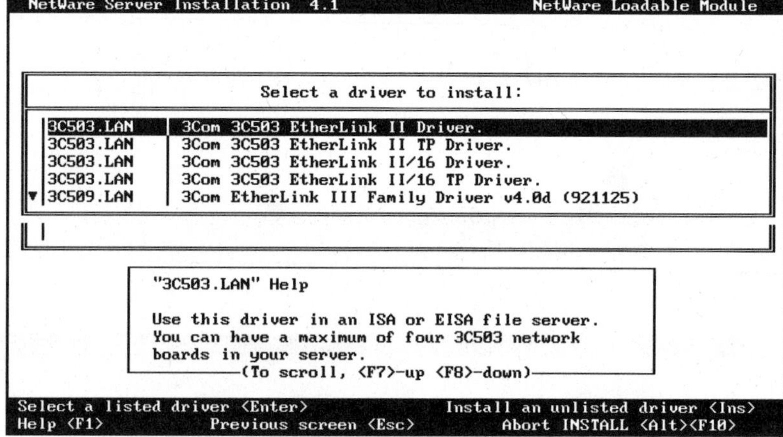

Figure 37.5

The Select a driver to install screen.

5. From the Select a driver to install list, choose the desired driver and press Enter. A prompt appears asking if you want to copy the files for this driver. Answer Yes to proceed. The Protocols, Parameters, and Actions screens for this driver appear next, as shown in figure 37.6.

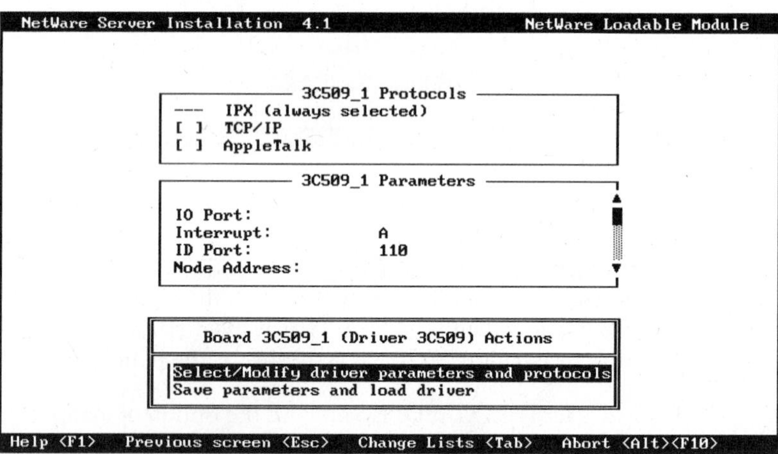

Figure 37.6

The Protocols, Parameters, and Actions screens for a new LAN driver.

6. To move between the Protocols, Parameters, and Actions screens, press the Tab key.

   The Protocols screen enables you to checkmark which protocols (in addition to IPX) you wish to enable for this board.

The Parameters screen is where you enter the hardware settings for this board. Settings include IO Port, Interrupt, DMA, Memory Address, and other pertinent settings.

From the Actions menu, you can move to the top screen (same effect as pressing the Tab key).

7. Choose Save parameters and load driver from the Actions menu, when done. The driver now loads. If there are any problems you are returned temporarily to the console prompt to view any pertinent error messages. When the driver has (or has not) loaded, you are returned to the Select a driver to install list where you can continue to load additional LAN drivers. Press Esc when done.

To unload a LAN driver, proceed as follows:

1. From the INSTALL main menu, select Driver options. The Driver options menu appears.
2. From the Driver options menu, select Configure Network Drivers. The Selected Network Drivers screen and the Additional Driver Actions menu appears.
3. From the Additional Driver Actions menu, select Deselect a Selected Driver. The cursor moves up to the Selected Network Drivers screen where you can select the driver to remove. The driver unloads at this point.

If you are running RCONSOLE, your screen freezes at this point if the LAN driver you unloaded was the one you were using to connect to the server.

Disk Options

The Disk options menu is used to prepare hard drives to be used with NetWare. When you select this from the INSTALL main menu, the Available Disk Options menu appears. This menu is shown in figure 37.7.

The first item on the Available Disk Options menu enables you to create and delete NetWare partitions and modify hot fix. When you add a new hard drive to the server, for example, use this menu option to create a NetWare partition on the new hard drive. To add and partition a new hard drive, proceed as follows:

1. From the INSTALL main menu, select Driver options. The Driver options menu appears.
2. From the Driver options menu, select Configure Disk and Storage Device Drivers. The Selected Disk Drivers screen and Additional Driver Actions menu appears.

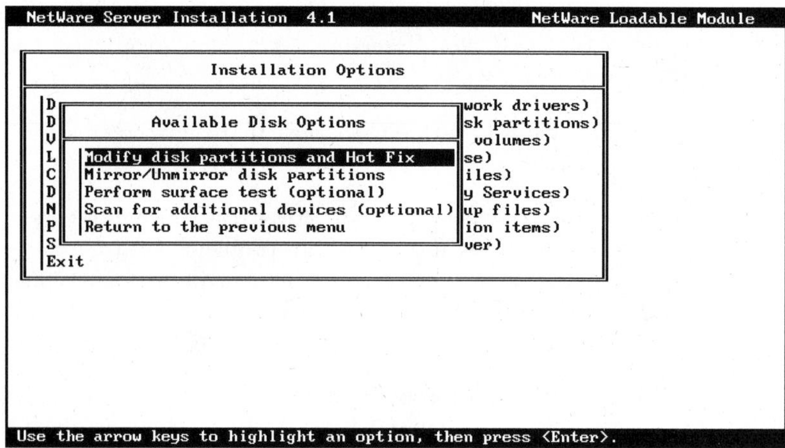

Figure 37.7
The Available Disk Options menu.

3. From the Selected Disk Drivers screen, verify that the driver for the new disk drive has been loaded. If not, select Load an Additional Driver and load the appropriate driver. Press Esc a few times to return to the INSTALL main menu.

4. From the INSTALL main menu, select Disk options. The Available Disk options menu appears.

5. From the Available Disk Options menu, select Modify Disk Partitions and Hot Fix. The Available Disk Drives list appears. Select the new hard drive from the list and press Enter. The Disk Partition Type screen and Disk Partition Options menu appears, as shown in figure 37.8.

6. If you see that there is no available disk space, from the Disk Partition Options menu select Delete any disk partition and select a partition that can be deleted. Many new drives come preformatted for DOS usage, for example. In this case, you would need to delete the DOS partition to make room for the NetWare partition.

7. From the Disk Partition Options menu, select Create NetWare disk partition. The Create Partition screen enables you to adjust the size of the NetWare data area as well as the size of the hot fix area. Press Esc to return to INSTALL and to create the partition. When prompted to save the partition information, enter Yes.

The Mirror/Unmirror disk partitions option of the Available Disk options menu enables you to set up drive mirroring. This option sets up a pair of NetWare partitions on different drives as mirrored sets.

To mirror one drive to another, proceed as follows:

1. From the INSTALL main menu, select Disk options. The Available Disk options menu appears.

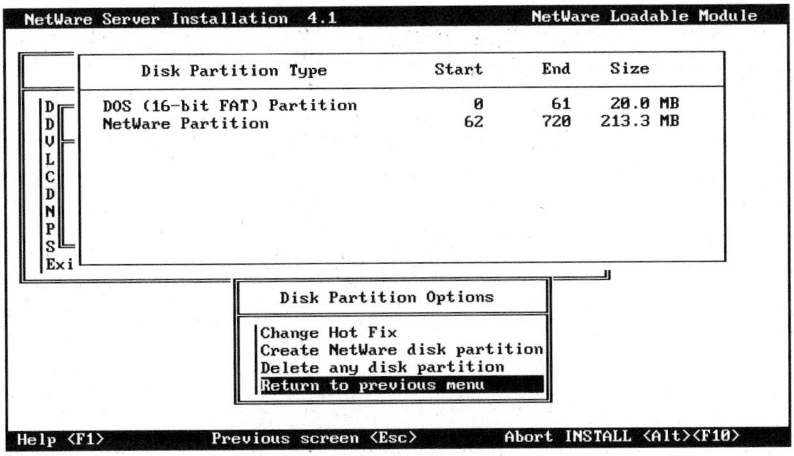

Figure 37.8

The Disk Partition Type screen and Disk Partition Options menu.

2. From the Available Disk options menu, select Mirror/Unmirror disk partitions. The Disk Partition Mirroring Status list appears.

3. From the Disk Partition Mirroring Status list, select the first hard drive in the set and press Enter. The Mirrored Disk Partitions screen appears, as shown in figure 37.9.

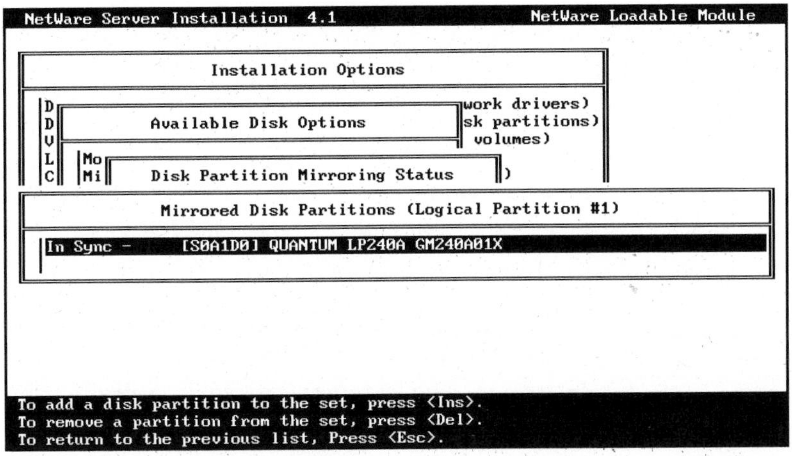

Figure 37.9

The Mirrored Disk Partitions screen.

4. From the Mirrored Disk Partitions screen, press Insert and select the second drive from the list. These two drives now act as a mirrored set. The status message at the left of each drive in the Mirrored Disk Partitions screen initially indicates Out of Sync. When all data from the first drive has been mirrored onto the second drive, this message changes to In Sync. Press Esc several times to return to the main INSTALL menu.

The two additional options of the Available Disk options menu are Perform surface test and Scan for additional devices. The surface test is based on an older NetWare DOS based utility, COMPSURF.EXE. This option performs a comprehensive surface test of the hard drive. The test updates the bad block table of the hard drive. No operating system (including NetWare) writes to any bad block identified by this test. Only the good portions of the drive are used.

The test takes between one and five minutes for every megabyte of disk space. You can perform either a destructive or non-destructive surface test. The destructive test is more thorough and more time consuming. The non-destructive test preserves any data that currently resides in the NetWare partition. This test is useful when you are installing a previously used hard drive and are unsure of its integrity.

The Scan for additional devices option is useful in reading devices that have been recently added to a SCSI bus, for example. You may have just added a new drive to an external expansion unit. This option causes NetWare to scan all disk buses for any new devices. You must be sure to load any necessary disk drivers before NetWare can recognize the new device.

Volume Options

The Volume options menu enables you to configure NetWare volumes. When you select this option, the Volume Name and Size list appears, as shown in figure 37.10.

To delete a volume, press Delete. Press the Insert key to add a new volume. If you press Enter, the Volume Information screen appears. From this screen you can enter any of the parameters indicated in table 37.1. Note that the Volume Block Size, Data Compression, and Block Suballocation parameters only can be adjusted when you are first installing a volume.

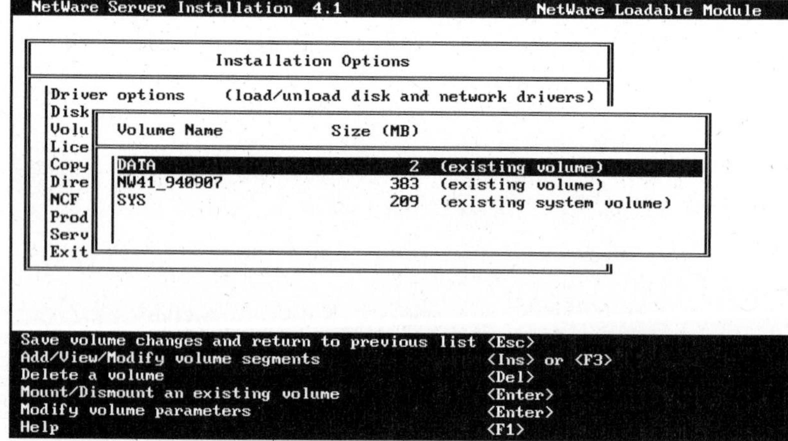

Figure 37.10
The Volume Name and Size menu.

TABLE 37.1
Volume Information Parameters

Parameter	Description
Volume Name	The name of the volume. The name of the first volume defaults to SYS.
Volume Block Size	The size of a disk block stored on this volume. It can only be adjusted upon installation of the volume.
Status	Mounted indicates the volume is mounted and possibly in use. Press Enter to change this to Dismount. A dismounted volume is not available to network users.
File Compression	On indicates this feature is enabled. Files that have not been accessed in a settable number of days automatically are compressed. This only can be adjusted upon installation of the volume.
Block Suballocation	On indicates that this feature is enabled. This allows more efficient usage of disk blocks. This only can be adjusted upon installation of the volume.
Data Migration	On indicates that the system migrates data that has not been accessed in a settable number of days off to another media.

When you delete a volume all data on that volume are erased. The disk space used for a deleted volume can be added to another existing volume.

To add disk space to an existing volume, proceed as follows:

1. From the INSTALL main menu, select Volume options. The Volume Name and Size list appears.

2. From the Volume Name and Size list, press Insert. The Volume Disk Segment List appears, as shown in figure 37.11.

3. From the Volume Disk Segment List, select the free space segment and press Enter. You see two options. If you select Make this segment a new volume, you assign the free space to a new volume. If you choose Make this segment part of another volume, you expand the space available to users of that volume.

4. After choosing Make this segment part of another volume, you see a list of volumes to which this space can be added. Select the desired volume and press Enter. You are returned to the Volume Disk Segment List where you can see that the segment has been added to the target volume.

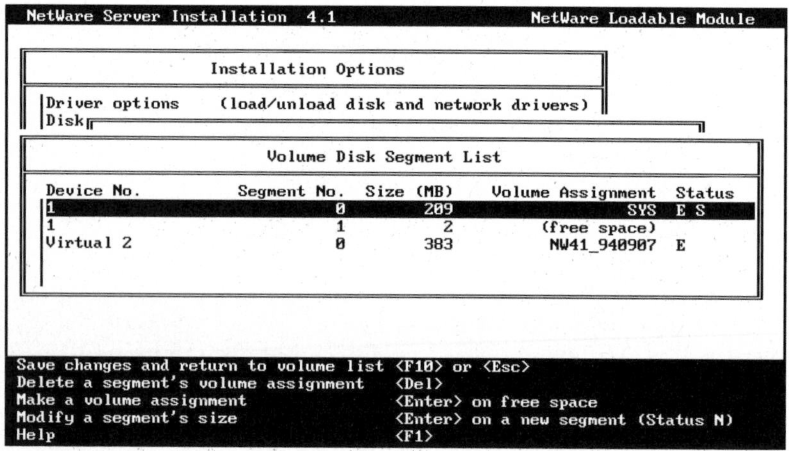

Figure 37.11
The Volume Disk Segment List.

5. The new space immediately is available to users accessing the volume. This operation has no impact on currently connected users. Press Esc to return to the main INSTALL menu and save volume changes.

To add a new volume, follow the procedure outlined previously (except choose the Make this segment a new volume option). Before you can save your changes, you must log in to the NDS as a user with at least Create object rights to the container to contain the volume. Once authenticated, you receive a confirmation message indicating that the volume object has been added to the NDS. The default location is the same container where the server object is located. You then see an option to mount the new volume. Once mounted, the new volume is available to network users with sufficient rights.

If you add free space to an existing volume from another hard drive, you have spanned the volume across multiple drives. This improves performance by causing NetWare to *stripe* data across the hard drives. This is a low level of RAID (Redundant Array of Independent Devices) technology.

License Option

The License Option is useful for the following two purposes:

- Upgrading your server license
- Installing a new server license

NetWare is sold with an *N* user license. This means that you can have *N* users logged in to this server before it starts refusing connections to new users. This is Novell's copyright protection scheme. If the number of users you want to have using this server is greater than your current server license, you must upgrade the license. If you go from a 50 user to a 100 user license, for example, you must now install the new license onto the server. The new license can be installed without having to reinstall the entire operating system.

In other cases, you may have restored an image file of a server, or may accidentally (let us hope!) have installed the same version twice. When the two identical servers communicate over the LAN, the duplication of server licenses is detected. A message Copyright Violation... appears on the server console. In addition, a broadcast goes out over the network informing all users that this has occurred. Needless to say, this is very annoying, not to mention embarrassing. Copyright violation can cause serious legal troubles. When a copyright violation is detected, the server licenses of both servers is immediately downgraded to a single user license. In this case, you need to re-install the server license on both servers affected.

To install the server license, proceed as follows:

1. From the main INSTALL menu, select License Option. The message screen shown in figure 37.12 appears.

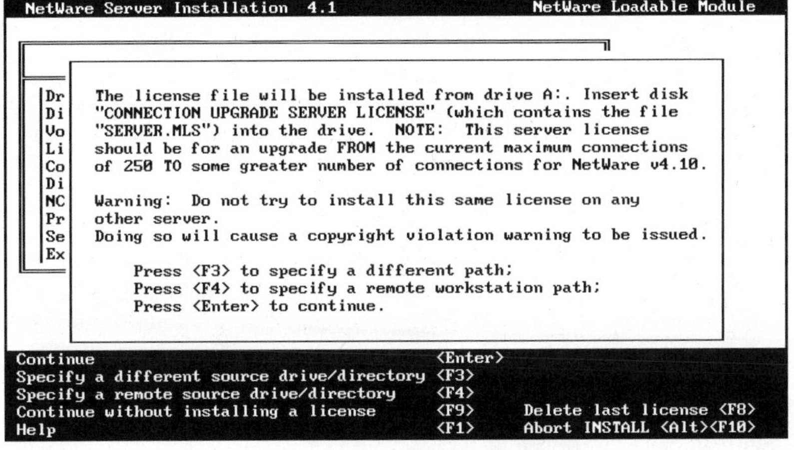

Figure 37.12

Installing a new server license.

2. Place the license disk in drive A and press Enter. If you are using RCONSOLE, you can place the license disk into drive A of the workstation. Press the F4 key to indicate the path on the workstation where the SERVER.MLS is located.

3. INSTALL reads the contents of the license disk, searching for the file SERVER.MLS. Once the license is installed, a message indicating success is displayed. Press Enter to return to INSTALL.

Copy Files Option

The Copy files option is used when installing updates or upgrades. Please note, however, that some upgrades or updates are installed using the Product options menu (described in a later section). The installation documentation accompanying the upgrade indicates which method is to be used.

The Copy files option reads data from the CD attached to the server (or from another volume on another server) and copies files into their respective directories on the server. In this fashion, files go into the LOGIN, PUBLIC, SYSTEM, and ETC directories.

When you first select this option, you see the message shown in figure 37.13.

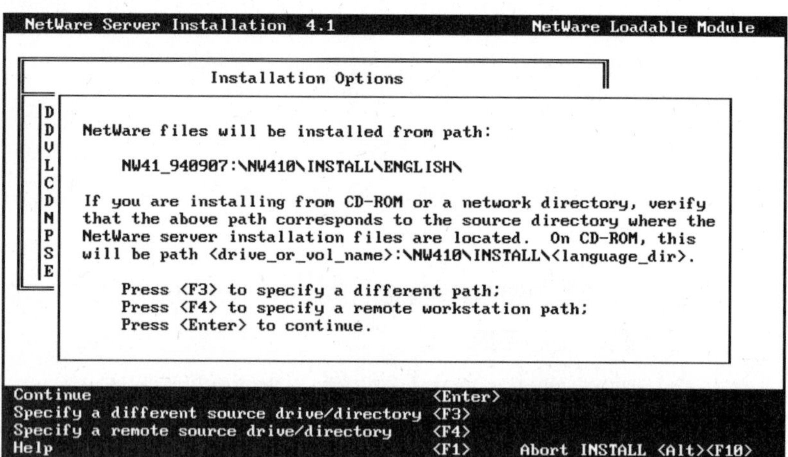

Figure 37.13
The Copy files option.

The default path indicated is the volume name of the CD used to install this version of NetWare. If you want to specify another path, press F3 and enter the correct volume and directory. If you are using RCONSOLE, you can press F4 and indicate a drive letter on another server, or a local drive and directory.

To use the CD or volume of another server, enter the server name, volume, and directory. In this case, you first are asked for a valid login name on that server. Once authenticated, you can start downloading files.

Once the CD or other volume has been read, the next option appears, as shown in figure 37.14.

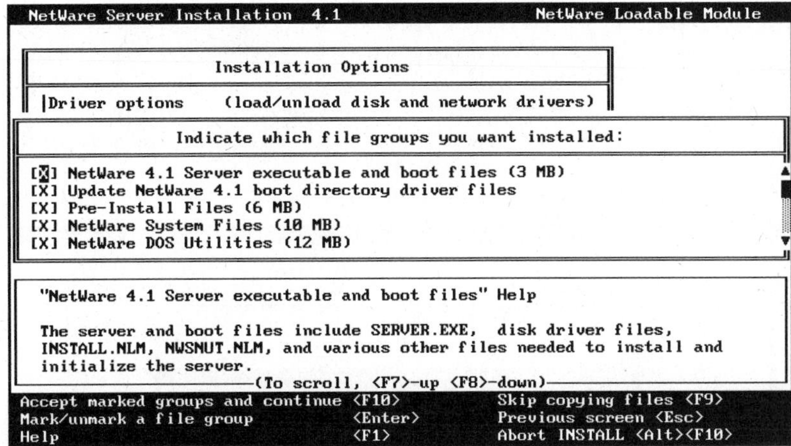

Figure 37.14

Copy files options - file groups list.

The list you see in the figure is the file groups list. Select the groups of files you want to download to your server by placing an X to the left, inside the square brackets ([ ]). Press the F10 key to start the file copy. Once the copy is in operation, a status screen showing the percentage of files copied displays.

In some cases, successful copy of upgrade files may be blocked by file or directory attributes. For example, if you want to upgrade the client installation directory, you may need to set the attributes to Read/Write for all files and directories under SYS:PUBLIC\CLIENT. In addition, you may need to remove the Rename Inhibit and Delete Inhibit attributes. This can be accomplished with the following FLAG command:

```
FLAG SYS:PUBLIC\CLIENT\*.* +rw -ri -di /sub /c
FLAG SYS:PUBLIC\CLIENT +rw -ri -di /do
```

The previous syntax adds the Read/Write attribute and subtracts the Rename Inhibit and Delete Inhibit attributes. The first command performs this operation for all files and directories under SYS:PUBLIC\CLIENT and performs it continuously. The second command performs the same operation for the SYS:PUBLIC\CLIENT directory itself.

Directory Options

The Directory Services Options menu is used to install, re-install, or remove NetWare Directory Services on this server. Other options include upgrading a NetWare 3.*x* bindery into the NDS, and adding mounted volumes to the NDS tree. The Directory Services Options menu is displayed in figure 37.15.

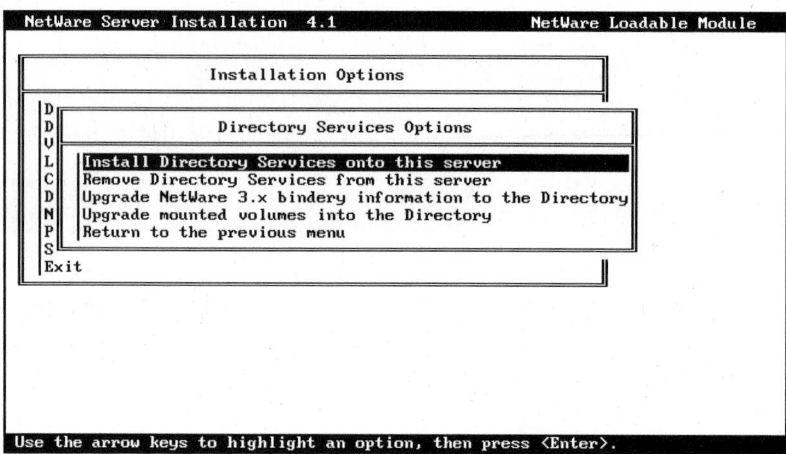

Figure 37.15
The Directory Services Options menu.

The Remove Directory Services option on this menu is extremely dangerous to the integrity of your NDS tree. Before NDS is removed you should first perform the following steps:

- ◆ Merge any NDS partitions stored on this server into the parent partition on another server.
- ◆ Remove any replicas of partitions stored on this server.
- ◆ If this server has a replica of the [root] partition, change the status of this replica to Read/Write and then remove it from the server.

Stop Removing NDS from a server that has a Master replica of any partition could cause corruption of your NDS tree. Be sure to merge any NDS partitions stored on this server into the parent or remove them entirely.

You now safely can remove NDS from this server. Be sure to backup your NDS before proceeding in case there is a problem.

To remove NDS from a server (assuming the previous steps have been performed), proceed as follows:

1. From the INSTALL main menu, select Directory options. The Directory Services Options menu appears.

2. From the Directory Services Options menu, select Remove Directory Services from this server. A bright pink warning message appears warning you of the dire consequences of removing NDS. Press Enter to continue. A prompt Remove Directory Services appears. Answer Yes to continue. A Directory Services Login/ Authentication screen appears.

3. From the Directory Services Login/Authentication screen, enter the appropriate NDS username and password. You see yet another bright pink warning message followed by another prompt asking if you wish to "Remove Directory Services Anyway?" Answer Yes to continue. NDS is removed from this server.

4. The last message, displayed in figure 37.16, tells you additional actions that must be performed to ensure the integrity of your NDS tree.

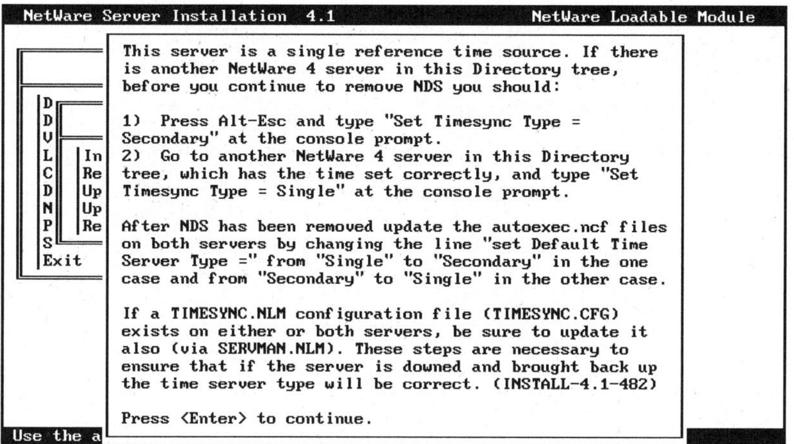

Figure 37.16

The final warning in removing Directory Services.

These additional actions include the following:

◆ Make sure there is at least one Primary, Single, or Reference time server servicing the tree.

◆ Modify the AUTOEXEC.NCF file with the new time information on any server in the tree modified.

◆ Update the TIMESYNC.CFG file (you can do so through SERVMAN.NLM).

Once NDS is removed from a server, it is no longer accessible by any means except from the server console itself. You then must install NDS in order to make the server useful again.

To install NDS on a server where NDS was removed, proceed as follows:

1. From the INSTALL main menu, select Directory options. The Directory Services Options menu appears.

2. From the Directory Services Options menu, select Install Directory Services onto this server. A dialog box asking you "Is this the first NetWare 4 Server?" appears.

   If there are other NetWare 4 servers and you want to connect to their tree, answer No, connect to existing NetWare 4 network.

   If this is the first server in the tree, answer Yes, this is the first NetWare 4 server. For the purposes of this illustration, assume Yes.

3. You now must enter the name of the new NDS tree. Enter a unique name and press Enter. The Choose a Time Zone screen appears.

4. From the Choose a Time Zone screen, locate your time zone and press Enter. The Verify/Enter Time Configuration Parameters dialog box appears, as illustrated in figure 37.17.

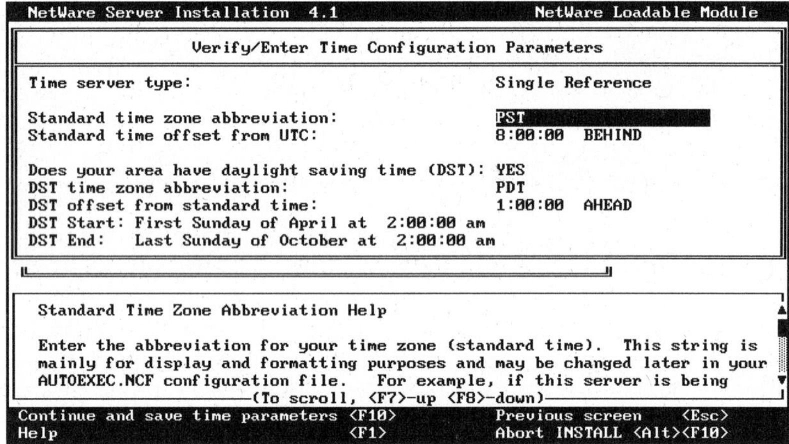

Figure 37.17
The Verify/Enter Time Configuration Parameters screen.

5. You now see a dialog box in which you can enter the first levels of your NDS tree. You can enter an Organization name, and up to 3 levels or Organizational Units. When done with this screen, press F10. Answer Yes to the prompt that asks, "Save and Continue?"

6. At this point, NDS is installed on the server. Any mounted volumes are registered with the tree. All volumes then are dismounted and remounted. Be sure to write down the complete name of the Admin user and the password.

   Press Esc to return to the main INSTALL menu.

The last two Directory Services options are used when upgrading a NetWare 3.*x* server to NetWare 4. The Upgrade NetWare 3.*x* Bindery Information to the Directory is used to read the bindery files of the upgraded NetWare 3.*x* server and place objects into the NDS. The Upgrade mounted volumes into the Directory is used to place NetWare 3.*x* volumes into the NDS. This option also can be used to enter a CD-ROM volume currently mounted into the NDS. You may want to do so for management purposes.

NCF Files Options

The NCF files options are used to create or edit the server's NCF (NetWare Configuration File) files—STARTUP.NCF and AUTOEXEC.NCF. The Create options take the current server environment and places this information into the NCF file selected. For example, in figure 37.18, you see the old STARTUP.NCF file that loads the driver IDE.DSK. When Create STARTUP.NCF File was selected, the old and new files are placed on the screen side-by-side. As you can see from the figure, the driver IDEATA.HAM was selected during a procedure earlier in this section, and now appears in the server's environment. To complete the change, use the Tab key to toggle to the old file. Use the F5 and F6 keys to mark the SET command. Use the Tab key to switch back to the new file, and use the Insert key to insert the SET command into the new file. Now you can press F10 to save the new file.

Once you have created the NCF files, you can use a DOS text editor on your workstation (with sufficient rights to SYS:SYSTEM) or EDIT.NLM at the server console to make changes to the files. You can also use INSTALL.NLM with the edit option.

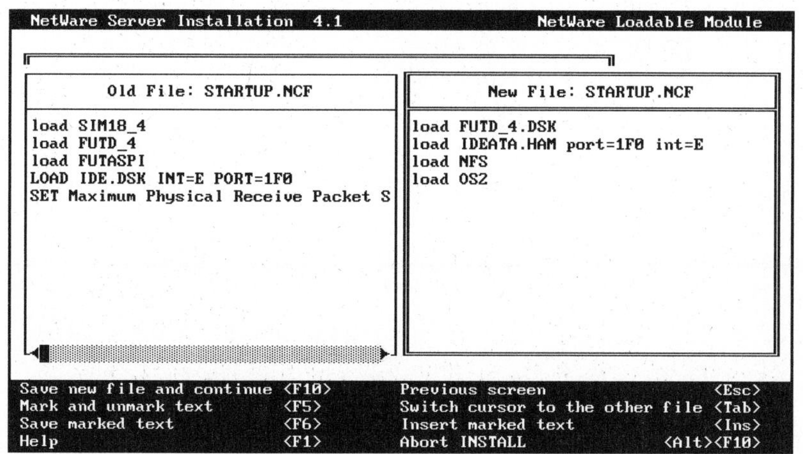

Figure 37.18

The Create STARTUP.NCF File option.

The Edit ...NCF File options are used to edit either of the server's two NCF files. The Upgrade a 3.1*x* AUTOEXEC.NCF File option is used during an upgrade from NetWare 3.*x* to 4.

Product Options

The Product options menu is used to install various products and perform actions associated with the NetWare 4 installation. Other products include NetWare for Macintosh, NetWare MHS Services, and others. The list of other product options from this menu is displayed in figure 37.19.

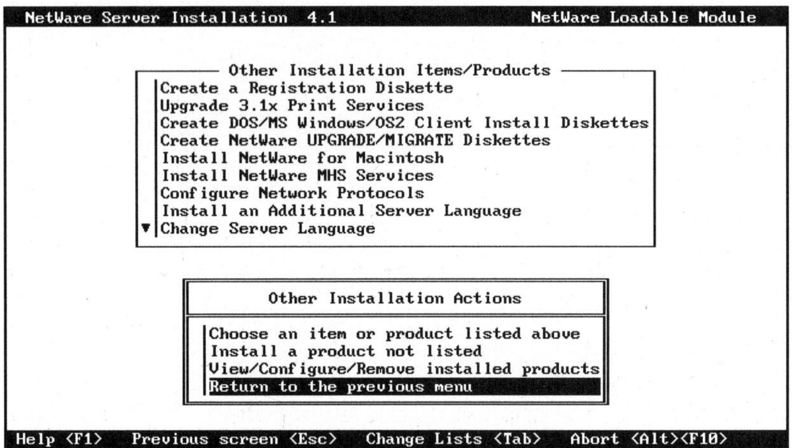

Figure 37.19
The Other Installation Items/Products screen and Other Installation Actions screen.

Table 37.2 summarizes the INSTALL product options.

Table 37.2
Product Options

Option	Description
Create a Registration Diskette	Prompts you for your company name and other information. This option then creates a registration diskette that you send to Novell in the provided mailer.
Upgrade 3.1*x* Print Services	Part of the process of upgrading from 3.1*x* to 4.1. Upgrades printing objects into NDS printing objects if you are using INSTALL.NLM to upgrade.
Create DOS/MS Windows/OS2 Client Install Diskette	Creates a set of installation diskette for client workstations.

Option	Description
Create NetWare UPGRADE/MIGRATE Diskettes	Creates a set of Upgrade or Migrate diskettes used to upgrade a NetWare 2.*x* or 3.*x* server to 4.1.
Install NetWare for Macintosh	Installs NetWare for Macintosh. NetWare 4.1 includes the software needed for a Macintosh client to access the server. This option installs the various NLMs needed on the server. You also, in a separate procedure, need to install client software on the Macintosh itself.
Install NetWare MHS Services	This options installs Basic MHS. This is a version of MHS that installs an MHS messaging server on the server. User mail then is stored on this server. This version of MHS does not enable transfer of mail outside of the network. You will need Global MHS for transfer to other services (Internet, for example). Also included with NetWare 4.1 is a version of First Mail, a simple user front end that uses MHS as its mail transport.
Configure Network Protocols	Loads INETCFG.NLM (discussed in the next section). This utility is used to configure LAN drivers and protocols.
Install an Additional Server Language	Installs language support other than English. Currently included with NetWare 4.1 are French, German, Italian, and Spanish.
Change Server Language	Changes the default language of this server. Normally, the default language is the language you selected when you first installed the server.
Install Online Documentation and Viewers	Installs the DynaText online documentation and viewing programs onto one of the server's hard drives. You can leave the documentation on CD if you have a CD player available on your network. Having the documentation on one of the server's hard drives gives you faster access.

In addition to the list summarized in table 37.2, the following actions are available from the Other Installation Actions menu:

Option	Description
Choose an item or product listed above	This option moves the cursor to the top of the screen, enabling you to select any of the options summarized in table 37.2.
Install a product not listed	This option enables you to install any product not listed. This includes NetWare for SAA, NetWare NFS, and other optional products.
View/Configure/Remove installed products	This option enables you to see which products are currently installed. You can select any product and press Delete to remove it from the server.

Server Options

Server options are available if you need to install a new 4.1 server or upgrade a 3.*x* or 4.*x* server to 4.1. This option is very similar to the Copy files option described previously. The difference is that the Install a New 4.1 Server option overwrites the existing installation and server files. The Upgrade a 3.*x* or 4.*x* Server to 4.1 option enables you to perform an upgrade from the server console.

Using INETCFG

The INETCFG.NLM (Internetwork Configuration) utility is used in NetWare 4.1 to configure network adapters and frame types, and to assign associated protocols. This is a menu-driven utility used from the server console. The INETCFG utility is a product of the Novell Internetworking Products Division, the group that produces the MultiProtocol Router (MPR). This group now supplies routing codes and utilities to the NetWare programmers in Provo, Utah.

To access INETCFG you can use either of the following two techniques:

- From the server console, type **LOAD INETCFG**
- From the INSTALL.NLM utility, select Product options, Configure Network Protocols

The INETCFG main menu is shown in figure 37.20.

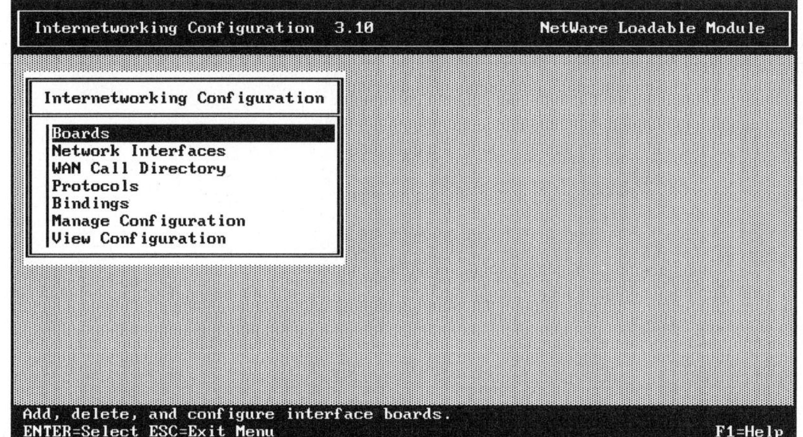

Figure 37.20
The INETCFG.NLM main menu.

The first time you load INETCFG you have the option to transfer any LAN driver configuration information from the AUTOEXEC.NCF file to the configuration files maintained by INETCFG. Once transferred, you cannot transfer them back. The INETCFG files cannot be edited using a text editor—all configuration must be done through the INETCFG utility. If you no longer want to use INETCFG you must reenter all LAN driver information manually.

The following excerpt from the AUTOEXEC.NCF file shows you the changes made when first loading INETCFG.NLM:

```
#LOAD EXP16 Port=300 Frame=Ethernet_802.2 Name=EXP16_8022
#BIND IPX exp16_8022 NET=01014088
load conlog
; Network driver LOADs and BINDs are initiated via
; INITSYS.NCF. The actual LOAD and BIND commands
; are contained in INITSYS.NCF and NETINFO.CFG.
; These files are in SYS:ETC.
sys:etc\initsys.ncf
```

You will note that the original LOAD and BIND commands used to initialize the LAN driver and bind it to a protocol have a remark character (#) placed in front of the line. The following is the INITSYS.NCF file created by INETCFG.NLM:

```
#! -- WARNING -- WARNING -- WARNING -- WARNING -- WARNING -- WARNING ----
#! This file was created by the Internetworking Configuration Console.
#! It is intended to be modified ONLY by the configurator (INETCFG.NLM).
#! Tampering with this file may cause severe malfunctioning of the system.
#! The configurator will check for tampering and abort if it is detected.
#! ---------------------------------------------------------------------
```

```
load snmp config=SYS:ETC
initialize system
```

The initialize system statement is what triggers configuration data maintained by INETCFG.

Table 37.3 summarizes the menu options available in INETCFG.NLM.

Table 37.3
INETCFG.NLM Menu Options

Option	Description
Boards	This contains configuration data on network adapters, high speed synchronous adapters, and other communications adapters in the server. This menu enables you to configure interrupts, I/O port addresses, memory addresses, and other hardware parameters.
Network Interfaces	For LAN adapters, there is a one-to-one correspondence between a Board and a Network Interface. For WAN adapters, this may not be the case. A high speed synchronous adapter may have several interfaces, with different data-link protocols associated with it. One interface could be PPP (Point to Point Protocol) adapter, for example. Another interface for the same board could be associated with the X.25 protocol.
WAN Call Directory	This is used to set up connections with remote sites with configuration data specific to the media being used.
Protocols	This menu option enables you to you configure the various protocols that may be in use on your server. Protocols include AppleTalk, IPX, TCP/IP, Source Routing, and an option for a user-specified protocol. If you have a newer OEM protocol, you would install the protocol from diskette.
Bindings	This menu associates a specific network and transport OSI layer protocol with a specific network interface defined previously. For example, you might associate IP with a LAN driver. This menu assigns the IPX network address or the IP address.

Option	Description
Manage Configuration	This menu is an odd collection of configuration parameters. These include SNMP (Simple Network Management Protocol) configuration data, importing or exporting the configuration to diskette (so that you can transfer the same settings to another server), configuring remote access by REMOTE.NLM, and an option to edit the AUTOEXEC.NCF file.
View Configuration	This menu option enables you to you view the configuration options you have enabled for specific menu options, or all INETCFG parameters you have configured.

Configuring IPX

To configure a network adapter for IPX, proceed as follows:

1. From the server console, load INETCFG as follows:

   LOAD INETCFG

   The INETCFG main menu appears.

2. From the INETCFG main menu, select Boards. The Configured Boards list appears.

3. From the Configured Boards list, press Insert and select the desired board from the list.

   If the board you want to add is not on the list, press Insert again. When prompted, add the full path in the New Driver input box, and press Enter. INETCFG reads configuration data from the indicated path and adds this board to the disk. The path you enter could be the volume and directory of the original NetWare 4.1 installation CD, or a disk provided by the manufacturer of your LAN adapter.

   Once the driver for the board has been entered, you see the Board Configuration dialog box, as shown in figure 37.21.

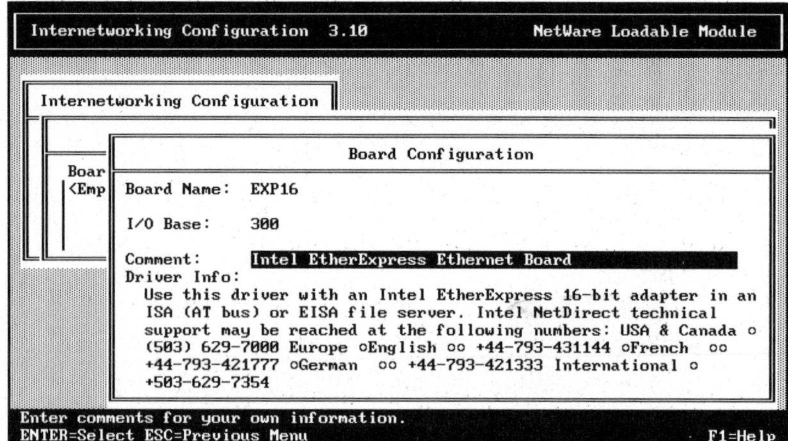

Figure 37.21
The Boards Configuration dialog box.

4. From the Board Configuration dialog box, enter an appropriate name for this board after the Board Name field. The name is used later as a reference, and appears when you type CONFIG from the server console prompt. The Comment field is for your reference only. Other settings, including I/O Base, Interrupt, IO Port, and other settings are specific to the board you have installed in your server.

   When done entering board configuration information, press Esc and save the data you have entered. Press Esc once again to return to the main menu of INETCFG.

5. From the INETCFG main menu, select Bindings. The Configured Protocol to Network Interface Bindings list appears.

6. From the Configured Protocol to Network Interface Bindings list, press Insert. You see a list of configured protocols from which to choose. Choose IPX and press Enter. You now see a list of boards from which to choose. Choose the board you want to assign to IPX and press Enter. The Binding IPX to a LAN Interface dialog box appears as shown in figure 37.22.

7. From the Binding IPX to a LAN Interface dialog box, enter the appropriate IPX Network Number and the desired Frame Type. If there are other servers on the same network, these settings must match the same settings in other servers. If unsure, go to another server and type CONFIG at the console. When done, press Esc and answer Yes to the prompt to save your information. Press Esc again to return to the INETCFG main menu.

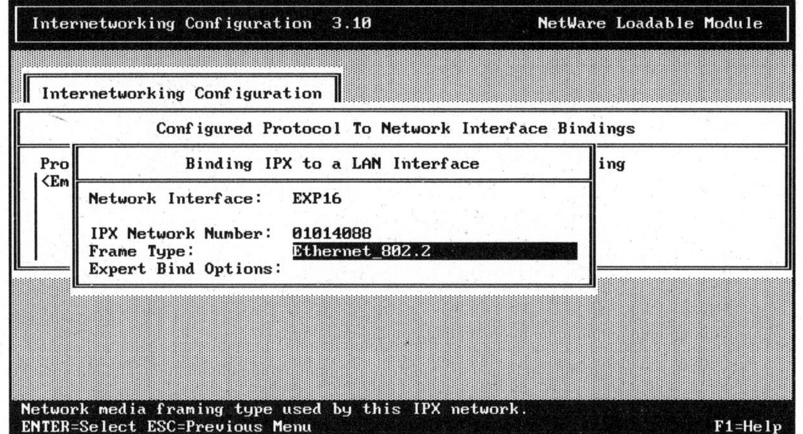

Figure 37.22

The Binding IPX to a LAN Interface dialog box.

8. From the INETCFG main menu, select View Configuration. From the View Configuration menu, select All INETCFG Commands. You can now verify that all commands are as you want. The resulting screen is similar to that shown in figure 37.23.

```
Internetworking Configuration  3.10                NetWare Loadable Module

            View (Read-Only) All INETCFG-Generated Commands
LOAD SNMP
LOAD EXP16 NAME=EXP16_E82 FRAME=Ethernet_802.2 PORT=300
LOAD SPXCONFG Q=1 A=540 V=108 W=54 R=10 S=1000 I=1200
BIND IPX EXP16_E82 net=01014088 seq=1
LOAD REMOTE NOVELL
LOAD RSPX

View all the "LOAD" and "BIND" commands (You cannot change them from here).
ESC=Exit Viewing                                                    F1=Help
```

Figure 37.23

The View All INETCFG-Generated Commands screen.

9. Press Esc to exit the viewing screen. Press Esc a couple of more times to exit INETCFG. Note that you must either bring the server down and restart it, or issue the following command to make your changes effective:

INITIALIZE SYSTEM

Configuring TCP/IP

The process for configuring a LAN adapter for TCP/IP is similar to that for IPX. If you plan to use the same LAN adapter for TCP/IP as you are using for IPX, it is loaded twice by INETCFG. You then have to assign it a frame type supported by TCP/IP. Supported TCP/IP frame types include the following:

- Ethernet_II (for Ethernet network adapters)
- Ethernet_SNAP (an advanced variation of Ethernet_II for Ethernet adapters)
- Token-Ring_SNAP (for token ring adapters)

To configure a network adapter for TCP/IP, proceed as follows:

1. From the server console, load INETCFG. The INETCFG main menu appears.
2. From the INETCFG main menu, select Boards. The Configured Boards list appears.

   If you plan to use the same board for TCP/IP as used for IPX, do not select another board. Skip the Boards option.
3. If you are using a different board for TCP/IP, from the Configured Boards list press Insert and select the desired board from the list. Press Esc to return to the INETCFG main menu.
4. From the INETCFG main menu, select Protocols. The Protocol Configuration menu appears. Be sure that TCP/IP is enabled.

   If not, select TCP/IP and press Enter. Press Esc and select Yes when asked to Update TCP/IP Configuration. You return to the Protocol Configuration menu where TCP/IP now appears Enabled.

   Press Esc in either case to return to the INETCFG main menu.
5. From the INETCFG main menu, select Bindings. The Configured Protocol to Network Interface Bindings list appears.
6. From the Configured Protocol to Network Interface Bindings list, press Insert. You see a list of configured protocols from which to choose. Choose TCP/IP and press Enter. You now see a list of boards from which to choose. Choose the board you want to assign to IPX and press Enter. The Binding TCP/IP to a LAN Interface dialog box appears, as shown in figure 37.24.

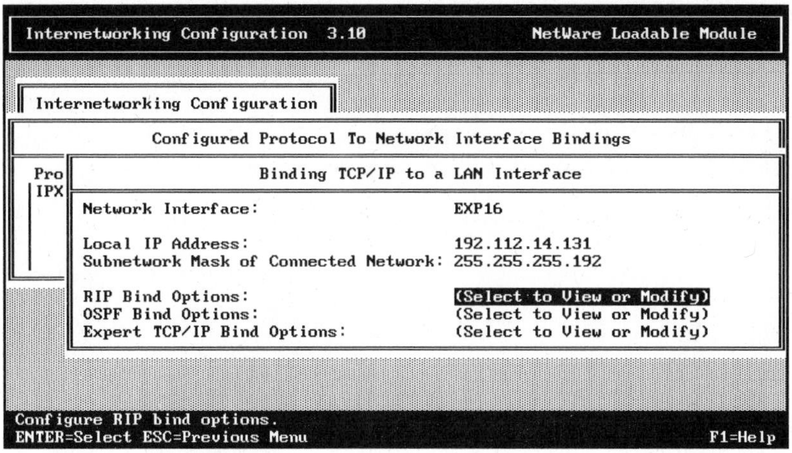

```
Internetworking Configuration  3.10                 NetWare Loadable Module

 Internetworking Configuration

            Configured Protocol To Network Interface Bindings
 Pro                     Binding TCP/IP to a LAN Interface
 IPX
      Network Interface:                     EXP16

      Local IP Address:                      192.112.14.131
      Subnetwork Mask of Connected Network:  255.255.255.192

      RIP Bind Options:                      (Select to View or Modify)
      OSPF Bind Options:                     (Select to View or Modify)
      Expert TCP/IP Bind Options:            (Select to View or Modify)

Configure RIP bind options.
ENTER=Select  ESC=Previous Menu                                       F1=Help
```

Figure 37.24

The Binding TCP/IP to a LAN Interface screen.

7. From the Binding TCP/IP to a LAN Interface dialog box, enter the appropriate Local IP Address and the Subnetwork Mask of Connected Network. The example shown in figure 37.24 shows a Class C IP address with a subnet mask other than the default.

   This menu also enables you to configure RIP (Routing Information Protocol), OSPF (Open Shortest Path First), and Expert TCP/IP bind options. These menu options are beyond the scope of this book. You can press F1 at any of these menus for further explanations.

   When done, press Esc and answer Yes to the prompt to save your information. Press Esc again to return to the INETCFG main menu.

8. From the INETCFG main menu, select View Configuration. From the View Configuration menu, select All INETCFG Commands. You can now verify that all commands are as you want. The resulting screen is similar to that shown in figure 37.25.

9. Press Esc several times to exit the viewing screen and to exit INETCFG. Remember that you must either down the server and restart it, or issue the initialize system command to make your changes effective.

Advanced IPX Configuration

NetWare 4.1 supports additional IPX features, including the following:

- SAP (Service Advertising Protocol) filtering
- NLSP (NetWare Link State Protocol)

Figure 37.25

Viewing all INETCFG commands with IPX and TCP/IP protocol support.

```
Internetworking Configuration  3.10                    NetWare Loadable Module

                View (Read-Only) All INETCFG-Generated Commands

LOAD SNMP
LOAD EXP16 NAME=EXP16_E82 FRAME=Ethernet_802.2 PORT=300
LOAD EXP16 NAME=EXP16_EII FRAME=Ethernet_II PORT=300
LOAD SPXCONFG Q=1 A=540 V=108 W=54 R=10 S=1000 I=1200
BIND IPX EXP16_E82 net=01014088 seq=1
LOAD Tcpip RIP=Yes Forward=No
BIND IP EXP16_EII ARP=Yes Mask=255.255.255.192 Address=192.112.14.131
LOAD REMOTE NOVELL
LOAD RSPX

View all the "LOAD" and "BIND" commands (You cannot change them from here).
ESC=Exit Viewing                                                        F1=Help
```

NLSP is an advanced form of routing that offers significant advantages over standard IPX routing using Novell's RIP (Routing Information Protocol). (The term "Novell's RIP" is used to distinguish from the form of RIP used by the Internet community.) NLSP uses a type of routing known as link state. In brief, an NLSP router stores a map of the entire network in its routing tables. When a change is made, it sends out only updated information. As a result, an NLSP router can provide more accurate routing information to its peers, the information can be provided faster, and more intelligent routing decisions can be made since all facts are known. Novell's RIP, on the other hand, uses what is known as distance vector routing. This form of routing simply measures distances between routers by hops. A hop is one router. This does not take into account the fact that the shorter path might include a slow line, and the longer path might be wired with FDDI network adapters. In addition, Novell's RIP causes routers to broadcast the entire contents of their routing tables to their neighbors every 60 seconds. This generates a substantial amount of network traffic. If you configure a NetWare 4.1 server for NLSP, it is backwards compatible with Novell's RIP.

SAP filtering is the process of disallowing specific types of services to come into this server or to go out from this server. The effect of this is that you can hide servers or services from segments of the network. SAP filtering also can reduce network traffic and is especially useful over a slow link.

To enable SAP filtering, proceed as follows:

1. From the server console, load INETCFG. The INETCFG main menu appears.

2. From the INETCFG main menu, select Protocols. The Protocol Configuration list appears.

3. From the Protocol Configuration list, select IPX. The IPX Protocol Configuration dialog box appears.

4. From the IPX Protocol Configuration dialog box select Advanced IPX and change the option to Enabled. This enables several advanced IPX parameters including Filter Support. Move Filter Support and change the option to Enabled. When done, the screen appears as shown in figure 37.26.

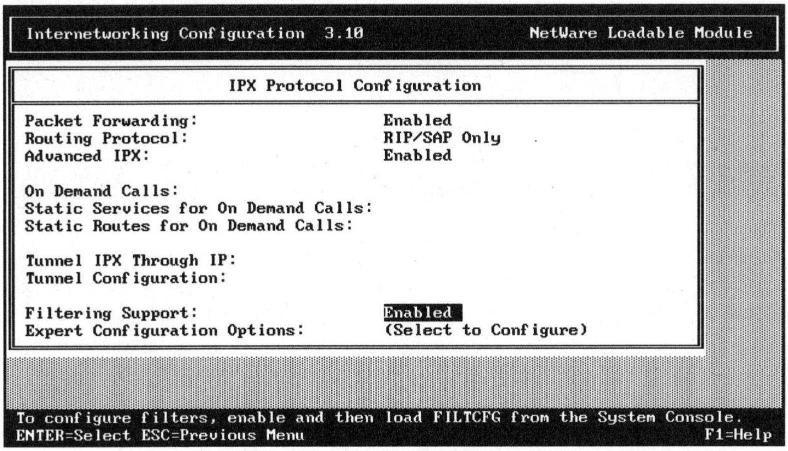

```
Internetworking Configuration  3.10                NetWare Loadable Module

                      IPX Protocol Configuration
Packet Forwarding:                          Enabled
Routing Protocol:                           RIP/SAP Only
Advanced IPX:                               Enabled

On Demand Calls:
Static Services for On Demand Calls:
Static Routes for On Demand Calls:

Tunnel IPX Through IP:
Tunnel Configuration:

Filtering Support:                          Enabled
Expert Configuration Options:               (Select to Configure)

To configure filters, enable and then load FILTCFG from the System Console.
ENTER=Select ESC=Previous Menu                                       F1=Help
```

Figure 37.26

The IPX Protocol Configuration dialog box.

5. At this point you can press Esc and answer Yes when prompted to save changes. SAP filtering has been enabled. You must now exit INETCFG and load the FILTCFG.NLM utility to configure which SAPs you want to filter. Press Esc several times to exit INETCFG. Be sure to restart the server to enable the changes you have made so far.

To configure SAP filtering, proceed as follows:

1. Restart the server so that any changes you have made so far become effective. You can proceed as follows:

   DOWN
   RESTART SERVER

2. Once the server has been restarted, load the FILTCFG.NLM utility as follows:

   LOAD FILTCFG

   The FILTCFG main menu appears, as shown in figure 37.27.

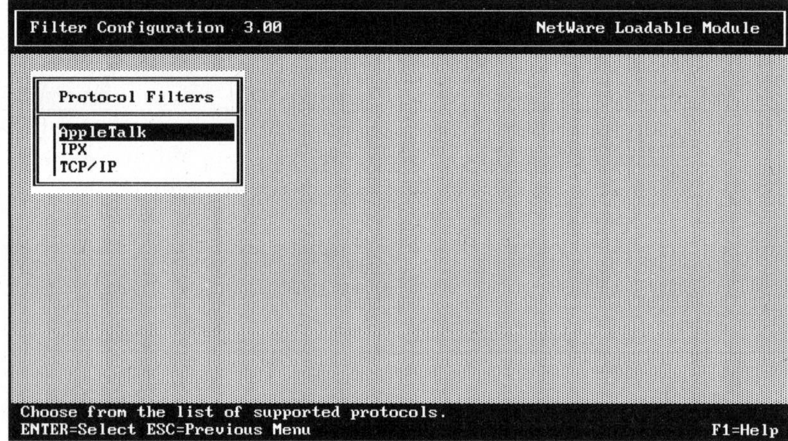

Figure 37.27
The Protocol Filters menu.

3. From the FILTCFG main menu, select IPX. The IPX menu appears. Initially all filters are Disabled. You can now select SAP Filters or RIP Filters. There are options for Incoming or Outgoing filters.

To prevent anyone on another network segment from seeing RCONSOLE advertisements, proceed as follows:

1. From the FILTCFG main menu, select IPX. The IPX menu appears.
2. From the IPX menu, select Outgoing SAP Filters and press Enter. The Outgoing SAP Filters dialog box appears. Change the Status field to Enabled. Change the Action field to Deny Services in Filter List. You must now configure the list of services to filter out. From the Outgoing SAP Filters dialog box, press Enter next to the Filters field. The Services Denied list appears.
3. From the Services Denied list, press Insert to add a service to the list. The Define Filter dialog box appears.
4. From the Define Filter dialog box, fill in the Service Name field with any name that is appropriate. For this illustration, enter **RCONSOLE Filter**. Move the cursor to the Service Type field. The default type is FFFF, which means All Services. Press Insert to define a service type. The Defined Service Types list appears, as shown in figure 37.28.
5. From the Defined Service Types list, locate the type for Remote Console. You note that this is type 0107 hex. Press Enter to add this type to the list. You then return to the Define Filter dialog box.

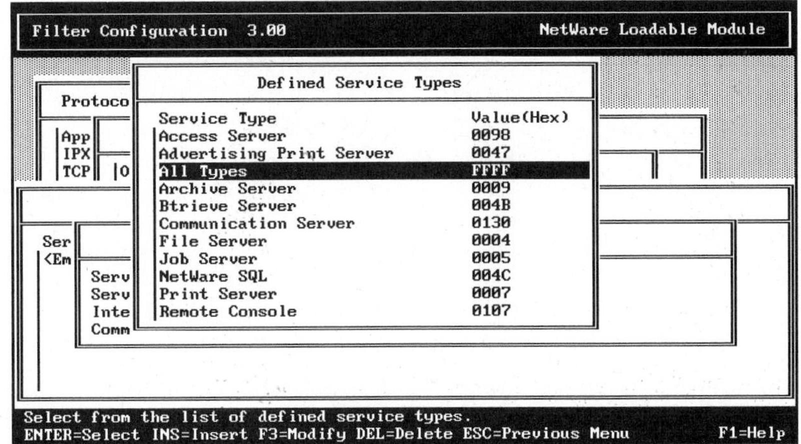

Figure 37.28

The Defined Service Types list.

6. Fill in the remaining fields in the Define Filter dialog box. The Interface field identifies which LAN or WAN interface is filtered. The Comment field should have some helpful description of the filter for future reference. When done, the screen should look something like that shown in figure 37.29.

   Press Esc to save the information. You return to the Services Denied list.

7. Press Esc several times to exit FILTCFG. Answer Yes when asked if you want to save your information. The filters you configured are now effective.

```
Filter Configuration 3.00                    NetWare Loadable Module

  Protocol Filters
  App                          IPX
  IPX
  TCP  |Out            Outgoing SAP Filters
                        Services Denied
  Ser                   Define Filter
  <Em
       Service Name: RCONSOLE Filter
       Service Type: 0107 (Remote Console)
       Interface:    EXP16
       Comment:      Filters outbound REMOTE/RCONSOLE advertising

Enter an optional short description.
ENTER=Select ESC=Previous Menu                                F1=Help
```

Figure 37.29

The Define Filter dialog box.

Getting the Latest Drivers

Getting the latest drivers for your NetWare servers can be a challenge. One of the most difficult and yet enjoyable tasks confronting the network Administrator is keeping up to date. This usually involves reading technical journals and periodicals. Many of the mainstream magazines (such as *PC Magazine* or *LAN Times*) carry worthwhile articles and product reviews. There is a growing number of books on NetWare and networking in general. *New Riders Publishing* is one among many fine publishers. Even reading computer ads can be revealing. A current trend, for example, is the drop in hard drive prices. For a long time the cost of a hard drive was over $1.00 per MB. Current prices are dipping below a price of $.50 per MB.

Among the greatest difficulties in keeping up with the latest drivers is finding out there is a driver related problem in the first place, and finding out whether or not the vendor has published an update. One of the best ways to find out current problems is to subscribe to either (or both) NetWire and the NSEPro.

NetWire

Some vendors have their own bulletin boards. This is a service where the vendor has a computer running bulletin board software, connected to a modem and phone line, available 24 hours a day, 7 days a week. There are many problems with such services, including the following:

- You must have a separate phone number available for each vendor.
- The vendor's phone lines only can handle a limited number of simultaneous calls.
- The cost is high if you live far away from the access number and have to pay long distance or international rates.
- Bulletin board software is not well-tested software and can easily lock up your system.

Many vendors, including Novell, have decided to seek a more comprehensive solution. The ideal is to have a 24 hour a day, 7 day a week service that can handle hundreds of calls an hour, is dependable, and is available to the greatest number of people. The solution is to go with an existing network provider such as CompuServe. Many other vendors, including Microsoft and Borland, have decided to go the same route.

NetWire is a service provided by Novell through CompuServe. *CompuServe* is a computer network that is like a commercial version of the Internet. CompuServe has many services available other than NetWire. Through CompuServe, for example, you

can go shopping, view airline schedules and purchase tickets, get stock quotes, and catch up on the latest news from API (Associated Press International). Novell's forum on CompuServe is called NetWire. Once you have access CompuServe using a PC, a modem, and terminal software (such as ProComm or the Windows Terminal), type the following:

GO NETWIRE

You are now connected to Novell's bulletin board. NetWire provides a series of informational areas. Of most interest to network Administrators are the Forums and the Libraries. Each forum or library has a CompuServe designation. Most NetWire forums or libraries start with the letter N. When wish to go to the NetWare 4.*x* forum, for example, you can issue the command:

GO NETW4X

The forums are places where technicians can post messages on various technical topics and read replies. There are around a dozen forums in NetWire. They are broken down roughly by product category. There are forums for the following:

- NetWare 3.*x*
- NetWare 4.*x*
- NetWare Clients
- Developers
- Hardware
- Vendors who sell NetWare related products
- UnixWare

The forums are a good place to find problems that other network Administrators are facing, and to get answers to problems you are facing.

The libraries are where the latest files, patches, fixes, and drivers are located. There is a library associated with some forums (such as the UnixWare forum). In addition, there are libraries for the following:

- User (non-Novell) Downloaded Files
- The Most Popular Novell Downloaded Files
- The Main Novell Library

Here is an example using a specially designed Windows interface for CompuServe. The interface is called NovCIM (Novell CompuServe Information Manager). It uses CompuServe's WinCIM and places the Novell NetWire main menu in the foreground. You can download a copy of this interface (for a price) by typing the following from CompuServe:

GO NOVCIM

In this example, you are using ARCServe to control backups on your server. You are experiencing problems and want to see if there is a patch or fix available. Assuming you find one, this example also shows you how to download the file.

1. From Windows Program Manager, access NovCIM. The NetWire main menu appears. This menu is shown in figure 37.30.

2. From the main menu, select Service/Support. The Service/Support menu appears.

3. From the Service/Support menu, select Files, Patches, and Fixes. The Files Area list appears.

4. From the Files Area list, select Novell File Library. Note that you could have used the following command to perform the same actions:

   GO NOVLIB

   The Novell Library Forum appears, as shown in figure 37.31.

5. From the Novell Library Forum, you can either select the Search icon (looks like books on a shelf with a magnifying glass), or from the Library menu, select Search. The Search for Files dialog box appears, as shown in figure 37.32.

   Note at the left is a list of areas to search. If you know the desired driver is not in certain areas, remove the checkmark to speed up the search. To the right you can search by File Name, Contributor (CompuServe ID of person who downloaded the file), or by Keyword(s). In addition, at the bottom right, you can limit the search by date.

6. When done specifying search criteria, choose the Search button. You will see a Library Search list showing you a list of files that match the criteria. Select the desired file.

   Choose Description to get information about a specific file. Choose Mark to mark the file for download when you are done. Choose Retrieve to download the file immediately. For the purposes of this illustration go ahead and download the file immediately. You are prompted for a local file name and directory before beginning the download. The Downloading File box appears indicating the remaining time.

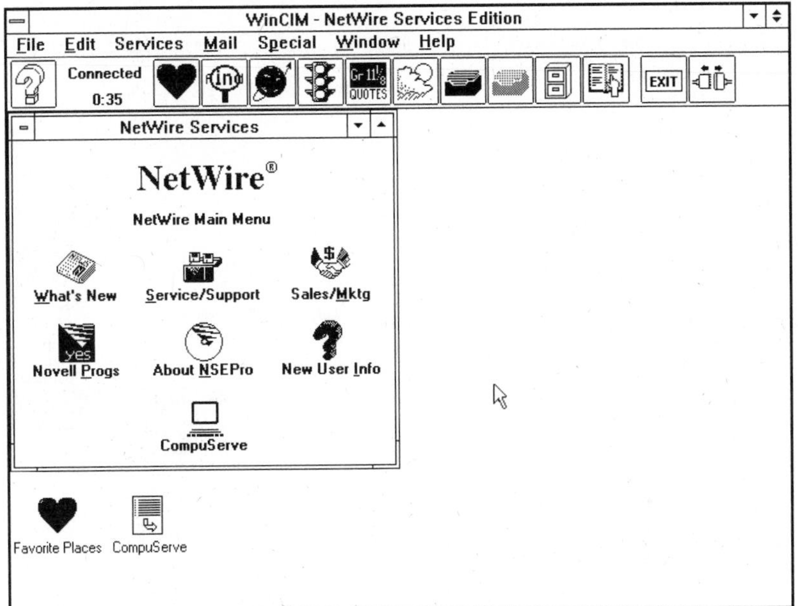

Figure 37.30
The NetWire main menu.

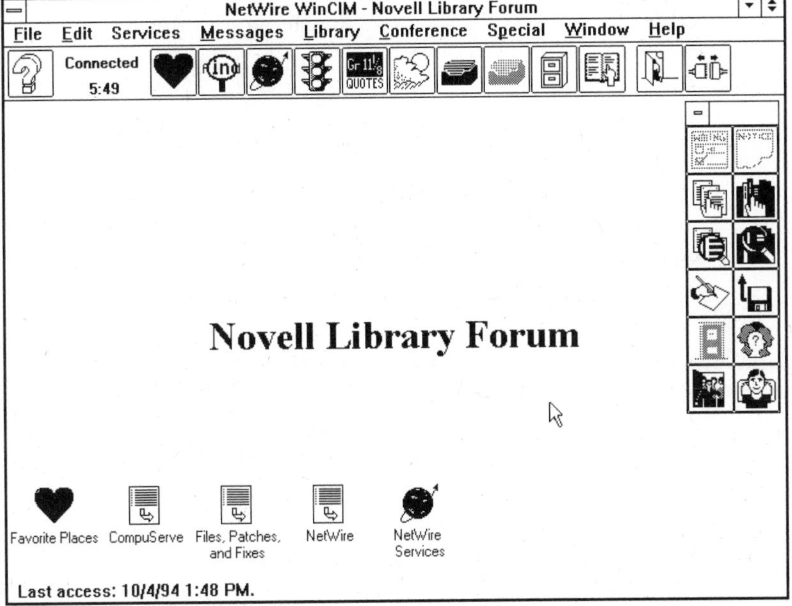

Figure 37.31
The Novell Library Forum.

Figure 37.32

The Search for Files dialog box.

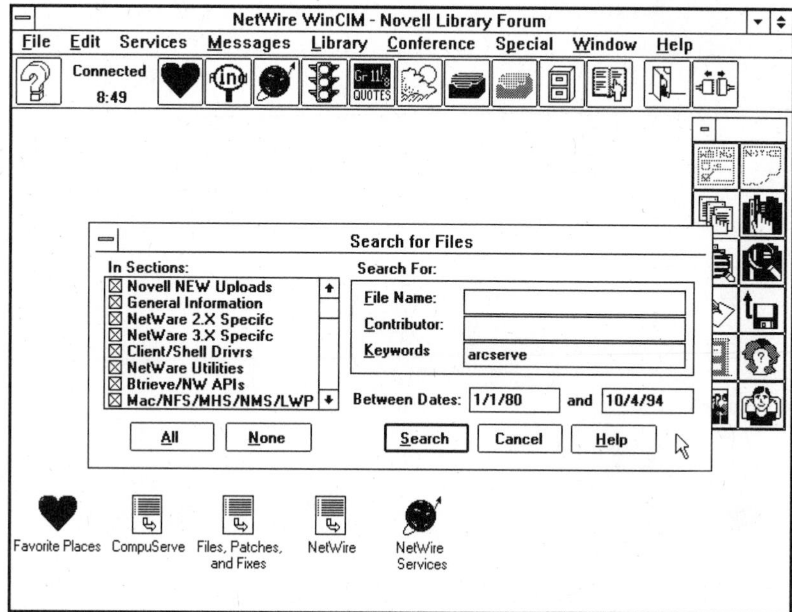

7. When done you can continue to browse CompuServe or exit the program. Remember, you are charged for every minute connected to CompuServe.

NSEPro

The NSEPro (Network Support Encyclopedia—Professional Edition) is available on a yearly subscription basis. The cost varies due to discounts and promotions. The full list price per year is around $1,400. The NSEPro is shipped on a CD, and contains a number of items, including the following:

- All NetWare manuals
- Application Notes (technical articles on NetWare specific topics written primarily by engineers)
- All files, patches, fixes, and drivers that are on CompuServe
- Product testing reports
- The Novell problem/resolution database

As you can see, the NSEPro is packed with good technical information. Imagine being able to carry around the complete NetWare manual set on a CD. The Application Notes are first published and sent to those with a subscription. A month or two later,

these same Application Notes get placed into the NSEPro and sent to all NSEPro subscribers. The Application Notes are usually related to specific NetWare applications. A typical issue has information on how to use CDROM.NLM, or how to implement time synchronization over a WAN, or an update on the latest client software.

The files, patches, fixes and drivers can be downloaded much as you would download from CompuServe and NetWire, except that you are not paying a per minute charge. If you frequently download files from NetWire it may be cost justified getting a subscription to the NSEPro.

When downloading a file from the NSEPro using the DOS interface, sometimes you cannot download the file, or view a graphic. The following is the solution to both problems:

1. Set a DOS variable NSE_DOWNLOAD before getting into the NSEPro. This variable must be set to the drive letter to which your NSEPro is mapped, and the directory that contains the downloadable files. If your NSEPro is mapped to a Search Drive X, you can set this variable as follows:

   ```
   SET NSE_DOWNLOAD = X:\DOWNLOAD
   ```

2. Start the NSEPro from a directory where you have Read, Modify, Create, Erase, and Write directory trustee rights. This could be your home directory on the server, or your local C drive. When the NSEPro goes to download a file (or produce a graphic), it writes a temporary file to your current directory. If you started the NSEPro while on the CD-ROM itself, you get an error message because the NSEPro cannot create a file on a Read Only medium.

The product testing reports indicate the results of testing various products using various configurations. Manufacturers pay a pretty penny to have Novell technicians put their products through the wringer. When a product is certified, the vendor legally can place the Yes NetWare Tested and Approved sticker on their packaging. In addition, the product testing report is included in the NSEPro. The advantage is that you can see under what conditions a product was tested, and if there are any qualifiers the Novell technicians noticed and recommended. This is a good way to do research prior to setting up a network. If you know that it has worked for Novell, you're one step ahead of the game.

The last item, the problem/resolution database, is a collection of problems reported and solved by Novell over the past several years. A search engine built into the NSEPro, based on Folio Infobase, enables you to search this database (as well as the manuals, Application Notes, and Product Testing bulletins) for words or phrases you enter. You see a hit list appear with Folio pages that contain the word or phrase you entered. You can then view each of the pages to see if there is an answer to your problem.

The problem/resolution database gives the date, version of software and equipment involved. There is a description of the problem followed by the solution. In many cases the solution is to download a patch or an update. In other cases it may be to change a jumper setting on a particular piece of hardware. Sometimes there is a conflict with the BIOS of a particular brand of computer and a BIOS update from the vendor solves the problem.

Although it is expensive, the NSEPro is a good investment, and may pay for itself in the time it saves you. In many cases you could qualify for a discount. If you are affiliated with a Novell Reseller, a Novell Authorized Education Center (NAEC), or a Novell Academic Education Partner (NEAP), or any of a number of other programs, you could receive the NSEPro either for free, or for a substantial discount. Contact you nearest Novell Reseller, NAEC, or NEAP for more information.

Update CDs

Novell ships updates to its operating systems on CD from time to time. In many cases you receive the update free of charge. You do not receive an update if you have not registered your version of NetWare. Take the time to perform the Create a Registration Diskette process in the Product options menu of INSTALL.NLM described previously.

To load the update you should follow the directions that come with the update. Usually there is a one page sheet describing the process. In most cases all you need to do is to load the INSTALL.NLM, and select the Copy Files option. In other cases you need to select the Product options menu, and select Install a product not listed.

Summary

This chapter showed you how to make configuration changes to a server. The chapter started with a discussion of INSTALL.NLM and its various menus and options. The Driver options menu enables you to load and unload disk or LAN drivers. This is the equivalent of issuing the LOAD command from the server console prompt. The Disk options menu enables you to partition a hard drive, set up mirroring, perform a surface test on a drive, and scan for new devices that you have installed since the server was last brought up. The Volume options menu enables you to create or delete volumes from hard drives with NetWare partitions. You also learned how to allocate free space to an existing volume. If a volume spans more than one hard drive efficiency is improved. License Option is used to upgrade your NetWare license, or restore a license after a copyright violation error. The Copy Files option is used to upgrade a server, or to finish an installation that was halted for some reason. Files are typically copied from the installation CD to the server's SYS: volume. This option

enables you to copy files from another server. The Directory options menu is used to install or remove NDS from the server. If you do so while a replica of a partition exists on this server, you could corrupt the NDS tree. It is advised to either remove the replica, or to merge the replica into its parent on another server. To see if there is a replica on this server, use PARTMGR.EXE or from NWADMIN.EXE select Tools, Partition Manager.

The NCF files option is used to create or update the server's NCF (NetWare Configuration File) files. When you select Create, INSTALL reads the server's current environment and places all possible information into the file selected. When you save a file after selecting create, the old file is overwritten. When you select Edit, the file is retained and you can make changes. The files affected are STARTUP.NCF and AUTOEXEC.NCF.

Product options enables you to perform a number of tasks. These include creating a Registration Diskette, upgrading NetWare 3.1*x* print services, creating client installation diskettes, creating upgrade or migrate diskettes, installing NetWare for Macintosh or MHS Services, installing language support files, changing the server's default language, and installing the online documentation. You also can install products not listed and call up the INETCFG utility.

The INETCFG utility is used to configure network adapters and protocols. It is a menu driven utility and makes multiple LAN cards and protocols much easier to manage. When done, the INITIALIZE SYSTEM command activates the parameters specified using INETCFG. You also can use this utility to enable SAP (Service Advertising Protocol) and RIP (Routing Information Protocol) filtering, and enable NLSP (NetWare Link State Protocol). The FILTCFG utility, an adjunct to INETCFG, is used actually to specify which SAP or RIP information is to be filtered. As you saw in the example, you can hide services from different portions of the network through filtering.

The last part of this chapter discussed how to obtain the latest drivers, patches, and fixes. Three sources were discussed—NetWire, NSEPro, and Update CDs. NetWire is Novell's bulletin board service based on CompuServe. The most popular areas are the forums and libraries. The forums are where you can post messages and read replies. The libraries contains downloadable files. The NSEPro has most of the Novell manual set, the same downloadables as on CompuServe, the Application Notes, and the problem/resolution database. The NSEPro may be more cost effective in the long run if you download many files or need quick fixes to problems. NetWire is more up-to-date. The last section briefly discussed how Novell ships periodic updates on CD.

The next chapter covers how to fine-tune your server. It focuses primarily on the SET commands.

Fine-Tuning the Server

NetWare 4.1 offers tremendous flexibility when you want to tune performance parameters. You can set over a hundred parameters. NetWare 4.1, left to its own devices, constantly allocates and deallocates resources. It adjusts to almost any environment over time. A time may come, however, when one or more resources available to the server become scarce—most commonly, memory. As you use the server more and more, NetWare allocates more resources. More often than not, you end up loading additional NLMs on the file server over time, including NLMs to perform scheduled backups, check for viruses, and handle different types of clients. The code portion of each NLM takes up memory on the file server. In addition, each NLM allocates memory for its own operation. After time, memory available to users can become scarce. Between the time memory is scarce and the time you eventually purchase and install additional memory, the server might not perform as well as in the past. This is the time to look at the way you can make minute adjustments in server performance parameters to allow optimal performance with minimal resources.

SET Commands

You use two primary tools to adjust server performance parameters: the SET command and the SERVMAN.NLM utility. You can access both of them from the file server console. This section discusses the SET commands. The following section discusses the SERVMAN.NLM utility.

You can issue the SET command from the file server console or through the SERVMAN utility. After you type **SET** at the console prompt, NetWare 4.1 lists the following configuration categories and asks which category you want to view:

```
EBDB:SET
Settable configuration parameter categories
  1. Communications
  2. Memory
  3. File caching
  4. Directory caching
  5. File system
  6. Locks
  7. Transaction tracking
  8. Disk
  9. Time
  10. NCP
  11. Miscellaneous
  12. Error Handling
  13. Directory Services
Which category do you want to view:
```

From a performance point of view, many of these parameters are closely associated. The SET commands for memory, file caching, and directory caching affect the server's memory performance. The SET commands for the file system, locks, and transaction tracking categories, for example, affect file system performance. Because of this interrelationship, the SET commands are grouped and discussed here as follows:

- ◆ Memory performance tuning
- ◆ File system performance tuning
- ◆ Communications performance tuning
- ◆ Operating system processes tuning
- ◆ Threshold and warning parameters

To change a SET parameter value, the general syntax is as follows:

```
SET parameter = New parameter value
```

To view a parameter's current setting, use this syntax:

```
SET parameter
```

Certain parameters cannot be set at the console prompt or in the AUTOEXEC.NCF file. You can set them only by entering the commands in the STARTUP.NCF file and restarting the server. These parameters include the following:

- Auto register memory above 16 MB
- Auto TTT backout flag
- Cache buffer size
- Maximum physical receive packet size
- Maximum subdirectory tree depth
- Minimum packet receive buffers
- Reserved buffers below 16 MB

You can also control or view these parameters by using the SET command.

Memory Performance Tuning for NetWare 4.1

NetWare 4.1 manages memory in a much more flexible manner than NetWare 2.*x*, or even NetWare 3.*x*. Generally, this memory management is transparent to the user, but you need to understand some principles that can help you troubleshoot problems in the event of a memory bottleneck.

The server memory is divided into three NetWare operating system application areas:

- File-cache buffer pool
- Allocated memory pool
- Code and data memory

Memory Pools

The file-cache buffer pool is used to store file blocks from the most frequently used files. Two pools, called *movable* and *nonmovable*, interact with the file-cache buffer pool. They obtain their memory from the file-cache buffer pool and, after they finish, return memory to it. The movable pool is used for system tables that change size, such as FATs (File Allocation Tables) and hash tables (used to index other tables). You can move tables and objects in the movable pool in memory to prevent excessive memory fragmentation. The nonmovable pool is used for NLMs.

The allocated memory and code/data pools grow or shrink according to actual demand. Memory not allocated to these pools and the operating system kernel is used for file caching. The code and data memory pool is used by NLMs and the data space they allocate.

The allocated memory pool is used for long-term memory needs such as directory cache buffers and packet receive buffers. A portion of it is static but the rest is semidynamic. Communications buffers are an example of allocated memory pool usage. When NetWare loads and initializes itself, it sets up a certain number of communication buffers. As network activity rises, NetWare allocates additional communication buffers to store the extra data packets. These buffers are allocated from allocated memory.

Note A *buffer* is an area of memory set aside for a special purpose. An example is a *packet receive buffer*. As the name implies, this type of buffer is an area of memory in which the file server stores incoming data packets.

The allocated memory (also referred to as *alloc memory*) pool is used to store information about the following:

- Drive mappings
- Service request buffers
- SAP tables
- Open/Lock files and semaphores
- User connection information
- NLMs
- Queue manager tables
- Messages queued for broadcasting

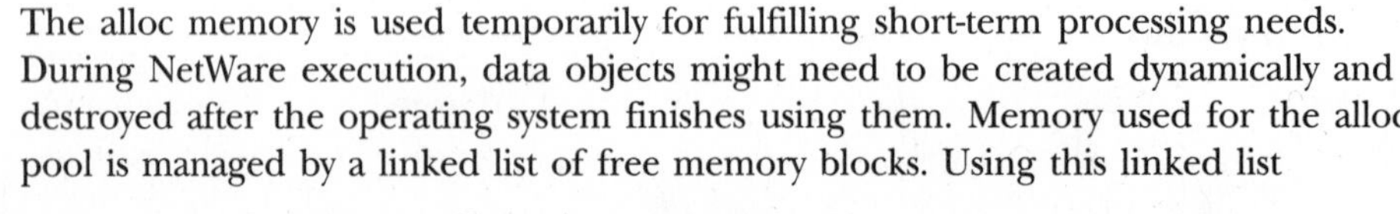

The alloc memory is used temporarily for fulfilling short-term processing needs. During NetWare execution, data objects might need to be created dynamically and destroyed after the operating system finishes using them. Memory used for the alloc pool is managed by a linked list of free memory blocks. Using this linked list

approach, the operating system can quickly find the memory it needs. When memory is needed, it is allocated from this free list. When released, it returns to the free memory list where it can be reused.

File caching also affects server memory performance. File caching allows you to keep data blocks from files that are being read or written to in RAM, thus speeding access to these files. File caching is independent of other caching techniques such as those used by disk-caching controllers. The file-caching tunable parameters deal with the number of file-cache buffers, concurrent disk writes, and disk synchronization (cache-write delays).

Setting Memory Parameters

To use parameters with the SET command, the SET command must precede the parameter, as shown in the following example:

```
SET ALLOC MEMORY CHECK FLAG = ON
```

The preceding command uses the SET command to set the flag that controls corruption checking in the Alloc memory area. The value expected for a parameter varies. Some parameters expect ON or OFF as values. Others expect a number. The following paragraphs describe some of the more important parameters used to adjust the server's use of memory.

```
SET AUTO REGISTER MEMORY ABOVE 16 MEGABYTES=[ON¦OFF]
```

EISA machines can support more than 16 MB of RAM. Under certain circumstances, you might need to use this parameter to allow NetWare to handle extra memory correctly. Setting this parameter in the STARTUP.NCF file lets NetWare register this memory when it first comes up. You cannot set this parameter at the console prompt or in the AUTOEXEC.NCF file. NetWare needs to know all the memory available when it first boots up. The default value is ON. If you use a board that can address only 24 bits of RAM, you might need to set this value to OFF, or you might have corrupted lower memory because 24 bits can address only 16 MB. Any higher address value maps to lower memory.

```
SET RESERVED BUFFERS BELOW 16 MEG = n
```

This parameter controls the number of file cache buffers set aside for devices that cannot access memory higher than 16 MB, including most ISA or MCA devices and/or boards that can address only 24 bits of RAM. You guarantee that a certain number of buffers are available to these devices by setting this parameter. Values range from 8 to 300 buffers, with a default of 16. You only can set this parameter in STARTUP.NCF.

```
SET GARBAGE COLLECTION INTERVAL = n
```

Garbage collection is the process of cleaning up fragmented memory. Memory returned to file cache (for example, when you unload an NLM), eventually becomes fragmented, The garbage collection process makes this memory available to new processes. *Garbage collection interval* refers to the maximum amount of time between collections, and can have values ranging from 1 minute to 1 hour. The default is 15 minutes.

The larger the value you specify, the longer the system waits between garbage collections. This frees the file server's CPU to perform other tasks. A shorter time period, on the other hand, causes the system to free up memory and make it available more quickly.

```
SET NUMBER OF FREES FOR GARBAGE COLLECTION = n
```

A *free* is when an NLM issues the command to release memory that it has allocated. The operating system tallies the number of times all NLMs issue such commands. When the tally reaches the number n you set using this parameter, the server begins another round of garbage collection. If you set this parameter low, the server performs garbage collection more often, which makes memory available more quickly to the various processes running on the server. The more often the server performs garbage collection, on the other hand, the more CPU power is used, which means that other processes suffer. This parameter can have values ranging from 100 to 10,000 frees. The default is 5,000.

```
SET MINIMUM FREE MEMORY FOR GARBAGE COLLECTION = n
```

This parameter specifies the minimum number of allocated memory bytes that need to be free before garbage collection can take place. In other words, the system does not perform garbage collection automatically unless the system needs this many bytes of allocated memory. Set this value low if you want garbage collection to occur more often yielding a small amount of memory. Set this value high if you have plenty of RAM and don't need garbage collection to occur as often. This parameter can have values ranging from 1,000 to 1,000,000 bytes. The default is 8,000.

Tuning the Server File System

File caching enables faster access of frequently used files by keeping the disk blocks in fast RAM for read and write operations. Write operations are performed in a delayed fashion, with the writes being done first. A background process writes these disk buffers (dirty buffers) to the disk during less critical moments but within the time specified by the Dirty Disk Cache Delay Time parameter.

File caching affects both memory and file system performance. The minimum file cache buffers parameter, discussed in the next section on memory performance tuning, affects both memory performance and file system performance.

Directory caching also plays an important role in file system performance, because it enables fast access to frequently used directories. Directory tables are kept in directory buffers in RAM, and the server uses a "least recently" algorithm to keep the directory entries in memory. When the server starts, NetWare starts with the minimum directory cache buffers (default is 20). When the minimum directory cache buffers is used up, the server must wait for a directory cache allocation wait time (default 2.2 seconds) before it can allocate another buffer. Under periods of sustained directory access, the number of directory entries could increase to fill the maximum directory cache buffers (default 500). As directory-cache buffers increase, the number of buffers available for file caching decreases. Hence, you have a trade-off between directory caching and file caching; balance is necessary for optimum performance.

File and Directory Caching

The following are SET parameters for file system performance.

```
SET MINIMUM FILE CACHE BUFFERS = n
```

You can use file caching to improve the performance of file I/O operations. NetWare uses memory that remains after allocation of the operating system and NLMs for file caching. In NetWare 4.1, you can set aside a certain amount of memory for file caching. The file-cache memory also acts as a memory reserve. The server draws on this memory reserve for its needs, but this creates a problem: you can severely deplete the file-cache memory, which can seriously affect server performance. You should always reserve a certain amount of memory for file caching (you can use this parameter to set the minimum amount reserved for file caching). If file I/O seems slow, or long delays and timeouts occur for network operations, the file cache may have fallen below the minimum value necessary for acceptable server performance. If such is the case, you should increase the value of this parameter. The default value for this parameter is 20, which also is the minimum value. You should gradually increase the number to a maximum of 1,000. If you use an extremely high value for this parameter, you might end up wasting memory and thereby impacting other critical data structures that need memory. The NetWare server should give a warning if the file-cache buffer reserve falls below the minimum level.

```
SET READ AHEAD ENABLED = [ ON ¦ OFF ]
```

The read ahead feature enables the operating system to automatically cache the next block when it accesses a file sequentially, which is very beneficial for network users. When a user is performing a database sort, for example, the data file is often accessed one record at a time from the top of the file to the bottom. Read ahead automatically caches the next block, even before the workstation actually asks for it. Read ahead is a background process that you can control using the next parameter. This feature is especially useful when reading from a CD-ROM mounted on the file server. The default is ON.

```
SET MAXIMUM CONCURRENT DISK CACHE WRITES= n
```

Unlike DOS, NetWare can perform several disk writes concurrently. One reason is that NetWare does not rely on the single-threaded BIOS on the machine to perform input/output (I/O). The disk drivers for NetWare allow multithreaded or concurrent I/O. A high value for this parameter makes write requests more efficient; a lower number makes read requests more efficient. One way to decide the way to set this parameter is to monitor the number of dirty cache buffers using MONITOR. If a majority of the buffers (70 percent or more) are dirty buffers, the writes are more predominant than reads, in which case, you can improve performance by increasing this parameter. The value ranges from 10 to 4,000, with a default of 50.

```
SET DIRTY DISK CACHE DELAY TIME= n
```

To improve disk I/O, the server performs delayed writes by writing first to RAM and then from RAM to disk during idle times. NetWare enables you to control the duration of this wait period. If you have many small requests, buffering the writes in RAM before writing them out to the disk is more efficient, especially if the write requests are contiguous sectors on the disk because you can combined these as a smaller number of disk writes. A disk-cache delay time that is too small is functionally equivalent to disabling the delayed write mechanism. Without delayed writes, server performance can suffer. The default value of 3.3 seconds is long enough for a typical mix of disk I/O operations that take place on the server. The value can range from 0.1 seconds up to 10 seconds. An extremely high value can make the server file system more vulnerable in the event of a server crash because many disk I/O operations would be in RAM and not committed to the disk.

```
SET MINIMUM FILE DELETE WAIT TIME= n
```

After you delete a file, that file is not purged immediately from the volume. This parameter controls the minimum amount of time a file should remain on the volume before being purged. Files that have been deleted are not purged for at least this specified time, even if the volume is full and the user is unable to create new files. The parameter value ranges from zero to seven days, with a default of 1 minute 5.9 seconds.

```
SET FILE DELETE WAIT TIME= n
```

After you delete a file, that file is not purged immediately from the volume. This parameter controls the amount of time a file remains on the volume before being purged. Files that have been deleted are not purged for the amount of time specified. After this time has expired, the server is free to purge these files. The server keeps at least 1/32nd of its disk space free and starts purging files (beginning with the oldest file) to meet this criterion. The parameter value ranges from zero seconds to seven days, and has a default of 5 minutes 29.6 seconds. A small value for this parameter can

slow down the server if many deletions are being made. A large value can adversely impact the availability of disk space if the server disks are almost full.

```
SET MINIMUM DIRECTORY CACHE BUFFERS= n
```

In NetWare, directories are cached in RAM for fast directory searches and directory updates. The directories are kept in directory cache buffers, whose minimum number is controlled by this parameter. This number must be high enough to perform most directory searches quickly. If the number is set too high, the unused portion is not available for file caching and other server operations. If the server responds slowly to directory searches, especially when it is first booted, monitor this number through the MONITOR.NLM. The delay could be because the minimum directory cache-buffers parameter is set too low and the server spends time allocating new directory buffers. The value ranges from 10 to 2,000, and has a default of 20.

```
SET MAXIMUM DIRECTORY CACHE BUFFERS= n
```

As the number of directory entries and files increases, the server allocates more directory-cache buffers to hold the directories. To prevent the situation from getting out of hand with all available space being used for directory caching, the server enables you to limit the maximum number of directory-cache buffers. If the file server continues to respond slowly, you can increase this parameter after consulting the MONITOR.NLM on the directory-cache usage. If the MONITOR.NLM reports a shortage of available RAM, and if this parameter is too high, you should reduce the parameter value. Because the server does not release memory automatically if this parameter value is reduced, you must reboot to free up the unused memory. The parameter value ranges from 20 to 4,000, with a default of 500.

```
SET DIRTY DIRECTORY CACHE DELAY TIME= n
```

You need to write out directory entries to disk that you modify in RAM to keep the directory on the server disk synchronized with changes in the file system. This parameter controls how long a directory entry can remain in RAM before it must be written to disk. Keeping this parameter high results in faster directory writes but also increases the chance of directory tables getting out of synch with those on disk in the event of a crash. A low value for this parameter reduces the possibility of corrupting directory tables, but the more frequent writes can reduce performance. The parameter value ranges from zero to ten seconds, with a default of 0.5 seconds. A zero setting disables the cache delay. Directory entries must be written immediately to disk, which causes slower directory writes.

```
SET MAXIMUM CONCURRENT DIRECTORY CACHE WRITES= n
```

To speed up directory operations, you can place several requests on the elevator mechanism. The elevator mechanism allows the disk head to move in continuous sweeps across the disk, which are more efficient than the random back-and-forth movements for disk I/O. This parameter controls the number of directory writes that you can queue on the elevator. A high value makes write requests more efficient; a lower number makes read requests more efficient. The parameter value ranges from 5 to 50, with a default of 10.

```
SET DIRECTORY CACHE ALLOCATION WAIT TIME= n
```

NetWare does not respond immediately to a demand for new cache buffers. It waits for a period of time before it satisfies this demand. This period of time, set by this parameter, is used to smooth out peak transient requests that might cause allocation of more DIRECTORY CACHE buffers than necessary. If the wait time is too low, the server seems too eager to satisfy transient loads and might allocate more DIRECTORY CACHE buffers than necessary. If the server delays too long to satisfy the request, it seems sluggish and seems to adapt slowly to user needs. The parameter value ranges from 0.5 second to 2 minutes, with a default of 2.2 seconds.

```
SET ALLOW DELETION OF ACTIVE DIRECTORIES = [ ON ¦ OFF ]
```

If this parameter is set to ON, a user who has sufficient trustee rights can delete a directory that another user might be using. A directory is considered to be in use if a user has a drive mapped to it, or is performing an action on the directory such as copying a file into or out of the directory. The default is ON.

File Compression Settings

File compression settings place limits on the file compression system. Unlike disk-doubling utilities such as Stacker, file compression occurs after a user accesses a file.

```
SET COMPRESSION DAILY CHECK STARTING HOUR = n
```

This parameter controls when file compression begins. You can force the system to immediately compress a file by flagging it with the "IC" (immediate compress) flag. Otherwise, the file is compressed automatically after a certain time interval (see "Days Untouched Before Compression" later in this chapter). Values range from 0 to 23. 0 is midnight, 1 is 1:00 a.m., and 23 is 11:00 p.m. The default is 0.

```
SET COMPRESSION DAILY CHECK STOP HOUR = n
```

This parameter controls when automatic file compression stops. You need to set this parameter if you have an automatically scheduled tape backup, for example, so you can be sure the file server is not compressing files while you are attempting a backup. On the other hand, if you want the server to be able to compress files with no time restrictions, set the STARTING HOUR (see above) and this parameter to the same value. The default is 6 (6:00 a.m.), and values range from 0 (midnight) to 23 (11:00 p.m.).

`SET MINIMUM COMPRESSION PERCENTAGE GAIN =` *`n`*

This parameter prevents the compression system from trying to compress a file if the percentage of disk savings is less than the value you assign. If, for example, you have a directory of ZIP files, the percentage you can gain by compressing them is very low (typically as low as 1 percent). Then it makes no sense to try to compress such files. By increasing the value of this parameter you can prevent the compression system from wasting time for little gain. Values range from 0 percent to 50 percent. The default is 2 percent.

`SET ENABLE FILE COMPRESSION = [` *`ON`* `¦` *`OFF`* `]`

This parameter, when set to OFF, stops the server from performing any file compression whatsoever. You set the default when you first install the file server.

`SET MAXIMUM CONCURRENT COMPRESSIONS =` *`n`*

This setting controls the number of compressions the file server can perform at the same time. A high setting speeds up the compression process, but takes CPU time away from other processes (such as servicing user requests on the network). Values range from 1 to 8. The default is 2.

`SET CONVERT COMPRESSED TO UNCOMPRESSED OPTION =` *`n`*

This option concerns the fate of an uncompressed file. The following options are available:

0	Always leave the file compressed.
1	If the compressed file is read only once within the boundaries set by the DAYS UNTOUCHED BEFORE COMPRESSION parameter, leave the file compressed. On any future access of the file leave uncompressed.
2	Always leave the file uncompressed.

If you want to conserve disk space, use option 0. If you want to leave the file uncompressed after being accessed once, use option 2. Values range from 0 to 2. The default is 1.

`SET DECOMPRESS PERCENT DISK SPACE FREE TO ALLOW COMMIT =` *`n`*

This setting represents the amount of disk space you must have free before NetWare can attempt to permanently uncompress a file. Set this value high if you are concerned that you have a large number of compressed files which, if uncompressed, could fill up the hard drive. Values range from 0 percent to 75 percent. The default is 10 percent.

```
SET DECOMPRESS FREE SPACE WARNING INTERVAL = n
```

This parameter sets the number of seconds between warning messages. The warning message controlled by this parameter tells you that not enough disk space remains to uncompress a file. The default setting is 31 minutes 18.5 seconds. Values can range from 0 seconds to 29 days, 15 hours, 50 minutes, 3.8 seconds.

```
SET DELETED FILES COMPRESSION OPTION = n
```

This command controls what happens to files that you have deleted. Options range from 0 to 2. Option 1 is the default.

0	Do not compress deleted files
1	Compress the next day
2	Compress immediately

Use option 2 if you do not plan to immediately recover a deleted file or want to conserve disk space. Go with option 0 if you or your users have a tendency to want to salvage deleted files soon after deleting them.

```
SET DAYS UNTOUCHED BEFORE COMPRESSION = n
```

This option sets the time period before automatic compression occurs. Set this option to the average number of days a file remains active. For example, in a law firm, when creating a legal document, you might determine that a document takes an average of 14 days from draft stage to final review. Values range from 0 (compress the same day) to 100,000 days. You can override this setting by using an "IC" (immediate compress) attribute on a file or directory. The default is 7 days.

Tuning Communications Performance

The communications parameters control characteristics of communication buffers. *Communication buffers* are areas in the server RAM dedicated for holding packets. The packets remain in memory before they are processed by the File Service Processes (FSPs).

The following sections describe how these SET parameters can affect the communications performance of a server.

```
SET MAXIMUM PHYSICAL RECEIVE PACKET SIZE= n
```

The size of a packet that you can transmit is determined by the network's physical access mechanism and driver limitations. On the server side, NetWare enables you to define the maximum size (*n*) of a packet that the file server can process. When a workstation makes a connection to the server, the packet size is negotiated based on

the settings of the network driver being used at the workstation. This parameter value needs to be large enough to accommodate the maximum packet size a workstation uses. The parameter value ranges from 618 to 24,682 bytes, with a default of 1,568 bytes (the optimum setting for Ethernet). Generally, a large packet size can speed communications but consumes more RAM. You can set this parameter only in the STARTUP.NCF file.

`SET MAXIMUM PACKET RECEIVE BUFFERS=` *`n`*

The server needs to keep a certain number of packet buffers in RAM to avoid being overrun by data. Normally, the server allocates receive buffers dynamically, based on its needs. NetWare enables you to set an upper limit on the number of packet receive buffers (*n*) the operating system can allocate. You can use the MONITOR.NLM to monitor current usage of this parameter. If this parameter is close to the maximum value, increase the value until you have at least one packet receive buffer per workstation. For OS/2 and MS Windows increase this value based on the number of simultaneously running network applications at the workstations. Allow for at least one buffer per application. You can also use the MONITOR.NLM to monitor the `No ECB available count` errors. If you are receiving reports of these errors, increase this parameter in increments of 10. For EISA and Micro Channel server machines, increase this parameter to allow for five to ten packet receive buffers per EISA/Micro Channel network board. If the number of file service processes MONITOR.NLM reports is close to maximum, you can increase the parameter maximum number of service processes to reduce the need for more packet receive buffers. The parameter value ranges from 50 to 4,000, and has a default of 100.

`SET MINIMUM PACKET RECEIVE BUFFERS=` *`n`*

NetWare enables you to set a minimum number of packet receive buffers (*n*) at the server. You can use the MONITOR.NLM to monitor current packet receive buffers. The default value is 50. Too few receive buffers cause the server to respond sluggishly when it first comes up. If you get `No ECB available count` errors through the MONITOR.NLM after the server boots, increase this parameter. For EISA and Micro Channel server machines, increase this parameter to allow for at least five packet receive buffers per EISA/Micro Channel network board. The parameter value ranges from 10 to 2,000.

`SET REPLY TO GET NEAREST SERVER = [` *`ON`* `¦` *`OFF`* `]`

This setting determines whether the file server responds to "Get Nearest Server" requests, which are generated by workstations first getting onto the network. For diskless workstations, for example, you might want to limit them to one physical server so that they can obtain their boot image files (default NET$DOS.SYS). The danger of only allowing one server to service requests is that if it goes down, you cannot get new workstations to log in unless you set this parameter on another server to ON. The default is ON.

```
SET NEW PACKET RECEIVE BUFFER WAIT TIME = n
```

NetWare enables you to set up a waiting period before a request for a new packet receive buffer is satisfied, to smooth out peak demands for receive buffers, and to allocate receive buffers for sustained network loads only. Otherwise, you end up with more receive buffers than you need for optimal performance. If the parameter is set to a high value, the server is slow to respond to sustained peak loads. If it is set too low, the server might respond too quickly to peak loads, and can end up allocating more receive buffers than you need. Novell recommends that this parameter not be changed for EISA bus master boards in the server. The parameter value ranges from 0.1 to 20 seconds, with a default of 0.1 second.

```
SET DELAY BETWEEN WATCHDOG PACKETS= n
```

This is the time interval (*n*) between watchdog packets sent from the server to the workstation after there is no response to the first watchdog packet. The watchdog packet is sent to see whether the workstation is still "alive" on the network. If this parameter is set too low, you can end up with excessive network traffic because the watchdog packet is sent to every station attached to the server. The parameter value ranges from 9.9 seconds to 10 minutes and 26.2 seconds, with a default of 59.3 seconds. Normally, the default value is adequate for most networks. For workstations and servers connected by wide area networks (WANs), you can increase the parameter value to avoid extra overhead and to account for extra delays. On a WAN, the setting of this parameter can be critical. Setting the delay too low causes a second watchdog packet to be sent without waiting to receive a response from the first. The delay between watchdog packets needs to be greater than the round-trip delay to the workstation.

```
SET DELAY BEFORE FIRST WATCHDOG PACKET= n
```

The server sends watchdog packets to a station that has been quiet for some time. NetWare enables you to set how long a server should wait before polling an inactive station; then a watchdog packet is sent as a probe to see whether the station is still alive. The parameter value ranges from 15.7 seconds to 14 days. The default is 4 minutes 56.6 seconds.

```
SET NUMBER OF WATCHDOG PACKETS= n
```

The NetWare server sends repeated watchdog packets if the workstation does not respond to a poll from the first watchdog packet. In a heavily congested network, the workstation response to a watchdog packet or the server watchdog packet can get lost. The NetWare server gives the workstation a few more chances (*n*) before declaring it dead and clearing the connection. The parameter ranges from 5 to 100, with a default value of 10. Setting a low delay between watchdog packets when the number of watchdog packets is high can cause excessive network traffic and affect the network performance.

Tuning Operating System Processes

A number of parameters deal with tuning the process scheduling time in the NetWare 4.1 operating system. These SET parameters for operating system processes are described in the following sections.

```
SET WORKER THREAD EXECUTE IN A ROW COUNT = n
```

This parameter places restrictions on the operating system scheduler. It represents the number of times the scheduler can consecutively schedule new work before allowing other existing threads to do their work. Values range from 1 to 20. The default is 10. Set this value high to allow the OS to handle more new requests at the cost of slowing down existing requests. Set this value low to force the server to finish existing work in a thread before dispatching new work.

```
SET UPGRADE LOW PRIORITY THREADS = [ON ¦ OFF]
```

If you set this command to ON, low priority threads (such as file compression) are upgraded to regular priority. The file server displays a warning message on the console which tells you to adjust this parameter if an ill-behaved NLM freezes a low priority thread. The default is OFF.

```
SET MAXIMUM SERVICE PROCESSES= n
```

In NetWare, file service processes are created on demand. You use service processes to handle incoming service requests from clients. NetWare enables you to set an upper limit on the number of file service processes (*n*) it can create. You can also use the MONITOR.NLM to monitor this number. Increase this parameter if the server is always near its maximum. Increasing the maximum service processes makes the file server able to respond to user requests more quickly. You do impact other processes, however, such as reading or writing to the hard drive, and RAM, slightly, because each service process requires buffer space. The parameter ranges from 5 to 100, and has a default value of 40.

```
SET NEW SERVICE PROCESS WAIT TIME= n
```

NetWare creates file service processes on demand. Under transient peak loads, too many file service processes can be created. NetWare enables you to smooth out transient demands for file service processes by setting up a waiting period. The parameter ranges from 0.3 seconds to 20 seconds, and has a default value of 2.2 seconds. This parameter prevents NetWare from reacting too quickly to peak loads and from allocating too many file service processes.

```
SET MAXIMUM OUTSTANDING NCP SEARCHES= n
```

Directory searches for existing files are common on a NetWare server because of the flexibility of NetWare's search-mode feature. Normally only one NCP search operation is permitted per workstation connection. If your applications support it, multiple NCP searches can speed up the application. This parameter enables you to set a limit on the maximum number of outstanding NetWare Core Protocol (NCP) searches at any time. The parameter ranges from 10 to 1,000, and has a default value of 51.

Threshold and Warning Parameters

NetWare 4.1 has many parameters that generate warning messages when their threshold values are crossed. These parameters do not affect the performance of the system directly, but are important for status alert messages and system operation. These SET threshold and warning parameters and their descriptions follow.

```
SET IMMEDIATE PURGE OF DELETED FILES=[ON¦OFF]
```

The SALVAGE utility enables you to salvage deleted files. When this parameter is set to ON, all files are immediately purged on deletion; that is, the salvage file feature is disabled. The default value (OFF) permits salvaging of deleted files.

```
SET VOLUME LOW WARN ALL USERS=[ON¦OFF]
```

NetWare enables users to be informed when a volume is almost full. The default value is ON: users are alerted when the volume is almost full.

```
SET VOLUME LOW WARNING THRESHOLD= n
```

NetWare enables you to set the number of free disk blocks (*n*) that remain on a volume before it issues a warning. To estimate this number, you must divide the desired free-space threshold by the disk-block size. The value for this parameter can range from 0 to 100,000 blocks, and has a default value of 256.

```
SET VOLUME LOW WARNING RESET THRESHOLD= n
```

The VOLUME LOW WARNING THRESHOLD parameter issues the first warning that disk space is low. NetWare enables you to set the number of disk blocks that must be freed (*n*) before a second warning is issued. You use this parameter to prevent repeated warning messages being sent if free space hovers around the threshold set by VOLUME LOW WARNING THRESHOLD. When the first warning VOLUME LOW WARN ALL USERS is issued, and users reduce disk space just below the threshold, having a warning message might not be desirable if disk-space utilization rises above the threshold. Actually, this process could repeat several times—dipping below the threshold and then rising again—and the repeated warning messages could be a source of great annoyance to the user. The value for this parameter can range from zero to 100,000 blocks, and has a default value of 256.

`SET MAXIMUM PERCENT OF VOLUME USED BY DIRECTORY= n`

NetWare enables you to set an upper limit on the percentage (*n*) of a volume that can be used as directory space. This percentage value ranges from 5 to 50, with a default value of 13.

`SET MAXIMUM PERCENT OF VOLUME SPACE`

NetWare 4.1 supports multiple file-name spaces such as are found in Macintosh, NFS, OS/2, and FTAM. These name spaces require extended attribute support. NetWare enables you to set and limit the percentage (*n*) of a volume that can be used for extended attribute storage. When the volume is being mounted, the setting becomes effective. This percentage value ranges from 5 to 50, with a default value of 13.

`SET MAXIMUM EXTENDED ATTRIBUTES PER FILE OR PATH= n`

NetWare enables you to set an upper limit on the number of extended attributes (*n*) that can be assigned to a file or path. This parameter setting affects all server volumes. The parameter value ranges from 4 to 512, with a default value of 16.

`SET MAXIMUM SUBDIRECTORY TREE DEPTH= n`

NetWare enables you to set the number of directory levels supported by the NetWare file system. The default value of this parameter is 25, even though some DOS applications cannot support more than 10 levels. The parameter value ranges from 10 to 100. You can set this parameter only from the STARTUP.NCF file; not from the console prompt.

`SET ALLOW UNENCRYPTED PASSWORDS=[ON¦OFF]`

When set to OFF, this parameter enables users to use encrypted passwords only. Use the OFF setting if all file servers are NetWare 4.1. If servers on the network are below NetWare 4.1, this parameter can be set to OFF to avoid login problems. If the servers are v2.12 and above, you can copy the NetWare 4.1 utilities to these servers and enable password encryption by keeping this parameter value OFF. For NetWare servers below v2.12 (such as NetWare v2.0a), this parameter should be set to ON.

`SET DISPLAY SPURIOUS INTERRUPT ALERTS=[ON¦OFF]`

NetWare alerts you to spurious interrupts. *Spurious interrupts,* caused by IRQ conflicts between devices on the server, generate the message `Spurious hardware interrupt <number> detected`. The default setting is ON because spurious interrupts need to be resolved for the proper functioning of the server. A value of OFF is provided as a convenience (to turn off the messages while waiting for a resolution of the problem).

`SET DISPLAY LOST INTERRUPT ALERTS=[ON¦OFF]`

NetWare alerts you about lost interrupts. This message is generated when a driver or adapter generates an interrupt request and then drops the request before the CPU can respond. This generates the message Interrupt controller detected a lost hardware interrupt. The default setting is ON because lost interrupts can degrade server performance. A value of OFF is provided as a convenience (to turn off the messages while waiting for a resolution of the problem). This usually indicates a driver or board problem.

```
SET DISPLAY DISK DEVICE ALERTS=[ON¦OFF]
```

NetWare alerts you to disk events such as a hard disk added, activated, deactivated, mounted, or dismounted. The default setting is OFF. Setting the parameter to ON during disk testing and debugging can yield potentially helpful information.

```
SET DISPLAY OLD API NAMES=[ON¦OFF]
```

Some of the API names are different in NetWare 4.1, and resource tracking was added for better monitoring and control of NLMs and their use of system resources. Also, resource tracking forces NLMs to release all their resources after they are unloaded. The default value of this parameter is OFF. Set this parameter to ON to monitor whether old APIs are being used. If older APIs are being used, contact the vendor of the software to get a more compatible version of the API.

```
SET HALT SYSTEM ON INVALID PARAMETERS = [ON¦OFF]
```

Setting this parameter to ON causes the server to stop when an invalid parameter or condition is detected. This can be set in AUTOEXEC.NCF or STARTUP.NCF. Set this value to ON when testing and debugging new NCF files. Set this value to OFF to allow the server to boot even though an anomalous condition arose. The default is OFF.

```
SET NCP PACKET SIGNATURE OPTION = n
```

This option sets the packet signature level of the file server. Packet signatures are created and added to every packet sent to the server if this feature is enabled. The server also can read incoming packet signatures. The rationale behind a packet signature is that in an unsecure environment, the server or client can require packet signatures to ensure the validity of every single transmission. Proper generation of a packet signature requires a valid initial authentication, and the VLM software on the workstation with the RSA.VLM and SECURITY.VLM components. If a "hacker" attempts to generate phony packets, the server detects this immediately and can shut down the phony connection. A high level of packet signature increases network security but degrades performance anywhere from 3 percent to 7 percent. Values can range from 0 to 3. The higher the level, the greater the level of security. The default is 1.

A breakdown of the packet signature levels on the server follows:

0	Disable packet signature
1	Add packet signatures only if requested by the client
2	Add packet signatures if the client can, but do not require them
3	Require packet signatures

Tuning Directory Services

There is a series of parameters that you can tune to affect or monitor the performance of Directory Services.

```
SET NDS trace to screen = abc
```

This parameter enables the NDS trace screen. The value for *abc* can be any text from 1 to 80 characters in length. You use the text to identify the trace and especially if you plan to log the NDS trace to a file. You must toggle to the NDS trace screen by pressing Alt+Esc or Ctrl+Esc (from the file server console), or Alt+F3 or Alt+F4 (from RCONSOLE). The NDS trace screen reveals NDS communications and synchronization activity. This is extremely useful when debugging NDS communications problems between servers in a tree.

```
SET NDS trace to file = [ ON ¦ OFF ]
```

When you set this value to ON, NDS trace information is logged to the file specified by the next parameter. The default is OFF. This option is extremely helpful when debugging NDS communications problems between servers in a tree.

```
SET NDS Trace Filename = filename
```

Use this option if you issue the SET NDS TRACE TO FILE = ON option. *filename* includes the directory and file name of the file on volume SYS: to contain the NDS trace log. The default is SYSTEM\DSTRACE.DBG. This file is always stored on volume SYS:.

```
SET NDS client NCP retries = n
```

This parameter sets the number of times a client can retry at the NCP protocol level before timing out a connection. You might need to increase this parameter if you have a busy, complex network and a workstation on a remote segment is having difficulty obtaining NDS services. The default value is 3. Values can range from 1 to 20.

```
SET NDS external reference life span = hours
```

Specifies the number of hours before an unused external reference is removed. The default is 192 hours. Values can range from 1 to 384 hours. Set this value low if you do not want replicas that are referenced from an external file server to remain on this file server. Set the value high if you find that your network has communications difficulties or a slow link and you want to allow the system to resolve its references.

```
SET NDS synchronization interval = minutes
```

This parameter specifies how long the server goes before performing a comprehensive NDS synchronization check. Increase this parameter to decrease NDS traffic on the network. Decrease this parameter to improve the integrity of an NDS tree that changes relatively frequently. The default is 30 minutes. Values can range from 2 to 1,440 minutes.

```
SET NDS synchronization restrictions = [OFF][ON, nnn, ..., nnn]
```

This sets a restriction on which versions of the NDS you want this server to synchronize with. The default is OFF, which tells this server to synchronize with any version of NDS. If you want to restrict synchronization to certain versions only, specify this by entering ON followed by the version numbers separated by commas. Version numbers should be entered as whole numbers. To find the version number, type the following command:

MODULES

Look for the DS.NLM module. You see something like the following:

```
DS.NLM
 NetWare 4.1 Directory Services
 Version 4.43  September 6, 1994
 Copyright 1993-1994 Novell, Inc. All rights reserved.
```

The preceding example shows this version of NDS to be 4.43. To restrict synchronization to this version only, enter the following command:

SET NDS synchronization restrictions = ON, 443

This parameter is useful if you have multiple versions of NDS and want to control which servers are synchronizing together. Having multiple versions of NDS in the same tree and not all servers set to synchronize together can be very dangerous. This parameter is also useful if you plan to extend the NDS and add object types of your own through the API programming tools, so you can cause servers running your version of NDS to synchronize only with each other. You can enter up to 132 characters in this field, including the word ON and the commas separating the version numbers.

```
SET NDS janitor interval = minutes
```

Sets the number of minutes between cycles of the NDS janitor process, analogous to the garbage collection process which sweeps up scattered server RAM. The default setting is 60 minutes. Values range from 1 to 10,080 minutes (7 days). Set this value high to save server processing power and performance. Set this value low to improve NDS integrity.

```
SET NDS backlink interval = minutes
```

This parameter sets the interval between checks off NDS back links. A *back link* is part of the way the NDS database is held together. You use a back link when the NDS needs move around in the tree. Consistency checking of this sort needs to take place for the sake of the integrity of the NDS. If you set the value low, the integrity of the NDS improves, but server and network performance suffers. If you set the value high, the server and the network encounters less overhead and has better performance, but the integrity of the NDS can suffer. If you do not make frequent changes to the NDS, you can set the value higher than the default. If your NDS tree has many partitions and replicas, and you make changes several times a day, you might want to set this parameter lower than the default. The default is 780 minutes. Values can range from 2 to 10,080 minutes (7 days).

```
SET NDS trace file length to zero = [ ON ¦ OFF ]
```

Set this parameter to ON to reset the NDS trace file. After you reset the file, the parameter automatically resets itself to the default value of OFF.

```
SET BINDERY CONTEXT = Container [; Container; ... Container]
```

This is an extremely important parameter for bindery emulation. Set this parameter to the container to offer when a bindery client accesses the server. The server must have a physical replica of a partition that contains the container specified. This command fails if any of the following are true:

- If *Container* does not exist
- If *Container* is not located in the replica that is physically stored on the server
- If the server has no NDS replica

When the parameter fails, you get an error message if the command is issued from the file server console. If you use SERVMAN.NLM to set this parameter, however, no error message appears.

Optionally, you might specify up to 16 containers separated by semicolons (;). Each container must be a valid NDS container name present in the replica stored on the server.

Using the SERVMAN.NLM Utility

SERVMAN.NLM is a utility that enables you to work with the console SET commands through an easily understandable menu interface. In addition, SERVMAN shows you some statistics not available in MONITOR. Figure 38.1 shows the SERVMAN main screen.

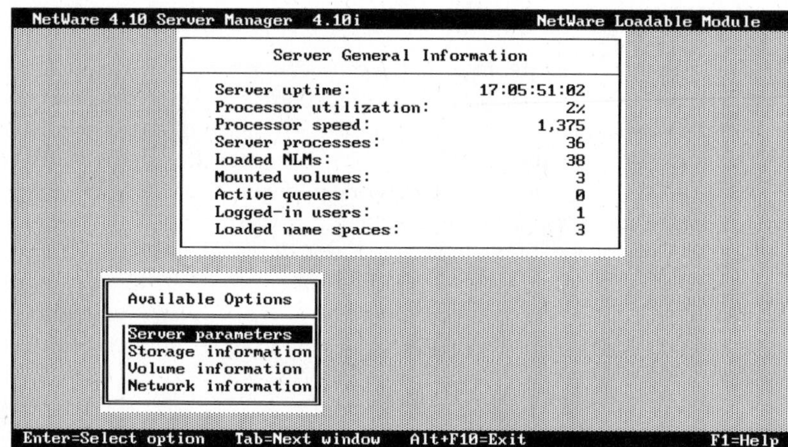

Figure 38.1
The SERVMAN main screen.

The General Information screen visible at the top contains general server statistics. Processor utilization, Server uptime, Server processes, and Users logged in correspond to similar statistics seen in the MONITOR utility. Additional General Information statistics include the number of NLMs loaded, number of volumes mounted, number of active print queues, and number of name space NLMs loaded.

The various main menu options are described in the next few sections.

Server Parameters

The Server parameters menu enables you to work with the SET commands using a convenient user interface. A list of the main SET categories appears in this menu. Here, you can select the desired category. All SET commands in this category appear at the top. At the bottom is an explanation of the command you have highlighted, along with the minimum, maximum, and current settings.

Press PgUp or PgDn to move up and down the list of settings for each category. Figure 38.2 shows the File System category. Note the scroll bar at the right, which indicates that more SET commands await unseen.

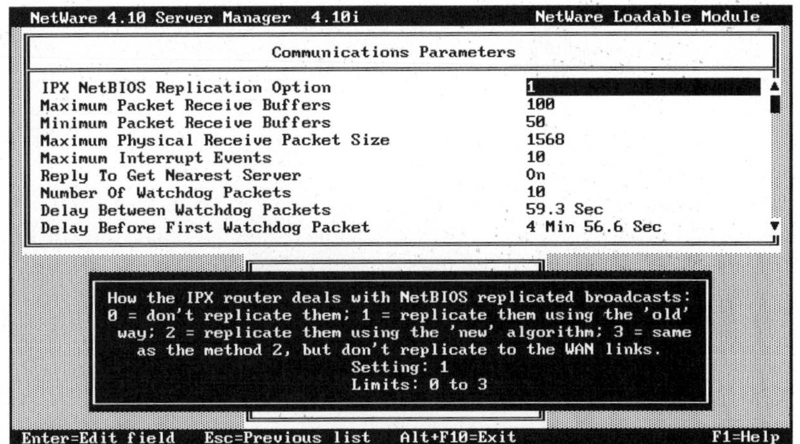

Figure 38.2
SERVMAN NLM Server Parameters—Communications Parameters.

After you exit the Console Set commands screen, you can save changes. SERVMAN saves them in the STARTUP.NCF or AUTOEXEC.NCF, to whichever file the command belongs. Any changes you make are immediately effective—just as if you issued the command from the console prompt.

The individual SET commands are covered in the section "Tuning NetWare 4.1 Performance" earlier in this chapter. Table 38.1 lists the SET commands by category.

TABLE 38.1
SERVMAN.NLM Server Parameters

Category	Commands
Communications	IPX NetBIOS Replication Option
	Maximum Packet Receive Buffers
	Minimum Packet Receive Buffers
	Maximum Physical Receive Packet Size
	Maximum Interrupt Events
	Reply To Get Nearest Server
	Number Of Watchdog Packets
	Delay Between Watchdog Packets
	Delay Before First Watchdog Packet
	New Packet Receive Buffer Wait Time
	Console Display Watchdog Logouts

continues

Table 38.1, Continued
SERVMAN.NLM Server Parameters

Category	Commands
Directory Caching	Dirty Directory Cache Delay Time Maximum Concurrent Directory Cache Writes Directory Cache Allocation Wait Time Directory Cache Buffer NonReferenced Delay Maximum Directory Cache Buffers Minimum Directory Cache Buffers Maximum Number Of Internal Directory Handles Maximum Number Of Directory Handles
Directory Services	NDS trace to screen NDS trace to file NDS Trace Filename NDS client NCP retries NDS external reference life span NDS synchronization interval NDS synchronization restrictions NDS servers status NDS janitor interval NDS backlink interval NDS trace file length to zero Bindery Context
Disk	Enable Disk Read After Write Verify Remirror Block Size Concurrent Remirror Requests Mirrored Devices Are Out Of Sync Message Frequency
Error Handling	Server Log File State Volume Log File State Volume TTS Log File State Server Log File Overflow Size Volume Log File Overflow Size Volume TTS Log File Overflow Size
File Caching	Read Ahead Enabled Read Ahead LRU Sitting Time Threshold Minimum File Cache Buffers Maximum Concurrent Disk Cache Writes Dirty Disk Cache Delay Time Minimum File Cache Report Threshold

Category	Commands
File System	Minimum File Delete Wait Time File Delete Wait Time Allow Deletion Of Active Directories Maximum Percent of Volume Space Allowed For Extended Attributes Storage Maximum Extended Attributes per File or Path Maximum Percent Of Volume Used By Directory Immediate Purge Of Deleted Files Maximum Subdirectory Tree Depth Volume Low Warn All Users Volume Low Warning Reset Threshold Volume Low Warning Threshold Turbo FAT Re-Use Wait Time Compression Daily Check Stop Hour Compression Daily Check Starting Hour Minimum Compression Percentage Gain Enable File Compression Maximum Concurrent Compressions Convert Compressed To Uncompressed Option Decompress Percent Disk Space Free To Allow Commit Decompress Free Space Warning Interval Deleted Files Compression Option Days Untouched Before Compression Allow Unowned Files To Be Extended
Locks	Open Callback Timeout Maximum Record Locks Per Connection Maximum Record Locks Maximum File Locks
Memory	Allow Invalid Pointers Read Fault Notification Read Fault Emulation Write Fault Notification Write Fault Emulation Garbage Collection Interval Number of Frees For Garbage Collection Minimum Free Memory For Garbage Collection Alloc Memory Check Flag Auto Register Memory Above 16 Megabytes Reserved Buffers Below 16 Meg

continues

Table 38.1, Continued
SERVMAN.NLM Server Parameters

Category	Commands
Miscellaneous	IPXFLT Log Errors To Disk Sound Bell For Alerts Replace Console Prompt With Server Name Alert Message Nodes Worker Thread Execute In A Row Count Halt System On Invalid Parameters Upgrade Low Priority Threads Display Relinquish Control Alerts Display Incomplete IPX Packet Alerts Display Old API Names Developer Option Display Spurious Interrupt Alerts Display Lost Interrupt Alerts Pseudo Preemption Count Global Pseudo Preemption Maximum Service Processes New Service Process Wait Time Automatically Repair Bad Volumes Allow Unencrypted Passwords
NCP	NCP File Commit Display NCP Bad Component Warnings Reject NCP Packets with bad components Display NCP Bad Length Warnings Reject NCP Packets with bad lengths Maximum Outstanding NCP Searches NCP Packet Signature Option Enable IPX Checksums Allow Change To Client Rights Allow LIP
Time	TIMESYNC ADD Time Source TIMESYNC Configuration File TIMESYNC Configured Sources TIMESYNC Directory Tree Mode TIMESYNC Hardware Clock TIMESYNC Polling Count TIMESYNC Polling Interval TIMESYNC REMOVE Time Source TIMESYNC RESET TIMESYNC Restart Flag TIMESYNC Service Advertising

Category	Commands
	TIMESYNC Synchronization Radius TIMESYNC Time Adjustment TIMESYNC Time Source TIMESYNC Type TIMESYNC Write Parameters TIMESYNC Write Value Time Zone Default Time Server Type Start Of Daylight Savings Time End Of Daylight Savings Time Daylight Savings Time Offset Daylight Savings Time Status New Time With Daylight Savings Time Status
Transaction	Auto TTS Backout Flag TrackingTTS Abort Dump Flag Maximum Transactions TTS UnWritten Cache Wait Time TTS Backout File Truncation Wait Time

Storage Information

The Storage information option screen shows much disk information at a glance. The information provided is a list that includes adapter information, device information, and partition information. If you press Enter for any one item in this list, you see specific information on that item. Figure 38.3 illustrates this screen showing information on the hard drive.

Adapter information gives you information on the disk controller in the file server, including the name of the DSK driver loaded, and configuration data, including interrupts, DMA channels, and port and memory addresses used.

Device information provides details on the devices attached to the controller. Device information is indented once from the adapter information. Details include the number of heads, cylinders, and sectors per track of each disk device. You also see the block size, device type (i.e., hard disk), and capacity (in bytes).

Partition information is again indented from the device information. Partition information includes the partition type (a number that represents types ranging from DOS to NetWare), size (in blocks), mirroring status (ON, OFF, or DISABLED), and the total number of Hot Fix blocks. You also see the partition offset (how far in on the hard drive it is), the number of mirrored partitions, the condition of the mirroring, and the number of Hot Fix blocks used.

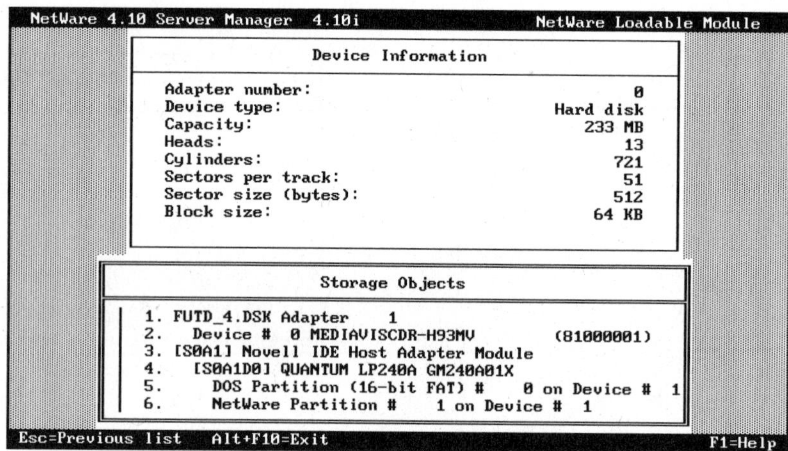

Figure 38.3
SERVMAN.NLM storage information.

Volume Information

The Volume Information menu gives you information pertaining to new features of NetWare 4.1. At the bottom of the screen is a list of your mounted volumes. Next to the name of each volume is its capacity in bytes, and the percentage of disk space on the volume in use (see fig. 38.4).

```
NetWare 4.10 Server Manager  4.10i                    NetWare Loadable Module

                       SYS: Volume Information

   File system name:                          NetWare 4.0 File System
   Loaded name spaces:                                       DOS, NFS
   Read only:                                                     Off
   Compression:                                                    On
   Sub allocation:                                                 On
   Sub allocation unit size:                                      512
   Migration:                                                     Off
   Migrated files:                                                  0
   Block size:                                                  32 KB
   Sectors per block:                                              64
   Total blocks:                                                6,688
   Free blocks:                                                 1,026
   FAT blocks:                                                      4
   Freeable limbo blocks:                                           1
   Non-freeable limbo blocks:                                       0
   Directory size (blocks):                                       246
   Directory entries:                                          31,488
   Used directory entries:                                     16,609
   Extended directory space:                                      512

Esc=Previous list   Alt+F10=Exit                                  F1=Help
```

Figure 38.4
The Volume Information screen.

Table 38.2 summarizes the statistics found on the Volume Information screen.

Table 38.2
SERVMAN.NLM Volume Information Statistics

Statistic	Description
File System Name	Shows the name of the file system on this particular volume, so you can quickly identify 4.1 file systems from other NetWare file systems.
Loaded Name Spaces	Which NAM modules are loaded and have been added to this volume. Name space modules include MAC, NFS, OS2, and OSI.
Read Only	ON or OFF. Indicates whether the status of the volume is Read Only. An option that you can set when mounting CD-ROM volumes.
Compression	ON or OFF. Tells you whether the file compression feature is enabled.
Sub Allocation	ON or OFF. Indicates the suballocation status of this volume.
Sub Allocation Unit	The size of a unit used for disk Size suballocation.
Migration	ON or OFF. Tells you whether the file migration feature is enabled for this volume.
Migrated Files	Number of files that have been physically removed from server's hard disk to another media via the Storage Management Services file migration feature.
Block Size	Block size in KB for this volume.
Sectors per Block	Indicates the number of subdivisions of a block on this volume.
Total Blocks	The total number of blocks on this volume.

continues

Table 38.2, Continued
SERVMAN.NLM Volume Information Statistics

Statistic	Description
Free Blocks	The number of blocks free out of the total number of blocks available on this volume.
FAT Blocks	Number of blocks used to store the File Allocation Table for this volume.
Freeable Limbo Blocks	Number of blocks usable if they can be freed. Blocks holding deleted files fall into this category. You can use the PURGE command to free such blocks.
Non Freeable Limbo Blocks	Blocks not used by the system, but not freeable either. You might be able to free up some of these blocks by running VREPAIR.
Directory Size (in blocks)	Current size of the Directory Entry Table on this volume. You can control the maximum size of the DET by using the SET command MAXIMUM PERCENT OF VOLUME USED BY DIRECTORY described earlier.
Directory Entries	Number of entries that can be made, given the current directory size. Each directory block can hold up to 32 slots.
Used Directory Slots	The number of directory slots currently used. This is the sum total of files and directories (plus some overhead) on this volume.
Extended Directory Space	The a.m.ount of space taken up by extended attributes. Extended attribute space is increased substantially when alternate name space support has been added to the volume.

Network Information

The Network Information screen is a summary of the information covered by the MONITOR.NLM. The information presented is summarized in table 38.3.

Table 38.3
SERVMAN.NLM Network Information Statistics

Statistic	Description
Packets transmitted	Total number of packets sent by this server
Packets received	Total number of packets received by this server
Packets waiting to be sent	Packets queued up by the server that cannot get onto the network. If this number is a substantial percentage of the Total Packets Transmitted, it indicates either that the network is too busy, that a card is malfunctioning, or that you need a faster, more efficient network card in the server.
Unclaimed packets	Packets where the protocol stack is unknown.
Get ECB buffers	Total number of Event Control Buffers allocated for incoming and outgoing information. An ECB is the programmer's term for *packet receive buffer.*
Get ECB requests failed	The total number of times the server failed to allocate an ECB. If this number is high relative to the statistic above, increase the *MAXIMUM PACKET RECEIVE BUFFERS* parameter.
Maximum number of LANs	Maximum number of LANs on the network.
Current number of LANs	Number of LANs currently on the network.
Loaded protocol stacks	Number of protocol stacks (i.e., IPX/SPX, TCP/IP, etc.) loaded.

The Network Information screen is shown in figure 38.5.

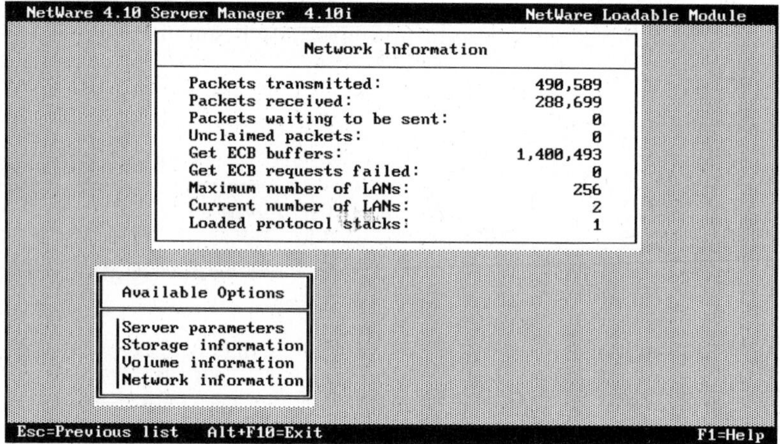

Figure 38.5
The Network Information screen.

Summary

This chapter covered what parameters to set and how to set them when you fine-tune the file server. The primary tool you use when you adjust the server are the SET commands, of which there are 13 different categories. When you issue the SET command from the file server console, you are given a list of categories. When you select a category, you are given a list of commands followed by explanations, current settings, and ranges of settings.

Each of the 13 SET command categories were covered, along with explanations and suggested settings for key SET parameters. The final part of the section covered an alternative way to work with the SET parameters: through the SERVMAN.NLM utility. Other menu areas in SERVMAN, including Storage Information, Volume Information, and Network Information, were also covered.

The next chapter covers monitoring the network for performance.

Monitoring Network Performance

Once you have your network up and running, your job is not finished. Now begins the ongoing task of keeping the network operating in top condition. The network will continue to change as the weeks and months go by. New users will be added. A new network segment could be created. You might join one LAN with another. New applications will be installed on the network. Users will shift work patterns as they adjust to the LAN. Like a person and like an organization, the network will grow and change.

Part of the challenge of being a network Administrator is to keep track of the day-to-day performance of the network. Part of what you can monitor has already been described in Chapter 36, "Monitoring the File Server." This chapter focuses on monitoring network events going to and from the file server.

Testing Cable

When a file server is not found or a workstation can no longer access the network, one of the first areas to test is the physical cabling. For a small network, start by disconnecting all nodes except for the file server and one workstation. If you are not able to log in, the problem might be the file server or your first section of cabling. After you have established a solid connection, start adding workstations, hubs, concentrators, and routers until you find the point of failure.

Bear in mind that the problem might not be related to cabling at all. Also check to ensure that the software settings match the hardware settings for all components in your file server or workstation.

For a DOS-based workstation, check the NET.CFG file. Do the settings in this file match the settings of your network adapter? You can also check the settings of the network adapter on the file server if you find that no workstations can access it. From the file server console, use the CONFIG command to display hardware settings for the network adapter. Make sure that the frame type settings for the workstations match that of the file server.

One indispensable tool for a network Administrator is a cable scanner. *Cable scanners* test the physical cabling for shorts and breaks. A *short* is caused when the "hot" wire has a connection with the "ground" wire. When this is the case, the electrical signal takes the path of least resistance (it takes the *shortest* path), which usually means that the signal never reaches its destination.

A cable scanner sends an electrical pulse into the cable and measures the amount of time before a returning pulse, a *reflection*, is detected. Based on various factors, the cable scanner is able to convert the amount of time into the distance the signal traveled. In this fashion, you can determine if there is a short or break in the cable. If you are measuring what is known to be a 200-foot length of cable, for example, and the cable scanner reports the distance to be only 5 feet, you know there is a problem.

Many types of cable scanners are available, and some are quite sophisticated. Microtest, Inc., for example, markets a line of cable scanners. One of the more popular cable scanners is the Compas, which is used to test twisted-pair or thin Ethernet cabling. The Compas is a hand-held device with a 128 by 64 graphic LCD readout. The menu-driven user interface is available in 10 different languages. It can test physical cabling and Ethernet data link level problems. In addition, it can be programmed to identify problems related to IPX, IP (and ARP), Banyan VINES, DECnet and LAT, APPI, as well as generic ISO protocols. It has a serial port to test serial communications and to receive programming changes. It can even be configured to provide a printout.

Cable scanner types include any of the following:

- Media specific. You must purchase a scanner that is designed for the type of cable or other media you are using.
- Scanners exist for a variety of types of coaxial cable, twisted-pair cable, and fiber optic cable.
- Different scanners are designed for Ethernet, token ring, Fiber Digital Distributed Interface (FDDI), and ARCnet.

Features of cable scanners include some or all of the following:

- TDR (Time Domain Reflectometry) tests (to determine the length of a cable based on the amount of time the signal takes to reflect back)
- Attenuation tests (to determine if the cable cannot pass an electronic signal without degradation)
- Mapping out the wiring of an installation
- Noise tests
- Cable grading (to see if the cable matches certain grade levels)
- Network traffic monitoring
- Tests for bad hubs or MAUs
- Tests for breaks and shorts
- SCR tests (Signal to Crosstalk Ratio)

LANalyzer for Windows

One of the primary tools for monitoring a network is a tool such as *LANalyzer for Windows*, a software utility that monitors network transmissions. This type of tool is also known as a *protocol analyzer*. Tools such as a cable tester monitor the physical layer of the OSI mode. A tool such as the LANalyzer monitors the network at the data link, network, transport, and even session layers of the OSI model.

Figure 39.1 shows the main screen (the dashboard) of the LANalyzer for Windows demonstrator. The demonstration running shows a workstation generating a large number of bad Cyclic Redundancy Check (CRC) errors.

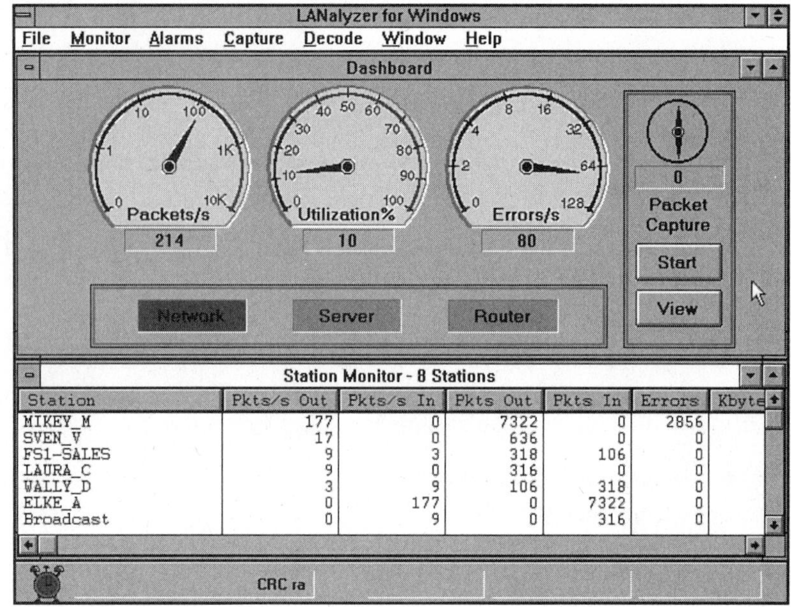

Figure 39.1
The Dashboard of the LANalyzer for Windows

The "dials" on the dashboard include the following:

- **Packet/s** indicates the current number of packets per second. A *packet* is a small unit of information transmitted on the network.
- **Utilization %** indicates the current utilization of the network. Networks can handle a certain amount of traffic, depending on their raw transmission rates and the amount of overhead required for the different types of network adapters used. Ethernet, for example, has a raw transmission rate of 10 mbps (million bits per second), with little overhead. Token ring can be configured at a rate of 16 mbps, but has a greater amount of overhead.
- **Error/s** indicates the number of errors per second.

At the right side of the screen are control buttons for initiating *packet capture*, which enables you to collect packets generated on the network into a capture buffer for later analysis. At the center of the screen are indicators for Network, Server and Router. When green, these indicate all is well. When red, they indicate a problem with either the network, server, or router. At the bottom of the screen is a list of statistics. These statistics are summarized in table 39.1.

Table 39.1
LANalyzer Statistics

Statistic	Description
Station	Displays the login name of the user at this workstation, or the node address if the login name is unknown.
Pkts/s Out	Packets per second being transmitted out of this station.
Pkts/s In	Packets per second being transmitted into this station.
Pkts Out	Total packets transmitted out of this station.
Pkts In	Total packets transmitted into this station.
Errors	The number of errors generated by this station.
Kbytes Out	The number of bytes in 1,024 (1 KB) increments transmitted out from this station.
Kbytes In	The number of bytes in 1,024 (1 KB) increments transmitted in to this station.
Bytes/s Out	The number of bytes per second transmitted out from this station.
Bytes/s In	The number of bytes per second transmitted into this station.
Address	The hardware (or Media Access Control) address of this station.

By clicking on any one of the statistical columns described above, you can cause LANalyzer to sort by this statistic. You can drag and drop a column into another location if you want to rearrange the order of the statistics as they appear from left to right. You can also resize any of the columns.

In this demonstration, the error condition is reported first in the Network category. By double-clicking on the Network button you can get the Network Alarms screen, as shown in figure 39.2. Alarms are generated when the LANalyzer reports a number of events that exceeds a threshold you can set (this is described in more detail later in this section).

You can press the Network Expert button for assistance with the problem reported. In this case, the Network Expert suggests that a large number of CRC errors most likely indicates a bad network card. The solution is to replace the bad card. You can have the LANalyzer locate the bad card by sorting according to the Errors statistics column. The station with the exceedingly large number of errors is the one with the bad card. The Network Expert also suggests that the problem could be due to faulty cabling.

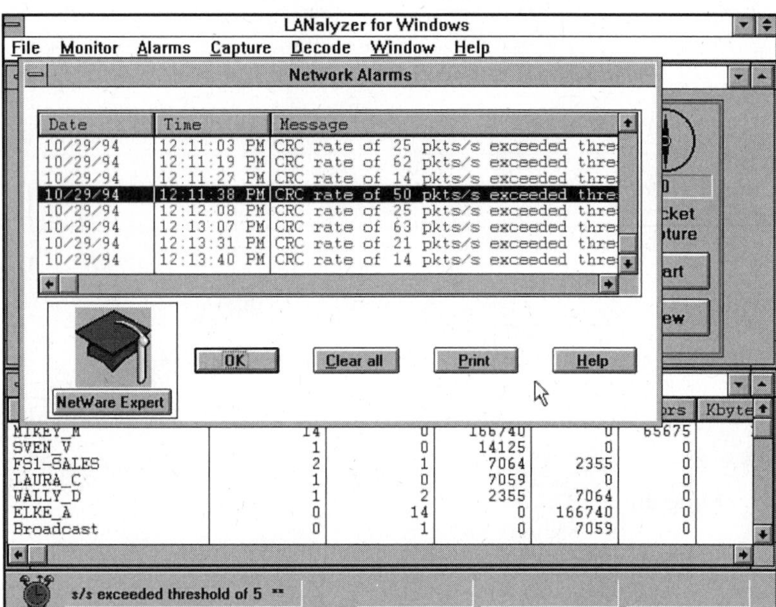

Figure 39.2
Network Alarms as shown in LANalyzer for Windows.

Monitoring Trends

One of the first things to do when your network is installed and functional is to gather baseline data on the network. *Baseline data* is information on what is considered normal for your network. Each network varies enough that it is safe to say that no two networks are alike. Compared to others, every network has a different number of computers, different network cards, and different mixtures of software being used. Perhaps most importantly, each network has different people using it.

The LANalyzer can be used to monitor network *trends*. You can view trends by selecting Trends from the Monitor menu. There are four types of trends that can be monitored. Each trend area represents a sampling of network events every 15 minutes. Trend graphs are generated, enabling you to scan forward and backward, viewing trend data over the period of time during which this graph was active. Figure 39.3 shows you a LANalyzer screen with all four trend graphs visible.

Trends are summarized in table 39.2.

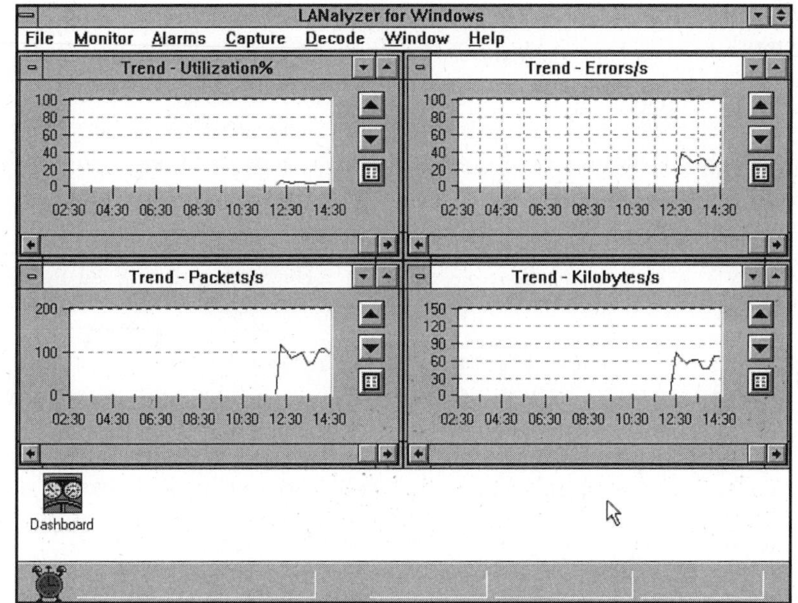

Figure 39.3
Trend Graphs Shown in LANalyzer for Windows

Table 39.2
LANalyzer Trends

Trend	Description
Packets/s	This network event represents the number of packets transmitted on the network segment per second. This trend should remain fairly constant. Even if there is a large number of workstations on the network, the rate should remain constant. Remember that the network only allows one workstation to transmit at a time. If you notice that this trend starts to decline, something is interfering with the speed of the network. If there is a bad Ethernet card, for example, the collision count increases. The more collisions there are, the less data is able to get through. This is mirrored in a declining Packets/s count.
Errors/s	This trend graph represents the number of errors per second generated on your network. As with other trends, the data is collected at 15-minute intervals and displayed on the trend graph. Errors collected include the following: ◆ **CRC/Alignment Errors.** Occurs when a network card transmits information and the receiving station reports a bad Cyclic Redundancy Check (CRC), a form of error

continues

Table 39.2, Continued
LANalyzer Trends

Trend	Description
	checking. Could indicate that the source network adapter is going bad. ◆ **Oversized Errors.** Indicates that packets over the maximum allowable size were received. Usually caused by a bad network adapter driver. ◆ **Fragment Errors.** This type of error is specific to Ethernet, and is usually a result of a collision. Excessive collisions result when the network is extremely busy. If you notice that these errors coincide with excessive utilization, consider splitting the network using routers or bridges to isolate traffic. ◆ **Jabber Errors.** "Jabbering" is when a network adapter transmits large amounts of meaningless information. This error is specific to Ethernet and usually coincides with CRC errors. Indicates a bad network adapter. Go to the Station Monitor screen and look for the station with a large number of errors to locate the likely suspect. ◆ **Undersized Packet Errors.** Occurs when data received is less than the minimum allowable size for your network. As with Oversized errors, this is caused by a faulty driver or a driver with bugs. You might see this when testing a Beta network adapter driver, for example. ◆ **Soft Errors.** Specific to token ring. Indicates internal errors or other errors related to the token ring specification. Go to the Station Monitor screen and look for the station with a large number of errors to locate the likely suspect. ◆ **Congestion Errors.** Specific to token ring, this error occurs when a receiving station runs out of internal buffer space in which to copy an incoming data frame. Possible causes include a station that is hung, an overloaded CPU, or a misconfigured LAN driver. ◆ **Internal Errors.** Reported by a token ring adapter, this error indicates problems with the hardware or firmware. Go

Trend	Description
	to the Station Monitor screen to locate the likely station and swap out the adapter card. ◆ **Abort Delimiter Errors.** Indicates a token ring adapter that aborts a frame transmission. The station usually has taken itself temporarily or permanently out of the ring due to an internal error condition. If this error persists in a station, it's a sign that the network adapter is malfunctioning. ◆ **A/C Errors.** Indicates that a station is unable to set bits in the token ring *frame status* byte. In this case, the station has recognized itself as the receiver of a data frame, or that it has received (copied) the frame, but is unable to set the necessary bits to inform the sender. Usually indicates a bad network adapter. ◆ **Beacon Error.** Indicates a problem with token ring cabling. The first station to detect the error condition sends out the beacon frame. It then identifies its "upstream" neighbor. You can sort through the Station Monitor table until you find the station generating an equal number of "downstream" beacon errors. The cable fault usually resides between these two stations. ◆ **Frequency Error.** Indicates a discrepancy between the adapter clock and the ring clock, and is difficult to isolate to a particular station. In most cases, the problem can be traced to an *Electro Magnetic Interference* (EMI) problem affecting the network.
Utilization%	This statistic indicates the percentage of utilization of your network. Every network has a theoretical maximum amount of traffic it can sustain, which is determined by the maximum transmission speed of the network adapters used on the stations on the network. FDDI, for example, has a theoretical maximum transmission of 100 mbps. LANalyzer takes this figure, performs some calculations, and determines the value for 100 percent. When the total traffic on the LAN saturates the LAN's capacity, a figure of 100 percent is achieved. A high value for utilization is not bad. In fact, it indicates that the network is being used. On the other hand, a healthy network has a

continues

Table 39.2, Continued
LANalyzer Trends

Trend	Description
	certain percentage unused. This additional capacity represents a "safety margin" in case temporary additional traffic is placed on the LAN. If utilization stands at 100 percent, then your network has no safety margin. If additional processing takes place, if the utilization is at 100 percent, users will notice sluggish performance, and the incidence of errors and possibly corrupted data will begin to rise.
Kilobytes/s	This trend indicates the throughput of your LAN. As mentioned above, network adapters have a theoretical maximum throughput rate. This statistic will show the actual throughput achieved on your LAN. It is estimated that Ethernet, for example, often only achieves 40 percent of its actual potential. This statistic is measured in kilobytes per second. Remember that most network adapters are rated in mega*bits* per second. Standard Ethernet adapters push 10 mbps. A full-length Ethernet frame is 1,524 bytes. An IEEE standard (802.3) Ethernet header occupies 28 bytes, leaving 1,500 bytes of data. This translates into a theoretical maximum of 1,250,000 bytes per second, approximately 2 percent of which represents overhead. In addition, a small gap is expected between transmissions because a transmitting Ethernet station is expected to wait for a period of time before determining that the network is free. With a conservative estimate, you could say that the expected amount of waiting and overhead information is 10 percent of the total. This brings down the expected transmission rate to 1,125,000 bytes per second. In reality, because there are collisions, waiting, and the fact that data frames are not always full, the actual throughput is substantially less than the theoretical maximum.

Setting Alarms

The alarm thresholds can be adjusted by selecting Thresholds from the Alarms menu. You should set alarm thresholds when you want to be notified of certain events. Each alarm monitors a different event. An alarm does not necessarily indicate a bad condition. Alarms that can be set include those summarized in table 39.3.

Table 39.3
LANalyzer Alarms

Alarm	Description
Packet/s	The number of packets per second. Monitor the network for a few days, activating the Packets per Second trend graph. This will collect information on the number of packets per second on your network. By observing the trend graph (described previously), you can get an idea of a typical number of packets per second. Set the alarm threshold at a rate of double the norm. If an alarm triggers, you will know that some anomalous condition has arisen.
Utilization%	This alarm is set when you want to be notified when the percent of network utilization exceeds a certain value. For example, when you want to know if the network utilization exceeds 50 percent. To know what value to set, you can monitor the Utilization% trend graph for a period of several days or weeks, as described previously.
Broadcasts/s	This tracks all packets that represent broadcasts. A broadcast packet is sent to all stations on the network. A typical broadcast packet in NetWare is a Server Advertising Protocol (SAP) packet. Workstations generate a broadcast when first attempting to attach to a server. Broadcast packets are part of the network overhead. They are administrative rather than working packets. When a workstation saves a file on a file server, it generates a data packet that accomplishes work. An example of administrative information is when a router exchanges information with another router. The more broadcasts you have, the less network capacity is available for work. If you have an excessive number of broadcasts, determined by your baseline figures, it could indicate router problems. Also, you might have loaded a new NLM that is generating a large number of broadcasts. In a NetWare 4 network, the number of broadcasts is reduced because much information is conveyed by NDS. NetSync and other utilities that rely on bindery emulation can cause the number of SAP broadcasts to increase.
Fragments/s	A *fragment* is a damaged packet, usually caused in an Ethernet network by a collision. This setting allows you to set a threshold for the number of Fragments per Second.
CRC Error/s	As mentioned above, CRC errors are often caused by bad network adapters. This setting represents the threshold you want to establish for the number of CRC errors generated per second.

continues

Table 39.3, Continued
LANalyzer Alarms

Alarm	Description
Server Overloads/min	This statistic represents the number of times a server was unable to respond to client requests. This could be caused by excessive server usage, too many users on the server, insufficient CPU capacity, or not enough RAM on the server, among other possibilities. You might be able to solve this problem by increasing the number of *packet receive buffers* on the server (see Chapter 38, "Fine-Tuning the Server").

Other alarms that can be set were previously described or are self explanatory. These are in the advanced category and include the following:

- Undersized (packet) errors
- Oversized (packet) errors
- Jabber errors
- Server down
- Router down

Detail Windows

LANalyzer for Windows enables you to display detail windows, which follow the same breakdown as Trend windows but display current information only. The *detail windows* pull network data every minute and plot the detail on a graph much like a trend graph. The graphs can be scaled up or down depending on the nature of the data presented. In the case of Errors/s, the breakdown of the errors recorded is presented at the bottom of the screen.

Figure 39.4 shows you a LANalyzer screen with two detail graphs visible. In this figure, you are viewing the results of Novell's Beaconing problem demo. As you can see, there was an initial flurry of errors reported. After the other token ring cards figured out that the problem was a break in the ring, network activity dropped to zero as no further transmissions were able to get through after the break.

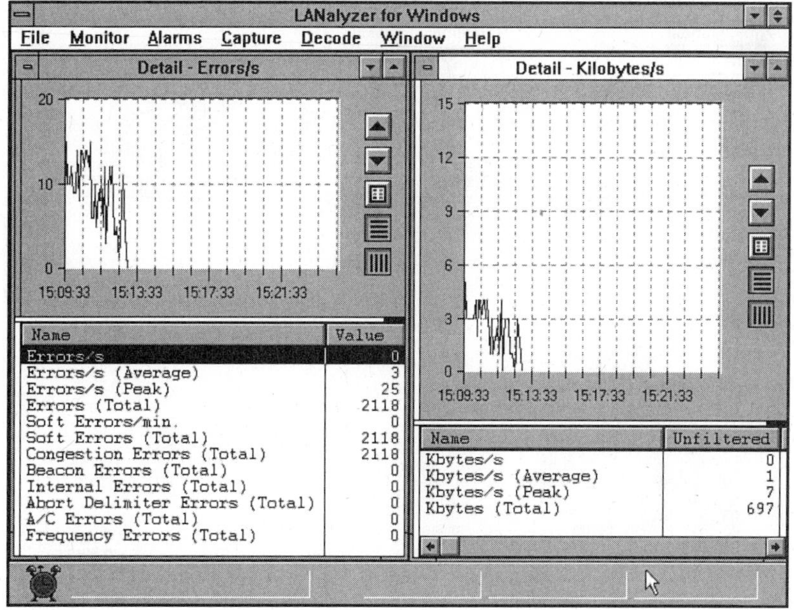

Figure 39.4

Detail graphs shown in LANalyzer for Windows.

Packet Capture

Packet capture is a feature that enables you to "capture" packets transmitted on the network and store them in a buffer. Captured packets can then be reviewed at your leisure. LANalyzer performs a decode of captured packets. Decoded packets are separated into their respective layers. At the bottom, you can see the data link layer, with media-specific information. The next layer up breaks down the packet by protocol. Upper layers include NetWare Core Protocol (NCP). You can see a hexidecimal dump of the contents of the packet. Packet capture is useful when debugging transmission problems between a workstation and a server, or all communications to and from a certain station. By setting a filter, you can filter captured packets by physical address or by protocol.

To invoke the packet capture, click on the Start button in the Packet Capture area of the LANalyzer for Windows dashboard. You will see the Packet Capture counter increment, as well as the "gauge" above the counter. When the colored area in the gauge is full, the packet buffer is full. To increase the size of the packet buffer and to select which packets are to be captured, click on either **C**apture, **O**ptions or **C**apture, **F**ilter. Figure 39.5 shows the packet capture decode screen.

As you can see in the figure, the decode screen consists of three smaller windows, as follows:

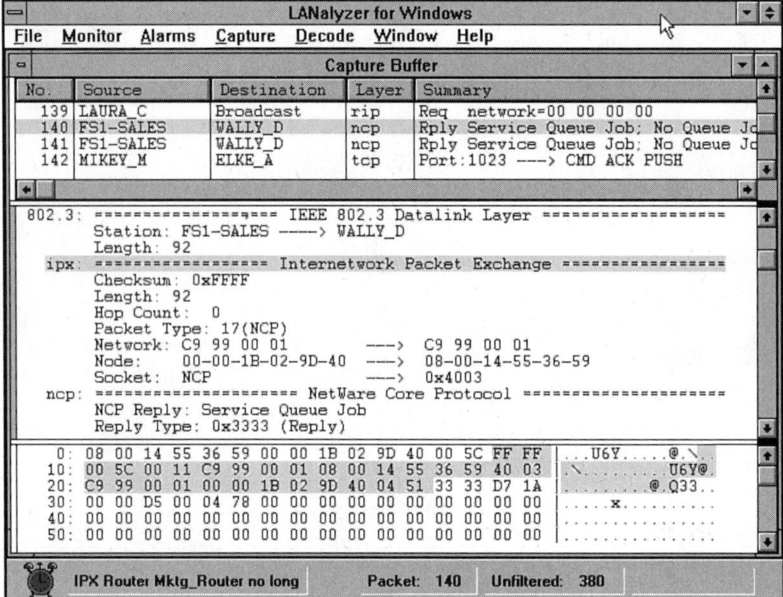

Figure 39.5

The LANalyzer for Windows Packet Capture Decode screen.

- **Capture buffer window.** You can scroll up and down and select a specific packet to decode.
- **Protocol decode window.** Shows you the various protocols. At the top is the lowest-level protocol. Protocols are progressively higher as you move down this window.
- **Hex display.** Shows you a hexidecimal display of the entire packet being decoded.

As you move down the capture buffer and select different packets, the display in the lower windows changes. The capture buffer window shows you the number of the packet (relative to the buffer), the source station, the destination station, the top layer for this packet, and a summary of the contents of the packet.

The protocol decode window shows you progress layers within the packet, starting with the data link layer. Note that the cursor changes to a "highlighter," enabling you to highlight portions of the packet. The highlight is reflected in the hex dump screen. If you highlight "802.3," for example, the 802.3 portion of both the protocol decode and the hex dump is highlighted.

The packet capture feature is an invaluable tool to see if two stations are communicating. It is also useful for the network segment as a whole to see if certain types (that is, TCP/IP) of information is being transmitted properly.

Accounting System: Gathering Statistics

You first learned about NetWare's accounting feature in Chapter 22, "Using Bindery Services." As you learned in that chapter, the accounting system is a way of collecting server specific information on how many minutes users have been logged in, blocks read, blocks written, and so forth. You learned how to install accounting and that this is one of the areas in which a network Administrator can manage from an NDS-based utility, even if the file server is only accessible through bindery services. In this section, you will learn how to use the accounting system to monitor network performance using the NETADMIN.EXE utility.

As discussed earlier, there are five areas that the accounting feature tracks, as follows:

- **Blocks Read** keeps track of the number of file caching blocks (4 KB) that are read. This statistic gives you an idea of the outgoing traffic from the server to clients.
- **Blocks Written** keeps track of the number of file caching blocks (4 KB) that are written. This statistic gives you an idea of the incoming traffic from the clients to the server.
- **Service Requests** is a total of the number of requests for services made by clients of this file server.
- **Connect Time** is the time, in minutes, users are logged onto the server.
- **Disk Storage** is the amount of disk space in use by users. This figure is a tally of the total size of files owned by specific users.

Of the statistics maintained by the accounting system, Blocks Read, Blocks Written, and Service Requests are discussed in this section. The other two are important, but not from the standpoint of monitoring network performance.

As with the LANalyzer, it is important initially to get a baseline for each of the three statistics mentioned above. The most effective way to do this is to set a charge rate of 1 for each of the three areas. The *charge rate* can be used for a departmental chargeback scheme or for cost accounting. This section does not focus on monetary issues. For further information, see the discussion on accounting in Chapter 22, "Using Bindery Services."

Setting User Account Balances

Before setting up a base charge rate, it is extremely important to alter the account balance of network users so that they can continue to use the server without being disconnected.

If you do not alter user account balances, and they have account balance limits set, they will be charged for using the server. When their account balance goes below zero, they will be disconnected from the server!

Because there is no way through the NetWare user management utilities to set a group of user account balances to allow unlimited credit, an automated solution must be used. The following code listings show a batch file and QBASIC program that performs four actions:

1. Runs NLIST to obtain the login name and last name of all users in the tree.
2. Produces a batch file that changes to each container and uses UIMPORT to update user accounts to allow unlimited credit.
3. Produces a series of user data files, one per container, to be used with UIMPORT.
4. Produces a UIMPORT control file.

The following is the batch file SETACCT.BAT that performs these listed actions:

```
@echo off
echo :  Title:          SETACCT.BAT
echo :  Date:           10-29-94
echo :  Author:         D. Bierer
echo :  Files:          SETACCT.TXT  = NLIST dump
echo :                  SETACCT.CTL  = UIMPORT control file
echo :                  SETACCxx.DAT = UIMPORT data files
echo :                  SETACCT2.BAT = Batch File to Call UIMPORT
echo :
echo :  Notes:  Sets all user accounts to unlimited credit with
echo :          a credit balance of 100,000
echo :
echo :          (1) Runs NLIST to dump user data to SETACCT.TXT
echo :          (2) Runs QBASIC program SETACCT.BAS which
echo :              produces files SETACCT.CTL, SETACCxx.DAT, and
echo :              SETACCT2.BAT
echo :          (3) Runs SETACCT2.BAT which changes context and
echo :              calls UIMPORT for each container
echo :          (4) Deletes temp files
echo :
echo :  Running NLIST
echo :
@echo on
```

```
CX [root]
NLIST user /s /d >SETACCT.TXT
@echo off
echo :
echo :  Run QBASIC program SETACCT.BAS
echo :
QBASIC /run SETACCT
echo :
echo :  Call SETACCT2.BAT batch file
echo :
CALL SETACCT2.BAT
echo :
echo :  Delete Temp Files
echo :
@echo on
DEL SETACC*.DAT
DEL SETACCT.CTL
DEL SETACCT.TXT
DEL SETACCT2.BAT
@echo off
echo :
echo :  Done
echo :
```

The following listing is the QBASIC program that scans the output file from the NLIST command issued above. This QBASIC program also produces a series of UIMPORT data files, one per container. It produces a batch file SETACCT2.BAT, which is called by the batch file shown previously. The SETACCT2.BAT file performs the CX command to change to each container in the tree, and uses UIMPORT to update user accounts to allow unlimited credit.

```
REM     Title:  SETACCT.BAS
REM     Date:   10-29-94
REM     Author: D. Bierer
REM     Notes:  Scans SETACCT.TXT file.  Produces a UIMPORT
REM             control file and a series of UIMPORT data files,
REM             one per container.  Along the way a batch file,
REM             SETACCT2.BAT is produced.  The batch file changes
REM             context to successive containers, and runs
REM             UIMPORT using the appropriate data file.
REM

REM     Set Variables
U = 0
```

```
REM     Open Files

OPEN "SETACCT.TXT" FOR INPUT AS #1
OPEN "SETACCT2.BAT" FOR OUTPUT AS #2

REM     Write out UIMPORT control file

OPEN "SETACCT.CTL" FOR OUTPUT AS #3
PRINT #3, "Import Control"
PRINT #3, "  Import Mode = U"
PRINT #3, "Fields"
PRINT #3, "  Name"
PRINT #3, "  Last Name"
PRINT #3, "  Allow Unlimited Credit"
CLOSE #3

1000    REM     If end of input file, bail out
IF EOF(1) THEN GOTO 4000

REM     Scan for container name

LINE INPUT #1, A$
A$ = UCASE$(A$)
X = INSTR(A$, "CURRENT CONTEXT")
IF X > 0 THEN GOSUB 3000

REM     Check to see if User

X = INSTR(A$, "USER:")
IF X > 0 THEN U$ = MID$(A$, X + 6)

REM     Check to see if Last Name

X = INSTR(A$, "LAST NAME:")
IF X > 0 THEN
     L$ = MID$(A$, X + 11)
     PRINT #3, CHR$(34); U$; CHR$(34); ","; CHR$(34); L$; CHR$(34); ",";
     ➥CHR$(34);
"YES"; CHR$(34)
END IF

GOTO 1000
```

```
3000    REM     Process Next Context

REM     Compose Context Name

C$ = "." + MID$(A$, X + 17)

REM     Write container name out as CX command to batch file

PRINT #2, "CX [ROOT]"
PRINT #2, "CX "; C$

REM     Open new UIMPORT data file

U = U + 1
IF U < 10 THEN
      F$ = "SETACC" + RIGHT$(STR$(U), 1) + ".DAT"
ELSE
      F$ = "SETACC" + RIGHT$(STR$(U), 2) + ".DAT"
END IF
CLOSE #3
OPEN F$ FOR OUTPUT AS #3
PRINT #2, "UIMPORT SETACCT.CTL "; F$

RETURN


4000    REM     Close Files and Exit
CLOSE #1
CLOSE #2
CLOSE #3
SYSTEM
```

As with other QBASIC programs in this book, these programs can be downloaded from the Macmillan Computer Publishing forum on CompuServe. After you access the MCP forum (GO MACMILLAN), you can find the files for this and other NRP networking books in the Networking and Comms library. You might have to make modifications to suit your environment.

Setting Baseline Charge Rates

After user accounts have been updated to allow unlimited credit, you can set the baseline charge rate to a factor of 1. To set up a charge rate of 1, proceed as follows:

1. Log in as a user with at least Supervisor rights to the file server object(s) you plan to work with.

2. From the DOS prompt, run NETADMIN. The main menu, NetAdmin Options, appears.

3. From the NetAdmin Options menu, select Manage Objects. The Object, Class menu appears.

4. From the Object, Class menu, browse the NDS tree until you locate the server object that you want to work with. Press Enter to select the server object. The Actions for NetWare Server: *server_name* menu appears, where *server_name* is the server's name.

5. From the Actions for NetWare Server: *server_name* menu, select View or edit properties of this object. The View or edit NetWare server menu appears.

6. From the View or edit NetWare server menu, select Accounting. The Accounting options menu appears, as shown in figure 39.6.

   If you have not yet installed accounting on this server, an initial menu appears asking if you want to "Install Accounting." If you have not, answer Yes.

7. From the Accounting options menu, select Block read charge rates. The Block read charge rates dialog box appears. You can see a 24-hour, 7-day grid. Each location on the grid represents a half-hour. The cursor can be located on the 8:00 a.m. Sunday location.

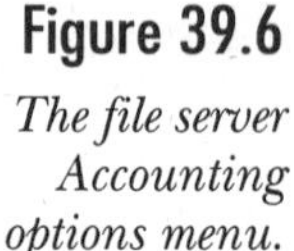

Figure 39.6

The file server Accounting options menu.

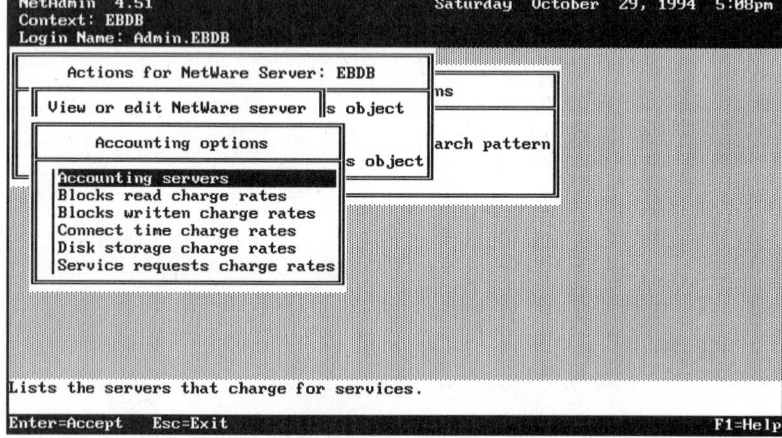

8. From the Block read charge rates dialog box, press F5. This enables you to highlight the entire grid. Press the End key. Note that the highlight now

stretches across the week, Sunday through Saturday, at the 8:00 a.m. time segment. The screen you should see to this point is illustrated in figure 39.7.

```
NetAdmin  4.51                              Saturday  October  29, 1994  5:13pm
Context: EBDB

       Blocks read charge rates                     Sun Mon Tue Wed Thu Fri Sat
                                          8:00       1   1   1   1   1   1   1
                                          8:30       1   1   1   1   1   1   1
                                          9:00       1   1   1   1   1   1   1
 Rate              Rate                   9:30       1   1   1   1   1   1   1
    Charge             Charge            10:00       1   1   1   1   1   1   1
  1 No charge       11                   10:30       1   1   1   1   1   1   1
  2                 12                   11:00       1   1   1   1   1   1   1
  3                 13                   11:30       1   1   1   1   1   1   1
  4                 14                   12:00       1   1   1   1   1   1   1
  5                 15                   12:30       1   1   1   1   1   1   1
  6                 16                   13:00       1   1   1   1   1   1   1
  7                 17                   13:30       1   1   1   1   1   1   1
  8                 18                   14:00       1   1   1   1   1   1   1
  9                 19                   14:30       1   1   1   1   1   1   1
 10                 20                   15:00       1   1   1   1   1   1   1
                                         15:30       1   1   1   1   1   1   1
           (Charge per block)            16:00       1   1   1   1   1   1   1

The time is military time.  13:00 is 1:00 pm.

Enter=Modify rates   F5=Mark   Esc=Exit                                   F1=Help
```

Figure 39.7

The Blocks read charge rates with 8:00 a.m. marked.

Press the PgDn key three times. You should see the time indicators to the left move forward in 8-hour increments. At this point, you should have the entire time grid highlighted.

9. After the entire grid is highlighted using the F5 and cursor movement keys, press Enter to establish a charge rate. The Select a charge rate screen appears. There are initially two choices: 1 No Charge and Other charge rate. Select Other charge rate. The New charge rate dialog box appears.

10. In the New charge rate dialog box, you can see the Multiplier and Divisor fields set to a value of 1. Press Esc to accept these values. You are returned to the Blocks read charge rate dialog box.

11. On the left side of the Blocks read charge rate dialog box, under the Rate/ Charge column, a value of 1/1 now appears. Press Esc to exit this screen and return to the Accounting options menu.

You can now proceed to add a charge rate of 1/1 at all times, to the Blocks Written and Service Requests categories.

Gathering Statistics

There are several ways to gather statistics from the accounting system. One technique is to use the utility ATOTAL.EXE provided in the SYS:SYSTEM directory of each server. ATOTAL scans the file NET$ACCT.DAT produced by the server-based accounting system and produces a total by category, day, and week. Following is a sample of the output produced by ATOTAL:

```
ACCOUNTING SERVICES TOTAL UTILITY
   Reading accounting records, please wait...
10/28/1994:
    Connect time:              6     Server requests:        3212
    Blocks read:            1409     Blocks written:
    Blocks/day:


10/29/1994:
    Connect time:            840     Server requests:       97814
    Blocks read:           23819     Blocks written:          556
    Blocks/day:


Totals for week:
    Connect time:            846     Server requests:      101026
    Blocks read:           25228     Blocks written:          556
    Blocks/day:
```

Note that only the categories where you have set an accounting charge rate are represented. In the example above, Blocks/Day is not represented because there is no charge rate assigned.

Another technique is to view individual account balances through NETADMIN.EXE or NWADMIN.EXE. To view users with an account balance below 0 using NWADMIN.EXE, proceed as follows:

1. Log in as a user with at least Browse object rights and Read rights to users' Account Balance property.

2. From Windows, run NWADMIN.EXE (the NetWare Administrator).

3. From the NWADMIN main menu, select Searc**h** from the **O**bject menu. The Search dialog box appears, as shown in figure 39.8.

   To search for all users with an account balance less than zero, enter the following values in the Search dialog box:

Start **F**rom	[root]
Search Entire Sub**t**ree	checkmarked
Search For	User
Property	Account Balance
Comparison	Less Than Or Equal To
Value	0

4. Click on OK to start the search. You will see a message indicating that a search from the [root] could take a long time. If you have a large tree and are willing to

wait, select Yes. Otherwise, restart the search procedure and limit where the search will start.

5. At this point, you can see a list of users whose account balances are less than 0.

A final technique to extract account information is to use output from the NLIST.EXE utility. Following are listings of a batch file that calls NLIST and a QBASIC (the inevitable) program, which picks out all users along with the value for their Account Balance property. The following sample program also summarizes account balances by container and gives a total at the bottom.

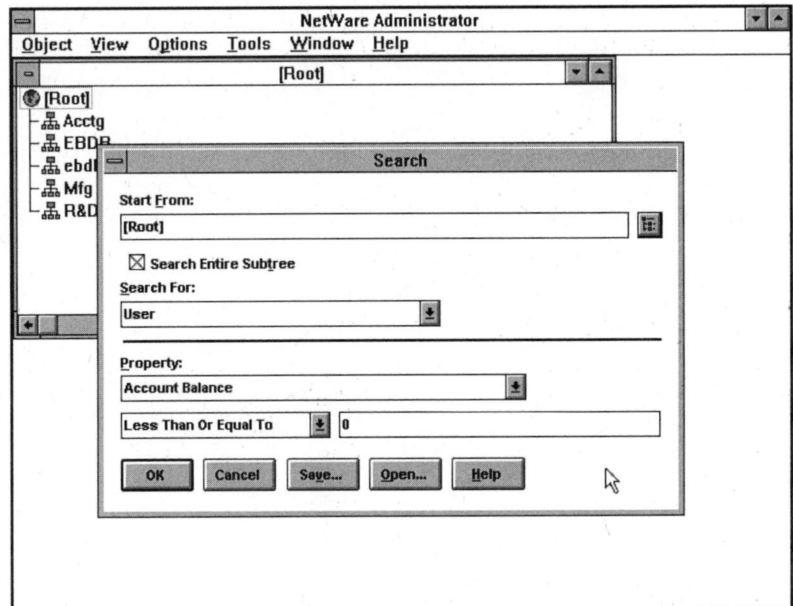

Figure 39.8

Searching for user accounts with a negative account balance.

The following is the batch file USRACCT.BAT, which calls NLIST and the QBASIC program:

```
@echo off
echo:  Title:             USRACCT.BAT
echo :  Date:             10-29-94
echo :  Author:           D. Bierer
echo :  Files:            USRACCT.TXT  = NLIST dump
echo :
echo :
echo :  Running NLIST
echo :
@echo on
```

```
cx [root]
NLIST user / s / d > USRACCT.TXT
@echo off
echo :
echo :  Run QBASIC program USRACCT.BAS
echo :
QBASIC /run USRACCT
echo :
echo :  Del Temp File
echo :
@echo on
DEL USRACCT.TXT
@echo off
echo :
echo :  Done
echo :
```

The following is the QBASIC program USRACCT.BAS, which scans the output produced by NLIST and produces a report file USRACCT.RPT:

```
REM     Title:  USRACCT.BAS
REM     Date:   10-29-94
REM     Author: D. Bierer
REM     Notes:  Scans USRACCT.TXT file.  Produces a report by user
REM             and by container of account usage.  Assumes account
REM             was initially set to zero.
REM

REM     Set Variables
T = 0
C = 0
F = 0

REM     Open Files

OPEN "USRACCT.TXT" FOR INPUT AS #1
OPEN "USRACCT.RPT" FOR OUTPUT AS #2

1000    REM     If end of input file, bail out
IF EOF(1) THEN GOTO 4000

REM     Scan for container name

LINE INPUT #1, A$
```

```
A$ = UCASE$(A$)
X = INSTR(A$, "CURRENT CONTEXT")
IF X > 0 THEN GOSUB 3000

REM     Check to see if User

X = INSTR(A$, "USER:")
IF X > 0 THEN U$ = MID$(A$, X + 6)

REM     Check to see if Account Balance

X = INSTR(A$, "ACCOUNT BALANCE:")
IF X = 0 THEN GOTO 1000

REM    Process User

Y = INSTR(A$, "-")
IF Y > 0 THEN
     B = VAL(MID$(A$, Y + 1))
ELSE
     B = VAL(MID$(A$, X + 16))
END IF
PRINT #2, CHR$(9); U$, B
T = T + B
C = C + B
GOTO 1000


3000    REM     Process Next Context

REM     Compose Context Name

C$ = MID$(A$, X + 17)

REM     Write container name out as CX command to batch file

IF F = 0 THEN
     F = 1
ELSE
     PRINT #2, "------------------------------------------------------"
     PRINT #2, "Container Total: ", C
     PRINT #2, "------------------------------------------------------"
     PRINT #2, ""
     PRINT #2, ""
```

```
    C = 0
END IF

PRINT #2, "-------------------------------------------------------"
PRINT #2, "Container: ", C$
PRINT #2, "-------------------------------------------------------"

RETURN


4000    REM     Close Files and Generate Report

PRINT #2, "Container Total: ", C
PRINT #2, ""
PRINT #2, ""
PRINT #2, "======================================================="
PRINT #2, "Total For All Containers: ", T
PRINT #2, "======================================================="

CLOSE #1
CLOSE #2

INPUT "Generate Report (Y/N)? ", A$
IF LEFT$(UCASE$(A$), 1) = "Y" THEN

     B = 0
     OPEN "USRACCT.RPT" FOR INPUT AS #1

     DO
          B = B + 1
          LINE INPUT #1, A$
          PRINT A$
          IF B > 24 THEN
               B = 0
               PRINT
               INPUT "Press ENTER to Continue...", A$
          END IF

     LOOP UNTIL EOF(1)
     CLOSE #1

END IF

SYSTEM
```

Network Management with Novell NMS 2.0

Another direction for network management is software that monitors the entire network. Network management systems have been available for the mainframe environment for the past 10 to 20 years. IBM has a system called NetView, for example, that provides for management of a complex Systems Network Architecture (SNA) network. Several minicomputer vendors, such as Digital Equipment Corporation (DEC), have provided enterprise management software. In TCP/IP-based networks, there are a variety of Simple Network Management Protocol (SNMP) management packages. Sun Microsystems and Hewlett Packard (HP), for example, both offer SNMP-based management packages.

In the LAN and WAN environments involving microcomputers, there are a growing number of network management packages. Most packages can be installed on a file server or workstation and can "listen" to network traffic. Many offer an analysis of network events, which can provide advice on how to optimize your network for best performance.

In this section, you learn about a network management package offered by Novell: the Network Management System v2.0 (NMS). This package is comprehensive and offers features you should consider when looking at the various network management packages available on the market.

NMS Overview

The NMS package consists of a series of NLMs, which need to be loaded on one or more file servers, and a monitor software program that should be run on a workstation. The basic NMS package gives you the NetExplorer utility, which loads on a file server. You also will see about a dozen 3 1/2-inch disks containing the monitoring software, which is installed on a workstation. Included in the main package are the client software, the monitoring software that runs on a workstation, and the NetExplorer software, which runs on a server.

The workstation that runs the monitoring software is called the *NMS Console*. The hardware requirements for the NMS console are fairly hefty, as follows:

- An 80386 or above computer
- VGA or above video adapter
- Windows 3.1 or above
- 12 MB of RAM free, including 510 KB of conventional memory

- 10 to 50 MB of hard drive space, depending on how many statistics you plan to store on the NMS console
- The DOS SHARE.EXE program

Requirements for the file server running the NetExplorer software are an additional 8 MB of RAM for NetExplorer and 20 MB of hard drive space. The requirements for NetExplorer Plus are 500 KB of RAM and 500 KB of disk space.

The purpose of the NMS console software is to enable you to monitor the network from a workstation, even if one or more servers are down. The NetExplorer software gathers network information and reports back to the NMS console. This software "explores" the network and returns a wealth of information that includes server name, and network and node addresses, among other things. NetExplorer Plus, also included with the basic package, can be installed on all other file servers. NetExplorer Plus enables you to gather precise information on nodes that use services on that file server. The additional information gathered by NetExplorer Plus includes workstation node addresses, user login names, and detailed token ring information (if you are using token ring).

The installation sequence for NMS is as follows:

1. Install the client software on the NMS console workstation. This software is a modified version of the standard NetWare Client software. There is an additional disk with TCP/IP support if you plan to monitor TCP/IP in addition to IPX.

2. Install the NMS console software. Because there are approximately twelve 3 1/2-inch disks, plan to spend 20 to 30 minutes completing the installation.

3. Install NetExplorer on a file server that you designate. The server names will appear on a list during the NMS console installation procedure. The designated server is updated from the NMS console workstation. The server's AUTOEXEC.NCF file will be modified, and a series of NLMs will be copied to a series of subdirectories. Only install NetExplorer on one file server.

   Optionally, you can install NetExplorer Plus software on other file servers, and it should be installed on all other file servers on the network. Doing so enables you to manage additional resources on each file server, including monitoring user activities on that server.

4. Install other NMS agents. There are a number of agent packages that work with NMS which are detailed later in this section. The most well-known agent is the LANalyzer Agent, which is a version of the LANalyzer, as described in the previous section, which runs as an NLM on a file server.

Network Autodiscovery

One of the first tasks you will want to have NMS perform is to "discover" your network. From the NMS console main menu, proceed as follows:

1. From the File menu, select Open. A pop-up menu appears with several choices.
2. From the pop-up menu, select Internet Map. A "map" of your network appears.

The Internet Map is put together from data provided by the NetExplorer software running on the designated file server. Information gathered includes networks, routers, and other devices, depending on what other NMS agents you have installed on your network. From the Internet Map, you can click on any network icon to get a more detailed view of that network. When you click on a network icon on the Internet Map, a Logical Map appears. Figure 39.9 shows both an Internet Map and a Logical Map from a demo provided with the NMS sales kit.

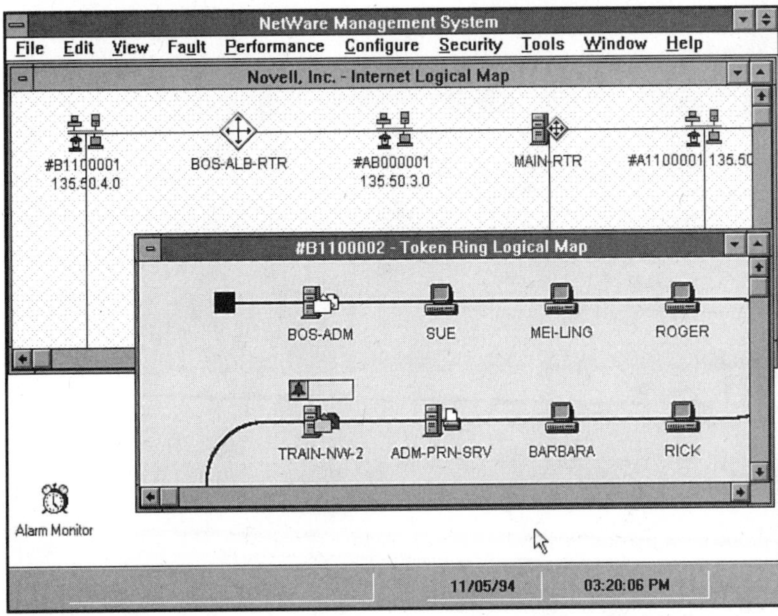

Figure 39.9

A demonstration of the Internet Map and Logical Map.

Notice in the figure that the Logical Map shows file servers, workstations, and other devices. You can set alarms for designated network events. When an alarm is triggered, a red bell appears at that location. In the figure, you can see that an alarm has been triggered in the TRAIN-NW-2 file server.

Locational Maps

NMS enables you to integrate a *Locational Map* into the network management database. You can use one of the predefined maps or incorporate your own map in *.BMP format (Bit Mapped image—used by Windows Paintbrush, for example). You could scan a map of your campus of buildings, for example, and incorporate this image into the management database. Locational Maps can go from large to small scale. You can see in figure 39.10 a series of interrelated locational maps. On the left is a map of California. In the middle is a map of the campus of buildings. On the right side is a map detailing the cubicles within an office of a specific building. By double-clicking on any one area, you can bring up the more detailed map. These maps are provided with the demo that accompanies the NMS sales kit.

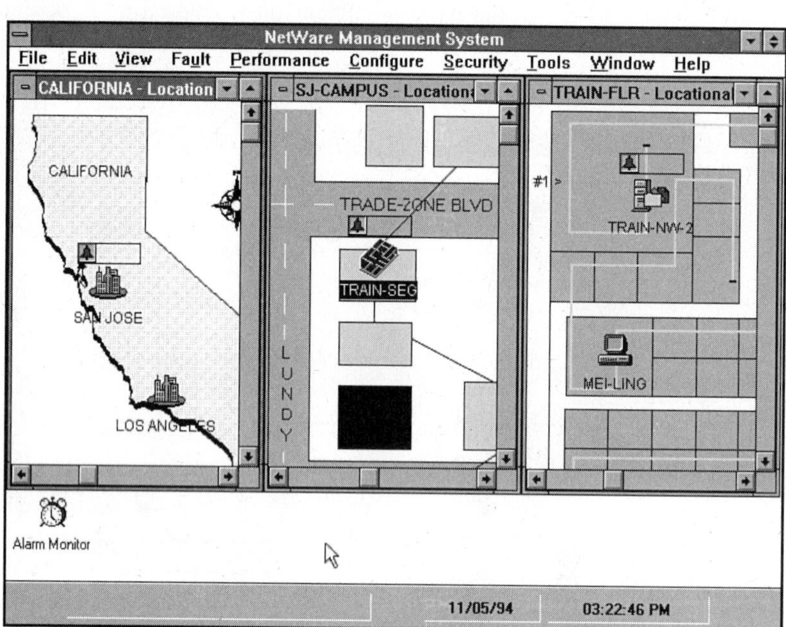

Figure 39.10
A demonstration of Locational Maps of increasing detail.

Configuring Alarms

You can configure a series of alarms in the NMS database. An alarm is generated when a network event exceeds a threshold you set. The number and variety of network events you can monitor depends on which NMS agents you have loaded. The LANalyzer Agent, for example, reports on low-level network events such as utilization, CRC errors, collisions (for Ethernet), or beaconing (for token ring). The Network Management Agent reports on server-specific events, such as low disk space, low server memory, CPU utilization, excessive number of packet receive buffers allocated, number of open files, and so forth.

Figure 39.11 shows the Alarm Disposition dialog box, an option available from the NMS console, Fault menu.

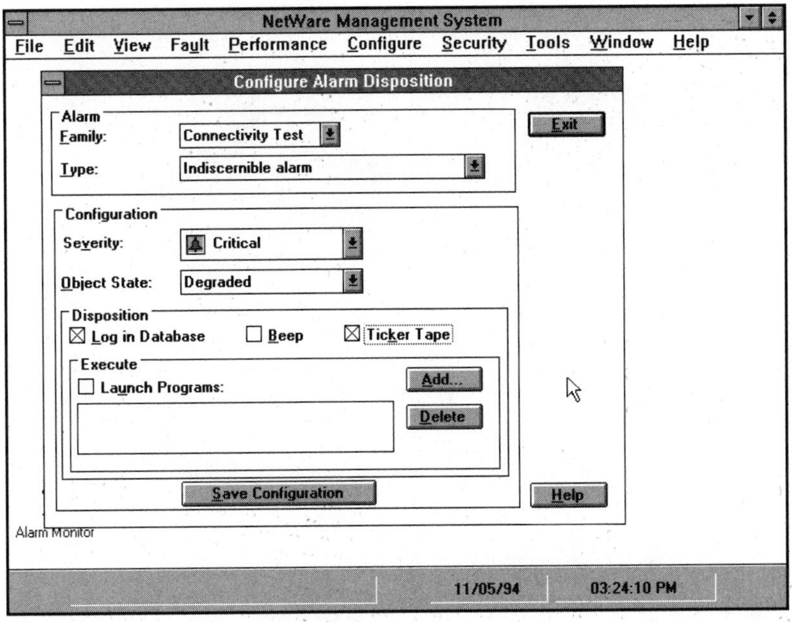

Figure 39.11

The Configure Alarm Disposition dialog box.

Figure 39.12 shows a demonstration list of reported alarms. As you can see from the figure, the date and time, notes, acknowledgments, alarm type, and alarm summary are included in the report. If you need assistance in interpreting the meaning or impact of a specific type of event reported, you can select the event and click on the NetWare Expert button—the button with the red graduation cap. The NetWare expert provides details on the nature of the alarm, possible causes, and suggested solutions.

Managing Routers

NMS can be used to diagnose and manage NetWare routers, which can include NetWare servers acting as routers, or routers such as Novell's MultiProtocol Router. Management comes through IPX diagnostics and the SNMP protocol. Any router that adheres to the SNMP protocol and has either a *Management Information Base version 1* (MIB-I) or MIB-II agent can be managed through NMS.

To have the NMS console query all routers, proceed as follows:

1. From the main NMS console menu, select View. A pop-up menu appears.

2. From the pop-up menu, select **A**ll. Another pop-up submenu appears. From the submenu, select **R**outers. The Query ... Routers list appears.

3. From the Query ... Routers list, select the desired router and either press Enter or double-click with the mouse. The System Details list for that router appears.

Figure 39.12

The Alarm Report list box.

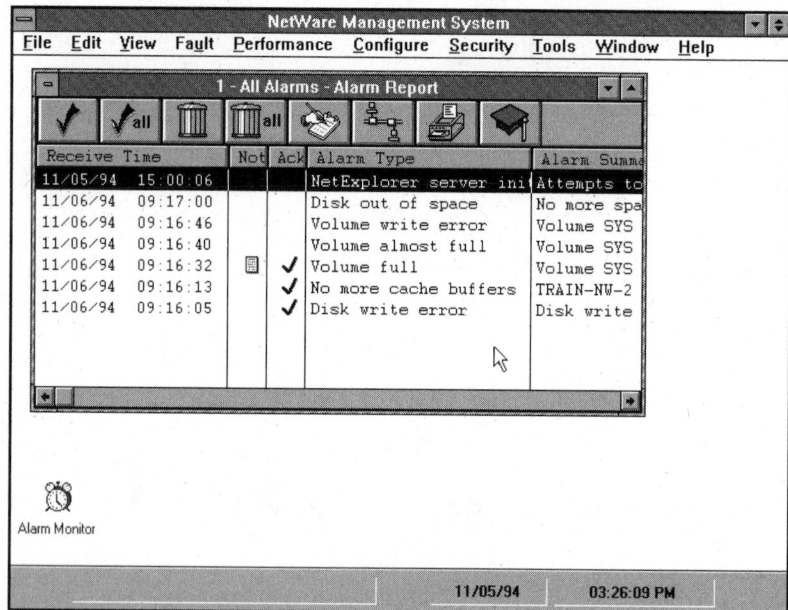

Figure 39.13 shows you sample Query ... Routers and System Details lists from the demo database included with the NMS sales kit. The Query ... Routers list gives you a list of routers, their status, a description of the router (entered by you when first building up the database), and the number of segments this router supports. The System Details list provides network addresses, the types of protocols supported, frame types, and Media Access Control (MAC) layer, which is also known as the node address.

Performance statistics are also available. NMS queries routers to gather information such as packets per second and errors, both inbound and outbound. These statistics can be displayed in the form of a graph, which updates in real time or reviews trends over a period of time. Bear in mind that the longer the time period, the more disk space is required on the NMS console workstation.

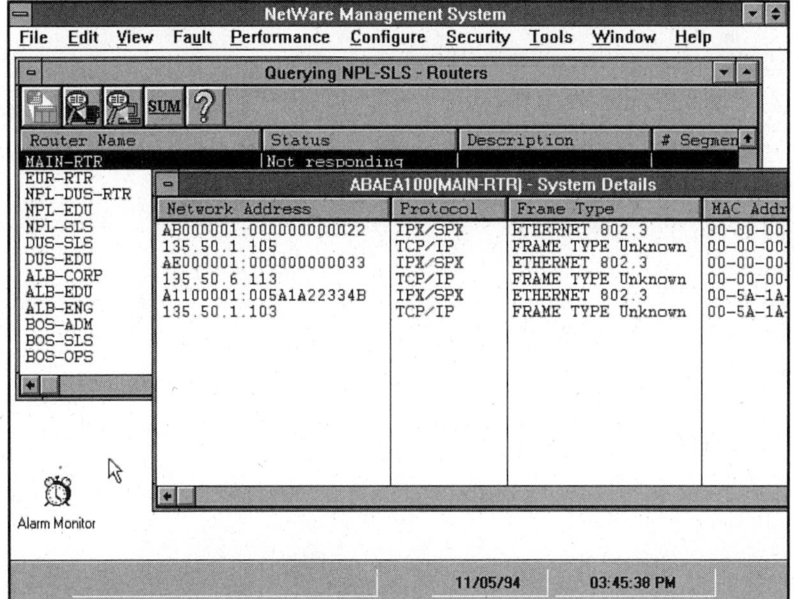

Figure 39.13

The Query ... Routers and System Details list boxes.

Connectivity Testing

One of the more important jobs of NMS is to test for connectivity. This simple test can save hours of troubleshooting in a complex network. You can select any device (such as a router or a file server) from any of the maps, and perform a connectivity test. Testing can be performed on a one-time-only basis, or you can elect to test periodically. You can create *test profiles,* which contain a set of specific devices to be tested. When you call the Connectivity Test option from the Fault menu, you can load and save different test profiles. When adding a device to the list of devices to be tested periodically, you can scan by name, IPX network address, node address, or IP address.

Figure 39.14 shows the result of a periodic connectivity test. As you can see from the figure, the protocol and MAC address are identified. The *Target* is the name as manually entered in the database, or "discovered" through the NetExplorer NLM running on a file server. The *Status* column indicates the result of the connectivity test. As you can see from the figure, the NMS console sent the target, SJF-ED1, 67 packets and did not receive any in return. The status returned the message `Response Timed Out`. As with most NMS lists, clicking on any given column causes the list to be sorted by that item. You can also drag and drop columns to rearrange their order.

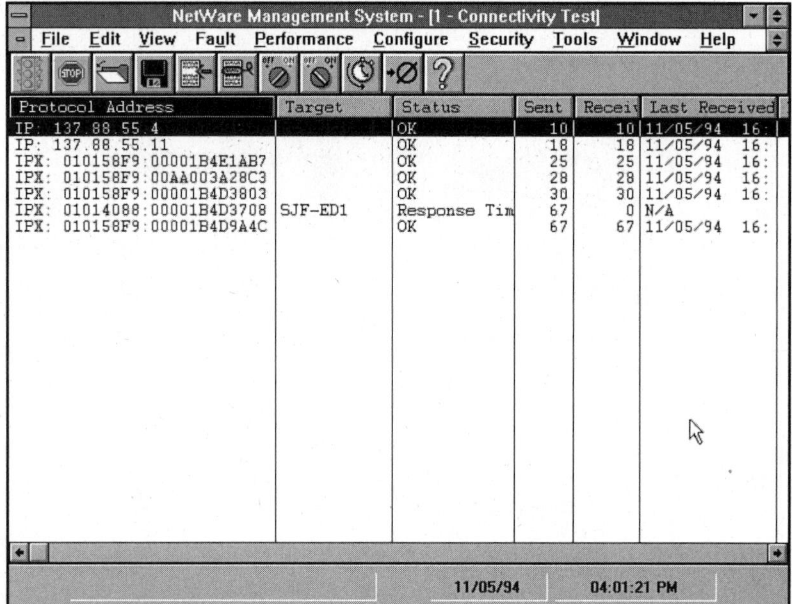

Figure 39.14
The Connectivity Test screen.

NetWare Expert

An invaluable feature offered with the basic NMS package is the *NetWare Expert*, which is a tutorial, an online help system, and a diagnostician all in one. When you first go to install NMS, you are presented with the option of installing the tutorial, which is a valuable tool that gets you up to speed on installing, configuring, and operating NMS. When you are using NMS, you can click on Help at any time and read about various features and functions. When a problem arises, select the NetWare Expert icon to receive a summary of the problem, a list of possible causes, and suggested corrections to make.

Figure 39.15 shows you the page from the tutorial that discusses using the NetWare Expert in conjunction with troubleshooting. As you can see from the figure, there is at the top of the screen a description of the error message you received. Keywords are highlighted in red. The results of the problem are shown under System Action. A list of areas to check in the NMS console can be found under User Action.

When the NetWare Expert cannot give a clear diagnosis of the problem, it will tell you to look in certain areas on the NMS console for more information. When you have gathered more statistics, you can return to the NetWare Expert for further diagnosis.

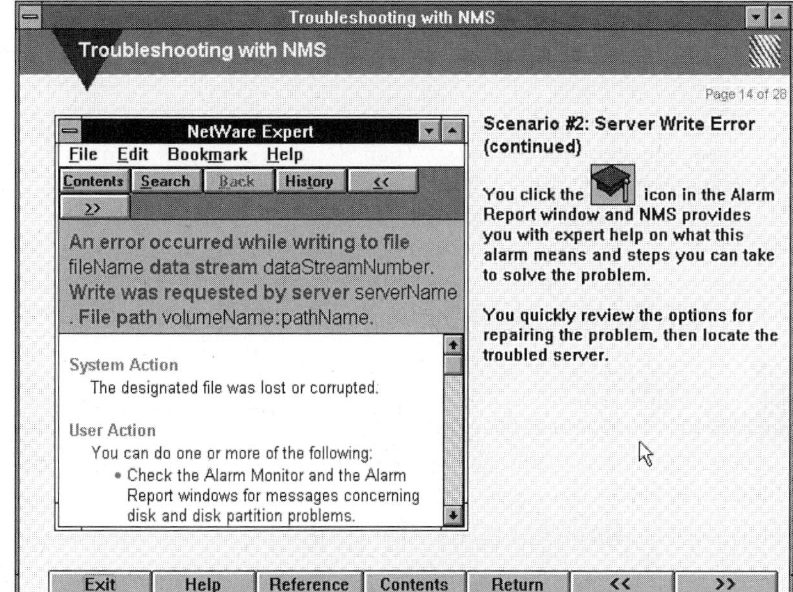

Figure 39.15
The NetWare Expert tutorial page.

Other Services and NMS Agents

Other services are available through optional NMS agents. These agents are offered by Novell and a number of third-party developers. The services available depend on the agent purchased. The following paragraphs summarize some of the available NMS agents and their vendors. These agents can be managed from the NMS console.

LANalyzer by Novell

As described previously, this is a full-blown version of the LANalyzer in NLM form. The agent runs on a file server and can be managed from the NMS console. You can view physical and data link layer events, scan for bad network adapters, track collisions and errors, and even capture packets.

NetWare Management by Novell

This agent can be installed on a file server to provide management and reporting capabilities. You can get a list of NLMs currently loaded, a report on memory usage, network adapter performance, and disk space free. You can generate graphs tracking inbound and outbound network traffic, and can set alarms when the number of open files, users logged in, files locked, or packets received exceeds a threshold you set.

NetWare Hub Management by Novell

This agent is used when your server has a managed hub. Intel Hub Cards and Cabletron Multi-Station Access Units (MAUs) are examples of managed hubs. This utility enables you to view the hubs graphically and monitor connections to the hub. You can gather statistics and immediately detect when a network adapter connected to a port on the hub has gone bad. You could even shut down a port on a hub through the NMS console. You can generate a real-time statistics graph of traffic through the hub.

MIB Browser and MIB Compiler by Novell

The basic NMS package includes a series of Management Information Base (MIB) tools that enables you to look through a MIB and even define your own events to be tracked. This tool enables you to extend the events that NMS will manage, and can be used to add third-party definitions to the NMS database.

PowerChute PLUS with SNMP Agent by American Power Conversion

This software package enables you to manage American Power Conversion (APC) Uninterruptible Power Supply (UPS) units connected to file servers managed by NMS. You can generate a graph of power spikes and brownouts monitored by the UPS. You can monitor the status of the UPS unit, for example, battery life remaining, and charge levels. The software also enables you to perform a test of the UPS from the NMS console.

LAN Automatic Inventory by Brightwork Development

This software package queries all computers and other devices on the LAN and generates an inventory database. Information collected includes the user name, operating system version, software versions, and equipment types. Equipment types inventoried include the number and nature of the system's hard and floppy drives, monitor, processor type, and keyboard. The amount of RAM, network adapter types, and additional information is collected. The software also detects changes to the network and automatically adds these to the database.

NETremote+ by Brightwork Development

This software package enables network administrators to "take over" the workstations of DOS or Windows users from the NMS console. In the case where a user has a problem using a certain application, for example, you could call up their display and watch as they perform an operation. Your keyboard is linked to theirs so that you could "step in" and use the application as if you were sitting at their workstation. In conjunction with a phone call, you could walk the user through a difficult operation.

NM Console by Eicon Technology

This product can manage an Eicon Technology Interconnect Server (ICS). An ICS is a computer with an Eicon board and software installed. From the NMS console, you can manage High Level Data Link Control (HDLC) or Synchronous Data Link Control (SDLC) connections to a mainframe. You can also manage X.25 or Frame Relay connections through the ICS. The software provides a graphical display of statistics, reports, and management capabilities.

NetWare Early Warning System (NEWS) by Frye Computer Systems

This package, offered by the same company that makes the Frye Utilities, automates the process of monitoring the network for critical events. It offers a more sophisticated version of the alarms that can be set through NMS. NEWS monitors over 50 major critical statistics and provides notification through a speech module, pager, e-mail, or fax.

NetWare Console Commander by Frye Computer Systems

This module enables you to schedule any NetWare 3.1*x* or above file server console command. From the NMS console, you are presented with a calendar. You can schedule commands to be executed at specific dates and times, enabling you to schedule backups, broadcast messages, disable logins, or issue any other server command.

Lancert Facilities Management (LFM) Systems by Lancert Technologies

This series of products enables you to manage external physical and electrical equipment through the NMS console. The *LFM Aircon* module can monitor the air conditioning system, enabling you to set alarms when the temperature of a room goes above or below predefined levels. The *LFM Secure* module monitors your security system, alerts you in case a computer cabinet has been opened, checks for break-ins, and even records when someone goes through a door with a secure keycard.

Router Manager for Cisco by StonyBrook Services

This module is a fully integrated router management utility that enables you to manage Cisco routers through the NMS console. It provides statistics, real-time graphs, and management capabilities.

Summary

This chapter gave you an overview of the various tools available for monitoring network performance. There was a description of tools to test cabling, and an example cited was the Compas offered by Microtest, Inc. This handheld device has jacks to plug into twisted-pair or thin coaxial Ethernet networks, and like other cable testers in general, can check for shorts and breaks, distance, noise, crosstalk, and bad hubs or MAUs.

The next section discussed LANalyzer for Windows, a protocol analyzer available from Novell. The LANalyzer analyzes network traffic and can provide real-time statistics, or over a period of time. It reports on packets per second, errors, and kilobytes per second, and gives you a report by node address. Statistics over a period of time are called trends. Trends that can be viewed include packets per second, errors, utilization, and kilobytes per second. By viewing trends and real-time statistics, you can determine baseline parameters for your network and determine the status of the network at any time.

LANalyzer also enables you to set alarms. An alarm is generated when a network event exceeds a value you set. The packet capture feature enables you to "capture" network packets into a buffer for analysis. You can perform a packet decode, which shows you a breakdown, by OSI layer, of any packet in the buffer. You can view data link level information, network information, and up the OSI model. The system can capture and decode a number of protocols, including IPX/SPX, TCP/IP, and AppleTalk.

The next area discussed was the accounting system. As you learned, this is server-specific and consists of five major areas: blocks read, blocks written, connect time, disk storage, and service requests. You can block off a period of time for any of the five areas and designate a charge rate. As you saw, a charge rate of 1/1 is useful for generating statistics. When setting up accounting, you must first determine and set user account balances. Provided was a batch file, along with a QBASIC program, which sets all user accounts in the tree to allow unlimited credit. If user account balances are not updated, the accounting system can cause users to be kicked off the network. Gathering statistics are possible through the ATOTAL.EXE utility or through NLIST.EXE. Because NLIST does not separate or total the figures, another QBASIC program and batch file were presented that generate a report by user by container, with totals.

The last portion of the chapter gave you an overview of a network management package, Novell's Network Management System (NMS). As you learned, NMS consists of a basic software package that installs on a workstation, and a number of NLMs that you run on the file servers. The workstation that runs the NMS software is called the NMS console. The file server component consists of the NetExplorer NLM, which runs on one file server, and NetExplorer Plus, which runs on all other file servers. The utilities gather data on the network and present it to the NMS console.

In addition to the basic NMS system, there are a number of Novell and third-party supplied agents that provide additional functionality. These agents include the LANalyzer Agent and the Network Management Agent by Novell, which provide more precise statistics and management capabilities for the network segment and servers. Other agents perform automatic inventory, and provide control over physical equipment, routers, high-speed links, and other devices.

NMS gives you tremendous control over the LAN and the physical environment surrounding and supporting the network. From a single NMS console, a network administrator can gather statistics, perform fine-tuning, and stay on top of any network problem.

The tools discussed in this chapter provide a way to prevent network problems before they even occur. You can generate baseline statistics for your network and use the tools discussed to monitor the current status of the network. Thresholds can be set, and alarms can be generated to warn you in case of problems. These tools enable you to get the "big picture" and more effectively manage the network.

Chapter 40 discusses another aspect of network management: how to set up and manage auditing.

Auditing the Network

NetWare 4.1 has the capability to audit a variety of events, ranging from the opening of a file to the changing of a user's security rights. Auditing can be performed by the network Administrator or by an independent third-party auditing firm. NetWare 4.1 enables you to fully monitor all aspects of network security. You can even audit the auditor!

There are dozens of reasons why your company would want to install auditing on the network. The following list gives you some of them:

- To monitor any changes in network security
- To know who is accessing certain files
- To monitor the activities of selected network users
- To keep a record of login and logout activity by date and time
- To justify getting a new printer or other network resources

Auditing is performed using the AUDITCON.EXE utility, which is located in the SYS:PUBLIC directory of each file server. The network

Administrator initially sets up auditing. Once initialized, any user with the auditing password can perform auditing functions. NDS events and file system events (volume auditing) are audited separately using different reports. Other volume auditing events include management of print queues and jobs within queues, file server brought up or down, volume mounts or dismounts, and bindery-based user events. Figure 40.1 shows the AUDITCON main menu.

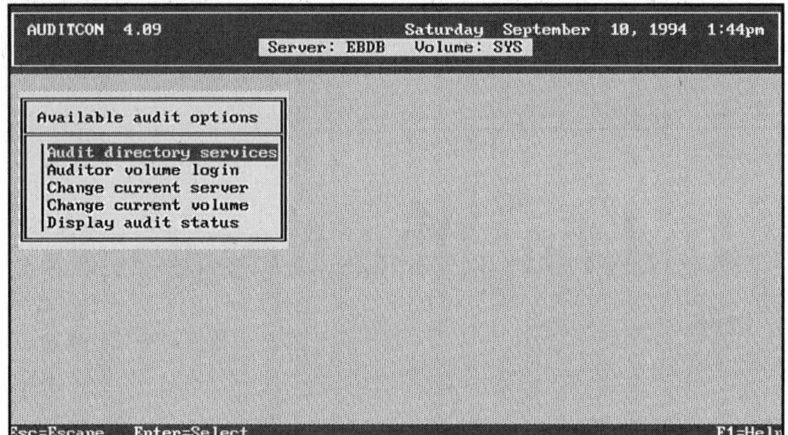

Figure 40.1
The AUDITCON main menu.

This chapter discusses the various aspects of auditing in NetWare 4.1.

Examining Auditing Considerations

Before setting up and performing network auditing, you must decide what you want to audit and why. AUDITCON enables you to audit NDS events and file system events. NDS events that can be audited include any changes to partitions, security equivalencies, the enabling, disabling, or deletion user accounts, logins and logouts, and so on. Auditing file system events is known as *volume auditing*. File system events include the creating, deleting, or renaming of files or directories, file opens, closes, or salvages. Other file system events that can be audited include printing events, file server events, and bindery based user events.

Volume Auditing and Directory Auditing

One decision you need to make is what type of auditing you want to perform. There are two main options available through AUDITCON: volume auditing and directory auditing. Volume auditing is available for individual volumes in your tree and must be

enabled separately for each volume. Volume auditing monitors events pertinent to the file system, the file server, print services (*Queue Management System*), and bindery services. Information collected by volume auditing is placed in an audit log. The *audit log* is a file maintained at the root of each volume where auditing is enabled. This file is hidden from all utilities and is considered always open. AUDITCON enables you to set limits on the size of the audit file.

Directory auditing audits directory services events. Directory events that can be audited are security related. Other events that can be audited are events that relate to changes in the NDS tree (partitioning, replication, creation, and modification of objects, and so forth). Directory auditing data is stored in the NDS itself.

Directory auditing is available on a per container basis. Auditing for a container must be enabled one container at a time. When you generate directory auditing reports, however, you are reporting for the entire NDS tree.

Enabling auditing for a high-level container does not enable auditing for lower-level containers. If you want to audit users in more than one container, you first must enable auditing for all desired containers.

Audit Files

There are several different kinds of audit files, as follows:

- **Audit file.** The Audit file is the file maintained for current auditing information. In the case of volume auditing, this is a hidden file at the root of the volume. In the case of directory auditing, the information is maintained as part of the NDS database.
- **Audit History file.** The Audit History file is a history of auditing actions and is used to audit the auditor. It contains the time when the Audit file was last reset and when an auditor logged into a volume or container for auditing.
- **Old Audit file.** The Old Audit file is a copy of the Audit file created when the Audit file is reset. The reset process copies current information into a separate file and clears the Audit file. This way you do not have to wade through too much information each time you view the Audit file. Resetting the Audit file also sets its size to zero. There is an Audit Files Maintenance option that enables you to make a copy of the Old Audit file.

AUDITCON File Event Options

One volume auditing consideration is determining how much auditing data you want to collect. AUDITCON offers three file event options. Each kind of file event enables you to set any of the following three options:

- Global
- User or File/Directory
- User and File/Directory

Global collects all data pertaining to the selected file event. If you select the file event File Open—Global, for example (from the AUDITCON main menu choose Auditor volume login, Auditing configuration, Audit by event, Audit by file events), the data that is entered into the volume audit log includes any instance of any user opening any file on that volume.

User or File/Directory is more selective because it collects data about events initiated by either a list of users you select, or data about events pertaining to a list of files (or directories) you select. If you select the file event File Open—User or File, for example, data entered into the volume audit log includes any file opens initiated by a list of users you select, or file opens of files you select.

User and File/Directory is the most selective—it collects data only when a user from a list you select opens a file from a list you select. If you select the file event File Open—User and File, for example, data entered into the volume audit log includes only file opens initiated by a list of users you select on files you select.

Figure 40.2 illustrates these three file event options. As you can see, the size of the audit log is largest for global, and smallest for user and file.

Other auditing options, such as Server Events or NDS auditing do not offer these three options. Other auditing options are simply on or off. When you want to monitor logins and logouts, for example, you simply turn on the event (from the AUDITCON main menu, select Audit directory services, Audit directory tree, choose the container to audit, Auditing configuration, Audit by DS events, then select Log in user and Log out user). Actual procedures to enable auditing are discussed in the next section.

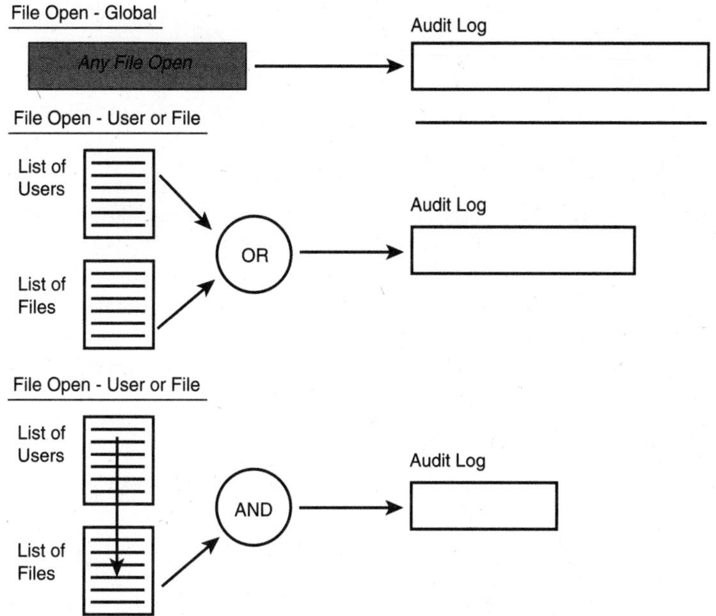

Figure 40.2
AUDITCON file event auditing options.

Auditing Reports

After you have decided what information you want to audit, consider what information you want to include in a report. As you learned earlier, you can collect a large amount of auditing data, or you can restrict the audit data you collect. After the data has been collected, you can create a series of report filters to restrict the amount of data included in the audit report. *Report filters* enable you to filter audit data by the following criteria:

- Date and time
- Specific directory event(s)
- Specific volume event(s)
- Include specific users
- Exclude certain users
- Include specific files or directories
- Exclude certain files or directories

You can create as many filters as are appropriate for your reporting needs. You can save or recall filters at any time. The report filter option is useful when you have a busy network and have generated a large amount of audit data.

Massaging of Report Files

The report data as generated by AUDITCON is not in a useful format. The following is an example of audit data generated from volume auditing:

```
14:05:28 Open file, event 27, PUBLIC\NLS\437_UNI.001, rights RE, status 0,
         user NOT_LOGGED_IN, connection 2
14:05:28 Open file, event 27, PUBLIC\NLS\437_UNI.001, rights RE, status 0,
         user NOT_LOGGED_IN, connection 2
14:05:28 Open file, event 27, PUBLIC\NLS\ENGLISH\SCHEMA.XLT, rights RE,
         status 0, user NOT_LOGGED_IN, connection 2
14:05:28 Open file, event 27, PUBLIC\NLS\ENGLISH\SCHEMA.XLT, rights RE,
         status 0, user NOT_LOGGED_IN, connection 2
14:06:16 Active connection, event 58, address 01014088:0080C7014103, status 0,
         user ALee.IND.EBDB, connection 6
14:06:16 Log out user, event 23, status 0,
         user ALee.IND.EBDB, connection 6
14:06:20 Active connection, event 58, address 01014088:0080C7014103, status 0,
         user BSAUNDER, connection 6
14:06:20 Open file, event 27, _NETWARE\0001B3C0.000, rights R, status 0,
         user BSAUNDER, connection 6
```

As you can see, such a report is not likely to persuade management that a new file server is justified. Third-party auditing utilities are expected to be forthcoming. In the meantime, however, it is the job of the network Administrator or the MIS staff to massage the data into a meaningful format, a task that can be accomplished with a simple BASIC or dBASE program, or a spreadsheet macro, for example. The section at the end of this chapter gives sample programs to produce various reports.

Who Should Perform Auditing?

Deciding who should perform auditing is a matter of some controversy in the network industry. Many network Administrators resent the implications behind hiring an outside auditor, which can be viewed as a lack of trust and can cause a rift between network Administrators and management. The Administrator of a Novell network traditionally had complete authority over all aspects of the network. NetWare 4.1 changes the balance of power considerably. Not only can network administration be delegated, but the ability to monitor changes to network security can be monitored through AUDITCON.

In a smaller network, the network Administrator is likely to be a person who performs auditing functions. The reasons for performing auditing are different in a smaller network, where the network Administrator usually is trying to gather statistics to justify the expense of the network or to justify additional network expenditures. In a large network, not only do network Administrators need to justify network expenditures, but security is an issue. The simple auditing task of monitoring user logins and logouts can generate useful security-related data. If a virus is discovered on the network, the auditor can review the auditing log to determine if a login occurred after normal working hours, for example. Unusual changes to the NDS tree can be detected to prevent a breach of security.

A pressing question is whether security changes to the network should be audited. In larger companies the answer is generally yes. If this is the situation, the network Administrator (or any user with Supervisor rights to the container object or volume object to be audited) can enable directory or volume auditing. After auditing is enabled, a designated user can access AUDITCON and change the auditing password. After the password has been changed, only those users with knowledge of the password can perform auditing for that specific volume or container. AUDITCON enables you to have different passwords for different volumes or containers. You can also configure AUDITCON to allow multiple auditors.

The auditor is an ordinary user who has knowledge of an auditing password. The auditor can perform auditing operations regardless of the rights assigned to (or revoked from) them by the network Administrator. Different events can be enabled, and reports can be generated even if the user has no rights to the audited object. The only exception is that this user must have at least Read file trustee rights to run the AUDITCON.EXE utility. In addition, the user must be a valid user in the NDS tree and have at least Browse object rights to the object to be audited.

To run AUDITCON.EXE, the auditor must also have Write, Create, and Erase directory trustee rights to the current directory. AUDITCON creates temporary files while reports are generated in the current directory. If the user does not have sufficient rights to the current directory, an error message is displayed when the report is generated. To satisfy this requirement, it is possible for the user to start AUDITCON from the local hard drive .

Computer networks have come of age. Auditing has been a standard in the financial sector for about 100 years. Auditing has been a standard in mainframe and minicomputer-based systems for the past few decades. NetWare 4.*x* introduced this feature to microcomputer-based LANs.

The next sections discuss the details of setting up and using NetWare 4.1 auditing.

Setting Up Auditing

The steps necessary to perform auditing are as follows:

- The network Administrator must enable auditing on all volumes and containers to be audited.
- Events to be audited must be configured.
- Auditing data is collected over a period of time.
- Report filters are created as needed.
- Audit report files are generated.
- Audit report files are massaged by external programming.

The first step in configuring the auditing environment is to enable auditing for each volume and container that you want to target. Before you can begin, you must log in as a user with Supervisor object rights to the volume or container object for which you plan to enable auditing. After logging in, type the following to manage auditing:

AUDITCON

Here is the procedure to enable volume auditing:

1. In the AUDITCON main menu, choose Change current server to select the server that contains the desired volume.

   In the AUDITCON main menu, choose Change current volume to select the desired volume. At the top center of the AUDITCON screen, the currently selected server and volume are confirmed.

2. After the desired server and volume are selected, choose Enable volume auditing in the AUDITCON main menu. You are prompted for the volume auditing password (see fig. 40.3).

3. The volume is ready for auditing.

The following is the procedure to enable directory auditing on an NDS container:

1. In the AUDITCON main menu, choose Audit directory services. The Audit directory services menu appears.

2. From the Audit directory services menu, choose Change session context to move to a container directly. Otherwise, choose Audit directory tree to browse the NDS tree structure. Your currently selected container is seen at the top of the screen. The Audit directory tree screen is shown in figure 40.4.

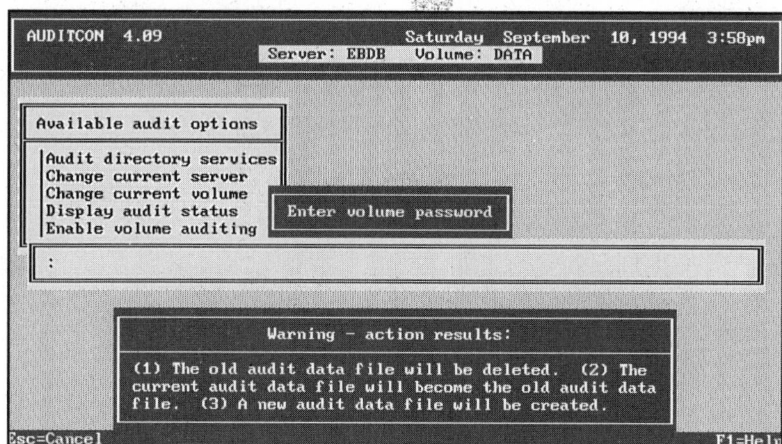

Figure 40.3

The Enable volume auditing password prompt.

3. From the Audit directory tree screen, select the desired container and press F10 to enable auditing. The Available audit options menu appears.

4. From the Available audit options menu, choose Enable container auditing to enable auditing for this container. You are prompted for the container auditing password. Enter the password and press Enter. Type the password a second time for confirmation and press Enter. The container is now ready for auditing.

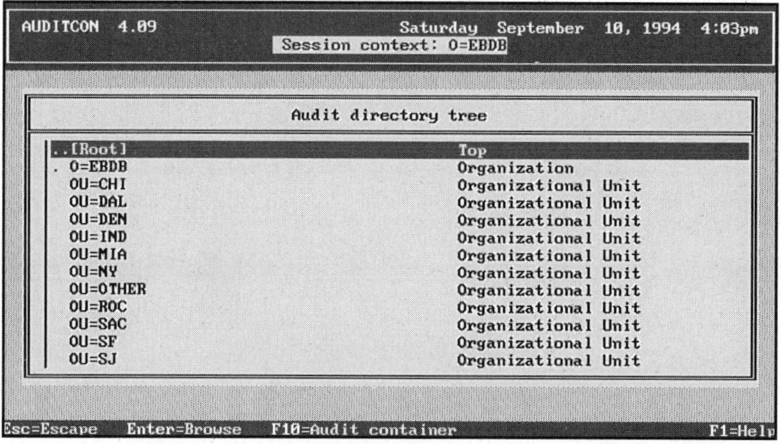

Figure 40.4

The Audit directory tree browse screen.

The next sections discuss how to configure volumes and containers for auditing.

Configuring Volume Auditing

After auditing for the desired volume has been enabled, the auditor can now configure which events should be audited. Before configuring volume auditing, the auditor must first type **AUDITCON**.

Here is the procedure to configure volume auditing:

1. From the AUDITCON main menu, choose Change current server to select the server that contains the desired volume.

2. From the AUDITCON main menu, choose Change current volume to select the desired volume. The currently selected server and volume are confirmed at the top center of the AUDITCON screen.

3. From the AUDITCON main menu, choose Auditor volume login. The Enter volume password input box appears. Enter the auditing password for this volume and press Enter. The Available audit options menu appears, as shown in figure 40.5.

4. From the Available audit options menu, choose Auditing configuration. The Auditing configuration menu appears, as shown in figure 40.6. Table 40.1 summarizes the options in the Auditing configuration menu.

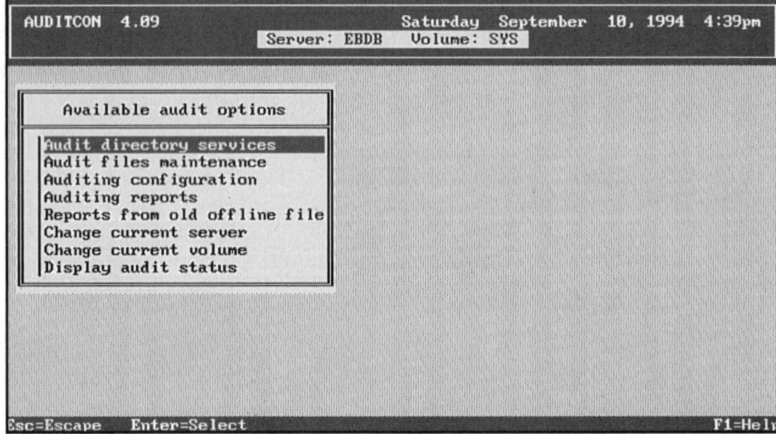

Figure 40.5
The Available audit options menu of the AUDITCON utility.

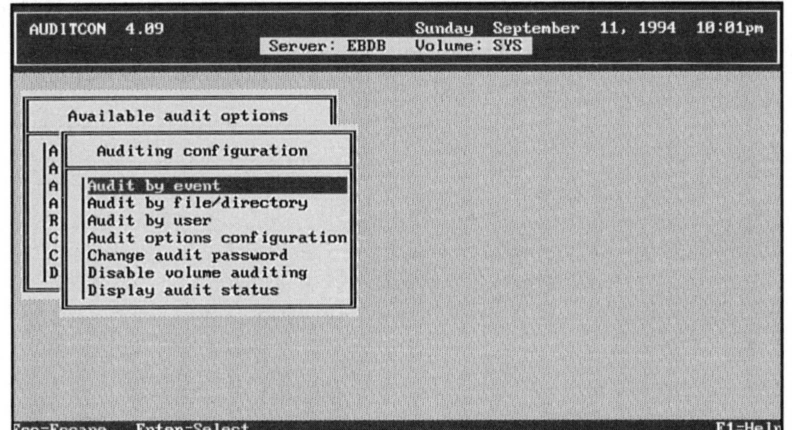

Figure 40.6
The Auditing configuration menu of the AUDITCON utility.

TABLE 40.1
Volume Auditing—Auditing Configuration Menu Options

Menu Option	Description
Audit by event	Brings up a sub menu with the following options: *Audit by file events* enables you to select different file events such as Open, Close, and other events related to files and directories. *Audit by QMS events* audits printing events such as create job, job finish, and remove job. *Audit by server events* audits file-server-related events. These include change date/time, down server, and volume dismount. *Audit by user events* tracks bindery user events such as log in user, remove trustee, and user space restrictions.
Audit by file/directory	Enables you to build list files and directories that you want to audit. Actions pertaining to these files and directories then are placed in the audit file, depending on other options selected (such as File Events).

continues

Table 40.1, Continued
Volume Auditing—Auditing Configuration Menu Options

Menu Option	Description
Audit by user	Gives you a list of bindery users to audit. The list you see in this menu are the users in the file server's bindery context. To add users to this list, add containers to the server's bindery context using the SET BINDERY CONTEXT = parameter. To audit other users, you must use directory auditing (discussed later).
Audit options configuration	Brings up a screen that enables you to set various parameters for this volume. Parameters include the maximum size of the audit file, audit file archiving parameters, and so on. These options are discussed in more detail in the "Auditing Maintenance" section.
Change audit password	Changes the auditing password. After the password has been changed, there is no way to audit the system without knowledge of the new password. By doing this, the auditor becomes independent of the network Administrator.
Disable volume auditing	Removes auditing from this volume. In this way, you can periodically audit or not audit volumes. When you re-enable volume auditing after using this option, the old audit information is overwritten.
Display audit status	Displays the current auditing status of the volume.

Table 40.2 summarizes the different events that can be audited. These options are available from the Audit by event menu described in table 40.1.

Table 40.2
Volume Auditing—Audit by Event Menu Options

Event Menu	Option	Description
File events (1)	Create directory	Tracks when a directory is created.
	Delete directory	Tracks when a directory is deleted.
	File close	Tracks when a file is closed after being used.
	File create	Tracks when a file is created.

Event Menu	Option	Description
	File delete	Tracks when a file is deleted.
	File open	Tracks when a file is opened. This is the preferred way to track when a file is accessed.
	File read	Tracks when a file is read. Tracks all NCP calls to read the file. In the audit file you will see every single read request for the file. If the file is 100 KB, for example, and your packet size is 1 KB, you will get 100 entries in the audit log for this one file—for each read request. If you want to track access of the file, choose File open.
	File rename/move	Tracks when a file is renamed.
	File salvage	Tracks when a file is recovered after being deleted.
	File write	Tracks when a file is written to.
	Modify directory entry	Tracks when a directory entry is changed.
QMS events	Queue attach server	Tracks when the print server connects to a queue.
	Queue create	Tracks creation of a print queue.
	Queue create job	Tracks when a new job has been placed in a print queue.
	Queue destroy	Tracks when a print queue is removed.
	Queue detach server	Tracks when a print server disconnects from the queue (when the print server goes down, for example).
	Queue edit job	Monitors changes to basic print job information (such as number of copies, banner/no banner, defer printing, and so on).

continues

Table 40.2, Continued
Volume Auditing—Audit by Event Menu Options

Event Menu	Option	Description
	Queue job finish	Identifies when a print job finishes printing.
	Queue service	Tracks the regular polling between the print server and queues serviced by its printers. Use this option only if you want to monitor communication between the print server and its queues. Otherwise, you'll see hundreds of entries for this routine task.
	Queue service abort	Tracks when the print queue service is aborted.
	Queue swap rights	Monitors any change of print queue rights.
	Queue remove job	Tracks when jobs are removed from the queue.
	Queue set job priority	Tracks when users change the service sequence of a job in the queue. You can see when operators move jobs ahead of other jobs.
	Queue set status	Tracks when a queue operator or network Administrator changes the status of a queue (which can be accomplished using PCONSOLE).
	Queue start job	Identifies when a job that has been created actually begins printing. Jobs that have begun will also appear during the Queue job service poll.
Server events	Change date/time	Tracks any change of the date or time from the file server console.
	Down server	Tracks when the server goes down.
	NLM add audit record	Tracks when an NLM running on the server adds a record to the audit file.

Event Menu	Option	Description
	NLM add user ID record	Tracks when an NLM running on the server adds a user to the NDS.
	Volume dismount	Tracks when a volume dismounts.
	Volume mount	Tracks when a volume is mounted. This and the Volume Dismount option are useful to track usage of a CD unit on the server. If you notice an excessive number of mounts and dismounts, consider adding a second CD unit.
User events (2)	Disable account	Tracks when a bindery user account is disabled for any reason.
	Grant trustee	Tracks when a bindery user is granted trustee rights.
	Log in user	Tracks when a bindery user logs in to the server.
	Log out user	Tracks when a bindery user logs out of the server.
	Remove trustee	Tracks when a bindery user has trustee rights removed.
	Terminate connection	Tracks when a bindery user connection is terminated.
	User space restrictions	Tracks when a bindery user has user space restrictions added or changed.

(1) Each event in this menu gives you the option Global, User and directory, and User or directory. As previously discussed, Global gives you the most data, and User and directory gives the least data. Please refer back to the "AUDITCON File Events Options" section.

(2) User events are only for bindery users. The users tracked by these options are user objects in the server's bindery context.

5. From the Audit configuration menu, choose the Audit by event menu. Choose any of the four categories: Audit by ... file events, ...QMS events, ... server events, or ... user events, as appropriate. Use the F8 key to switch all events on or off. Use the cursor keys to select individual events and the F10 key to switch the event on or off. Press Esc when finished.

6. From the Audit configuration menu, choose the Audit by file/directory menu to choose specific files or directories to audit. To audit the AUDITCON.EXE utility, for example, proceed as follows:

    a. Select the PUBLIC subdirectory and press Enter.

    b. Select the AUDITCON.EXE file and press F10.

    c. Continue to select files and directories as desired. Press Esc when done.

7. From the Audit configuration menu, choose the Audit by user menu to choose specific bindery users to audit.

8. You are now done configuring this volume for auditing. To exit AUDITCON, press Esc several times. Press Alt+F10 to exit immediately.

Configuring Directory Auditing

The procedure for configuring directory (NDS) auditing is simila–r to that of configuring volume auditing. The network Administrator first must enable the containers to be audited before the auditor is free to configure them. The auditor can be any user with Browse object rights to the target container(s). Before configuring directory auditing, the auditor first must type **AUDITCON**.

Here is the procedure to configure directory auditing:

1. From the AUDITCON main menu, choose Audit directory services. The Audit directory services menu appears.

2. From the Audit directory services menu, choose Change session context to move directly to a container. Otherwise, select Audit directory tree to browse the NDS tree structure. Your currently selected container is shown at the top of the screen.

3. From the Audit directory tree screen, select the desired container and press F10 to configure auditing. The Available audit options menu appears.

4. Before you can start configuring directory auditing for this container, you first must log in. From the Available audit options menu, choose Auditor container login. You are prompted for the container auditing password. After the appropriate password has been entered, press Enter. The Available audit options menu (see fig. 40.7) expands to include the options summarized in table 40.3.

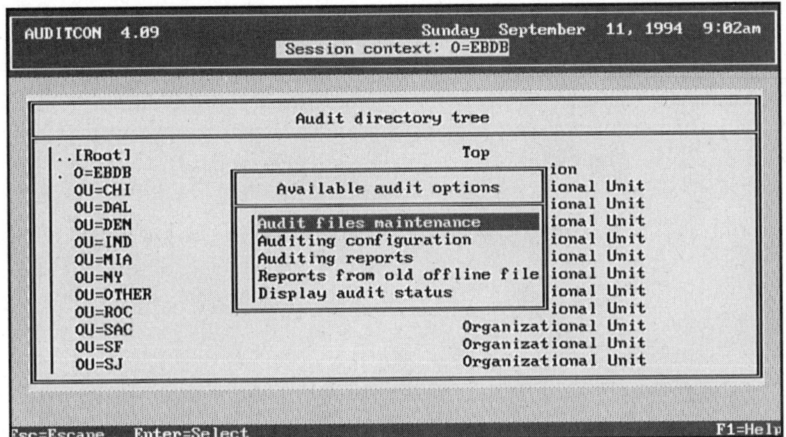

Figure 40.7

The Available audit options menu.

Table 40.3
Directory Auditing—Available Audit Options

Menu Option	Description
Audit files maintenance	Enables you to reset the audit file and perform operations on old audit files. These options are discussed in more detail in the "Auditing Maintenance" section.
Auditing configuration	Brings up the primary configuration menu, which includes the following options: Audit by DS events, Audit by user, Audit options configuration, Change audit password, Disable container auditing, and Display audit status. These options are summarized in table 40.4.
Auditing reports	Generates audit reports to a file or to the screen.
Reports from old offline file	Enables you to generate reports from an older audit file that you created at a previous time.
Display audit status	Displays the current status of auditing for this container.

Table 40.4 summarizes the options available in the Auditing configuration menu.

TABLE 40.4
Directory Auditing—Auditing Configuration Menu Options

Configuration Menu	Option	Description
Audit by DS events	Abort partition	Tracks when the partitioning operation was aborted.
	Add entry	Tracks when an entry is added to the NDS.
	Add partition	Tracks when a new partition is created.
	Add replica	Tracks when a partition is replicated.
	Change ACL	Tracks changes to the Access Control List (ACL). This is a critical indication that security rights have been changed.
	Change password	Tracks when someone changes a password.
	Change replica type	Tracks when the type of a replica is changed (from Read/Write to Master).
	Change security also equals	Tracks whenever a change an object's Security Also Equals property occurs. This occurs when a user changes to the security level of another user, for example.
	Change security equivalences	Tracks security equivalencies (to whom this object is equal in security).
	Change station restrictions	Tracks changes in physical login location restrictions.
	Disable user account	Tracks when a user account has been disabled.
	Enable user account	Tracks when a user account has been enabled.
	Intruder lockout change	Tracks changes in the intruder lockout status.

Configuration Menu	Option	Description
	Join partitions	Tracks when partitions have been joined.
	Log in user	Tracks when users log in.
	Log out user	Tracks when users log out.
	Move entry	Tracks when an object is moved to another container.
	Receive replica update	Tracks when Master replicas of partitions receive updates from Read/Write replicas.
	Remove entry	Tracks when an object is removed from the tree.
	Remove partition	Tracks when a partition is removed.
	Remove replica	Tracks when a replica is removed.
	Rename object	Tracks when an object is renamed.
	Repair time stamps	Tracks when time stamps are repaired (could indicate problem with time synchronization).
	Send replica update	Tracks when Master replicas of partitions send updates to Read/Write replicas. Useful when checking the integrity of the NDS over a WAN.
	Split partition	Tracks when a partition is split. Useful when trying to coordinate the creation of partitions. Generally, only one Administrator should be creating partitions and replicas within a single tree.
	User locked	Tracks when a user account has been locked. Could be from the Intruder Detection system.
	User unlocked	Tracks when a user account is unlocked after a lockout.

5. From the Audit by DS events menu, choose the NDS event that you want to audit and press F10 to enable auditing. Press F10 again to disable auditing for that event. Press F8 to enable auditing for all NDS events. When finished, press Esc to return to the Auditing configuration menu.

6. From the Auditing configuration menu, choose Audit by user to select users that you want to audit. The Audit directory tree users screen appears. Browse the NDS tree and select the users you want to audit. Press F10 to enable auditing of that user. When finished, press Esc to return to the Auditing configuration menu. Answer Yes when prompted whether you want to Save user audit changes.

7. You have now completed the directory auditing configuration. Press Esc several times or press Alt+F10 to exit AUDITCON.

Generating Audit Reports

After some time has elapsed, you will be ready to generate reports. (Do not expect to generate a report immediately: a network event must occur before you can produce a report.) The information you configured for auditing has now accumulated in either the volume audit file or in the NDS database. The reports menus for volume and directory auditing are the same. They both include the following primary options:

- Display audit status
- Edit report filter
- Report ... (sends report to a file)
- View ... (sends report to the screen)

The Auditing reports menu for volume auditing is displayed in figure 40.8.

To reach the volume Auditing reports menu, proceed as follows:

1. From the AUDITCON main menu, choose Change current server to select the server that contains the desired volume. From the AUDITCON main menu, choose Change current volume to select the desired volume. The currently selected server and volume are confirmed at the top center of the AUDITCON screen.

2. From the AUDITCON main menu, choose Auditor volume login. The Enter volume password input box appears. Enter the auditing password for this volume and press Enter. The Available audit options menu appears.

3. From the Available audit options menu, choose Auditing reports. The Auditing reports menu appears.

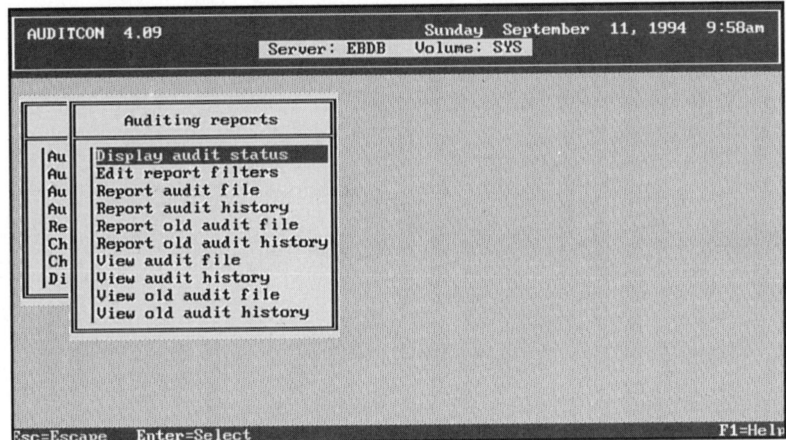

Figure 40.8

The Auditing reports menu.

To reach the directory Auditing reports menu, proceed as follows:

1. From the AUDITCON main menu, choose Audit directory services. The Audit directory services menu appears.
2. From the Audit directory services menu, choose Change session context to move directly to a container. Otherwise, choose Audit directory tree to browse the NDS tree structure. Your currently selected container is shown at the top of the screen.
3. From the Audit directory tree screen, select the desired container and press F10 to configure auditing. The Available audit options menu appears.
4. Before you can start configuring directory auditing for this container, you first must log in. From the Available audit options menu, choose Auditor container login. You are prompted for the container auditing password. After the appropriate password has been entered, press Enter. The Available audit options menu appears with additional options.

If you set all auditing passwords the same, you will only have to log in once to either volume auditing or directory auditing. If your passwords are different, you will have to log in to each volume and container separately.

continues

If you log in to volume auditing, container auditing, or both, and stay in AUDITCON, you will not be asked to log in to auditing again until you exit AUDITCON.

5. From the Available audit options menu, choose Auditing reports.

Note that auditing reports cannot be printed from AUDITCON. To generate a printout, you must do the following:

1. From the Auditing reports menu, select one of the Report ... options.
2. Enter a file name and path.
3. Exit AUDITCON when the report is finished.
4. Use NPRINT to send the report file to a print queue.

The next sections discuss each of the primary auditing reports options.

Audit Status

The first auditing report option is Display audit status. When you choose this option, the AUDIT STATUS screen appears, as shown in figure 40.9. Options include the following:

- **Auditing status** is either on or off, indicating whether auditing has been enabled for this volume or container.
- **Audit file size** is the current size of the audit file in bytes.
- **Audit file size threshold** is the size that the file is allowed to reach before warning messages are displayed.
- **Audit file maximum** size is the maximum size that the audit file is allowed to reach.
- **Audit history file size** is the current size of the Audit History File.
- **Audit record count** is the total number of entries in the audit file.
- **History record count** is the number of records in the Audit History File.

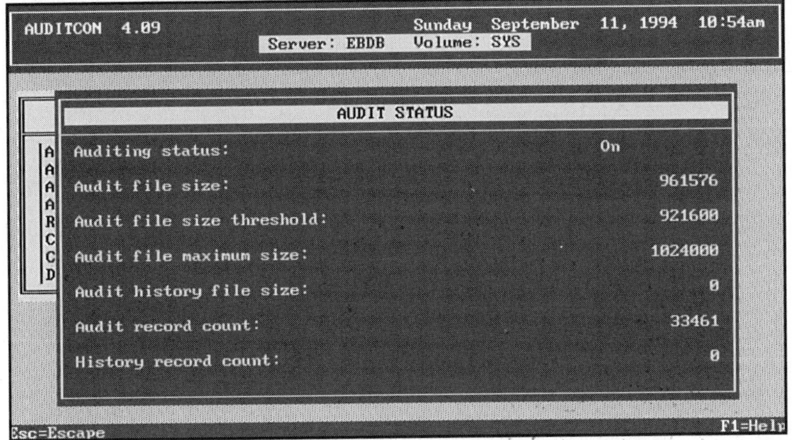

Figure 40.9

The Audit Status screen.

Report Filters

You can create report filters by selecting the Edit report filters option from the Auditing reports menu. A *report filter* is a restriction on information generated from any of the audit files. Create a new filter by pressing Insert. The Edit report filter menu appears, as shown in figure 40.10.

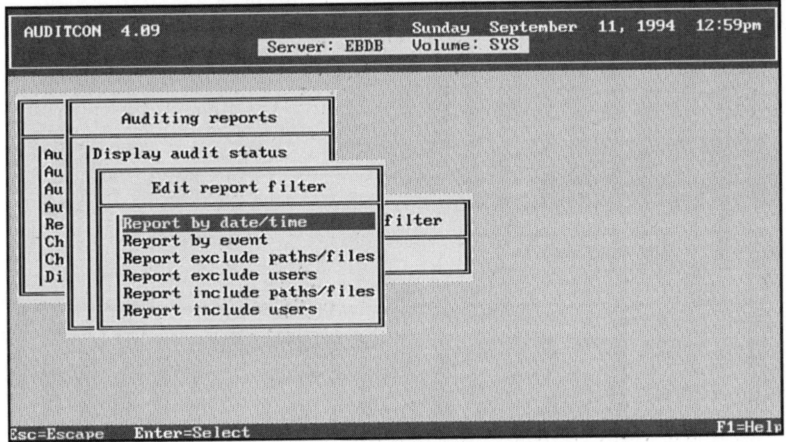

Figure 40.10

The Edit report filter menu.

With the Edit report filter menu, you can create restrictions on the amount of data generated in the report. Restrictions include by date and time, by event, by users, and by paths and files. The next sections summarize report filter options.

Report by Date/Time

The Report by date/time option enables you to set up a filter by date, time, or both. You can specify a starting and ending date and time for the report. The only events reported are those recorded during (and including) the indicated dates and times.

To set up a filter by date and/or time, proceed as follows:

1. From the Edit report filter menu, choose Report by date/time. The Report by date/time list appears.

2. From the Report by date/time list, press Insert. The Report by date/time dialog box appears, as show in figure 40.11.

3. In the Report by date/time dialog box, enter the desired Start date, Start time, End date, and End time. AUDITCON verifies that the date is accurate. If you enter **9-31-94**, for example, an error message alerts you that this is an invalid date (September only has 30 days).

4. When you finish entering dates and times, press Esc. You are returned to the Report by date/time list where a new entry appears with the selected dates and times. You can continue to add date and time restrictions until you have the desired dates and times for your report. Press Esc once again to return to the Edit report filter menu.

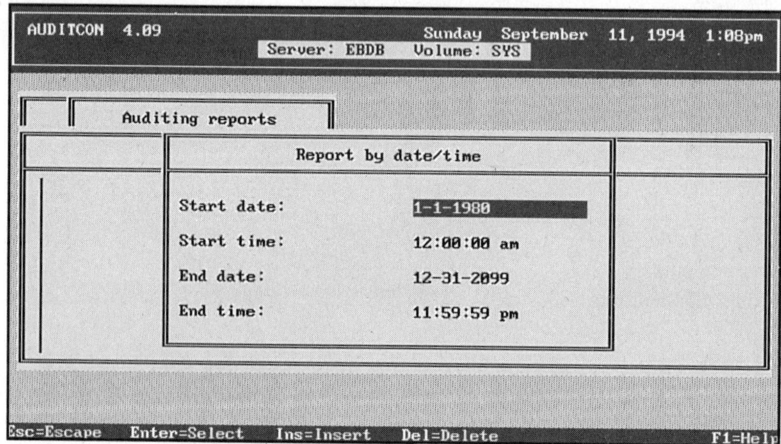

Figure 40.11
The Report by date/time dialog box.

Report by Event

You can select which events you want to report by clicking on Report by event from the Edit report filter menu. The menu that appears, as shown in figure 40.12, is similar to the menu used to configure auditing.

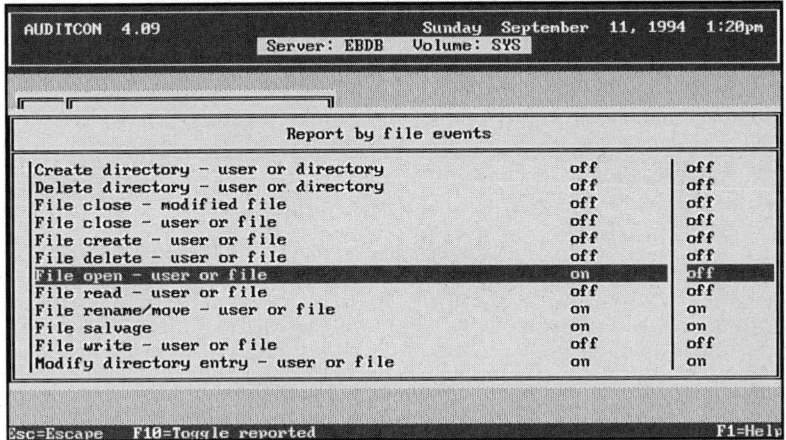

Figure 40.12

The Report by file events dialog box.

The difference is that two columns with on or off values are displayed. The first column represents whether this event has been configured for auditing.

- ◆ If this event is configured on, any event of this type will be recorded in the audit file and can be reported.
- ◆ If this event is configured off, even if you switch it on for reporting, no data will appear.

Select the event to be reported and press the F10 key. The value in the second column, to the far right of the screen, switches between on and off. An example of this screen is shown in figure 40.12.

Press Esc when finished. You can continue to select any events that are appropriate for your report. When done, press Esc again to return to the Edit report filter menu.

Report Include or Exclude Paths/Files

When you choose Report exclude paths/files from the Edit report filter menu, press Insert to add a directory or file to the list. This list causes AUDITCON not to report any data on files or directories in this list. Click on Report include paths/files from the Edit report filter menu to add specific directories or files to the list. The following rules hold true for these options:

- ◆ If no files or directories are on the Exclude list, AUDITCON assumes all files and directories should be reported.
- ◆ If some files or directories are on the Exclude list, AUDITCON assumes all files and directories should be reported except those on the list.
- ◆ If no files or directories are on the Include list, AUDITCON assumes all files and directories should be reported.
- ◆ If some files or directories are on the Include list, AUDITCON assumes no files and directories should be reported except those on the list.

To exclude a file or directory, proceed as follows:

1. From the Edit report filter menu, choose Report exclude paths/files. The Report exclude paths/files list appears.
2. From the Report exclude paths/files list, press Insert. You are prompted for a directory or file name (including its complete path). If unsure of where the directory or file is located, press Insert again and browse through the directory structure.

   Wild cards are permissible. If you want to have all batch files excluded, for example, type ***.BAT** into the list.
3. After you have entered or found the name of the directory or file, press Enter. The directory or file appears on the list and is excluded from the report.

To include a file or directory, proceed as follows:

1. From the Edit report filter menu, choose Report include paths/files. The Report include paths/files list appears.
2. From the Report include paths/files list, press Insert. You are prompted to enter a directory or file name (including its complete path). If unsure of where the directory or file is located, press Insert again and browse through the directory structure.

   Wild cards are permissible. If you want to have all executable files included, for example, type ***.EXE** into the list.
3. After you have typed or found the name of the directory or file, press Enter. The directory or file appears on the list and is included in the report.

You must remove the asterisk from the Report include paths/files list if you want to have *only* those files and directories on the list included in the report. Otherwise, the effect of the asterisk is to have *all* files and directories included.

When you have finished including or excluding files or directories, press Esc to return to the Edit report filter menu.

Report Include or Exclude Users

The Report exclude users or the Report include users options in the Edit report filter menu serve a similar purpose to that of including or excluding files. Users on the Exclude list do not appear in the report. Users on the Include list do appear in the report.

To exclude a user, proceed as follows:

1. From the Edit report filter menu, choose Report exclude users. The Report exclude users list appears.

2. From the Report exclude users list, press Insert. You are prompted for the name of the user to be excluded. If unsure of the user name, press Insert again and browse through the user list.

   When generating a volume auditing report, the list of users are those in the server's bindery emulation contexts. When generating a directory auditing report, the list of users consists of any user in the NDS tree.

   Wild cards are permissible. If you want to exclude only users whose login names begin with the letter B, for example, add **B*** to the list.

3. After you have the desired user name(s), press Enter. The user names that appear on the list are excluded from the report.

To include a user, proceed as follows:

1. From the Edit report filter menu, choose Report include users. The Report include users list appears.

2. From the Report include users list, press Insert. You are prompted for the user to be included. If unsure of the user name, press Insert again and browse through the user list.

   When generating a volume auditing report, the list of users are those in the server's bindery emulation contexts. When generating a directory auditing report, the list of users are those in the NDS tree.

Wild cards are permissible. If you want to include only users whose login names begin with the letter D, for example, add **D*** to the list.

3. Once you have entered the desired user name(s), press Enter. The user names appear on the list and are included from the report.

Report File

The Report audit file, Report audit history, Report old audit file, and Report old audit history options enable you to generate an audit report to a file. A printed report can be generated outside of AUDITCON. When you select any of the four Report ... options, you are asked to Enter report destination file name. Enter the drive, directory, and file name of the report file and press Enter. You are then presented with a list of report filters. Choose a filter and press Enter. AUDITCON generates the requested report.

Files that can be reported include the following:

- Audit file
- Audit History file
- Old Audit file
- Old Audit History file

You must have Write, Create, and Erase directory trustee rights in the directory where the report file is to be created. You also must have these rights in your current directory. If there is a problem, AUDITCON reports that it is unable to create the report file.

If you plan to report either of the Old files, you will see a list of files ordered by the date they were created. This is the date that the auditor chose to reset the Audit or Audit History file.

View File

The View ... options are similar to the Report ... options except that the report appears on screen instead of in a file. The Audit History file is shown in figure 40.13. As you can see, dates are displayed across the top, followed by events for that day. While viewing a file, you have the option of selecting a report filter that you created earlier.

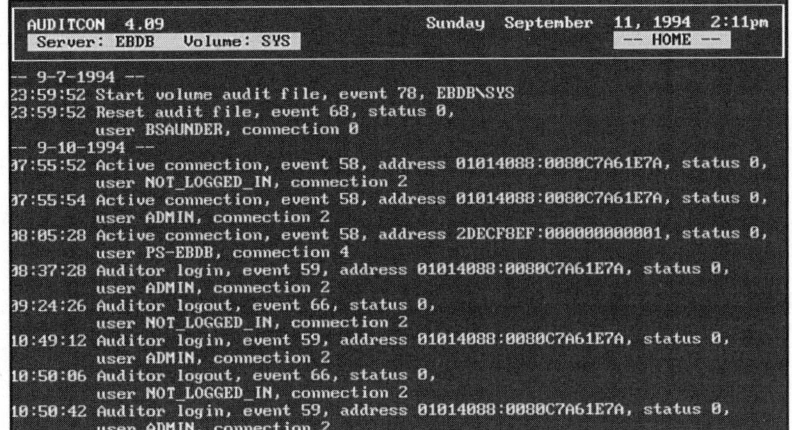
```
AUDITCON  4.09                              Sunday  September  11, 1994  2:11pm
 Server: EBDB   Volume: SYS                                   -- HOME --
-- 9-7-1994 --
23:59:52 Start volume audit file, event 78, EBDB\SYS
23:59:52 Reset audit file, event 68, status 0,
        user BSAUNDER, connection 0
-- 9-10-1994 --
07:55:52 Active connection, event 58, address 01014088:0080C7A61E7A, status 0,
        user NOT_LOGGED_IN, connection 2
07:55:54 Active connection, event 58, address 01014088:0080C7A61E7A, status 0,
        user ADMIN, connection 2
08:05:28 Active connection, event 58, address 2DECF8EF:000000000001, status 0,
        user PS-EBDB, connection 4
08:37:28 Auditor login, event 59, address 01014088:0080C7A61E7A, status 0,
        user ADMIN, connection 2
09:24:26 Auditor logout, event 66, status 0,
        user NOT_LOGGED_IN, connection 2
10:49:12 Auditor login, event 59, address 01014088:0080C7A61E7A, status 0,
        user ADMIN, connection 2
10:50:06 Auditor logout, event 66, status 0,
        user NOT_LOGGED_IN, connection 2
10:50:42 Auditor login, event 59, address 01014088:0080C7A61E7A, status 0,
        user ADMIN, connection 2
```

Figure 40.13

The View audit history screen.

If you happen to press Insert when selecting a filter on the way to generating a Report... or View... of an audit file, the Edit report filter menu appears. You are not allowed to save any changes when exiting this menu—you cannot create and save a report filter when going to report or view an audit file. If you want to edit and save a report filter, you must use the Edit report filter menu option.

Fields in an Audit Report

As you saw in the previous example, the fields in an audit report are extremely cryptic. The next section, "Using External Programming to Massage Audit Reports," discusses how to extract information to make it more presentable. This section discusses the contents of the report.

The following is a sample of a directory audit report:

```
11:34:06 Active connection, event 58, address 01014088:0080C7A61E7A, status 0,
         user CN=Admin.O=EBDB, replica 1
12:49:30 Log in user, event 109, address 01014088:0080C7014103, status 0,
         user CN=BSaunder.OU=NY.O=EBDB, replica 1
15:03:26 Log out user, event 110, status 0, user CN=BSaunder.OU=NY.O=EBDB,
         replica 1
```

A volume audit report example follows:

```
14:24:06 Queue job service, event 35, queue Q_MAIN, job , type 0, status 213,
         user PS-EBDB, connection 3
14:24:06 Queue job service, event 35, queue Q_MAIN, job , type FFFF, status 213,
         user PS-EBDB, connection 3
14:26:24 Open file, event 27, PUBLIC\NDIR.EXE, rights RE, status 0,
         user ADMIN, connection 5
```

Each record in the audit report begins with a timestamp. The first eight characters of each line is a timestamp in 24-hour format. Subsequent fields are separated by commas. The next two fields in the report are related. Following the timestamp is a description of the event, followed by the event code. In the first example, you see `Active connection` followed by `event 58`. You can see from this that event code 58 means "Active connection." An *active connection* is when a logical attachment to the server was active at the time the audit process was configured. New logins and logouts are also reported if configured.

The fields that follow (fields 4 through the end of the line) vary depending on the nature of the event. In the case of a Log in user event, for example, the fields following the event number indicate the following:

- Network and node address from where the user logged in
- Login status (0 = successful login)
- Complete NDS user name
- Replica used to authenticate the login

In the case of a QMS event, fields 4 through 9 (the fields which follow the event code) indicate the following:

- Name of the print queue being polled (queue Q_MAIN).
- Nature of the queue service. In the previous example, this is `job`.
- The type of poll. The 0 indicates the first query, and FFFF indicates the last query for this poll.
- Status code (status 213).
- User name. If this is a routine service poll, the user name is the name of the print server (user PS-EBDB).
- Connection number for that user (connection 3).

As you can see from the samples, there is no indication of date. The only indication of date is the start date you indicate in a report filter. After that, it is up to you to keep track of when the timestamp goes past 23:59:59 (11:59:59 p.m.).

Using External Programming To Massage Audit Reports

The first step in developing a program to massage the audit report data file is to parse the data into some sort of database or table. Because the nature of the fields, beginning with the fourth field, can vary widely, you need to parse the data into some sort of generic field. Alternatively, you can analyze the type of event and make a logical decision on which field to place the data. If the event is related to logins and logouts, for example, you know that one of the fields will have the username. You can create a field USERNAME, and have your program parse for the letters "CN=" or the keyword "user."

Here is a sample QBASIC program PARSE.BAS that parses the audit file and produces an ASCII comma delimited file. In the comma delimited file, each field is enclosed in quotes and a comma separates fields. The comma delimited file can then be imported into dBASE using the APPEND FROM ... DELIMITED option, or into a spreadsheet, such as Excel, using the CSV (Comma Separated Values) format. The program also produces a number in front of each line that represents the day. Because the audit report does not include date information, the program starts with "0," which represents the first day. As the report moves into the next day, the day counter is incremented. "1" represents the second day, "2" the third day, and so forth. In a dBASE program you can use date arithmetic to assign a start date to the first day. The day counter can then be added to the start date to arrive at the correct date.

```
REM
REM     Title:              PARSE.BAS
REM     Date:               9-14-94
REM     Author:             D. Bierer
REM     Notes:              Parses file produced as AUDITCON report
REM     Inputs:             i$ = Input Filename
REM     Outputs:            o$ = Output Filename
REM
REM
REM     Input Syntax:
REM             QBASIC /RUN parse < input_filename
REM
```

```
REM     Input file has the following syntax:
REM             1st line = name of audit file
REM             2nd line = name of output file
REM                         use "&&" if you only want output to screen
REM
REM     Outputs a total of 20 fields
REM

REM
REM     Initialize variables
REM
maxfields = 16
day = 0
inhour = 0
prevhour = 0

REM
REM     1st line of input_filename has name of input file
REM     2nd line (optional) of input_filename has name of output file
REM
INPUT "Enter Name of Input File ", i$
INPUT "Enter Name of Output File or &&& for Screen Output ", o$

REM
REM     If no input filename, error
REM
IF i$ = "" THEN
     GOSUB 3000
     RETURN
END IF

REM
REM     Add end flag and reopen for input
REM
OPEN "A", 1, i$
PRINT #1, "::END::"
CLOSE #1
OPEN "I", 1, i$

REM
REM     If no output filename, assume output to scrn
REM
```

```
IF LEFT$(o$, 1) = "&" THEN
     scrn = 1
ELSE
     scrn = 0
     OPEN "O", 2, o$
END IF

REM
REM     Parse input file
REM
100
IF EOF(1) THEN 2000
LINE INPUT #1, l$
IF LEN(l$) <= 8 THEN 2000

REM
REM     Check for End of File
REM
200
m$ = ""
IF EOF(1) THEN 300
LINE INPUT #1, m$

REM
REM     Check to see if ":" in LINE2
REM
300
IF INSTR(m$, ":") > 0 THEN
     IF LEN(l$) <= 8 THEN 2000
     GOSUB 4000
     l$ = m$
     GOTO 200
END IF
l$ = l$ + m$
IF LEN(l$) <= 8 THEN 2000
GOTO 200

REM
REM     Close Files and Quit
REM
2000    CLOSE #1
2010    IF scrn > 0 THEN PRINT "Done..." ELSE CLOSE #2
```

```
2020    SYSTEM

REM
REM     Display Help scrn if Error
REM
3000
PRINT "-----------------------------------------------------------------------"
PRINT
PRINT "  Unable to open input file..."
PRINT
PRINT "  Usage:"
PRINT "         QBASIC /RUN parse < input_filename"
PRINT
PRINT "    Input file INPUT_FILENAME has the following syntax:"
PRINT "             1st line = name of audit file"
PRINT "             2nd line = name of output file"
PRINT "                        use && if you only want output to screen"
PRINT
PRINT "    Outputs a total of 20 fields per line"
PRINT
PRINT "-----------------------------------------------------------------------"
RETURN

REM
REM     Process Line
REM
4000

REM
REM     Initialize variables
REM
u$ = ""

REM
REM     Get hour
REM
inhour = VAL(LEFT$(l$, 2))

REM
REM     Process change of day
REM
```

```
5000
IF inhour < prevhour THEN day = day + 1
prevhour = inhour

REM
REM     Output day
REM
u$ = CHR$(34) + STR$(day) + CHR$(34) + CHR$(44)

REM
REM     Output time
REM
u$ = u$ + CHR$(34) + LEFT$(l$, 8) + CHR$(34) + CHR$(44)

REM
REM     Output event description
REM
u$ = u$ + CHR$(34) + MID$(l$, 10, INSTR(l$, CHR$(44)) - 10) + CHR$(34) +
CHR$(44)

REM
REM     Output event number
REM
x = INSTR(l$, "event")
IF x >= LEN(l$) THEN
     u$ = u$ + CHR$(34) + "00" + CHR$(34) + CHR$(44)
ELSE
       u$ = u$ + CHR$(34) + MID$(l$, x + 6, INSTR(x, l$, ",") - x - 6) +
CHR$(34) + CHR$(44)
END IF

REM
REM     Output remainder of data
REM
x = INSTR(l$, "event")
pos1 = INSTR(x, l$, CHR$(44)) + 1
pos2 = INSTR(pos1, l$, CHR$(44))
fieldcnt = 4

REM
REM     Keep appending fields until end of string is reached
REM
```

```
4500
IF pos2 = 0 OR pos2 >= LEN(l$) OR pos1 = pos2 THEN GOTO 4600

REM
REM     Pull next field and get rid of leading blanks
REM
a$ = MID$(l$, pos1, pos2 - pos1)
4550
IF LEFT$(a$, 1) = " " THEN
     a$ = MID$(a$, 2)
     GOTO 4550
END IF


REM
REM     Surround field with quotes and a comma, reposition pointers
REM
u$ = u$ + CHR$(34) + a$ + CHR$(34) + CHR$(44)
pos1 = INSTR(pos2, l$, CHR$(44)) + 1
pos2 = INSTR(pos1, l$, CHR$(44))
fieldcnt = fieldcnt + 1
GOTO 4500

REM
REM     Output last field
REM
4600
u$ = u$ + CHR$(34) + MID$(l$, pos1) + CHR$(34) + CHR$(44)
fieldcnt = fieldcnt + 1

REM
REM     Pad remaining fields
REM
4700
u$ = u$ + CHR$(34) + " " + CHR$(34) + CHR$(44)
fieldcnt = fieldcnt + 1
IF fieldcnt < maxfields THEN 4700
u$ = u$ + CHR$(34) + " " + CHR$(34)

REM
REM     Output to File if OK
REM
```

```
IF scrn = 0 THEN PRINT #2, u$ ELSE PRINT u$

RETURN
```

The following is a dBASE IV program (ACCESS.PRG) that imports the comma delimited file produced by PARSE.BAS into a database file (ACCESS.DBF). The program prints a report, sorted by user, of which files he opened and when.

The preceding PARSE.BAS program consistently produces an output of 20 fields per line. The first four fields are as follows:

- ◆ Day number, starting with 0
- ◆ Time
- ◆ Event description
- ◆ Event number

The remaining fields vary. If there was no data to correspond with a field, the PARSE.BAS program produces a null value (“ ”). Here is the dBASE program:

```
*      Title:     ACCESS.PRG
*      Date:      10/15/94
*      Author:    D. Bierer
*      Notes:     Produces a report, by user, of which files they opened
*      Files:     ACCESSIN.TXT = Temp file to input parameters into PARSE.BAS
*                 ACCESSOU.TXT = Output file for PARSE.BAS
*                 ACCESS.DBF   = Existing database
*                 ACCESS.FRM   = Report Format File
*


*
*      Set Environment
*
SET CENTURY ON
SET TALK OFF
SET SAFETY OFF

*
*      Ask user which file is to be used for input
*
CLEAR
mcorrect = .F.
```

```
mfile = SPACE(20) + "AUDITDAT.TXT"
mdate = DATE()
mprint = .F.
minput = "Y"
*
*     Loop Until User Input is Correct
*
DO WHILE .NOT. mcorrect
     @ 07,10 SAY "Enter Report Parameters"
     @ 08,10 SAY "---------------------"
     @ 10,10 SAY "Enter Name of Audit File: "
     @ 10,42 GET mfile PICTURE "!!!!!!!!!!!!!!!!!!!!!!!!!!!!!!!!!"
     @ 11,10 SAY "Enter Starting Date of Report: "
     @ 11,42 GET mdate PICTURE "99/99/9999"
     @ 12,10 SAY "Report to Printer (Y/N)? "
     @ 12,42 GET mprint PICTURE "Y"
     @ 13,10 SAY "Is this correct (Y/N/Q)? "
     @ 13,42 GET minput PICTURE "!"
     READ
     *
     *     Quit if "Q"
     *
     IF minput = "Q"
          RETURN
     ENDIF
     mcorrect = IIF(minput = "Y", .T., .F.)
ENDDO

*
*     Test ACCESSIN.TXT Temporary File
*
mAccessfile = 0
mAccessfile = FCREATE("ACCESSIN.TXT", "W")
IF mAccessfile = 0
     ?
     ? "Error Writing to ACCESSIN.TXT Temporary File..."
     RETURN
ENDIF
mcorrect = FCLOSE(mAccessfile)
```

```
IF .NOT. mcorrect
     ?
     ? "Error Writing to ACCESSIN.TXT Temporary File..."
     RETURN
ENDIF

*
*     Test ACCESSOU.TXT Temporary File
*
mAccessfile = 0
mAccessfile = FCREATE("ACCESSOU.TXT", "W")
IF mAccessfile = 0
     ?
     ? "Error Writing to ACCESSOU.TXT Temporary File..."
     RETURN
ENDIF
mcorrect = FCLOSE(mAccessfile)
IF .NOT. mcorrect
     ?
     ? "Error Writing to ACCESSOU.TXT Temporary File..."
     RETURN
ENDIF

*
*     Check AUDITCON input file for PARSE.BAS
*
mfile = LTRIM(mfile)
minputfile = 0
minputfile = FOPEN(mfile, "R")
IF minputfile = 0
     ?
     ? "Error Opening " + mfile + "..."
     RETURN
ENDIF
mcorrect = FCLOSE(minputfile)
IF .NOT. mcorrect
     ?
     ? "Error Opening " + mfile + "..."
     RETURN
ENDIF
```

```
*
*     Produce input file for PARSE.BAS.  Write
*     Access filename
*
RUN echo &mfile >ACCESSIN.TXT
RUN echo ACCESSOU.TXT >>ACCESSIN.TXT
RUN echo ... >>ACCESSIN.TXT

*
*     Call QBASIC and run the PARSE.BAS program
*     File INPUT.TXT provides Audit File and Access Filenames
*          Input File = value of variable MFILE
*          Access File = temp file ACCESS.TXT
*
CLEAR
?
? "Running QBASIC Parse Program..."
RUN qbasic /run parse.bas <ACCESSIN.TXT

*
*     Append the input into AUDIT.DBF and erase temp file
*
USE Access EXCLUSIVE
ZAP
APPEND FROM AccessOu.txt DELIMITED

*
*     Sort the data by username
*     Change FIELD16 to date by adding DAY to MDATE entered above
*     NOTE: this requires a knowledge of where to expect the
*          username in the input data (field4)
*      NOTE: Event number 27 = Open File
*
SORT ON field4, day, time TO Access2 FOR event_num = 27
USE Access2
REPLACE field16 WITH DTOC(mdate + day)

*
*     Produce the report
*
```

```
IF mprint
     REPORT FORM Access TO PRINT
ELSE
     REPORT FORM Access
ENDIF
USE

*
*     Erase Temp Files
*
ERASE Access2.DBF
ERASE AccessIn.txt
ERASE AccessOu.txt

RETURN
```

Here is the database structure used by the program:

```
Structure for database: F:\DATA\NRP\INSIDE4\ACCESS.DBF
Number of data records:       0
Date of last update   : 10/16/1994
Field  Field Name  Type        Width    Dec    Index
    1  DAY         Numeric         2                N
    2  TIME        Character       8                N
    3  EVENT       Character      28                N
    4  EVENT_NUM   Numeric         3                N
    5  FIELD1      Character      40                N
    6  FIELD2      Character      40                N
    7  FIELD3      Character      40                N
    8  FIELD4      Character      40                N
    9  FIELD5      Character      40                N
   10  FIELD6      Character      40                N
   11  FIELD7      Character      40                N
   12  FIELD8      Character      30                N
   13  FIELD9      Character      20                N
   14  FIELD10     Character      20                N
   15  FIELD11     Character      20                N
   16  FIELD12     Character      20                N
   17  FIELD13     Character      20                N
   18  FIELD14     Character      20                N
   19  FIELD15     Character      20                N
   20  FIELD16     Character      20                N
** Total **                      512
```

The last example, LOGINS.XLM, is an Excel macro that imports a file LOGIN.CSV produced by PARSE.BAS, which produces a chart tracking the number of logins by date. The chart produced is illustrated in figure 40.14.

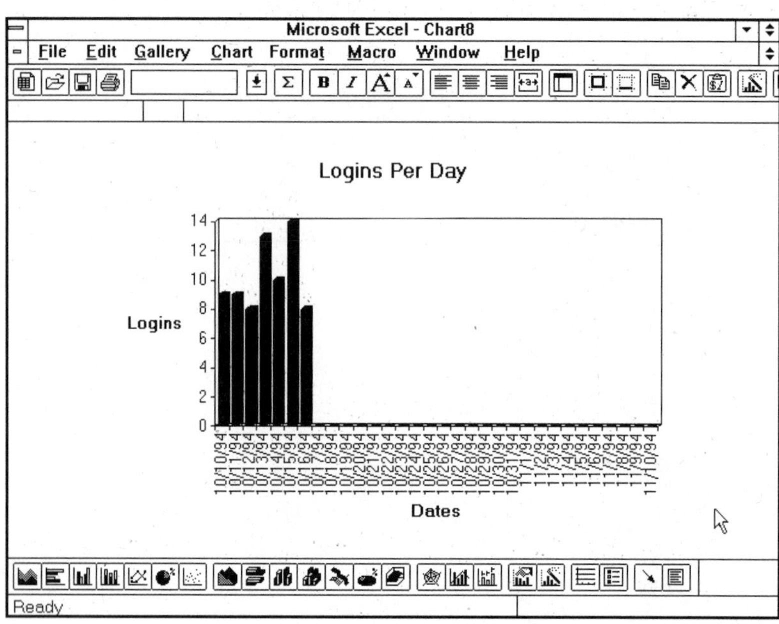

Figure 40.14
An Excel chart produced by LOGINS.XLM.

To run the macro, you must first parse the Audit file into a file of type CSV (Comma Separated Values). Proceed as follows:

1. From the DOS prompt, create a parameter file as follows:

```
COPY CON in_filename
audit_filename
output_filename.CSV

<Ctrl+Z>
```

in_filename is the name of the parameter file to feed to PARSE.BAS. *audit_filename* is the name of the Audit file you produced in AUDITCON. The default is AUDITDAT.TXT. *Output_filename.CSV* is the name of the file to load into Excel.

To stop the COPY CON command and create the file, press Ctrl+Z, or press the F6 key, and then press ENTER. A new parameter file is now created.

2. Run PARSE.BAS with the parameter file as follows:

   ```
   QBASIC /RUN PARSE.BAS <in_filename>
   ```

   You now have a parsed file in CSV format.

3. From Windows, run Excel. The Excel main menu appears.

4. From the Excel main menu, run the macro.

Here is a printout of the macro. You also can download this file from the Macmillan Computer Publishing forum on CompuServe. After you access the forum (GO MACMILLAN), you can find the files for this and other networking books in the Networking and Comms library.

```
LOGINS (L)
=OPEN("F:LOGIN.CSV")
=SELECT.END(4)
=SELECT("R[2]C")
=FORMULA("=NOW()-R[-2]C")
=FORMAT.NUMBER("m/d/yy")
=DEFINE.NAME("DDATE","=R109C1")
=SELECT("R[-108]C")
=SELECT.END(2)
=SELECT("RC[2]")
=FORMULA("0")
=SELECT("RC[1]")
=FORMULA("=RC[-1]+1")
=COPY()
; Note that in the next line, the macro assumes
; 31 days.  If you wish to chart a longer period
; of time, change the RC[30] to a larger number
=SELECT("RC[1]:RC[30]")
=PASTE()
=CANCEL.COPY()
=SELECT("R[1]C[-2]")
=FORMULA("=IF(R[-1]C1=R1C,IF(R[-1]C4=109,1,0),0)")
=DEFINE.NAME("FIRST","=R2C19")
=COPY()
=SELECT("RC:R[107]C[31]")
=PASTE()
=CANCEL.COPY()
```

```
=SELECT("R[1]C")
=SELECT.END(4)
=SELECT("R[1]C")
=FORMULA("=DDATE+R[-109]C")
=FORMAT.NUMBER("m/d/yy")
=SELECT("R[1]C")
=FORMULA("=SUM(R[-109]C:R[-2]C)")
=SELECT("R[-1]C:RC")
=COPY()
=SELECT("RC:R[1]C[31]")
=PASTE()
=CANCEL.COPY()
=NEW(2,2)
=GALLERY.3D.COLUMN(1)
=ATTACH.TEXT(1)
=FORMAT.FONT(0,1,FALSE,"MS Sans Serif",12,TRUE,FALSE,FALSE,FALSE)
=FORMULA("=""Logins Per Day""")
=ATTACH.TEXT(2)
=FORMAT.FONT(0,1,FALSE,"MS Sans Serif",10,TRUE,FALSE,FALSE,FALSE)
=FORMULA("=""Logins""")
=ATTACH.TEXT(4)
=FORMAT.FONT(0,1,FALSE,"MS Sans Serif",10,TRUE,FALSE,FALSE,FALSE)
=FORMULA("=""Dates""")
=SELECT("")
=RETURN()
```

Maintaining Audit Files

A certain amount of auditing maintenance should be performed. The key points are as follows:

- Limiting the audit file in size
- Enabling multiple auditors to use AUDITCON at the same time
- Resetting the audit file

To limit the volume audit file's size, proceed as follows:

1. From the AUDITCON main menu, choose Change current server to select the server that contains the desired volume. From the AUDITCON main menu, choose Change current volume to select the desired volume. The currently selected server and volume are confirmed at the top center of the AUDITCON screen.

2. From the AUDITCON main menu, choose Auditor volume login. The Enter volume password input box appears. Enter the auditing password for this volume and press Enter. The Available audit options menu appears.

3. From the Available audit options menu, choose Auditing configuration. The Auditing configuration menu appears.

4. From the Auditing configuration menu, choose Audit options configuration. The Audit configuration dialog box appears, as shown in figure 40.15.

5. As you can see from the Audit configuration dialog box, the default size of the volume audit file is 1 MB (1,024,000 bytes). Press Enter and use the backspace key to erase this number. Enter the desired size for the audit file, and then press Enter to register the change.

6. Press Esc several times (or press Alt+F10) to exit AUDITCON.

Table 40.5 summarizes the other options in the Audit configuration dialog box.

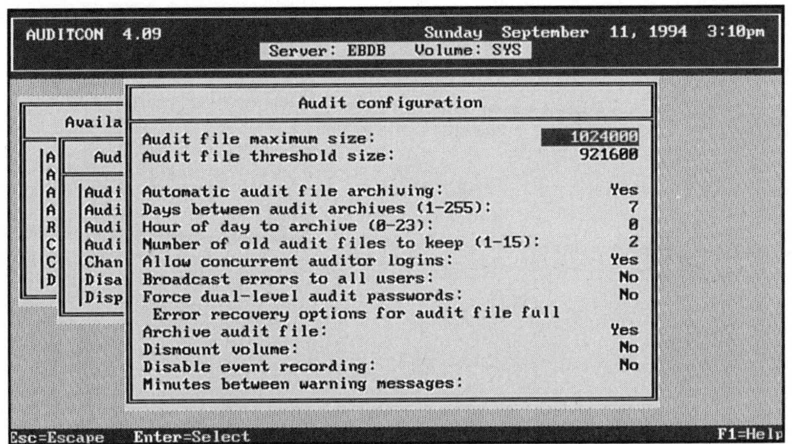

Figure 40.15

The Audit configuration dialog box.

Table 40.5
Audit Options Configuration

Menu Option	Description
Audit file maximum size	Size in bytes the audit file is allowed to reach.
Audit file threshold size	Size the audit file can reach before warning messages (or other Error recovery options) are activated.
Automatic audit file archiving	Answer Yes if you want NetWare to automatically reset the audit file after it reaches its maximum size. The file then becomes an Old Audit File. Answer No if automatic archiving violates the security policy of your organization. In extreme cases, set Automatic archiving to No and Dismount volume to Yes to prevent the system from being used if auditing is not available.
Days between audit archives	You can set the number of days, from 1 to 255, before the system automatically archives the audit file. This is only valid if Automatic archive is set to Yes.
Hour of day to archive	If set to Yes, sets when the automatic archive is to take place. The default of 0 indicates midnight.
Number of old audit files to keep	You can set the number of old archive files to maintain, from 1 to 15.
Allow concurrent auditor logins	If set to Yes, you can have more than one auditor using AUDITCON at the same time.
Broadcast errors to all users	Set this option to Yes to send broadcast messages to all users when the audit file is greater in size than the value indicated in the Archive file threshold size field.
Force dual-level audit passwords	If set to Yes, the auditor must know one password to perform auditing and another password to use this dialog box (the Audit

Menu Option	Description
	configuration dialog box). This is an additional level of security that tends to restrain the abilities of the auditor somewhat.
Archive audit file	If set to Yes, causes the automatic archive to take place if the audit file reaches maximum size before the Days between audit archives value has been reached.
Dismount volume	In extreme cases (such as top secret government installations or organizations with high security requirements), set this value to Yes; doing so ensures that the volume is not used if it cannot be audited.
Disable event recording	Set this value to Yes if you do not want to archive the audit file and do not care if auditing is taking place.
Minutes between warning messages	Adjusts the number of minutes between messages if the audit file exceeds the size set by the Threshold size parameter.

The same audit options configuration is available for directory auditing. The size of the audit file is especially critical because this data is stored in the NDS database. NDS data is then replicated throughout the network to all replicas of the partition that contain the containers being audited. To minimize the amount of data going across the network during the NDS replica update process, set the size of the audit file to a lower value. You can compensate for the loss of audit data by setting Automatic Archiving to Yes and increasing the number of old audit files to keep.

The audit file is reset automatically if you set the Automatic archiving parameter to Yes. You might want to reset the file manually in some cases. The following is the procedure for directory auditing:

1. From the AUDITCON main menu, choose Audit directory services. The Audit directory services menu appears.

2. From the Audit directory services menu, choose Change session context to move directly to a container. Otherwise, choose Audit directory tree to browse the NDS tree structure. Your currently selected container appears at the top of the screen.

3. From the Audit directory tree screen, select the desired container and press F10 to configure auditing. The Available audit options menu appears.

4. Before you can reset the directory auditing file, you must first log in. From the Available audit options menu, choose Auditor container login. You are prompted for the container auditing password. After you type the appropriate password, press Enter. The Available audit options menu appears with additional options.

5. From the Available audit options menu, choose Auditing configuration. The Auditing configuration menu appears.

6. From the Auditing configuration menu, choose Audit files maintenance. The Audit files maintenance menu appears (see fig. 40.16).

7. From the Audit files maintenance menu, choose Reset audit data file. The contents of the current audit file are copied into the old audit file. The current audit file is cleared. Press Esc several times (or Alt+F10) to exit AUDITCON.

Table 40.6 summarizes the other options in the Audit files maintenance menu.

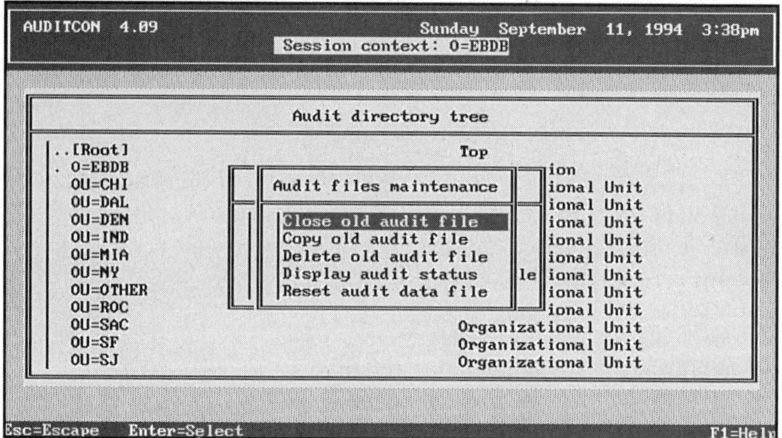

Figure 40.16
The Audit files maintenance menu.

Table 40.6
Audit Files Maintenance Menu

Menu Option	Description
Close old audit file	Updates the status of the old audit file from open to closed. NetWare 4.1.0*x* networks keep this file hidden and always open to prevent tampering. This option closes the file so that it can be copied. You do not need this option for old audit files in NetWare 4.1*x* networks.

Menu Option	Description
Copy old audit file	Enables you to copy the old audit to another file name and location for storage. This is wise if you want to maintain a history of the system for an extended period of time to establish baseline performance statistics. The file is copied in its original compressed, encrypted format.
Delete old audit file	Deletes an old audit file.
Display audit status	Displays the status of auditing in this container or volume.
Reset audit data file	Copies the contents of the current audit file to an old audit file. Clears the contents of the current audit file.

The Audit files maintenance menu for volume auditing is identical in appearance. The volume auditing menu only affects the audit files maintained at the root of the volume. The directory Audit files maintenance menu affects the audit files maintained in the NDS database.

Auditing the Auditor

Sometimes you need to audit the auditor, such as when you have outside auditors and want to keep them honest. To audit the auditor, you can generate a report of the Audit History file. The data contained in the Audit History file report simply indicates when the auditor used AUDITCON and when the audit file was reset. If you find that the audit file has been reset whenever the outside auditor comes to review your network, you might want to determine why. With automatic archiving, there is no reason to reset the audit file.

The following is an example of the Audit History file:

```
14:23:52 Start volume audit file, event 78, EBDB\SYS
14:23:52 Reset audit file, event 68, status 0,
         user PS-EBDB, connection 0
14:24:06 Active connection, event 58, address 2DECF8EF:000000000001, status 0,
         user PS-EBDB, connection 3
14:26:18 Active connection, event 58, address 01014088:0080C7A61E7A, status 0,
         user ADMIN, connection 5
14:26:18 Auditor logout, event 66, status 0, user ADMIN, connection 5
14:27:46 Auditor login, event 59, address 01014088:0080C7A61E7A, status 0,
         user ADMIN, connection 5
```

Summary

This chapter gave you a detailed coverage of NetWare 4.1 auditing. You learned several reasons why you might need to set up auditing, including monitoring security changes, monitoring activity of users and files, and justifying network usage. Auditing is performed using the AUDITCON.EXE utility. The procedure to set up auditing is for the network Administrator to enable auditing. A user with at least Browse object rights to the container or volume to be audited can then perform auditing.

There are two types of auditing: volume and directory. Volume auditing monitors activities related to the file system, server, printing, and bindery users. Directory auditing monitors activities relating to the NDS tree. Directory auditing must be enabled one container at a time. Directory auditing reports report on the entire NDS tree.

You learned about the four types of audit files. The Audit file maintains current information on volumes or containers. The Old Audit file is an archive of the current audit file. The Audit History file contains information on who used AUDITCON and when. The Old Audit History file is an archive of the Audit History file.

Volume auditing enables you to decide how much data to put into the audit file. The three file events options are: Global, User or File, and User and File. Global places the most information in the audit file. User and File only places information into the audit file when a user you selected uses one of the files you selected.

As you learned, the steps involved in setting up auditing include: enabling volume or container auditing; configuring which events, users, files and directories should be audited; and generating reports. The last portion of this chapter gave you step-by-step procedures on how to perform these activities.

The reports section showed you how to create a report filter. The filter enables you to limit according to date and time, users, and event, and which data appears in the report. The report file itself is somewhat cryptic. You learned how to decode the report data. Another section showed you sample external programs in QBASIC language, dBASE, and Excel, which massage the data into a useful format.

You then learned about audit file maintenance, how to set the maximum audit file size, and how to reset the audit file. The last section discussed how to audit the auditor by generating a report on the audit history file.

Part X

Backing Up, Disaster Planning, and Troubleshooting

New Riders Publishing
INSIDE
SERIES

Protecting Your Network Files

This chapter focuses on how to protect your network in case of a disaster. Several considerations should go into the bigger picture. Remember the end result: the company must keep going in order for it to remain financially viable.

One way to remain financially viable is to develop a good disaster recovery plan. This involves taking preventative measures to minimize the impact of a disaster and having various contingency plans ready. Planning a good, solid backup strategy is a critical component in any disaster recovery plan. This chapter goes into detail on how to plan and perform your backups. NetWare's SBACKUP utility and one of the most popular backup packages on the market, Cheyenne Software's ARCServe, are discussed.

Another strategy is to completely duplicate your file server. This chapter discusses file server duplexing, also known as SFT (System Fault Tolerance) Level III. Finally, to correct problems that might occur with the NDS, the DSREPAIR.NLM utility is discussed.

Developing a Disaster Recovery Plan

Here is the story of two different companies and how they each handled disasters. The first company, XYZ Clothing, produces a line of women's clothing. They have a factory outlet in San Francisco, California. They have a network with workstations at each cashier's station, connected to a cash drawer. They are running point-of-sale software that enables them to produce an invoice for customers, take payments, record payments in a central accounts receivables file, and deduct items purchased from a central inventory file. All workstations connect to a file server that maintains the central files.

A power outage hit their section of the city during a busy Saturday morning. All electricity in the building went out. A set of emergency generators came on line providing power to sets of emergency lights and a ventilation system. All computers were off-line. The file server, on a UPS (Uninterruptible Power Supply), closed all open files and came down gracefully within half an hour of the power outage. The cashiers took out pads of receipts which they kept at their stations, and wrote customer receipts and processed the purchases of customers remaining in the store. When power was restored several hours later, the receipts were manually keyed into the computer and the central files were updated.

The second company, ABC Video, has retail outlets in 12 different locations in the San Diego, California area. Each location has 6 workstations on a network. Each network is connected to the central office, using a router, where central accounting and inventory files are maintained. Four workstations are located at the cashier's counters around the store. Of the remaining two workstations, one is used by management and the other is used as a router.

A power outage hit parts of the city leaving several of the locations without power. One location had two dozen customers inside the store at the time of the outage. The staff in this location rushed around frantically, resetting breakers and checking power lines in a vain attempt to restore power. Customers were starting to line up, videos in hand, waiting to check out and go home. The grumbling and complaining grew louder and louder. Finally, a bold customer asked the clerk behind the cash register, "Why don't you just write a receipt?" The clerk replied that he had no receipts to give. The customer asked, "Why don't you just write down my name and membership number and let me rent the video?" The clerk replied, "I can't do that. I must record your membership number and video bar code into the computer. It's company policy."

The stalemate continued for another 10 minutes. Finally, frustrated by the staff's refusal to rent them videos, customers started to leave, grumbling and complaining. One customer even tried to hand the staff money saying he'd pay them double the amount to rent a cherished video. This offer also was met with refusal. The customer

left, sadly shaking his head and muttering about the state of American businesses who refused to take money offered to them. Many people were angry and vowed never to return.

You might have had similar experiences yourself. You must stop and think for a second, "Which one of these stories best describes my company?" Are you prepared to continue to operate if there is a power outage or other disaster, or will your company be unable to conduct business? This section focuses on how to plan for disaster.

The Cost of Downtime

Estimating the cost of downtime will convince you of the need to develop a good disaster recovery plan. *Downtime* is the time the computer system is inaccessible. The cost of downtime can be measured in the following ways:

- The combined wages of workers who cannot work while the computer system is down
- The combined wages of workers for work that was lost
- Present and future lost revenue
- The cost involved in bringing the system back up

The wages of workers who cannot work while the system is down is fairly easy to calculate. In addition to these wages, you must also take into account time spent on work that was lost. If the crash occurred at 3:00 p.m., for example, and the last good backup was from midnight, there are 15 potential hours of lost work per employee depending on how many shifts are in operation at your company.

Present and future lost revenue might be more difficult to calculate. If your company is a law firm, for example, an important document may not be completed, resulting in an attorney missing a court-imposed deadline. This could cause the company to lose a case that could result in a malpractice lawsuit, or future lost business.

Note: Law firms can reduce their malpractice insurance premiums by having an accepted computerized calendar system with a good backup.

The costs involved in bringing the system back up vary depending on what type of warranties or other coverage you have, and what the going rates are in your area. These costs also include the cost of replacement parts and labor.

Here is an example of how to calculate the cost of downtime. This example is for a computer graphic company of 40 employees. In this example, the computer system crashed on Friday at 2:00 p.m. The last good backup was taken at 2:00 a.m. that morning. The company's hours are from 8:00 a.m. to 5:00 p.m. Because the repairs were estimated to take 4 hours, most employees left for the day. The average rate of pay is $20 per hour.

Lost Wages:	$20/hour×40 employees×3 hours = $2,400
Lost Work:	$20/hour×40 employees×6 hours = $4,800
Lost Revenue:	missed a deadline that resulted in the loss of a contract = $5,000
Cost of Labor:	$125/hour×4 hours = $500
Cost of Parts:	new hard drive = $1,000
Total Cost:	$13,700

In this case, the company got off easy. In many cases, the lost revenue, although difficult to measure, can be quite significant. When a good disaster recovery plan is not in effect, the amount of time required to bring the system back up is much greater than 4 hours. In some cases, an esoteric part may have to be ordered, taking days or weeks, instead of hours. On the other hand, with the proper precautions, the failure of one component can result in only minutes of downtime with no data or files lost.

Contingency Planning

As much as possible, you must be prepared for various contingencies. As a network Administrator, be prepared for the possibility that the network is unavailable. Contingency planning involves the following two phases:

- ◆ Taking preventative measures to avoid a disaster
- ◆ Developing a plan of action for various contingencies

The second item is covered in the section, "What To Do If...?." The first item involves any of the following items:

- ◆ Disk mirroring, duplexing, and drive arrays
- ◆ Mirrored file servers
- ◆ Setting a regular, reliable, backup system
- ◆ Rotating the backup media and taking some media offsite
- ◆ Setting up UPS units and power filters on key network components

- Having sufficient spare parts on hand
- Physically securing key network components
- Providing for network security against unauthorized intruders

Backup considerations and mirroring file servers are covered later in this chapter. This section covers the other items on the previous list.

Disk Mirroring, Duplexing, and Drive Arrays

Disk drive units can be mirrored. *Mirroring* involves adding a second, identical, hard drive to the file server. You can use the INSTALL.NLM utility to mirror one drive to another. (See Chapter 37, "Making Configuration Changes," for a detailed description.) In this situation, if the first drive fails, the second drive is available and can immediately take over. The advantage of this is that network users experience no downtime. The disadvantage is that these solutions are expensive.

Drive *duplexing* is where you have complete redundancy in the disk channel. This involves the following:

- Two disk host bus adapters in the file server
- Pairs of hard drives
- Physically separate drive bays
- Separate power supplies
- Two sets of drive cables

With drive duplexing, if any component in one of the disk channels fails, the second channel takes over. The advantage over mirroring is greater speed (having two separate disk channels results in improved disk read performance). In addition, you are not reliant on a single disk channel, as with mirroring.

Another approach is a drive array. A *drive array,* as explained in Chapter 11, "Hardware Configuration," consists of a series of hard drives which can cover for each other if one of them fails. Drive arrays typically utilize RAID (Redundant Array of Inexpensive Devices) level 3 or 5. In a drive array, you have superior performance over mirroring or duplexing because all drives are put to work equally. If any single drive fails, the other drives are able to rebuild the lost information. If the drive array also has hot swap capability, an extra drive is standing by online, and will take over in the event of the failure of one of the drives actively participating in the array.

You can also duplex two drive arrays. This would result in the redundancy of duplexing, with the superior performance of a disk array. Combine this with the hot swap capability, and you have the best possible redundant system short of mirroring with another file server (discussed later in this chapter).

Setting Up UPS Units and Line Filters on Key Network Components

An *Uninterruptible Power Supply* (UPS) is a battery connected to a power supply, which lasts anywhere from 15 minutes to several hours, with an online recharging system. When you plug the UPS unit into an AC power source, most units available now start dispensing power from the battery while receiving a continuous charge from the AC power source. This way, if the AC power source fails, the battery continues to provide power.

You also must connect a monitoring cable between a port on the UPS unit and the file server. The monitoring cable normally comes with the UPS unit, although it sometimes must be ordered separately. The connection to the file server can be to a serial port, a parallel port, a mouse port, or a special adapter card that comes with the UPS. In addition, you need to load monitoring software on the file server. The monitoring software monitors the port to which the monitoring cable is connected. When a power loss is sensed, the UPS sends a signal through the monitoring cable. The monitoring software reacts by issuing a warning message, waiting for a designated period of time, and bringing the server down. The advantage to this arrangement is that open files on the file server are closed, and all disk writes currently residing in file server cache are written to the file server's hard drives before the server goes down. This prevents file corruption and loss of data.

You also may want to connect key network components to a UPS. Critical hubs, bridges, or routers may need to remain running in the event of a power loss. External disk drive units connected to the file server should be connected to the UPS. You also may want to connect one or two critical workstations to a UPS. Many UPS vendors provide inexpensive UPS units that can be connected to workstations. If your network has remote communications, it might be necessary to connect modems to a UPS.

When connecting components to the UPS, it is not necessary to connect monitors or printers. These devices drain considerable power and can be connected later if necessary. Without the monitor connected, the UPS connected to the file server may give you 20 to 50 percent more time. The same applies to computers acting as bridges or routers. There is no need to connect these monitors to a UPS. Most UPS units provide many outlets. Leave an outlet free in case you need to connect a monitor temporarily.

A *line filter* is a power strip with electronic components designed to prevent power surges from destroying equipment. Most UPS units have a line filter built into their circuitry. A variation of a line filter is called a *surge protector*. The line filter is designed

to provide "clean" power to electrical equipment. In the case of computer equipment, this can mean the difference between having equipment survive power surges or being destroyed. An example of when a line filter is useful is during a thunderstorm. During a thunderstorm, lightning bolts can hit the building, sending a surge of electricity through the wiring. Any computers that are not protected by a line filter or UPS unit are vulnerable to the surge. A power surge can cause electrical components to short out, rendering the equipment inoperable.

Line filters are relatively inexpensive. They can be purchased for as little as $20, and can go up to $200 or more. Be careful when selecting a line filter. Some line filters tested by *Consumer Reports* were found, under certain conditions, to break down completely. Protective components in these particular units fused together and were found to amplify the power surge, causing twice as much damage!

A line filter is not a substitute for a UPS unit. A good line filter provides protection against a power surge, but provides no protection against a power shortage. In the case of a power shortage, the UPS provides power through its battery. In the case of a power surge, the line filter prevents excess voltage from getting through to your equipment.

Having Sufficient Spare Parts On Hand

The importance of this point cannot be overemphasized. In the case where key components fail, having sufficient spare parts on hand can save your company much downtime. An entire thin Ethernet network can be brought down by a bad terminator. The cost of a terminator varies from $.50 to $5.00. Think of the time it would take you to go out and purchase a terminator. What store carries terminators? Clerks in most stores would think you meant to purchase a video of the famous movie starring Arnold Schwartzenegger. Plan ahead and have several terminators on hand (and we don't mean Arnold!) in case of emergency.

Other spare parts that are useful to a network Administrator include the following:

- Network adapters
- Network cabling
- Hubs (MAUs if in a token ring network)
- Connectors (T-connectors, for example)
- Hard drives
- Floppy drives
- CD-ROM drives

- Keyboards (some computers will not boot without the keyboard!)
- Bootable DOS disks with FDISK, FORMAT, a text editor, and some sort of backup and restore utility
- NetWare workstation installation disks
- Monitors
- Computers
- RAM
- Disks
- Modems

This list is by no means complete. Think about the components that go into your network. Keep the list reasonable. If you have 12 workstations, for example, one extra computer may be appropriate. If you have 1,000 workstations, on the other hand, you may find yourself going through a computer a week! (The more computers you have, the more you may want to consider an on-site service contract. Consult your local computer reseller about such contracts.)

Physically Securing Key Network Components

Network components should be physically secured. This is especially important in areas of the country prone to natural disasters like earthquakes. The file server, for example, should be securely mounted in a rack, on a sturdy table, or in a steady holder on the floor. Wires should be tied down. In an office wired for twisted pair, for example, wherever possible run the wires through walls and provide data jacks for each computer. When the computer needs to be moved you can simply disconnect the jack and move it to a new location without disrupting the network.

To protect against earthquake damage, each unit should be physically bolted to its surface and shock mounted. There is not much you can do if the entire rack falls to the floor during an earthquake. The floor itself might give out! You can use rubber spacers and padding to protect the unit as much as possible against shock.

In the case of flooding, waterproofing the equipment would be ideal, but probably won't work. Instead you can make sure all units are well off the floor. In a multi-story building, place key equipment on an upper story. Do not place computers on the floor in flood zones. In many cases, the flooding is mainly confined to the floor, and any height you can lift the computer equipment increases its chances of surviving. Also, in flood zones, be sure to connect electronic equipment to power strips that shut off in case of a short. When the flood hits, electricity shorts out due to the conductivity characteristics of water. If your computer equipment is not properly

protected, the short can cause your computer's power supply to burn out, possibly taking more sensitive components (such as RAM) with it.

Providing for Network Security Against Unauthorized Intruders

Another type of disaster is when a hacker breaks into your network. There are no guidelines to clearly identify the type of person who is a hacker. Hackers vary from disgruntled former employees to bored teenagers looking for an electronic thrill. Many dire consequences can result. The hacker may be content to simply roam through your system to satisfy some curiosity. In other cases, critical files are damaged or viruses are introduced. Company secrets could be stolen to the advantage of the competition.

There are two primary guidelines to protect against unauthorized intruders:

- Keep your employees happy
- Keep the file servers in a locked room

Happy employees are less inclined to bring harm to their companies. Unhappy employees, on the other hand, account for a good amount of intentional or unintentional damage to the company. Corporate espionage is a reality, and the competition often takes advantage of such situations.

Anyone with the right knowledge who has physical access to the file server can gain access to company data. Novell clearly states in their documentation that they cannot guarantee the security of a network where physical access to the file server is available. If this is the case, anyone could gain access to data on the file server by rebooting it with a DOS disk and using the Norton Tools to view the contents of the hard drive.

It also is important to limit access to the file server console. The RCONSOLE.EXE utility is located in the SYS:SYSTEM directory of any given file server. It is important to limit who has directory trustee rights to this directory. The remote password should be carefully guarded. It is possible for a hacker to get a copy of RCONSOLE from the NetWare 4 installation CD. RCONSOLE does not have to be run from the server. The hacker is not able to access a server without the remote password.

You can use the REMOTE ENCRYPT command, as described in Chapter 36, "Monitoring the File Server," to produce an encrypted remote password. This protects against hackers attempting to locate the remote password. Even if they locate and read the LDREMOTE.NCF file, the password is unreadable.

Users on the network also should guard their passwords. Many unauthorized network intrusions result in careless use of passwords. Employees give their passwords to co-workers when working on common projects. In some cases, employees post their passwords on their monitors.

The selection of a good password is a highly developed art. There are password generators that produce a near meaningless stream of letters and numbers that can be used for passwords. The problem with this approach is that such passwords are not easily remembered. This leads to the password being written down, which means that it can be found by unauthorized personnel. The opposite extreme is where network users use passwords based on some well-known aspect of their personal lives. Parents choose the names of their children. Pet owners choose the names of their pets. A good solution to both problems is to produce passwords that are a combination of two words that have no relationship joined by a random punctuation character. The following are some examples:

- zebra;wall
- bill-donut
- target!comic

As you can see, the combinations of words above is meaningless, and the punctuation characters are chosen at random. Yet these passwords are relatively easy to remember.

NetWare also provides a number of features and utilities that can be used to monitor your network for unauthorized intruders. These features have been discussed in other chapters in the book. They include the following:

- Auditing
- Accounting
- Intruder detection

In addition, there are a number of user properties that can be set for maximum security. These include the following:

- Minimum password length of no less than 5 characters.
- Passwords should change at least every 3 months.
- New passwords should be unique.
- Grace logins should remain at 6 or less.
- The number of concurrent connections should be limited to 1 if possible. Certain users may need an increase to 2 or 3.
- Login time restrictions should be set.
- For workstations with sensitive equipment or located in unsecured areas, you can set station restrictions.

Here is a glossary of terms used in the previous section:

Unique passwords occur when the new password must be different from the last 8 passwords.

Grace logins indicate a certain number of additional logins after your password has expired.

Concurrent connections are when a user logs in under the same user name from several different physical locations.

Time restrictions are when you set times during which users can log in. If they login outside of these times, or are logged in past the restriction, the system logs them out.

Station restrictions are a limitation by protocol, network address, or node address.

Another potential threat to the network is in the area of long distance connectivity. Access given to remote dial-in users must be carefully guarded. In most cases you can set up access servers to dial back the remote user. This enables you to control the locations of your remote users, and gives you a record of access (your phone bill).

Access to the company network through the Internet is a difficult problem. The advantage to the Internet is that many people can access your network, increasing your potential market. On the other hand, there are no regulations on the Internet. Hackers love to hang out on the Internet, taking every possible opportunity to ransack company data files. One technique involves setting up a firewall. You can program routers using SAP and RIP filtering, to see only certain portions of your network. The server that is on the Internet should only have data that is meant to be publicly accessible. This server is then placed on the other side of a firewall of routers that do not enable it to see other servers on the network.

Packet Signature

Other problems arise when company data passes through a PDN (Public Data Network). The Internet is, in a sense, the largest PDN in the world. There also are private PDNs for lease through such organizations as AT&T, MCI, CompuServe, and others. This approach gives you a less expensive alternative to running your own fiber optic lines across the country. The disadvantage is that there are many points at which unauthorized parties could tap into your communications. NetWare 4 provides a solution in the form of packet signatures. This technique involves setting an option in the NET.CFG file of each workstation that needs to communicate across a PDN as follows:

```
NetWare DOS Requester
Signature Level = n
```

n is a number from 0 to 3. On the file server console, issue the following command:

```
SET NCP PACKET SIGNATURE OPTION = n
```

Again, *n* is a number from 0 to 3. Packet signature, if enabled, causes the workstation to add a signature to each packet transmitted. The signature is based on the security key and credential already generated during the initial login process, and other factors such as the node address, date and time. The signature on each packet is different. Only the security keys available on the workstation and server are able to properly decode and validate the signature. If an unauthorized workstation tries to hack its way into your network where packet signatures are enabled, the unauthorized workstation is immediately detected and disconnected.

Packet signature degrades network performance. Not only is the header of each packet marginally larger (meaning that the percentage of data per packet decreases), but the workstations perform additional processing for each packet transmitted. The server must perform extra processing to validate each signed packet.

Only use packet signatures if you have security problems or if security is necessary for your network environment.

Packet signature is enabled by setting a level at both the workstation and file server. Table 41.1 summarizes the combined settings. Set the packet signature option on the server in the STARTUP.NCF file. From the file server console you can only increase the packet signature option once the server has booted up.

Table 41.1
Packet Signature Combinations

Workstation Setting	Server Setting	Description
0	0	If both the workstation and server set packet signature to 0, neither are required to sign packets.
0	1 or 2	The server enables an unsecure workstation to log in but processes packet signatures if the workstation requires it.
0	3	The workstation cannot log in to a server that requires packet signature.

Workstation Setting	Server Setting	Description
1	1	Either workstation or server signs packets if requested. Level 1 does not request signature. This is the default setting.
1	2 or 3	Server requests packet signature. Workstation signs all packets where the requesting server has a level of 2 or 3.
2	1, 2, or 3	Servers with level of 1, 2, or 3 are capable of signing packets. A workstation with a level of 2 signs all packets where the server is capable of signing packets.
3	1, 2, or 3	Packet signature is required. Workstations with this level cannot communicate with servers with level of 0. Servers with level of 0 are considered unsecure.

What To Do If ... ?

One of the tasks delegated to a network Administrator is to provide an accessible, working network at all times. When a disaster occurs, the network Administrator who cannot provide access to key applications and files will probably not survive.

Taking preventative measures, as discussed previously, goes a long way towards protecting your network from damage. If a disaster occurs, however, you need a well-defined plan of action. The goal of the company as a whole should be, "How can we continue to do business?" Remember the stories of the two companies. Company XYZ Clothing continued to do business. No profit was lost during the power outage. ABC Video, on the other hand, had no plan, and lost perhaps thousands of dollars in revenues. Worse yet, the company may have lost future business after having ineptly handled the problem.

The goal of the network Administrator during a disaster is first, to survive. (If you are dead or injured, you are not doing yourself or the company any favors!) Your next task is to ensure that your co-workers are in a safe position. Once you and your co-workers have achieved a degree of safety, your task is to see how you can continue to provide services to either customers or to co-workers.

It is a good exercise for network Administrators to take the time to come up with a list of possible (or more probable) disasters. You can call this the What If...? list. The following are some possible What Ifs:

- What if there is an earthquake?
- What if there is a flood?
- What if there is a hurricane?
- What if there is a fire?

Now that you have a good-sized list, the next step is to list what would be affected in each situation. This step takes some thought. You think of various aspects of your business and relate them to the disaster situation. Here is an example for ABC Clothing mentioned previously:

Effects of an Earthquake on ABC Clothing:

1. Loss of retail outlet building
2. Loss of headquarters building
3. Loss of personnel through injury or death
4. No electricity
5. Equipment damage

You can then take each item and start to detail problems that stem from that cause. To again use ABC Clothing as an example, the following are expanded lists from the previously mentioned items:

Effects of an Earthquake on ABC Clothing:

4. No electricity
    - A. Network will go down
    - B. No computers available for cashiers
    - C. Files on file server may become corrupted
    - D. Financial records will be unavailable
5. Equipment damaged
    - A. Hard drives on file server
    - B. Network hubs and routers
    - C. Some or all computers

Once the expanded list is completed, you can start to develop a plan to cover each expanded item. The answer to 4B above, for example, "No computers available for cashiers," could be covered by placing receipt books at each cashier's station. Item 4C, "File on file server may become corrupted," could be handled by setting up NetWare's TTS (Transaction Tracking System) on critical files, and by maintaining a good backup. Item 4D, "Financial records will be unavailable," can be handled by keeping a weekly or monthly paper or microfiche printout of company financial records. These records could then be kept in a fireproof safe in two different locations.

In a situation where the network is not functional, your job is to bring it back up to a working condition as quickly as possible. If you are sure you can bring the network up within a reasonable amount of time, you should proceed to do so. If it appears that it will take a considerable length of time to bring the network up (days or weeks, for example), you will have to develop an alternative plan.

Manual Operations

Another consideration is what sort of manual operations might be necessary to keep business going. The following is a list of examples:

- Receipt books
- Source documents on paper or microfiche
- Data entry forms
- Printed or microfiche copies of company records
- Typewriters (remember those?)
- The most important consideration is this: BUSINESS DOES NOT STOP!

Take note of the main function of your network. What do people do on the network? What are the key tasks your network performs for your company? The following are some suggestions:

- E-mail
- Shared applications
- Shared data
- Shared printers

E-mail is one of the main uses of computer networks. How can you continue to provide this service without the network? One suggestion is to look back to the 1950s when companies did not have access to a computer. How did people communicate with co-workers? One suggestion is to use the telephone system more extensively.

Most phone providers have excellent disaster recovery systems and fallback options. Telephone service usually is the first of the electronic services to be restored. Many phone companies offer a Centrex system where the phone switching equipment and voice mail equipment is maintained by the phone company and is not at your site. In the event of a disaster at your site, the phone company can provide the same services to your new or temporary site. All your voice mail messages will not be lost. Falling back to an even older form of communications, you might revive the custom of placing message pads on people's desks and hanging up one or more bulletin boards around the office.

Shared applications are a common use for networks. These enable several people to contribute to a single project, and they save money through the purchase of a single multi-user license rather than through a number of single user copies. In the case of a disaster you will not have access to the network version. You may want to allocate enough budget for several single-user copies of the software. These could be installed on strategically placed computers so that people could continue to do their work.

These are some suggestions to get you thinking about your situation. Take the time to go through the steps mentioned previously and develop a comprehensive plan of action for your company. Once you have done so, have co-workers or management review your ideas and make suggestions. It also is important to schedule some dry runs to test the plan of action to the extent that is possible.

Planning the Backup

As mentioned previously, a good backup scheme is essential in case of a disaster. There are several elements that go into a good backup scheme:

- Reliable, easy to use backup software
- A reliable, adequate backup device
- A well-defined backup plan or procedure

The world's best backup system is no good if you lose your backup disks or tapes in the same disaster that claimed your network. You also need to decide exactly what to backup. This section discusses these elements as well as other considerations.

How Much Data Do You Need To Backup

Before setting up your backup system and developing a procedure, you need to identify the following:

- Which files and directories need to be backed up?
- How much data (in bytes) needs to be backed up?
- How often should data be backed up?

Before you learn about backup schemes, you must make a decision about how much data you wish to backup. Files on your file server can be broken down into two categories: application files and data files. As you might imagine, *application files* are binary executables or overlay libraries. *Data files* include configuration files used with applications, documents, spreadsheets, databases, and other files created by users as they do their work.

Application files tend to remain fairly static. This type of file does not change on a day-to-day basis. In the worst case you might end up upgrading an application every 6 months to a year, sometimes even longer. Data files, on the other hand, change frequently. You need to determine how much new data is generated on your network each day, and how often data files change. In a mail order company, for example, hundreds of calls might be received each day, generating thousands of bytes of information on new leads, updates to inventory files, and changes to the accounting files. Software companies produce hundreds of lines of new code and thousands of bytes of new object code each day. A large law firm could produce megabytes of legal documents each day.

The frequency of backup depends on what is an acceptable risk and cost associated with not backing up. You first need to determine the cost of losing data for a given period of time. (See the "Cost of Downtime" section.) You must take into account any penalties that might accrue because some document missed a deadline. Accounting departments must file certain forms with the IRS at certain time periods throughout the year. A missed deadline caused by a network disaster might cost the company several thousand dollars in late fees and penalties. A law firm that misses a deadline for filing a certain document might ultimately lose their case on a technicality. This would result in a possible negligence lawsuit, lost business and a bad reputation in the legal community.

On the other hand, if you go to the extreme of backing up every hour, for example, you impair the smooth functioning of the network. There are backup systems that immediately backup any new file saved to the file server. These systems tend to be expensive and hurt file server performance. Another solution is to combine a daily backup system with disk mirroring or duplexing.

Types of Backups

There are two main types of backups: the full backup, and the partial backup.

The *full backup*, also known as the *full system backup*, backs up every file on the file server regardless of type. This type of backup is very simple to implement and simple to restore. The disadvantage is that it takes a long time to backup your entire system. This type of backup also is wasteful since certain files, such as application files, do not change frequently and do not need to be backed up.

In a *partial backup*, you only backup selected files on your system. The selection of files can be made automatically. When you backup a file, the backup software clears a bit in the DET (Directory Entry Table) known as the archive bit. When this bit is clear, the backup software knows that this file has been backed up. A full backup clears the archive bit of every file on the server. When a file has been changed or a new file is created, the archive bit is set. This informs the tape backup software that this file needs to be backed up.

The following are the three variations of partial backup:

- Incremental backup
- Differential backup
- Backup of selected files

In the case of *incremental backups*, only files where the archive bit is set are backed up. Once the backup takes place, the archive bit is cleared. In a *differential* backup, the archive bit is not cleared. Rather, the differential backup backs up all files where the archive bit is set. The effect of a differential backup is that all files modified or newly created since the last full backup will be backed up. *Selected files* is when you inform the backup software that you plan to backup the files on a list every time regardless of the status of the archive bit. The process of backing up these files may or may not clear the archive bit, but this does not affect this type of backup. Figure 41.1 illustrates these types of backups.

As you can see in Step 1 in the figure, a user updates a file. The archive bit is set. After a full backup (Step 2), the archive bit is clear. In Step 3, the user again updates the file, setting the archive bit. After an incremental backup (Step 4), the archive bit is cleared.

In Step 5, the user updates a file setting the archive bit. After a full backup (Step 6), the archive bit is clear. In Step 7, the user again updates the file, setting the archive bit. A differential backup is performed (Step 8), which does not set the archive bit.

Full and Incremental Backups

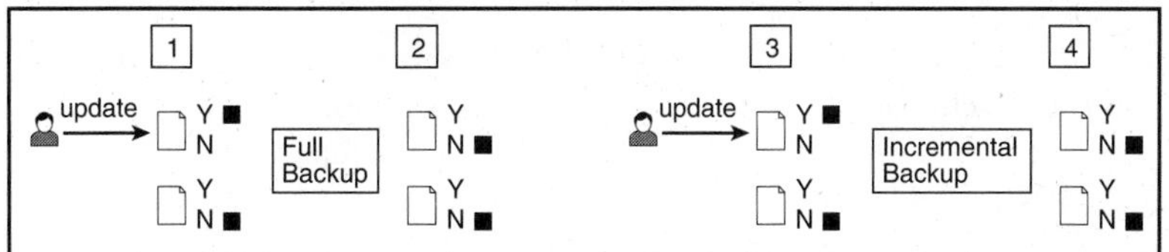

Full and Differential Backups

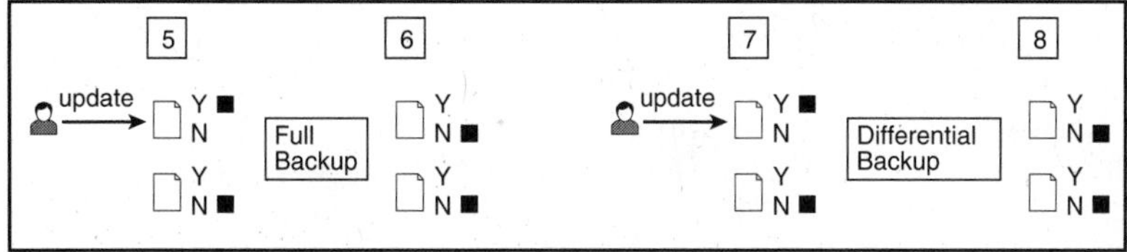

Legend: Y = Archive Bit is Set
N = Archive bit is Clear

Figure 41.1

The status of the archive bit after different types of backup.

Media Rotation Schemes

Media refers to the tapes, disks, or other type of storage. The phrase *media rotation* means "do not use the same disk or tape all the time." Car owners are advised to rotate their tires on a regular basis. The idea is that all 4 tires of the car wear evenly. The same principle applies to the media used to store your backups, whether they be disks or tapes.

There are several types of rotation schemes. Many are mathematically derived and quite complex. The backup software you use to schedule your backups often enforces certain media rotation schemes. In this section you learn about two types of media rotation schemes: a simple scheme and a complex scheme.

Simple Media Rotation Scheme

A simple, yet effective, media rotation scheme involves labeling a set of disks or tapes, one for each day of the week. At the end of each week you perform a full backup. Each day you perform a differential backup. The media is rotated daily. At the beginning of the next week you start to recycle the media, reusing the set from the past week.

This scheme is very simple, and accomplishes the following purposes:

- The same media is not constantly used
- You cannot lose any more than one day of data

- If there is a problem with one of the tapes or disks during a restore, you can go to the previous day

The disadvantage to this scheme is that if you lose the full backup, you are not able to restore. This is because the differential backup, although faster than a full backup, still requires a full backup before you can restore the differential backup.

Complex Media Rotation Scheme

The complex rotation scheme is similar to the simple rotation scheme mentioned previously and involves a weekly full backup. Each weekly backup is then pulled out of the rotation until the end of the month. The monthly backup is pulled out of rotation until the end of the year. The yearly backup is permanently archived. This scheme protects the full backups. The yearly archive is useful if you need to obtain data from previous years. For example, if your company undergoes an IRS audit, records from up to the past 7 years might have to be pulled.

The following is an outline of the complex rotation scheme:

1. At the beginning of the week, perform a full backup and label the media WEEK1.

2. Each day perform a differential backup and label the media according to the day of week.

3. At the beginning of the next week, store the media from the previous week in a safe place. Take the MONDAY media and label it WEEK*x* where "x" is the current week number (1 to 4). Perform a full system backup.

4. Reuse the daily backup media. Relabel the TUESDAY media MONDAY. Relabel the WEDNESDAY media TUESDAY, etc. Use a new media on the last day of the week.

5. At the end of the month, take the media labeled WEEK1 and relabel it MONTH1. Perform a full system backup. Store this media in a safe place. Start the monthly procedure as in Step 1, reusing existing tapes.

6. At the end of the year, take the media labeled MONTH1 and relabel it YEAR1. Perform a full system backup. Restart the weekly and monthly backup cycle starting with Step 1.

The advantage of this system is that it saves full backups on a weekly basis. You have several fallback points in case media goes bad, is destroyed, or lost. This system also pulls media out of the rotation for weeks or months at a time so that all media are used less often.

Off-Site Storage of Backups

In conjunction with the complex rotation scheme described above, you can take media off site on a regular basis. The reasoning behind this is to safeguard company data in case of a disaster. The disaster might claim the entire office or building. In this case, if the backup media is kept in the office or building, it is lost as well. By taking media off site you ensure greater security of your data.

Off-site rotation can be combined with the WEEK*x*, MONTH*x* and YEAR*x* media mentioned in the scheme previously. When you perform the first full backup for WEEK1, take the media off site. When you get to WEEK2, take the media off site and return WEEK1. This way you have backup media on site *and* off site.

Types of Backup Systems

There are several different types of backup systems available. The most popular uses tape for media. Other types of systems use a form of CD that can be written to once (WORM—Write Once Read Many), and magneto-optical devices. A *magneto-optical* device uses a special type of disk that is rigid and has a capacity close to that of a CD.

This section discusses tape backup software. For a discussion of tape backup hardware and other types of systems that can be used for backup, refer to Chapter 1, "Elements of a Simple Network."

SBACKUP

The SBACKUP.NLM utility is provided with NetWare to meet federal standards for network operating systems. It is a simple, rather inelegant, backup software package that simply does the job. When SBACKUP was introduced in NetWare 3.*x*, a new backup architecture was envisioned. The name for the architecture was SMS (Storage Management Services). The idea behind this architecture is that vendors of backup hardware or software would only have to write their software and hardware drivers for SMS. As long as the hardware drivers or backup software were SMS compliant, you theoretically could use any vendor's hardware with any vendor's software. This strategy has worked out to a certain extent and most vendors adhere to the SMS specifications.

SBACKUP runs on a file server and uses a tape unit directly connected to the file server. This is referred to as *server based backup*. Server based backup has the following advantages:

- Backing up files on that server takes place quickly and does not tie up the network

- A workstation is not tied up
- Network security is maintained because you do not have to leave an unattended backup workstation logged with rights to all files and directories

The other backup type is workstation-based backup. In the case of workstation-based backup, the backup unit is connected to a workstation. At the end of each day, the user at this workstation runs a special program or batch file to start the backup. If the backup is scheduled for a later time, the workstation must remain logged in, unattended, with a user name with rights to all files and directories on the server. This poses a security breach. Another problem with workstation-based backup is that a tremendous amount of network traffic is generated as files are copied from the server to the backup unit on the workstation. An advantage to this technique is that if the network is down, files can be restored to this workstation and transferred to other computers quickly.

Part of the difficulty in working with SBACKUP lies in the number of NLMs required for its operation. These NLMs fall into the following three categories:

- Main menu (SBACKUP.NLM itself)
- Target Service Agent (TSA) NLMs
- Device drivers

The TSA modules are loaded on each backup target. A *target* is a computer to be backed up. The *host* is the file server with the tape drive and is running SBACKUP. The host identifies and can backup any device with TSA modules loaded. *Device drivers* are drivers loaded at the host to service the controller and backup device. If you have a Conner tape unit and a Bustek controller, for example, you would need device drivers for each. As you can see from table 41.2, SBACKUP supports a variety of TSA devices including other NetWare file servers (from version 2.2 and above), DOS and OS/2 workstations, and the NDS.

Table 41.2 summarizes the supporting NLMs.

Table 41.2
SBACKUP.NLM Supporting NLMs

Category	NLM	Description
Main Menu	SBACKUP.NLM	This is the main backup menu utility. When you load this NLM, you see a menu giving you backup and restore choices.

Category	NLM	Description
Target Service Agents	TSA220.NLM	Target service agent for a NetWare 2.2 file server.
	TSA311.NLM	Target service agent for a NetWare 3.11 file server.
	TSA312.NLM	Target service agent for a NetWare 3.12 file server.
	TSA400.NLM	Target service agent for a NetWare 4.0*x* file server.
	TSA410.NLM	Target service agent for a NetWare 4.1*x* file server.
	TSADOS.NLM	Identifies target service agents loaded on DOS client workstations, and reports to SBACKUP.NLM. DOS workstations must run TSASMS.COM.
	TSANDS.NLM	Target service agent for the NDS. You must load this if you plan to backup the NDS tree on your network.
	TSAPROXY.NLM	A future enhancement that enables a non-SMS supported file system to be backed up.
	TSAOS2.NLM	Identifies target service agents loaded on OS/2 client workstations and reports to SBACKUP.NLM. The OS/2 workstation can configure its local TSA driver through the NetWare for OS/2 Client software.
	TSASMS.COM	Local target service agent you must load on the DOS workstation.
Device Drivers	TAPEDAI.DSK	Generic SCSI driver for any ASPI compatible SCSI controller. You also must load the SCSI controller software.
	MNS16S.NLM MNS8MM.DSK MNSDAT.DSK	Software to drive Mountain Network Solutions SCSI controllers and tape backup units.

continues

Table 41.2, Continued
SBACKUP.NLM Supporting NLMs

Category	NLM	Description
	PS2SCSI.DSK	Software to drive IBM PS/2 SCSI tape units.
	AHA14*xx*.DSK AHA15*xx*.DSK AHA16*xx*.DSK AHA77*xx*.DSK ASPITRAN.DSK	Adaptec SCSI controller software. Drives the various Adaptec SCSI controllers.

For NetWare 2.2 file servers you need to create a special ASCII text file.

```
SYS:SYSTEM\TSA\TSA_V2X.LST
```

In this file, enter the names of all NetWare 2.2 file servers, one server name per line, that you plan to backup. TSA220.NLM reads this file and uses it to make a connection to the NetWare 2.2 file servers. This is necessary because the interaction between the NetWare 2.2 file server and TSA220.NLM is not dynamic as with the other TSA drivers.

The following is the procedure for performing a backup using SBACKUP:

1. From the file server console, load the device driver(s) appropriate for your system.

2. Issue the following commands:

   SCAN FOR NEW DEVICES
   LIST DEVICES

   This ensures that all devices are visible to SBACKUP. You will see a message on the file server console that is similar to the following message:

```
EBDB:SCAN FOR NEW DEVICES
EBDB:LIST DEVICES
13. Device # 2 ARCHIVE_PYTHON_MUL8 (40030000).
1. Device # 0 MEDIAVISCDR-H93MV    (81000001).
3. [S0A1D0] QUANTUM LP240A GM240A01X.
EBDB:
```

3. Load the desired TSA drivers. The following is the type of response you see if you load the TSA410.NLM (Target Service Agent for NetWare 4.10), and TSANDS.NLM (Target Service Agent for the NDS tree):

```
EBDB:load tsa410
Loading module TSA410.NLM
 NetWare 4.10 Target Service Agent
 Version 4.02i  September 1, 1994
 Copyright 1994 Novell, Inc. All rights reserved.
 Auto-loading module SMDR.NLM
 NetWare SMS Data Requestor
 Version 4.02e  August 12, 1994
 Copyright 1994 Novell, Inc. All rights reserved.
 Auto-loading module SPXS.NLM
 NetWare STREAMS SPXII Protocol
 Version 4.01g  August 30, 1994
 (C) Copyright 1992-1994 Novell, Inc.
 All Rights Reserved.
EBDB:load tsands
Loading module TSANDS.NLM
 NetWare Directory Target Service Agent v4.0
 Version 4.00  March 21, 1994
 Copyright 1994 Novell, Inc. All rights reserved.
EBDB:
```

4. Load SBACKUP. You will see the Main Menu, as shown in figure 41.2.

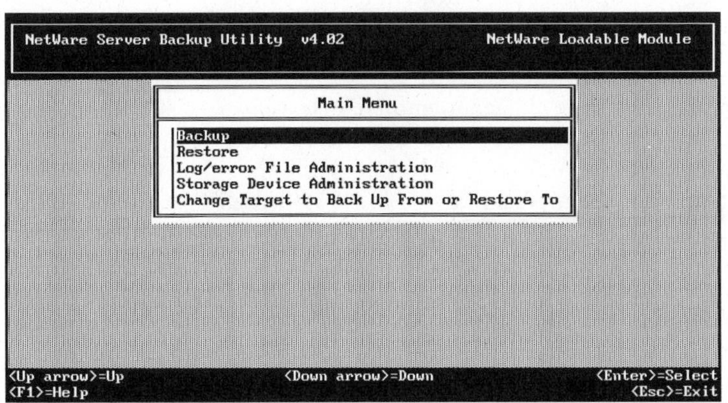

Figure 41.2
The SBACKUP.NLM Main Menu.

5. From the SBACKUP Main Menu, select Backup. You will see a menu asking you to select a target. For the purpose of this illustration, select NetWare 4.0 Directory. This is to backup the NDS tree.

6. You are prompted to enter a valid user name. This user must have at least Browse NDS object rights to all objects in the tree. Because this is the default for [public], it is not difficult to meet this requirement. In addition, this user must have Read rights to All Properties starting at [root]. When you have entered a valid user name and password, a green box appears on screen informing you that you are connected to the target.

7. Next, you must select a device and associated media. If you have only one tape unit on the file server, this choice is made for you automatically. Otherwise, select the device and media from the list and press Enter.

8. The next prompt asks you for the location of the backup log and error files. The default is SYS:SYSTEM\TSA\LOG. Enter a new location or press Enter to accept the default.

9. Your next choice is to perform a full or custom backup. The custom backup option lets you select what you want to backup. You can include and exclude specific objects or containers. The full option backs up all objects in the tree.

   When using SBACKUP to backup the file system, a similar choice appears. In this case you are able to include or exclude specified files and directories.

10. Once the type of backup has been determined and what you want to backup has been established, the next screen asks for a backup description. This goes into the backup log file for future identification in case you need to restore data.

    Press F10 to begin the backup.

11. You can now elect to start the backup immediately, cancel, or schedule the backup for a later date and time. Make your choice and press Enter. You are then asked to enter a name for the label. This name should be transcribed onto a label and attached to the media. It also is used by SBACKUP to identify the backup in the future. Enter an appropriate name and press Enter.

12. The backup now takes place (if you elected to start the backup now), or at the scheduled time. Figure 41.3 shows you the SBACKUP screen as the backup is in progress.

Once the backup is complete, you must exit SBACKUP and unload modules in the reverse order of which they were loaded. This is very important because of inter-module dependencies. Unloading modules out of order can cause the server to crash.

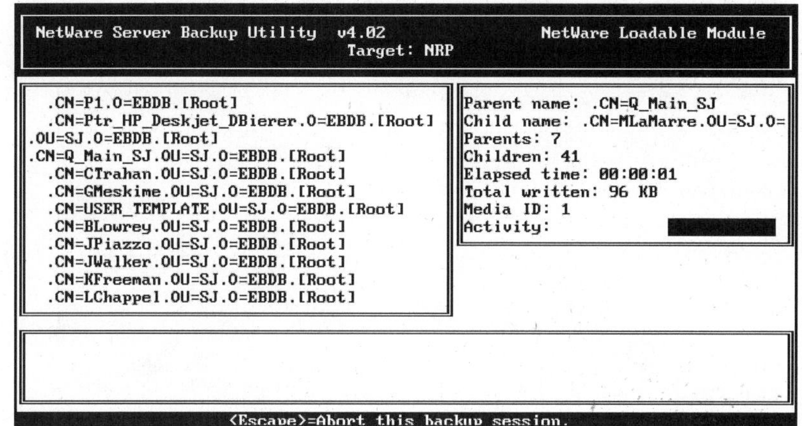

Figure 41.3

Backup of the NDS in progress.

ARCServe

One of the most popular third-party backup software packages in use today is ARCserve by Cheyenne Software, Inc. ARCserve is a software package designed for use with a wide variety of tape drives and host bus adapters. It is designed to install either on a workstation or a file server. The software manages tape drives located either on a server or a workstation. It features the capability to schedule unattended backups and to generate reports on backup activity. An *unattended backup* is where you schedule the backup for a certain date and time. You can then place a tape in the tape drive and go home. Unattended backups are generally scheduled for times when the least number of people are working on the network. For example, you might schedule a weekly full backup at 2:00 a.m. on Sunday morning.

Figure 41.4 shows you the main menu of ARCserve.

The ARCserve Quick Start menu guides you through your first backups with an easy to use visual interface. The Quick Start menu, shown in Figure 41.5, inventories all possible backup targets. Targets are file servers, DOS based workstations, Macintoshes, and UNIX workstations, with the necessary target software loaded(provided with ARCserve). Any target that has a NetWare TSA module loaded will also be recognized. To produce a backup you select the desired target from the list shown at the bottom left, and click on the To Tape button.

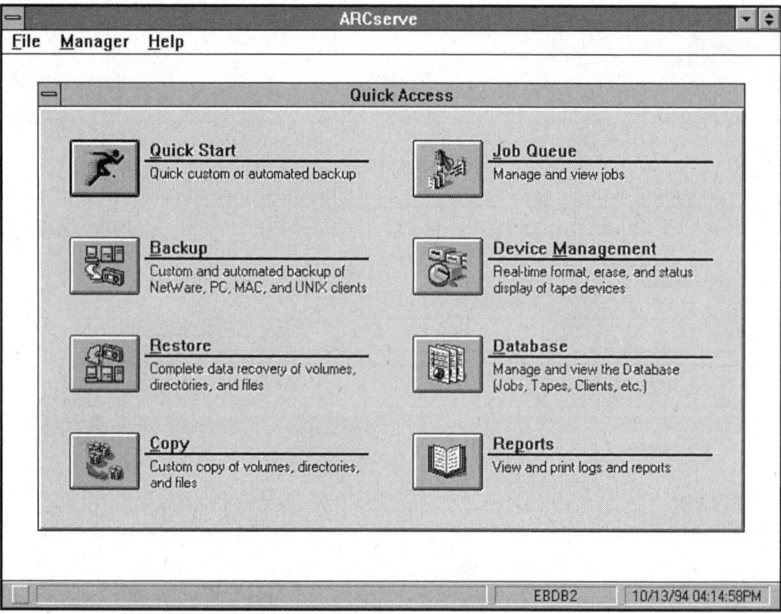

Figure 41.4

The ARCserve main menu.

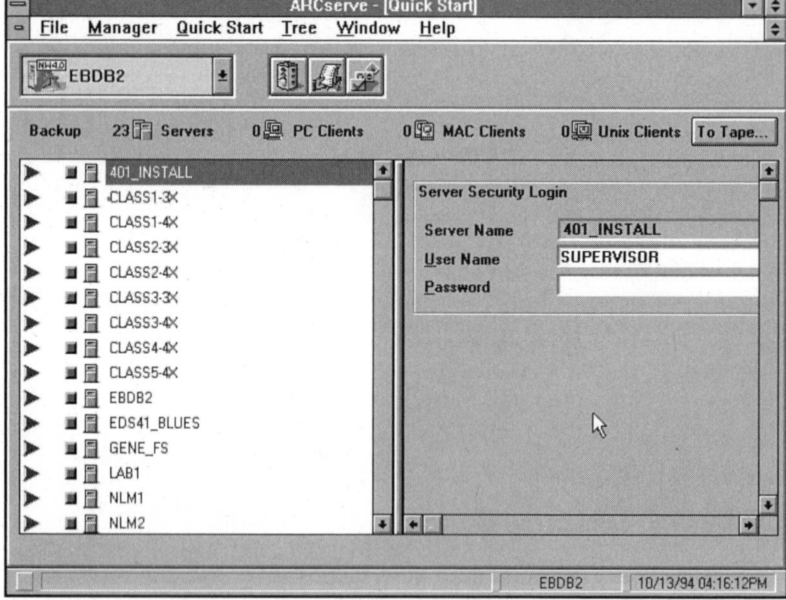

Figure 41.5

The ARCserve Quick Start menu.

The ARCserve Auto Pilot feature, shown in figure 41.6, lets you set up a complete backup system. Choices available in the Method drop down box include Full, Incremental, and Differential backups. Figure 41.6 shows the defaults when you select Differential. This particular scheme is based on the archive bit of the files to be backed up. As you can see, the default has a full backup take place on Friday. There is no backup on Saturday or Sunday. Monday through Thursday, there is a differential backup. As with the complex media rotation scheme discussed previously, tapes cycled include 4 daily backups Monday through Thursday, 5 weekly backups and 12 monthly backups, for a total of 21 tapes (assuming 1 tape per backup). You also notice an optional feature, Grooming. This feature, if enabled, causes ARCserve to remove files that have not been used in over 6 months after retaining 3 copies (on 3 different backups) of the file.

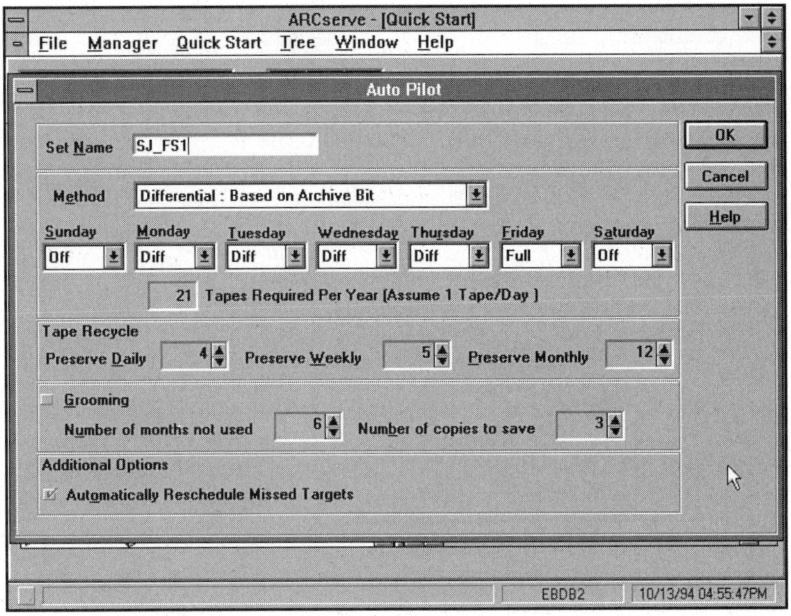

Figure 41.6

The ARCserve Auto Pilot menu.

ARCserve also features a number of NLMs that run on the file server. After the initial installation of the product is completed, the files ASTART.NCF and ASTOP.NCF are created. These files contain the command needed to start or stop ARCserve. The ARCserve Tape Server module is shown in figure 41.7.

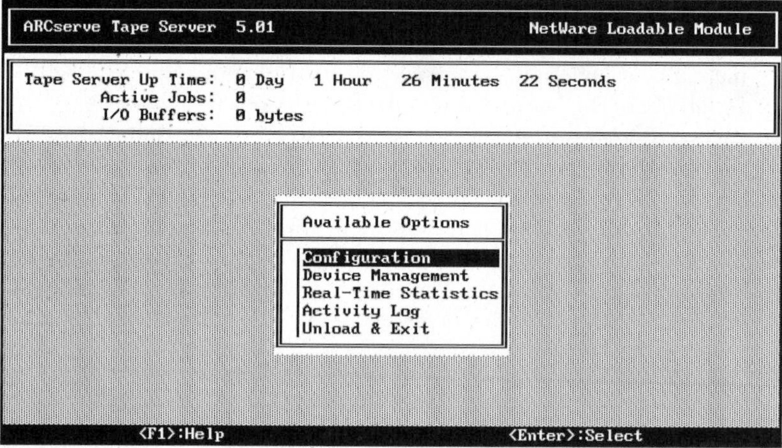

Figure 41.7
ARCserve Tape Server module running on a file server.

From the ARCserve Tape Server menu, you can view device configuration and statistics. You also can bring up a menu that enables you to format, erase, retain, and test the tape unit, among other options. Another utility that runs on the file server, simply called ARCserve, enables you to deactivate ARCserve, view statistics and logs, and configuration information. This menu enables you to view the status of jobs that are queued to run. Much like NetWare's PSERVER, this module lets you view backup jobs in progress or scheduled for a future date and time.

The Configuration menu, available from the ARCserve module, is shown in figure 41.8. As you can see, there are many configurable options available in ARCserve. Further discussion of these options is beyond the scope of this book.

```
ARCserve  v5.01  (5     user)                     NetWare Loadable Module

                              Configuration

Maximum # Concurrent Jobs:                                        16
Statistics broadcast & update frequency (seconds):                1
Minimum Cache Buffers Required to Start Jobs (%):                 10
Preserve Log File Information For <n> Days:                       30

Notify Owner at end of job:                                       Yes
Turn off all messages to workstations:                            No
Overwrite ANY tape in drive:                                      No
Use SMS logic for DOS and MAC files also:                         No
Change to ARCserve message screen on Alerts:                      Yes
Disable Writing to the ARCserve Database:                         No
Disable Writing to the ARCserve Activity Log:                     No

Skip files Larger than 2 GB:                                      No
Use 512 Byte Packet to Communicate with WS Agent:                 No

          <F1>:Help          <F2>:Save          <Esc>:Exit
```

Figure 41.8
The ARCserve Configuration menu.

Using DSREPAIR

The DSREPAIR.NLM utility can be used if you run into problems with the NDS. This utility replaces the BINDFIX.EXE utility used with bindery-based versions of NetWare. DSREPAIR can be used to make repairs and adjustments on the NDS. It repairs inconsistencies to the NDS and fixes problems caused with other servers when replicas are down or unavailable.

Do not run DSREPAIR casually. NetWare 4.1 has much better NDS synchronization than does NetWare 4.0x. It should only be necessary to run DSREPAIR when an unusual condition has arisen (such as a server crash or a critical network failure).

The DSREPAIR main menu is displayed in figure 41.9. As you can see, the main menu options are very simple. The Unattended full repair option enables you to perform an NDS repair without having to interact with the system. The View/Edit repair log file option lets you see the results of the repair. The Advanced options menu lets you perform detailed NDS repairs.

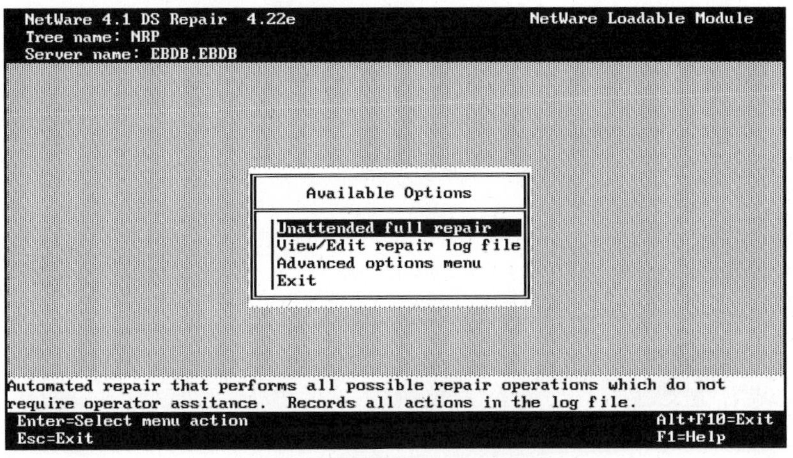

Figure 41.9
The DSREPAIR.NLM main menu.

Unattended Full NDS Repair

You may want to perform a repair on the NDS database if you experience the symptoms of a corrupted NDS database. These symptoms include the following:

- ◆ You cannot create, delete, or modify objects even though you have sufficient rights.

- You have unknown objects appearing in the tree that do not disappear of their own accord after all servers are synchronized.
- You cannot create, merge, or modify partitions.

If you experience some or all of these problems, you are most likely experiencing problems related to NDS corruption. Corruption of the NDS can occur for many different reasons. The NDS is a distributed database. The recommended procedure to safeguard the NDS is to replicate NDS partitions onto several different file servers. This form of fault tolerance also causes another problem—what happens if a server with a replica of an important portion of the NDS crashes?

When this happens, the other servers with replicas of the same partitions stored on the crashed server attempt to re-synchronize with it. The attempt fails, of course. In the meantime, however, the status of all partitions affected is in doubt. Any efforts to change the status of a partition, to merge it into its parent, or further subpartition it are not effective. This is a simplification, of course, since the outcome of partitioning operations depends on the status of the replicas of partitions on the server that is down. Any of the replicas that are Masters cause problems for the other servers. Ordinary changes to the containers and leaf objects within the partitions affected take place. Operations that involve partitioning are impacted. DSREPAIR can be used to resynchronize the remaining servers, and to make a replica on another server a Master.

To perform the unattended repair, type the following from the file server:

LOAD DSREPAIR

From the DSREPAIR main menu, select Unattended full repair. The repair begins. While the repair is in progress, the NDS database is locked. Any attempts to affect the partition are rejected. Figure 41.10 shows a repair in process.

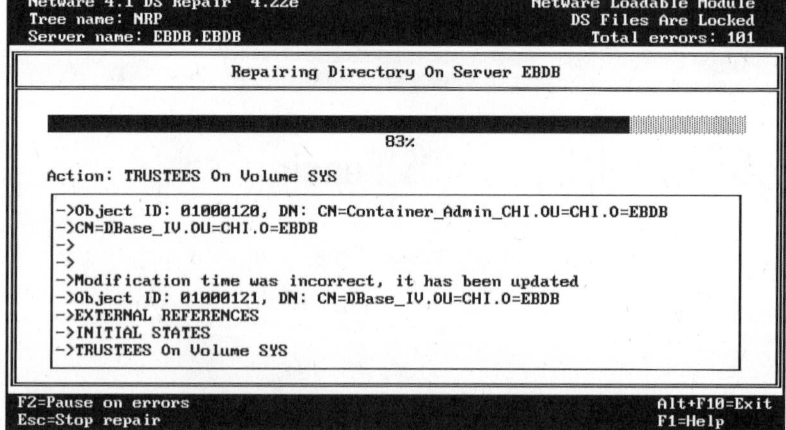

Figure 41.10
DSREPAIR.NLM—Unattended full repair in process.

Alternatively, you can load DSREPAIR with the unattended option as follows:

LOAD DSREPAIR -U

Viewing the DSREPAIR Repair Log

Once the full repair is complete, you may want to review the log file. The log file is stored by default in SYS:SYSTEM\DSREPAIR.LOG. The name and location of this file can be changed in the Advanced Options menu.

To view the repair log, from the DSREPAIR main menu, select View/Edit repair log file. The following are some excerpts from the log:

```
/***************************************************************************/
Netware 4.1 Directory Services Repair 4.22e
Log file for server "EBDB.EBDB" in tree "NRP"
Verifying / Updating Global Schema
Start: Sunday, October 9, 1994  5:18:39 PM Local Time
Checking server: CN=EBDB.O=EBDB
Schema on server: CN=EBDB.O=EBDB is up-to-date.
Checking server: CN=EBDB312.OU=NY.O=EBDB
   Performing SCHEMA upgrade
Error -625 upgrading schema.
Checking server: CN=EBDB312.OU=SJ.O=EBDB
   Performing SCHEMA upgrade
Error -625 upgrading schema.
*** END ***
/***************************************************************************/
Netware 4.1 Directory Services Repair 4.22e
Log file for server "EBDB.EBDB" in tree "NRP"
** Automated Repair Mode **
Repairing Local Database
Start: Sunday, October 9, 1994  5:19:57 PM Local Time
RECORDS
Opening temporary files
STRUCTURE
SCHEMA
Generating Schema Cache
Master   : NRP
Modification time was incorrect, it has been updated
Object ID: 010000B3, DN: NRP

Modification time was incorrect, it has been updated
```

```
Object ID: 010000B4, DN: O=EBDB
...
Modification time was incorrect, it has been updated
Object ID: 01000121, DN: CN=DBase_IV.OU=CHI.O=EBDB
EXTERNAL REFERENCES
INITIAL STATES
TRUSTEES On Volume SYS
TRUSTEES On Volume OTHER
TRUSTEES On Volume NW410DOC
Checking mail directories
Removing invalid mail directory "10010003"
Removing invalid mail directory "C8000009"
Removing invalid mail directory "4010004"
Checking stream syntax files
Removing invalid stream file "00005140.000"
Removing invalid stream file "00003A80.000"
...
Removing invalid stream file "0001FE00.000"
Repair process completed, total errors found = 126
Finish: Sunday, October 9, 1994  5:20:38 PM Local Time
Total repair time: 0:00:41
** Automated Repair Mode **
Repairing server network addresses
Start: Sunday, October 9, 1994  5:20:38 PM Local Time

Checking server: EBDB312.SJ.EBDB
Could not find a net address in SAP for this server
Error - Could not connect -625
Checking server: EBDB312.NY.EBDB
Could not find a net address in SAP for this server
Error - Could not connect -625
Checking server: EBDB.EBDB
Found a network address property on the server object:
Address Type= (IPX), data[12]= 2DECF8EF000000000010451
Checking server address in Replica ID: 4, [Root]
** Automated Repair Mode **
Repairing replica ring
Start: Sunday, October 9, 1994  5:21:34 PM Local Time
Replica Ring for replica: [Root]
Remote server's local ID: 010000B5
Remote server's replica root ID: 010000B3
Remote server name is: EBDB.EBDB
```

```
OK - Authenticated to server
** Automated Repair Mode **
Finish: Sunday, October 9, 1994  5:21:34 PM Local Time
Total repair time: 0:01:38
```

As you can see from the repair log, the following errors were detected and repaired:

- The servers EBDB312.NY.EBDB and EBDB312.SJ.EBDB were unavailable and therefore operations pertaining to them failed. These servers are NetWare 3.12 servers synchronized with the NetWare 4.1 server through NetSync.
- Modification times for some objects were incorrect. This could be because a series of updates were occurring by two workstations performing operations on the same objects at the same time. This also could be a result of improper time synchronization.
- There were invalid mail directories. These directories are for bindery-based users who may have been deleted.
- Invalid stream files were removed. These files are part of the NDS database. (You can view these files by using the RCONSOLE menu option Directory Scan. Look at the SYS:_NETWARE directory.)

DSREPAIR Advanced Options

DSREPAIR can be used to perform individual options, some of which are visible in the previous sample repair log. The Unattended full repair option is used in most cases. The advanced options are used for fine-tuning and when you need assistance on specific issues or problems on your network. Table 41.3 summarizes the DSREPAIR advanced options.

TABLE 41.3
DSREPAIR.NLM Advanced Options

Menu Item	Options	Description
Log File and Login Configuration	Current File Size	The current DSREPAIR log file in bytes.
	Reset the Log File?	When you press Enter, the DSREPAIR log file is deleted. The next time you run DSREPAIR, the file is started again.

continues

Table 41.3, Continued
DSREPAIR.NLM Advanced Options

Menu Item	Options	Description
	Log Output to a File?	The default is Yes. If you select No, the output of the DSREPAIR operation is not logged to a file. This is marginally faster and takes less disk space.
	Log File Filename	The volume, directory, and filename of the DSREPAIR log file.
	If File Already Exists?	This option enables you to choose between the default, Append to existing file, or you can choose to Overwrite existing file. The Append... option lets you maintain an ongoing log.
	Administrator Name	Before you can begin a repair you must supply a valid NDS name here.
	Password	This is where you enter the password for the valid NDS name supplied above.
Repair Local DS Database		Options in this menu pertain to the repair operation on the NDS files physically residing on this server. After selecting the appropriate options, press F10 to begin the local repair.
	Pause on Errors?	The default is No. If you select Yes, DSREPAIR pauses on every error detected.
	Validate Trustee IDs?	If you select the default, Yes, DSREPAIR proceeds to compare and validate user object ID numbers with the ID numbers associated with trustee rights stored in the DET (Directory Entry Table)

Menu Item	Options	Description
		on every volume located on this server. This is a worthwhile option but can be extremely time consuming on large volumes. Select No to save time. Select Yes to maintain the integrity of your file system security.
	Validate Mail Directories?	If you select the default of Yes, DSREPAIR deletes directories under SYS:MAIL for bindery users who no longer exist.
	Validate Stream Syntax Files?	If set to the default of Yes, DSREPAIR checks the existing stream syntax files (such as login scripts) if they corre spond with valid users.
	Rebuild Operational Schema?	This is a final effort that rebuilds the NDS database on this server. This option is not recommended and should remain at the default of No. You may need to set it to Yes if directed to do so by Novell tech support.
	Exit Automatically Upon Completion?	The default is No. If set to Yes, DSREPAIR unloads upon completion of the repair that reopens the NDS database. Set this option to Yes if you expect a lengthy repair and want to leave the site.
Servers Known to this Database		This option provides a list of servers known to DSREPAIR. Any repair operations (with the exception of Repair Local DS Database) are performed on all servers listed.

continues

Table 41.3, Continued
DSREPAIR.NLM Advanced Options

Menu Item	Options	Description
View Remote Server ID List		Gives you a list of remote servers and their NDS identification numbers (used internally by NDS). If you do not see a list of remote servers there are several possibilities: This is the only server in the tree. There are no replicas of the NDS data residing on this server. There is a communica tions problem that prevents this server from seeing other NDS servers.
Replica and Partition Operations		This option gives you a list of replicas stored on this server. When you press enter on any given replica, another menu appears, giving you the options listed next.
	View Replica Ring	Gives you a list of file servers that have a copy of the replica you selected. A *replica ring* is a series of file servers that have copies of the same replica. One server can belong to several replica rings.
	Synchronize the Replica and Report Status	Forces all servers in the replica ring for this replica to synchronize. They exchange all data, compare timestamps, and update their local databases. This option then displays a report showing you the outcome of this operation. Use this option if you are experiencing problems with a specific NDS partition.
	Repair All Replicas	Causes DSREPAIR to repair all replicas stored on this server.

Menu Item	Options	Description
	Repair Selected Replica	Causes DSREPAIR to repair the replica you selected.
	Schedule Immediate Synchronization	This option is similar to the Synchronize Replica and Report Status option described above. There is no report, however, and the synchronization is not forced. Rather, the file server schedules the synchronization process at its earliest convenience (usually within a couple of seconds, depending on how busy the file server is).
	Send All Objects to Every Replica in the Ring	Causes the server to dump all objects in this replica to all other servers participating in the replica ring. This does not force synchronization. This is a way of manually exchanging NDS data between servers. The other servers may or may not act on this data depending on timestamps and replica status.
	Receive All Objects from the Master to this Replica	Causes the server in the replica ring with the Master replica to dump all its objects to this server.
	Repair Time Stamps and Declare a New Epoch	This option sets all NDS updates to the current time. A new epoch is declared on the Master replica (see the Note below). All Read/Write or Read Only replicas receive an immediate update from the Master.
	Cancel Partition Operation	Cancels a partition operation in progress. This menu option may not be effective if the

continues

Table 41.3, Continued
DSREPAIR.NLM Advanced Options

Menu Item	Options	Description
		operation has progressed too far.
	Display Replica Information	Displays the contents of the DSREPAIR log.
	View Entire Replica Name	Displays the complete replica name of up to 256 characters.
Security Equivalence Synchronization		This option causes DSREPAIR to stop every time it needs to make a security adjustment in order to complete a repair. A menu option appears asking you to add the equivalent, to delete the equivalent, or leave the security equals alone.
Global Schema Update	Update All Server's Schema	This option repairs the NDS schema (database structure) on all servers in the tree.
	Update the Root Server Only	This option repairs the NDS schema (database structure) only on the server that contains the master replica of the root partition.
View/Edit Repair Log File		Displays the contents of the DSREPAIR log file.
Create a Database Dump File		Creates a compressed, encrypted, copy of the NDS database. This is useful if you are experiencing problems with your NDS tree and need Novell tech support to examine your structure and diagnose problems.

An *epoch* is a marker. When a new epoch is declared, all NDS updates with a timestamps from the previous epoch are ignored. Only updates with a timestamp from the current epoch are processed. An analogy is when you place bets at a Roulette Wheel. While the ball is rolling you can place a bet. Once the ball reaches a certain place in the wheel, the croupier declares that no further betting is allowed. In a similar fashion, while the current epoch is in force, NDS updates are allowed. When a new epoch is declared, updates under the previous epoch are ignored.

Understanding SFT III—Server Duplexing

Novell offers a strategy for protecting all aspects of a file server—even the file server itself. This is known as SFT (System Fault Tolerance) Level III, also known as mirrored servers. Many solutions to the problem of what to do if your server itself has a failure have been available in the past. The traditional approach is to have a workstation available that can be used as a server in a crisis. This approach relies on having a good backup and on the good graces of the person who is currently using this computer. Using the traditional approach, if the main file server crashes and the problem cannot be repaired, NetWare is installed on the designated workstation, and the last backup is restored. This process is time consuming and does not enable recovery of all new work generated since the last backup.

A second approach is to have another server online, already installed and ready to go. Critical data is copied to this server from time to time. This approach was automated a few years ago with a product called LAN Shadow. This software package monitored all updates to the primary server and took a copy of that update. When the primary server failed, the shadow server was ready to take over. The main problem with this solution is that it doubled the amount of network traffic.

Figure 41.11 illustrates Novell's server mirroring solution, called SFT III. As you can see in the figure, two servers are installed. You need a copy of NetWare 4.1 and a NetWare 4.1 SFT III License Disk. Both computers should be identical (or similar, if possible) for best performance. They should have similar CPUs, 16 MB or more of RAM, similar versions of DOS, similar video boards and monitors, and similar hard drives. Each server must have an MSL (Mirrored Server Link) adapter that is directly connected. In addition, each server should have one or more LAN cards to connect to the network.

Figure 41.11
SFT III connectivity.

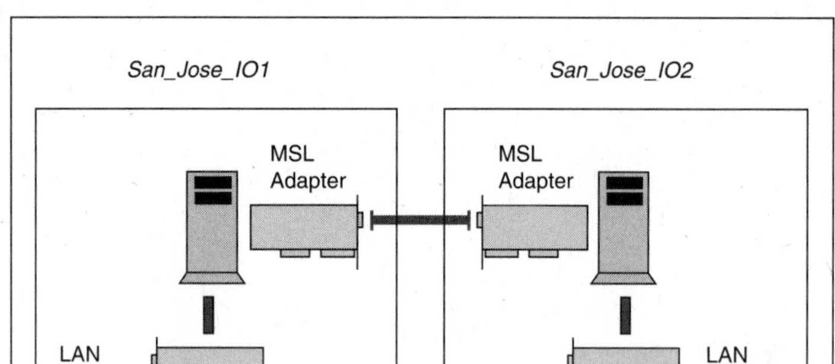

During the installation, an MS Engine (Mirrored Server Engine) name is assigned. This is the equivalent to a file server name. SFT III then creates two additional unique IO Engine (Input/Output Engine) names, one for each server. The convention is to take the MS Engine name and add _IO*n* where *n* is 1 or 2. In the figure you see an MS Engine name of San_Jose. The IO Engine names are San_Jose_IO1 and San_Jose_IO2. Three internal IPX network addresses are assigned—one for each IO Engine, and one for the MS Engine. The installation process then converts the SERVER.EXE file of each computer to MSERVER.EXE.

The first server is installed much like a standard NetWare 4.1 server. During the installation, however, you select the option, NetWare 4.1 SFT III. After supplying SFT III specific information (such as the MS Engine name), the installation proceeds much like a NetWare 4.1 installation. The MSL drivers are installed much like LAN drivers.

The second SFT III server is installed after the first. The first server must be fully installed, and up and running. Both servers must be connected through the LAN and through the MSL adapters. During the installation of the second server, INSTALL runs the ACTIVATE SERVER utility. This causes the memory of both servers to synchronize. At this point, both server consoles show the same INSTALL screen.

Four files are used for startup instead of the traditional STARTUP.NCF and AUTOEXEC.NCF. They are the following:

- IOSTART.NCF loads disk drivers, the MSL drivers, names the IO Engine, and assigns an IPX network address for the IO Engine. There is one IOSTART.NCF file for each mirrored server.

- IOAUTO.NCF points to the INITSYS.NCF file. It contains commands that are very similar to the AUTOEXEC.NCF file. There is one IOAUTO.NCF file per mirrored server.

- MSAUTO.NCF contains MS Engine specific commands as well as assigning an internal IPX network address to the MS Engine.

- MSSTART.NCF contains SET parameters specific to the MS Engine.

When the SFT III servers are in operation, workstations only see one server. The server is identified by its MS Engine name. You can login and perform operations just as if there were only a single server. If one of the servers crashes, the other server automatically takes over after a short (measured in seconds) delay.

Any updates to one mirrored server automatically are transferred to the second server using the MSL connection. This has the advantage of high speed, and does not tie up the LAN. The file server consoles of the servers are tied together (this is why you need similar monitors). Use Alt+Esc to toggle between the MS engine, and IO Engine 1 and 2 screens.

Summary

This chapter gave you an overview of the concerns and considerations behind backing up critical files and planning for disaster. The first part of the chapter dealt with developing a disaster recovery plan. A discussion of the cost of downtime demonstrated that not having a good plan can be expensive. The section on contingency planning showed you that there are several steps you can take in order to prevent a disaster in the first place. These steps include setting up disk mirroring, duplexing, or using RAID technology. Several other suggestions were offered as well. A UPS unit is desirable to ensure that the file server, or other key network components, do not lose power. A list of spare parts to have on hand was suggested. Physically securing key network components to forestall the effects of earthquakes, floods, and high winds also was recommended.

Another section dealt with how to secure the network from unauthorized intruders. The discussion included creating passwords that use words and punctuation in unusual combinations. Certain recommendations regarding password lengths, password changes, and other restrictions were discussed. The key to good security is to have enough restrictions to discourage the casual intruder, and yet not so many as to discourage people trying to do an honest day's work!

Packet signature levels were discussed. You learned what the different levels on workstations and file servers indicate.

The other key component in planning is developing a plan on What to do if ...? The two case studies were discussed. Some contingency plans included bringing back certain manual operations such as using typewriters and having receipt books ready. The key to such planning is to remember that business does not stop.

The central portion of this chapter deals with backups. The first thing you learned is to determine what should get backed up and how often. You learned about the main types of backup—full, incremental and differential. You were then introduced to two different types of media rotation schemes. The simple scheme involved having one set of media for each day and rotating them the next week. A more complex scheme involved daily, weekly, monthly, and yearly backups. Media was rotated out of the cycle on a systematic basis to prevent media failure, to provide for an archive, and for off-site storage.

Two backup software systems were discussed—SBACKUP, included with NetWare 4, and ARCserve, a third-party software package. You learned how to perform a backup using SBACKUP and Novell SMS architecture. You were then introduced to ARCserve and were given a quick tour of its features. With ARCserve you quickly can schedule unattended backups. The Auto Pilot feature enforces the rules presented in the complex media rotation scheme discussed above. ARCserve consists of a Windows based component that you run on a workstation, and a series of NLMs that are loaded on the server with the tape backup unit.

You also learned about the DSREPAIR.NLM utility and how it can be used to repair problems experienced with the NDS. You learned about the unattended repair feature, log files and reports, as well as advanced options.

The last section discussed NetWare 4.1 SFT III. As you learned, this feature enables you to have a duplicate server on-line receiving updates. If any problems are experienced with the primary, this secondary server takes over. The updating takes place over a private LAN created by connecting an MSL adapter in each server to the other. Each server has an IO Engine name. The two servers combined are seen as a single server with an MS Engine name.

The next chapter discusses the impact of computer viruses on a network.

Virus Protection

Computer viruses have been quietly working away at the "innards" of many computers for the past couple of decades. The first known virus was invented as an experiment at the Massachusetts Institute of Technology (MIT). This virus wrote itself into a position in core memory. It then wrote two copies of itself and activated them. Before long, the virus was using all computer memory and all processor power. The computer operators at MIT ultimately had to shut down the system and meticulously bring it up, manually removing the virus one component at a time.

The attention of the American public became riveted on computer viruses with the widely publicized Michelangelo virus scare of 1991 and 1992. The virus was first reported in April, 1991, in Sweden and the Netherlands. It is timed to activate on March 6. Many reports hit the press around this date, and many computer users were sweating as the dreaded day came and went. Many people set their system clocks to a date other than March 6. More concerned computer users did not use their computers at all that day. Sales of antivirus programs skyrocketed. The vendors of the virus programs came under public scrutiny. Many people thought, "If they write antivirus software, isn't it possible that they created the viruses in the first place?"

The Michelangelo virus scare might have wrought more harm than good. Although it did raise public awareness of the virus threat, when said threat failed to materialize, many people began to think that computer viruses were a hoax. Many more individuals bought one virus protection program and continue to rely on it to this day. Unfortunately, many people—not just hackers—now take part in writing viruses. These antisocial programmers come from all walks of life. The author of a computer virus might be a bored high school student (or even younger!), an angry former employee, a college student contriving a prank, or a publicity seeker.

Since that mass-media–fueled virus scare, an entire industry has been born. Many companies and consultants now are versed in virus protection. Large software corporations, including Microsoft, Symantec, and Novell, include antivirus software in their product lines. The National Computer Security Association (NCSA) was founded in 1989 primarily to organize computer professionals against the threat of computer viruses. Many current reports predict that computer viruses are not only here to stay, but will pose a greater and greater threat.

A Brief Overview of Viruses

Computer viruses, or simply *viruses*, are software programs designed to be irritating or harmful to computer systems. The first viruses were designed as computer science experiments. During the late 1960s and 1970s, a fascination developed around the idea of a virus, an organism that infects a host and replicates itself. This idea captured the imagination of the computer community and a race ensued to see who could produce a program that emulated the behavior pattern of a living organism. One offshoot of this effort was the branch of computer science known as artificial intelligence. Another offshoot was the computer virus.

One variation of the computer virus, known as a *worm*, or tapeworm, grows in size, unlike the computer virus, which makes copies of itself. This particular development was shortlived, however, because a worm is relatively easy to spot and eradicate.

The following section addresses the impact of viruses on the various computers in your network. The first discussion focuses on the impact of viruses on DOS workstations. The next discussion is about the network and file servers, and is followed by a discussion of non-DOS workstations.

Virus Cleanup

Virus cleanup can be a messy business. Sometimes, you have to write off the contents of your hard disk as lost. You might find it handy to have a copy of the NetWare 2.*x* COMPSURF.EXE utility, which performs a low-level format of the hard disk and

which you can set to overwrite every disk block with a uniform bit pattern. A faster variation of COMPSURF is the NetWare 2.2 ZTEST.EXE utility. ZTEST overwrites the first 10 cylinders of a hard drive with a uniform bit pattern. Many viruses infect the master boot record of the hard drive, which is on track 0. Most SCSI adapters come with either a utility built into the ROM BIOS, or are available on a disk which performs a low-level format of any attached drives.

Less drastic measures include running a commercial antivirus cleanup routine. The risk you run here is that the program might report success, but the virus (or another virus) might still remain. Usually before you begin the cleanup, cold-booting your computer with a known good, write-protected DOS disk removes any memory resident viruses and eliminates the potential of loading the virus from the master boot record on the hard drive. Also, because the floppy disk is write-protected, any efforts by a virus to infect the floppy disk are defeated mechanically.

You sometimes can use FDISK to restore the master boot record. Running the command FDISK /MBR restores the master boot record on your hard drive. You can use the DOS SYS command to restore the COMMAND.COM and DOS system files to an uninfected state.

A simple preventative measure is to rename your executable files so that they have an extension other than EXE or COM. When you need to execute a file, you could create a batch file to rename the file so that it has its former EXE or COM extension. After you finish executing the file, you could then rename it *back* to the other extension again. Certain advantages accompany this technique, as well as obvious disadvantages. For example, it would be impossible with Windows programs. Also, before you could rename a file, you would need to have the Modify right, which could expose that directory to further virus infection if you are on the network. The advantage to this simple technique is that when some virus programs initially try to infect your hard or floppy disk, they look specifically for programs with *.EXE or *.COM extensions.

Viruses occasionally change the nature of the FAT or boot sector. If you attempt to cleanup after the virus, attempting to copy files from the infected hard drive could well be doomed to fail. Damage to the FAT often can be repaired by using a utility such as Norton Disk Doctor.

Virus Categories

Patricia M. Hoffman (mentioned in the "Other Sources" section later in this chapter) has compiled a comprehensive database of known viruses. In it, she develops four main categories of computer virus:

- Boot sector infectors

- Multipartite
- Polymorphic
- Stealth viruses

Boot Sector Infector Viruses

A *boot sector infector* virus resides in the boot sector of a floppy or hard drive. The boot sector is the first sector of a hard disk or floppy disk. If a computer boots up using an infected disk, formatted as a system or boot disk, the virus is read into RAM (and activated) along with any other *bootstrap loader code.* The bootstrap loader code is the program which initializes DOS and some basic computer functions. The virus then proceeds to infect any disks that are not write-protected. Hard disks can become infected as well as floppy disks.

Boot sector infector viruses often write the original boot sector bootstrap loader program to another area of the hard drive, which makes them hard to detect because after they load themselves, they refer the operating system to the original bootstrap loader. The computer then appears to be operating normally.

A typical symptom of a boot sector infector virus is that the amount of RAM reported by CHKDSK is 1 KB or more less than the amount of RAM physically installed in the computer, because most boot sector infector viruses take up 1 KB to 2 KB of RAM.

An example of a boot sector infector virus is the Alameda virus, discovered in 1987. The original virus infected only 5 1/4-inch floppy disks. Alameda infects the boot sector of the disk and relocates the original boot sector to track 39. The virus was programmed to intercept the Ctrl+Alt+Del warm reboot command and at that point increment a counter. Subsequent variations of this virus cause a format of drive C when the counter reaches a particular number of warm boots, which varies from 30 to 500. Most of the commercially available antivirus utilities work for cleaning up this virus, or sometimes using the SYS command works because it overwrites the boot sector of a floppy or hard drive.

Other boot sector viruses produce the following problems and symptoms:

- Cause most or all files on the disk to appear missing
- Prevent you from booting the computer when using the infected disk
- Display a message upon bootup, such as:

```
Non-system...
```

or

```
Red State, Germ Offensive. AIRCOP.
```

- Change disk volume label to a nonsensical label, such as:

  ```
  Brain
  ```

- Destroy FAT, effectively preventing access to all files on the disk
- Disable the COM1 and LPT1 ports after a specific number of warm boots
- Decrease total system and/or free memory RAM by 1 KB to 2 KB

Multipartite Viruses

The *multipartite virus* is characterized by the way it infects more than one file at a time. Viruses of this type infect both EXE or COM files, as well as the boot sector or partition table of a disk. Multipartite viruses are less common than boot sector infector viruses.

An example of a multipartite virus is Flip. It was first discovered in West Germany in July, 1990. It infects EXE, COM and OVL files, as well as the boot sector of hard or floppy drives. This memory-resident virus usually occupies around 3 KB RAM. After files become infected, their length increases from 2 KB to 3 KB, and some might be damaged or corrupted. The most visible symptom of Flip is that the video display of any infected computer "flips" horizontally between 4:00 and 5:00 p.m. on the second day of any month. A far worse problem is that hard drives that have a partition size greater than 32 MB might have the partition size reduced to less than 32 MB.

To clean up Flip, use the "clean" function of most commercial antivirus packages, or delete the infected files. Be sure to use a known good copy of DOS on a write-protected floppy disk to reboot your computer before cleanup.

Other multipartite viruses can produce the following problems and symptoms:

- Alter small portions of the partition table (as small as 1 or 2 bytes) and then write themselves into another part of track 0
- Infect any program that you execute, open, or copy. If you copy, the source *and* target get infected
- Increase the size of program files from 2 KB to 3 KB
- Set the seconds field of the last modified time of the file to 60

- Play a melody continuously after a certain period of time has elapsed (for example, the Invader virus does so after 30 seconds)
- Overwrite the first track of the hard drive when user presses Ctrl+Alt+Del
- Produce file allocation errors on infected files
- Overwrite the master boot record

Polymorphic Viruses

Polymorphic viruses use a complex encryption scheme that makes them extremely difficult to detect.

An example of a polymorphic virus is Tequila, thought to have originated in Switzerland and first reported in April, 1991. The Tequila virus uses a complex garbling and encryption method to avoid detection. After it infects a system, it checks whether the master boot sector is infected. The virus writes an unencrypted version of itself to the last 6 sectors of the hard drive and modifies the master boot record so that it activates upon the next bootup. Here, the virus does not activate nor infect other programs. The next time you boot the system, the virus becomes memory-resident and moves the return of interrupt 12, which prevents the virus from being overwritten in memory. It hooks interrupts 13 and 21. DOS CHKDSK shows 3 KB less RAM than you should have. Infected programs increase in size by slightly more than 2 KB. A directory scan of an infected program does not show any change in the program's date, time, or size when Tequila is resident in RAM. CHKDSK starts to report file allocation errors, and CHKDSK /F can result in file corruption. Four months after the date of infection, a graphic and the message, `Execute: mov ax, FE03 / int 21. Key to go on!` appears. If you execute this program (in DEBUG), you see the message, `Welcome to T. Tequila's latest production ... BEER and TEQUILA forever!`.

You can clean up polymorphic viruses by deleting the infected files, using a commercial virus cleanup program, or replacing the master boot record. To replace the master boot record, type the following command:

FDISK /MBR

Other viruses can cause the following symptoms and problems:

- Decrease the RAM that CHKDSK reports by 2 KB to 4 KB
- Display a V-shaped graphic on-screen after a certain number of disks have been infected, and then hang the system
- Cause the video image to be flipped horizontally on the second day of any month, sometime between 4:00 and 5:00 p.m.

- Cause an increase in the size of infected files from 1 KB to 3 KB in size
- Cause the system to hang
- Append the following text to the end of infected .DOC files: `OOPS! Hope I didn't ruin anything!!! Well, nobody reads these stupid DOCS anyway!`
- Overwrite the first 4 sectors of cylinders 0 through 29 of the hard drive on March 15 and November 1
- Increase the year of the file by 100
- Cause sluggish program response and execution
- Cause file allocation errors to be reported when the virus is memory-resident
- Cause the contents of the video display to appear to "shake" and the message `-=> T.R.E.M.O.R. was done by NEUROBASHER ...` to appear on the monitor, after which the system returns to normal

Stealth Viruses

Stealth and "sub stealth" viruses are difficult to detect because they exhibit little or no visible symptoms until the final (usually fatal) activation. One type of virus which could be included in this category hides the increase in file length and changes the file date and time. In addition, stealth viruses load infected programs into memory in a "clean" state so that they behave normally, making initial virus detection difficult. Another characteristic of stealth viruses is that they infect all program files executed or even opened, so the virus tends to spread rapidly.

An example of a stealth virus is SVC 6.0, which originated in the former USSR in 1991. SVC 6.0 resides in the top portion of the first 640 KB of RAM and uses slightly more than 4 KB of RAM. It hooks interrupts 8 and 21 (the same interrupt used by the older NETX shell), and resides in track 0 of the hard drive. It alters the first three bytes of the master boot record on the hard drive and infects any EXE or COM file you open or execute. When you read programs into memory, the virus "cleans" them so that they appear to operate normally. Later, variants of the virus cause the infected file's date and time to appear the same as the original date and time. SVC 6.0 also qualifies as multipartite because it infects EXE and COM files, and the master boot record.

To clean up such viruses, use a clean write-protected DOS disk to reboot your system or run commercial antivirus software. If necessary, delete the infected files.

Characteristics, problems, and symptoms of stealth viruses include the following:

- Hide memory usage from CHKDSK
- Hide alterations to the partition table when the virus is in memory in order to present an uninfected view of the partition table
- Hide size increases in program files as long as virus is memory-resident
- Lock the system keyboard if you use a virus checker while the virus is memory-resident
- Cause CHKDSK /F to report slow cross-linking of files as lost sectors or cross links
- Make data files appear fine on infected systems, but appear to be corrupted on uninfected (or cleaned up) systems
- Hang the system on September 22
- Cause sectors to be marked bad in the FAT—some viruses move the original master boot record to these sectors and write themselves to the original master boot record
- Increase file sizes by an additional 1 KB to 2 KB
- Overwrite random disk sectors with virus code that corrupts any file occupying those sectors
- Decrease available system memory reported by CHKDSK from 2 KB to 6 KB of RAM
- Alter the system date and time format (for example, from "mm/yy/dd" to "yyyy#mm#dd")
- Cause CHKDSK to report errors on infected files
- Cause sluggish response to DOS DIR command
- Move original pointers for executables and substitute with pointers to virus code; after virus is cleaned, attempts to copy infected files result in the file not being copied properly
- Overwrite the first few tracks of each disk
- Cause the system to hang and a message to appear: `That rings a bell, no? From Cursy`

- Display the message `Invalid Drive Specification` after booting from a clean, uninfected disk
- Cause the system to hang on January 5 and a message to appear: `type Happy Birthday Joshi`
- Sounds a tone on the system speaker between 10:00 and 11:00 a.m.
- Cause the speaker to emit a clicking sound when you press keys
- Display `Disk Boot Failure` messages when you boot from infected floppy disks
- Set the seconds field to 58
- Corrupt the hard drive on the 18th of any month

How Viruses Affect DOS Workstations

Viruses affect workstations in several different ways. The worst way is when a virus destroys all the files and data on your hard drive. In addition, a virus can infect all floppies read from or written to an infected workstation.

One simple DOS computer virus creates a program that has the same prefix as an executable residing on your system and uses the extension COM. The shadow program is then hidden, using the DOS hidden file attribute. When you go to execute the program, DOS first executes the hidden program that has the COM extension. This shadow program then generally installs itself into RAM before executing the actual program that has the extension EXE. Viruses of this type are relatively easy to spot. At the DOS workstation, to produce a list of all files in all subdirectories (hidden or otherwise), and redirect the results into a file TEST1.TXT, type the following command:

ATTRIB C:*.COM /S >TEST1.TXT

The file attributes for TEST1.TXT are listed at the left. Watch for any files that have the H (Hidden) or S (System) attributes. Then, to produce a list of all files that are not hidden or system files, and to place the results into a file TEST2.TXT, type the following command:

DIR C:*.COM /S >TEST2.TXT

You can then compare the two files and determine any differences. If you discover additional files on the first list (produced by the ATTRIB command), be suspicious. Why are these files hidden? You might then want to compare those files to files that have the EXE extension. To do so, type the following command:

DIR C:*.EXE /S >TEST3.TXT

Other viruses are more insidious and damaging. Some viruses alter the DOS command interpreter file COMMAND.COM. These viruses then load into RAM every time you boot up the computer. Other viruses infect executable files or overlays (such as Windows Dynamic Link Library files). These viruses are activated every time you run the infected executable program. Other viruses affect the boot sector of the hard drive. These viruses generally damage your capacity for storing and retrieving files.

Figure 42.1 shows the effects of the Cascade virus. The Cascade virus falls into the irritating category. It causes the letters on your screen to "fall" to the bottom one by one. After a certain point your computer becomes difficult to use because letters do not remain on screen.

```
FIG3300.PCX    FIG3311.PCX    ~DOC0002.TMP   FIG3312.PCX    FIG3313.PCX
FIG3314.PCX    CHAP33.ZIP     FIG3501.SRC    FIG3505.BAT    FIG3502.SRC
FIG3503.DAT    FIG3501.DAT    FIG3503.SR     FIG3504.SRC    FIG3502.DAT
MENU_O.BAT     FIG350 .DA     CHAP35.ZIP     FIG3505.TXT    FIG3506.BAT
FIG1502.TXT    CHAP0 4        CHAP2  Z P     ACCESS.DBO     CHAP20.ZIP
CHAP42.Z P     Q.BATB ZIP     I.TXT2. I      CATALOG.CAT    UNTITLED.CAT
CHAP41 Z P     CHAP43.  IP    ACCESS.FRMC    ACCESS.FR      ACCESS.FR
FIG6.B. I      CHAP25.Z       FIG251 .       CREATEST       TEST.PRG
FILE.1AT       FILE.2.Z       FILE.30 PR     TEST.DBF G     TEST.DBT O
CREATESTID O   TEST.DBO       799066.L       TEST.MDX.P     883261.TM
883261.D.T     TEST.FRMIP     TEST.FRGOG     VOLAUD.FIL     TEST.FRO
TODO.DOCB B    VOLAUD.HIST    VOLAUD.OLDG    CHAP17.ZIPR    BAC .BA  P
FIG2203.PCX    FIG2202.PCX    FIG2204.PC     FIG2220.PC     FIGK218TPCX
FIG2207.PCX    FIG2210.PCX    CHAP13   O X   FIG22 5. CX    FIG 2 8.PC
FIG2206.PCX    FIG2212.PCX    FIG221.DPCX    CH P30   P     CHA 20..O X
E TIM TE.XLS   FIG 0 3.XLS    FIG10 1. C      I 108.ZIPX    FIG  0  XC
F G19 1.XL     PRI T N . LS   A.TXT04.X S     . X  5.XLS     ND 006  LS
A  E  .D KS    FIG 2 3 PX     FIG 21  P       I 2    . C     I  2 1 PCX
 S 2 A . C     P R1  BGSCX    FI  22  P         2            I 2  7 P
 I   0  BCX       N 0 .PC        215 .         A               2    .  T
 CC SS9 P X       2 I A GX      G2P    LX    F G               P   D
FIG 21.DO  ile(sFA S 13.  12,58  HAPe    C   B T T0          E  1   .
CHAP229.P      AIG2E..PR  8, 8  TEM ]4. C    F G 215 P       F G2 2 .
FIG371263Cf    )CCE2212,3     5Cbyt s2ZIPX   FIG 216.PCX     F G221 . CX
F:\DATA\NRP\INSIDE4>SS89,71  7 4[bytes.free  CHAP37.ZIPXG    AUDITFIL TX
```

Figure 42.1

Effects of the Cascade virus on an infected computer.

How Viruses Affect the Network

The impact of viruses on the network is not as severe as on workstations. A virus that attempts to infect the boot sector of a drive mapped to a NetWare volume is doomed to fail for the same reason you cannot use the DOS FORMAT command to format a NetWare drive: The only way you can gain access to the file server's hard drive is by using the workstation shell and the NetWare operating system. Any commands you try to use to directly access the file server's hardware are not translated.

Here are some points to consider:

- The server can become a carrier for computer viruses. Files infected on a workstation can get stored on the server and, in turn, infect other workstations. Even if the server itself is immune to infection through its workstations, it can still carry the virus to all workstations.

- An infection could occur on the file server's DOS partition. If a bad disk was used to install the server in the first place, it can infect a server if you boot first under DOS. Under these circumstances, any file on the DOS partition can get infected, including COMMAND.COM. If you have a server that has an infected DOS partition, you can lose all the files on your hard drives through boot sector contamination.
- NetWare might not boot because of a virus in memory or a corrupted SERVER.EXE file. If you suspect a virus on the file server's DOS partition, watch as the server boots up. If you spot a message that indicates that NetWare was unable to load at a certain address in RAM, a virus might be the culprit. When NetWare detects a RAM resident program, it attempts to load above the TSR. NetWare normally loads in extended RAM above DOS high memory (the first 64 KB of RAM)—if it cannot, a warning message appears, and it tries to load anyway.

How Viruses Affect Non-DOS Workstations

Non-DOS workstations are certainly not exempt from virus infection. Many of the early viruses that infected microprocessor-based workstations were designed for the Macintosh. Most of the early Macintosh viruses were nondestructive—best described as irritating pranks. One virus, for example, caused the letters on-screen for a certain word-processing document to "drop out" of the document one-at-a-time. After 5 to 10 minutes expired, the screen would look like a piece of Swiss cheese. Letters would be missing and you could see a jumble of letters in a "heap" at the bottom of the screen.

Similarly, UNIX has born its share of computer viruses. Newer operating systems such as OS/2 and Windows NT have not seen many viruses simply because fewer disgruntled programmers are familiar with these systems.

UNIX has an advantage over DOS in that executable files can have any file name. As long as the file has the "x" attribute, you can execute it in UNIX. Many DOS-based viruses specifically search out files that have the extension COM or EXE. Because a UNIX executable file name has no specific extension (no extension at all, as a matter of fact!) invasion by a virus is more difficult.

UNIX also manages memory differently than does DOS. The UNIX world has no such thing as a *terminate-and-stay-resident* (TSR) program. You can run any UNIX program in the background, so in a sense, all UNIX programs are TSR. The system Administrator on a UNIX system can obtain a detailed breakdown of any program running on the system at any time, which makes viruses easy to detect.

One form of virus in UNIX adds a cron job to the system crontabs file. The cron utility schedules tasks repetitively at specified dates and times, requiring high-level security. Only a user who had sufficient rights could insert such a virus. The UNIX cron daemon would then run the virus at the designated date and time. Tracking a task placed in a crontabs file, however, is fairly easy, and an alert system Administrator could detect the virus using cron within 24 hours.

Workstation Protection

Virus protection at the workstation consists of several levels:

- Carefully check the source of all software loaded onto the workstation
- Use virus scanning utilities regularly
- Use memory-resident virus prevention programs

The first consideration is to check all software that you load onto the workstation in the first place. If the software is a copy or you have obtained it from a bulletin board, you might want to do a virus scan on the executable before you ever use the program. Bulletin boards and shareware have gotten bad press in recent years. Shareware is a wonderful concept. Many excellent programs have first become popular as shareware. Just because a program is shareware does not mean it has a virus.

On the other hand, bulletin boards and the Internet are easy targets for propagators of viruses. The virus often is propagated without the knowledge of the person downloading the program in the first place. Other times, the person downloading the program might intentionally be embedding a virus into the program.

You can use virus scanning programs such as the Norton AntiVirus program or the SCAN utility from McAfee Associates on a regular basis to scan the workstation for viruses. You should make a point to keep your virus scanning programs up-to-date. The false sense of security you have when your virus scanning program reports no viruses is very dangerous. Out-of-date antivirus software might not be able to detect the latest generation of computer viruses. Most vendors offer regular updates to their antivirus software. McAfee Associates, for example, offers a license that provides a year of updates to the virus profile files that come with the SCAN utility.

One good way to ensure that regular scanning of your workstations occurs is to build it into your login scripts. You could, for example, set up the login script to perform a scan every Friday before 10:00 a.m. You could add the following commands to your container login script:

```
IF "%DAY_OF_WEEK" = "FRIDAY" AND "%HOUR24" < "10" THEN
    MAP INS S1:=SYS:APPS\ANTIVRUS
    #SCAN C:
    MAP DEL S1:
END
```

This set of statements causes the SCAN utility to scan drive C every Friday before 10:00 a.m. The preceding example assumes that the SCAN utility is located in a directory named SYS:APPS\ANTIVRUS and that users have Read and File Scan directory trustee rights to this directory. (Any additional rights could allow a virus to infect the antivirus program.)

Virus prevention programs are loaded in the CONFIG.SYS or AUTOEXEC.BAT files. These programs remain memory-resident in your workstation, safeguarding against the intrusion of a virus. The first thing such programs do is to check immediately for the presence of a virus in RAM or in the boot sector of the workstation. After assuring that all is well, the virus prevention program remains vigilant, continuously monitoring system activity and attempting to detect the presence of a virus. Such programs intercept any attempts to erase your hard drive, or to alter an existing EXE or COM file. In a Macintosh, the virus protection software is located in the System Folder and monitors against similar activities.

The disadvantage of having a virus protection program is that it takes up RAM that you could be using for other applications. Antivirus programs also take up CPU time, which decreases workstation performance. Sometimes such programs are intrusive. When you want to format a new hard drive, for example, the antivirus program usually tries to stop you.

Another good way to protect workstations is to maintain a small dosage of prevention. Because most viruses are memory-resident, they steal away a certain amount of RAM from your system. You can use the DOS CHKDSK utility to obtain the current amount of RAM available on your system. If you notice a decrease in available RAM and you have not added or revised your system, a virus might be present.

Following is a batch file, DETECT.BAT, that calls CHKDSK and redirects the output to a text file \DETECT.TMP. A small QBASIC program is then called that compares the "total memory" and "bytes free" lines in a CHKDSK output for differences from values stored in a file \DETECT.TXT. If this is the first time you run this batch file, press Y when prompted to save the "total memory" and "bytes free" values.

```
echo off
echo :    Title:         DETECT.BAT
echo :    Date:          10/25/94
echo :    Author:        Doug Bierer
echo :    Notes:         Calls CHKDSK and redirects output to \DETECT.TMP.
echo :                   Then calls QBASIC program DETECT.BAS which compares
echo :                   results with results stored in \DETECT.TXT.
echo :                   If there is a difference, you are notified.
echo :
echo :    Running CHKDSK Utility
echo :
```

```
chkdsk >\detect.tmp
echo :
echo :    Running QBASIC Program DETECT.BAS
echo :
qbasic /run detect
echo :
echo :    Done...
echo :
```

The following is the QBASIC program DETECT.BAS:

```
REM
REM   Title:     DETECT.BAS
REM   Date:      10/25/94
REM   Author:     D. Bierer
REM   Notes:     Takes output from CHKDSK, a file \DETECT.TMP,
REM              and looks for "lost allocation units" found;
REM              it also compares original TOTAL and FREE bytes
REM              of memory.
REM   Files:     Original results are in \DETECT.TXT
REM              Also writes new values to \DETECT.TXT if user says so
REM              File \DETECT.TMP is assumed to have CHKDSK output
REM

PRINT "Checking CHKDSK Output for Memory Inconsistencies..."

REM   Set Values
REM       N = 0 if \DETECT.TXT not found, or if write new values = True
REM       T = 0 if Total Memory line does not match
REM       F = 0 if Free Bytes line does not match

N = 1
T = 0
F = 0

REM   Check for \DETECT.TXT

ON ERROR GOTO 2000
OPEN "\DETECT.TXT" FOR INPUT AS #1

REM   Input Values
REM       L$ = Lost Allocation Units
REM       T$ = Total Memory
```

```
REM       F$ = Memory Free

LINE INPUT #1, L$
LINE INPUT #1, T$
LINE INPUT #1, F$
CLOSE #1
T$ = UCASE$(T$)
F$ = UCASE$(F$)


1000
REM   Open \DETECT.TMP for input
OPEN "\DETECT.TMP" FOR INPUT AS #1

1500
IF EOF(1) THEN 3000
LINE INPUT #1, A$
A$ = UCASE$(A$)

REM   Check for "Lost Allocation Unit" count and increment counter

X = INSTR(A$, "LOST")
IF X > 0 THEN
    Z = VAL(LEFT$(A$, X))
    L = VAL(L$) + Z
    PRINT
    PRINT "Lost Allocation Units Found:", Z
    PRINT "Total Lost Allocation Units:", L
    PRINT "This could indicate a virus infection..."
    PRINT
    L$ = STR$(L)
END IF

REM   Check for "Total Bytes Memory" and compare
X = INSTR(A$, "TOTAL BYTES MEMORY")
IF X > 0 THEN
    IF A$ = T$ THEN
        T = 1
    ELSE
        T2$ = A$
    END IF
END IF
```

```
REM   Check for "Bytes Free" and compare
X = INSTR(A$, "BYTES FREE")
IF X > 0 THEN
    IF A$ = F$ THEN
        F = 1
    ELSE
        F2$ = A$
    END IF
END IF

REM   Loop Back to Next Line Input

GOTO 1500


2000
REM   Sets values if \DETECT.TXT does not exist
IF ERR = 53 THEN
    N = 0
    L$ = "0"
    T$ = "0"
    F$ = "0"
ELSE
    PRINT "Unexpected Error..."
    RETURN
END IF
GOTO 1000


3000
REM
REM   End of File
REM
CLOSE #1

REM   Print Analysis

IF T = 0 THEN
    PRINT
    PRINT "Original:", T$
    PRINT "New:", T2$
    PRINT
```

```
    PRINT "If the new TOTAL MEMORY is less, this could indicate the"
    PRINT "presence of a virus..."
    PRINT
    PRINT "If the new amount is more and you have adjusted your"
    PRINT "memory usage, or if this is the first time you have"
    PRINT "run this program, do you wish to update the files"
    PRINT "with the new value (Y/N)?"
    INPUT A$
    IF UCASE$(LEFT$(A$, 1)) = "Y" THEN
        T$ = T2$
        N = 0
    END IF
ELSE
    PRINT "Total Memory Value Checks Out OK..."
END IF

IF F = 0 THEN
    PRINT
    PRINT "Original:", F$
    PRINT "New:", F2$
    PRINT
    PRINT "If the new BYTES FREE is less, this could indicate the"
    PRINT "presence of a virus..."
    PRINT
    PRINT "If the new amount is more and you have adjusted your"
    PRINT "memory usage, or if this is the first time you have"
    PRINT "run this program, do you wish to update the files"
    PRINT "with the new value (Y/N)?"
    INPUT A$
    IF UCASE$(LEFT$(A$, 1)) = "Y" THEN
        F$ = F2$
        N = 0
    END IF
ELSE
    PRINT "Bytes Free Value Checks Out OK..."
END IF

REM   Write \DETECT.TXT if None Exists, or to update values

IF N = 0 THEN
    OPEN "\DETECT.TXT" FOR OUTPUT AS #1
    PRINT #1, L$
```

```
    PRINT #1, T$
    PRINT #1, F$
    CLOSE #1
END IF
SYSTEM
```

Server Protection

Virus protection on the file server consists of several possible procedures:

- Limiting the number of times users log into the server with full SUPERVISOR trustee rights from the root of the volume
- Using a virus-scanning utility to scan the server's DOS partition for viruses
- Scanning each program before installing it on the server
- Using virus-scanning utilities on a regular basis
- Loading an antivirus NLM on the file server

Each time you log in to the server with full Supervisor directory trustee rights from the root of the volume, you place your server at risk. If you are the network Administrator, you should have a separate user ID with which to log in to the server as a user who has limited rights. If you log in as a user having full Supervisor trustee rights, and your workstation is infected with a virus, you potentially can infect every file on the server! If you log in as a user who has limited rights, you can impact only those files and directories where you have Read, Write, File Scan, Create, Erase, and Modify at a minimum. If you have Access Control and/or Supervisor rights, the virus in an infected workstation is given the same rights.

To do a virus scan on the file server's DOS partition, follow the same procedure as for scanning a workstation. You must bring down the file server and reboot it with a known good, write-protected bootable DOS disk. Place the write-protected disk with the virus scanning software into the file server's floppy drive, and execute the scan utility on drive C.

As when you work with workstations, be aware of the source of the program you plan to install on the file server. Scan the program disks before you install. You should then scan the application program files immediately after installation and prior to execution.

You should regularly use virus scanning programs on each of the file server's volumes. Usually, you can use the same programs you use to scan a workstation. If you plan to locate virus scanning programs on the server, it is very important to limit user rights to the directories that contain the antivirus programs. Because the antivirus program is an executable, it too is subject to infection just like any other program. For maximum protection of antivirus software on the server, take the following steps:

- Give users only Read rights to the directory that contains the antivirus software. You can then create batch files in other directories (such as SYS:PUBLIC) to invoke the antivirus software by name. The reason not to give File Scan rights is to prevent users from seeing the names and dates of the antivirus software.
- Change the names of the antivirus utilities. It is conceivable that some viruses deliberately seek these programs out to try to neutralize them.
- After you change the names, use the FLAG.EXE command to assign Read Only attributes to the utilities.

Antivirus NLMs on the file server are geared to perform several actions. Typically, you can access a menu interface from the file server console. From this menu, most vendors will allow you to perform a scan of the file server. Although similar to a scan from a workstation logged into the server using a workstation-based virus scan utility, performing the action from the server on the server introduces no additional network traffic and is faster.

In addition, many server-based antivirus packages offer the following features:

- Monitoring the network for possible virus intrusions
- "Registering" executables on the server
- Scheduling regular virus scans
- Handling possibly infected files

You can set server-based virus utilities to monitor the network for possible virus intrusions. Such utilities perform a virus scan of any file of a specified type that is copied to the network or modified. The types of files checked vary. Many server-based virus utilities enable you to configure the types of files to scan. Others have a preset list. The lists usually include files that have the extensions of EXE and COM. In addition, many utilities now check files that have the following extensions: DLL (Windows library files), OVL (overlay files), BIN (binary files), and SYS (system files). The disadvantage of having the virus NLM monitor for possible viruses is reduced server performance.

The method by which server-based virus utilities register executable files is usually to use a form of CRC or checksum, which involves reading the file and producing one or two numbers that you can enter into a file for future reference. During scheduled scans, the file is reread and compared with its original checksum. If the new and old numbers do not match, it means the file has been modified, possibly by a virus.

A classic registration program, available on CompuServe and the Internet, is VALIDATE.EXE by McAfee Associates. VALIDATE.EXE checks the file(s) or directories specified and produces two hexadecimal numbers. You could easily write a QBASIC program to take the output of this program and compare it with a database you maintain. Because most virus programs can do this anyway, however, writing such a program is not necessary.

Following is the output of the VALIDATE.EXE utility:

```
F:\APPS\VIRUS>validate.exe c:\windows\*.dll
Validate version 2.00 Copyright  McAfee, Inc. 1994. All rights reserved.
(408) 988-3832 EVALUATION COPY
Directory of C:\WINDOWS\

CAS    DLL    5648 09-02-93 12:06p  440E  CE51
FAXABLE DLL  377312 09-02-93 12:09p  667F  DA5E
VBRUN100 DLL  271264 05-10-91  1:00a  404C  B7A8
VBRUN200 DLL  356992 10-21-92  0:00a  9474  E4DC
VBRUN300 DLL  394384 04-28-93  0:00a  FE14  1C4E
CCMGR  DLL   13357 09-03-93  3:04p  C589  DDC6
MORICONS DLL  118864 03-10-92  3:10a  AB9A  5D38
PBRUSH  DLL   6766 03-10-92  3:10a  7F50  0885
RECORDER DLL   10414 03-10-92  3:10a  A19B  F5EB
CGMZV  DLL  609118 08-26-93  4:07p  0DB7  9E6C
MCIOLE  DLL   11776 11-19-93  0:00a  B630  91C8
CTL3D  DLL   19568 06-06-93  9:31p  9700  1A5D

    12 file(s) were validated

F:\APPS\VIRUS>
```

Much like unattended backups, you can usually set up virus programs on the server to perform scheduled virus scans. You can have the utility perform a virus check at a time early in the morning, for example, when it will not affect the primary operations of your company.

Another feature you find in many server-based antivirus programs is the capability to handle infected files. Most programs give you the option to send out a message to one or more users if you discover an infected file. Usually, you would keep a log of virus scans. You can configure most antivirus programs to delete or relocate infected files and can then later go through the scan log to determine which files need to be examined or reinstalled.

Antivirus Software

Because the major virus scares of the past few years, many antivirus software companies have sprung into existence. Owing to the trend toward "consolidation" (i.e., mergers and acquisitions of smaller software companies by larger software companies) in the software industry, most of the major players in the operating system business have written or have licensed antivirus software. Microsoft, for example, licenses antivirus software from Central Point Software, Inc.

Several types of antivirus software are available, including DOS-based utilities that you can execute from the DOS command prompt. Most of the major software players have released Windows versions as well. This section gives you an overview of the major antivirus software packages on the market today.

McAfee Associates

McAfee Associates is a private computer security consulting company based in Santa Clara, California. Phone number: (408) 988-3832. McAfee Associates was one of the first companies to specialize in the detection and eradication of computer viruses. McAfee Associates has both a bulletin board (408/988-4004), and a forum on CompuServe (GO MCAFEE). McAfee Associates' Internet address is support@mcafee.com.

McAfee Associates is noted primarily for its SCAN program. This program, updated approximately every quarter, scans any DOS drive (including NetWare-mapped drive letters) for viruses. The program first scans memory to see if a virus has lodged itself in RAM. It then proceeds to check the entire drive indicated for the presence of viruses. This utility works very quickly and produces a report at the end that indicates any viruses detected. The utility checks for the presence of viruses in COM, EXE, DLL, OVL, BIN, and SYS files.

Following is a sample showing the output produced when running the SCAN.EXE program:

```
G:\APPS\VIRUS>scan c:
Scan V.2.1.1 Copyright  McAfee, Inc. 1994. All rights reserved.
(408) 988-3832 EVALUATION COPY

Virus data file V2.1.211 created 09/26/94 23:50:20
No viruses found in memory.
Scanning C:
Scanning file ...
```

```
Summary report on C:

File(s)
    Analyzed: .............  2495
    Scanned: ..............   479
    Possibly Infected: .....    0
Master Boot Record(s):..........    1
    Possibly Infected:......    0
Boot Sector(s):................    1
    Possibly Infected:......    0


Time: 00:00.42

Thank you for choosing to evaluate VirusScan from McAfee. This version
of the software is for Evaluation Purposes Only and may be used for up
to 30 days to determine if it meets your requirements. To license the
the software, or to obtain assistance during the evaluation process,
please call (408) 988-3832, or contact your local authorized agent
(see the file AGENTS.TXT for a current list). If you choose not to
license the software, you need to remove it from your system. All use
of this software is conditioned upon compliance with the license terms
set forth in the LICENSE.TXT file.

G:\APPS\VIRUS>
```

In addition to the SCAN program, McAfee offers an NLM which you can run on a NetWare file server called NETSHLD.NLM (NETShield). This software package consists of an NLM that you load on your NetWare file servers. After you install NETShield, you can configure it to scan your network periodically, watching especially for executable files copied to the network by users. NETShield offers options that enable you to configure to send out a warning message to all or selected users if a virus infected file is found. After NETShield detects a virus, it can log this to a file, and even can move the infected file to a "quarantined" area of the network.

Figure 42.2 shows the main screen for NETShield running on a file server.

In addition to the options already mentioned, you can upload the latest list of viruses uncovered by McAfee Associates to NETShield, generate a report, schedule when and how often to scan for viruses, and create a checksum file for files on your server.

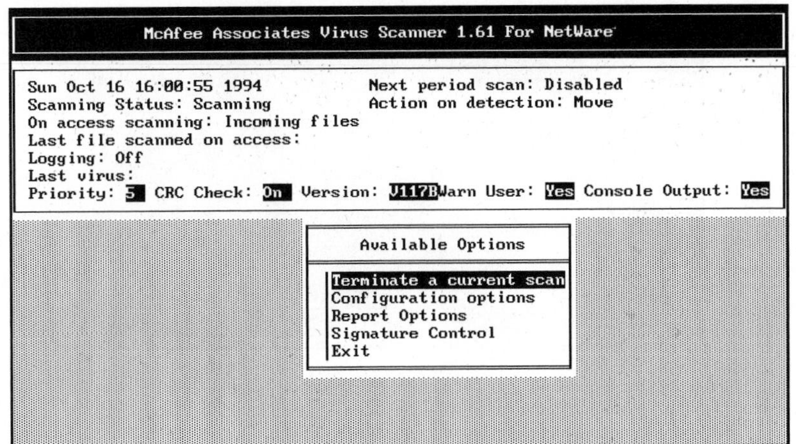

Figure 42.2

McAfee Associates NETShield utility running on a file server.

Other software offered by McAfee Associates includes the following:

- CLEANUP software to clean up detected viruses
- VSHIELD software to protect against virus contamination in the first place
- SENTRY software to alert you of the presence of a virus

Note McAfee Associates offers free evaluation copies of its software on its bulletin board (and CompuServe forum). The software is designed to self-destruct in 30 days. If you do not plan to license the software from McAfee, be sure to remove it from your system.

Microsoft Anti-Virus/Central Point Software

Included with Microsoft's MS-DOS 6.*x* versions is a special version of Central Point Software's antivirus utility. This utility is also included in PC-Tools. There are two components to the package as included in MS-DOS 6.*x*:

- MSAV.EXE is a virus scanner/cleaner invoked from the DOS command prompt
- VSAFE.COM is a memory resident program which protects the workstation against virus activities
- MWAV.EXE is invoked from within Windows

Both utilities will search for viruses and perform virus cleanup. Figure 42.3 shows you the main screen for the MWAV.EXE utility.

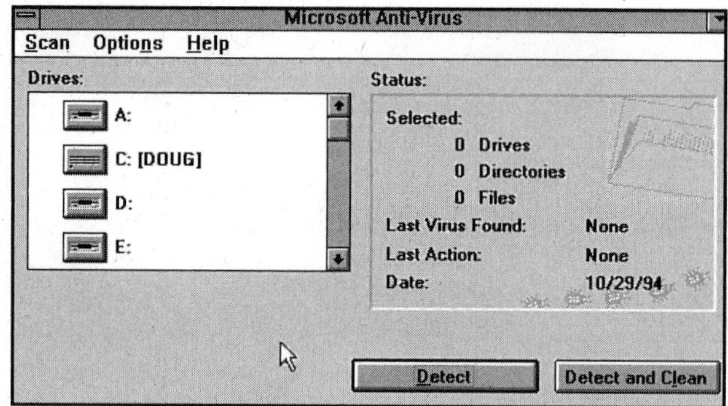

Figure 42.3

Microsoft Anti-Virus for Windows included in MS-DOS 6.x.

To scan for viruses, first select a drive letter. Microsoft Anti-Virus will read the drive and load a count of files and directories into memory. To check for viruses, press the Detect button, or, from the Scan menu, select Detect. The utility will then check the designated drive for virus infected files. The first time a scan operation is performed, Microsoft Anti-Virus will check RAM for the presence of a virus.

You can also select the Detect and Clean option, which combines a virus scan with a cleanup activity if any viruses are detected. Otherwise, if a virus is detected, you will be prompted to perform an immediate cleanup. Once the operation is completed you will see a summary window which shows you the total number of files and directories checked, and total numbers of files infected and cleaned.

Figure 42.4 shows you the detect operation in action on a floppy disk.

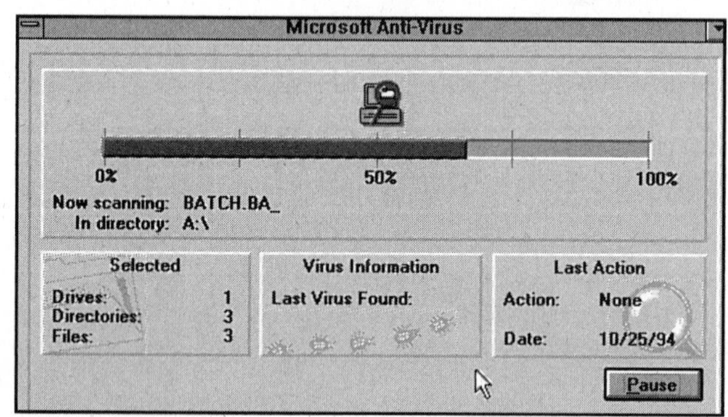

Figure 42.4

Microsoft Anti-Virus for Windows detecting viruses.

The detect operation creates a list of file checksums with the extension *.MS. These files are stored in each directory on each drive. Microsoft Anti-Virus uses these files to more quickly check for files which have been altered. You will be prompted during a scan if a file which has been altered is detected.

The Options menu lets you set whether or not to create these checklist files. Other options include whether or not to set the audible alarm which goes off when a virus has been detected, to check for *stealth* viruses (viruses that do not produce immediate symptoms and take certain actions to make themselves invisible to detection), whether or not to delete infected files, and whether or not to prompt when a virus has been detected.

Figure 42.5 shows you the list of viruses for which Microsoft Anti-Virus checks.

Virus List

Virus Name	Type	Size	#
Ada	File	2600	1
Adolph	File	1720	1
AIDS	Trojan	13312	4
Ha Ha Ha trojan			
Taunt			
AIDS II	Trojan	8064	1
AIDS Information	Trojan	120000	1
AirCop	Boot	512	2
Red State			
Afri	File	109	1
Agiplan	File	1536	2
Alabama	File	1560	2
Amilia	File	1614	1
Amoeba	File	1392	1

OK | Print | Search for: | Find Next | Info

Figure 42.5
The Microsoft Anti-Virus for Windows virus list.

This list can be reached from the Scan menu by selecting Virus List. When you select the Info button you can get a short description of the virus. This list shows the names, size, and number of variants of this type of virus. Unfortunately, the total number of variants, and the total number of viruses, increases daily.

The most comprehensive list of viruses is maintained by a consultant, Patricia Hoffman, and is called VSUM (see below). This list had, as of August 1994, 2,632 recorded viruses and their variants.

Microsoft's DOS based virus scanner is MSAV.EXE. If you invoke the utility with the /P option, it operates strictly at the command prompt. Otherwise you will see the menu interface shown in figure 42.6.

Select the Select a Drive option to change between drives A, C, or any other drive letters you have available, including drives mapped to the network. When you select the Detect option, MSAV first scans memory for RAM resident viruses, and then checks files on the indicated drive. Figure 42.7 shows you this operation in progress.

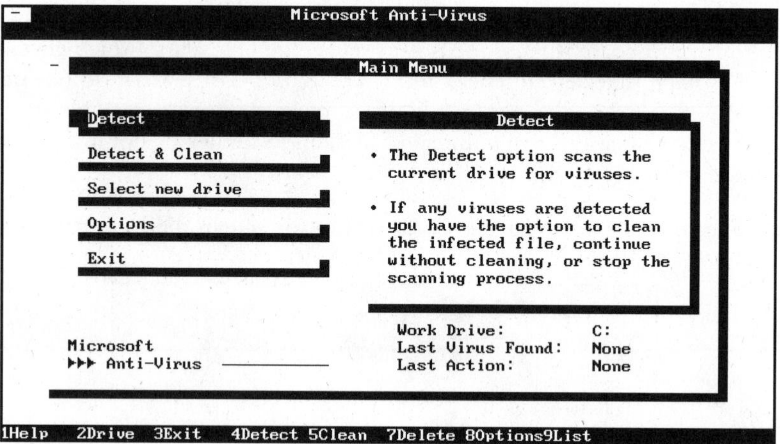

Figure 42.6
The Microsoft Anti-Virus for DOS main menu.

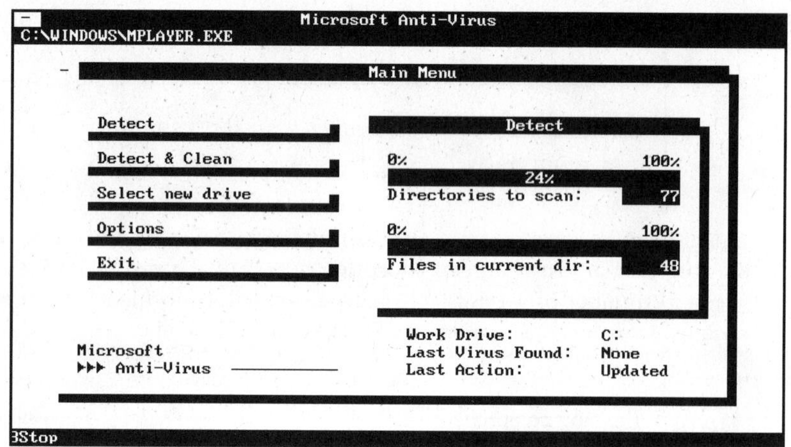

Figure 42.7
The Microsoft Anti-Virus for DOS detect operation in progress.

If the checksum of a file has changed since the last time the *.MS file was updated, you will receive a Verify Error. In many cases, you simply updated the file, such as CONFIG.SYS, or perhaps you have copied a more recent version. If you wish to ignore the verify error, select Update. This option updates the file checksum in the *.MS file in that directory. Otherwise you can either select Repair, which goes into virus cleanup, or Continue or Stop which ignores the message.

The VSAFE.COM utility is designed to load into the RAM of your workstation as it boots up. Place the command:

```
C:\DOS\VSAFE.COM
```

into your AUTOEXEC.BAT file to activate this utility. Once active, the VSAFE utility constantly monitors your computer for the presence of viruses. It first checks RAM, an operation that is performed again whenever a new program is loaded into RAM. It also checks all files that you open or access. VSAFE protects the boot sector of both your hard and floppy disks. It can also place a "write-protect" on files preventing you (or a virus) from writing any information without being prompted. VSAFE takes approximately 23 KB of conventional RAM, and 23 KB of extended RAM. It also slows workstation performance by a small percentage.

Norton AntiVirus

Peter Norton, like McAfee, was very early on the market with antivirus software. Norton sold his name to Symantec where he maintains an office. The Norton AntiVirus package for workstations is included in the Norton Desktop for Windows. There is also a server based version which includes both an NLM which runs on the file server as well as a Windows-based workstation component. The Norton server based software, Norton AntiVirus for NetWare, has many of the same features as described for McAfee's NetShield above. One unique feature is the ability to block an infected workstation from logging into the network in the first place. The user is denied access, and the network and node address goes into a log file on the server. The network Administrator is notified of this information along with the type of virus.

When you install the Norton AntiVirus for NetWare software, the default directory is SYS:SYSTEM\NAVNLM. To run the antivirus NLM on the file server you may wish to add this directory to the file server's search path as follows:

```
SEARCH ADD SYS:SYSTEM\NAVNLM
LOAD NAV.NLM
```

The last line above loads the Norton AntiVirus NLM software (NAV.NLM) on the file server. You will see a menu as shown in figure 42.8. Once the software starts running, it starts scanning files copied into and out of the file server's hard drives.

```
Norton AntiVirus for NetWare - Version 1.0
NLM Status
Status:                      Enabled       11-03-94 - 6:06:38 pm
CPU Load:                    1%
Total Files Scanned:         10
Total Infected Files:        0
Enabled Since:               November  3, 1994 - 5:51:27 pm
Last Activity for Server: EBDB
 11-03-94 5:51:27 pm: Enabled
 SYS:\PUBLIC\NCOPY.EXE
Real-time Status
Direction: Incoming and Outgoing files
File Type: Scan DOS executables
Look For:  Known viruses
Last Infected File
Virus:
User:
Time:
File:
Action:
<F2>Enable NLM  <F3>Disable NLM  <F4>Begin scan  <F5>Stop scan  <F10>Unload
```

Figure 42.8

The Norton AntiVirus for NetWare main menu as seen from the file server console.

Table 29.1 summarizes the fields visible in figure 42.8.

TABLE 29.1
NAV.NLM (Norton AntiVirus NLM) Server Menu Options

Section/ Menu Option	Description
	NLM Status
Status	Displays the status of the antivirus software on the server.
CPU Load	Current overall CPU utilization. This is the same statistic as seen in the main screen for MONITOR.NLM. This is so that you can gauge the effect of the antivirus software on the server.
Totals Files Scanned	Displays the total files scanned by the NLM since it was last loaded.
Total Infected Files	Displays the total number of files infected of the files scanned.
Enabled Since	Date and time NAV.NLM was loaded.
Last Activity for Server	Displays the name of the server scanned, the date and time, and file name of the file last scanned.

Section/ Menu Option	Description
	Real-Time Status
Direction	Indicates which files are scanned. *Incoming* indicates files copied to the server. *Outgoing* indicates file copied from the server.
File Type	Types of files which NAV.NLM will scan. The default is *Scan DOS executables.* This includes *.EXE and *.COM files.
Look For	What NAV.NLM is looking for.
	Last Infected File
Virus	The virus type of the last infected file found.
User	Username of the user who copied the infected file to or from the server.
Time	The time the infected file was copied.
File	File name of the infected file.
Action	The action NAV.NLM took upon detecting the virus.

Once the server software has been loaded, you can load the workstation portion of the Norton AntiVirus for NetWare software. The main menu of the workstation portion of the package is shown in figure 42.9.

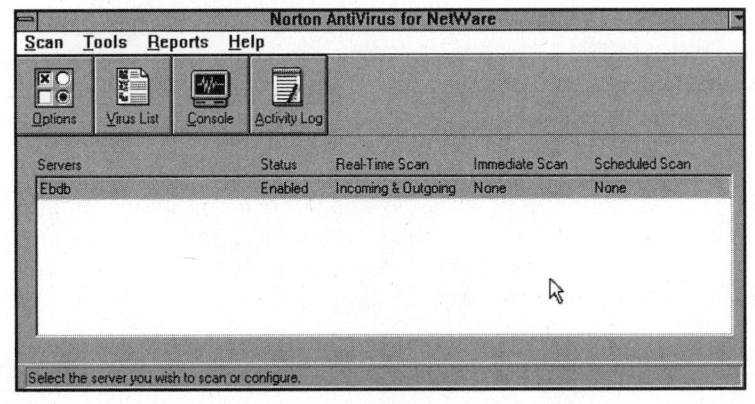

Figure 42.9

The Norton AntiVirus for NetWare workstation software main menu.

The Scan menu has an option Selected Server which causes NAV.NLM to scan the server selected on the list. You can also cancel a scan if you decide its impact on network activities is too great. Scans should be scheduled for periods where few or no users are logged into the network. Under the Tools menu, you can select Inoculation, which registers a "fingerprint" of a file in a database. This is similar to the checksum or CRC techniques described above when discussing VALIDATE.COM. The *Inoculation* process registers all files you indicate. You can use wild cards and include subdirectories. For Item you could enter *EBDB/SYS:*, and place a checkmark in the Include Subdirectories field. This would cause NAV.NLM to inoculate all files on volume SYS: of file server EBDB. This process enables NAV.NLM to very quickly determine whether or not a file has been altered.

The four toolbar items are: Options, Virus List, Console, and Activity Log. The Options dialog box is shown in figure 42.10.

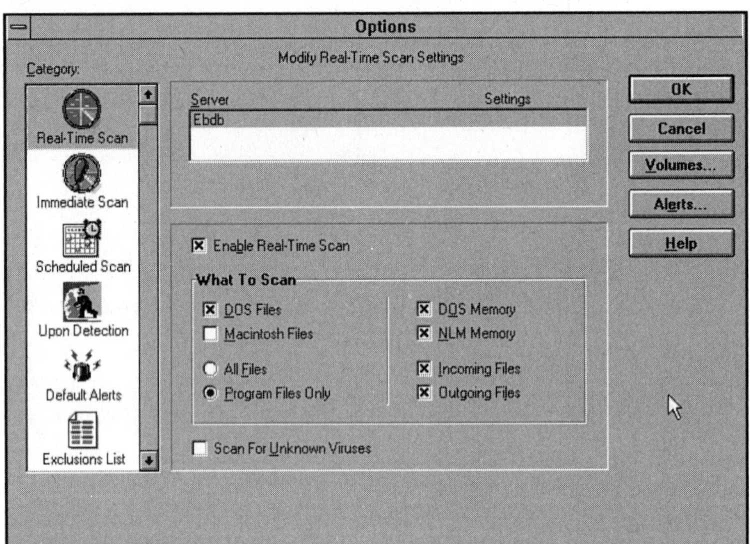

Figure 42.10

The Norton AntiVirus for NetWare Options dialog box

The categories include the following:

- **Real Time Scan.** Controls what NAV.NLM does all the time when running. You can tell NAV.NLM what types of files to scan (DOS or Macintosh, All files or Program files only), and whether or not to scan incoming and/or outgoing files. In some cases, you may wish to only scan *incoming* files since these represent the greatest danger to the network.

- **Immediate Scan.** Starts a scan when you click on the OK button.

- **Scheduled Scan.** Enables you to control when the server performs its virus scans. Using this option you can schedule NAV.NLM to perform any of a number of different scans at different time periods. You could schedule a complete scan of all files weekly, and a daily scan of program files, for example.

  The Scan for Unknown Viruses option works with the Inoculation feature. First you must inoculate all files you wish to protect. When the Scan for Unknown Viruses option is checkmarked, NAV.NLM will check inoculated files against their "fingerprints."

  The Add Schedule ... dialog box is shown in figure 42.11.

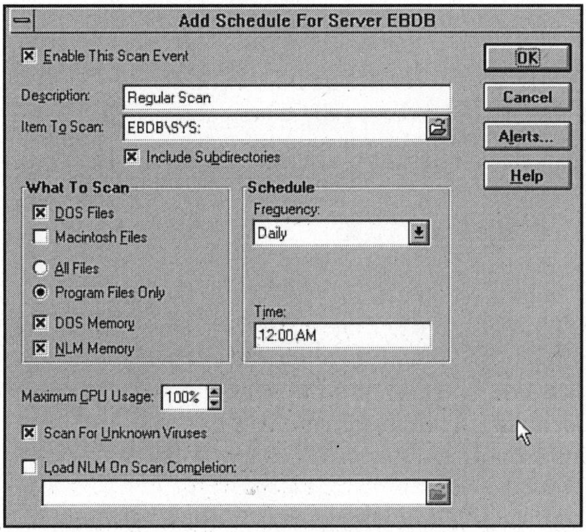

Figure 42.11

The Norton AntiVirus for NetWare Add Schedule ... dialog box.

- **Upon Detection.** Describes actions to take once a virus has been detected. These actions can include deleting the file, moving it to a designated subdirectory, deny access to the file, loading an NLM, or even forcing the offending workstation to logout.

  When an unknown virus is detected (when the "fingerprint" of a file fails to match its registered "fingerprint"), you have the same options as above. In addition you can instruct NAV.NLM to ignore a file which has not been inoculated. It is a good idea to not inoculate files which will be changed on a regular basis. These include word processing documents, spreadsheets, graphics files, among other types of data files.

- **Default Alerts.** Enables you to configure the defaults for alerts.

- **Exclusions List.** Instructs NAV.NLM to exclude certain files or subdirectories from being scanned. You select which type of scan to exclude. You could scan for known viruses but not unknown viruses, for example. You can also set a time limit on the exclusion. If you plan to perform some system upgrades for the next week, for example, you could exclude all files in the subdirectory you plan to upgrade for a period of 7 days.

In the case of any of the types of scan mentioned above, you can have certain actions take place. These are controlled by selecting the Alerts button. An *alert* is a broadcast message. You can configure who receives this message. A warning can be set to all users, the network Administrator, selected users, the file server console, or a log file. In addition, you can send messages through e-mail using MHS, or to a pager (once this feature is configured).

From the main menu you can also select **V**irus List. This brings up a list of "known" viruses. You can scroll down the list and view the types of viruses NAV.NLM protects against. As of April, 1994, there are 2,555 viruses on the list. Select the **I**nfo button to read about the virus. Information includes the name, aliases, what the virus infects (for example: master boot record), and whether or not it is common. There is also a characteristics grid and additional comments.

The **C**onsole option, from the main menu, allows you to view the same information as is presented on the NAV.NLM menu from the file server console. The **A**ctivity Log option displays NAV.NLM activity. Activity includes virus scans, infected files detected, when NAV.NLM was loaded or unloaded on the file server, and configuration changes.

Other Software and Sources

Novell DOS 7 includes a version of the SDSCAN.EXE utility (Search and Destroy Virus Scanner) licensed from Fifth Generation Software. This utility is DOS based and very easy to use. It operates quickly, both searching and cleaning virus infections.

Cheyenne Software produces a server-based antivirus utility called InocuLAN. It consists of a series of NLMs which run on the file server. This utility has many of the same features as the products discussed above. What makes this product unique is that it can be incorporated into backups using Cheyenne's ARCserve server-based backup software.

As you can see in figure 42.12, the backup options screen for an ARCserve backup session includes an option **I**nocuLAN Virus Scan. If you select this option, a virus scan will occur prior to the backup.

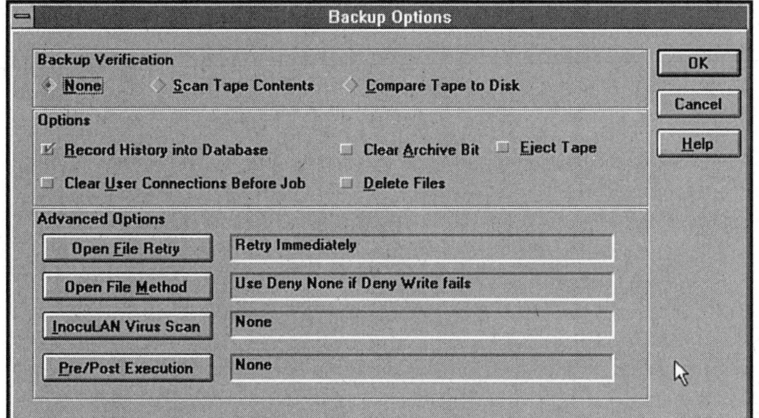

Figure 42.12

The ARCserve Backup Options dialog box showing the InocuLAN Virus Scan option.

In addition to these programs, there are numerous antivirus software packages. Patricia M. Hoffman is an antivirus specialist who certifies antivirus programs. She has compiled a comprehensive database of viruses. At her research facility are thousands of "trapped" live viruses. Antivirus software is checked against the "real thing" and the results are compiled. The database can be obtained from the McAfee Associates bulletin board (or CompuServe forum). It comes in the form of a ZIP file of over one megabyte in size. When expanded, the file contains a 2 MB database of known viruses, antivirus software certification results, and a hypertext style viewing program VSUM.EXE. Ms. Hoffman can be contacted at 408-988-3773. Her bulletin board number is 408-244-0813.

Summary

In this chapter, you were given a detailed look at computer viruses. One of the most common techniques for cleaning an infected system is to reboot with a "clean" write-protected floppy disk. You can then run an antivirus protection program to detect and clean viruses. Files infected by stealth viruses may be lost, however.

The next portion of this chapter described the four main types of viruses as defined by a well-known antivirus specialist, Patricia Hoffman. Boot sector infector viruses infect the boot sector of the hard drive. Multipartite viruses infect more than one area of a disk. Such viruses often infect the boot sector of a hard drive as well as an executable program file. Polymorphic viruses employ an encryption scheme that make them difficult to detect. Stealth viruses are among the most insidious. These viruses hide their effects on the infected system.

The effect of a virus on a DOS workstation is to attach itself to an executable file. When this file is run, the virus loads itself into RAM. In some cases, a virus will infect COMMAND.COM, the main DOS interpreter. In other cases, the virus attacks the boot sector of the hard drive.

In the case of the network, the DOS partition of the file server itself may be infected. In other cases, an infected file may be copied to the server. In the latter case, the network becomes a carrier for infected files. If the server's DOS partition is not infected, most virus programs are not capable of harming the server. Because the server is running NetWare, the boot sector is not accessible from a workstation.

Non-DOS workstations are not impacted as heavily as DOS workstations simply because not as many non-DOS systems which are easily affordable exist. Macintosh computers have been fairly heavily hit with viruses. UNIX systems are not easily infected, as is the case with OS/2 and Windows NT.

To protect the workstation from infection perform a virus scan on a regular basis. It is important to keep virus scanning software up to date. In many cases, network Administrators have been lulled into a false sense of security. The newer "stealth" viruses may be infecting workstations that are being scanned by outdated antivirus software. A simple antivirus QBASIC program and an accompanying batch file were presented in this chapter that can be installed into the AUTOEXEC.BAT file of a workstation.

To protect the server there are a number of antivirus software packages that are file server based. The server itself must be physically protected. Server based antivirus software can then be set up to perform regular virus scans. One of the best forms of server protection is to set up a rigorous set of security rights. If users have only Read and File Scan rights to the application programs, there is little chance these files can become infected.

Some of the commercially available antivirus software packages were reviewed towards the end of this chapter. You learned about the McAfee associates SCAN and NETShield antivirus utilities. The Microsoft Antivirus utility MSAV for DOS, and MWAV for Windows, is included with MS-DOS version 6.0 and above. It quickly scans the hard drive, or mapped network drive, for viruses. There is also a utility, VSAFE.COM, which can be loaded memory resident. VSAFE protects the workstation against virus-like activities, such as attempts to alter the master boot record of the workstation's hard drive.

The Norton AntiVirus software from Symantec is available on the workstation through the Norton Desktop for Windows package. There is another version, Norton AntiVirus for NetWare (NAV.NLM), which is installed on a file server. NAV.NLM is loaded on a file server and works with a workstation software component.

Unfortunately, viruses are a real threat to the computer professional. Ignoring the threat is very risky. As a network Administrator, you must keep on top of the problem by taking effective, workable, preventative action. You must also be prepared to deal with an actual infection. Keeping antivirus software up-to-date and staying informed on the latest reported developments is extremely important.

APPENDIX

Windows: A Brief Tutorial

This appendix should be subtitled "A Network Administrator's Survival Guide." The advent of Windows 3.0 caused a massive software revolution in the PC/DOS world. The graphical interface suddenly was in, and text-based applications were out. As the interface has matured, many software developers have jumped on the Windows bandwagon, extolling the virtues of the graphical-user interface—Windows is now firmly rooted in the PC world and appears to be here to stay. A working knowledge of Windows is vital for network Administrators to stay current in their jobs. With the advent of NetWare 4, Novell released two critical Windows-based utilities, which now make network management and navigation possible without ever having to leave Windows.

This appendix is designed to give network Administrators who are not familiar with Windows a working knowledge of the interface. This appendix provides tips on how to navigate Windows with or without a mouse. Basic Windows features are explained, and an occasional tip, trick, and technique are presented.

For further information on using Windows, consult one of the many books available on this subject, including *Inside Windows, Platinum Edition,* published by New Riders Publishing.

Understanding Program Manager

Several programs are run when you first load Windows. These include basic Windows engines, such as WIN.COM and WIN386.EXE. After the basic engines are loaded, Program Manager (PROGMAN.EXE), Windows' graphical menuing system, is run. At this point you should see several typical Windows program groups such as Main, and Accessories. Programs are organized in groups. Each group is defined by a file with the extension GRP.

The program groups contain icons that identify the individual programs. An *icon* is a pictorial representation of the program; they often incorporate the logo of the software publisher. Below the icon is a terse description that identifies the icon either by application or with a brief phrase.

You can run Windows programs through Program Manager by using either of two simple methods. The first involves selecting the icon, which you can do by clicking on it or by using the arrow keys. The title under the icon is highlighted when the icon is selected. After the icon is selected, you can execute the program by pressing Enter. The second simple method is to double-click on the icon; this executes the program automatically.

Program Manager can load the types of applications identified in table A.1.

Table A.1
Program Manager Executables

Type of Executable	File Name Extension	Description
Windows	EXE	Uses the Windows graphical environment application.
DOS	EXE or COM	Runs a DOS session out of Windows application. Windows first sets up a unique virtual machine for the session, allocating a preset amount of RAM.
DOS	PIF	Runs a DOS session out of Windows application. Windows consults the PIF file for information about this application. Use the PIF Editor to set a variety

Type of Executable	File Name Extension	Description
		of factors including foreground/background priority, amount of RAM allocated, video display environment, and so on.
Batch file	BAT	Runs any DOS batch file. Windows first sets up a unique virtual machine and then runs a DOS shell for the batch file.

Some Windows executables have their own definition files called *initialization files*. These files have the extension INI. The PROGMAN.INI file has a list of program groups defined for your computer. By default, INI files are located in the WINDOWS directory.

Each icon has a set of properties associated with it. Properties can be adjusted by selecting the icon, and either pressing Alt+Enter or choosing **F**ile, **P**roperties. Either method will display the Program Item Properties dialog box, shown in figure A.1.

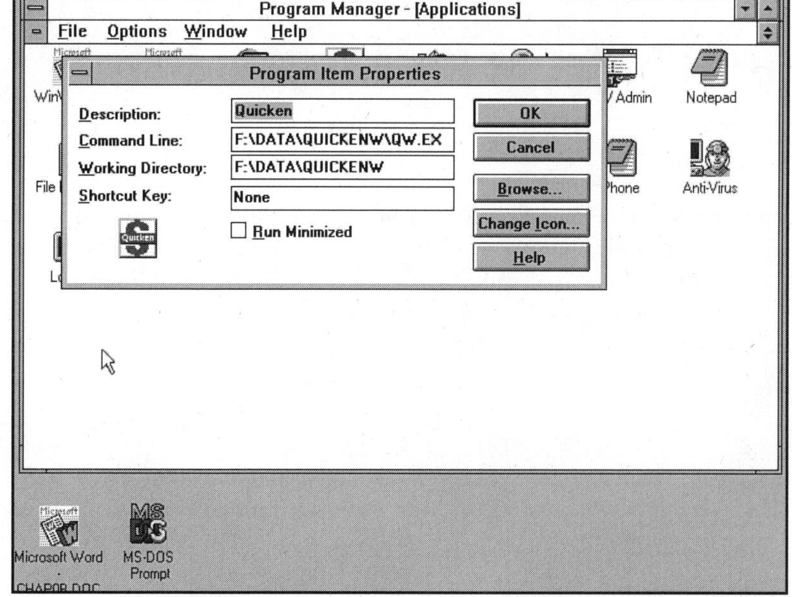

Figure A.1

The Program Item Properties dialog box.

The fields shown in the Properties dialog box are as follows:

- The Description field contains the text that appears under the icon.
- Command Line identifies the command that will be executed. Note that if the drive letter is a NetWare drive mapping, this application will not be accessible until you are logged in to the network.
- Working Directory indicates the directory Windows changes prior to running the application. This can be a directory other than that indicated by the Command Line field.
- Shortcut Key is used to identify a keystroke sequence that will activate this program without having to navigate around Program Manager. To change this field, enter a letter or other keystroke. Windows will add Ctrl+Alt in front of the letter or keystroke. If you press Q, for example, Windows will activate the application when you press Ctrl+Alt+Q.
- You should place a check mark in the Run Minimized field if you want to have this application continue to run even if the application window has been minimized. A *minimized* window appears as a small square at the bottom of the screen with the application's icon to identify it.

Examining Windows Buttons and Other Controls

One of the trademark features of Windows and Windows applications is the array of iconified controls. These include buttons, scroll bars, drop-down boxes, and list boxes among other controls. This section gives you an overview of what some of these controls are and how they operate.

Action Buttons

Most Windows applications feature the 3D effect. 3D controls have the appearance of being three-dimensional. When a button is shaded on its bottom and right side, it is considered to be in the out position, which in most cases corresponds with off. When you either click once on the button or press the spacebar, the button appears to be in the in position. When a button is pushed in, it appears lighter than other buttons, and the shading switches to the top and left sides of the button. A button that is pushed in is usually considered on. Some buttons stay in when pushed; other buttons appear to move in then out, but remain in the out position.

Figure A.2 shows three action buttons from Microsoft Word for Windows. The button labeled **B** indicates boldface, the button labeled *I* indicates italic, and the button labeled u indicates underline. In this figure, *italic* is selected (the *I* button is in the on position), whereas boldface and underline are not selected (the **B** and u buttons are in the off position).

Figure A.2

Three action buttons, with the middle button in the on position.

The most common Windows controls are *action buttons,* which, as their name implies, are used to take some sort of action. They usually stay in the out position when pressed. Action buttons also can be used to confirm some sort of operation. An example of an action button is the button that appears after a server broadcast message, such as the one in figure A.3. The message appears in a dialog box, and an action button labeled OK appears underneath. You must click on the action button to continue.

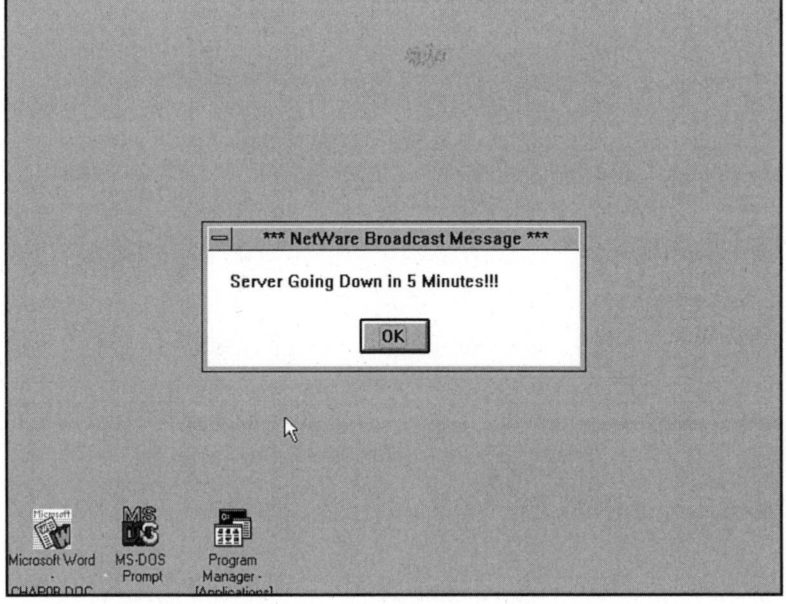

Figure A.3

A server broadcast message indicating the OK action button.

Action buttons can be "pressed" in several ways:

- ◆ Click once on the button with the mouse.
- ◆ Use the Tab key to select the button and press the spacebar.
- ◆ If the button has a bold border, it is the default action button. Press Enter to select the default.

Radio Buttons

Radio buttons give users a series of either/or choices. These buttons appear in a series, typically in a vertical arrangement. When you press one of a series of radio buttons, that button becomes active and all other buttons in the series become inactive.

The term *radio button* comes from pre-digital car radios. When you pressed the button corresponding to a radio station, any other buttons were pushed out.

Figure A.4 illustrates a horizontal series of radio buttons from the NWUSER utility. In this example, the radio buttons have icons illustrating their functions. The four buttons displayed represent Drive Connections, Printer Connections, NetWare Connections, and Send Messages. The Printer Connections radio button (the second from the left) is selected in the figure.

Figure A.4
NWUSER radio buttons with the second button from the left selected.

Drop-Down Boxes

Drop-down boxes are used to gather controlled user input. They are identified by an input box where you can enter text, and by a button with a downward-pointing arrow to the right of the input box. This type of box appears in two different styles. The first style enables you to either select the drop-down button at the right to scroll through a list of choices, or to type a choice not on the list. The other style only allows a choice from the list.

As with any list in Windows, you can type the first letter or number in a list of choices. When you type a character the cursor moves to the first item in the list that begins with the letter or number you typed. In certain lists, only the letter you type will appear. If this is the case, press either the Up or Down arrow to activate the drop-down box.

Figure A.5 illustrates a drop-down box with a list of numeric choices. To register a choice, click on an item in the list or type it in the input field. Use the Tab key or the mouse to move out of the drop-down box to the next field you wish to edit. The choice you selected will now be displayed in the input box of the drop-down box. Note that the choices presented in a drop-down box will vary and will often depend on choices selected in other fields.

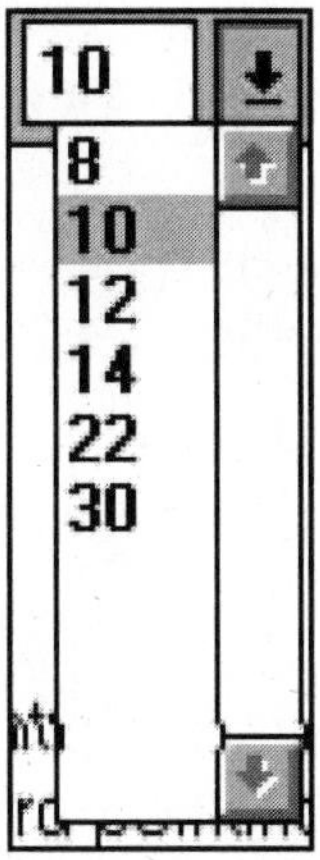

Figure A.5

A drop-down box with a list of numbers displayed.

A variation of the drop-down box is a field where you have a small up and down arrow to the right of the input field. In this variation, sometimes called a *spin box*, you can press the up or down arrow to increment or decrement a value or to move between choices in a list. This variation on the drop-down box conserves screen real estate. A drop-down box covers up other fields and could be less desirable under certain circumstances. Figure A.6 shows you this variation.

Figure A.6

Variation on the drop-down box where arrows increment or decrement values.

Note A *list box* is a variation on a drop-down box that appears with a list of items, perhaps after some sort of search has been instituted. The items also might be choices in a menu.

Scroll Bars

Scroll bars appear to the right of and underneath program windows, list boxes, and text boxes when the length or width of the on-screen object exceeds the amount of on-screen room. Scroll bars are used to move up and down a lengthy login script, for example.

The following list describes the three ways you can navigate around the screen by using scroll bars. Refer to figure A.7, which illustrates a scroll bar and directions for its use.

- **Scroll bar buttons.** A scroll bar button appears within each scroll bar. To use the scroll bar, center your mouse pointer on the button that appears in the scroll bar. While pressing the left mouse button, drag the scroll bar button up or down. Let go of the mouse button when you have moved the scroll bar button to the desired position. The items in the list box, or the text on screen next to the scroll bar, will move "up" or "down" with the scroll bar button.

- **Arrow buttons.** Arrow buttons are located at the top and bottom of the scroll bar. Clicking once on an arrow button moves you up or down one line (or item) at a time. When you click on an arrow button and hold the mouse button down, you continuously move up or down the list until you release the mouse button.

- **Clicking on the scroll bar.** You also can click on the scroll bar, rather than the scroll bar button, to change your position within the document or list. The position of the button in the scroll bar indicates your viewing position in the document or list. If the scroll bar button is at the top of the bar, you are at the top of the document or list. Click above or below the scroll bar button to page up or down inside the document or list.

Note Scroll bars can also be horizontal. In this case, dragging the scroll bar button will move the contents of the associated list or text box left or right.

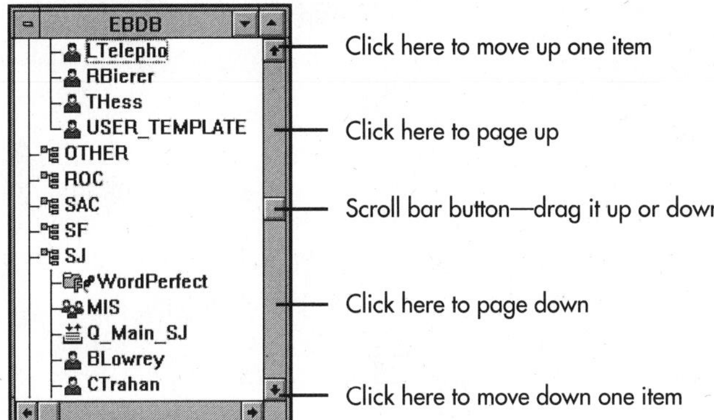

Figure A.7

Directions for using a scroll bar next to a list box.

You also can use the keyboard to move up and down on-screen. Pressing the up- and down-arrow keys moves up or down one item or line at a time, whereas pressing the PgUp and PgDn keys moves up or down one screen.

Hot Keys

Hot keys are shortcuts used to activate menus, menu items, and dialog box choices. When used with menus, hot keys are a fast alternative to browsing through a series of menus, and can minimize use of the mouse. Any given Windows menu can be accessed with a hot key if the menu name appears with an underlined letter. If this is the case, press and hold the Alt key. Then, while still holding the Alt key, press the underlined letter to display the drop-down menu. You now can release both keys. To access the **F**ile menu, for example, press Alt+F. The File menu drops down.

As a convention, when you see a keyboard action listed as Alt+O, for example, it means the following:

- Press and hold the Alt key
- While holding the Alt key, also press the O key

After you have accessed a drop-down menu, you can choose items on the menu by again observing underlined letters. Type any of the underlined letters (*without* holding pressing Alt) to access a submenu. From the File menu of most Windows programs, for example, you can press the letter O to access the **O**pen option.

Some submenu options are identified by additional shortcut keys. If this is the case you can directly access the submenu item without first accessing its drop-down menu.

Figure A.8 illustrates the Object menu from the NWADMIN utility. You can access this menu by pressing Alt+O. From the Object menu, you can print an object by pressing P. To print an object without first going to the Object menu, however, press and hold the Ctrl key and the letter P.

You will often see hot keys in dialog boxes as well. Inside a dialog box, the hot key follows the same convention as in a menu: the hot key will be underlined. As when you access a menu (the File menu for example), press and hold the Alt key, then press the underlined key to access the desired dialog box item.

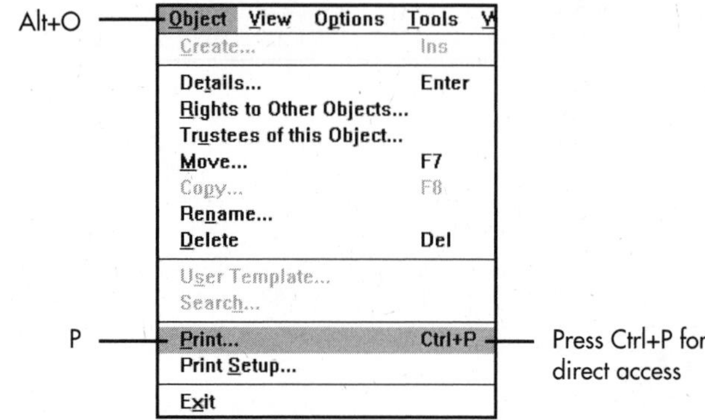

Figure A.8

Using a shortcut key to access the Object menu's Print command.

Moving and Resizing Windows

Part of the art of using Windows involves knowing how to move and resize windows. Windows can be moved at any time while working within the Windows environment. The contents of the window will move with the window itself, unchanged relative to the new position of the window.

Windows programs use two types of windows: application windows, and document windows. An *application window* is generated when you first invoke an application, and a *document window* is created within an application. Another way of phrasing this is that a document window is a child process of an application window. Options for moving and resizing apply to both document and application windows.

You might decide to move or resize a window in order to view multiple processes at the same time. Windows applications that run in 386 Enhanced mode will continue to run even if they are not selected. Some applications do not fare well when running in the background. The section "Examining Windows Navigation" later in this chapter discusses moving between windows.

Moving a Window

To move a window with a mouse, proceed as follows:

1. Locate the window's *title bar,* the line located at the top of the window that contains the title of the window. Position the pointer anywhere on the title bar. Be sure not to place the pointer on any of the buttons or controls to the right and left of the title bar.

2. Press and hold the left mouse button. While continuing to press and hold the left mouse button, drag the title bar to the new position. An outline of the window follows your movements, giving you an idea of where the new window will be located.

3. Once the final position has been selected, release the mouse button.

To move a window using the keyboard, proceed as follows:

1. Select the application's Control menu button, the button located at the upper left corner of the window. Using the keyboard you can access this button by pressing Alt+spacebar.

   Or, if you are attempting to move a document window (created by the application), select the document's Control menu button (upper left corner of the document subwindow). To access the document's Control menu by the keyboard, press Alt+-. The Control menu appears, as shown in figure A.9.

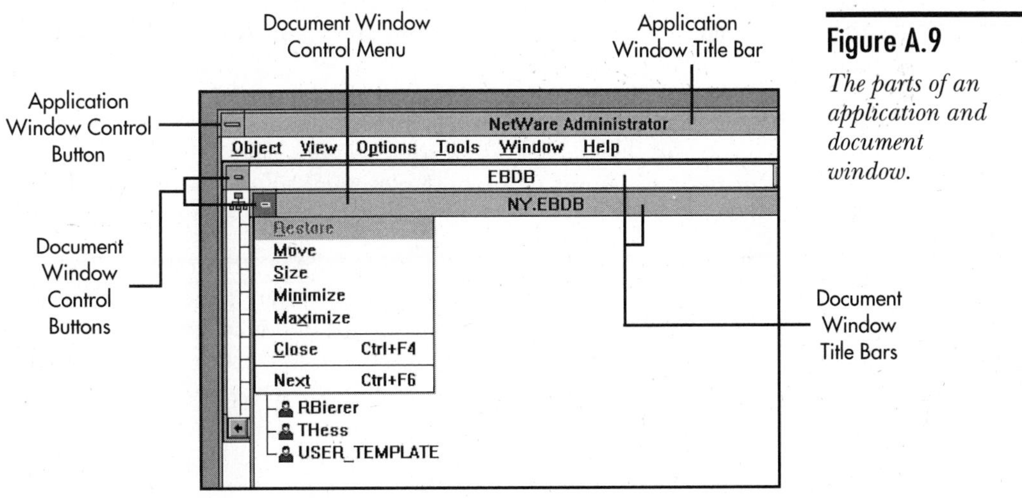

Figure A.9

The parts of an application and document window.

2. From the application or document Control menu, choose **M**ove. The pointer will change to a shape resembling a cross with arrowheads pointing up, down, right, and left. You can use the arrow keys to move the window to the desired location. As you move, an outline of the window will move with you, giving you an idea of the final location of the window.

3. When you have moved to the final location, press Enter.

Resizing a Window

Resizing a window is similar to moving a window. When you resize a window to a smaller size, you will be able to see less information at one time, but you can have multiple windows in view at once. When resizing a window to a smaller size, scroll bars will appear to the right and at the bottom of the window if there is more information in the window than is visible in its new size.

You cannot move or resize a window that has been maximized. If the window is maximized and you want to move or resize it, press the Restore button to bring it back to its original dimensions. Once restored, the window can now be moved or resized.

To resize a window using the mouse, proceed as follows:

1. Move the pointer to any edge of the window you want to resize, and the pointer will change to a double-headed arrow. The arrows point left and right when next to the left or right borders, and up and down when next to the top or bottom borders.

2. Click the left mouse button and hold it down while moving the mouse in the desired direction for the window. The border follows the mouse movements, giving you an idea of what the new window size will be. Release the mouse button and the window is now resized.

3. Alternatively you could position the pointer on any of the four corners. The pointer then changes to a slanted double pointer, indicating that you can move up, down, right, or left. Click the left mouse button and hold it down while repositioning the mouse. The corner of the window, along with the two borders that intersect at that corner, will move along with the mouse movements. Release the mouse button when done.

To resize a window using the keyboard, proceed as follows:

1. Activate the application's Control menu if you want to move the application window, or the document's Control menu if you want to move just the document window. (Refer to the second set of steps within the preceding section, "Moving a Window.")

2. From either Control menu, choose **S**ize. The pointer will change to a shape resembling a cross with arrow heads pointing up, down, right, and left. You can use the arrow keys to change the window to the desired size. As you move, an outline of the border or corner moves with you, giving you an idea of the final size of the window.

3. When you have moved to the final location, press Enter. The window is now resized.

Minimize, Maximize, and Restore

Windows can be *maximized,* meaning expanded to full size, or *minimized,* meaning shrunk down to an icon. A maximized window gives you the largest possible viewing area. This is convenient for desktop publishing, drawing programs, word processing, and so on. A minimized program is "out of the way." This is useful when there are other tasks you want to perform, and you want to temporarily get a program out of the way but not leave it entirely. When minimized, the program can still be active (depending on what settings you have enabled in the 386 Enhanced settings); it is just not displaying any information to you.

A minimized application does not use any fewer resources than if it were not minimized.

The maximize button is at the upper right corner of the Windows screen, with an upward-pointing triangle. The minimize button is immediately to the left of the maximize button, with a downward-pointing triangle. When a window has already been maximized, the maximize button changes to a restore button, which switches a window from maximized to whatever its previous dimensions were the last time you resized it. Note that both application and document windows can have maximize, minimize and restore buttons.

The restore operation brings the window to a state between that of maximized and minimized. When you restore from either a maximized or minimized state, the window changes to the size you last resized it to.

Figure A.10 illustrates an application and a document window in which these buttons appear, and table A.2 summarizes maximize, minimize, and restore operations.

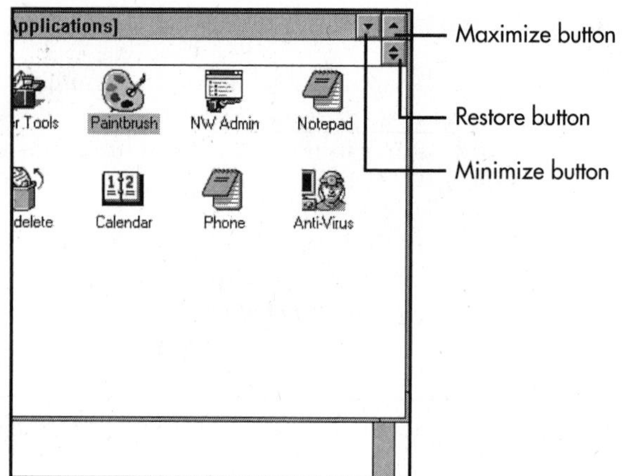

Figure A.10
A maximize, minimize, and restore button.

Table A.2
Maximize, Minimize, and Restore Window Operations

Operation	Input Device	Action
Maximize	Mouse	Click on the maximize button.
	Keyboard	Application window: Press Alt+spacebar, then press X. Document window: Press Alt+-,then press X.
Minimize	Mouse	Click on the minimize button.
	Keyboard	Application window: Press Alt+spacebar, then press N. Document window: Press Alt+-, then press N.
Restore from Maximized	Mouse	Click once on the restore button.
	Keyboard	Application window: Press Alt+spacebar, then press R. Document window: Press Alt+-, then press R.
Restore from Minimized	Mouse	Double-click on the minimized icon.
	Keyboard	Press and hold the Alt key. While holding the Alt key press the Tab key until you see a box with the title of the minimized program appear on the screen. Release both keys.

Using Windows Menus

Windows menus come in the form of pull-down menus and toolbars. Pull-down menus are visible after selecting an item from the menu bar. The *menu bar* is a series of words immediately under a window's title bar. As mentioned earlier, each menu word has one character underlined: the hot key that can be used to access the menu.

Figure A.11 illustrates the elements of the Windows menu system.

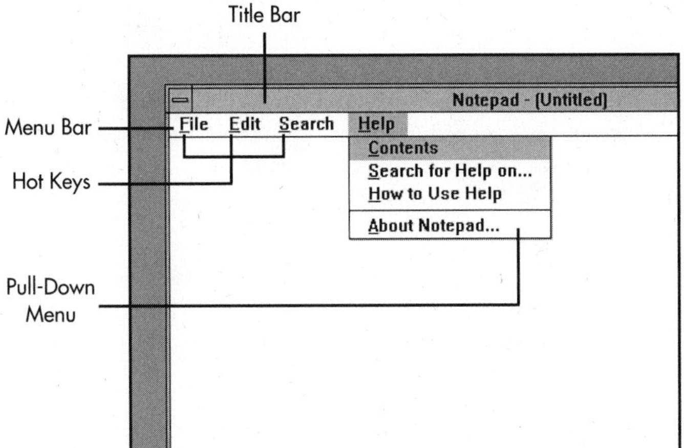

Figure A.11

The elements of a typical Windows menu.

Pull-Down Menus

The menu bar represents a point of contact between you and the pull-down menus. Pull-down menus are identified by a word on the menu bar line. They can be selected by either clicking on one of the words on the menu bar, or by pressing and holding the Alt key and then pressing the underlined letter (the hot key).

After the pull-down menu is visible, you can select an item on the menu by any of these methods:

- Use the arrow keys to move up or down the menu and press Enter on the desired option.
- Press the hot key that corresponds with the underlined letter in the desired menu option.
- Double-click on the menu option.

Some pull-down menu items have submenus. These are indicated with a right arrow next to the item on the pull-down menu. If you have used the arrow keys to highlight the menu item, press the right-arrow key to display the submenu off to the side. Using the mouse, click on the item that calls the submenu, or slide the pointer to the right to access the submenu.

If the menu item acts as a toggle switch, press Enter or click on the item. A check mark appears next to the item, indicating it is now active. Press Enter or click again to remove the check mark.

Toolbars

Many Windows applications use a toolbar to replace or supplement a pull-down menu system. A *toolbar* is a series of action buttons with an icon on the front (see fig. A.12). To activate an item with a mouse, click on the desired toolbar button. The toolbar button will appear to push inwards, and then will appear to spring back out. The desired action will then take place.

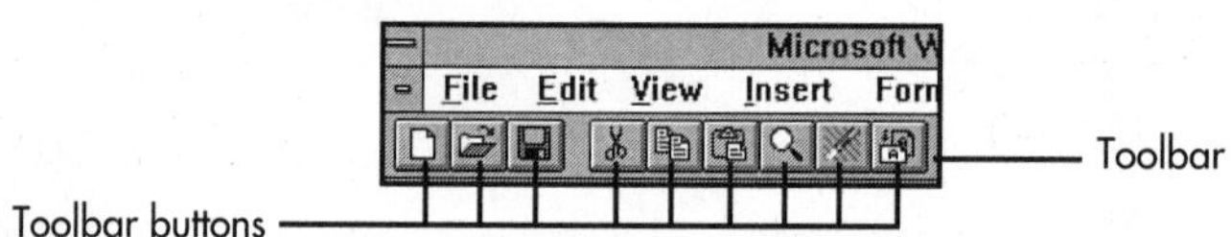

Figure A.12
A portion of the toolbar from Microsoft Word for Windows.

To access a toolbar button with the keyboard, you must use the Tab key to move the faint highlight to the desired toolbar button, then use the spacebar to activate the button. In some cases you will not be able to access the toolbar buttons using the keyboard.

Examining Windows Navigation

Moving around in Windows is an important skill for network Administrators. When troubleshooting Windows applications, a solid knowledge of how to navigate inside an application, around dialog boxes, and between applications will save you time (and possible embarrassment!).

Movement Inside a Text Window or Dialog Box

A *text window* is a window where you can enter or modify blocks of text. Movement with the mouse inside a text window consists of simply repositioning the mouse pointer and clicking once. When in the form of an I beam, the pointer can be used to select blocks of text. When the pointer is at the left side of the window and is in the shape of a diagonal arrow pointing to the upper right, it can be used to select a line of text. Press and hold the left mouse button and move the mouse down to select multiple lines of text. When the mouse is pointing to a scroll bar, a button, the title bar, the menu bar, or the toolbar, the shape changes to an arrow pointing to the upper left. When in this shape, the pointer can be use to activate a button or take action.

Using the keyboard to move around varies depending on whether you are in a text window or some sort of dialog box. A *dialog box* is an input screen in which you can enter data, perform searches, print data, and so on. Movement in either of these situations is summarized in tables A.3 and A.4.

TABLE A.3
Keyboard Navigation Inside a Text Window

Keystroke	Action
Up arrow	Moves one row up
Down arrow	Moves one row down
Right arrow	Moves one character to the right
Left arrow	Moves one character to the left
Page Up	Moves to the previous screen
Page Down	Moves to the next screen
Home	Moves to the beginning of the line
End	Moves to the end of the line
Ctrl+up arrow	Moves to the beginning of the paragraph
Ctrl+down arrow	Moves to the beginning of the next paragraph
Ctrl+right arrow	Moves to the beginning of the next word

continues

Table A.3, Continued
Keyboard Navigation Inside a Text Window

Keystroke	Action
Ctrl+left arrow	Moves to the previous word
Ctrl+Page Up	Moves to the top of the screen
Ctrl+Page Down	Moves to the bottom of the screen
Ctrl+Home	Moves to the beginning of the document
Ctrl+End	Moves to the end of the document

Table A.4
Keyboard Navigation Inside a Dialog Box

Keystroke	Action
Right arrow	Moves one character to the right
Left arrow	Moves one character to the left
Up arrow	Moves to the previous field or row of fields
Down arrow	Moves to the next field or row of fields
Tab	Moves to the next field or action button

Movement between Windows

Equally important for the harried network Administrator is the ability to move between windows. Using the mouse, it is simply a matter of clicking once on any part of the target window. If the window is not in view, you can double-click in the area below the Program Manager to display the Task List (described later). From Program Manager, you can choose Window to move to any of the program groups. From inside an application, choose Window to move to windows created by the application.

To move between windows using the keyboard, press Alt+Tab; a dialog box identifying the next window appears. When you let go of both the Tab and Alt keys, you will be moved to that window. Pressing Alt+Tab again and letting go switches you to the

window you were in prior to the current window. By continuing to hold the Alt key and pressing the Tab key repeatedly, you can cycle through all open windows. Another method of cycling through open windows is to use the Alt+Esc key combination.

Ctrl+F6 moves you to the next document window within an application. Ctrl+Tab moves you to the next program group in the Program Manager. Ctrl+Esc brings up the Task List (described next).

Task List

The *Task List* is a dialog box that shows a list of the currently active windows (see fig. A.13). You can move to any of the windows by double-clicking on its name in the list, or by selecting the desired task and choosing Switch To. Choosing End Task closes the selected application. Cascade causes the task windows to arrange themselves on-screen in a staggered fashion. Tile causes the task windows to be arranged so that all are visible on-screen, arranged as a series of small windows.

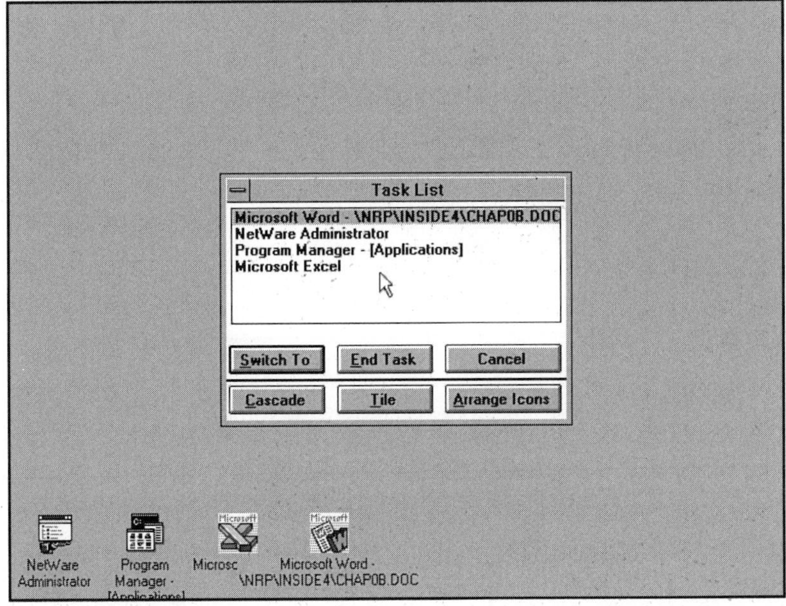

Figure A.13

The Windows Task List.

As mentioned earlier, you can access the Task List using either of the following methods:

- Double-click on the area below the Program Manager
- Press Ctrl+Esc

Click Once or Twice?

Part of the art of using Windows is knowing when to click the mouse button once and when to click twice. When you read a manual or other book explaining a Windows application, the term *click* is used to indicate clicking the left mouse button one time. The term *double-click* tells you to click the left mouse button twice in rapid succession. If your double-clicks are not rapid enough, Windows will treat them as two separate clicks.

Table A.5 summarizes common actions and how many times to click the left mouse button.

Table A.5
How Many Times To Click the Mouse

Action	Mouse Clicks
Open an item in a list box	Double
Activate an action button	Single
Activate a menu item	Single
Restore an icon	Double
Close a window	Double on the Control menu button
Select a field in a dialog box	Single

Editing, Cutting, and Pasting

Windows offers a credible cutting and pasting capability. You can cut sections of text and paste them into another position within a text editing window or between Windows applications. This section gives you a look at these capabilities.

Understanding Input Fields

One of the first things to notice about a Windows input field is whether you have the field selected. After the field is selected, observe the shape of the cursor. If there is no cursor, you are not in either input or editing mode. If this is the case, use the mouse to click on the input box, or press Tab until the input box is highlighted. The editing cursor is a straight line. When using the mouse, the pointer changes from an arrow to a cursor shaped like the capital letter I.

Inside the input field, editing keys similar to those in text editing boxes are available. You can press Home or End, for example, to move to the beginning and end of the input field. Likewise, you can press Ctrl+right arrow and Ctrl+left arrow to move to the beginning of the next or previous words, respectively.

Selecting Text

In Windows, the phrase *selecting text* refers to the process of highlighting a block of text. After text has been selected, it can be cut and pasted. To select text with the mouse, position the mouse pointer at the beginning of the desired block of text. Press and hold the left mouse button, move the pointer to the end of the target block of text, then let go of the mouse button. The target block of text is now selected. Many text editors offer the capability to select a word by double-clicking on it.

After text has been selected, any key you press causes the block to disappear and to be replaced with what you type. Many hours of work have been lost this way; however, you can use this to your advantage if you truly want to replace text. Select the text to be replaced, and start typing. The old text disappears with the first new keystroke.

When operating within a dialog box with input fields, press Tab to move between fields. You will see that the text in an input field is selected when you move to that input box. This enables you to replace all the text in an input field. If you want to edit only one or a few characters in an input field, first use the left or right arrow keys to remove the highlight. Any cursor movement will move the highlight.

To select text with the keyboard, press and hold the Shift key. While holding the Shift key, press any of the arrow keys (left, right, up, or down). The highlighted area expands, following the direction of the arrow. To select an entire line, move the cursor to the beginning of the line by pressing Home, then press Shift+End.

Edit boxes often will enable you to perform manipulations on selected text. The Windows Write utility, for example, enables you to change fonts, boldface, underline, or italics, among other operations, to any selected text.

Cutting and Copying Text

After you have selected a block of text, you can *cut* the text, which removes the text from its original position and places it in a paste buffer. The text then can be reinserted using the paste operation (described later).

To cut text with the mouse, follow this procedure:

1. Select the text by dragging the cursor over the desired text while holding down the left mouse button.
2. From the Edit menu of the application, choose Cut. The block of text is removed and placed in a paste buffer.

To cut text with the keyboard, proceed as follows:

1. Select the text by holding down the Shift key and moving the cursor with any arrow key, Home, End, and so on. The desired text becomes highlighted.
2. Press Ctrl+X to cut the block of text.

The copy operation is similar to the cut operation with these exceptions:

- From the Edit menu choose Copy, or, with the keyboard, press Ctrl+C.
- The selected text will not disappear. Instead, a copy of the text is placed in the paste buffer, and the original text remains intact.

Pasting Text

After text has been either cut or copied, you can paste it into another part of the window or into another window. To paste text proceed as follows:

1. Reposition the cursor to the new location.
2. Choose Paste from the Edit menu, or press Ctrl+V.

The text stored in the paste buffer appears at the cursor position. You can continue to paste if you want to create multiple copies of the block of text.

The "paste buffer" in Windows is the *Clipboard*. This is an application, called Clipboard Viewer, which can be accessed from the Program Manager Main Windows group. Any text that you cut or copy is first placed in the Clipboard. You can then access this application through the Program Manager and make additional edits before pasting the contents into another location.

The Clipboard also holds the contents of the screen when the Print Screen key is pressed. This is useful when documenting Windows-based procedures.

Understanding Windows Program Operations

Windows runs programs in a rather strange fashion. One of the selling points of Windows 3.*x* is that it manages memory dynamically, without the user having to be concerned with such memory issues as the availability of conventional and upper memory. Windows 3.*x* places Windows applications in extended RAM and takes care of how much memory is available and how it is managed.

One of the weakest points about Windows is that it runs on top of DOS. As a result, Microsoft has embarked on several "next generation" Windows products. One of these is Windows NT. The other two notable products are code-named Chicago and Daytona. *Chicago* is the successor to Windows 3.1 and will be shipped with the name Windows 95. Windows 95 will no longer be dependent on DOS, but will still target the desktop market. So that it can run on PCs with fairly limited memory, Windows 95 will lack some of the advanced features of Windows NT such as security.

Daytona will be the next generation of Windows NT and will combine the new desktop of Windows 95 with the advanced operating system features of Windows NT. Both Windows NT and Windows 95 incorporate an improved file system and cold boot loader. DOS functions are written into the Windows interface, and will no longer be needed to boot or operate the computer.

Windows 3.*x*, which is available and in use today, presents a problem because of its reliance on DOS. DOS is designed to have applications run in the first 640 KB of RAM. The remaining 384 KB of RAM was originally allocated as space for device drivers and video memory. As programs continued to increase in size, DOS became a "memory trap." Programmers found it more and more difficult to accomplish certain tasks, including implementing a high-resolution graphical interface, in 640 KB.

The first memory solutions used what we now refer to as *expanded memory*. Expanded memory operates by switching banks of RAM in and out of buffers maintained between the 640 KB and 1 MB areas of the computer memory map. Later improvements introduced extended memory. *Extended memory* is mapped by the computer past the 1 MB area.

With large programs, DOS programmers had to design their programs to operate in part out of the base 640 KB of RAM, avoid the next 384 KB of RAM, and continue to operate in either expanded or extended memory. Windows 3.*x* broke this barrier to a certain extent by taking over memory management for applications. Any application written to run in Windows is designed to run entirely (or mostly) in extended RAM.

Swap Files

If Windows determines that you have too many programs running for the amount of extended RAM available, a process that originated in the UNIX environment in the 1970s called virtual memory is used. This process involves swapping portions of RAM out onto a hard drive to make room for additional programs in RAM. During the installation process, Windows has you create a swap file. The size of the swap file is added to the amount of extended RAM installed in your computer to create a total amount of virtual memory.

There are two types of Windows swap files: permanent and temporary. The permanent swap file resides permanently on your hard drive and is used when Windows is in operation. The temporary swap file is created when Windows first loads and is deleted when you exit Windows. The advantage to a permanent swap file is that the disk space is allocated all at once, and is contiguous. Information is located physically in adjacent tracks and sectors on your hard drive, and can be read and written to quickly. A temporary swap file might not necessarily be located on contiguous disk blocks; therefore, reads and writes to a temporary swap file are not as efficient as to a permanent swap file. Because the temporary swap file must be built when Windows first starts, Windows takes longer to load. On the other hand, a temporary swap file is less subject to corruption because it is created each time you load Windows. Because the temporary swap file is deleted upon exiting Windows, less disk space is taken on a permanent basis.

Windows and DOS Applications

Windows applications take advantage of Windows resources. These resources include the following:

- Memory management
- Access to Windows devices such as printers and modems
- The capability to exchange information dynamically (Dynamic Data Exchange)

Windows applications run in a single virtual machine. DOS applications run in their own separate virtual machines. The advantage to this arrangement for Windows applications is that all Windows applications can share the same resources and exchange data, whereas DOS applications are isolated from each other. You can set the amount of relative time Windows allocates to processes running in foreground and in background. A highlighted window indicates your application is active. Any active application is in the foreground, and other processes are running in the background. The exception to this is that when one Windows application is in the foreground, all Windows applications are in the foreground because they all share the same virtual machine.

Windows allocates time to processes in slices. The time allocated to a slice is set by using the Control Panel's 386 Enhanced option. All Windows applications currently running on your computer share the same timeslice. DOS applications are given separate and distinct timeslices. The more DOS applications you have running under Windows, the more your Windows applications will suffer when running in background. You can adjust this balance by increasing the number of time slices indicated in the Windows in Background field.

Index

Symbols

B

C

D

E

G

H

I

J–K

L

M

N

O

P

Q

R

S

T

U

V

W

X–Y–Z

Fold Here

PLACE
STAMP
HERE

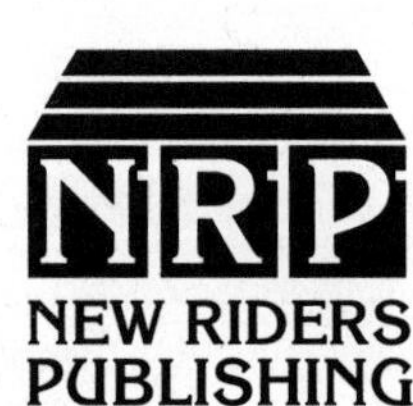

New Riders Publishing
201 West 103rd Street
Indianapolis, Indiana 46290
USA

Inside NetWare 4.1

REGISTRATION CARD

Fill out this card to receive information about future NetWare books and other New Riders titles!

Name ______________________________ **Title** ____________________

Company ____

Address ____

City/State/ZIP ____

I bought this book because: _____________________________

____

I purchased this book from:

☐ A bookstore (Name ___________________________)

☐ A software or electronics store (Name ______________)

☐ A mail order (Name of Catalog ____________________)

I purchase this many computer books each year:

☐ 1–5 ☐ 6 or more

I currently use these applications: _______________________

____

____

____

I found these chapters to be the most informative: ___________

____

I found these chapters to be the least informative: ___________

____

Additional comments: __________________________________

____

☐ I would like to see my name in print! You may use my name and quote me in future New Riders products and promotions. My daytime phone number is: ____________________

New Riders Publishing 201 West 103rd Street • Indianapolis, Indiana 46290 USA

Fold Here

PLACE
STAMP
HERE

New Riders Publishing
201 West 103rd Street
Indianapolis, Indiana 46290
USA

GET CONNECTED
to the ultimate source of computer information!

The MCP Forum on CompuServe

Go online with the world's leading computer book publisher! Macmillan Computer Publishing offers everything you need for computer success!

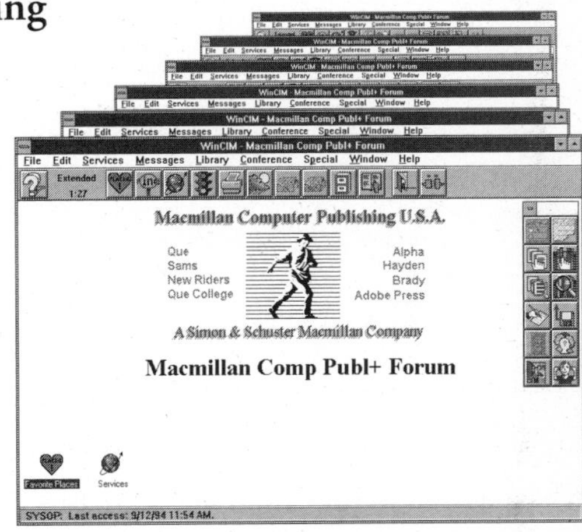

Find the books that are right for you!

A complete online catalog, plus sample chapters and tables of contents give you an in-depth look at all our books. The best way to shop or browse!

- Get fast answers and technical support for MCP books and software
- Join discussion groups on major computer subjects
- Interact with our expert authors via e-mail and conferences
- Download software from our immense library:
    - Source code from books
    - Demos of hot software
    - The best shareware and freeware
    - Graphics files

Join now and get a free CompuServe Starter Kit!

To receive your free CompuServe Introductory Membership, call **1-800-848-8199** and ask for representative #597.

The Starter Kit includes:

- Personal ID number and password
- $15 credit on the system
- Subscription to *CompuServe Magazine*

Once on the CompuServe System, type:

GO MACMILLAN

for the most computer information anywhere!

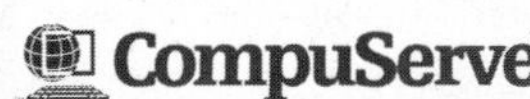